BY THE EDITORS OF
CONSUMER GUIDE®

More Favorite Brand Name Recipes Cookbook

BEEKMAN HOUSE
New York

Contents

Library of Congress Catalog Card Number: 83-62604
ISBN: 0-517-41445-7
This edition published by:
Beekman House
Distributed by Crown Publishers, Inc.
One Park Avenue
New York, New York 10016
Manufactured in the United States of America
10 9 8 7 6 5 4 3 2
Cover Design: Linda Snow Shum
Cover Photography: Petroff Photography

Introduction

You loved our first collection—the FAVORITE BRAND NAME RECIPE COOKBOOK—and wanted more. MORE FAVORITE BRAND NAME RECIPES COOKBOOK, compiled by the Editors of CONSUMER GUIDE®, contains over 2,000 all new recipes; not one is repeated from our first collection. Also included are over 65 taste-tempting color photographs.

Take a quick glance through this all new cookbook of America's favorite recipes. You'll discover 20 chapters on everything from Soups and Salads to Main Dishes and Desserts. So many of your best-loved recipes are here, including the ones you may have seen (and wish you had saved) on the box tops, side panels and labels of food packages or in newspaper and magazine advertisements.

We have included recipes for the Microwave Oven. Watching your diet? See the Low Calorie recipes and the Low Sodium recipes, even among the nutritious snacks and scrumptious desserts. You will find a wide selection of ethnic recipes—Mexican, Chinese, Italian, French and others—that are so easy to prepare and that will add variety to your menus. American cooking is definitely "in." And we have chosen favorite regional recipes ranging from New England to California and from Maine to Texas.

CONSUMER GUIDE® Food Editors have worked closely with the home economists from major food companies in order to complete this wonderful new collection of brand name recipes. Without exception, all of the recipes have been kitchen-tested by our country's leading food manufacturers to make this your permanent reference to what are and what will be classic favorites, such as taco and spinach salads, veal parmigiana, fried rice, Impossible Pies, delicious open-face sandwiches and marvelous desserts. For wonderful new recipes, such as Tofu-Vegetable Sauté, Noodles Primavera, Apricot Barbecued Spareribs and one of our favorites—Chocolate Peanut Ripple Cake—just look in the index. We have terrific beverage recipes, both alcoholic and nonalcoholic. There are satisfying main dishes, soups, stews and chowders, delectable cakes, pies, cookies and more. Prepare the Two Time World Champion Chili; add to this one of the wonderful vegetable salads, a loaf of Cheesy Mexican Bread or the delicious Bohemian Casserole Bread and you have a super meal.

How to Use This Cookbook

The book is divided into 20 chapters from appetizers to beverages, making it easy to find your favorite recipes. Most of the chapters also have subgroups for easy reference; for example, the Poultry chapter is separated into "Chicken," "Turkey," etc. In addition, recipes of a similar type have been grouped together, such as recipes that use chicken breasts.

The Index. Our readers tell us they often remember the brand name or the major food ingredient of their favorite recipe, rather than the exact title. Our recipes, therefore, are listed in the index (1) by brand name and (2) under major food categories, such as "beef," as well as (3) by recipe title.

Directory of Food Manufacturers. For the convenience of our readers, we have included an address directory of all food manufacturers listed in the book (see Acknowledgments). Any questions or comments regarding the recipes should be directed to the individual manufacturers for prompt attention.

CONSUMER GUIDE® wishes to thank all of the participating food companies for their excellent contributions; we believe this collection contains some of the best and most popular brand name recipes. Of course, by printing these recipes, CONSUMER GUIDE® is not endorsing particular brand name foods.

So here it is—an easy to use, giant reference book of your favorite brand name recipes. We know this book will be used again and again in the years to come and will bring compliments from family and friends.

Recipes Shown on Cover:

1. Vegetable Chowder, *page 38*
2. Chocolate Peanut Ripple Cake, *page 249*
3. Lime Soda, *page 337*
4. Sea Breeze Salad, *page 164*
5. Pickle Swizzles, *page 340*
6. Two Story Pizza, *page 202*
7. Chocolate Finger Cookies, *page 283*
8. Fudge-Filled Bars, *page 293*
9. Chinese Pepper Steak, *page 106*
10. Chicken Sate, *page 50*

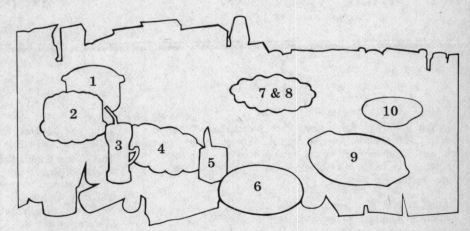

Appetizers

First Course — Cold

CUCUMBER APPETIZER

1 large cucumber, peeled, pitted, sliced
Salt
1 cup DANNON® Plain Yogurt
1 small onion, sliced
1 clove garlic, mashed
½ teaspoon fresh mint, chopped
Juice of ½ lemon
Lettuce leaves
Walnuts, for garnish

Season sliced cucumber with salt. Allow to stand for 10 to 15 minutes. Drain off any liquid residue. To cucumbers, add yogurt, sliced onion, garlic, mint and lemon juice. Toss well. Arrange on lettuce leaves and garnish with walnuts.   *Serves 2 as appetizer*

EGGPLANT CAPONATA

1 large eggplant, cut into ¾-inch cubes
1½ tablespoons salt
1 cup finely chopped celery
1 cup finely chopped onion
2 cloves garlic, minced
½ cup BERTOLLI® Olive Oil
1¼ cups BERTOLLI® Spaghetti Sauce
¼ cup pimiento-stuffed olives, cut into fourths
3 tablespoons pine nuts
1½ tablespoons drained capers
3 anchovies, minced
2 tablespoons BERTOLLI® Red Wine Vinegar
2 teaspoons sugar
⅛ teaspoon crushed red pepper

Sprinkle eggplant with salt; let stand 30 minutes. Rinse; pat dry. Sauté eggplant, celery, onion and garlic in oil in Dutch oven until eggplant is browned, about 10 minutes. Stir in remaining ingredients; heat to boiling. Reduce heat; simmer 15 minutes. Spoon into bowl; refrigerate until cold.

HOLIDAY HAM MOLD

½ cup water
1 tablespoon unflavored gelatin (1 envelope)
1 cup chicken broth, hot
1 stalk celery
1 quarter of medium onion
1 medium sweet pickle
¼ teaspoon cream-style horseradish
2 cans (4½ oz. each) deviled ham
⅔ cup prepared HIDDEN VALLEY ORIGINAL
    RANCH® Salad Dressing

In a medium bowl, mix gelatin with cold water. Add hot chicken broth and stir until gelatin is dissolved. Cool. In a blender or food processor chop celery, onion and pickle. Blend with horseradish and deviled ham. Stir in Salad Dressing and cooled gelatin mixture. Pour into a 2-cup mold. Refrigerate several hours. Serve, sliced thin, as an appetizer.   *Makes 8 to 10 servings*

MINTED MELON

1 large cantaloupe or honeydew melon
3 Tbsp. HIRAM WALKER Creme de Menthe
    (White)
1 Tbsp. lemon juice
12 thin slices prosciutto ham
Lemon and lime wedges

Halve melon. Remove seeds. Cut each half into 6 slices; remove rind. Wrap each slice with prosciutto. Mix Creme de Menthe and lemon juice; drizzle over melon. Chill. Serve with lemon and lime wedges.   *12 appetizers*

SALMON ANTIPASTO

15½ oz. can DEMING'S Red Sockeye Salmon*
2 stalks celery, sliced into 1 in. pieces
2 carrots sliced lengthwise into 3 in. sticks
2-3 cups cauliflower flowerets
2-3 cups broccoli flowerets
¼ pound fresh mushrooms, cleaned and sliced
10 oz. can artichoke hearts, drained and halved
16 oz. can whole green beans, drained
16 oz. bottle Italian Dressing & Marinade
Cherry tomatoes
Stuffed or ripe olives
Crisp crackers or toast points

Drain salmon and break into bite size pieces in small bowl. Sprinkle with 3 Tbsp. dressing; cover and chill for 2 hrs. Cook celery, carrots, cauliflower, and broccoli in small amount of water until tender-crisp. Drain and place in shallow container with mushrooms, artichoke hearts and green beans. Pour remaining dressing over all until vegetables are well coated; cover and chill. When ready to serve, remove vegetables and salmon from marinade and arrange attractively on a platter with cherry tomatoes, olives and crisp crackers or toast points.   *Serves 10-12*

*DOUBLE Q, GILLNETTERSBEST or HUMPTY DUMPTY Salmon may be substituted.

SASHIMI

2 pounds fresh filleted tuna, striped bass or sea bass,
    skinned
3 cups shredded lettuce
Watercress for garnish
2 tablespoons wasabi (Japanese horseradish powder)
    OR dry powdered mustard
Water
½ cup KIKKOMAN Soy Sauce

Cut fish into pieces about 1½ inches long, 1 inch wide and ¼-inch thick. Arrange attractively on bed of shredded lettuce on large serving plate. Garnish with crisp watercress. Cover plate with plastic wrap and refrigerate until ready to serve. Meanwhile, blend wasabi or mustard with small amount of water to form a smooth paste; cover and let stand 5 minutes. Press together and form into a cone-shaped ball; place on side of fish on serving plate or divide equally into serving bowls. Pour about 2 tablespoons soy sauce into separate dipping dishes, allowing one for each person. Let each person mix as much wasabi into soy sauce as desired. Dip cold fish pieces into soy sauce mixture before eating.   *Makes 4 to 6 servings*

TUNA MOSAIC PÂTÉ

2 cans (6½ or 7 ounces each) tuna
½ cup soft bread crumbs
¼ cup milk
¼ cup lemon juice
1 small onion, grated
2 eggs
½ teaspoon dried leaf tarragon
¼ teaspoon salt
Dash pepper
3 thin lemon slices, peeled
14 whole, fresh green beans, uncooked
3 medium whole carrots, cooked
½ cup frozen peas, thawed
Black olives

Drain tuna. In large bowl of electric mixer, combine tuna, bread crumbs, milk, lemon juice, grated onion, eggs, tarragon, salt and pepper, beat until tuna is finely flaked. Center a row of lemon slices in bottom of a 7⅜ × 3⅝ × 2¼-inch loaf pan. Spread thin layer of tuna mixture in pan; layer green beans lengthwise over tuna mixture, leaving spaces between beans. Spread thin layer of tuna over beans, pressing mixture between the beans. Arrange carrots lengthwise over tuna; cover with tuna mixture. Add peas; cover with tuna; press down firmly. Bake in a 375°F. oven 45 minutes. Cool and refrigerate several hours or until chilled through. Turn out onto serving plate; garnish with slivers of black olives.   *Yield: 6 to 8 appetizer servings*

Favorite recipe from **The Tuna Research Foundation Inc.**

SHRIMP COCKTAILS FOR FOUR

1 can (4½ ounces) **LOUISIANA BRAND Shrimp**
1 tablespoon lemon juice
Lettuce

Sauce:

⅔ cup chili sauce or tomato catsup
1 tablespoon prepared horseradish
1 tablespoon lemon juice
⅓ cup chopped celery

Drain shrimp. Cover with ½ cup cold water; add lemon juice. Refrigerate 2 hours or longer. Drain well; arrange in cocktail glasses on crisp lettuce. Combine sauce ingredients; serve over shrimp.

SHRIMP COCKTAIL

2 lbs. **ATALANTA Shrimp**, raw, shelled, deveined

Bring salted water (1 tsp. salt per quart of water) to a boil in a kettle. Add the shrimp. When water reboils cook shrimp 3-4 minutes. Chill and serve with cocktail sauce or Dill Sauce.*
                                        Yield: 8 Servings

*DILL SAUCE

1 cup Sour cream
1 tsp. Dried dill or 1 Tbsp. Fresh dillweed
3 Tbsp. Lemon juice

Mix well sour cream, dill and lemon juice.

SEVICHE

1 pound sole *or* haddock, fresh or frozen, thawed, cut
    into bite-size pieces
⅔ cup **REALIME® Lime Juice from Concentrate**
¼ cup sliced green onions
2 tablespoons chopped pimiento
2 tablespoons water
1 clove garlic, finely chopped
1 teaspoon salt
¼ teaspoon black pepper
Dash hot pepper sauce
2 cups shredded lettuce

In medium bowl, combine all ingredients except lettuce. Cover and refrigerate 6 hours or overnight. (**REALIME®** ''cooks'' fish.) Drain; serve on lettuce. Refrigerate leftovers.
                        Makes about 2 cups, 6 servings

First Course — Hot

GRAPEFRUIT DELUXE
(Low Calorie)

1 grapefruit
Artificial sweetener to equal 2 teaspoons sugar
¼ teaspoon cinnamon
¼ teaspoon **ANGOSTURA® Aromatic Bitters**

Cut grapefruit in half. Loosen each section from skin and membrane. Sprinkle sweetener, cinnamon and **ANGOSTURA® Bitters** over each half. Bake at 350° F. (moderate oven) for 4 minutes or until heated throughout.   *Yield: 2 Servings*

BROILED GRAPEFRUIT TOPPINGS

Top each **SUNKIST® Grapefruit** half with **one** of the following:

2 tsp. brown sugar
1 Tbsp. maple-flavored syrup *or* apricot preserves
2 tsp. orange, almond *or* coffee-flavored liqueur
2 tsp. sugar and 1 tsp. rum
2 tsp. sugar and dash ground cinnamon
1 Tbsp. *each* peanut butter and honey
1 Tbsp. *each* brown sugar and chopped nuts

Place in broiler 4 to 5 inches from source of heat. Broil until bubbly (cold broiler 6 to 8 minutes **or** preheated broiler 3 to 4 minutes).

BROILED GRAPEFRUIT

2 large grapefruit
½ cup light brown sugar, firmly packed
2 tablespoons butter, melted
⅓ cup **GIROUX® Grenadine Syrup**

Cut each grapefruit in half, crosswise. Pick out the seeds and cut out the core. Then, with a sharp knife, cut around each section to loosen the flesh from the membrane and skin. Sprinkle each half with brown sugar and butter. Finally, spoon some grenadine over each half. Place on a baking sheet and broil in a preheated broiler, under a moderate heat, about 10 minutes or until lightly browned. Serve at once for dessert or as a first course.

ROCK LOBSTER PETITES WITH CAPER MAYONNAISE

Drop 12 frozen **SOUTH AFRICAN ROCK LOBSTER Petites (2 oz. size)** into boiling salted water. When water reboils, cook tails 2 minutes. Drain immediately and drench with cold water. Cut away underside membrane and remove meat in one piece. Reserve shells. Cut rock lobster into crosswise slices. Arrange slices in shell. Mix ½ cup mayonnaise with ⅔ cup sour cream, and 3 tablespoons each of catsup and drained capers. Serve with petites.

Favorite recipe from **South African Rock Lobster Service Corp.**

CLAM FRITTERS

1 can (10-oz.) **BUMBLE BEE**® Whole Baby Clams
2 eggs, lightly beaten
½ cup milk
¾ cup flour
1 teaspoon baking powder
Salt and pepper to taste
Hot oil for sautéing
Tartar sauce

Drain clams, reserving ½ cup liquid. Mince clams. Combine clams, reserved liquid, eggs, milk, flour, baking powder, salt and pepper. Drop batter by one measuring tablespoon into hot oil. Brown 4 or 5 minutes, turning once. Serve with tartar sauce.

Makes 24 fritters or 4 servings

OLD BAY IMPERIAL CRAB

Mix together lightly with your hands, the following:

1 can (12-ounce) lump or flake crab meat
4 Tablespoons mayonnaise
1 teaspoon finely chopped parsley
1 Tablespoon finely chopped celery
Juice of one lemon
1 Tablespoon Worcestershire sauce
1 teaspoon prepared mustard
½ teaspoon grated lemon rind
½ teaspoon **BALTIMORE SPICE OLD BAY Seasoning**

Heat 2 teaspoons of butter or margarine and pour into crab mixture turning it lightly with a fork so that flakes do not break. Place in baking shells, dot with butter or margarine, sprinkle bread crumbs, add a pinch of paprika and a slice of bacon on top of each. Bake in a hot oven (400°F) until hot 'n bubbly (approximately 15 minutes).

KING CRAB ROYAL

10 to 12 ounces **ALASKA King Crab** split legs, thawed if necessary
¼ cup butter, melted
1 tablespoon lemon juice
2 teaspoons grated onion
1 clove garlic, crushed
1 tablespoon finely chopped parsley
¼ teaspoon *each* salt and crushed tarragon
Dash bottled hot pepper sauce

Remove crab meat from shells and cut into bite-size pieces for easier serving; return to shells. Combine remaining ingredients and brush over crab. Broil 3 to 5 inches from heat 3 to 4 minutes; brush occasionally with sauce.

Makes 4 main dish servings or 8 appetizer servings
Favorite recipe from the **Alaska Seafood Marketing Institute**

THE BROTHERS PRAWNS

1 large clove garlic, chopped
¼ medium onion, chopped
2 tablespoons olive oil
½ lb. prawns, shelled and deveined
Salt and pepper to taste
2 teaspoons flour
⅔ cup **THE CHRISTIAN BROTHERS**® Chablis
2 tablespoons **THE CHRISTIAN BROTHERS**® Brandy
2 tablespoons minced parsley

Sauté garlic and onion in olive oil over medium-high heat until limp. Add prawns and sauté over high heat for 1 minute or until pink. Season with salt and pepper. Add flour and toss to mix. Add chablis and brandy and boil, uncovered, 4 minutes or until sauce is reduced and glossy. Mix in parsley. *Makes 4 servings*

SEASHELL OYSTER APPETIZER

1 can (8 oz.) **BUMBLE BEE**® Whole Oysters
3 slices bacon
¼ cup chopped green onion
3 tablespoons bread crumbs
½ teaspoon paprika
⅛ teaspoon garlic powder

Drain oysters. Finely dice bacon. Combine oysters, bacon, green onion, bread crumbs, paprika and garlic powder. Spoon into 12 (3-inch) coquille shells or baking shells. Arrange on a jelly roll pan. Broil 4 inches from heat source 4 to 5 minutes.

Makes 12 appetizers

Appetizers — Hot

PAT BOUTONNET'S ARTICHOKE NIBBLES

2 (6-ounce) jars **CARA MIA Marinated Artichoke Hearts**
1 small onion, finely chopped
1 garlic clove, minced
4 eggs, beaten
¼ cup fine breadcrumbs
¼ teaspoon salt
⅛ teaspoon pepper
⅛ teaspoon oregano
⅛ teaspoon hot pepper seasoning
2 cups shredded sharp Cheddar cheese
2 tablespoons minced parsley

Preheat oven to 325°F. Drain marinade from 1 jar of artichoke hearts into medium skillet. Drain second jar and discard marinade (or reserve for use in salads). Chop artichokes and set aside.

Heat marinade; add onion and garlic and sauté until onion is limp, about 5 minutes. Combine eggs, breadcrumbs, salt, pepper, oregano and hot pepper seasoning. Fold in cheese and parsley. Add artichokes and sautéed onion mixture, blending well.

Pour into 9-inch square glass baking dish. Bake about 30 minutes. Allow to cool briefly before cutting into 1-inch squares. (Can also be served cold.) *4 to 6 servings*

Note: May be prepared a day or two ahead and reheated 10 to 12 minutes.

HIDDEN TREASURES

1 can (3 oz.) **BinB® Mushroom Crowns,**
  drained—reserving broth
1 package (10 oz.) refrigerated biscuits
¼ cup grated Parmesan cheese

Drain buttery broth from mushrooms. Reserve broth. Blot excess moisture from mushroom crowns with paper towels. Separate biscuits and cut each one into fourths. On floured board, press biscuit quarters into rounds and wrap one around each crown. Brush wrapped mushrooms with buttery broth and roll in Parmesan cheese. Bake on greased cookie sheet in preheated 400°F. oven for 10-12 minutes.   *Makes about 2 dozen appetizers*

FRENCH-FRIED MUSHROOMS

1 egg
½ cup evaporated milk
½ teaspoon salt
⅓ cup flour
1 cup packaged cornflake crumbs
40 medium DOLE® Fresh Mushrooms
Oil for frying
Lemony Tartar Sauce*

Beat egg, milk and salt until blended. Place flour and cornflake crumbs on separate pieces of waxed paper. Cut stems from mushrooms to ¼-inch. Save stems to use in soups, if desired. Roll mushrooms in flour, dip in egg mixture and roll in cornflake crumbs. Pour 1½ to 2 inches oil in electric skillet or heavy saucepan. Heat oil to 375°F. Gently drop mushrooms into hot oil a few at a time. Fry until golden, about 1 minute on each side. Remove with a slotted spoon and drain on paper towels. Serve with Lemony Tartar Sauce.   *Makes 40 hors d'oeuvres*

*LEMONY TARTAR SAUCE

¾ cup mayonnaise
¼ cup sweet pickle relish
1 tablespoon lemon juice
½ teaspoon dill weed

Combine all ingredients. Serve as a dip for French-Fried Mushrooms.

CHAFING DISH MUSHROOMS

½ cup butter
1½ pounds large mushrooms, stems removed
1 medium onion, chopped
2 teaspoons LAWRY'S® Garlic Salt
1 cup dairy sour cream
Paprika

Melt butter in electric skillet at 250°F. Add mushroom caps, round side up. Sprinkle Garlic Salt over mushrooms until completely covered (additional Garlic Salt may be needed); add onion; cover, leaving vent open. Simmer at 250°F 10 to 15 minutes, depending upon size of mushrooms. Stir once. Drain butter. Fold in sour cream and sprinkle with paprika. (The butter can be used to season another vegetable or to sauté the mushroom stems.)
    Makes 8 servings

MUSHROOM APPETIZER

¾ cup corn flake crumbs
2 teaspoons onion salt
2 egg whites, well beaten
¼ cup water
1 quart (about) MAZOLA® Corn Oil
½ pound fresh mushrooms, sliced

Mix together crumbs and onion salt. Mix together egg whites and water. Pour corn oil into heavy, sturdy, flat bottomed 3-quart saucepan or deep fryer, filling utensil no more than ⅓ full. Heat over medium heat to 375°F. Dip mushrooms in egg mixture and then coat with crumbs. Carefully add to oil in single layer. Fry 1 to 2 minutes or until crisp and lightly browned. Drain on absorbent paper. Serve hot.   *Makes about 45 appetizers*

FRENCH'S® STUFFED MUSHROOMS

30 large size fresh mushrooms (about 1 lb.)
Salt and FRENCH'S® Pepper
¼ cup minced green onions
¼ cup butter or margarine
¼ cup sherry
¼ cup water
¾ cup FRENCH'S® Big Tate Mashed Potato Flakes
⅓ cup grated Parmesan cheese
FRENCH'S® Paprika

Remove caps from mushrooms; arrange, hollow side up, in buttered shallow baking dish. Season with salt and pepper. Chop mushroom stems; cook, with onion, in the ¼ cup butter 4 to 5 minutes, until tender, stirring occasionally. Remove from heat; add sherry and water. Stir in potato flakes and cheese to make a stiff mixture. Place a generous spoonful in each mushroom cap; sprinkle with paprika. Bake in 375° oven 15 minutes, until hot. Serve as hors d'oeuvres.

MICROWAVE METHOD:
Mushrooms can be prepared and stuffed ahead of time. Refrigerate until serving time. Cover loosely with wax paper. Cook on HIGH 3 minutes; rotate pan ½ turn and cook 2 to 3 minutes, until piping hot.

PESTO STUFFED MUSHROOMS

12 large fresh mushrooms
6 oz. sweet Italian bulk sausage
1 clove garlic, minced
6-8 Tbsp. Pesto Butter*

Remove mushroom stems and chop fine; mix with sausage and garlic. Sauté, breaking into small bits with fork until meat is lightly browned. Heap each mushroom cap with sausage filling and top generously with Pesto Butter. Place in shallow baking pan. Bake in moderate oven 20 minutes.   *4-6 appetizer portions*

*PESTO BUTTER

Make a Pesto Butter simply by blending 3 parts **ARMANINO FARMS Freeze-Dried Pesto for Pasta** with 8 parts soft butter.

VARIATION:

Fill mushroom cavities with **ARMANINO FARMS Frozen** or **Freeze-Dried Pesto** prepared according to package directions and place in shallow baking pan. Bake at 350° for 15-20 minutes.

MUSHROOMS OF THE FOREST
(Champignons Du Bois)

18 medium-size mushrooms
3 Italian sausages
2 green onions, thinly sliced
1 Tbsp. olive oil
½ cup **PAUL MASSON®** Burgundy Wine
Salt and pepper to taste
Grated Parmesan cheese

Remove stems from mushrooms and set aside for other recipes. Gently clean mushroom caps. Remove sausage from casings and combine with remaining ingredients (not mushrooms or Parmesan) in saucepan. Cook over low heat for 5 minutes, stirring occasionally. Cool to room temperature and stuff mushrooms. Sprinkle with grated Parmesan, place on cookie sheet and broil 6 inches from heat until bubbly (about 3 minutes).

WASHINGTON POTATO SKINS

6 large (4 to 5 lbs.) **WASHINGTON RUSSET** Potatoes
Oil
¼ cup flour
Seasoned salt to taste

Scrub potatoes; rub lightly with oil. Pierce with fork. Bake at 400°F. 50 to 60 minutes or until tender. Cool. Cut potatoes in half lengthwise; scoop out pulp leaving ¼-inch shell. Pulp may be used for mashed potatoes or reserved for other use. Cut shells crosswise into 1-inch strips. Dip in flour; shake off excess. Deep-fry in oil heated to 375° F. 2 minutes or until lightly browned. Drain on absorbent paper towels. Sprinkle to taste with seasoned salt. Serve as an appetizer or accompany with dairy sour cream and minced green onion for dipping if desired.

Makes about 60 potato skins

To Reheat: Place fried skins on baking sheet. Bake at 375° F. about 10 minutes.

Favorite recipe from the **Washington State Potato Commission**

BAKED POTATO SKINS

4 baked potatoes
4 tablespoons melted butter or margarine
½ cup shredded Cheddar cheese
½ cup **DURKEE** Bacon Bits
½ cup sour cream

Cut baked potatoes into quarters lengthwise; scoop out pulp, leaving ¼-inch shell. Brush shells with melted butter. Bake shells at 350° for 10 minutes. Sprinkle with cheese and bacon bits. Bake just until cheese is melted, 1 to 2 minutes. Serve with a dollop of sour cream and a garnish of more bacon bits.

Makes 4 servings as a side dish or 16 hors d'oeuvres

ZUCCHINITIZERS

2 pounds small zucchini squash
¼ cup **SEAGRAM'S V.O.**
4 tablespoons flour
½ teaspoon salt
3 tablespoons butter
1 tablespoon salad oil
16 Melba rounds or crackers
Powdered tarragon

Wash but do not peel zucchini; discard stem ends. Cut into 16 slices; cover with **SEAGRAM'S V.O.** Let stand 1 hour; drain. Combine flour and salt; coat marinated zucchini slices. Heat butter and oil; sauté zucchini slices until golden on both sides. Place on Melba toast rounds or crackers; sprinkle with tarragon.

Makes 16

SPINACH BALLS

2 packages (10 ounces each) Frozen **STOKELY'S® Chopped Spinach**
2 medium-size onions, chopped
6 eggs, unbeaten
2 cups herb-seasoned stuffing mix
½ cup grated Parmesan cheese
¼ cup butter or margarine, melted
1 teaspoon salt
1 Tablespoon garlic salt
½ teaspoon thyme
Pepper to taste

Preheat oven to 350°F. Thaw spinach and place in large sieve. Drain spinach thoroughly, squeezing out as much water as possible. Add spinach to remaining ingredients; mix well. Shape mixture into balls the size of walnuts. Bake on greased jelly-roll pan 20 minutes. Serve promptly.

About 60 appetizers

Note: Spinach balls may be wrapped and frozen, then thawed 1 hour before baking.

FRIED CHEESE CUBES

Assorted natural cheeses, cut in ½-inch cubes*
Beaten egg
Fine dry bread crumbs
CRISCO® for deep frying

If using soft cheeses, shape crust around the soft center as much as possible. Dip cheese cubes in beaten egg, then coat with crumbs. Repeat dipping in egg and crumbs for a second layer. (A thick coating prevents cheese from leaking through during frying.) Fry, a few cubes at a time in deep **CRISCO®** heated to 365° till cubes are golden, about ½ minute. Serve warm.

*Use soft cheeses with a crust (Camembert or Brie), semi-hard cheeses (Bel Paese or brick), or hard cheeses (Cheddar, Edam, and Gouda).

CHEESY WALNUT PINWHEELS

1 cup **BISQUICK®** Baking Mix
¼ cup cold water
1 package (3 ounces) cream cheese, softened
1 tablespoon mayonnaise or salad dressing
¼ cup shredded Cheddar cheese
¼ cup finely chopped walnuts
2 tablespoons finely chopped onions

Mix baking mix and water until soft dough forms; beat vigorously 20 strokes. Gently smooth dough into ball on floured cloth-covered board. Knead 5 times. Roll dough into rectangle, 12 × 9 inches.

Mix remaining ingredients; spread over dough to within ¼ inch of edges. Roll up tightly, beginning at 12-inch side. Seal well by pinching edge of dough into roll. Wrap and refrigerate until thoroughly chilled, at least 2 hours.

Heat oven to 400°. Cut roll into ¼-inch slices. Arrange slices, cut sides down, on greased cookie sheet. Bake until golden brown, 10 to 12 minutes.

About 40 appetizers

BRIE EN CROÚTE

1 egg yolk
1 **PEPPERIDGE FARM®** Frozen "Bake It Fresh"
  Puff Pastry Sheet
2 small Brie or Camembert

Beat egg yolk with 1 tablespoon water. Thaw puff pastry 20 minutes, then unfold. Cut pastry sheet into 4 squares. Roll out 1 pastry square until it is approximately ½ inch larger than the circle of cheese. Place Brie in center of circle and trim edges leaving a ½ inch border. Brush border with egg mixture. Roll second square of pastry until it is large enough to fit over the cheese again allowing the ½ inch border. Place over the circle of cheese and press to seal. Repeat with remaining pastry and cheese. If desired, decorate with cutouts made from pastry scraps (heart-shapes, crescents, twists etc.) and apply with egg mixture.

Brush *top only* with egg and place on an ungreased cookie sheet in the middle of a preheated 375° oven. Bake for 20 minutes or until golden brown. Serve warm or at room temperature.

Makes 12 servings

TORTILLA CHEESE ROLLS

1 (5 oz.) jar process cheese spread with jalapeños
1½ cups (6 oz.) **SARGENTO Shredded Colby Cheese**
4 (8-inch) flour tortillas
1 (4 oz.) jar sliced pimientos, drained well
1 (4 oz.) can diced green chilies, drained

Combine cheeses in bowl or food processor fitted with plastic blade. Spread one tortilla evenly with ¼ of cheese mixture to within ½ inch of border. Top with second tortilla then spread with ¼ more of cheese mixture and sprinkle with ½ of green chilies and ½ of sliced pimientos. Roll tortillas as tightly as possible being careful not to let tortilla slide forward. Finished roll should be about 2 inches in diameter. Wrap tightly in foil.

Make second roll using remaining ingredients. Place wrapped rolls in refrigerator and chill at least 3 hours or overnight. Remove foil and slice rolls into ¼ inch thick rounds. Place on greased baking sheets and bake in 375° oven for 15 to 20 minutes, or until lightly crisp on top. *Makes about 24 appetizers*

WHEAT GERM HERB BALLS

1¾ cups unsifted **ROBIN HOOD®** All Purpose Flour
½ cup **KRETSCHMER** Regular Wheat Germ
2 cups grated sharp Cheddar cheese
1 cup softened butter or margarine
¾ tsp. thyme leaves, crushed
¼ tsp. dry mustard
Wheat germ for topping

Combine flour and ½ cup wheat germ on wax paper. Stir to blend. Beat cheese, butter, thyme and mustard together until well-blended. Add blended dry ingredients to cheese mixture, mixing to combine. Shape into 1-inch balls. Dip half of each ball in remaining wheat germ. Place dipped-side up on ungreased baking sheets. Bake at 400° for 10-12 minutes until lightly browned. Remove from baking sheet. Cool on rack. *Makes 4½ dozen appetizers*

BAKED APPETIZER TRAY

Put 1-16 oz. can of beanless chili into 8-inch cake pan. Top with 2 cups shredded Jack or Cheddar cheese. Surround with 12 to 36 **JENO'S®** Mexican Style Snack Rolls on a baking sheet. Bake at 375°F. for 15 minutes until Rolls sizzle and cheese is melted.

Serves 6 to 10

CHEESE BACON SNACKS

1 loaf **RHODES™** Frozen Bread Dough, thawed
⅓ cup butter or margarine, melted
2 cups shredded Cheddar or American cheese
½ pound fried bacon, crumbled

Let dough rise until almost doubled in size. Press into or roll out to fit greased 15 × 10-inch pan. Cover with melted butter. Sprinkle with cheese and bacon. Cover; let rise in warm place until light, about 30 minutes. Bake in a 375°F. oven for 20 to 25 minutes, or until golden brown. Cut into bars and serve warm.

SMOKE FLAVOR CHEESE AND BACON PINWHEELS

Trim the brown crust from an unsliced loaf of white bread. Slice bread lengthwise in ¼-inch strips.

Season a package of Cream Cheese with ½ teaspoon of **FIGARO LIQUID BARBECUE SMOKE**; add celery salt and garlic salt to taste. Blend well.

Spread mixture on bread strips; roll them like a jelly roll. Chill, then cut into one-inch slices. Surround each slice with a narrow strip of thin bacon. Toast in moderate oven until bacon is crisp.

EASY CHEESE FONDUE

1 clove garlic
1 cup **LANCERS®** Vinho Branco Wine
2 cups (½ lb.) grated sharp natural Cheddar cheese
2 cups (½ lb.) grated natural Swiss cheese
2 tablespoons flour
2 tablespoons **ARROW®** Kirsch Brandy
French bread, cut into bite-sized cubes

Rub fondue pot with garlic. Discard garlic. Pour wine into pot and heat until just simmering. Combine cheeses and flour. Sprinkle cheese, one handful at a time, into wine, stirring constantly until cheese is blended into a smooth sauce and bubbly. Stir in Kirsch. Spear bread, dip into fondue, and swirl in a figure 8 motion. If fondue should get too thick, thin with a little heated wine.

CHEESE FONDUE

1 clove garlic
¾ lb. Jarlsberg cheese, shredded
¾ lb. Gruyere cheese, shredded
1¼ cups **Soave BOLLA** Wine
3 tablespoons kirsch
3 teaspoons cornstarch
Dash nutmeg
French bread

Rub heavy saucepan and fondue pot with a garlic clove which has been sliced in half. In small container mix kirsch, cornstarch and nutmeg. Set aside. Heat wine in saucepan until it begins to bubble. Add cheese gradually, stirring constantly. Keep heat moderately high, but don't bring quite to boil. When cheese is melted, add kirsch mixture to it. Transfer the fondue to a fondue pot over low heat. It will thicken as it sets.

Never make ahead of time. Serve with French bread cut into 1-inch cubes with the crust on one side, and fondue forks.

BAKED SWISS CHEESE FONDUE
(Using Roman Meal® Bread)

3 Tbsp. margarine
⅓ cup chopped green pepper (½ medium pepper)
¼ cup chopped onion
3 Tbsp. flour
½ tsp. salt
¼ tsp. thyme
1½ cups milk
1 cup (4-oz.) shredded Swiss cheese
2 eggs, separated
3 cups cubed **ROMAN MEAL® Bread** (5–6 slices)
½ medium green pepper, cut in rings

Grease a 1½-quart casserole or spray with non-stick, vegetable oil. In 2-quart saucepan, melt margarine over medium heat; sauté chopped green pepper and onion until tender. Stir in flour, salt and thyme. Add milk gradually; cook until thick, stirring constantly. Add cheese, stir until melted. Remove from heat. Beat egg yolks slightly. Slowly stir ¼ cup hot sauce into yolks; return to sauce. Mix in bread cubes. Beat egg whites until stiff; fold into bread mixture. Pour into prepared baking dish; garnish with green pepper rings. Bake in moderate oven (325° F) about 45 minutes or until puffed and golden. Serve immediately.

Makes 5 cups. Serves 4 to 6

Nutrients per serving (⅕ recipe): 308 calories, 15g protein, 21g carbohydrates, 19g fat, 138 mg cholesterol, 588 mg sodium

CHICKEN KABOBS
(Yakitori)

3 pounds chicken breasts
1 pound chicken livers
1 bunch green onions, cut into 1-inch lengths
1 cup **KIKKOMAN Soy Sauce**
¼ cup sugar
1 tablespoon salad oil
2 cloves garlic, crushed
¾ teaspoon ground ginger (OR 1 tablespoon grated fresh ginger root)

Skin and bone chicken, keeping meat in one piece; cut into 1-inch lengths. Thread bamboo skewers each with a chicken piece, a green onion piece, and a chicken liver piece. Blend together soy sauce, sugar, oil, garlic and ginger. Place kabobs in large shallow baking pan; pour sauce over. Brush each kabob thoroughly with sauce. Marinate about 1 hour and remove; reserve marinade. Broil 5 inches below preheated broiler 3 minutes on each side, brushing with reserved marinade after turning.

Makes about 4 dozen appetizers

CHICKEN LIVERS HONG KONG
(Low Calorie)

1 pound (about 12) chicken livers
1 can (8 oz.) water chestnuts, drained and halved
2 tablespoons **LEA & PERRINS Worcestershire Sauce**
1 tablespoon dry sherry
1 tablespoon soy sauce
1 teaspoon garlic powder
½ teaspoon salt
¼ teaspoon ground ginger

Cut chicken livers in half; place in a medium bowl. Stir in remaining ingredients. Cover and refrigerate for 1 hour. On wooden picks skewer a piece of liver and a water chestnut half. Place on a rack in a broiler pan. Broil under a preheated hot broiler until cooked as desired, about 2 minutes on each side.

Calorie Count: About 58 calories per hors d'oeuvre

BARBECUED WINGS

1 pkg. **HOLLY FARMS® Chicken Wings**
1 16-oz. jar bottled BBQ sauce

Preheat oven to 350°F. Place wings in baking dish. Cover well with BBQ sauce. Cover and bake for 1 hour or until tender.

GLAZED MINI RIBS

6 pounds or 2 racks of spareribs
Water
1 jar (8.5-oz.) **SMUCKER'S Low Sugar Blackberry Spread**
¾ cup catsup
¼ cup bottled steak sauce
1 teaspoon dry mustard
1 clove garlic, minced

Have the butcher cut the ribs crosswise through the bones to form 2½-to-3-inch wide strips. Boil 3-4 quarts of water in large stockpot. Place the ribs in pot, making sure there is enough water to cover. Reduce heat to simmer; cover; simmer ribs over low heat until fork tender, about 25 minutes. Drain. (Ribs can be cooked ahead and refrigerated.) Just before serving, line two jelly-roll pans or broiler pans with foil. Cut strips of ribs into individual ribs. Arrange in a single layer in pans. Broil, 1 pan at a time, about 4 inches from heat source for 10 minutes, turning once.

Meanwhile, in a small saucepan, combine remaining ingredients for the glaze. Heat to boiling; simmer over low heat for 10 minutes. Brush ribs with glaze and continue to broil, turning and basting frequently, for about 5 more minutes.

Serve ribs in a chafing dish over a heat source or place on a plate and keep warm on an electric hot tray. *Makes 12 appetizers*

ORIENTAL RIBLETS

½ cup soy sauce
½ cup dry sherry
½ cup water
¼ cup brown sugar
2 tablespoons lemon juice
2 cloves garlic, crushed
1 capful **ADOLPH'S® 100% Natural Tenderizer—Seasoned**
2 pounds pork riblets, cut into individual ribs

In a large bowl, thoroughly blend first 7 ingredients. Add riblets, making certain marinade covers meat. Marinate 1 hour, turning occasionally. Broil 5 inches from heat about 8 minutes per side or until done. *Makes 6 servings as an appetizer*

APPETIZER SPARERIBS

2–3 lb. spareribs, cut into small serving size pieces
Garlic salt and pepper
¾ cup **IRISH MIST® Liqueur**
½ cup *each* catsup and **GREY POUPON Dijon Mustard**

Place spareribs, fat side up, on rack in shallow baking pan. Sprinkle with garlic salt and pepper. Bake in preheated 350°F oven 1 hour. While ribs are baking, mix remaining ingredients. Broil ribs, turning and basting frequently with sauce, 45 minutes or until tender and well glazed. *Serves 12*

SOUTH SEAS PORK TIDBITS

1 envelope **LIPTON® Onion Soup Mix**
3 tablespoons lime juice
2 tablespoons water
1 teaspoon ground ginger
1½ pounds boneless pork, thinly sliced and cut into
    1-inch squares

In large shallow baking dish, blend onion soup mix, lime juice, water and ginger; add pork. Cover and marinate in refrigerator, turning occasionally, 4 hours or overnight.

Remove pork, reserving marinade. Thread pork on 6-inch skewers; brush with marinade. Broil, turning occasionally, 15 minutes or until done.   *Makes about 6 dozen appetizers*

HOLIDAY MEATBALLS

Meatballs:
2 pounds lean ground beef
1 tablespoon seasoned salt
1 tablespoon brown sugar
¾ cup water
2 teaspoons lemon peel
1 8-oz. package **BORDO Imported Diced Dates**
Sauce:
3 10¾ oz. cans condensed tomato soup
1½ soup cans of water
¾ cup brown sugar
3 tablespoons lemon juice
1 8-oz. package **BORDO Imported Diced Dates**

Meatballs: Mix ground beef and remaining meatball ingredients until well blended and dates are dispersed through mixture. Set aside.

Sauce: Place tomato soup in a large (5-6 quart), heavy saucepan. Add water, brown sugar and lemon juice. Mix well. Bring to a slow boil, uncovered, over medium heat. Then simmer. Stir occasionally.

Using about 1 teaspoon of meat mixture, shape with hands into balls and drop into simmering liquid. Repeat until meat mixture is used. Simmer meatballs in sauce, uncovered, 15 minutes. Add dates. Mix carefully. Simmer an additional 15 minutes, stirring every 5 minutes, until sauce thickens.

Serves 8-10 as a hearty appetizer

ZIPPY MEATBALL APPETIZERS

1 egg, beaten
¾ cup soft bread crumbs (about 1 slice of bread)
¼ cup chili sauce
½ teaspoon salt
½ teaspoon instant minced onion
⅛ teaspoon garlic powder
¾ pound ground beef
⅓ cup **CRISCO®**
Bottle barbeque sauce

In a bowl, combine the egg, crumbs, chili sauce, salt, instant minced onion, and garlic powder. Add ground beef and mix thoroughly. Shape mixture into about 30 small meatballs. In large skillet, brown meatballs slowly on all sides in hot **CRISCO®**. Continue cooking till meatballs are done, shaking skillet to turn meatballs. Keep meatballs hot; serve on wooden picks and dip in warmed barbeque sauce.   *Makes about 30 meatballs*

SAUSAGE COCKTAIL BALLS

Mix 1 pound **TENNESSEE PRIDE® Hot Country Sausage** and 1 pound **TENNESSEE PRIDE® Mild Country Sausage**. Form sausage into bite-size balls. Set aside. Mix 1 cup currant jelly or apple jelly with ½ cup prepared mustard. Heat mixture until jelly is almost dissolved. Add sausage balls and simmer for 30 minutes. Serve with toothpicks.

COMFORT® MEAT BALLS

1 pound ground chuck
¾ cup herb seasoned stuffing
¼ cup chili sauce
1 egg, slightly beaten
¼ cup **SOUTHERN COMFORT®**
¼ teaspoon salt
2 tablespoons butter or margarine

Mix stuffing and salt into ground chuck. Combine egg, chili sauce and **SOUTHERN COMFORT®**. Pour mixture into meat and mix well. Form into small balls. Melt butter in large skillet. Brown meat balls on all sides over medium high heat. Turn heat down slightly; put lid on skillet and cook 5 minutes more.

SAUSAGE WITH HOT MUSTARD SAUCE

8 ounce package **SWIFT PREMIUM® BROWN 'N SERVE™ Sausage Links**

Cut sausage links into halves. Brown according to package directions. Keep hot on hot tray or in chafing dish. Spear sausage pieces with smooth wooden picks. Serve with Hot Mustard Sauce* for a dip.   *Yield: 20 appetizers*

*HOT MUSTARD SAUCE

2 tablespoons butter or margarine
1 tablespoon flour
½ teaspoon salt
⅛ cup water
1 beef bouillon cube
⅓ cup Dijon-style mustard
2 teaspoons horseradish
2 tablespoons sugar

Melt butter in a saucepan. Stir in flour and salt. Gradually add water. Add bouillon cube, mustard, horseradish and sugar. Stir and cook until sauce thickens.   *Yield: 1½ cups*

BARBECUED SAUSAGE SNACKS

2 (12-ounce) packages **BOB EVANS FARMS®**
    Sausage Patties
1 medium onion, diced
1 stalk celery, diced
2 Tbsp. dark brown sugar
2 Tbsp. cider vinegar
Pinch dried tarragon
½ cup chili sauce

Cook patties until done. Drain on absorbent paper and cut each patty into eight pieces. Keep warm, pour off drippings. Add remaining ingredients to pan and simmer five minutes, stirring occasionally. Add sausage tidbits and heat through. Serve hot with toothpicks.

SAUSAGE AND HORSERADISH CANAPÉS

16 slices white bread*
½ lb. **HILLSHIRE FARM**® **Polska Kielbasa** or **Smoked Sausage**, chopped
5 Tbsp. sour cream
2 to 3 Tbsp. prepared horseradish (to taste)
1 tsp. flour

CONVENTIONAL METHOD:
Cut 2 (2-inch) circles from each slice of bread, using biscuit cutter or juice glass. Toast 1 side of bread round under broiler. Meanwhile, mix together sausage, sour cream, horseradish, and flour. Spread untoasted side of each bread circle with sausage mixture. Bake at 450° for 10 minutes.   *Makes 32 canapés*

MICROWAVE METHOD:
Toast both sides of bread; microwave canapés, uncovered, HIGH, 2 to 2½ minutes, rotating dish once.

*Round Melba toast may be substituted; do not toast.

STEAMED MEAT-FILLED DUMPLINGS

1 lb. ground beef or pork
1 can (8-oz.) **LA CHOY**® **Water Chestnuts**, drained, chopped fine
¼ cup chicken broth
¼ cup cornstarch
¼ cup parsley, chopped fine
1 green onion, chopped fine
1 tablespoon sugar
1 tablespoon minced fresh or prepared ginger
1 tablespoon **LA CHOY**® **Soy Sauce**
1 teaspoon salt
1 teaspoon dry sherry
2 packages (1 lb. each) egg roll wrappers (available in freezer section of supermarkets)

Combine all ingredients except egg roll wrappers in large mixing bowl; blend well. Using sharp knife or kitchen scissors, trim corners from egg roll wrappers to make them round. Place 2 tablespoons meat mixture in center of each circle and gather up sides of egg roll wrapper about filling, twisting to seal. Flatten top slightly.

Arrange dumplings in steamer and steam over boiling water 25 to 30 minutes. Remove dumplings and place on serving platter. Serve hot.   *About 30 dumplings*

Note: Dumplings can be cooked ahead of time, refrigerated or frozen, and reheated over steam at serving time.

KIELBASA BITES

¾ cup chili sauce
¾ cup grape jelly
½ tsp. (scant) cinnamon
½ tsp. (scant) nutmeg
½ tsp. (scant) ginger
4 tsp. red wine
2 tsp. (heaping) prepared mustard
1½ tsp. soy sauce
1½ lb. **HILLSHIRE FARM**® **Polska Kielbasa**, cut into 1½-inch pieces

Mix together chili sauce, jelly, cinnamon, nutmeg, ginger, wine, mustard, and soy sauce in saucepan or chafing dish until mixture can be smoothly blended. Add **Polska Kielbasa** and heat until sausage is hot. Serve with toothpicks.   *Makes 48 pieces*

SAUSAGE ROLLUPS

1 (9-inch) **BANQUET**® **Frozen Pie Crust Shell**
½ pound bulk hot pork sausage

Pop frozen piecrust out of foil pan and place upside down on sheet of waxed paper to thaw, about 10 minutes. Flatten thawed pie crust by gently pressing down. Spread sausage evenly on top of crust to ½ inch from edge. Begin at one end and roll up pie crust jellyroll style. Cut off excess crust ½ inch from each end. Slice roll into ½-inch slices. Arrange slices with cut edge flat on cookie sheet. Bake in 350°F oven for 15 to 20 minutes, until crust is browned. Serve warm.   *Makes 12 pinwheel appetizers*

APPETIZER FRANKS WITH MUSTARD SAUCE

Mustard Sauce*
1 lb. **WILSON**® **Western Grillers** or **Jumbo Franks**

Prepare mustard sauce. Keep warm. Cut each frank into 6 pieces. Place in baking pan. Bake in 350°F oven 5 minutes or until heated through. Serve with toothpicks.   *48 appetizer servings*

*MUSTARD SAUCE

Place ¾ cup evaporated milk and ¼ lb. sliced American cheese in a small saucepan. Heat over medium heat, stirring constantly, until cheese is melted. Stir in ¼ cup prepared mustard until smooth. Keep warm.

SAUCY FRANKS

1 lb. **VIENNA BEEF**® **Cocktail Franks**
1 10½ oz. can condensed tomato soup
1 cup water
1 medium onion, chopped
½ tsp. salt
⅛ tsp. pepper

Preheat oven to 350°. Place franks in baking dish. Combine remaining ingredients and pour over franks. Bake, covered, 30 minutes.   *6 servings*

SAUCY BOURBON BITES

1 cup firmly-packed **COLONIAL**® **Light Golden Brown Sugar**
1 cup bourbon
1 cup chili sauce
2 pounds frankfurters, cut into bite-size pieces

Preheat oven to 325°. In 2-quart casserole, combine sugar, bourbon and chili sauce; stir in frankfurters. Bake, uncovered, 1½ hours, stirring once during baking. (OR, simmer in large skillet, on top of range, 30 to 45 minutes; stir occasionally.) Serve hot in chafing dish. Refrigerate leftovers.

Makes 8 dozen appetizers

Tip: Flavor is improved if made a day ahead; reheat before serving.

BARBECUE FRANK APPETIZERS

SWIFT PREMIUM® Franks
Thick Barbecue Sauce* or your favorite BBQ sauce

Cut franks into bite-size pieces. Insert a smooth wooden pick into each piece. Heat in Thick Barbecue Sauce in a chafing dish. Or, place hot barbecue sauce in small bowl and use as a dip for the frank bites.

*THICK BARBECUE SAUCE

2 small onions, finely chopped
2 tablespoons vinegar
2 tablespoons Worcestershire sauce
1 teaspoon chili powder
¾ cup catsup
¾ cup water
½ teaspoon salt

Combine all ingredients in a skillet. Cover and simmer about 30 minutes. Remove cover and simmer 10 to 15 minutes or until thick. *Yield: About 1 cup sauce*

NACHOS

*FRESH AZTECA® NACHO CHIPS

Cut **AZTECA® Corn Tortillas** into quarters and let dry in open air at least ½ hour. Fry in ¼″ hot oil or deep fat fry until golden brown.

NACHOS CON QUESO

Place fresh **AZTECA®** Nacho Chips on a cookie sheet. Top each with 1 Tbsp. shredded Cheddar and a small piece of canned jalapeño pepper. Heat 350° for 3 minutes.

NACHO REFRITO

Place fresh **AZTECA®** Nacho Chips on a cookie sheet. Spread with refried beans. Top with 1 Tbsp. shredded Cheddar, piece of jalapeño and a dab of sour cream. Heat 350° for 3 minutes.

NACHOS RANCHERO

Place fresh **AZTECA®** Nacho Chips on a cookie sheet. Top each with 1 tsp. Salsa Ranchero* and 1 Tbsp. shredded Cheddar. Heat 350° for 3 minutes.

SALSA RANCHERO

Melt in Saucepan:

    3 Tbsp. melted butter or margarine

Fry: 1 clove garlic, minced
      1 green pepper, seeded and chopped
      1 medium onion, chopped

Add: 1 16 oz. can tomatoes
      1 jalapeño pepper (canned), rinsed in cold water and
         chopped
      ¼ tsp. salt
      Dash fresh ground pepper

Cook 15 minutes. This sauce can be used as a dip for fried tortilla chips. Store in refrigerator.

LA COCINA® CHILI CHIP NACHOS

Just spread **LA COCINA®** Chili Chips in a shallow baking dish or on a cookie sheet, and top with a generous portion of **LA COCINA®** Aged Cheddar Cheese Sauce (and **LA COCINA®** Sliced Jalapeño Peppers for extra spicy flavor if you wish); place under the broiler until the cheese is bubbling.

BEAN DIP NACHOS

1 10½-ounce can **FRITOS®** Brand Jalapeño Bean Dip
DORITOS® Brand Tortilla Chips
Jalapeño peppers, sliced
Sharp Cheddar cheese, sliced or coarsely grated

Spread **DORITOS®** Brand Tortilla Chips with **FRITOS®** Brand Jalapeño Bean Dip. Arrange on baking sheet. On each chip place a slice or mound of grated cheese. Top with slice of jalapeño pepper. Bake at 400°F. until cheese melts. Serve hot.

QUESADILLA SUPREMO

Mix together ½ cup shredded lettuce with ½ cup of your favorite guacamole or the tasty guacamole recipe that follows. Set aside.

Butter one side of **VAN DE KAMP'S®** Flour Tortilla and toast under broiler. When tortilla is a crisp golden brown on top, remove from oven and turn it over. Top with 2 cups grated Monterey Jack cheese and sprinkle with 1 tablespoon *each* of diced green chiles, pimiento and bell pepper. Place under broiler until cheese is melted. Cut into 8 pie-shaped pieces and top center with guacamole. Garnish with a black olive.

EASY GUACAMOLE

Combine 1 mashed avocado, ¼ cup sour cream, ¼ cup green chili salsa (sauce), ½ teaspoon lemon juice, pinch of salt and a pinch of garlic powder. Stir until smooth. Serve with the Quesadilla, your favorite chips or taquitos.

PICCOLO PIZZA TARTS

1 8-oz. container butterflake-type dinner rolls
¾ cup tomato sauce
1 cup mozzarella cheese, shredded
2 3½ oz. packages **HORMEL** Sliced Pepperoni
Small muffin tin, cups 1½″ × 1″

Heat oven to 375°. For each tart remove two layers from rolls. Flatten in hand and gently pull out to a 4″ circle. Ease into muffin cups. To each cup add 1 tsp. sauce, 2 pepperoni halves crisscrossed and 1 tsp. cheese. Top with two pepperoni halves, crisscrossed. Bake for 18-20 minutes, until deep golden brown on tops and sides of tarts. Remove from oven. Let cool slightly in tins for 5-10 minutes. Serve warm.

HAPPY HOUR PIZZA

1 jar (14 oz.) **RAGÚ'®** Pizza Quick Sauce, with Mushrooms
24 slices cocktail rye bread (2″ diameter), lightly toasted
6 slices cooked, crumbled bacon
⅔ cup (about 3 oz.) crumbled blue cheese
¼ cup sliced Spanish olives

Preheat broiler. Spoon 1 teaspoon **Pizza Quick Sauce** onto each bread slice. Evenly top with bacon, blue cheese and olives. Broil 5″ from heat 5-6 minutes or until cheese melts.

Makes 24 appetizers

RUMAKI

¾ lb. chicken livers
Canned water chestnuts
1 Tbsp. soy sauce
1 cup **THE CHRISTIAN BROTHERS®** Ruby Port
Bacon slices, cut in half

Cut livers into bite-size pieces; cut water chestnuts in half. Marinate for one hour or more in combined soy sauce and wine. Wrap bacon around liver and water chestnut; secure with wooden toothpick. Broil slowly until crisp. May be assembled ahead of time.
20-24 appetizers

NEW YEAR'S DATE RUMAKI

2 dozen **SUN WORLD®** Pitted Dates
Soy sauce
1 dozen water chestnuts
12 slices bacon

Marinate dates in soy sauce for 1-2 hours. Wrap one date and ½ water chestnut in half a bacon slice. Fasten with wooden pick. Broil until bacon is done. Serve hot as appetizers.

STICKS RUMAKI

1 pkg. **TYSON® CHICK'N QUICK™** Chick'n Sticks
Water chestnuts, sliced
Bacon slices
Soy sauce

Cook Chick'n Sticks according to package directions. Cube sticks and marinate with water chestnut slices in soy sauce for 5 minutes. Top each cube with a water chestnut slice and wrap with bacon. Broil 10 minutes.
Makes approximately 36 pieces

ELEGANT CRAB MEAT BALLS

2 cans (6 to 7 ounces each) crab meat
1 cup fresh bread crumbs
3 tablespoons **HOLLAND HOUSE®** Sherry Cooking
  Wine
1 tablespoon lemon juice
1 tablespoon grated onion
1 teaspoon dry mustard
½ teaspoon salt
Pepper to taste
Bacon slices (about 12), cut in halves

Drain and flake crab meat; combine with remaining ingredients except bacon; mix well. Shape into walnut-size balls. Wrap with bacon; secure with toothpicks. Broil under medium heat until bacon is crisp, about 10 minutes, turning to brown evenly. Garnish with parsley and lemon.
Makes about 2 dozen

JAC KING KRAB GARLIC BUTTER HORS D'OEUVRE

1 (6-oz.) package **JAC King Krab Simulated Crab
  Legs**
2 Tbsp. unsalted butter
Dash of garlic salt
1 Tbsp. Parmesan cheese
1 tsp. lemon juice (fresh)
½ tsp. finely chopped parsley

Heat skillet to 175°. Cut **JAC King Krab Simulated Crab Legs** into 1-inch pieces. Melt butter in a skillet and add diced **King Krab** and heat until warm. Sprinkle garlic salt to taste, follow with lemon juice and Parmesan cheese. Heat for approximately 1 minute, sprinkle with fresh chopped parsley and serve at once.
Serves 6

HONEY-BUTTER SCALLOPS

1 package (7 ounces) **MRS. PAUL'S®** Light Batter
  Scallops
¼ cup butter
¼ cup honey

Prepare **MRS. PAUL'S®** Light Batter Scallops as directed on package. Heat butter and honey in small saucepan until melted. Add cooked **MRS. PAUL'S®** Light Batter Scallops. Stir until scallops are coated. Remove scallops with toothpicks and serve immediately.

SHRIMP TURNOVERS

2 tablespoons butter
¼ cup chopped scallions
2 cloves garlic, minced
⅛ teaspoon ground black pepper
1 pound raw shrimp, cleaned and finely chopped
¼ cup **Manto Liqueur** by **METAXA®**
1 tablespoon fine dry bread crumbs
5 sheets filo pastry (16" × 12")
PLANTERS Peanut Oil

Melt butter in a large skillet over medium heat. Add scallions, garlic and pepper; sauté 1 to 2 minutes. Mix in shrimp and sauté until pink and liquid in skillet evaporates; stir occasionally. Remove from heat. Add **Manto Liqueur** by **METAXA®** and bread crumbs; toss lightly.

Cut each sheet of filo pastry into five 12-inch long strips. (Keep filo pastry strips covered with a damp cloth to prevent drying while shaping turnovers.) Place a rounded teaspoon of shrimp filling at end of each strip. Fold one corner of each strip over filling, bringing corner to opposite side of strip. Continue folding entire length of strip to encase filling in triangular shaped turnovers. Moisten edges of pastry triangles with water to seal.

Deep fry in **PLANTERS Peanut Oil** that has been heated to 400° F. for 3 minutes, or until golden. Serve immediately. Garnish with scallion brushes if desired.
Makes 25 turnovers

SHRIMP MIAMI

2 pounds shrimp, fresh or frozen
¼ cup olive or salad oil
2 teaspoons salt
½ teaspoon white pepper
¼ cup extra dry vermouth
2 tablespoons lemon juice

Thaw frozen shrimp. Peel shrimp, leaving the last section of the shell on. Remove sand, veins and wash. Preheat electric frying pan to 320°F. Add oil, salt, pepper, and shrimp. Cook for 8 to 10 minutes or until shrimp are pink and tender, stirring constantly. Increase temperature to 420°F. Add vermouth and lemon juice. Cook one minute longer, stirring constantly. Drain. Serve hot or cold as an appetizer or entree.
Makes 6 servings

Favorite recipe from the **Gulf and South Atlantic Fisheries Development Foundation, Inc.**

MANDARIN SHRIMP

½ lb. **ATALANTA Frozen Shrimp**, raw, shelled, deveined
½ lb. Mandarin orange sections
¼ cup scallions, ½ inch pieces
¼ cup butter, melted

On skewers, alternate shrimp, orange section, scallion and shrimp. Brush with butter and broil 4 minutes on each side.

Yield: 6 Servings

SEAFOOD HORS D'OEUVRES

1 package (7 ounces) **MRS. PAUL'S® French Fried Scallops** or
1 package (6 ounces) **MRS. PAUL'S® French Fried Shrimp**
1 pound sliced bacon, partially cooked

Prepare **MRS. PAUL'S® French Fried Scallops** or **French Fried Shrimp** as directed on package. Wrap each scallop or shrimp with one slice of bacon. Secure with toothpick. Broil approximately 6-8 inches from heat source for about 1 minute on each side or until bacon is crisp. Watch closely so bacon will not burn.

TUNA CHILI CON QUESO

1 tablespoon butter or margarine
¼ cup chopped onion
1 can (1 pound) tomatoes, drained and cut up
1 bay leaf
2 tablespoons flour
¼ cup milk
1 can (4 ounces) green chilies, drained, seeded, and chopped
1 cup (4 ounces) shredded Monterey Jack or mild Cheddar cheese
1 can (6½ or 7 ounces) **STAR-KIST® Tuna**, drained
¼ teaspoon salt
Corn Chips

Melt butter in a medium saucepan. Sauté onion until tender. Add tomatoes and bay leaf. Simmer 5 minutes, stirring occasionally. Mix flour and milk to make a paste. Add to saucepan. Simmer 5 minutes. Remove bay leaf. Add green chilies and cheese. Stir until cheese melts. Stir in **STAR-KIST® Tuna** and salt. Keep warm and serve with corn chips.

Yield: about 2½ cups

Appetizers — Cold

GALLO® SALAME AND TROPICAL FRUIT TRAY

24 slices **GALLO® Italian Dry Salame**
8 oz. cream cheese, at room temperature
⅓ cup sour cream
2 Tbsp. each chopped shallots or green onions and chopped parsley
Salt and pepper to taste
Dash **TABASCO® Sauce**
1 large pineapple
2 papayas
1 basket of strawberries
4 bananas
1 lime, cut in wedges

Beat until blended cream cheese, sour cream, shallots, parsley, salt and pepper to taste, and **TABASCO®**. Spread spoonful on one side of each **GALLO® Salame** slice and roll to form cone shapes. Skewer with toothpicks and place at end of tray. Peel and slice pineapple (into spears), papaya, and banana (diagonally). Clean strawberries. Arrange fruits on the tray with **GALLO® Italian Dry Salame**. Garnish with lime wedges.

Serves 6 to 8

COCKTAIL TOSTADAS
(Tohs-Tah-Dahs)

Small round fried corn tortillas (3 inch) or packaged tortilla chips
1 can refried beans
1 lb. **JIMMY DEAN® Taco Filling**
Guacamole
2 large tomatoes
Shredded lettuce
Parmesan or other grated cheese
Jalapeños, sliced

Optional (additional garnishes):
Sour cream
Taco sauce or picante sauce

Brown taco filling as directed. Drain on paper towels. Spread on each tortilla about 1 Tbsp. refried beans. Top with 1 Tbsp. meat mixture. Add a few pieces of tomato, a layer of lettuce and a mound of guacamole. Garnish with cheese and a slice of jalapeño. Add sour cream and taco or picante sauce if desired.

CHEESE STICKS OLÉ

2 sticks pie crust mix
4-oz. (1 cup) shredded **FISHER Cheese's TACO-MATE®**
¼ tsp. dry mustard
2 tsp. paprika

Prepare pie crust mix according to package directions. Stir in remaining ingredients until mixture forms a ball. Roll out on floured surface to 16 x 12 x ¼-inch rectangle. Cut into sticks ½-inch wide and 4-inches long. Place on ungreased baking sheet. Bake in hot oven (425°) for 10 to 12 minutes or until golden brown. Remove from baking sheet; cool.

Makes 96 sticks

MEXICAN CUCUMBER STICKS

Peel 1 **CALAVO®-BURNAC Cucumber** cut in half. Put a stick through each piece of cucumber (sucker-wise), dip in lemon juice, sprinkle with salt & roll in a mixture of cayenne pepper, paprika and chili powder.

STUFFED CELERY

2 packages (3 oz. each) cream cheese
½ cup **SKIPPY® Creamy** or **Super Chunk Peanut Butter**
¼ cup sesame seeds, toasted
2 teaspoons milk
2 teaspoons soy sauce
¼ teaspoon ground ginger
Celery stalks

In small bowl stir cream cheese and peanut butter until blended; mix in sesame seeds, milk, soy sauce and ginger. Stuff celery stalks and cut to desired size.

Makes about 1½ cups

Note: May also be served as a spread on crackers.

STUFFED CELERY ELITE

1 5-ounce jar bacon-cheese spread
1 package **FRITO-LAY® Brand Green Onion Dip Mix**
4 celery sticks

Combine cheese spread with **FRITO-LAY® Brand Green Onion Dip Mix**. (If mixture is too firm to spread, thin with 1 to 2 tablespoons milk.) Fill celery sticks with cheese spread. Chill and cut into desired lengths.

BUDDIG STUFFED CELERY

1 3-ounce package cream cheese, softened
2 tablespoons blue cheese, crumbled
1 tablespoon cream
¼ cup chopped **BUDDIG Smoked Sliced Beef** or **Ham**
Celery sticks

Combine all ingredients, except celery. Dry celery and fill with beef mixture.

SAVORY STUFFED MUSHROOMS

24 medium mushrooms
⅓ cup seeded and finely chopped tomato
¼ cup finely chopped green pepper
2 tablespoons sliced scallions
⅓ cup low-calorie Italian dressing
SNACK MATE Chive 'n Onion or **Cheese 'n Bacon Pasteurized Process Cheese Spread**

1. Remove stems from mushroom caps; chop stems and blend with tomato, green pepper and scallions. Place mushroom caps and vegetable mixture in baking dish.
2. Pour dressing over mushroom caps and vegetable mixture. Cover and refrigerate at least 4 hours or overnight, turning mushroom caps occasionally. Drain caps on paper towels before stuffing.
3. Spoon vegetable mixture evenly into mushroom caps. Garnish with **SNACK MATE Cheese**.   *Makes 24 mushrooms*

MILLIONAIRE MUSHROOMS

1 can (3 oz.) **BinB® Mushroom Crowns**, drained
1 jar (6 oz.) marinated artichoke hearts, undrained
1 tablespoon chopped pimiento

Combine crowns, artichoke hearts with liquid and pimiento. Cover and chill overnight; stir now and then. Drain and serve with wooden picks.

MUSHROOM HORS D' OEUVRES

⅓ cup rice wine vinegar
1 tablespoon sugar
2 teaspoons **KIKKOMAN Soy Sauce**
Dash monosodium glutamate
1 can (4 oz.) whole mushrooms, drained
Toasted sesame seed

Thoroughly combine vinegar, sugar, soy sauce and monosodium glutamate. Pour over mushrooms and sprinkle with sesame seed. Marinate 30 to 60 minutes. Remove from sauce and serve with wooden picks. OR: Pour sauce over drained whole water chestnuts; marinate overnight in refrigerator.

Makes about 2 dozen appetizers

TOMATO TEASERS

1 pint cherry tomatoes
½ pound bacon, cooked and crumbled
¼ teaspoon **TABASCO®**

Cut out small hole in the top of each tomato. Combine crumbled bacon with **TABASCO®**. Spoon bacon mixture into tomatoes. Serve with food picks.   *Yield: About 24 tomatoes*

TINY TOMATO PLEASERS

½ cup **SHOAL LAKE Pure Canadian Wild Rice**
1 pint cherry tomatoes
3-4 strips bacon
¼ teaspoon **TABASCO®** (optional)
½ cup mayonnaise

Cook wild rice according to basic package directions. Fry bacon crisp. Drain and crumble. Cut out small hole in top of each tomato and scoop out center. Combine bacon, wild rice, mayonnaise, and **TABASCO®**. Spoon mixture into tomatoes, serve on lettuce bed.

Fills 20-24 tomatoes

CANAPÉ A LA CAVALIER

Upon white bread, cut in fancy shapes, spread a mixture of equal parts of **AMBER BRAND Deviled SMITHFIELD Ham** and **PHILADELPHIA BRAND Cream Cheese**. Decorate with slices of stuffed green olives.

WATER CHESTNUT CANAPÉS

1 package **FRITO-LAY® Brand Garlic and Onion Dip Mix**
1 3-ounce package cream cheese, softened
¼ cup milk
¼ cup diced green pepper
¼ cup diced pimiento
¼ cup chopped slivered almonds
½ cup diced cooked chicken or turkey breasts
1 8-ounce can whole water chestnuts

Drain chestnuts and slice. Combine **FRITO-LAY® Brand Garlic and Onion Dip Mix**, cream cheese and milk. Add pepper, pimiento, almonds, chicken or turkey. Mix well. Place mounds of mixture on top of each chestnut slice. Chill and serve cold.

Makes 30 appetizers

CAVIAR CROÛTES

14 slices regular white bread
Softened butter or margarine
1 pkg. (3 oz.) cream cheese and chives, softened
3 Tbsp. (1½ oz.) **ROMANOFF® Caviar***
2 tsp. lemon juice
14 pimiento strips

With two-inch biscuit cutter, cut out two rounds from each bread slice. Spread half the slices with soft butter. With one-inch cutter, cut out center of remaining rounds. Place one rim on each whole round and spread with butter. Place on cookie sheet; bake at 400°F (hot oven) about ten minutes until browned. Cool. Divide cheese into centers. Combine caviar and lemon juice and spoon over cheese. Garnish with pimiento.   *Makes 14*

***ROMANOFF® Red Salmon Caviar** suggested.

CELERY AND EGGS

2 cups finely chopped celery with leaves
6 hard-boiled eggs, chopped
3 tablespoons oil
1 teaspoon salt
¼ teaspoon pepper
1 small onion, chopped
Paprika
SUNSHINE® Crackers

Combine first six ingredients, and mix. Chill and serve, topped with paprika, on assorted **SUNSHINE® Crackers.**

DANISH CHIPWICH

1⅓ cups crab meat (flaked fine)
¼ cup mayonnaise
¼ cup finely chopped pickled onions
Hard cooked egg
Green pepper
Olives
Large **JAYS Potato Chips**

Stir mayonnaise and onions into crab meat. Spread on large crisp Potato Chips and garnish with olive slices or green pepper strips and hard cooked egg slices.

ANCHOVY CANAPÉ

HI HO CRACKERS®
Anchovy paste
Thinly sliced fresh mushrooms
Lemon juice
Anchovy filets
Minced chives

Spread crackers with layer of anchovy paste. Add a layer of mushrooms that have been marinated in lemon juice. Place anchovy filet on top. Sprinkle with chives. Serve on **HI HO CRACKERS®.**

CHEESY CUCUMBER APPETIZERS

Spread Milwaukee party rye slices with **KAUKAUNA® Cheese Garden Vegetable Buttery Spread™**. Top each with cucumber slice. Sprinkle with snipped fresh chives or parsley.

SALMON CANAPÉS
(Low Calorie)

½ cup canned red salmon, drained and flaked
1 tablespoon low calorie mayonnaise
⅛ teaspoon dill weed
12 **OLD LONDON® Melba Rounds**
3 slices **BORDEN® LITE-LINE® Pasteurized Process Cheese Product**, quartered
12 thin slices cucumber
Parsley

In small bowl, combine salmon, mayonnaise and dill; mix well. On top of each Melba round, place a cheese product piece, a cucumber slice, 2 teaspoons salmon mixture and parsley. Serve immediately. Refrigerate leftovers.   *Makes 12 snacks*

Calories: Prepared as directed, provides approximately 440 or 36 per snack. (Values by product analyses and recipe calculations.)

CRACKER TOPPINGS

HAM 'N CHEESE

Top **SOCIABLES Crackers** with small ham rolls and sliced olives. Garnish with **SNACK MATE Sharp Cheddar Pasteurized Process Cheese Spread.**

HARVEST SQUARES

Top **TRISCUIT Wafers** with thin slices of red and yellow apples. Garnish with **SNACK MATE Cheese 'n Bacon Pasteurized Process Cheese Spread.**

FRUIT 'N CHEESE SPECIAL

Top **ESCORT Crackers** with Mandarin orange segments and halved green grapes. Garnish with **SNACK MATE American Pasteurized Process Cheese Spread.**

SHRIMPLY DELICIOUS

Top **Buttery Flavored Sesame Snack Crackers** with thin cucumber slices and cooked small shrimp. Garnish with **SNACK MATE Chive 'n Green Onion Pasteurized Process Cheese Spread.**

BACON 'N EGG

Top **SESAME WHEATS Snack Crackers** with crumbled cooked bacon, chopped hard-cooked egg and parsley sprigs. Garnish with **SNACK MATE Cheddar Pasteurized Process Cheese Spread.**

CANAPÉ AND SANDWICH SPREAD

1½ cups finely chopped cooked **SOUTH AFRICAN ROCK LOBSTER Meat** (6-2 oz. tails)
⅓ cup celery, finely chopped
1½ tablespoons drained sweet pickle relish
6 stuffed olives, finely chopped
2 tablespoons chives
2 teaspoons lemon juice
2 hard-cooked eggs, finely chopped
1 teaspoon salt
Pepper to taste
½ cup mayonnaise

Mix all ingredients and chill.

Yield: Enough spread for 8 sandwiches or 24 canapés

EGG AND BEET STACK-UPS
(Low Calorie)

1 medium hard-cooked egg, sliced
8 **OLD LONDON® Melba Rounds**
2 slices **BORDEN® LITE-LINE® Pasteurized Process Cheese Product**, quartered
8 slices pickled beets, well drained
Parsley

On top of each Melba round, layer a cheese product piece, a beet slice, an egg slice and parsley. Serve immediately. Refrigerate leftovers.   *Makes 8 snacks*

Calories: Prepared as directed, provides approximately 277 or 35 per snack. (Values by product analyses and recipe calculations.)

MOCK HERRING
(Low Calorie/Low Fat)

2 medium onions, sliced
2 stalks celery, cut into 1-inch pieces
1 small eggplant, peeled and cut into long strips, 1-inch wide
1 cup plain low-fat yogurt
1 tablespoon lemon juice
1 packet SWEET 'N LOW®
¼ teaspoon salt
⅛ teaspoon ground cloves
1 bay leaf

Steam onions and celery in vegetable steamer over boiling water 5 to 6 minutes. Add eggplant and steam about 5 minutes, or until soft but not mushy. Remove vegetables to bowl and set aside to cool. In separate bowl, combine remaining ingredients; mix gently with cooled vegetables. Remove bay leaf. Chill thoroughly. Serve on whole-grain bread or crackers. *About 3½ cups*

Per Serving (⅓ cup): Calories: 30; Fat: 1g

ROQUEFORT COCKTAIL BALLS

¼ lb. ROQUEFORT Cheese
1 tablespoon chopped celery
1 tablespoon chopped scallions
½ cup sour cream
Paprika

In an electric blender or with a fork, blend **ROQUEFORT Cheese**, celery, scallions and sour cream. Shape into small balls, the size of a walnut, and sprinkle with paprika. Chill.
Makes about 2 dozen balls

Favorite recipe from the **Roquefort Association, Inc.**

ALMOND PEPPERONI CHEESE BALL

8 oz. cream cheese
10 oz. Cheddar cheese spread
2 Tbsp. sour cream
18 slices HORMEL Pepperoni
Sliced almonds for garnish

Mix together softened cream cheese, Cheddar spread and sour cream. On waxed paper form mixture into a ball. Add in 12 slices of pepperoni chopped into eighths. Garnish with whole pepperoni slices and almonds thrust into ball.

CHEESE BALL

Two 8-oz. pkg. cream cheese, softened
2 cups (8 oz.) shredded Swiss cheese
One 8-oz. can crushed pineapple, well drained
3 crisply cooked bacon slices, crumbled
¼ cup finely chopped celery
1 teaspoon Worcestershire sauce
¼ teaspoon salt
1 cup QUAKER® 100% Natural Cereal, coarsely crushed

Beat together cream cheese and Swiss cheese, mixing until well blended. Stir in pineapple, bacon, celery, Worcestershire sauce and salt; mix well. Chill until firm. Shape to form 1 large or 2 small balls; chill. Just before serving, roll ball in cereal, coating well. Serve with crackers or raw vegetables, as desired.
Makes about 12 servings

SAUSAGE CREAM CHEESE BALLS

4 oz. JIMMY DEAN® Sausage
8 oz. cream cheese
1 tablespoon chopped green olives
Parmesan cheese

Crumble and slowly cook sausage over medium heat in skillet. Drain off excess fat. Mix cooked sausage with cream cheese. Add chopped olives. Form into bite-size balls. Roll in Parmesan cheese. Serve on toothpicks.
Makes approximately 1½ dozen balls

BEEFY CHEESE BALL

1 2½-oz. jar ARMOUR STAR® Sliced Dried Beef, rinsed, finely chopped
1 8-oz. pkg. cream cheese, softened
¼ cup dairy sour cream
¼ cup grated Parmesan cheese
1 teaspoon prepared horseradish
Assorted crackers

Combine ¼ cup dried beef, cream cheese, sour cream, Parmesan cheese and horseradish; blend thoroughly. Refrigerate mixture 15 minutes. Form into ball and roll in remaining dried beef. Chill thoroughly. Serve as an appetizer with crackers.

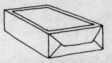

SESAME CHEESE LOG*

1 package (8 oz.) cream cheese, softened
1 package (4 oz.) blue cheese, crumbled
½ cup butter or margarine, softened
½ cup chopped pitted green olives
2 tablespoons LEA & PERRINS Worcestershire Sauce
1 tablespoon chopped chives
1 tablespoon chopped parsley
¼ cup toasted sesame seed

In a small mixing bowl combine all ingredients except sesame seed; blend well. Shape into a log or ball; roll in sesame seed. Chill. Serve as an hors d'oeuvre with assorted crackers.
Yield: 1 cheese log

Note: To toast sesame seed sprinkle seeds in a shallow baking pan. Place in a preheated moderate oven (375° F.) for 8 to 10 minutes or until golden, tossing occasionally.

*May be prepared in advance of serving.

PISTACHIO SHERRY CHEESE BALL

3 cups (about 12-oz.) shredded sharp Cheddar cheese
1 package (8-oz.) cream cheese, softened
1 to 2 tablespoons dry sherry
1 teaspoon Dijon mustard
3 drops bottled hot pepper sauce
¼ cup chopped shelled Pistachios from California
Crackers or vegetable slices

Combine cheeses, sherry, mustard and hot pepper sauce in mixer bowl; beat until thoroughly combined. Chill about ½ hour or until firm enough to handle. Form into ball; roll in pistachios. Serve with crackers or vegetables. *Makes one 4-inch ball*

Favorite recipe from **California Pistachio Commission**

DILLED CHICKEN AND CHEESE BALL

1 package (8-ounces) cream cheese, softened
1 can (5-ounces) SWANSON Mixin' Style Chicken
⅓ cup finely chopped cucumber
¼ cup chopped green onions
2 tablespoons finely chopped green pepper
1 teaspoon lemon juice
¼ teaspoon dried dill weed, crushed
½ cup chopped parsley

In bowl, beat cheese until smooth; stir in remaining ingredients except parsley. Shape into ball; roll in parsley. Chill. Serve on crackers or cucumber slices or use to stuff celery.

Makes about 2 cups, 8 servings

SHRIMP LOG

1 package (8 ounces) cream cheese, softened
1 cup minced cooked shrimp
2 tablespoons cocktail sauce
2 tablespoons chopped stuffed olives
2 tablespoons minced onion
⅓ cup chopped parsley
PEPPERIDGE FARM® Goldfish Thins and Butter Thins Crackers

Stir cream cheese until smooth. Blend in cooked shrimp, cocktail sauce, olives and onion. Shape into a log and garnish with parsley. Chill thoroughly. To serve, spread on **Butter Thins** and **Goldfish Thins**.   *Makes about 1½ cups*

DORMAN'S® CHEESE RIBBONS

Spread 4 slices DORMAN'S® Natural Swiss Cheese with DORMAN'S® Dorelle Cheese Spread. Stack, and top with fifth slice of Swiss Cheese. Refrigerate until firm and cut 1-inch squares. Arrange on sides on serving plate so ''ribbons'' show. If desired, center plate with hot pepper relish or with a bunch of stemmed watercress.   *Makes 12 squares*

HORS D'OEUVRES WITH DANISH NATURAL CREAM CHEESE

From center of plate outward:

1. Sandwich small rectangular slices of Danish Natural Cream Cheese with fruit flavor between 2 pecan halves.
2. Halve black pitted olives crosswise. Press together again with a slice of Danish Natural Cream Cheese with Herbs & Spices.
3. Cut a ½ inch slice of Danish Cream Cheese with fruit flavor. Then cut into 10 equal rectangles. Roll each in chopped almonds. Cut a ½ inch slice of Danish Natural Cream Cheese with Herbs & Spices. Then cut into 10 equal rectangles. Roll each in coarse black pepper, chopped chives, or paprika.

Favorite recipe from the **Denmark Cheese Association**

BLACK WALNUT CHEESE LOGS

2 cups coarsely chopped black walnuts OR California walnuts
⅓ cup butter, softened, divided
1 teaspoon curry powder
3 cups grated SARGENTO Muenster OR Monterey Jack Cheese
½ cup SARGENTO Crumbled Blue Cheese
1 teaspoon Dijon OR prepared mustard
1 teaspoon paprika

Spread walnuts in shallow pan; dot with 2 tablespoons butter. Sprinkle with curry powder. Bake in preheated 300 degree oven for 20 minutes, stirring occasionally to toast evenly. Remove from oven; cool.

Chop 1 cup walnuts finely, reserving remaining nuts. Using electric mixer, blend remaining softened butter, cheeses, mustard, and paprika. Stir in finely chopped walnuts. Divide mixture in half. Turn each half onto sheet of foil; shape each into a log. Roll logs in reserved walnuts; wrap in foil. Refrigerate until firm. To serve, place logs on cutting board; spread on crackers or party rye bread.

Note: Logs may be made up to 2 days ahead.

PORT WINE CHEESEBALL

1 (8-oz.) cream cheese, softened
1 (12-oz.) container WOODY'S® Cheddar Cheese with Port Wine, room temperature
1 (8½-oz.) can crushed pineapple, drained
1 tablespoon sugar
¼ cup finely chopped green pepper
1 cup finely chopped walnuts

Blend all ingredients together except walnuts; chill thoroughly. Shape into a ball and roll in nuts. Wrap in foil until ready to serve.

ECKRICH® HONEY LOAF PICK-UPS

Slice ECKRICH® Honey Loaf into bite-size squares. Alternate several slices of Honey Loaf with cubes of cheese and slices of olives on cocktail picks.   *An 8-ounce package of Honey Loaf will make about 25 Pick-Ups*

APPETIZER WEDGES
(Low Calorie)

Remove stack of meat from an 8 ounce package of OSCAR MAYER 90% Fat-Free Beef Honey Roll. Cut into eight pie-shaped wedges. Separate wedges into 5 slices each. Top each with an onion and secure with pick.   *Makes 16 wedges*

Calories: 25 each

OLD FASHION ROLL-UPS

Combine one 3-ounce package softened cream cheese with 1 tablespoon finely chopped green onion. Spread on slices of ECKRICH® Old Fashion Loaf. Roll slices like a jelly roll. Chill well. Cut each roll into four bite-size pieces and spear each with a party pick.   *One package Old Fashion Loaf makes 32 pieces*

CREAM CHEESE SALAMI WEDGES

5 slices salami (approximately 4″ in diameter)
1 3-ounce package cream cheese, softened
2 tablespoons milk
1 teaspoon lemon juice
½ teaspoon monosodium glutamate
½ teaspoon prepared mustard
¼ teaspoon salt
1 teaspoon horseradish
2 tablespoons finely crushed FRITOS® Brand Corn Chips

Blend cheese with milk. Add remaining ingredients except salami slices. Spread on slices of salami, placing one on top of the other to form a stack. Chill. Slice in wedges.   *Makes 12 wedges*

CREAMY BEEF ROLL-UPS

1 8-oz. pkg. cream cheese, softened
2 Tbsp. prepared horseradish
1 2½-oz. jar **ARMOUR STAR® Sliced Dried Beef**, rinsed

Combine cream cheese and horseradish. Spread mixture on double dried beef slices; roll up. Chill. *10 to 12 appetizers*

VARIATION:

Substitute ¼ cup chopped green onions for horseradish.

CANADIAN BACON ROLL-UPS

¼ lb. **COUNTRY SMOKED MEATS Canadian Bacon**, sliced thin
6 green onions
1 8-oz. pkg. cream cheese

Take one slice of Canadian Bacon, lay flat and spread with cream cheese. Roll this around one green onion. Slice into ½" pieces. *Makes about 72 Roll-Ups*

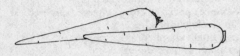

SLICED MEAT ROLL-UPS
(Low Calorie)

Remove stack of meat from an 8 ounce package of **OSCAR MAYER 93% Fat-Free Peppered Loaf**. Cut stack in half diagonally. Wrap half slices around pickle spear, celery, carrots or other crisp vegetables. Secure with pick. *Makes 20 roll-ups*

Calories: 20 each

BUDDIG BANDS

Bowl of favorite coleslaw
BUDDIG Smoked Sliced Ham or **Turkey Ham**
Colored toothpicks

Carefully separate **BUDDIG Ham** into individual slices. Top with coleslaw and roll up. Fasten with colored toothpicks and cut into 1-inch lengths.

PARTY PINWHEELS
(Low Calorie)

Spread 1 pkg. (8 oz.) **OSCAR MAYER 95% Fat-Free Luxury Loaf** with 3 ounces imitation cream cheese. Roll first slice, join meat edges to start second slice, and continue to roll 4 slices into log. Repeat using remaining 4 slices. Wrap and chill; cut into ¼-inch slices. *Makes 32 pinwheels*

Calories: 15 each

PICKLE PINWHEELS

Cold cuts, thinly sliced (salami, bologna, ham)
HEINZ Sweet Gherkins or **Baby Dills** (whole), **HEINZ Sweet** or **Dill Pickles** (Spears)
Cheese, at room temperature for ease in spreading and rolling (cream cheese, cheese spreads, sliced mozzarella, process cheese slices)

Select thin, straight pickles and set out on paper towel. Spread cream cheese or cheese spread on a slice of meat. Cover with a slice of cheese or another slice of meat. Spread top slice with cream cheese or cheese spread. Lay pickle at edge; roll jelly-roll fashion. Wrap each roll tightly in plastic film; chill several hours or overnight. Slice rolls crosswise into ¼ inch rounds. Arrange pinwheels on platter. Serve with assorted crackers.

CHICKEN—HAM PINWHEELS

4 teaspoons **GREY POUPON Dijon Mustard**
½ teaspoon tarragon
¼ teaspoon *each* salt and pepper
1 clove garlic, crushed
4 boneless, skinless chicken filets, pounded thin
4 thin slices baked ham

In small bowl, combine mustard, tarragon, salt, pepper and garlic. Spread mixture on chicken breasts. Top with ham slice. Roll. Place seam side down in baking dish. Bake in 350°F oven 30 minutes. Wrap and chill. Slice each roll in 5 or 6 slices. Arrange on serving plate. *Makes about 24 pinwheels*

FIREBRAND® PINWHEELS

1 package **FIREBRAND® Beef Strips**
3 ounce package cream cheese, softened
1 teaspoon lemon juice
¼ teaspoon dry mustard
1 teaspoon horseradish

Blend cheese, lemon juice, mustard and horseradish until smooth. Cook beef strips according to package directions. Drain. Spread cheese mixture on cooked beef strips. Roll and fasten with 2 wooden picks. Cut between picks into halves and serve. *Yield: 30 to 34 pinwheels*

BUDDIG PIN WHEELS

1 3-ounce package cream cheese, softened
1 tablespoon grated onion
1 teaspoon horseradish
Dash Worcestershire sauce
1 package **BUDDIG Smoked Sliced Beef** or **Ham**

Blend cream cheese, onion, horseradish and Worcestershire sauce until of spreading consistency. Carefully separate slices of **BUDDIG Beef** or **Ham** and spread with cheese mixture. Roll as for jelly roll and fasten with toothpicks. Chill. Just before serving, slice into ½-inch slices.

GOURMET DEVILED EGGS

8 hard cooked eggs
¼ cup mushrooms, chopped fine
⅓ cup cooked **SHOAL LAKE Pure Canadian Wild Rice**
2 Tbsp. finely chopped ripe olives
2 Tbsp. pickle relish
Salt and pepper to taste
Mayonnaise to moisten

Shell and half the eggs. Combine the remaining ingredients with the egg yolks and mix well. Spoon the yolk mixture back into the egg whites and garnish with fresh parsley. *Yield: 16 servings*

CURRIED EGGS

1 can (3½-oz.) **BUMBLE BEE® Solid White Tuna**
1 dozen eggs, hard-cooked, peeled
1 cup mayonnaise
2 tablespoons chopped green onion
¼ to ½ teaspoon curry powder
¼ teaspoon garlic powder
Paprika

Drain tuna. Slice eggs in half lengthwise. Remove yolks leaving whites intact. Combine tuna, egg yolks, mayonnaise, onion, curry and garlic powder. Mash and stir until smooth. Pipe or spoon into egg whites. Sprinkle with paprika. Refrigerate until ready to serve.
Makes 24 curried eggs

STUFFED EGGS A LA POLONAISE

6 hard cooked eggs, shelled
½ cup ground **ATALANTA/KRAKUS/POLKA Polish Ham**
¼ cup mayonnaise
1 teaspoon dry mustard
½ teaspoon chopped capers
½ teaspoon lemon juice
¼ teaspoon salt

Mash yolks of eggs with a fork. Blend in remaining ingredients, except egg whites. Refill whites with mixture. Garnish with paprika or capers.
Makes 12 appetizers

HOLLAND HOUSE®
CHICKEN LIVER PÂTÉ

Melt 3 Tbsp. butter or margarine in skillet. Sauté 1 lb. chicken livers with 1 cup finely chopped onions and 2 crushed garlic cloves. When livers lose pinkness, add ⅓ cup **HOLLAND HOUSE® Marsala Cooking Wine**. Cook approx. 2 mins. Remove from heat. Combine liver mixture with 3 oz. cream cheese, 1 Tbsp. butter, ½ tsp. tarragon, ½ tsp. dry mustard and dash Worcestershire sauce in electric blender. Mix until smooth. Pour into crock and chill before serving.

PARTY COUNTRY PÂTÉ

1 pound finely ground pork
½ pound finely ground veal
⅔ cup finely chopped boiled ham
½ cup chopped black olives
½ cup ground blanched almonds
1 cup fresh bread crumbs
⅓ cup **B&B Liqueur**
1 egg
1 clove garlic, crushed
1 teaspoon rosemary
½ teaspoon salt
½ teaspoon thyme
1 tablespoon margarine or butter
Parsley

In a large bowl combine pork, veal, ham, olives and blanched almonds. Soften bread crumbs in **B&B Liqueur** and add with egg, garlic, rosemary, salt and thyme to meat mixture; thoroughly mix together.

Coat the bottom and sides of a 5-cup mold or an 8½ × 4½ × 2½-inch loaf pan with margarine. Fill with meat mixture, pressing down firmly. Bake at 350°F. for 1½ hours. Drain. Cover pâté with foil and weight down with a heavy can. Refrigerate 12 hours.

Unmold pâté onto serving plate. Serve pâté at room temperature, garnished with parsley sprigs.   *Makes 1 4-cup mold*

HALFTIME PÂTÉ

⅓ cup toasted chopped almonds
4 strips **WILSON® Bacon**, fried crisp and crumbled
½ cup mayonnaise
1½ cups grated sharp Cheddar cheese
1½ tablespoons finely chopped onion

Combine all ingredients in a small bowl. Serve with your favorite crackers.

SHRIMP MOUSSE

½ cup **COFFEE RICH® Frozen Non-Dairy Creamer**, thawed
2 envelopes unflavored gelatin
1 (10¾-ounce) can tomato soup
1 (8-ounce) package cream cheese, softened
1 cup finely chopped celery
½ cup finely chopped green pepper
1 teaspoon minced onion
2 tablespoons lemon juice
½ teaspoon salt
¼ teaspoon Worcestershire sauce
Dash of **TABASCO® Sauce**
1 pound cooked shrimp, cut into small pieces

1. Combine non-dairy creamer and unflavored gelatin in a medium saucepan. Heat over medium heat, stirring, until gelatin is completely dissolved.

2. Add soup to saucepan; blend well.

3. Add cream cheese. Continue to heat over medium heat, stirring constantly, until cream cheese is melted and thoroughly blended.

4. Remove saucepan from heat. Allow mixture to cool.

5. Stir in celery, green pepper, onion, lemon juice, salt, Worcestershire, **TABASCO®**, and shrimp, when mousse has cooled.

6. Pour mixture into an oiled 5-cup mold. Refrigerate several hours or overnight until firm.

7. To serve, unmold onto a serving platter and serve with assorted crackers.

DORMAN'S® MUENSTER MOUSSE

½ envelope (1½ teaspoons) unflavored gelatine
¼ cup white wine
¼ cup boiling water
3 scallions, chopped
½ cup PLUS 1 tablespoon heavy cream
1 egg
1 teaspoon salt
1 tablespoon cognac, optional
3 slices **DORMAN'S® Muenster Cheese**
Sliced almonds

Sprinkle gelatine over wine; let stand until softened. Add boiling water; stir until dissolved. In electric blender container, combine dissolved gelatine and remaining ingredients except sliced almonds. Blend 10 seconds. Pour into a 1½ cup mold. Chill in refrigerator until firm. Unmold and garnish with sliced almonds.
Serves 6

ANCHOVY AND SWEET PEPPER

1 flat can of anchovies
2 sweet red peppers (pimientos)
8 Tbsp. of **FILIPPO BERIO Olive Oil**
1½ Tbsp. of **FILIPPO BERIO Wine Vinegar**

Cut pimiento into slices about ½-inch wide and 3-inches long. Take out filets of anchovies from can and drain off the oil. Place one anchovy on each strip of pimiento, rolling them together into a circle and piercing them with a toothpick to hold them firm. Place them in a serving dish. Mix the **FILIPPO BERIO Olive Oil** and **Wine Vinegar** thoroughly and pour over pimiento and anchovy rolls. Serve with Melba crackers.

STEAK TARTARE

1 pound raw, ground beef (top round, sirloin or fillet)*
2 egg yolks
½ teaspoon salt
½ teaspoon Worcestershire sauce
¼ teaspoon pepper
½ cup finely chopped green onions or scallions
¼ cup finely chopped parsley
1 to 3 finely chopped anchovy fillets
Capers
Anchovy fillets
PEPPERIDGE FARM® Butter and **Goldfish Thins Crackers**

Mix beef, egg yolks, salt, Worcestershire sauce, pepper, onions and parsley. Add chopped anchovies to taste. Shape meat mixture into a ball; place on serving platter and flatten slightly. Garnish top with capers and anchovy fillets and surround with crackers.

Makes 8 to 10 servings

*Note: Have butcher grind meat at least three times.

Dips & Spreads

BANANA CURRY DIP

1 cup mashed banana (3 medium)
1 container (8 ounces) plain yogurt
2 teaspoons minced onion
1 teaspoon curry powder
¼ teaspoon salt
1 pineapple, peeled and cut into spears
1 cucumber, cut into slices
1 pound cooked shrimp

Combine bananas, yogurt, onion, curry powder and salt in small bowl. Chill at least 1 hour. Serve with pineapple, cucumber and shrimp. *Yield: 1⅔ cups dip.*

Favorite recipe from **The Banana Bunch**

ORIGINAL RANCH DIP

1 pint sour cream
1 packet **HIDDEN VALLEY ORIGINAL RANCH® Salad Dressing**

Combine sour cream and Salad Dressing mix; stir to blend. Chill. For variety add any one of the following ingredients in amounts to satisfy taste: dill weed, well-drained minced clams, shrimp or crab. *Makes 2 cups dip*

DIETERS STRAWBERRY DIP

1 cup ripe strawberries, halved
⅓ cup **DOMINO® Confectioners 10-X Powdered Sugar**
1 cup low fat cottage cheese

Place all ingredients in blender and blend until smooth, or beat with electric mixer until smooth. Use as Basic Fruit Dip.

Makes 1⅔ cups

Note: All dips, toppings and sauces should be refrigerated if not used immediately after preparation.

PEANUT BUTTER DIP

1 cup dairy sour cream
½ cup **JIF® Creamy Peanut Butter**
2 tablespoons prepared mustard
1 teaspoon prepared horseradish
⅛ teaspoon salt
Rippled potato chips or crackers

In a bowl, stir together the sour cream, **JIF®**, mustard, horseradish, and salt. Serve with potato chips or crackers.

Makes 1½ cups

SURPRISE DIP

1 cup sour cream
1 tsp. lemon juice
4 Tbsp. (2 oz.) **ROMANOFF® Caviar***

Combine all ingredients. Cover and chill. Serve with unsalted crackers or raw vegetable relishes. *Makes about 1 cup dip*

Note: Yogurt lovers may substitute 1 cup plain whole milk yogurt.

***ROMANOFF® Black Lumpfish** or **Whitefish Caviar** suggested.

ANGOSTURA® VEGETABLE DIP

1 pint sour cream
1 package (2.3 oz.) Russian salad dressing mix
2 teaspoons **ANGOSTURA® Aromatic Bitters**

Mix all ingredients together and blend well. *Yield: 2 cups*

ROQUEFORT SOUR CREAM DIP

Combine 1 cup dairy sour cream, ¼ cup crumbled **ROQUEFORT**, 1 scant tablespoon prepared mustard and 1 tablespoon capers; mix well. *Makes over 1 cup of basic dip*

Favorite recipe from the **Roquefort Association, Inc.**

ALPINE AVOCADO DIP

1 medium avocado, peeled and seeded
1 cup (8-ounces) **BORDEN® LITE-LINE® Plain Yogurt**
1 tablespoon chopped onion
1 teaspoon **REALEMON® Brand Lemon Juice from Concentrate**
½ teaspoon garlic salt
¼ teaspoon hot pepper sauce

In small bowl, mash avocado. Stir in remaining ingredients (mixture will be lumpy). Chill thoroughly to blend flavors. Serve with assorted chips. *Makes 1½ cups*

DILLY OF A DIP

Chop **CLAUSSEN Kosher Pickles** to make ¾ cup. Combine with 1 cup sour cream, 2 tablespoons pickle brine, 1 tablespoon chopped onion and ¼ teaspoon dill weed. Chill. Serve with fresh vegetables and chips or as a topping for potatoes and fish.

BUFFET DIP

1 clove garlic
¼ cup catsup
¼ cup sour cream*
1½ teaspoons sweet basil
½ teaspoon horseradish
¼ teaspoon salt
¼ teaspoon **TABASCO®**

Rub bowl with cut clove of garlic; discard garlic. Combine remaining ingredients and blend thoroughly. Chill. Serve with seafood cocktails, crisp raw vegetables or corn chips.

Makes about ½ cup

*Or substitute ¼ cup whippping cream and 1 teaspoon lemon juice or vinegar whipped to desired consistency.

VARIATION:

For an interesting flavor variation, add ¼ cup minced clams and blend thoroughly with other ingredients.

CLAM CHEESE DIP

Mix together:

12 oz. cream cheese, softened
1 - 10 oz. can **HIGH LINER® Clams**, reserving juice
½ garlic clove, minced
1 Tbsp. lemon juice

Add enough clam juice to make the mixture the right consistency for dipping. Excellent with **HIGH LINER® Shrimp** or **Breaded Scallops.**

HORSERADISH DIP

1 can (15½ oz.) **BUMBLE BEE® Pink Salmon**
1 package (8 oz.) cream cheese, softened
¼ cup dairy sour cream
¼ cup prepared horseradish
½ teaspoon salt
⅛ teaspoon garlic powder
Crisp romaine lettuce
Paprika
Crackers
Celery sticks

Drain salmon. Remove skin, if desired. Mash bones. Beat cream cheese, sour cream, horseradish, salt and garlic powder until smooth. Beat in salmon and bones until blended. Arrange romaine lettuce in a bowl. Spoon in salmon mixture. Sprinkle with paprika. Serve with crackers and celery sticks.

Makes 6 to 8 servings

"KETCH" A CLAM DIP

Blend ⅓ cup **HEINZ Tomato Ketchup** gradually into 1 package (8-ounces) cream cheese, softened. Stir in 1 teaspoon lemon juice, ⅛ teaspoon garlic powder, 1 can (6½-ounces) minced clams, drained. Cover; chill.

Makes about 1½ cups

CLAM AND CHEESE DUNK

2 Tbsp. lemon juice
1 8-oz. package cream cheese
1 tsp. salt
1½ tsp. Worcestershire sauce
½ tsp. paprika
2 oz. **DUBONNET Blanc Wine**
1 7½-oz. canned minced clams, well drained

Blend all ingredients and store in a tightly covered container in the refrigerator. As this dunk is made with seafood, it should not be kept more than 24 hours.

YOUR OWN SHRIMP DIP

1 can (4½ ounces) **LOUISIANA BRAND Shrimp**
2 teaspoons instant onion flakes
1 chicken bouillon cube
2 packages (3 ounces each) cream cheese
½ teaspoon Worcestershire sauce
¼ teaspoon hot pepper sauce
1 tablespoon lemon juice
2 tablespoons minced fresh parsley

Drain shrimp and chop coarsely. Soften onion flakes and dissolve bouillon cube in ⅓ cup hot water. Combine with cheese and work to a smooth dip consistency. Add all other seasonings and shrimp.

Makes 1¾ cups

BLACK BEAN DIP

1 can (11 oz.) condensed black bean soup
¼ cup dairy sour cream
¼ cup minced onion
1 clove garlic, minced
4 teaspoons **LEA & PERRINS Worcestershire Sauce**
2 tablespoons chopped parsley

In a medium bowl mash soup. Stir in remaining ingredients except parsley. Cover and chill for 1 hour. Spoon into a serving bowl. Garnish with parsley. Serve with corn chips or crackers.

PIMIENTO CHEESE DIP

2 cups (8 oz.) shredded process pimiento cheese
½ cup sour cream
1 package (3 oz.) cream cheese, softened
½ cup **OLD EL PASO® Taco Sauce**
1 can (4 oz.) **OLD EL PASO® Chopped Green Chilies**
4 slices bacon, crisp-cooked, drained and crumbled
⅛ teaspoon cayenne pepper
OLD EL PASO NACHIPS® Tortilla Chips

In small mixing bowl, combine pimiento cheese, sour cream, cream cheese, taco sauce and green chilies. Beat until light and fluffy. Stir in crumbled bacon and pepper. Chill. Serve with vegetable dippers and/or **NACHIPS®**.

ZESTY PARTY DIP

Blend ⅓ cup **HEINZ Tomato Ketchup**, 3 tablespoons milk, ½ teaspoon prepared horseradish, ¼ teaspoon salt into 1 package (8 ounces) softened cream cheese. Stir in ⅓ crumbled blue cheese. Cover; chill.

Makes about 1½ cups

BLUE CHEESE DIP OR DRESSING

1 pkg. (8 oz.) cream cheese, softened
½ teaspoon garlic salt (or as desired)
2 tablespoons lemon juice
½ cup **MILNOT®**
½ cup (approx. 4 oz.) crumbled blue cheese

Beat cream cheese until fluffy, add garlic salt and lemon juice gradually, then add **MILNOT®**. Blend well. Fold in crumbled blue cheese. Serve as a dip or on vegetable salads.

Yield: approx. 2 cups

COTTAGE CHEESE DIP

1 cup **BREAKSTONE'S®** Smooth and Creamy Style Cottage Cheese
¼ cup **KRAFT** Creamy Cucumber Dressing
2 crisply cooked bacon slices, crumbled
1 tablespoon green onion slices

Combine all ingredients; mix well. Chill. Serve with vegetable dippers.

1¼ cups

RICOTTA CHEESE DIP

1 lb. ricotta cheese
1 Tbsp. soft butter or margarine
2 Tbsp. horseradish
1 cup diced celery
1 Tbsp. chopped chives
2 Tbsp. dry onion soup mix
1 tsp. sugar
½ cup chopped sweet pickle
1 (4-oz.) **Family Pak BUDDIG** diced **Pastrami** or **Corned Beef**

Mix well. Refrigerate for one hour.

LOW-CAL CHEESE SPREAD/DIP
(Low Calorie/Low Cholesterol)

1 cup low-fat cottage cheese
1 packet **BUTTER BUDS®**
1 tsp. horseradish
1 Tbsp. Worcestershire sauce
4 tsp. minced onion
1 tsp. caraway seeds
Salt and pepper
Paprika (optional)

In blender, mix cheese until smooth. Add **BUTTER BUDS®**, horseradish, Worcestershire, onion; mix. Remove from blender, stir in caraway, salt and pepper. Garnish with paprika if desired. Serve on crackers, as dip for crudités.

About 1 cup

> Calories: 16 per oz. (2 Tbsp.)
> Cholesterol: .001 g per oz. (2 Tbsp.)

TASTY CHEESE DIP

Blend ½ cup **HEINZ Tomato Ketchup**, ½ cup dairy sour cream, 1 teaspoon grated onion into 1 jar (8 ounces) pasteurized process cheese spread. Cover; chill.

Makes about 2 cups

PARISIAN DIP

1 package (8 oz.) cream cheese, softened
3 ounces **ROQUEFORT Cheese**
3 tablespoons heavy cream
1 teaspoon chopped chives
½ teaspoon Worcestershire sauce

To the softened cream cheese, add the **ROQUEFORT Cheese**, cream, chopped chives and the Worcestershire sauce. Mix until well blended. Place in a bowl and sprinkle with additional chives. Serve with potato chips.

Makes about 1½ cups

Favorite recipe from **Roquefort Association, Inc.**

CREAMY BACON DIP

1 cup **SEVEN SEAS®** Creamy Bacon Dressing
3 oz. cream cheese, softened
¼ cup sour cream

Blend Creamy Bacon Dressing, cream cheese and sour cream. Refrigerate. Serve with your favorite raw vegetables.

Makes 1½ cups

TABASCO® DIP PIQUANTE

1 package (8 ounces) cream cheese
½ teaspoon **TABASCO®**
3 tablespoons mayonnaise
1 tablespoon horseradish
1 teaspoon minced onion
¼ teaspoon celery salt

Soften cream cheese in mixing bowl. Add **TABASCO®** and mayonnaise and beat until smooth. Stir in remaining ingredients. Use as dip for potato chips, pretzel sticks, Melba toast or crackers.

Makes about 1¼ cups

Note: The flavor improves on standing. Keep in refrigerator several hours before serving.

GALLO® SALAME PARTY DIP

6 ounces **GALLO® Italian Dry Salame**
12 ounces sour cream

Finely chop **GALLO® Italian Dry Salame**. Measure by weight both chopped **GALLO® Salame** and sour cream before mixing to insure 1 part **GALLO® Salame** to 2 parts sour cream. Mix well. Refrigerate minimum of 2 hours for firmness. Serve on celery, crackers, sliced cucumbers, cauliflower, cherry tomatoes, or chips.

SPINACH BEEF DIP

1 10-oz. pkg. frozen chopped spinach, thawed
1 8-oz. pkg. cream cheese, softened
1 cup mayonnaise
½ cup chopped green onions
1 tablespoon dillweed
1 2½-oz. jar **ARMOUR STAR®** Sliced Dried Beef, rinsed, chopped
Assorted crackers

Combine spinach, cream cheese, mayonnaise, green onions and dillweed in container of electric blender; process on high speed 1 to 2 minutes or until smooth and creamy. Fold in dried beef. Chill. Serve with crackers.

3 cups

PEPERONI WHIP

5 ounce package **SWIFT PREMIUM® PEPERONI®**
2 packages (3 ounces each) cream cheese
½ cup whipping cream, whipped
4 tablespoons chopped parsley

BLENDER METHOD:
Hold peperoni under running hot water and remove skin. Slice into ¼ inch slices; then in half. Grind on ''low'' or ''chop'' speed. Add cream cheese, whipped cream and parsley. Blend until just mixed; stopping blender to scrape down sides if necessary. Serve with crackers, Melba toast or toasted party rye bread.

FOOD PROCESSOR METHOD:
Cut skinned peperoni into small chunks. Using cutting blade, chop peperoni and remove from bowl. Chop parsley and remove. Cut cream cheese into cubes and process until smooth. Add peperoni and parsley to cheese. Process to mix. Remove from bowl and combine with whipping cream.   *Yield: 2 cups*

HAM STICKS WITH YOGURT DILL DIP
(Low Calorie)

Cut contents of one 8 ounce package of **OSCAR MAYER 95% Fat-Free Ham Steaks** into julienne strips. For dip, mix 1 (16 oz.) container plain yogurt with ½ tsp. dill weed and 2 tsp. dehydrated minced onion. Chill.   *Makes 8 servings*

Calories: One serving (¼ cup dip; ½ ham steak) contains 50 calories.

SAVORY EGG DIP

1 cup dairy sour cream
3 hard-cooked eggs, chopped
1 tablespoon instant minced onion
1 teaspoon Italian salad dressing mix

Combine all ingredients. Cover; refrigerate to blend flavors. Serve with assorted vegetable dippers.
Makes approx. 1½ cups dip

Favorite recipe from the **American Egg Board**

PEANUT BUTTER CHILI DIP

½ cup **SKIPPY® Super Chunk Peanut Butter**
½ cup chili sauce
1 tablespoon horseradish
1 tablespoon lemon juice

In small bowl stir together peanut butter, chili sauce, horseradish and lemon juice. Cover; refrigerate. Serve with raw vegetables.
Makes about 1 cup

GREEN GODDESS DIP

½ cup mayonnaise
½ cup sour cream
2 teaspoons lemon juice
1 teaspoon anchovy paste
1 clove garlic, cut up
¼ cup coarsely chopped parsley
¼ cup sliced green onion
½ teaspoon onion powder
¼ teaspoon tarragon
1 package (27 oz.) **BANQUET® Frozen Fried Chicken Wing Portions**

Place all ingredients except chicken into blender container or food processor. Process until smooth. Chill several hours. Heat chicken wing portions on cookie sheet in 375°F oven for 25 minutes, until hot and crisp. Serve hot chicken with dip for appetizers.
Makes 1 cup dip

MYSTERY HORS D'OEUVRE-RELISH

Snip 1 cup pitted dates into sixths. In a saucepan, combine with ½ cup chili sauce, 1 teaspoon grated orange rind, ½ cup orange juice, 2 tablespoons chopped onion, 1 teaspoon minced, seeded canned green chiles **or** 1 or more teaspoons green salsa sauce, 1 oz. unsweetened chocolate, grated; bring to rolling boil, stirring often; remove from heat; stir in ¼ cup coarsely chopped **BLUE RIBBON® Natural Almonds**, roasted. Chill. Serve with corn chips.
Makes 1¾ cups

GUACAMOLE

2 medium ripe avocados, seeded and peeled
2 tablespoons **REALIME® Lime Juice from Concentrate**
1 tablespoon finely chopped onion
1 teaspoon seasoned salt
¼ teaspoon hot pepper sauce
¼ teaspoon garlic powder

In medium bowl or blender, mash avocados. Add remaining ingredients; stir well. Chill thoroughly to blend flavors. Serve with tortilla chips or fresh vegetables. Garnish as desired.
Makes about 1½ cups

VARIATIONS:

Add one or more of the following ingredients to Guacamole: sour cream, crumbled bacon, coarsely chopped water chestnuts, chopped tomato, chopped mild or hot green chilies.

OLÉ GUACAMOLE DIP

1 ripe avocado, mashed
¼ cup dairy sour cream
½ teaspoon fresh grated **SUNKIST® Lemon** peel
1 tablespoon fresh squeezed **SUNKIST® Lemon** juice
½ teaspoon instant minced onion
½ teaspoon garlic salt
¼ teaspoon salt
¼ teaspoon chili powder
Dash hot pepper sauce
1 small tomato, diced

In bowl, combine all ingredients; mix well. *Makes about 2 cups*

HOT ARTICHOKE 'N HERBS DIP

⅓ cup **WISH-BONE® Sour Cream & Italian Herbs Dressing**
1 package (9 oz.) frozen artichoke hearts, thawed and coarsely chopped
¼ cup grated Parmesan cheese
Buttered bread crumbs
Suggested dippers—raw carrot or celery sticks, whole mushrooms or sliced zucchini

Preheat oven to 350. In blender or food processor, combine **Sour Cream and Italian Herbs Dressing**, artichokes and cheese; process at high speed until blended. Turn into 2-cup casserole, top with bread crumbs. Bake 30 minutes or until heated through. Serve with Suggested Dippers.   *Makes about 2 cups dip*

HOLIDAY CRAB DIP

1 (6-oz.) package **WAKEFIELD®** Crabmeat
1 (8-oz.) package softened cream cheese
⅓ cup mayonnaise
1 teaspoon prepared mustard with horseradish
1½ tablespoons dried onion
½ teaspoon seasoned salt
1 tablespoon coarsely chopped parsley
Dash of garlic powder

Thaw crabmeat, drain and separate into small chunks. Blend well cream cheese, mayonnaise, mustard, onion and seasoned salt. Fold in parsley, garlic powder and crabmeat. Serve hot or cold with crisp relishes or crackers.

Makes 1¾ cups

HOT ONION DIP

1 can (10½ ounces) **CAMPBELL'S Condensed Cream of Onion Soup**
1 package (8 ounces) cream cheese, softened
2 tablespoons chili sauce
1 tablespoon chopped hot cherry peppers

With electric mixer or rotary beater, gradually blend soup into cream cheese. Beat just until smooth (overbeating makes dip thin). Stir in chili sauce and peppers; chill. Serve with crackers or chips.

Makes about 2 cups

SPINACH AND YOGURT APPETIZER

1 pound spinach, washed, drained, stemmed and coarsely chopped
½ cup water
3 tablespoons olive oil
1 small onion, finely chopped
1 cup **DANNON® Plain Lowfat Yogurt**
1 small clove garlic, crushed, or to taste
½ teaspoon crushed dried mint
Salt and freshly ground black pepper to taste
2 tablespoons finely chopped toasted walnut meats

In a heavy saucepan combine the spinach with the water and bring to a boil over high heat. Reduce the heat to low, cover, and simmer 10 minutes. Drain and squeeze the spinach dry. In a heavy skillet heat the oil over moderate flame. Add the onion and sauté until golden, stirring frequently. Add the spinach and sauté a few minutes. Remove from the heat.

In a mixing bowl combine the yogurt, garlic, mint, and salt and pepper until well blended. Gradually stir in the contents of the skillet and mix thoroughly. Taste for seasoning. Transfer to a serving bowl, cover, and chill. Serve sprinkled with the walnuts.

Serves 4

HOT SPINACH DIP

1 (10-ounce) package frozen chopped spinach, thawed and well drained
1 (8-ounce) package cream cheese, softened
½ cup milk
2 tablespoons margarine or butter
2 teaspoons **WYLER'S® Chicken-Flavor Instant Bouillon**
⅛ teaspoon ground nutmeg
1 tablespoon **REALEMON®** Lemon Juice from Concentrate
OLD LONDON® Melba Rounds

In medium saucepan, combine cheese, milk, margarine, bouillon and nutmeg; cook and stir over low heat until thickened and smooth. Stir in spinach; heat through. Remove from heat. Stir in **REALEMON®**. Serve hot in chafing dish with Melba rounds. Refrigerate leftovers.

Makes 2 cups

HOT SAUSAGE-BEAN DIP

½ pound **TENNESSEE PRIDE® Country Sausage**
1 16-ounce can pork and beans in tomato sauce
2 ounces sharp process American cheese, shredded (½ cup)
2 tablespoons catsup
½ teaspoon prepared mustard
Few drops bottled hot pepper sauce

Cook **TENNESSEE PRIDE® Country Sausage** in skillet until it loses its pink color; stir to break up sausage and drain off fat. In blender combine sausage with beans, shredded cheese, catsup, mustard and hot pepper sauce; blend till smooth, stopping occasionally to scrape down sides. Return to skillet. Heat. Serve with corn chips or assorted crackers.

Makes 2½ cups

HOLIDAY-SAUSAGE STROGANOFF DIP

1 clove garlic
2 lbs. **JIMMY DEAN® Sausage**
4 Tbsp. flour
2 cups beef broth
2 onions chopped (medium)
1 cup mushrooms sliced (canned or fresh)
½ stick butter
2 tsp. soy sauce
2 Tbsp. Worcestershire
1 tsp. dry mustard
Salt-pepper-paprika
TABASCO® to taste
2 cups sour cream
Party rye or pumpernickel bread toasted

Rub large skillet with garlic; heat and brown sausage. Crumble sausage with a fork. Sprinkle sausage with flour; add beef broth. Simmer until slightly thickened & set aside. Sauté onions and mushrooms in butter until onions are tender. Add onions, mushrooms and seasonings to sausage mixture. Cook until mixture bubbles—remove from heat and add sour cream. Keep hot in chafing dish. Serve with toasted party rye or party size pumpernickel.

(To double recipe, use only 3 onions. Freezes well before adding sour cream.) If you have leftovers, pour over rice.

Makes approximately 1½ qts.

CREAMY CHILE CON QUESO DIP

1 cup **MERKT'S Cheddar Cheese Spread**
1 cup **MERKT'S Buttery Swiss Cheese Spread**
1 cup sour cream
1 12-oz. can chopped green chilles or banana peppers, drained
1 small can black olives, drained & sliced
1 med. tomato, peeled & chopped

Mix the cheeses with sour cream & half of the chopped peppers. In a small baking dish, spread some of the chopped chilles on bottom. Spread the cheese mixture & cover with remaining peppers. Sprinkle with the sliced olives & chopped tomatoes. Bake in 375° oven for 20-25 min. or until cheeses are melted. Serve hot. Decorate with tortilla chips.

HOT BEAN AND CHEESE DIP

1 11½-ounce can condensed bean with bacon soup
1 cup (4 ounces) shredded sharp American cheese
¼ cup chopped green chilies
1 teaspoon instant minced onion
Dash garlic powder
¼ cup water
LA FIESTA™ Tortilla Strips

In saucepan, combine soup, cheese, chilies, onion, garlic powder, and water. Heat slowly, stirring constantly, till heated through. Transfer to fondue pot or small chafing dish. Keep warm over fondue or chafing dish burner. Add water to thin, as necessary. Serve with tortilla strips for dippers.   *Makes about 2 cups dip*

ZIPPITY-DO-DIP

1 15-oz. can **GEBHARDT® Refried Beans**
½ teaspoon **GEBHARDT® Chili Powder**
3 dashes **GEBHARDT® Louisiana Style Hot Sauce**
2 tablespoons onion, chopped fine
¼ cup sour cream
Salt to taste

Combine all ingredients in bowl and mix well. Chill at least one hour to blend flavors. Serve with corn chips.

CREAMY CHILI BEAN DIP

¼ pound pork sausage
1 small onion, minced
½ cup chopped tomatoes, fresh or drained canned
1 can (15-oz.) **NALLEY®'S Hot Chili With Beans**
1 pkg. (8-oz.) cream cheese, softened
1 cup sour cream
Garnish with green pepper and pimiento

Fry sausage and onion; drain off fat. Stir in tomatoes and Chili. Heat, mashing beans with fork; simmer 15 minutes. Blend in cheese and sour cream; heat thoroughly. Pour into bowl; garnish. Serve warm with **NALLEY®'S Chips**, use cold for sandwich spread. (Freezes well.)   *Makes 1 quart*

SPICY COCKTAIL DIP

1 bottle chili sauce (12 oz.)
2 Tbsp. lemon juice
2 Tbsp. salad oil
1 Tbsp. cider vinegar
2 tsp. brown sugar
1 tsp. dehydrated onion flakes
½ tsp. dry mustard
½ tsp. hot pepper sauce
½ tsp. salt

Combine ingredients in saucepan, heat to boiling and simmer 5 minutes. Serve with **JENO'S® Egg Rolls**.   *Makes 1¼ cups*

MILD PEPPER DIP

1¾ cups (16 oz.) **KAUKAUNA® Cheese Mild Pepper Buttery Spread™**
1 can (4 oz.) chopped green chilies, drained
¼ cup chopped ripe olives
¼ cup chopped green onions
¼ cup dairy sour cream
Bread sticks or tortilla chips

Heat cheese in medium saucepan over low heat until melted. Blend in remaining ingredients except bread sticks or chips. Serve hot with bread sticks or chips.   *Makes 3 cups*

HOT SHRIMP DIP

1 package (8-ounces) cream cheese, cut in chunks, softened
1 can (4-ounces) cocktail shrimp, rinsed, drained, chopped
¼ cup minced onion
1 teaspoon **MORTON® NATURE'S SEASONS® Seasoning Blend**
1 teaspoon milk
1 teaspoon prepared horseradish
Slivered almonds (optional)
Assorted crackers

Day Before Serving or Early in Day: Mix cream cheese, shrimp, onion, seasoning blend, milk, and horseradish until well blended. Place mixture in 2-cup, oven-proof baking dish. If desired, top with slivered almonds. Store, covered, in refrigerator.

Just Before Serving: Bake in preheated 375°F oven 15 minutes, or until heated through. Serve hot with crackers.
    Makes about 2 cups dip

HOT CHEESY SHRIMP DIP
(Microwave Recipe)

1 pound raw, peeled and deveined shrimp
½ cup margarine or butter
½ cup finely chopped onions
¼ cup finely chopped bell pepper
1 pound diced American process cheese
1 teaspoon sherry
½ cup catsup
1 tablespoon Worcestershire sauce
¼ teaspoon pepper
2 drops liquid hot pepper sauce

Chop shrimp. In a large mixing bowl combine shrimp, margarine and vegetables. Cover and cook on HIGH for 5 minutes. In another bowl, combine remaining ingredients. Cover and cook on MEDIUM for 4 minutes stirring twice. Combine both mixtures and reheat on LOW for 2 minutes. Serve hot with crackers, chips or fresh fruit wedges.   *Makes 3 cups dip*

Favorite recipe from **National Marine Fisheries Service**

HOT BEEF DIP
(Microwave Recipe)

1 package or jar (2½ ounces) dried beef
1 cup cold water
1 package (8 ounces) cream cheese
½ cup grated Parmesan cheese
¼ cup chopped green onion
¼ cup sour cream
¼ cup salad dressing or mayonnaise
1 tablespoon instant parsley flakes

Cut dried beef up in small pieces with kitchen shears. Combine with water, cover, and cook on High (full power) for 3 minutes; drain. Heat cream cheese in 1-quart covered casserole on Medium (50% power) for 2 to 3 minutes or until soft. Stir in remainder of ingredients. Cover and heat on High for 3 to 4 minutes or until bubbly. Stir and serve as a hot dip for crackers and vegetables or chill and serve as cheese spread.

Favorite recipe from the **Iowa Beef Industry Council**

CUCUMBER SPREAD

1 pound creamed cottage cheese
1 package (3 ounces) cream cheese, softened
1 package (.56 ounce) green onion dip mix
½ cup minced cucumber
½ cup minced watercress

Blend cottage cheese and cream cheese till thoroughly combined. Blend in remaining ingredients; chill. Serve on **PEPPERIDGE FARM® Goldfish Thins Crackers**.

Makes about 2 cups spread

CREAM CHEESE SPREAD

Soften 1 (3 oz.) package of cream cheese and mix in 2 tablespoons mayonnaise, 1 tablespoon minced onion, 2 tablespoons of chopped pecans, ½ teaspoon salt.

Favorite recipe from **National Pecan Marketing Council**

CARAWAY CHEESE SPREAD

2 cups (8 ounces) shredded Cheddar cheese
½ cup **MEADOW GOLD® Cottage Cheese**
¼ cup (½ stick) **MEADOW GOLD® Butter**, softened
1 teaspoon caraway seeds
1 teaspoon each: finely chopped onion, prepared mustard
½ teaspoon soy sauce
Chopped parsley

In mixing bowl, combine above ingredients except parsley. Beat until well blended. Chill mixture several hours. Shape into round ball; roll in chopped parsley.

TANGY CHEESE SPREAD

2 cups shredded Cheddar cheese
¼ cup blue cheese, crumbled
8 oz. cream cheese
⅓ cup **BÉNÉDICTINE Liqueur**
½ teaspoon onion powder

Combine Cheddar cheese, blue cheese and cream cheese in a small bowl of electric mixer. Beat at low speed until thoroughly blended. Add **BÉNÉDICTINE** and onion powder; continue beating 2 more minutes until creamy. Pack into 6 (4 oz.) ramekins or one 3 cup crock. Serve with assorted crackers.

BLUE CHEESE SPREAD

1 cup **COFFEE RICH® Frozen Non-Dairy Creamer**, thawed
1 envelope unflavored gelatin
½ cup blue cheese (4 ounces)
2 (8-ounce) packages cream cheese, softened
¼ cup chopped fresh parsley
¾ teaspoon onion salt
1 teaspoon Worcestershire sauce

1. In a medium saucepan, stir unflavored gelatin granules into non-dairy creamer. Let stand for one (1) minute. Heat over medium heat, stirring, until gelatin is completely dissolved. Remove from heat.
2. In medium bowl or food processor container, blend crumbled blue cheese with softened cream cheese.
3. Add chopped parsley, onion salt and Worcestershire to cheese mixture. Mix well. *(Continued)*

4. Add non-dairy creamer/gelatin mixture to cheese mixture. Blend thoroughly.
5. Pour mixture into a well-oiled 3-cup mold or bowl. Chill several hours or overnight until firm.
6. To serve, unmold onto a serving platter or tray. Surround with fresh fruit slices such as pears as well as an assortment of fresh vegetables, or, serve with assorted crackers.

SHARP GOUDA SPREAD

1 (8-oz.) round real baby Gouda or Edam cheese, at room temperature
½ cup finely chopped smoked sliced beef
¼ cup real dairy sour cream
2 tablespoons pickle relish
2 teaspoons prepared horseradish

Slice top of wax on Gouda or Edam into 8 sections, leaving sides and bottom intact; peel wax back to form petals. Carefully remove cheese from shell, keeping shell intact. Beat cheese until smooth; add beef, sour cream, pickle relish and horseradish. Refill shell. Serve at room temperature with sliced apples and assorted crackers.

Yield: 1½ cups

Favorite recipe from **American Dairy Association**

CHEDDAR CHEESE WITH HORSERADISH SPREAD

2 cups (8 ounces) finely shredded Cheddar cheese
⅓ cup **BEST FOODS®/HELLMANN'S® Real Mayonnaise**
1 tablespoon horseradish
Dash **TABASCO®**
Salt
Pepper
⅓ cup whole almonds, blanched, split and toasted or ⅔ cup pecan halves
Assorted crackers

Mix together cheese, real mayonnaise, horseradish, **TABASCO®**, salt and pepper to taste. Chill. Shape flat on serving plate to resemble pine cone. Place rounded edge of nuts into cheese in uneven rows. Serve with assorted crackers. *Makes 1 cup*

PLOWMAN'S CHEESE SPREAD

Beat until smooth and well blended 1 large package (8 oz.) softened cream cheese, 1½ cups shredded sharp Cheddar cheese, ¼ cup **ALMADÉN Mountain White Chablis** wine, 1 teaspoon paprika, ½ teaspoon garlic salt and a dash of cayenne. Serve the nippy cheese spread from a stoneware crock to lavish on crusty whole wheat bread or wedges of a tart apple.

Makes about 2 cups

CHAMPAGNE GORGONZOLA SPREAD

Blend to a smooth paste ½ pound mellow Gorgonzola, ¼ pound sweet butter, and cayenne pepper to taste. Moisten the spread with ¾ cup **CLICQUOT YELLOW LABEL Champagne** and serve with crackers or any good bread.

ROQUEFORT & CREAM CHEESE CHICKEN SPREAD

1 pkg. (1¼ oz.) **ROQUEFORT Cheese**
1 pkg. (3 oz.) cream cheese
¼ cup sour cream
Few grains cayenne
¼ teaspoon salt
Few drops **TABASCO®**
1 jar (3½ oz.) boned chicken, finely chopped

Mix the cheeses, sour cream and seasonings together until thoroughly blended. Add the finely chopped chicken. Serve on crackers.   *Makes 1 cup*

Favorite recipe from **Roquefort Association, Inc.**

FISHERMEN'S BEST SPREAD

2 envelopes **KNOX® Unflavored Gelatine**
½ cup cold water
1 cup boiling water
2 cups (16 oz.) sour cream
1 cup **WISH-BONE® Thousand Island Dressing**
2 cans (7 oz. ea.) tuna or salmon, drained and flaked*
¼ cup finely chopped onion
1 teaspoon dill weed

In large bowl, sprinkle unflavored gelatine over cold water; let stand 1 minute. Add boiling water and stir until gelatine is completely dissolved. With wire whip or rotary beater, blend in sour cream and Thousand Island dressing. Fold in remaining ingredients. Turn into 6-cup mold or bowl; chill until firm.
Makes about 5½ cups spread

*Substitution: Use canned shrimp or crabmeat.

Note: Recipe can be halved. Turn into 3-cup mold or bowl.

SALMON SPREAD

1 package (8 ounces) cream cheese, softened
¼ pound smoked salmon, finely chopped
½ cup chopped green onion
2 tablespoons dairy sour cream
1 tablespoon lemon juice
⅛ teaspoon freshly cracked black pepper
½ cup chopped parsley

Blend all ingredients except parsley until well mixed. Refrigerate until ready to serve. Spread on **PEPPERIDGE FARM® Goldfish Thins Crackers** and sprinkle with chopped parsley.
Makes about 1½ cups spread

SALMON CHEESE SPREAD A LA B&B

1 package (8 oz.) cream cheese, softened
3 tablespoons **B&B Liqueur**
1 can (7¾ oz.) pink salmon, drained and flaked
¼ cup sliced green onions

In a small bowl blend cream cheese and **B&B Liqueur**. Mix in salmon and onions. Cover and refrigerate 2 hours or overnight. Serve as a spread on toast points or cocktail size bagels.
Makes 1½ cups

TUNA APPLE CHEESE SPREAD

1 can (6½ or 7 ounces) tuna in vegetable oil
1 package (3 ounces) cream cheese, softened to room temperature
1 small or ½ large apple, unpeeled, chopped
¼ cup chopped walnuts
2 tablespoons chopped parsley
2 tablespoons milk
½ teaspoon lemon juice
¼ teaspoon ground nutmeg

Drain excess liquid from tuna. In medium bowl, break tuna into fine flakes. Add remaining ingredients; mix well. Use as spread for party sandwiches.   *Yield: About 2 cups*

Favorite recipe from **The Tuna Research Foundation Inc.**

GINGERED HAM SPREAD

2 diced cooked **ATALANTA/KRAKUS/POLKA Polish Ham**
½ cup Mandarin oranges, cut-up
¼ cup chopped toasted almonds
¼ cup seedless grapes, cut-up
2 tablespoons minced green pepper
½ teaspoon garlic salt
⅛ teaspoon pepper
½ cup mayonnaise or salad dressing
Assorted breads

Combine all ingredients, except bread. Blend well and chill until ready to serve. Spread on breads.   *Makes about 10 servings*

Soups

CONSOMMÉ BOMBAY
(Low Calorie)

3 cups chicken stock
3 cups tomato juice
1 Tbsp. fresh lemon juice
1 tsp. SUPEROSE® Liquid Fructose
⅛ tsp. salt
⅛ tsp. curry powder
2 whole cloves
8 thin lemon slices for garnish

Combine all ingredients except the lemon slices in a saucepan and bring to a boil. Reduce heat and simmer for 10 minutes. To serve, place a thin slice of lemon on top of each bowl of consommé.

Makes 8 servings

Each serving contains approximately: 20 calories

BORSCHT

4 cups water
1 envelope LIPTON® Onion Soup Mix
4 medium beets, pared, quartered
1 tablespoon sugar
1 tablespoon lemon juice
Dairy sour cream

In medium saucepan, bring water to a boil; stir in **LIPTON® Onion Soup Mix**, beets, sugar and lemon juice. Simmer covered 30 minutes or until beets are tender. Remove beets and cool slightly. Grate beets coarsely; return to saucepan. Serve hot or chilled topped with sour cream.

Makes 4 to 6 servings

BLACK BEAN SOUP

2 cups black beans
8 cups cold water
3 medium-sized onions, chopped
3 stalks celery, chopped
¼ cup butter
2 bay leaves
2 tablespoons parsley, chopped
1 ham bone
½ teaspoon salt
⅛ teaspoon freshly ground black pepper
⅔ cup DRY SACK® Sherry
Salt and freshly ground pepper to taste
2 hard-boiled eggs
2 lemons

Place beans in a soup kettle. Cover with water and soak overnight. Drain beans, return to soup kettle, and simmer in 8 cups of water until soft. Sauté onions and celery in butter until golden and transparent. Add to the soup kettle onions, celery, bay leaves, parsley, ham bone, salt and pepper. Continue to cook, covered, over medium-low heat for 3 hours, adding more water from time to time if the soup becomes thick. Remove ham bone and bay leaves. Mix soup in a blender until smooth. Return to soup kettle, and add **DRY SACK®**, and cook over low heat until hot. Add salt and pepper to taste. Garnish individual dishes with slices of hard-boiled egg white and circles of lemon.

Serves: 8

MEXICALI BEAN POT

1 package (12 ounces) dry chick peas
Water
1 cup chopped ham (about 4 ounces)
1 tablespoon margarine or butter
2½ teaspoons MORTON® NATURE'S SEASONS® Seasoning Blend
½ teaspoon ground cumin
1 medium onion, sliced, separated into rings
1 can (6 ounces) tomato paste

Day Before Serving: Place chick peas in 3-quart saucepan or Dutch oven. Pour 6 cups boiling water over peas. Let soak 1 hour. Drain. Add 6 cups fresh water. Cover and simmer about 1½ hours, or until chick peas are tender. Sauté ham in margarine. Stir in remaining ingredients; add to chick peas. Cover and simmer 45 minutes longer. Refrigerate.

About 20 Minutes Before Serving: Reheat, covered, until hot and bubbly. Spoon into soup bowls. *Makes 8 cups*

RICH ONION SOUP

2 pounds onions, sliced
6 tablespoons butter
2 tablespoons corn oil
½ teaspoon sugar
½ teaspoon dry mustard
3 tablespoons flour
2 quarts beef broth
1½ cups HOLLAND HOUSE® White Cooking Wine
Salt and pepper to taste
French bread slices, toasted
Gruyere cheese slices

In large kettle, cook onions with butter and oil over low heat for 30 minutes, stirring occasionally. Add sugar and mustard; cook 30 minutes longer. Blend in flour. Stir in broth and wine and cook 30 minutes more. Season to taste. To serve, ladle into crocks; top with bread and Gruyere slices. Bake in 450° oven until cheese is bubbly. Sprinkle with Parmesan cheese, if desired.

CLASSIC FRENCH ONION SOUP

4 cups thinly sliced sweet onions
1 clove garlic, finely chopped
¼ cup margarine or butter
5½ cups water
⅓ cup dry sherry *or* white wine *or* water
8 teaspoons WYLER'S® Beef-Flavor Instant Bouillon *or* 8 Beef-Flavor Bouillon Cubes
6 (¾-inch thick) slices French bread, buttered and toasted
6 (8 × 4-inch) slices Swiss cheese, cut in half crosswise

In large saucepan, cook onions and garlic in margarine until golden brown. Add water, sherry and bouillon; bring to a boil. Reduce heat; cover and simmer 30 minutes to blend flavors. Place soup in 6 ovenproof soup bowls. Top each serving with a bread slice and cheese. Broil until cheese melts. Serve immediately. Refrigerate leftovers. *Makes 6 servings*

FRENCH ONION SOUP

Boil 1 rounded teaspoon instant minced onions with each cup of water until tender (about 3 minutes), add 1 envelope or (1 teaspoon) **ROMANOFF® MBT® Onion Broth Mix** for each cup (6 oz.) . . . top each serving with round of toast . . . sprinkle with 1 teaspoon grated Parmesan cheese.

BROCCOLI SOUP

1 lb. broccoli, fresh or frozen
1 tablespoon instant onion flakes
1 teaspoon salt
¼ teaspoon white pepper
1 tablespoon flour
1 teaspoon sweet basil (optional)
1⅓ cups water
1 chicken bouillon cube
1 can (13-oz.) **MILNOT®**

Fresh broccoli should be washed, trimmed, and broken into small pieces. Place broccoli in medium saucepan; add next 7 ingredients. Cover and bring to boil; simmer until tender, 10-15 minutes. Remove some flowerets and set aside for garnish. Puree or blend remaining broccoli, return to heat, and stir in **MILNOT®**. Heat to serving temperature.   *Makes 4 cups*

VARIATIONS:

Asparagus, mushrooms, or zucchini can be substituted for broccoli.

CARROT SOUP WITH PEAS

½ stick butter
1 pound carrots, shredded
8 green onions, minced
1 cup finely chopped potatoes
1 small clove garlic, minced
⅓ teaspoon dried tarragon
¼ teaspoon dried chervil
¼ teaspoon dried marjoram
¼ teaspoon dried thyme
1½ quarts chicken stock
3 cups **COFFEE RICH® Frozen Non-Dairy Creamer**
1 (10-oz.) pkg. frozen tiny peas, thawed
Salt and pepper to taste

1. In a heavy stockpot, melt ½ stick butter over medium-low heat.
2. Add shredded carrots, green onions, potatoes, minced garlic and seasonings. Cover and cook, stirring occasionally, until vegetables are wilted, about 10 minutes.
3. Add chicken stock and boil uncovered over medium-high heat until potatoes are tender, about 15 minutes more.
4. Transfer mixture to food processor or blender in batches. Puree.
5. Return to pot and reheat.
6. Gradually stir in **COFFEE RICH®** and peas. Continue cooking until soup is just heated through.
7. Season to taste with salt and pepper.

Yield: 20 (4-oz.) servings

GREEN CHILE SOUP

2 tablespoons butter or margarine
1 tablespoon oil
4 to 5 cloves garlic, finely chopped
1 medium onion, chopped
2 teaspoons paprika
4 cups chicken broth
1½ pounds tomatoes, chopped
1 4-ounce can diced green chiles
¼ teaspoon chili powder
Salt and pepper to taste
2 8-ounce or 1 16-ounce container **Plain DANNON® Yogurt**
4 ounces Jack or Cheddar cheese, shredded
1 tablespoon chopped cilantro or parsley

Melt butter in large stock pot; add oil. Sauté garlic until lightly browned. Remove garlic and set aside. Add onion to butter; sauté until soft. Add paprika; sauté 1 minute. Add chicken broth, tomatoes, chiles, chili powder, salt and pepper. Bring to a boil; reduce heat and simmer 20 minutes. Stir in yogurt slowly; heat thoroughly over low heat. Add reserved garlic. Ladle into soup bowls; sprinkle with cheese and cilantro.   *Serves 6*

CREAM OF SPINACH SOUP

1 package **Chicken Noodle** or **Chicken Vegetable Homemade SOUP STARTER™**
4 cups water
2 cups milk
10-ounce package frozen chopped spinach, thawed
2 to 4 tablespoons freshly squeezed lemon juice, optional
Ground nutmeg for garnish

In a large saucepan or Dutch oven combine **SOUP STARTER™** ingredients and 4 cups water. Bring to a boil; reduce heat, cover and simmer 35 minutes, stirring occasionally. Add milk and spinach. Stir and cook until heated. If desired, add lemon juice to taste. Serve in bowls with nutmeg garnish.   *Yield: 6 cups*

GREEN GARDEN SOUP
(Low Calorie/Low Cholesterol)

6 cups chicken stock
1 onion
1 clove
1 celery stalk, without leaves
1 bay leaf
¼ teaspoon thyme
½ cup chopped watercress
1 cup chopped fresh spinach
¼ teaspoon **SWEETLITE™ Liquid Fructose**
⅛ teaspoon freshly ground black pepper
½ teaspoon fresh lemon juice
2 tablespoons plain low-fat yogurt

1. Pour the chicken stock in a large saucepan or soup kettle.
2. Stick the clove in the onion and add it to the chicken stock; add the celery, bay leaf and thyme.
3. Bring to a boil, reduce heat and simmer, covered, for 1 hour.
4. Remove the clove from the onion and the bay leaf and discard.
5. Put all other ingredients in the saucepan in a blender container and blend until smooth.
6. Add the watercress, spinach, fructose, pepper and lemon juice and blend until the watercress and spinach are the desired size flecks in the soup.

(Continued)

7. Serve immediately or chill and serve cold. Just before serving, hot or cold, put 1 teaspoon of yogurt on the top of each serving.
Makes 6 servings

Note: If reheated, the watercress and spinach will lose their fresh tangy flavor.

Each serving contains approximately: ½ vegetable exchange, 13 calories, .8 mg. cholesterol

CREAM OF SORREL SOUP

3 Tbsp. butter or margarine
1 medium onion, chopped
1 medium potato, peeled and diced
1 (14-oz.) can chicken broth
1 cup **SEBASTIANI VINEYARDS Chenin Blanc Wine**
4 cups finely shredded sorrel
⅔ cup heavy cream
Salt & pepper to taste

Melt butter in a 4-quart saucepan over medium heat. Add onion and cook until limp. Add diced potato, chicken broth, and **Chenin Blanc.** Cover and simmer for 20 minutes, or until potato mashes easily. Stir in sorrel and cook 3 minutes longer. In a blender whirl the mixture, a small amount at a time until pureed and smooth. Return to heat and stir in heavy cream, salt, pepper. Do not boil.
Makes 2 quarts

SNAPPIEST TOMATO SOUP

½ cup chopped onion
½ cup butter or margarine
5 cans (6-oz. each) **SNAP-E-TOM Tomato Cocktail** or 3 (10-oz.) cans
1 teaspoon **A.1. Steak Sauce**
1 cup croutons

In a medium saucepan, sauté onion in butter until transparent. Slowly add **SNAP-E-TOM** and **A.1.** Stir and continue cooking until it begins to boil. Reduce heat and simmer for another 10 minutes. Serve hot, garnished with croutons.
Serves 4

CREAMY TOMATO SOUP

½ cup minced onion
2 Tbsp. butter
¼ pound cream cheese
2 cups milk
2 cans **MANISCHEWITZ Tomato Soup** or **MANISCHEWITZ Tomato And Rice Soup**
⅛ tsp. garlic powder

In a saucepan, sauté onion in butter until tender but not brown. Mash cream cheese, gradually add milk and beat until smooth. Blend in soup and garlic powder. Heat, stirring frequently, but do not boil. Garnish with minced parsley.
Serves 4-6

QUICK LUNCHEON SOUP
(Low Calorie)

1 (12-oz.) can **DIET SHASTA® Ginger Ale**
1 (18-oz.) can tomato juice
¼ cup diced green pepper
½ cup diced celery
1 teaspoon instant minced onion
1 teaspoon salt
1 cup drained canned or cooked fresh green beans

Simmer all ingredients except green beans together until vegetables are tender-crisp, about 10 minutes. Add green beans and heat a few minutes longer.
Makes about 4 cups

35 calories per serving

PINK GREEN GODDESS SOUP

1 can (4-oz.) **ORTEGA Whole Green Chiles**
1 can (10½-oz.) condensed cream of tomato soup
1½ cups milk
2 stalks celery, chopped
½ cup sour cream
Croutons

Remove seeds from chiles. Place undiluted soup, chiles, milk and celery in blender; blend until semi-smooth. Pour this mixture into saucepan to heat over medium heat; do not bring to boil. Remove from heat and stir in sour cream. Serve warm and garnish with croutons.
Serves 4-6

VARIATION:

To create a new idea in soups, add 1 (6-oz.) can kernel corn to soup as it heats and substitute grated Jack cheese for toasted croutons as garnish. Or try this soup chilled. After blending, chill in refrigerator, serve in bowls garnished with tiny buds of fresh cauliflower.

TOMATO-SPINACH SOUP

2 cups **PREGO Spaghetti Sauce**
2½ cups water
3½ cups trimmed fresh spinach, chopped (about ¼ pound)
1 cup diced potato
2 tablespoons chopped fresh basil or 1½ teaspoons dried basil leaves, crushed
2 tablespoons chopped parsley
1½ teaspoons lemon juice
½ teaspoon ground nutmeg

In 3-quart saucepan over high heat, heat all ingredients to boiling. Reduce heat to low. Cover; simmer 20 minutes.
Makes 6 servings or 6 cups

TOMATO ZUCCHINI SOUP

2 cups unpeeled, diced zucchini
½ cup chopped onion
1 tablespoon olive oil
4 cups tomato juice
1 14½-ounce can chicken broth
3 tablespoons **HENRI'S TAS-TEE® Dressing**
2 tablespoons lime juice
1 teaspoon sugar
½ teaspoon salt
⅛ teaspoon hot pepper sauce
Parsley for garnish

1. In 2-quart saucepan, sauté zucchini and onion in olive oil.
2. Add tomato juice, chicken broth, **HENRI'S TAS-TEE® Dressing,** lime juice, sugar, salt, and hot pepper sauce.
3. Cover and simmer until vegetables are tender. Serve hot. Garnish with parsley.
Makes 6 ½-cup servings

FRENCH VEGETABLE SOUP
(Low Sodium)

1½ cups water
2 cups diced fresh tomatoes
1 cup sliced fresh mushrooms
¼ cup diced onion
¼ cup diced fresh zucchini
¼ cup sliced fresh carrot
1 teaspoon onion powder
½ teaspoon basil leaves, crushed
1 teaspoon **LEA & PERRINS Worcestershire Sauce**

In a medium saucepan bring water to a boil. Add tomatoes. Simmer, covered, until tomatoes are soft and turn into a broth, about 20 minutes. Add mushrooms, onion, zucchini, carrot, onion powder and basil. Simmer, covered, until vegetables are tender, about 10 minutes. Add **LEA & PERRINS Worcestershire Sauce**. Simmer, covered, until flavors are blended, about 2 minutes. Remove from heat. Remove 1 cup of the vegetables; place in the container of an electric blender. Blend at high speed until smooth. Return mixture to saucepan and mix well. Heat until hot.
Yield: 2 portions

51 mg. sodium per portion

HALLOWEEN ALPHABET VEGETABLE SOUP

2½ cups water
1 can (10½-oz.) beef broth
1 can (8-oz.) tomato sauce
1 envelope **FRENCH'S® Italian Style Spaghetti Sauce Mix**
1 cup each finely chopped carrots and celery
1 can (8½-oz.) cream style corn
1 cup finely chopped zucchini or yellow squash
¼ cup alphabet macaroni

Combine water, beef broth, tomato sauce, spaghetti sauce mix, carrots, celery, and corn in large pan. Simmer, covered, 15 minutes. Add zucchini and macaroni; cover and simmer 20 minutes longer, stirring occasionally.
8 servings

RONZONI® MINESTRONE
(Low Calorie)

1 (15-oz.) jar **RONZONI® Lite 'n' Natural All-Purpose or Marinara Sauce**
1 (16-oz.) pkg. **RONZONI® Small Shells #23 or Elbows #35**
1 clove garlic, minced
1 medium onion, chopped
2 Tbsp. chopped fresh parsley
¾ cup diced celery
1 Tbsp. olive oil
1 (16-oz.) can tomatoes
1 cup coarsely shredded cabbage
3 beef bouillon cubes
8 cups water
2 tsp. salt
¼ tsp. pepper
¼ tsp. celery salt
¼ tsp. basil
1 Tbsp. soy sauce
1 (16-oz.) can red kidney beans
Parmesan cheese

Cook **RONZONI® Small Shells or Elbows** per package directions. In a large soup pot, sauté garlic, onion, parsley and celery in the olive oil until lightly browned. Add sauce, tomatoes, cabbage, bouillon cubes, water and seasonings and cook uncovered 30-45 minutes. Add drained kidney beans and drained cooked pasta. Simmer 10 more minutes. Taste and add more salt and/or basil if necessary. When serving, sprinkle Parmesan cheese over each bowl.
Serves 10

245 calories per serving

STILWELL GUMBO

In a 2-quart saucepan, combine one package frozen **STILWELL Vegetable Gumbo Mixture**, one (16-ounce) can whole tomatoes (cut up, with juice), ¼ cup water, 1 Tbsp. oil, 1¼ tsp. salt and ¼ tsp. pepper. Bring to a boil, cover, reduce heat and simmer 12 to 15 minutes or until vegetables are tender.   *Makes 8 servings*

Note: If desired, add one can (4½-oz.) drained chicken or shrimp. May be served over rice.

VEGETABLE SOUP ORIENTAL
(Low Calorie)

5 beef bouillon cubes
5 cups boiling water
2 teaspoons **LEA & PERRINS Worcestershire Sauce**
1 teaspoon soy sauce
1 cup thinly sliced carrots
½ cup sliced scallions or green onions
2½ cups (½ lb.) sliced mushrooms
¼ pound torn spinach

In a medium saucepan combine bouillon cubes, water, **LEA & PERRINS,** and soy sauce. Bring to boiling point, stirring to dissolve bouillon cubes. Add carrots and scallions. Return to boiling point. Reduce heat and simmer, covered, for 10 minutes. Add mushrooms and spinach. Cover and simmer 5 minutes longer.

Calorie Count: About 36 calories per 1 cup serving

CHICKEN AND VEGETABLE SOUP
(Low Calorie/Low Sodium/Low Cholesterol)

3½ cups water
4 cups diced fresh tomatoes
¼ cup instant minced onion
1 teaspoon basil leaves, crushed
1 teaspoon paprika
¾ teaspoon instant minced garlic
¼ teaspoon salt
1/16 teaspoon ground black pepper
1½ cups sliced fresh mushrooms
¾ cup diced fresh zucchini
¾ cup sliced fresh carrots
1 cup diced cooked chicken
2 tablespoons red wine

In a medium saucepot, bring water to a boil. Add tomatoes, minced onion, basil, paprika, minced garlic, salt and black pepper. Reduce heat and simmer, covered, until tomatoes are soft, about 20 minutes. Add mushrooms, zucchini and carrots; simmer, covered, until vegetables are tender, about 8 minutes. Remove 1 cup of the vegetables and broth to the container of an electric blender; blend until pureed. Return to saucepot. Add chicken and wine; simmer, covered, until hot, about 2 minutes.

Yield: about 6 cups

Per cup: 102 calories, 125 mg sodium, 19 mg cholesterol

Favorite recipe from **The American Spice Trade Association**

CHICKEN SOUP

1 **EMPIRE Stewing Chicken**, about 4 or 5 pounds
3½ quarts water
1 tablespoon salt
3 stalks celery
1 parsley root
2 onions
3 sprigs dill
3 sprigs parsley

Clean the chicken thoroughly. Combine in a deep saucepan with the water and onions. Bring to a boil and cook over medium heat for 1½ hours. Add remaining ingredients. Cover and cook over low heat one hour longer, or until chicken is tender. Remove chicken and strain soup. *Makes about 2 to 2½ quarts of soup*

NOODLE EGG DROP SOUP

2 cans (10¾ ounces each) condensed chicken broth
4 cups water
1½ cups (4 ounces) **SKINNER® Fine Egg Noodles**, uncooked
2 eggs, slightly beaten
2 tablespoons chopped parsley
2 tablespoons butter

Bring chicken broth and water to a boil. Gradually add noodles, stirring occasionally; cook 8 minutes. Reduce heat to low; stir in eggs. Simmer 3 minutes longer. Remove from heat; stir in parsley and butter. *4 servings*

EGG DROP SOUP

6 cups water
2 tablespoons **WYLER'S® Chicken-Flavor Instant Bouillon** *or* 6 Chicken-Flavor Bouillon Cubes
2 tablespoons cornstarch
½ teaspoon monosodium glutamate, optional
1 egg, well beaten
Chopped green onions

In medium saucepan, combine water, bouillon, cornstarch and monosodium glutamate if desired. Cook, stirring constantly until bouillon dissolves. Slowly pour in egg; stir. Heat through. Garnish with onions. Refrigerate leftovers. *Makes about 1½ quart*

CHICKEN SOUP WITH CHEESE DUMPLINGS

1 can (19-ounces) **CAMPBELL'S Chunky Old Fashioned Chicken Soup**
½ cup biscuit mix
2 tablespoons finely shredded sharp Cheddar cheese
1 teaspoon chopped parsley
2 tablespoons milk

1. In 2-quart saucepan over medium heat, heat soup to boiling.
2. Meanwhile, in small bowl with fork, stir remaining ingredients until mixture forms soft dough. Drop by heaping teaspoons onto boiling soup. Reduce heat to low; cover. Cook 15 minutes or until dumplings are done.
3. Ladle into soup bowls. *Makes 2 servings*

CHICKEN CUCUMBER SOUP

2 large cucumbers, peeled
2 tablespoons butter or margarine
5 cups chicken stock or canned chicken broth (regular strength)
½ teaspoon grated fresh ginger
1 green onion, thinly sliced
Salt and pepper
½ cup dry white wine (Chablis or Sauterne)
Cucumber slices

Cut cucumbers into quarters, remove seeds, and chop finely. Sauté chopped cucumbers in butter 1 minute. Add chicken stock, ginger and onion. Season to taste with salt and pepper. Simmer 15 minutes. Stir in wine and reheat quickly. Garnish with thin cucumber slices. *Makes 6 servings*

Favorite recipe from the **Hawaiian Ginger Growers Association**

QUICK CHICKEN SOUP WITH NEW MILL® KLUSKI

1 quart seasoned chicken broth
½ cup diced, cooked carrots
½ cup diced, cooked chicken meat
1 Tbsp. chopped parsley
3 ounces **NEW MILL® KLUSKI Noodles**

Bring broth, carrots and chicken meat to a boil in a large saucepan. Add **NEW MILL® KLUSKI**. Simmer for 15 minutes. Add parsley and serve.

Serves 4 to 6

MEATBALL SOUP FLORENTINE

½ pound ground beef
¼ cup fine dry bread crumbs
1 egg, slightly beaten
2 tablespoons grated Parmesan cheese
2 tablespoons chopped parsley
½ teaspoon salt
1 tablespoon olive oil
1 can (10¾-ounces) **CAMPBELL'S Condensed Beefy Mushroom Soup**
1 can (10¾-ounces) **CAMPBELL'S Condensed Tomato Soup**
1½ soup cans water
1 cup sliced zucchini squash
½ cup carrots cut in thin sticks (2-inch)
1 small clove garlic, minced
½ teaspoon basil leaves, crushed
1 cup cooked small shell macaroni
½ cup chopped fresh spinach

Mix *thoroughly* beef, bread crumbs, egg, cheese, parsley and salt; shape firmly into 24 meatballs. In large saucepan, brown meatballs in oil. Add remaining ingredients except macaroni and spinach. Cover; bring to boil. Reduce heat; simmer 10 minutes or until done. Stir occasionally. Add macaroni and spinach; heat.

Makes about 7 cups, 4 servings
For 14 cups, double all ingredients

SAVORY PORK SOUP

2 pounds boneless pork shoulder, cut into 1-inch cubes
¼ cup all-purpose flour
¼ cup cooking oil
1 bunch green onions, sliced
2 cloves garlic, minced
2 (16-ounce) cans tomatoes
2 (10½-ounce) cans beef broth
1 (16-ounce) jar small boiled onions, drained
1 (6-ounce) can cocktail vegetable juice
½ cup water
3 stalks celery, sliced into 1-inch pieces
2 medium yellow squash, sliced
1 bay leaf
1 tablespoon dried parsley flakes
1 teaspoon salt
½ teaspoon seasoned pepper

Dredge pork cubes in flour, coating well. Heat oil in a Dutch oven; brown cubes on all sides in hot oil. Add green onions and garlic; cook over medium-high heat for one minute, stirring constantly. Add remaining ingredients; bring to a boil. Reduce heat; cover and simmer for 1 to 1½ hours, stirring occasionally. Remove bay leaf.

Yield: 3 quarts

Favorite recipe from **National Pork Producers Council**

ITALIAN FRESH TOMATO AND SAUSAGE SOUP

2 pounds Florida tomatoes
3 tablespoons oil
¼ pound sweet Italian sausage links, cut in ¼-inch slices
1 cup chopped onions
6 cups beef broth
½ teaspoon Italian seasoning
½ teaspoon sugar
½ teaspoon salt
½ cup raw regular cooking rice

Use tomatoes held at room temperature until fully ripe. Drop tomatoes into boiling water for 30 seconds; remove skins. Dice tomatoes (makes about 3 cups); set aside. In a medium saucepan heat oil until hot; add sausage; brown on both sides, about 5 minutes. Remove from pan and set aside. Add onions; sauté until tender, about 5 minutes. Add beef broth, Italian seasoning, sugar and salt. Bring to a boil; add rice and reserved tomatoes. Simmer, covered, until rice is tender, about 20 minutes. Add reserved sausage, simmer, covered, for 2 minutes.

Yield: about 8 cups

Favorite recipe from **Florida Tomato Exchange**

SAUSAGE AND VEGETABLE SOUP
(Microwave Recipe)

12 ounces "fully-cooked" smoked link sausage, cut into ½-inch slices
1 medium potato, grated
1 large carrot, cut into 1½ × ⅛-inch strips
1 medium onion, chopped
3½ cups water
¾ teaspoon salt
¼ teaspoon celery seed
2 dashes crushed red pepper
2 cups coarsely chopped cabbage
2 tablespoons snipped parsley

Combine potato, carrot, onion, water, salt, celery seed and red pepper in 2-quart microwave-safe bowl. Cover with plastic wrap, venting one corner and microwave at HIGH 12 minutes, stirring every 6 minutes. Stir cabbage and sausage into vegetables, cover with plastic wrap, vent and microwave at HIGH 4 minutes. Stir in parsley, cover with plastic wrap, vent and microwave at HIGH 4 minutes.

4 servings

Favorite recipe from **National Live Stock & Meat Board**

HUNGARIAN GOULASH SOUP

1 cup chopped onion
2 cloves garlic, finely chopped
2 tablespoons margarine or butter
2 tablespoons paprika
1 pound beef stew, cut into 1-inch pieces
8 cups water
1 (16-ounce) can tomatoes, undrained
2 tablespoons WYLER'S® Beef-Flavor Instant Bouillon *or* 6 Beef-Flavor Bouillon Cubes
1 teaspoon sugar
½ teaspoon marjoram leaves
⅛ teaspoon pepper
1 cup pared, diced potatoes
1 cup chopped green pepper

In large saucepan or Dutch oven, cook onion and garlic in margarine until tender. Add paprika; stir until onions are coated. Stir in remaining ingredients except potatoes and green pepper. Bring to a boil; reduce heat and simmer uncovered 1 hour or until beef is tender. Add potatoes and green pepper; cook 20 minutes or until potatoes are tender. Refrigerate leftovers. *Makes about 2 quarts*

GOLDEN CHEESE SOUP

¼ cup water
2 tablespoons real butter
1 package (10-oz.) frozen whole kernel corn
½ cup shredded carrot
¼ cup chopped onion
⅛ teaspoon pepper
2 cans (10¾-oz. each) condensed cream of potato soup
2 cups real milk
1 cup (4-oz.) shredded real Cheddar cheese
½ cup (2-oz.) shredded real Provolone cheese
1 cup broccoli flowerets, cooked (optional)

Combine water, butter, corn, carrot, onion and pepper in 3-quart saucepan. Cover; simmer 10 minutes. Add soup, milk, cheeses and broccoli, stirring until cheese melts. Bring to serving temperature over low heat. *Yield: about 7½ cups*

Favorite recipe from **American Dairy Association**

EASY BEER-CHEESE SOUP

2 cans (10½-ounces each) condensed cream soup, such as celery, mushroom or chicken
1 teaspoon Worcestershire sauce
¼ teaspoon seasoned salt
¼ teaspoon paprika
2 cans or bottles (12-ounces each) STROH'S Beer
2 cups shredded Cheddar cheese (8-ounces)
Garnish (optional)

1. In a saucepan, mix soup and seasonings. Add beer gradually while stirring. Heat to simmering.
2. Add cheese. Heat slowly, stirring constantly until cheese is melted.
3. Pour into soup bowls or cups. Garnish as desired with croutons, bacon bits, minced parsley or chives.

7 cups, about 8 servings

MERKT'S "COMPANY'S COMING" SOUP

½ cup **MERKT'S Swiss Cheese Spread**
½ cup **MERKT'S Cheddar Cheese Spread**
3 cups water
2 chicken bouillon cubes
1 cup diced carrots
1 cup diced celery
½ teaspoon white pepper
2 tablespoons sugar
½ teaspoon **AC'CENT®**
2 tablespoons butter
2 cups hot milk
¼ cup flour

Bring water and bouillon cubes to boil in large kettle. Add celery, carrots, white pepper, sugar and **AC'CENT®**. Cover, simmer 10 minutes, until vegetables are tender.

Melt butter in large saucepan, blend in flour. Stir in hot milk gradually. Stir constantly over medium heat until smooth. Stir in cheeses until melted. Add to vegetables; heat through but do not boil.

Cooking sherry may be added to taste.   *Serves 12 people*

VEGETABLE CHEESE CHOWDER

1 cup thinly sliced celery
1 cup thinly sliced carrots
½ cup minced onion
¼ cup butter
¼ cup flour
1 teaspoon salt
⅛ teaspoon white pepper
3 cups milk
1 cup (4-ounces) shredded **COUNTY LINE®** Colby or
  Cheddar Cheese
2 tablespoons minced parsley

In large heavy saucepan, cook celery, carrots and onion in butter until tender. Stir in flour, salt and pepper. Gradually add milk, mixing well. Stir over low heat until slightly thickened. Add cheese, stirring until cheese melts. Sprinkle with parsley.

1 quart

MEXICORN CHOWDER

2 tablespoons butter
2 tablespoons flour
1 (10½ oz.) can condensed chicken broth
1 cup milk
1 tablespoon minced onion
1 can mexicorn
1 (2¼ oz.) can **LINDSAY®** Sliced Ripe Olives
⅛ teaspoon fine herbs

Melt butter and blend in flour. Stir in chicken broth gradually. Add milk and onion and cook, stirring until mixture boils thoroughly. Add corn, drained ripe olives and herbs. Serve hot.

Makes about 3 cups

OVEN BAKED VEGETABLE CHOWDER

PAM® No-Stick Cooking Spray
5 large eggs (1 cup)
2 tablespoons enriched all-purpose flour
2½ cups reconstituted nonfat dry milk, scalded
3½ cups mashed cooked carrots (about 12)
2 cups diced cooked potatoes (about 2)
1½ cups shredded sharp Cheddar cheese
½ cup chopped parsley
¼ cup minced onion
1 teaspoon salt
⅛ teaspoon pepper
⅛ teaspoon nutmeg

Coat a 2-quart round casserole with **PAM® No-Stick Cooking Spray** according to directions.

In a large mixing bowl, beat together eggs and flour until well mixed. Add remaining ingredients, stirring to blend. Pour into casserole. Set in pan of hot water. Bake in a 375°F moderate oven for 1 hour. Spoon into soup bowls.   *Makes 8 servings*

Calories per serving: 223

CREAMY CORN AND SAUSAGE CHOWDER

1 cup chopped green pepper
½ cup chopped onion
¼ cup butter or margarine
1 can (10¾-ounces) condensed cream of potato soup
3 cups milk
1 tablespoon Worcestershire sauce
1 tablespoon chicken-flavor instant bouillon
1 pound **MR. TURKEY®** Smoked Turkey Sausage,
  cut into ½-inch pieces
1 can (16-ounces) cream-style corn
2 cups shredded Cheddar cheese

Sauté green pepper and onion in butter in large saucepan 5 minutes. Stir in potato soup, milk, Worcestershire sauce, and bouillon. Heat to boiling, reduce heat and simmer uncovered for 10 minutes. Stir in sausage and corn; simmer 15 minutes. Stir in cheese until melted.   *Makes 4 servings (2 cups each)*

HEARTY POTATO CHOWDER

2 cups diced pared potatoes
½ cup sliced carrots
1 teaspoon salt
2 cups water
2 tablespoons chopped onion
2 tablespoons **MEADOW GOLD®** Butter
2 tablespoons all-purpose flour
¼ teaspoon paprika
⅛ teaspoon pepper
2 cups **MEADOW GOLD®** Viva 2% Low Fat Milk
2 slices crisp bacon, crumbled

In medium saucepan, cook potatoes and carrots in salted water until tender. In medium skillet, cook onion in butter for 3 to 5 minutes. Add flour and seasonings; mix well. Gradually stir in milk. Add to potato mixture in saucepan. Stir over low heat until slightly thickened. Top with crumbled bacon.   *4 to 5 servings*

VEGETABLE CHOWDER

¼ cup **MAZOLA® Corn Oil Margarine**
1 cup chopped onion
1 clove garlic, minced
1 cup chopped celery
4 cups beef bouillon
3 cups peeled, cubed potatoes
1 can (16-oz.) tomatoes
1 can (17-oz.) corn, undrained
2 cups sliced carrots
½ teaspoon salt
½ teaspoon ground thyme
½ teaspoon celery seed
2 tablespoons **ARGO®/KINGSFORD'S® Corn Starch**
¼ cup water

In 5-quart Dutch oven or saucepot, melt margarine over medium heat. Add onion and garlic and cook until transparent. Add celery, bouillon, potatoes, tomatoes, corn, carrots, salt, thyme and celery seed. Bring to boil over medium heat. Cover and simmer 30 minutes, or until vegetables are tender. Stir together corn starch and water until smooth. Add to soup. Stirring constantly, bring to boil over medium heat, and boil 1 minute.

Makes about 3½ quarts

CORN CHOWDER

6 slices **WILSON® Western Hearty Cut Bacon**
½ cup onion, chopped
1 stalk celery, sliced
2 medium potatoes, peeled and cubed
1 (17-oz.) can whole kernel corn
½ cup water
½ teaspoon salt
¼ teaspoon pepper
3 tablespoons flour
1½ cups milk

Cut bacon in 1-inch pieces. Cook in a large saucepan until crisp. Remove bacon. Reserve 2 tablespoons drippings in pan. Add onion and celery. Sauté until onion is tender. Add potatoes, corn and liquid, water, salt and pepper. Bring to a boil. Reduce heat; cover and simmer 15 minutes or until potatoes are tender. Combine flour and ¼ cup milk in a small bowl until smooth. Stir in remaining milk. Pour into corn mixture. Cook over medium heat, stirring constantly, until mixture comes to a full boil. Stir and boil 1 minute. Stir in bacon. Heat 5 minutes.   *Makes about 6 cups*

NEW ENGLAND CLAM CHOWDER

2 cans (10-oz. each) **BUMBLE BEE® Whole Baby Clams**
¼ pound salt pork, finely chopped
1 medium onion, chopped
3 medium potatoes, peeled and diced
Water
Dash pepper
2 cups milk
1 tablespoon butter

Drain clams, reserving liquid. In large saucepan, sauté salt pork until golden. Add onion and cook until tender, about 5 minutes. Add potatoes; cook, stirring occasionally, about 5 minutes. Combine reserved clam liquid with enough water to make 2 cups liquid;

add to pan along with pepper. Cook, covered, until potatoes are tender, about 20 minutes. Add milk, clams and butter. Heat through. Do not boil.   *Makes about 2 quarts*

FISH SOUP
(Zuppa di Pesce)

½ cup finely sliced onion
2 cloves garlic, minced
¼ cup **BERTOLLI® Olive Oil**
2½ cups **BERTOLLI® Spaghetti Sauce With Clams**
1½ teaspoons grated lemon rind
¼ teaspoon fennel seeds, crushed
⅛ teaspoon pepper
1 bottle (8-ounces) clam juice
¾ cup **BERTOLLI® Orvieto Wine**
¾ cup water
4 celery leaves, minced
1½ pounds whitefish, cod, snapper or flounder (use 3 kinds)
1 can (8-ounces) clams, undrained
1 tablespoon minced parsley

Sauté onion and garlic in oil in Dutch oven until tender. Stir in spaghetti sauce, lemon, fennel and pepper; heat to boiling. Reduce heat; simmer 10 minutes.

Heat clam juice, wine, water and celery leaves to boiling in saucepan. Reduce heat; simmer 10 minutes. Stir into sauce with remaining ingredients; simmer until fish is tender, about 10 minutes.

Makes 6 servings (1 cup each)

ALASKA POLLOCK CHOWDER

1 pound Alaska pollock fillets
¼ cup chopped bacon
2 tablespoons bacon drippings
2 garlic cloves, finely chopped
1 can (1 pound 12 ounces) stewed tomatoes
2 cans (8 ounces each) tomato sauce
2 cups water
2 cups Potatoes O'Brien Mix
¼ teaspoon thyme
Liquid hot pepper sauce to taste
¼ cup soy sauce
½ cup dry Vermouth (optional)

Thaw fish if frozen. Cut into one-inch pieces. Fry bacon until crisp, reserving 2 tablespoons bacon drippings. Add garlic and cook with reserved bacon drippings until tender. Add remaining ingredients except fish and Vermouth. Cover and simmer 30 minutes. Add fish and Vermouth. Cook an additional 10 minutes. Sprinkle with parsley.   *Makes 6 servings*

Favorite recipe from **National Marine Fisheries Service**

CONCH CHOWDER

1½-2 lb. conch, cleaned
½ lb. lean salt pork or bacon, finely chopped
2 medium onions, sliced
1½ tsp. finely chopped garlic
4 medium tomatoes, peeled, seeded and chopped
1 large boiling potato, peeled and cut into ½-inch cubes
1 Tbsp. uncooked long-grain rice
3 bay leaves
1 qt. water
1 (13-oz.) can evaporated milk

Put conch meat through the finest blade of a food grinder or chop in a food processor and set aside. Sauté salt pork or bacon until crisp and brown. Add onions and garlic and cook, stirring often, until soft but not brown. Stir in conch, tomatoes, potato, rice, bay leaves and water. Bring to a boil, then reduce heat and simmer, partially covered for 1 hour. Pour in evaporated milk and stir until heated through, but do not allow to come to a boil. Remove bay leaves.   *Serves 4-6*

Favorite recipe from **Rhode Island Seafood Council**

FISHERMAN'S WHARF CIOPPINO

1 can (13-oz.) **BUMBLE BEE® Solid White Tuna**
1 can (10-oz.) **BUMBLE BEE® Whole Clams**
2 large cloves garlic, pressed
1 large onion, chopped
1 green bell pepper, seeded, chopped
¼ pound **DOLE® Fresh Mushrooms**, sliced
3 tablespoons chopped parsley
¼ cup olive oil
1 can (28-oz.) whole tomatoes, chopped
1 bottle (8-oz.) clam juice
1 chicken bouillon cube, crumbled
2 cups dry red wine
⅓ cup tomato paste
1 teaspoon oregano, crumbled
1 teaspoon sugar
½ teaspoon salt
¼ teaspoon pepper
1 pkg. (6-oz.) frozen baby shrimp, thawed

Drain tuna. Drain clams, reserving liquid. In a Dutch oven, sauté garlic, onion, bell pepper, mushrooms and parsley in olive oil. Add reserved clam liquid, tomatoes and liquid, clam juice, bouillon cube, red wine, tomato paste and seasonings to sautéed vegetables. Simmer, uncovered 35 minutes. Add tuna, clams and shrimp; cook until heated through.   *Makes 2 generous quarts*

TASTY BUDDIG BISQUE

1 cup sliced mushrooms
¾ cup sliced onions
½ cup chopped green pepper
3 tablespoons butter or margarine
2 cans (11-oz.) Cheddar cheese soup
2½ cups milk
1 cup light cream
1 teaspoon paprika
¼ teaspoon pepper
1 (4-oz.) **Family Pak BUDDIG Smoked Sliced Ham**, sliced
1 (4-oz.) **Family Pak BUDDIG Smoked Chopped Turkey**, sliced
3 tablespoons sherry

CONVENTIONAL METHOD:
Sauté mushrooms, onions and green pepper in butter or margarine in 3-quart saucepan until tender. Stir in all remaining ingredients except sherry and simmer gently 10 minutes. Stir in sherry and serve.   *Serves 6*

MICROWAVE METHOD:
Cook mushrooms, onions and green pepper in 3-quart casserole for 3 to 4 minutes. Stir in all remaining ingredients except sherry and cook on medium high (70%) for 6 to 8 minutes. Stir in sherry and serve.   *Serves 6*

CHEESE BISQUE

2 cups (8 ounces) shredded **OLD CANADIAN Cheese**
½ stick (¼ cup) butter or margarine
¼ cup chopped onion
¼ cup flour
½ teaspoon dry mustard
⅛ teaspoon white pepper
1 teaspoon Worcestershire sauce
2 chicken bouillon cubes
2 cups water
¼ cup *each* chopped green pepper, chopped celery and shredded carrot
1 quart milk
Croutons*

Melt butter in large saucepan; add onion and cook about 3 minutes. Blend in flour, mustard, pepper, Worcestershire sauce, bouillon, water, green pepper, celery and carrot. Simmer, covered, 10 minutes. Add milk and heat almost to boiling. Add cheese and stir until cheese is melted. Serve hot topped with croutons.
                                                          Yield: 7 cups

*CROUTONS

Lightly toast 1 cup (½-inch) bread cubes. Combine 2 tablespoons melted butter and ½ teaspoon garlic salt. Pour over croutons and toast until golden.

THRIFTY FISH BISQUE

1 lb. boneless pieces of fish (sole, flounder or any other lean fish)
3 tablespoons margarine or butter
2 tablespoons chopped green onions
2 tablespoons chopped chives
1 tablespoon flour
3 cups milk
2-4 tablespoons **GOLD SEAL Dry Sauterne Wine**
½ cup heavy cream
Salt and white pepper to taste

Sauté onions and chives in melted butter in large, heavy-duty pot. Then remove the onions and chives and reserve. Stir the flour into the melted butter, cook for 3 minutes, then add milk, stirring constantly, until just before boiling. Stir in fish, onions and chives, and cook, stirring frequently, until fish flakes apart. Take the pot from the heat and add cream, salt, pepper and Dry Sauterne. Then pour into serving tureen and dust with paprika.

KRAB BISQUE

1 pkg. (6-oz.) **JAC King Krab Simulated Crab Legs** (cut and separate)
1 can condensed cream of celery soup
½ soup can of milk
½ soup can of water
½ cup celery, finely chopped

Blend soup, milk and water. Add **Krab Meat** and celery to mixture and chill thoroughly before serving.

CHEESY VEGETABLE BISQUE

½ cup chopped carrots
½ cup sliced celery
⅓ cup chopped onion
1 small clove garlic, minced
2 tablespoons butter or margarine
2 cups chicken stock or broth
3 cups milk
3 tablespoons flour
1½ cups shredded **JARLSBERG Cheese**
1 egg yolk
1 cup cooked corn
1 cup cooked peas
2 tablespoons chopped parsley

In large deep saucepan, cook carrots, celery, onion and garlic in butter until tender. Add chicken broth. Cover and simmer 10 minutes. Blend ⅓ cup milk with flour. Add remaining 2⅔ cup milk to broth. Bring to boil. Add flour mixture. Heat, stirring until thickened. Reduce heat. Add cheese. Blend in egg yolk and vegetables. Heat, do not boil. Sprinkle with parsley.

Makes 8 servings

GAZPACHO
(Cold Spanish Soup)

3 slices bread
3 tablespoons olive oil
2 cloves garlic, minced
1 can (28 ounces) **REDPACK Whole Tomatoes in Juice**
1 tablespoon chicken soup base concentrate*
¼ cup rosé wine
Pinch of salt
1 large cucumber, peeled and finely grated
Juice of 1 lemon
Parsley or cilantro

In blender whir broken up bread to make fresh breadcrumbs. Heat olive oil in skillet; sauté garlic until golden brown; add bread crumbs and mix well. Remove bread mixture from pan and place in deep bowl; add tomatoes and chicken soup base. Use pastry cutter or fork to blend thoroughly. Stir in wine, salt and cucumber. Refrigerate to chill. Serve cold garnished with lemon juice and parsley or cilantro. *Makes about 5 cups thick soup*

***Note:** 2 chicken bouillon cubes may be substituted.

LOW CALORIE GAZPACHO

4 **WASA® Lite Rye Crispbread Slices**
1 clove garlic
1 small onion, chopped
3 large tomatoes, peeled and cut into large chunks
1 cucumber, peeled and cut into thick slices
1 small green pepper, seeded and coarsely chopped
2 tablespoons salad oil
2 tablespoons lemon juice
1 cup clam juice
½ teaspoon oregano
Salt and pepper
Celery salt

Combine garlic, onion, tomatoes, cucumber, green pepper, oil, lemon juice, clam juice, oregano and 1 **Lite Rye** slice in a blender and whirl at chop speed until finely chopped. Pour into serving bowl and season to taste with salt and pepper. Chill for several hours or until icy cold. Sprinkle remaining **Lite Rye** slices with celery salt. Break slices into bite-size pieces. When ready to serve, spoon Gazpacho into individual bowls. Place 1 or 2 ice cubes into each serving. Sprinkle **Lite Rye** pieces over each serving.

Serves 6

101 calories per serving

COLD SWISS CHARD SOUP

1 bunch Swiss chard, chopped
½ cup chopped celery
4 green onions, chopped
2 Tbsp. fresh parsley
1 clove garlic, minced
⅛ tsp. each oregano, dill weed and pepper
2 chicken bouillon cubes
2 Tbsp. olive oil
2 cups water
1 cup **PAUL MASSON® Chablis Wine**
3 Tbsp. grated Parmesan cheese

Simmer Swiss chard, celery, onions, parsley, garlic, seasonings, bouillon cubes, oil and water 20 minutes; add wine. Heat 10 more minutes. Blend soup in processor or blender until pureed; blend in cheese. Chill. *6 servings*

Poultry

Chicken

HOLIDAY STUFFED ROASTER

½ cup chopped celery
¼ cup sliced green onion
7 tablespoons butter or margarine
2 cups coarse dry bread crumbs
1 cup chopped drained raw oysters
¼ cup oyster liquid
2 tablespoons chopped fresh parsley
½ teaspoon salt
½ teaspoon poultry seasoning
⅛ teaspoon pepper
1 PERDUE® Oven Stuffer Roaster

Sauté celery and onion in 6 tablespoons butter until tender. Remove from heat. Blend in bread, oysters, oyster liquid, parsley and spices. Pre-heat oven to 350°F. Stuff bird with oyster mixture. Tie legs together. Dot with remaining 1 tablespoon butter. Season with salt and pepper.

Roast 2¼ to 2¾ hours for 5-6 pound bird; 2½ to 3 hours for 6 to 7 pound bird.

BARBECUED CHICKEN ORIENTAL

Make a basting sauce of ½ cup salad oil, ½ cup COLGIN HICKORY LIQUID SMOKE, 1 #2 can tomato juice, ½ cup dry wine, 5 drops liquid pepper seasoning, dash of soy sauce, juice of one lemon, salt and pepper to taste.

Brush sauce on the split chicken or chicken breast before cooking. Baste the chicken frequently. Cook well done to a golden brown. Try this sauce baste for your outdoor charcoal broil.

LEMON BARBECUED CHICKEN

½ cup lemon juice
2 teaspoons grated lemon peel
2 teaspoons oil
1 teaspoon MORTON® Table Salt
1 teaspoon ginger
1 teaspoon paprika
½ teaspoon onion powder
½ teaspoon black pepper
2 broiler-fryers, each about 3 pounds, cut up

Early in Day: In shallow baking dish, mix all ingredients, except chicken. Add chicken, turning to coat all sides. Cover and refrigerate.

About 1 Hour Before Serving: Prepare outdoor grill for barbecuing. Place chicken on grill over medium coals. Grill 45 minutes, or until tender, turning occasionally. *Makes 8 servings*

OVEN BAKING VARIATION:

Marinate chicken as above. Bake in baking dish at 375°F for 1 hour, or until tender.

HONEY 'N' SPICE BARBECUE CHICKEN

½ cup HEINZ 57 Sauce
¼ cup honey
2 to 2½ pounds broiler-fryer pieces
Melted butter or margarine

Combine 57 Sauce and honey. Place the chicken pieces on broiler pan or grill; brush with melted butter, then 57 Sauce-honey mixture. Broil or grill until chicken is tender, turning and basting frequently with honey mixture. *Makes 4-5 servings*

Note: For a flavorful sauce to serve over slices of ham or meat loaf, combine 2 parts HEINZ 57 Sauce and 1 part honey.

SOUTHLAND'S FAMOUS BARBECUED CHICKEN

1 jar (10 ozs.) DURKEE Famous Sauce
¾ teaspoon DURKEE Dry Mustard
2 teaspoons lemon juice
¼ cup vinegar
2¼ teaspoons Worcestershire sauce
2 2½- to 3-pound broiler-fryers, split in half
¼ cup melted margarine

Combine all ingredients except chicken and margarine. Brush chickens inside and out with melted margarine. Place cavity side down on grill about 4 inches above hot coals. Turn chicken about every 10 minutes for a total of 45 to 60 minutes, brushing with margarine each time. During the last 10 minutes cooking time, baste both sides with sauce. For broiling inside: Place chickens skin side up on rack of broiler pan. Brush with margarine. Place pan 7 to 9 inches from broiler unit. Turn chicken about every 10 minutes for a total of 45 to 50 minutes, brushing with margarine each time. During the last 10 minutes cooking time, baste both sides with sauce.

Makes 4 servings

TEXAS BARBECUE CHICKEN

4 lbs. frying chicken (meaty pieces)
Oil for frying
1 can (15-oz.) NALLEY®'S Chili Without Beans
1 cup tomato juice
¼ cup minced onion
2 Tbsp. lemon juice
1 Tbsp. Worcestershire
2 tsp. sugar
1 tsp. salt
1 cup pitted ripe olives

Brown chicken in oil; drain. Remove to shallow baking dish. Combine remaining ingredients and simmer 5 minutes. Pour sauce over chicken; cover with foil and bake in 350° oven 30 minutes. Uncover and bake 20 minutes or until chicken is tender, basting several times. Arrange chicken on platter. *(Good in a rice ring!)* Stir a little water into sauce and pour over chicken.

Makes 5 or 6 servings

HICKORY SMOKED BAR-B-QUE CHICKEN

1 1½- to 2-lb. chicken, quartered
1 3½-oz. bottle **WRIGHT'S Hickory Liquid Smoke**™
1 cup hot water
Barbecue sauce

Place chicken pieces in a shallow dish. Combine liquid smoke and water. Marinate chicken in liquid smoke solution for 15 minutes, turn chicken pieces and marinate for additional 15 minutes. (Smaller pieces require shorter marinating time.)

Remove chicken from marinade, drain and place on a baking pan. Bake uncovered in a 325° F oven for 45 to 50 minutes.

Dip or brush chicken with barbecue sauce and bake an additional 10 to 15 minutes. (Chicken may be cooked on an outdoor grill.)   *Makes 4 servings*

CRISPY FRIED CHICKEN

2½ to 3 lb. cut-up frying chicken (or use chicken parts)
CRISCO® Shortening for deep frying

Seasoned Flour:
1½ cups all-purpose flour
1 tablespoon garlic salt
1½ teaspoons black pepper
1½ teaspoons paprika
¼ teaspoon poultry seasoning

Combine all ingredients; set aside.

Crispy Batter:
⅔ cup all-purpose flour
½ teaspoon salt
⅛ teaspoon pepper
1 beaten egg yolk
¾ cup flat beer* or water

Combine flour and seasonings in medium bowl. Combine egg yolk and beer or water. Add gradually to dry ingredients.

Heat **CRISCO®** to 365° in deep saucepan or deep fryer to a depth of about 2 inches. Moisten chicken pieces. Dip in seasoned flour, then batter, then back in seasoned flour. Fry in hot **CRISCO®** for 15 to 18 minutes or until well browned. Drain on paper toweling.   *4 servings*

*If you are using beer and batter becomes too thick, add a little extra beer.

NEW HAMPSHIRE FRIED CHICKEN

1 cup flour
⅓ cup **ARGO®/KINGSFORD'S® Corn Starch**
1 teaspoon salt
⅛ teaspoon paprika
2 eggs
1 cup milk
1 broiler-fryer chicken, cut in parts
1 quart **MAZOLA® Corn Oil** (about)

In medium bowl stir together flour, corn starch, salt and paprika. Add eggs, stirring with fork until all ingredients are moistened. Gradually stir in milk just until combined. Dip chicken pieces in batter. Pour corn oil into heavy, sturdy, flat bottomed 3-quart saucepan or deep fryer, filling utensil no more than ⅓ full. Heat over medium heat to 350°F. Carefully add chicken a few pieces at a time. Fry about 15 minutes, or until juices run clear when pierced with a fork. Drain on paper towels.

Makes 4 servings

TERIYAKI SESAME FRIED CHICKEN

1 package (2 lb.) **BANQUET® Heat and Serve Frozen Fully Cooked Fried Chicken**
2 tablespoons teriyaki sauce
1 tablespoon sesame seeds

Place chicken on shallow baking pan. Brush with teriyaki sauce. Sprinkle sesame seeds on top. Heat in 375°F oven 30 to 35 minutes or until hot.   *Makes 5 servings*

CHICKEN MARYLAND

3 pounds frying chicken pieces
½ cup **KIKKOMAN Teriyaki Sauce**
2 eggs
6 tablespoons water, divided
½ cup flour
1½ cups dry bread crumbs
Vegetable oil for frying

Gravy:
2 tablespoons flour
1 cup milk
1 cup water
1 tablespoon **KIKKOMAN Soy Sauce**

Place chicken and teriyaki sauce in large plastic bag; press air out and close top securely. Refrigerate 8 hours or overnight; turn bag over occasionally. Beat eggs together with 2 tablespoons water. Remove chicken from marinade; coat with ½ cup flour. Dip into egg mixture; then roll in bread crumbs. Pour enough oil in large frying pan or electric frying pan to measure ¼ inch; heat to 350°F. Brown chicken pieces on all sides in hot oil over medium heat. Remove chicken; pour off and discard oil. Return chicken to pan; pour in remaining 4 tablespoons water. Cover and simmer 20 minutes, or until chicken is tender. Remove chicken; keep warm while preparing gravy. Blend together flour and milk; stir into pan drippings with water and soy sauce. Cook until mixture boils and thickens, stirring constantly. Serve gravy with chicken.

Makes 4 to 6 servings

OVEN FRIED CHICKEN

¼ cup butter or margarine
2 cups **PEPPERIDGE FARM® Herb Seasoned Stuffing**, crushed
1 teaspoon salt
2- to 3-pound chicken, cut up
1 egg
1 tablespoon water

Gravy:
1 can (10¾-oz.) chicken gravy
½ cup sour cream

Preheat oven to 425° F. Put butter in shallow baking pan and place in oven until melted. Meanwhile combine crushed stuffing and salt in a plastic bag.

Dip chicken parts into egg that has been beaten with water. Then shake, a few pieces at a time, in bag until well coated. Place chicken, skin side down, in melted butter. Do not layer in pan. Bake, uncovered, 30 minutes, turn and continue baking for 15 minutes.   *Serves 4*

GRAVY:
Combine canned gravy with sour cream and heat to just below boiling.

CHEDDAR CHICKEN

1 3-pound **HEALTH VALLEY®** Cut-Up Chicken, thawed and patted dry
½ cup **HEALTH VALLEY®** Safflower Oil
½ teaspoon each of: crushed basil and oregano leaves
¼ cup chopped onion
1 garlic clove, minced
1 cup (½ can) **HEALTH VALLEY®** Tomato Sauce
1 cup (½ can) **HEALTH VALLEY®** Mushroom Soup
½ cup (¼ can) **HEALTH VALLEY®** Chicken Broth
2 cups (⅔ package) shredded **HEALTH VALLEY®** Raw Milk Cheddar Cheese
½ cup wheat germ

In a large skillet, heat oil and brown chicken on all sides. Remove chicken, then pour off all but 1 tablespoon of oil. Sauté herbs and vegetables; add chicken, tomato sauce, mushroom soup, and chicken broth. Simmer for one hour.

Mix cheese and wheat germ.

When ready to serve, place chicken and vegetable-soup-sauce mixture on bed of cooked **HEALTH VALLEY®** Spaghetti and cooked **HEALTH VALLEY®** Green Peas, top with mixture of cheese and wheat germ and place under broiler until cheese is melted and lightly browned.

Serve on a heated platter over a bed of **HEALTH VALLEY® Frozen Spinach**, cooked five minutes and drained.

Total Preparation Time: 1½ hours   *Yield: 4 to 6 servings*

TANDOORI CHICKEN
(Low Calorie/Low Fat)

1 2½- to 3-pound broiler-fryer, cut up
1 teaspoon cayenne
1 teaspoon paprika
¼ cup lemon juice
6 tablespoons red wine vinegar
¾ cup chopped onions
¼ cup chopped pimiento
¾ cup plain low-fat yogurt
1 packet **BUTTER BUDS®**, mixed with ¼ cup hot water
¼ teaspoon ginger

Preheat oven to 375°F. Wash, dry, and skin chicken. Prick in several places with sharp knife point. Arrange chicken in glass baking dish. In separate bowl, mix cayenne and paprika with lemon juice and vinegar. Rub into chicken. Refrigerate 1 hour. In blender container, combine onions, pimiento, yogurt, **BUTTER BUDS®**, and ginger. Cover and process at medium speed 10 seconds. Pour yogurt mixture over chicken. Bake 40 to 50 minutes, or until tender. Baste frequently with yogurt mixture while cooking.   *4 servings*

Per Serving (¼ chicken): Calories: 245; Fat: 6g

Note: By using **BUTTER BUDS®** instead of butter in this recipe, you have saved 188 calories and 70 mg cholesterol per serving.

CHICKEN IN RED WINE
(Coq au Vin)

Cut two 2-pound broilers into serving pieces. Rub with salt, black pepper, paprika, and a little nutmeg. Dredge in flour in a large shallow casserole. Brown ½ pound salt pork cut in finger-size strips. Add 24 whole small white onions, peel and brown lightly. Add chicken, brown on all sides, turning frequently.

Discard fat from casserole. Pour over chicken 3 tablespoons warmed brandy and ignite the spirit. When flame dies, pour in 1 bottle of **BOLLA Bardolino Wine**. Add 1 lump of sugar, 12 whole mushrooms, and a bouquet garni (2 sprigs of fresh parsley, 2 mashed garlic cloves, 2 sprigs of rosemary, and 1 large bay leaf). Cover and cook in oven (375°F) for 45 minutes or until tender. Remove bouquet garni and serve from casserole.

Serves 4 to 6

SOUVERAIN® PAELLA

1 (3 pound) broiler-fryer chicken, cut up
⅓ cup **PLANTERS Peanut Oil**
¾ cup chopped onion
1 clove garlic, minced
2 cups long grain rice
4 cups water
4 chicken bouillon cubes
2 teaspoons salt
½ teaspoon paprika
¼ teaspoon ground saffron
2 pounds fresh shrimp with tails, shelled and deveined
1 package (10 oz.) frozen artichoke hearts, defrosted
2 cups fresh cut green beans
2 medium tomatoes, peeled and chopped
1 cup **SOUVERAIN®** Chardonnay
12 small clams, scrubbed

Debone chicken breast and cut into 5 pieces. In a large skillet heat **PLANTERS Peanut Oil** over medium high heat. Add chicken pieces and sauté until golden brown. Remove chicken from skillet. Add onion and garlic to skillet and cook until tender. Stir in rice until grains are well coated. Remove skillet from heat.

In a Dutch oven bring water to a boil. Mix in bouillon cubes, salt, paprika and saffron. Stir in chicken, rice mixture, shrimp, artichoke hearts, green beans and tomatoes. Simmer over medium high heat for 15 minutes. Cover and chill until ready to use.

Stir **SOUVERAIN® Chardonnay** into mixture in Dutch oven; place clams on top. Cover and simmer 20 to 25 minutes, or until most of the liquid is absorbed. Serve immediately.

Makes 8 servings

SOUTH OF THE BORDER CHICKEN

⅓ cup **LAND O LAKES®** Sweet Cream Butter
1 cup crushed corn chips
1 tsp. *each* dried green onion and chili powder
¼ tsp. hot pepper sauce
3 to 3½ lb. frying chicken, cut into 8 pieces
¼ cup **LAND O LAKES®** Sweet Cream Butter
1 Tbsp. cornstarch
16-oz. can stewed tomatoes, undrained
4-oz. can chopped green chiles, undrained
½ cup pitted, sliced (¼ inch) ripe olives
¼ cup water
1 tsp. *each* garlic salt and chili powder

Preheat oven: 350°. In ungreased 13x9 inch (3 qt.) baking dish melt ⅓ cup butter in preheated oven (5 to 7 min.). Meanwhile, in 9 inch pie pan combine crushed corn chips, green onion and 1 tsp. chili powder; stir to blend. Add hot pepper sauce to melted butter; stir to blend. Dip chicken pieces into melted butter, then roll into seasoned crumbs to coat. Place chicken, skin side up, in same baking dish; sprinkle with remaining crumb mixture. Bake near center of 350° oven for 65 to 80 min. or until chicken is fork tender. Meanwhile, in heavy 2-qt. saucepan melt ¼ cup butter over med. heat (4 to 5 min.). Add cornstarch; stir to blend. Add remaining ingredients; stir to blend. Cook over med. heat, stirring occasionally, until mixture comes to a full boil (7 to 10 min.). Boil 1 min. To serve, pour hot sauce over chicken.

Yield: 4 to 6 servings

CHICKEN AND YELLOW RICE
(Arroz con Pollo)

2½-3 pounds of your favorite **COOKIN' GOOD**™
  Parts
1 teaspoon salt
Juice of 1 lime
2 medium onions, chopped
1 medium green pepper, chopped
2 cloves garlic, pressed
½ cup tomato sauce or 1 ripe tomato chopped
¼ cup of olive or vegetable oil
3 cups chicken broth
1 can (8 oz.) sweet peas
1 can (4 oz.) pimientos
2 tablespoons parsley, chopped
1 pound rice
½ teaspoon saffron
2 teaspoons salt
¼ teaspoon black pepper

Cut chicken in small serving pieces. Sprinkle with 1 teaspoon of salt and lime juice. Set aside for 1 hour. Heat oil in a large heavy skillet over medium heat. Add garlic, chopped onions and green pepper. Cook over medium heat until onion is tender, but not browned. Add tomato sauce or chopped tomato and parsley. Cook 5 minutes, stirring often. Add chicken broth, half of the sweet peas with its liquid, saffron, pepper, and salt. Bring to a boil. Add rice. Cover and simmer about 20 minutes or until rice is tender and liquid is absorbed. If extra liquid is needed add additional broth. Serve garnished with peas and pimientos.   *Serves 4*

CHICKEN MOLE

Chicken:
⅓ cup unsifted flour
3 measuring tablespoons chili powder, divided
2 measuring teaspoons salt
½ measuring teaspoon pepper
2 broiler-fryers (2½ to 3 pounds each), cut up
3 measuring tablespoons vegetable oil
1 cup chopped onion
3 garlic cloves, minced
¼ cup water

Chocolate Mole Sauce:
1 10-ounce can tomatoes and green chilies
1 cup tomato puree
1 6-ounce package (1 cup) **NESTLÉ**® **Semi-Sweet**
  Real Chocolate Morsels
1 measuring teaspoon chicken-flavored instant bouillon
  (or 1 cube, crushed)

Garnish:
1 cup chopped peanuts

CHICKEN:
In a large bowl or plastic bag, combine flour, 1 measuring table-spoon chili powder, the salt and pepper. Add chicken pieces (2 to 3 at a time); coat well. Heat oil in a large skillet; brown half the chicken pieces on all sides over medium heat. Drain thoroughly on paper towels. Repeat with remaining chicken. In same skillet, sauté onion and garlic until golden. Return chicken to skillet. Add the water; simmer, covered, over medium heat about 35 to 40 minutes or until chicken is tender. Transfer to a serving platter and top with Chocolate Mole Sauce (below). Garnish each serving with chopped peanuts.   *(Continued)*

CHOCOLATE MOLE SAUCE:
In a small saucepan, combine tomatoes and green chilies, tomato puree, **NESTLÉ**® **Semi-Sweet Real Chocolate Morsels**, remaining chili powder and bouillon. Cook over low heat until morsels melt and sauce is heated through.
                   Makes 6 to 8 servings and 3⅓ cups sauce
Note: This mole is milder in flavor than a traditional Mexican mole.

VERSATILE CHICKEN

1 (3-pound) broiler-fryer chicken, cut up
¾ cup buttermilk
1 tablespoon **WYLER'S**® **Chicken-Flavor Instant**
  Bouillon
½ teaspoon oregano leaves, optional
1 cup unsifted flour
1 to 2 teaspoons paprika
¼ cup melted margarine or butter

Rinse chicken; pat dry with paper towels. In a 1-cup measure, combine buttermilk, bouillon and oregano. Mix well. Let stand 10 minutes; stir. Place chicken in large bowl. Pour bouillon mixture over chicken; toss to coat. Let stand at least 30 minutes to blend flavors. In paper or plastic bag, combine flour and paprika. Add chicken, a few pieces at a time; shake to coat. Place in 13x9-inch baking dish. Drizzle with margarine. Bake uncovered in preheated 350° oven for 1 hour or until golden. Refrigerate leftovers.
                                                    Makes 4 servings

Tip: To fry chicken, omit melted margarine; fry in vegetable oil.

CHICKEN RATATOUILLE

2 tablespoons butter or margarine
1 small clove garlic, crushed
1 medium eggplant, cubed
2 medium zucchini, sliced
2 medium onions, sliced
2½ pounds cut-up chicken
1 envelope **SHAKE 'N BAKE**® **Seasoned Coating**
  Mix for Chicken–Barbecue Style

Melt butter in a 13 × 9-inch baking pan; stir in garlic. Add vegetables; stir to coat with butter. Bake at 350° for 10 minutes. Meanwhile, coat chicken pieces with seasoned coating mix as directed on package. Sprinkle any remaining mix evenly over vegetables. Top with chicken pieces and bake 50 minutes longer or until chicken and vegetables are tender.   *Makes 4 servings*

LA SAUCE® CHICKEN CACCIATORE

1 2½ to 3-lb. chicken, cut up
2 tablespoons vegetable oil
1 jar **LA SAUCE**® **Chicken Baking Sauce—Italian**
  Style
¼ cup dry white wine
1 tablespoon sugar, if desired
Hot cooked spaghetti

In large fry pan, brown chicken in oil on medium heat 15 minutes. Remove chicken from skillet; reserve drippings. In same skillet, combine ⅓ cup reserved drippings, **LA SAUCE**®, wine and sugar; place chicken pieces on top. Simmer, covered, on low heat 30 minutes, stirring occasionally. Serve on spaghetti.   *4 servings*

CHICKEN CACCIATORE

2 tablespoons olive oil
2½-pound broiler-fryer, cut into parts
2 cups sliced fresh mushrooms
½ cup green pepper, cut in squares
½ cup finely chopped onion
¼ cup finely chopped celery
1 cup **PREGO Spaghetti Sauce**
½ cup dry red wine
½ cup water
1 tablespoon drained capers

In 10-inch skillet over medium-high heat, in hot olive oil, cook chicken until well-browned on all sides. Remove chicken. To drippings in skillet, add mushrooms, green pepper, onion and celery. Cook 5 minutes, or until tender. Stir in spaghetti sauce, wine, water and capers. Return chicken to skillet. Heat to boiling. Reduce heat to low. Cover; simmer 30 minutes. Uncover; cook 15 minutes more or until chicken is fork-tender. If necessary, spoon off fat. *Makes 6 servings*

EASY CHICKEN CACCIATORE

1 clove garlic, minced
1 medium green pepper, sliced into ¼" strips
2 tablespoons vegetable oil
1 chicken (2½-3 pounds), cut up
1 jar (15½ oz.) **RAGU® Spaghetti Sauce**
½ package (16 oz. size) seashell pasta, cooked and drained

Preheat oven to 350°F. In a large skillet, sauté garlic and pepper in oil until tender; remove and set aside. Brown chicken on both sides; cook 30 minutes or until tender. Add spaghetti sauce and green peppers; simmer, covered, 10 minutes. Place pasta in an 11" × 7" baking dish; spoon chicken and sauce over pasta. Bake, covered, 20 minutes or until bubbly. *Serves 4*

CHICKEN ROMA

1 broiler-fryer chicken (2½ to 3 pounds), cut into pieces
4 cups **KELLOGG'S CORN FLAKES® Cereal**, crushed into fine crumbs
1 teaspoon salt
¼ teaspoon pepper
2 tablespoons chopped parsley
½ teaspoon crushed oregano
1 clove garlic, crushed
½ cup light cream or undiluted evaporated milk
Fresh lemon wedges

Wash chicken pieces and dry thoroughly. Combine finely crushed **CORN FLAKES® Cereal**, salt, pepper, parsley, oregano and garlic. Dip chicken pieces into cream or undiluted evaporated milk, then roll in seasoned **CORN FLAKES® Cereal** crumbs until evenly coated. Place chicken pieces skin side up in a single layer in a well-greased shallow baking pan; do not crowd pieces. Bake in preheated oven (350° F.) about 1 hour, or until drumstick is tender when pierced with a fork. No need to cover pan or turn chicken while cooking. Serve with fresh lemon, if desired. *Makes 4 to 5 servings*

® Kellogg Company

PESTO CHICKEN AND RICE

2 chickens, 3 pounds each, quartered
Salt and pepper
¾ cup melted butter or margarine
1 package **ARMANINO FARMS Frozen** or **Prepared Freeze-Dried Pesto**
5 cups cooked rice
2 tablespoons instant minced onion
1 can (13¾-ounces) chicken broth
1 clove garlic, minced

Prepare Pesto Sauce according to package instructions (adding oil, grated Parmesan cheese and water). Sprinkle chicken quarters with salt and pepper. Combine butter and Pesto Italian Green Herb Sauce. Mix half of the mixture with the rice, onion and garlic. Spread rice into a greased 9 × 13-inch baking pan. Top with chicken skin side up. Pour chicken broth evenly over chicken. Brush remaining Pesto Italian Green Herb Sauce mixture over chicken. Bake uncovered in a preheated oven 350° F for one hour or until chicken is tender. *Makes 6 to 8 servings*

BRACE OF BIRDS SARONNO

2 chickens, 4 pounds each
Salt and pepper

Stuffing:
2 tablespoons butter or margarine
1 onion, chopped
2 cups sliced celery
2 teaspoons fines herbes
6 cups cooked brown rice (1 pound raw)
½ cup chopped pecans
⅓ cup **AMARETTO DI SARONNO®** Liqueur
½ cup golden raisins

Glaze:
¼ cup melted butter or margarine
½ cup **AMARETTO DI SARONNO®** Liqueur
1 teaspoon grated orange rind

Sauce:
¼ cup flour
2 cups orange juice

Sprinkle chickens inside and out with salt and pepper. In a saucepan, heat 2 Tbsp. butter or margarine and sauté onion until golden. Stir in celery and fines herbes and sauté for 5 minutes. Stir in brown rice, pecans, ⅓ cup **AMARETTO DI SARONNO®** and raisins. Season to taste with salt. Stuff chickens with mixture. Sew or skewer openings. Roast in a shallow roasting pan in a preheated moderate oven (350° F) for 1½ to 2 hours, or until chickens are tender. While chickens are roasting, baste them with a mixture of ¼ cup melted butter or margarine, ½ cup **AMARETTO DI SARONNO®** and orange rind. Baste them every 30 minutes. Remove chickens to a warm serving platter. Place roasting pan on top of range and stir flour into pan juices. Gradually stir in orange juice. Scrape loose all brown particles and stir until sauce bubbles and thickens. Season to taste with salt and pepper. Spoon sauce over each serving. Garnish chickens with watercress and orange slices. *Makes 8 to 10 servings*

ORANGE TERIYAKI CHICKEN

2 broiler-fryer chickens, (2½ pounds each, quartered)
1 can (6 ounces) frozen concentrated orange juice
    thawed and undiluted
¼ cup soy sauce
2 tablespoons chopped onion
1 tablespoon vegetable oil
2 teaspoons AC'CENT® Flavor Enhancer
½ teaspoon ground ginger
½ teaspoon hot pepper sauce

Combine concentrated orange juice, soy sauce, onion, oil, **AC'CENT®**, ginger, and hot pepper sauce. Marinate chicken at least 3 hours, refrigerated, turning once. Broil 40 minutes or grill slowly, 6 to 8 inches away from source of heat 30 to 45 minutes. Turn chicken several times during cooking, brushing frequently with remaining marinade.   *Yield: 6 servings*

MANDARIN CHICKEN

3 pounds chicken pieces
1 (11-ounce) can Mandarin orange sections, drained
1 red onion, thinly sliced
1 (8-ounce) bottle **HENRI'S Beefsteak French Dressing**

1. Preheat oven to 350° F.
2. Place chicken pieces in 9 × 13-inch baking dish. Arrange orange sections and onion rings on top of chicken. Pour on **HENRI'S Beefsteak French Dressing**.
3. Bake uncovered 45 minutes to 1 hour or until done.

Serves 4

CHICKEN MARRAKESH

5 lbs. frying chicken, cut up
¼ cup butter
2 tablespoons olive oil
½ teaspoon garlic powder
1 teaspoon salt
½ teaspoon coarsely ground black pepper
⅛ teaspoon cayenne pepper
⅛ teaspoon powdered saffron
1 teaspoon summer savory
2 tablespoons chopped fresh parsley
1 large onion, thinly sliced
1 lemon cut into 8 wedges
½ cup stuffed green olives
1 can (1 lb. 4 oz.) **DOLE® Pineapple Chunks**

Sauté chicken in butter and olive oil in a heavy Dutch oven. Sprinkle with garlic powder, salt, black pepper, cayenne pepper, saffron, summer savory and parsley, turning chicken pieces to coat. Add onion and lemon wedges. Turn heat to simmer; cover and cook very slowly 1½ hours. Remove chicken pieces to heated serving platter (chicken will be *very* well-cooked). Halve olives lengthwise; drain pineapple chunks. Stir into pan juices until heated through. Pour over chicken to serve.

Makes 4 to 6 servings

CHICKEN JAMBALAYA

1 (4 lb.) chicken, cut up
⅓ cup salad oil
2 tablespoons butter
2 cups chopped onion
½ cup chopped celery
½ cup chopped green pepper
1 tablespoon **TRAPPEY'S® Steak Sauce**
½ teaspoon **TRAPPEY'S® Pepper Sauce**
4 cups hot water
½ cup chopped parsley
½ cup chopped green onion
2 cups rice (raw)
2 teaspoons salt

Lightly sprinkle chicken with salt and pepper. Brown in oil and butter in deep saucepan. Remove chicken. Add onion, celery and green pepper, cook until soft. Stir in **TRAPPEY'S® Steak** and **Pepper Sauces** and add chicken. Cover, simmer until chicken is tender. Add remaining ingredients, bring to boil. Lower heat. Cover, simmer until rice is cooked (about 1 hour).   *Serves 6*

CHICKEN DOLORES RICE-A-RONI®

2½-3 lb. frying chicken, cut up
¼ cup oil
1 pkg. **GOLDEN GRAIN® Spanish RICE-A-RONI®**
2 cups hot water
1 can (1 lb.) tomatoes, cut up
1 can (3¼-oz.) pitted ripe olives, drained
Dash **TABASCO® Sauce**

Brown chicken in oil. Cook slowly until tender, about 30 minutes; remove from pan. Brown rice-vermicelli mixture in oil. Stir in water, contents of flavor packet, tomatoes, olives and **TABASCO®**. Arrange chicken on top. Cover, simmer 15 minutes.

Makes 5 servings

STAGE COACH CHICKEN

⅔ cup prepared **HIDDEN VALLEY ORIGINAL RANCH® Salad Dressing**
1 egg, slightly beaten
1 2½ to 3-pound broiler-fryer, cut-up
⅓ cup all purpose flour
1 teaspoon salt
¼ teaspoon pepper
1 cup cornflake crumbs
¼ cup butter or margarine, melted

In a bowl, combine Salad Dressing and egg; set aside. Rinse chicken with water and drain well. Dredge chicken pieces in flour mixed with salt and pepper; dip in Salad Dressing-egg mixture; roll in cornflake crumbs. Arrange chicken pieces in a broiler pan, lined with foil if desired. Drizzle with butter. Bake at 350°F. for 50 minutes to 1 hour or until fork tender. *Makes 4 to 6 servings*

TROPICAL CHICKEN
(Low Calorie/Low Fat)

2½ lbs. quartered chicken parts
8 oz. can crushed pineapple packed in unsweetened juice
½ cup **ESTEE® Granulated Fructose**
2 Tbsp. lemon juice
1 tsp. dry mustard powder

Preheat oven to 375°F. Remove excess fat from beneath skin and cut chicken into parts. Rinse each piece in cold water and pat dry.

(Continued)

Mix pineapple with its juice, fructose, lemon juice and mustard together in small bowl. Place chicken on rack in shallow baking pan. Spread pineapple mixture over each piece of chicken, approx. 2 tablespoons each. Bake for 20 minutes, then remove from oven to baste again. Bake 20 minutes and baste again. Return to oven for final 20 minutes of baking. Pour pineapple sauce and drippings from baking pan into bowl and chill. Skim fat, then return to sauce pan to reheat. Serve sauce over chicken.   *Makes 6 servings*

NUTRITION INFORMATION

Calories	Carbohydrates	Protein	Fat	Cholesterol	Sodium
185	22g	28g	3g	55mg	64 mg

DIABETIC EXCHANGE INFORMATION

Fruit	Meat
2	4 (med. fat)

CHICKEN AVOCADO A LA ORANGE

⅓ cup flour
1½ teaspoons salt
Dash pepper
¾ teaspoon curry powder
1 teaspoon chili powder
1 (2-pound) chicken, cut in pieces
¾ cup melted butter
2 cups orange juice
1 tablespoon grated orange rind
1 cup pecan halves
2 to 2½ cups cooked rice
1 medium-sized **CALAVO®** Avocado, sliced
1 medium-size orange, sliced

Put flour, salt, pepper, curry powder, and chili powder in paper bag. Dip chicken pieces in melted butter, drop them in bag and coat pieces with flour by shaking them in bag. Broil or fry chicken in remaining butter until well done. Meanwhile, blend flour left in bag with orange juice and beat until thickened. Stir in orange rind and pecan halves. Arrange rice on serving platter and pour most of orange sauce over rice. Place avocado slices and orange slices in a row down the middle of the rice. Place chicken pieces along each side of the center. Spoon remaining sauce over avocado and orange slices.   *Makes 6 to 8 servings*

SHERRIED CHICKEN

½ cup flour
4 packets **ROMANOFF® MBT®** Instant Chicken Broth
½ teaspoon basil leaves, crushed
¼ teaspoon white pepper
1 chicken (2½-3 lb.) cut into serving pieces
1 cup vegetable oil
1 cup milk
1½ cups water
¼ cup sherry
1 jar (2½-oz.) sliced mushrooms, drained

Combine flour, 2 packets **MBT®**, basil, and pepper; coat chicken with mixture. Brown in oil, about 5 minutes each side; remove chicken. Drain all but 3 tablespoons oil. Stir in ¼ cup of remaining flour mixture. Gradually stir in milk, water, sherry, mushrooms, and remaining 2 packets **MBT®**. Heat and stir until thickened. Place chicken on top; cover and simmer 30 minutes. Serve over hot cooked rice or noodles.   *Makes 4 servings*
(about 2-3 pieces chicken each)

CHICKEN WITH SOUR CREAM MUSHROOM SAUCE

1 package (32-oz.) **BANQUET® Heat and Serve Frozen Fully Cooked Fried Chicken**
½ cup lemon juice
8 ounces mushrooms, sliced
1 medium onion, sliced
2 tablespoons butter or margarine
3 tablespoons flour
1 cup chicken broth
½ teaspoon salt
¼ teaspoon pepper
¼ cup dairy sour cream

1. Place chicken in 12 × 8-inch baking dish. Sprinkle lemon juice over each piece. Heat in 375°F oven for 35 to 40 minutes, or until hot.
2. Meanwhile, in saucepan, cook mushrooms and onion in butter until tender. Sprinkle with flour.
3. Stir in broth, salt, and pepper. Heat to boiling, stirring frequently.
4. Remove pan from heat. Stir in sour cream.
5. Serve sauce with hot chicken.   *Makes 5 servings*

CHICKEN PAPRIKA

3 tablespoons **MAZOLA®** Corn Oil
2 whole broiler-fryer chicken breasts, halved
8 small white onions
4 carrots, cut into 2-inch pieces
1½ cups chicken bouillon
1 tablespoon paprika
½ teaspoon salt
¼ teaspoon pepper
2 tablespoons **ARGO®/KINGSFORD'S®** Corn Starch
2 tablespoons water
½ cup plain yogurt

In large skillet heat corn oil over medium heat. Add chicken; brown well on both sides, about 15 minutes. Remove chicken. Add onions; cook about 5 minutes. Remove onions and excess oil from skillet. Return chicken and onions. Add carrots, bouillon, paprika, salt and pepper. Cover; simmer 30 minutes or until chicken and vegetables are tender. Remove chicken and vegetables to serving platter. Keep warm. Mix corn starch and water. Stir into bouillon. Stirring constantly, bring to boil over medium heat and boil 1 minute. Remove from heat; with wire wisk stir in yogurt until smooth. Pour sauce over chicken.
Makes 4 servings

CHICKEN ROLLS

4 chicken breasts, split and boned
1 teaspoon green onion, finely chopped
1 teaspoon parsley, finely chopped
Butter or margarine
Flour
1 egg
Corn flakes or cracker crumbs
½ cup **BRONTE** Sherry
Salt

Place chicken between waxed paper and pound each piece as thin as possible. Place green onions, parsley, 1 pat of butter on each piece of chicken. Roll up and dip in flour, egg and corn flakes or cracker crumbs. Let stand in refrigerator over-night (or at least for one hour). Place in shallow pan with a stick of butter and sherry. Bake at 350° for 1½-2 hours. Baste occasionally. Salt to taste.

HONEY-GOLD CHICKEN

4 chicken breasts, quartered
1 cup **GOLDEN DIPT® Chicken Seasoned Coating Mix**
1 tsp. salt
½ tsp. pepper
1 6-oz. can frozen lemonade concentrate
¼ lb. butter
½ cup honey
1 lemon, cut in wedges
Parsley sprigs

Dip chicken breasts in mixture of dry ingredients. Melt butter in shallow pan in 400° oven. Place chicken in pan, coating it with butter. Bake 30 minutes; turn. Combine lemonade concentrate with honey. Pour over chicken; bake 45 minutes at 325°, turning and basting every 15 minutes. When chicken is fork-tender, transfer to warm platter, garnish with lemon wedges and parsley.

Serves 4

CHICKEN BREASTS ROMANO

3 whole chicken breasts, split in half
3 tablespoons seasoned flour
¼ cup shortening
¼ cup onion, finely chopped
2 cups **LIBBY'S® Tomato Juice**
2 tablespoons Romano cheese
1 tablespoon sugar
½ teaspoon salt
½ teaspoon garlic salt
½ teaspoon oregano
¼ teaspoon basil
1 teaspoon vinegar
1 can (3-oz.) sliced mushrooms
1 tablespoon fresh parsley, minced
1 cup shredded American or Cheddar cheese

Shake chicken breasts in a bag with salt and pepper seasoned flour to coat evenly. In large skillet brown the chicken in the shortening. Remove chicken from skillet. Discard all but 1 tablespoon shortening. Add onions and lightly brown. Add tomato juice which has been combined with Romano cheese, sugar, salt, garlic salt, oregano, basil, vinegar, mushrooms and parsley. Cover and simmer 45 minutes or until chicken is tender and sauce is the consistency of gravy. Sprinkle with shredded cheese before serving.

Yields 6 servings

CHEESY COOKIN' GOOD™ CHICKEN ROLLS

2 large **COOKIN' GOOD™ Chicken Breasts**, boned, halved and skin removed
2 slices of Swiss cheese
1 tablespoon spicy mustard
½ cup seasoned bread crumbs
Melted butter or margarine approx. ½ cup
Paprika
Parsley

Arrange sliced Swiss cheese over chicken breasts. Trim if necessary. Lightly spread mustard over cheese and roll starting at narrow end. Secure with toothpicks. Dip first into melted butter or margarine then into bread crumbs. Sprinkle with paprika and parsley. Place rolls on a baking dish. Microwave for 6-8 minutes or 15 minutes in toaster oven or conventional oven at 350°F. Serve with herbed rice and a crisp salad.

Serves 4

CHICKEN BREASTS À LA JUDITH

3-4 whole chicken breasts, split, boned, and skinned
2 tablespoons butter (or margarine)
1 teaspoon salt
¼ teaspoon white pepper
½ cup **ARROW® Apricot Flavored Brandy**
1 large clove garlic, minced
2 tablespoons minced shallots (or onion)
1 teaspoon tarragon
1 cup heavy cream
1 tablespoon lemon juice

In large skillet, brown chicken in butter until cooked. Sprinkle with salt and pepper. Pour ¼ cup Brandy over chicken. Ignite carefully. When flame dies, remove chicken to heated serving platter. To drippings in pan, add garlic, shallots, remaining Brandy, tarragon, cream, and lemon juice. Cook, stirring, until sauce is reduced and slightly thickened. Place chicken breasts on bed of wild rice, if desired. Pour sauce over all. Serve immediately.

Serves 6-8

CHICKEN ROLLS SPECIAL

3 large chicken breasts (2¼ to 2½ pounds), skinned, boned, and halved lengthwise
6 thin slices boiled ham
3 slices mozzarella cheese, halved
½ cup fine dry bread crumbs
2 tablespoons snipped fresh parsley
Flour
1 egg, beaten
CRISCO® Shortening for deep frying
Sauce*

Place chicken pieces, boned side up, between two pieces of clear plastic wrap. Working from center out, pound lightly to 5 × 5 inches. Peel off wrap. Place a ham slice and half slice of cheese on each cutlet, cutting to fit. Roll meat as for jelly roll, tucking in sides. Secure with wooden picks. Combine bread crumbs and parsley. Coat each roll with flour; dip in beaten egg; roll in crumb mixture. Fry in deep **CRISCO®** heated to 340° till golden, about 5 minutes. Remove wooden picks and keep warm in 325° oven till served. Serve with Sauce.

Makes 6 servings

*SAUCE

Melt 2 tablespoons **CRISCO®**. Stir in 3 tablespoons flour, 2 teaspoons instant chicken bouillon granules or 2 chicken bouillon cubes, and ⅛ teaspoon paprika. Stir in 1 cup water and ½ cup light cream or milk. Cook and stir till mixture thickens and bubbles. Stir in 2 tablespoons chopped pimiento. Cook 1 minute.

CHICKEN IN CHABLIS

Bone, skin and halve 2 whole chicken breasts (about 2 lbs. total as purchased) to make 4 pieces. Sprinkle on all sides with salt and nutmeg. In a frying pan brown chicken on both sides in 2 tablespoons butter or margarine.

Add 2 tablespoons finely chopped onion, ¼ pound mushrooms, quartered and ⅔ cup **ALMADÉN Mountain White Chablis** wine. Bring to boiling, cover, reduce heat and simmer for 15 minutes.

Remove chicken to a warm serving dish, bring pan juices to boiling and cook, stirring until liquid is slightly reduced. Remove from heat. Stir in a mixture of 1 teaspoon cornstarch and 2 teaspoons water. Return to heat and cook, stirring, until thickened. Spoon sauce and mushrooms over chicken.

Makes 2 servings

CHICKEN SCALLOPINE CALIFORNIA STYLE

1 can (17 ounces) apricot halves
2 whole chicken breasts, boned, skinned and flattened
Salt and pepper
¼ cup flour
2 tablespoons butter or margarine
½ cup sliced celery
1 small onion, sliced
1 tablespoon soy sauce
¼ teaspoon ground ginger

Drain apricots reserving ½ cup syrup. Sprinkle chicken with salt and pepper; dust with flour. In large skillet, brown chicken in butter on both sides. Place in shallow baking dish. Sauté celery and onion in pan drippings until tender but crisp. Place 'cots and vegetables in dish with chicken. Combine reserved syrup, soy sauce and ginger in skillet; heat to boiling. Pour over chicken and vegetables. Bake in 350° F. oven 20 minutes.

Makes 4 servings

Favorite recipe from **California Apricot Advisory Board**

CHICKEN WITH TANGY LEMON GRAVY

1 cup sliced onion
1 cup thinly sliced carrots
1 cup thinly sliced celery
1 lemon, sliced
1 clove garlic, minced
1½ teaspoons salt
½ teaspoon dried thyme leaves
¼ teaspoon pepper
3 whole broiler-fryer chicken breasts, halved
¼ cup **MAZOLA® Corn Oil Margarine**, melted
1 pound zucchini, thinly sliced
2 tablespoons **ARGO®/KINGSFORD'S® Corn Starch**
1½ cups cool chicken bouillon or water

In shallow roasting pan mix together onion, carrots, celery, lemon, garlic, salt, thyme and pepper. Place chicken, skin side up, on top. Pour melted margarine over chicken. Bake in 375°F oven 30 minutes. Add zucchini, bake 30 minutes longer or until vegetables are tender. Remove chicken, zucchini and lemon to serving platter. Mix corn starch and bouillon until smooth; pour into pan. Stirring constantly, bring to boil over medium heat and boil 1 minute. Serve with chicken and vegetables.

Makes 4 to 6 servings

Note: 1 broiler-fryer chicken, cut up, may be substituted for chicken breasts.

Makes 4 servings

GINGER PEACH CHICKEN

3 cups sliced peeled peaches, divided
⅓ cup **KARO® Light Corn Syrup**
2 tablespoons lime juice
1 tablespoon **ARGO®/KINGSFORD'S® Corn Starch**
½ teaspoon ground ginger
½ teaspoon salt
¹⁄₁₆ teaspoon pepper
3 chicken breasts, boned, skinned, halved

In blender container place 2 cups of the peaches, corn syrup and lime juice; cover. Blend on high speed 30 seconds or until smooth. In small saucepan stir together corn starch, ginger, salt and pepper. Gradually stir in peach mixture until smooth. Stirring constantly, bring to boil over medium heat and boil 1 minute. Arrange chicken and remaining 1 cup sliced peaches in greased 10 × 6 × 2-inch baking dish. Spoon peach sauce over chicken and peaches. Bake in 400°F oven 25 to 35 minutes or until chicken is tender. If desired, serve over rice.

Makes 4 to 6 servings

CHICKEN WITH ARTICHOKE HEARTS

2 cloves garlic, minced
3 tablespoons butter or vegetable oil
3 skinless and boneless chicken breasts, cut into 1-inch strips
2 jars (6-oz. each) marinated artichoke hearts, rinsed and drained
¼ cup chicken stock or dry white wine
Salt, to taste
Freshly ground pepper, to taste
2 tablespoons fresh lemon juice
1 teaspoon grated lemon peel
1 jar (15½-oz.) **RAGU'® Spaghetti Sauce**
½ package (16-oz. size) spaghetti, cooked and drained
¼ cup sliced black olives
Lemon slices

In a large skillet, lightly sauté garlic in butter or oil. Add chicken and brown on both sides; drain fat. Add artichokes, chicken stock or wine, salt and pepper; simmer 5 minutes or until most of the liquid evaporates. Add lemon juice and peel; keep warm and set aside. In a saucepan, simmer sauce until heated through. Top spaghetti with sauce, chicken mixture and olives. Garnish with lemon slices.

Serves 4

PAPAYA CHICKEN

6 chicken breasts, boned and skinned
½ cup cornstarch
¼ teaspoon pepper
½ teaspoon salt
3 tablespoons pure vegetable oil
1 cup fresh orange juice
¼ cup fresh lime juice
1 cup granulated sugar
1 teaspoon grated orange rind
1 clove garlic, crushed
2 teaspoons ground ginger
1 teaspoon soy sauce
1 tablespoon cornstarch mixed with 2 teaspoons water
½ cup slivered almonds, toasted
2 ripe **CALAVO® Papayas**
½ cup coconut, toasted
Hot cooked rice

Clean chicken breasts with damp cloth. Place in paper sack with ½ cup cornstarch, pepper and ½ teaspoon salt. Shake until thoroughly coated. In a large frying pan, brown chicken in heated oil until tender. Once chicken is lightly browned, turn to lower heat.

Meanwhile, in separate saucepan, combine juices, sugar, orange rind, garlic, ginger and soy sauce with cornstarch mixture; stir over low heat until thickened. Pour thickened sauce over chicken, add toasted almonds. Cover and simmer 15 minutes.

Before serving, cut papayas in half, pare and remove seeds. Slice lengthwise.

To serve, place hot cooked rice in 9 × 14-inch serving dish with chicken breasts and almonds on top. Place papaya slices across top. Spoon remaining sauce over all and sprinkle with toasted coconut.

Makes 6 servings

ITALIAN FRIED CHICKEN

6 chicken breasts, boned and skinned
1 box any flavor crushed **HAIN® No-Salt Crackers**
1 tsp. oregano
1 tsp. marjoram
½ tsp. pepper
1 Tbsp. parsley flakes
½ cup whole wheat flour
2 eggs, beaten
2 Tbsp. water
¼ cup **HAIN® Garlic 'N' Oil**
½ cup **HAIN® Safflower Oil**

Crush crackers into fine meal and place in medium bowl. Mix in oregano, marjoram, pepper and parsley flakes. In second bowl, beat two eggs with water. In third bowl, place whole wheat flour. In skillet, heat Garlic 'N' Oil and Safflower Oil to 350°F. Dredge each chicken breast in flour; then dip in egg mixture and, lastly, coat with cracker mixture. Fry chicken in hot oil mixture 5-7 minutes each side. Place fried chicken in 8-inch × 10-inch baking dish and heat in oven at 350°F for 30 minutes.

BREAST OF CHICKEN EN CROÛTE

2 chicken breasts, boned, skinned and cut in half
Salt, pepper, oregano
1 package (10 ounces) frozen chopped spinach, thawed
    and squeezed dry
1 teaspoon minced garlic
3 tablespoons processed cheese spread
1 package (17¼ ounces) **PEPPERIDGE FARM®**
    "Frozen Bake It" Fresh Puff Pastry
4 slices ham
1 egg beaten with 1 teaspoon water
½ pint sour cream

Sprinkle chicken breasts lightly with salt, pepper and oregano. Combine spinach, garlic and cheese spread and season to taste with salt and pepper. Thaw pastry sheets 20 minutes, then unfold. Cut each sheet into 4 squares. On a lightly floured surface, roll first square until it's slightly larger than the chicken breast. In center of pastry place a slice of ham folded in half, ¼ of the spinach mixture and a chicken breast. Roll second square of pastry only enough to cover chicken breast and border of the first sheet. Press edges together firmly to seal and trim with pastry wheel. If desired, use scraps to decorate pastry and attach with beaten egg. Repeat with remaining chicken and pastry. Place on baking sheet; brush top with egg and bake in preheated 375° oven for 30 minutes or until golden brown. Serve with sour cream.

Makes 4 servings

CHICKEN SATAY

1 pound boneless chicken breasts
1 teaspoon ground caraway seed
1 teaspoon ground coriander seed
1 to 2 cloves garlic, crushed
1 tablespoon brown sugar
2 tablespoons soy sauce
2 teaspoons fresh lemon juice
Salt and pepper to taste
Peanut Butter Satay Sauce*

Cut chicken in ¾-inch cubes. Combine remaining ingredients, pour over chicken and allow to marinate 1 hour or longer. Thread chicken pieces on bamboo or wood skewers. Broil over a charcoal fire (or in broiler) for 10 minutes, turning several times. Serve with Peanut Butter Satay Sauce.

(Continued)

*PEANUT BUTTER SATAY SAUCE

½ cup water
3 tablespoons **SUPERMAN™ Creamy Peanut Butter**
Few drops **TABASCO® SAUCE**
2 tablespoons lemon juice

Combine ingredients and whisk lightly to combine. Serve cold, do not heat.

CHICKEN SATE

3 tablespoons soy sauce
2 tablespoons **MAZOLA® Corn Oil**
1 tablespoon lemon juice
½ teaspoon curry powder
1 clove garlic, minced or pressed
1 pound boned, skinned chicken breasts, cut in 1-inch
    cubes
Peanut Butter Sauce*

In small bowl stir together soy sauce, corn oil, lemon juice, curry and garlic. Add chicken; toss to coat well. Cover; refrigerate at least 2 hours. Drain; reserve marinade. Rinse bamboo skewers in water; thread with chicken cubes. Broil about 6 inches from source of heat, turning and basting frequently with reserved marinade, about 5 minutes or until tender. Serve with Peanut Butter Sauce.

Makes 4 servings

*PEANUT BUTTER SAUCE

In 1-quart saucepan heat 1 teaspoon **MAZOLA® Corn Oil** over medium heat. Add ¼ cup sliced green onions, 1 teaspoon minced ginger root and ¼ to ½ teaspoon crushed dried red pepper. Stirring frequently, cook 1 minute. Stirring constantly, add ½ cup **SKIPPY® Creamy** or **Super Chunk Peanut Butter**. Gradually stir in 1 cup water and 1 tablespoon soy sauce until well blended. Stirring constantly, bring to boil until mixture thickens. Serve hot or at room temperature with chicken kabobs.

Makes about 1½ cups

CHICKEN CASHEW

2 teaspoons **WYLER'S® Chicken-Flavor Instant
    Bouillon** *or* **2 Chicken-Flavor Bouillon Cubes**
1¾ cups boiling water
2 tablespoons soy sauce
5 teaspoons cornstarch
2 teaspoons light brown sugar
¼ teaspoon ground ginger
2 whole chicken breasts, split, boned and cut into
    bite-size pieces (about 1½ pounds)
2 tablespoons vegetable oil
2 cups sliced fresh mushrooms (about 8 ounces)
½ cup sliced green onions
1 small green pepper, sliced
1 (8 ounce) can sliced water chestnuts, drained
½ cup cashew nuts
Hot cooked rice

In small saucepan, dissolve bouillon in water. Combine soy sauce, cornstarch, sugar and ginger; stir into bouillon mixture. In large skillet, brown chicken in oil. Add bouillon mixture; cook and stir until sauce is slightly thickened. Stir in remaining ingredients except nuts and rice; simmer uncovered 5 to 8 minutes, stirring occasionally. Remove from heat; stir in ¼ cup nuts. Serve over rice. Garnish with remaining nuts. Refrigerate leftovers.

Makes 4 servings

CHINESE CHICKEN WITH CHERRIES

2 whole boned, skinned chicken breasts
½ cup sugar
2 Tablespoons cornstarch
2 Tablespoons plus 1 teaspoon lemon juice
2 Tablespoons water
2 Tablespoons vegetable oil, divided
1 package (14 ounces) **Frozen STOKELY'S® Chinese Style Stir-Fry Vegetables**
1 cup **Frozen STOKELY'S® Dark Sweet Cherries,** thawed
Soy sauce

Cut chicken into 1-inch cubes. Combine sugar, cornstarch, lemon juice and water; blend until smooth. Set aside. Heat 9- or 10-inch skillet or wok over high heat (a drop of water will sizzle). Pour 1 Tablespoon oil in wide, circular motion inside rim of pan. Tilt pan to coat surface; add chicken and stir-fry about 1½ minutes, or until chicken turns white. Push chicken to side. Remove seasoning packet from vegetables and reserve; add frozen vegetables to pan. Pour remaining oil around rim of pan quickly. Toss vegetables to coat each piece. Cover and cook 3 minutes, stirring once midway. If vegetables begin to stick, reduce temperature slightly or add 1 teaspoon oil. Sprinkle reserved seasoning packet over mixture and blend. Cook about 30 seconds more. Push vegetables and meat to sides. Give reserved sauce a quick stir and pour into center of pan. When it comes to a boil, stir in vegetables and chicken. Add cherries; stir, remove from heat and serve with soy sauce.

4 servings

CHICKEN LEMONAISE

3 whole chicken breasts, halved, skinned, boned
¾ cup **BEST FOODS®/HELLMANN'S® Real Mayonnaise**
½ cup fine dry bread crumbs
5 tablespoons **MAZOLA® Corn Oil Margarine**
½ cup chopped onion
3 tablespoons flour
1½ cups water
3 chicken-flavored bouillon cubes
¼ cup chopped parsley
3 tablespoons lemon juice

Brush chicken with ¼ cup real mayonnaise; coat with bread crumbs. In skillet melt 3 tablespoons of the margarine over medium heat. Cook chicken, 3 pieces at a time, 15 minutes or until tender; keep warm. In saucepan sauté onion in 2 tablespoons margarine. Stir in flour until well blended. Gradually stir in water. Add bouillon cubes, parsley and lemon juice. Cook and stir until mixture boils. Add ½ cup real mayonnaise; cook and stir until hot. Spoon sauce over chicken.

Makes 6 servings

OVEN-FRIED CHICKEN DRUMSTICKS

10 chicken drumsticks
½ cup dry bread crumbs
2 teaspoons **MORTON® NATURE'S SEASONS® Seasoning Blend**
⅓ cup oil

About 1 Hour Before Serving: Combine bread crumbs and seasoning blend. Roll chicken in bread crumb mixture. Pour oil in 15½-by 10½-inch jelly roll pan. Arrange chicken in pan. Bake at 400°F. for 30 minutes. Turn chicken. Continue baking for 20 more minutes, or until tender. Drain on paper towels.

Makes 10 drumsticks

CHICKEN THIGHS PARMIGIANA
(Microwave Recipe)

6 **COUNTRY PRIDE® Broiler-fryer Chicken Thighs,** boned and skinned
1 egg, beaten
¼ cup water
1 cup fine dry bread crumbs
3 tablespoons butter or margarine
2 cans (8 oz. each) tomato sauce
1 clove garlic, minced
½ teaspoon salt
½ teaspoon dried leaf basil
½ teaspoon dried leaf oregano
¼ cup grated Parmesan cheese
4 oz. mozzarella cheese, cut into 6 slices

Flatten chicken thighs by pounding between two pieces of waxed paper. Beat egg with ¼ cup water in small shallow dish. Dip chicken thighs in egg, then in bread crumbs. In 12 x 7½ x 2-inch glass baking dish melt butter in microwave oven 1 minute. Place thighs top side down in dish. Cook in microwave oven 10 minutes. Turn thighs over and turn dish. Cook 10 minutes longer. Mix tomato sauce, garlic, salt, basil and oregano; pour over chicken and cover with waxed paper. Cook 5 minutes. Turn dish, uncover, sprinkle with Parmesan cheese, and place a cheese slice on each chicken thigh. Cook 2 to 5 minutes, until chicken is tender and cheese melts. Let stand 3 to 5 minutes before serving. Total cooking time: 30 minutes.

Yield: 6 servings

CHICKEN LEGS WITH LEMON AND GARLIC

4 whole **PERDUE® Chicken Legs** with thighs attached
½ cup melted butter
2 large garlic cloves, crushed
1 lemon, halved
Salt and freshly ground pepper
Paprika

Combine butter and garlic. Rub chicken legs with lemon and sprinkle with salt, pepper and paprika. Place legs on rack in roasting pan and brush liberally with garlic butter. Cook 6-8 inches under heat for 10 minutes. Turn and baste. Cook for 10 minutes. Turn again, baste and cook until tender and golden brown. Brush with remaining garlic butter before serving. Place ½ inch of water in bottom of roaster pan to prevent dripping fat from burning. This recipe is also excellent when cooked on outdoor grill.

Makes 4 servings

GLAZED DRUMSTICKS

1 pkg. **HOLLY FARMS® Drumsticks**
1 tsp. salt
¼ cup honey
1 Tbsp. soy sauce
1 Tbsp. all-purpose flour
½ cup cold water

Preheat oven to 350°F. Place drumsticks in shallow baking dish. Bake for 45 minutes. Combine salt, soy sauce, honey and baste chicken. Cover chicken and baste occasionally while cooking for an additional 15 minutes or until tender. Remove chicken to serving dish, pour pan juices in small skillet. Blend ½ cup cold water into flour, stir into pan juices. Cook, stirring constantly, until thickened and bubbly. Serve sauce with drumsticks.

LEMON CHICKEN ORIENTAL

1 garlic clove, minced
2 tablespoons butter or margarine
4 chicken legs with thighs, separated
2 teaspoons salt
¼ teaspoon pepper
2½ cups chicken broth
1 cup **UNCLE BEN'S® CONVERTED® Brand Rice**
2 tablespoons lemon juice
1 small sweet red or green pepper, cut into julienne
   strips
⅓ cup sliced green onions with tops
1 tablespoon soy sauce
1 package (10 oz.) frozen broccoli spears, partially
   thawed
1 tablespoon cornstarch
½ cup cold water

Sauté garlic in butter in 10-inch skillet 2 to 3 minutes. Season chicken with 1 teaspoon of the salt and the pepper. Add chicken to skillet; brown on all sides over medium heat. Reduce heat; cover and cook until chicken is tender, about 25 minutes. While chicken is cooking, bring chicken broth to a boil in medium saucepan. Add rice, 1 tablespoon of the lemon juice and remaining 1 teaspoon salt. Cover and simmer 20 minutes. Remove from heat. Stir in red pepper and green onions; let stand covered until all liquid is absorbed, about 5 minutes. When chicken is tender, remove and keep warm; pour off all but 1 tablespoon fat. Add soy sauce and the remaining 1 tablespoon lemon juice to drippings. Add chicken and broccoli to skillet. Cover and simmer 5 minutes. Spoon rice onto serving platter; arrange chicken and broccoli on rice. Combine cornstarch and water; stir into pan drippings. Cook and stir until thickened. Pour sauce over chicken, broccoli and rice.

Makes 4 to 6 servings

EL PASO CHICKEN LEGS

4 cups corn chips, crushed
1½ teaspoons chili powder
½ teaspoon onion powder
¼ teaspoon garlic powder
6 broiler-fryer chicken legs
¼ cup **BEST FOODS®/HELLMANN'S® Real
   Mayonnaise**

CONVENTIONAL METHOD:
In shallow dish or on sheet of waxed paper combine first 4 ingredients. Rinse chicken and pat dry. Brush all sides with Real Mayonnaise; coat with chip mixture. Place skin-side-up in shallow roasting pan. Bake in 425°F oven 45 minutes or until fork-tender.

Makes 6 servings

MICROWAVE METHOD:
Place 3 legs in oblong glass baking dish with thickest parts toward outside of dish. Microwave with full power 20 minutes, rotating dish after 10 minutes. Let stand 5 minutes. Repeat.

CHICKEN LEGS DIJONNAISE

Juice of 1 lemon
½ teaspoon tarragon leaves
1 tablespoon Dijon mustard
4 tablespoons soft butter
6 chicken legs
Salt

Mix together first four ingredients and let sit at room temperature for half an hour to allow flavors to blend. With fingers carefully lift up skin from chicken legs to make space for mustard-butter mixture. Allow one teaspoon of mixture for filling second joint area and one teaspoon for drumstick area. Place filling between skin and meat and then press down skin to spread filling evenly in area. Salt chicken legs and broil, 6 to 8 inches from source of heat, turning twice until completely cooked.

Makes about six servings

Favorite recipe from **Food and Wines from France**

ZIPPY COOKIN' GOOD™ LIVERS

4 slices of bacon
1 pound of **COOKIN' GOOD™ Livers**
1 medium onion, sliced

Sauce:
½ cup ketchup
2 tablespoons of brown sugar
1 tablespoon Worcestershire sauce
1 tablespoon lemon or lime juice
1 tablespoon prepared mustard
1 clove of crushed garlic or ¼ teaspoon of garlic powder
¼ teaspoon pepper

In an electric skillet or large frying pan, cook bacon until crisp; remove to drain on absorbent paper. In bacon fat sauté onion until tender; add livers and sauté until livers are no longer pink. While livers are cooking prepare sauce in a small mixing bowl by combining remaining ingredients, stirring to blend well. Pour sauce over livers and simmer until hot and bubbly. Serve with bacon crumbled over the top.   *Serves 2-3*

CHICKEN WINGS MEXICANA

12 **PERDUE® Chicken Wings**
2 tablespoons oil
1 medium onion, chopped
½ cup chopped green pepper
1 medium clove garlic, minced
1 can (16 ounces) whole tomatoes
1½ cups water
1 cup raw long grain rice
1 teaspoon salt
½ teaspoon chili powder
1 package (10 ounces) frozen peas, partially thawed

Wash chicken; pat dry. In Dutch oven, brown chicken in oil and cook onion, green pepper and garlic until onion is tender. Add tomatoes, water, rice, salt and chili powder. Bring to boil. Reduce heat, cover and simmer 30 minutes or until chicken and rice are tender. Add peas. Cook 5 minutes longer.   *Serves 4*

CHICKEN LITTLE

1 package (12-oz.) **WEAVER® Frozen Chicken
   Rondelets**, original flavor
1 package (6-oz.) herb-seasoned stuffing mix
4 slices jellied cranberry sauce, ½-inch thick; cut with
   chicken cookie cutter

In oven-proof bowl, combine stuffing mix ingredients as listed on package. Bake in oven while baking chicken patties at 425°F for 15 minutes. Place patties on serving platter; mound stuffing on top. Garnish with cranberry sauce cutouts.   *4 servings*

Cornish Hens

BEST EVER BARBECUED CORNISH HENS

4 PERDUE® Fresh Cornish Game Hens
1 cup ketchup
2 tablespoons brown sugar
2 tablespoons cider vinegar
1 tablespoon Worcestershire sauce
1 teaspoon prepared mustard
¼ teaspoon garlic salt
2 tablespoons grated onion
1 small clove garlic, minced

In saucepan, combine all ingredients, except Cornish hens. Simmer 5 minutes, stirring frequently. Halve Cornish hens and remove backbones. Season with salt and pepper. Arrange hens cut side down, on greased grill, 3 to 5 inches from coals. Turn and brush with prepared sauce every 5 minutes until hens are done, about 20 minutes. *Makes 4 servings*

LEMON BUTTER CORNISH

4 TYSON® Cornish Game Hens
Vodka
8 thin slices lemon
8 thin slices butter
2 tsp. salt
1 tsp. white pepper
2 tsp. crushed tarragon
1½ sticks butter, melted
2 tsp. finely grated lemon rind
1 Tbsp. lemon juice
1½ cups chicken broth
2 Tbsp. heavy cream
½ cup sour cream
1 Tbsp. parsley

Coat Cornish Hens with vodka inside and out; let rest 15 minutes. Carefully loosen skin over the breast with fingers making a pocket. Place 2 slices lemon and 2 slices butter in the skin pocket of each hen. Season inside and out with mixture of salt, white pepper, and tarragon. Coat with Lemon Basting Sauce (butter, rind and lemon juice). Place in roasting pan with chicken broth to cover the bottom. Bake at 450° F; cook for 15 minutes. Baste. Reduce heat to 375° F; cook for 30-45 minutes or until done. Remove Cornish Hens from pan. For sauce, reduce pan liquids to ½ quantity; add cream, sour cream and parsley. Simmer to thicken. *Serves 4*

PEKING CORNISH HENS WITH SCALLION SAUCE

4 PERDUE® Fresh Cornish Game Hens
6 cups water
¼ cup honey
4 ¼-inch thick slices fresh ginger
Scallion Sauce:
½ cup soy sauce
2 tablespoons sherry
2 tablespoons orange juice
1 teaspoon grated orange rind
1 teaspoon sugar
2 scallions, thinly sliced

Remove giblets. Pat hens dry. Bring water to a boil in large saucepan. When boiling, add honey and stir. One at a time, lower each bird into honey bath, quickly turning it completely over to evenly coat with liquid. Immediately remove and place a slice of ginger in each bird. Let hens dry on metal rack for 10 minutes. Place in roasting pan with wings folded back, but do not tie legs together or truss. Cook in preheated 350° F. oven for 1 hour until tender. Combine Sauce ingredients and serve with hens. *Makes 4 servings*

CORNISH ITALIANO

2-3 TYSON® Cornish Game Hens (halved)
1½ tsp. sage
1 tsp. rosemary
1 tsp. garlic powder
1 tsp. salt
⅛ tsp. pepper
2 Tbsp. butter
2 Tbsp. olive oil
1 cup dry white wine
1 Tbsp. flour

Mix dry seasonings and rub game hens inside and out. In Dutch oven melt butter and oil and brown hens on all sides. Add wine, cover and simmer until tender (approximately 45 minutes). Remove hens to platter, cover and keep warm.

Mix flour with ½ cup warm water and add to pan juices for Cornish sauce. Serve with noodles mixed with sour cream and Parmesan cheese.

POLYNESIAN GAME HENS

6 TYSON® Cornish Game Hens
1½ cups honey
1½ cups prepared mustard
⅓ cup lemon juice
1 Tbsp. curry powder
Paprika
Rice or Chinese noodles
Fresh pineapple, garnish

Rinse hens, pat dry, and season with salt and pepper inside and out. Place in shallow baking pan. Baste hens with sweet and sour sauce (honey, mustard, lemon juice and curry powder). Bake 45-60 minutes in preheated oven at 400°F. Last 10 minutes, spoon mixture oven hens again and sprinkle with paprika. Serve with rice or Chinese noodles. Garnish with fresh pineapple. *Serves 6*

Turkey

QUICK TURKEY STROGANOFF

2 lb. JENNIE-O® White, Dark, or Combination Pan Roast, prepared according to pkg. directions
2 tablespoons butter or margarine
1 cup chopped onion
1 cup dairy sour cream
Cooked rice, egg noodles, or mashed potatoes

Cube turkey. Sauté onion in butter; stir in turkey. Prepare gravy according to gravy packet directions; stir into turkey mixture. Add sour cream; cook over low heat just until warm. Serve over hot cooked rice, noodles, or mashed potatoes.

About 8 servings

TURKEY ON THE GRILL

To prepare covered grill (kettle or wagon): Open all dampers and leave open during cooking. Make a drip pan using a double thickness of heavy duty foil or use a disposable foil pan. Put pan on bottom rack or to one side of firebox. Place 25 to 30 briquets on each side of drip pan. Ignite briquets and burn 15 to 20 minutes or until covered with gray ash.

To prepare turkey: Thaw **SWIFT PREMIUM® BUTTER-BALL® Turkey** according to directions in folder. Free legs and tail from tucked position. Remove neck and giblets. Rinse turkey and drain. Draw skin over neck and hold in place by twisting wing tips behind back. Do not stuff. (Stuffing can be baked in a disposable foil pan on the grill beside the turkey during the last hour of cooking.) Retuck legs and tail. Brush turkey with oil. Insert roast meat thermometer into the center of the thickest part of the thigh, not touching the bone.

To cook turkey: Place unstuffed turkey on top rack. Put lid on grill. Add 4 or 5 briquets to each side every hour of cooking to maintain heat. (If grill is equipped with a thermometer, use enough briquets to maintain a temperature of 300° to 350°F). Check for doneness after 2½ hours for a 12- to 14-pound turkey; the internal temperature should be 180° to 185°F.

Covered electric or gas grills: Follow manufacturer's directions for setting up grill. Set temperature control at 300° to 350°. Preheat 15 to 20 minutes. Place turkey on a rack in a shallow pan and put on grill rack. Close grill lid. Adjust heat controls to maintain desired temperature. Check for doneness after 2½ hours.

TURKEY A LA B&B

1 oven-ready turkey (10-12 pounds)
6 ounces **B&B Liqueur**
2 tablespoons melted **FLEISCHMANN'S Margarine**
1 teaspoon salt
½ teaspoon paprika
¼ teaspoon rosemary leaves, crushed
¼ teaspoon thyme leaves, crushed
⅛ teaspoon white pepper

Place turkey on rack in shallow roasting pan. Combine **B&B Liqueur**, **FLEISCHMANN'S Margarine**, salt, paprika, rosemary, thyme and pepper. Brush turkey skin with **B&B** mixture. Roast at 325°F. about 25 minutes per pound. Roast to 190°F.-195°F. on meat thermometer, or until drumstick and thigh move easily and thick part of drumstick feels soft. Baste frequently with **B&B** mixture. When turkey is done remove to warm platter. Strain juice from roasting pan; skim off fat. Serve juice over sliced meat.   *Makes 2 servings per pound*

TURKEY WITH CARROT STUFFING

2 packages **STOVE TOP® Chicken Flavor Stuffing Mix**
3 cups shredded carrots (6 medium)
1 cup chopped green pepper
½ cup butter or margarine, cut in pieces
3½ cups hot water
8- to 12-pound turkey
Salt

Place contents of Vegetable/Seasoning Packets, carrots, green pepper and butter in large bowl. Add hot water; stir to blend and partially melt butter. Add Stuffing Crumbs; stir just to moisten. Do not stuff turkey until ready to roast. Rinse turkey with cold water.
(Continued)

Sprinkle neck and body cavities with salt and stuff lightly with prepared stuffing. Truss and roast at 350° for 3½ to 4½ hours. Place any remaining stuffing in small baking dish; bake at 400° for 15 minutes.   *Makes about 12 servings*

ROAST TURKEY WITH PRUNE WALNUT STUFFING

1 (9-10 lb.) turkey, defrosted
7 cups stuffing cubes (herb-seasoned package)
1 cup boiling water
1 medium onion finely chopped
¾ cup **CHIFFON® Margarine**
½ cup **SEVEN SEAS® Buttermilk Recipe™ Dressing**
1 cup prunes, cut into quarters
½ cup very coarsely chopped walnut pieces
Extra **Buttermilk Recipe™ Dressing**

Sauté onion in **CHIFFON®**. Plump prunes in boiling water and add onion and nuts. Mix in stuffing cubes. Salt and pepper to taste. Stuff turkey loosely. Roast according to directions on wrapping. Baste turkey twice with Dressing while roasting.

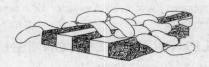

FRUITED-SAUSAGE STUFFING

1 pound bulk pork sausage
½ cup chopped celery
½ cup chopped onion
3 cups coarsely chopped fresh cranberries
1 can (8 ounces) undrained crushed pineapple
1½ cups water
1 package (8 ounces) **PEPPERIDGE FARM® Herb Seasoned Stuffing**

In a skillet, brown pork sausage, stirring to break into bits. Add celery and onion. Cook until tender, stirring frequently. Combine with remaining ingredients.   *Use to stuff 12 to 14 pound turkey*

MEXICAN FIESTA TURKEY WINGS

1 package (2 to 3 lb.) **LOUIS RICH™ Fresh Turkey Wings**
1 cup water
1 can (15 oz.) tomato sauce with tomato bits
1 package (1¼ oz.) taco seasoning mix
1 cup (4 oz.) shredded Cheddar cheese

Remove skin that stretches between the joint of each wing; separate wing into two pieces. Rinse turkey and pat dry.

Skillet Method: Place turkey and water in skillet; bring to a boil. Cover; turn down heat. Simmer 2 hours. Pour off liquid. In small bowl combine tomato sauce and taco mix; pour over turkey. Simmer, covered, 15 minutes; sprinkle with cheese. Cover; heat 3 to 5 minutes more or until cheese melts.

Oven Method: Place turkey and water in casserole or Dutch oven; cover and bake in 350°F oven 2 hours. Remove from oven; pour off liquid. In small bowl combine tomato sauce and taco mix; pour over turkey. Bake, uncovered, 25 minutes; top with cheese and bake 5 minutes more or until cheese melts.
Makes 2 to 4 servings

AMBER GLAZE FOR BARBECUED TURKEY WINGS
(Low Calorie)

1 package (2 to 3 lbs.) **LOUIS RICH**™ Fresh Turkey Wings
1 cup water
Glaze:
1 jar (8½ oz.) low sugar apricot spread
2 teaspoons soy sauce
1½ teaspoons dry mustard

Cut out skin between the joint of each wing; separate wing into two pieces. Rinse and pat dry.
Oven BBQ: Place turkey and water in casserole or Dutch oven; cover and bake in 350°F oven 2 hours. Pour off liquid. In small bowl combine glaze ingredients; pour over turkey. Bake, uncovered, 30 minutes more.
Outdoor BBQ: Several hours or day ahead cook turkey as above 2 hours, refrigerate. Grill turkey over hot coals about 20 minutes, occasionally brushing with glaze.   *Makes 4 servings*

Calories: 280 calories per serving.

"OLD FAVORITE" TURKEY BARBECUE
Barbecue Sauce:
2 parts lemon-lime type soda water
1 part soy sauce
1 part cooking oil
Optional:
Garlic powder—¼ tsp. per quart
Horseradish powder—½ tsp. per quart

Make enough marinade to cover meat.
BARBECUING: **NORBEST**® Turkey wing sections and breast meat are excellent for barbecues. Soak meat in marinating sauce for approximately two hours. Place charcoal in a pile on grill and ignite charcoal briquets with solvent, available at most gas stations, or commercial lighting fluid. Use at least one pint of starter for each ten pounds of briquets. Allow approximately 20 minutes for starter to burn and grey ashes to appear on outside briquets. Scatter briquets evenly over grill. Place marinated turkey meat on hot grill, skin side up. Rotate about every 10 to 15 minutes until turkey is cooked, usually about one hour. Cooked turkey can be placed back in marinating sauce and kept hot until time to serve. Breast meat can be sliced crosswise in ¼- to ½-inch slices.
One pound of barbecued turkey will serve approximately 3 people

VARIATION:

BAKING: **NORBEST**® Turkey dark meat can be baked or roasted in the oven at 350°F. Meat is done when the thermometer registers 185°F or when drumstick feels soft when pressed with thumb and forefinger.

TURKEY A L'ORANGE

1 pkg. (1-2 lbs.) **LOUIS RICH**™ Fresh Turkey Breast Tenderloins
1 Tbsp. firmly packed brown sugar
2 tsp. cornstarch
½ cup orange juice
1½ tsp. lemon juice
1 tsp. butter
Fresh orange slices, for garnish
1 Tbsp. brandy, optional*

Place tenderloins on broiler pan; broil 5 inches from heat 20 minutes, turning once. Meanwhile, combine sugar and cornstarch in saucepan. Add juices and butter; cook, stirring constantly, over medium heat until sauce thickens and boils. To serve, garnish turkey tenderloins with orange slices. Pour sauce over turkey.
Makes 2 servings

*Heat brandy in small pan over low heat until it begins to sizzle along sides of pan when tilted. Remove from heat; using a long match, light brandy; pour over tenderloins.

SWEET 'N SPICY TURKEY KABOBS

2 lb. **JENNIE-O**® Brand Fully Cooked Turkey Breast, cut into 1-inch cubes
2 large green peppers, cut into 1-inch cubes
½ medium pineapple, cut into ½ × 1-inch wedges
8 to 16 large whole fresh mushrooms
About ¾ cup thick spicy French dressing
1 large tomato, cut into 8 wedges

Thread turkey cubes, green pepper cubes, pineapple wedges, and mushrooms onto 8 skewers. Brush all sides generously with dressing. Broil or grill over hot coals, turning and basting often with dressing. Thread tomato wedge onto each skewer during last 5 minutes of grilling.   *Makes 8 kabobs*

Note: You may substitute other **JENNIE-O**® Turkey products in this recipe.

TURKEY BREAST Á LA GREQUE

1 package (4 to 5 lbs.) **LOUIS RICH**™ Fresh Turkey Breast Half
1 package (8 oz.) cream cheese, softened
1 can (3 oz.) real bacon bits
2 slices fresh bread, finely chopped
¼ cup chopped fresh parsley
1 teaspoon instant minced onion
½ teaspoon oregano
⅛ teaspoon garlic powder
1 egg, beaten

Rinse turkey and pat dry. With knife, loosen lining under skin, pulling skin back to expose meat. Leave skin attached along one edge. In large bowl combine remaining ingredients. Spread mixture on area where skin was removed. Replace skin; secure with poultry skewers or toothpicks. Place skin side up in shallow, foil-lined roasting pan. Insert meat thermometer into center of thickest part of muscle, taking care not to touch bone. Bake in 325°F oven 1½ hours. Baste with pan drippings; cover loosely with foil. Bake one hour longer until thermometer registers an internal temperature of 170°F. Remove from oven, let stand 10 minutes before slicing.   *Makes 8 to 10 servings*

Note: For 2 to 4 lb. breast half or portion, prepare as above. After basting and covering, bake 30 minutes more.

TURKEY ON TURKEY GLAZE

Prepare roast turkey according to your favorite method. During last hour of roasting brush every 15 minutes with following mixture: 1 cup **WILD TURKEY LIQUEUR**®, 1 Tbsp. each lemon juice and soy sauce. Also delicious on chicken, duck, game, lamb, pork and ham.

Duck

CRISP DUCKLING À L'ORANGE

1 (4 to 5 lb.) duckling, thawed
3 tablespoons **LEA & PERRINS Worcestershire Sauce**, divided
2 teaspoons salt
3 navel oranges, divided
2 tablespoons butter or margarine
2 tablespoons orange liqueur
1 clove garlic, crushed
2 tablespoons flour
1 can (10½-oz.) condensed chicken broth
2 tablespoons port wine
2 tablespoons sugar

Remove giblets from cavity of duckling; reserve liver for later use. Wash, drain and pat duckling dry. Combine 1 tablespoon of the **LEA & PERRINS** and salt; brush mixture inside cavity and on outer skin. Thinly peel 2 of the oranges. Place peelings inside cavity. Tie legs and tail together. Skewer neck. Prick the skin every ½-inch around the thigh, back and lower breast with a fork. Place on a rack in a roasting pan, breast side up. Roast in a preheated oven 425° F for 30 minutes. Reduce heat to 375° F and roast 1½ hours longer or until the legs move freely. Pour off fat from pan every 30 minutes and prick the skin occasionally.
SAUCE:
To prepare orange sauce grate the peel from the remaining orange (makes about 2 tablespoons). Cut off remaining outer white membrane from the three oranges and carefully remove the sections, saving juice; set aside. Reserve ¼ cup of orange juice. In a medium skillet melt butter. Add reserved liver and sauté until lightly browned. Remove liver; set aside. Stir in orange liqueur and heat 2 minutes. Add reserved grated orange peel, 1 tablespoon of the **LEA & PERRINS** and garlic; cook 3 minutes longer, stirring frequently. Remove from heat and stir in flour. Gradually add reserved orange juice, broth, wine, sugar and remaining 1 tablespoon **LEA & PERRINS**. Cook, stirring frequently, until thickened and smooth. Dice reserved liver and add to sauce along with orange sections. Heat and serve with duckling.
Yield: 4 portions

ROAST DUCKLING WITH ORANGE SAUCE

2 ducklings, 4 to 5 pounds each
1 teaspoon salt
3 cups Florida orange juice, divided
½ cup honey
3 tablespoons cornstarch
2 teaspoons grated orange peel
4 Florida oranges, peeled and sectioned

Rinse ducklings and pat dry. Sprinkle ducklings inside and out with salt. Close cavity with skewers; truss legs. Pierce duckling skin with a fork in several places around the perimeter of the breast and on the back. Place on rack in roasting pan. Roast in a 350°F oven 2 to 2½ hours (meat thermometer inserted on inside of thigh should read 170°F when done). Use 1 cup orange juice to brush ducklings during roasting. Combine honey with ½ cup orange juice; baste ducklings with honey glaze during last 30 minutes of roasting. Remove ducklings to heated serving platter; keep warm. To prepare orange sauce, drain off all fat from pan drippings (there should be about 1 cup drippings). Combine cornstarch with remaining 1½ cups orange juice. Pour into pan with drippings. Add grated peel. Bring to a boil. Simmer 2 minutes until gravy thickens, stirring constantly. Strain. Stir in orange sections. Serve sauce with ducklings.
Yield: 6 to 8 servings

Favorite recipe from **Florida Department of Citrus** and **National Duckling Council**

MEXICAN-STYLE DUCKLING WITH PINEAPPLE ORANGE SAUCE

2 frozen ducklings (4 to 5 pounds each) defrosted and cut into halves or quarters
1 teaspoon salt
⅓ cup sugar
2 tablespoons cornstarch
1 can (8 ounces) pineapple tidbits or chunks
1 cup diced orange sections
⅓ cup light corn syrup
⅓ cup water
2 tablespoons grated orange rind
1 tablespoon lemon juice
6 to 8 drops **TABASCO® Sauce**, or as desired
Onion Rice (recipe follows)
Toasted slivered almonds, optional
Avocado and fresh pineapple slices for garnishing, if desired

Wash, drain and dry duckling. Sprinkle both sides with salt. Place duckling pieces, skin side up, on rack in a roasting pan. Bake in moderate oven (350°F.) until meat is tender and skin is brown and crisp, about 2 hours. Turn several times during roasting ending with skin side up. Combine and mix sugar and cornstarch in saucepan. Drain pineapple tidbits or chunks and orange sections; save juices. Add juices, corn syrup and water; stir until free of lumps. Cook until clear and thickened, stirring constantly. Stir in orange rind, lemon juice and **TABASCO® Sauce**. Add pineapple and orange; heat through. Serve duckling with Onion Rice. Sprinkle with almonds; garnish with avocado and fresh pineapple slices, if desired.
Makes 4 servings

*ONION RICE

½ cup chopped onion
2 tablespoons cooking oil
1 cup long grain rice
Water
1 teaspoon salt
1 chicken bouillon cube

Cook onion in oil until tender, but not brown. Stir in rice. Add amount of water called for on package label, salt and bouillon cube. Bring to a boil. Cover and simmer until tender, about 15 minutes.
Yield: 4 servings

Favorite recipe from **National Duckling Council**

ROAST DUCK WITH CHAMBORD SAUCE

Take a 4 to 5 lb. duck, trim excess fat, season with salt and pepper. Prick skin to allow fat to drain. Roast duck, along with chopped giblets at 450° for 1½ hours.

Pour off all but 2 tablespoons of fat from the roasting pan. Add 1 carrot, 1 onion, 1 tomato, coarsely chopped, and sauté for 10 minutes. Add 1 cup brown stock (or canned beef broth). Scrape pan to loosen all the brown bits and then strain this duck sauce into a container.
(Continued)

Melt 3 tablespoons sugar and 1 tablespoon butter in a saucepan and cook, stirring until the mixture is brown. Add ⅓ cup cider vinegar and continue to cook until the mixture is reduced by half. Pour in the duck sauce and reduce heat to simmer. Add one 10 oz. package of defrosted frozen raspberries and ¼ cup **CHAMBORD Liqueur**. Simmer for 10 minutes. Serve over duck.

SPIT-ROASTED DUCKLING WITH OLIVE BARBECUE SAUCE

1 frozen duckling (4½ to 5 pounds), defrosted
½ teaspoon garlic salt
½ cup catsup
½ cup water
¼ cup chopped onion
3 tablespoons red wine vinegar
1 clove garlic, cut in half
1½ teaspoons sugar
¼ teaspoon paprika
½ cup sliced stuffed olives

Wash, drain and dry duckling. Sprinkle neck and body cavities with garlic salt. Skewer neck skin to back. Truss duckling compactly. Tie wings against breast. Tie legs together loosely, looping cord around tail. Insert rotisserie spit lengthwise through duck cavities on a slight angle; balance and tighten holding prongs. Roast on rotisserie over moderate to low heat until meat on drumstick is very tender, about 2½ hours. While duckling is roasting, prepare sauce. Combine catsup, water, onion, vinegar, garlic, sugar and paprika; simmer about 20 minutes. Remove garlic. Baste duckling with sauce frequently during last 30 minutes of roasting. Stir olives into remaining sauce; heat. Serve with duckling. *Makes 3 to 4 servings*

Favorite recipe from the **National Duckling Council**

KAHLÚA® PEKING DUCK

1 or 2 frozen ducks, 3½ to 4 lb. each (1 duck serves 2)
1 cup **KAHLÚA® Coffee Liqueur**
4 1″ slices peeled fresh ginger root or ½ tsp. ground ginger
½ tsp. brown gravy base
⅛ tsp. red food coloring
¼ cup Hoi Sin (sweet bean paste)
2 Tbsp. soy sauce
1 tsp. sesame oil or peanut oil

Wash ducks inside & out under cold running water; pat dry with paper towels. Place ducks in shallow baking dish. Combine **KAHLÚA®**, ginger root, gravy base and food coloring; pour over ducks. Let ducks marinate 1 hour at room temperature, turning now & then. Remove ducks, reserving marinade.

For crisper skin hang ducks. Cut a 20″ length of cord for each duck and tie an end around each neck. If the duck skin at the neck has been cut away, loop cord under wings. Suspend birds so they have plenty of air. Let hang 1 to 3 hours to dry. Remove cord, place ducks breast side down on rack in shallow roasting pan. Roast ducks in slow oven (325°) 45 minutes; turn ducks breast side up to roast 45 minutes or till done. (If breasts get excessively brown, cover loosely with foil).

SAUCE:
To reserved **KAHLÚA®** marinade, add Hoi Sin, soy sauce and oil, stirring to blend. Bring to boil stirring occasionally; reduce heat and simmer 5 minutes or till thickened. Keep warm to serve with duck.

DUCKLING QUARTERS, CAL-HAWAIIAN STYLE

1 frozen duckling, defrosted and quartered
½ teaspoon garlic salt
½ teaspoon ginger
1 can (1 pound 4 ounce) pineapple chunks
⅓ cup sugar
2 tablespoons cornstarch
¼ teaspoon salt
¼ cup catsup
¼ cup vinegar
1 teaspoon soy sauce
1 medium green pepper, cut in chunks
1 medium tomato, cut in wedges
6 green onions, cut in ½ inch lengths (½ cup)
4 servings hot, fluffy, seasoned and buttered rice
¼ cup chopped macadamia nuts or almonds, optional

Wash, drain and dry duckling quarters. Sprinkle both sides with garlic salt and ginger. Place quarters, skin side up, on rack in roasting pan. Bake in slow oven (325 degrees F.) until drumsticks are very tender, about 40 minutes per pound. While duckling is roasting drain pineapple chunks; save 1 cup syrup. Combine sugar, cornstarch and salt. Add pineapple syrup, catsup, vinegar and soy sauce; mix well. Cook stirring constantly until thickened and clear. Use ½ cup sauce for spooning over duckling quarters for last 30 minutes of cooking time. Just before serving, heat remaining sauce. Add pineapple chunks, green pepper, tomato and onion; stir to coat with sauce. Heat just until vegetables are hot. Serve with duckling quarters and rice sprinkled with macadamia nuts or almonds if desired. *Makes 4 servings*

Favorite recipe from **National Duckling Council**

Meat

Beef

CENTRAL PARK KABOBS

1½ pounds boneless chuck steak, cut into 1½″ cubes
1½ teaspoons **ADOLPH'S® 100% Natural Meat Tenderizer-Seasoned**
1 can (8 oz.) tomato sauce
¼ cup brown sugar
2 tablespoons prepared mustard
1 teaspoon horseradish
1 medium green pepper, cut into 1″ cubes
1 large onion, cut into wedges
6 cherry tomatoes
6 mushroom caps

Moisten meat with water. Sprinkle evenly on all sides with tenderizer and pierce deeply with a fork. (Use no salt.) In a saucepan, combine next four ingredients; heat through. Arrange meat on skewers, alternating with vegetables.

To barbecue: Grill kabobs 3″ from heat about 15 minutes for medium, basting and turning frequently.

To cook indoors: Broil kabobs 4-5″ from heat about 14 minutes for medium, basting and turning frequently.   *Serves 6*

DELISH-KABOBS

1 envelope **LIPTON® Onion Soup Mix**
1 cup dry red wine
¼ cup oil
1 tablespoon soy sauce
1 clove garlic, finely chopped
2-pound boneless round steak, cut into 2-inch cubes
12 mushroom caps
½ pint cherry tomatoes
2 small green peppers, cut into chunks

In large shallow baking dish, combine **LIPTON® Onion Soup Mix,** wine, oil, soy sauce and garlic; add beef. Cover and marinate in refrigerator, turning occasionally, 4 hours or overnight.

On skewers, alternately thread beef, mushrooms, tomatoes and green peppers. Grill or broil, turning and basting frequently with remaining marinade, until done.   *About 6 servings*

COMPANY KABOBS

Sweet 'n Sour Sauce*
1½ lb. ground beef
¾ cup **QUAKER® Oats** (quick or old fashioned, uncooked)
1 egg, beaten
1 teaspoon salt
¼ teaspoon pepper
1 clove garlic, minced
18 pineapple chunks reserved from canned pineapple
1 green pepper, cut into 1-inch chunks
6 green onions, cut into 2-inch pieces
12 medium mushrooms

Prepare Sweet 'n Sour Sauce; set aside. Heat oven to 350°F. Combine ground beef, oats, egg, salt, pepper and garlic; mix well. Shape meat mixture around pineapple chunks to make 18 meatballs. Alternate green pepper, meatballs, green onion and mushrooms on six 12 to 14-inch skewers. (To be sure meatball stays on skewers, thread through pineapple in center.) Place kabobs on rack in shallow roasting pan. Bake about 20 minutes. Brush with Sweet 'n Sour Sauce; continue baking 10 minutes or until desired doneness. Serve over rice with additional Sweet 'n Sour Sauce, if desired.   *Makes 6 kabobs*

*SWEET 'N SOUR SAUCE

1 8-oz. can pineapple chunks in unsweetened pineapple juice
1 tablespoon cornstarch
½ cup maple flavored table syrup
¼ cup vinegar
2 tablespoons soy sauce
2 tablespoons catsup
1 clove garlic, minced

Drain pineapple; reserve ¼ cup juice. Set aside pineapple chunks for Company Kabobs. In small saucepan, combine pineapple juice and cornstarch; mix well. Add remaining ingredients. Bring to a boil. Reduce heat. Simmer, stirring frequently, until thickened and clear.   *Makes about 1 cup*

KOOFTAH KABOBS

1 can (1 lb., 4 oz.) **DOLE® Sliced Pineapple**
2 lbs. ground chuck
½ cup bread crumbs
3 tablespoons soy sauce
2 tablespoons instant minced onions
2 teaspoons garlic salt
1 teaspoon curry powder
½ teaspoon ground cumin
1 large green bell pepper

Drain pineapple well, reserving all syrup. Add pineapple syrup to ground chuck along with bread crumbs, soy sauce, onions, garlic salt, curry and cumin. Mix well. Form into 20 meatballs. Cut green pepper, remove seeds and cut into 15 chunks. On each of 5 long skewers thread a piece of green pepper, a meatball, a slice of pineapple, a meatball, and repeat ending with a pepper chunk. Broil on grill 12 minutes on first side; turn and grill 8 minutes longer.   *Makes 5 generous servings*

BEEF AND VEGETABLE KABOBS

½ cup olive or salad oil
2 tablespoons red wine vinegar
1 tablespoon **MORTON® NATURE'S SEASONS® Seasoning Blend**
2 pounds boneless, tender beef, cubed for kabobs
½ pint cherry tomatoes
8 ounces fresh mushrooms, halved
4 medium onions, quartered
3 medium green peppers, cut into eighths
Pita or French bread rolls

Early in Day: In a large bowl, combine oil, vinegar, and seasoning blend; add beef cubes. Cover and refrigerate, stirring occasionally.

About 45 Minutes Before Serving: Prepare outdoor grill for barbecuing. Drain beef cubes, reserving marinade. On eight 18-inch skewers, alternately thread beef with vegetables. Heat reserved marinade to boiling; remove from heat. Brush beef and vegetables with marinade. Barbecue kabobs over medium coals 20 minutes for medium doneness, turning occasionally and brushing with marinade. Spoon into pita pockets or split rolls.

Makes 8 servings

OVEN BROILING METHOD:
Prepare kabobs as above. Place kabobs on rack in broiler pan. Broil 20 to 25 minutes to desired doneness, turning occasionally and brushing with marinade. Serve as above.

KABOBS INTERNATIONAL

1½ pounds ground beef chuck
1 cup **NABISCO 100% Bran Cereal**
⅓ cup finely chopped onion
¼ cup water
1¾ teaspoons salt
2 cloves garlic, crushed
¼ teaspoon ground black pepper

Basting Sauce:
½ cup red wine vinegar
3 tablespoons vegetable oil
¾ teaspoon oregano

Vegetables:
2 small zucchini, cut in 1-inch pieces
18 whole fresh mushrooms
1 (4-ounce) jar **DROMEDARY Pimiento Pieces**, drained

1. In medium bowl, combine beef, **NABISCO 100% Bran Cereal**, onion, water, 1½ teaspoons salt, 1 clove garlic and pepper; mix until well blended. Moisten hands with cold water and shape mixture into 24 1-inch meatballs. Set aside.
2. In small bowl, make Basting Sauce by blending vinegar, oil, oregano, ¼ teaspoon salt and 1 clove garlic.
3. Carefully thread 6 skewers, alternating meatballs, zucchini, mushrooms and pimientos; brush well with sauce. Grill or broil in oven about 7 to 10 minutes or until desired doneness, turning occasionally and basting with remaining sauce.
4. If broiling in oven, serve with pan juices. *Makes 6 servings*

BEEF AND VEGETABLE KABOBS WITH SESAME LIME MARINADE

1½ pounds top round of beef, cut in 1½-inch cubes
2 tablespoons sesame seeds
¼ cup lime juice
2 tablespoons vegetable oil
1 tablespoon soy sauce
2 cloves garlic, finely minced
½ teaspoon **TABASCO® Pepper Sauce**
2 medium zucchini, cut in 1-inch pieces
8 cherry tomatoes
2 medium onions, parboiled, cut in quarters

Place meat in a bowl or plastic bag. Combine sesame seeds, lime juice, oil, soy sauce, garlic and **TABASCO® Pepper Sauce**; pour over meat. Cover. Refrigerate at least 5 hours or overnight. Arrange 3 or 4 pieces of meat on each skewer. Reserve marinade. Arrange vegetables on separate skewers, alternating pieces of zucchini, tomato and onion. Brush meat and vegetables with marinade. Grill, allowing 15 to 20 minutes for meat and 10 to 12 minutes for vegetables. Baste meat and vegetables often during grilling. Turn occasionally. *Yield: 4 servings*

SPICY SHORT RIBS

3 pounds short ribs of beef
¼ cup all-purpose flour
2 tablespoons shortening
1 cup beef broth or bouillon
½ cup **SMUCKER'S Apricot Preserves**
2 tablespoons brown sugar
2 tablespoons vinegar
¼ teaspoon ground allspice
¼ teaspoon ground cinnamon
¼ teaspoon ground cloves
1 tablespoon cornstarch
1 tablespoon cold water

Remove as much excess fat from ribs as possible. Dust ribs with flour. Melt shortening in a Dutch oven or large heavy skillet. Place ribs in skillet; brown well on all sides. Pour off excess drippings. Combine broth, preserves, brown sugar, vinegar, and spices. Pour over ribs. Cover and cook over low heat about 2½ hours, or until ribs are tender, turning ribs occasionally during cooking time. With a spoon, skim as much fat as possible from top of sauce. Combine cornstarch and water to make a smooth paste. Stir into sauce and cook, stirring, until sauce is clear and lightly thickened.

Makes 4 to 6 servings

Good Idea: This is particularly good made a day in advance. Do not thicken. Refrigerate and, when cold, remove all fat from top of sauce and meat. Just before serving, heat, then thicken with cornstarch paste as above.

CATTLEMEN'S RIBS & BEANS

4 lb. beef short ribs
2 tsp. salt
½ tsp. pepper
½ tsp. dried leaf oregano
½ tsp. dried leaf basil
2 Tbsp. chili powder
2-4 Tbsp. vegetable oil
1 large onion, sliced
2 garlic cloves, minced
2 cups red wine
2 (15½-oz.) cans **JOAN OF ARC® Fancy Red Kidney Beans**, drained

Preheat oven to 350°F. Trim excess fat from ribs. In a small bowl, combine salt, pepper, oregano, basil and chili powder. Mix well. Rub seasonings into ribs, covering all sides. Heat 2 tablespoons oil in a medium skillet. Brown ribs in oil until golden brown on all sides. Remove ribs and set aside. Add remaining oil if needed. Sauté onion and garlic in oil until onion softens. Cover bottom of a shallow 4-quart casserole with sautéed onion mixture. Place ribs on top of onion. Pour in wine. Cover and bake until ribs are fork tender, 1½ to 2 hours. Add beans. Cover and bake 30 minutes longer. Remove ribs and place on a warmed platter. Stir beans into pan juices before spooning around ribs. *Makes 6 to 8 servings*

ZINFANDEL BEEF RIBS

½ cup water
½ cup **ALMADÉN Zinfandel Wine**
1 teaspoon dried thyme, crushed
½ garlic clove, crushed
½ teaspoon lemon pepper
2 pounds beef short ribs

In Dutch oven or heavy skillet, combine water, wine, thyme, garlic and lemon pepper. Add ribs. Cover and simmer for 1¼ hours. Drain, reserving liquid.

Grill over slow coals 15 to 20 minutes (or broil in oven a few minutes on each side, watching carefully). Turn frequently and brush on reserved liquid.   *Serves 4*

BARBECUED STEAK

Cover surface of a thick steak with prepared mustard. Moisten **LESLIE Rock Salt** and press into mustard on steak to form a thick coating. Place in a basket grill. Broil over a glowing fire quite close to heat. When cooked to desired degree of doneness, crack off salt crust and place on a buttered platter to carve.

SAUCY LEMON-PEPPERED STEAKS

2 beef loin, top loin or tenderloin steaks
2 teaspoons lemon pepper
1 tablespoon butter or margarine
1 tablespoon vegetable oil
Salt
2 tablespoons chopped green onions
1 tablespoon butter or margarine
2 teaspoons flour
½ cup whipping cream
1 tablespoon brandy

Pat steaks dry with paper toweling. Sprinkle both sides of steak with lemon pepper, pressing it into the meat; cover. Let stand 30 minutes. Heat 1 tablespoon butter and the oil in large skillet. Brown steaks 3 to 4 minutes on each side. Remove to hot platter; sprinkle with salt and keep warm. Pour fat from skillet. Cook and stir green onions in 1 tablespoon butter 1 minute; mix in flour. Gradually stir in cream and brandy. Cook and stir until bubbly. Pour over steaks. Serve immediately.   *Makes 2 servings*

Favorite recipe from **Oregon Beef Council**

STEAK STRIP BONANZA
(Microwave Recipe)

1 pound beef top round steak, cut ¾-inch thick
1 can (10-ounces) tomatoes
1 cup thinly sliced carrots
½ cup chopped onion
½ teaspoon basil leaves
¼ teaspoon oregano leaves
2 tablespoons flour
1 teaspoon salt
⅛ teaspoon cumin
⅛ teaspoon pepper
1 tablespoon oil
1 cup thinly sliced zucchini

Slice top round steak in strips ⅛-inch or less thick and 2- to 2½-inches long. Break up tomatoes; drain liquid into 1½-quart microwave-safe bowl. Add carrots, onion, basil and oregano to liquid; cover and microwave at HIGH 4 minutes, stirring after 2 minutes. Combine flour, salt, cumin and pepper; dredge steak strips. Add

oil to 11¾ × 7½-inch or 8 × 8-inch microwave-safe baking dish or casserole; spread steak strips in layer over bottom. Cover and cook at MEDIUM 6 minutes, stirring every 3 minutes. Stir in carrot mixture, tomatoes and zucchini. Cover and continue cooking at MEDIUM 12 minutes, stirring every 3 minutes. Cover and let stand 3 minutes.   *4 servings*

Note: Partially freeze steak to facilitate slicing into thin strips.

Favorite recipe from **National Live Stock & Meat Board**

STEAKS ITALIANO

3 tablespoons vegetable oil
1 medium onion, sliced
1 medium green pepper, chopped
8 rump steaks (about 1 pound), pounded to ¼-inch thick
1 jar (15½ oz.) **RAGU'® Homestyle Spaghetti Sauce,** any flavor
Salt and pepper, to taste
1½ cups (6 oz.) shredded mozzarella cheese

In large skillet, sauté onion and green pepper in oil until onion is translucent; remove from skillet. Add steaks to skillet and brown quickly on both sides. Return onion and pepper to skillet. Add **Homestyle Spaghetti Sauce**, salt and pepper; simmer 10 minutes. Sprinkle evenly with mozzarella. Cover and simmer 8-10 minutes more. Serve on pasta.   *Serves 4*

STEAK ROLLS

1½ pounds round steak, cut ½ inch thick
6 tablespoons shortening
¼ cup finely chopped onion
1½ cups day-old bread crumbs
1 cup crushed **JAYS Potato Chips**
½ cup chopped celery
½ teaspoon salt
¼ teaspoon poultry seasoning
Dash of nutmeg
1 tablespoon water
1 can condensed mushroom or tomato soup mixed with can of water

Remove bone from meat. Pound meat to flatten with edge of saucer or meat pounder. Cut into 4 pieces. Lightly brown onion in 3 tablespoons shortening. Add bread, chips, celery, seasonings and water. Place ¼ of the mixture on each piece of meat. Roll up and fasten with skewer or wooden pick. Flour and brown in remaining fat. Dilute soup with soup-can of water and pour over meat in skillet. Sprinkle with salt, pepper and nutmeg. Cover and simmer over low heat 1½ hours or until tender.   *4 servings*

COOKOUT CHUCK STEAK

2 beef chuck blade steaks, cut ¾ inch thick (approximately 4 pounds)
1 envelope **LIPTON® Beefy Onion Soup Mix**
½ cup dry red wine
¼ cup red wine vinegar
1 tablespoon Worcestershire sauce
1 can (8 ounces) tomato sauce
¼ cup brown sugar
1 tablespoon chili powder
¼ teaspoon cumin, if desired

Combine beefy onion soup mix, wine, vinegar and Worcestershire sauce. Place steaks in utility dish or plastic bag; add marinade, turning to coat steaks. Cover dish or tie bag securely and marinate in refrigerator 6 to 8 hours (or overnight), turning at least once. Drain marinade from meat and combine with tomato sauce, brown sugar, chili powder and cumin, if desired, in small saucepan; cook slowly 10 minutes, stirring occasionally. Place steaks on grill so surface of meat is 4 inches from heat. Broil at moderate temperature 7 to 10 minutes on each side, depending upon degree of doneness desired (rare or medium). Brush steaks with sauce occasionally while broiling. *6 to 8 servings*

Favorite recipe from the **Iowa Beef Industry Council**

GALLO® SALAME STUFFED STEAK CONTINENTAL

8 slices **GALLO® Italian Dry Salame**
1⅓ lbs. top round or sirloin, cut ¾ inch thick
2 ounces Gruyere or Samsoe cheese, sliced
Salt and pepper to taste
½ tsp. crumbled dried oregano
2 Tbsp. butter, divided
¼ lb. mushrooms, sliced
¼ cup diced **GALLO® Italian Dry Salame**
1 clove garlic, minced
1 tsp. grated lemon peel
¼ cup each dry red wine and beef stock
2 Tbsp. chopped parsley

Cut steak into four serving size pieces. Cut a pocket in side of each, to within ½ inch of the other side. Tuck cheese and **GALLO® Salame** slices inside pockets. Add salt, pepper, and oregano. Brown steak in butter in frying pan; turn to brown both sides and cook until medium rare. Place on warm platter. Add remaining butter to pan and sauté mushrooms, diced **GALLO® Italian Dry Salame**, garlic and lemon peel for one minute. Spoon over meat. Add wine and stock to the pan and deglaze pan juices. Spoon sauce over meat and sprinkle with parsley.

Serves 4

PEPPER STEAK

1½ pounds beef round steak, cut ½ inch thick
¼ cup **CRISCO® Shortening**
1 can (8 ounces) tomatoes
1¼ cups water
½ cup chopped onion
1 small clove garlic, crushed
1 teaspoon salt
⅛ teaspoon pepper
2 teaspoons Worcestershire sauce
3 tablespoons Brown Roux*
2 large green peppers

Partially freeze meat and cut meat in strips 3 inches long and ¼ inch wide. In large skillet, brown meat strips in hot **CRISCO®**; drain off excess fat. Drain tomatoes, reserving liquid. Add reserved liquid, the water, onion, garlic, salt, and pepper to meat in skillet. Cover and simmer 50 to 60 minutes or till meat is tender. Uncover and stir in the Worcestershire sauce. Stir in the Brown Roux. Cook and stir till thickened and bubbly. Cut the green peppers in 2-inch long strips and add to meat along with the drained tomatoes which have been cut up. Simmer 5 minutes more. Serve over hot cooked rice. *Makes 6 servings*

(Continued)

*BROWN ROUX

Blend 1 cup **CRISCO® Shortening** and 1 cup flour till smooth. Stir in 2 tablespoons **KITCHEN BOUQUET®**. Refrigerate the mixture in a covered container till needed for gravy-making. To use the roux, combine 3 tablespoons roux for each cup of liquid (pan juices plus water) for gravy of medium thickness. Blend the roux into the liquid; cook and stir till gravy thickens and bubbles. Season gravy as desired with salt and pepper.

PEPPER STEAK, ISLE OF SKYE

1 sirloin steak, about 3 lbs.
2 tablespoons whole black peppercorns, crushed
2 tablespoons oil
2 tablespoons wine vinegar
½ teaspoon sugar
3 tablespoons **JOHNNIE WALKER RED Scotch**, warmed

Rub each side of steak with crushed peppercorns. Combine oil and vinegar; pour over steak. Turn steak to coat both sides; let stand at room temperature 2 to 3 hours. Broil about 7 minutes each side for medium rare. Place on heated platter. Sprinkle with sugar, pour on **JOHNNIE WALKER RED** and ignite. Slice when flames go out. *4 to 6 servings*

TARA STEAK DIANE

1 lb. boneless sirloin steak, ¼" thick
GREY POUPON Dijon Mustard
Freshly ground pepper
3 tablespoons butter (or margarine)
¼ cup finely minced shallots
1 medium clove garlic, finely minced
1 cup sliced fresh mushrooms
1 teaspoon steak sauce
1 tablespoon capers
½ cup beef broth
¼ cup **IRISH MIST® Liqueur**

Pound steak to ⅛" thickness. Coat one side with mustard. Sprinkle with pepper. Roll steak to coat both sides with mustard. Set aside. In large skillet, melt butter. Cook shallots and garlic until soft. Stir in mushrooms, steak sauce, 1 teaspoon mustard, capers and broth. Cook to reduce slightly. Unroll steak. Place in sauce and cook as desired, turning once. Pour **IRISH MIST®** over all and ignite carefully. When flame dies, serve immediately. *Serves 2*

BUDGET STEAK WITH HORSERADISH SAUCE

1 bottle (12 oz.) chili sauce
2 tablespoons horseradish
1 tablespoon fresh lemon juice
1 teaspoon Worcestershire sauce
1 chuck steak (about 2 pounds), cut 1" thick
2 teaspoons **ADOLPH'S® 100% Natural Meat Tenderizer, Unseasoned**

In bowl, combine first 4 ingredients. Chill, if desired, to improve flavor. Moisten steak with water; sprinkle evenly with half the tenderizer and pierce deeply with a fork. Repeat on other side. (Use no salt.) Broil steak 4 to 5 inches from heat about 7 minutes per side for medium. Serve steak with sauce.

Serves about 4

WOODLAND ONION CHUCK STEAK

2½ to 3-pound boneless chuck steak
1 envelope **LIPTON® Onion** or **Beefy Onion Soup Mix**
1 cup sliced mushrooms
Heavy-duty aluminum foil (about 18" × 18")

Place steak on foil; sprinkle both sides with onion soup mix, then top with mushrooms. Wrap foil loosely around steak, sealing edges airtight with double fold. Place seam-side up on grate over hot coals, about 5 inches from heat. Grill 1 hour or until beef is tender.   *Makes about 6 servings*

THE WESTERN LITE BROIL

1 to 1½ pounds beef top round, sirloin or flank steak
½ cup soy sauce
¼ cup water
2 tablespoons lemon juice
2 tablespoons honey
2 green onions, chopped
¼ teaspoon garlic powder
1 tablespoon toasted sesame seeds

Combine soy sauce, water, lemon juice, honey, green onions and garlic powder, stir thoroughly. Pour marinade over steak, turn to coat both sides thoroughly. Cover and marinate in refrigerator 48 hours, turn occasionally. Broil or grill only to medium rare. Cut across the grain into thin slices and sprinkle lightly with sesame seeds.   *Makes 3 servings per pound*

Favorite recipe from **Oregon Beef Council**

LONDON BROIL

1 beef flank steak (1¼ to 1¾ pounds)
¼ cup salad oil
1 tablespoon lemon juice
1 clove garlic, crushed
½ teaspoon salt
¼ teaspoon pepper

Combine salad oil, lemon juice, garlic, salt and pepper for marinade. Place steak in plastic bag or flat utility dish and pour marinade over it. Close bag securely or cover pan with foil and refrigerate 4 to 6 hours or overnight, turning occasionally. Pour off and reserve marinade. Place steak on grill and broil at moderate temperature for 5 minutes. Turn, brush with marinade and broil 5 minutes or to desired doneness (rare or medium). To carve, slice diagonally across grain in thin strips.   *4 servings*

Favorite recipe from **Iowa Beef Industry Council**

MARINATED LONDON BROIL

1½ pound flank, round or shoulder steak
½ cup **LEA & PERRINS Steak Sauce**
4 teaspoons lemon juice
2 teaspoons **LEA & PERRINS Worcestershire Sauce**
¼ teaspoon salt

Place steak in a shallow glass pan. Prick with fork tines on both sides. To prepare marinade combine **LEA & PERRINS Steak Sauce**, lemon juice, **LEA & PERRINS Worcestershire Sauce** and salt. Pour over steak coating both sides. Marinate for 1 hour. To cook over charcoal, place steak on a rack over hot coals until done as desired, 10 to 15 minutes for medium, turning and brushing often

with marinade. To broil, place on a rack in a broiler pan under a preheated hot broiler until done as desired, 10 to 15 minutes for medium, turning and brushing occasionally with marinade.
                    Yield: 4 to 6 portions

GALLO® SALAME BEEF SPIEDINI

16 slices **GALLO® Italian Dry Salame**
1 lb. thinly sliced steak or roast, cut ³⁄₁₆-inch thick
Salt and freshly ground pepper to taste
½ tsp. crumbled dried oregano
4 ounces Gruyere, Samsoe, or Fontinella cheese
2 Tbsp. butter, melted
1 clove garlic, minced

Cut meat slices in rectangles, approximately 3 inches by 5 inches. Sprinkle with salt, pepper, and oregano. Lay a slice of **GALLO® Italian Dry Salame** on each. Thinly slice cheese and lay a piece on top. Roll up and skewer, placing 4 meat rolls on each skewer. Melt butter and garlic and brush over meat rolls. Broil or barbecue over hot coals, turning until cooked through, about 6 minutes.
                    Serves 4

Note: If desired, alternate cherry tomatoes, green pepper squares, and 1-inch chunks of sourdough French bread dipped in garlic butter on skewers. Brush vegetables with additional garlic butter and broil until bread turns golden brown.

SAUTÉED BEEF

1 cup fresh mushrooms, sliced
3 tablespoons butter or margarine
3 tablespoons minced green onions
½ teaspoon thyme
2 tablespoons butter or margarine
1 tablespoon cooking oil
3 pounds beef tenderloin tips
¼ cup **HOLLAND HOUSE® Marsala Cooking Wine**
½ cup beef bouillon
1 cup heavy cream
2 teaspoons cornstarch
2 tablespoons softened butter or margarine
Salt, freshly ground pepper to taste

Melt 3 tablespoons butter or margarine in a small skillet; sauté mushrooms for 5 minutes. Add green onions and thyme and cook 1 minute more. Remove to side dish. In the same skillet, add 2 tablespoons butter or margarine and the cooking oil and quickly brown beef, a few pieces at a time. Remove beef to side dish; discard fat in skillet. Pour Marsala and bouillon into skillet and boil down rapidly to ⅓ cup. Blend cornstarch with 1 tablespoon heavy cream. Add remaining cream and cornstarch mixture to Marsala broth; simmer for one minute. Add mushroom mixture; when blended with sauce add beef. Cover skillet and simmer for 3 to 4 minutes. Prior to serving, add softened butter or margarine and baste meat until it is absorbed. Add salt and pepper to taste and serve.   *Serves 4 to 6*

SWISS STEAK

½ cup sifted **E-Z-BAKE Flour**
3 teaspoons salt
½ teaspoon pepper
2 pounds round steak (1½ inches thick)
3 tablespoons fat
1 small onion, minced
2 cups tomatoes

Mix flour, salt and pepper. Pound into steak with tenderizer or potato masher. Brown in fat in heavy skillet. Add onions to tomatoes. Boil 5 minutes. Pour over steak. Bake in moderate oven (350°F.) 2 hours.

RONZONI® SWISS STEAK

1 (15-oz.) jar **RONZONI® Lite 'n' Natural Meat Flavored Sauce**
8 oz. **RONZONI® Ziti #2 or Mostaccioli #86**
1 lean chuck steak (1½ lb.) about 1-inch thick
½ cup flour
1½ Tbsp. corn oil
½ cup water
1 cup bouillon made with 2 cubes
1 large onion, sliced
1 clove garlic, minced
½ tsp. salt
¼ tsp. pepper
½ tsp. seasoned salt

Dredge steak on both sides with flour. Heat oil in Dutch oven or large skillet and brown steak on each side. Add remaining ingredients except pasta. Cover and simmer over low heat for one hour or until meat is tender. After steak has been simmering for ½ hour, cook **RONZONI® Pasta** per package directions. When steak is tender, serve over pasta. *Serves 5*

415 calories per serving

CANTONESE FLANK STEAK

½ pound flank steak
2 Tablespoons cornstarch
1 teaspoon sugar
½ teaspoon ginger
½ cup dry sherry
2 Tablespoons soy sauce
⅓ cup water
1 teaspoon plus 1 Tablespoon vegetable oil, divided
1 package (14 ounces) **Frozen STOKELY'S® Cantonese Style Stir Fry Vegetables**

Cut flank steak across the grain into paper-thin strips.* Place in glass dish. Blend cornstarch, sugar, ginger, sherry, soy sauce, and water to make marinade. Pour marinade over meat. Refrigerate, covered, 2½ hours. Remove meat from marinade and drain, reserving marinade. Heat 9- or 10-inch skillet or wok over high heat (a drop of water will sizzle). Pour 1 teaspoon oil in wide, circular motion inside rim of pan. Tilt pan to coat surface. Add half the meat and stir-fry about 3 minutes. Remove to warm serving dish. Cook remaining meat about 3 minutes and remove to serving dish. Remove seasoning packet from vegetables and reserve. When skillet is again very hot, spread frozen vegetables evenly in pan. Pour 1 Tablespoon oil in pan in circular motion and stir into vegetables quickly, coating each piece. Sprinkle reserved seasoning packet over vegetables and add 2 Tablespoons water and reserved marinade in circular motion. Cook and stir about 30 seconds until vegetables and seasonings are blended. Cover and cook 1 minute, return meat to skillet, stir, and cook 1 minute more. Serve immediately. *4 servings*

*Note: For easier slicing, partially freeze flank steak.

BEEF BURGUNDY

1½ pounds round steak, cut in 1½-inch cubes
1 cup dry red wine
1 small onion, quartered
½ pound (about 2 cups) small mushrooms
4 tablespoons **FLEISCHMANN'S Unsalted Margarine**
3 cups sliced onion
2 cups diced carrots
¼ cup chopped parsley
2 cloves garlic, crushed
½ teaspoon ground marjoram
½ teaspoon thyme, crushed
¼ teaspoon pepper
1 bay leaf
1¼ cups water
2 tablespoons flour

Combine beef, ¾ cup wine and onion. Cover; refrigerate overnight. Drain beef cubes; set aside. Strain and reserve liquid. Sauté mushrooms in 3 tablespoons margarine until lightly browned; remove and set aside. Add beef; cook until well browned. Remove and set aside. Sauté sliced onion, carrots, parsley and garlic in remaining 1 tablespoon margarine until onions are tender. Add meat, marjoram, thyme, pepper, bay leaf, marinade and 1 cup water. Cover and simmer 2 hours, or until meat is tender. Dissolve flour in remaining ¼ cup water; add to beef mixture. Add mushrooms and cook until mixture thickens, about 5 minutes. Stir in remaining wine. *Makes 6 servings*

ALL AMERICAN POT ROAST

¼ cup **MAZOLA® Corn Oil**
1 (4-lb.) boneless beef chuck roast
1 cup chopped onion
1 cup sliced celery
2 cloves garlic, minced or pressed
3 cups beef bouillon
¼ cup catchup
1 teaspoon salt
½ teaspoon dried thyme leaves
¼ teaspoon pepper
6 medium potatoes, peeled, quartered
4 carrots, peeled, cut in 2-inch pieces
½ pound green beans
¼ cup **ARGO®/KINGSFORD'S® Corn Starch**
¼ cup water

In Dutch oven or large saucepot heat corn oil over medium heat. Add meat; brown on all sides. Add onion, celery, garlic, bouillon, catchup, salt, thyme and pepper. Cover; bring to boil. Reduce heat and simmer 2 hours. Add potatoes and carrots. Cover; simmer ½ hour or until meat and vegetables are tender. Add green beans and simmer 10 minutes longer or until tender-crisp. Remove meat and vegetables to platter. Stir together corn starch and water until smooth. Add to liquid in Dutch oven. Stirring constantly, bring to boil over medium heat and boil 1 minute. Serve gravy over meat and vegetables. *Makes about 6 servings*

POT ROAST

3 to 4 lbs. lean beef
2 large onions, sliced
1 lemon, sliced
2 Tbsp. sugar
1 Tbsp. ginger (may be omitted)
1 Tbsp. salt
12 whole black peppercorns
4 Tbsp. fat
2 Tbsp. flour
1½ cups **DUBONNET Rouge Apertif Wine**

The day before it is to be cooked, buy a solid piece of lean beef rump, bottom round, shoulder or chuck. Place meat in deep bowl, and add all of the above ingredients except fat and flour. The meat should be more than half covered with **DUBONNET Rouge**. Let it stand 18 to 24 hours in a cold place, turning occasionally during the day. Remove meat from liquid, drain thoroughly, then brown all over in 2 Tbsp. hot fat in heavy skillet. Add wine in which meat was marinated, cover kettle and simmer 3 to 4 hours. Add a little **DUBONNET Rouge** if it cooks dry. When tender lift meat out, and strain liquid in pot. In the kettle melt 2 Tbsp. fat, stir in the flour and brown lightly. Add the liquid and cook, stirring until slightly thickened. (If too thick, then mix with hot water to desired consistency). Taste, add more salt if needed, put meat back into gravy and heat 5 minutes longer. Serve sliced on hot platter, pouring gravy over roast.   *Makes 4 servings*

ITALIAN POT ROAST

1 chuck roast, about 3 pounds
2 to 3 tablespoons grated Parmesan cheese
2 tablespoons oil
2⅓ cups water
2 cans (6-oz. each) tomato paste
1 envelope (1¾-oz.) **FRENCH'S® Thick, Homemade Style Spaghetti Sauce Mix**
¼ cup Burgundy or other dry red wine, if desired
1 bag (16-oz.) unseasoned European style mixture of vegetables such as broccoli, cauliflower and red pepper
Cooked spiral or other macaroni

Coat roast with cheese. Brown in oil in large skillet or Dutch oven-type pan; pour off excess fat. Add water, tomato paste, sauce mix and Burgundy, stirring to blend. Cover and simmer 1½ to 2 hours, or until tender. Add vegetables; cook 15 minutes. Slice roast and serve with vegetables and sauce on macaroni.   *8 to 10 servings*

POLYNESIAN POT ROAST

1 can (8½ oz.) pineapple tidbits
2 tablespoons brown sugar
½ teaspoon ground ginger
½ cup chopped onion
⅓ cup cider vinegar
3 tablespoons soy sauce
2 tablespoons oil
1 tablespoon **LEA & PERRINS Worcestershire Sauce**
5-pound beef chuck arm pot roast
1 can (10½ oz.) condensed beef broth
1½ teaspoons salt
3 cups peeled sweet potato chunks
2 tablespoons cornstarch
2 tablespoons cold water

Combine pineapple, brown sugar, ginger, onion, vinegar, soy sauce, oil and **LEA & PERRINS**. Place beef in a snug-fitting bowl or doubled plastic bag. Pour pineapple mixture over meat. Cover or fasten. Refrigerate for 12 hours, mixing or turning once. Place beef and the pineapple marinade in a large saucepot or Dutch oven. Add broth and salt. Bring to boiling point. Reduce heat and simmer, covered, for 1½ hours. Add sweet potatoes. Simmer, covered, for ½ hour. Remove beef to a warm platter. Blend cornstarch with water. Stir into liquid in saucepot. Cook and stir until sauce thickens. Serve hot with the pot roast.

COLONIAL POT ROAST

2 tablespoons vegetable oil
1 3-pound boneless beef chuck roast
Salt and pepper
1 can (16 ounces) **STOKELY'S FINEST® Stewed Tomatoes**
1 teaspoon sugar
1 teaspoon oregano
1 package (28 ounces) **Frozen STOKELY'S® SIZE WIZE® Vegetables Sized for Roast**
All-purpose flour (optional)

Heat oil in Dutch oven. Season meat with salt and pepper and brown on all sides over medium heat, about 15 minutes. Add tomatoes, sugar, and oregano. Cover and simmer 2½ to 3 hours. Add vegetables and continue cooking, covered, 1 hour, or until meat and vegetables are tender. Lift meat and vegetables from pan with slotted spoon. If gravy is desired, measure sauce from Dutch oven. Add 2 tablespoons flour to each cup of drippings; blend and return to Dutch oven. Heat, stirring constantly, until thickened. Adjust seasoning. Serve with meat and vegetables.

4 to 6 servings

BOILED DINNER, CALIFORNIA STYLE

1 beef cross rib pot roast, about 3½ pounds
1 tablespoon oil
1 (13¾ oz.) can beef broth
½ cup California brandy
½ bay leaf
¼ teaspoon thyme, crumbled fine
2 pounds small red-skinned potatoes
½ pound small boiling onions
½ pound small carrots
1 pound zucchini, quartered
1 small cabbage, cut in wedges
2 tablespoons cornstarch

Brown beef on all sides in oil. Add broth, ¼ cup brandy, bay leaf and thyme, and bring to a boil. Cover and cook slowly until meat is almost tender, 2½ to 3 hours. Add potatoes, onions and carrots. Cover and cook 20 minutes, until almost tender. Add zucchini and cabbage, and cook 5 to 10 minutes longer. Remove meat and vegetables to serving platter and keep warm. Skim fat from broth, and remove bay leaf. Mix cornstarch with remaining ¼ cup brandy, and stir into broth remaining. Cook, stirring, until sauce boils and thickens. Turn into serving bowl, and pass separately.

Makes 6 servings

Favorite recipe from the **California Brandy Advisory Board**

GERMAN SAUERBRATEN

4 lb. boneless beef rump, sirloin tip or round bone chuck
1½ cups vinegar
1 cup COCA-COLA®
¾ cup water
3 onions, peeled and sliced
2 stalks celery, sliced
2 carrots, sliced
10 whole black peppers
10 whole cloves
3 bay leaves
2 tablespoons sugar
1½ tablespoons salt
3 tablespoons oil or shortening

Two to four days before serving, wipe meat with damp cloth, then place it in a large plastic bag. In bowl, thoroughly combine remaining ingredients except oil and pour over meat. Fasten bag tightly and lay flat in a 13 × 9-inch pan. Refrigerate, turning bag each day. (If you like a sour sauerbraten, let meat marinate four days.)

When ready to cook, remove meat (saving marinade) and dry well. Rub surface lightly with flour. Heat oil or shortening in Dutch oven and slowly brown meat well on all sides. Add 1 cup of the marinade liquid plus some of the vegetables and bay leaves. Cover tightly and simmer on surface heat or in a 350° oven for 3 to 4 hours until meat is fork-tender. If needed, add more marinade during cooking to keep at least ½-inch liquid in the Dutch oven. Remove meat and keep warm until ready to slice. Strain drippings into a large measuring cup; add several ice cubes; let stand a few minutes for fat to separate. Remove fat, then make gravy.
Makes 8 servings

Gravy:
3 cups drippings plus strained marinade
5 tablespoons flour
5 tablespoons ginger snap crumbs

Combine above ingredients in Dutch oven, stir and cook about 5 minutes over medium heat until gravy is thickened. Taste for seasonings. *Makes 3 cups gravy*

Note: Plan ahead because it takes days to properly marinate.

BEEF AND SAUSAGE LOAF

½ cup chopped onion
2 tablespoons chopped green pepper
2 tablespoons butter or margarine
2 beaten eggs
⅓ cup tomato juice
½ cup quick-cooking rolled oats
1 teaspoon salt
¼ teaspoon dry mustard
1½ pounds ground beef
½ pound TENNESSEE PRIDE® Country Sausage

Cook onion and green pepper in butter until tender but not brown. Combine eggs with next 4 ingredients and cooked vegetables. Add beef and sausage and mix well. Pat mixture into 8½ × 4½ × 2½-inch loaf dish. Bake at 350° for 1½ hours. Remove from oven and pour off excess fat. Let meat stand in pan several minutes before slicing. *Makes 8 servings*

H.J.'S FAMILY MEAT LOAF

1½ pounds ground beef
1 cup soft bread crumbs
1 egg, slightly beaten
½ cup chopped onion
⅓ cup HEINZ Tomato Ketchup
1 teaspoon salt
⅛ teaspoon pepper

Combine ingredients thoroughly. Form into a loaf (8″ × 4″ × 1½″) in shallow baking pan. Bake in 350°F oven, 1 hour. Let stand 5 minutes before slicing to serve hot or refrigerate and slice cold for sandwiches. *Makes 6 servings*

MONA LINDSAY®'S OLIVE MEATLOAF

2 lb. lean ground beef
1 cup chopped onions
1 clove garlic, crushed
3 bacon slices, halved
¼ tsp. pepper
½ tsp. each basil, oregano and salt
1 can (6 oz.) LINDSAY® Pitted Black Ripe Olives, drained
1 can (8 oz.) tomato sauce

In large bowl, thoroughly mix all ingredients except LINDSAY® Olives, tomato sauce and bacon. Mix in LINDSAY® Olives, reserving 5 for garnish. In a 9 x 13-inch baking pan, shape mixture into a 4 x 12-inch rounded loaf. Pour tomato sauce over loaf. Lay bacon slices across loaf. Bake in 350° F. oven 1 hour 15 minutes. Garnish with reserved LINDSAY® Olives. Slice to serve hot or cold. *Makes 8 servings*

ORIENTAL MEAT LOAF

2 pounds ground beef
1 can (8 oz.) water chestnuts, thinly sliced
4 green onions & tops, chopped
3 bread slices, finely shredded
¼ cup KIKKOMAN Soy Sauce
1 egg
1 clove garlic, crushed

Thoroughly combine all 7 ingredients until blended. Lightly pack into 9 × 5-inch loaf pan. Bake in 350°F. oven 1 hour or until meat is thoroughly cooked. Let stand 10 minutes before slicing.
Makes 4 to 6 servings

CREOLE MEAT LOAF

½ cup chopped onion
½ cup chopped celery
¼ cup chopped green pepper
2 tablespoons butter or margarine
1¼ cups HEINZ Tomato Ketchup
1½ pounds lean ground beef
1 cup soft bread crumbs
1 egg, slightly beaten
½ teaspoon salt

Sauté onion, celery and green pepper in butter until vegetables are tender. Stir in ketchup; combine ½ cup this mixture with ground beef, bread crumbs, egg and salt. Form into loaf (8×4×1½-inches) in shallow baking pan. Bake in 350°F oven, 1 hour. Let stand 5 minutes before slicing. Serve remaining sauce, cold or heated, over meat loaf. *Makes 6 servings*

TANGY MEAT LOAF

½ cup catsup
2 tablespoons brown sugar
½ teaspoon powdered mustard
4 teaspoons Worcestershire sauce
2 teaspoons seasoned salt
1½ teaspoons onion powder
¼ teaspoon garlic powder
¼ teaspoon ground black pepper
1 egg
2 tablespoons finely chopped green pepper
1½ cups **WHEAT CHEX®** Cereal
1½ pounds ground beef

In large bowl combine catsup, brown sugar and mustard. Reserve 4 tablespoons mixture for topping.

To remaining mixture, add Worcestershire, salt, onion and garlic powders, pepper and egg. Blend well. Stir in green pepper and **CHEX®**. Let stand 5 minutes. Break up **CHEX®**. Add ground beef. Mix well. Shape into loaf in shallow baking pan. Bake in 350° oven 65 minutes. Spread top with reserved catsup mixture. Bake additional 15 minutes.   *Makes about 6 servings*

CHEESE FLAVORED MEAT LOAF

½ cup **POLLY-O®** Bread Crumbs
1 tablespoon chopped fresh parsley
½ cup **POLLY-O®** Grated Parmesan or **Romano Cheese**
2 eggs
1 small onion, chopped
Salt and pepper to taste
½ pound lean ground beef
¼ pound lean ground pork
¼ pound lean ground veal
1 container (15-ounces) **POLLY-O®** Ricotta Cheese
1 (16-ounce) package **POLLY-O®** Bacon

Preheat oven to 375°. Thoroughly combine bread crumbs, parsley, grated cheese, 1 beaten egg, onion, salt and pepper. Blend with meat gently, being careful to handle meat as little as possible. Mix ricotta with remaining egg and blend well. Line bottom of a loaf pan with strips of bacon. Place half of meat in pan. Spread ricotta mixture over meat and top with remaining meat. Press edges firmly so ricotta does not seep out. Bake 35 minutes.

6 servings

VARIATION:

Place slices of **POLLY-O® Mozzarella** and sliced hard-cooked egg in center of meat loaf instead of ricotta mixture.

Note: Bacon slices, placed under a meat loaf, will prevent meat from sticking to pan, but bacon flavor will not be transferred to meat. If you want to add bacon flavor to meat, place a few slices of bacon on top of meat loaf during baking.

TOFU AND MUSHROOM MEATLOAF

½ pkg. (16-oz.) **AZUMAYA** Japanese-Style Tofu
1 lb. ground chuck
1 egg
¼ cup **KIKKOMAN** Soy Sauce
½ cup soft bread crumbs
½ teaspoon marjoram
½ teaspoon rubbed sage
¼ cup chopped green onion
Soy-Mushroom Sauce*

Mix all ingredients except Soy-Mushroom Sauce in bowl. Form into dome-shaped loaf in 8- or 9-inch pie plate. Spoon a little Soy-Mushroom Sauce over loaf. Bake at 350° 1 hour, glazing loaf with a little additional Sauce after ½ hour. Transfer baked loaf to serving plate. Pour remaining Sauce over top. Cut into wedges to serve.   *Makes 4 servings*

*SOY-MUSHROOM SAUCE

Combine 1 can (3-oz.) sliced mushrooms, 2 teaspoons cornstarch, 1 tablespoon brown sugar and 2 tablespoons soy sauce in saucepan. Cook, stirring until mixture comes to boil and is thickened.

RICE FILLED TERIYAKI MEATLOAF

Meatloaf:
2 lb. lean ground beef
6 tablespoons A.1. Steak Sauce
3 tablespoons *each* soy sauce and **REGINA Cooking Sherry**
1 tablespoon dark brown sugar
2 eggs, beaten
1 cup dry bread crumbs
1 medium clove garlic, crushed

Rice Filling:
1 medium onion, sliced
⅓ cup sliced celery
1 tablespoon butter (or margarine)
1 can (8 oz.) sliced water chestnuts, drained
½ cup drained bean sprouts
1 egg, beaten
⅔ cup rice, cooked
½ teaspoon salt

Lightly combine meatloaf ingredients. Set aside. In small saucepan, cook onion and celery in butter until onion is soft. Mix in remaining ingredients. Pat ½ meat mixture in 9 x 9 x 2-inch pan. Spread rice filling evenly over meat. Pat remaining meat carefully over filling. Bake in preheated 350° F oven 1 hour. Let stand 5 minutes. Cut in squares.   *Makes 9 servings*

SOUTHERN BEEF ROLL

Biscuit Dough*
2 cups ground cooked beef
2 cups gravy
2 tablespoons minced onion
2 tablespoons chopped green pepper (optional)

Roll dough into rectangle about ⅓ inch thick. Combine meat, 1 cup gravy and vegetables. Spread beef mixture on dough; roll up as for jelly roll. Bake in a hot oven (400°F.) about 30 minutes or until lightly browned. Cut in thick slices and serve with the extra gravy.

*BISCUIT DOUGH

2 cups E-Z BAKE Flour
3 teaspoons baking powder
1 teaspoon salt
¼ cup shortening
¾ cup milk

Mix together flour, salt, baking powder, and cut in shortening. Add enough milk to make a soft dough. Roll out on floured board and cut as directed in recipe.

TAVERN MEATBALLS

1 pound ground beef
1 clove garlic, pressed
½ cup bread crumbs
3 tablespoons prepared mustard
1 tablespoon Worcestershire sauce
1 teaspoon salt
2 tablespoons vegetable oil
1 medium onion, sliced
1 can (10¾ oz.) beef broth
1 cup dairy sour cream
1 tablespoon flour
1 tablespoon chopped parsley
1 bag (1 lb.) **BUD OF CALIFORNIA® Shredded Cabbage**

Combine beef, garlic, crumbs, mustard, Worcestershire and salt. Form into about 25 meatballs. In a large skillet, heat oil and brown meatballs on all sides. Remove meatballs from skillet. Drain excess skillet dripping reserving 2 teaspoons. Add onions and sauté until soft. Combine beef broth, sour cream and flour. Pour into skillet. Add meatballs. Cover and simmer 30 minutes. Stir in parsley. Steam cabbage 3 to 5 minutes until cabbage is tender-crisp. Arrange cabbage on a serving platter. Spoon meatballs over all. Serve immediately. *Makes 4 servings*

MEATBALLS IN MEAT SAUCE
(Polpette al sugo)

1 ounce salt pork, chopped
¼ cup **BERTOLLI® Olive Oil**
1 clove garlic, minced
1½ pounds ground beef
1½ pounds ground pork
4 cups **BERTOLLI® Spaghetti Sauce**
½ cup **BERTOLLI® Chianti Classico Wine**
⅛ teaspoon pepper
½ cup grated Parmesan cheese
⅓ cup dry bread crumbs
2 eggs
1 tablespoon minced chives
1 teaspoon dried basil leaves
½ teaspoon each salt and pepper

Sauté salt pork in oil in Dutch oven until crisp. Add garlic and ⅓ of the meats; sauté until meats are brown; drain excess fats. Stir in sauce, wine and pepper; heat to boiling. Reduce heat; simmer 20 minutes.

Mix remaining ingredients; form into 20 meatballs. Stir into sauce; simmer covered 30 minutes. *Makes 4 servings*

MEATBALLS AND GRAVY

1 pound ground beef
1 egg, slightly beaten
¼ cup fine dry bread crumbs
2 tablespoons salad oil
1 can **FRANCO-AMERICAN Brown Gravy with Onions**
Cooked rice

1. In medium bowl, combine beef, egg and crumbs; shape into 16 meatballs.
2. In 10-inch skillet over medium heat in hot salad oil, brown meatballs; spoon off fat. Add gravy.
3. Reduce heat to low; cover, simmer 20 minutes or until done. Stir occasionally. Serve with rice. *Makes 4 servings*

SWEDISH MEATBALLS

Meatballs*
1¾ cups beef broth
¼ cup dry sherry
½ teaspoon dill weed
⅛ teaspoon pepper
2 tablespoons **ARGO®/KINGSFORD'S® Corn Starch**
½ cup skim milk

Prepare meatballs. Broil 6 inches from source of heat 5 to 6 minutes or until browned. Drain on paper towels. In large skillet stir together broth, sherry, dill and pepper. Add meatballs. Bring to boil, reduce heat; cover and simmer 10 to 15 minutes or until tender. In small bowl stir together corn starch and milk until smooth. Stir into meatball mixture. Stirring constantly, bring to boil over medium heat and boil 1 minute. If desired, serve over noodles. *Makes 6 servings*

*MEATBALLS

In medium bowl stir together 2 tablespoons **ARGO®/KINGSFORD'S® Corn Starch**, ¼ cup dry sherry, ½ teaspoon salt and ¼ teaspoon ground nutmeg until smooth. Add 1½ pounds ground beef round, ¼ cup finely chopped onion and ¼ cup chopped parsley; mix well. Let stand 10 minutes. Shape into 36 (1-inch) meatballs.

ASIAN MEATBALLS AND SAUCE

1 can (10 ounces) beef broth, undiluted
⅓ cup dry sherry
2 tablespoons cornstarch
1 tablespoon soy sauce
1 teaspoon granulated sugar
1 pound lean ground beef
1 can (8 ounces) water chestnuts, finely chopped
2 tablespoons soy sauce
½ teaspoon ground ginger
¼ teaspoon garlic powder
1 egg, beaten
2 tablespoons vegetable oil
1 cup diagonally sliced celery
⅓ pound fresh mushrooms, sliced (about 2 cups)
½ cup **BLUE DIAMOND® Blanched Whole Almonds** (Almonds, toasted, see Index)
1 large tomato, cut into wedges
¼ cup sliced green onion
Hot steamed rice

Mix together beef broth, sherry, cornstarch, the 1 tablespoon soy sauce and sugar; set aside.

Mix together beef, water chestnuts, the 2 tablespoons soy sauce, ginger, garlic powder and egg; shape into 1-inch balls. Heat 1 tablespoon of the oil in a large skillet; brown meatballs and remove from skillet.

Add remaining tablespoon oil to skillet; add celery and sauté over medium-high heat 2 to 3 minutes; add mushrooms and continue sautéing until celery is tender-crisp.

Add broth mixture and cook, stirring, over medium heat until mixture thickens. Add meatballs to sauce, cover and cook for 10 minutes. Stir in almonds and tomato wedges; heat through. Pour into serving dish and sprinkle with green onions. Serve with hot steamed rice. *Makes 4 servings*

MEATBALL STROGANOFF

1¾ cups water, divided
1 envelope (about 1.3 oz.) onion soup mix, dry, divided
4½ teaspoons Worcestershire sauce
¾ teaspoon salt, divided
1 pound ground beef
¾ cup **Instant** or **Regular RALSTON®**
1 can (4 oz.) mushroom stems and pieces, undrained
⅓ cup all-purpose flour
1 container (8 oz.) dairy sour cream
¼ cup snipped parsley

Combine ½ cup water, ½ envelope (about 3 tablespoons) soup mix, Worcestershire sauce and ½ teaspoon salt. Stir in ground beef and **RALSTON®**. Mix thoroughly. Shape into 24 balls (use about 2 tablespoons mixture for each). Place on sided baking sheet. Bake in 400° oven about 20 minutes or until done. Turn midway. Drain on absorbent paper. Meanwhile, in large saucepan combine ¾ cup water, remaining ½ envelope soup mix and undrained mushrooms. Bring to boil. Cover. Reduce heat and simmer 5 minutes. Mix together remaining ½ cup water, flour and remaining ¼ teaspoon salt. Slowly stir into hot mixture. Heat until boiling and thickened, stirring frequently. Stir in sour cream until blended. Add parsley and meatballs. Heat thoroughly. Serve over noodles, linguini or rice.

Makes 4-5 servings

SAUERBRATEN MEATBALLS

1 pound lean ground round
¼ cup soft-coarse **HI HO CRACKER®** Crumbs
¼ cup minced onion
Freshly ground black pepper
2 tablespoons water
7 tablespoons lemon juice
2 tablespoons margarine
2½ cups beef broth
¼ cup brown sugar
¾ cup **SUNSHINE®** Gingersnap Crumbs

Combine meat, cracker crumbs, onion, pepper, 2 tablespoons of water and 3 tablespoons lemon juice. Mix well and form into 1-inch balls. In a skillet, heat margarine and brown meatballs. Remove from pan. To the drippings in the pan, add broth and remaining lemon juice. Bring to a boil and stir in sugar and gingersnap crumbs. Add meatballs to the sauce and simmer covered for 10 minutes. Stir and cook uncovered 5 minutes longer. Serve over noodles and sprinkle with poppy seeds.

Yield: 6 servings

YULETIDE MEATBALLS

1½ pounds ground beef
½ cup dry bread crumbs
1 tablespoon **FRENCH'S®** Instant Minced Onion
1 teaspoon **FRENCH'S®** Parsley Flakes
½ teaspoon **FRENCH'S®** Ground Thyme
2 eggs
Stuffed green olives
1 tablespoon oil
1 envelope (¾-oz.) **FRENCH'S®** Mushroom Gravy Mix
1 cup water
1 cup milk

CONVENTIONAL METHOD:

Combine ground beef, bread crumbs, onion, parsley, thyme and eggs. Shape into 1½-inch meatballs, enclosing an olive in the center of each. Brown in oil in large skillet; pour off excess fat. Stir together gravy mix, water and milk; pour over meatballs in skillet. Cover and simmer 30 minutes. Garnish with sliced olives, if desired.

6 servings

MICROWAVE METHOD:

Arrange meatballs in a 12 × 8-inch glass baking dish. Microwave on HIGH 7 to 10 minutes, or until firm and no longer pink, rearranging once or twice during cooking. Pour off excess fat. Reduce milk to ½ cup; combine with gravy mix and water and pour over meatballs. Cover with wax paper and microwave on MEDIUM 5 to 8 minutes, until sauce is thickened, stirring once or twice.

SWEET 'N SOUR MEATBALLS

½ pound ground beef
½ pound ground pork
½ cup seasoned breadcrumbs
1 egg
2 tablespoons milk
½ teaspoon garlic powder
½ teaspoon salt
¼ teaspoon pepper
2 tablespoons vegetable oil
1 jar (15½ oz.) **RAGÚ®** Spaghetti Sauce, any flavor
½ cup finely chopped onion
¼ cup vinegar
2 tablespoons Worcestershire sauce
2 tablespoons brown sugar
2 teaspoons prepared mustard
3 cups cooked rice

In a large bowl, combine first 8 ingredients; mix thoroughly. Shape into 1 inch meatballs. In a large skillet, brown meatballs in hot oil; drain fat. Add next 6 ingredients; stir gently. Simmer, partially covered, 30 minutes or until meatballs are done. Serve over rice.

Serves 4

SWEDISH MEATBALLS SUPREME

BETTY CROCKER® POTATO BUDS® Instant
   Mashed Potatoes (enough for 2 servings)
1 pound ground beef
1 medium onion, chopped (about ½ cup)
½ cup dry bread crumbs
1 egg, beaten
1 tablespoon vegetable oil
2 tablespoons margarine or butter
2 tablespoons all-purpose flour
1 can (10¼-ounces) beef consommé
1 cup evaporated milk

Heat oven to 400°. Prepare mashed potatoes as directed on package for 2 servings except—decrease water to ⅓ cup and omit butter. Mix potatoes, ground beef, onion, bread crumbs and egg. Shape into 1-inch balls. Bake meatballs in oil in rectangular pan, 13 × 9 × 2-inches, until brown, about 20 minutes; drain. Heat margarine in 2- or 3-quart saucepan until melted; stir in flour. Cook over low heat until smooth and bubbly; stir in consommé. Heat to boiling over medium heat, stirring constantly. Add meatballs; reduce heat. Simmer uncovered 10 minutes; stir in milk. Cook until heated through, 2 to 3 minutes. Serve over hot cooked rice, noodles or mashed potatoes if desired.

4 or 5 servings

HIGH ALTITUDE DIRECTIONS (3500 to 6500 feet): No adjustments are necessary.

THE GIANT OF HAMBURGERS

Wine Barbecue Sauce:
⅔ cup catchup
⅔ cup prepared mustard
⅔ cup dry red wine
¼ cup packed brown sugar
¾ teaspoon **TABASCO® Pepper Sauce**, divided

Hamburger:
2 pounds ground beef
1 teaspoon salt
1 tablespoon grated onion
1 tomato, chopped
⅔ cup chopped cucumber
⅔ cup chopped green pepper

In a small saucepan combine catchup, mustard, wine, sugar and ½ teaspoon **TABASCO®**. Simmer, uncovered, 20 minutes. In a large bowl mix ground beef with salt, onion and remaining ¼ teaspoon **TABASCO®**.

Shape into 1 large hamburger. Place on broiler pan, baste with Wine Barbecue Sauce and broil 6 inches from heat for 12 to 15 minutes on each side, basting occasionally with sauce, until desired doneness is reached. In a small bowl combine tomato, cucumber and green pepper. Serve on top of hamburger along with remaining barbecue sauce.

Yield: 8 servings

ROYAL HAMBURGERS

1 lb. chopped beef
1 teaspoon chopped parsley
1 tablespoon minced onion
2 tablespoons grated parmesan or romano cheese
½ clove garlic, minced
4 slices **MIGLIORE® Mozzarella**
2 tablespoons Sherry
2 tablespoons tomato paste, dissolved in 1 cup warm
   water
1 can peas, drained
Dash of pepper, salt to taste

Mix first 5 ingredients together. Form 8 thin hamburger patties. On four of these place a slice of **MIGLIORE® Mozzarella** cheese; top these patties with remaining patties and pinch edges together to enclose cheese. Sprinkle enough salt in a heavy frying pan to cover bottom with a thin coating. Heat pan very hot. Place stuffed hamburgers on salt. Brown one side, turn, brown other side. Lower heat and wet hamburgers with sherry. Pour dissolved paste over them. Cover and simmer until hamburgers are done. Add peas, five minutes before serving, to heat thoroughly with hamburgers and sauce.

BACON STROH'S BURGERS

10 slices bacon
2½ lb. ground beef
1 beaten egg
3 Tbsp. **STROH'S Beer**
⅓ cup bread crumbs
¼ cup green pepper, finely chopped
¼ cup finely chopped onions
2 Tbsp. catsup
2 tsp. prepared horseradish
2 tsp. prepared mustard
1 tsp. salt
¼ tsp. pepper
10 hamburger buns, split and toasted

Cook bacon in a skillet till *almost* done. Cut strips in half, reserve. Place ground beef in a separate bowl. Add egg, beer, bread crumbs, green pepper, onions, catsup, horseradish, mustard, salt and pepper. Mix well. Shape into ten 4-inch patties. Arrange patties in a greased wire grill basket. Place two half-slices of bacon criss-crossed atop each burger to form an "X". Close basket. Grill burgers over medium coals, turning often, for 18 to 20 minutes, or to desired doneness. Serve on toasted buns.

Makes 10 servings

STUFFED HAMBURGER PATTIES

1½ pounds hamburger
1½ tsp. salt
1 cup **BELL'S® Ready Mixed Stuffing**
1 medium onion, grated
½ cup soft butter or margarine
2 Tbsp. lemon juice
¼ tsp. black pepper
Dash cayenne

Mix hamburger and salt. Divide into 12 equal parts. Flatten with rolling pin until about 5 inches in diameter. Leave each pattie on paper. Combine remaining ingredients. Divide among six patties. Top each with a pattie and press edges together with fork. Flip onto hot broiler pan and broil under medium heat until brown. Turn carefully with pancake turner and broil on other side.

6 patties

MOCK BACON FILETS

4 slices **JOHN MORRELL® Bacon**, partially cooked
2 lbs. ground beef
¼ cup chopped green pepper
¼ cup chopped onion
½ cup chili sauce
1 teaspoon Worcestershire sauce
1 teaspoon sweet basil
½ teaspoon salt
⅛ teaspoon black pepper
2 cups sliced fresh mushrooms
2 tablespoons butter or margarine
Wooden picks
Savory Tomato Sauce*

Combine beef, pepper, onion, chili and Worcestershire sauces, basil, salt and pepper in bowl; mix well. Form mixture into 8 patties; set aside. In small skillet, sauté mushrooms in butter over low heat until soft; drain. Spoon small amount of mushrooms on center of four patties; cover each with remaining four patties and seal edges. Wrap bacon slice around each filet; secure with pick. Place on rack in shallow pan; spoon Savory Tomato Sauce over each patty. Bake in preheated 350° oven, 45 minutes. Garnish with sautéed whole mushrooms.

Yield: 4 servings

*SAVORY TOMATO SAUCE

8 oz. can tomato sauce
6 oz. can tomato paste
½ teaspoon Worcestershire sauce
½ teaspoon sweet basil
½ teaspoon parsley
4 drops hot red pepper sauce
Pinch garlic salt
Pinch thyme

Combine all ingredients in bowl; mix well.

Yield: 1¼ cups

TERIYAKI BURGERS

1 can (8¼ oz.) pineapple slices
3 tablespoons soy sauce
1 tablespoon catsup
½ teaspoon marjoram leaves, crushed
⅛ teaspoon garlic powder
¼ teaspoon ground ginger
¼ cup finely chopped onion
1 pound ground beef
1½ cups **RICE CHEX® Cereal** crushed to ½ cup
1½ teaspoons packed brown sugar, divided
1 tablespoon butter or margarine

Drain pineapple, reserving juice. In large bowl combine soy sauce, catsup and 1 tablespoon pineapple juice. Remove 3 tablespoons of mixture. Set aside.

To mixture in large bowl add marjoram, garlic powder and ginger. Blend well. Add onion, ground beef and **CHEX®** crumbs. Mix thoroughly. Shape into 6 patties. Add ½ teaspoon brown sugar to reserved soy sauce mixture. Grill or broil to desired doneness, brushing with reserved sauce.

Meanwhile, in medium-size skillet sauté pineapple slices in remaining 1 teaspoon brown sugar and butter. Serve on top burgers.   *Makes 6 burgers*

CREOLE LIVER

1 (8-oz.) can tomato sauce with tomato bits
¼ cup chopped green pepper
¼ cup chopped celery
¼ cup chopped onion
¼ cup water
¼ teaspoon basil
Dash of pepper
1 slice of bacon
½ pound sliced beef liver (about ½-inch thick)
1 cup hot cooked rice

Combine tomato sauce, green pepper, celery, onion, water, basil and pepper in small saucepan. Simmer over low heat for 15 minutes. Meanwhile, cook bacon until crisp in a medium skillet. Remove bacon and crumble into sauce; reserve bacon drippings. Brown liver in bacon drippings; about 2 minutes on each side over medium heat. Place liver on cutting board and slice into narrow strips, about ½-inch wide. Return liver to skillet; add creole sauce and rice. Gently stir to blend ingredients and simmer for an additional 5 minutes.   *2 servings*

Favorite recipe from **Iowa Beef Industry Council**

MEXICAN LIVER

6 slices bacon
¾ cup onions, chopped
1 clove garlic, minced
¼ cup flour
1½ teaspoons chili powder
1 teaspoon salt
1½ lb. liver, cut in thin strips
1 can (16 oz.) **FURMAN'S® Whole Tomatoes**
1 can (16 oz.) **FURMAN'S® Whole Kernel Corn**, drained
Hot cooked rice

In large skillet cook bacon until crisp. Reserve 3 tablespoons drippings in skillet. Crumble bacon and set aside. Cook onions and garlic in drippings until onions are tender but not brown, about 5 minutes. Combine flour, chili powder and salt. Cut liver into thin strips, toss in flour mixture to coat. Add liver to onions and brown quickly on all sides. Stir in bacon, undrained tomatoes and corn. Simmer covered until mixture is heated through. Serve over cooked rice.   *Serves 6*

Veal

OSSO BUCO

4 rounds **PROVIMI® Osso Buco**
Flour, seasoned with salt and pepper, for dredging
4 Tbsp. butter
½ cup onion, chopped
1 medium carrot, chopped
½ cup celery, chopped
1 clove garlic, finely chopped
½ cup white wine
Enough seasoned stock to cover veal half way
2 Tbsp. tomato puree (optional)

Roll veal rounds thoroughly in seasoned flour. Melt butter in heavy skillet and brown veal on all sides. Add remaining ingredients and bring mixture to a boil, then reduce heat. Cover and simmer gently about 1½ hours, turning veal once while cooking. Place veal on serving platter and spoon some broth over it.   *Serves 2*

VEAL PARMESAN

⅓ cup flour
1 teaspoon salt
1 teaspoon dry parsley flakes
1 teaspoon basil
¼ teaspoon pepper
¼ cup grated Parmesan cheese
2 pounds veal cutlet, cut ½-inch thick
1 egg
1 tablespoon water
½ cup **PURITAN® Oil**
2 tablespoons chopped onion
1 cup (8-oz.) can tomato sauce
⅓ cup (4-oz. can) sliced mushrooms
¼ cup sherry, if desired

Mix first six ingredients and place in large plastic or paper bag. Cut veal into serving pieces, dip in egg beaten with water, then shake in bag with flour mixture. Brown meat on both sides in hot **PURITAN® Oil** in a heavy skillet. Remove meat. Add onion, tomato sauce, mushrooms and any remaining flour mixture to skillet. Stir until mixture bubbles. Add meat; cover and cook over low heat for about 45 minutes, until meat is tender. Stir in sherry, if desired.   *4-5 servings*

CONTINENTAL VEAL CUTLETS

2 cups fresh bread crumbs
¾ teaspoon *each* oregano, basil, and garlic salt
1 lb. Italian-style veal cutlets
2 eggs, lightly beaten
Oil for frying
1 can (7 oz.) **ORTEGA Green Chile Salsa**
¼ cup grated Parmesan cheese

Combine bread crumbs, oregano, basil and garlic salt. Dip veal cutlets in eggs. Coat egg-covered cutlets with seasoned crumbs; quickly sauté in skillet in oil until golden brown on both sides. Lay cutlets in shallow baking pan. Pour salsa over cutlets and top with cheese. Bake in preheated oven (350°) for 15-20 minutes, or until heated through. Do not overcook. *Serves 4-6*

VEAL WITH GREEN PEPPERS AND BLACK MUSHROOMS

A. Thinly slice:
  ½ lb. veal cutlet
B. Cut in matchstick shreds:
  6 soaked **CHINA BOWL**® **Black Mushrooms***
  1 large, seeded green pepper
C. Finely chop:
  1 clove garlic
  3 slices **CHINA BOWL**® **Fresh Ginger**
D. Mix chow sauce in a bowl:
  2 Tbsp. **CHINA BOWL**® **Chinese Light Soy Sauce**
  2 Tbsp. **CHINA BOWL**® **Chinese Cooking Wine** or dry sherry
  1 tsp. sugar
  1 tsp. corn starch
  ½ tsp. salt
  ¼ tsp. **CHINA BOWL**® **Taste Powder-MSG** (optional)
E. Cooking: Pour 2 Tbsp. peanut or vegetable oil into a wok or large skillet over high heat and, as oil starts to smoke, add garlic and ginger and stir fry for 30 seconds. Add veal and stir fry for 2 minutes more. Stir chow sauce, add to wok along with vegetables, reduce flame to medium and stir fry for 2 minutes.

Optional: Add ¼ tsp. **CHINA BOWL**® **Sesame Oil** just before completing cooking. Serves 4 when included in a Chinese family-style meal of 2 other main dishes and rice.

*These dried mushrooms will keep indefinitely when stored in a covered jar or closed plastic bag in a dry, cool place.

Note: This dish is equally good with pork or beef, but substitute **CHINA BOWL**® **Dark Soy Sauce** for the **Light** when making chow sauce.

DRY SACK® VEAL FRENCH

¾ to 1 pound fresh thinly sliced veal cutlet
Vegetable oil
1 cup flour
3 eggs
Dried parsley flakes
Fresh Parmesan cheese
White pepper
Salt
Garlic powder
4 lemons, cut in half
Butter
2 tablespoons chicken flavored instant bouillon
5 ounces **DRY SACK**® **Sherry**
5 ounces water

Beat 3 eggs in medium size bowl. Cover with dried parsley flakes. Grate fresh Parmesan cheese on top of parsley until covered. Mix well. Add white pepper, salt and garlic powder to taste.

Pound veal until paper thin and cut into 4-inch pieces. Heat 1 inch of vegetable oil in large 12-inch electric frying pan to 350°. Coat veal with flour first, then dunk in egg batter and fry until golden brown. When fried to desired color, remove from pan and discard oil. Wipe pan clean. *(Continued)*

Replace veal in pan. Place 1 pat of butter on each piece of veal. Sprinkle about 2 tablespoons of instant bouillon on the veal. Reheat pan to 350°. Pour in **DRY SACK**® **Sherry. Flambé.** Shake pan. Add water. Squeeze lemons onto veal. Let sauce come to a boil, making sure instant bouillon is well-blended with sauce. Remove veal. Pour sauce into serving container and pour on veal as desired.

VEAL SCALLOPINI

2 pounds veal round, sliced ½-inch thick
LAWRY'S® **Seasoned Salt**, to taste
LAWRY'S® **Seasoned Pepper**, to taste
Flour
½ cup butter
½ pound fresh mushrooms, sliced
1 large onion
1 sprig fresh parsley
¼ teaspoon each: rosemary and oregano
½ teaspoon **LAWRY'S**® **Seasoned Salt**
¼ teaspoon **LAWRY'S**® **Seasoned Pepper**
1 cup dry white wine
1 tablespoon sugar

Sprinkle meat with Seasoned Salt and Seasoned Pepper; dredge in flour. Melt ¼ cup of butter in large skillet and brown meat slowly on both sides; remove to platter and keep warm. Sauté mushrooms in 2 tablespoons of butter until just golden; remove from pan and set aside. Finely chop together onion and parsley, add rosemary and oregano; sauté in remaining 2 tablespoons of butter until onion is golden brown. Add mushrooms, Seasoned Salt, Seasoned Pepper, wine and sugar; cook just until heated through. Spoon over meat and serve immediately. *Makes 6 to 8 servings*

VEAL PICCATA ALLA PROGRESSO

1½ pounds veal leg (scallopini) sliced ⅛-inch thick (about 12 slices)
1 egg, lightly beaten
1¼ cups **PROGRESSO Italian Style Bread Crumbs**
½ cup **PROGRESSO Olive Oil**
¾ cup dry white wine
1 tablespoon lemon juice
½ teaspoon salt
⅛ teaspoon ground black pepper
Lemon wedges

With a meat mallet lightly pound veal between two sheets of waxed paper or clear plastic wrap. Dip veal in egg then in bread crumbs, pressing bread crumbs into meat; arrange on jelly-roll pans; place in freezer for 5 minutes. In a large skillet heat olive oil. Add veal a few pieces at a time; brown about 2 minutes on each side. Remove and keep warm. Into drippings left in skillet, stir wine, lemon juice, salt and black pepper. Bring to the boiling point. Reduce heat and simmer, uncovered, until sauce is reduced to about ⅓ cup, about 5 minutes. Serve about 1 tablespoon sauce over each serving of 2 pieces of veal. Serve with lemon wedges. Sprinkle with chopped parsley, if desired. *Yield: 6 portions*

VARIATION:

Substitute boned, skinned and halved chicken breasts for the veal leg.

VEAL ELIZABETTA

4 Tbsp. butter
4 Tbsp. olive oil
Flour
12 thin slices veal scallopini
2 cloves garlic, minced or mashed
4 anchovy fillets
2 dozen pitted Italian olives
4 whole, peeled, canned tomatoes, drained
4 leaves fresh basil or 1 tsp. dried basil
1 sprig parsley, chopped
Salt and pepper to taste
2 Tbsp. capers
½ cup **SEBASTIANI VINEYARDS** Cabernet Sauvignon Wine

Heat butter and oil in large, heavy skillet. Pass veal through flour and shake off excess. Sauté meat for 1 minute on each side. Set aside.

Sauté garlic, anchovies, and olives for 1-2 minutes, mashing anchovies with fork. Add tomatoes, basil, and parsley and heat to boiling, breaking up tomatoes with a fork. Reduce heat. Add salt, pepper, capers, wine and meat and simmer on low heat for 5 minutes. *Serves 4*

BLANQUETTE DE VEAU, NAPOLÉON

2 tablespoons each oil and butter
2 lbs. boneless veal, cut in 1-inch cubes
1 medium onion, finely chopped
1 garlic clove, crushed
1 lb. small mushrooms, quartered
Salt and pepper, to taste
⅛ teaspoon nutmeg
1 bay leaf
1 can (5 oz.) water chestnuts, thinly sliced
1 cup chicken broth or bouillon
¼ cup **MANDARINE NAPOLÉON** Brandy
1 cup sour cream, at room temperature

Heat oil and butter in a casserole or Dutch oven and brown veal cubes lightly on all sides. Don't crowd the pan and remove cubes as they brown. Add onion, garlic and mushrooms to pan and sauté until lightly gold. Return meat to pan, stir and sprinkle with salt, pepper and nutmeg. Add bay leaf, water chestnuts and broth to pan. Cover and bake in preheated 350°F. oven until meat is tender, about 1¼ hours. Add **MANDARINE NAPOLÉON**, stir and bake, uncovered, 15 minutes more. Remove casserole from oven. Stir 2 or 3 tablespoons of the pan juices into the sour cream, then add sour cream mixture to pan. Stir. Place pan over low heat on top of range and cook just until sauce is heated through.
6 servings

VEAL BOLOGNESE

6 large slices of veal cut about ¼ inch thick
Freshly ground black pepper
2 egg yolks
1 cup breadcrumbs
Butter
6 thin slices prosciutto
6 slices Gruyère cheese
½ cup **HOLLAND HOUSE® Sherry Cooking Wine**
Parsley sprigs

On a cutting board pound veal cutlets with a meat mallet or the side of a cleaver until they are about ⅛ inch thick. Dry veal with paper towels, sprinkle with freshly ground pepper. Dip in beaten egg yolks, cover them thoroughly with breadcrumbs. In a skillet melt enough butter to cover the bottom of pan. Brown veal cutlets over fairly high heat (no more than 3 minutes on each side). Remove from skillet and place in baking dish. Cover each cutlet with slices of prosciutto and Gruyère. Add Sherry to skillet and deglaze, scraping the pan to loosen any brown bits of breadcrumbs which may adhere to the bottom and sides. Pour contents of skillet over veal in baking dish and place in a preheated 350° oven. Bake for about 5 minutes or until cheese is melted. Remove from oven and garnish with parsley sprigs. *Makes 6 servings*

DORMAN'S® SWISS VEAL DORMANDIA

1 slice white bread, crust removed
¼ cup white wine
1 lb. ground veal
1½ teaspoons salt
¼ cup chopped onion
1 egg
1 package (6 oz.) **DORMAN'S®** Swiss Cheese, divided
5 or 6 midget sweet gherkins
2 tablespoons vegetable oil
1 cup water
1 tablespoon flour, plus additional flour for coating
¼ cup cold milk

Soak bread in wine until completely absorbed. Combine veal, soaked bread, 1 teaspoon salt, 1 tablespoon chopped onion and egg; mix well. Spread mixture onto large sheet of waxed paper into a rectangle ½-inch thick. Cover with cheese slices. Place gherkins along narrow edge of meat. Starting at this end, roll meat layer up, jelly-roll fashion. If necessary, use waxed paper to help roll meat. Gently slice roll into 5 equal pieces. Coat rolls with flour. In a medium-size skillet, heat oil. Sauté remaining 3 tablespoons chopped onion until tender. Add water and ½ teaspoon salt; bring to a boil. Add veal rolls; bring to a boil. Lower heat; cover and steam for 15 minutes. Remove rolls; keep warm. Dissolve flour in cold milk. Add to skillet, stirring constantly. Bring to a boil. Grate remaining cheese in electric blender. Add to sauce; continue stirring until cheese melts. Serve sauce with warm veal rolls. *Makes 5 servings*

SKEWERED VEAL LIVER AND BACON

4 **PROVIMI®** Veal Liver Slices, thawed
8 slices bacon, cut in half
1 Golden Delicious apple, cored, cut in eighths
¼ cup butter, melted
1 tsp. lemon juice
1 tsp. chopped parsley
½ tsp. Worcestershire sauce

Cut thawed liver slices into 2 inch pieces. Wrap each piece with bacon. Thread onto skewers alternately with apple wedges. Combine remaining ingredients; brush on meat and apples. Broil 4 minutes. Turn and brush again. Broil 3 minutes until bacon is crisp. Serve over rice pilaf. *Makes 4 servings*

Lamb

MARINATED LAMB STEAKS

½ cup **BOGGS® Cranberry Liqueur**
¼ cup olive oil
2 tablespoons catsup
1 tablespoon brown sugar
¼ teaspoon oregano
1 tablespoon lemon juice
2 cloves garlic, crushed
2 lbs. shoulder or leg lamb steaks

In medium bowl, combine all ingredients except lamb. Arrange steaks in shallow glass dish. Pour marinade over meat. Cover. Refrigerate several hours or overnight, turning steaks occasionally. Drain. Broil until cooked as desired. *Serves 4-6*

SAVORY ROAST LAMB

1 leg of lamb (6 to 7 lbs.)
2 thin slices of ham
1 teaspoon salt
1 tablespoon minced parsley
1 peppercorn
1 to 2 garlic cloves
2 tablespoons **POMPEIAN Olive Oil**

Combine salt, parsley, peppercorn and garlic; mash to a paste. Blend in **POMPEIAN Olive Oil**. Spread this mixture over the ham. Cut ham into thin slivers. Force deep gashes in lamb with sharp thin knife; force ham strips into the holes. Brush meat all over with additional **POMPEIAN Olive Oil** and roast at 325° until meat thermometer registers 150° (pink), about 25 minutes to the pound for medium well done. *Serves 6*

BARBECUED LAMB, SONOMA STYLE

¾ cup olive oil
½ cup red wine vinegar
½ cup **SEBASTIANI VINEYARDS Cabernet Sauvignon Wine**
1 (4-oz.) can chopped green chiles
6 cloves garlic, minced or mashed
4 tsp. Italian seasoning
2 Tbsp. hot mustard
1 leg of lamb, 6 lbs. or more, boned and butterflied
1 (4-oz.) can tomato sauce
3 Tbsp. honey

Combine oil, vinegar, wine, chiles, garlic, Italian seasoning and mustard. Mix well. Place lamb in shallow dish and pour mixture over it. Turn to coat topside. Cover and marinate overnight, turning again once.

To barbecue, remove meat from marinade and prepare basting sauce by blending tomato sauce and honey into marinade and stirring well. Barbecue marinated lamb over double layer of hot coals for 8-10 minutes on each side, basting frequently until done.

Note: The marinade in this recipe removes some of the strong lamb flavor.

LEG OF LAMB WITH COFFEE

1 leg of lamb, about 5 pounds
1 clove garlic, slivered
Juice of ½ lemon
Salt and pepper
2 teaspoons rosemary
2 cups coffee with cream and sugar
½ cup **JACQUIN'S Coffee Brandy**

With the tip of a small knife, pierce lamb all over fatty side and insert slivers of garlic. Rub lamb with lemon juice, salt and pepper. Sprinkle with rosemary. Place fatty side up on a rack in a roasting pan and roast in a 325° oven for 15 minutes per pound. After the first half hour of roasting, pour coffee over lamb. Continue roasting, basting occasionally with liquid in pan. When lamb is done, transfer it to a serving platter. Skim fat from pan juices; add **JACQUIN'S Coffee Brandy**; set pan over heat and bring to a boil while scraping up the brown bits. Taste for seasoning. Serve in a sauceboat with the lamb. *Serves 6*

LAMB ITALIANO

¼ cup butter or margarine
2 Tbsp. Worcestershire sauce
1 tsp. garlic powder
2 tsp. **BALTIMORE SPICE OLD BAY Seasoning**
4 lamb chops or 2 pounds boneless/shoulder
Green pepper slices

Heat oven to 450°. Arrange lamb chops on broiler pan. Combine remaining ingredients except green pepper and brush onto meat. Garnish with green pepper slices. Roast 30 minutes for chops and 45 minutes for shoulder. *4 servings*

JAMAICAN FRUIT LAMB CHOPS

7 to 8 medium loin lamb chops
1 can (16 oz.) **DEL MONTE Lite Apricot Halves**
2 tsp. coffee crystals
Dash salt and pepper
2 Tbsp. chopped parsley

In large skillet, brown meat. Drain fruit reserving liquid in small saucepan. Heat liquid; stir in coffee to dissolve. Pour over meat; simmer 15 to 20 minutes, turning frequently. Add salt, pepper, fruit and parsley. Cover and heat through. *3 to 4 servings*

MINTED LAMB CHOPS

4 blade or shoulder lamp chops, ¾" thick, trimmed
ADOLPH'S® 100% Natural Tenderizer, Unseasoned*
3 tablespoons butter
3 tablespoons Worcestershire sauce
2 tablespoons cognac or brandy (optional)
1 tablespoon lemon juice
1 teaspoon parsley
1 teaspoon mint leaves

Moisten chops with water; sprinkle evenly with tenderizer and pierce deeply with a fork. Repeat on other side. (Use no salt.) Broil 6" from heat, about 6 minutes per side for medium. While lamb chops are broiling, combine next 6 ingredients in a saucepan. Simmer 5 minutes. Pour sauce over chops and serve immediately. *Serves 4*

*Use approximately 1 teaspoon per pound of meat

HEARTY LAMB SHANKS

¼ cup all-purpose flour
1 teaspoon seasoned salt
½ teaspoon pepper
¼ teaspoon garlic powder
4 lamb shanks
2 tablespoons cooking oil
½ cup chopped onion
½ cup chopped carrot
¼ cup chopped celery
1 tablespoon chopped parsley
½ teaspoon rosemary
½ teaspoon salt
1 (1 lb.) can whole tomatoes
1 cup **LINDSAY® Pitted Ripe Olives**

Combine flour, seasoned salt, pepper and garlic powder. Coat shanks with flour mixture; reserve remaining flour. Heat oil in heavy skillet; brown shanks and remove from skillet. Add onion, carrot, celery, parsley, rosemary and salt to skillet and sauté lightly. Add tomatoes, ripe olives, and lamb shanks. Cover and simmer 2 to 2½ hours or until shanks are tender. Remove shanks to warm platter. Combine remaining flour mixture with a little cold water and add to pan. Cook, stirring until thickened. Pour over shanks.   *Makes 4 servings*

MEXICAN LAMB

6 lamb shanks
1½ teaspoons salt
1 teaspoon pepper
½ teaspoon garlic powder
1 large onion, chopped
2 cups milk
3 jars (8-oz.) junior peaches
4 teaspoons **ANGOSTURA® Aromatic Bitters**
½ teaspoon marjoram
Pinch thyme
¼ teaspoon rosemary
⅓ cup raisins
Cooked rice
Cling peach slices

Rub lamb shanks with salt, pepper and garlic powder. Place in large pan, cover with boiling water and simmer until almost tender, about 45 minutes. Remove shanks and trim off meat, discarding bones. Cut meat into bite-size pieces. Place lamb in large skillet and add onion and milk. Simmer all together gently until the milk is almost absorbed. Add junior peaches, **ANGOSTURA® Aromatic Bitters**, marjoram, thyme, rosemary and raisins. Heat together slowly, stirring occasionally, for about 20 minutes. To serve, arrange hot cooked rice on large platter, spoon meat mixture over top, and garnish with peach slices.
Yield: 6 servings

MEXICANA LAMB

4-5 lbs. lamb, cut into 1½″ cubes
4 cloves garlic, minced
2 teaspoons oregano
2 cans (7 oz. each) **ORTEGA Green Chile Salsa**
Salt and pepper
2 tablespoons red wine vinegar
3 tablespoons oil

Combine all ingredients, except lamb. Pour over lamb cubes in a glass or enamel dish and mix thoroughly; cover and let stand overnight in refrigerator. Place lamb cubes on skewers and barbecue, basting with remaining marinade.   *Serves 6*

MOROCCAN LAMB
(Low Calorie)

1½ pounds lean lamb, cubed
Flour to coat lamb
2 tablespoons corn oil
2 buds garlic, minced
2 onions, coarsely chopped
1 cup chicken stock, boiling
4 tomatoes, diced
6 prunes, pitted and chopped
2 bay leaves, crushed
2 teaspoons paprika
½ teaspoon salt
¼ teaspoon freshly ground black pepper
1 tablespoon **SWEETLITE™ Liquid Fructose**
¼ cup plain low-fat yogurt

1. Put the cubed lamb in a paper bag with the flour. Shake until the lamb is well coated with the flour.
2. Heat the corn oil in a large skillet with a lid.
3. Brown the lamb well on all sides.
4. Add the garlic and onions and cook until soft.
5. Add the boiling chicken stock and all other ingredients except the yogurt. Mix well, cover and simmer for 1 hour or until the lamb is tender. Add more stock if necessary.
6. Remove from the heat and stir in the yogurt.
Makes 6 servings

Each serving contains approximately:
  3 low-fat meat exchanges
  1½ vegetable exchanges
  ½ fruit exchange
  223 calories
  83.8 mg cholesterol

KAHLÚA® SESAME LAMB

2 tbsp. toasted sesame seeds
1 tsp. dry mint
½ tsp. paprika
¼ tsp. salt
½ cup **KAHLÚA® Coffee Liqueur**
¼ cup lemon juice
2 pounds lean boneless lamb
4 strawberries
Fresh pineapple wedges
Cracked wheat pilaf

Blend sesame seeds, mint, paprika and salt together with mortar and pestle or in blender. Combine with **KAHLÚA®** and lemon juice. Measure out 2 tablespoons for basting, save remainder for dipping sauce. Cut lamb in 1½-inch chunks (12 to 16 pieces). Thread on skewers. Broil about 7 inches from heat for 10 minutes. Turn once and baste with the 2 tablespoons sauce during cooking. Place a strawberry on each skewer for decoration. Serve with reserved sauce. Accompany lamb with fresh pineapple wedges and cracked wheat pilaf, if desired.   *Makes 4 servings*

KIDNEYS IN SHERRY

2 tablespoons **PLANTERS** Peanut Oil
½ cup chopped onion
1 pound lamb kidneys, skinned and quartered
¼ cup **DRY SACK®** Sherry
½ teaspoon salt
Scant ¼ teaspoon pepper

Heat **PLANTERS** Peanut Oil in a skillet; add onion and sauté until golden. Add lamb kidneys and sauté until browned. Add **DRY SACK®** Sherry, salt and pepper; stir to combine. Cook about 4 minutes or until tender; stir occasionally.

Makes 8 servings

Pork

ROAST PORK WITH ORANGE GLAZE
(Low Calorie)

1 cup orange juice
1 tsp. curry powder
½ cup **ESTEE®** Granulated Fructose
2 cloves crushed garlic
Black pepper, freshly ground
¼ cup corn oil
4 lb. pork shoulder, boneless butt
Water
3 Tbsp. cornstarch

Mix first six ingredients together in small bowl. Trim excess fat from pork roast. Place roast in plastic bag or shallow pan, and cover with the marinade. Let meat marinade in refrigerator one to three hours.

Set oven to 375°F. Remove roast from marinade and place on rack in open roasting pan. Pour ½ cup water into bottom of pan. Baste roast with ¼ cup marinade every 30 minutes for first hour. Add more water to roasting pan when needed. Cover meat with foil when it becomes very brown and crispy, and lower oven temperature to 350° F. Cook for 45 minutes per pound, or until internal temperature is 185°F.

Remove roast from oven. Chill drippings and skim fat. Mix ½ cup water and 3 Tbsp. cornstarch until blended. Reheat gravy, and gradually add cornstarch. Heat until thickened. Serve gravy with sliced meat. Season to taste with **ESTEE® Salt-Free Meat Seasoning**.

Makes 12 servings, 3 oz. meat + 2 Tbsp. gravy per serving

NUTRITION INFORMATION

Calories	Carbohydrates	Protein	Fat	Cholesterol	Sodium
190	10g	21g	8g	120mg	55mg

DIABETIC EXCHANGE INFORMATION

Fruit	Meat
1	3

KIWIFRUIT TERIYAKI PORK

Place a loin of boneless pork on a rack in a shallow pan. Rub with salt and pepper. Sprinkle on rosemary. Roast at 350° for 2-2½ hours. Mix ½ cup each of ketchup and soy sauce, ¼ cup honey, 1 crushed garlic clove. Use as basting last 45 minutes.

Transfer to a heated platter. Surround meat with **CALAVO® Kiwifruit** slices and halves. Garnish with banana or ti leaves.

ROAST PORK ALLA TOSCANA

1-4 pound loin of pork
½ clove garlic, slivered
1-8 oz. can tomato sauce
½ cup vinegar
½ cup brown sugar
¼ cup **AMARETTO from GALLIANO®** Liqueur

Use small pointed knife to make deep incisions in pork; insert garlic slivers. Place pork in uncovered pan and roast at 450° for 15 to 20 minutes. Reduce heat to 350°, continue cooking pork for 2 hours or until done. While pork is cooking combine remaining ingredients in saucepan. Simmer until slightly thickened. Half an hour before roast is done, drain fat from roasting pan. Spoon about ½ of sauce over meat and baste. After 15 minutes add remaining sauce; continue basting until done.

Serves 6 to 8

ROAST PORK WITH CHESTNUTS

Center cut loin of pork, 6-8 chops
Salt and pepper
⅛ teaspoon dill weed
⅛ teaspoon crushed thyme
4 shallots, minced
1 (10½-ounce) can beef broth
⅓ cup dry white wine
2 (1-pound each) cans **RAFFETTO®** Chestnuts
2 tablespoons flour
¼ cup brandy

Sprinkle loin of pork with salt and pepper. Rub with dill weed and crushed thyme. Place meat, fat side up in a shallow roasting pan and roast in 350° oven 1½ hours. Add shallots, beef broth, white wine, and drained chestnuts to pan. Roast another 30 minutes or until the meat thermometer reaches 180°F. Remove meat and chestnuts to a platter and keep warm. Skim excess fat from juices in pan. Stir together flour and brandy. Stir mixture into juices in pan. Cook over low heat, stirring constantly, until sauce bubbles and thickens. Serve with slices of pork and chestnuts.

6-8 servings

ORANGE GLAZED SMOKED PORK

½ cup firmly packed brown sugar
2 tablespoons **ARGO®/KINGSFORD'S®** Corn Starch
¼ teaspoon ground cinnamon
¼ teaspoon ground cloves
3 cups orange juice
1 (2 lb.) smoked pork shoulder roll (butt)
6 small sweet potatoes (about 1½ lb.), pared, halved
1 package (11 oz.) mixed dried fruit (2 cups)

In 2-quart saucepan stir together sugar, corn starch, cinnamon and cloves until well mixed. Gradually stir in juice until smooth. Stirring constantly, bring to boil over medium heat and boil 1 minute. In 13 × 9 × 2-inch baking pan place pork, potatoes and fruit. Spoon orange sauce over all. Bake in 325°F oven, basting frequently, 2 hours or until temperature on meat thermometer reaches 170°F and potatoes are tender.

Makes 6 servings

PORK TENDERLOINS IN SOUR CREAM SAUCE

1-2 lb. **FARMLAND FOODS, INC.**™ **Pork Tenderloin**, sliced ½-inch thick
¾ teaspoon dried sage, crushed
½ teaspoon salt
Dash pepper
2 tablespoons shortening
1 medium onion, sliced
1 beef bouillon cube
¼ cup boiling water
1 cup sour cream
1 tablespoon all-purpose flour

Slice meat and rub with a mixture of sage, salt, and dash pepper. Brown lightly on both sides in hot shortening. Drain off excess fat; add onions. Dissolve bouillon cube in ¼ cup boiling water. Pour over meat. Cover and simmer 30 minutes or until meat is done. Remove meat. Prepare gravy by combining sour cream and flour in small bowl. Slowly stir in meat drippings. Return mixture to skillet; cook and stir just until boiling. Add water until gravy is desired consistency. Place meat on noodles and spoon on gravy.

Serves 4 to 6

ORANGE SPICED PORK CHOPS

6 pork chops, 1-2 inches thick
⅓ cup **DOMINO®** Liquid Brown Sugar
½ cup water
3 tablespoons frozen orange juice concentrate, thawed
1 teaspoon dry mustard
¼ teaspoon ground ginger
1 orange, sliced

Preheat oven to 375°F. Place pork chops in large shallow baking dish, 13 × 9-inch. To make sauce, combine **DOMINO®** Liquid **Brown Sugar**, water, orange juice concentrate, mustard and ginger. Pour over pork chops. Bake 20 minutes. Turn chops and baste with sauce. Bake 25 minutes. Top with orange slices, brush with sauce and bake 15 minutes longer or until chops are tender. To serve, place chops on warmed platter. Spoon over sauce. Garnish with orange slices.

Makes 6 servings

SWEET SOUR PORK CHOPS

6 rib pork chops, ½-inch thick
1 tablespoon shortening
Salt and pepper
½ cup **HEINZ Tomato Ketchup**
½ cup pineapple juice
1 tablespoon brown sugar
1 tablespoon lemon juice
2 tablespoons minced onion
1 teaspoon **HEINZ Worcestershire Sauce**
½ teaspoon salt
⅛ teaspoon ground cloves

Brown chops in shortening; drain excess fat. Sprinkle lightly with salt and pepper. Combine ketchup and remaining ingredients; pour over chops. Cover; simmer 45 minutes, basting occasionally, or until meat is tender. Skim excess fat from sauce.

Makes 6 servings (about 1 cup sauce)

PORK CHOPS CALIFORNIAN

4 pork chops, 1-inch thick
1 envelope **LIPTON®** Onion Soup Mix
1 can (16 oz.) peach halves, drained (reserve syrup)
¾ cup water
2 tablespoons lemon juice
½ teaspoon ground ginger
¼ teaspoon ground cinnamon
Strawberries or currant jelly

In large skillet, brown pork chops well; drain. In medium bowl, combine **LIPTON®** Onion Soup Mix, reserved syrup, water, lemon juice, ginger, and cinnamon; add to skillet. Simmer covered 40 minutes, turning pork chops occasionally. Add peach halves cut side up and top with a strawberry or fill with currant jelly; simmer covered an additional 5 minutes. Arrange on a platter.

Makes 4 servings

WESTERN PORK CHOPS

2 tablespoons **MAZOLA®** Corn Oil Margarine
4 shoulder or center pork chops (about 1½ lb.)
1 cup chopped green pepper
1 cup chopped onion
1 can (8 oz.) tomato sauce
½ cup **KARO®** Light or Dark Corn Syrup
¾ teaspoon chili powder

In medium skillet melt margarine over medium heat. Add pork chops; cook until brown on all sides, about 10 minutes. Remove chops from skillet. Add peppers and onion; cook until tender, about 5 minutes. Stir tomato sauce, corn syrup and chili powder into skillet; add chops. Simmer, uncovered, about 30 minutes or until pork chops are tender. If desired, serve over cooked noodles and garnish with parsley.

Makes 4 servings

PENANG PORK CHOPS

2 tablespoons red wine vinegar
1 tablespoon **FRENCH'S®** Worcestershire Sauce
½ teaspoon **FRENCH'S®** Lemon Peel
½ teaspoon **FRENCH'S®** Tarragon Leaves
½ teaspoon **FRENCH'S®** Thyme Leaves
2 dashes **FRENCH'S®** Cayenne Pepper
⅛ teaspoon **FRENCH'S®** Ground Nutmeg
2 tablespoons oil
¾ cup chicken broth
4 to 6 pork chops, cut ¾ to 1 inch thick
Cooked rice
Strips of fresh lemon peel, if desired

Combine vinegar, Worcestershire sauce, lemon peel, tarragon, thyme, cayenne, nutmeg, 1 tablespoon oil, and chicken broth; pour over chops and refrigerate 1 to 2 hours. Drain chops, reserving marinade. Brown chops in remaining oil in skillet; pour off excess fat. Add marinade and simmer, covered, 50 minutes, or until tender. Serve on rice, garnished with strips of fresh lemon peel.

4 to 6 servings

MICROWAVE METHOD:
Prepare marinade *reducing chicken broth to ¼ cup and oil to 1 tablespoon. Sprinkle chops with ¼ to ½ teaspoon salt.* Place chops, meaty side out, in shallow casserole; marinate. Cover with plastic wrap and microwave on MEDIUM 10 minutes. Rearrange chops with pink areas facing out. Recover and microwave 6 minutes. Rearrange chops again and microwave 2 to 10 minutes or until chops are no longer pink near the bone.

EASY PORK CHOPS AND RICE BAKE

5 pork chops, ½ inch thick
1 tablespoon cooking oil
1 cup **UNCLE BEN'S® CONVERTED® Brand Rice**
1 can (10½ ounces) beef broth
1 cup sliced carrots
½ cup chopped onion
2 tablespoons steak sauce
1 tablespoon salt
¼ teaspoon pepper
½ teaspoon basil

Brown pork chops in oil. In a 2-quart baking dish (12″ × 8″ × 2″) add rice, beef broth, one soup can of water, carrots, onions, steak sauce, salt, pepper and basil. Arrange pork chops over rice mixture. Cover and bake in 350°F. oven 45 minutes. Uncover and continue baking 10 minutes more or until all water is absorbed.

Makes 5 servings

DEL MONTE PEACHY PORK CHOPS

6 loin pork chops, 1-inch thick
1 Tbsp. butter or oil
½ cup chopped onion
½ cup chopped green pepper
1 can (16 oz.) **DEL MONTE Lite Peach Halves**
1 cup beef broth
1½ tsp. thyme
1 tsp. dry mustard
¼ tsp. garlic powder
Dash salt
Dash pepper
6 green pepper rings (sliced crosswise)

In skillet, brown meat in butter and remove from pan. Sauté onion and pepper. Drain fruit reserving ½ cup liquid. Return meat to pan; add broth, reserved liquid, thyme, mustard, garlic powder, salt and pepper. Cover and simmer 45 minutes. Garnish each chop with peach half and pepper ring. Sprinkle with chopped parsley, if desired.

6 servings

SUCCESS® SWEET-SOUR PORK CHOPS

6 rib pork chops, ½ inch thick
1 tablespoon shortening
Salt and pepper
½ cup catsup
½ cup pineapple juice
1 tablespoon brown sugar
1 tablespoon lemon juice
2 tablespoons minced onion
1 teaspoon Worcestershire sauce
½ teaspoon salt
⅛ teaspoon ground cloves
2 bags **SUCCESS® Rice**

Brown pork chops in shortening, drain excess fat. Sprinkle lightly with salt and pepper. Combine catsup and next 7 ingredients; pour over the pork chops. Cover; simmer 45 minutes, basting occasionally or until meat is tender. Skim excess fat from sauce.

Prepare rice according to package directions. Serve pork chops and sauce on bed of rice.

SPANISH STYLE PORK CHOPS

4 rib pork chops, cut ¾ to 1-inch thick
1 tablespoon cooking oil
1 medium onion, sliced thin
Salt
Pepper
1 can (15½ ounces) **AUNT NELLIE'S® Sloppy Joe Sandwich Sauce**
⅓ cup beef bouillon
2 tablespoons flour
½ cup sliced pimiento stuffed olives

Trim excess fat from meat. In large skillet, brown chops well in hot oil. Remove chops. In same skillet, cook onion until crisp-tender; drain off fat. Return chops to skillet. Season with salt and pepper. Cover with onions. Combine Sandwich Sauce, bouillon and flour; pour over chops. Add olives. Cover. Simmer 1½ hours or until meat is tender.

4 servings

SOUTHERN PORK CHOPS

4 to 6 pork chops, cut about ¾ inch thick
1 envelope regular cream of mushroom soup mix
½ cup **JIF® Peanut Butter**
2 cups water
1 medium onion, sliced
½ green pepper, cut into strips

Trim excess fat from chops; heat the fat in a skillet till about 1 tablespoon drippings accumulates. Remove fat trimmings. Brown the chops well in the hot fat. Remove chops from skillet.

Blend the dry soup mix and **JIF®** into the pan drippings. Gradually add water, stirring till smooth. Bring to boiling; reduce heat and add pork chops, onion slices, and green pepper strips. Cover and simmer for 45 to 50 minutes or till pork is tender. Serve from the skillet or remove chops and some of the vegetables to a warm platter. Spoon off any excess fat from gravy; add a little **KITCHEN BOUQUET®** to the gravy, if desired, for rich color. Season to taste with salt and pepper. Serve gravy with pork chops.

Makes 4 to 6 servings

PEACHY PORK CHOPS
(Low Calorie)

6 lean pork chops (about 2 pounds)
½ teaspoon freshly ground pepper
1 can (1 pound) juice-packed peach halves
3 packets **SWEET 'N LOW®**
2 teaspoons lemon juice
¼ teaspoon cinnamon
¼ teaspoon ginger
3 whole cloves
2 teaspoons all-purpose flour

Carefully trim away any visible fat from chops. Season chops with pepper and brown in large non-stick skillet. Drain off fat. Drain peaches, reserving ½ cup juice. Combine juice with **SWEET 'N LOW®**, lemon juice, and spices. Pour over pork; cover tightly. Simmer gently over very low heat, about 45 minutes, or until pork is well cooked, turning chops once. Remove chops to serving platter and keep warm. Add peaches to liquid in skillet. Cover and heat through, about 5 minutes. Place one peach half on each chop. Mix flour with remaining juice and stir into pan juices. Heat and stir until sauce thickens, about 5 minutes. Remove cloves. Pour sauce over chops.

6 servings

PER SERVING (1 pork chop): Calories: 180   Protein: 18g
Carbohydrate: 7g   Fat: 9g   Sodium: 400mg

SATURDAY NIGHT SUPPER

4 center cut pork chops, thinly sliced
1 tablespoon oil
1 28-ounce can **B&M® Brick Oven Baked Beans**
2 tablespoons apple jelly
2 teaspoons water
8 apple slices
Cinnamon

In a skillet, brown chops evenly in oil, about 10 minutes each side. Drain chops on paper towels. Pour beans into a 2 quart casserole and place chops on top of beans. Bake at 350°F. for 45 minutes. In a small bowl, combine jelly and water. Baste chops with this mixture and arrange apple slices on top. Sprinkle with cinnamon. Return to oven and continue baking for another 15 minutes.

Makes 4 servings

GLAZED PORK CHOPS

¾ cup apricot *or* peach preserves
1 (8-ounce) bottle Russian salad dressing
1 tablespoon **WYLER'S® Beef-Flavor Instant Bouillon** *or* 3 **WYLER'S® Beef-Flavor Bouillon Cubes**
1 tablespoon instant minced onion
1½ pounds pork chops
Salt and pepper
Flour
Vegetable oil

Preheat oven to 300°. In medium saucepan, combine preserves, dressing, bouillon and onion. Cook and stir until bouillon dissolves; simmer uncovered 15 minutes. Sprinkle chops lightly with salt and pepper; coat with flour. Fry in small amount of oil until golden. Drain. Arrange in shallow baking dish; spoon sauce evenly over chops. Bake 20 minutes or until hot. Garnish as desired. Refrigerate leftovers.

Makes 4 to 6 servings

LIME GLAZED PORK CHOPS

⅓ cup **KARO® Dark Corn Syrup**
½ teaspoon grated lime rind
⅓ cup lime juice
1 tablespoon soy sauce
¼ teaspoon ground cloves
6 pork chops, 1-inch thick

In small bowl stir together corn syrup, lime rind, lime juice, soy sauce, and cloves. Grill pork chops about 6 inches from source of heat 30 minutes turning once. Baste with lime mixture. Grill 30 minutes longer turning and basting frequently or until pork is tender when pierced with fork and nicely glazed.

Makes 4 servings

PORK CHOP HOMINY

4 pork chops (½-inch thick)
3 tablespoons minced onion
2 tablespoons minced green pepper
3 tablespoons butter or margarine, melted
1 can (1 lb. 13-oz.) **VAN CAMP'S® Hominy**, drained
1 can (10¾-oz.) cream of mushroom soup
⅓ cup milk
¼ teaspoon salt

Place pork chops, onion and green pepper in skillet with butter; brown. Meanwhile, place drained Hominy in a greased 10 × 6 × 2-

inch dish. Top with chops. Blend together remaining ingredients in skillet drippings and pour over chops. Bake, covered, at 350°F for 1 hour. Remove cover and bake 15 minutes longer.

Makes 4 servings

BARBECUED PORK STEAKS

3-4½ lb. **FARMLAND FOODS INC.™ Shoulder Butt Pork**, sliced into steaks 1-1½" thick

Barbecue Sauce:
1½ teaspoons salt
½ cup chopped onion
1 tablespoon shortening
⅓ cup light brown sugar
1 teaspoon Worcestershire sauce
¼ teaspoon celery seed
1 cup catsup
¾ cup water
⅓ cup vinegar

Barbecue Sauce: To prepare barbecue sauce, cook onion in shortening until tender, stirring frequently. Stir in remaining ingredients and simmer for 20 minutes.

Broil steaks on your outdoor grill or in your broiler until both sides are brown. Continue cooking with moderate heat until tender, basting frequently with this or your favorite barbecue sauce.

Serves 6 to 8

Note: Other cuts that may be used in this recipe are the **FARMLAND FOODS, INC.™ Leg-O-Pork and Center Cut Loin.**

HICKORY SMOKED BAR-B-QUE RIBS

4 to 5 lbs. pork ribs (spareribs or backribs)
1 3½ oz. bottle **WRIGHT'S Hickory Liquid Smoke™**
2½ quarts water
Favorite barbecue sauce

Combine liquid smoke and water in a large pot. Bring to a boil; add the ribs and reduce heat and simmer 1½ to 2 hours. Use exhaust fan to eliminate cooking odor. Remove ribs from liquid, cool. Ribs may be refrigerated or frozen for future use.

Dip or brush ribs with barbecue sauce. Place in a 400 degree oven for 15 to 20 minutes. For crusty ribs, broil for 3 to 5 minutes.

Makes 4 servings

Note: Ribs may be prepared in a browning bag. Place ribs in a single layer in a large size oven cooking bag in a baking pan. Add 1 bottle of smoke and 1 quart water. Close bag with tie and with a fork make 4 small holes in the top. Bake in a 325° oven for 1½ hours. Complete as directed.

APRICOT BARBECUED SPARERIBS

2 large strips spareribs (about 3½ pounds), with bones cracked for easy handling
2 tablespoons olive or vegetable oil
1 medium-size onion, grated (¼ cup)
1 clove garlic, finely minced
½ cup honey
½ cup catsup
½ cup **COLONIAL CLUB Apricot Liqueur**
¼ cup Worcestershire sauce
1½ tablespoons soy sauce
1½ teaspoons dry mustard
1 tablespoon bottled meat concentrate
¼ teaspoon leaf oregano, crumbled
¼ teaspoon black pepper
Salt

Bake spareribs in moderate oven (350 degrees) for 45 minutes. Prepare sauce; combine oil, onion, garlic, honey, catsup, **COLONIAL CLUB Apricot Liqueur**, Worcestershire sauce, soy sauce, mustard, meat concentrate, oregano and pepper in large saucepan; stir well and simmer for 30 minutes. Taste; add salt, if needed. Baste spareribs with sauce and bake at 350 degrees for 1 hour, basting several times during baking time.

PEACH BARBEQUED SPARE RIBS

4 lbs. spare ribs
Onions

Arrange ribs in flat roasting pan. Cover with thinly sliced onions. Add water to bottom of pan. Cover with foil and bake at 350° for 1 hour. Drain and marinate for 4 hours in:

½ cup soy sauce
¼ cup catsup
½ cup **HIRAM WALKER Peach Flavored Brandy**
2 cloves garlic, crushed and finely chopped

Bake in 350° oven for 30-35 minutes. Glaze with honey mixture:

3 tsp. honey
1 Tbsp. marinade sauce

Raise heat to 450° for 5 minutes only. Garnish with onion rings.
Serves 6 to 8

SWEET AND TANGY BARBECUED SPARERIBS

4 pounds pork spareribs, cut into serving-size pieces
1½ teaspoons salt
¼ cup honey
2 tablespoons **LEA & PERRINS Worcestershire Sauce**
2 tablespoons soy sauce
2 tablespoons catsup
2 tablespoons water

Sprinkle both sides of the ribs with salt. Place on a rack in a baking pan. Bake in a preheated very hot oven (450 F.) for 20 minutes, turning once. Reduce oven heat to moderate (350 F.). Cook until almost tender, about 20 minutes longer. To prepare barbecue sauce combine remaining ingredients; blend well. Brush over ribs. Cook 30 minutes longer, brushing and turning frequently.

SIERRA RANCH RIBS

4 pounds country-style spareribs, trimmed and cut into serving pieces
Water
1 can (8 oz.) tomato sauce
1 cup chopped onion
½ cup **KARO® Dark Corn Syrup**
¼ cup cider vinegar
2 tablespoons Worcestershire sauce
1 teaspoon salt
1 teaspoon monosodium glutamate
1 teaspoon dry mustard
½ teaspoon chili powder

In 5-quart kettle place spareribs; add water to depth of 1". Cover. Bring to boil over high heat; reduce heat and boil gently 1 hour or until ribs are fork tender. In 1-quart saucepan mix together remaining ingredients. Bring to boil; reduce heat; simmer 10 minutes. Drain ribs. Brush generously with sauce.　　*(Continued)*

To grill: Place ribs 6″ from source of heat, basting and turning frequently, about 15 minutes or until browned.
To broil: Place ribs on broiler pan. Broil 4″ from source of heat, basting occasionally, about 10 minutes on each side. If desired, heat remaining sauce and serve with ribs.
Makes 6 to 8 servings

ZESTY RIBS

5 lb. spareribs, cracked, cut in 3 rib portions
1 can (lb.) tomato sauce
¼ cup minced onion
2 Tbsp. soy sauce
1 tsp. salt
¼ tsp. pepper
¼ tsp. ground cloves
½ cup **MARUKAN® Seasoned Gourmet Rice Vinegar**
½ cup vegetable oil

Parboil spareribs. In medium bowl, combine tomato sauce, soy sauce, onion, salt, pepper and cloves with vinegar and oil. Place ribs in bowl and marinate for several hours. Broil, brushing frequently with marinade sauce, about 30 minutes until tender and crisp.

SAUCY SPARERIBS

1 envelope **LIPTON® Onion Soup Mix**
1½ cups water
⅓ cup honey
¼ cup soy sauce
2 tablespoons sherry
1 teaspoon ginger
4 pounds spareribs, cut into serving pieces

In large shallow baking dish, combine all ingredients except spareribs; add spareribs. Cover and marinate in refrigerator, turning occasionally, at least 3 hours.

Preheat oven to 350°. Remove spareribs, reserving marinade. Place ribs on rack in foil-lined baking dish. Bake, turning and basting occasionally with marinade, 1¼ hours or until spareribs are done.　　*Makes about 6 servings*

EASY OVEN BARBECUE RIBS

Brush ribs liberally with **FIGARO LIQUID BARBECUE SMOKE**. Relax, allow 30 minutes for flavor to penetrate. Salt and pepper. Fry salt pork in pan until brown, remove and place ribs in pan of hot grease and quickly fry brown. Pour ½ cup of water in pan and for each pound of ribs, add one teaspoon of **FIGARO LIQUID BARBECUE SMOKE**. Place lid on pan and cook in oven about 350°. Baste often while cooking. Uncover pan about 30 minutes before done.

COOKIES SURPRISE BAR-B-Q RIBS

Place pork or beef ribs in a roasting pan. For every six pounds of ribs add 1 (12-oz.) can of beer. Cover and bake at 325 degrees until tender. Remove from pan and drain well. Place on a flat baking sheet and cover with **COOKIES Bar-B-Q Sauce**. Return to 275 degree oven for 30 minutes or until hot.

TANGY PORK KABOBS

**1 JOHN MORRELL® TABLE TRIM® Pork
Tenderloin**, cut horizontally into 8, 1 inch pieces
Large, whole fresh mushrooms
Green pepper squares
Red sweet pepper squares *or*
whole tomatoes, quartered
Par-boiled onions, quartered
½ cup chili sauce
¼ cup sugar
2 Tbsp. lemon juice
2 tsp. Worcestershire sauce
½ to 1 tsp. chili powder
Hot cooked rice

Thread pork pieces onto 2 skewers, leaving space between each so they will cook evenly. Thread alternating pieces of green pepper, red pepper, mushrooms and onions onto 2 separate skewers. Blend together remaining ingredients except rice. Spread on meat and vegetables. Place pork kabobs on broiler rack in pan and broil 3 to 4 inches from heat for 20 to 25 minutes, or until done. Baste meat frequently with sauce, turning several times. During the last 10 minutes, place vegetable kabobs on broiler rack. Turn once and baste with sauce. Serve pork and vegetable kabobs over hot cooked rice.   *Serves 3-4*

SWEET AND SOUR PORK WITH CRANBERRIES

1 pound lean pork cut into 1 inch cubes
Salt and pepper
1 egg
¼ cup cornstarch
¼ cup consommé
6 tablespoons flour
Peanut oil, ½ inch deep
½ cup OCEAN SPRAY® Cranberry Juice Cocktail
½ cup OCEAN SPRAY® Whole Berry Cranberry
Sauce
1 green pepper, diced
1 large onion, diced
2 zucchini, diced

Sprinkle pork cubes with salt and pepper. In a bowl, beat egg with cornstarch, consommé and flour. Dip pork into mixture. Fry pork in peanut oil until richly browned and cooked. Drain cubes on absorbent paper. In a saucepan, heat cranberry juice and cranberry sauce until smooth. Pour all of the oil out of the skillet leaving only 1 tablespoon in skillet. Sauté (over very high heat) green pepper in oil for 20 seconds. Add onion and sauté another 20 seconds. Add zucchini and sauté another 20 seconds. Stir in cranberry mixture. Add pork cubes and bring mixture just to a boil. Season to taste with salt and pepper.   *Serves 4*

SWEET SOUR PORK

Drain, reserving juice:
1 can (15¼ oz) DEL MONTE Pineapple Chunks In
Its Own Juice
Thinly slice:
¾ cup onion
¾ cup green pepper
½ cup celery
1 lb. pork butt
Dissolve in reserved juice:
2 Tbsp. cornstarch   *(Continued)*

Add:
½ cup firmly packed brown sugar
½ cup water
⅓ cup vinegar
2 Tbsp. soy sauce
1 tsp. instant beef bouillon
⅛ tsp. ground ginger
Set aside. Heat in skillet or wok:
2 Tbsp. peanut or salad oil

Sauté pork, stirring constantly, until tender. Remove; set aside. Sauté vegetables, stirring constantly, until tender. Add pineapple chunks, pork and cornstarch mixture. Cook, stirring constantly, until sauce thickens and is translucent. Cover and keep warm. Serve over hot rice.

JOHN'S GOURMET PORK BURGERS

2 GOLDEN PRAIRIE Iowa Pork Burgers
(approximately ¼ pound each)
1 Tbsp. chopped (frozen) spinach
1 Tbsp. mushroom pieces
1 tsp. minced black olives
Pepper to taste
1 Tbsp. zesty Italian dressing
1½ tsp. grated Parmesan cheese
¼ tsp. seasoned salt
2 Tbsp. grated Monterey Jack cheese

In a small bowl combine Italian dressing, spinach, mushrooms, olives, pepper, Parmesan cheese and salt. Stir until well blended and set aside.

Thaw burgers in refrigerator. Make an indentation in the center of each burger. Add mixture to the center of one burger and cover with one tablespoon grated Monterey Jack cheese. Cover with remaining burger and pinch edges together.

Grill and top with remaining Monterey Jack cheese melted over the burger. Garnish with alfalfa sprouts and black olive.

SPICY SAUSAGE PATTIES
(Low Sodium)

1 teaspoon sugar
1 teaspoon DURKEE Rosemary Leaves
¾ teaspoon DURKEE Ground Coriander
½ teaspoon DURKEE Ground (Rubbed) Sage
¼ teaspoon DURKEE Ground Mustard
¼ teaspoon DURKEE Ground Black Pepper
¼ teaspoon DURKEE Paprika
¼ teaspoon DURKEE Ground Nutmeg
Dash DURKEE Ground Red Pepper
1 pound ground pork
¼ cup water
1 egg white

Place sugar and spices in blender container; blend on high speed 3 minutes. Mix thoroughly with ground pork, water, and egg white. Shape into patties. Broil, bake or fry as usual.
                                         Makes 4 patties

About 82 mg sodium per patty

Ham

HAM IN A CAN

Preheat oven to 325°F. Remove the key from the can (either 3 lb. or 5 lb.) **DUBUQUE ROYAL Buffet Oval Canned Ham**. Punch holes around *top* edge of can with beer can opener (every inch or so, all the way around the can). Place ham in oven and bake for one hour. Remove from oven and pour juice out of can through holes in lid. (DO NOT OPEN THE CAN.)

Mix together:

½ cup of dark corn syrup
½ to ¾ cup of B-B-Q sauce and garlic salt to taste

Pour this mixture into the holes in lid of can. Bake another 2-2½ hours. Remove from oven, pour off sauce, and open can.

HAM TAHITI

HORMEL CUREMASTER® Ham (about 2 lbs.)
Fresh pineapple slices, trimmed of rind
¼ cup butter
¼ Tbsp. cornstarch
1 cup pineapple juice
1 tsp. curry powder
1 Tbsp. chutney

Cut 5 slices half-way into ham, bake as directed. For glaze melt butter in a small saucepan, blend in cornstarch, pineapple juice, curry powder and chutney. Cook and stir until thickened. After 25 minutes of baking, insert half slices of pineapple into cuts in ham. Glaze and continue baking and glazing. To serve, arrange ham on platter with pineapple top.

HAM WITH APRICOT GLAZE

(Prosciutto Cotto con Conserva di Apricot)

1 jar (12 oz.) apricot preserves
1 tablespoon lime juice
1 teaspoon whole cloves
½ cup **LIQUORE GALLIANO®**
1-6 to 8 pound cooked ham

In small saucepan, heat apricot preserves, lime juice, cloves and **LIQUORE GALLIANO®**.

Place ham on rack in shallow roasting pan. Bake at 325° 30 minutes. Remove from oven. Remove any rind; smooth fat. Score in diamond pattern, if desired. Return to oven. Bake 1½ hours longer, basting or brushing frequently with apricot glaze.

Serves 8-10

CARAMELLA GLAZED HAM

10-12 lbs. precooked ham
Whole cloves
1½ cups **ARROW® Caramella Caramel Vanilla Liqueur**

Score ham and stud with cloves. Bake in preheated 350°F. oven for 3 hours. During last 45 minutes of baking, pour Caramella over ham every 15 minutes to glaze. Serve with Caramella Fruit Sauce.*

(Continued)

*CARAMELLA FRUIT SAUCE

1 cup seedless raisins
1 cup dried apricots
1½ cups **ARROW® Caramella Caramel Vanilla Liqueur**
½ cup water

In medium saucepan, combine all ingredients. Bring to a boil. Reduce heat. Simmer, covered, 45 minutes or until fruit is tender and plump. Cool. Serve plain or over vanilla ice cream. May also be served as an accompaniment with pork, chicken, ham, Cornish Game hen, turkey, or lamb.

VERY MERRY HAM

1 can (5 lb.) **RATH® Hickory Smoked Ham**
1 cup apricot preserves
2 egg yolks, slightly beaten
Maraschino cherry halves
Pecan halves

Heat ham on wire rack as directed on can. Last 20 minutes of heating time, remove ham from oven; increase temperature to 350°F. Score fat surface of ham in diamond pattern. Put 1 cherry or pecan half in center of each diamond. Combine preserves and egg yolks. Carefully spoon over decorated top and spread on sides of ham. Heat ham 15 minutes more. (Do not baste.)

Makes 14 4-oz. servings

HAM-ON-THE-SPIT

1 can (5 lb.) **RATH® Hickory Smoked Ham**
Glaze:
1 can (6 oz.) frozen orange juice concentrate, thawed
¾ cup honey
¼ cup prepared mustard
¼ cup butter or margarine
1 tablespoon soy sauce
2 tablespoons dry sherry
½ teaspoon ground ginger

HEATING HAM:
Remove ham from can; put all jellied ham juices in small saucepan. Push spit lengthwise through ham and test for balance; tighten prong screws. Tie heavy white cord around ham in center and at ends to help ham keep its shape. Insert meat thermometer at slight angle in center of ham. Be sure tip does not touch spit and thermometer will clear hood and coals as spit turns. Attach spit, turn on motor and lower hood, if any. Rotate ham for 1½ to 2 hours (figure 20 to 25 minutes per pound) or to 140° F. internal temperature on meat thermometer. Baste ham with heated jellied ham juices and pan drippings.

GLAZING HAM:
Meanwhile, prepare Orange-Honey Glaze: Combine thawed orange juice concentrate, honey, mustard, butter, soy sauce, sherry and ginger in small saucepan. Last ½ hour of heating time, turn off motor and remove spit from grill. Score ham, if desired; then return spit to grill and restart. Brush ham several times with heated Orange-Honey Glaze.

Makes 14 4-oz. servings ham and about 1½ cups glaze

HONEY GLAZED HAM AND FRUIT

2 lb. **WILSON®** Masterpiece Ham
2 tablespoons butter, melted
2 tablespoons lemon juice
½ cup honey
¼ teaspoon ground cloves
4 slices pineapple, quartered
1 banana, sliced
½ cup canned Mandarin orange segments

Heat oven to 350°F. Place ham in small roasting pan and bake as directed on package. 30 minutes before ham should be done, remove from oven. Score lightly. Combine butter, lemon juice, honey and cloves. Spoon about half of mixture over ham. Bake 20 minutes. Arrange pineapple, banana and oranges around ham. Pour remaining honey mixture over fruit and ham. Bake 10 minutes longer. Serve slices of ham topped with fruit. Serve with corn muffins and petite peas.   *Makes 6 to 8 servings*

MILWAUKEE GLAZE HAM

HORMEL CURE/81® Half Ham
½ cup brown sugar
2 Tbsp. prepared mustard
¼ cup beer or ale
2 slices each of American and Swiss cheese

Bake ham as label directs. Mix brown sugar and prepared mustard; stir to a paste. Gradually add in beer, stirring until well blended. Brush part of mixture over ham 45 minutes before it is done. Repeat frequently during remainder of baking time. When ham is done, remove from oven. Decorate with 1¼" triangles of Swiss and American cheese. Return to oven; heat briefly till cheese softens.

DIJON BAKED HAM

8-10 lb. precooked ham
Whole cloves
⅓ cup *each* **GREY POUPON** Dijon Mustard and apricot preserves
1 cup orange juice
2 tablespoons light brown sugar

Score ham and stud with cloves. Bake in preheated 350°F oven for two hours. While ham is baking, combine remaining ingredients in medium saucepan. Simmer, uncovered, 10 minutes. Brush ham with sauce every 15 minutes during last 45 minutes of baking. Serve remaining sauce with ham.

CELEBRITY® HONEY-ALMOND BAKED HAM

1 can (3 pounds) **Imported CELEBRITY®** Ham
½ cup apricot jam
½ cup sliced almonds
3 tablespoons honey
½ teaspoon ground ginger
⅛ teaspoon almond extract

Place ham on baking pan. Preheat oven to 350 degrees F. Combine remaining ingredients in small bowl. Spread mixture over top and sides of ham. Bake 45 minutes, basting sides occasionally with glaze in pan.

ROSY GLOW HAM GLAZE

8 lb. precooked ham
Whole cloves
1 can (16-oz.) jellied cranberry sauce
1 cup **BOGGS®** Cranberry Liqueur

Score ham and stud with cloves. Bake in 350°F oven 2½ hours. Beat together cranberry sauce and **BOGGS®**. During last 45 minutes of baking, baste with sauce every 15 minutes to glaze. Serve remaining glaze with ham.   *Makes 3 cups*

BAKED HAM BATTILANA

10 lb. **CELEBRITY®** Hungarian Ham, oval-shaped
½ cup Dijon mustard
½ cup dark molasses
2 cups ginger ale
1 cup apple juice
1 cup dry sherry

Ham Glaze:*
1 cup currant jelly
1 cup orange marmalade
½ cup **GRAND MARNIER** Liqueur

After combining molasses and mustard, use a pastry brush to spread mixture over the ham. Place the ham in a shallow baking pan. Then pour ginger ale, apple juice, and sherry wine over the meat, and cover the pan with aluminum foil. Placing the ham into a 350° oven, let it simmer 1 hour. Pour glaze over the ham, and return it, covered, to the oven for 15 minutes more. Garnish with the topping of your choice.   *Serves 15-20*

*HAM GLAZE

Mix all three ingredients together.

SPICED APRICOT GLAZE AND SAUCE FOR HAM

1 cup apricot preserves
⅓ cup sherry or apricot juice
½ teaspoon ground nutmeg
¼ teaspoon ground cinnamon
¼ teaspoon ground cloves

Combine apricot preserves and sherry. Blend in nutmeg, cinnamon and cloves. To glaze **SWIFT PREMIUM® HOSTESS® Ham**, spoon ⅓ cup apricot mixture over ham during last 10 minutes of heating in oven.

Serve remainder as sauce for sliced ham.   *Yield: 1⅓ cups*
(⅓ cup to glaze ham plus 1 cup sauce for 6 to 8 slices ham)

INDIVIDUAL HAM WELLINGTONS

1½-2 lbs. boneless fully-cooked ham
1 pkg. (17¼ oz) frozen puff pastry
2 tablespoons Dijon mustard
½ cup natural almonds (skins on), chopped
⅓ cup diced green onions
Egg Wash
Cherry Sauce*

1. Cut two ¾-inch slices from ham, then divide each slice into 2 individual servings. Remove sharp corners and fat edges from ham portions to form more shapely Wellingtons; reserve trimmings.
2. Chop ham trimmings and combine with almonds and onions to make a stuffing. (Food processor can be used to chop ham, almonds, and onions in a few on-off pulses).   *(Continued)*

3. Thaw pastry sheets about 20 minutes; unfold one sheet at a time. Use rolling pin, if necessary, to make a smooth pastry sheet large enough to cover 2 Wellingtons. Divide sheet in half. Spread mustard over pastry surface.

4. Pat some stuffing on top of each piece of ham. Then place ham on pastry so seam will join on underside of ham and mustard is on the inside. Wrap ham in pastry, trimming pastry so seams join without wide overlaps. Seal seams by dampening pieces to be joined with water and pinching edges together.

5. Place Wellingtons on ungreased baking sheet. Decorate with cherry fruit and leaf designs cut from pastry. (The top of a cake decorating tip makes a good cherry shape). Wellingtons may be refrigerated up to 3 hours at this point.

6. Before baking, brush pastry with 1 egg beaten with 1 teaspoon water. Bake in preheated 425°F. oven for 15 minutes, then reduce temperature to 350°F for 20-25 minutes or until pastry is puffed and golden brown. Shield any portions of pastry that brown too rapidly with foil. If total baking time is shortened, interior of pastry may still be doughy and meat may not be hot enough.

7. Ladle cherry sauce over Wellingtons.

Makes 4 servings

*CHERRY SAUCE

1 can (21 oz) cherry pie filling
⅔ cup prepared mincemeat
¼ cup red wine or orange juice
2 tablespoons high-proof liqueur or brandy (optional)

Combine ingredients in saucepot. Heat through but do not boil. For a spectacular presentation, place sauce in serving dish, pour on liqueur that has been warmed slightly and set aflame with long-stemmed match.

Note: This recipe can easily be multiplied or divided for fewer or more servings. Each package of puff pastry contains two individually wrapped sheets; each sheet encases two Wellingtons.

Favorite recipe from the **Western New York Apple and New York Cherry Growers**

GRILLED HAM STEAKS MANDARIN

4 ½-inch slices from 3-lb. **HORMEL BLACK LABEL®
Ham**
2 Tbsp. cooking oil
1 medium onion, sliced
1 green pepper, cut in 1 inch chunks
13-oz. can pineapple chunks
1 cup chicken bouillon
¼ cup vinegar
¼ cup brown sugar
2 Tbsp. cornstarch
2 Tbsp. soy sauce
½ cup mandarin orange sections

Place cooking oil in small skillet; sauté green pepper and onion about 5 minutes; remove. Heat ½ cup of liquid from pineapple in skillet with bouillon, brown sugar and vinegar. Add cornstarch and soy sauce, stirring constantly, until sauce thickens. Add fruit and vegetables; keep warm. Grill ham steaks 3 minutes per side. Serve with sweet sour mixture.

BANANA BAKED HAM SLICES

2 **ATALANTA/KRAKUS/POLKA Ham Slices,** ½-inch thick
⅓ cup orange juice
¼ cup dark corn syrup
½ teaspoon grated orange peel
2 large bananas, quartered
2 tablespoons toasted sesame seeds

Slash edges of ham slices at 2 inch intervals. Place in shallow baking pan. Combine orange juice, corn syrup and orange peel. Brush over ham slices. Bake at 350° F. for 20 minutes, basting twice with orange mixture. Brush bananas with syrup and place on ham. Sprinkle with sesame seeds. Bake 30 minutes longer or until bananas are lightly browned.

Makes 6 servings

HAM WAIKIKI

1 can (1 lb. 4 oz.) pineapple slices
1 tablespoon cornstarch
1 tablespoon **LEA & PERRINS Worcestershire Sauce**
1 teaspoon ground ginger
3-pound ready-to-eat ham steak

Drain pineapple; set aside slices and juice separately. In a small saucepan combine cornstarch with **LEA & PERRINS** and ginger. Blend in reserved pineapple juice (about 1 cup). Cook and stir over moderate heat until thickened. Place ham on a rack in a broiler pan. Brush pineapple juice mixture over ham. Place under a preheated hot broiler for 10 minutes, brushing once more. Turn ham. Add reserved pineapple slices to broiler rack. Brush ham and pineapple slices with pineapple juice mixture. Broil until ham and pineapple are well glazed, about 10 minutes, brushing once more.

8 to 10 servings

HAM SLICES BAKED WITH GIROUX® GRENADINE

2 thick ham slices
Whole cloves
1 cup **GIROUX® Grenadine Syrup**
1½ teaspoon allspice
½ teaspoon pepper

Cut slashes in fat around ham to keep it from curling, and stud the meat with cloves. Place in roasting pan. Mix the grenadine syrup with allspice and pepper and pour over the ham. Bake uncovered in a preheated 350°, or moderate, oven for 45 minutes or until meat is very tender. Baste very often.

Serves 6

HAM AND RICE STIR-FRY

1 tsp. vegetable oil
5 slices (5 oz.) **KAHN'S® Cooked Ham,** cut into thin strips
1 can (8 oz.) sliced water chestnuts, drained
2 green onions, chopped (approx. ¼ cup)
2 tsp. soy sauce, divided
1 cup cooked rice
Chinese Sauce (optional; see index)

Heat oil in large nonstick skillet. Add ham, water chestnuts, green onions and 1 tsp. soy sauce. Cook over medium heat, stirring occasionally, until ham is browned and slightly crisp, about 10 minutes. Add cooked rice and remaining 1 tsp. soy sauce to ham mixture. Continue cooking until rice is heated through. Serve with Chinese Sauce if desired.

Makes 2 servings

Calories: 246 calories per serving

SLAVIC HAM KABOBS

3 pounds cooked ATALANTA/KRAKUS/POLKA Polish
    Ham, cut into 1-inch cubes
3 apples, cut in wedges
6 apricots, halved and seeded
3 green bananas, cut into 1½ inch pieces
1 jar (10 ounces) grape jam
2 tablespoons honey
¼ teaspoon curry powder
⅛ teaspoon ground ginger

Arrange ham, apples, apricots and bananas on skewers. In a small
saucepan, combine jam, honey, curry and ginger. Heat, stirring,
until jam is melted and sauce is heated. Grill kabobs 3 to 5 inches
from heat, basting with grape sauce. Turn and baste several times
until heated through. Serve hot on cooked rice.

Makes 6 servings

Note: For classic ham kabobs alternate cherry tomatoes, mushroom caps and green pepper squares with cubes of ham.

HAMBALLS WITH PINEAPPLE SAUCE

Hamballs:
24 ounces OSCAR MAYER Ham, ground
8 ounces lean ground pork
1 cup soft bread crumbs
¼ cup finely chopped onion
2 eggs, slightly beaten
½ cup milk

Sauce:
1 can (8½ oz.) crushed pineapple
½ cup firmly packed brown sugar
1 tsp. cornstarch
⅓ cup catsup
⅓ cup vinegar
2 Tbsp. soy sauce
½ tsp. ginger

3 cups hot cooked rice

Preheat oven to 350°. Combine hamball ingredients in bowl; mix
well. Shape into 2-inch balls and place in a 9 x 13 inch shallow
baking pan. To make sauce, empty can of crushed pineapple into
bowl. Mix brown sugar with cornstarch; add to pineapple. Stir in
remaining ingredients. Pour sauce over hamballs and bake 50
minutes. Serve over hot cooked rice.

Makes about 18. Allow 3 per serving

Note: These can be made into 1-inch appetizer balls as well.

HAMKEBAB

3 lb. EXCELSIOR™ Ham
1 lb. fresh mushrooms, medium-sized
8 cherry tomatoes
2 fresh peppers, one green, one red
1 large tomato
½ cup peanut oil
8 bamboo skewers

Sauce:
1 cup mayonnaise
½ cup heavy cream, whipped
2 tablespoons horseradish

Soak the bamboo skewers in cold water for one hour. Meanwhile,
cut ham and peppers into 1-inch cubes and squares. Remove
mushroom stems.
    Leaving at least an inch of space on one end, mount chilled
skewers, alternating mushrooms, tomatoes, ham and pepper chunks.
After readying a cooking dish, insert skewer ends all around large
tomato, brush each skewer with peanut oil (this prevents burning).
Now, place onto an electric grill until lightly singed.
    Mix and whip sauce ingredients. Sprinkle with paprika, if de-
sired and dip-a-bob.   *Serves 8*

GLAZED CANTONESE HAM PATTIES

¾ lb. ground ham
¼ lb. lean ground pork
¾ cup soft bread crumbs
¼ cup chopped onion
2 tablespoons chopped green pepper
½ cup LA CHOY® Water Chestnuts, chopped
½ teaspoon dry mustard
1½ teaspoons LA CHOY® Soy Sauce
1½ teaspoons prepared horseradish
2 tablespoons LA CHOY® Sweet & Sour Sauce
½ cup buttermilk
1 egg, beaten
Additional LA CHOY® Sweet & Sour Sauce
Pimiento strips

Combine ham, pork, bread crumbs, onion, green pepper, water
chestnuts, dry mustard, soy sauce, horseradish, and Sweet & Sour
Sauce. Add buttermilk and egg; mix lightly. Shape into eight
patties. Bake at 350 degrees for 25 minutes. Brush tops lightly
with additional Sweet & Sour Sauce; bake 5 minutes more. Garnish with pimiento strips.   *8 servings*

Fish & Shellfish

Fish

GRILLED PANFISH WITH FRESH VEGETABLE SAUCE

6 (6 to 8 ounce) pan-dressed yellow perch, catfish, croaker, black sea bass, or other small pan-dressed fish, fresh or frozen
2 tablespoons margarine, melted
1 teaspoon salt
3 strips bacon, diced
6 large green onions, sliced (about 1 cup)
½ cup chopped green pepper
1½ cups chopped fresh tomato
6 to 8 pitted ripe olives, sliced
½ teaspoon garlic salt
Dash pepper

Thaw fish if frozen. Clean, wash, and dry fish. Cover head and tail with foil. Brush fish inside and out with melted margarine. Sprinkle with ½ teaspoon salt. Place fish in well-greased, hinged wire grills. Cook about 5 inches from moderately hot coals for 6 to 8 minutes. Baste with melted margarine. Turn and cook 7 to 10 minutes longer or until fish flakes easily when tested with a fork. Brush fish with melted margarine as needed. While fish is cooking, fry bacon until crisp; remove bacon bits and drain on paper towels. Add onion and green pepper to drippings; cook until onion is tender, but not brown, 3 to 4 minutes. Add tomatoes, ripe olives, remaining ½ teaspoon salt, garlic salt, and pepper; cook until tomatoes are heated, but still hold their shape. Sprinkle with bacon bits. Serve immediately over cooked fish.

Makes 6 servings

Note: For a Mexican-style sauce add 1 to 3 tablespoons chopped jalapeno peppers with tomatoes before heating.

Favorite recipe from the **National Marine Fisheries Service**

BAKED WHOLE FISH WITH MUSHROOMS

3½ pounds whole striped bass, rainbow trout or red snapper
Flour
Salt and pepper
3 tablespoons **BERTOLLI® Olive Oil**
2 tablespoons butter
1 rib celery, thinly sliced
1 medium carrot, thinly sliced
8 ounces mushrooms, thinly sliced
¼ cup minced parsley
2 tablespoons **BERTOLLI® Orvieto Wine**
¼ teaspoon each salt and pepper
1⅓ cups **BERTOLLI® Spaghetti Sauce With Mushrooms**
¼ cup sliced green onions
Lemon wedges

Coat fish with flour; sprinkle with salt and pepper. Sauté in oil and butter in large skillet until brown; remove. Sauté vegetables, except green onions, wine, salt and pepper 5 minutes. Spread ⅔ vegetables on oven-proof platter; spoon ⅔ cup sauce over. Stuff fish with remaining vegetables; arrange on platter. Spoon remaining sauce on fish; bake at 425° until fish is tender, about 20 minutes. Sprinkle with onions; garnish with lemon.

Makes 4-6 servings

ACAPULCO FILLETS

BOOTH® 14 or 16 oz. **Fish Fillets**
¼ cup butter
1 tablespoon chili sauce
1 teaspoon lemon juice
1 tablespoon chopped parsley
1 teaspoon Worcestershire sauce
1 tomato, sliced

Place fillets in single layer on heavy duty aluminum foil large enough to fold and seal over all ingredients. Melt butter and add remaining ingredients except tomato. Spoon over fillets and top with tomato slices. Fold and seal edges tightly. Bake in a preheated 400°F oven for 30-40 minutes or until fish flakes easily with a fork. Serve on a heated platter garnished with parsley.

BEER BATTER FISH

1 pound fish fillets or cooked large shrimp
3 to 4 tablespoons **BISQUICK® Baking Mix**
1 cup **BISQUICK® Baking Mix**
½ cup beer
1 egg
½ teaspoon salt
Soy sauce or vinegar

Heat fat or oil (1½ inches) in heavy saucepan or deep-fat fryer to 350°. Lightly coat fish with 3 to 4 tablespoons baking mix; reserve. Mix 1 cup baking mix, the beer, egg and salt until smooth. Dip fish into batter, letting excess drip into bowl. Fry fish until golden brown, about 2 minutes on each side; drain. Serve hot with soy sauce.

3 or 4 servings

PAN FRIED FILLETS WITH GINGER SAUCE
(Low Calorie)

1 package **VAN DE KAMP'S® Today's Catch Cod** or **Fish Fillets**
2 Tbsp. oil
1 tsp. minced fresh ginger
1 green onion, thinly sliced
3 Tbsp. shredded or diced bamboo shoots
⅛ tsp. five-spice powder
2 tsp. cornstarch
½ cup chicken stock
3 Tbsp. soy sauce
2 tsp. sherry

Heat oil in skillet or wok and fry fillets 5 minutes on each side until light golden. Remove from heat and sprinkle ginger, green onion, bamboo shoots and five-spice powder over fish. Dissolve cornstarch in chicken stock, soy sauce and sherry. Pour over fish and bring quickly to a boil. Cover and simmer gently for 5 minutes. Serve with steamed rice.

Serves 2

Calories: 225 calories per serving

BEER BATTER BARBECUE

1 (12-oz.) package **BOOTH**® Beer Batter French
   Fried Fish Fillets (or Crunchy Corn Batter French
   Fried Fish Fillets)
1 (8-oz.) can tomato sauce
2 tablespoons brown sugar
¼ teaspoon salt
2 tablespoons Worcestershire sauce
1 tablespoon salad oil
2 teaspoons prepared mustard
Grated cheese (optional)

Combine all ingredients in bowl, except the fish fillets. Place
frozen fish fillets on well-greased rack over moderately hot coals
and grill 10 minutes. Turn and brush with barbecue sauce. Grill
10-15 minutes; do not overcook. If desired, sprinkle with your
favorite cheese and cook 1-2 minutes to melt cheese.

PARMESAN CRUMB FILLET

1 pound **BOOTH**® Fish Fillets (whiting, ocean
   catfish, turbot)
¼ cup melted butter or margarine
1 teaspoon lemon juice
1 teaspoon Worcestershire sauce
2 teaspoons instant minced onion
1 tablespoon dry bread crumbs
1 tablespoon grated Parmesan cheese

Defrost fillets. Place in a single layer in a greased baking dish.
Combine butter, lemon juice, Worcestershire sauce, onion, bread
crumbs and cheese. Blend well and spread over fish. Bake in
preheated 350°F oven for 20-25 minutes, until fish flakes easily
with a fork.

LEMON BUTTERED FISH

¼ cup margarine or butter
¼ cup **REALEMON**® Reconstituted Lemon Juice
¼ cup water
1 teaspoon **WYLER'S**® Chicken-Flavor Instant
   Bouillon *or* 1 **WYLER'S**® Chicken-Flavor Bouillon
   Cube
¼ teaspoon thyme leaves or dill weed
1 pound fish fillets, fresh or frozen, thawed (turbot, sole,
   perch, haddock, salmon or flounder)
Salt and pepper
Paprika

In large skillet, combine margarine, **REALEMON**®, water,
bouillon and thyme; heat until margarine is melted and bouillon is
dissolved. Add fish; cover and simmer 6 to 8 minutes or until fish
flakes with fork. Season with salt and pepper; garnish with paprika. Refrigerate leftovers. *Makes 3 to 4 servings*

GREEK FILLETS
(Ocean Perch)

1 lb. **BOOTH**® Block Frozen Fillets
1 tablespoon softened butter or margarine

Let fillets stand at room temperature 30 minutes. Cut into four
equal portions and place on greased aluminum foil. Spread softened butter or margarine on fish and wrap securely. Bake 30-35
minutes at 450°F. or until fish flakes easily with a fork. While fish
is baking prepare sauce.* *(Continued)*

*GREEK SAUCE

1 cup sliced celery
½ cup minced onion
¼ cup butter or margarine (or combination of half olive
   oil and half butter or margarine)
1 can (16 oz.) stewed tomatoes, cut up
1 can (3.2 oz.) sliced ripe olives, drained
¼ teaspoon garlic powder
3-4 drops liquid hot pepper sauce
2-3 tablespoons white wine (optional)
¾ cup Feta cheese, crumbled

Melt butter or margarine; sauté celery and onion. Add tomatoes
and liquid and rest of ingredients except cheese. Simmer 10-15
minutes. Just before serving, remove sauce from heat and blend in
Feta cheese. Serve immediately over steamed fillets.

Serves 3-4

FISH FILLETS PAPRIKASH

1 package (14 ounces) **MRS. PAUL'S**® French Fried
   Fish Fillets
3 tablespoons butter or margarine
¼ cup onions, diced
1 tablespoon flour
1 teaspoon paprika
1 cup milk
¾ cup sour cream
½ teaspoon salt
½ teaspoon parsley flakes
1 package (8 ounces) egg noodles, cooked according to
   package directions

Prepare **MRS. PAUL'S**® French Fried Fish Fillets according to
package directions. Sauté onion in butter over medium heat until
soft. Stir in flour and paprika and cook over low heat for 2-3
minutes. Gradually add milk and salt, heat until thickened.
Remove from heat and stir in sour cream. Place noodles on serving
dish. Arrange fish fillets on noodles and spoon sauce over fish
fillets. Garnish with parsley flakes. *Serves 6*

BUTTERCRISP FISH FILLETS

1 lb. fish fillets
½ cup flour
1 egg, well beaten
¼ cup butter
1 cup **3-MINUTE BRAND**® Oats
1 tsp. salt
¼ tsp. pepper
½ tsp. paprika
¼ tsp. ground thyme
Oil for deep frying

Tartar Sauce:

¼ cup plain yogurt
¼ cup chili sauce
2 Tbsp. lemon juice
1 Tbsp. finely chopped onion
2 Tbsp. finely chopped dill pickle or pickle relish

Wash and dry fillets. Dip each piece in flour, then in egg and set
aside. Melt butter in a skillet. Add oats, salt, pepper, paprika and
thyme. Stir over medium heat until oats are lightly browned. Roll
the fillets in the oat mixture and fry in 375°F. deep oil until golden
and crisp (about 3 to 5 minutes). Drain on paper towels. Combine
ingredients for tartar sauce and mix well. Serve with fried fish.

FISH COQUILLE

1 can (4 oz.) sliced mushrooms
Water
¼ cup dry white wine
2 tablespoons minced onion
1 tablespoon LEA & PERRINS Worcestershire Sauce
⅛ teaspoon salt
1½ pounds fresh or frozen fish fillets, cut into chunks
1 package (1 oz.) white sauce mix
1¼ cups milk
2 tablespoons grated Parmesan cheese
2 tablespoons chopped parsley
2 tablespoons diced pimiento
½ cup soft bread crumbs
1 tablespoon butter or margarine, melted

Drain mushrooms, reserving liquid; set mushrooms aside. Add sufficient water to mushroom liquid to measure 1 cup. In a medium saucepan combine mushroom liquid, wine, onion, LEA & PERRINS, and salt. Bring to boiling point. Add fish. Simmer, uncovered, until fish flakes, about 15 minutes. With a slotted spoon remove fish from the saucepan; set aside. Into liquid in the saucepan stir white sauce mix, milk, and cheese. Cook and stir until thickened. Return fish to sauce. Stir in reserved mushrooms along with the parsley and pimiento. Simmer, uncovered, for 5 minutes, stirring occasionally. Spoon into individual baking shells or casseroles. Combine bread crumbs with butter; sprinkle over fish mixture. Bake in a preheated hot oven (400 F.) until bubbly, about 10 minutes. *6 servings*

CUCUMBER-DILL FILLETS

1 package (1⅛-oz.) DURKEE Roastin' Bag Creamy–Dill Sauce Mix for Fish
1 pound unbreaded fish fillets (thawed if frozen)
1 cup finely chopped cucumber
⅔ cup water
1 tablespoon DURKEE Instant Minced Onion
2 teaspoons lemon juice

CONVENTIONAL METHOD:
Preheat oven to 350°. Place roasting bag in a baking dish 1½ to 2-inches deep and large enough to contain entire bag. Place fish in bag. Spoon cucumber over fish. Combine sauce mix with remaining ingredients; pour over fish and cucumber in bag. Close open end of bag with twist tie. Cut 4 small holes along the top of bag. Place on rack in lower half of oven, leaving at least 10 inches between rack positions to allow for expansion of bag. Bake in preheated 350° oven for 20-25 minutes. Cut top of bag; remove fish to serving platter and spoon sauce and cucumber over fish.
Makes 3 to 4 servings

MICROWAVE METHOD:
Prepare according to recipe, except fasten open end of bag with a string. Microwave on HIGH 7-9 minutes, rotating dish ½ turn half way through cooking time. Allow to stand, unopened, 5 minutes before serving. Times can vary depending on particular oven being used; check manufacturer's manual for more specific cooking time charts.

HERB-TOPPED FISH FILLETS
Topping:
20 PREMIUM Saltine Crackers, crushed (about 1 cup crumbs)
2 tablespoons chopped parsley
2 tablespoons snipped fresh dill or 2 teaspoons dried dill weed
(Continued)

Fish Fillets:
¼ cup FLEISCHMANN'S Margarine
1 clove garlic, crushed
¼ cup lemon juice
1½ pounds flounder, sole or whiting fillets, cut into serving pieces

For topping, combine crushed PREMIUM Saltine Crackers, parsley and dill. Toss to mix well; set aside.
Preheat oven to 400°F. In small skillet, over low heat, melt FLEISCHMANN'S Margarine. Sauté garlic 1 to 2 minutes; stir in lemon juice. Brush fish fillets lightly on both sides with lemon mixture; place fish on shallow baking tray. Toss remaining lemon-mixture with prepared crushed crackers. Spoon crumb mixture evenly over surface of each portion of fish. Bake 8 to 10 minutes, depending on thickness of fish, until fish flakes easily. Serve with steamed vegetables. *Makes 6 servings*

FILLETS VALARIAN

1 pound BOOTH® Fish Fillets
1 teaspoon instant minced onion
½ teaspoon dry mustard
¼ teaspoon dill
Salt and pepper to taste
2 teaspoons water
1 teaspoon lemon juice
¼ cup mayonnaise
1 cup sliced mushrooms sautéed in 2 tablespoons butter
Paprika

Place fillets in single layer on heavy duty aluminum foil large enough to fold and seal over all ingredients. Combine onion, mustard, dill, salt and pepper with water and let stand 10 minutes. Add lemon juice and mayonnaise, blending well. Spoon over fillets; top with mushrooms and sprinkle with paprika. Fold and seal edges tightly. Bake in preheated 400°F oven for 30-40 minutes or until fish flakes easily with a fork. Serve on heated platter garnished with sliced lemon.

LEMON FISH AND RICE AMANDINE

2¼ cups water
¼ cup lemon juice
1 cup UNCLE BEN'S® CONVERTED® Brand Rice
1 teaspoon salt
⅛ teaspoon nutmeg
4 green onions with tops, sliced
1 pound frozen fish fillets, thawed
Salt (optional)
Paprika (optional)
¼ cup butter or margarine, melted
1 lemon, thinly sliced
¼ cup toasted sliced almonds

Bring water and lemon juice to a boil in saucepan; stir in rice, salt and nutmeg. Cover tightly and simmer 20 minutes. Remove from heat. Let stand covered until all liquid is absorbed, about 5 minutes. Stir green onions into rice. Spoon rice into 12 × 8-inch baking dish. Arrange fish over rice; sprinkle lightly with salt and paprika, if desired. Pour butter evenly over fish; arrange lemon slices over fish. Sprinkle almonds around lemon slices. Cover loosely with aluminum foil. Bake at 400°F. 12 to 15 minutes or until fish flakes easily. *Makes 6 servings*

BROILED FILLETS WITH ALMOND-MUSHROOM SAUCE

1 lb. **BOOTH®** Block Frozen Fillets, thawed
1-2 tablespoons butter or margarine
Salt and pepper

Sauce:
¼ lb. fresh mushrooms, sliced or 1 can (4-oz.)
   mushrooms, drained
1½ tablespoons butter or margarine
2 tablespoons lemon juice
2 tablespoons white wine
¼ teaspoon Worcestershire sauce
¼ cup almond slivers
⅓ teaspoon Dijon mustard

Place thawed fillets on greased broiler pan. Brush with melted butter or margarine. Salt and pepper to taste. Broil 6 inches from heat for 4-6 minutes or until fish flakes easily with a fork. Prepare Sauce while fish is cooking.

SAUCE:
Melt 1½ tablespoons butter and sauté mushrooms 1-2 minutes. Add remaining ingredients and simmer gently about 5 minutes. Serve immediately over broiled fillets.

WRAPPED FARM-RAISED CATFISH WITH CREAM CHEESE STUFFING

4 farm-raised catfish fillets (6 to 8 ounces each), fresh
   or frozen
½ teaspoon salt
¼ teaspoon pepper
1 teaspoon lemon juice
1 cup fresh bread crumbs
3 tablespoons cream cheese
1 tablespoon lemon juice
1 tablespoon chopped celery
1 tablespoon chopped onion
1 teaspoon dehydrated parsley
1 teaspoon ground thyme
½ teaspoon salt
¼ teaspoon pepper
8 slices bacon
Lemon slices
Pimiento strips

Thaw fish if frozen. Season with ½ teaspoon salt and ¼ teaspoon pepper. Sprinkle fish with 1 teaspoon lemon juice. Combine bread crumbs, cream cheese, 1 tablespoon lemon juice, celery, onion, parsley, thyme, ½ teaspoon salt and ¼ teaspoon pepper. Divide stuffing into four portions. Place one portion of stuffing at one end of each fillet of fish. Roll fish around stuffing. Fry bacon until cooked, but not crisp. Wrap 2 slices of bacon around each fillet; secure with a toothpick. Place fish rolls in a lightly greased baking dish. Bake in a moderate oven, 350°F., for 15 to 20 minutes or until fish flakes easily when tested with a fork. Garnish with lemon slices and pimiento strips. *Makes 4 servings*

Note: Remove toothpicks before serving.

Favorite recipe from the **Catfish Farmers of America**

POACHED FARM RAISED CATFISH IN EMERALD BAY SAUCE

2 pounds farm raised catfish fillets, fresh or frozen
3 tablespoons margarine or butter
⅓ cup sliced green onions
⅔ cup chicken broth
¼ cup dry white wine
¼ cup mint-flavored apple jelly
2 tablespoons brandy
¼ teaspoon salt
Emerald Bay Sauce*
⅓ cup cashew nuts, halves, toasted and salted

Thaw fish if frozen. In a large skillet melt margarine. Add onion and cook for 2 minutes. Add broth, wine, jelly, brandy and salt. Simmer uncovered for 10 minutes. Place fish in a single layer in skillet with broth mixture. Cover and poach for approximately 7 to 8 minutes or until fish flakes easily when tested with a fork. Remove fish to a warm platter reserving poaching liquid. Pour Emerald Bay Sauce over fish. Sprinkle cashews over fish.
Makes 6 servings

*EMERALD BAY SAUCE

Reserved poaching liquid
¾ cup sour cream
1¼ cups seedless green grapes

Boil the poaching liquid over medium heat until reduced to ½ cup. Blend in sour cream. Stir in grapes. Heat until hot.

Favorite recipe from **Catfish Farmers of America**

FARM-RAISED CATFISH SESAME WITH LEMON PARSLEY SAUCE

2 pounds **FARM FRESH®** Catfish Fillets, fresh or
   frozen
1 teaspoon salt
¼ teaspoon white pepper
¼ cup all-purpose flour
1 egg, beaten
2 tablespoons milk
½ cup finely crushed saltine cracker crumbs
3 tablespoons sesame seed
Cooking oil for frying
Lemon Parsley Sauce*

Thaw catfish if frozen. Season catfish with salt and pepper. Coat lightly with flour. Combine egg and milk. Combine cracker crumbs and sesame seed. Dip catfish into egg mixture and roll in crumb mixture. Place catfish in a single layer in hot oil in a large fry pan. Fry at a moderate heat, 360° F, approximately 4 to 5 minutes. Turn carefully and cook 4 to 5 minutes longer or until brown and catfish flakes easily when tested with a fork. Drain on absorbent paper. Serve Lemon Parsley Sauce over catfish.
Makes 6 servings

*LEMON PARSLEY SAUCE

⅓ cup finely chopped onion
¼ cup finely chopped parsley
¼ cup lemon juice

Combine all ingredients in saucepan. Heat to boiling. Serve over catfish.

BAKED FISH CONTINENTAL

2 tablespoons instant minced onion
2 tablespoons water
½ teaspoon basil leaves, crushed
½ teaspoon paprika
⅛ teaspoon garlic powder
2 tablespoons salad oil
1½ tablespoons lemon juice
1 pound cod fillets
1 teaspoon **MADELINE'S Low Sodium Seasoning**

Preheat oven to 350° F. Combine minced onion and water; let stand for 10 minutes to soften. Stir in basil, paprika, garlic powder, oil and lemon juice. Place fish fillets in a greased 10 × 6 × 2-inch baking pan. Pour herb mixture over top. Bake until fish flakes easily with a fork, about 15 minutes. Sprinkle with **MADELINE'S Low Sodium Seasoning** just before serving.

Yield: 4 portions

BARBECUED COD FILLETS

2 pounds fresh cod fillets or other fresh fish fillets
2 tablespoons chopped onion
1 clove garlic, finely chopped
2 tablespoons melted fat or oil
1 can (8-oz.) tomato sauce
2 tablespoons sherry
½ teaspoon salt
¼ teaspoon oregano
3 drops liquid hot pepper sauce
Dash pepper

Cook onion and garlic in fat until tender. Add remaining ingredients except fish and simmer for 5 minutes, stirring occasionally. Cool. Cut fillets into serving size portions and place in a single layer in a shallow baking dish. Pour sauce over fish and let stand for 30 minutes, turning once. Remove fish, reserving sauce for basting. Place fish in well-greased, hinged wire grills. Cook about 4 inches from moderately hot coals for 8 minutes. Baste with sauce. Turn and cook for 7 to 10 minutes longer or until fish flakes easily when tested with a fork.

Serves 6

Favorite recipe from **Maine Department of Marine Resources**

HALIBUT STEAKS WITH ALMOND-CAPER SAUCE

4 halibut steaks, about 1-inch thick
1 tablespoon butter or margarine, melted
Salt and pepper
2 tablespoons butter or margarine
2 tablespoons all-purpose flour
½ cup milk
½ cup dairy sour cream
2 teaspoons lemon juice
2 tablespoons capers, drained
⅓ cup **BLUE DIAMOND® Blanched Slivered Almonds**, toasted*

Arrange halibut in lightly buttered baking dish; brush with the 1 tablespoon melted butter; sprinkle with salt and pepper. Bake in 450 degree F. oven about 20 minutes, or until fish flakes. *Do not overcook.*

(Continued)

Melt the 2 tablespoons butter in saucepan; add flour and cook, stirring, 2 to 3 minutes. Add milk and cook, over medium heat, until thickened, stirring constantly. Remove from heat; stir in sour cream, lemon juice, capers, and ¼ cup of the almonds. (Sauce may be kept warm over low heat, but *do not boil*.) Pour sauce over fish and garnish with remaining almonds.

Makes 4 servings

MICROWAVE METHOD:
Pat fish dry. Melt the 1 tablespoon butter in 11 × 7-inch baking dish for 30 to 45 seconds; tilt dish to distribute. Arrange fish in a single layer with thickest portions towards edges of dish; cook, uncovered, 3½ minutes; turn fish over, cover with plastic wrap and cook 2 to 3 minutes more or until fish flakes when pierced with fork. Remove fish to warmed serving platter; cover.

Melt the 2 tablespoons butter in 4-cup glass measure for 30 to 45 seconds. Stir in flour and cook 1 minute. Gradually blend in milk and cook, uncovered, 1 to 1½ minutes or until thickened, stirring after each 30 seconds. Stir in sour cream, lemon juice, capers, and ¼ cup of the almonds. Cook 30 seconds to 1 minute or until heated through, stirring after 30 seconds.

*To Toast Almonds: Spread in single layer in shallow pan. Bake, stirring often in 300° F. oven 15 minutes, or until they begin to turn color. *Don't wait for them to become golden brown.* After removing the almonds from the oven, their residual heat will continue to toast them slightly.

FLOUNDER NOUVELLE

3 tablespoons **MAZOLA® Corn Oil**, divided
1 cup chopped onions
1 clove garlic
¼ cup dry white wine
½ teaspoon salt
¾ pound flounder fillets (4 small)
3 medium carrots, cut in match-stick pieces
3 ribs celery, cut in match-stick pieces

In medium skillet heat 1 tablespoon of the corn oil over medium heat. Add onion and garlic. Cook, stirring frequently, 5 minutes. Place onion mixture, wine and salt in blender container; cover. Blend on high speed 15 seconds or until smooth. Beginning with tail end roll each flounder fillet lengthwise; place in 1-quart shallow baking pan. Spoon onion mixture over fish. Bake uncovered in 375°F oven 20 minutes. Meanwhile, heat remaining 2 tablespoons of the corn oil in skillet over medium heat. Add carrots and celery. Cook, stirring frequently, 5 minutes. Spoon over fish. Bake 5 minutes longer or until fish flakes easily.

Makes 4 servings

MICROWAVE METHOD:
In 2-quart microproof bowl place 1 tablespoon of the corn oil, onions and garlic. Microwave with full power 2 minutes, stirring once. Place onion mixture, wine and salt in blender container; cover. Blend on high speed 10 seconds or until pureed. In 2-quart microproof bowl place remaining 2 tablespoons corn oil, carrots and celery. Microwave 2½ minutes, stirring once. Beginning with tail end roll each flounder fillet lengthwise; place in 8 × 8 × 2-inch microproof baking dish. Spoon onion mixture over fish; top with carrot and celery mixture. Cover with waxed paper. Microwave 7 to 8 minutes rotating dish twice or until fish flakes easily.

Makes 4 servings

JAPANESE STIR-FRY FISH

1 tablespoon soy sauce
1 tablespoon sherry wine or water
2 teaspoons cornstarch
1 package (12 oz.) frozen flounder fillets, thawed and cut in strips*
2 tablespoons oil
1 package (10 oz.) **BIRDS EYE**® **Japanese Style Stir-Fry Vegetables**
1 small garlic clove, crushed

Combine soy sauce, sherry and cornstarch. Add fish and mix to coat all strips. Let stand for 10 minutes. Sauté fish in oil in large skillet for 1 or 2 minutes; keep warm. Prepare vegetables in separate clean skillet as directed on package, adding garlic with the vegetables. Arrange fish in center.

Makes 3¾ cups or 3 servings

*Or use ¾ pound fish fillets, cut in strips.

FLOUNDER CARIBE

1 pound **BOOTH**® **Flounder Fillets**
1 (10½-oz.) can condensed tomato soup
⅓ cup diced green pepper
¼ cup diced onion
¼ teaspoon thyme
1 teaspoon Worcestershire sauce
2 tablespoons white wine

Defrost fillets. Roll up and place in a single layer in a buttered baking dish. Combine tomato soup (undiluted), green pepper, onion, thyme, Worcestershire sauce and white wine. Pour over fish and bake in a preheated 350°F oven 20-25 minutes, until fish flakes easily with a fork.

LEMON DELIGHT FISH FILLETS

4 sole or haddock fillets (about 1 pound)
Salt and pepper
2 tablespoons fresh squeezed lemon juice
Fine dry bread crumbs (seasoned or plain)
2 tablespoons butter or margarine
2 tablespoons salad oil
⅓ cup light cream or half & half
1 teaspoon fresh grated lemon peel
1 avocado, sliced
Whole or chopped salted cashew nuts
SUNKIST® **Lemon**, cut in half-cartwheels
Parsley

Sprinkle fillets with salt, pepper and 1 tablespoon lemon juice; let stand 5 to 10 minutes. Coat fillets with bread crumbs. In large skillet, heat butter and oil. Sauté fillets (3 to 4 minutes on each side) until lightly browned and fish flakes easily with fork. Remove fillets to serving dish; sprinkle with remaining 1 tablespoon lemon juice. Keep warm. Add cream and lemon peel to pan drippings. Bring to boil, stirring constantly until slightly thickened; spoon over fillets. Top with avocado slices and nuts. Serve with lemon half-cartwheels. Garnish with parsley.

Makes 4 servings

BAKED HADDOCK IN CUCUMBER SAUCE

2 pounds frozen haddock fillets, thawed
2 tablespoons **MEADOW GOLD**® **Butter**, melted
¼ teaspoon salt
⅛ teaspoon each: pepper, paprika
¼ cup sliced green onions
¼ cup (½ stick) **MEADOW GOLD**® **Butter**
¼ cup flour
1 teaspoon salt
1 container (8 ounces) **MEADOW GOLD**® **Plain Lowfat Yogurt**
1 cup chopped, pared cucumber, drained

Pat fillets dry with paper toweling; arrange in shallow baking dish. Brush with melted butter; sprinkle with ¼ teaspoon salt, pepper and paprika. Cook onions in ¼ cup butter for 2 to 3 minutes. Remove from heat. Add flour and salt; mix well. Stir in yogurt. Cook, stirring constantly, until mixture begins to boil. Stir in cucumber. Spoon sauce over fillets. Bake at 350° for 30 minutes, or until hot and bubbly.

6 to 8 servings

POACHED HADDOCK WITH MUSSELS

2 pounds haddock, cod or other thick fillets, fresh or frozen
4 pounds mussels in shells (about 4 dozen)*
1 cup dry white wine
1 cup water
1 small onion, sliced
½ teaspoon salt
½ cup whipping cream
¼ cup margarine or butter
Dash white pepper
Dash nutmeg
2 tablespoons chopped parsley
Parslied potatoes
1 cup each of zucchini, carrots and celery, cut julienne style
Margarine or butter for cooking vegetables

Thaw fillets if frozen. Cut into serving-size portions. Clean mussels in cold water. Scrub shells with a stiff brush, rinsing thoroughly several times. Combine wine, water, and onion in large pan; bring to simmering stage. Add cleaned mussels. Cover and steam about 5 minutes or until shells open. Remove mussels from shells; set aside. Strain cooking liquid into a large skillet. Add fillets and salt. Cover and simmer 8 to 10 minutes or until fish flakes easily when tested with a fork. Transfer fillets to warm platter; keep warm. Reduce cooking liquid to ½ cup. Stir in whipping cream, ¼ cup margarine or butter, pepper and nutmeg; simmer until sauce thickens slightly. Add mussels and parsley; heat. Spoon mixture over fillets. Serve with parslied potatoes and julienne strips of zucchini, carrot, and celery sautéed in margarine or butter, stirring constantly just until tender.

Makes 6 servings

*If desired clams may be substituted for mussels.

Favorite recipe from the **National Marine Fisheries Service**

LAND O' LAKES CLASSIC SALMON STEAKS
(Low Sodium)

Topping:
½ cup **LAND O LAKES® Unsalted (Sweet) Butter**, softened
1 tsp. lime juice
¼ tsp. dill weed
⅛ tsp. pepper

4 salmon steaks (1" thick)
1 lime, cut into 8 slices

Combine all topping ingredients until well blended. Place salmon steaks on greased broiler pan. Spread one side of each steak with 2 tsp. topping. Broil 5" away from heat for 5 to 6 min. or until lightly browned. Turn steaks over and top each steak with 2 lime slices. Continue broiling 5 to 6 min. or until salmon flakes with fork. To serve, place lime slices beside steak and top each steak with 1 Tbsp. topping.   *Yield: 4 servings*

Sodium: 153 mg/serving

FISH STEAKS MINCEUR
(Low Calorie/Low Sodium)

¾ cup water
¾ cup dry white wine
1 teaspoon dried leaf thyme
1 bay leaf
¼ teaspoon **TABASCO® Pepper Sauce**
1 large carrot, cut in julienne strips
1 zucchini, cut in julienne strips
1 red pepper, cut in julienne strips
1 leek (white portion only), cut in julienne strips
4 halibut or salmon steaks (about 1½ pounds)
1 egg yolk

In large skillet combine water, wine, thyme, bay leaf and **TABASCO® Sauce**. Bring to a boil. Add carrot, zucchini, red pepper and leek. Arrange fish steaks on top of vegetables. Reduce heat. Cover. Simmer 10 to 12 minutes until fish flakes easily with a fork. Transfer fish steaks to heated serving platter. Remove vegetables from skillet and reserve. Reduce poaching liquid to ¾ cup. Strain. Pour into container of electric blender. Add 1 cup reserved vegetables and egg yolk. Cover. Process until smooth. Spoon sauce around fish steaks on serving platter. Arrange remaining vegetables on top of fish.   *Yield: 4 servings*

Halibut: 112 mg sodium per serving
252 calories per serving

POMPANO WITH GRAPES

3 lbs. **FIN BRAND Pompano Fillets**
1 cup white wine
1½-2 lbs. white seedless grapes
Salt and pepper to taste

Marinate fish 30 minutes in white wine. Cut grapes in half and spread them in baking pan. Place fillets on grape bed and pour wine over them. Bake in 350 degree F oven 20 minutes or until fish flakes easily when tested with a fork. Baste once or twice with wine from pan. Salt and pepper to taste after cooking.

ORIGINAL PORTLAND POLLOCK-BURGERS

1 pound fresh pollock fillets
½ teaspoon salt
Dash of pepper
1 cup fine bread crumbs
½ cup flour
2 eggs
Cooking oil

Cut fillets into 3-inch squares. Place flour on waxed paper and in a separate bowl mix the remaining dry ingredients. Beat eggs well. Roll fish squares in the flour, dip in the beaten eggs and roll in the dry mixture. Heat cooking oil until hot and fry fish squares for 3 or 4 minutes, or until golden brown; turn carefully and fry the same length of time. Place pollock-burgers on paper toweling to absorb extra oil. Serve on toasted hamburger buns, as is or with tartar sauce.   *Serves 5*

Favorite recipe from **Maine Department of Marine Resources**

SOLE AMANDINE

1 - 14 oz. pkg. **HIGH LINER® Sole Fillets**
¾ cup blanched almonds
6 Tbsp. butter
Flour
Salt
Pepper

Melt butter in skillet over medium high heat. Dust frozen fish with flour and season to taste with salt and pepper. Place in skillet. Cut ¼ cup of almonds into slivers, leaving the remainder whole. Sprinkle almonds in pan around fish, stirring them to prevent burning. Turn fish once while frying. Fry approximately 6-8 minutes each side. To serve, pour almond butter over fish. Garnish with parsley and lemon wedges.   *Serves 3-4*

SOLE FILLETS NORMANDE

1 pound sole fillets
Salt and pepper
2 tablespoons scallions, chopped
½ teaspoon tarragon
1 cup **Soave BOLLA Wine**
3 tablespoons flour
3 tablespoons butter
2 egg yolks
¾ cup heavy cream
Clam juice
Few drops lemon juice

Garnish:
½ pound sautéed, sliced mushrooms
½ pound large shrimp, boiled and shelled

Season fillets with salt, pepper and tarragon. Sprinkle on chopped scallions and roll up, securing with toothpicks. Arrange in shallow buttered baking dish. Pour in wine. Cover with lid or foil. Poach in 375° oven, 15-20 minutes, until flaky. Drain and reserve liquid from fish. Melt butter in saucepan. Add flour and cook gently two minutes. To reserve liquid, add clam juice to make 1½ cups. Add this to roux, stirring with wire whisk until smooth and boiling. Simmer 3 minutes. Beat egg yolks with cream. Gradually stir several tablespoons sauce into egg yolk mixture, then return all to saucepan stirring and bringing almost to a boil. Add a few drops of lemon juice.

Arrange drained fish on warm platter. Coat with sauce. Arrange mushrooms and shrimp to garnish.

GREEN GIANT® STUFFED SOLE FILLETS

10-oz. pkg. **GREEN GIANT® Rice Originals Frozen Herb Butter**
4 frozen sole fillets (about 1 lb.), thawed
4 teaspoons butter or margarine
½ cup dry white wine

Heat oven to 375°F. Cook rice pouch according to package directions; cool slightly.

Place two fillets together, one on top of the other; slice in half diagonally. Repeat with remaining fillets. Make a center lengthwise cut almost to the ends down each top fillet. Place top-slit fillets to side; spread about 3 tablespoons cooked rice over each bottom fillet. Replace top fillets over rice; spoon 2 tablespoons cooked rice down center slit of each. Place 1 teaspoon butter on top of each stuffed fillet. Arrange in 13 × 9-inch (3-quart) baking dish. Pour wine around stuffed fillets. Cover and bake at 375°F for 25 to 30 minutes or until fish flakes easily with fork. *4 servings*

NUTRITION INFORMATION PER SERVING

SERVING SIZE: ¼ OF RECIPE		PERCENT U.S. RDA PER SERVING	
Calories	300	Protein	35
Protein	23 g	Vitamin A	60
Carbohydrate	13 g	Vitamin C	2
Fat	17 g	Thiamine	15
Sodium	595 mg	Riboflavin	8
Potassium	370 mg	Niacin	20
		Calcium	*
		Iron	6

*Contains less than 2% of the U.S. RDA of this nutrient.

CHILE STUFFED FILLET OF SOLE

1 small onion, chopped
2 tablespoons butter (or margarine)
1 cup fresh bread crumbs
1 can (4 oz.) **ORTEGA Diced Green Chiles**
1 egg, lightly beaten
Salt and pepper to taste
6 fillets of sole (approximately 2 lbs.)
1 can (10½ oz.) condensed Cheddar cheese soup

Sauté onion in butter. In a bowl, mix bread crumbs, chiles, and onion. Stir in egg and salt and pepper. Spread some of this mixture evenly over each fillet, roll and fasten each with a toothpick. Set, seam side down, in well-greased 6″ x 9″ x 2″ baking pan. Bake, uncovered, in preheated oven (350°) for 15 minutes. Drain excess liquid. Spoon undiluted soup over fillets and continue baking for 15 minutes, or until fish flakes. Serve hot. *Serves 6*

LIME BAKED FILLETS

3 tablespoons butter
1 pound sole fillets
2 tablespoons fresh Florida lime juice
Salt and pepper
¼ teaspoon *each* dried tarragon and chives
4 lime wedges

Melt butter in shallow baking pan. Arrange fillets in pan, turning to coat both sides with butter. Drizzle lime juice over fish. Sprinkle with salt, pepper, and crushed herbs. Cover pan with foil. Bake in 350 degree oven 10 to 15 minutes. Serve at once, pouring juices over each serving. Garnish with wedges of lime. *Makes 3 to 4 servings*

Favorite recipe from **Florida Lime Administrative Committee**

COCONUT-CRUSTED SOLE WITH SWEET-SOUR SAUCE

2 pounds sole, flounder, or other thin fillets, fresh or frozen
2 cups moderately fine buttery cracker crumbs
1 cup flaked coconut
2 eggs, beaten
2 tablespoons evaporated milk
½ teaspoon salt
½ cup cooking oil (about)
Sweet-Sour Sauce*
Fresh in-season fruit garnish, optional

Thaw fillets if frozen; cut in serving size portions. Combine cracker crumbs and coconut. Combine eggs, milk and salt. Dip fish in egg mixture; drain and coat well with cracker-coconut mixture. Heat 2 to 3 tablespoons oil in a 12-inch skillet. Arrange fillets in single layer in skillet. Fry over moderate heat for 5 to 8 minutes or until browned on both sides and fish flakes easily when tested with a fork, turning fillets only once. Repeat process to fry remaining fish. Drain on absorbent paper. Serve with Sweet-Sour Sauce. Garnish with in-season fruits, if desired. *Makes 6 servings*

*SWEET-SOUR SAUCE

½ cup apricot or plum preserves
¼ cup catsup
¼ cup light corn syrup
2 tablespoons lemon juice
¼ teaspoon ginger

Combine ingredients; simmer 2 to 3 minutes. Serve over fish. *Makes about 1 cup sauce*

Favorite recipe from **National Marine Fisheries Service**

SKEWERED FILLETS

1 (1-lb.) package **BOOTH® Atlantic Sole or Flounder Fillets**
½ cup melted butter or margarine
Bread crumbs
Salt
Pepper
Grated Parmesan cheese

Thaw fillets and separate. Pat dry with paper towels. Dip in melted butter or margarine and roll in bread crumbs. Roll fillet up and pierce with a skewer. Grill over moderately hot coals on a well-greased rack, 5-10 minutes, turning once. Just before fillets are completely cooked, season with salt and pepper and sprinkle generously with grated Parmesan cheese.

TASTY FRIED FILLETS

1 (14-oz.) pkg. **BOOTH® IQF Sole or Flounder Fillets**
1 bottle Italian salad dressing
1 cup flour
2 eggs
2 Tbsp. water or milk
1 cup corn flake crumbs

Beat eggs and add milk or water. Dip thawed fillets first in Italian dressing, then flour, egg mixture and finally corn flake crumbs. Let coated fillets stand 5-10 minutes before frying. Pan-fry in a skillet with ⅛-inch oil, over medium heat. Cook 3-4 minutes per side or until fish flakes easily with a fork.

STUFFED SOLE FILETS
(Low Calorie)

4 slices filet of sole (about ¾ pound)
2 teaspoons seasoned salt
½ teaspoon pepper
1 tablespoon chopped green onion
½ teaspoon dill weed
1 (12-oz.) can **DIET SHASTA®** Lemon-Lime
⅓ cup chopped celery
1 small bay leaf
½ teaspoon whole allspice
1 tablespoon lemon juice
1 teaspoon vinegar

Sprinkle fish with 1½ teaspoons seasoned salt, the pepper, onion and dill. Roll up each slice to enclose seasoning; skewer with wooden pick. Combine remaining ½ teaspoon salt with all remaining ingredients in small skillet. Bring to a boil. Place fish rolls in liquid, reduce heat to simmering and cook gently until tender, about 10 minutes.   *Makes 2 servings of 2 filets each*

143 calories per serving

FILET OF SOLE EN CROUTE

4 small filets of sole
Salt, pepper, thyme, tarragon
2 tablespoons butter or margarine
½ cup julienne onions
½ cup julienne mushrooms
½ cup julienne carrots
1 package (17¼ ounces) **PEPPERIDGE FARM®**
    Frozen "Bake It Fresh" Puff Pastry Sheets
1 egg, beaten

Sprinkle sole filets lightly with salt, pepper, thyme and tarragon and refrigerate. Melt butter in skillet; cut vegetables into narrow matchstick-like strips (julienne) and add to skillet. Season with salt and pepper and cook briefly, 3-5 minutes. Vegetables should remain crisp.

Allow puff pastry sheets to thaw for 20 minutes, then unfold and cut each sheet into 4 squares. On a lightly floured surface, roll first square until it's slightly larger than the filet. Place filet in center of pastry, spoon ¼ of the julienne mixture on top. Roll second square of pastry only enough to cover sole filet and border of the first sheet. Firmly press down edges to seal and trim excess with pastry wheel. If desired, use scraps to decorate pastry and attach with beaten egg. Repeat with remaining sole filets and pastry.

Place on baking sheet, brush top with beaten egg and bake in preheated 375° oven for 25-30 minutes or until golden brown.
Makes 4 generous servings

NORDIC STUFFED FILLETS

1 cup chopped mushrooms
2 tablespoons butter or margarine
⅓ cup sliced green onions
1 cup small broccoli florets
¼ cup fine dry bread crumbs
1½ cups shredded **NOKKELOST** Cheese
6 sole fillets (about 2 pounds)
Salt and pepper to taste
Paprika
2 tablespoons melted butter or margarine
2 tablespoons lemon juice

In skillet, brown mushrooms in butter and cook onions and broccoli until just tender. Remove from heat. Stir in bread crumbs and

1 cup **NOKKELOST** Cheese. Divide broccoli mixture among fillets. Roll up. Secure with toothpicks. Place seam side down in buttered shallow baking dish. Season with salt and pepper. Sprinkle with paprika. Drizzle butter over sole. Sprinkle with lemon juice. Bake at 400° F for 20 minutes or until fish is done. Top with remaining ½ cup cheese. Bake until cheese melts.
Makes 6 servings

RED SNAPPER IN ORANGE SAUCE

2 lbs. **FIN BRAND Red Snapper**
3 Tbsp. orange juice
1 Tbsp. grated orange rind
5 Tbsp. butter or margarine (melted)
1 tsp. lemon juice
Salt and pepper to taste
Dash of nutmeg

Place fillets in a single layer in well-greased baking pan. Combine remaining ingredients and pour over fish. Bake in 350 degree F oven 25-30 minutes or until fish flakes easily when tested with a fork. Remove to warm serving platter, pour any sauce remaining in the pan over fish and garnish with parsley.

CONFETTI FISH FILLETS

2 lbs. red snapper fillets
2 cups **MALT-O-MEAL®** Toasty O's
1 tsp. lemon-pepper seasoning
5 Tbsp. butter, melted
1½ cups shredded cheddar cheese
1 fresh tomato, diced
½ cup sliced green onions
1½ cups sliced fresh mushrooms

Cut fish into serving size pieces. Pour **Toasty O's** into blender; blend on slow speed until evenly crumbled. Combine crumbled **Toasty O's** with lemon-pepper seasoning in a flat dish. Dip fillet pieces first in butter, then in **Toasty O's** mixture to coat thickly. Place on baking sheet or broiler pan. Bake at 450° for about 15 minutes until fish flakes easily with fork. Meanwhile, combine cheese and tomato. Sauté green onion and mushrooms in remaining butter until just tender. Combine with cheese. Spoon over fillets and return to oven just to melt cheese.

Makes 6 servings

MINTED TROUT

4 whole, pan-dressed rainbow or lake trout, fresh or
    frozen (about 5 ounces each)
2 cups fresh mint leaves, lightly packed or ½ cup
    crushed dried mint
2 teaspoons salt
½ cup olive or salad oil
4 strips of bacon

Thaw trout; wash and pat dry. Mash fresh mint with salt to release the flavor; add oil. When using dried mint, mix with salt and oil. Fill the cavity of the trout with mint mixture. Wrap each trout with one strip of bacon; secure with wooden picks. Broil over charcoal, or under the broiler, or pan-fry for 4 to 5 minutes on each side until bacon is cooked and fish flakes easily when tested with a fork.
Makes 4 servings

Favorite recipe from **National Marine Fisheries Service**

FISH CREOLE

1 can (8 oz.) stewed tomatoes
1 teaspoon **KITCHEN BOUQUET®**
¼ teaspoon sugar
¼ teaspoon thyme, crumbled
¼ teaspoon curry powder
1 lb. fresh or thawed frozen white fish
Salt to taste
Parsley (optional)

Combine tomatoes, **KITCHEN BOUQUET®**, sugar, thyme and curry powder, breaking up large tomato pieces with spoon. Cut fish into 4 portions. Place in shallow baking pan. Spoon tomato mixture over top. Cover pan with lid or foil. Bake in 450° oven for 15 minutes or until fish flakes with fork. Sprinkle with minced parsley, if desired. Salt to taste. Serve with rice, spooning pan juices over. Cooking time: 15 minutes.   *Makes 4 servings*

WHITEFISH WITH CLAM SAUCE

1 cup **BERTOLLI®** Spaghetti Sauce with Clams
½ cup **BERTOLLI®** Soave Wine
1½ pounds whitefish fillets
Flour
Salt and pepper
3 tablespoons **BERTOLLI®** Olive Oil
12 cherrystone clams, steamed
¼ cup minced chives

Heat sauce and wine to boiling in saucepan. Reduce heat; simmer 10 minutes. Coat fish with flour; sprinkle with salt and pepper; sauté in oil in skillet until tender, about 8 minutes. Spoon ½ the sauce on serving plate; arrange fish and clams on sauce. Spoon remaining sauce over; garnish with chives.

Makes 4 servings

BUTTERY FISH ROLL-UPS
(Low Calorie)

1 pound white fish fillets
12 fresh or frozen asparagus spears, each about
    5-inches long
½ cup water
2 tablespoons white wine
1 teaspoon chopped fresh parsley
⅛ teaspoon thyme
Freshly ground pepper to taste
1 packet **BUTTER BUDS®**
Paprika

Preheat oven to 350°F. Split fillets into 4 serving pieces. Cook asparagus spears in water until tender and crisp, about 5 minutes. Do not overcook. Reserve ¼ cup liquid. In saucepan, combine asparagus liquid, wine, parsley, thyme, pepper, and **BUTTER BUDS®**. Heat on low until **BUTTER BUDS®** dissolve.

Brush each fillet with sauce. Depending on size of fillet, arrange 1 to 2 asparagus spears on top of each fillet. For easier handling, split asparagus spears lengthwise. Roll fillet from thin to thick end. Secure with toothpicks. Place in lightly greased baking dish. Pour remaining sauce over fish rolls. Bake, covered, about 20 minutes. Remove from oven and preheat broiler. Uncover fish and baste with pan juices. Sprinkle fish lightly with paprika. Broil 2 or 3 minutes, or until golden brown. Remove toothpicks just before serving. Pour remaining pan juices over fish rolls.   *4 servings*

(Continued)

PER SERVING (1 fish roll):	Calories: 105	Protein: 18g
Carbohydrate: 3g	Fat: trace	Sodium: 285mg

Note: By using **BUTTER BUDS®** instead of butter in this recipe, you have saved 188 calories and 70 mg cholesterol per serving.

SALMON A LA KING

1 can (1 pound) salmon
¼ cup chopped green pepper
¼ cup melted fat or oil
¼ cup flour
½ teaspoon salt
Dash pepper
2½ cups salmon liquid and milk
¼ cup chopped pimiento
Corn bread, biscuits, or toast

Drain salmon, reserving liquid. Break salmon into large pieces. Cook green pepper in fat until tender. Blend in flour, salt, and pepper. Add salmon liquid and milk gradually and cook until thick, stirring constantly. Add pimiento and salmon; heat. Serve over corn bread, biscuits, or toast.   *Serves 6*

Favorite recipe from **National Marine Fisheries Service**

SALMON A LA KING WITH SPINACH NOODLES

3 quarts water
3 teaspoons salt
1 tablespoon oil
4 cups **AMERICAN BEAUTY®** Spinach Egg Noodles
    or 6 cups **Extra Wide Egg Noodles**
1 tablespoon chopped onion
1 tablespoon margarine or butter
⅓ cup flour
1 teaspoon salt
Dash pepper
3 cups milk
1 tablespoon chopped pimiento
7¾-oz. can salmon
3 hard-cooked eggs, sliced

Boil water in large deep pot with 3 teaspoons salt and oil (to prevent boiling over). Add noodles; stir to separate. Cook uncovered after water returns to a full rolling boil for 6 to 7 minutes. Stir occasionally. Drain and rinse under hot water.

In large saucepan, cook onion in margarine until tender. Stir in flour, salt and pepper until well blended. Add milk all at once. Cook until thickened, stirring constantly. Stir in pimiento, salmon and eggs; cook until heated through. Serve over cooked spinach egg noodles.   *6 servings*

High Altitude—Above 3500 Feet: Cooking times may need to be increased slightly for noodles.

NUTRITION INFORMATION PER SERVING			
SERVING SIZE: ⅙ of recipe		Percent U.S. RDA	
Calories	620	Per Serving	
Protein	28	Protein	42
Carbohydrate	80	Vitamin A	17
Fat	20	Vitamin C	2
Sodium	670	Thiamine	35
Potassium	485	Riboflavin	35
		Niacin	34
		Calcium	25
		Iron	21

SALMON IN POTATO SHELLS
(Low Calorie)

	Calories
1-15½ oz. can HUMPTY DUMPTY Chum Salmon*	554
3 large baking potatoes (approx. 8 oz. ea.)	418
½ cup skim milk	45
1 teaspoon dried dill weed	—
1 teaspoon garlic salt	—
¼ teaspoon pepper	—
Paprika	—
	1017

Drain salmon and flake. Bake potatoes as usual; cool slightly. Cut in half lengthwise and scoop out cooked potato, leaving shell intact. Beat cooked potato with skim milk until fluffy; add more milk if necessary. Stir in salmon, dill, garlic salt and pepper. Spoon into potato shells and sprinkle with paprika. Return to hot oven and bake until heated through.   *Makes 6 servings*

Calories per half = Approx. 169

*DEMING'S, DOUBLE Q or GILLNETTERSBEST Salmon may be substituted.

SALMON BURGERS

3-oz. package MANISCHEWITZ Potato Pancake Mix
2 eggs
1 cup water
1 pound can salmon, drained and flaked
1 Tbsp. minced parsley
Oil for frying

Combine potato pancake mix with eggs and water as directed on box, using the 2 eggs instead of the usual 1. Blend in salmon and parsley. Heat oil, ⅛-inch deep, in a large skillet. Drop salmon mixture, by large spoonful, into skillet. Brown on both sides.   *Makes 10*

BASIC BEST SALMON LOAF

1 can (15½-oz.) salmon
2 cups soft bread crumbs
⅓ cup finely minced onion
¼ cup milk
2 eggs
2 tablespoons minced parsley
1 tablespoon lemon juice
¼ teaspoon *each* salt and dill weed
Dash pepper

Drain salmon, reserving 2 tablespoons liquid; flake. Combine all ingredients. Place in well-greased 8½ × 4½ × 2½-inch loaf pan or shape into loaf on greased baking pan. Bake at 350°F 45 minutes.   *Makes 4 to 6 servings*

VARIATION:
SALMON PATTIES

Prepare salmon mixture as above. Shape into eight 1-inch thick patties. Pan-fry on both sides in 2 tablespoons oil or butter until golden brown.

Favorite recipe from **Alaska Seafood Marketing Institute**

SALMON PATTIES

1 can (16 ounces) salmon
½ cup chopped onion
2 tablespoons CRISCO® Shortening
⅔ cup fine dry bread crumbs
2 eggs, beaten
¼ cup snipped fresh parsley
1 teaspoon dry mustard
3 tablespoons CRISCO® Shortening
Lemony-Cheese Sauce*

Drain salmon, reserving ⅓ cup liquid; discard bones and skin; flake meat. Cook onion in 2 tablespoons CRISCO® till tender. Add reserved liquid, ⅓ cup of the crumbs, eggs, parsley, mustard, and salmon; mix well. Shape mixture into 6 patties; roll in remaining bread crumbs. In skillet, melt 3 tablespoons CRISCO®. Brown patties over medium heat; turn and brown other side. Serve with Lemony-Cheese Sauce.   *Serves 6*

*LEMONY-CHEESE SAUCE

In saucepan, melt 2 tablespoons CRISCO®; stir in 2 tablespoons flour, ½ teaspoon salt, and dash pepper. Add 1 cup milk; stir over low heat until thickened. Stir moderate amount of hot mixture into 2 beaten egg yolks. Return to hot mixture. Stir in ½ cup shredded sharp process American cheese and 2 tablespoons lemon juice till cheese melts.

SALMON CURRY
(Low Calorie)

	Calories
1 15½-oz. can Pink DOUBLE Q Pink Salmon*	554
1 cup chicken broth	12
½ cup chopped onion	22
½ cup chopped green pepper	16
1 clove garlic, minced	—
1 teaspoon curry powder	6
¼ cup flour	128
1 cup skim milk	90
2 cups cubed cantaloupe or other suitable melon	96
1 teaspoon lemon juice	4
¼ teaspoon salt	—
Chopped parsley	—
	928

Drain salmon; separate into bite size pieces. Combine chicken broth, onion, green pepper, garlic and curry powder in saucepan and cook until onion is tender. Stir flour into milk and add to chicken broth; cook, stirring until sauce is smooth and thickened. Add salmon, melon, lemon juice and salt; cook a few minutes longer. Serve over hot cooked rice if desired and garnish with parsley.   *Makes 5 servings*

Calories per serving = Approx. 186

*GILNETTERSBEST, HUMPTY DUMPTY or DEMING'S Salmon may be substituted.

SALMON LOAF WITH SAUCE

Loaf:
1 can (15½ oz.) salmon, drained (reserve ¼ cup liquid)
⅓ cup finely chopped onion
2 tablespoons butter or margarine
1 can (10¾ oz.) condensed cream of celery soup, undiluted, divided
2 eggs, beaten
2 tablespoons lemon juice
¾ cup **Instant or Regular RALSTON®**
2 tablespoons snipped parsley
1 teaspoon dry mustard
⅛ teaspoon pepper

Sauce:
3 tablespoons milk
¼ teaspoon lemon juice
⅛ teaspoon Worcestershire sauce
1 tablespoon snipped parsley

LOAF:

To prepare loaf, preheat oven to 350°. Grease 8½ x 4½ x 2½-inch loaf pan. Line bottom with greased wax paper. Remove skin and bones from salmon. Flake fine. Sauté onion in butter about 5 minutes or until tender. Add to salmon. Reserve ½ cup undiluted soup for sauce. Combine remaining soup with salmon. Add reserved salmon liquid and remaining ingredients. Mix well. Pour into loaf pan. Bake about 50 minutes or until lightly browned and firm.

Makes 6 servings

SAUCE:

To prepare sauce, in small saucepan combine reserved ½ cup soup and sauce ingredients. Place over low heat until heated through. Stir occasionally. Serve with salmon loaf.

SPINACH PICKLE SALMON ROLL

¼ cup butter or margarine
½ cup flour
1¾ cups milk
½ teaspoon salt
Dash pepper
Dash cayenne
5 egg yolks
5 egg whites
⅛ teaspoon cream of tartar
1 package (9 ounces) frozen creamed spinach, thawed
1 can (16 ounces) salmon, drained and flaked
¾ cup chopped dill pickles
Dilled Sour Cream*

Grease a 15½" × 10½" jelly roll pan. Line bottom with waxed paper; grease and flour. Melt butter in saucepan; mix in flour. Gradually stir in milk, salt, pepper and cayenne; cook, over medium heat, stirring constantly, until sauce boils. Remove from heat. Beat egg yolks; stir in small amount of sauce and return to saucepan. Cool to lukewarm. Beat egg whites and cream of tartar until stiff but not dry; fold into sauce. Spread evenly in prepared pan. Bake in 400° F. oven 30 minutes.

While roll is baking, combine spinach, salmon and pickles in medium saucepan; heat to simmering. Remove from heat.

Loosen edge of roll with sharp knife; invert onto clean towel. Carefully peel off paper. Spread filling on top. Roll jelly roll fashion from long sides. Serve immediately with Dilled Sour Cream.

Makes 8-10 servings

(Continued)

*DILLED SOUR CREAM

Combine 1 cup sour cream and 2 tablespoons dill pickle liquid.

Note: Roll can be prepared ahead of time and then heated in 200° F. oven 30 minutes.

Favorite recipe from **Pickle Packers International**

TUNA CROQUETTES

3 tablespoons **CRISCO® Shortening**
¼ cup flour
⅔ cup milk
2 tablespoons finely chopped onion
1 tablespoon snipped parsley
2 teaspoons lemon juice
¼ teaspoon salt
Dash pepper
Dash paprika
2 cans (6¼ or 7 ounces each) tuna, drained and flaked
⅔ cup fine dry bread crumbs
1 egg, beaten
1 package (8 ounces) frozen peas with cream sauce
CRISCO® Shortening for deep frying

In saucepan, melt the 3 tablespoons **CRISCO®**. Blend in the flour. Add the milk. Cook and stir till thickened and bubbly. Add the onion, parsley, lemon juice, salt, pepper, and paprika; stir in the tuna. Cover and chill thoroughly, about 3 hours. With wet hands, shape tuna mixture into 8 cones, using about ¼ cup for each. Roll in crumbs. Dip into a mixture of beaten egg and 2 tablespoons water; roll in crumbs again. Prepare peas with cream sauce according to package directions; keep hot. Meanwhile, fry a few croquettes at a time in deep **CRISCO®** heated to 350° till brown and hot, about 3 minutes. Drain on paper toweling. Spoon pea sauce over croquettes.

Makes 4 servings

TUNA VERACRUZ

1½ tablespoons olive oil
1 clove garlic, minced
1 onion, thinly sliced
1 can (1 pound) whole tomatoes, drained, crushed
1 tablespoon tomato paste
1 small bay leaf
¼ teaspoon dry oregano
10 green olives with pimiento, cut in half
1 tablespoon capers
4 ounces canned whole green chilies, cut in strips
½ teaspoon hot pepper sauce
2 tablespoons lemon juice
1 12½ or 13 ounce can **CHICKEN OF THE SEA® Tuna**, drained
4 cups cooked white rice

Pour olive oil into heavy 12 inch skillet. Sauté garlic and onions over moderate heat for 3 to 5 minutes. Add tomatoes, tomato paste (freeze leftover tomato paste for future use), bay leaf, oregano, olives, capers, chilies, hot pepper sauce, and lemon juice.

Cook, stirring, over moderate heat for 15 minutes or until mixture is thick and some of the liquid has evaporated. Add tuna and heat thoroughly.

Prepare rice according to package directions. Serve at once, or refrigerate and reheat before serving.

Serves 4

ORIENTAL SWEET AND SOUR TUNA

1 8-ounce can pineapple chunks, packed in natural juice
1 tablespoon cornstarch
¼ teaspoon salt
¼ cup cider vinegar
2 tablespoons **SWEETLITE**™ **Fructose**
2 teaspoons soy sauce
½ cup sliced fresh mushrooms
½ bell pepper thinly sliced
½ onion thinly sliced
1 6-ounce can water chestnuts, drained and thinly sliced
2 7-ounce cans white tuna packed in water, drained
2 cups cooked rice

Drain the juice from the pineapple chunks and pour it in a large saucepan. Add the cornstarch, salt and vinegar and stir until the cornstarch is completely dissolved. Place the pan on medium heat and cook, stirring constantly, until the sauce has thickened. Add all other ingredients except the tuna and cooked rice. Cook until the vegetables are done but still crisp—about 5 minutes. Break the tuna into bite sized chunks and add it to the other ingredients. Mix well and serve each portion over ½ cup of the cooked rice.

Makes 4 servings

EATWELL® MACKEREL LOAF

1 can **EATWELL**® **Mackerel**
¾ cup bread crumbs
¾ cup milk
½ cup coarsely chopped gherkins or pickle relish
2 eggs
1½ teaspoons salt
1½ Tbsp. melted butter or margarine

1 teaspoon minced onion
1½ cups medium white sauce
2 hard cooked eggs, sliced
6 stuffed olives, sliced

Flake mackerel. Add crumbs, milk, gherkins, eggs, salt and melted butter or margarine. Mix well. Pack into greased loaf pan. Set in shallow pan of hot water and bake in moderate oven (350°) about 30 minutes or until loaf becomes firm. Turn out on hot platter. Add onion to white sauce and pour over loaf. Arrange egg slices on top with an olive slice on top of each.

CHEESY FISH STICKS

1 (1-lb.) package **BOOTH**® **Fish Sticks**
1½ tablespoons butter or margarine
4 teaspoons flour
¼ teaspoon salt
Dash white pepper
¾ cup milk
1 (4-oz.) package shredded Cheddar cheese
Crumbled bacon bits

Bake fish sticks according to package directions. While fish sticks are baking, prepare cheese sauce. Melt butter or margarine in saucepan. Blend in flour and seasonings. Add milk gradually and bring to boil, stirring constantly. Cook for 1 minute. Add Cheddar cheese and allow to melt. Pour cheese sauce over baked fish sticks; top with crumbled bacon bits. Return to oven for a few minutes until lightly browned.

Shellfish

CRAB & MUSHROOM CASSEROLE

¼ cup butter or margarine
¼ cup chopped onion
¼ cup chopped celery
½ pound mushrooms, sliced
3 tablespoons flour
½ teaspoon salt
Dash ground ginger
2 cups **WELCH'S**® **White Grape Juice**
2 egg yolks, slightly beaten
1 pound crabmeat

Melt butter in large skillet. Add onion, celery and mushrooms and cook until just tender. Blend in flour, salt and ginger. Add white grape juice and cook and stir until thickened. Add a little of the hot sauce to the egg yolks, return to sauce and cook until heated through. Add and mix in crabmeat. Pour into shallow 1½ quart baking dish. Bake in 350° oven about 30 minutes.

Makes 6 servings

CRAB MEAT NEWBURG

6 Tbsp. butter
3 Tbsp. flour
¾ tsp. salt
Dash of cayenne pepper
2 cups milk
½ cup heavy cream
3 egg yolks slightly beaten
2 Tbsp. tomato paste
3 cans **HIGH SEA**® **Crab Meat**

Melt 3 Tbsp. butter in double boiler. Blend in flour, salt, and cayenne pepper and cook for 5 minutes. Remove top section of boiler from heat and gradually add milk, stirring until smooth. Replace top section over simmering water and cook for 45 minutes, stirring often. Combine cream with beaten egg yolks and ½ cup of white sauce. Pour back into boiler, stir and cook for 2 more minutes. Add tomato paste and mix well. Melt remaining 3 Tbsp. butter in a sauce pan, add drained crab meat, and heat over a low fire about 3-4 minutes, adding sherry and brandy during last minute. Stir into heated sauce and serve. *Serves 6*

LEMON LUAU MUSHROOM & CRABMEAT

2 teaspoons **HOUSE OF TSANG**® **Lemon Luau Seasoning**
2 cups fresh mushrooms, sliced
2 cups crab meat
2 cloves garlic, lightly mashed
2 tablespoons peanut oil or butter
2 tablespoons dry sherry (optional)

Heat wok at medium heat for 2 minutes. Pour in oil and wait a few seconds. Brown garlic and stir in mushrooms and **Lemon Luau Seasoning**, cook 2 minutes. Add in crab meat, cook another 2 minutes. Pour in sherry, stir well and serve.

Serves 2 with rice

BAKED SQUASH WITH SEAFOOD STUFFING

2 small acorn squash
3 Tbsp. margarine
¾ cup finely chopped celery
3 Tbsp. finely chopped onions
¾ cup crab, shrimp or tuna (drain if canned)
½ tsp. salt
¼ tsp. pepper
½ tsp. Worcestershire sauce
2 cups **ROMAN MEAL® Bread Cubes** (3 to 4 slices)
¾ cup (3 oz.) grated Cheddar cheese

Clean squash. Cut in half; remove seeds and strings. Brush 1 Tbsp. of the margarine over bottom of 9 × 9 × 2-inch baking dish. Place squash, cut side down, in dish. Cover; bake until tender in moderate oven (375°) about 30 minutes. Meanwhile, sauté celery and onion in remaining margarine until tender. In medium bowl combine seafood, salt, pepper, Worcestershire, bread and ¼ cup of the cheese. When squash is tender, scoop meat out of shell; mash and season with ½ tsp. salt, ¼ tsp. pepper and 1 Tbsp. milk. Line shells with mashed squash. Place ¾ cup stuffing in each squash half; top with remaining cheese. Return to baking dish cut side up. Cover; bake at 350° F. about 25 minutes.

IMPOSSIBLE SEAFOOD PIE

1 package (6 ounces) frozen crabmeat or shrimp,* thawed and drained
1 cup shredded process sharp American cheese (about 4 ounces)
1 package (3 ounces) cream cheese, cut into about ¼-inch cubes
¼ cup sliced green onions
1 jar (2 ounces) chopped pimiento, drained, if desired
2 cups milk
1 cup **BISQUICK® Baking Mix**
4 eggs
¾ teaspoon salt
Dash of nutmeg

Heat oven to 400°. Grease pie plate, 10x1½ inches. Mix crabmeat, cheeses, onions and pimiento in plate. Beat remaining ingredients until smooth, 15 seconds in blender on high or 1 minute with hand beater. Pour into plate. Bake until knife inserted in center comes out clean, 35 to 40 minutes. Cool 5 minutes.   *6 to 8 servings*

*1 can (6 ounces) crabmeat, drained and cartilage removed, or 1 can (4½ ounces) shrimp, well rinsed and drained, can be substituted for the frozen crabmeat or shrimp.

VARIATION:

*IMPOSSIBLE TUNA PIE

Substitute 1 can (6½ ounces) tuna, drained, for the crabmeat.

JAPANESE STEAMED ROCK LOBSTER

3 pkgs. (8 oz. ea.) frozen **SOUTH AFRICAN ROCK LOBSTER Tails**
6 mushrooms, cut into slices
6 scallions, cut into long thin strips
1 cup thinly sliced celery
1 bunch broccoli, trimmed and cut into flowerets
1 tablespoon soy sauce
1 envelope dehydrated chicken broth
¼ cup water

With scissors remove thin underside membrane. Push a bamboo skewer lengthwise through tail to prevent curling. Place a colander over boiling water in a large pot, or use a steamer. Put rock lobster tails into colander and place vegetables on top and around tails. Mix soy sauce, broth and water and brush over tails and vegetables. Cover pot and let steam for 20 minutes or until vegetables are tender-crisp and tail meat has lost its translucency and is opaque. Serve with fried rice.   *Yield: 6 servings*
Favorite recipe from **South African Rock Lobster Service Corp.**

SOUTH AFRICAN ROCK LOBSTER THERMIDOR

6 (3 oz. ea.) **SOUTH AFRICAN ROCK LOBSTER Tails**
1 tablespoon whole pickling spice
Boiling water
¼ cup butter
⅓ cup flour
1 can (10½ oz.) condensed chicken broth
¾ cup heavy cream
2 tablespoons sherry
1 tablespoon brandy
2 cans (4 oz. each) button mushrooms, drained
Salt and pepper
¼ cup grated Parmesan cheese

Parboil frozen rock lobster tails by dropping into boiling salted water to which pickling spice has been added. When water reboils, drain immediately and drench with cold water. Cut away underside membrane and remove meat. Dice. Reserve shells. Melt butter and stir in flour. Gradually stir in chicken broth and cream. Add sherry and brandy. Cook over low heat stirring constantly until sauce bubbles and thickens. Fold in mushrooms and diced rock lobster. Season to taste with salt and pepper. Reheat and then spoon mixture into reserved rock lobster shells. Sprinkle with Parmesan cheese and broil until golden brown. Garnish with parsley sprigs.   *Yield: 6 servings*

SCALLOPS AU GRATIN

4 **BAYS® English Muffins**
1 pound scallops (sliced in half)
1 cup chicken stock
4 tablespoons salted butter
¼ cup chopped green pepper
¼ cup chopped onion
¼ teaspoon paprika
3 tablespoons all-purpose flour
1 cup whipping cream
1 pimiento, chopped (approx. ¼ cup)
2 tablespoons sherry
¼ teaspoon salt
Dash pepper
Dash nutmeg
Parmesan cheese
Bread crumbs
Butter

Put scallops and chicken stock in a large frying pan and poach until scallops are opaque. Remove scallops. Reserve 1 cup of the poaching liquid. In the same frying pan, melt butter and sauté green pepper and onion, over low heat, until soft. Turn up heat to medium; stir in paprika and flour. Stir constantly for about 1 minute. Take pan off heat and stir in reserved poaching liquid and cream. Return pan to the heat and stir constantly until mixture thickens and comes to a full boil. Add pimientos, sherry, salt, pepper and nutmeg. Stir well. Fold in cooked scallops. Keep
(Continued)

mixture warm. Toast and lightly butter 4 **BAYS® English Muffins**. Place two halves in each of four au gratin dishes. Pour ⅔ cup of the scallop mixture in each dish. Sprinkle with parmesan cheese and bread crumbs. Dot with butter. Broil until lightly browned and bubbly. Serve immediately. *Serves 4*

COCONUT FRIED SHRIMP

1 lb. small raw shrimp, shelled and deveined
⅓ cup lemon juice
½ tsp. salt
⅓ tsp. ground ginger
3 tsp. curry powder
1¾ cups flour
2 tsp. baking powder
1¼ cups skimmed milk
½ cup **COCO CASA® Cream of Coconut**
3½ oz. can flaked coconut
Fat for frying

Marinate shrimp in lemon juice, salt, ginger and curry powder for 1 to 2 hours. Drain well. Prepare batter of 1½ cups flour, baking powder, milk and Cream of Coconut. Coat shrimp with remaining flour; dip in prepared batter and then dip lightly into flaked coconut. Fry in deep fat (hot) about 2-3 minutes. Fry only about 6 shrimp at a time.

BATTER-FRIED SHRIMP

2 eggs
½ cup milk
1 cup all-purpose flour, stirred before measuring
1 teaspoon baking powder
1 teaspoon salt
2 teaspoons cooking oil
2 pounds fresh or frozen whole shrimp
Oil or shortening for deep-fat frying
Orange Sauce (recipe follows)
Grape-Horseradish Sauce (recipe follows)
Plum Hot (recipe follows)

Beat together eggs and milk until frothy. Sift together flour, baking powder, and salt. Add to egg mixture; add oil and beat until mixture is smooth and well-blended. Set aside. Remove shells from shrimp, leaving tails on. If shrimp are frozen, remove shells under running cold water. Cut partway through lengthwise along outside curve. Lift out vein; wash shrimp and flatten so they stay open. Drain well on paper towels. Place enough oil or shortening to more than cover shrimp in a deep-fat fryer or kettle and heat to 375°F. Dip shrimp into batter, one at a time, and fry, a few at a time, about 4 minutes, or until golden brown and puffy. Drain on paper towels. Serve immediately with Orange Sauce, Grape-Horseradish Sauce, or Plum Hot. *Makes 6 servings*

ORANGE SAUCE

1 cup **SMUCKER'S Sweet Orange Marmalade**
1 clove garlic
1 piece whole ginger root or ½ teaspoon ground ginger

In a saucepan, combine all ingredients and cook over low heat, stirring constantly, until mixture bubbles. Remove garlic and ginger root. *Makes about 1 cup*

GRAPE-HORSERADISH SAUCE

1 cup **SMUCKER'S Grape Jelly**
1 tablespoon prepared horseradish
¼ cup ketchup

Combine all ingredients. *Makes about 1 cup*

(Continued)

PLUM HOT

1 cup **SMUCKER'S Plum Preserves**
1 to 2 cloves garlic, as desired, very finely minced
2 teaspoons soy sauce
¼ teaspoon pepper

In a saucepan, combine all ingredients and cook over low heat, stirring occasionally, at least 5 minutes, or until garlic is cooked. Remove from heat and cool slightly. *Makes about 1 cup*

TEMPURA

Vegetable oil
3 cups **BISQUICK® Baking Mix**
1½ cups water
2 eggs
½ pound shelled and deveined fresh shrimp, 1 can (7 ounces) large shrimp, rinsed and drained, or 1 package (8 ounces) frozen shrimp, thawed
½ pound sole fillet, cut into 1½-inch pieces
1 cup pared eggplant strips, 2 x ¼-inch
1 cup parsley sprigs
4 ounces mushrooms, cut into halves
2 carrots, cut into 2 x ¼-inch strips
1 green pepper, cut into 2 x ¼-inch strips
Sauce*
Shredded radish, drained

Heat oil (1 inch) in electric skillet or wok to 350°. Beat baking mix, water and eggs with hand beater until smooth. Pat shrimp, sole and vegetables dry with paper towel. Dip into batter, allowing excess batter to drip into bowl. Fry several pieces at a time in hot oil, turning once, until golden brown, 2 to 3 minutes; drain on paper towel. Dip into Sauce, then into radish. *6 servings*

*SAUCE

Mix ¼ cup soy sauce, ¼ cup white wine vinegar and 1 tablespoon finely chopped green onion.

Note: Tempura can be made ahead. Wrap in aluminum foil and refrigerate or freeze no longer than 24 hours. To reheat: Heat oven to 400°. Place refrigerated or frozen food on ungreased cookie sheet. Heat until hot, refrigerated food about 15 minutes, frozen food about 25 minutes; drain on paper towel.

SHRIMP ELEGANT

3 tablespoons butter or margarine
⅓ cup finely chopped onion
1 garlic clove, minced
1 small can sliced mushrooms, drained
½ cup chopped green pepper
1 pound **BOOTH® Peeled and Deveined Shrimp**, frozen
1 (10½-oz.) can condensed Cheddar cheese soup
⅓ cup half-and-half
¼ cup dry sherry

Melt butter in large saucepan; sauté onion, garlic, mushrooms and green pepper until tender but not brown, about 5 minutes. Add shrimp and sauté another 5-7 minutes. Drain off liquid. Stir in soup; gradually blend in half-and-half and wine. Cook, stirring occasionally until heated through. Serve over rice.

BEER-BROILED SHRIMP

¾ cup **COORS® Beer**
3 tablespoons cooking oil
2 tablespoons snipped parsley
4 teaspoons Worcestershire sauce
1 clove garlic, minced
½ teaspoon salt
⅛ teaspoon pepper
2 pounds large shrimp, unshelled

Combine **COORS®**, oil, parsley, Worcestershire, garlic, ½ teaspoon salt and ⅛ teaspoon pepper. Add shrimp; stir. Cover; let stand at room temperature for 1 hour. Drain, reserving marinade. Place shrimp on well-greased broiler rack; broil 4 to 5 inches from heat for 4 minutes. Turn; brush with marinade. Broil 2 to 4 minutes more or till bright pink.

Makes 6 servings

SHRIMP CREOLE

2 Tbsp. butter or margarine
¾ cup chopped onion
½ cup chopped green pepper
¼ cup chopped celery
1 6-oz. can tomato paste
2 cups water
2-3 tsp. **BALTIMORE SPICE OLD BAY Seasoning,**
  depending on heat preference
1 tsp. salt
1 bay leaf, whole or crushed
2 cups cleaned cooked shrimp
3 cups hot cooked rice or spaghetti

In 10″ skillet sauté onion and green pepper in butter until tender. Stir in remaining ingredients except shrimp and rice or spaghetti. Cook over low heat stirring occasionally, about 20 minutes. Stir in shrimp; heat through about 5-8 minutes. Serve over rice or spaghetti.

6 servings

CURRIED SHRIMP WITH APPLES

4 Tbsp. butter (or margarine)
1½ cups **LUCKY LEAF® Sliced Apples**
3 or 4 tsp. curry powder
¼ cup flour
3¾ cups milk
2 tsp. salt
4 cups cooked, cleaned shrimp (2 lbs. in shell)
5 cups hot cooked rice
Paprika

Melt butter in skillet. Add coarsely diced apples and simmer a few minutes. Mix flour and curry powder and stir into apples. Slowly add milk. Cook while stirring until thick. Add salt and shrimp and heat slowly. Serve with hot fluffy rice sprinkled with paprika.

Serves 8

SHRIMP TERIYAKI

2 lb. **ATALANTA Frozen Shrimp,** raw, shelled,
  deveined
1 cup pineapple juice
6 Tbsp. soy sauce
½ cup vegetable oil

Marinate shrimp in juice, soy sauce and oil for 20 minutes. Drain and broil shrimps 4 minutes on each side. Serve with rice.

Yield: 6 servings

SHRIMP SCAMPI WITH ZUCCHINI

½ cup **LAND O LAKES® Sweet Cream Butter**
¼ cup chopped fresh parsley
2 Tbsp. chopped onion
1½ tsp. garlic salt
½ tsp. dill weed
1 Tbsp. lemon juice
24 fresh, med. size (3-inch) green shrimp, shelled,
  deveined, rinsed
2 cups (2 med.) sliced (¼-inch) zucchini
Cooked, hot rice

In heavy 10-inch skillet melt butter over med. heat (3 to 6 min.). Add remaining ingredients *except* rice; stir to blend. Cook over med. heat, stirring occasionally, until shrimp and zucchini are tender (5 to 7 min.). To serve, spoon 6 shrimp with zucchini and butter sauce over cooked rice.

Yield: 4 servings

SPEEDY SHRIMP ORIENTAL

1 pound **BOOTH® Tender Young Shrimp,** frozen
2 10-oz. packages frozen Chinese vegetables

Cook shrimp according to package directions; drain. In large saucepan cook vegetables as directed on the package. Add cooked shrimp to vegetables and heat through. Serve over rice or Chinese noodles.

PEPPERS & SHRIMP

1 package (6 ounces) **MRS. PAUL'S® Fried Shrimp**
1 tablespoon vegetable oil
1 medium green pepper, cut into bite size strips
3 scallions with tops, chopped
1 medium tomato, chopped in small pieces
⅛ teaspoon ginger
¼ teaspoon garlic powder
1 tablespoon soy sauce
¼ cup water
1 tablespoon cornstarch
½ cup chicken broth
2 cups cooked rice

Prepare **MRS. PAUL'S® Fried Shrimp** as directed on package. Sauté green pepper and scallions in vegetable oil for approximately 5 minutes. Add remaining ingredients except cornstarch, chicken broth and rice. Blend cornstarch and chicken broth; add to pan and simmer mixture until thickened. Place cooked shrimp on rice and pour sauce on top.

Serves 4

SHRIMP JAMBALAYA

12 oz. **BOOTH® Peeled & Deveined Shrimp,**
  uncooked
½ green pepper, chopped
3 slices bacon, diced
½ garlic clove, minced
½ onion, chopped
¼ tsp. Worcestershire sauce
¼ tsp. chili powder
Salt and pepper to taste
1 lb. can tomatoes
1½ cups rice, cooked

Fry bacon; add green pepper, onion and garlic and cook until tender. Pour off grease and add seasonings and tomatoes. Simmer

15 minutes. Add shrimp and cook 5-7 minutes or until shrimp are pink and have lost their translucency. Do not overcook as shrimp will become tough. Serve over hot cooked rice.

STIR FRIED SHRIMP AND VEGETABLES

Stir fry 1 pound of any frozen oriental style vegetable mix in 2 tablespoons of hot oil. Cook for 2 minutes. Add 6 ounces thawed **BRILLIANT Cooked Shrimp** and heat 1 additional minute. Serve with white or fried rice. Serve with duck sauce, soy sauce and sharp mustard. *Serves 3-4*

GLAZED SHRIMP KABOBS WITH FRUITY GLAZE

2 pounds raw large shrimp (14 to 15 per pound), fresh or frozen
18 lime or lemon wedges

Sauce:
½ cup apricot preserves
½ cup orange juice
½ cup lemon juice
¼ cup honey
1 tablespoon cornstarch
2 to 3 drops hot pepper sauce
1 teaspoon chopped fresh or dried mint, optional
Fruit Kabobs (banana slices, orange wedges, fresh pineapple chunks, and melon chunks), optional

Thaw shrimp if frozen. Peel raw shrimp leaving tails on. Remove sand veins and wash. Thread the following on metal or bamboo skewers: a lime or lemon wedge, 3 shrimp, a lime or lemon wedge, 3 more shrimp and another citrus wedge. Cover tails of shrimp with aluminum foil. Place kabobs on a tray, cover and refrigerate until ready to cook. Prepare sauce.

SAUCE:
Combine preserves, orange and lemon juice, honey, cornstarch, and hot pepper sauce; stir until no cornstarch lumps remain. Cook until sauce thickens slightly, stirring constantly; simmer 3 to 4 minutes.

Broil kabobs on hibachi or in the oven (see below). Serve with favorite fresh fruit kabobs, if desired. *Makes 5 to 6 servings*

Shrimp Kabobs Cooked on Hibachi or Small Grill: Assemble kabobs as directed. Arrange kabobs on well-greased hibachi. Brush with sauce; sprinkle with mint, if desired. Cook about 4 inches from moderate heat about 5 minutes. Brush with sauce; sprinkle with mint if desired. Turn and cook 4 to 5 minutes longer or until shrimp is cooked, turns pink and is lightly browned. Remove foil from tails. Serve any remaining sauce with kabobs.

Shrimp Kabobs Broiled in Oven-Broiler: Assemble kabobs as directed. Place kabobs on well-greased broiler pan. Brush with sauce; sprinkle with mint, if desired. Broil about 4 inches from source of heat for 5 minutes. Turn, brush with sauce and sprinkle

with mint, if desired. Broil 4 to 5 minutes longer or until shrimp is cooked, turns pink and is lightly browned. Remove foil from tails. Serve any remaining sauce with kabobs.

Favorite recipe from **National Marine Fisheries Service**

VERACRUZ SHRIMP

1 pound fresh medium shrimp
1 large green pepper
3 tablespoons vegetable oil, divided usage
1 small onion, chopped
1 can (4 oz.) **OLD EL PASO®** Chopped Green Chilies
1 jar (16 oz.) **OLD EL PASO®** Taco Sauce
2 medium tomatoes, chopped
12 pimiento stuffed olives
1½ teaspoons capers
¼ teaspoon cumin
1 bay leaf
1 teaspoon salt
½ teaspoon sugar
Lime juice
Hot cooked rice

Peel shrimp and remove veins; set aside. Cut green pepper into 1½ x ½-inch strips. Heat 1 tablespoon oil in a large skillet. Add green pepper and onion. Cook until onion is translucent. Add green chilies, taco sauce, tomatoes, olives, capers, cumin, bay leaf, salt, and sugar. Bring to a boil. Reduce heat and simmer for 10 minutes. Heat 2 tablespoons of oil in a large skillet. Add shrimp. Cook over medium heat stirring constantly about 3 minutes or until shrimp turns pink. Sprinkle a few drops of lime juice over shrimp. Add sauce. Cook 2 minutes longer. Serve immediately over hot rice. *Makes 4 servings*

SHRIMP ORIENTAL

¼ cup margarine or butter
2 cups sliced fresh mushrooms (about 8 ounces)
1 cup sliced celery
½ cup finely chopped onion
8 ounces raw shrimp, peeled and deveined
⅓ cup **REALEMON®** Lemon Juice from Concentrate
2 tablespoons brown sugar
1 tablespoon soy sauce
¼ teaspoon ground ginger
1 tablespoon cornstarch
¼ cup water
1 (6 ounce) package frozen pea pods, thawed
Hot cooked rice

In large skillet, melt margarine. Add mushrooms, celery and onion; cook until onion is transparent. Stir in shrimp; cook about 3 minutes. Combine **REALEMON®**, sugar, soy sauce and ginger; stir into shrimp mixture. Blend cornstarch with water; gradually stir into shrimp mixture. Add pea pods; bring to a boil. Cook and stir about 1 minute. Serve over rice with additional soy sauce if desired. Refrigerate leftovers. *Makes 4 servings*

Main Dishes

SUMMER MIXED GRILL

MEAT KABOBS

½ cup **WISH-BONE® Italian Dressing**
¼ cup dry white or red wine
1 teaspoon thyme
2 bay leaves
1½ pounds pork, chicken, lamb or beef cubes
Bacon slices (optional)

In large shallow baking dish, blend real Italian dressing, wine, thyme and bay leaves; add meat cubes. Cover and marinate in refrigerator, turning occasionally, 4 hours or overnight. Remove meat, reserving marinade. On skewers, alternately thread meat cubes and bacon. Grill or broil, turning and basting frequently with reserved marinade until done.   *Makes about 6 servings*

VEGETABLE KABOBS

½ cup **WISH-BONE® Italian Dressing**
1 teaspoon finely chopped dill weed
3 cups assorted fresh vegetables

In large shallow baking dish, combine all ingredients. Cover and marinate in refrigerator, turning occasionally, 4 hours or overnight. Remove vegetables, reserving marinade. On skewers, alternately thread vegetables. During last 10 minutes of meat kabob cooking time, begin to grill or broil. Turn and baste frequently with reserved marinade until done.   *Makes about 6 servings*

CURRIED KABOBS WITH LEMON MARINADE

2 lbs. lamb, pork, or beef, cut into 2-inch cubes
½ cup **MINUTE MAID® 100% Pure Lemon Juice**
¼ cup salad oil
2 Tbsp. grated onion
1 clove garlic, crushed
1 tsp. ground ginger
1 tsp. salt
1½ tsp. curry powder
½ tsp. cayenne pepper
16 fresh mushroom caps
2 large green peppers, seeded and cut into 1-inch squares
2 Tbsp. butter
16 cherry tomatoes
4 onions, quartered
32 pineapple chunks (16-oz. can)

Place the meat cubes in a glass dish; cover with a marinade made of **MINUTE MAID® 100% Pure Lemon Juice**, oil, and seasonings. Marinate for at least 4 hours. When ready to cook the kabobs, sauté the mushrooms and peppers in butter over medium heat and remove the meat from the marinade. Using skewers 12 inches or longer, assemble 8 kabobs, alternating meat, vegetables, and pineapple on the skewers. Grill over medium heat or 2-3 inches from heat in a broiler 10-15 minutes, turning and brushing with marinade several times. Serve over cooked brown rice.
Yield: 8 servings

TROPICAL KABOBS

1 lb. **JIMMY DEAN® Special Recipe Sausage**
1 small can (8½ oz.) sliced pineapple, drained (reserve syrup)
1 Tbsp. brown sugar
1 Tbsp. vinegar
1 Tbsp. soy sauce
1 tsp. cornstarch
4 green onions, cut into 2-inch pieces
1 green pepper, cut into 2-inch pieces

Shape sausage into 24 balls. Place in glass bowl. Mix reserved pineapple syrup, brown sugar, vinegar and soy sauce until sugar is dissolved. Pour over meatballs and refrigerate at least 3 hours.

Drain marinade from meatballs into small saucepan; stir in cornstarch. Cook, stirring constantly, until mixture thickens and boils. Boil and stir 1 minute. Remove sauce from heat and set aside.

Cut pineapple slices into quarters. On each of six metal skewers, alternate 4 meatballs with pineapple pieces and vegetables; brush kabobs with part of sauce. Grill over medium fire for 20 minutes. Brush occasionally with sauce and gently push with fork to turn. Serve with rice.

RUSSIAN BEEF STROGANOFF WITH WILD RICE

1 cup uncooked **CHIEFTAIN Wild Rice**
4 cups cold water
1 teaspoon salt
2 lbs. sirloin steak (or round steak)
½ cup butter or margarine
1 lb. fresh mushrooms, sliced
2 large sweet onions, chopped
2 8-oz. cans tomato sauce
1 cup cultured sour cream
1 teaspoon salt
2 teaspoons Worcestershire sauce
Dash pepper

Cook wild rice as in basic preparation*. Cut meat in very thin slices; brown in butter. Add mushrooms and onions; remove from heat. Combine tomato sauce, sour cream and seasonings; add to meat mixture. Cover and simmer for one hour. Serve over buttered hot wild rice.

*BASIC PREPARATION:
1. Wash wild rice thoroughly with warm tap water; rinse and drain in strainer until water runs clear. Can also pre-soak several hours.
2. Place wild rice in medium sauce pan with 4 cups cold water and 1 teaspoon salt and bring to boil. Chicken or beef broth can be substituted for the water.
3. Simmer covered for about 45 minutes until tender but not mushy. Cooking time may vary some.
4. Drain and rinse.

PENNY-WISE STROGANOFF

1 package (1½ oz.) **DURKEE Roastin' Bag Pot Roast Gravy Mix**
2 pound chuck steak, thinly sliced
1 large onion, sliced thin
2 jars (4½ oz. each) sliced mushrooms, drained
½ cup dry red wine
½ cup water
1 cup sour cream

Preheat oven to 350°. Place chuck steak, onion, and mushrooms in oven cooking bag. Combine gravy mix with wine and water. Pour over meat. Close end of bag with twist-tie. Place in a baking dish 1½ to 2 inches deep and large enough to contain entire bag. Punch 4 small holes along top of bag. Place on rack in lower half of oven, leaving at least 10 inches between rack positions to allow for expansion of bag. Roast in preheated 350° oven for 1½ hours. Cut top of bag; remove meat and gravy to serving dish; stir in 1 cup sour cream. *Makes 5 to 6 servings*

BEEF STROGANOFF A LA NEW MILL® KLUSKI

¼ cup flour
¼ tsp. pepper
½ tsp. salt
1 pound beef sirloin cut into thin strips
¼ cup shortening
1 can condensed cream of chicken soup
1 Tbsp. Worcestershire sauce
1 (4-ounce) can sliced mushrooms, drained
¾ cup dairy sour cream
4 cups **NEW MILL® KLUSKI Noodles,** uncooked

In plastic bag, shake strips of sirloin with flour, salt and pepper. In large skillet, brown the floured strips of meat in hot shortening. Add the cream of chicken soup, mushrooms, and Worcestershire sauce. Simmer, covered, for 20 minutes. Stir in sour cream. Heat through, but do not boil.

Cook Kluski Noodles in rapidly, boiling salted water as directed on package. Drain. Serve stroganoff over the Kluski Noodles.

MAZOLA® BEEF STROGANOFF

2 tablespoons **MAZOLA® Corn Oil**
2½ pounds boneless beef chuck, cut into ¼-inch thick strips, ½-inch wide
½ pound mushrooms, sliced
1 cup finely chopped onion
2 cloves garlic, minced
1 can (28 oz.) plum tomatoes in juice
2 teaspoons salt
½ teaspoon pepper
⅓ cup **ARGO®/KINGSFORD'S® Corn Starch**
½ cup dry white wine
1 cup dairy sour cream
½ cup chopped parsley

In large skillet heat corn oil over medium heat. Add meat ¼ at a time; brown quickly on both sides. Remove meat. Add mushrooms, onion and garlic; sauté 5 minutes or until tender. Add tomatoes, salt and pepper. Simmer 10 minutes. Stir together corn starch and wine until smooth. Stir into tomato mixture. Stirring constantly, bring to boil over medium heat and boil 1 minute. Remove from heat. Stir in sour cream and parsley; add meat.
Makes 6 to 8 servings

BEEF STROGANOFF

1 (1½-lb.) round steak
2 packets **ROMANOFF® MBT® Instant Beef Broth**
¼ teaspoon garlic powder
2 tablespoons vegetable oil
½ cup chopped onion
1 jar (2½-oz.) sliced mushrooms, drained
1¼ cups water
½ teaspoon salt
2 tablespoons flour
1 cup sour cream
2 teaspoons Worcestershire sauce

With edge of saucer or meat cleaver, pound **MBT®** and garlic powder into meat. Cut meat, across the grain, into ½-inch strips. Brown quickly in hot oil; remove. Stir in the onion and mushrooms; sauté until onion is tender. Return meat to skillet and add 1 cup water and the salt. Bring to a boil; cover and simmer 45 minutes. Combine flour with the remaining ¼ cup water and stir into meat mixture. Continue to heat until thickened. Blend in sour cream and Worcestershire; heat gently. Serve over hot, cooked noodles or rice. *Makes 4 servings (about 1 cup each)*

BEEF STUFFED ZUCCHINI
(Low Calorie)

1 cup **DIET SHASTA® Ginger Ale**
2 beef bouillon cubes
1 large fresh tomato, diced (about 1 cup)
½ cup chopped onion
1 teaspoon seasoned salt
⅛ teaspoon pepper
1 teaspoon oregano, crumbled
¾ pound ground chuck
4 medium-size zucchini (about 5-inches long, 1 lb.)
¼ cup grated American cheese (optional)

Combine **DIET SHASTA®** with the next six ingredients. Simmer together 5 minutes. Brown beef in skillet. Add ¼ cup of the sauce to meat and set aside. Rinse, trim and discard stem ends from zucchini. Add zucchini to sauce and simmer, covered, 10 minutes. Cut off top of each zucchini and scoop out a little of the squash to make a shell. Add trimmings to sauce. Arrange zucchini in shallow casserole, fill with meat mixture and spoon sauce over all. Sprinkle with cheese, if desired, and bake in a 350°F oven about 20 minutes. *Makes 2 servings of two zucchini each*

287 calories per serving

STUFFED ZUCCHINI

3 lb. zucchini
1 lb. ground beef
3 tablespoons **A.1. Steak Sauce**
¼ cup chopped onion
1 clove garlic, minced
1 cup (4 oz.) shredded mild Cheddar cheese
1 jar (16 oz.) spaghetti sauce
½ cup dry bread crumbs

In boiling salted water, cook zucchini 3 minutes. Drain. Cut in half lengthwise. Scoop out seeds to form shell. Set aside. In large skillet, brown beef until crumbly. Drain. Mix in **A.1.,** onion, garlic, spaghetti sauce and ½ cheese. Fill zucchini. Arrange in 13 x 9 x 2-inch baking pan. Combine bread crumbs with remaining cheese. Sprinkle on top. Bake in preheated 350° F oven 35 minutes.
Serves 6

MISSION RICE-A-RONI® PEPPERS

1 pkg. **GOLDEN GRAIN® Chicken Flavor RICE-A-RONI®**
2½ cups water
1½ cups grated Monterey Jack cheese
2 eggs, separated
3 large green peppers
1 can (10-oz.) green chili sauce

Prepare **RICE-A-RONI®** as directed on package except use 2½ cups water. Remove from heat; stir in cheese. Quickly add beaten egg yolks; cool slightly.

Halve peppers and remove centers. Blanch in boiling water 5 minutes; drain.

Beat egg whites with a pinch of salt until stiff. Fold into **RICE-A-RONI®** mixture. Fill each pepper half with ⅔ cup **RICE-A-RONI®** mixture. Arrange in baking dish with small amount of hot water on bottom. Bake at 350°F for 25 minutes. Top with green chili sauce.   *Makes 6 servings*

MEXICAN STUFFED PEPPERS

2 medium green peppers
Boiling salted water
1 can (8 oz.) kidney beans
¼ pound ground beef
½ teaspoon chili powder
1 tablespoon oil
¾ teaspoon salt
¾ cup MINUTE® Rice
6 tablespoons grated Cheddar cheese
1 can (8 oz.) stewed tomatoes
½ teaspoon chili powder

Cut peppers in half lengthwise and remove stems and seeds. Cook in boiling salted water for 10 minutes, or until just tender. Drain and set aside.

Drain beans, reserving liquid. Add water to liquid to make ¾ cup. Brown beef lightly with ½ teaspoon chili powder in oil in small skillet; add salt and the measured liquid. Bring to a boil; stir in rice, cover and simmer 5 minutes. Stir in ¼ cup of the cheese and spoon meat mixture into peppers. Pour tomatoes, the kidney beans and ½ teaspoon chili powder into the skillet. Place stuffed peppers in the skillet; sprinkle with remaining cheese. Cover and simmer 5 minutes.   *Makes 2 servings*

BEEFED-UP PEPPERS
(Microwave Recipe)

1½ pounds ground beef
4 green peppers
½ cup chopped onion
1 teaspoon salt
⅛ teaspoon pepper
1 cup cooked rice
1 can (11-ounces) condensed Cheddar cheese soup
1 egg
¾ teaspoon dill weed
¼ cup milk
½ teaspoon Worcestershire sauce

Cut peppers lengthwise in half; remove seeds and membrane. Place pepper cups on large microwave-safe plate, cut side down; cover with waxed paper and microwave at HIGH 3 minutes. Rotate plate ½ turn and continue cooking at HIGH 2 minutes. Combine ground beef and onion; arrange in a ring in all-plastic sieve or small colander. Place sieve in bowl; microwave at HIGH 3 minutes. Stir to break up beef. Continue cooking at HIGH 3 minutes; stir after removing from oven. Sprinkle salt and pepper over beef; combine with rice, ⅔ cup soup, egg and dill weed. Combine remaining soup with milk and Worcestershire sauce in glass custard cup and place in center of plate. Divide beef mixture into 8 portions, press one portion in each pepper cup, rounding the top; place in circle on plate. Microwave at HIGH 6 minutes, rotating ¼ turn every 2 minutes.   *4 to 6 servings*

Favorite recipe from **National Live Stock & Meat Board**

STUFFED PEPPER MATES

4 green peppers
¾ cup cooked rice
1 pound ground beef
1 (12-oz.) can stewed tomatoes, drained
¼ cup butter
1 envelope onion soup mix
4 slices **FISHER Cheese's SANDWICH-MATE® Singles**

Cut off tops of green peppers; remove seeds. Cook peppers 5 minutes in salted boiling water. Drain and set aside in covered pot. Brown the beef, then mix well with the cooked rice, tomatoes, butter and onion soup mix. Fill peppers with the mixture; place in baking dish. Pour ¼-inch hot water into dish and bake at 350° for 25 minutes. Now, place **FISHER Cheese's SANDWICH-MATE® Singles** atop each green pepper; return to oven and bake an additional 5 minutes.   *Yield: 4 servings*

JARLSBERG STUFFED PEPPERS

6 large green peppers
Boiling salted water
1 pound ground beef
1 cup chopped mushrooms
1 cup zucchini, sliced and quartered
½ cup chopped onion
1 medium clove garlic, minced
1 teaspoon salt
¼ teaspoon basil, crushed
1 cup cooked rice
2 cups shredded **JARLSBERG Cheese**
1½ cups tomato sauce (optional)

Cut peppers in half lengthwise; remove stem, seeds and membrane. Wash inside and out. Cook peppers in boiling salted water 5 minutes; drain.

Meanwhile, in skillet brown meat, stirring to break into bits. Add mushrooms, zucchini, onion, garlic, salt and basil. Cook until vegetables are tender; stir often. Remove from heat; stir in rice and 1½ cups **JARLSBERG Cheese**.

Lightly stuff pepper halves with cheese mixture. Place cut side up in buttered shallow baking dish. If desired, spoon tomato sauce over peppers. Cover and bake at 350° F for 40 minutes. Uncover, add remaining cheese and bake 5 minutes longer.

Makes 6 servings

STUFFED CABBAGE
(Low Calorie)

2 medium-size onions, cut in chunks
1 large head cabbage
2 pounds lean ground veal or beef
Freshly ground pepper to taste
1 teaspoon garlic powder
2 cups tomato juice, divided
4 packets SWEET 'N LOW®
2 tablespoons lemon juice

In large saucepan, cook onions and cabbage in boiling water about 5 minutes. Drain, leaving onions in saucepan and removing cabbage. Mix ground meat with pepper, garlic powder, and ½ cup tomato juice. Divide in 18 portions. Separate cabbage leaves and place a portion of meat on each. Roll up and fasten with toothpick. Place in saucepan with onions. Stir SWEET 'N LOW® and lemon juice into remaining tomato juice. Pour over all. Cover and gently simmer 1 hour, or until cabbage is tender and meat is cooked through. *18 servings*

Calories: 110 per serving (1 cabbage roll)

BEEFY STUFFED CABBAGE

12 large cabbage leaves
1 can (16 ounces) stewed tomatoes
1 tablespoon lemon juice
1 tablespoon brown sugar
½ teaspoon AC'CENT® Flavor Enhancer
¼ teaspoon dry mustard
2 cans (4½ ounces each) UNDERWOOD® Corned Beef Spread
2 cups cooked rice
¼ cup chopped onion

Preheat oven to 350°F. In a covered saucepan, in 1 inch boiling water, cook cabbage leaves 5 minutes; drain; set aside. In a bowl, stir together tomatoes, lemon juice, brown sugar, flavor enhancer and dry mustard; set aside. In a small bowl, mix together corned beef spread, rice and onion. In center of each cabbage leaf, place portion of meat mixture. Fold 2 sides of leaf toward center; from narrow edge of leaf roll up jelly roll fashion. Place filled leaves, seam side down, in a 1½-quart shallow casserole. Spoon sauce over rolls. Bake covered 45 minutes.

Makes 4 to 6 servings

SWEET 'N LOW® HUNGARIAN GOULASH
(Low Calorie/Low Fat)

1½ pounds cubed lean beef
2 medium onions, sliced
1 can (1 pound) whole tomatoes
1 can (8 ounces) tomato sauce
1½ tablespoons paprika
1 packet SWEET 'N LOW®
Freshly ground pepper to taste
3 cups cooked (6 ounces uncooked) whole-wheat or spinach noodles
1 cup plain low-fat yogurt

In medium-size non-stick saucepan, brown beef on all sides. Remove beef and set aside. In same saucepan, cook onions until transparent. Return beef to pan and add tomatoes, tomato sauce, paprika, SWEET 'N LOW®, and pepper. Cover and simmer over very low heat 1 hour. Uncover slightly and let simmer 30 minutes, or until meat is tender and sauce has reduced a little. Meanwhile, prepare noodles according to package direction, omitting salt.
(Continued)

Remove goulash from heat. Stir in yogurt. Reheat to serving temperature without boiling. Serve over hot noodles.
Per Serving (1¼ cups): Calories: 230; Fat: 5g   *6 servings*

Note: If you don't own a non-stick saucepan, you can spray your saucepan with a non-stick coating agent.

HUNGARIAN GOULASH

3 lbs. lean beef chuck
2 tablespoons margarine
2 cups chopped onions
1 clove garlic, minced
1 tablespoon paprika
2½ teaspoons salt
½ teaspoon caraway seeds
½ cup COCA-COLA®
¼ cup dry red wine
4 ripe tomatoes
3 tablespoons flour
Hot cooked noodles

Cut beef into 1-inch cubes, discarding bone and fat. In a Dutch oven, melt margarine and add meat, stirring to brown on all sides. Remove meat cubes as they brown. Sauté onions and garlic in the drippings until they are soft. Stir in paprika, salt, and caraway seeds; cook 1 minute. Stir in meat, COCA-COLA®, wine, and peeled, cut-up tomatoes. Cover tightly; simmer about 1¼ hours or until meat is fork-tender. Blend flour with a little water to make a smooth paste; stir into goulash. Stir and cook 3 to 5 minutes until gravy is thickened. Serve with hot noodles.
Makes 6 cups goulash or 8 servings

SKILLET BEEF, TOMATOES AND MACARONI

½ pound ground beef
1 can (15½ ounces) AUNT NELLIE'S® Sloppy Joe Sandwich Sauce
1 small clove garlic, minced
¾ teaspoon salt
⅛ teaspoon each: crushed basil, celery salt, ground oregano, ground thyme
2 cups cooked macaroni

In large skillet, cook beef until lightly browned. Pour off excess fat. Stir in remaining ingredients. Simmer, covered, for 5 minutes, stirring occasionally.
3 to 4 servings

CHINESE SLICED BEEF

½ cup julienne-cut carrots
½ cup diced celery (½-inch dices)
1 medium onion, sliced
1 cup frozen peas
2 teaspoons soy sauce
1 package (32 oz.) BANQUET® Gravy and Sliced Beef Frozen Heat and Serve Buffet Supper Main Dish
Hot rice

Place carrots, celery, and onion in boiling water for 5 minutes. Drain and place in a 2-quart oblong baking dish. Add frozen peas and soy sauce. Remove frozen gravy and sliced beef from foil tray and place into baking dish on top of vegetables. Heat in 400°F oven for 25 minutes. Separate beef slices and stir gravy and vegetables. Heat additional 15 minutes, until bubbly. Serve with hot rice.
Makes 6 servings

BEST BEEF HASH

2 tablespoons butter or margarine
1 cup cubed cooked roast beef
1½ cups cubed raw potato (about 2 medium potatoes)
2 tablespoons chopped onion
¼ cup water
½ teaspoon instant beef bouillon granules
½ teaspoon salt
¼ teaspoon pepper

Melt butter or margarine in small skillet. Add remaining ingredients and mix well. Cover and cook over low heat until potatoes are fork-tender, about 10 minutes. Uncover and cook 5 minutes longer. *2 servings*

Favorite recipe from **Iowa Beef Industry Council**

CHINESE PEPPER STEAK

1 to 1½ lb. boneless top round or sirloin steak
2 tablespoons oil
1 clove garlic, minced
1 teaspoon salt
1 cup canned undiluted beef broth (bouillon)
1 cup thinly sliced green pepper strips
1 cup thinly sliced celery
¼ cup thinly sliced onions
½ cup **COCA-COLA**®
2 medium, ripe tomatoes
2½ tablespoons corn starch
¼ cup **COCA-COLA**®
1 tablespoon soy sauce
Hot cooked rice

Trim all fat from meat and cut into pencil-thin strips. In deep skillet or Dutch oven, heat oil, garlic and salt. Add meat and brown over high heat about 10 minutes, stirring occasionally with a fork. Add beef broth, cover and simmer 15 to 20 minutes, or until meat is fork-tender. Stir in green pepper, celery, onions and ½ cup **COCA-COLA**®. Cover; simmer 5 minutes. Do not overcook; vegetables should be tender-crisp. Peel tomatoes, cut into wedges, gently stir into meat. Blend corn starch with the ¼ cup **COCA-COLA**® and soy sauce. Stir into meat and cook until thickened, about 1 minute, stirring lightly with fork. Serve over hot rice. *Makes 6 (¾ cup) servings*

KRISPY® AMERICAN CHOPPED SUEY

½ pound ground lean beef
2 tablespoons shortening
⅓ cup diced onion
½ cup diced celery
1 (10½ ounce) can tomato puree
1 (8 ounce) can spaghetti sauce
2½ cups coarsely crushed **SUNSHINE**® **KRISPY**®
   Saltine Crackers
1 egg, beaten
1 cup grated American cheese
1 cup milk
2 tablespoons minced parsley
1 teaspoon salt

Heat oven to 325°F. Brown beef in shortening, breaking it with a spoon into small bits. Add onion, celery, tomato puree and

spaghetti sauce. Cook, uncovered, over low heat for 20 minutes. Combine crushed cracker crumbs, beaten egg, grated cheese, milk, parsley and salt. Stir **KRISPY**® **Cracker** crumb mixture into tomato mixture. Pour into a greased 1½-quart baking dish. Bake, uncovered, at 325°F. for 40 minutes.

Yield: 4 to 5 generous servings

SOUPER SKILLET ZITI

1 pound ground beef
1 envelope **LIPTON**® **Beef Flavor Mushroom** or
   Onion-Mushroom Soup Mix
2 cans (16 oz. ea.) whole tomatoes, undrained
2 cups water
1½ teaspoons oregano
3 cups uncooked ziti macaroni (about 8 oz.)
⅓ cup grated Parmesan cheese
Mozzarella cheese

In large skillet, brown ground beef; drain. Add beef flavor mushroom soup mix and tomatoes blended with water and oregano. Bring to a boil, then stir in uncooked macaroni; simmer covered, stirring occasionally, 20 minutes or until macaroni is tender. Stir in Parmesan cheese and top with mozzarella cheese.

Makes about 6 servings

BEEF SUKIYAKI IN WOK
(Low Calorie)

1 medium onion, sliced
1 pound beef sirloin, cut in thin strips
1 teaspoon salt
¼ teaspoon pepper
1 tablespoon vinegar
½ pound fresh mushrooms, sliced
½ cup sliced celery
½ cup green pepper strips
1 (12 oz.) can **DIET SHASTA**® Lemon-Lime
3 tablespoons soy sauce
1 beef bouillon cube, crumbled
1 (16 oz.) can bean sprouts, drained
1 (4⅔ oz.) can bamboo shoots, drained
1 (8 oz.) can water chestnuts, drained and sliced

Sauté onion in large skillet until softened. Add beef strips. Cook and stir over high heat until lightly browned. Sprinkle with salt, pepper and vinegar. Add mushrooms, celery and green pepper. Cook 5 minutes. Add all remaining ingredients and simmer 5 minutes. *Serves 5 or 6*

Calories: 151 per serving

LIPTON® NEW ENGLAND
BOILED DINNER

3 to 3½ pound boneless beef pot roast (rump, chuck or
   round)
2 envelopes **LIPTON**® **Onion** or **Beef Flavor**
   Mushroom Soup Mix
1½ quarts water
4 medium potatoes, quartered
4 medium carrots, quartered
½ medium head cabbage, cut into wedges

In Dutch oven, add roast and **LIPTON® Onion Soup Mix** blended with water. Bring to a boil, then simmer covered, 2 hours. Add vegetables; continue cooking covered an additional 20 minutes or until beef and vegetables are tender.

Makes about 6 servings

NEW ENGLAND BOILED DINNER

4 lb. corned brisket of beef
½ lb. salt pork
3 quarts boiling water
½ cup **DOMINO® BROWNULATED® Sugar**
3 bay leaves
1 medium clove garlic
6-8 medium potatoes, peeled (about 2 lb.)
6-8 medium carrots, peeled (about 1 lb.)
6 medium onions
6-8 parsnips, peeled (about 1 lb.), optional
1 medium cabbage, cut in wedges (about 2 lb.)

Wash beef and place in Dutch oven or large heavy saucepan. Add salt pork, water, sugar, bay leaves and garlic. Bring to boil. Skim surface. Cover and simmer 3 hours. Add vegetables except cabbage, cut into serving size pieces. Cook 10 minutes longer. Add cabbage and cook 10 minutes longer or until vegetables are tender.* If desired, serve with hot mustard, horseradish and green tomato pickles.

Yield: 6-8 servings

*Use liquid from brisket as stock for vegetable soup.

SOUTHERN SMOTHERED STEAKS

4 cubed steaks
Flour (about ½ cup)
¼ cup oil
Seasoned salt
Pepper
1 medium onion, sliced
1 can (15-oz.) **VAN CAMP'S® Spanish Rice**
1 teaspoon sugar
1 teaspoon parsley flakes

Coat cubed steaks with flour. In large skillet, brown steaks in oil; remove to 9×9×2-inch baking dish. Sprinkle with seasoned salt and pepper. Sauté onion slices in skillet drippings; add Spanish Rice and sugar. Pour Rice mixture over steaks; sprinkle with parsley flakes. Bake, uncovered, at 325°F for 45 to 55 minutes.

Makes 4 servings

BEEF AND CHICKEN SUPREME

1½ cups sliced fresh mushrooms (about 4 ounces)
3 tablespoons butter or margarine
5 tablespoons flour
4 teaspoons **FRENCH'S® Prepared Yellow Mustard**
2 cups milk
1½ cups cubed cooked chicken
1 jar or package (about 2½-oz.) chipped dried beef, sliced
1 medium size avocado, peeled and sliced
6 baked patty shells (10-oz. pkg. frozen patty shells)

Cook mushrooms in butter; blend in flour and mustard. Gradually stir in milk; cook, stirring, until mixture comes to a boil and thickens. Gently stir in chicken, beef, and avocado pieces; heat through, spoon hot mixture immediately into patty shells.

6 servings

SKILLET BARBECUED CORNED BEEF

1 can (12 oz.) **LIBBY'S® Corned Beef**
1 cup shredded carrots, lightly packed
1 jar (12 oz.) chili sauce
1½ teaspoons Worcestershire sauce
6 toasted hamburger buns
Midget gherkins and carrot curls, garnish

Crumble corned beef into a heavy skillet. Add carrots, chili sauce and Worcestershire sauce; stir to mix well. Heat until bubbly. Reduce heat and cover; simmer, stirring occasionally, for 30 minutes. Serve on toasted hamburger buns. Garnish each with a midget gherkin tucked inside a carrot curl if desired.

Yields 6 sandwiches

CORNED BEEF AND CABBAGE

1 4-pound corned beef
Cold water
½ bottle **SOUVERAIN® White Wine**
¼ teaspoon peppercorns
¼ teaspoon bay leaves
½ teaspoon parsley
1 medium size onion, chopped
1 large carrot, sliced
1 can of small white potatoes
1 2-pound cabbage, cut in quarters

Wash corned beef thoroughly. Put it into a large pot and cover with equal parts of water and **SOUVERAIN® White Wine**. Add all other ingredients except cabbage. Simmer very gently for 3 hours. Skim when a scum rises. Wash cabbage well, add to pot and simmer for a further 20 minutes, or until the cabbage is cooked.

Serves six

NO-BAKE MEATLOAF

¾ cup water
2 tsp. salt
2 beef bouillon cubes
¾ cup **3-MINUTE BRAND® Oats**
3½ oz. box lemon gelatin
12 oz. can corned beef
¼ cup chopped onion
3 Tbsp. prepared mustard
½ tsp. celery seed
1 cup ice water
¼ cup finely chopped green pepper

Combine ¾ cup water, salt and bouillon cubes in a saucepan. Bring to a boil. Stir in oats and gelatin and remove from heat. Stir until gelatin and bouillon cubes are dissolved. Cool. Cut corned beef into very thin slices. Stack slices and cut through again, resulting in very thinly chopped pieces. Combine with onion, mustard and celery seed, mixing lightly with fork. Beat oatmeal-gelatin mixture at high speed of an electric mixer for a few seconds. Add ice water and beat again. Add about a fourth of the corned beef mixture at a time, beating on high speed after each addition. When very well mixed, stir in green pepper with a fork and pour into a buttered 1 quart baking dish or ring mold. Refrigerate until firm. Serve on a lettuce leaf with crackers.

BUDDIG CORNED BEEF HASH

3 (2½-oz.) packages of **BUDDIG Corned Beef** or **Pastrami** cut into ½-inch squares separated for easy mixing
½ cup cooking oil
16 oz. frozen diced, O'Brien style potatoes
Salt and pepper to taste
6 poached eggs (optional)
Chili sauce (optional)

Heat cooking oil in large skillet. Carefully add potatoes (you may cover with aluminum foil in the beginning to speed up cooking). Stir and continue cooking until the potatoes are slightly brown. Add the **BUDDIG** meat and cook until the meat is thoroughly heated. Add salt and pepper to taste. Divide into 6 portions with poached egg on each (optional) and serve with chili sauce for those who wish the condiment.   *Serves 6*

TAS-TEE TOSTADAS

6 tortillas
2 avocados, peeled, pitted and mashed
¼ cup **HENRI'S TAS-TEE® Dressing**
¼ cup finely chopped onion
⅛ teaspoon hot pepper sauce
1½ cups shredded lettuce
12 thin slices roast beef
3 medium tomatoes, chopped
1 cup grated mild Cheddar cheese
Chili powder or taco sauce

1. Fry tortillas in hot oil until crisp and lightly browned. Drain. Set aside.
2. Combine avocados, **HENRI'S TAS-TEE® Dressing,** onion and hot pepper sauce. Mix well.
3. Spread each crisp tortilla with the avocado-**HENRI'S TAS-TEE® Dressing** mixture.
4. Top with lettuce, beef slices, chopped tomato and cheese.
5. Sprinkle with chili powder or taco sauce to taste.
          Makes 6 tostadas

MEATY LOAVES

1 (one pound) loaf **BRIDGFORD Frozen Bread Dough** (White or Honey Wheat)
1½ lbs. ground beef
¾ cup oats, uncooked
1 cup grated cheese (Cheddar or Jack)
½ onion, chopped
1 egg
Salt & pepper
2 Tbsp. butter, melted
3 Tbsp. grated Parmesan cheese

Let frozen dough thaw to room temperature 2½-3½ hours, or overnight in refrigerator. Mix remaining ingredients for meat loaf except butter and Parmesan. Shape into 6 equal patties approximately 4 inches in diameter. Cook in conventional oven approximately 20 minutes at 350°F. or in microwave oven 10 minutes. Drain off grease. Cut thawed loaf into 6 equal pieces. On lightly floured board roll each piece into a circle approximately 6 inches in diameter. Place one partially cooked meat patty in center of each piece of dough. Fold ends over patty and seal. Place seam side down on lightly greased cookie sheet. Brush loaves with butter (at this point grated Parmesan cheese can be sprinkled over loaves). With sharp knife make small cuts in top of dough. Bake in 375° oven 20-25 minutes or until golden brown. Serve with mixed vegetables and beverage for a balanced meal.

VARIATIONS:

TURKEY

3 cups cooked turkey, ground
1 cup stuffing
¾ cup gravy
½ onion, chopped
3 Tbsp. grated Parmesan cheese
Salt & pepper

Mix ingredients together and shape into patties approximately 4 inches in diameter. Wrap dough pieces around turkey. Follow above baking directions.

HAM

3 cups cooked ham, ground
2 cups grated cheese (Cheddar or Jack)
1 egg
½ onion, chopped
3 Tbsp. grated Parmesan cheese

Mix ingredients together and shape into patties approximately 4 inches in diameter. Wrap dough pieces around ham. Follow above baking directions.

PORK CHOW MEIN

1 lb. **WILSON® Recipe Ready Brand Boneless Pork Tenderloin**
2 tablespoons soy sauce
⅛ teaspoon ground ginger
4 green onions, cut in 1 inch pieces
¼ cup oil
½ cup sliced celery
1 cup thinly sliced mushrooms
½ cup julienne carrots
1 cup French cut green beans
1 tablespoon cornstarch
¾ cup chicken broth
8 oz. Chinese egg noodles (or regular egg noodles if you cannot find Chinese), cooked

Cut tenderloin in ¼ inch thick slices. Combine 1 tablespoon soy sauce and ginger in a small bowl. Add pork and green onions. Toss to mix. Let stand 10 minutes. Heat 2 tablespoons oil in a large skillet or a wok over high heat. Add pork and cook and stir until meat loses its pink color. Remove from pan. Add remaining 2 tablespoons oil. Add celery, mushrooms, carrots and green beans. Cook and stir 3 minutes. Return meat to pan. Combine 1 tablespoon soy sauce and cornstarch. Stir in chicken broth. Stir into vegetable mixture. Heat, stirring constantly, until mixture comes to a full boil. Reduce heat and cook 3 to 5 minutes or until pork is done. Serve over egg noodles.   *Makes 4 servings*

PORK AND SAUERKRAUT SENSATION

Two 1 lb. cans sauerkraut
2 tablespoons bacon drippings or oil
1 large onion, chopped
1 apple, chopped
6 peppercorns
1 cup chicken broth
1 cup dry white wine or water
6 **WILSON® Smoked Pork Loin Chops**
1 lb. **WILSON® Smoked, Beef or Polish Sausage**

Rinse sauerkraut and drain. Place bacon drippings in Dutch oven or large skillet with a lid. Add onion and sauté until tender. Add drained sauerkraut, apple, peppercorns, chicken broth and wine or water. Cover and simmer 1 hour. Nestle chops into sauerkraut around the edges. Lightly score sausage. Place on top of sauerkraut. Cover and simmer ½ hour. Serve this sauerkraut dish with boiled potatoes and spicy mustard.

Makes 6 servings

HAM WITH NOODLES AND SOUR CREAM

2 cups cubed (½-inch) **SWIFT PREMIUM® HOSTESS® Ham** in Round Can
1 (4-ounce) can mushrooms
¼ cup chopped onion
2 tablespoons butter or margarine
¼ teaspoon salt
¼ teaspoon paprika
⅛ teaspoon pepper
¼ cup chopped green pepper
4 ounces (about 2 cups) uncooked noodles
1½ cups water
1 cup sour cream
Parsley

Drain mushrooms well and reserve the liquid. Panfry mushrooms, onion and ham in butter about 5 minutes. Add salt, paprika and pepper. Stir in green pepper. Arrange noodles on top of ham. Pour in mushroom liquid and water. Cover and simmer for about 15 minutes. Uncover and cook for another 15 minutes. Stir in the sour cream and cook uncovered for 5 minutes. Serve immediately garnished with parsley.

Yield: 4 servings

HEARTY SKILLET SUPPER

2 tablespoons butter or margarine
10 oz. pkg. frozen corn
9 oz. pkg. frozen cut green beans
1 tablespoon flour
10¾ oz. can condensed cream of chicken soup
½ cup dairy sour cream
2 cups **JENNIE-O® Turkey Ham**, cut into ¼ × 2-inch strips
1 cup (4 oz.) cubed Cheddar or American cheese

In large skillet, combine butter and vegetables. Cover and cook about 5 minutes, stirring occasionally, until tender-crisp. Blend in flour. Stir in soup, sour cream, and ham. Cook and stir over low heat just until hot and thickened. Sprinkle with cheese; heat just until cheese begins to melt.

About 6 servings

PENNSYLVANIA DUTCH VEGETABLE SKILLET

3 cups cabbage chunks (about 1-inch)
3 medium-size carrots, thinly sliced
2 cups small broccoli flowerets
1 red pepper, sliced, or ½ cup sliced pimiento
8 ounces cooked ham, cut in cubes (about 1½ cups)
½ cup water
1 can (20-oz.) sliced pineapple
⅓ cup firmly-packed brown sugar
¼ cup cider vinegar
1 tablespoon **FRENCH'S® Worcestershire Sauce**
½ teaspoon salt
4 teaspoons cornstarch

In large skillet, layer cabbage, then carrots, broccoli, pepper slices, and ham cubes; pour on ½ cup water. Cover, bring to a boil and simmer 5 minutes or until vegetables are crisp-tender. Drain pineapple, saving ¾ cup juice. Combine brown sugar, vinegar, Worcestershire sauce, salt, and cornstarch; mix thoroughly. Stir into the ¾ cup pineapple juice. Cut 6 slices of pineapple in half and add, with juice mixture, to skillet. Heat to boiling, stirring constantly, until sauce thickens. Serve immediately. *4 servings*

Note: Serve with hot cooked rice and chow mein noodles, if desired.

SUMMER STIR-FRY

1 package (6-oz.) **OSCAR MAYER Smoked Cooked Ham**
2 tablespoons vegetable oil
¼ teaspoon garlic powder
1 package (16-oz.) frozen mixed vegetables
1 small onion, cut into wedges
1 package (6-oz.) frozen pea pods and water chestnuts
1 cup (2-oz.) sliced fresh mushrooms

Sauce:
1 bottle (8-oz.) Russian salad dressing
2 tablespoons soy sauce

Cut ham into ½-inch strips. Set aside. Heat oil in wok or skillet on medium-high 3 minutes; add garlic, mixed vegetables and onion. Stir-fry vegetables 5 minutes until tender-crisp. Add remaining vegetables and ham continuing to stir-fry 3 to 5 minutes more. Combine sauce ingredients. Serve with stir-fry. *4 servings*

SPINACH SUPPER RING

1 loaf **RHODES™ Frozen Honey Wheat** or **White Bread Dough**, thawed as directed
2 (10-oz.) packages chopped frozen spinach, thawed and very well drained
½ lb. sliced pepperoni or chopped cooked ham
1 (2½-oz.) jar sliced mushrooms, drained or ½ cup sliced fresh mushrooms
1½ cups (6 oz.) shredded mozzarella cheese
1 egg white
1 tablespoon water
2 to 3 teaspoons sesame seeds, optional

Let dough rise until nearly doubled. Preheat oven to 350°F. Roll and pat out dough to a 10 × 15-inch rectangle. Sprinkle spinach over surface. Top with pepperoni, mushrooms, and cheese.

Starting from long side, roll as for jelly roll. Pinch along seam to seal. Form a ring and pinch open ends together. Place in greased and floured 10-inch pie or cake pan or on a greased baking sheet, seam side down.

Beat egg white with water. Brush over surface of ring; sprinkle with sesame seeds. Make 5 or 6 slashes 1 to 1½ inches long on top of ring to let out steam.

Bake 30 to 40 minutes or until nicely browned. Serve hot from the oven.

Makes 6 to 8 servings

HAM 'N SWEETS SKILLET DINNER

¼ cup finely chopped onion
¼ cup butter or margarine
2 tablespoons flour
1 15¼-oz. can pineapple chunks, drained, reserving syrup
⅓ cup water
⅓ cup brown sugar, packed
1 29-oz. can sweet potatoes, drained, sliced
5 ARMOUR STAR® Ham Patties

Cook onion in butter or margarine 2 to 3 minutes; stir in flour. Add reserved syrup and water; cook, stirring constantly, until thickened. Stir in pineapple and brown sugar. Top with sweet potatoes and ham patties. Cook, covered, 20 to 25 minutes or until heated through. Preparation time: 35 minutes   *5 servings*

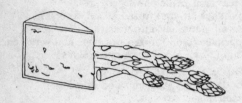

CREAMED HAM AND ASPARAGUS IN PARMESAN PUFF RING

2 tablespoons butter or margarine
¼ cup finely chopped onion
2 tablespoons flour
½ teaspoon salt
¼ teaspoon pepper
1 cup milk
½ cup cream
½ cup shredded Swiss cheese
2 tablespoons grated Parmesan cheese
2 cups ½″ cubes WILSON® Ham
1¼ cups 1″ pieces cooked fresh or frozen asparagus

Melt butter in medium saucepan. Add onion and sauté until tender. Stir in flour, salt and pepper until thoroughly blended. Add milk and cream. Cook over medium heat, stirring constantly, until mixture thickens and comes to a full boil. Stir and boil 1 minute. Reduce heat. Stir in cheeses, until melted. Stir in ham and asparagus. Cook until ham is heated. Serve over toast, biscuits or in Parmesan Puff Ring*.   *Makes 4 to 6 servings*

*PARMESAN PUFF RING

¾ cup water
6 tablespoons butter
¾ cup flour
½ teaspoon salt
3 eggs
¼ cup grated Parmesan cheese

Heat oven to 400°F. Bring water and butter to a full boil in a medium saucepan over medium heat. Add flour and salt all at once. Stir vigorously until mixture forms a ball and leaves the sides of the pan. Add eggs, one at a time, beating well after each addition. After adding the last egg, stir vigorously 1 minute. Stir in 3 tablespoons Parmesan cheese. Butter a 9″ pie pan or shallow casserole. Spoon dough in a ring around the bottom of the pan, leaving the center open. Sprinkle with remaining 1 tablespoon Parmesan cheese. Bake 35 minutes or until lightly browned. Serve as a bread or fill center with Creamed Ham and Asparagus.   *Makes 6 servings*

HAM & POTATO SKILLET FEAST

1-12 oz. can HORMEL Ham Patties (Cut into halves)
2 Tbsp. margarine or butter
1 pkg. BETTY CROCKER® Scalloped Potatoes
2 medium carrots (sliced)
2¾ cups water
⅔ cup milk
½ tsp. dried basil leaves (crushed)
¼ tsp. garlic salt
⅛ tsp. pepper
1 small zucchini (thinly sliced)
1 medium tomato (chopped)

Cook ham patties in margarine in 10-inch skillet until light brown. Remove ham patties; stir in potatoes, Sauce Mix, carrots, water, milk, basil, garlic salt and pepper. Heat to boiling, stirring frequently; reduce heat. Cover and simmer, stirring occasionally, 20 minutes. Stir in zucchini and tomato; top with ham patties. Cover and cook 10 minutes longer.   *6 servings*

TURKEY AND RICE MEDLEY

¼ cup diagonally sliced celery
¼ cup green pepper strips
1 small clove garlic, minced
¼ teaspoon ground ginger
2 tablespoons butter or margarine
1 can (18¾ ounces) CAMPBELL'S Chunky Turkey Soup
2 tablespoons water
1 tablespoon cornstarch
1 can (10 ounces) mandarin orange segments, drained
Cooked rice

In saucepan, cook celery and green pepper with garlic and ginger in butter until tender. Add soup. Blend water and cornstarch until smooth; stir into soup mixture. Cook, stirring until thickened. Add oranges; heat. Serve with rice.   *Makes about 3 cups*

POLYNESIAN TURKEY AND NOODLES

2 cups cubed cooked turkey
1 egg, slightly beaten
¼ cup cornstarch
2 tablespoons cooking oil
1 can (13½ ounces) pineapple chunks, drained (reserve juice)
½ cup sugar
½ cup cider vinegar
1 medium green pepper, cut in strips
2 tablespoons cornstarch
¼ cup water
1 teaspoon soy sauce
4 large carrots, cooked and cut in 1-inch pieces
8 ounces (5 cups) MUELLER'S® Klops® Egg Noodles

Dip turkey pieces in egg; roll in ¼ cup cornstarch until coated. In skillet, brown turkey pieces in oil; remove and set aside. Add enough water to reserved pineapple juice to make 1 cup; add to skillet along with sugar, vinegar and green pepper. Heat to boiling, stirring constantly. Reduce heat; cover and simmer 2 minutes. Blend 2 tablespoons cornstarch and ¼ cup water; stir into skillet. Heat, stirring constantly, until mixture thickens and boils; cook 1 minute. Stir in pineapple chunks, soy sauce, carrots, and turkey pieces; heat. Meanwhile, cook noodles as directed on package; drain. Serve turkey over noodles.   *4 to 6 servings*

IDEAL EGG SPAGHETTI WITH CHICKEN CACCIATORE

1 medium stewing chicken
¼ cup vegetable oil
1 green pepper, chopped
½ lb. mushrooms
2 onions, chopped
1 clove garlic, chopped (optional)
Salt and pepper to taste
1-8 oz. tomato sauce
1 can (No. 303) tomatoes, chopped
¼ cup Sherry wine
1 pkg. (12-oz.) **IDEAL Egg Spaghetti**

Cut chicken into segments and brown in vegetable oil using large skillet. Remove chicken and use pan to sauté green pepper, mushrooms, onions and garlic. In a large saucepan pour tomatoes and all other ingredients except chicken, **IDEAL Egg Spaghetti** and Sherry wine. Bring to a boil. Add chicken and Sherry wine. Allow to simmer with cover about 30 minutes. Cook **IDEAL Egg Spaghetti** according to package directions, and drain. Serve with sauce arranging chicken in the middle of plate.   *Serves 4-6*

CHICKEN CHOP SUEY

1 cup diagonally sliced celery
1 medium onion, sliced
3 tablespoons vegetable oil
1 tablespoon instant chicken bouillon crystals
1 cup water
1 tablespoon cornstarch
1 jar (2½ oz.) sliced mushrooms
1 green pepper, sliced
1 can (5 oz.) water chestnuts, drained and sliced
1 can (16 oz.) bean sprouts, drained
2 cups cooked, cubed chicken
2 tablespoons soy sauce
2 bags **SUCCESS® Rice**, cooked

Sauté celery and onion in oil about 3 minutes. Blend chicken bouillon crystals and cornstarch with water. Stir into celery-onion mixture. Heat until slightly thickened. Stir in mushrooms, green pepper, water chestnuts, bean sprouts, chicken, and soy sauce. Cover and steam 5 minutes. Serve over hot rice.
Makes 8 servings (about 1 cup each)

CHICKEN A LA MERLINO'S SPINACH NOODLES

¼ cup margarine
1 Tbsp. chopped onion
¼ cup green pepper, diced
¼ cup flour
½ tsp. salt
1 cup chicken stock
1 cup milk
½ cup light cream
1½ cups diced, cooked chicken
2 Tbsp. diced pimiento
½ cup cooked peas
1 Tbsp. sherry wine
4 cups **MERLINO'S Spinach Noodles**

Sauté green pepper and chopped onion in margarine until tender. Blend in flour and salt. Gradually stir in chicken stock and milk. Cook, stirring constantly, until mixture comes to a boil. Stir in light cream, cooked chicken, pimiento, peas and sherry. Heat thoroughly. Cook Spinach Noodles as directed on package in boiling, salted water until tender. Drain. Serve chicken over Spinach Noodles.   *Serves 4-6*

CREAMY CHICKEN PECAN

6 patty shells or croissants
¼ cup margarine
½ cup chopped onions
½ cup diced green pepper
4-oz. can mushrooms
1 cup coarsely chopped pecans
2 Tbsp. diced pimiento
1½ cups White Sauce (Thick)*
1½ cups diced cooked chicken

Melt margarine; add onions and green peppers and sauté until onions are tender. Add remaining ingredients except patty shells and heat. Ladle chicken mixture into and over prepared shells or croissants.   *Makes 6 servings*

*WHITE SAUCE (THICK)

4½ Tbsp. butter or margarine
6 Tbsp. all-purpose flour
½ tsp. salt
Dash white pepper
1½ cups milk

Melt butter in saucepan over low heat. Blend in flour, salt and dash white pepper. Add milk all at once. Cook quickly, stirring constantly, until mixture thickens and bubbles. Remove sauce from heat when it bubbles.   *Makes 1½ cups*

Favorite recipe from **National Pecan Marketing Council**

CHICKEN WITH SOUR CREAM GRAVY

2 tablespoons butter or margarine
1 cup sliced onion
1 can (14¾-ounces) **FRANCO-AMERICAN Chicken Gravy**
2 cups cubed cooked chicken
½ cup sour cream
¼ teaspoon paprika
Generous dash pepper
Cooked noodles

In 3-quart saucepan, over medium heat, in hot butter, cook onion until tender. Stir in remaining ingredients except noodles. Heat thoroughly; stirring occasionally. Serve over noodles.
Makes 4 cups or 8 servings

DICED CHICKEN IN SOUR CREAM

2 cups cooked diced chicken
1 8-ounce carton sour cream
2 teaspoons grated onion
¼ cup chopped sweet pickle
Salt and pepper
JAYS Whole Potato Chips

In top of double boiler heat sour cream and chicken. (Never let water boil in bottom of boiler.) Add onion, pickle, salt and pepper to taste. Serve over whole potato chips and garnish as desired.
4 servings

RANCH CHICKEN

1 3-pound (4 cups) chicken
1 medium onion, peeled and left whole
1 rib celery
2 teaspoons salt
1 10½-ounce can cream of chicken soup
⅔ cup tomatoes with chilies
4 cups **FRITOS® Brand Corn Chips**
2 cups grated American cheese
1 cup chopped onion
2 tablespoons shortening

In kettle cook chicken until tender with onion, celery, salt and enough water to cover. Bone chicken and cube. Strain broth, reserving 1⅓ cups.

Sauté chopped onion in shortening. Add soup, tomatoes, and broth. Simmer 5 minutes.

In electric skillet, spread a layer of chicken, **FRITOS® Brand Corn Chips**, sauce and cheese. Repeat, ending with cheese. Cover and cook at 250° F. for 20 minutes. Lower temperature to 200° F. and continue cooking for 40 minutes.

Makes 6 to 8 servings

GINGER CHICKEN WITH PEANUTS

½ to ¾ pound cubed raw chicken
1 tablespoon soy sauce
1 teaspoon cornstarch
2 tablespoons oil
1 package (10 oz.) **BIRDS EYE® Japanese** or **Chinese Style Vegetables With a Seasoned Sauce**
¼ cup water
½ teaspoon ginger
2 tablespoons salted peanuts

Combine chicken and soy sauce in bowl; stir in cornstarch. Sauté chicken in hot oil in skillet until just tender, about 3 or 4 minutes. Remove from pan. Add vegetables, water and ginger to skillet. Bring to a *full* boil over medium heat, separating vegetables with a fork and stirring frequently. Reduce heat; cover and simmer 2 minutes. Add chicken and heat. Sprinkle with peanuts. Serve over hot cooked rice, if desired. *Makes about 3 cups or 3 servings*

CHINESE SKILLET DINNER

22 **PREMIUM Saltine Crackers**
2 tablespoons butter or margarine
1 cup diagonally sliced celery
¼ cup sliced scallions
1 (19-ounce) can chunky chicken with rice soup
2 cups cubed cooked chicken
1 (10-ounce) package frozen chopped broccoli
2 tablespoons lemon juice
Soy sauce, optional

1.   Finely roll 7 **PREMIUM Saltine Crackers** to yield about ¼ cup crumbs; set aside. Using a sharp serrated knife, thinly slice remaining 15 saltines; set aside.
2.   In large skillet, over medium heat, melt butter or margarine; sauté celery and scallions about 5 minutes, or until tender.
3.   Add soup, chicken, broccoli and lemon juice; over medium heat, bring to a boil. Cover; reduce heat; simmer about 5 minutes, or until broccoli is tender-crisp. Blend in saltine crumbs.
4.   *To Serve*: Spoon into serving bowl; if desired, sprinkle with soy sauce. Arrange sliced saltines in center.

Makes 5 to 6 servings
(Continued)

MICROWAVE METHOD:
Finely roll and thinly slice **PREMIUM Saltine Crackers** as in Step 1. In 3-quart microwave-proof bowl, microwave butter or margarine, celery and scallions 4 minutes, stirring after 2 minutes, until vegetables are tender. Add remaining ingredients, except saltines, and, if desired, soy sauce; cover with plastic wrap. Microwave at 100% power 6 minutes, stirring every 2 minutes, until broccoli is tender-crisp. Blend in saltine crumbs; serve as in Step 4.

CHICKEN AND CHINESE PEAPODS

1 frying chicken, boned and cut in small pieces
2 tablespoons cornstarch
2 slices fresh ginger, slivered
1 package **KUBLA KHAN Chinese Peapods**
3 tablespoons oil
¾ teaspoon salt
½ teaspoon monosodium glutamate

Dredge chicken in cornstarch. Sauté ginger in oil on high heat. Sauté chicken in oil. When chicken is done, in about 8 minutes, add Chinese Peapods and seasoning. Sauté for 10 minutes on high heat. Serve at once. *Serves 4*

ELEGANT CHICKEN AND SHRIMP

¼ cup butter or margarine
8 oz. sliced fresh mushrooms
¼ cup sliced green onions
2 Tbsp. unsifted all purpose flour
1 cup half-and-half
2 Tbsp. dry sherry
1 cup **KAUKAUNA® Cheese Sharp Cheddar Buttery Spread™**
2 cups cubed, cooked chicken
1 cup cooked shrimp
2 Tbsp. snipped fresh parsley
2 Tbsp. diced pimiento
Hot cooked rice

Melt butter in large skillet. Add mushrooms and green onions. Sauté over low heat until tender. Blend in flour until smooth. Add half-and-half and sherry. Stir constantly until mixture boils and thickens. Stir in cheese until melted. Blend in chicken and shrimp. Heat to serving temperature. Stir in parsley and pimiento before serving. Serve over hot cooked rice. *Makes 4-5 servings*

MEXICAN CHICKEN ROLLS

2 whole chicken breasts, split, skinned and boned
1 4 oz. can **S&W® Whole Green Chili Peppers**
4 tsp. chopped **S&W® Olives**
½ cup shredded Monterey Jack cheese
1 egg, slightly beaten
1 cup crushed tortilla chips
¼ cup vegetable oil
1 1⅝ oz. envelope enchilada sauce mix
½ cup water
1 16 oz. can **S&W® Mexican Style Stewed Tomatoes**
½ cup shredded Cheddar cheese

Pound chicken breasts to flatten. On each breast, put 1 chili pepper, 1 teaspoon chopped olives and 2 tablespoons Monterey Jack cheese. Roll-up the breasts tightly and secure with toothpicks. Dip each roll into egg, then into crushed chips to coat. Heat oil in skillet and brown chicken rolls lightly. Place rolls in a shallow casserole dish. Prepare enchilada sauce according to package directions, only using ½ cup water and **Mexican Style Stewed Tomatoes**. Pour sauce over chicken rolls. Bake at 350° for 35-40 minutes. Sprinkle Cheddar cheese over top and bake an additional 5 minutes or until cheese is bubbly. *Serves 4*

FLAKY CRESCENT CHICKEN WELLINGTON

10-oz. pkg. frozen chopped spinach, cooked and well drained
2 cups chopped cooked chicken or 2 (5-oz.) cans boned chicken, drained and flaked
3 hard-cooked eggs, chopped
½ cup finely chopped dill pickle (reserve 2 tablespoons liquid for sauce)
⅓ cup finely chopped celery
2 (8-oz.) cans **PILLSBURY Refrigerated Quick Crescent Dinner Rolls***
¼ cup **PARKAY Margarine** or butter, melted
½ teaspoon dry mustard

Sauce:
1 cup dairy sour cream
2 tablespoons reserved dill pickle liquid

Heat oven to 350°F. Grease cookie sheet. In large bowl, combine spinach, chicken, eggs, dill pickle and celery. Set aside. Unroll 1 can of dough into 2 long rectangles. Overlap long sides ½ inch; firmly pressing edges and perforations to seal. Press or roll to form 12x9-inch rectangle. Combine margarine and mustard; brush half over dough. Spread half the chicken mixture over seasoned margarine to within 1 inch of edges. Starting at longest side, roll up; pinch seam and ends to seal. Place seam-side-down on one side of prepared cookie sheet. Repeat with second can of dough and remaining filling. Cut 2-inch diagonal slashes at 2-inch intervals across tops of Wellingtons. Bake at 350°F for 18 to 28 minutes or until deep golden brown. Cool slightly. Remove from pan; place on serving plate. In small bowl, combine sauce ingredients. Slice to serve; serve with sauce. *8 to 10 servings*

*Tips: For best results, keep dough refrigerated until ready to use. To reheat, cover loosely with foil; heat at 350°F. for 15 to 20 minutes.

HIGH ALTITUDE—Above 3500 Feet: No change.

NUTRITION INFORMATION PER SERVING
SERVING SIZE: ⅒ of recipe

		Percent U.S. RDA Per Serving	
Calories	320		
Protein	15 g	Protein	25%
Carbohydrate	22 g	Vitamin A	45%
Fat	19 g	Vitamin C	8%
Sodium	830 mg	Thiamine	10%
Potassium	290 mg	Riboflavin	10%
		Niacin	20%
		Calcium	6%
		Iron	10%

STIR-FRY CHICKEN FILLETS WITH ZUCCHINI

1 12-oz. package **TYSON® CHICK 'N QUICK™ Breast Fillets** (8-12 pieces)
¼ cup oil
2 cloves crushed garlic
3 Tbsp. soy sauce
½ cup bamboo shoots
½ cup canned mushroom slices
2 cups diced zucchini
2 Tbsp. cornstarch in ½ cup water
Roasted slivered almonds

Stir-fry chicken fillets over high heat with garlic and oil for 3 to 4 minutes. Add soy sauce and continue stirring for several minutes. Add zucchini, mushrooms, and bamboo shoots, cover and cook a few minutes.

Add cornstarch paste and stir for about 1 minute. Garnish with roasted slivered almonds. *Yield: 4-6 servings*

PAELLA

2 cups cubed cooked chicken
1 pound medium or large shrimp, peeled, leaving tails on and deveined
1 pound **ECKRICH® Smoked Sausage**, sliced into 1-inch pieces
1 cup chopped onion
1 to 2 cloves garlic, chopped
¼ cup olive or vegetable oil
3 cups water
1½ cups uncooked long grain rice
1 (16-ounce) can stewed tomatoes
2 tablespoons **WYLER'S® Chicken-Flavor Instant Bouillon** or 6 Chicken-Flavor Bouillon Cubes
2 to 3 teaspoons paprika
¼ to ½ teaspoon cayenne pepper
½ teaspoon black pepper
¼ teaspoon saffron or ground turmeric
1 (10-ounce) package frozen green peas, thawed
1 (2-ounce) jar sliced pimiento, drained

In Dutch oven, cook sausage, onion and garlic in oil until onion is tender. Stir in chicken, water, rice, tomatoes, bouillon, paprika, peppers and saffron. Bring to a boil; reduce heat and simmer covered 20 minutes. Stir in shrimp; cover and cook 5 minutes longer. Stir in peas; cover and cook until heated through, about 5 to 10 minutes. Garnish with pimiento. Refrigerate leftovers. *Makes 8 to 10 servings*

JAMBALAYA

½ cup chopped onion
¾ cup green pepper strips
1 garlic clove, minced
3 tablespoons butter or margarine
1 pound slivered raw chicken or turkey
½ pound slivered cooked ham
½ teaspoon thyme
½ teaspoon salt
¼ teaspoon pepper
1 can (8-oz.) whole peeled tomatoes
¼ cup chili sauce
2¼ cups water
2¼ cups **MINUTE® Rice**

Sauté onion, green pepper and garlic in butter in large skillet until tender but not browned. Add chicken and sauté for about 5 to 8 minutes. Add ham, thyme, salt, pepper, tomatoes, chili sauce and water. Bring to a boil. Stir in rice. Cover and simmer 5 to 8 minutes or until most of liquid is absorbed. *Makes 6 servings*

BAYOU JAMBALAYA

1 medium onion, sliced
½ cup chopped green pepper
1 clove garlic, minced
1 cup uncooked regular white rice
¼ cup butter or margarine
1 cup **HEINZ Tomato Ketchup**
2½ cups water
4 teaspoons **HEINZ Apple Cider Vinegar**
1 teaspoon salt
⅛ teaspoon cayenne
1 cup cubed cooked ham
½ pound raw, peeled, deveined shrimp

In large skillet, sauté first 4 ingredients in butter until onion is transparent. Stir in ketchup and remaining ingredients except shrimp. Cover; simmer 25-30 minutes or until rice is tender. Add shrimp; continue to simmer, tossing mixture gently with a fork, until shrimp is tender (about 5 minutes).

Makes 4-6 servings (about 6 cups)

QUICK SHRIMP CHOW MEIN

1½ cups diagonally-sliced celery
1 cup sliced onions
1 large green pepper, cut in slivers
12 ounces peeled, deveined raw shrimp
2 tablespoons vegetable oil
1 can (16 ounces) fancy mixed Chinese vegetables
1 can (10¾ ounces) condensed cream of chicken soup
3 tablespoons soy sauce
¼ teaspoon pepper
⅓ cup sliced pimientos
3 cups hot cooked **BLUE RIBBON Rice**
1 can (3 ounces) rice noodles *or* chow mein noodles

Sauté celery, onions, green pepper and shrimp in oil until vegetables are tender crisp and shrimp are pink. Add Chinese vegetables, soup, soy sauce, pepper and pimientos. Heat thoroughly. Serve over beds of fluffy **BLUE RIBBON Rice** and sprinkle with noodles.

Makes 6 servings

MANDARIN TUNA AND CASHEWS

⅓ cup sugar
2 tablespoons cornstarch
½ teaspoon ground ginger
½ cup sherry
⅓ cup soy sauce
⅓ cup water
2 tablespoons cider vinegar
5 tablespoons vegetable oil, divided
1 clove garlic, minced
4 green onions, thinly sliced
1 large green pepper, cut into ½-inch pieces
1 cup celery, cut into ½-inch pieces
1 can (8 oz.) sliced water chestnuts, drained
¾ cup dry roasted whole cashews
1 can (13 oz.) **CHICKEN OF THE SEA® Solid White Tuna**, drained*
Chow mein noodles

In small bowl combine sugar, cornstarch and ginger. Blend in sherry, soy sauce, water, vinegar and 2 tablespoons oil. Set aside.

In large skillet or wok heat remaining 3 tablespoons oil. Add garlic, onions, green pepper, celery and water chestnuts. Stir-fry** 3 minutes. Add cashews. Stir-fry 1 minute. Reduce heat to medium. Stir soy sauce mixture. Add to skillet. Gently stir in tuna. Bring to a boil. Heat and stir until thickened and glossy. Serve over noodles.

Makes 4 to 5 servings

*Tuna packed in oil or water may be used, based on personal preference.

**Cook and stir over high heat.

ROYAL SARDINES CREOLE

1 cup chopped green pepper
¾ cup chopped onion
¾ cup sliced celery
1 clove garlic, crushed
3 Tbsp. cooking oil
2 cups canned tomatoes
1 can tomato paste mixed with 6 Tbsp. water
½ tsp. salt
¼ tsp. thyme
1 bay leaf, crushed
Dash of cayenne
2 cans **KING OSCAR Sardines**, drained

Cook pepper, onions, and celery and garlic in the oil until tender. Add tomatoes, tomato paste and seasonings. Simmer 25 minutes, stirring occasionally. Fold in sardines carefully to keep their shape. Serve over hot rice.

Serves 6 to 8

IMPOSSIBLE LASAGNE PIE

½ cup small curd creamed cottage cheese
¼ cup grated Parmesan cheese
1 pound ground beef, cooked and drained
1 cup shredded mozzarella cheese (4 ounces)
1 teaspoon dried oregano leaves
½ teaspoon dried basil leaves
1 can (6 ounces) tomato paste
1 cup milk
2 eggs
⅔ cup **BISQUICK® Baking Mix**
1 teaspoon salt
¼ teaspoon pepper

Heat oven to 400°. Grease pie plate, 10x1½ inches. Layer cottage cheese and Parmesan cheese in plate. Mix cooked beef, ½ cup of the mozzarella cheese, the oregano, basil and tomato paste; spoon evenly over top. Beat milk, eggs, baking mix, salt and pepper until smooth, 15 seconds in blender on high or 1 minute with hand beater. Pour into plate. Bake until golden brown and knife inserted in center comes out clean, 30 to 35 minutes. Sprinkle with remaining cheese. Cool 5 minutes.

6 to 8 servings

HIGH ALTITUDE DIRECTIONS (3500 to 6500 feet): No adjustments are necessary.

SUPER SIMPLE CANADIAN BACON PIE

2 cups cubed **COUNTRY SMOKED MEATS Canadian Bacon**
1 jar (4½ oz.) sliced mushrooms, drained
½ cup sliced green onions
½ teaspoon salt
1 cup shredded natural Swiss cheese
1½ cups milk
¾ cup packaged biscuit mix (**BISQUICK®**)
3 eggs

Heat oven to 400°. Grease pie plate, 10 × 1½ inches. Sprinkle Canadian Bacon cubes, mushrooms, onions, salt and cheese in pie plate. Beat remaining ingredients until smooth, 15 seconds in blender on high or 1 minute with hand beater. Pour into plate. Bake until knife inserted between center and edge comes out clean, 30 to 35 minutes. Cool 5 minutes.   *6 to 8 servings*

IMPOSSIBLE HOT DOG 'N CHEESE PIE

1 pound frankfurters, sliced
⅓ cup chopped onion, if desired
1½ cups milk
¾ cup **BISQUICK® Baking Mix**
3 eggs
1½ cups shredded Cheddar cheese (about 6 ounces)

Heat oven to 400 degrees. Grease rectangular pan, 13×9×2-inches. Layer frankfurters and onion in pan. Beat milk, baking mix and eggs until smooth, 15 seconds in blender on high or 1 minute with hand beater. Pour into pan. Sprinkle with cheese. Bake until knife inserted in center comes out clean, about 30 minutes. Cool 5 minutes. Serve with catsup and mustard if desired.   *6 to 8 servings*

Favorite recipe from **The National Hot Dog & Sausage Council**

DUTCH PANTRY PIE

Pastry:
2 cups sifted flour
1½ tsp. salt
½ cup **WESSON® Oil**
2 Tbsp. undiluted evaporated milk
2 Tbsp. water

Mix flour and salt. Measure oil, milk and water in same cup (but don't stir). Pour all at once into flour; stir until mixed. Press into smooth ball. Cut in halves; flatten slightly. Place one half between two sheets of waxed paper, 12″ square. Roll out gently to edges of paper, (dampen table top to prevent slipping). Peel off top paper. If dough tears, mend without moistening. Lift paper and pastry by top corners. Place paper-side-up in 9″ pie pan. Peel off paper. Fit pastry into pan. Roll out top crust same way.

Filling:
4 slices American cheese (¼ lb.), cubed
1 cup undiluted evaporated milk
2 cups cooked potatoes, chopped
¼ cup chopped green onions and tops (or use dry onions)
2 Tbsp. chopped green pepper or pimiento
¼ to ½ tsp. salt
¼ tsp. pepper
1 can **SPAM® Luncheon Meat**, cubed

Heat oven to 425°F. Melt cheese in milk, stirring constantly. Mix with all remaining ingredients, except **SPAM® Luncheon Meat**. Spread in pastry-lined pan. Top with cubed **SPAM® Luncheon Meat**. Trim bottom crust. Place top crust over, gently peel off paper. Turn upper crust under lower crust and seal by pressing edges together. Flute. Make 3 or 4 slashes near center. Bake 35-40 minutes. Serve hot, with Sauce.*   *Makes 6 to 8 servings*

*SAUCE

Heat together 1 can undiluted soup (mushroom, tomato, chicken or celery) and ½ cup undiluted evaporated milk.

CHICKEN POT PIE

4 cups chicken stock
1 cup diced carrots
1 cup peas, fresh or frozen
½ cup chopped celery
½ cup chopped onion
½ teaspoon salt
½ teaspoon black pepper
4 cups cooked diced chicken (or turkey)
¼ cup white flour
½ cup cold water
1 recipe, Pastry for Chicken Pot Pie*
Melted margarine

1. Pour the chicken stock in a large pot. Add the carrots, peas, celery and onion and bring to a boil. Boil for 10 minutes. Add the salt, pepper and cooked chicken and continue to cook until the chicken is heated through.
2. Combine the flour and water and form a paste. Slowly add to the chicken mixture, stirring constantly until slightly thickened.
3. Line a 3-quart casserole with pastry and pour the filling into the casserole. Place the top layer of pastry over the filling and seal the edges as you would a pie. (Or place the filling into twelve individual ramekins 4½″ in diameter and place pastry circles over the top of each.) Cut several small slashes in the top of the crust and brush with melted margarine.
4. Bake in 375° oven for 45 minutes.   *Makes 12 servings*

*PASTRY FOR CHICKEN POT PIE

1 cup warm low-fat milk
1 package active dry yeast (check the date on the package)
2 eggs lightly beaten
1 package **BATTER-LITE® Natural Sourdough Bread Mix**
5 cups unbleached white flour
1 teaspoon salt
2 tablespoons **SWEETLITE™ Fructose**
½ cup unmelted corn oil margarine

1. Pour the warm milk into a large warm mixing bowl and sprinkle the yeast over the top of it. Stir until the yeast is dissolved, about 5 minutes.
2. Add the lightly beaten eggs and **BATTER-LITE® Natural Sourdough Bread Mix** and mix well.
3. Combine 4 cups of the flour with the salt and fructose in a warm bowl. Using a pastry blender (or 2 knives), cut the margarine into the flour mixture until it looks like coarse corn meal.
4. Form a well in the center of the flour mixture and pour the sourdough mixture into it. Mix well.
5. Turn onto a floured board and knead the dough, adding the remaining flour mixture until the dough is no longer sticky and is easy to handle.
6. Roll ¾ of the dough to form the lining of a 3-quart casserole dish and ¼ of the dough to form the top crust (or make 12 4½″ circles to cover individual pot pies).

Makes 12 individual 4½″ circles or a top and bottom crust for a casserole

MUSHROOM STROGANOFF PIE

**1 pkg. (7½ oz.) GOLDEN GRAIN® Stroganoff
  RICE-A-RONI®**
½ lb. fresh mushrooms, sliced
2 Tbsp. butter
1 lb. lean ground beef
¼ cup sour cream
1 Tbsp. chopped parsley or chives

Prepare **RICE-A-RONI®** as directed for meatless side dish. Sauté mushrooms in butter; drain liquid and stir into cooked rice. Press ground beef into bottom and sides of 10-inch pie pan; spread rice mixture over meat. Bake, uncovered, at 325°F. for 15 minutes. Cool slightly, cut into 6-8 wedges, garnish with sour cream and parsley.

BEEFY CHEESE PIE

1 lb. lean ground beef
½ cup onions, finely chopped
¼ cup catsup
¼ tsp. pepper
½ cup celery, chopped
1 cup sharp Cheddar cheese, shredded
¼ cup cornflake crumbs (optional)
1 egg
¾ cup cornflake crumbs
½ tsp. garlic salt
¼ tsp. salt
2 Tbsp. margarine
1-16 oz. can VEG-ALL® Mixed Vegetables, drained

Combine ground beef, egg, onion, ¾ cup cornflake crumbs, catsup, garlic salt, pepper and salt. Press meat mixture into bottom and sides of a 9 inch pie pan. Bake in a preheated oven at 400 degrees for 15 minutes, remove from oven and drain. Reduce heat to 350 degrees.

While meat is baking, in a small skillet sauté celery in 2 Tbsp. margarine. Remove from heat and add the cheese and **VEG-ALL® Mixed Vegetables**. Toss lightly and spoon over top of meat. Sprinkle with the cornflake crumbs if desired. Return to oven and continue baking for about 10-15 minutes. Cut in wedges to serve.
Serves 5-6

MEAT 'N TATER PIE

2 cups KELLOGG'S® RICE KRISPIES® Cereal
1 teaspoon salt
¼ teaspoon pepper
1 tablespoon catsup
⅓ cup milk
¼ cup chopped onion
1 lb. ground beef
1 egg
2 cups seasoned, very stiff mashed potatoes
2 tablespoons margarine or butter, melted
½ cup shredded American cheese
Paprika

1. In large mixing bowl, combine 1 cup of the **KELLOGG'S® RICE KRISPIES®** Cereal, the salt, pepper, catsup, milk and onion. Beat well. Add ground beef. Mix until combined. Press evenly in 9-inch pie pan to form meat shell. Set aside.
2. In small mixing bowl, beat egg slightly. Add potatoes. Stir

until combined. Spread potato mixture evenly over meat mixture.
3. Bake at 350°F for 35 minutes. While pie is baking, crush the remaining 1 cup cereal to ½ cup. Combine with melted margarine.
4. Remove pie from oven. Sprinkle cheese evenly over potato mixture. Top with cereal mixture. Bake about 10 minutes longer or until cheese melts. Sprinkle with paprika.
Yield: 6 servings

® Kellogg Company

IMPOSSIBLE TACO PIE

1 pound ground beef
1 medium onion, chopped (about ½ cup)
1 envelope (1¼ ounces) taco seasoning mix
1 can (4 ounces) chopped green chilies, drained
1¼ cups milk
3 eggs
¾ cup BISQUICK® Baking Mix
2 tomatoes, sliced
**1 cup shredded Monterey Jack or Cheddar cheese
  (4 ounces)**

Heat oven to 400°. Grease pie plate, 10 x 1½ inches. Cook and stir ground beef and onion in 10-inch skillet until beef is brown; drain. Stir in taco seasoning mix (dry). Spread in plate; sprinkle with chilies. Beat milk, eggs and baking mix until smooth, 15 seconds in blender on high or 1 minute with hand beater. Pour into plate. Bake 25 minutes. Top with tomatoes; sprinkle with cheese. Bake until cheese is golden brown and knife inserted in center comes out clean, 8 to 10 minutes longer. Cool 5 minutes. Serve with sour cream, chopped tomatoes and shredded lettuce if desired.
6 to 8 servings

SALT FREE CHILI POWDER
(Low Sodium)

2 tablespoons DURKEE Paprika
2 teaspoons DURKEE Imported Oregano
1¼ teaspoons DURKEE Ground Cumin
1¼ teaspoons DURKEE Garlic Powder
¾ teaspoon DURKEE Ground Red Pepper
¾ teaspoon DURKEE Onion Powder

Mix all ingredients thoroughly. Store in *airtight* container. Use as desired.
Makes 4 tablespoons

About .59 mg. sodium per teaspoon

TURKEY CHILI

**2 cups diced, roasted SWIFT PREMIUM®
  BUTTERBALL® Turkey**
1 cup chopped onion
½ cup chopped celery
1 clove garlic, minced
2 tablespoons butter or margarine
10¾ ounce can condensed cream of tomato soup
8 ounce can tomato sauce
1 tablespoon chili powder
¼ teaspoon salt
2 cans (16 ounces each) kidney beans

Panfry onion, celery and garlic in butter until lightly browned. Stir in soup and sauce, turkey, chili powder and salt. For a future meal, pour half the mixture into a 1 pint freezer container. Cool, label and freeze.
(Continued)

To serve: Add one 16 ounce can kidney beans with liquid to remaining mixture. Cook, uncovered, over low heat, simmering gently for 30 minutes.   *Makes 3 to 4 servings*

To serve frozen Chili: Thaw chili, add remaining can of kidney beans and follow same procedure as above.

Makes 3 to 4 servings

VEGETARIAN CHILI

⅓ cup **MAZOLA® Corn Oil**
2 cups coarsely chopped onion
2 medium green peppers, cut into 1-inch strips
  (2 cups)
3 cloves garlic, minced or pressed
3 cups coarsely shredded carrots
1 large zucchini, diced (2 cups)
1 cup sliced celery
3 cans (1 lb. each) tomatoes, undrained, coarsely
  chopped
2 cans (4 oz. each) hot green chilies, drained, minced
1½ teaspoons salt
1 teaspoon crushed dried red pepper
1 teaspoon dried oregano leaves
2 cans (1 lb. each) white and/or red kidney beans,
  drained
1 can (1 lb.) pinto beans, drained

In 8-quart saucepot heat corn oil over medium heat. Add onion, green peppers and garlic. Stirring occasionally, cook 5 minutes or until tender. Stir in carrots, zucchini, celery, tomatoes, chilies, salt, red pepper and oregano. Stirring occasionally, cook over medium heat 30 minutes. Add beans; cook 30 minutes longer. If desired, serve over rice.   *Makes about 12 (1-cup) servings*

Note: Chili may be frozen in tightly covered containers. Thaw completely before heating.

CHILLY DAY CHILI

2 medium onions, chopped
1 green pepper, coarsely diced
1 tablespoon salad oil
2 pounds lean ground beef
1 can (1 pound) tomatoes
1 can (15 ounces) tomato sauce
½ cup **HEINZ Tomato Ketchup**
1 tablespoon chili powder
2 teaspoons salt
¼ teaspoon pepper
2 cans (15½ ounces each) kidney beans, partially
  drained

In large kettle or Dutch oven, sauté onions and green pepper in oil until tender. Add beef stirring lightly to break up. Cover; simmer about 30 minutes or until meat loses color. Drain excess fat. Add tomatoes and next 5 ingredients. Simmer, uncovered, 30 minutes, stirring occasionally. Add kidney beans; simmer an additional 15 minutes.   *Makes 10-12 servings (about 2½ quarts)*

Note: Recipe is a mild flavored chili. Additional chili powder may be added for a spicier dish.

TEXAS-STYLE CHILI

3 pounds beef cubes for stew, cut into small pieces
¼ cup vegetable oil
1½ cups chopped onion
1 cup chopped green pepper
3 cloves garlic, chopped
2 (28-ounce) cans whole tomatoes, undrained and
  broken up
2 cups water
1 (6-ounce) can tomato paste
8 teaspoons **WYLER'S® Beef-Flavor Instant Bouillon**
  or 8 **Beef-Flavor Bouillon Cubes**
2 tablespoons chili powder
1 tablespoon ground cumin
2 teaspoons oregano leaves
2 teaspoons sugar

In large kettle, brown meat in oil, one-third at a time. Remove meat from pan; cook onion, green pepper and garlic until tender. Add meat and remaining ingredients; bring to a boil. Reduce heat; cover and simmer 1½ hours or until meat is tender. Serve with corn chips and shredded cheese if desired. Refrigerate leftovers.
Makes about 4 quarts

TEXAS CHILI

½ pound lean ground beef
½ cup chopped onion
½ cup chopped green pepper
¼ cup chopped celery
1 package (1¼ ounces) chili seasoning mix
1 can (8 ounces) **STOKELY'S FINEST® Tomato
  Sauce**
1 can (15 ounces) **STOKELY'S FINEST® Dark Red
  Kidney Beans**
For garnish: chopped onion, chopped green pepper,
  grated cheese, or commercial sour cream

Place beef, onion, green pepper, and celery in large skillet. Cook over medium heat, stirring constantly, until meat is browned and vegetables are tender. Drain excess fat. Stir in remaining ingredients, cover, and simmer 30 minutes. Top with chopped onion, chopped green pepper, grated cheese, or sour cream.   *4 servings*

MICROWAVE METHOD:
Crumble beef in 1½-quart casserole. Add onion, green pepper, and celery. Microcook, covered, 6 minutes, stirring twice. Drain excess fat. Stir in remaining ingredients, cover, and microcook 5 minutes, stirring once. Top with chopped onion, chopped green pepper, grated cheese, or sour cream.

COORS® SPICY CHILI

2 strips bacon
2 pounds beef chuck, diced
2 (12-ounce) cans **COORS® Beer**
2 tablespoons chili powder
1 tablespoon dried oregano, crushed
1 tablespoon ground cumin
½ teaspoon cayenne pepper
2 teaspoons Worcestershire sauce
1 tablespoon cornmeal or masa harina
Cooked pinto beans

Cook bacon till crisp; drain, reserving drippings in pan. Crumble bacon; set aside. In drippings, brown meat. Add next 6 ingredients and 1 teaspoon *salt*. Bring to boiling; reduce heat. Simmer, covered, 45 minutes. Combine cornmeal and ¼ cup *water*. Stir into hot mixture; add crumbled bacon. Return to boiling. Reduce heat; simmer, covered, 15 minutes. Serve with beans.   *Serves 8*

RIO GRANDE CHILI

2 tablespoons salad oil
1 medium onion, chopped
1 clove garlic, crushed
1 pound ground beef
2 teaspoons salt
1 teaspoon paprika
2 teaspoons chili powder
2 cans (1 pound each) kidney beans
½ cup bean liquid
1 can (1 pound) seasoned stewed tomatoes
1 can (6 ounces) tomato paste
½ teaspoon sugar
¾ teaspoon TABASCO® Pepper Sauce
1 can (12 ounces) whole kernel corn, drained

Heat oil in large skillet; add onion and garlic and cook until yellow, but not brown. Add ground beef; sprinkle with salt, paprika and chili powder. Cook meat until brown, breaking up with a fork. Drain kidney beans and discard all but ½ cup liquid; reserve beans. Stir in bean liquid, tomatoes, tomato paste, sugar and TABASCO®. Cover and simmer 30 minutes. Add kidney beans and corn; simmer 15 minutes longer, stirring occasionally. Serve with rice if desired, and a bottle of TABASCO® Sauce on the side. *Yield: About 6 servings*

SOUTH OF THE BORDER STYLE

¼ cup chopped onion
¼ cup chopped green pepper
1 tablespoon butter or margarine
2 15-ounce cans (4 cups) BROADCAST® Chili with Beans
1 12-ounce can (1½ cups) whole kernel corn, drained
1 4½-ounce can (¾ cup) chopped ripe olives
1 4-ounce package (1 cup) shredded sharp Cheddar cheese
1 package corn muffin mix

In large skillet, cook onion, and pepper in butter till tender. Stir in chili, corn, and olives; bring to boiling. Add cheese; stir to melt. Pour into 11 x 7 x 1½-inch baking pan.

Prepare muffin mix according to package directions. Spoon dough in diagonal bands across top of casserole; (bake any remaining dough in muffin pans and freeze for later use). Bake at 400° for 15 to 20 minutes. *Serves 8*

TWO TIME WORLD CHAMPION CHILI

4 tablespoons GEBHARDT®'S Chili Powder
2 tablespoons cumin
1 tablespoon paprika
1 teaspoon oregano
1 teaspoon sugar
1 teaspoon molé poblano
1 teaspoon coriander
4 beef bouillon cubes
1 cup chopped onion
1 cup cubed pork
1 cup cubed chuck steak
2 cups ground round steak
⅓ cup tomato sauce
2 teaspoons masa harina
1 cup beer
10 cloves garlic
Cooking oil to brown meat

Combine beer, bouillon cubes and spices. Let simmer. Brown meat, onions, garlic in small amount of oil. Add to spice mixture and cook for three hours.

Dissolve masa harina in hot water and add to chili. Add tomato sauce at end of cooking cycle.

Note: For hotter chili add ground chili peppers to taste.

CHILI 'N CORN BREAD

½ cup sliced celery
½ cup chopped onion
2 tablespoons chili powder
1 medium clove garlic, minced
2 tablespoons butter or margarine
1 can (10¾ ounces) CAMPBELL'S Condensed Tomato Soup
2 cans (about 15 ounces each) kidney beans, undrained
1½ cups quick-cooking rice, uncooked
1¼ cups shredded Cheddar cheese
Corn bread
Sliced green pepper
Sliced onion

In saucepan, cook celery and onion with chili powder and garlic in butter until tender. Add soup, beans, rice, and cheese. Bring to boil; cover. Reduce heat; simmer 10 minutes or until rice is done. Stir often. Serve with corn bread. Garnish with additional cheese, green pepper, and onion. *Makes about 6 cups*

VARIATION:

TORTILLA CHIPS

Omit corn bread. Serve with taco flavor tortilla chips.

CHILI ENCHILADAS

Tortillas*
½ pound ground beef
2 tablespoons chopped onion
1 can (15½ ounces) chili (without beans)
¼ teaspoon salt
¼ teaspoon crushed red pepper
Dash of pepper
Margarine or butter, melted
⅓ cup chopped onion
1½ cups shredded process American cheese (about 6 ounces)

Heat oven to 350°. Prepare Tortillas. Cook and stir ground beef and 2 tablespoons onion in 10-inch skillet until beef is brown; drain. Stir in chili, salt, red pepper and pepper. Heat to boiling; reduce heat. Cover and simmer 10 minutes.

Brush both sides of tortillas with melted margarine. Place 1 tablespoon chili mixture, 1 teaspoon onion and 1 teaspoon cheese in center of each tortilla. Roll up; place in 2 rows in ungreased rectangular baking dish, 12x7½x2 inches. Spoon remaining chili mixture over rolled tortillas, being careful to cover each. Sprinkle remaining onion and cheese over chili mixture. Bake until cheese is melted, about 15 minutes. *4 servings*

*TORTILLAS

Mix 1 cup BISQUICK® Baking Mix and ¼ cup water. Turn onto lightly floured board. Knead 1 minute. Shape dough into 8 balls. Roll each ball into 5-inch circle on board dusted with cornmeal. Cook on ungreased griddle until light brown. Turn; cook other sides until light brown. Stack tortillas, covering with damp towel to keep them soft.

HIGH ALTITUDE DIRECTIONS (3500 to 6500 feet): Use boiling water to make Tortillas. Continue as directed. Bake about 20 minutes.

CALIFORNIA ENCHILADAS

1 can (15 oz.) tomato sauce
1 clove garlic, finely chopped
1½ teaspoons hot pepper sauce
½ pound Monterey Jack or Muenster cheese
1½ cups cut-up cooked chicken
1 cup **LIPTON**® California Dip (see Index)
1 can (4 oz.) green chilies, drained and chopped
12 tortillas, softened
1 large green pepper, cut into 12 thin strips

Preheat oven to 375°. In small saucepan, combine tomato sauce, garlic and ½ teaspoon hot pepper sauce; simmer 15 minutes.

Cut cheese into 12 strips (4 x ¾ x ¼ inch) and reserve; shred remaining cheese (should equal about ½ to ¾ cup).

In large bowl, combine shredded cheese, chicken, California Dip, chilies, and remaining hot sauce. Place 2½ tablespoons mixture on each tortilla; roll up and place seam-side down in greased 2-quart oblong baking dish. Top each tortilla with 1 tablespoon prepared sauce, a cheese strip, and a green pepper strip. Bake 15 minutes or until cheese is melted. Serve with remaining sauce. *Makes 4 to 6 servings*

GROUND BEEF ENCHILADAS

1 pound lean ground beef
½ cup chopped onion
1 can (8¼ ounces) refried beans
1 can (10 ounces) enchilada sauce
2 teaspoons **KITCHEN BOUQUET**®
1½ teaspoons oregano, crumbled
½ teaspoon salt
4 full shakes **TABASCO**® or to taste
4 flour tortillas
½ cup grated Cheddar cheese

Sauté beef and onion in skillet over high heat for 5 minutes or until beef is cooked. Mix in beans, 2 tablespoons enchilada sauce, **KITCHEN BOUQUET**®, oregano, salt and **TABASCO**®. Remove from heat. Dip tortillas into some of the remaining enchilada sauce. Divide beef mixture evenly onto tortillas. Roll to enclose filling. Place seam-side down in 2-quart baking dish. Pour any remaining enchilada sauce over top. Sprinkle with cheese. Cover with lid or foil. Bake in a 350° oven for 15 minutes or until heated through. Dollop with sour cream and sprinkle with minced parsley if desired. Cooking time: 20 minutes. *Makes 4 servings*

TUNA ENCHILADAS DEL MAR

1 cup oil
12 corn tortillas
30 ounces enchilada sauce
1 12½ or 13 ounce can **CHICKEN OF THE SEA**® **Tuna**, drained and flaked
1 cup scallions, minced
½ pound grated Monterey Jack cheese

Preheat oven to 350°. Place oil in skillet, heat until hot. Quickly fry 12 tortillas in oil one at a time, until soft (about 4 seconds to a side). *(Continued)*

Remove from oil and drain on paper towels. When ready to assemble the enchiladas, dip each tortilla in enchilada sauce. Place 1 tablespoon flaked tuna in center of tortilla, add 1 generous tablespoon cheese, scallions and 2 tablespoons enchilada sauce.

Roll enchiladas and place seam side down in a greased 9 × 12 baking dish. Top with remaining enchilada sauce, sprinkle with remaining cheese and bake at 350° for 20 minutes.

Garnish with sour cream, black olives, avocado slices and tomato wedges. Serve at once.

Serves 6 (2 enchiladas per serving)

CHICKEN TACOS

1 jar **LA SAUCE**® Chicken Baking Sauce—Mild Mexican Style
2 cups chopped or shredded cooked chicken
8 taco shells, heated
½ head lettuce, shredded
1 cup chopped tomato
1 cup (4 oz.) shredded Cheddar cheese

In saucepan, combine **LA SAUCE**® and chicken; cook on low heat 10 minutes. Spoon chicken mixture into taco shells; top with lettuce, tomato and cheese. *8 tacos*

TACOS ALCHILI

Heat mixture of equal parts **WOLF**® Brand Chili and refried beans, spoon into taco shell. Cover with lettuce, tomato, and grated cheese. Add picante sauce.

SAUSAGE AND VEGETABLES ALFRESCO

3 Tbsp. olive oil or butter
¼ cup chopped onions
¼ cup chopped green pepper
½ lb. fresh mushrooms, sliced
2 cups broccoli flowerettes, chopped asparagus, zucchini squash or green peas
1 Tbsp. chopped pimiento
¼ tsp. garlic powder
1 tsp. oregano
1 pound **HILLSHIRE FARM**® Smoked Sausage or Italian Smoked Sausage, cut into bite-sized pieces
¾ cup Parmesan cheese
Salt
Pepper
Cooked and buttered pasta

Stir-fry onions, green pepper, mushrooms, green vegetables, pimiento and seasonings in oil over medium high heat until crisp-tender (about 4 minutes). Add sausage and cook over medium heat until sausage is heated through, about 5 minutes, stirring often. Mix in ½ cup cheese, salt and pepper to taste. Serve over buttered pasta. Sprinkle with remaining ¼ cup cheese.

Yield: 4-6 servings

MICROWAVE METHOD:
Combine olive oil, onions and green pepper in a large glass bowl or casserole. Microwave, uncovered, HIGH, 3 minutes, stirring once. Add mushrooms, green vegetables, pimiento, garlic, oregano and sausage. Microwave, uncovered, HIGH, 3-5 minutes or until hot and crisp-tender, stirring once. Stir in ½ cup of cheese, salt and pepper to taste. Serve over buttered pasta. Sprinkle with remaining ¼ cup cheese.

STIR-FRY PINEAPPLE BROWN 'N SERVE™

8 ounce package **SWIFT PREMIUM® Original BROWN 'N SERVE™ Sausage Links**
1 pound 4 ounce can pineapple chunks in juice, drained—reserve ¾ cup juice
1 cup sliced celery
1 green pepper cut into chunks
1 cup sliced fresh mushrooms
¼ cup water
1 tablespoon cornstarch
½ teaspoon ginger
¼ cup dry sherry
2 medium-size tomatoes cut into wedges
½ cup blanched almonds, optional

Cut sausage into halves lengthwise. Brown in skillet or electric wok. Add celery, green pepper and mushrooms. Stir-fry until vegetables are tender-crisp, about 5 to 6 minutes. Combine reserved pineapple juice, water, cornstarch, ginger and sherry. Mix well. Add to skillet, stirring constantly. Cook until liquid thickens. Stir in pineapple chunks and tomatoes. Cook an additional 2 to 3 minutes. Sprinkle with almonds, if desired.

Yield: 4 to 5 servings

GERMAN SAUSAGE SKILLET

6 slices bacon
1 medium (about 2 pounds) firm head green cabbage, cut into 6 wedges and cored
1 medium onion, chopped
2 Tbsp. sugar
¼ cup water
1 tsp. minced garlic
1 tsp. seasoned salt
½ tsp. crushed red pepper (optional)
2 tsp. caraway seed
1 lb. **HILLSHIRE FARM® Polska Kielbasa**, cut into 6 pieces

In a large skillet, fry bacon until crisp. Remove. Add the following ingredients to the drippings: cabbage, onion, sugar, water and spices. Cook, covered, over medium heat, 10-15 minutes, stirring several times. Add **Polska Kielbasa**. Return cover and continue to cook 10-15 minutes or until the sausage is heated. Top with reserved bacon, crumbled.

Yield: 6 servings

MICROWAVE METHOD:
Place bacon in a 2 qt. glass baking dish. Microwave, covered with a paper towel, HIGH, 5-6 minutes or until crisp. Remove bacon and drain. Stir the following ingredients into the drippings: onion, sugar, water, and spices. Add cabbage wedges. Microwave, covered, HIGH, 8 minutes. Move cabbage wedges to the side of the dish. Place sausage in the center. Microwave, covered, HIGH, 5-10 minutes or until sausage is hot and cabbage is tender. Top with reserved bacon, crumbled.

FALL-BAKED APPLES FILLED WITH SAUSAGE

1 lb. **JIMMY DEAN® Special Recipe Sausage**
4 Tbsp. minced onion
4 large cooking apples
½ cup brown sugar
¼ tsp. cinnamon
Bread crumbs

Preheat oven to 350°. Butter a shallow pan. Cut a slice from the top of apples. Scoop out core and pulp leaving shells ¾ inch thick. Chop the core and combine it and the minced onion with the sausage. Sauté the sausage mixture, breaking the meat with a fork, cooking until the rawness disappears. Mix in bread crumbs. Sprinkle the apple shells with half the brown sugar and cinnamon, and stuff firmly with the sausage mixture. Sprinkle with the remaining sugar and cinnamon. Bake for 40 minutes or until apples are tender.

Serves 6

TUSCANY SAUSAGE SKILLET

8 sweet Italian sausages (about 1 lb.) sliced
⅓ cup water
1 package (10 oz.) **BIRDS EYE® Italian Style Vegetables with a Seasoned Sauce**

Brown sausages well in skillet. Add water and simmer 5 minutes. Move sausages to one side of skillet. Add vegetables. Bring to a *full* boil over medium heat, separate vegetables with a fork; stir frequently. Reduce heat; cover and simmer for 2 minutes.

Makes about 3½ cups or 3 servings

SAUSAGE FIESTA

1 (8-ounce) package **SWIFT PREMIUM® BROWN 'N SERVE Sausage Links**
2 medium-sized onions, cut into rings
Large green bell pepper, cut into julienne strips
Large red bell pepper, cut into julienne strips
½ pound fresh mushrooms, sliced
¼ teaspoon salt
⅛ teaspoon ground black pepper
¾ cup white wine or chicken bouillon
1 (13¾-ounce) can chicken broth
1 cup long grain uncooked rice
⅛ to ¼ teaspoon ground saffron

Brown sausage in large skillet. Remove. Wipe out excess drippings. Add vegetables; cooking until tender crisp or to desired doneness. Stir in salt, black pepper and wine. Add sausage and heat just until boiling.

While vegetables are cooking bring chicken broth and rice to a boil in a medium-sized saucepan. Reduce heat to simmer; cover, cook 15 to 20 minutes or until tender. Stir in saffron. Serve with sausage mixture.

Yield: 5 servings

TREET® HAWAIIAN

1 12-oz. can **ARMOUR STAR TREET®**
4 pineapple fingers, reserving syrup
1 16-oz. can sweet potatoes, drained
¼ cup brown sugar, packed
Dash of ground cloves

Heat oven to 375°. Make 4 lengthwise slits in **ARMOUR STAR TREET®** to within ½ inch of bottom. Place one pineapple finger in each slit. Place in 1½-qt. casserole; arrange potatoes around meat. Combine ½ cup reserved pineapple syrup, brown sugar and cloves; pour over meat and potatoes. Bake at 375°, 40 minutes. To serve, cut **TREET®** and pineapple crosswise.

4 servings

MICROWAVE METHOD:
Make 4 lengthwise slits in **ARMOUR STAR TREET®** to within ½-inch of bottom. Place one pineapple finger in each slit. Place in 1½-qt. casserole; arrange potatoes around meat. Combine ½ cup reserved syrup, brown sugar and cloves; pour over meat and potatoes. Cook, covered, 5 to 6 minutes. Let stand, covered, 5 minutes. To serve, cut **TREET®** and pineapple crosswise.

WORLDS FASTEST LASAGNA

Brown in skillet:
>½ lb. mild Italian sausage (May substitute hamburger)

Drain grease. Add:
>1 15½ oz. jar spaghetti sauce

Mix:
>1½ lb. ricotta cheese
>¼ cup Parmesan cheese
>1 egg
>1 Tbsp. parsley flakes
>1 tsp. salt

Slice:
>½ lb. mozzarella cheese

Get out:
>2 AZTECA® Super Size Flour Tortillas

Using a 10″ skillet with ovenproof handle, place 1 tortilla in skillet. Top with one half ricotta, one half mozzarella, and one half the sauce. Repeat, forming a second layer. Bake in 375° oven 30 minutes. Let stand 10 minutes before serving (You may use square baking pan instead of skillet. Place tortilla in pan, tearing up second tortilla to fill in corners. Proceed as above).

Makes 6 servings

SAUCEY FRANK 'N CABBAGE ROLLS

>½ pound ECKRICH® Jumbo Beef Franks
>8 green cabbage leaves
>¼ cup chopped onion
>¼ cup diced fresh mushrooms
>2 tablespoons chopped green pepper
>2 tablespoons chopped celery
>1 tablespoon butter
>1 teaspoon salt
>½ teaspoon garlic powder
>⅛ teaspoon pepper
>1½ cups cooked brown rice
>1 can (10¾ ounces) tomato soup

Slice franks in half lengthwise; set aside. Cook cabbage leaves in salted water for 5 minutes; drain well. In medium skillet, cook onion, mushrooms, green pepper, and celery in butter for 3 minutes. Remove from heat and stir in seasonings and rice. Divide filling evenly between cabbage leaves. Top each with frank half; roll up. Place cabbage rolls, seam side down, in shallow baking dish. Combine tomato soup and ⅓ cup water. Pour over cabbage rolls. Bake, uncovered, at 350° for 30 minutes.   *4 servings*

Calories: 354 calories per serving.
1 serving = (2 cabbage rolls, ¼ cup sauce.)

GERMAN BRAND WIENERS 'N KRAUT

>1 lb. pkg. JOHN MORRELL® German Brand Wieners
>2 cans (14 oz. each) sauerkraut, drained
>3 cups of beer
>1 large onion, thinly sliced
>½ cup thinly sliced celery

Place kraut and beer in a large saucepan and bring to a boil; reduce heat and simmer, covered, for 20 minutes. Add **German Brand Wieners**, onion and celery. Bring to a boil, reduce heat and then simmer another 20 minutes. To serve, place kraut mixture on heated serving dish and top with **German Brand Wieners**.

Yield: 6 servings

CREOLE FRANKS ON CHIPS

>8 large frankfurters (1 pound), cut in ½-inch pieces
>3 tablespoons butter, margarine, bacon drippings, or vegetable oil
>1 large onion, chopped (1 cup)
>½ cup chopped green pepper
>1 can (1 pound, 12 ounce) tomatoes
>1 teaspoon chili powder
>1 teaspoon salt
>2 teaspoons sugar
>Dash of pepper
>**JAYS Potato Chips**

Brown frankfurters in fat or oil; remove. Sauté onion and green pepper in remaining fat or oil until tender; add tomatoes, chili powder, salt, sugar, and pepper; cover. Simmer 25 minutes; add frankfurters; simmer 5 minutes longer. Serve hot on potato chips.

Makes 6 servings

BEANY VEGETARIAN "MEATBALLS"

>1 can (10½-oz.) HAIN® Natural Onion Bean Dip
>1 cup shredded carrots
>1 cup uncooked rolled oatmeal
>1 jar (16-oz.) HAIN® Natural Spaghetti & Cooking Sauce

In bowl, combine and mix Bean Dip, carrots, rolled oats, and 2 Tbsp. of the Spaghetti Sauce. Grease hands lightly and form mixture into 2-inch balls. Place in baking dish. Bake at 350°F for 30 minutes and remove from oven. Top with remaining Spaghetti Sauce and bake for an additional 15 minutes. Serve with spaghetti or in sandwiches.

Makes 16

Stews

ITALIAN BEEF STEW
(Manzo Stufato)

>3 tablespoons PROGRESSO Olive Oil
>3 pounds beef shoulder, cut into 2-inch cubes
>1 cup chopped onions
>¼ pound sliced cooked ham, slivered
>1 clove garlic, minced
>1 can (28 oz.) PROGRESSO Recipe-Ready Crushed Tomatoes
>2 tablespoons PROGRESSO Wine Vinegar
>2 teaspoons basil leaves, crumbled
>2 teaspoons salt
>¼ teaspoon ground black pepper
>1 can (14 oz.) artichoke hearts in brine, drained
>1 package (10 oz.) frozen peas, thawed

In a large heavy ovenproof saucepot or a Dutch oven heat oil until hot. Add beef a few pieces at a time, brown on all sides. Remove beef from saucepot; set aside. To saucepot add onions, ham and garlic; sauté over moderate heat for 2 minutes. Add tomatoes, vinegar, basil, salt and black pepper; mix well. Return beef to pot. Cover and bake in a preheated slow oven (325 F.) until beef is fork-tender, about 2½ hours. Strain off fat. Add artichoke hearts and peas. Cover and bake 15 minutes longer. Serve with fettuccine noodles, if desired.

Yield: 8 portions

SAVORY BEEF STEW

1½ pounds beef stew meat, boneless, cut in 1½-inch cubes
¼ cup flour
1 teaspoon salt
¼ teaspoon basil
¼ teaspoon savory or marjoram
⅛ teaspoon pepper
3 tablespoons vegetable oil
2 onions, sliced
1 can or bottle (12-ounces) **STROH'S Beer**
½ cup water
1 bay leaf
5 medium potatoes (1⅔ pounds)
1 pound carrots (8 to 10) or ½ pound each parsnips and carrots

1. Dredge meat in mixture of flour, salt, basil, savory and pepper. Reserve excess flour. Brown meat in oil. Add onions, beer, water and bay leaf. Cover and simmer 1½ hours.
2. Pare potatoes, cut into large cubes. Slice carrots and/or parsnips. Add vegetables to stew. If necessary, add a little more water.
3. Cover and simmer 1 hour more, or until meat and vegetables are tender. Make smooth paste of reserved flour mixture and a little water. Stir into stew during last 10 minutes of cooking. Remove bay leaf. *6 servings*

Note: The alcohol boils off early in the cooking, so the dish may be served to children.

HARVEST BEEF & SAUSAGE STEW

2 slices bacon
½ cup unsifted flour
1 pound beef cubes for stew
3 cups water
2 medium apples, pared and chopped
1 medium onion, cut into wedges
4 teaspoons **WYLER'S® Beef-Flavor Instant Bouillon** *or* **4 Beef-Flavor Bouillon Cubes**
½ teaspoon thyme leaves
4 medium carrots, pared and cut into strips
1 (1-pound) head cabbage, cut into wedges
½ pound link smoked sausage, sliced

In Dutch oven, cook bacon until crisp; reserve drippings. Remove and crumble; set aside. In paper or plastic bag, mix ¼ cup flour and beef; shake to coat. Brown beef in bacon drippings. Combine water and ¼ cup flour; mix well. Add flour mixture, apples, onion, bouillon and thyme to beef. Bring to a boil. Reduce heat; cover and simmer 1 hour. Stir in carrots; simmer 20 minutes. Add cabbage and sausage; continue cooking 40 minutes or until vegetables are tender. Garnish with bacon. Refrigerate leftovers.
Makes 4 to 6 servings

BUCK'S COUNTY BEEF STEW

3 tablespoons corn oil
2 pounds stewing beef, cut in 2-inch cubes
1 beef bouillon cube
2 teaspoons salt
1 bay leaf
¼ teaspoon crushed dried thyme leaves
4½ cups water
6 carrots
12 small white onions
¼ cup **ARGO®/KINGSFORD'S® Corn Starch**

In skillet heat corn oil over medium heat. Add beef; brown on all sides. Add next 4 ingredients and 4 cups of the water. Cover; bring to boil. Reduce heat; simmer 1½ hours. Add carrots and onions. Simmer ½ hour or until tender. Mix corn starch and ½ cup water. Stir into beef mixture. Bring to boil, stirring constantly; boil 1 minute. *Makes 6 servings*

Note: Lamb may be substituted for beef.

BALTIMORE SPICE BEEF STEW

¼ cup flour
1 Tbsp. **BALTIMORE SPICE OLD BAY Seasoning**
1½ lb. beef stew meat, cut in 1½-inch cubes
2 Tbsp. oil
½ cup chopped onions
3½ cups hot water
1 (8½-oz.) can small white whole onions, drained
4 carrots, pared and sliced
3 medium potatoes, pared and quartered
1 (1-lb.) can green beans, drained
½ cup peas
2 beef bouillon cubes
1 Tbsp. **BALTIMORE SPICE OLD BAY Seasoning**

Mix flour and 1 tablespoon **BALTIMORE SPICE OLD BAY Seasoning**; shake with beef cubes in paper bag to coat meat. Heat oil in 4-quart heavy stock pot. Brown beef. Add chopped onions; cook 5 minutes. Drain fat. Add hot water; heat to boiling. Add vegetables and bouillon cubes; reduce heat. Cover and simmer until vegetables are tender, about 45 minutes. Near end of cooking, season with remaining tablespoon of **BALTIMORE SPICE OLD BAY Seasoning.**

BEEF STEW

2 pounds stewing beef, cut into 1-inch cubes
1 cup **HENRI'S Beefsteak French Dressing**
2 cups beef broth
½ cup cold water
¼ cup flour
4 potatoes, peeled and cut into 1½-inch cubes
1½ cups thinly sliced carrots
2 onions, quartered
Salt and pepper to taste

1. Marinate beef in **HENRI'S Beefsteak French Dressing** in refrigerator for 2 hours.
2. Preheat oven to 350° F.
3. Add beef broth to marinated meat and bake in a 9 × 13-inch pan, uncovered, 1½ hours or until meat is tender.
4. Combine cold water and flour, mix until smooth. Stir into meat juices. Add vegetables and seasonings. Cover and continue baking for 45 minutes or until vegetables are tender.
Makes 6 (1-cup) servings

STEW 'N BISCUIT BAKE

1 can (24 oz.) **DINTY MOORE® Beef Stew**
¼ cup dairy sour cream
1 cup biscuit mix
¼ cup water

In 1½ quart casserole, combine stew and sour cream. Bake in 425° F oven. Meanwhile, in small bowl, stir biscuit mix and water to make a soft dough. Drop by spoonfuls into hot stew. Bake about 20 minutes until biscuits are lightly browned. *2 to 3 servings*

CALIFORNIA BEEF STEW

2 tablespoons salad oil
2 pounds beef, suitable for stew, cut in 1½-inch cubes
1 tablespoon **LAWRY'S® Seasoned Salt**
½ teaspoon **LAWRY'S® Seasoned Pepper**
1 bay leaf
2 cups water
1 cup dry red wine
1 bunch carrots
12 small boiling onions
3 medium zucchini
2 large tomatoes
2 tablespoons flour
¼ cup water

Heat oil in Dutch oven. Add beef cubes and brown thoroughly on all sides. Add Seasoned Salt, Seasoned Pepper and bay leaf. Stir in 2 cups water and wine. Bring to a boil, reduce heat, cover and simmer about 1 hour and 15 minutes. Meanwhile, peel carrots and cut in 2-inch lengths. Peel onions and pierce each end with a fork so they will retain their shape when cooked. Cut zucchini in about four diagonal pieces. Peel and quarter tomatoes. Combine flour and ¼ cup water. After beef has simmered 1 hour and 15 minutes, add carrots. About 10 minutes later add onions and zucchini. Continue simmering until meat and vegetables are tender, about 20 minutes. Add tomatoes and flour-water mixture. Combine carefully but thoroughly. Bring to a boil, reduce heat and simmer 2 to 3 minutes. Serve immediately. *Makes about 6 servings*

BEEF STEW BOURGUIGNONNE

1 cup mushrooms, quartered
½ cup diced onion
¼ teaspoon pepper
½ teaspoon garlic powder
¾ cup Burgundy wine
1 teaspoon vinegar
2 tablespoons catsup
1 package (32 oz.) **BANQUET® Beef Stew Heat and Serve Frozen Buffet Supper Main Dish**

In a 2-quart oblong baking dish place mushrooms, onion, pepper and garlic powder. Stir in wine, vinegar and catsup. Remove frozen beef stew from foil tray; place in baking dish on top of wine mixture. Heat in 400°F oven for 25 minutes. Stir stew thoroughly. Heat for additional 15 minutes, until mixture is bubbly.
Makes 6 servings

MAIN DISH BEEF STEW

2½ pounds beef chuck
2 tablespoons cooking oil
2 teaspoons salt
2 teaspoons chili powder
¼ teaspoon pepper
1 (1 lb.) can whole tomatoes
1 clove garlic, crushed
1 cup **LINDSAY® Pitted Ripe Olives**
3 large onions
3 large carrots
¾ cup celery
2 tablespoons cornstarch
¼ cup water

Cut beef into one-inch cubes. Heat oil; add beef and brown slowly. Add 1½ teaspoons salt, chili powder, pepper, canned tomatoes and garlic. Bring to boil. Reduce heat; cover and cook gently 1½ to 2 hours or until beef is almost tender. Drain ripe olives. Peel and quarter onions. Clean carrots and celery. Cut in 2-inch lengths. Add ripe olives, onions, celery and carrots to meat. Sprinkle with remaining ½ teaspoon salt. Continue to cook, covered, 30 to 40 minutes or until vegetables are tender. Mix cornstarch with water. Add to meat and vegetables; cook, stirring, until thickened.
Makes 6 servings

RIO GRANDE STEW

2 pounds beef cubes for stew
Flour
¼ cup vegetable oil
4½ cups water
1 (16-ounce) can stewed tomatoes, undrained
2 medium onions, cut into wedges
7 teaspoons **WYLER'S® Beef-Flavor Instant Bouillon** *or* **7 Beef-Flavor Bouillon Cubes**
1 teaspoon ground coriander, optional
1 teaspoon ground cumin
1 teaspoon oregano leaves
¼ teaspoon garlic powder
1 bay leaf
1 cup sliced carrots
2 ears fresh or thawed frozen corn, cut into chunks
1 small head cabbage, cut into wedges (about 1 pound)
1 (4-ounce) can chopped mild green chilies, drained

In paper or plastic bag, add meat, a few pieces at a time, to flour; shake to coat. In Dutch oven, brown meat in oil. Add remaining ingredients except carrots, corn, cabbage and chilies. Bring to a boil. Reduce heat; cover and simmer 1½ hours. Add remaining ingredients; cook 30 minutes longer or until vegetables are tender. Remove bay leaf. Refrigerate leftovers. *Makes 8 servings*

CANTONESE BEEF STEW

1 lb. round steak, cut in 2 inch strips
1 clove garlic, minced
1 Tbsp. cooking oil
2 cups stock or 1 bouillon cube mixed with 2 cups water
1 Tbsp. **CHINA BEAUTY® Soy Sauce**
½ tsp. sugar
¼ tsp. salt
¼ tsp. thyme or ginger
1 cup green onions, cut in 1 inch pieces
1 pkg. frozen green peas
1 cup sliced celery
1 small can **CHINA BEAUTY® Water Chestnuts**, drained and sliced
1 can **CHINA BEAUTY® Bean Sprouts**, drained
2 diced tomatoes
1 Tbsp. cornstarch

Sauté beef and garlic in oil until lightly browned. Add 1 cup of stock, and the seasonings. Cover and cook slowly until meat is tender, about 45 minutes. Add onions, peas and celery and cook for 5 minutes more, then add water chestnuts, bean sprouts and tomatoes; Heat through. Combine remaining cup of stock with cornstarch, mix with stew and simmer until sauce is clear and thickened; add more soy sauce if desired. Serve with chow mein noodles or rice. *4-5 servings*

PORK STEW ORIENTAL

1 pound (1 inch cubes) pork shoulder
1 to 2 tablespoons shortening
1¼ cups water
1 medium onion, quartered
Dash pepper
3 medium carrots, cut in ½ inch diagonal slices
1½ cups diagonally sliced celery
1 can (8 ounces) water chestnuts, halved
1 jar (12 ounces) **HEINZ Home Style Pork Gravy**
2 tablespoons soy sauce
1 tablespoon cornstarch
1 tablespoon water

Brown pork in shortening; drain excess fat. Add water, onion and pepper. Cover; simmer 45 minutes. Add carrots, celery and water chestnuts; stir in gravy and soy sauce. Cover; simmer an additional 20 minutes or until meat and vegetables are tender. Thicken with a mixture of cornstarch and water. Serve stew in a bowl topped with chow mein noodles or a mound of rice, if desired.

Makes 4-5 servings (about 5½ cups)

FLAVORFUL PORK STEW

1¼ pounds boneless pork shoulder, cut into 1¼-inch
   pieces
3 tablespoons all-purpose flour
1 teaspoon salt
⅛ teaspoon pepper
1 tablespoon shortening
1¼ cups water
¾ teaspoon curry powder
1½ cups celery pieces
12 pitted prunes
2½ cups cooked cauliflowerettes, drained

Combine flour, salt and pepper; mix well. Dredge pork in flour mixture. Reserve excess flour mixture. Brown pork in shortening in a large skillet. Pour off drippings. Add 1 cup water, cover tightly, and cook over low heat for 30 minutes. Stir in curry powder. Add celery; cover and continue cooking for 15 minutes. Combine reserved flour with remaining ¼ cup water, mixing well. Stir into pork mixture; add prunes and continue cooking for 15 minutes or until meat and celery are done, stirring occasionally. Stir cauliflowerettes into pork mixture and heat through.

Makes 4 servings

Favorite recipe from **National Pork Producers Council**

BROWN VEAL STEW WITH CASHEWS

3 tablespoons butter or margarine
2 lb. boneless lean veal, cut into 1-inch cubes
1 teaspoon salt
½ teaspoon pepper
1 small bay leaf, crumbled
1 garlic clove, crushed
1 medium onion, chopped
1 celery stalk, chopped
1½ cups **FISHER® Chopped Salted Cashews**
2 fresh ripe tomatoes, peeled and chopped*
1½ cups water
1 teaspoon flour
1 teaspoon Worcestershire sauce

Melt butter in a deep, heavy skillet. Add veal, salt, pepper, bay leaf, garlic, onion and celery. Cook over moderate heat, stirring frequently, until meat is well browned on all sides. Add cashews, tomatoes and water. Cover loosely and simmer over low heat for 1 hour. Blend flour and Worcestershire sauce; stir into meat mixture. Cook uncovered, stirring occasionally, until thickened. Simmer over lowest heat without stirring for 20 minutes. Serve immediately over rice. *6 servings*

*Tip: Two whole canned tomatoes may be substituted for fresh.

DICED VEAL STEW

1 pkg. (12-oz.) **PROVIMI® Diced Veal**, thawed
3 Tbsp. butter
2 medium onions, cut in eighths
½ lb. fresh mushrooms, sliced
1 clove garlic, minced
1 Tbsp. flour
1¼ cups water
1 tsp. chicken seasoned stock base
2 carrots, sliced
1 leek, sliced
1 stalk celery, sliced
1 cup frozen peas
1 tsp. lemon juice
1 egg yolk
½ cup heavy cream
½ tsp. salt

Bouquet Garni:
1 bay leaf
1 sprig parsley
⅛ tsp. thyme, tied in cheesecloth

Lightly brown diced veal in butter. Add onions, mushrooms and garlic, cook 10 minutes. Sprinkle flour over meat; stir to blend. Add water, salt, bouquet garni, broth stock base and vegetables. Cover and simmer, stirring occasionally, until meat is tender—about 30 minutes. Remove bouquet garni; stir in lemon juice. Beat egg yolk and cream together. Stir small amount of hot mixture into yolk mixture; return all to pan. Heat and stir until mixture is bubbly and slightly thickened. *Makes 4 servings*

CHICKEN STEW

1 package (12-oz.) **BANQUET® Breaded Chicken
   Nuggets**
½ green pepper, chopped (about ½ cup)
1 small onion, chopped (about ½ cup)
2 tablespoons vegetable oil
1 can (16-oz.) whole peeled tomatoes, chopped
1 package (10-oz.) frozen cut okra, thawed
1 can (8-oz.) tomato sauce
1 bay leaf
1 teaspoon Worcestershire sauce
Dash ground red pepper

CONVENTIONAL METHOD:
Prepare chicken nuggets according to conventional oven package instructions. In large skillet, sauté green pepper and onion in oil until green pepper is tender-crisp. Stir in tomatoes, okra, tomato sauce, bay leaf, Worcestershire sauce and pepper. Heat to boiling; simmer covered, 10 minutes or until okra is tender-crisp, stirring occasionally. Remove bay leaf. Top chicken with vegetable mixture. *Makes 4 servings*

MICROWAVE METHOD:
Omit oil. In 3-quart round glass casserole, place green pepper and onion. Cover with plastic wrap. Heat on HIGH 2 to 3 minutes or until green pepper is tender-crisp. Stir in tomatoes, okra, tomato sauce, bay leaf, Worcestershire sauce and pepper. Heat on HIGH

5 to 7 minutes or until okra is tender-crisp, stirring occasionally. Remove bay leaf. Let stand covered. Prepare chicken nuggets according to microwave package instructions. Remove paper towels. Top chicken with vegetable mixture.

SPANISH CHICKEN STEW

1 5-lb. stewing chicken, whole or cut up
3 tablespoons **POMPEIAN Olive Oil**
1 tablespoon salt
12 small whole new potatoes, peeled
2 carrots, diced
1½ cups water
1 package frozen peas
1 package frozen artichoke hearts
2 tablespoons flour

Place chicken in **POMPEIAN Olive Oil** in large, heavy pot. Add salt, cover, turn heat low as possible and steam chicken in **POMPEIAN** for 1 hour. (Chicken should not brown.) Add potatoes, carrots and water; cover, continue cooking over lowest heat 1 hour longer or until chicken is very tender, adding water if necessary. Add frozen peas and artichokes, cook until frozen blocks can be broken up, cook 5 minutes longer. Skim fat from top of sauce. Mix flour with liquid from pot to make thin paste, add this to sauce, and cook until sauce is smooth and thickened. Serve vegetables with chicken on large platter.   *Makes 12 servings*

CAJUN SHRIMP STEW

3 lb. whole shrimp
2 tablespoons butter
1 tablespoon salad oil
3 tablespoons flour
1 cup chopped onion
½ cup chopped green pepper
1 cup chopped celery
2 cloves garlic, minced
1 can (8-oz.) tomato sauce
½ can water
2 tablespoons chopped parsley
¼ teaspoon sugar
¼ teaspoon thyme
2 thin slices lemon
TRAPPEY'S® Worcestershire Sauce
Salt
TRAPPEY'S® Pepper or MEXI-PEP® Sauce

Peel, devein, and wash shrimp. Heat butter and oil in large skillet; sauté shrimp 5 minutes. Remove shrimp. Lower heat; stir in flour until light brown. Add onion, green pepper, celery; sauté until soft. Stir in garlic, tomato sauce and water. Simmer five minutes. Add shrimp and remaining ingredients and seasonings to taste. Cover, simmer 15 minutes. Serve over hot rice.   *Serves 4*

CRABMEAT VEGETABLE STEW

2 tablespoons **PLANTERS Peanut Oil**
1 small onion, grated
¼ pound fresh mushrooms, thinly sliced
2 medium tomatoes, skinned and chopped
½ pound flaked crabmeat
½ teaspoon salt
Dash ground red pepper
1 cup milk
1 cup heavy cream
1 tablespoon chopped parsley
1 teaspoon chopped chives
¼ cup **DRY SACK® Sherry**

Heat oil in a saucepan over medium heat; add onion and cook and stir for about 1 minute. Add mushroom slices and continue cooking for about 3 minutes. Mix in tomatoes and cook for 5 minutes. Stir in crabmeat, salt, red pepper, milk and cream; heat until mixture *just* comes to a boil. Mix in parsley, chives and **DRY SACK® Sherry**. Serve at once.   *Serves: 6*

HADDOCK STEW

4 tablespoons butter
1 medium onion, chopped
4 tablespoons flour
1 teaspoon celery salt
½ teaspoon white pepper
3 cups **COFFEE RICH® Frozen Non-Dairy Creamer**
1 cup water
1 tablespoon salt
1 quart water
1 pound frozen haddock, thawed
3 carrots, sliced
2 potatoes, diced
1 (10-ounce) package frozen peas, slightly thawed

1. In a 1½-quart saucepan, sauté onion in butter until tender. Add flour, celery salt and white pepper, stirring until mixture thickens.
2. Gradually add non-dairy creamer, then 1 cup water, stirring constantly, until mixture simmers. Set aside.
3. In a soup kettle, heat 1 quart of water with 1 tablespoon salt to boiling. Add haddock, and return to boil. Reduce heat and simmer until fish is tender, about 10 minutes. Using a slotted spoon, transfer fish to a platter. Set aside.
4. Add carrots to soup kettle. Boil 5 minutes.
5. Add potatoes to soup kettle and boil until vegetables are tender, about 10 minutes more.
6. Add peas and cook about 3 minutes. Adjust seasoning.
7. Add creamer mixture to soup kettle and blend thoroughly. Flake haddock into small pieces and return to soup kettle. Heat through and serve.

Casseroles

SMOKE FLAVOR CASSEROLE OF CHOPS

6 loin veal, lamb or pork chops, 1 inch thick
1 cup diced carrots
1 tsp. minced parsley
1 cup thinly sliced onion
1 cup peas
FIGARO LIQUID BARBECUE SMOKE

Roll chops in flour and brown in a little hot fat in frying pan. Place one-half of vegetables in a deep casserole; add 1 cup of boiling salted water and 1 teaspoon minced parsley. Brush chops on both sides with **FIGARO LIQUID BARBECUE SMOKE.** Lay chops on top of vegetables and cover with remaining vegetables. Cover casserole and cook 1 hour in 375° oven.

PORK AND CHEESE BAKE

4 ounce package **TREASURE CAVE® Blue Cheese,** crumbled
¼ cup chopped onion
¼ cup chopped green pepper
2 tablespoons butter or margarine
¼ cup flour
1 teaspoon salt
2 cups milk
1 tablespoon Worcestershire sauce
3 or 4 drops **TABASCO® Sauce**
8 ounce package medium egg noodles, cooked and drained
8 rib pork chops, cut ½ inch thick
2 tablespoons shortening
Salt and pepper

Sauté onion and green pepper in butter in skillet until tender. Stir in flour and salt. Gradually add milk. Heat to boiling, stirring constantly; boil 1 minute. Add cheese, Worcestershire and **TABASCO® Sauce.** Combine with noodles. Spread noodles in a 1½ quart rectangular baking dish. In a skillet, brown chops in shortening. Season with salt and pepper. Place chops on top of noodles. Cover. Bake in a 350°F. oven 35 to 45 minutes.

Yield: 8 servings

Note: When crumbled, a 4 ounce package of **TREASURE CAVE® Blue** equals about 1 cup.

ALMOND CRAB CASSEROLE

1 (6 oz.) pkg. **WAKEFIELD® Crabmeat**
1 can condensed cream of mushroom soup
1 cup chopped celery
¼ cup chopped onion
1 (3 oz.) can chow mein noodles
1 (8 oz.) can water chestnuts, drained and sliced
⅓ cup toasted, slivered almonds
1 (4 oz.) can mushroom pieces
1 teaspoon Worcestershire sauce

Thaw and drain crabmeat and retain liquid. Stir together soup, celery, onion, noodles, water chestnuts, mushrooms and Worcestershire sauce. Fold in crabmeat and crab liquid. Spoon into greased 1½ quart casserole dish. Top with almonds and bake in 350° F. oven for 20-30 minutes or until hot and lightly browned.

SHRIMP AND CRAB MEAT CASSEROLE
(Microwave Recipe)

1 pound raw, peeled and deveined shrimp
1 pound lump, blue crab meat
½ cup chopped green pepper
½ cup chopped onion
½ cup chopped celery
1 cup mayonnaise
½ teaspoon salt
¼ teaspoon pepper
1 teaspoon Worcestershire sauce
1 teaspoon paprika
½ cup grated Cheddar cheese
½ cup dry bread crumbs

In a 3-quart casserole, cook shrimp, green pepper, onion and celery in 1 cup water on HIGH for 5 minutes, stirring once. Drain and fold in remaining ingredients except cheese and bread crumbs. Sprinkle top with cheese and crumbs. Cook on MEDIUM for 4 minutes, turning dish once. *Makes 6 servings*

Favorite recipe from **National Marine Fisheries Service**

HERBAL ARTICHOKE-SHRIMP BAKE

2 (4½ oz.) cans **S&W® Deveined Medium Size Whole Shrimp,** drained
2 (14 oz.) cans **S&W® Small Artichoke Hearts,** drained and halved
6 green onions, sliced
2 Tbsp. chopped fresh parsley
½ tsp. each basil, marjoram and dill weed
2 Tbsp. French dressing
1 (8 oz.) can **S&W® Tomato Sauce**
2 Tbsp. lemon juice
1 Tbsp. cornstarch
2 Tbsp. dry sherry
1 cup grated Cheddar cheese
Dash paprika

Drain and rinse shrimp. Soak in ice cold water for 20 minutes. Place artichokes, green onions, parsley, herbs, French dressing, tomato sauce and lemon juice in a saucepan. Mix cornstarch with dry sherry and add into artichoke mixture to thicken. Bring mixture to a low boil and simmer for 3-4 minutes. Pour into a shallow casserole. Drain shrimp and arrange on top of artichoke mixture. Sprinkle with grated cheese. Cover and bake at 350° for 15 minutes. Serve over rice. *Serves 4 to 6*

FISH STICKS AU GRATIN

1 10 oz. package **VAN DE KAMP'S®** **Fish Sticks** (or any small package of **VAN DE KAMP'S®** fish products)
3 medium potatoes, sliced ⅛ inch
4 tablespoons butter or margarine
2 tablespoons flour
1½ cups grated Cheddar cheese
1 cup milk
Pepper
Salt

Preheat oven to 450°. Peel and slice potatoes. Heat milk over medium setting until hot. In a 2 quart casserole dish layer potato slices, 1 tablespoon flour, 2 tablespoons butter or margarine, salt, pepper, ½ cup milk, ½ cup cheese. Repeat. Place fish on top and cover with remaining cheese. Bake covered 20 minutes, remove lid and continue baking for 20 minutes. *Makes 4 servings*

SEAFOOD-NOODLE CASSEROLE

2 pounds fresh flounder or other fish fillets
3 tablespoons melted margarine or cooking oil
1 can (3½-oz.) French fried onions
4 cups (4-oz. raw weight) medium noodles, cooked and drained
1 can (4-oz.) sliced mushrooms, drained
¼ cup chopped pimientos
2 cans (10¾-oz. each) condensed Cheddar cheese soup
1 cup milk
1 teaspoon salt
1 teaspoon paprika
1 teaspoon Worcestershire sauce

Cut fish into 1-inch pieces. Cook fish in 10-inch fry pan in melted margarine or cooking oil, turning fish carefully until firm. Reserve ½ cup onions for topping. Combine fish, noodles, mushrooms, pimientos and remaining onions in large mixing bowl. Combine soup, milk and seasonings in saucepan. Heat and stir until smooth. Pour over fish mixture and stir carefully. Pour into shallow, 2-quart, round casserole or 12 × 8 × 2-inch baking dish. Bake in a moderate oven, 350°F, 30 minutes or until mixture is hot and bubbles around edge. Sprinkle the reserved ½ cup onions around edge of baking dish 5 minutes before end of baking time. *Makes 6 to 8 servings*

Favorite recipe from **Maine Department of Marine Resources**

BROCCOLI FISH CASSEROLE

10 oz. pkg. of frozen broccoli, thawed
1 to 1½ lb. fish fillets, thawed
6 oz. **FISHER Cheese's CHEEZ-OLA®** **Loaf**, sliced
1 teaspoon oregano
⅛ teaspoon powdered thyme
¼ cup corn oil
2 medium onions, chopped
½ green pepper, chopped
2 tablespoons flour
⅛ teaspoon pepper
1½ cups skim milk

Arrange broccoli in bottom of lightly oiled 13 × 8 × 2″ baking dish. Top with layer of fish and layer of **CHEEZ-OLA®**. Sprinkle with oregano and thyme. Heat oil on low heat and cook onions and green pepper until tender. Stir in flour and pepper. Add milk and cook, stirring constantly, until thickened. Pour over fish and **CHEEZ-OLA®** and bake at 400 degrees F. for 25 minutes or until fish flakes easily. *Serves 4*

FAMILY TUNA CASSEROLE

1½ cups **KELLOGG'S®** **40% BRAN FLAKES Cereal**
2 teaspoons margarine or butter, melted
1 cup (4 oz.) shredded American cheese
1 can (6½ oz.) chunk light tuna in water, well-drained and flaked
1 can (10½ oz.) condensed cream of mushroom soup
⅓ cup milk
2 cups egg noodles, cooked and drained
½ cup cooked peas
½ cup thinly sliced celery
2 tablespoons chopped pimiento

1. Toss 1 cup of the **KELLOGG'S®** **40% BRAN FLAKES Cereal** with the melted margarine. Set aside for topping. Set aside ½ cup of the cheese.
2. Stir together remaining cereal, remaining cheese, tuna, soup and milk. Stir in noodles, peas, celery and pimiento. Spread in 10 × 6 × 2-inch glass baking dish. Sprinkle with cereal topping.
3. Bake at 350°F for 25 minutes. Top with reserved cheese. Bake about 5 minutes longer or until cheese melts and tuna mixture is thoroughly heated. *Yield: 6 servings*

® Kellogg Company

TUNA CASSEROLE

2 cans (7 oz. each) tuna, drained and flaked
2 hard cooked eggs, chopped
½ cup **BEST FOODS®/HELLMANN'S®** **Real Mayonnaise**
2 tablespoons chopped parsley
1 teaspoon lemon juice
½ teaspoon dry mustard
½ cup fresh bread crumbs
1 tablespoon **MAZOLA®** **Corn Oil Margarine**, melted

Stir together tuna, eggs, real mayonnaise, parsley, lemon juice and mustard. Spoon into 4 individual casseroles or shells. Toss together bread crumbs and margarine. Sprinkle over tuna mixture. Bake in 375°F oven 15 minutes or until heated. *Makes 4 servings*

SEA SHELL CASSEROLE

1 can (6½ oz.) **BUMBLE BEE®** **Chunk Light Tuna**
1 cup shredded Cheddar cheese
¼ cup pimiento strips
8 ounces (4¼ cups) large sea shell macaroni
1 package (9 oz.) frozen cut broccoli
1 can (15 oz.) tomato sauce with tomato bits
1 teaspoon vinegar
½ teaspoon basil, crumbled
½ teaspoon salt
¼ teaspoon onion powder

Drain tuna. Combine with cheese and pimiento, and set aside. Cook macaroni in boiling salted water as package directs, for 10 minutes. Add broccoli, and cook 4 minutes longer. Drain well. Combine tomato sauce, vinegar, basil, salt and onion powder. Mix with macaroni and broccoli. Turn into shallow 2-quart baking dish. Center with tuna mixture. Cover dish. Bake in a 350°F oven about 30 minutes, until piping hot. *Makes 4 to 6 servings*

TUNA/NOODLE CASSEROLE
(Low Sodium)

1 can (6½ oz.) FEATHERWEIGHT® Tuna Chunks
1 can (7½ oz.) FEATHERWEIGHT® Cream of
  Mushroom Soup
2 cups cooked noodles
⅓ cup FEATHERWEIGHT® Colby or Cheddar
  Cheese, grated
¼ cup FEATHERWEIGHT® Imitation Mayonnaise
½ cup celery, chopped
¼ cup onion, chopped
2 Tbsp. green pepper, chopped
2 Tbsp. pimiento, chopped
¼ tsp. FEATHERWEIGHT® Salt Substitute
1 Tbsp. lemon juice

Combine all of the ingredients and place in a casserole dish. (Optional: Top with sliced almonds) Bake at 350°F. for 30-35 minutes.   *Serves 4-5*

Approx.	Calories	Protein (Grams)	Fat (Grams)	Carbohydrate (Grams)	Sodium (Mgs.)
½ cup serving	145	8	8	11	26

BAKED APPLE TUNA CASSEROLE

¼ cup butter (or margarine)
½ cup diced celery
½ cup chopped onion
¼ cup diced green pepper
1 - #2 can LUCKY LEAF® Sliced Apples
1 can cream of mushroom soup
2 - 6½ oz. cans tuna
1 small jar pimientos
½ cup milk
2 cups cooked rice - cooked according to pkg.
  directions
½ tsp. salt
Dash of pepper
½ cup crushed croutons

In a large saucepan melt butter or margarine; add celery, onion and green pepper. Cook until tender but not brown. Add apples, soup, tuna, and pimientos. Gradually stir in milk. Add rice, salt and pepper. Mix well. Turn into a well greased 2½ qt. casserole dish. Sprinkle crushed croutons over top. Bake in 375° oven for 30 minutes or until heated thoroughly.

RUS-ETTES SPUD-SKIN TUNA PIE
(Microwave Recipe)

3 cups of frozen RUS-ETTES Spud-Skins or
  RUS-ETTES Rumple Spud-Skins
1 can (10¾ oz.) condensed cream of celery soup
1 can (6½ or 7 oz.) tuna, drained and flaked
¼ cup milk
¼ cup chopped green pepper
1 Tbsp. lemon juice
2 tsp. finely chopped fresh dill weed or 1 tsp. dried dill

Arrange frozen RUS-ETTES Spud-Skins on bottom and along sides of 1 quart shallow baking dish. Cover with plastic wrap. Microwave on high for 5 minutes. In large bowl combine soup, tuna, milk, green pepper, lemon juice, dill weed; mix well. Spoon over potatoes. Cover with plastic wrap. Microwave on high 5 minutes. Let stand 10 minutes before serving.

Yield: 4-6 servings

ORIENTAL CASSEROLE

1 3-oz. can chow mein noodles
1 can cream of mushroom soup
¼ cup water
1 can chunk tuna
Salt and pepper to taste
⅓ cup FISHER® Cashew Nuts
1 cup diced celery
¼ cup diced onion
¼ cup chopped green pepper

Oven 325°. Set aside ½ cup noodles. Combine remaining noodles with other ingredients and place in 1½ quart casserole. Sprinkle with ½ cup reserved noodles and some of the cashew nuts. Bake at 325° for 40 minutes.

TUNA-BACON BAKE

7-oz. package CREAMETTES® Macaroni (2 cups
  uncooked)
¼ cup chopped onion
6 tablespoons butter or margarine
6 tablespoons flour
½ teaspoon salt
¼ teaspoon pepper
3 cups milk
1 cup process American cheese, grated
1 can (7-oz.) tuna, drained and flaked
2 tablespoons tomato catsup
1 teaspoon Worcestershire sauce
4 slices bacon
1 tomato, sliced

Prepare CREAMETTES® according to package directions. Drain. Sauté onion in butter until tender. Add flour, salt and pepper; cook, stirring constantly, for 2 minutes. Do not brown. Add milk; cook till smooth and thickened. Stir in cheese until melted. Combine macaroni, cheese sauce, tuna, catsup and Worcestershire. Pour into 11 × 7 × 1½″ casserole and top with bacon. Bake at 350° for 15 minutes. Turn bacon and add tomato slices. Bake an additional 15 minutes.   *6-8 servings*

CHIPOTLE CHICKEN

2 cups chopped cooked chicken
2 Tablespoons slivered almonds
2 Tablespoons dark seedless raisins
2 Tablespoons sliced ripe olives
1 (15-oz.) can HUNT'S® Tomato Sauce Special
1 large clove garlic, minced
1½ Tablespoons brown sugar, packed
¼ cup vinegar
1 teaspoon paprika
1 teaspoon WESSON® Oil
½ teaspoon hickory-flavored salt
¼ teaspoon liquid smoke
⅛ teaspoon crushed red pepper
1 dozen corn tortillas
1½ cups shredded Monterey Jack cheese

In a medium bowl, combine chicken, almonds, raisins and olives; toss lightly; set aside. Blend together in a small bowl, HUNT'S® Tomato Sauce Special, garlic, brown sugar, vinegar, paprika, oil, hickory salt, liquid smoke and red pepper. In a 1½ quart greased casserole, arrange alternate layers of tortillas, chicken mixture, sauce mixture and cheese, *reserving ½ cup cheese for top layer*. Bake at 375°F 30 to 35 minutes.   *Makes 6 to 8 servings*

RED CROSS® TUNA-YOGURT MACARONI BAKE

1½ cups **RED CROSS®** Macaroni, Ready-cut
1 Tbsp. salt
3 quarts boiling water
1 can condensed cream of mushroom soup
1 cup (8-ounces) plain yogurt
1 cup canned peas, drained (or use frozen)
1 (10-ounce) package cauliflower, partially thawed
1 can (6½-ounces) tuna, drained and flaked
⅛ tsp. thyme
Dash pepper
½ cup shredded Cheddar cheese

Gradually add **RED CROSS®** Macaroni and salt to boiling water. Cook, uncovered, stirring occasionally, until tender. Drain in colander. Rinse with cold water, set aside.

Thinly slice the partially thawed cauliflower. Combine the Macaroni, condensed cream of mushroom soup, yogurt, peas, cauliflower, thyme, tuna fish and pepper. Mix well. Put in a greased 1½-quart casserole. Top with the Cheddar cheese. Bake in 400° oven for 20 minutes.   *Serves 4*

CHEESE-CLOUD CASSEROLE

1 cup each mayonnaise and sour cream
1 Tbsp. lemon juice
1 Tbsp. finely chopped onion
½ tsp. curry powder, or to taste
⅛ tsp. cayenne pepper
1 cup frozen peas, thawed
6 cups cooked, cubed chicken, turkey or ham*
5 cups (about 1 lb) shredded **Danish Fontina** or **Creamy Havarti Cheese**
6 egg whites
½ tsp. cream of tartar
Parsley or watercress sprigs for garnish

In large bowl, blend mayonnaise, sour cream, lemon juice, onion, curry and cayenne pepper. Fold in peas, poultry and a little less than half of cheese. Spoon into buttered, shallow, oven-to-table dish; cover and bake in preheated 300 degree oven for about 20 minutes, until warm. Remove dish from oven. Meanwhile, beat egg whites with cream of tartar until stiff peaks form. Gradually sprinkle and fold in remaining cheese. Spoon meringue onto warm mixture forming 6-8 mounds. Increase oven temperature to 400 degrees. Return dish to oven and bake 8-10 minutes or until meringue is golden brown. Garnish with parsley or watercress. Serve at once with crisp French bread.   *Makes 6-8 servings*

*Note: If leftover poultry or ham does not measure 6 cups, substitute cooked vegetables for amount lacking.

Favorite recipe from the **Denmark Cheese Association**

COMPANY CHICKEN CASSEROLE

3 large chicken breasts, split
1 teaspoon salt
¼ teaspoon pepper
2 to 3 tablespoons **PURITAN®** Oil
1 can cream of chicken soup
¾ cup white wine
4-ounce can mushroom stems and pieces, drained
5-ounce can water chestnuts, drained and sliced
2 tablespoons chopped green pepper
¼ teaspoon thyme
Cooked rice, if desired

Preheat oven to 350°. Sprinkle chicken with salt and pepper and brown in hot **PURITAN®** Oil. Place skin side up in an 11½ × 7½ × 1½-inch baking dish. Blend soup into drippings in skillet, then gradually stir in the wine. Add drained mushrooms, water chestnuts, green pepper and thyme. Heat to boiling, then pour around chicken. Cover baking dish with foil. Bake at 350° for 25 minutes; uncover and bake 25 to 35 minutes longer, until chicken is tender. Serve with hot rice, if desired.   *6 servings*

EASY CHICKEN DIVAN

1 (4⅝-ounce) can SNACK MATE American Pasteurized Process Cheese Spread
½ cup milk
4 ounces packaged cream cheese (half 8-ounce package)
½ teaspoon Worcestershire sauce
½ teaspoon ground nutmeg
2 (10-ounce) packages frozen broccoli spears, thawed
2 cups diced cooked chicken (about ½ pound)

CONVENTIONAL METHOD:
1. Preheat oven to 325°F. Lightly grease 2-quart shallow baking dish. In medium saucepan, combine SNACK MATE Cheese, milk, cream cheese, Worcestershire sauce and nutmeg. Cook over very low heat, stirring constantly, until smooth and very hot, about 3 minutes.
2. Arrange thawed broccoli in baking dish; top with diced cooked chicken; pour sauce evenly over chicken. Bake 20 minutes or until piping hot.   *Makes 6 servings*

MICROWAVE METHOD:
1. In 1½-quart microwave-proof casserole, combine SNACK MATE Cheese, milk, cream cheese, Worcestershire sauce and nutmeg. Cover with lid or plastic wrap; microwave at 100% power 1½ minutes, stirring to blend every 30 seconds.
2. Lightly grease 2-quart shallow microwave-proof casserole; arrange broccoli spears in casserole, flower ends towards center. Cover with plastic wrap, leaving one corner open. Microwave at 100% power 8 to 10 minutes, rotating a half turn every 3 minutes, until broccoli is tender.
3. Drain broccoli; arrange spears, stem ends towards center; top with diced cooked chicken; pour sauce evenly over chicken.
4. Re-cover with plastic wrap, leaving one corner open; microwave at 100% power 7 to 10 minutes, rotating a half turn after 4 minutes, until piping hot.

UNCLE BEN'S® CHICKEN CASSEROLE WITH WILD RICE

1 package (6 ounces) **UNCLE BEN'S®** Original Long Grain & Wild Rice
2 cups hot water
1 frying chicken, cut up
Salt and pepper, to taste
1 can (10¾ ounces) condensed cream of mushroom soup
½ cup milk
½ cup slivered almonds
1 tablespoon butter or margarine

Combine contents of rice and seasoning packets and water in a 2½ quart casserole. Season chicken with salt and pepper to taste. Arrange on top of rice mixture. Bake, covered, 1¼ hours at 375 F., or until chicken is tender. Combine soup and milk. Sauté almonds in butter or margarine until lightly browned. Pour soup mixture over chicken in casserole. Sprinkle top with almonds. Return to oven and bake uncovered until hot and bubbly.   *Makes 6 servings*

ORIENTAL CHICKEN AND RICE CASSEROLE

1 bag SUCCESS® Rice
2 cups cubed, cooked chicken
1 tablespoon soy sauce
2 tablespoons lemon juice
1 can (1-lb.) bean sprouts, drained
1 cup finely chopped celery
¾-1 cup mayonnaise
1 can (5 oz.) water chestnuts, drained and sliced
¼ cup finely chopped green onion
½ teaspoon salt
⅛ teaspoon black pepper
1 can (3-oz.) chow mein noodles

Cook bag of rice according to package directions. Drain. While rice is cooking, sprinkle chicken with soy sauce and lemon juice. Add the bean sprouts, celery, mayonnaise, water chestnuts, onion, salt and pepper. Add the rice. Mix well and pour into a buttered 2-quart casserole dish. Bake, uncovered, at 375°F. for 15 minutes. Sprinkle with noodles. Bake 5 more minutes.

Makes 8 servings (about 1 cup each)

SUPER ITALIAN SUPPER

1 package WEAVER® Italian Style Seasoning Fried Chicken
4 cups thinly sliced zucchini
½ cup sliced onion
¼ cup grated Parmesan cheese
½ teaspoon garlic salt
8 slices tomato

Place chicken in center of shallow baking dish (13 × 9-inch). Combine zucchini, onion, Parmesan and garlic salt; arrange mixture in each end of baking dish. Bake at 425°F for 25 minutes. Place tomato slices on top of zucchini; bake 10 minutes longer.

4 to 6 servings

CHILL-FIGHTING CHICKEN AND CHICK PEA CASSEROLE

3½-4 pounds chicken parts, washed and dried thoroughly
GOYA® ADOBO All Purpose Seasoning
8 slices bacon, cut in half
3 cans (16-oz. each) GOYA® Chick Peas (Garbanzos), drained
12 small white onions, peeled
18 baby carrots, frozen and defrosted
2 medium green peppers, halved, seeded and cut into wide strips
2 cloves garlic, minced
1 can (8-oz.) GOYA® Spanish Style Tomato Sauce
1½ cups chicken bouillon made with cubes
1 cup dry white wine
1 tablespoon tomato paste
1 tablespoon GOYA® SOFRITO Sauce
1 teaspoon salt
½ teaspoon pepper
½ teaspoon thyme
1 bay leaf, crumbled

Sprinkle chicken liberally with GOYA® ADOBO All Purpose Seasoning. Set aside. In large frying pan, sauté bacon until crisp. Remove, drain on paper towel and reserve. Leave drippings in pan. Brown chicken on all sides, a few pieces at a time, in bacon drippings and place in a 4-quart casserole or a skillet with a heat-proof handle. (To heat-proof handle, wrap aluminum foil tightly around it.) Spoon drained chick peas over and around chicken. Discard all but 3 tablespoons drippings from frying pan and sauté onions, carrots, green peppers and garlic. Add tomato sauce, chicken bouillon, wine, tomato paste, SOFRITO, salt, pepper, thyme and bay leaf. Bring to a boil. Reduce heat and simmer for 5 minutes to develop flavor. Pour tomato mixture over chicken and chick peas. (Up to this point the dish may be prepared ahead, covered and refrigerated. Bring back to room temperature before baking.) Place covered casserole in 350 degree oven and bake for 1 hour or until chicken is done. Uncover and sprinkle with reserved bacon. Bake another 15 minutes.

Serves 6

MACARONI MEDITERRANEAN

1 (7-ounce) package *or* 2 cups uncooked CREAMETTES® Elbow Macaroni, cooked as package directs and drained
2 cups cubed cooked chicken or turkey
½ pound hard salami, cubed (about 2 cups)
1 (10-ounce) package frozen green peas, thawed
¾ cup chopped onion
2 tablespoons margarine or butter
½ cup sliced pitted ripe olives
1½ cups milk
1 (10¾-ounce) can condensed cream of mushroom, chicken or celery soup
1 teaspoon salt
1 cup (4 ounces) shredded Cheddar cheese

Preheat oven to 350°. In small saucepan, cook onion in margarine until tender. In large bowl, combine all ingredients except cheese; mix well. Turn into greased 3-quart baking dish. Cover; bake 40 minutes. Uncover; top with cheese and bake 5 minutes longer. Refrigerate leftovers.

Makes 8 to 10 servings

CHICKEN TORTILLA CASSEROLE

2 or 3 whole chicken breasts
1 package VAN DE KAMP'S® Corn Tortillas
1 onion, chopped
1 small can green chilies, chopped
2 cups grated Monterey Jack cheese
1 can (10¾ ounces) cream of mushroom soup
1 can (10¾ ounces) cream of chicken soup
1 soup can water or chicken broth
1 clove garlic

Cook chicken in water until tender; cut or shred into bite size pieces. Mix onion, chilies, soups, water or broth and garlic together with chicken in saucepan. Bring to boil; then remove from heat. Cut tortillas into 1″ pie shaped pieces. Layer tortillas, chicken soup mixture and cheese alternately to make 6 layers in a large casserole. Bake 45 minutes in 350° oven uncovered.

POLYNESIAN CASSEROLE

40 SUNSHINE® HI HO® Crackers
1 cup chopped onion
2 cups cooked chicken, chopped
1 (10½ ounce) can cream of mushroom soup
½ cup water
1 (1 pound) can bean sprouts, drained
1 cup coarsely broken cashew nuts
3 pears, halved and cored

Break crackers into medium-coarse crumbs; there should be about 2 cups. Spread half the crumbs over bottom of a shallow 2-quart casserole. Combine remaining ingredients, except pears, and pour evenly over a layer of crumbs. Sprinkle remaining crumbs over top. Arrange pears on top, cut side down. Bake in preheated moderate oven (350°F) for about 45 minutes or until pears are tender. Time will depend on size and ripeness of pears. Serve immediately.   *Yield: 6 servings*

CHICKEN MAC 'N CHEESE

1 small onion, chopped (about ½ cup)
¼ teaspoon crushed oregano leaves
1 package (32-oz.) **BANQUET® Macaroni and Cheese Buffet Supper Main Dish**
1 package (12-oz.) **BANQUET® Breaded Chicken Sticks**
1 small tomato, chopped (about ¾ cup)

CONVENTIONAL METHOD:
In 2-quart oblong baking dish, place onion and oregano. Remove macaroni and cheese from foil tray; place in dish with onion mixture. Heat in 400°F oven 25 minutes. Stir mixture. Top with chicken sticks and tomato. Heat an additional 20 minutes or until hot.

MICROWAVE METHOD:
In 2-quart oblong glass baking dish, place onion and oregano. Remove macaroni and cheese from foil tray; place in dish with onion mixture. Cover with plastic wrap. Heat on HIGH 10 to 12 minutes or until thawed. Stir mixture. Top with chicken sticks and tomato. Heat, uncovered on HIGH 6 to 8 minutes or until hot, rotating dish once. Let stand 2 to 3 minutes before serving.

Makes 6 servings

CHICKEN-CHEESE RAVIOLI CASSEROLE

3 tablespoons cooking oil
1 tablespoon butter or margarine
1 broiler-fryer chicken, cut into serving pieces
¼ cup chopped onion
¼ cup chopped green pepper
1 can (6 oz.) sliced mushrooms, drained
2 cans (15 oz. each) **CHEF BOY-AR-DEE® Cheese Ravioli in Beef and Tomato Sauce**
¼ cup chopped pimiento
1 cup light cream
Hot pepper sauce
1 package (10 oz.) Chinese pea pods
3 tablespoons toasted slivered almonds

Combine cooking oil and butter. Heat in medium sized skillet. Fry chicken parts until lightly browned. Remove browned parts to warm platter. Sauté onion and pepper in remaining butter. Add drained sliced mushrooms and **Cheese Ravioli in Beef and Tomato Sauce**. Cover; simmer for 5 minutes. Add pimiento, light cream and hot pepper sauce. Stir gently. Cook Chinese pea pods according to package directions. Add to Ravioli mixture. Arrange chicken on top; cover. Bake for 45 minutes in 350 F oven. Garnish with toasted almonds.   *Serves 4 generously*

CHICKEN CHOW MEIN CASSEROLE

3 Tbsp. butter or margarine
⅓ cup chopped onion
¼ cup chopped green pepper
½ cup mushrooms
¼ cup flour
1 can **CHINA BEAUTY® Chicken Chop Suey** or **Chow Mein**
1 cup milk
1¼ tsp. **CHINA BEAUTY® Soy Sauce**
1 chopped hard boiled egg
2 cups cooked plain noodles
1 can crushed **CHINA BEAUTY® Chow Mein Noodles**

Make a sauce by heating the butter or margarine in pan, add onion and pepper, cooking until onion browns. Add mushrooms and cook several minutes. Blend in flour, add milk, soy sauce, hard boiled egg, and heat until thoroughly blended. In a greased casserole, layer the cooked noodles, Chicken Chop Suey or Chow Mein, the sauce, making two layers of each. Cover with crushed Chow Mein Noodles. Bake in a moderate oven, 350° F., for 30-35 minutes.   *Serves 8*

TAMALE POLLO CASSEROLE

1 cup finely crushed corn chips
1 15 oz. can **WOLF® Brand Tamales**
1 10 oz. can **WOLF® Brand Plain Chili**
1½ cups chopped cooked chicken
1 8 oz. can whole kernel corn, undrained
1 4 oz. can chopped can chopped green chilies, drained
1 cup (4 oz.) shredded Cheddar cheese

Sprinkle corn chips evenly onto bottom of 8-inch square baking dish. Unwrap tamales; arrange over corn chips. Combine remaining ingredients except cheese; mix well. Spoon over tamales. Bake in preheated moderate oven (350°F.) 20 minutes. Sprinkle with cheese; continue baking about 5 minutes. Serve with sour cream.
Serves 5 to 6

VIVA CHICKEN TORTILLA

2 tablespoons chicken broth or water
2 cartons (6 ounces each) **YOPLAIT® Plain Yogurt** (about 1⅓ cups)
1 can (10¾ ounces) condensed cream of mushroom soup
1 can (10¾ ounces) condensed cream of chicken soup
1 jar (8 ounces) green salsa
1 medium onion, finely chopped
12 corn tortillas, cut into 1-inch strips
4 cups cut-up cooked chicken
4 cups shredded Cheddar cheese (16 ounces)
Spanish stuffed olives, sliced

Heat oven to 350°. Butter rectangular baking dish, 13x9x2 inches; spoon broth into dish. Mix yogurt, soups, salsa and onion. Layer ⅓ of the tortilla strips, 1⅓ cups of the chicken, about 1⅓ cups of the soup mixture and 1⅓ cups of the cheese in dish; repeat 2 times. Bake uncovered 40 minutes. Let stand 10 to 15 minutes before serving. Garnish with olives.   *8 servings*

SWISS HAMLETS

1 package (8-oz.) **OSCAR MAYER Chopped Ham**
4 slices Swiss cheese, 4 inches square
1 package (10-oz.) frozen broccoli spears, thawed
Toothpicks
1 package (1-oz.) white sauce mix
¼ cup sour cream
1 tablespoon prepared mustard
¼ teaspoon dill weed

Top 2 slices of meat with slice of cheese and ¼ of broccoli; roll and secure with toothpicks. Place in small shallow baking dish. Repeat. Prepare white sauce mix according to package directions. Stir in remaining ingredients. Top meat with sauce. Bake in 350°F oven about 30 minutes. Remove toothpicks before serving.

2 servings

HAM BALLS IN PEACH HALVES POLSKA

2 cups ground **ATALANTA/KRAKUS/POLKA Polish Ham**
½ pound ground lean pork
1 cup crushed cornflakes
2 tablespoons light brown sugar
¼ teaspoon ground nutmeg
½ cup evaporated milk
1 egg, slightly beaten
8 canned cling or fresh peach halves
2 tablespoons butter or margarine

In bowl, combine ham, pork, cornflakes, sugar, nutmeg, milk and egg. Blend well; shape into balls to fit into peach halves. Place in greased shallow baking pan. Bake at 350° F. for 30 minutes; turn occasionally.

Place peach halves in pan, cut side up. Dot with butter. Bake 15 minutes longer. To serve, place ham ball in each peach half.

Makes 4 servings

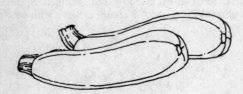

ZUCCHINI-BEEF CASSEROLE

½ lb. **AZUMAYA Japanese Noodles** (Futo-udon, wide noodles)
½ cup chopped green onion
1 lb. lean ground beef
1 zucchini, chopped or ¼ lb. fresh spinach, chopped
¼ lb. mushrooms, sliced
1 can (8-oz.) tomato sauce
1 tablespoon **KIKKOMAN Soy Sauce**
1 teaspoon grated fresh ginger root
½ teaspoon oregano, crumbled
¼ teaspoon thyme, crumbled
½ cup grated Parmesan cheese

Cook noodles as package directs, drain. Stir in green onion; set aside. Combine beef, zucchini and mushrooms in skillet. Cook until beef is browned. Remove from heat. Stir in tomato sauce, soy sauce, ginger, oregano and thyme. Place cooked noodles in bottom of 2-quart baking dish. Top with meat mixture. Sprinkle with cheese. Bake at 375° for 20 minutes or until heated through.

Makes 4 servings

EASY ITALIAN CASSEROLE

1 lb. pork sausage
1 lb. ground beef
1 cup chopped onion
1 teaspoon Italian Seasoning
½ teaspoon garlic powder
1 (29½ oz.) can **HUNT'S® MANWICH® Sloppy Joe Sauce**
1 cup water
1 (16-oz.) pkg. shell macaroni, cooked and drained
2 cups grated mozzarella cheese
½ cup grated Parmesan cheese

In a large skillet, cook pork and beef until it loses redness; drain fat. Add onion, Italian seasoning and garlic powder; cook until onion is soft. Add **MANWICH®** and water; simmer 5 minutes. In a 3-quart casserole, layer *half* the meat mixture, macaroni and both cheeses. Repeat layers using *remaining* meat, macaroni, and cheeses. Bake at 350° F 30 minutes.   *Makes 6 to 8 servings*

ALL-IN-ONE CASSEROLE

1⅓ cups water
2 tablespoons margarine or butter
½ cup milk
1⅓ cups **HUNGRY JACK® Mashed Potato Flakes**
1 lb. ground beef
½ cup chopped onion
10¾-oz. can condensed tomato soup
16-oz. can **GREEN GIANT® Cut Green Beans**, drained
¼ teaspoon oregano leaves
¼ teaspoon garlic salt
⅛ teaspoon pepper
Paprika

Heat oven to 350°F. In medium saucepan, heat water and margarine to rolling boil; remove from heat. Add milk and flakes; stir to desired consistency. Set aside. Brown ground beef and onion in large skillet; drain. Add soup, green beans, oregano, garlic salt and pepper; mix until well blended. Spoon into 1½-quart casserole; top with mashed potatoes. Sprinkle with paprika. Bake at 350°F. for 15 to 20 minutes or until thoroughly heated.

HIGH ALTITUDE—Above 3500 Feet: No change.   *4 servings*

SPICY BAKED CASSEROLE
(Low Sodium)

1 can (8 oz.) **FEATHERWEIGHT® Vegetable-Beef Soup**
½ pound hamburger
¼ cup onion, chopped
2 Tbsp. green pepper, chopped
⅓ cup **FEATHERWEIGHT® Chili Sauce**
½-1 cup noodles, cooked
⅛ tsp. **FEATHERWEIGHT® K-Salt**
Dash pepper

Brown hamburger, add onion and green pepper. Cook a few minutes. Stir in remaining ingredients. Pour into casserole dish. Bake at 350° F for 30 minutes.   *Serves 3*

MONTERREY CASSEROLE

1 pound ground beef
2 tablespoons chopped onion
¾ teaspoon seasoned salt
2 8-ounce cans tomato sauce
2 cups grated Cheddar cheese
4 cups **DORITOS® Brand Taco Flavor Tortilla Chips**
½ cup ripe olives

Cook beef in skillet for 5 minutes until crumbly and light in color. Add onion, salt and tomato sauce. Simmer for 5 minutes.

Place 3 cups of **DORITOS® Brand Taco Flavor Tortilla Chips** in a 2-quart baking dish. Sprinkle 1 cup cheese over the **DORITOS® Brand Taco Flavor Tortilla Chips**.

Pour meat sauce over the above and top with remaining cheese. Garnish with remaining cup of **DORITOS® Brand Taco Flavor Tortilla Chips**.

Bake at 350° F. for 15 minutes. Top with ripe olives before serving.   *Makes 4 to 6 servings*

SAVORY BEEF 'N MACARONI CASSEROLE

1 pkg. (7-oz.) or 2 cups uncooked **CREAMETTES® Elbow Macaroni**
1 pound ground beef
½ cup chopped celery
½ cup chopped onion
3 Tbsp. flour
2 cups milk
¼ cup **KIKKOMAN Soy Sauce**
½ tsp. basil, crumbled
2 cups shredded Cheddar cheese (about 8 oz.)
1 pkg. (10-oz.) frozen peas and carrots, corn or peas

Cook macaroni as package directs for baked dishes; drain and set aside. Thoroughly brown meat with celery and onion over medium heat. Sprinkle flour evenly over meat mixture and stir in to blend. Gradually stir in milk, soy sauce and basil. Bring to boil; stir in cheese. Cook and stir until cheese melts. Combine macaroni, meat and cheese mixture and frozen vegetables in large bowl or pan. Turn into 3-quart baking dish or 13 × 9-inch baking pan. Bake at 350° F 35 minutes. Serve with additional soy sauce as desired.
Makes 6 to 8 servings

ITALIAN HAMBURGER DEEP DISH

1½ pounds ground beef
1½ teaspoons salt
⅛ teaspoon pepper
1 clove garlic, finely chopped
BETTY CROCKER® POTATO BUDS® Instant Mashed Potatoes (enough for 8 servings)
2 tablespoons instant minced onion
1 teaspoon dried oregano leaves
3 or 4 tomatoes, sliced
4 ounces mozzarella cheese, shredded or sliced

Heat oven to 350°. Butter rectangular baking dish, 12x7½x2 inches, or 2-quart round casserole. Cook and stir ground beef, salt, pepper and garlic in 10-inch skillet until beef is brown; drain.
(Continued)

Prepare potatoes as directed on package for 8 servings except—stir in onion and oregano. Layer half each of the potato mixture, beef mixture, tomato slices and cheese in dish; repeat. Bake uncovered 30 minutes.   *6 to 8 servings*

SEVEN LAYER DINNER

3 medium potatoes, sliced
2 packets **HERB-OX® Onion Flavored Instant Broth and Seasoning**
1 can (12 ounces) whole kernel corn
1 pound ground beef
½ pound fresh green beans, sliced, or 1 package (10 ounces) frozen green beans
2 medium onions, sliced
1 green pepper, slivered
1 can (1 pound) tomatoes

Fill a greased 4-quart casserole with layers of vegetables and meat in the order given, sprinkling each layer with some of the instant broth. Bake in a moderate oven (350°F.) about 2 hours.
Makes 6 servings

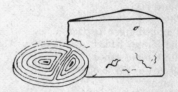

BAKED ROLLER COASTER RING AROUND

4 eggs
2 cans (15 oz. each) **CHEF BOY-AR-DEE® Roller Coasters With Tiny Meatballs**
2 cups milk
Nutmeg
¼ cup chopped pimiento, drained
1 cup grated Cheddar cheese
3 tablespoons instant minced onion
1 medium onion, thinly sliced

Place baking pan (suitable for holding 6½ cup ring mold) with 1″ water in it, in oven. Set oven for 350°F. Beat eggs lightly. Combine with remaining ingredients, saving 6 to 8 meatballs from **Roller Coasters** for garnish. Stir gently. Pour in well-greased ring mold or spring pan. Place in water in baking pan. Bake for 55 minutes or until inserted knife comes out clean. Allow to set for 10 minutes. Unmold; garnish with onion slices and meatballs.
Serves 8

ONION, BEEF, MUSHROOM CASSEROLE

1 pound beef
Flour
2 tablespoons fat
1 (4-oz.) can mushrooms
Water
Salt and pepper
¼ teaspoon Worcestershire sauce
1 can (No. 303) **TAYLOR'S Whole Onions**

Dredge bite-size cubes of beef in flour; brown in fat. To liquid drained from mushrooms, add enough water to make one cup; add to beef and stir until thick and smooth. Add mushrooms and seasonings. Place onions in casserole, and top with meat mixture. Bake covered in slow oven (325°F.) two hours or until meat is tender.

SOUR CREAM CHILI BAKE

1 pound ground beef
¼ cup chopped onion
1 can (16 ounces) kidney beans, drained
1 can (15 ounces) tomato sauce
1 envelope (1¼ ounces) taco seasoning mix
1 cup (4 ounces) shredded Cheddar cheese
3½ cups corn chips
1¼ cups **MEADOW GOLD® Sour Cream**

Cook ground beef and onion until meat is browned and onion is tender; drain. Stir in beans, tomato sauce, taco seasoning mix and ¾ cup cheese. Sprinkle 2½ cups corn chips in bottom of 8 × 8 × 2-inch baking dish. Cover with beef mixture. Bake at 350° for 20 to 25 minutes. Spread sour cream over chili. Top with remaining corn chips and cheese. Bake 3 to 4 minutes longer.

6 to 8 servings

LAND O' LAKES CORNBREAD MEXI-CASSEROLE

1 lb. ground beef
⅓ cup chopped onion
⅓ cup chopped green pepper
16-oz. can kidney beans, undrained
15-oz. can tomato sauce
½ cup sliced (⅛") ripe olives
1 Tbsp. sugar
2 tsp. chili powder
1 tsp. salt
¼ tsp. garlic powder

Cornbread Topping:

2 cups (8-oz.) shredded **LAND O LAKES® Process American Cheese** (reserve 1 cup)
½ cup yellow cornmeal
½ cup all-purpose flour
2 tsp. baking powder
¼ tsp. salt
⅔ cup milk
1 egg
2 Tbsp. **LAND O LAKES® Sweet Cream Butter**, softened

Preheat Oven: 425°F. In heavy 10" skillet brown ground beef with onion and green pepper; drain well. Stir in kidney beans, tomato sauce, olives and seasonings. Cook, covered, over med. heat for 15 min. Meanwhile, prepare cornbread topping*

*CORNBREAD TOPPING

In med. bowl combine 1 cup cheese (reserve remaining 1 cup cheese) and remaining ingredients; stir to combine.

Pour ground beef mixture into 12 × 8" baking dish; top with dollops of cornbread topping, spreading to edges. Bake near center of 425° oven for 20 to 25 min. or until cornbread topping is golden brown. Remove from oven and sprinkle with remaining 1 cup cheese.

Yield: 6 (1 cup) servings

CHILLI MAN® TACO CASSEROLE

1 package (approx. 6 oz.) corn chips
1 can (20 oz.) **CHILLI MAN® Chilli with Beans**
1 can (16 oz.) stewed tomatoes
1 jalapeño pepper, chopped (optional)
½ cup sliced black olives, optional
1 cup (4 oz.) shredded cheese (brick, Cheddar, etc.)

Crush half the corn chips and line an 8-inch casserole dish. Add: layer of Chilli, spoon over the tomatoes, sprinkle with olives and jalapeño pepper, top with remaining chips and cheese. Bake in 350° oven about 30 minutes or until bubbly and brown.

Makes about 8 servings

CHILI CASSEROLE

1 pound ground beef
½ cup chopped onion
1 tablespoon chili powder
1 teaspoon salt
¼ teaspoon oregano
1 can (30 ounces) **ROSARITA® Refried Beans**
1 can (16 ounces) stewed tomatoes
6 ounces Monterey Jack cheese
2 cups slightly broken tortilla chips

Brown beef and onion in skillet. Add chili powder, salt and oregano. Stir in beans and tomatoes. Remove from heat. Shred cheese, reserving ½ cup for topping. Spoon ½ of beef mixture into 2-quart casserole. Sprinkle with half of cheese; top with half of tortilla chips. Repeat layers. Bake at 350° for 20 minutes. Sprinkle with reserved ½ cup of cheese. Bake 5 minutes longer or until cheese has melted and mixture is bubbly.   *8 servings*

CHILLI MAN® AND RICE BAKE

1 can (15-oz.) **CHILLI MAN® Chilli With Beans**
1 can (15-oz.) Spanish rice
1 pkg. (7½-oz.) corn muffin mix
1 cup (4-oz.) shredded cheese
1 jalapeño pepper, chopped (optional)
½ cup **MILNOT®**

Spread Chilli on bottom of 8-inch casserole dish; spoon rice on top of Chilli. Blend muffin mix, cheese, jalapeño pepper, and **MILNOT®**; layer over rice. Bake in 375° oven for 25-30 minutes or until crust is brown.   *Makes 4-6 servings*

MEXICAN BEEF CASSEROLE

1 (7-ounce) package or 2 cups uncooked **CREAMETTES® Elbow Macaroni,** cooked as package directs and drained
1 pound lean ground beef
¾ cup chopped green pepper
¾ cup chopped onion
1 clove garlic, finely chopped
2 cups hot water
1 (16-ounce) can tomatoes, cut up and undrained
1 (6-ounce) can tomato paste
1 (12-ounce) can whole kernel corn, drained
¼ cup pitted ripe olives, sliced if desired
1 (8-ounce) can tomato sauce
2 teaspoons chili powder
1 teaspoon oregano leaves
1 teaspoon salt
⅛ teaspoon ground cumin, optional
Corn chips
½ cup (2 ounces) shredded Cheddar cheese

Preheat oven to 350°. In large skillet, brown meat; pour off fat. Add green pepper, onion and garlic; cook and stir until tender. Stir in cooked macaroni, water, tomatoes, tomato paste, corn and olives. Pour into 3-quart shallow baking dish (13x9-inch). Stir together tomato sauce and seasonings; pour over macaroni mixture. Bake 25 to 30 minutes or until hot; top with corn chips and cheese. Bake 5 minutes longer or until cheese melts. Refrigerate leftovers. *Makes 8 servings*

CHILI JACK CASSEROLE

1 med. onion, finely chopped
1 Tbsp. butter or oil
1 can (8-oz.) tomato sauce
½ tsp. oregano, crushed
2 eggs, slightly beaten
¾ cup half and half (light cream)
2 cups coarsely crushed NALLEY®'S Corn Chips
1 cup diced Monterey Jack cheese
2 cans (15 oz. each) NALLEY®'S Chili With Beans
1 cup sour cream
½ cup shredded cheddar cheese

Sauté onion in butter. Stir in tomato sauce, oregano; simmer 5 minutes. Mix eggs with half and half; gradually stir in tomato mixture. In 2-quart casserole, make layers using *half* the corn chips, Chili, Jack cheese and tomato mixture. Repeat layers. Spoon on dollops of sour cream; top with cheddar cheese. Bake at 350° for 30 minutes. (Add 5 to 10 minutes if mixture is cold.) *Makes 6 generous servings*

CANADIAN BACON CASSEROLE

2 cups diced COUNTRY SMOKED MEATS
  Canadian Bacon
2 cups cooked rice
1 can asparagus soup
1 4-oz. can mushrooms
2 tablespoons chopped onions
2 tablespoons chopped green pepper
1½ cups shredded cheddar cheese
½ cup milk
¾ cup cereal flakes
3 tablespoons melted butter

Mix all ingredients together except flakes and butter in casserole. Top with cereal flakes, which have been mixed with melted butter. Bake at 350° for 30 minutes.

APPLE SIZZ-N-RICE CASSEROLE

12 ounce package SIZZLEAN®
2⅔ cups cooked rice
⅓ cup chopped onion
½ cup orange juice
1⅓ cups cubed apples
⅓ cup raisins, plumped
⅛ teaspoon cinnamon
¾ teaspoon brown sugar

Cook rice according to package directions, substituting ½ cup of orange juice for ½ cup water. Cut half of the SIZZLEAN® slices into 1 inch pieces. In a skillet over medium heat cook SIZZLEAN® pieces until well browned. Pour off all but 1 teaspoon of drippings. Cook onion in drippings until tender. Add apples, raisins, cinnamon, sugar and rice. Mix well. Place in greased 2-quart casserole. Place whole strips of SIZZLEAN® over all. Bake in a 375°F oven about 35 minutes.

QUICKIE BEAN BAKE

½ cup GRANDMA'S® Unsulphured Molasses
3 tablespoons vinegar
3 tablespoons prepared mustard
½ teaspoon TABASCO® Pepper Sauce
3 cans (1 pound each) baked beans in tomato sauce
1 can (1 pound) kidney beans, drained
½ pound frankfurters, cut in 1-inch pieces
1 cup diced cooked ham
1 medium onion, chopped, divided

Mix molasses, vinegar, mustard and TABASCO®. Add to baked beans, kidney beans, frankfurters and ham in 3-quart casserole. Add half of chopped onion; mix well. Bake in 375°F. oven 1 hour. Stir before serving. Sprinkle remaining chopped onion around edge of casserole. *Yield: 8 servings*

BARBECUE-BEAN CASSEROLE

2 lbs. canned baked beans
1 lb. 2 oz. JAMES RIVER SMITHFIELD Pork or
  Beef Barbeque
6 oz. JAMES RIVER SMITHFIELD Barbeque
  Sauce
Bread crumbs
2 Tbsp. butter

Place beans in casserole dish; cover with Barbeque. Pour Barbeque Sauce over casserole; sprinkle with bread crumbs and pats of butter. Cook in 400° F oven for about 25 minutes or until brown. *Serves 6*

PEACHY BEAN CASSEROLE

1 can (16 ounces) VAN CAMP'S® Brown Sugar Beans
2 Tablespoons STOKELY'S FINEST® Tomato
  Catsup
¼ cup peach preserves
2 Tablespoons chopped onion
¼ teaspoon soy sauce
4 chicken thighs or breasts

Preheat oven to 350°F. Combine beans, catsup, preserves, onion, and soy sauce in a 10 × 6 × 2-inch baking dish. To coat chicken pieces evenly with sauce, nestle chicken in bean mixture, skin side down, then turn pieces skin side up; cover and bake 1 hour. Uncover and bake an additional 30 minutes, basting chicken with sauce occasionally. *4 servings*

BRUNCH CASSEROLE

1 lb. BOB EVANS FARMS® Roll Sausage
1 (8-oz.) can refrigerated crescent dinner rolls
2 cups (8-oz.) shredded mozzarella cheese
4 eggs, beaten
¾ cup milk
¼ tsp. salt
⅛ tsp. pepper

Crumble sausage in a medium skillet; cook over medium heat until brown, stirring occasionally. Drain well.

Line bottom of buttered 13 × 9 × 2-inch baking dish with crescent rolls, firmly pressing perforations to seal. Sprinkle with sausage and cheese.

Combine remaining ingredients; beat well and pour over sausage. Bake at 425° for 15 minutes or until set. Let stand five minutes; cut into squares and serve immediately. *Serves 6 to 8*

SWEET RED BEAN AND SAUSAGE BAKE

1½ pounds sweet Italian sausage or sweet & hot
  sausage mixed
2 cans (16-oz. each) GOYA® Red Kidney Beans,
  drained
2 large green peppers, seeded and chopped
1 teaspoon GOYA® ADOBO All Purpose Seasoning
1 teaspoon oregano
½ teaspoon salt
1 cup chili sauce
4 tablespoons apple jelly

Cook sausage in a skillet containing ¼-inch of water until water disappears. Continue cooking, turning frequently, until sausage is golden brown on all sides. Roll and cut into ½-inch slices. Layer half of drained beans in bottom of a 2-quart casserole. Top with half of sliced sausages and half of the green pepper. Sprinkle with half the seasonings. Repeat. Heat chili sauce and apple jelly in small saucepan until jelly is melted. Pour over top. Poke a few holes into the mixture to allow sauce to permeate. Bake at 350 degrees for 25 minutes.   *Serves 4*

COUNTRY COOKING CASSEROLE

1-12 oz. can HORMEL Sausage Patties—Hot
1-15 oz. can HORMEL Chili Beans in Chili Sauce
1-15 oz. can blackeyed peas
1-17 oz. can green lima beans
1-15 oz. can golden (or white) hominy (optional) or
  substitute another choice of beans if desired
2 Tbsp. dehydrated onion flakes
1 tsp. celery seed (optional)
½ cup packed brown sugar
½ cup barbecue sauce
⅓ cup all-purpose flour

In large pan, over medium heat, thicken beans, peas and juices with flour. Add onion, celery seed, sugar and barbecue sauce. Pour into large casserole or baking dish. Lay patties on top. Bake in moderate oven (350°F) 30-35 minutes, or until hot and bubbly.
                    Serves 6

SAUSAGE SPINACH BAKE

1 pound bulk pork sausage
¼ cup green pepper, chopped
¼ cup onion, chopped
2 jars (4½ oz. each) GERBER® Strained Creamed
  Spinach
¾ cup milk
2 eggs
2 cups bread crumbs
1 can (8 oz.) water chestnuts, drained and chopped
1 cup sour cream
⅓ cup salad dressing
1 tablespoon prepared mustard
1 tablespoon sugar
2 teaspoons dried parsley

In skillet cook sausage, green pepper and onion until browned; drain off fat. In medium bowl combine spinach, milk, and eggs; mix well. Stir in bread crumbs and water chestnuts. Add sausage and mix well. Turn mixture into 13 × 9 × 2 inch baking pan. Bake uncovered in preheated 350°F. oven for 20 minutes. Combine sour cream, salad dressing, mustard, and sugar. Spread over sausage mixture. Sprinkle with parsley flakes. Bake 5-7 minutes longer or until topping is hot.   *Yield: 8 servings*

SAUSAGE STROGANOFF

1 lb. USINGER Smoked Polish Sausage Links
2 tablespoons drippings
½ cup sliced green onions
1 cup (8 oz.) sour cream
1 can (6 oz.) tomato paste
1 tablespoon flour
½ teaspoon salt
¼ teaspoon pepper
6 oz. egg noodles, cooked
Parmesan Cheese

Preheat oven to 325°F. Cook sausages and cut half of the links into bite size pieces. Sauté onions in drippings until tender. Blend together sour cream, tomato paste, flour and seasonings. Add noodles, sausage pieces and onions. Place in 2-qt. casserole, sprinkle generously with Parmesan Cheese, and top with remaining whole links. Bake for 25 minutes.   *6 servings*

COUNTRY CASSEROLE

1½ pounds ground sausage meat
6 thin slices of onion
2 cups SEALTEST® Cottage Cheese
½ teaspoon oregano
1 (7½-ounce) can tomato sauce
Sugar

Form the sausage meat into six flat cakes. Brown thoroughly on both sides over medium heat. Drain. Arrange them in an oven-proof casserole.

Place a slice of onion on each sausage cake. Mix cottage cheese with oregano. Divide equally on top of each sausage cake. Top each one with some of the tomato sauce. Sprinkle with a couple of pinches of sugar. Bake in a preheated 350° oven 25 to 30 minutes or until piping hot.   *6 servings*

HOMESTYLE PASTA BAKE

1 pound ziti or elbow macaroni
1 egg
1 pound cottage cheese
½ teaspoon FRENCH'S® Italian Seasoning
½ pound Italian sausage*
1 envelope (1¾-oz.) FRENCH'S® Thick, Homemade
  Style Spaghetti Sauce Mix
2 cans (6-oz. each) tomato paste
2½ cups water
1½ cups shredded mozzarella cheese

Cook and drain macaroni. Lightly beat egg in large mixing bowl; stir in cottage cheese, Italian seasoning, and the cooked macaroni. Spoon into greased 13 x 9-inch baking dish. Cover loosely with foil. Bake at 350° for 30 minutes. Meanwhile, cut sausage in 1-inch pieces and brown in large saucepan, stirring frequently. Add sauce mix, tomato paste, and water. Cover and simmer 15 to 20 minutes, stirring occasionally. Spoon about half the sauce on top of macaroni; sprinkle with mozzarella cheese. Bake, uncovered, 10 to 15 minutes. Cut in squares and serve with remaining sausage and sauce.   *8 to 10 servings*

*If preferred, omit sausage. Brown 1 pound ground beef and add to spaghetti sauce.

SPICY SOUTHWESTERN CASSEROLE

8 PERDUE® Franks
2 (15-ounce) cans chili
1 cup yellow cornmeal
2 teaspoons baking powder
1½ teaspoons salt
2 eggs
⅔ cup melted butter or margarine
1 cup sour cream
2 cups canned niblets-style corn, drained
¼ pound grated Monterey Jack or Cheddar cheese
1 (4-ounce) can chopped green chilies, drained

Cut Franks in half lengthwise. Place chili in bottom of a buttered 7×14×2-inch baking dish. Arrange Franks, cut side down, on top of chili. In medium size mixing bowl, mix dry ingredients. Add eggs, butter, and sour cream and blend thoroughly. Fold in corn. Sprinkle half of the cheese and green chilies over the layer of Franks. Top with half of the corn mixture. Sprinkle with remaining cheese and chilies and finish with a layer of corn mixture. Smooth the top with a spatula. Bake in the middle of a preheated 375° oven for 35 to 40 minutes, or until top is lightly browned and toothpick inserted in corn layers comes out clean. *Serves 6-8*

WIENER ENCHILADA CASSEROLE

OSCAR MAYER Lard
10 tortillas
1 package (1 lb.) OSCAR MAYER Wieners
1 can (15 oz.) enchilada sauce
1 can (6 oz.) tomato paste
½ cup finely chopped onion
½ cup (2 oz.) shredded Cheddar cheese

Preheat oven to 350°F. Melt lard in a skillet to a depth of ½-inch. Heat. Dip each tortilla in the hot lard (375°F) just long enough to soften, about 5 seconds. Drain on absorbent paper. Roll a tortilla around each wiener. Place one inch apart in greased 13x9x2-inch pan, lapped sides down. Combine enchilada sauce, tomato paste and onion. Pour sauce over wiener enchiladas in pan. Bake for 30 minutes. To serve, spoon sauce over top of wiener enchiladas and sprinkle with cheese. *Makes 5 servings*

GLAZED FRANKS 'N BEANS

1 can (16-ounces) CAMPBELL'S Pork & Beans
6 frankfurters
2 tablespoons brown sugar
1 teaspoon prepared mustard
½ teaspoon Worcestershire sauce

1. Pour beans into a 10×6-inch baking dish.
2. Using a sharp knife, make about 5 diagonal slashes ½-inch deep in each frankfurter. Arrange frankfurters cut-side up on beans.
3. In small bowl, combine remaining ingredients. Spread on frankfurters.
4. Bake at 375°F for 20 minutes until beans are hot and frankfurters are glazed. *Makes 4 servings*

BEANS AND FRANKS

3 Tablespoons chopped onion
2 Tablespoons butter or margarine
1 can (1 lb. 15-oz.) VAN CAMP'S® Pork and Beans
6 wieners, sliced penny style
⅓ cup brown sugar
1 teaspoon prepared mustard
1 teaspoon celery salt

Sauté onion in butter until tender. Combine onion with remaining ingredients in a 2-quart casserole. Bake, uncovered, at 350°F for 40 minutes, stirring occasionally. *Makes 6 servings*

PIZZA CASSEROLE WITH R·F® SHELMACS

1 pound box of R·F® Shelmacs
¼ cup margarine
1 quart (2 pounds) spaghetti sauce
¼ tsp. oregano
¼ tsp. pepper
¼ tsp. basil
½ pound mozzarella cheese, shredded
¼ pound pepperoni, thinly sliced
Miscellaneous pizza toppings optional: green pepper, mushrooms, onions, etc.

Cook a one pound box of R·F® Shelmacs according to package directions; drain. In a mixing bowl, combine the hot pasta with margarine (cut into pieces). Toss until the pasta is coated with the margarine. Add spaghetti sauce, oregano, basil, and pepper. Mix well. Pour into a 13-inch × 9-inch baking dish. Top with shredded mozzarella cheese. Bake in 350° oven for 10 minutes. Remove and add slices of pepperoni and other toppings, if desired. Bake for another 10 minutes. Let cool for 5 minutes before cutting. *Serves 8*

MACARONI & BEANS ITALIANO

½ cup chopped onion
½ cup chopped green pepper
1 medium zucchini, cut into ⅛-inch slices
3 tablespoons margarine or olive oil
¾ cup HEINZ Tomato Ketchup
¾ cup water
1 teaspoon salt
½ teaspoon oregano leaves
¼ teaspoon garlic salt
⅛ teaspoon pepper
1 can (1 pound) HEINZ Vegetarian Beans in Tomato Sauce
1½ cups cooked macaroni
Grated Parmesan cheese

Sauté first 3 ingredients in margarine until tender. Stir in ketchup and next 5 ingredients. Combine with beans and macaroni in a 1½-quart casserole. Bake in 375°F. oven, 35-40 minutes. Stir occasionally. Serve with Parmesan cheese.
Makes 4-5 servings (about 4½ cups)

MICROWAVE METHOD:
Power Level—HIGH. Omit margarine. Decrease salt to ½ teaspoon and pepper to dash. Place onion, green pepper and zucchini in a 1½-quart casserole. Cover casserole with plastic film, turning one edge back slightly to vent. Microwave 6 minutes or until vegetables are tender. Stir in ketchup and remaining ingredients except Parmesan cheese. Cover; microwave 5 minutes, stirring once. Stir and let stand, covered, 5 minutes. Serve with Parmesan cheese.

BAKED ZITI AND CHEESE

½ pound sweet Italian sausage
1 cup sliced mushrooms
1 cup green pepper slices, cut into 2-inch lengths
⅓ cup chopped onion
½ cup butter or margarine
⅓ cup unsifted all-purpose flour
2¼ cups milk
2 cups shredded Cheddar cheese
½ cup grated Parmesan or Romano cheese
½ teaspoon each salt and pepper
3 cups (8 ounces) SAN GIORGIO® Cut Ziti, uncooked

Bake sausage at 350° for 30 minutes; cool. Slice sausage in thin pieces; set aside.

Sauté mushrooms, green pepper and onion in butter or margarine in 3-quart saucepan until tender, but not brown; remove vegetables from pan and set aside. Blend flour into butter or margarine in saucepan; gradually stir in milk. Cook and stir constantly over medium low heat until mixture begins to boil. Boil and stir 1 minute. Add 1½ cups Cheddar cheese and Parmesan or Romano cheese, salt and pepper; stir until cheese is melted and mixture is smooth. Set aside and keep warm.

Cook **Cut Ziti** according to package directions for 10 minutes; drain well. Stir cooked **Cut Ziti**, reserved sausage slices and reserved sautéed vegetables into the cheese sauce. Pour mixture into a buttered 2-quart casserole or baking dish. Sprinkle with remaining ½ cup Cheddar cheese. Cover with aluminum foil and bake at 350° for 20 minutes. Remove foil; bake about 10 to 15 minutes longer or until top is browned.   *4 to 6 servings*

WHEAT GERM RATATOUILLE CASSEROLE

4 slices bacon, diced
½ medium eggplant, cut into ½-inch cubes
1 medium onion, cut into wedges
1 medium zucchini, sliced
⅔ cup KRETSCHMER Regular Wheat Germ
2 cups (8-oz.) grated Monterey Jack cheese
2 medium tomatoes, sliced
1 can (8-oz.) tomato sauce
¼ cup water
½ - 1 tsp. oregano leaves, crushed
½ tsp. marjoram leaves, crushed
¼ tsp. rosemary leaves, crushed
¼ tsp. salt

Fry . . . . bacon in large skillet until almost crisp.
Add . . . . . . eggplant, onion and zucchini. Sauté until eggplant is tender, about 10 minutes.
Place . . . . . half the vegetables in 4 individual casseroles (1½ - 2 cups).
Spoon . . . . wheat germ on vegetables.
Sprinkle. . . with half the cheese.
Top . . . . . . with tomatoes and remaining vegetables.
Combine . . tomato sauce, water and seasonings. Pour over vegetables.
Sprinkle. . . with remaining cheese.
Bake . . . . . uncovered at 375° for 20 minutes until hot.
    Makes 4 servings

SLIM HERB MAC AND CHEESE

1 (7 oz.) package or 2 cups uncooked CREAMETTES® Elbow Macaroni, cooked as package directs and drained
¼ cup low calorie margarine
¼ cup unsifted flour
1 teaspoon dry mustard
1 teaspoon garlic salt
¼ to ½ teaspoon basil leaves
½ teaspoon paprika
2 cups skim milk
8 slices low calorie cheese cut into small pieces
2 teaspoons corn flake crumbs
Chopped parsley

Preheat oven to 350. In small saucepan, over low heat, melt margarine; stir in flour, mustard, salt, basil and paprika. Gradually stir in milk; cook and stir until thickened. Add cheese product; cook and stir until melted. Remove from heat; stir in cooked macaroni. Turn into 1½ quart baking dish; top with crumbs. Bake 20 minutes or until bubbly. Garnish with parsley. Refrigerate leftovers.   *Makes 8 servings*

CASSEROLE MILANO

½ cup commercial sour cream
3 Tablespoons all-purpose flour
¼ cup chopped onion
2 teaspoons prepared mustard
1 can (10¾ ounces) condensed cream of celery soup, undiluted
2 cups cooked ham, cut into ½-inch cubes
1 package (16 ounces) Frozen STOKELY'S® Vegetables Milano®
⅓ cup dry bread crumbs
2 Tablespoons grated Parmesan cheese
2 Tablespoons butter or margarine, melted
½ teaspoon paprika

Preheat oven to 350°F. Combine sour cream, flour, onion, mustard, and soup in 2-quart casserole, blending thoroughly. Stir in ham and vegetables, spreading mixture evenly in casserole. Mix bread crumbs, cheese, butter, and paprika; sprinkle over casserole. Bake, covered, 1 hour.   *4 servings*

MICROWAVE METHOD:
Combine sour cream, flour, onion, mustard, and soup in 2½-quart covered casserole, blending thoroughly. Stir in ham and vegetables, spreading mixture evenly in casserole. Cover and microcook 15 minutes, stirring every 5 minutes (including just before topping is added). Mix bread crumbs, cheese, butter, and paprika; sprinkle over casserole and cook, uncovered, an additional 2 minutes.

Note: Use a slightly larger casserole when you make a recipe in the microwave oven. That way you will have room to stir and food will cook more evenly.

Egg Dishes

TUBETTINI DEVILED EGGS

¼ cup (2 ounces) **SAN GIORGIO® Tubettini**, uncooked
6 hard-cooked eggs
⅓ cup cottage cheese
2 teaspoons milk
2 teaspoons prepared mustard
2 tablespoons sweet pickle relish or chopped pickle

Cook Tubettini according to package directions; drain well. Cool. (Rinse with cold water to cool quickly; drain well.)

Slice eggs in half; remove yolks. Combine yolks, cottage cheese, milk, mustard and relish or chopped pickle; blend well by hand or process in blender or food processor until smooth. Stir in cooled Tubettini; fill egg whites with macaroni mixture. Chill.

12 eggs

DEVILED EGGS WITH CRAB

1 package (6 ounces) snow crab or other crabmeat, frozen or 1 can (6½ ounces) crabmeat
6 hard-cooked eggs
3 tablespoons finely chopped celery
4 heaping tablespoons mayonnaise
1 teaspoon dry mustard
¼ teaspoon salt
Dash pepper
1 teaspoon finely chopped parsley
⅛ teaspoon oregano
⅛ teaspoon garlic powder
4 drops Worcestershire sauce

Thaw crabmeat if frozen. Drain canned crabmeat. Remove any remaining shell or cartilage. Peel eggs and cut in half lengthwise. Remove yolks, put in bowl and mash well. Add celery, mayonnaise and seasonings. Add crabmeat and mix well. Stuff egg whites with yolk mixture. Chill before serving.

Makes 1 dozen

Favorite recipe from the **National Marine Fisheries Service**

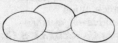

RAGU´® SCRAMBLED EGGS D'ITALIA
(Low Calorie)

1 small yellow squash, thinly sliced
1 small onion, thinly sliced
3 tablespoons butter or margarine (reserve 2 tablespoons)
1 jar (15½ oz.) **RAGU´® Classic Combinations®
Spaghetti Sauce, flavored with Sausage & Peppers**
Salt, to taste
Pepper, to taste
4 large eggs, beaten with 2 tablespoons water

In a medium skillet, lightly sauté squash and onion in 1 tablespoon butter until onion is translucent. Add 1 cup sauce, salt and pepper, simmer 5 minutes and set aside. In a large skillet, scramble eggs in reserved butter. Serve eggs topped with vegetable-sauce mixture.

Serves 4

213 calories per serving

SAUSAGE RING WITH MUSHROOM SCRAMBLED EGGS

1 pound bulk sausage
¾ cup fine dry bread crumbs
½ teaspoon basil
1 tablespoon **LAWRY'S® Minced Onion with Green Onion Flakes**
1 egg, beaten

Combine all ingredients and mix thoroughly. Press into a 7-inch ring mold; bake in a 350°F. oven 15 minutes. Drain fat. Continue baking an additional 15 to 20 minutes or until done. Drain any fat. Invert on heated serving dish and fill center with Mushroom Scrambled Eggs.*

Makes 4 to 6 servings

*MUSHROOM SCRAMBLED EGGS

6 eggs
½ teaspoon **LAWRY'S® Seasoned Salt**
¼ teaspoon **LAWRY'S® Seasoned Pepper**
¼ teaspoon **LAWRY'S® Pinch of Herbs**
2 tablespoons butter or margarine
1 can (2 oz.) sliced mushrooms, drained
2 tablespoons milk

Combine all ingredients and beat well. Melt butter in skillet; add egg mixture. Cook over medium heat until bottom starts to get firm. Lower heat, stir until desired doneness is reached.

Makes 3 to 4 servings

PAPAYA'S OMELETTE

½ soft **CALAVO® Papaya**, seeded and cut into widthwise wedges
1 tablespoon cream sherry
1 tablespoon brandy
½ cup sour cream
2 tablespoons brown sugar
2 tablespoons butter or margarine
6 eggs
¼ teaspoon salt
1 tablespoon cold water
10 strawberries, hulled and cut into halves (save 2 for garnish)

Place papaya wedges, cream sherry and brandy into shallow bowl. Cover and allow to marinate overnight.

In small bowl, whip sour cream until fluffy; gradually add brown sugar; set aside. Break the eggs into a medium bowl; add salt and cold water. Beat eggs briskly for 25 to 30 seconds—just enough to blend the yolks and whites.

Melt 1 tablespoon butter in 7-inch omelette pan. When butter begins to foam, add ½ of the eggs. As edges of omelette set, tilt pan and lift edges of omelette with spatula to move cooked portion toward center of pan. Allow uncooked egg to run under firm portion. Continue to tilt and move eggs until the omelette is firm. Place ½ of marinated papaya and ½ of halved strawberries on one side of the omelette; fold other side over into half moon shape to cover the filling. Repeat with remaining butter, eggs and fruit for second omelette.

To serve spoon sour cream topping over each omelette; garnish with whole strawberry.

Makes 2 omelettes

EGG-STUFFED CELEBRITY® SLICED HAM ROLL

8 eggs, slightly beaten
½ cup milk
½ teaspoon salt
½ teaspoon chopped chives
⅛ teaspoon pepper
¼ cup butter or margarine
1 (3-ounce) package soft cream cheese
6 slices **CELEBRITY® Ham**

Blend eggs, milk, salt, chives and pepper. Using large skillet, melt butter or margarine. Add the eggs and cook. Stir until just set. Stir small pieces of cream cheese into eggs. With ham slices flat, spoon eggs onto each slice, then roll the ham slice. Seam side of roll should be placed face down on serving platter. Garnish with hot tomato slices and parsley.

TROPICAL OMELET

Fruit Sauce:

1 can (17-ounce) **STOKELY'S FINEST®** Fruit Cocktail
⅓ cup orange juice
1 tablespoon honey
2 teaspoons lemon juice
2 teaspoons cornstarch
½ banana, sliced

Omelet:

6 eggs
2 tablespoons milk
½ teaspoon salt
Dash pepper
2 tablespoons butter or margarine

FRUIT SAUCE:
Drain fruit cocktail reserving 2 tablespoons liquid. In saucepan, blend reserved fruit cocktail liquid with orange juice, honey, lemon juice, and cornstarch. Cook over medium heat, stirring constantly, until thickened and bubbling. Stir in fruit cocktail and banana; heat until warmed through. Keep warm while preparing omelet.

OMELET:
You may wish to make one large omelet or three individual omelets. To prepare: beat together eggs, milk, salt, and pepper. Melt butter in pan(s) for making omelet; when butter bubbles, add egg mixture to pan. Reduce heat to low and cook without stirring. As mixture begins to set, gently lift edges, allowing thin uncooked portion to flow to bottom. Cook until eggs are set. Remove to serving platter. Top with fruit filling and fold omelet in half. Serve at once.   *1 large or 3 individual omelets*

Note: Sprinkle Tropical Omelet with shredded Cheddar cheese for an added taste treat.

VEGETABLE-CHEESE OMELET

1 package (10 oz.) **BIRDS EYE® AMERICANA RECIPE®** Vegetables, Wisconsin Country Style
½ cup diced cheddar cheese
6 eggs
¼ teaspoon salt
2 tablespoons milk or water
2 tablespoons butter or margarine

Prepare vegetables as directed on package. Stir in cheese and the topping and keep warm. Beat eggs with salt and milk. Heat butter in skillet. Add egg mixture and cook over medium heat. Run a spatula slowly around the edge to allow uncooked portion to flow underneath. When omelet is set but still glossy, top with vegetable mixture and cook 1 to 2 minutes longer. Loosen with spatula, fold over and turn onto platter.   *Makes 3 servings*

Note: ¼ cup of the cooked vegetables may be reserved and spooned over filled omelet as garnish, if desired.

BUDDIG OMELETS

6 eggs
⅓ cup milk
½ teaspoon salt
Dash pepper
Select one (2½-oz.) package of either **BUDDIG Pastrami, Corned Beef, Ham** or **Beef** and dice
2 tablespoons butter or margarine

With a fork, beat together eggs, milk, salt and pepper. Heat the meat in skillet with butter or margarine. Add the egg mixture. Cook over low heat, lifting edges and tipping skillet so uncooked egg flows under cooked mixture. When mixture is set, fold over and serve. If you desire a softer omelet, remove from skillet by tipping it on to a plate before the eggs set too hard.

VARIATIONS:

WESTERN OMELET

Sauté ½ cup of green peppers diced and ½ cup of onions chopped. Sauté until the vegetables are soft and then add the **BUDDIG** meat of your choice and proceed with the above directions.

MEXICAN OMELET

Prepare the **BUDDIG** omelet according to the directions above and then spoon Taco Sauce on top before serving.

STEAK AND POTATO OVEN OMELET

3 tablespoons butter or margarine
½ cup sliced green onion
½ teaspoon basil leaves, crushed
1 can (19-ounces) **CAMPBELL'S Chunky Steak 'N Potato Soup**
1 medium tomato, cut into wedges
6 eggs, separated
¼ teaspoon cream of tartar
¼ cup water
¼ teaspoon salt
Dash pepper
½ cup shredded Cheddar cheese

1. In 2-quart saucepan over medium heat, in 1 tablespoon hot butter, cook onion with basil until tender. Add soup and tomato. Heat thoroughly; stir occasionally.
2. In large bowl with mixer at high speed, beat egg whites until foamy. Add cream of tartar; beat until whites form stiff peaks. Preheat oven to 350°F.
3. In small bowl with mixer at high speed, beat yolks with water, salt and pepper until light and fluffy. With rubber spatula carefully fold into beaten egg whites.
4. In oven-safe 10-inch skillet, over medium heat, melt remaining

butter. Add egg mixture; cook until underside of omelet is golden, about 3 minutes.

5. Place skillet in oven and bake 10 minutes, or until surface is golden and springs back when pressed lightly with finger. Sprinkle with cheese. Serve immediately.

6. To serve cut omelet into six wedges. Serve ½ cup soup mixture over each wedge. *Makes 6 servings*

OMELETTE WITH GORGONZOLA

½ cup heavy cream
2 oz. **Gorgonzola LOCATELLI® Cheese**
Dash nutmeg
2 tablespoons butter
8 eggs, beaten

Combine over hot (not boiling) water, heavy cream, **Gorgonzola LOCATELLI®** and nutmeg. Cook until cheese melts and mixture is smooth and creamy. In large skillet, melt butter. Pour in eggs; cook over moderate heat until omelette begins to set up. Pour cheese mixture over top. Cover; cook over low heat until omelette is completely set. Fold and serve. *Makes 4-6 servings*

HAMBURGER OMELETS FU YUNG

6 eggs, separated
¾ pound ground beef
1¼ teaspoons **LAWRY'S® Seasoned Salt**
½ teaspoon **LAWRY'S® Seasoned Pepper**
2 tablespoons minced parsley
½ cup minced onion
2 tablespoons butter

Beat egg yolks until thick and lemon colored. Blend in ground beef, **Seasoned Salt**, **Seasoned Pepper**, parsley and onion. Beat egg whites until stiff peaks form. Fold whites into meat mixture. Melt butter in electric skillet at 320°F. or in skillet over low heat. For each omelet use a scant ¼ cup. Cook about 3 minutes on each side or until browned. Use additional butter for frying if necessary. *Makes about 18*

THE INCREDIBLE OMELET ALMONDINE

4 eggs
¼ cup water
1 teaspoon sugar
Salt
2 tablespoons butter
½ cup sliced almonds
½ to ⅔ cup dairy sour cream or yogurt
2 tablespoons strawberry or other fruit preserves

Mix eggs, water, sugar and salt with fork. Set aside. In 8-inch omelet pan or skillet over medium-high heat, toast almonds in butter until golden, about 1 to 2 minutes, stirring frequently. Spoon almonds and about half the butter into a bowl; then put 3 tablespoons almonds back in pan. Pour in half the egg mixture which should set at edges at once. Carefully push cooked eggs to center and tip and tilt pan so uncooked eggs can flow to bottom. While top is still moist and creamy-looking, fill with half of the sour cream and preserves. Fold omelet over filling and turn out onto plate. Keep warm while preparing remaining omelet. Put 3 tablespoons toasted almonds and remaining butter in pan. Add remaining egg mixture and cook and fill as above. Garnish with remaining toasted almond slices. *2 servings*

Favorite recipe from **American Egg Board**

MEXICAN CHEESE OMELET

2 tablespoons butter, melted
2 tablespoons flour
1 cup milk
¼ teaspoon ground cumin
1 (9-oz.) stick **HOFFMAN'S® Hot Pepper Cheese,** cubed
Your Favorite Plain Omelet

Combine butter, flour, milk and ground cumin. Cook over medium heat until thickened, stirring constantly. Reduce heat to low and add cheese. Continue stirring until cheese is melted. Spoon over omelet. *Makes 2 cups*

SIZZLEAN® FRITTATA

6 strips **SIZZLEAN®**, cut into 1-inch pieces
1 small onion, finely chopped
¼ cup chopped green pepper
1 tomato, peeled and chopped
6 eggs, slightly beaten

In a heavy 9-inch ovenproof skillet, cook pork breakfast strips, onion and green pepper until pork breakfast strips are cooked, about 7 minutes over medium heat. Turn mixture into a bowl to cool. Add chopped tomato and eggs.

Pour mixture back into skillet and cook over low heat until edges of frittata pull away from pan. To cook top, broil 4 inches from heat source until center is firm and top is lightly browned. Cut into 6 wedges and serve at once. *Yield: 6 servings*

LONG GRAIN AND WILD RICE FRITTATA

6 slices bacon
2⅓ cups water
1 package (6 ounces) **UNCLE BEN'S® Original Long Grain & Wild Rice**
1 medium zucchini, chopped (about 1 cup)
1 teaspoon salt
1 medium tomato, chopped
8 eggs
¾ cup dairy sour cream
½ cup grated Parmesan cheese

Fry bacon in 10-inch ovenproof skillet*; remove and reserve. Drain all but 2 tablespoons drippings. Add water, and contents of rice and seasoning packets to skillet. Bring to a boil. Cover tightly and cook over low heat until all water is absorbed, about 25 minutes. While rice is cooking, sprinkle zucchini with salt; let stand at least 10 minutes. Press out excess moisture. Stir zucchini and tomato into rice in skillet; press into even layer. Beat eggs with sour cream; pour over rice mixture. Crumble reserved bacon; sprinkle bacon and cheese over egg mixture. Bake at 375° F. 25 to 30 minutes or until firm and puffy. Let stand 5 minutes; cut into wedges. *Makes 6 servings*

*If ovenproof skillet is not available, prepare rice and vegetable mixture in skillet; spoon into well-greased deep 10-inch pie dish. Pour egg mixture over rice; sprinkle with bacon and cheese and bake at 350° F. until firm and puffy, about 30 minutes.

EGGS BENEDICT SUPREME

12 Holland Rusk
12 thin slices baked ham, heated
Mushroom Sauce*
12 thin slices tomato
12 poached eggs
Hollandaise Sauce**

On each rusk, place ham. Spoon Mushroom Sauce over ham. Top with tomato and egg. Spoon Hollandaise Sauce over egg.

Serves 6

*MUSHROOM SAUCE

½ cup butter or margarine
½ cup finely chopped fresh mushrooms
1 tablespoon finely minced onion
1 large clove garlic, minced
2 tablespoons flour
¼ teaspoon salt
⅛ teaspoon pepper
1 cup beef broth
¼ cup **REGINA Cooking Burgundy**
½ cup finely minced baked ham

In medium skillet, melt butter. Add mushrooms, onion and garlic. Cook until onion is soft. Stir in flour. Cook 2-3 minutes. Mix in remaining ingredients. Bring to boil. Spoon over ham in Eggs Benedict Supreme.

**HOLLANDAISE SAUCE

4 egg yolks
½ teaspoon salt
2 tablespoons **GREY POUPON Dijon Mustard**
½ cup butter, melted

In blender, combine egg yolks, salt and mustard. While continuing to blend, *slowly* add butter until thoroughly combined. Serve immediately over Eggs Benedict Supreme.

PORK BURGER BENEDICT

Place broiled or grilled **GOLDEN PRAIRIE Iowa Pork Burger** on toasted English muffin halves. Top each with poached eggs and cover with Hollandaise sauce. Garnish with black olive slice.

EGGS BENEDICT VARIATION

6 **BAYS® English Muffins**
12 eggs, poached
6 ounces thinly sliced ham cut into 12 slices
1 (28-ounce) can peeled tomatoes, drained and chopped (1½ cups)
½ cup juice from canned tomatoes
1 tablespoon dehydrated minced onions
1 tablespoon butter
¼ teaspoon salt
¼ teaspoon garlic salt
⅛ teaspoon ground black pepper
Easy Blender Hollandaise Sauce*
Minced Parsley

Toast muffins and keep warm. Poach eggs and drain. Drain tomatoes; reserve ½ cup liquid. In medium saucepan combine tomatoes, reserved juice, minced onions, butter, salt, garlic salt and ground black pepper. Simmer over medium-high heat for fifteen minutes, stirring frequently. Remove from heat; keep warm. Make Easy Blender Hollandaise Sauce.

(Continued)

*EASY BLENDER HOLLANDAISE SAUCE

2 sticks butter
4 egg yolks
1 tablespoon lemon juice
1 tablespoon water
Salt
White pepper

Melt butter until bubbling. Remove from heat. In blender place egg yolks, lemon juice, water and salt and pepper to taste. Blend at high speed for 30 seconds. Open top of blender and slowly pour in hot butter in a thin stream. Hollandaise Sauce will be thick and creamy.

To assemble top each muffin half with a slice of ham. Then add 2 tablespoons of the tomato mixture. Make a well to hold egg. Place a poached egg on each half. Top with Hollandaise Sauce. Sprinkle with minced parsley. Serve with steamed broccoli.

Serves 6, two halves per serving

SCOTCH EGGS

¾ pound bulk pork sausage
12 hard-cooked eggs
1 egg, beaten
⅓ cup fine dry bread crumbs
Fat for deep frying

Divide sausage into 12 equal portions (1 oz. each). Shape each portion into patty and wrap completely around 1 hard-cooked egg, pressing edges together to seal. Dip sausage-wrapped eggs in beaten egg; then roll in bread crumbs until completely coated. Cook eggs in preheated 375°F. deep fat until golden brown and heated through, 7 to 9 minutes. Drain on absorbent paper. Serve hot or cold.

6 servings

Favorite recipe from the **American Egg Board**

EGG CROQUETTES

1 can (10¾ ounces) **CAMPBELL'S Condensed Cream of Celery Soup**
8 hard-cooked eggs, finely chopped
¼ cup fine dry bread crumbs
2 tablespoons finely chopped onion
2 tablespoons finely chopped parsley
Dash pepper
2 tablespoons shortening
⅓ to ½ cup milk

Mix *thoroughly* 2 tablespoons soup, eggs, bread crumbs, onion, parsley and pepper. Shape *firmly* into 8 croquettes or patties. (If mixture is difficult to handle, chill before shaping.) Roll in additional bread crumbs. In skillet, brown croquettes in shortening. Meanwhile, in saucepan, combine remaining soup and milk. Heat; stir occasionally. Serve with croquettes.

Makes 6 to 8 servings

MAKE-AHEAD EGG BAKE

1 pound bulk pork sausage
6 eggs, beaten
2 cups light cream or half-and-half
1 cup (4-oz.) shredded Cheddar cheese
1 teaspoon salt
1 teaspoon **DURKEE Ground Mustard**
1 can (2.8-oz.) **DURKEE French Fried Onions**

Fry sausage until crumbly and brown; drain well. Add remaining ingredients except French fried onions and mix well. Stir in ½ can onions. Pour mixture into a greased 9 × 13-inch baking dish. Refrigerate 8 hours or overnight. Bake at 350° for 45 minutes. Sprinkle with remaining onions and bake 5 minutes longer. Remove from oven and let stand 15 minutes before serving.

Makes 6 servings

SKILLET EGGS FLORENTINE

¼ cup butter or margarine
1 large onion, thinly sliced (1 cup)
2 tablespoons flour
2 cups milk
½ teaspoon **TABASCO® Pepper Sauce**
¼ teaspoon salt
Pinch nutmeg
1 can (4 ounces) sliced mushrooms, drained
1 package (10 ounces) frozen chopped spinach, thawed, drained
8 eggs

In large skillet melt butter; sauté onions until golden. Stir in flour; cook 1 minute. Gradually add milk; stir until mixture boils and thickens. Stir in **TABASCO® Sauce**, salt and nutmeg. Add mushrooms and spinach. With back of a spoon make 8 indentations in spinach mixture. Break one egg into each well. Cover. Cook about 5 minutes until egg whites are set. *Yield: 4 servings*

SURPRISE EGGS

STOKES® Green Chile Sauce with Pork
Eggs
English Muffins
Grated longhorn cheese
Optional ingredients*

Empty 2 cans **STOKES® Green Chile Sauce with Pork** into an electric skillet or a 10-12 inch skillet on top of range and heat to bubbling. Make a slight hole with a spoon and drop eggs one at a time into each hole, 4 or 5 eggs can be cooked at one time. Cover with a lid and simmer for approximately 3 or 4 minutes depending on your preference for degree of doneness. Remove with a large spoon and serve on an English muffin. Grated cheese and onion may be added.

*Optional serving suggestions: over a bed of cooked rice, toasted bread or warm flour tortilla.

HUEVOS RANCHEROS

4 tablespoons oil, divided
¼ cup minced onion
1 can (1 lb.) tomatoes, broken up
2 teaspoons **LEA & PERRINS Worcestershire Sauce**
½ teaspoon salt
½ teaspoon sugar
½ teaspoon chili powder
12 tortillas
6 tablespoons butter or margarine, divided
12 eggs, divided
1 ripe avocado, peeled, pitted, and chunked

In a medium saucepan heat 1 tablespoon of the oil. Add onion; sauté for 1 minute. Add tomatoes, **LEA & PERRINS**, salt, sugar, and chili powder. Bring to boiling point. Reduce heat and simmer, uncovered, for 15 minutes. In a large skillet heat remaining 3 tablespoons oil. Add tortillas, 3 at a time; fry lightly, about 1 minute. Drain tortillas on paper towels; keep hot. In the same skillet melt 2 tablespoons of the butter. Crack 4 eggs into the skillet; fry lightly. Repeat, using remaining butter and eggs. Place an egg on each tortilla. For each serving spoon tomato sauce on an individual serving plate; place 2 egg-topped tortillas over sauce. Garnish with avocado chunks. *6 servings*

EGGS SAN REMO

1 clove garlic (or equivalent garlic powder)
½ cup chicken stock (or ½ cup water and chicken flavored bouillon)
1½ tablespoons butter or margarine
1 tablespoon flour (plus additional flour for tomatoes)
½ cup **MILNOT®**
4 thick slices underripe tomato
2 eggs, poached
4 or more tablespoons grated Parmesan or shredded Cheddar cheese
Fat for frying

Simmer clove of garlic in chicken stock about 3 minutes; remove garlic. Make a sauce: melt butter, stir in tablespoon of flour, blend in chicken stock, stir in **MILNOT®**. Continue cooking and stirring until sauce is thickened.

Dip tomatoes in flour. Sauté quickly in small amount of fat until browned on both sides; place in shallow baking dish. Place one poached egg on two tomato slices. Pour sauce over eggs, sprinkle with cheese. Place under broiler until cheese melts.

Yield: 2 servings

"CREOLE" EGG AND KIDNEY BEAN QUICKIE

1 cup onions, chopped
2 cloves garlic, minced
2 tablespoons olive oil
¼ cup **GOYA® SOFRITO Sauce**
1½ cups chicken broth made with bouillon cubes
1 teaspoon salt
½ teaspoon black pepper
3 cans (16-oz.) **GOYA® White Kidney Beans**, drained
½ cup black olives, diced
¼ cup **GOYA® Red Pimientos**, diced
4-6 eggs

In a 10-inch skillet sauté onions and garlic in olive oil until soft. Add **GOYA® SOFRITO**, chicken broth, salt and pepper and simmer for 5 minutes. Carefully stir in white kidney beans, black olives and pimiento. Bring to a boil, reduce heat and simmer for 5 minutes to blend flavors. While simmering, break one egg at a time into a cup and carefully slide the egg into an indentation on top of the beans. Cover and heat gently until the eggs are set.

Serves 4-6

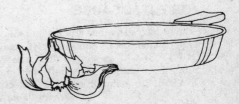

HAM EGG FOO YUNG
(Low Calorie)

4 eggs
1 cup bean sprouts
3 oz. (3 slices) **KAHN'S®** Cooked Ham, cut into small pieces
2 green onions, thinly sliced (approx. ¼ cup)
1 can (2½ oz.) sliced mushrooms
1 Tbsp. soy sauce
1 tsp. vegetable oil
Chinese Sauce* (optional)

Beat eggs well. Add bean sprouts, ham, green onions, mushrooms and soy sauce; mix well. Heat 1 tsp. oil in an 8-inch nonstick skillet. Pour in egg mixture. Scramble eggs until partially set; then press down on egg mixture with spatula to form appearance of an omelette. When evenly set, turn to brown other side. Invert onto serving plate. Serve with Chinese Sauce if desired.

Makes 2 servings

Calories: 246 calories per serving

*CHINESE SAUCE

2 tsp. cornstarch
½ cup beef broth
1 Tbsp. soy sauce

Mix all ingredients together and heat, stirring constantly. Boil 1 minute. Serve with Ham Egg Foo Yung.

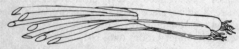

EGGS FU YUNG

2 strips bacon, diced
½ lb. green beans, cut into 1-inch julienne strips
5 eggs
2 cups fresh bean sprouts, chopped
½ cup chopped green onion
1 teaspoon **KITCHEN BOUQUET®**
½ teaspoon salt
¼ teaspoon ground ginger
Vegetable oil
Oriental Sauce*

Sauté bacon and beans in large skillet over medium-high heat for 5 minutes or until bacon is cooked and beans are tender-crisp. Remove from heat. Beat eggs with fork in mixing bowl. Lift bacon and beans from skillet with slotted spoon, leaving drippings in pan and add to eggs. Add bean sprouts, onion, **KITCHEN BOU-QUET®**, salt and ginger. Pour ¼ to ⅓ cup mixture into drippings in warm skillet. Cook over moderate heat, scraping liquid portion to center as it cooks. Turn and cook other side until browned. Transfer to serving plate and keep warm. Continue with remaining egg mixture, adding oil as needed. Spoon sauce over stack of egg cakes. Pass remaining. Cooking time: Approximately 20 minutes.

Makes 2 to 3 servings (8 patties)

*ORIENTAL SAUCE

Drain liquid from 1 can (3 oz.) sliced mushrooms into saucepan. Add ⅓ cup water, 1 tablespoon cornstarch, 1 teaspoon **KITCHEN BOUQUET®** and ¼ teaspoon salt in sauce pan. Cook over medium-high heat, stirring constantly until mixture thickens and comes to a boil. Stir in mushrooms and 2 tablespoons sherry.

Makes about 1 cup

Quiche

ASPARAGUS CHEESE QUICHE

3 eggs, beaten
1 cup heavy cream
2 tablespoons finely minced onion
½ cup shredded Jack cheese
¼ teaspoon salt
⅛ teaspoon pepper
¼ teaspoon basil
2 tablespoons **GREY POUPON** Dijon Mustard
1 cup cooked, well-drained cut asparagus
1 unbaked 9-inch pie shell

In medium bowl, combine all ingredients except pie shell. Pour into pie shell. Arrange 8 asparagus spears on top of mixture, if desired. Bake in preheated 375°F oven 40 minutes or until knife inserted in center comes out clean. Allow to cool 5 minutes before serving.

Serves 6-8

GREEN CHILIES QUICHE

1 (9-inch) **BANQUET®** Frozen Pie Crust Shell
1 can (4 oz.) chopped green chilies, drained
¼ cup ripe olives, quartered
1 cup (4 oz.) shredded Cheddar cheese
3 eggs
½ cup milk

Spread green chilies over bottom of pie crust. Place olives on top of chilies. Sprinkle cheese on top. Beat together eggs and milk; pour over cheese. Bake on cookie sheet in 375°F oven 30 to 35 minutes or until knife inserted 2 inches from edge comes out clean. Let stand 10 minutes before serving.

Makes 1 pie

TOMATO QUICHE

2 medium-sized Florida tomatoes
Pastry for one crust 9-inch pie
4 eggs
1½ cups milk
2 cups shredded Swiss cheese
½ cup chopped onions
1¼ teaspoons salt
¼ teaspoon ground black pepper

Hold tomatoes at room temperature until fully ripe. Cut one into small dice; slice the second tomato. Set both aside separately. Roll pastry to fit a 9-inch pie pan. Fit pastry into pan and flute edges. Prick bottom and sides of pastry. Refrigerate for 10 minutes. Bake in a preheated very hot oven (450°F) until golden, about 8 minutes. Remove pie shell. Reduce oven temperature to slow (325 F).

In a medium bowl lightly beat eggs. Stir in milk, cheese, onions, salt, black pepper and reserved diced tomato. Pour into baked pie shell. Bake in slow oven for 30 minutes. Top with reserved sliced tomatoes. Bake until a knife inserted in center comes out clean, about 25 minutes longer. Let pie stand at room temperature for 10 minutes before cutting.

Yield: One 9-inch pie

Favorie recipe from **Florida Tomato Exchange**

BROCCOLI QUICHE

Crust:
1 cup 3-MINUTE BRAND® Quick Oats or 3 packets
  Regular Flavor HARVEST BRAND® Instant
  Oatmeal
1 cup all-purpose flour
½ teaspoon salt
½ cup butter or margarine

Filling:
3 eggs
½ cup milk or light cream
⅔ cup chopped broccoli
⅔ cup shredded Swiss cheese
½ cup cooked and diced ham
1 tablespoon finely chopped onion or minced dried onion

CRUST:
Stir together oats, flour and salt. Cut in butter till crumbly. Pat dough in bottom and up sides of a quiche dish or 9-inch pie plate; set aside.

FILLING:
Combine eggs and milk; mix well. Stir in remaining ingredients. Pour into prepared crust. Bake in a 350°F. oven for 35 to 40 minutes or till a knife inserted near center comes out clean. Let stand 10 minutes before cutting into wedges.

Makes 6 main-dish servings

Note: To make **Bite-size Broccoli Quiches,** follow the above recipe *except* double all crust ingredients and pat dough in bottom and up sides of 1¾-inch muffin cups. Spoon about 1 tablespoon filling in each cup, and bake in a 350°F. oven about 20 minutes.

Makes 32 appetizers

ITALIAN ZUCCHINI CRESCENT PIE

4 cups thinly sliced, unpeeled zucchini
1 cup coarsely chopped onion
½ cup margarine or butter
½ cup chopped parsley or 2 tablespoons
  McCORMICK®/SCHILLING® Parsley Flakes
½ teaspoon salt
½ teaspoon McCORMICK®/SCHILLING® Black
  Pepper
¼ teaspoon McCORMICK®/SCHILLING® Garlic
  Powder
¼ teaspoon McCORMICK®/SCHILLING® Sweet
  Basil Leaves
¼ teaspoon McCORMICK®/SCHILLING® Oregano
  Leaves
2 eggs, well beaten
8 oz. (2 cups) shredded CASINO Brand Natural
  Muenster or KRAFT Natural Mozzarella Cheese
8-oz. can PILLSBURY Refrigerated Quick Crescent
  Dinner Rolls
2 teaspoons Dijon or KRAFT Pure Prepared Mustard

Heat oven to 375°F. In 10-inch skillet, cook zucchini and onion in margarine until tender, about 10 minutes. Stir in parsley and seasonings. In large bowl, blend eggs and cheese. Stir in vegetable mixture.

(Continued)

Separate dough into 8 triangles. Place in ungreased 11-inch quiche pan, 10-inch pie pan or 12x8-inch baking dish; press over bottom and up sides to form crust. Spread crust with mustard. Pour vegetable mixture evenly into crust.

Bake at 375°F. for 18 to 20 minutes or until knife inserted near center comes out clean. (If crust becomes too brown, cover with foil during last 10 minutes of baking.) Let stand 10 minutes before serving. Cut into wedges to serve; serve hot. *6 servings*

Tips: If using 12x8-inch baking dish, separate dough into 2 long rectangles; press over bottom and 1 inch up sides to form crust. To reheat, cover loosely with foil; heat at 375°F. for 12 to 15 minutes.

HIGH ALTITUDE—Above 3500 Feet: No change.

NUTRITION INFORMATION PER SERVING
SERVING SIZE: ⅙ of recipe

		PERCENT U.S. RDA	
Calories	482	PER SERVING	
Protein	9 g	Protein	15%
Carbohydrate	24 g	Vitamin A	37%
Fat	39 g	Vitamin C	28%
Sodium	985 mg	Thiamine	14%
Potassium	350 mg	Riboflavin	28%
		Niacin	10%
		Calcium	35%
		Iron	10%

HAM & ASPARAGUS QUICHE

1 (9-inch) unbaked pie shell
1 (4-oz.) package sliced ham
1 (10-oz.) package frozen asparagus spears, defrosted, drained
1 cup whipping cream
¾ cup milk
3 eggs
¼ cup SEVEN SEAS® Buttermilk Recipe™ or
  SEVEN SEAS® Buttermilk Recipe Country
  Spice™ Dressing
½ teaspoon salt
¼ teaspoon white pepper
¼ cup green onion tops, finely chopped

Slice ham into ¼-inch julienne. Cut asparagus spears into ½-inch diagonal pieces. Beat eggs slightly; add cream, milk, dressing, seasoning and onion tops. Distribute ham and asparagus evenly over bottom of pie shell. Pour in filling. Bake 25-30 minutes at 375°F. *6-8 servings*

CRUMB-CRUSTED HAM AND CHEESE PIE

1½ cups of fine crumbs, using WASA® Golden Rye
  (about 15 slices)
½ cup melted butter or margarine
1½ cups grated Swiss cheese (6 ounces)
1½ tablespoons flour
¾ cup finely chopped smoked cooked ham*
4 eggs, well beaten
1 teaspoon salt
½ teaspoon pepper
½ teaspoon dry mustard
Dash nutmeg

Combine crumbs and butter. Mix well and press mixture firmly into bottom of a buttered 9-inch pie pan. Mix cheese and flour, and sprinkle into pan. Combine remaining ingredients and beat until smooth. Pour mixture into pan. Bake in a preheated oven (350 degrees) for 40 to 45 minutes, until top of pie is golden brown and puffed.

*Left over beef or chicken may be substituted.

QUICHE

12 slices **RATH® BLACK HAWK Bacon**, cut into small
   pieces and browned
1 cup shredded Swiss cheese
½ cup minced onions
4 eggs
2 cups light cream
Dash sugar
4-5 drops hot pepper sauce
Pastry for 1 crust, 9-10 inch pie, uncooked

Sprinkle **RATH® BLACK HAWK Bacon**, Swiss cheese and
onion into pastry-lined pie pan. Beat eggs together, stir in light
cream, sugar and hot pepper sauce. Pour over bacon, cheese and
onions. Bake in 375° F. oven 50 to 55 minutes or until knife
inserted into pie comes out clean. Let stand 5 to 10 minutes before
cutting into wedges.

SAUSAGE QUICHE

Pastry for 9-inch shell
6 oz. **MR. TURKEY® Smoked Sausage**, thinly sliced
4 oz. shredded Swiss or Gruyere cheese
4 eggs, slightly beaten
2 cups light cream or half-and-half
1 teaspoon salt
Dash of pepper

Line deep 9-inch pie pan or quiche dish with pastry. Sprinkle half
the sausage in bottom of pastry. Add cheese. Combine eggs,
cream, salt and pepper; pour into pastry. Sprinkle remaining sausage on top. Bake in hot oven (400° F) 30 to 40 minutes until
quiche puffs in center. Cool 5 minutes before cutting.   *Serves 6*

SHRIMPLY DELICIOUS QUICHE

¾ pound raw, peeled and deveined rock shrimp, fresh
   or frozen
1 tablespoon salt
2 cups water
1½ cups sliced fresh mushrooms
⅔ cup sliced green onion
¼ cup butter or margarine, melted
4 eggs, well beaten
1½ cups half-and-half cream
1 teaspoon salt
⅛ teaspoon dry mustard
1 cup shredded mozzarella cheese
2 unbaked 9-inch pie shells

Thaw rock shrimp if frozen. Add salt to water and bring to a boil.
Place shrimp in boiling water; cook 30 seconds. Drain. Rinse
under cold running water for 1 to 2 minutes. Remove any remaining particles of sand vein. Chop rock shrimp.

   Cook mushrooms and green onions in butter until tender, but
not brown. Combine eggs, half-and-half, salt and dry mustard;
beat until smooth. Layer half of the rock shrimp, half of the
mushroom mixture and half of the mozzarella cheese in each pie
shell. Pour half of the egg mixture into each pie shell.

   Bake in a hot oven, 425°F, for 15 minutes; reduce heat to 300°F
and continue to bake for 30 minutes or until knife when inserted in
the center of quiche comes out clean. Let stand 15 minutes before
serving.   *Makes 6 servings*

Favorite recipe from **National Marine Fisheries Service**

BUTTERMILK QUICHE

1 pkg. any flavor **HAIN® Crackers**, crumbled
3 Tbsp. **HAIN® Safflower Oil**
1 cup chopped chicken or turkey
½ cup sliced mushrooms
¼ cup chopped onion
1 cup shredded raw milk Cheddar cheese
4 eggs
1 cup milk
1 cup **HAIN® Buttermilk Style Dressing**

Place crushed crackers in bowl. Add oil and mix well. Place
mixture in 9- or 10-inch pie pan and press into sides with fork.
Bake at 350°F for 10 minutes. Cool. Into cooled cracker crust,
place chicken or turkey, mushrooms, onions, and cheese. In bowl,
mix together eggs, milk and Dressing. Pour over mixture in pie
pan. Bake at 400°F for 30-40 minutes, or until knife inserted
comes out clean.   *Makes 6 servings*

NUTRITIONAL INFORMATION: 1 serving = 1 slice. Each
serving contains approximately 570 calories, 22 grams protein, 25
grams carbohydrate, 43 grams fat.

SUPERB SALMON QUICHE

1 unbaked 9-inch pastry shell
1 can (15½ oz.) **BUMBLE BEE® Alaska Sockeye Red
   Salmon**
3 large eggs
1 cup small curd cream style cottage cheese
2 teaspoons Dijon mustard
¾ teaspoon salt
½ cup half & half
1 can (4 oz.) sliced mushrooms
½ cup shredded carrot
¼ cup thinly sliced green onion
Parsley

Partially bake pastry shell on lower rack of 375°F oven 15 minutes. Meanwhile drain salmon, reserving 2 tablespoons liquid.
Break salmon into chunks. Beat eggs with cottage cheese, mustard
and salt. Add half & half, salmon liquid and undrained mushrooms. Stir in carrot, onion and salmon. Ladle into partially baked
pastry shell. Return to oven and bake 45 minutes longer, or until
set in center. Let stand 10 minutes. Garnish with parsley sprig. Cut
into wedges and serve warm.   *Makes 6 to 8 servings*

SHRIMP QUICHE

1 9-inch partially baked pie shell
½ lb. **ATALANTA Shrimp**, cooked, diced
¼ cup scallions, sliced
Pinch pepper
1 cup heavy cream
3 eggs
2 tomatoes, fresh, sliced
¼ cup Swiss cheese, grated
2 Tbsp. butter

Sauté scallions in butter. Add shrimp and pepper and cook for 2
minutes. Set aside. Beat together eggs and cream. Spread shrimp
mixture in bottom of pie shell. Pour cream mixture over shrimp.
Top with slices of tomato and sprinkle with cheese. Bake in 375°
oven for 25 minutes.   *Yield: 6 servings*

Pasta & Rice

Pasta

DORMAN'S® AMERICANA NOODLES

1½ teaspoons salt
½ medium-size head green cabbage, shredded
2 tablespoons butter
1 small onion, diced
2 tablespoons light cream
6 slices **DORMAN'S® American Singles**, grated in electric blender
2 cups cooked hot noodles
1 teaspoon poppy seeds
4 slices cooked bacon, crumbled

Sprinkle salt over shredded cabbage. Place in colander; let drain 40 minutes. In a large-size skillet, melt butter. Sauté drained cabbage until it becomes light green. Add onion; sauté until tender. Add cream, cheese, noodles and poppy seeds; toss gently. Sprinkle with crumbled bacon. *Makes 6 servings*

NOODLES PRIMAVERA

½ (12-oz.) pkg. **AMERICAN BEAUTY® Wide Egg Noodles**
¼ cup butter or margarine
1 clove garlic, minced
1 cup chopped onions
1 cup thinly sliced carrots
1 cup frozen peas
1 small bunch fresh broccoli, cut into 1-inch pieces, or 10-oz. pkg. frozen chopped broccoli, thawed and drained
4½-oz. or 2 (2½-oz.) jars **GREEN GIANT® Whole Mushrooms**, drained
½ teaspoon basil leaves
¼ teaspoon seasoned salt
1 medium zucchini, cut into 1½-inch lengths and quartered
Grated Parmesan cheese

Cook noodles to desired doneness as directed on package. In large skillet, melt butter over low heat. Stir in garlic and onions; sauté for 2 minutes. Add remaining ingredients except zucchini and Parmesan cheese; sauté until tender-crisp, about 5 minutes, stirring occasionally. Add zucchini; sauté an additional 5 minutes. Combine cooked noodles and vegetables; toss lightly. If desired, sprinkle with Parmesan cheese. *8 (1-cup) servings*

HIGH ALTITUDE—Above 3500 feet: Cooking time may need to be increased slightly for noodles.

THE KING'S NOODLE

3 cups cooked, drained egg noodles
2 cans **KING OSCAR Sardines**, drained, reserving oil
¼ cup melted butter
2 Tbsp. lemon juice
Salt
Parsley
Lemon wedges

Combine reserved sardine oil, salt, butter, lemon juice. Stir into cooked noodles. Place mixture in serving dish. Garnish with sardines around edges, and if you wish, parsley. Serve with lemon wedges.

POSH PASTA

1 package (1½ oz.) **LAWRY'S® Spaghetti Sauce Mix With Imported Mushrooms**
1 can (6 oz.) tomato paste
1⅔ cups water
½ cup red wine
3 to 4 half chicken breasts, boned, skinned and cut into ½ × 2-inch strips (approximately 1½ cups)
6 ounces noodles or other pasta
1 can (8½ oz.) artichoke hearts, drained *OR* 1 package (10 oz.) frozen artichoke hearts, cooked according to package directions

In medium saucepan, combine **Spaghetti Sauce Mix With Imported Mushrooms**, tomato paste, water and wine; blend thoroughly. Cook, uncovered, for 10 minutes. Add chicken and simmer 15 minutes. Meanwhile, cook noodles according to package directions. Just before serving, add artichoke hearts to sauce and heat through. Serve over cooked noodles. *Makes 4 to 6 servings*

LASAGNE

2 pounds ground chuck
2 cloves garlic, minced
3 large onions, chopped
1 tablespoon oil
1 tablespoon Italian Herbs*
¼ cup butter
1 tablespoon salt
¼ teaspoon pepper
¼ cup flour
1 cup hot water
1 cup red wine
1 can (16 ounce) **REDPACK Tomato Puree**
1 can (28 ounce) **REDPACK Whole Tomatoes in Juice**
1 package (16 ounce) lasagne noodles
4 cups grated Monterey Jack cheese
1 container (16 ounce) ricotta cheese**

Brown meat, garlic and onions in oil. Sprinkle with 2 teaspoons Italian Herbs. Remove from pan. Melt butter, add salt, pepper and remaining Herbs; stir in flour. Add water, wine, tomato puree and liquid from whole tomatoes. Cook, stirring until sauce thickens. Break up tomatoes; add to sauce with juice. To bake, use two pans, (11¾x7½x1¾-inch) or 1 pan (18 x 12 x 2-inch). Pour sauce to cover bottom of pan(s). Arrange uncooked lasagne noodles to fit pan. Cover lasagne with more sauce. Add layer of meat mixture, grated cheese and ricotta. End with top layer of lasagne. Cover with remaining sauce and top with grated cheese. Bake covered at 375 degrees F. for 45 minutes. Uncover and continue baking 20 minutes. Let stand before serving. Garnish with chopped parsley, if desired. *Serves 15*

*Available in grocery store spice section.
**Small curd cottage cheese may be substituted.

SPANISH NOODLES

2 Tbsp. oil
1 med. onion, chopped
½ med. green pepper, chopped
½ cup chopped celery
1 lb. ground beef
2 8-oz. cans tomato sauce
2 8-oz. cans water
1 Tbsp. brown sugar
2 Tbsp. **MARUKAN® Rice Vinegar (Genuine Brewed)**
1 tsp. salt
6 oz. of noodles uncooked

Heat oil in large skillet. Sauté vegetables in skillet until golden brown and slightly transparent. Push the vegetables to one side of the skillet. Add meat and brown lightly. Add remaining ingredients and mix together. Cover. Bring the mixture to boil over full flame. Adjust to simmer and continue cooking 25 to 30 minutes.

LASAGNA WITH MUSHROOMS

1 (8-ounce) package **CREAMETTE® Italian Style Lasagna,** cooked as package directs and drained
1 pound lean ground beef *or* Italian sausage
1 cup chopped onion
3 cloves garlic, finely chopped
3½ cups tomato juice
8 ounces fresh mushrooms, sliced (about 2 cups)
1 (6-ounce) can tomato paste
1 tablespoon Worcestershire sauce
1 teaspoon oregano leaves
½ teaspoon salt
⅛ teaspoon pepper
1 (15- or 16-ounce) container ricotta cheese
1 cup grated Parmesan cheese
2 cups (8 ounces) shredded Mozzarella cheese
Parsley flakes

In large saucepan, brown meat; pour off fat. Add onion and garlic; cook and stir until onion is tender. Stir in tomato juice, mushrooms, tomato paste and seasonings. Cover; simmer 30 minutes, stirring occasionally. In 3-quart shallow baking dish (13 × 9-inch), layer half each of the cooked lasagna noodles, sauce, ricotta cheese, grated cheese and mozzarella cheese. Repeat layering; top with parsley. Cover tightly with foil; bake in preheated 350° oven 30 minutes or until bubbly. Uncover; bake 15 minutes longer. Remove from oven; let stand 20 minutes before serving. Refrigerate leftovers.   *Makes 8 servings*

EASY LASAGNE

1 pound ground beef
½ cup chopped onion
1 clove garlic, finely chopped
1 package **BETTY CROCKER® HAMBURGER HELPER® Mix for Lasagne**
2 cups hot water
1 can (16 ounces) whole tomatoes
1½ cups dry cottage cheese (small curd)
1 cup shredded mozzarella cheese (about 4 ounces)

Cook and stir ground beef, onion and garlic in 10-inch skillet until beef is brown; drain. Stir in Macaroni, Sauce Mix, water and tomatoes (with liquid); break up tomatoes with fork. Heat to boiling, stirring constantly; reduce heat. Cover and simmer, stirring occasionally, 15 to 20 minutes. Stir in cottage cheese; sprinkle with mozzarella cheese. Cover and cook over low heat until cheese is melted, 2 to 3 minutes.   *6 to 8 servings*

HIGH ALTITUDE DIRECTIONS (3500 to 6500 feet): Increase hot water to 2½ cups and simmer time to 25 to 30 minutes.

LASAGNA ROLL-UPS

1 pound sweet Italian sausage
½ cup chopped onion
1 crushed garlic clove
1⅓ cups (two 6-ounce cans) **CONTADINA® Tomato Paste**
1⅔ cups water
1 teaspoon oregano leaves
½ teaspoon basil leaves
⅔ cup (10-ounce package) cooked, thoroughly drained, frozen chopped spinach
2 cups (1 pint) ricotta cheese
1 cup grated Parmesan cheese
1½ cups (6 ounces) shredded mozzarella cheese
1 slightly beaten egg
½ teaspoon salt
¼ teaspoon pepper
8 cooked, drained lasagna noodles

Remove casings from sausage; crumble. Brown sausage with onion and garlic in saucepan. Pour off excess fat. Add tomato paste, water, oregano, and basil. Cover; boil gently 20 minutes. Combine spinach, ricotta cheese, Parmesan cheese, *1 cup mozzarella cheese*, egg, salt, and pepper in medium bowl. Mix thoroughly. Spread about ½ cup mixture on each noodle. Roll up. Place seam-side down in 12 x 7½ x 2-inch baking dish. Pour sauce over rolls. Top with *remaining ½ cup mozzarella cheese*. Bake in moderate oven (350° F.) 30-40 minutes, or until heated through.
Makes 6 to 8 servings

MUSHROOM LASAGNA

3 cans (3 oz.) **BinB® Broiled in Butter Sliced Mushrooms,** drained—reserving broth
1 package (16 oz.) lasagna noodles
1 package (8 oz.) cream cheese, softened
3 cups cottage cheese
1 tablespoon parsley flakes
½ teaspoon salt
½ teaspoon basil
¼ teaspoon oregano
⅛ teaspoon garlic powder
1 can (15 oz.) tomato sauce
¾ cup grated Parmesan cheese

Drain mushrooms, reserving buttery broth. Combine cream cheese, cottage cheese, salt, garlic powder and parsley. Set aside. Combine buttery broth, oregano, basil and tomato sauce and simmer about 10 minutes. Layer noodles and cheese mixture in buttered 9 inch × 13 inch shallow baking dish. Sprinkle each layer with 1 can of mushroom slices, tomato sauce and ¼ cup Parmesan cheese. Bake, uncovered, in preheated 350°F. oven for 30 minutes. Uncover and continue for 15 minutes.

Makes 8 to 10 servings

TURKEY LASAGNE

8 ounces **MUELLER'S®** Lasagne
1 can (10¾-ounces) condensed cream of chicken soup
1 can (10¾-ounces) condensed cream of mushroom
 soup
1 cup grated Parmesan cheese
1 cup sour cream
1 cup finely chopped onion
1 cup sliced ripe olives
¼ cup chopped pimiento
½ teaspoon garlic salt
2 to 3 cups diced cooked turkey
2 cups (8 ounces) shredded process American cheese

Cook lasagne as directed on package; drain. Meanwhile, blend soups, Parmesan cheese, sour cream, onion, olives, pimiento and garlic salt; stir in turkey. Spread one-fourth turkey mixture over bottom of 13 × 9 × 2-inch baking pan. Alternate layers of lasagne, turkey mixture and American cheese three times, ending with American cheese. Bake at 350°F for 40 to 45 minutes. Let stand 10 minutes before cutting. *8 servings*

TUNA LASAGNE

2 cans (6½ or 7 ounces) **STAR-KIST® Tuna**
½ cup chopped onion
2 cloves garlic, minced
1 can (15 ounces) tomato sauce
1 can (6 ounces) tomato paste
1 teaspoon sugar
1 teaspoon dried leaf oregano
½ teaspoon dried leaf basil
1 tablespoon lemon juice
½ package (8 ounces) lasagna noodles, cooked according
 to package directions
2 cups (1 pound) small curd creamed cottage cheese or
 ricotta cheese
1 pound mozzarella cheese, thinly sliced
1 cup (4 ounces) grated Parmesan cheese

Drain 1 tablespoon oil from **STAR-KIST® Tuna** into medium saucepan. Add onion and garlic. Cook until tender. Add tomato sauce, tomato paste, sugar, oregano, basil, and lemon juice. Simmer uncovered 45 minutes. Remove from heat, stir in **STAR-KIST® Tuna**. Spoon a small amount of sauce over bottom of a 13 × 9 × 2-inch baking dish or shallow 3-quart casserole. Add layers of one-third noodles, one-third sauce, half the cottage cheese, and one-third mozzarella cheese . . . Repeat, ending with layers of noodles, sauce, and mozzarella cheese. Sprinkle Parmesan cheese over top. Bake in 350° oven 30 minutes. Let stand 10 minutes before serving. *Yield: 8 servings*

LOW-CALORIE MANICOTTI

12 manicotti shells
1 container (8 ounces) dry-curd cottage cheese
1 container (8 ounces) part-skim ricotta cheese
1 cup (about 4 ounces) grated mozzarella cheese
2 eggs
½ cup low-fat milk
2 packets **BUTTER BUDS®**
¼ cup chopped fresh parsley
1 teaspoon oregano
½ teaspoon garlic powder
¼ teaspoon white pepper
Tomato Sauce*

Preheat oven to 350°F. Prepare manicotti shells according to package directions. Drain. Cool quickly in cool water. In large bowl, combine cheeses, eggs, and milk and mix well. Blend in **BUTTER BUDS®**, parsley, oregano, garlic powder, and pepper. Stuff shells with cheese mixture. Coat bottom of baking dish with Tomato Sauce. Place filled manicotti shells on top of sauce. Cover shells with remaining sauce. Bake, covered, 40 to 45 minutes.
6 servings

PER SERVING (2 shells): Calories: 275 Protein: 17gm
Carbohydrate: 37gm Fat: 5gm Sodium: 660mg

Note: By using **BUTTER BUDS®** instead of butter in this recipe, you have saved 250 calories and 93 mg cholesterol per serving.

*TOMATO SAUCE

1 tablespoon vegetable oil
½ cup chopped green pepper
½ cup (1 medium-size) chopped onion
2 medium-size garlic cloves, minced
1 can (1 pound 12 ounces) peeled tomatoes, chopped
½ cup water
1 can (6 ounces) tomato paste
¼ cup chopped fresh parsley
1 packet **BUTTER BUDS®**, made into liquid
1 teaspoon basil
1 teaspoon thyme
¼ teaspoon freshly ground pepper

Heat oil in large saucepan or skillet. Add green pepper, onion, and garlic and sauté until tender. Add tomatoes, water, tomato paste, parsley, **BUTTER BUDS®**, basil, thyme, and pepper. Mix well. Simmer, covered, 25 to 30 minutes, stirring frequently.
About 4 cups

PER SERVING (½ cup:) Calories: 70 Protein: 2gm
Carbohydrate: 10gm Fat: 2gm Sodium: 140mg

Note: By using **BUTTER BUDS®** instead of vegetable oil in this recipe, you have saved 114 calories per serving.

HOMESTYLE CANNELONI CLASSICO

1½ pounds ground beef
1 small onion, chopped
1 package (10 oz.) frozen chopped spinach, cooked
 and squeezed dry
1½ cups (6 oz.) shredded mozzarella cheese, divided
½ cup bread crumbs
1 egg, slightly beaten
¼ cup grated Parmesan cheese, divided
1 teaspoon oregano
½ teaspoon salt
¼ teaspoon black pepper
1 jar (15½ oz.) **RAGU'®** Homestyle Spaghetti Sauce,
 any flavor
½ pound (about 8) lasagne noodles, cooked and
 drained

Preheat oven to 350°F. In large skillet, brown beef; add onion and sauté until translucent. Pour off fat. Add spinach, 1 cup mozzarella, bread crumbs, egg, ½ cheese and seasonings. Mix well; set aside. In 11 x 7-inch baking dish, spread 1 cup **Homestyle Spaghetti Sauce.** Cut each lasagne noodle in half crosswise. Place quarter cup of filling on each noodle half; roll and place seam-side down in baking dish. Pour remaining sauce over canneloni; sprinkle with remaining cheeses. Cover tightly with foil; bake 30 minutes. Uncover, bake 5 minutes more. *Serves 8*

MANICOTTI WITH FOUR CHEESES

½ cup butter or margarine
1 large onion, minced
1 lb. mushrooms, sliced
½ cup flour
4 cups milk
1 cup **SARGENTO Grated Parmesan and Romano Blend Cheese**
Salt and pepper
12 manicotti shells
15 oz. **SARGENTO Ricotta Cheese**
1 cup (4 oz.) **SARGENTO Shredded Cheese for Pizza (Mozzarella)**
1 cup **SARGENTO Grated Parmesan and Romano Blend Cheese**
½ cup finely chopped walnuts
¼ cup chopped parsley
3 eggs
Dash nutmeg

In a saucepan melt butter and sauté onion and mushrooms for 5 minutes. Stir in flour. Gradually stir in milk. Stir over low heat until sauce bubbles and thickens. Stir in Parmesan/Romano cheese, salt, and pepper to taste. Set aside. Cook manicotti shells according to package directions. Drain and cover with cold water. In a bowl, mix ricotta, mozzarella, grated cheese, walnuts, parsley, and eggs. Season to taste with salt, pepper and a dash of nutmeg. Drain manicotti noodles and stuff with cheese mixture. Place shells side by side in a greased shallow baking dish. Spoon sauce over. Bake in a preheated hot oven (400°F) for 20 to 25 minutes or until bubbly and lightly brown. Makes 12 manicotti.

Serves 6

SPAGHETTI ITALIANO

1 lb. ground beef
1 medium onion, chopped
½ green pepper, chopped
1 can (1-lb. or 2 cups) whole tomatoes, cut up
1 can (6-oz.) tomato paste
1 can (6-oz.) water
1 can (4-oz.) mushroom stems and pieces, undrained
2 teaspoons Worcestershire sauce
1 bay leaf
1 teaspoon salt
¼ teaspoon oregano
¼ teaspoon pepper
7-oz. package **CREAMETTE® Spaghetti**
2 tablespoons butter or margarine
Parmesan cheese

Brown meat, onion and green pepper till tender. Drain excess fat. Add all ingredients except spaghetti, butter and cheese. Simmer uncovered for 1 hour. Remove bay leaf. Prepare **CREAMETTE® Spaghetti** according to package directions. Drain. Toss with butter. Serve sauce over spaghetti with Parmesan cheese.

4 servings

VARIATION:

Spaghetti with meatballs: Prepare sauce as above, omitting ground beef. Combine beef, ½ cup chopped onion, 1 teaspoon salt, ¼ teaspoon pepper, ⅛ teaspoon garlic powder. Shape into 16 meatballs. Brown in 2 tablespoons oil. Drain. Add meatballs to sauce during last 25 minutes of cooking.

SPAGHETTI AL PESTO

8 ounces (½ package) **LA ROSA® Spaghetti**
1 clove garlic, minced
⅓ cup olive oil
1 cup firmly packed fresh basil leaves OR parsley sprigs
½ cup grated Parmesan cheese
2 tablespoons pine nuts OR coarsely chopped walnuts
1 tablespoon butter
½ teaspoon salt
⅛ teaspoon pepper
Additional grated Parmesan cheese

Cook garlic in olive oil until lightly browned. Combine with remaining ingredients in electric blender; blend at high speed to a pastelike consistency, about 1 minute. Cook Spaghetti as directed on package; drain. Serve sauce over cooked Spaghetti with additional Parmesan cheese.

Serves 4

Note: To prepare Al Pesto by hand, crush basil or parsley with a mortar and pestle until pastelike. Work in salt and pepper, garlic, nuts and butter. Add olive oil a little at a time. Mix in the ½ cup grated Parmesan cheese.

CELEBRATION SPAGHETTI

1 tablespoon olive oil
2 medium zucchini, sliced
2 cups fresh mushrooms, sliced
1 medium green pepper, sliced
1 cup California Ripe Olives, sliced
1 (28-ounce) can tomatoes, broken up
2 (6-ounce) cans tomato paste
¼ cup **FRIGO® Parmesan Cheese Wedge**, grated
1 teaspoon salt
½ teaspoon sweet basil leaves
¼ teaspoon pepper
1 (1 pound) package **CREAMETTE® Spaghetti**
2 tablespoons softened butter or margarine
FRIGO® Parmesan Cheese Wedges, grated

In large skillet heat oil. Sauté zucchini, mushrooms, green pepper and olives. Add tomatoes, tomato paste, Parmesan cheese, salt, basil and pepper. Simmer 15 minutes. Prepare **CREAMETTE® Spaghetti** according to package directions. Drain. Toss with softened butter; arrange on warm platter. Pour on sauce and top with grated Parmesan.

8-10 servings

This recipe is from **CREAMETTES®**, **FRIGO® Cheese** and the **California Olive Industry**

SPAGHETTI WITH TOMATO SAUCE

2 large onions
1 clove garlic
⅓ cup parsley fresh cut leaves
Dried mushroom
½ cup **FILIPPO BERIO Olive Oil**
1 lb. spaghetti
½ lb. chopped meat (optional)
3 cups strained Italian Plum Tomatoes OR
1½ cup tomato sauce and 1 cup water
1 tsp. salt
½ tsp. pepper

Sauté onions in **FILIPPO BERIO Olive Oil** only till light brown. Add garlic finely cut or clove cut in half which can be removed. When cooled, add tomato puree. Bring to a boil. Simmer for 20 minutes, add parsley, dried mushroom broken up, salt and freshly ground pepper. Let simmer an additional 10 minutes and serve with freshly prepared spaghetti. A fresh ripe tomato cut into small pieces may be added to the sauce while simmering.

VARIATION:

Meat Sauce—When sauce comes to a boil, the chopped meat may be added.

Note: Sauce may simmer from 40 minutes to 2 hours. If tomatoes are very watery, cook until sauce has desired consistency.

MILANO MEDLEY

1 package (16 ounces) **Frozen STOKELY'S®**
   Vegetables Milano®
1 cup water, divided
2 Tablespoons vegetable oil
4 teaspoons cornstarch
1 Tablespoon sugar
1 Tablespoon instant minced onion
¾ teaspoon salt
½ teaspoon garlic salt
Dash pepper
¼ cup white vinegar
2 medium-size tomatoes, quartered
¼ cup walnut pieces
Spaghetti noodles, cooked

Cook vegetables in ½ cup water 8 to 9 minutes; drain and set aside. Combine ½ cup water, oil, cornstarch, sugar, onion, salt, garlic salt, pepper, and vinegar in medium-size skillet. Cook, stirring constantly, until thickened. Add reserved vegetables, tomatoes, and walnuts; stir until coated with sauce. Cover and cook until heated through, 1 to 2 minutes. Serve over spaghetti noodles. *6 servings*

SPAGHETTI WITH GARLIC AND OLIVES

6 ounces (½ package) **HEALTH VALLEY® Whole**
   Wheat Spaghetti
½ cup chopped walnuts
½ cup chopped ripe olives
¼ cup chopped pimiento
¼ cup chopped parsley
½ teaspoon dried sweet basil
3 tablespoons **HEALTH VALLEY® Safflower Oil**
1 teaspoon minced garlic
2 cups (⅔ package) grated **HEALTH VALLEY® Raw**
   Milk Medium Cheddar Cheese

Cook spaghetti according to directions on package. While spaghetti is cooking, combine in a bowl the walnuts, olives, pimiento, parsley and basil.

When spaghetti is done, drain immediately into a large colander. In the empty kettle, heat oil and add garlic. Sauté briefly without permitting to brown. Add spaghetti and toss to mix thoroughly. Turn into a hot serving platter, top with nut-herb mixture, sprinkle cheese over all, and serve immediately.

If desired, it can also be served with diced, browned **HEALTH VALLEY® Italian Sausages**, crumbled, cooked **HEALTH VALLEY® Bacon** or a handful of **HEALTH VALLEY® Shrimp** (thawed and drained). Total Preparation Time: 30 minutes.
Yield 4 to 6 servings

SPAGHETTI WITH MEAT SAUCE

1½ pounds **FOULDS' Spaghetti**
2½ tablespoons salt
6-9 quarts boiling water
½ pound sweet Italian sausage, cut up
2 medium onions, quartered
2 cloves garlic
1 small rib celery, halved
1 small carrot, quartered
3 sprigs parsley
1½ pounds ground beef
1 can (28 ounces) tomatoes
2 jars (15½ ounces each) marinara sauce

FOOD PROCESSOR METHOD:
Gradually add spaghetti and salt to rapidly boiling water so that water continues to boil. Cook uncovered, stirring occasionally, until tender. Drain in colander. While spaghetti is cooking, process, until finely chopped, sausage, onions, garlic, celery, carrot and parsley with cutting blade in food processor. Brown sausage mixture and ground meat in Dutch oven or large pot. Add tomatoes and marinara sauce. Heat to boiling. Serve with spaghetti. *Makes 12 servings*

CONVENTIONAL METHOD:
Finely chop sausage, onions, garlic, celery, carrot and parsley. Proceed as above.

SPAGHETTI AND MEAT BALLS WITH ENRICO'S SPAGHETTI SAUCE

Prepare the meat balls as follows:

   1 lb. beef cubes ground
   ½ lb. shoulder pork ground
   1½ teaspoons salt
   ½ teaspoon black pepper
   ½ cup bread crumbs moistened with water
   ½ cup grated Italian style cheese
   1 teaspoon parsley
   1 medium onion, minced
   1 clove garlic, minced
   1 egg slightly beaten

Mix all above ingredients thoroughly. Shape into medium size balls and brown in about 3 tablespoons of fat. Add a little water to keep the meat balls from sticking and simmer for 15 minutes.

Add 1 jar of **ENRICO'S Spaghetti Sauce** and simmer just 5 minutes more. While the meat balls are simmering prepare the spaghetti by plunging it into rapidly boiling salted water for about 7 minutes or until tender. Drain and place on a flat dish or platter. Pour the **ENRICO'S Spaghetti Sauce** with meat balls over the spaghetti and sprinkle with grated Italian style cheese, if desired.
Four to six servings

SUMMER-SPAGHETTI WITH SAUSAGE AND ZUCCHINI

1 lb. **JIMMY DEAN® Sausage**
2 cans condensed cream of mushroom soup
1 cup milk
4 or 5 cups zucchini (about 1½ lbs.) quartered and sliced
¼ lb. mushrooms, sliced
¼ cup sliced green onions
½ tsp. salt
¼ tsp. pepper
1 lb. spaghetti
Parmesan cheese

Brown sausage in large skillet. Break up with fork. Add zucchini, mushrooms, green onions and sauté a few more minutes. Stir in soup, milk, salt and pepper. Cook over medium heat 15 minutes or until zucchini is tender. (Add more milk if the mixture becomes too thick). Cook spaghetti. Drain. Toss sausage mixture with cooked spaghetti & sprinkle generously with parmesan cheese.

Serves 6

RED CLAM SAUCE AND SPAGHETTI

2 10-oz. cans **GEISHA® Brand Whole Baby Clams**
  and liquid
1 cup minced onions
1 minced clove garlic
2 tablespoons olive oil
1 8-oz. can tomato sauce
1 6-oz. can tomato paste
1 No. 2½ can Italian tomatoes
1 teaspoon salt
⅛ teaspoon pepper
½ teaspoon sweet basil
½ teaspoon oregano
1 tablespoon chopped parsley
1 pound spaghetti (cooked as label directs)
Parmesan cheese (optional)

In Dutch oven sauté onions and garlic in oil until tender. Add tomato sauce, tomato paste, tomatoes, salt, pepper and basil. Cook stirring occasionally until mixture has cooked down about two-thirds and is very thick (about 2 hours). Add clams and their liquid, oregano and parsley. Cook about 10 minutes longer. Serve over hot spaghetti. Sprinkle with cheese if desired.

Makes 4 to 6 servings

BUTTERY PASTA WITH SHRIMP

3 cups cooked spaghetti (7 oz. uncooked spaghetti)
¾ cup **LAND O LAKES® Sweet Cream Butter**
1 cup (1 med.) chopped green pepper
½ cup (1 small) chopped onion
2 (12 oz.) pkgs. frozen cocktail size (1½ inch) shrimp
  (not breaded), thawed, drained
1½ tsp. garlic powder
½ tsp. *each* salt and oregano leaves
¼ tsp. pepper
2 cups (2 med.) cubed (½ inch) tomatoes
Grated Parmesan *or* Romano cheese

Have ready cooked spaghetti; set aside. In heavy 3-qt. saucepan melt butter over med. heat (5 to 7 min.). Add remaining ingredients *except* tomatoes and Parmesan cheese; stir to blend. Cook over med. heat (5 to 7 min.). Add cooked spaghetti; stir to blend. Continue cooking over med. heat, stirring occasionally, until

spaghetti is heated through (3 to 5 min.). Remove from heat; add tomatoes. Cover; let stand 1 min. or until tomatoes are heated through. To serve, sprinkle with Parmesan cheese.

Yield: 6 (1½ cups) servings

TURKEY TETRAZZINI

6 slices roasted **SWIFT PREMIUM®
  BUTTERBALL® Turkey**
½ stick (¼ cup) butter
⅔ cup sliced onion
¼ cup flour
1 teaspoon salt
¼ teaspoon white pepper
½ teaspoon poultry seasoning
¼ teaspoon dry mustard
2 cups milk
⅔ cup shredded sharp Cheddar cheese
2 tablespoons chopped pimiento
2 tablespoons sherry
4-ounce can mushrooms, stems and pieces, undrained
7-ounce package spaghetti, cooked, drained
⅓ cup shredded sharp Cheddar cheese

Melt butter in saucepan. Sauté onion in butter until tender. Blend in flour and seasonings. Remove from heat. Gradually add milk. Stirring constantly, cook until mixture thickens. Add ⅔ cup cheese and pimiento, stirring until cheese melts. Add sherry and mushrooms and liquid to cheese sauce. Place a layer of spaghetti in a 12 x 7½ inch (2 quart) casserole. Cover with a layer of turkey and a layer of sauce. Repeat, finishing with a layer of sauce. Sprinkle ⅓ cup cheese over top. Bake in a 400°F oven about 25 minutes.

Yield: 6 servings

Note: Casserole may be assembled in advance and frozen. To serve, heat, covered, in a 350°F oven for 1½ hours or until hot.

FETTUCCINI CARBONARA

¼ pound bacon
1 box (12 ounces) **SAN GIORGIO® Fettuccini,**
  uncooked
¼ cup butter or margarine, softened
½ cup whipping cream, at room temperature
½ cup grated Parmesan cheese
2 eggs, slightly beaten
2 tablespoons snipped parsley

Sauté bacon until crisp; drain well and crumble. Cook Fettuccini according to package directions. Drain well and place in warm serving dish large enough for tossing. Add crumbled bacon, butter or margarine, whipping cream, grated cheese, eggs and parsley; toss until Fettuccini is well coated. Serve.

PASTA WITH CARBONARA SAUCE

4 eggs
¼ cup butter or margarine
¼ cup cream
1 lb. fettucini or spaghetti
2 (3½ oz.) pkg. **HORMEL Sliced Pepperoni**
1 cup Parmesan cheese, grated
¼ cup snipped fresh parsley
Pepper to taste

Let eggs, butter or margarine and cream stand at room temperature for 2-3 hours. Beat together eggs and cream just until blended. Add pasta to a large amount of boiling, salted water. Cook 10-12 minutes or until tender, but firm. Drain well. *(Continued)*

Heat an ovenproof serving dish in a 250°F. oven. Turn pasta into heated serving dish. Toss pasta with butter and pepperoni. Pour egg mixture over and toss until pasta is well coated. Add cheese and parsley; toss to mix. Serve immediately.

Makes 10-12 side dishes or 4-5 main servings

FETTUCCINE ALFREDO

1 package RONZONI® Extra Long Fettuccine
½ cup grated Parmesan cheese
⅔ cup light cream (sour cream may be substituted)
¼ lb. butter (preferably sweet)
1 egg yolk

Cook noodles according to directions on the panel. While noodles are cooking, beat egg yolk lightly with fork and add to cream. Melt butter. Place drained, hot noodles in warm serving bowl or platter. Pour over the noodles egg and cream mixture, melted butter and about half of the grated cheese. Toss noodles with fork and spoon until well blended, adding balance of cheese a little at a time while tossing. Top with additional grated cheese, if desired, and serve immediately.

FETTUCCINE ALLA PAPALINA

¼ cup butter or margarine
½ pound fresh mushrooms, sliced, or 1 can (8 ounces) sliced mushrooms, drained
1 cup chopped onion
1 pound cooked ham, diced
1 recipe White Sauce Base*
¼ cup milk
¼ cup grated Parmesan cheese
½ pound fettuccini noodles, cooked and drained
1 tablespoon chopped fresh parsley

In large skillet, melt butter; sauté mushrooms and onions until tender. Add ham; mix well. In small saucepan, make White Sauce Base. Stir in ¼ cup additional milk and Parmesan cheese. Add ham mixture; heat until bubbly, stirring constantly. Serve over hot noodles. Garnish with parsley and additional grated Parmesan cheese, if desired. *Yield: 4 servings*

*WHITE SAUCE BASE

2 tablespoons butter or margarine
2 tablespoons flour
¼ teaspoon salt
½ teaspoon TABASCO® Pepper Sauce
1 cup milk

Melt butter in saucepan over low heat. Blend in flour, salt and TABASCO®. Gradually stir in milk. Cook over medium heat, stirring constantly, until sauce thickens and comes to a boil. Simmer for 1 minute, continuing to stir. *Yield: About 1 cup*

TOMATO AND BASIL FETTUCCINI

¼ cup chopped onion
1 clove garlic, minced
¼ cup olive oil
3½ cups (28-ounce can) peeled tomatoes (with liquid)
6 fresh basil leaves, chopped or 1 tablespoon dry basil
1 teaspoon salt
½ teaspoon pepper
1 box (12 ounces) SAN GIORGIO® Fettuccini, uncooked
Parmesan cheese (optional)

Sauté onion and garlic in oil in medium skillet until onion is tender, but not brown. Chop tomatoes into small pieces; reserve liquid. Add tomatoes, tomato liquid, basil, salt and pepper; bring to boil over medium heat. Reduce heat; simmer, uncovered, 15 to 20 minutes, stirring occasionally. Cook Fettuccini according to package directions; drain well. Immediately toss hot Fettuccini with tomato basil sauce in large serving dish. Garnish with Parmesan cheese, if desired. Serve.

4 to 6 servings

PASTA AMARETTO DI AMORE®

½ cup PLANTERS Slivered Almonds
¼ cup butter
1 cup sliced fresh mushrooms
2 cups shredded fontina cheese
½ cup dairy sour cream
¼ cup AMARETTO DI AMORE® Liqueur
½ package (8 oz.) spinach linguini, cooked and drained
¼ cup minced fresh parsley (optional)

In a medium skillet, sauté PLANTERS Slivered Almonds in 2 tablespoons butter over medium heat until golden. Remove almonds and reserve. Add remaining 2 tablespoons butter to skillet and sauté mushrooms. Mix mushrooms, cheese, sour cream and AMARETTO DI AMORE® Liqueur into cooked linguini. Toss well and place over low heat to warm through. Mix in almonds, reserving a few for garnish. Toss with parsley if desired and serve immediately.

LINGUINE WITH CLAM SAUCE

2 tablespoons margarine or butter
1 tablespoon peanut oil
3 cloves garlic, finely minced
¼ cup half and half
¼ cup B&B Liqueur
2 cans (6½ oz. each) chopped clams, drained
¼ teaspoon salt
¼ cup chopped parsley
1 package (8 oz.) linguine, cooked according to package directions

Heat margarine and peanut oil in a skillet over medium heat. Add garlic and sauté 2 minutes, or until tender. Remove skillet from heat; stir in half and half, B&B Liqueur, clams and salt. Return skillet to heat and cook and stir until mixture is heated through. Do not boil. Toss clam sauce and parsley with drained hot linguine and serve. *Makes 4 servings*

LINGUINE QUICKIE PESTO SAUCE

1 lb. RONZONI® Linguine #17 or Spaghetti #8
1 cup parsley finely chopped
½ cup basil finely chopped
½ cup pine nuts (optional)
2 cloves garlic finely chopped
½ cup olive oil
¼ cup water
½ cup Parmesan cheese
Dash pepper

Cook linguine as directed on package. While macaroni is cooking blend in mixing bowl parsley, basil, pine nuts, and garlic. When blended thoroughly together add olive oil, water, Parmesan cheese, and pepper. Mix. Combine mixture with cooked linguine; serve hot.

FUSILLI SUPREME

3 cups (8-ounces) **SAN GIORGIO® Cut Fusilli**, uncooked
1 clove garlic, minced
½ cup butter or margarine
2 cups cubed cooked turkey or ham
¾ cup (4-ounce can) sliced mushrooms, undrained
¼ cup chopped parsley
¼ cup dry white wine or apple juice
⅔ cup milk
½ cup grated Parmesan cheese
Dash pepper

Cook Cut Fusilli according to package directions; drain. Meanwhile, sauté garlic in 2 tablespoons butter or margarine in medium skillet about 1 minute. Add turkey or ham, mushrooms, parsley and wine or apple juice. Cook, stirring constantly, about 3 minutes or until turkey is lightly browned or ham becomes pink; set mixture aside in small bowl. Melt remaining 6 tablespoons butter or margarine in skillet; add milk, cheese and pepper and cook, stirring constantly, over low heat until cheese melts and sauce is smooth. Remove from heat. Gently toss hot Fusilli with cheese sauce and meat mixture until coated; serve.

About 4 servings

IDEAL CHOO CHOO-WHEELS WITH MEAT SAUCE

1 Tbsp. salad oil
1 small onion, chopped
1 clove garlic, finely chopped
1-lb. ground beef
½ tsp. salt
⅛ tsp. pepper
1 tsp. oregano
Dash of cinnamon
1-8 oz. can tomato sauce
1 (No. 303) can tomatoes
1 pkg. **IDEAL Choo Choo-Wheels**
Parmesan cheese

Heat salad oil over medium heat. Add onion, garlic and beef. Cook, stirring beef until browned. Add tomatoes and cook for 5 minutes. Add tomato sauce, salt, pepper, oregano, cinnamon and simmer for 30 minutes stirring occasionally. Meanwhile, cook **IDEAL Choo Choo-Wheels** according to package directions. Drain. Serve **IDEAL Choo Choo-Wheels** topped with meat sauce, sprinkled with Parmesan cheese.   *Serves 4-6*

MOSTACCIOLI MEDLEY

1½ cups thinly sliced carrots
1 cup thinly sliced celery
⅓ cup chopped onion
1 clove garlic, minced
2 tablespoons olive or vegetable oil
2 to 3 cups cubed cooked turkey or ham
1¾ cups (16-ounce can) tomatoes in tomato juice, undrained, cut into small pieces
1¾ cups (15-ounce can) tomato sauce
1 cup dry white wine or apple juice
¼ cup chopped parsley
½ teaspoon basil
½ teaspoon salt
¼ teaspoon pepper
3 cups (8 ounces) **SAN GIORGIO® Mostaccioli**, uncooked

Sauté carrots, celery, onion and garlic in oil until tender, but not brown. Stir in remaining ingredients except Mostaccioli. Simmer, uncovered, 20 minutes to blend flavors. Cook Mostaccioli according to package directions; drain. Toss with hot sauce mixture; serve.   *About 4 servings*

MOSTACCIOLI MOSTA

1 pound ground beef
1 cup onion, chopped
1 (16-ounce) can tomatoes, broken up
2 (8-ounce) cans tomato sauce
1 cup California Ripe Olives, coarsely chopped
¼ cup **FRIGO® Parmesan Cheese Wedge**, grated
1 teaspoon seasoned salt
½ teaspoon oregano leaves
¼ teaspoon crushed red pepper
1 (1 pound) package **CREAMETTE® Mostaccioli**
2 tablespoons softened butter or margarine
1 cup **FRIGO® Mozzarella Cheese**, grated

In large skillet cook ground beef and onion; drain excess fat. Add tomatoes, tomato sauce, olives, Parmesan cheese, seasoned salt, oregano and crushed pepper. Simmer 15 minutes. Prepare **CREAMETTE® Mostaccioli** according to package directions. Drain. Toss with softened butter. Arrange in a 3-quart shallow baking dish; pour on meat sauce; top with Mozzarella. Place under broiler 2 to 3 minutes until cheese melts.   *8-10 servings*

This recipe from **CREAMETTES®**, **FRIGO® Cheese** and the **California Olive Industry**

Rice

PERFECT PILAF

1 cup sliced fresh mushrooms (about ¼ pound)
½ cup fine noodles, broken in pieces
2 tablespoons butter or margarine
1 can (14½-oz.) **SWANSON Ready-to-Serve Chicken or Beef Broth**
½ cup raw regular rice

In saucepan, brown mushrooms and noodles in butter; stir often. Add broth and rice. Cover; bring to boil. Reduce heat; cook over low heat 20 minutes or until done. Stir occasionally.

Makes about 3 cups, 6 servings

ALMOND HERB PILAF

½ cup chopped onion
1 clove garlic, minced or pressed
1 tablespoon butter
1 cup long grain rice
2 cups beef broth
1 teaspoon marjoram
1 teaspoon basil
½ teaspoon salt
¾ cup **BLUE DIAMOND® Sliced Natural Almonds**, toasted

Sauté onion and garlic in butter until soft. Add rice and cook, stirring, for 1 minute. Add beef broth, marjoram, basil, and salt. Bring to a boil. Reduce heat to low, cover, and cook 20 minutes or until all liquid is absorbed. Remove from heat and let stand, covered, 5 minutes. Stir in almonds.   *Makes 4 to 6 servings*

MUSHROOM RICE PILAF

2 tablespoons butter or margarine
1 cup chopped celery
¼ cup chopped onion
1 envelope **LIPTON® Beef Flavor Mushroom Mix**
1½ cups packaged pre-cooked rice
2 cups water

In large skillet, melt butter and cook celery and onion until tender. Add **LIPTON® Beef Flavor Mushroom Mix**, rice, and water; bring quickly to a boil. Simmer, stirring frequently, 5 minutes or until water is absorbed.   *Makes about 6 servings*

RICE MILAN STYLE

¼ cup butter
½ cup onion, chopped
1 lb. rice, uncooked
½ cup dry white wine
5 cups beef or chicken stock
1 cup grated **LOCATELLI® Genuine Pecorino Romano** or **Parmesan Cheese**
¼ cup butter
Saffron (if desired)
Dash salt

In large skillet, melt ¼ cup butter; sauté onions until golden brown. Add rice, wine and 1 cup stock; mix well. Bring to boil; lower heat and simmer, covered, adding stock, one cup at a time, as the rice absorbs it. Cook until rice is tender (about 30 minutes). Add **LOCATELLI® Genuine Pecorino Romano** or **Parmesan Cheese**, ¼ cup butter, saffron and salt; mix well. Continue cooking until cheese melts (about 5 minutes). Serve hot.   *Makes 4-6 servings*

WHITE RISOTTO WITH MUSHROOMS

½ pound fresh mushrooms, sliced
1 garlic clove
1 tablespoon olive or vegetable oil
2 tablespoons butter or margarine
1 cup thinly sliced onion
1 cup **UNCLE BEN'S® CONVERTED® Brand Rice**
2¼ cups chicken broth
¼ cup dry white wine
1½ teaspoons salt
¼ teaspoon white pepper
¼ cup freshly grated Parmesan cheese
2 tablespoons chopped parsley

Sauté mushrooms and garlic in olive oil in 10-inch skillet until mushrooms are tender, but not brown. Remove and reserve mushrooms; discard garlic. Add butter to skillet. Sauté onion until tender. Add rice; cook, stirring constantly, 5 minutes. Add chicken broth, mushrooms, wine, salt and pepper. Bring to boil; reduce heat. Cover tightly and simmer 20 minutes. Remove from heat. Stir in cheese and parsley. Let stand, covered, until all liquid is absorbed, about 5 minutes.   *Makes 6 servings*

CHINESE FRIED RICE

½ cup diced green onion
1 cup diced celery
3 tablespoons butter or margarine
1 jar (2½ oz.) sliced mushrooms, drained
1 bag **SUCCESS® Rice**, cooked
2 tablespoons soy sauce
1 egg, well beaten

Sauté onion and celery in butter until tender. Stir in mushrooms, rice and soy sauce. Cook 10 minutes over medium low heat, stirring occasionally. Stir in beaten egg and cook until egg is done. If desired, serve with extra soy sauce.
Makes 4 servings (about ⅔ cup each)

FRIED RICE

¼ cup cooking oil
2 eggs, well beaten
½ cup green onions cut in 2-inch matchsticks
1 - 1 lb. can bean sprouts, drained
3 cups cooked, unsalted rice
2 tsp. **BALTIMORE SPICE OLD BAY** Seasoning
6 Tbsp. soy sauce
4 oz. can sliced mushrooms, drained, or 4 oz. fresh mushrooms, sliced*
8 oz. cooked shrimp or cooked and julienned pork, beef, chicken or ham

Heat 1 Tbsp. oil in wok or 10-inch skillet. Add eggs, scramble and remove from wok.

Heat remaining 3 Tbsp. oil in wok. Add onions and bean sprouts, stir fry about 2 minutes. Add remaining ingredients to the wok. Stir fry until heated throughout. Toss with eggs. Serve.

*If fresh mushrooms are used, add to wok and cook partially before adding bean sprouts and onions.

BROWNED RICE WITH CASHEWS

PAM® No-Stick Cooking Spray
⅔ cup rice
2 tablespoons chopped scallions
2 tablespoons chopped cashews
1⅓ cups water
½ teaspoon salt
Few grains pepper

Coat inside of medium saucepan with **PAM® No-Stick Cooking Spray** according to directions; heat over medium heat. Add rice, scallions and cashews; cook and stir until rice is lightly browned. Stir in water, salt and pepper; bring to a boil. Cover and simmer over low heat 15 minutes or until rice is tender.
Makes 4 servings

Calories per serving: 128

KOOPS SPANISH RICE

¼ lb. bacon
1 small onion
3 cups cooked rice
2 (8-oz.) cans tomato sauce
1 tsp. **KOOPS' Extra Strong Mustard**

Cut bacon in small pieces; brown lightly; remove grease; add finely chopped onion; brown lightly. Add remaining ingredients and simmer for five minutes. Serve hot.

CHILI CHEESE RICE

1 cup enriched uncooked long-grain rice
16 ounces plain yogurt
6 ounces chopped green chilies
Salt
Pepper
2 ounces COUNTY LINE® Cheddar Cheese, cubed
4 ounces COUNTY LINE® Monterey Jack Cheese,
   sliced and cut into strips

Cook rice in medium-size saucepan following label directions. Stir in yogurt and chilies, small amounts of salt and pepper, and COUNTY LINE® Cheddar Cheese and COUNTY LINE® Monterey Jack Cheese. Cover and allow the cheeses to melt.

Serves 6

RICE OLÉ

2 slices bacon
⅓ cup chopped onion
¼ cup finely chopped green pepper
1½ cups water
2 envelopes LIPTON® Tomato Cup-a-Soup
1 cup uncooked instant rice
½ teaspoon garlic salt

In medium skillet, cook bacon until crisp; drain, reserving 2 tablespoons drippings. Crumble and reserve bacon. Add onion and green pepper to skillet; cook until tender. Add water and bring to a boil. Stir in instant tomato soup mix, rice, garlic salt and reserved bacon; cover and remove from heat. Let stand 5 minutes.
Note: Recipe can be doubled.   *Makes 3 to 4 servings*

BAKED RICE WITH CHEESE

1-6 oz. package SHOAL LAKE Pure Canadian Wild
   Rice
1 Tbsp. butter
½ onion chopped
¼ tsp. garlic powder
2 tsp. Worcestershire sauce
1 Tbsp. minced parsley
1½ cups chicken broth
⅔ cup dry wine
1 cup cubed sharp Cheddar cheese

Melt butter in a skillet; add onions and cook until tender. Stir in the wild rice and continue cooking until rice is golden. Add garlic powder, Worcestershire sauce, parsley, chicken broth and wine. Heat to boiling. Stir in the cheese. Turn into a buttered 1½ quart casserole and bake in a 350° oven for 2 hours. Serve hot as a meat accompaniment.   *Serves 6*

MUSHROOM ALMOND RICE

1 cup long grain rice
2 cups chicken broth or bouillon
2 tablespoons butter or margarine
½ pound mushrooms, sliced
1 clove garlic, minced or pressed
½ cup BLUE DIAMOND® Blanched Slivered
   Almonds, toasted
¼ cup minced parsley
Salt and pepper

Combine rice and broth in a saucepan and cover; bring to a full boil; reduce heat and simmer for 20 minutes. Do not remove cover. Remove pan from heat and steam another 20 minutes.

Just before serving, heat butter until bubbly in a large skillet; add mushrooms and garlic and sauté quickly. After rice has steamed, add to mushrooms along with almonds and parsley; mix well. Salt and pepper to taste.   *Makes 4 to 6 servings*

OYSTER CONFETTI RICE

1 can (8-oz.) BUMBLE BEE® Whole Oysters
½ pound boned pork shoulder
1 tablespoon vegetable oil
1 medium green bell pepper, seeded, chunked
1 small onion, diced
1 clove garlic, pressed
1 can (8-oz.) water chestnuts, drained
1 can (14½-oz.) chicken broth
2 medium tomatoes, seeded, chopped
1 cup uncooked brown rice
1 teaspoon thyme, crumbled
¾ teaspoon salt
½ teaspoon turmeric
1 medium zucchini

Drain oysters, reserving 1 tablespoon liquid. Slice pork into thin strips. Brown in oil. Stir in green pepper, onion and garlic; sauté until onion is soft. Coarsely chop water chestnuts. Add to skillet along with reserved oyster liquid, chicken broth, tomatoes, rice, thyme, salt and turmeric. Cover and simmer 30 minutes. Shred zucchini (should have about 1 cup). Stir in zucchini, then oysters. Cover and cook until heated through.   *Makes 4 to 6 servings*

PACIFIC ISLES RICE

2 tablespoons butter or margarine
¾ cup chopped celery
1½ cups uncooked instant rice
1½ cups hot water
1 envelope LIPTON® Onion Soup Mix
1 can (4 oz.) sliced mushrooms (optional)

In medium saucepan, melt butter and cook celery over low heat until crisp-tender. Add remaining ingredients. Bring to a boil; reduce heat and simmer, uncovered, about 5 minutes.

Makes about 6 servings

HOLIDAY RICE WITH APRICOTS

3 cups water
1 cup enriched long grain rice
1 cup pared, chopped, raw apple
½ cup raisins
¼ cup chopped onion
1 teaspoon salt
¼ cup chopped, soft, dried apricots
¼ cup HENRI'S Sweet 'N Saucy French Dressing
2 tablespoons margarine

1. Bring water to a boil. Add rice, apples, raisins, onions and salt. Cover pan, reduce heat and simmer until rice is tender.
2. Stir apricots, HENRI'S Sweet 'N Saucy French Dressing and margarine into rice mixture. Cover pan, let stand 10 minutes.
3. Serve hot or cold.   *Makes 6 (1-cup) servings*

Salads & Salad Dressings

Main Course

TURKEY SALAD IN POPOVERS

2 teaspoons lemon juice
1 apple, pared and cut into bite-size pieces
4 cups cut-up cooked turkey or chicken
½ cup diagonally sliced celery
⅓ cup slivered almonds
½ teaspoon salt
1 cup mayonnaise or salad dressing
½ teaspoon curry powder
1 to 2 tablespoons milk
Popovers*
2 slices bacon, crisply fried and crumbled, if desired

Sprinkle lemon juice over apple. Mix apple, turkey, celery and almonds; sprinkle with salt. Mix mayonnaise, curry powder and milk. Toss mayonnaise mixture with turkey mixture; refrigerate. Prepare Popovers. Just before serving, split popovers; fill with salad. Garnish with bacon.   *6 servings*

*POPOVERS

1 cup **GOLD MEDAL WONDRA® Flour**
½ teaspoon salt
1 cup milk
2 eggs, slightly beaten

Heat oven to 450°. Generously grease six (6-ounce) custard cups or 8 medium muffin cups, 2½ × 1¼ inches. Mix all ingredients with fork just until smooth (do not overbeat). Fill custard cups about ½ full. Bake 20 minutes. Decrease oven temperature to 350°. Bake until deep golden brown, 20 minutes longer. Immediately remove from cups.

Note: To freeze popovers, immediately remove from cups. Cut small slit in side of each to allow steam to escape; cool. Wrap and freeze no longer than 2 weeks. To serve, heat frozen popovers on ungreased cookie sheet in 350° oven 5 to 8 minutes.

TURKEY HAWAIIAN

3 whole fresh pineapples
2½ cups cooked cubed **JENNIE-O® Turkey**
1 cup green seedless grapes
½ cup sliced celery
½ cup coarsely chopped nuts
1 can (8 oz.) Mandarin oranges, drained
1 cup dairy sour cream
¼ cup firmly packed brown sugar
Walnut halves, if desired

Cut pineapples in half. Remove fruit; cut into bite-size pieces. Combine pineapple pieces and remaining ingredients, except walnut halves. Spoon mixture into pineapple shells. Garnish with walnut halves, if desired.   *6 servings*

CALIFORNIA TURKEY SALAD

Salad:
2 pounds **JENNIE-O® Fully Cooked Turkey Breast,** cubed
1 cup sliced celery
1 cup sliced ripe olives
½ cup toasted slivered almonds
Leaf lettuce
3 small avocados, each cut into 12 slices*
4 medium oranges, peeled and sectioned
12 strawberries, halved
Green seedless grapes**

Dressing:
1½ cups vegetable oil
½ cup light wine or cider vinegar
3 tablespoons sugar
2 teaspoons each salt and minced parsley
½ teaspoon each dry mustard, basil, and pepper
1 garlic clove, minced

In medium bowl, combine all Dressing ingredients. Refrigerate at least one hour. Shake before serving. In large bowl, combine turkey, celery and olives. Assemble salads by lining six plates with lettuce, spooning on about one cup of turkey mixture and garnishing the top with slivered almonds and grapes. Surround salad with avocado slices, orange sections, strawberry halves and additional grapes or whole olives. Drizzle with Dressing.
Makes 6 salads

  *Dip avocado slices in lemon juice to prevent discoloring.
  **A combination of red and green grapes may be used.
You may substitute other **JENNIE-O®** turkey products in this recipe.

MOLDED TURKEY SALAD

2 envelopes unflavored gelatin
½ cup cold water
3 cups boiling water
3 **HERB-OX® Chicken Bouillon Cubes** or 1 tablespoon **HERB-OX® Instant Chicken Style Bouillon**
2 cups cooked turkey or chicken, chopped
1 onion, grated
⅓ cup chopped celery
1 tablespoon chopped parsley
2 tablespoons mayonnaise
2 tablespoons cream (any type)

Sprinkle gelatin on cold water, let stand 5 minutes. Add boiling water and bouillon cubes or instant bouillon, stir over low heat until gelatin is dissolved. Cool until aspic is thick and syrupy. Swirl enough thickened mixture in a chilled 5-cup pan or mold to coat bottom and sides. Chill until set. Combine remaining ingredients, blend well. Add ½ cup aspic, adjust seasoning. Fill aspic-lined pan smoothly, add remaining aspic. Chill until firm, unmold to serve.   *Makes 4 to 6 servings*

DIETER'S TURKEY CITRUS SALAD
(Low Calorie)

1 cup cubed roast **SWIFT PREMIUM®
    BUTTERBALL®** Turkey
1 cup fresh grapefruit sections
½ cup fresh orange sections
½ small head lettuce, broken into bite-size pieces
Low calorie dressing
4 leaves garden lettuce or endive

Toss together lightly turkey, fruit and lettuce with enough dressing to coat. Serve on lettuce leaves arranged on 2 salad plates.

Yield: 2 servings

CHICKEN SALAD WITH WHITE WINE DRESSING

White Wine Dressing*
2 cups coarsely chopped cooked chicken
¼ cup toasted blanched almonds, chopped
¼ cup chopped celery
2 teaspoons capers, chopped
¼ cup plain yogurt
1½ teaspoons lemon juice
½ teaspoon salt
⅛ teaspoon ground pepper
Lettuce cups

Prepare White Wine Dressing. Pour dressing over chicken and allow to marinate about 1 hour; drain chicken thoroughly. Combine marinated chicken, almonds, celery, and capers in a bowl. Mix yogurt, lemon juice, salt, and pepper; add to bowl and toss lightly until thoroughly mixed; chill. To serve, spoon salad into lettuce cups.

About 4 servings

*WHITE WINE DRESSING

½ cup **CRISCO®** Oil
¼ cup dry white wine
2 tablespoons vinegar
1 teaspoon sugar
¼ teaspoon salt
¼ teaspoon basil

Combine all ingredients in a screw-top jar. Cover tightly and shake vigorously to blend well. Store covered in refrigerator. Shake well before using.

About ⅔ cup

LOW-CAL HOT APPLE CHICKEN SALAD
(Low Calorie)

2 cups cooked, diced chicken
2 cups diced, unpeeled red apple
½ cup sliced celery
¼ cup chopped onion
1 can cream of chicken soup
1 tsp. sage (optional)
½ tsp. salt
¼ tsp. pepper

Combine chicken, apple, celery and onion in a 1½-quart baking dish. In small bowl, combine remaining ingredients, mixing until well blended. Pour into baking dish, stirring to combine all ingredients. Bake at 350°F. for 35-40 minutes or until hot and bubbly.

Yield: 6 servings

Calories: 166 each serving

Favorite recipe from the **Michigan Apple Committee**

SAVORY TANGERINE CHICKEN SALAD

½ cup mayonnaise or salad dressing
Grated peel of 1 **SUNKIST®** Tangerine
¼ tsp. curry powder *or* poultry seasoning
¼ tsp. seasoned salt
2 cups cubed cooked chicken
2 **SUNKIST®** Tangerines, peeled, segmented, seeded
½ cup chopped celery
¼ cup chopped green pepper
¼ cup toasted slivered almonds

In large bowl, combine mayonnaise, tangerine peel, curry powder and seasoned salt. Stir in remaining ingredients; chill. Serve on salad greens, if desired.

Makes 4 servings (about 3½ cups)

FRUITED CHICKEN SALAD

10-oz. pkg. **AMERICAN BEAUTY®** Large
    SHEL-RONI®
1 cup mayonnaise
1 teaspoon salt
1 teaspoon dry mustard
½ teaspoon paprika
3 (5-oz.) cans boned chicken or 2 cups cubed, cooked
    chicken
2 cups melon balls or cubes
20-oz. can pineapple chunks, drained
⅓ cup sliced almonds, toasted

Cook shells to desired doneness as directed on package. Drain and rinse under cold water. In large bowl, combine mayonnaise, salt, mustard and paprika; stir until well blended. Fold in remaining ingredients, except almonds. Refrigerate 2 to 3 hours to blend flavors. Serve on lettuce leaves; sprinkle almonds over top before serving.

6 servings

HIGH ALTITUDE—Above 3500 Feet: Cooking times may need to be increased slightly.

BRANDIED CHICKEN-VEGETABLE SALAD

2 (10½ oz.) cans condensed chicken broth
2 envelopes plus 2 teaspoons unflavored gelatin
½ cup California Brandy
3 tablespoons white wine vinegar
½ teaspoon salt
3 drops **TABASCO®** Sauce
1 cup sliced yellow crook-neck squash
1 cup fresh or frozen peas
1 small avocado, sliced
1½ cups shredded cooked chicken
¼ cup diced pimiento
¼ cup sliced green onion
½ cup shredded carrot

Chill broth before opening cans, so any fat can be removed easily. Remove and discard fat. Sprinkle gelatin over ½ cup broth and let stand 5 minutes to soften. Heat remaining broth, add gelatin and stir until dissolved. Stir in brandy, vinegar, salt and **TABASCO®**. Cool until mixture begins to thicken slightly.

Meanwhile, cook squash about 5 minutes, until tender-crisp, and peas 5 to 10 minutes. Drain well, keeping separate.

When gelatin is cooled and lightly thickened, turn about ½ cup into oiled 6½ cup ring mold, and set in shallow pan of ice water. Arrange avocado slices around bottom and side of mold, and let stand until gelatin is set to hold in place. Mix about 1 cup of the gelatin mixture with chicken, pimiento and onion, and spoon into mold. Chill a few minutes, then add squash and about ½ cup more of the gelatin mixture. Chill again, and add peas and more gelatin, then carrots with remaining gelatin. Chill firm, at least 3 hours.

At serving time, unmold, and garnish with lettuce. Serve plain or with mayonnaise or dairy sour cream. *Makes 6 servings*

Note: For perfect layers, chill each until just set in pan with ice water before adding next layer.

Favorite recipe from the **California Brandy Advisory Board**

CONFETTI MAIN DISH SALAD

1 cup uncooked long grain rice
1¾ cups water
5 tablespoons **KIKKOMAN Soy Sauce**, divided
1½ cups cooked pork, beef or chicken, cut into strips
1 cup thinly sliced green onions & tops
10 cherry tomatoes, halved
3 tablespoons vegetable oil
2 tablespoons vinegar
1 teaspoon sugar

Measure rice, water and 3 Tbsp. soy sauce into saucepan. Cook rice according to package directions; omit salt. Cool completely. Combine rice, meat, green onions and tomatoes in large bowl. Mix together remaining 2 Tbsp. soy sauce, oil, vinegar and sugar; stir until sugar dissolves. Pour over rice mixture; toss to combine. Cover and chill at least 2 hours before serving.

Makes 4 to 6 servings

TANGY CHICKEN SALAD

3 cups chopped cooked chicken
⅓ cup **B&B Liqueur**
2 cups halved seedless green grapes
1 cup sliced celery
⅓ cup chopped green pepper
1 can (8 oz.) chunk pineapple, drained
½ cup coarsely chopped walnuts
1 cup mayonnaise
Lettuce cups

Combine chicken and **B&B Liqueur** in a small deep bowl. Cover and chill 1 hour. In a large bowl combine chicken mixture, grapes, celery, green pepper, pineapple and walnuts. Toss thoroughly with mayonnaise. To serve lightly pile into individual lettuce cups.

Makes 6 servings

CHICKEN SALAD A LA TARRAGON
(Low Calorie)

2 cups diced cooked chicken
1 cup sliced celery
2 tablespoons finely chopped green pepper
1 tablespoon finely chopped green onion
2 teaspoons chopped pimiento
Salt
Crisp lettuce
Creamy Tarragon Dressing*

Combine chicken, celery, green pepper, onion and pimiento. Salt to taste. When ready to serve, spoon onto crisp lettuce on chilled salad plates. Pass Creamy Tarragon Dressing.

Makes 4 servings

Calories: 216 per serving   *(Continued*

*CREAMY TARRAGON DRESSING

Beat ¾ cup instant nonfat dry milk with ½ cup **DIET SHASTA® Ginger Ale** until fluffy. Crumble 1 chicken bouillon cube into ¼ cup tarragon flavor vinegar. Add to first mixture beating until thick. Add 1 teaspoon dry mustard, ½ teaspoon crumbled tarragon leaves, ¼ teaspoon paprika, 1 teaspoon onion powder, ½ teaspoon salt and 1 tablespoon chopped parsley. Stir to blend and serve at once. *Makes about 2 cups*

Calories: 43 per serving

COBB SALAD WITH PEPPY FRENCH DRESSING

1 medium head lettuce, coarsely broken
2 cups coarsely chopped watercress leaves
3 hard-cooked eggs, quartered
½ pound bacon, cooked and crumbled
2 medium avocados, peeled, pitted and sliced
2½ cups cut-up cooked chicken
1 tablespoon chopped chives
Lettuce

Combine all ingredients in bowl except lettuce; mix lightly. Line large or individual salad bowls with crisp lettuce. Add salad mixture. If desired, garnish with tomato wedges. Serve with Peppy French Dressing*, and, if desired, additional **TABASCO®**.

Yield: 4 quarts, about 6 to 8 servings

*PEPPY FRENCH DRESSING

⅔ cup salad oil
⅓ cup vinegar
¼ cup catchup
½ teaspoon dry mustard
½ teaspoon paprika
½ teaspoon **TABASCO® Pepper Sauce**
⅛ teaspoon salt
½ teaspoon sugar
2 tablespoons crumbled blue cheese

Combine all ingredients in jar with tight cover. Shake to mix well.

Yield: 1¼ cups

GERMAN CHICKEN AND POTATO SALAD

4 slices bacon
2 tablespoons flour
1 cup water
¼ cup wine vinegar
1 teaspoon sugar
⅛ teaspoon pepper
4 cups sliced cooked potatoes
2 cans (5 ounces each) **SWANSON Chunk White or Thigh Chicken**
¼ cup chopped green pepper
¼ cup chopped onion

In skillet, cook bacon until crisp; remove and crumble. Pour off all but ¼ cup drippings; blend in flour. Cook a few minutes, stirring constantly. Remove from heat. Add water, a little at a time, stirring until smooth after each addition. Add vinegar, sugar and pepper. Cook, stirring until thickened. Add bacon and remaining ingredients. Heat; stir occasionally.

Makes about 5 cups, 4 servings

TROPICAL CHICKEN SALAD

4 cups cooked cubed chicken or turkey
2 large oranges, peeled, sectioned and drained
1½ cups cut-up fresh pineapple, drained
1 cup seedless white grape halves
1 cup chopped celery
¾ cup mayonnaise or salad dressing
¼ cup **REALEMON® Lemon Juice from Concentrate**
1 teaspoon ground ginger
½ teaspoon salt
½ to ¾ cup cashew nuts

In large bowl, combine chicken, fruit and celery. Chill. In small bowl, combine remaining ingredients except cashews. Chill. Just before serving combine chicken mixture, dressing and nuts. Serve in hollowed out pineapple shells or on lettuce leaves. Refrigerate leftovers.   *Makes about 2 quarts*

"END OF A SUNNY DAY" SALAD

3 cups cooked rice
1 bottle (8 oz.) **WISH-BONE® Russian Dressing**
¼ cup finely chopped green onions
1 can (8 oz.) pineapple chunks in natural juice, drained
   (reserve 1 tablespoon juice)
1 tablespoon soy sauce
¾ tablespoon ground ginger
2 cups cubed cooked chicken*
2 medium green peppers, cut into 1-inch chunks
1 can (8½ oz.) water chestnuts, drained and sliced

In medium bowl, combine rice, ⅓ cup red Russian dressing, green onions, and reserved pineapple juice. Pack into lightly greased 3 or 4-cup ring mold; chill.

In medium bowl, combine remaining ⅔ cup red Russian dressing, soy sauce, and ginger. Add chicken, green pepper, pineapple, and water chestnuts; chill, tossing occasionally, at least 2 hours.

To serve, unmold rice ring and fill center with salad mixture. Serve, if desired, on fresh lettuce or spinach leaves.
                    Makes about 4 servings

*VARIATIONS:

Use 2 cups leftover cooked turkey, beef, or pork.

HOME STYLE RUBY CHICKEN SALAD

3 medium **TEXAS RUBY RED Grapefruit**, chilled
1 broiler-fryer chicken (2 to 2½ lbs.) quartered or 2 cups
   cooked chicken
2 teaspoons salt
½ cup yogurt
¼ cup mayonnaise
⅛ to ¼ teaspoon dill weed
½ cup chopped celery
4 to 5 tablespoons chopped green onions
¼ cup ripe olives

In medium saucepan, place chicken, 1 teaspoon salt, and cover with water. Heat to boiling. Cover, reduce heat and simmer for 40 minutes. Remove chicken and cool slightly. When cool enough to handle, cut chicken into bite-size pieces. Discard bones and skin.

Meanwhile cut grapefruit in half crosswise; cut around each section to loosen from membrane or use serrated grapefruit spoon. Remove sections from shell and cut into bite-size pieces; drain well. Scrape remaining membrane from shells. Refrigerate until ready to use.   *(Continued)*

In medium bowl, combine yogurt, mayonnaise, 1 teaspoon salt and dill weed; stir well. Add grapefruit, chicken, and remaining ingredients; toss lightly. Spoon about ¾ cup chicken mixture into each grapefruit shell. Cover and chill until ready to serve.
                    6 servings

Favorite recipe from the **Texas Citrus Industry**

BEST FOODS®/HELLMANN'S® CHINESE CHICKEN SALAD

1 broiler-fryer chicken
2 ribs celery
1 carrot
1 teaspoon salt
1 bay leaf
1 small onion
1 cup water
1 can (8½ oz.) water chestnuts, drained (1 cup)
1 can (8½ oz.) bamboo shoots (1 cup)
2 ribs celery, sliced
2 canned pimientos, chopped
2 green onions, thinly sliced
¾ cup **BEST FOODS®/HELLMANN'S® Real Mayonnaise**
2 tablespoons soy sauce
1 tablespoon lemon juice
1 quart torn lettuce pieces

Cook chicken with celery, carrot, salt, bay leaf, onion and water about 40 minutes or until tender. Cool; remove skin and bones and cut into bite-size pieces. Mix water chestnuts, bamboo shoots, sliced celery, pimiento, green onion and chicken. Toss lightly; cover and chill. Mix together Real Mayonnaise, soy sauce and lemon juice; chill. Just before serving toss chicken mixture with dressing. Serve salad on a bed of torn lettuce pieces.
                    Makes 4 to 6 servings

Note: If desired, serve dressing on the side instead of tossing with chicken mixture.

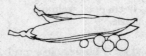

ARROZ CON POLLO SALAD

1 cup chopped onion
1 tablespoon vegetable oil
2⅔ cups water
1 cup **UNCLE BEN'S® Select Brown Rice**
2 teaspoons chili powder
2 teaspoons salt
½ cup vegetable oil
2 tablespoons vinegar
2 cups diced cooked chicken
1 package (10 ounces) frozen peas, cooked and drained
½ cup ripe olive slices
2 soft California avocados
1 medium tomato, chopped, chilled

Cook onion in oil in large saucepan until tender but not brown. Add water and bring to a boil. Stir in rice, chili powder and 1 teaspoon salt. Cover tightly and cook over low heat until all liquid is absorbed, about 50 minutes. Combine oil, vinegar and remaining salt, mixing well; stir into hot cooked rice with chicken, peas and olives. Chill. To serve, peel, seed and coarsely chop 1½ avocados, reserving remaining half for garnish. Stir chopped avocado and tomato into rice mixture. Top with reserved avocado slices.
                    Makes 6 main dish servings

WHEAT GERM STUFFED TOMATO SALAD

1 whole chicken breast, boned, skinned and diced
1 Tbsp. butter or margarine
4 large, firm, ripe tomatoes
¾ cup **KRETSCHMER Regular Wheat Germ**
⅓ cup chopped green onion
⅓ cup chopped green pepper
¾ tsp. curry powder
½ tsp. thyme leaves, crushed
½ tsp. salt
⅛ tsp. pepper

Sauté chicken in butter until tender (about 5 minutes). Cut thin slice from tops of tomatoes. Scoop out pulp, leaving shells intact. Dice tomato tops and pulp. Drain. Combine all ingredients *except* tomato shells. Mix well. Spoon mixture into shells. Serve on lettuce garnished with avocado wedges and ripe olives if desired.
Makes 4 servings

Note: To serve hot, place in shallow baking pan and bake at 350° for about 25 minutes until hot. Top with yogurt if desired.

CHARM CITY SALAD

⅔ cup salad oil
⅓ cup **HEINZ Wine Vinegar**
1 tablespoon chopped parsley
½ teaspoon salt
Freshly ground black pepper
3 cups lump crab meat
Lettuce slices, chilled
2 tomatoes, cut into wedges
3 hard-cooked eggs, quartered

Combine first 5 ingredients in jar. Cover; shake vigorously. Chill to blend flavors. Arrange crab meat on lettuce slice; garnish with tomato and egg. Shake dressing again before spooning over salad.
Makes 6 servings

SUMMERTIME SALAD MARINADE

Dressing:
½ cup **PLANTERS Peanut Oil**
⅓ cup white wine vinegar
¼ cup **DRY SACK® Sherry**
1 tablespoon Dijon mustard
½ teaspoon tarragon leaves
¼ teaspoon salt
⅛ teaspoon ground black pepper

2 cups blanched sliced zucchini, chilled
1 pound medium shrimp, shelled, cooked and chilled
1½ cups shredded cooked chicken, chilled
½ cup thinly sliced onion
1 tablespoon **DROMEDARY Sliced Pimientos**
Crisp lettuce leaves

DRESSING:
Combine peanut oil, vinegar, **DRY SACK® Sherry**, mustard, tarragon, salt and pepper. Mix well. Divide prepared dressing into 3 separate bowls.

Place zucchini and shrimp in separate bowls with dressing. Combine chicken, onion and pimientos; place in 3rd bowl of dressing. Toss each combination well. Place bowls in refrigerator and marinate 30 minutes. Spoon individual salads onto lettuce leaves.
Serves: 6

ALOHA CRAB SALAD

1 (6-oz.) pkg. **WAKEFIELD® Crabmeat**
1 fresh pineapple
1 ripe avocado
1 tablespoon lemon juice
⅓ cup sliced water chestnuts
1 finely chopped green onion
1 cup mayonnaise
¼ teaspoon curry powder

Thaw crabmeat, drain and separate into chunks. Halve pineapple lengthwise and remove core; scoop out fruit and cut into chunks. Peel avocado and coarsely dice; sprinkle with lemon juice. Toss together pineapple chunks, water chestnuts, avocado, green onion and crabmeat. Spoon into pineapple shells and garnish with mayonnaise seasoned with curry.
Serves 4 to 5

SHRIMPARONI SALAD

7-oz. package **CREAMETTES® Macaroni** (2 cups uncooked)
1 package (10-oz.) frozen, cooked shrimp
1½ cups celery, diced
¾ cup cucumber, diced
½ cup mayonnaise
1 tablespoon onion, grated
1 teaspoon seasoned salt
½ teaspoon pepper
1 hard-cooked egg, sliced
Cucumber slices
Radish roses

Prepare **CREAMETTES®** according to package directions for salad use. Drain. Defrost shrimp according to instructions on the package. Combine macaroni, shrimp, celery, cucumber, mayonnaise, onion, salt and pepper. Chill before serving. Garnish with egg slices, cucumber and radishes.
6 servings

ARTICHOKE SURPRISE SALAD

7-oz. package **CREAMETTES® Macaroni**, (2 cups uncooked)
1 package (9 oz.) frozen artichoke hearts
1 can (5½-oz.) lobster, shrimp or crabmeat, drained and flaked
½ cup French dressing
½ cup mayonnaise
1 teaspoon salt
½ teaspoon basil
¼ teaspoon pepper
Lettuce
½ cup sliced radishes

Prepare **CREAMETTES®** according to package directions for salad use. Drain. Prepare artichoke hearts according to package directions. Drain. Combine all ingredients except lettuce and radishes. Chill. Serve in lettuce lined bowl. Garnish with radishes.
6 servings

Calories: 177 per serving

VARIATION:

One 7-oz. can tuna may be added. Water-packed tuna will increase calories to 219 per serving. Oil-packed tuna will increase calories to 242 per serving. Shrimp, crabmeat, ham or chicken may be added. Adjust the calories for the addition.

PALM BEACH SALAD

1 12-ounce bag **BOOTH®** Peeled and Deveined
 Shrimp
⅓ cup mayonnaise
⅓ cup heavy cream, whipped
½ cup mandarin orange sections
3 tablespoons chopped nuts
3 tablespoons coconut
2-3 drops **TABASCO®** Sauce
¼ teaspoon salt
Lettuce leaves

Boil shrimp according to package instructions. Drain, rinse and
chill. Combine the rest of the ingredients except lettuce leaves
thoroughly. Fold in shrimp. Chill for one hour. Serve on lettuce
leaves.

SPICY SHRIMP SALAD

1 pound medium shrimp, shelled and deveined
1 cup sour cream
¼ cup **RAGU'®** Spaghetti Sauce
1½ teaspoons lemon juice
1 teaspoon grated onion
1 teaspoon horseradish
½ teaspoon Worcestershire sauce
TABASCO® Sauce
Salt, to taste
Pepper, to taste

In a large saucepan, bring 1 quart of water to a boil. Add shrimp,
simmer 2-4 minutes or until shrimp turns pink; drain and chill.
Combine remaining ingredients, cover and chill. To serve, toss
shrimp with dressing. Spoon over shredded lettuce and garnish with
lemon slices.
Serves about 4

SHRIMP SALAD POLYNESIAN

1 lb. **ATALANTA** Frozen Shrimp, cooked, peeled,
 deveined
1 large red apple, cored and cubed
1½ cups pineapple chunks
½ lb. grapes, green, seedless
1 cup yogurt, plain
1 Tbsp. curry powder
3 Tbsp. lemon juice
Lettuce leaves, Bibb or Romaine, as needed

Combine yogurt, curry powder and lemon juice. Mix well. Combine shrimp, cubed apple, pineapple chunks and grapes. Toss
gently with yogurt dressing. Serve on lettuce leaves.
Yield: 4 servings

MUSHROOM-CLAM DINNER SALAD
(Low Calorie)

½ cup **DIET SHASTA®** Orange
½ teaspoon minced garlic
1 tablespoon vinegar
1 teaspoon celery salt
⅛ teaspoon white pepper
1 teaspoon basil leaves, crushed
½ teaspoon thyme leaves, crushed
1 (6½ oz.) can minced clams, drained
1 cup finely chopped fresh mushrooms
¼ cup chopped green pepper
4 medium or small tomatoes
Crisp lettuce

Combine **DIET SHASTA®** with garlic, vinegar, salt, pepper,
basil and thyme. Simmer about 5 minutes until liquid is reduced to
about ¼ cup. Pour over drained clams and mushrooms. Chill
several hours or overnight. Add green pepper. Cut tomatoes partially through to open like flowers. Arrange on crisp lettuce and
spoon mushroom-clam mixture over each.
Makes 4 servings

THE DELICIOUS SARDINE SALAD

2 cans **KING OSCAR Sardines,** drained
2 large delicious apples, peeled, cored, chopped
2 large oranges, peeled and cut into bite-size pieces
1 large sweet Spanish onion, peeled and chopped
½ cup walnuts, chopped
½ cup sour cream
¼ cup lemon juice
1 tsp. chopped chives
Lettuce
Parsley

In large salad bowl, toss together sardines, apple, orange, onion,
walnuts. Make dressing by mixing together sour cream, lemon
juice, chives. Pour dressing over salad and toss gently. Serve on
bed of lettuce and garnish with parsley.
Serves 6

DELUXE FARM-RAISED CATFISH AND FRESH SPINACH SALAD

2 pounds skinned farm-raised catfish fillets, fresh or
 frozen
1 quart boiling water
1 tablespoon salt
1 lemon, cut in half
1 tablespoon lemon juice
1 pound fresh spinach
1 cup sliced red onion
½ cup sliced pitted ripe olives
1 cup sliced fresh mushrooms
3 slices bacon, diced
1 teaspoon all-purpose flour
¼ cup red wine vinegar
¼ cup water
1 teaspoon sugar
1 teaspoon salt
¼ teaspoon pepper
¼ teaspoon Dijon mustard
2 hard-cooked eggs, cut into fourths

Thaw fish if frozen. Combine boiling water, 1 tablespoon salt and
lemon. Place fillets in water. Cover and return to the boiling point.
Reduce heat and simmer for 8 to 10 minutes or until fish flakes
easily when tested with a fork. Drain. Flake fish into bite size
pieces and sprinkle with lemon juice. Remove large stems from
spinach and break into bite size pieces. In a large salad bowl
combine fish, spinach, onion, olives and mushrooms. Fry bacon
until crisp. Blend flour into bacon drippings. Add vinegar, water,
sugar, 1 teaspoon salt, pepper, and mustard, stirring constantly
until slightly thick. Pour sauce over fish mixture and toss. Garnish
with egg.
Makes 6 servings

Favorite recipe from the **Catfish Farmers of America**

SALMON VEGETABLE SALAD
(Low Calorie)

	Calories
1 (15½ oz.) can **DOUBLE Q** **Pink Salmon***	554
1½ cups finely shredded green cabbage	33
1½ cups finely shredded red cabbage	33
1 cup diced green pepper	32
1 cup shredded carrot	46

Dressing:

1 cup low calorie plain yogurt	61
1 tablespoon vinegar	2
½ teaspoon dry mustard	—
½ teaspoon celery seed	—
	761

Drain salmon and separate into bite size pieces. Combine cabbage, green pepper and carrot and mound on four salad plates. Top with salmon. Combine salad dressing ingredients and spoon over salmon. *Makes 4 servings*

Calories per serving = Approx. 190

***DEMING'S, GILLNETTERSBEST** or **HUMPTY DUMPTY Salmon** may be substituted.

SALMON PASTA SALAD

8 oz. pkg. small shell macaroni
1¼ cups Italian Dressing & Marinade
2 Tbsp. lemon juice

Cook macaroni according to package directions, drain—combine with dressing and lemon juice and chill 1 hr.

To Serve:
15½ oz. can **GILLNETTERSBEST Red Sockeye Salmon***
1½ cups sliced celery
2 medium tomatoes, cubed
2 green onions, chopped
2 hard cooked eggs, chopped
Ripe olives
Parsley

Drain salmon and separate into bite size chunks. In a salad bowl, combine salmon, macaroni, celery, tomato, green onion and egg. Garnish with ripe olives and parsley. Sprinkle additional dressing over salad and toss gently. *Serves 6-8*

***DEMING'S, DOUBLE Q** or **HUMPTY DUMPTY Salmon** may be substituted.

TOSSED FISH SALAD*

2½ cups water
¼ cup plus 1 teaspoon **LEA & PERRINS Worcestershire Sauce**, divided
2 tablespoons lemon juice
4 teaspoons onion powder
1½ teaspoons salt, divided
2 pounds cod or halibut fillets
1 cup cherry tomatoes, halved
1 cup thinly sliced celery
4 hard-cooked eggs, diced
½ cup mayonnaise
1 tablespoon sweet pickle relish
½ teaspoon garlic powder

In a medium skillet combine water, ¼ cup of the **LEA & PERRINS**, lemon juice, onion powder and 1 teaspoon of the salt. Bring to boiling point. Add fish. Reduce heat and simmer 12 to 15 minutes or just until fish flakes. Cool fish in liquid. Drain, flake and chill. In a salad bowl combine flaked fish, tomatoes, celery and eggs. Mix mayonnaise, relish and garlic powder with remaining 1 teaspoon **LEA & PERRINS** and ½ teaspoon salt. Spoon into fish mixture; toss gently. Serve on crisp lettuce, or in avocado halves, if desired. *Yield: 6 to 8 portions*

*May be prepared in advance of serving.

SALMON 'N RICE SALAD

3 cups cooked rice
1 (7¾-oz.) can salmon, drained, flaked
½ cup celery slices
½ cup creamy cucumber dressing
¼ cup chopped pimiento
¼ cup green onion slices
⅛ teaspoon pepper
1 cup cherry tomato halves
½ cup chopped cucumber

Combine rice, salmon, celery, dressing, pimiento, onion and pepper; toss lightly. Pack into 4-cup ring mold; chill. Unmold. Combine tomatoes and cucumber; toss lightly. Fill center of mold with vegetable mixture. Garnish with cucumber and serve with additional dressing, if desired. *4 to 6 servings*

VARIATION:

One 6¾- or 7-oz. can of tuna may be substituted for salmon.

Favorite recipe from **The Association for Dressings and Sauces**

ORIENTAL TUNA SALAD

1 package **BETTY CROCKER® TUNA HELPER® Mix for Creamy Noodles 'n Tuna**
3 cups hot water
1 cup diagonally sliced celery
1 can (8 ounces) water chestnuts, drained and sliced
1 can (6½ ounces) tuna, drained
1 package (6 ounces) frozen Chinese pea pods, thawed and drained
1 jar (2 ounces) sliced pimientos, drained
¼ cup vegetable oil
3 tablespoons vinegar
1 tablespoon soy sauce
2 teaspoons sugar
½ teaspoon pepper
¼ to ½ teaspoon ground ginger

Heat Noodles, Sauce Mix and water to boiling in 10-inch skillet, stirring constantly. Reduce heat; cover and simmer, stirring occasionally, 10 minutes. Simmer uncovered 5 minutes longer; cool 5 minutes. Mix celery, water chestnuts, tuna, pea pods and pimientos in large bowl. Mix remaining ingredients; toss with tuna mixture. Stir in noodle mixture. Serve immediately, or if desired, cover and refrigerate until chilled, at least 3 hours.

4 or 5 servings

HIGH ALTITUDE DIRECTIONS (3500 to 6500 feet): Increase hot water to 3¼ cups and first simmer time to 15 minutes.

TUNA FRUIT SALAD PLATTER

1 cup strawberries
2 oranges, peeled and sliced
2 bananas, sliced
1 avocado, peeled and sliced
1 small bunch green grapes
1 small bunch dark grapes
2 cans (6½ or 7 ounces each) tuna in vegetable oil

On a large platter arrange fruit and tuna chunks. Garnish with fresh mint sprigs. Serve with Poppy Seed Dressing* or Orange Ginger Dressing.**   *Yield: 4 to 6 servings*

*POPPY SEED DRESSING

½ teaspoon dry mustard
1 teaspoon salt
1 teaspoon grated onion
⅓ cup honey
2 tablespoons cider vinegar
¾ cup salad oil
2 teaspoons poppy seeds

In a 2-cup measuring cup mix mustard, salt and grated onion. Beat in honey, vinegar and oil. Add poppy seeds and stir. Serve over Tuna Fruit Salad.   *Yield: 1¼ cup dressing*

**ORANGE GINGER DRESSING

1½ cups sour cream
⅓ cup mayonnaise
¼ teaspoon grated orange rind
2 tablespoons orange juice
1 tablespoon finely chopped candied ginger
2 teaspoons sugar
⅛ teaspoon salt

In a small bowl, mix all ingredients. Chill 1 hour. Serve over Tuna Fruit Salad.   *Yield: 2 cups dressing*

Favorite recipe from the **Tuna Research Foundation Inc.**

CHICKEN OF THE SEA® MEDITERRANEAN TUNA SALAD

½ cup olive oil
¼ cup lemon juice
½ teaspoon salt
¼ teaspoon oregano leaves, crushed
⅛ teaspoon ground pepper
1½ quarts torn salad greens
2 cucumbers, sliced
6 green onions, thinly sliced
8 radishes, sliced
16 pitted ripe olives
1 can (13 oz.) CHICKEN OF THE SEA® Solid White (albacore) Tuna, drained
3 tomatoes, quartered
2 cups (8 oz.) crumbled feta cheese

For dressing, combine oil, lemon juice, salt, oregano and pepper. Chill. In salad bowl combine greens, cucumbers, onions, radishes and olives. Just before serving pour dressing over greens. Toss. Add remaining ingredients. Toss lightly.

Makes 6-8 servings

SEA BREEZE SALAD

1 (7-ounce) package CREAMETTE® Shells, or 2 cups CREAMETTES® Elbow Macaroni, uncooked
1 (7-ounce) can tuna, drained and flaked
1 tomato, sliced
1 medium cucumber, sliced
½ cup California Ripe Olives, sliced
¼ cup green pepper, diced
¼ cup red onion rings
1 teaspoon seasoned salt
½ cup BERNSTEIN'S Italian with Cheese Dressing or BERNSTEIN'S Italian Dressing and Marinade

Prepare CREAMETTE® Shells according to package directions. Drain. Combine remaining ingredients with cooked shells; mix well. Chill. Toss before serving.   *6-8 servings*

This recipe from **CREAMETTES®**, the **California Olive Industry** and **BERNSTEIN'S Salad Dressings**.

COTTAGE TUNA SALAD
(Low Calorie/Low Fat)

1 can (6½ ounces) tuna, packed in water, drained
1 cup low-fat cottage cheese
¼ cup chopped celery
¼ cup chopped green onion
2 tablespoons chopped fresh parsley
1 tablespoon capers
¼ cup plain low-fat yogurt
1 tablespoon lemon juice
½ teaspoon dry mustard
1 packet SWEET 'N LOW®
¼ teaspoon freshly ground pepper
¼ teaspoon salt

In medium bowl, combine tuna, cottage cheese, celery, green onion, parsley, and capers. Mix remaining ingredients in separate bowl. Add to tuna mixture and mix thoroughly. Cover and chill.

4 servings

Per Serving (½ cup): Calories: 115; Fat: 1g

TUNA SALAD NIÇOISE

1 can (13-oz.) BUMBLE BEE® Solid White Tuna
1 pound red potatoes
Boiling water
1 cup cooked green beans, cut in 2-inch pieces
½ cup pitted black olives
¾ cup olive oil
½ cup white wine vinegar
1 teaspoon salt
1 teaspoon tarragon, crumbled
½ teaspoon onion powder
½ teaspoon garlic powder
¼ teaspoon pepper
1 small head butter lettuce, wash and separate leaves
2 tomatoes, cut in wedges
2 hard-cooked eggs, cut in half
1 can (1-oz.) anchovies

Drain tuna. Cook potatoes in boiling water until tender-crisp. Drain. Cool slightly. Slice crosswise about ¼-inch thick. Arrange in 3-quart shallow casserole dish along with green beans and olives. Combine olive oil, vinegar, salt, tarragon, onion and garlic powders, and pepper in a screw-top jar. Shake well. Pour one-half over vegetables. Cover; refrigerate 2 hours. Toss lettuce with ¼ cup remaining dressing. Arrange lettuce on salad platter. Drain marinated vegetables; reserve marinade. Spoon potatoes in center of platter. Arrange beans, olives, tomatoes, eggs and anchovies around potatoes. Arrange tuna on platter. Spoon remaining dressing over entire salad.   *Makes 4 servings*

PASTA-TUNA SALAD

1 cup **BEST FOODS®/HELLMANN'S® Real Mayonnaise**
2 tablespoons red wine vinegar
Dash pepper
4 ounces twist macaroni (1 cup), cooked, drained
1 can (7-oz.) tuna, drained, flaked
1 cup cooked peas
1 cup sliced celery
½ cup chopped red onion
¼ cup snipped dill or 1 tablespoon dried dill weed

In large bowl stir together Real Mayonnaise, vinegar and pepper until smooth. Add macaroni, tuna, peas, celery, onion and dill. Toss to coat well. Cover; refrigerate at least 2 hours to blend flavors.   *Makes 4 servings*

VARIATION:

PASTA-HAM SALAD

Follow recipe for Pasta-Tuna Salad. Substitute 1¼ cups diced cooked ham for tuna.

TUNA CRACKED WHEAT SALAD

2½ cups water
1 package (8 ounces) wheat pilaf mix
¼ cup lemon juice
¼ cup salad oil
2 cans (6½ or 7 ounces each) tuna in vegetable oil
1 cucumber, pared, seeded and diced
½ cup diced pared carrot
⅓ cup sliced scallions
¼ pound mushrooms, sliced
1 tomato, chopped
½ cup sliced pitted ripe olives
½ cup chopped parsley
½ teaspoon salt
½ teaspoon **TABASCO® Pepper Sauce**
Salad greens

In medium saucepan bring water to boil. Add pilaf mix, reduce heat, cover and simmer 15 minutes. Remove from heat; stir in lemon juice and oil. Let stand at room temperature until cool. Stir in remaining ingredients except salad greens. Cover and chill several hours. Turn into bowl lined with salad greens. Serve with Yogurt Dressing.*   *Yield: 6 to 8 servings*

*YOGURT DRESSING

2 containers (8 ounces each) plain yogurt
⅛ teaspoon **TABASCO® Pepper Sauce**
4 teaspoons chopped fresh mint or ¼ teaspoon dried dill weed

In a small bowl mix together yogurt, **TABASCO®** and mint; chill.   *Yield: 2 cups dressing*

PICNIC TUNA-SEASHELL SALAD

⅔ cup dairy sour cream
⅔ cup mayonnaise or salad dressing
¼-½ teaspoon salt
⅛ teaspoon ground white pepper
⅛ teaspoon dill weed
1 can (9¼ oz.) **CHICKEN OF THE SEA® Chunk Light Tuna**, drained and flaked
4 ounces (1 cup raw) small seashell macaroni, cooked and drained
4 ounces (1 cup) diced Muenster cheese
½ cup chopped celery
¼ cup sliced stuffed olives
¼ cup thinly sliced sweet gherkins
¼ cup sliced green onions with tops
¼ cup chopped cucumber
2 tablespoons chopped green pepper

In a large bowl, combine sour cream, mayonnaise, salt, pepper and dill weed. Add remaining ingredients. Toss gently to coat. Chill several hours to blend flavors. If desired, serve on lettuce leaves; garnish with tomato wedges or green pepper rings.   *Makes about 5½ cups*

CALIFORNIA TUNA FRUIT SALAD PLATTER

2 cans (6½ or 7 ounces) **STAR-KIST® Tuna**, drained
1 small cantaloupe, pared and cut in wedges
1 avocado, peeled and cut in wedges
1 small pineapple, pared, cored, and cut in strips or chunks
2 large bananas, cut in chunks
1 can (1 pound, 14 ounces) whole unpeeled apricots, drained
Small cluster of grapes
Watercress or escarole
Pineapple-Lime Cream Dressing*

Break **STAR-KIST® Tuna** into large chunks and arrange with fruit on large platter. Garnish with watercress or escarole. Serve immediately with Pineapple-Lime Cream Dressing.   *Yield: 6 to 8 servings*

*PINEAPPLE-LIME CREAM DRESSING

¼ cup sugar
2 tablespoons cornstarch
½ teaspoon salt
¼ teaspoon curry powder
⅛ teaspoon ground ginger
1½ cups pineapple juice
4 egg yolks, slightly beaten
½ teaspoon grated lime rind
¼ cup lime juice
⅔ cup sour cream or yogurt
½ cup mayonnaise

In a saucepan, mix sugar, cornstarch, salt, curry powder, and ginger. Stir in pineapple juice. Cook, stirring constantly until mixture boils and thickens. Stir a small amount of hot mixture into egg yolks. Stir warmed egg yolks into sauce and cook over very low heat for 2 minutes, stirring constantly. Stir in remaining ingredients and chill.   *Yield: 2 cups*

CALIFORNIA SALAD

1 small head iceburg lettuce
½ head romaine lettuce
4 VIENNA® Franks, cut crosswise
4 slices Swiss cheese, cut in julienne strips
2 green onions, chopped
1 small can ripe olives, cut crosswise
1 large tomato, cut in wedges
Croutons

Break lettuce into bite-size pieces. When ready to serve, combine ingredients in a chilled bowl. Toss with a clear French dressing.

Serves 4

GALLO®-RIOUS LAYERED SALAD

1 cup elbow macaroni
4 cups shredded lettuce
4 carrots, sliced
10 oz. pkg. frozen peas
1 small red onion, sliced
3 oz. GALLO® Italian Dry Salame, julienned strips
1½ cups mayonnaise
1½ tsp. dill weed
½ tsp. salt
½ cup shredded Swiss cheese

Cook macaroni as directed on package; drain and chill. In 3 quart clear glass salad bowl, layer lettuce, carrots, macaroni, peas, onion, and salame. Combine mayonnaise, dill weed and salt; mix well. Spread evenly over top of salad. Sprinkle with cheese. Cover and chill several hours or overnight.

6-8 servings

HAM RICE SLAW

2 cups cubed ARMOUR STAR® Ham
2 cups cooked rice
1 cup chopped celery
1 hard-cooked egg, finely chopped
1 medium tomato, chopped
¼ cup grated carrot
¼ cup chopped green pepper
¼ cup chopped sweet pickle
¾ cup mayonnaise
¼ teaspoon salt

Combine all ingredients; mix lightly. Chill. Preparation time: 20 minutes.

6 to 8 servings

TROPICAL HAM SALAD

3 cups OSCAR MAYER Ham cubes (½″) OR 2 packages (8 oz. each) OSCAR MAYER Ham Slices cut into ½″ cubes
1 can (1 lb.) orange and grapefruit sections, chilled
¼ cup flaked coconut
Lettuce leaves
1 avocado, peeled and cut into wedges

Dressing:

½ cup (4 oz.) sour cream
1½ teaspoons sugar
½ teaspoon horseradish
¼ teaspoon salt
Dash dry mustard

Drain orange and grapefruit sections, reserving 1 tablespoon liquid. Gently combine orange and grapefruit sections with ham, avocado wedges and coconut in bowl. Spoon ham and fruit mixture onto lettuce leaves.

DRESSING:
Whip sour cream until fluffy, about 1 minute. Fold in 1 tablespoon orange and grapefruit liquid and remaining ingredients. Serve with salad.

Makes 4 servings

HAM & CHEESE SALAD

1 package FRENCH'S® Au Gratin Potatoes
2 cups chopped celery
1½ to 2 cups diced cooked ham
½ cup mayonnaise
½ cup undrained sweet pickle relish
Lettuce

Simmer potato slices from package in about 3 cups water 15 minutes, until tender. Drain and chill. Combine with celery and ham. Stir together mayonnaise, pickle relish, and seasoning mix from package of potatoes; add to potato mixture. Toss lightly and chill. Serve on lettuce.

6 servings

HOT HAM PATTIES, MACARONI AND CHEESE SALAD

1-12 oz. HORMEL Ham Patties (Cut into bite-sized pieces)
¼ cup margarine
½ cup chopped green pepper
¼ cup chopped onion
¼ cup flour
2 cups milk
1-7 oz. pkg. cooked shell or elbow macaroni
8 oz. (2 cups) shredded sharp Cheddar cheese
4 Tbsp. sweet pickle relish
2 Tbsp. cider vinegar
1½ tsp. salt

In large saucepan, over medium heat, cook ham pieces until lightly brown and hot. Remove from pan—set aside—add margarine to saucepan and cook green pepper and onion until tender. Stir in flour. Slowly add milk, stirring constantly until sauce thickens. Blend in cooked macaroni, cheese, relish, vinegar, salt and ham pieces. Continue cooking until cheese is melted and macaroni is heated through.

Serves 6-8

HAM STUFFED AVOCADOS

½ cup mayonnaise or salad dressing
2 tablespoons catsup or chili sauce
1 tablespoon vinegar
⅛ teaspoon garlic salt
1½ cups diced WILSON® Ham
½ cup thinly sliced celery
¼ cup chopped green pepper
1 hard cooked egg, chopped
2 avocados

To make dressing, combine mayonnaise, catsup, vinegar and garlic salt. In another bowl, combine ham, celery, green pepper and egg. Stir in 2 tablespoons of the dressing. Chill at least 1 hour. Cut avocados in half and remove pit. Spoon about ½ cup ham mixture into each cavity. Serve remaining dressing with the avocados.

Makes 4 servings

TRADE WINDS SALAD

1 (7-ounce) package *or* 2 cups uncooked
 CREAMETTES® Elbow Macaroni, cooked as
 package directs, rinsed and drained
1 tablespoon margarine or butter
2 tablespoons brown sugar
1 (12-ounce) can luncheon meat, cubed
1 (15½-ounce) can pineapple chunks, drained,
 reserving 2 tablespoons liquid
1 cup (4 ounces) cubed process American cheese
½ cup chopped green pepper, optional
½ cup mayonnaise or salad dressing
1 (8-ounce) container sour cream *or* pineapple yogurt
½ teaspoon salt
Lettuce leaves

In large skillet, melt margarine with brown sugar; add luncheon
meat. Cook and stir until golden brown. In large bowl, combine
cooked macaroni, luncheon meat, pineapple, cheese and green
pepper. Stir together mayonnaise, sour cream, reserved pineapple
liquid and salt. Add to macaroni mixture; mix well. Chill thoroughly. Serve on lettuce garnished as desired. Refrigerate leftovers. *Makes 8 servings*

CELEBRATION SALAD

Cooked asparagus spears
Bottled Italian dressing
8 ounces (2 cups) **MUELLER'S® Elbow Macaroni**
¾ cup mayonnaise
2 tablespoons ketchup
½ teaspoon prepared horseradish
¼ teaspoon dry mustard
2 tablespoons sliced scallions
2 cups slivered cooked ham
1 cup sliced celery
Watercress
Cherry tomatoes

Marinate asparagus in Italian dressing over night, or at least 3 to 4
hours. Cook macaroni as directed on package; drain. Rinse with
cold water; drain again. In bowl blend mayonnaise, ketchup,
horseradish, mustard and scallions; toss in macaroni, ham and
celery. To serve, arrange asparagus spears on platter; top with
macaroni salad. Garnish with watercress and cherry tomatoes.
6 servings

CHUNK HAM POTATO SALAD

2 medium potatoes, cooked and sliced
2 Tbsp. Italian salad dressing
1 Tbsp. snipped parsley
1 can **HORMEL Chunk Ham**, flaked with fork
3 cups salad greens (lettuce, spinach, romaine, endive,
 etc.) torn into bite-size pieces
3 hard-cooked eggs, quartered
¾ cup Swiss cheese strips
½ cup sliced pitted ripe olives
¼ cup chopped green onion
½ cup Italian salad dressing

In salad bowl, sprinkle potatoes with 2 tablespoons salad dressing
and parsley. Marinate, covered, in refrigerator for several hours or
overnight. Layer remaining ingredients except Italian dressing.
Just before serving, pour ½ cup Italian dressing over salad and toss
lightly. *Makes 4 servings*

TACO SALAD

1 pound lean ground beef
1 envelope taco sauce mix
¾ cup water
1 head lettuce, chopped
1 bunch green onions, chopped
1 tomato, cut in wedges
2 cups sliced ripe olives
¼ pound shredded sharp Cheddar cheese
HENRI'S Beefsteak French Dressing
1 (4-ounce) can chopped green chilies
1 (8-ounce) package taco-flavored corn chips

1. Brown lean ground beef. Drain off excess fat. Stir in taco
seasoning mix and water. Simmer uncovered 10-15 minutes.
2. In salad bowl, layer lettuce, green onions, tomato, and ripe
olives.
3. Top with meat mixture, and shredded cheese.
4. Add chopped chilies to **HENRI'S Beefsteak French Dressing**. Serve salad with corn chips and top with **HENRI'S Beefsteak French Dressing**. *Serves 4-6*

MICROWAVE TACO SALAD

Sauce:
1 pound ground beef
1 cup chopped onion
1 pound processed cheese food (**VELVEETA**-type),
 cubed
½ to 1 can (4 ounces) chopped green chilies
1 tomato, chopped

Salad Ingredients, choose several and add to lettuce:
Ripe olives, sliced
Green pepper, chopped
Green or red onion, chopped or in rings
Avocado, chopped
Kidney beans, drained
Tomato, chopped

1 medium head lettuce, torn in bite-size pieces
1 bag (7 to 8 ounces) corn chips

SAUCE:
Crumble ground beef in 2-quart casserole dish. Add onion and
cover. Microwave on High (full power) for 4 to 5 minutes, stirring
once; drain. Add cubed cheese and microwave on High, covered,
3 to 4 minutes or until melted. Stir in chilies and tomato and cook
one minute.

SALAD:
Combine lettuce and your choice of salad vegetables. Place on
individual serving plates. Top with slightly crushed corn chips.
Top with hot beef/cheese mixture.
Makes 4 main dish servings

VARIATION:
Prepare sauce as directed and serve with corn chips as a hot dip.

Favorite recipe from the **Iowa Beef Industry Council**

AUNT NELLIE'S® TACO SALAD

1 pound ground beef
1 can (15½-ounces) **AUNT NELLIE'S® Sloppy Joe Sandwich Sauce**
⅛ cup (or to taste) diced green chilies
¼ teaspoon each: ground cumin, salt
3 cups shredded lettuce
2 small tomatoes, sliced in thin wedges
¾ cup sour cream
2 tablespoons sliced green onion
Tortilla chips

In large skillet, brown beef; drain. Stir in sandwich sauce, chilies, cumin and salt. Simmer, uncovered, 10 minutes. Stir often. For each salad, arrange tortilla chips on plate. Top with lettuce, tomato wedges, meat sauce, sour cream and onion.   *6 servings*

SOUTHWESTERN SALAD BOWL

½ head lettuce shredded
1 pound ground beef
½ teaspoon salt
1 medium onion, chopped
1 15-ounce can kidney beans, drained
1 cup grated American cheese
2 medium tomatoes, cut in wedges
½ cup ripe olives
2 cups **DORITOS® Brand Taco Flavor Tortilla Chips**
Tomato Sauce*

Sauté beef, salt and onion in skillet. Add drained beans; heat through. In a large salad bowl, layer in order: lettuce, **DORITOS® Brand Taco Flavor Tortilla Chips**, beef and bean mixture, cheese and Tomato Sauce*. Repeat. Garnish with tomato wedges, ripe olives, cheese and whole **DORITOS® Brand Taco Flavor Tortilla Chips**.   *Makes 6 servings*

*TOMATO SAUCE

1 8-ounce can tomato sauce
½ medium onion, chopped fine
½ medium tomato, cut into small pieces
¼ teaspoon chili powder

Mix together and simmer for 10 minutes.

MEXICAN-STYLE TACO SALAD

4 cups coarsely chopped iceberg lettuce
1 pint cherry tomatoes, halved
½ cup pimiento-stuffed green olives, sliced
1 large green pepper, cored and diced (about 1 cup)
1½ cups coarsely shredded Cheddar cheese
1 pound ground beef round
¾ cup chopped onion
1 can (20 ounces) red kidney beans, drained
2 tablespoons red wine vinegar
2 teaspoons ground cumin seed
2 teaspoons chili powder
½ teaspoon salt
¼ teaspoon pepper
1½ cups **PEPPERIDGE FARM® Cheddar-Romano** or **Sour Cream and Chive Croutons**
1½ cups plain yogurt or sour cream

Arrange lettuce, tomatoes, olives, pepper and cheese on a large platter. Chill up to 12 hours. Heat a large skillet over moderately high heat. Add beef and onion and cook, stirring frequently, until beef is browned and onion is soft. Add beans, vinegar, cumin, chili, salt and pepper. Cook 3 to 4 minutes longer, stirring constantly, until most moisture has evaporated. Cover loosely and let stand 30 minutes. *Just before serving*, spoon meat mixture on top of lettuce mixture; sprinkle with croutons and serve with yogurt or sour cream.   *Makes 6 main-dish servings*

BETTY CROCKER® TACO SALAD

1 pound ground beef
1 package **BETTY CROCKER® HAMBURGER HELPER® Mix for Cheeseburger Macaroni**
3⅓ cups hot water
2 to 3 teaspoons chili powder
1 large clove garlic, crushed
Dash of cayenne pepper, if desired
6 cups shredded lettuce
1 medium green pepper, chopped (about 1 cup)
2 medium tomatoes, chopped (about 1½ cups)
⅓ cup sliced green onions (with tops)
¼ cup sliced ripe olives

Cook and stir ground beef in 10-inch skillet until brown; drain. Stir in Macaroni, Sauce Mix, water, chili powder, garlic and cayenne pepper. Heat to boiling, stirring constantly; reduce heat. Cover and simmer, stirring occasionally, 15 minutes. Uncover and cook 5 minutes longer.

Place lettuce, green pepper, tomatoes, onions and olives in large bowl; toss with ground beef mixture. Serve immediately or, if desired, cover and refrigerate until chilled, at least 4 hours. Serve with tortilla chips and dairy sour cream if desired.
    6 to 8 servings

HIGH ALTITUDE DIRECTIONS (3500 to 6500 feet): Increase hot water to 3½ cups and simmer time to 20 minutes.

ZESTY MEAT 'N POTATO SALAD

1 cup (8 oz.) **BREYERS® Plain Yogurt**
¼ cup mayonnaise
½ teaspoon salt
Dash of pepper
½ teaspoon dry mustard
1 teaspoon prepared horseradish
1 tablespoon lemon juice
3 cups sliced, hot cooked potatoes (about 1 pound)
½ cup thinly sliced scallions
1 cup diced celery
¼ cup finely chopped dill pickle
3 diced hard cooked eggs
2 cups cubed cooked roast beef, ham, or pork

1. Combine yogurt, mayonnaise, salt, pepper, mustard, horseradish, and lemon juice. Pour over hot potatoes. Cool.
2. Add scallions, celery, pickle, eggs, and meat. Chill.
    Makes 6 cups or 5 to 6 servings

CONFETTI EGG SALAD

4 hard-cooked eggs, diced
¼ cup mayonnaise
2 tablespoons diced green pepper
2 tablespoons diced pimiento
2 teaspoons **LEA & PERRINS Worcestershire Sauce**

Combine all ingredients. Chill.   *2 servings*

TEXAS BEEF SALAD

One 12-ounce **RATH®** **Breakfast Beef**, cut into small
   pieces and browned
1 head lettuce, chopped
1 medium onion, minced
4-5 tomatoes, diced
1 can pinto beans, rinsed and drained
1 cup Cheddar cheese, grated
¼ cup catsup
⅛ teaspoon chili powder
¼ teaspoon oregano

Dressing:
½ cup hot or mild taco sauce
½ cup mayonnaise

1 bag taco-flavored tortilla chips, crushed.

Combine first 9 ingredients. Add dressing and mix well. Add
crushed tortilla chips just before serving.

DILLED BEEFEATER'S SALAD

1 quart torn lettuce leaves
¾ pound roast beef strips (about 2 cups)
3 small boiled potatoes, sliced
¼ pound mushrooms, thinly sliced
½ cup sliced celery
6 red or green pepper rings
Beefeater Dressing*
6 dill pickle fans**

Put lettuce in large shallow salad bowl. Arrange roast beef,
potatoes, mushrooms, celery and pepper rings on top of greens.
Before serving, toss with Beefeater Dressing. Serve in individual
salad bowls and add a dill pickle fan.   *Makes 6 servings*

*BEEFEATER DRESSING

Combine and mix well ⅔ cup salad oil, ½ cup sliced dill pickles, ¼
cup dill pickle liquid, 1 tablespoon lemon juice, 1¼ teaspoons salt,
1 teaspoon dry mustard, 1 teaspoon Worcestershire sauce, ½
teaspoon thyme and a few grains pepper.

Dill Pickle Fans: Cut dill pickles into 4 lengthwise slices
without cutting through pickle end. Spread out sections to form
"open fan."

Favorite recipe from **Pickle Packers International**

BACON CHEESE SALAD

3 or 4 hard cooked eggs
6 to 8 slices bacon
1 head lettuce
3 or 4 green onions
1 slice dry toast
1 clove garlic, cut in half
2 cups **SEALTEST®** **Cottage Cheese**
French Dressing to taste

Peel, then chop eggs coarsely. Fry bacon until crisp, drain on
paper and crumble coarsely.
   Tear lettuce into bite-size pieces. Chop green onions. Rub toast
on both sides with a clove of garlic. Cut into small cubes. Place
croutons in the bottom of a salad bowl. Then add lettuce and
sprinkle with onions. Cover and refrigerate until ready to serve.
   To serve, toss lettuce mixture with French Dressing. Spread
cottage cheese on top and sprinkle with crumbled bacon and eggs.
     6 servings

CONTINENTAL EGG SALAD

8 hard-cooked eggs,* chopped
½ cup chopped celery
½ cup shredded carrots
¼ cup mayonnaise or salad dressing
1 tablespoon chopped chives
½ teaspoon seasoned salt
6 tomatoes
Shredded carrots, optional
Chopped chives, optional

Combine eggs, celery, carrots, mayonnaise, chives and seasoned
salt; mix until blended. Cut tomatoes in 6 sections almost to stem
end; fill each with approximately ⅓ cup egg salad. Garnish with
carrots and chives, if desired.   *Makes 6 servings*

*HARD-COOKED EGGS

Cover EGGS in pan with enough WATER to come at least 1 inch
above eggs. Cover; bring rapidly just to boiling. Turn off heat; if
necessary remove pan from unit to prevent further boiling. Cover;
let stand in hot water 15 minutes for large eggs—adjust time up or
down accordingly for other sizes. Cool eggs immediately and
thoroughly in cold water—shells are easier to remove and dark
surface is prevented on yolks. To remove shell: Crackle shell by
tapping gently all over. Roll egg between hands to loosen shell;
then peel, starting at large end. Holding egg under running cold
water or dipping in bowl of water helps to ease off shell.

Favorite recipe from the **American Egg Board**

EGG SALAD TO YOUR TASTE

6 eggs, hard-cooked, peeled and finely diced
½ cup small curd cottage cheese, drained
¼ cup **HENRI'S TAS-TEE®** **Dressing, HENRI'S**
   Chopped Chive Dressing, or HENRI'S Creamy
   Dill Dressing
2 tablespoons finely chopped celery
1½ teaspoons yellow prepared mustard
½ teaspoon salt
2 tablespoons chopped dill pickle or dill relish
   (optional)

1. Combine all ingredients and chill.
2. Serve stuffed in a tomato, or on a lettuce leaf, or in an open-
face sandwich.   *Makes 2 cups filling*

WISH-BONE® PASTA PRIMAVERA SALAD

½ pound rotelle macaroni*
1 cup (8 oz.) **WISH-BONE®** **Sour Cream & Italian**
   Herbs Dressing
¼ cup milk
2 tomatoes, coarsely chopped
1 cup sliced mushrooms
½ cup pitted ripe olives
1 green or red pepper, cut into thin strips

Cook macaroni according to package directions; drain and rinse
with cold water until completely cool. In large bowl, blend sour
cream and Italian herbs dressing with milk; stir in tomatoes,
mushrooms, olives and green pepper. Add macaroni and toss well;
chill.   *Makes about 4 servings*

Substitution: Use ½ pound ziti or shell macaroni.

MAMA MIA MACARONI SALAD

2 cups salad macaroni, uncooked (4 cups cooked)
1 can (3 oz.) **BinB® Sliced Mushrooms**, undrained
1 package (10 oz.) frozen Italian green beans, cooked
2 tablespoons vegetable oil
2 tablespoons wine vinegar
½ teaspoon salt
¼ teaspoon each basil, oregano, celery seed
⅛ teaspoon pepper
Sliced pepperoni (4 oz.), cut in small pieces
¼ cup mayonnaise

Cook macaroni according to package directions. Drain. Cook green beans until tender-crisp and drain. Combine mushrooms including buttery broth, oil, vinegar, salt, basil, oregano, celery seed and pepper. Toss lightly with macaroni, pepperoni, and beans. Chill well. Just before serving, toss with mayonnaise.

Serves 4 to 5

MACARONI MEDLEY

2 cups uncooked elbow macaroni
1 medium cucumber, peeled, chopped
½ cup chopped onion
2 tablespoons chopped parsley
2 tablespoons chopped pimiento
1½ cups **HEINZ Apple Cider Vinegar**
¾ cup granulated sugar
1 tablespoon salad oil
1 teaspoon **HEINZ Mild Mustard**
¾ teaspoon salt
½ teaspoon pepper
½ teaspoon garlic powder

Cook macaroni following package directions. Drain; rinse in cold water; drain again. In large bowl, combine cooked macaroni, cucumber and next 3 ingredients. In large jar, combine vinegar and remaining ingredients; cover; shake well to blend. Pour over macaroni mixture; toss. Cover; refrigerate overnight.

Makes 6-8 servings (about 6½ cups)

NOTE: Macaroni will keep about a week when stored tightly covered in the refrigerator.

GREEK ROTINI SALAD

3 cups **SAN GIORGIO® Rotini**, uncooked
2 tablespoons lemon juice
½ cup olive oil or vegetable oil
½ teaspoon salt
¼ teaspoon pepper
¼ teaspoon dried oregano
1 clove garlic, crushed
2 tomatoes, cut into wedges
1 cucumber, peeled and thinly sliced
1 cup thinly sliced green pepper strips
12 black olives or Greek olives
1½ cups (6 ounces) crumbled Feta cheese
8 red radishes, thinly sliced
¼ cup (about 4) green onions, sliced
2 tablespoons chopped parsley

Cook Rotini according to package directions; drain well. Cool. (Rinse with cold water to cool quickly; drain well.)
  Combine lemon juice, oil, salt, pepper, oregano and crushed garlic in screw top jar or small bowl. Shake well or whip with wire whisk until blended and of a thick and creamy consistency. Chill.

(Continued)

Combine cooled Rotini, tomato wedges, cucumbers, green peppers, olives, Feta cheese, radishes, green onions and parsley in large bowl. Pour dressing over salad and toss gently to coat pasta and vegetables evenly. Serve immediately.   *6 to 8 servings*

MACARONI-CHEDDAR SALAD

1 cup elbow macaroni, uncooked
1 cup cubed Cheddar cheese
½ cup chopped celery
¼ cup chopped green pepper
2 tablespoons chopped onion
2 tablespoons chopped pimiento
¾ cup mayonnaise
⅓ cup sweet pickle relish
1 tablespoon vinegar
1 teaspoon mustard
½ teaspoon dill weed
¼ teaspoon salt
¾ cup **SALAD CRISPINS®, AMERICAN STYLE**

Cook macaroni according to package directions; rinse, drain and cool. Combine mayonnaise, pickle relish, vinegar, mustard, dill weed and salt. Toss together macaroni, cheese, celery, green pepper, onion and pimiento. Top with mayonnaise mixture and toss to coat macaroni. Chill several hours. Top with **SALAD CRISPINS®** before serving.   *Makes 6 servings*

SUMMER MACARONI SALAD

2 cups (8-ounces) **SKINNER® Elbow Macaroni**, uncooked
1 cup mayonnaise or salad dressing
½ cup finely chopped celery
⅓ cup finely chopped carrot
1 hard-cooked egg, chopped
¼ cup minced onion
2 tablespoons sweet pickle relish
¾ teaspoon dry mustard
¼ teaspoon salt
⅛ teaspoon pepper
Dash paprika

Cook Elbow Macaroni according to package directions; drain well. Cool. (Rinse Elbow Macaroni with cold water to cool quickly; drain well.) Combine cooled Elbow Macaroni with remaining ingredients and toss lightly. Chill.   *4 to 6 servings*

SEAFOOD SALAD WITH CRAB LOUIS DRESSING

3 quarts water
3 teaspoons salt
1 tablespoon oil
2½ cups **AMERICAN BEAUTY® SHEL-RONI®**
6-oz. pkg. frozen cooked crab, thawed and drained
10-oz. pkg. frozen cooked shrimp, thawed and drained
½ cup sliced celery
½ cup quartered ripe olives
½ cup chopped green pepper
¾ cup chili sauce
½ cup mayonnaise
5 tomatoes, cut in sixths
Lettuce leaves

Boil water in large deep pot with salt and oil (to prevent boiling over). Add **SHEL-RONI®**; stir to separate. Cook uncovered after water returns to a full rolling boil for 10 to 11 minutes. Stir occasionally. Drain and rinse under cold water.

In large bowl, combine cooked **SHEL-RONI®**, crab, shrimp, celery, olives and green pepper; cover and refrigerate for at least 1 hour. In small bowl, combine chili sauce and mayonnaise. Cover and refrigerate for at least 1 hour.

Line individual salad bowls with lettuce leaves. Place 1 cup of salad in each bowl. Garnish each salad with 3 tomato wedges and serve with dressing.   *10 servings*

HIGH ALTITUDE—Above 3500 Feet: Cooking times may need to be increased slightly for **SHEL-RONI®**; no additional changes.

NUTRITION INFORMATION PER SERVING
SERVING SIZE: 1/10 of recipe

		Percent U.S. RDA	
Calories	294	Per Serving	
Protein	15g	Protein	23
Carbohydrate	30g	Vitamin A	21
Fat	13g	Vitamin C	41
Sodium	663mg	Thiamine	14
Potassium	359mg	Riboflavin	8
		Niacin	13
		Calcium	7
		Iron	15

AVOCADO ITALIANO

1 package (7-ounces) **CREAMETTES®** Elbow
  Macaroni (2 cups uncooked)
1/3 cup Italian salad dressing
1½ tsp. lemon juice
1½ tsp. salt
¼ tsp. pepper
¼ cup each sliced green onions and radishes
¼ cup each diced green pepper and carrots
¼ cup each coarsely chopped black olives and celery
2 California Avocados, peeled and pitted (1½ avocados
  cut in chunks; ½ avocado sliced into crescents)

Cook **CREAMETTES® Macaroni** according to package directions; drain and chill in cold water for 5 minutes. Drain cooled macaroni; mix with Italian salad dressing, lemon juice, salt and pepper. Stir in onions, radishes, green pepper, carrots, black olives, and celery. Cover and refrigerate at least 2 hours. Carefully mix in avocado chunks. Gently toss salad. Serve on a bed of lettuce topped with avocado crescents.

This recipe from **CREAMETTES®** and **California Avocado Commission.**

CURRY MACARONI SALAD

1 package (8 oz.) macaroni (2 cups uncooked)
1 tablespoon butter or margarine
1½ teaspoons curry powder
1 cup finely chopped onion
1 cup thinly sliced celery
¼ cup raisins
½ cup dairy sour cream
¼ cup mayonnaise
¼ cup **KIKKOMAN Soy Sauce**
1 tablespoon lemon juice

Prepare macaroni according to package directions for salad use; drain and turn into medium-size bowl. Melt butter in small pan. Stir in curry and onion; cook and stir over high heat 1 minute. Combine onion mixture with macaroni, celery and raisins. Blend together sour cream, mayonnaise, soy sauce and lemon juice; add to macaroni mixture and toss to combine. Cover and chill at least 2 hours to allow flavors to blend. Just before serving, stir thoroughly.   *Makes 6 to 8 servings*

Vegetable

MAJESTIC LAYERED SALAD

1 quart torn spinach
2 cups mushroom slices
1½ cups red onion rings
2 (10-ounce) packages frozen peas, cooked, drained
1 cup mayonnaise
½ teaspoon sugar
½ teaspoon curry powder
2 crisply cooked bacon slices, crumbled

In a 2½-quart salad bowl, layer spinach, mushrooms, onions, and peas. Combine mayonnaise, sugar and curry powder. Spread over salad to seal. Cover; refrigerate overnight. Top with bacon before serving.   *Serves 8*

Favorite recipe from **The Association for Dressings and Sauces**

MARINATED VEGETABLE SALAD

1/3 cup **WISH-BONE® HERB CLASSICS™** Herbal
  Italian Dressing
Suggested Fresh Vegetables*

In large bowl, combine classic herbal Italian dressing with Suggested Fresh Vegetables. Cover and marinate in refrigerator, turning occasionally, 4 hours or overnight.
                    Makes about 1 quart salad

*Suggested Fresh Vegetables—Use any combination of the following, uncooked, to equal 1 quart: sliced mushrooms, carrots, cucumbers or celery; tomato wedges; cauliflowerets or broccoli flowerets.

GREEK SALAD

1 head lettuce
2 medium tomatoes
1 onion, sliced
1 chopped green pepper
1 cucumber, sliced
½ cup **POMPEIAN Olive Oil**
¼ cup vinegar
Fillets of anchovies or herring

Section lettuce. Add quartered tomatoes, onion, pepper, cucumber. Salt, pepper to taste; mix well. Add **POMPEIAN Olive Oil** and vinegar; toss lightly. Garnish with anchovies or herring bits.
                    Serves 6

DAD'S FAVORITE SALAD

1 large head romaine lettuce
1 can (15¼ ounces) red kidney beans, drained
1 large cucumber, pared and cubed
1 small carrot, pared and shredded
1 bottle (8 ounces) chunky blue cheese dressing
2 tablespoons dry sherry
¼ teaspoon **TABASCO® Pepper Sauce**

Wash romaine, dry, and tear into bite-size pieces, removing coarse ribs. In a large bowl combine romaine, kidney beans, cucumber, and carrot. Mix blue cheese dressing, sherry and **TABASCO®** in small bowl; serve with salad.   *Yield: 6 to 8 servings*

SEVEN LAYER SALAD

1 large head lettuce
½ cup chopped green pepper
¼ cup sliced green onion
2 cups sliced celery
1 (10-oz.) package frozen green peas
2 cups mayonnaise
2 tablespoons sugar
1 (4-oz.) package **SARGENTO Fancy Shred Cheddar Cheese**
8 slices crumbled, crisp-cooked bacon

Break lettuce into large bowl. Add green pepper, onion, and celery in layers. Cook frozen peas according to package directions. Drain. Add peas as next layer. Cover peas with mayonnaise and sprinkle with sugar. Top with shredded cheese and bacon. Chill 8-12 hours. *Serves 8*

Note: Before preparation: all ingredients must be dry

WESTERN SALAD BOWL

½ lb. **WILSON® Bacon**
1 head romaine or iceberg lettuce
2 tomatoes, cut in wedges
1 cup shredded Cheddar cheese
3 green onions, sliced
¼ cup coarsely chopped ripe olives
Avocado Dressing*

Cook bacon until crisp. Drain and crumble. Remove outside leaves from lettuce and use to line a large shallow salad bowl. Chop remaining lettuce. Place on lettuce leaves. Arrange tomato wedges near edge of lettuce. Sprinkle cheese in a circle just inside the tomatoes. Follow with a circle of bacon, one of green onion and one of ripe olives. Leave about a 4″ space in the center. Chill until serving time. Spoon Avocado Dressing into center. If desired, sprinkle with bacon and green onion.

Makes 6 to 8 servings

*AVOCADO DRESSING

Cut 1 large ripe avocado in half. Remove pit and peel. Mash until smooth. Stir in 1 tablespoon lemon juice, ½ cup dairy sour cream, ¼ teaspoon garlic salt, ¼ teaspoon salt, ⅛ teaspoon pepper and a dash ground red (cayenne) pepper. Refrigerate.

SIZZLEAN® 'N VEGETABLE SALAD

7 to 8 slices **SWIFT SIZZLEAN®**, cut into ½ inch pieces
10 ounce package frozen mixed vegetables, prepared according to packaged directions
2 cups torn lettuce
½ cup chopped celery
3 green onions, sliced
1½ tablespoons vinegar
2 hard-cooked eggs, sieved

Panfry **SIZZLEAN®** until crisp. Remove with slotted spoon and drain on paper towel. Combine **SIZZLEAN®**, mixed vegetables, lettuce, celery and onion in large bowl. Add vinegar to **SIZZLEAN®** drippings in skillet. Heat just until flavors are blended, about 4 to 5 minutes. Pour over vegetables and toss lightly. Garnish with sieved eggs. *Yield: 5 cups, 4 to 5 servings*

VEGETABLE PEPPERONI SALAD

1 package (16 ounces) **Frozen STOKELY'S® Vegetables Milano®**
1 medium-size head lettuce, torn
2 tomatoes, cut in wedges (optional)
4 ounces mozzarella cheese, cubed
2 hard-cooked eggs, diced
½ cup thinly sliced pepperoni
¼ cup sliced scallion (green onion)
2 Tablespoons sliced black olives
½ cup Italian dressing
Salt and pepper to taste
1 jar (4 ounces) **STOKELY'S FINEST® Sliced Pimientos**, drained

Cook frozen vegetables according to package directions, drain, and cool. In a large salad bowl, combine all ingredients except dressing, salt, pepper, and pimientos. Toss mixture lightly with dressing, season to taste, and garnish with pimientos. *8 servings*

SUMMER SALAD SUPREME

2 cups chopped tomato
1 cup thick sliced cucumber
1 can (3 oz.) **BinB® Sliced Mushrooms**, undrained
3 tablespoons vegetable oil
3 tablespoons wine or cider vinegar
1 clove garlic, minced
1 teaspoon salt
Dash pepper
Lettuce
3 tablespoons blue cheese, crumbled (optional)

Place tomato, cucumber and mushrooms, including buttery broth in bowl. Combine remaining ingredients except cheese and lettuce and pour over vegetables. Chill several hours. To serve, sprinkle with cheese and place on lettuce.

Makes 3¼ cups or 4 to 6 servings

CAESAR SALAD

12 cups torn romaine lettuce leaves (about 1½ pounds)
¼ cup olive oil
2 tablespoons lemon juice (about 1 medium lemon)
1 medium garlic clove
½ teaspoon **MORTON® Table Salt**
¼ teaspoon dry mustard
⅛ teaspoon coarse black pepper
1 cup unseasoned croutons
¼ cup grated Parmesan cheese
1 egg, beaten
1 can (2 ounces) anchovy fillets, rolled

Early in Day: Place lettuce in large salad bowl; cover with wet paper towels and refrigerate. Combine oil, lemon juice, garlic, table salt, mustard, and pepper. Cover and let stand until serving time.

Just Before Serving: Remove garlic clove. Stir dressing well. Add dressing to salad; toss lightly. Add croutons and cheese; toss. Add egg; toss well. Garnish with rolled anchovy fillets. Serve immediately. *Makes 8 servings*

FRIENDLY CITY SALAD

⅔ cup salad oil
⅓ cup **HEINZ Wine Vinegar**
2 teaspoons dry mint leaves
½ teaspoon salt
⅛ teaspoon pepper
8 cups torn salad greens, chilled
10 cherry tomatoes, halved
1 cup cubed brick cheese
½ cup sliced pitted ripe olives
¼ cup chopped onion

Combine first 5 ingredients in jar. Cover; shake vigorously. Chill to blend flavors. Shake again before tossing with salad greens and remaining ingredients.   *Makes 8 servings (about 8 cups)*

LOW CALORIE LITE RYE CAESAR SALAD

6 **WASA®** Lite Rye Crispbread Slices
Garlic powder
2 quarts bite-size assorted greens—romaine,
    watercress, Bibb or Boston lettuce
1 small red onion, cut into rings
1 cucumber, unpeeled and sliced paper thin
½ cup low calorie Italian salad dressing
¼ cup (2-ounces) crumbled blue cheese

Sprinkle **Lite Rye** slices with garlic powder and rub into each slice. Break slices into bite-size pieces. In a large salad bowl, combine greens, onion rings and cucumber slices. Chill. Just before serving, toss salad with salad dressing. Sprinkle top of salad with crumbled blue cheese and pieces of **Lite Rye**.

Serves 6

91 calories per serving

HEALTHY CAESAR SALAD

1 small clove garlic, crushed
Caesar Salad Dressing*
2 heads romaine lettuce, torn into bite-size pieces (about
    3 quarts)
Garlic Croutons**
¼ cup Parmesan cheese

Rub bottom of salad bowl with garlic. Add Caesar Salad Dressing. Add lettuce and Garlic Croutons; toss gently until greens are coated. Add cheese; toss again and serve immediately.
Makes 4 to 6 servings

*CAESAR SALAD DRESSING

Place 1 small clove garlic, crushed in ⅓ cup **MAZOLA® Corn Oil**. Let stand several hours. Remove. In small bowl with whisk beat together garlic corn oil, 2 tablespoons lemon juice, 2 tablespoons water, 1 tablespoon white wine vinegar, 1 egg white, 1 teaspoon Worcestershire sauce, ¼ teaspoon salt and ¼ teaspoon pepper until well blended.   *Makes about ⅔ cup*

**GARLIC CROUTONS

Place 1 small clove garlic, crushed, in ¼ cup **MAZOLA® Corn Oil**. Let stand several hours. Remove. In large skillet heat garlic corn oil over medium heat. Add 4 slices bread, crusts removed and cut into cubes; toss to coat. Place in shallow baking pan. Bake in 400°F oven 10 to 12 minutes or until golden brown.
Makes about 1 cup

CAVIAR VEGETABLE BOWL

2 cucumbers, peeled
2 tomatoes, peeled
2 carrots, pared
¼ cup grated sweet onion and juice
1 pkg. (3 oz.) cream cheese, softened
1 cup sour cream
¼ cup mayonnaise
1 Tbsp. lemon juice
4 Tbsp. (2 oz.) **ROMANOFF® Caviar***
Lettuce leaves

Cut cucumbers in half lengthwise, scoop out seeds. Cut in one-fourth inch thick slices. Halve tomatoes, discard seeds and juice and cut meat into three-fourths inch pieces. Cut carrots into julienne strips. (Food processor may be used.) Stir onion into cream cheese. Blend in sour cream, mayonnaise and lemon juice. Fold in three tablespoons of the caviar and combine with vegetables. Chill. Serve in lettuce-lined bowl garnished with remaining caviar.   *Makes 6 servings*

***ROMANOFF® Black Lumpfish** or **Whitefish** suggested.

CABBAGE SALADA

1 (15½-oz. can) **JOAN OF ARC® Fancy Red Kidney
    Beans**, drained
1 (15-oz. can) **JOAN OF ARC® Garbanzo Beans**,
    drained
½ small head cabbage, cut in 1-inch cubes
¼ cup chopped onion
2 Tbsp. coarsely chopped green pepper
1 clove garlic, minced
1½ tsp. salt
½ tsp. dry mustard
½ tsp. sugar
1 tsp. pepper
5 slices bacon
¼ cup oil
¼ cup vinegar

Place red kidney and garbanzo beans, cabbage, onion and green pepper in large bowl; mix well. Combine oil, vinegar, garlic, salt, dry mustard, sugar and pepper. Pour dressing over bean mixture, tossing lightly to combine. Cover and chill 4 to 6 hours; stir occasionally. Cut bacon into ½- to 1-inch pieces and cook in large frying pan until crisp; remove to absorbent paper. Toss vegetables before serving; garnish with bacon.   *Makes 6 servings*

CHINESE GARDEN SALAD

½ cup vinegar
¼ cup water
¼ cup sugar
4 teaspoons salt
1½ teaspoons monosodium glutamate
¼ teaspoon minced garlic
¼ teaspoon black pepper
2 tablespoons diced red pepper
2 tablespoons finely diced onion
2 cans (1 lb. each) **LA CHOY® Fancy Bean Sprouts**,
    drained
¼ cup vegetable oil

Heat water and vinegar in sauce pan. Stir in sugar, salt, monosodium glutamate and garlic. Pour seasoned mixture over Bean Sprouts, peppers and onions. Stir; let cool. Add vegetable oil, toss lightly and serve. Chill for best results.   *Yield: 6 Servings*

CALIFORNIA SALAD, STROGANOFF

1 head **ICEBERG** Lettuce
1 cup Brussels sprouts
1½ cups cauliflowerets
Marinade*
1 can (1 lb.) sliced beets
Stroganoff dressing**

Core, rinse and thoroughly drain lettuce; chill in disposable plastic bag or crisper. Cook Brussels sprouts and cauliflowerets in boiling salted water just until tender. Drain well and cut vegetables in halves. Toss gently with about ¼ cup Marinade; chill. Drain beets and toss with about 3 tablespoons Marinade; chill. When ready to serve, line individual chilled salad plates with outer leaves of lettuce. Shred remaining lettuce and divide among plates. Drain vegetables. Arrange beets and cauliflower in circle on each plate, with a ring of Brussels sprouts in center. Fill center with Stroganoff Dressing.   *Makes 4 servings*

*MARINADE

Combine ⅓ cup corn oil, 1½ tablespoons white wine vinegar, 1 tablespoon dry sherry, ½ teaspoon seasoned salt, ⅛ teaspoon *each* dry mustard and dill weed, and a generous dash pepper. Shake together well in small covered jar.

**STROGANOFF DRESSING

Stir 1½ tablespoons Marinade and ¼ teaspoon seasoned salt into ½ cup dairy sour cream.

Favorite recipe from the **California Iceberg Lettuce Commission**

SALAD ROUGE

1 can (4 oz.) **ORTEGA Whole (or Sliced) Pimientos**
1½ cups fresh mushrooms, sliced
¾ cup black pitted olives, sliced
½ cup pine nuts (or sliced walnuts)
1 can (4 oz.) tiny shrimp (optional)
1 cup prepared Italian salad dressing
6-8 lettuce leaves (Bibb lettuce is preferred)

Drain and chop pimientos; place in glass dish with mushrooms, olives, nuts and drained shrimp. Pour dressing over vegetables, nuts, and shrimp; stir to coat. Place in refrigerator at least 2-3 hours (8 hours preferred). To serve, remove with slotted spoon to drain excess marinade and place in lettuce cups on salad plates. Garnish with additional strips of pimientos or curly parsley. An unusual salad idea which can be served as an appetizer as well.   *Serves 6-8*

SCANDINAVIAN CUCUMBER SALAD

½ cup **LIPTON®** California Dip*
1 tablespoon vinegar
1 teaspoon sugar
½ teaspoon salt
¼ teaspoon dill weed
2 large cucumbers, thinly sliced

In medium bowl, combine all ingredients; chill.
                    About 4 servings

VARIATION:

Substitute raw cauliflowerets for the cucumbers.

*LIPTON® CALIFORNIA DIP

In small bowl, blend 1 envelope **LIPTON® Onion Soup Mix** with 2 cups (16 oz.) sour cream; chill.

ORIENTAL BROCCOLI AND BEAN SPROUT SALAD

2 lb. fresh broccoli
½ lb. fresh mushrooms, cleaned
1 can (16 oz.) **LA CHOY®** Bean Sprouts, rinsed and drained
⅓ cup cider vinegar
⅓ cup salad oil (not olive oil)
2 teaspoons catsup
1 teaspoon salt
Freshly ground black pepper to taste

Cut broccoli florets from stalks. Pare stalks and cut into ¼-inch slices. Cook broccoli stalks in boiling water 1 minute; rinse under cold water and drain. Cook florets 2 minutes in boiling salted water; rinse with cold water and drain. Combine cooked broccoli with mushrooms and bean sprouts. Blend remaining ingredients, pour over vegetables, mixing well. Marinate 1 hour in refrigerator. Serve on crisp lettuce leaves.   *8 servings*

WHEAT GERM VEGGIE SALAD

1 can (7-8¾ oz.) whole kernel corn, drained
⅓ cup **KRETSCHMER Regular Wheat Germ**
⅓ cup finely sliced green onion
⅓ cup minced parsley
⅓ cup chopped carrots
⅓ cup chopped celery
3 Tbsp. cooking oil
2 Tbsp. lemon juice
½ tsp. basil leaves, crushed
¼ tsp. oregano leaves, crushed
¼ tsp. salt
Salad greens
Sliced cucumber

Combine all ingredients *except* salad greens and cucumber. Mix well. Line salad bowl with greens. Spoon corn mixture into center of greens. Garnish with cucumber.   *Makes 4 servings*

MIDDLE EASTERN YOGURT SALAD

2 medium tomatoes, sliced thin
1 medium cucumber, sliced wafer thin
1 cup plain yogurt
Salt to taste
2 tablespoons **HOLLAND HOUSE®** White Cooking Wine
1 teaspoon white wine vinegar
2 scallions, chopped

Rub cucumbers with salt; rinse and drain. Rinse and drain again after 10 minutes. Mix wine, vinegar and yogurt together in a large bowl. Add tomatoes and cucumbers. Toss lightly. Sprinkle with chopped onion. Chill.   *Serves 2 to 4*

ORIENTAL CUCUMBER SALAD

2 medium-size cucumbers, peeled and seeded
2 teaspoons salt
¼ cup distilled white vinegar
1 tablespoon sugar
1 tablespoon water
1½ teaspoons **KIKKOMAN Soy Sauce**
¼ teaspoon grated fresh ginger root *OR* ⅛ teaspoon ground ginger

Cut cucumbers into thin slices; place in bowl and sprinkle with salt. Let stand at room temperature 1 to 2 hours. Drain and squeeze out excess liquid. Combine vinegar, sugar, water, soy sauce and ginger in serving bowl; add cucumbers and mix well. Chill thoroughly before serving.   *Makes 4 servings*

COOL CORN SALAD

¼ cup commercial sour cream
¼ cup mayonnaise
1 tablespoon prepared mustard
2 teaspoons white vinegar
1 teaspoon sugar
¼ teaspoon salt
⅛ teaspoon pepper
1 can (17 ounces) **STOKELY'S FINEST® Whole Kernel Golden Corn**, drained
1 jar (2 ounces) **STOKELY'S FINEST® Sliced Pimientos**, drained and diced
2 carrots, peeled and grated
½ cup diced onion

In medium-size bowl, make dressing by combining sour cream, mayonnaise, mustard, vinegar, sugar, salt, and pepper. Add remaining ingredients and toss to blend. Cover and refrigerate at least 1 hour.   *4 to 6 servings*

HUNGARIAN CUCUMBERS

2 large cucumbers
1 large onion
Ice water
Salt
¼ cup **POMPEIAN Olive Oil**
¼ cup tarragon vinegar
1 cup sour cream
Dash cayenne
Parsley (garnish)

Peel cucumbers, score with fork, slice thin as possible. Slice onion same way. Place alternate layers in shallow dish, sprinkling each layer with salt. Cover with ice water and chill 2 to 3 hours. Drain, rinse with running water, drain again. Mix **POMPEIAN Olive Oil** and vinegar, pour over vegetables, marinate 2 to 3 hours. Drain. Arrange on platter, alternating cucumber and onion slices. Pour on sour cream. Sprinkle with cayenne. Garnish with parsley.   *Serves 6*

WILTED LETTUCE

4 cups leaf lettuce
3 tablespoons **PURITAN® Oil**
⅓ cup cider vinegar
3 tablespoons bacon bits
2 tablespoons sugar
1 teaspoon salt
¼ teaspoon pepper

Tear lettuce into pieces. Bring remaining ingredients to a boil. Reduce heat and simmer 2 to 3 minutes. Pour hot mixture over lettuce in a bowl and toss to coat evenly.   *4 servings*

VARIATION:

HOT SLAW

Follow above recipe but substitute 4 cups shredded cabbage for lettuce.

CHOPPED EGGPLANT SALAD

1 large eggplant
¾ teaspoon salt
3 tablespoons oil
1 medium onion, diced
2 tablespoons white vinegar
1 to 2 tablespoons sugar
½ tablespoon garlic powder
SUNSHINE® Crackers

Core eggplant, and wrap in aluminum foil. Bake at 350°F. for 45 minutes, or until soft. Cool and peel skin. Chop eggplant, salt, oil, onion, vinegar, sugar, and garlic powder. Refrigerate for one to two hours. Season again if needed. Serve with assortment of **SUNSHINE® Crackers**.   *Yield: 6 servings*

CHEESE-CAPPED ICEBERG

1 package (8 oz) cream cheese, softened
¾ cup **BEST FOODS®/HELLMANN'S® Real Mayonnaise**
½ cup chopped pimiento-stuffed olives
2 tablespoons minced green onion
1 medium head iceberg lettuce
¼ cup catchup
2 teaspoons cider vinegar
¾ teaspoon chili powder
Dash hot pepper sauce

In small bowl with mixer at medium speed beat cream cheese until light and fluffy. Stir in ¼ cup Real Mayonnaise, olives and onion. Remove core from lettuce. Hollow out center leaving 1-inch shell. Fill with cheese mixture. Seal in plastic bag or aluminum foil. Stir together ½ cup Real Mayonnaise and remaining ingredients; cover. Chill lettuce and dressing overnight. Cut lettuce into 6 wedges; serve with dressing.

Makes 6 servings

SPINACH-CHEDDAR TOSS

1 **DARIGOLD Egg**, hard cooked and sliced
½ cup olives, sliced
1 small head lettuce, torn into pieces
2 cups torn spinach leaves
1 cup (4 oz.) **DARIGOLD Red Boy Cheese**, shredded
4 slices bacon, cooked crisp, drained and crumbled
½ cup Light Style Salad Dressing*, heated

Pour heated Light Style Dressing over the ingredients. Toss and serve immediately.   *Makes 6 servings*

*LIGHT STYLE SALAD DRESSING
(Low Calorie)

1 pkg. salad dressing mix (use one that calls for 1 cup mayonnaise and 1 cup buttermilk)
½ pint **DARIGOLD Sour Cream**
3 Tbsp. **DARIGOLD Powdered Buttermilk**
1 cup water

To make a low calorie dressing, substitute **DARIGOLD Sour Cream** and **DARIGOLD Powdered Buttermilk** in a package mix that calls for mayonnaise and fresh buttermilk. Blend all ingredients listed above together.   *Makes 1 pint dressing*

Calories: Approximately 18 calories per tablespoon.

ORIENTAL SPINACH SALAD

Ginger-Soy Dressing*
5 ounces spinach, torn into bite-size pieces
¼ cup sliced water chestnuts
1 green onion (with top), thinly sliced
BAC*Os® Imitation Bacon

Prepare Ginger-Soy Dressing; toss with spinach, water chestnuts and onion. Sprinkle with imitation bacon.   *6 servings*

*GINGER-SOY DRESSING

2 tablespoons vegetable oil
1 tablespoon vinegar
2 teaspoons honey
1 teaspoon soy sauce
¼ teaspoon ground ginger

Shake all ingredients in tightly covered container.

LEMON-ZESTY SPINACH SALAD

1 lb. fresh spinach
1 16-oz can Chinese vegetables without celery, drained and rinsed
⅔ cup salad oil
¼ cup sugar
¼ cup catsup
¼ cup **MINUTE MAID® 100% Pure Lemon Juice**
¼ cup Worcestershire sauce
2 Tbsp. coarsely chopped onion, or 1 Tbsp. instant minced onion
6 slices crisp bacon, crumbled
6 large fresh mushrooms, sliced

Wash spinach thoroughly, drain and tear into bite-size pieces. Combine spinach and Chinese vegetables in a large bowl, cover tightly and chill. Combine next 6 ingredients in an electric blender and blend well; store in refrigerator. At serving time, pour dressing over vegetables, add sliced mushrooms, and sprinkle bacon on top; toss lightly.   *Yield 6-8 servings*

LITE SPINACH SALAD

6 cups spinach leaves
1 can (16 oz.) **DEL MONTE Lite Sliced Peaches**, drained
1 can (15½ oz.) **DEL MONTE Sockeye Red Salmon**
½ cup sliced water chestnuts
6 cherry tomatoes, halved
Gingered Dressing*

Thoroughly clean spinach, drain and tear into bite-size pieces. Combine ingredients and serve with Gingered Dressing.

*GINGERED DRESSING

½ cup oil
2 Tbsp. vinegar
1 Tbsp. lemon juice
¼ tsp. garlic powder
¼ tsp. ground ginger
Dash salt
Dash pepper

Thoroughly blend all ingredients.   *4 servings*

TOMATOES VINAIGRETTE

3 to 4 tomatoes, sliced
1 cup **PURITAN® Oil**
⅓ cup wine vinegar
2 teaspoons oregano
1 teaspoon sugar
1 teaspoon salt
1 teaspoon dried parsley flakes
½ teaspoon pepper
½ teaspoon dry mustard
2 cloves garlic, crushed
6 green onions, minced

Arrange tomato slices in square glass baking dish. Combine remaining ingredients, except green onions, and pour over tomatoes. Cover, chill at least 2 to 3 hours, basting occasionally. Before serving, top with minced green onions.   *6 servings*

TOMATO CHILE FILL-UPS

6 large, firm tomatoes
1 large avocado
1 can (4 oz.) **ORTEGA Diced Green Chiles**
3 tablespoons mayonnaise
1 teaspoon lemon juice
1 tablespoon finely chopped celery
1 tablespoon minced onion
Lettuce

Wash tomatoes and scoop out pulp (reserve pulp). Set tomatoes upside down to drain while you mash and mix avocado with 4 tablespoons of chiles (reserve remaining chiles), 2 tablespoons of the mayonnaise, lemon juice, celery and onion. Fill tomatoes with mayonnaise-vegetable mixture. Set stuffed tomatoes on salad plates lined with lettuce leaves. Mix tomato pulp and reserved chiles with additional mayonnaise for dressing. Serve dressing separately in a bowl.   *Serves 6*

VARIATION:

Add canned baby shrimp to stuffing or use as a garnish ring around base of tomatoes for a change of pace. Create additional variations by using your favorite garnish.

GAZPACHO SALAD

Dressing:
½ cup **REGINA Red Wine Vinegar**
1 cup olive oil
1 can (7 oz.) **ORTEGA Green Chile Salsa**
1 teaspoon oregano
1 teaspoon basil
2 bay leaves
½ teaspoon rosemary
½ teaspoon salt

Salad:
3 medium tomatoes, sliced
1 medium red onion, thinly sliced
1 can (7 oz.) **ORTEGA Whole Green Chiles**, sliced crosswise
1 cucumber, thinly sliced
Bibb lettuce
Croutons
Cooked, crumbled bacon
Freshly grated Jack cheese

Thoroughly combine all dressing ingredients. In large bowl, layer tomatoes, onion, chiles and cucumber. Drizzle with dressing. Cover. Refrigerate 3-4 hours. Drain. Serve on lettuce. Garnish with croutons, bacon and cheese.   *Serves 8*

GAZPACHO GARDEN SALAD

½ cup vegetable oil
⅓ cup **REALEMON**® Lemon Juice From Concentrate
2 cloves garlic, finely chopped
1½ teaspoons salt
¼ teaspoon pepper
1 medium green pepper, seeded and diced
2 medium, firm tomatoes, diced
1 medium cucumber, peeled, seeded and diced
½ cup sliced green onion

In 1-pint jar with tight-fitting lid, combine oil, **REALEMON**®, garlic, salt and pepper; shake well. In narrow 1-quart glass container, layer ½ each of the green pepper, tomato, cucumber and onion; repeat layering with remaining vegetables. Pour dressing over salad. Chill 4 hours to blend flavors.   *Makes 8 servings*

VERY GREEN SALAD

2 packages (10 ounces each) frozen green peas
¼ cup chopped scallions
1 cup sliced celery
1 head Boston lettuce

Cook peas according to package directions, drain, and mix with scallions, celery, and ¼ cup Green Mayonnaise*. Cover and chill until ready to serve. To serve, separate lettuce leaves into cups and place on 6 salad plates. Spoon salad into lettuce cups and serve with remaining mayonnaise.   *6 servings*

*GREEN MAYONNAISE

1 cup water
10 fresh spinach leaves
1 tablespoon chopped chives
¼ cup watercress leaves
¼ cup chopped parsley
1 teaspoon dried leaf tarragon
1 egg
¼ teaspoon dry mustard
½ teaspoon salt
1 tablespoon lemon juice
½ teaspoon **TABASCO**® Pepper Sauce
1 cup salad oil

In medium saucepan combine water, spinach leaves, chives, watercress, parsley and tarragon. Place over medium heat, bring to a boil and boil 3 minutes. Drain well and turn into container of electric blender. Add egg, dry mustard, salt, lemon juice and **TABASCO**®. Cover and process until smooth. Remove cover and while blender is running, very gradually add oil in a thin steady stream or 1 tablespoon at a time, continuing to blend until all oil is absorbed. Chill.   *About 1¼ cups*

Note: To make Green Mayonnaise with commercial mayonnaise, measure 1 cup mayonnaise into small bowl and blend in 1 tablespoon lemon juice, ¼ teaspoon dry mustard, ½ teaspoon **TABASCO**® Pepper Sauce, ¼ cup chopped watercress, ¼ cup chopped parsley, 1 tablespoon chopped chives and ½ teaspoon dried tarragon.

TWIN BEAN SALAD

1 can (16 oz) pinto beans, drained (2 cups)
1 can (15 oz) garbanzo beans, drained (2 cups)
½ cup sliced pitted ripe olives
½ cup chopped green pepper
¼ cup chopped onion
¼ cup chopped green chilies
¼ cup **BEST FOODS**®/**HELLMANN'S**® Real Mayonnaise
2 tablespoons cider vinegar
1 teaspoon sugar
1 teaspoon salt
¼ teaspoon chili powder
⅛ teaspoon garlic powder
⅛ teaspoon pepper

Toss together beans, olives, green pepper, onion and chilies. Stir together Real Mayonnaise, vinegar, sugar, salt, chili powder, garlic powder and pepper. Add to bean mixture tossing until well mixed. Chill 1 hour.   *Makes about 5 cups*

ACAPULCO SALAD

Drain:
    1 can (2¼ oz.) sliced ripe olives
    1 can (8½ oz.) garbanzo beans
    1 can (8¾ oz.) **DEL MONTE Whole Kernel Family Style Corn** (Reserve liquid for other recipe uses)
Using sharp knife, shred:
    ½ head iceberg lettuce
Thinly slice:
    1 bunch radishes
Toss ingredients with:
    Bottled green goddess dressing

Season with garlic salt and pepper to taste. Garnish with shredded Cheddar cheese.

THREE BEAN SALAD

In large bowl, blend ¼ cup **DOMINO**® Liquid Brown Sugar, ½ cup cider vinegar and 1 tsp. salt. Add 1 can (1 pound) drained cut green beans; 1 can (1 pound) drained red kidney beans; 1 package (10 ounces) frozen baby lima beans, cooked and drained; ½ cup chopped onion and ¼ cup chopped green pepper. Toss to mix well. Chill.

TANGY BEAN SALAD

½ cup white vinegar
½ cup sugar
½ cup vegetable oil
½ cup chopped onion
½ cup chopped green pepper
1 can (16 ounces) **STOKELY'S FINEST**® Cut Green Beans, drained
1 can (15½ ounces) **STOKELY'S FINEST**® Cut Wax Beans, drained
1 can (15 ounces) **STOKELY'S FINEST**® Dark Red Kidney Beans, drained
Red onion rings (optional)

Combine vinegar, sugar, oil, onion, and green pepper in large bowl and mix well. Drain all beans and add to dressing. Toss gently and marinate in refrigerator for at least 4 hours or overnight. Serve in bowl lined with lettuce. May be garnished with onion rings.
     10 servings

LIMA GARLIC SALAD

1 package (10 ounces) frozen lima beans, cooked and drained
1½ cups cherry tomatoes, cut in half
1 medium purple onion, sliced and separated into rings
1 medium green pepper, cored, seeded and cut into strips
½ cup sliced black olives
½ cup olive oil
2 tablespoons lemon juice
1 large clove garlic, minced
½ teaspoon salt
¼ teaspoon basil, crushed
1 cup PEPPERIDGE FARM® Cheddar and Romano Croutons
Lettuce leaves
Chopped parsley

In a large bowl, combine vegetables. Blend oil, lemon juice, garlic, salt and basil. Pour over vegetables; toss to blend. Cover and refrigerate at least 2 hours. To serve, spoon over lettuce leaves and sprinkle with croutons. Garnish with parsley.
Makes 4 to 6 servings

DELICATESSEN SALAD

1 can (1 pound) cut green beans, drained
1 can (1 pound) cut yellow beans, drained
1 can (1 pound) green lima beans, drained
1 can (15 to 15½ ounces) garbanzos, drained*
½ cup chopped green pepper
½ cup chopped onion
1 can (4 ounces) pimiento, chopped (½ cup)
½ cup salad oil
½ cup HEINZ Wine or Apple Cider Vinegar
½ cup granulated sugar
1 tablespoon salt
1 teaspoon pepper

Combine first 7 ingredients in large glass bowl. Combine salad oil and remaining ingredients in jar; shake vigorously. Pour dressing over bean mixture; toss well. Cover; marinate overnight in refrigerator, stirring occasionally. Serve as a meat accompaniment, relish or drain well and serve in lettuce cups as a salad.
Makes about 7½ cups
*1 can (15½ to 17 ounces) kidney beans, drained may be substituted.
Note: One package of each (9 ounces) frozen cut green beans, yellow beans, and (10 ounces) green lima beans may be substituted. Cook the frozen beans according to package directions.
Makes about 7½ cups

RED KIDNEY BEAN SALAD

1 cup cubed cheese—American, Cheddar, etc.
⅓ cup chopped green pepper
⅓ cup chopped celery
2 tablespoons chopped onion
2 hard cooked eggs, chopped
1 can (15 oz.) red kidney beans, drained
½ cup MILNOT®
1½ tablespoons lemon juice or vinegar
½ teaspoon salt
Dash of pepper
4 tablespoons chili sauce
Salad greens

Place cheese, green pepper, celery, onion, eggs, and beans in bowl. Combine MILNOT®, lemon juice, salt, pepper, and chili sauce. Blend until smooth. Pour over vegetables and toss until well coated. Line bowl with salad greens, heap salad on top. Garnish with onion and green pepper rings.
Yield: approximately 6 servings

LEA & PERRINS KIDNEY BEAN SALAD

1 can (15 oz.) kidney beans, drained
½ cup bottled French dressing
¼ cup minced onion
1½ tablespoons LEA & PERRINS Worcestershire Sauce

Combine all ingredients. Toss, cover, and chill.
3 to 4 servings

BASIC POTATO SALAD

¾ cup finely chopped onion
¼ cup lemon juice
1 tablespoon salt
½ teaspoon dry mustard
¼ teaspoon pepper
4 pounds potatoes, boiled in jackets, peeled and cubed
1½ cups chopped celery
½ cup chopped green pepper
2 cups BEST FOODS®/HELLMANN'S® Real Mayonnaise

Stir together onion, lemon juice, salt, mustard and pepper. Pour over hot potatoes tossing to coat evenly. Cover and refrigerate about 1 hour. Stir in celery, green pepper and Real Mayonnaise. Chill.
Makes 10 (1 cup) servings

VARIATIONS:

HAM AND CHEESE POTATO SALAD

Follow directions for Basic Potato Salad adding 2 cups cooked, cubed ham and 1 cup cubed Cheddar cheese.
Makes 13 (1 cup) servings

HOT POTATO SALAD

Follow directions for Basic Potato Salad adding 2 pounds cooked kielbasy, cut in ¼-inch slices. Place in 4-quart casserole. Sprinkle top with ½ cup fine dry breadcrumbs and ½ cup grated Cheddar cheese. Bake in 350°F oven 15 minutes or until heated.
Makes 14 (1 cup) servings

APPLE-CHEESE POTATO SALAD

Follow directions for Basic Potato Salad adding 4 cups diced apples, ¼ cup crumbled bleu cheese, 2 tablespoons lemon juice and 1 teaspoon celery seed.   *Makes 14 (1 cup) servings*

CONFETTI POTATO SALAD

Follow directions for Basic Potato Salad adding 1 cup each chopped zucchini, cucumber, radish and carrot.
Makes 14 (1 cup) servings

HERB POTATO SALAD

Follow directions for Basic Potato Salad adding ¼ cup chopped parsley, ½ teaspoon dried chervil and ½ teaspoon dried tarragon leaves to marinade. Substitute 1 cup dairy sour cream for 1 cup of the Real Mayonnaise.   *Makes 10 (1 cup) servings*

CANYON STYLE POTATO SALAD

5 cups diced potatoes, cooked in chicken broth
½ cup sliced celery
1 cup prepared **HIDDEN VALLEY ORIGINAL RANCH® Salad Dressing**
1 tablespoon prepared mustard
2 tablespoons sweet pickle relish, drained
2 tablespoons sliced green onion
1 teaspoon salt
¼ teaspoon pepper
¼ cup sliced radishes

In a bowl, combine potatoes and celery. Mix together Salad Dressing, mustard, pickle relish, green onion, salt and pepper. Pour over potatoes and celery; toss gently. Cover and refrigerate. Garnish with radishes or toss in just before serving.

Makes 8 to 10 servings

HARVEST POTATO SALAD

8 medium red potatoes (2½ pounds)
1 pound frankfurters
2 tablespoons vegetable oil
¾ cup chopped onion
½ cup chopped celery
3 tablespoons flour
1 tablespoon sugar
½ teaspoon salt
1 teaspoon dry mustard
⅛ teaspoon pepper
1 cup chicken broth
⅓ cup white vinegar
¼ cup parsley, minced
¾ cup **SALAD CRISPINS®**, Italian Style

Cook potatoes, with skins on, in boiling salted water until tender. Peel and slice the drained potatoes. Cut each slice in half. Brown frankfurters in oil. Remove from skillet. Drain and combine with potatoes. Sauté onion and celery in oil remaining in skillet until soft. Blend in flour, sugar, salt, dry mustard and pepper. Stir until bubbly. Add chicken broth and vinegar. Cook and stir until mixture thickens. Pour over potatoes. Sprinkle with parsley. Toss lightly. Top with **SALAD CRISPINS®**. Serve hot.

Makes 8 Servings

CONTINENTAL POTATO SALAD

1½ pounds (4 cups) peeled, cooked and diced potatoes
1 pound (3 cups) diced, raw zucchini squash
½ pound sliced fresh mushrooms
1 tomato, diced
¼ cup sliced scallions
½ cup olive or salad oil
2 tablespoons **LEA & PERRINS Worcestershire Sauce**
4 teaspoons lemon juice
1¼ teaspoons salt
1 small clove garlic, crushed
¼ teaspoon coarse ground black pepper
¼ teaspoon oregano leaves

In a large salad bowl combine potatoes, squash, mushrooms, tomato and scallions; set aside. Combine oil, **LEA & PERRINS**, lemon juice, salt, garlic, black pepper and oregano; mix well. Pour over vegetable mixture; toss well. Chill thoroughly. Just before serving, sprinkle with pignola nuts, if desired.

Yield: 6 to 8 portions

*May be prepared in advance of serving.

ROQUEFORT POTATO SALAD

Dressing:
⅓ cup olive oil
1 tablespoon tarragon vinegar
2 tablespoons cider vinegar
2 tablespoons minced shallots
1 teaspoon Dijon mustard
1 tablespoon finely minced parsley
Salt and pepper

Salad:
20 small potatoes (about 2 pounds)
1 head leafy lettuce
¼ cup **ROQUEFORT**, crumbled
¼ cup half-and-half or cream
6 slices bacon, cooked and crumbled
2 tablespoons minced fresh or dried chives
½ bunch watercress or parsley

Mix together all dressing ingredients and set aside.

Steam or boil potatoes in their jackets until tender, about 20 to 30 minutes. While still warm, slice potatoes into bowl. Pour ¼ cup of dressing over potatoes and mix gently.

Line large platter with lettuce leaves. Arrange potatoes over lettuce. Add cheese and half-and-half to remainder of dressing and spoon over potatoes. Sprinkle with cooked crumbled bacon and minced chives. Garnish with watercress.

Makes 6 servings

Favorite recipe from **The Potato Board**

HILL COUNTRY POTATO SALAD

6 medium red potatoes, unpeeled
1 teaspoon salt
½ cup diced raw bacon
½ cup diced onion
1½ teaspoons cornstarch or flour
4 teaspoons **IMPERIAL Granulated Sugar**
1 teaspoon salt
¼ teaspoon pepper
¼ cup cider vinegar
½ cup water
¼ cup minced onion
2 tablespoons snipped parsley
1 teaspoon celery seeds
½ cup sliced radishes, optional
Celery leaves

About 1 hour before serving, cook potatoes in their jackets in boiling water with 1 teaspoon salt in covered saucepan until fork tender, about 35 minutes. Peel and dice or partially mash potatoes. In small skillet, fry bacon until crisp. Add diced onion and sauté until tender but not brown. In bowl, mix cornstarch or flour, **IMPERIAL Granulated Sugar**, 1 teaspoon salt and the pepper. Stir in vinegar and water until smooth. Add to bacon; simmer, stirring until thickened. Pour hot dressing over potatoes and add ¼ cup minced onion, parsley, celery seeds and radishes. Serve lightly tossed and garnished with celery leaves.

Serves 4 to 6

Note: Potatoes may be diced or sliced rather than mashed but mashing allows a more even penetration of seasonings.

GREEN 'N GOLD SALAD

1 package **BETTY CROCKER®** Julienne Potatoes
1 package (10 ounces) frozen green peas, rinsed and drained
1 medium stalk celery, sliced (about ½ cup)
1 small onion, chopped (about ¼ cup)
½ cup ½-inch cubes Cheddar cheese
Dash of salt
½ cup mayonnaise or salad dressing
Lettuce leaves

Prepare potatoes as directed on package for Stove-Top Method. Pour into large bowl; cover and refrigerate until chilled. Stir remaining ingredients except mayonnaise and lettuce into potatoes; toss with mayonnaise. Cover and refrigerate at least 2 hours. Serve on lettuce leaves.   *6 servings*

CREAMY HOT SLAW

½ cup butter or margarine
1 medium head cabbage, shredded
2 medium onions, chopped
1 cup (8 oz.) **WISH-BONE®** Sour Cream & Bacon Dressing
1 teaspoon caraway seeds

In large saucepan, melt butter and cook cabbage and onions until tender. Remove from heat; stir in remaining ingredients.
Makes about 6 servings

SOUR CREAM COLE SLAW

1 cup **MEADOW GOLD®** Sour Cream
2 tablespoons sliced green onion
2 tablespoons vinegar
1½ teaspoons salt
¼ teaspoon ground mustard
⅛ teaspoon pepper
1 small head cabbage, shredded (about 7 cups)

Combine first six ingredients, mixing well. In large bowl, gently toss cabbage and sour cream mixture. Cover. Chill 1 to 2 hours.
6 to 8 servings

SWEET AND TART SALAD

3 cups shredded cabbage
1½ cups chopped apple
½ cup Celery Seed Dressing*

Toss together cabbage and apple. Pour on dressing and toss lightly to coat evenly.   *6 servings*

*CELERY SEED DRESSING

½ cup sugar
1 teaspoon dry mustard
1 teaspoon salt
4½ tablespoons cider vinegar
1 teaspoon grated onion
1 cup **CRISCO®** Oil
1 tablespoon celery seed

Mix sugar, mustard, and salt. Blend in 2 tablespoons of the cider vinegar and the grated onion. Gradually beat in **CRISCO®** Oil. Beat until thick and light. Slowly beat in the remaining cider vinegar. Stir in celery seed. Pour into a screw-top jar. Cover tightly and shake vigorously to blend well. Store covered in refrigerator. Shake well before using.   *About 1⅔ cups*

COUNTRY COLE SLAW

3 cups shredded cabbage
2 tablespoons shredded carrot
2 tablespoons diced onion
2 tablespoons diced green pepper
½ cup dairy sour cream
2 tablespoons **JIF®** Peanut Butter
2 teaspoons sugar
1 teaspoon salt
2 teaspoons tarragon vinegar

In a large bowl, combine cabbage, carrot, onion, and green pepper. Mix sour cream, **JIF®**, sugar, salt, and vinegar. Pour over vegetables and toss well. Top with more shredded carrot, if desired.   *Serves 8*

CRISP OVERNIGHT SLAW
(*Low Calorie*)

1½ teaspoons **PILLSBURY SWEET* 10®** or ¼ cup **PILLSBURY SPRINKLE SWEET®**
½ teaspoon celery salt
½ teaspoon garlic salt
2 tablespoons lemon juice
2 tablespoons vinegar
3 cups (½ medium head) shredded cabbage
¼ cup chopped green pepper
1 stalk celery, chopped
3 to 4 green onions, sliced
5 to 6 radishes, sliced

In large bowl, combine sweetener, celery salt, garlic salt, lemon juice and vinegar. Add remaining ingredients except radishes; toss lightly. Cover and chill at least 4 hours. Before serving, add radishes.   *6 servings*

Tip: If desired, chopped cucumber, zucchini or halved cherry tomatoes may be added with cabbage.

NUTRITION INFORMATION PER SERVING

SERVING SIZE: ⅙ of recipe		PERCENT U.S. RDA	
Calories	20	PER SERVING	
Protein	1 g	Protein	*
Carbohydrate	4 g	Vitamin A	*
Fat	1 g	Vitamin C	50
Sodium	295 mg	Thiamine	2
Potassium	160 mg	Riboflavin	*
		Niacin	*
		Calcium	2
		Iron	*

*Contains less than 2% of the U.S. RDA of this nutrient.

MRS. SMITH'S SAVORY SLAW

1 cup plain low-fat yogurt
2 tablespoons mayonnaise
1 teaspoon sugar
½ teaspoon salt
⅛ teaspoon pepper
4 **CAPE GRANNY SMITH Apples**, divided
1 medium zucchini, shredded (2 cups)
2 cups shredded cabbage
1 small onion, chopped (¼ cup)

In a large bowl combine yogurt, mayonnaise, sugar, salt and pepper. Core and shred two apples. Add shredded apples, zucchini, cabbage and onion to dressing; toss gently to coat. Core and slice remaining two apples. Arrange apple slices on a serving plate and top with salad mixture.   *Yield: 4 servings*

TROPICAL COLE SLAW
(Low Calorie)

1 head cabbage, finely shredded
1 cup (½ pint) sour cream
1 cup crushed, fresh pineapple or canned in natural juice
1 tablespoon cider vinegar
1 tablespoon **SWEETLITE**™ **Liquid Fructose**

1. Put the shredded cabbage in a colander and run cold water over it to wash it. Dry thoroughly.
2. Combine all other ingredients in a large bowl and mix thoroughly.
3. Add the washed, thoroughly dried cabbage to the mixture in the bowl and mix it thoroughly again.   *Makes 8 servings*

Each serving contains approximately:
   ½ fruit exchange
   1 fat exchange
   65 calories
   32 mg cholesterol

TANGY TANGERINE COLESLAW
Dressing:
¼ cup salad oil
Grated peel of ½ **SUNKIST®** Tangerine
Juice of 1 **SUNKIST®** **Tangerine** (¼ cup)
Juice of ½ **SUNKIST®** **Lemon**
2 Tbsp. honey
1 Tbsp. toasted sesame seed (optional)

1 small head cabbage, cut in long thin shreds (about 5 cups)
2 to 3 **SUNKIST®** **Tangerines**, peeled, segmented, cut in half, seeded
½ cup raisins
¼ cup chopped nuts

DRESSING:
In jar with lid, combine oil, tangerine peel and juice, lemon juice, honey and sesame seed; shake well.

In large bowl, combine cabbage, tangerines, raisins and salad dressing; chill. To serve, add chopped nuts; toss gently.
Makes 6 servings (about 7 cups)

RICE SALAD INDIENNE

3 cups cold cooked long grain rice
1 cup fresh bean sprouts
½ cup thinly sliced green onion
½ cup **BLUE DIAMOND®** **Blanched Slivered Almonds**, toasted*
Curry Dressing (recipe follows)

Combine rice, bean sprouts, onion and almonds; add Curry Dressing and toss to mix well.   *Makes 4 to 6 servings*

*To Toast Almonds: Spread in single layer in shallow pan. Bake, stirring often in 300°F. oven 15 minutes, or until they begin to turn color. *Don't wait for them to become golden brown.* After removing the almonds from the oven, their residual heat will continue to toast them slightly.

CURRY DRESSING

Mix together ½ cup mayonnaise, ¼ cup plain yogurt, 2 tablespoons chopped chutney, 1 tablespoon soy sauce, 1 teaspoon curry powder and ¼ teaspoon ground ginger.
Makes about 1 cup

APRICOT RICE SALAD

1 can (16 oz.) **DEL MONTE** Lite Apricot Halves
1 Tbsp. soy sauce
1 tsp. oil
1 tsp. vinegar
1 clove garlic, minced
½ tsp. oregano
¼ tsp. ground ginger
2 cups cooked rice
½ cup diced cooked ham
¼ cup diced green pepper
¼ cup sliced green onion
Lettuce
Alfalfa sprouts
Parsley sprigs

Drain fruit reserving liquid for other recipe uses. In salad bowl, combine soy sauce, oil, vinegar, garlic, oregano and ginger. Stir in rice, ham, pepper and onion. Serve on lettuce-lined plates. Garnish with 2 to 3 apricot halves, sprouts and parsley sprigs.
4 servings

CARROT-RAISIN RICE SALAD

1 cup coarsely shredded carrots
½ cup sliced celery
¼ cup raisins
2 tablespoons finely chopped onion
1½ cups chilled, cooked **UNCLE BEN'S®** **CONVERTED®** Brand Rice
½ cup mayonnaise
½ cup sour cream
1½ teaspoons lemon juice

Add carrots, celery, raisins, and onion to chilled rice. Combine mayonnaise, sour cream and lemon juice. Stir into rice mixture. Cover and chill before serving.   *Makes 4 servings*

SHIRLEY'S WILD RICE AND KIDNEY BEAN SALAD

1½ cups uncooked **CHIEFTAIN** Wild Rice
1 cup mayonnaise
1 can drained kidney beans
½ cup diced celery
1 small chopped green pepper
1¼ teaspoons salt
¾ teaspoon pepper
1 small chopped onion

Cook rice as in basic method.* Combine all ingredients and chill.
10 servings

*BASIC METHOD

1. Wash wild rice thoroughly with warm tap water; rinse and drain in strainer until water runs clear. Can also pre-soak several hours.
2. Place wild rice in medium sauce pan with recommended amount of salted water and bring to boil. Chicken or beef broth can be substituted for the water.
3. Simmer covered for about 45 minutes until tender but not mushy. Cooking time may vary some.
4. Drain and rinse.

INTERNATIONAL RICE SALAD

1 bag **SUCCESS®** Rice
1 can (8 oz.) English peas, drained
1 cup cubed or shredded Swiss cheese
⅓ cup mayonnaise
¼ cup minced pimiento
1 or 2 green onions, sliced
1 tablespoon Dijon mustard

Cook bag of rice according to package directions. Drain bag and empty rice into mixing bowl. Add the remaining ingredients and toss lightly. Chill. Serve on lettuce leaves or garnish with hard cooked egg, crumbled bacon, or tomato wedges.

Makes 6 servings (about ½ cup each)

RICE SALAD VINAIGRETTE

2 cups cooked, cold rice
1 cup sliced carrots
1 cup raw green beans, cut into 1 inch pieces
1 cup raw snow peas
1 cup sliced mushrooms
½ cup sliced radishes
¼ cup sliced green onions
¾ cup oil
1 egg, slightly beaten
¼ cup wine vinegar
1½ teaspoons Dijon mustard
¼ teaspoon salt
⅛ teaspoon pepper
1 cup **PEPPERIDGE FARM®** Herb Seasoned Croutons

In a bowl, combine rice with vegetables. Combine oil, egg, vinegar, mustard, salt and pepper. Pour over rice mixture: toss to blend. Cover and refrigerate at least 2 hours. To serve, spoon onto serving dishes and sprinkle with seasoned croutons.

Makes 6 to 8 servings

NAPA VALLEY BROWN RICE SALAD

1 cup **UNCLE BEN'S®** Select Brown Rice
1⅓ cups dry white wine
⅓ cup vegetable oil
⅓ cup lemon juice
2 tablespoons sugar
1 teaspoon salt
1 garlic clove, minced
Dash of pepper
2 medium zucchini, thinly sliced
1½ cups sliced fresh mushrooms
1 small red onion, cut into thin rings
2 medium tomatoes, chopped

Cook rice according to package directions, substituting 1⅓ cups wine for 1⅓ cups of the water, and omitting butter. Transfer to large bowl. Combine oil, lemon juice, sugar, salt, garlic and pepper, mixing well; stir into rice. Stir in zucchini, mushrooms, and onion. Chill at least 4 hours. To serve, stir in tomatoes.

Makes 8 to 10 servings, about 8 cups rice salad

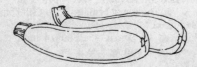

CUCUMBER-ORANGE SALAD

1 head **California ICEBERG Lettuce**
1 cup white vinegar
¼ cup sugar
1 tablespoon finely grated orange peel
2 teaspoons salt
½ teaspoon white pepper
½ cup vegetable oil
¼ cup chopped fresh parsley
3 cucumbers (European or hot-house preferred), thinly sliced
3 oranges, thinly sliced
¼ cup toasted sesame seeds

Core, rinse and thoroughly drain lettuce. Refrigerate in plastic bag or plastic crisper. Combine vinegar, sugar, orange peel, salt and pepper in blender. Cover and blend until sugar is dissolved. With blender running, slowly pour in oil. Stir in parsley. Place cucumbers in shallow glass or plastic dish. Pour marinade over. Cover and refrigerate overnight.

To serve: Cut lettuce into bite-size chunks to measure 6 cups. (Refrigerate remainder for future use.) Place chunks in shallow bowl. Drain cucumbers, reserving marinade. Drizzle half of marinade over lettuce; toss gently. Arrange cucumbers over lettuce in alternate rows with orange slices. Drizzle with remaining marinade; sprinkle with sesame seeds.   *Makes 6 to 8 servings*

Favorite recipe from **California Iceberg Lettuce Commission**

BIRD OF PARADISE SALAD

1 cup plain yogurt
2 tablespoons freshly squeezed lime juice
1 tablespoon brown sugar
6 **CAPE GRANNY SMITH Apples**
3 cups cantaloupe melon balls
3 cups watermelon balls

In a medium bowl combine yogurt, lime juice and brown sugar. Using a melon ball cutter, cut apple balls from four apples. Cut remaining two apples into six wedges each. Cut each wedge into three layered v-shaped slices. Reassemble the wedges, spreading out slightly to resemble "feathers" (see color photo). Arrange apple, cantaloupe and watermelon balls on a serving platter. Surround with apple "feathers". Serve with yogurt dressing.

Yield: 4 servings

GRAPEFRUIT ARTICHOKE AND GREENS SALAD

1-14 ounce can artichoke hearts, drained
Italian Dressing*
3 cups torn leaf lettuce
3 cups torn escarole
2 pink grapefruit, peeled and sectioned

Halve artichokes. Pour ¼ cup Italian Dressing* over artichokes; chill, covered, 3 to 4 hours or overnight. Place leaf lettuce and escarole in salad bowl. Arrange grapefruit sections and artichoke hearts atop leafy greens. Serve with Italian Dressing*.

Serves 8
(Continued)

*ITALIAN DRESSING

⅔ cup red wine vinegar
⅓ cup salad oil
½ teaspoon celery seed
¼ teaspoon onion salt
¼ teaspoon monosodium glutamate
⅛ teaspoon crushed red peppers

Combine ingredients in jar; cover and shake well before serving.
Makes 1 cup

Favorite recipe from the **Leafy Greens Council**

ROSY GRAPEFRUIT SALAD
(Low Calorie)

½ teaspoon unflavored gelatin
2 teaspoons lemon juice
1 large grapefruit
¼ cup grapefruit juice
¾ cup **DIET SHASTA® Wild Raspberry**
1 drop anise extract
3 cloves
Dash salt
1 tablespoon frozen orange juice concentrate
Crisp lettuce
Cottage cheese

Soften gelatin in lemon juice. Remove peel from grapefruit and section fruit over a bowl to catch any juice; squeeze juice from membranes left from sectioning fruit. Combine ¼ cup grapefruit juice with **DIET SHASTA®**, anise, cloves, salt and orange juice concentrate. Boil rapidly to reduce to ½ cup; remove cloves. Add gelatin, stirring until dissolved. Combine with grapefruit sections and chill. Arrange lettuce on chilled salad plates and spoon cottage cheese in center. Serve, topped with grapefruit.
Makes 4 servings

GRAPEFRUIT/ALMOND SALAD
(Low Calorie/Low Sodium)

1 can (16 oz.) **FEATHERWEIGHT® Grapefruit Segments**, drained
¼ cup blanched almonds, sliced
¼ cup dates, chopped
1 green pepper, cut into rings

Sweeten to taste with **FEATHERWEIGHT® Sweetening**. **FEATHERWEIGHT® Salad Dressing** (optional). Toss all together and chill.
Serves 4-5

Approx.	Calories	Protein (Grams)	Fat (Grams)	Carbohydrate (Grams)	Sodium (Mgs.)
½ cup serving	75	1	2	7	4

FROZEN FRUIT SALAD

1 package (3¾ ounces) instant vanilla pudding mix
1 cup mayonnaise
½ cup milk
2½ tablespoons lemon juice
1 can (30 ounces) fruit cocktail, drained
1 medium banana, peeled, sliced
2 cups **FIRESIDE Miniature Marshmallows**
1 cup whipping cream, whipped
⅓ cup coarsely chopped pecans

Beat pudding mix, mayonnaise, milk and lemon juice until smooth and thickened. Fold in remaining ingredients. Spoon into 13 x 9 x 2-inch pan. Cover; freeze. Let stand at room temperature 15 minutes before serving.
12 servings

SOLO® FROZEN FRUIT SALAD

1-8 oz. package cream cheese, softened
½ tsp. salt
1 cup mayonnaise
3 Tbsp. lemon juice
1 jar (16 oz.) **SOLO®** Strawberry Glaze or pkg. **SOLO®** Strawberry Glaze Dry Mix
1 can (15 oz.) crushed pineapple, drained
2 bananas, sliced
½ cup chopped nuts
1 cup whipping cream
¼ cup sugar

Mix cream cheese, salt, mayonnaise, lemon juice and **SOLO® Glaze** until well blended. Add pineapple, bananas and nuts. Whip cream until thick, adding sugar 1 tablespoon at a time. Combine whipped cream and cream cheese mixture. Pour into 9″ × 13″ pan and freeze until firm.
Serves 16

TWO FINGERS® FRUIT SALAD

1 small fresh pineapple
2 navel oranges
6 kiwi fruit
3 medium-size bananas
3 cups halved strawberries
Lettuce
TWO FINGERS® Creamy Fruit Dressing*

With large heavy knife, peel pineapple; remove eyes with small knife, and cut pineapple into chunks, removing core (should measure about 3 cups). Peel kiwis, and slice crosswise. Peel and slice bananas. Peel and break oranges into sections. Arrange fruits in groups on lettuce-garnished plate. Pass Creamy Fruit Dressing.
Makes 6 servings (about 1½ cups each)

Substitute any fresh, in-season fruits for those suggested, keeping an eye on color, texture and flavor variety.

*TWO FINGERS® CREAMY FRUIT DRESSING

¼ cup sugar
1½ tablespoons flour
¾ teaspoon dry mustard
¼ teaspoon salt
¾ cup orange juice
¼ cup **TWO FINGERS®** Tequila
1 tablespoon lime juice
1 large egg, beaten
½ cup plain yogurt

Mix sugar, flour, mustard and salt together well in 1-quart saucepan. Gradually stir in orange juice, mixing until smooth. Add tequila and lime juice. Stir over moderate heat until mixture comes to a boil. Cook for 1 minute, stirring constantly, until mixture is thickened. Stir a little of the hot mixture into beaten egg. Combine with remaining mixture, and cook about 30 seconds longer over very low heat, stirring briskly. Remove from heat; cool. When cold, stir in yogurt.
Makes 1½ cups dressing

Serve poured over individual fruit salads, or as a dip for individual fruit pieces.

FESTIVE FRUIT SALAD

1 cup dairy sour cream
2 Tbsp. brown sugar
Grated peel of 1 SUNKIST® Tangerine
3 to 4 SUNKIST® Tangerines, peeled, segmented, seeded (about 2 cups)
1 apple, unpeeled, cubed
1 pear, unpeeled, cubed
1 banana, sliced
1 cup seedless grapes
½ cup coarsely chopped nuts

In large bowl, combine sour cream, brown sugar and tangerine peel. Stir in remaining ingredients; chill. Serve on salad greens, if desired.   *Makes 6 servings (about 5½ cups)*

BOGGS® WALDORF SALAD

⅓ cup mayonnaise
1 teaspoon sugar
¼ cup BOGGS® Cranberry Liqueur
1 teaspoon finely grated lemon rind
1 tablespoon lemon juice
3 medium delicious apples, cored, diced
½ cup thinly sliced celery
¼ cup coarsely chopped walnuts

In medium bowl, combine mayonnaise, sugar, BOGGS®, lemon rind and lemon juice. Mix in apples, celery and nuts. Chill overnight. Serve on bed of lettuce, if desired.   *Serves 6*

LEMONY APPLE-BRAN SALAD

½ cup lemon yogurt
1 tablespoon finely snipped fresh parsley
2 cups cubed, unpared red apples (about ½ lb., 1 to 2 medium-size)
½ cup thinly sliced celery
½ cup halved red grapes
½ cup KELLOGG'S® ALL-BRAN® or KELLOGG'S® BRAN BUDS® Cereal
6 lettuce leaves

Stir together yogurt, parsley, apples, celery and grapes. Cover and chill thoroughly. At serving time, stir in KELLOGG'S® ALL-BRAN® Cereal. Serve on lettuce leaves.

Yield: 6 servings

® Kellogg Company

AVOCADO SURPRISE SALAD

2 medium avocados
2 oranges
1 large grapefruit (or 1 11-oz. can grapefruit sections, drained)
1 head lettuce, washed and crisped
1 can (4 oz.) ORTEGA Sliced Pimientos
6 black pitted olives, sliced
1 can (7 oz.) ORTEGA Green Chile Salsa

Peel, seed, and slice avocados, oranges and grapefruit. Alternate sections of fruits on individual plates lined with leaves of crisp lettuce (lettuce can also be shredded for easier eating). Garnish with strips of pimientos and black olives. Serve salsa in separate dish for salad dressing. You'll find the salsa a natural for salad dressing and a perfect match for avocados in particular.

Serves 4-6

EMERALD SALAD WITH YOGURT DRESSING

3 CAPE GRANNY SMITH Apples, cored and cubed (about 4 cups)
2 cups honeydew melon balls
2 cups green grapes, halved
2 kiwi fruit, pared and thinly sliced
¼ cup orange juice

In large bowl combine all ingredients; mix well. Cover. Chill. Serve with Yogurt Dressing.*   *Yield: 8 servings*

*YOGURT DRESSING

2 containers (8 ounces each) plain yogurt
3 tablespoons confectioners' sugar
2 tablespoons orange juice
½ teaspoon grated orange peel
¼ teaspoon ground cinnamon
⅛ teaspoon ground mace

In a bowl, combine all ingredients; mix well. Spoon over fruit salad.

FRUIT, AVOCADO & CHEESE SALAD

1 medium head Boston lettuce
1 clove garlic
2 grapefruits
1 large navel orange
2 medium avocados
1 container (15 oz.) MIGLIORE® Ricotta
3 tablespoons lemon juice
3 tablespoons olive oil
1 teaspoon sugar
¾ teaspoon salt
Dash of pepper

Wash and drain lettuce and tear into bite-size pieces. Rub inside of large salad bowl with garlic. Add lettuce. Peel grapefruit and orange; cut into sections. Cut avocados in half lengthwise, remove pits and peel. Slice avocados and sprinkle with 2 tablespoons lemon juice. Arrange fruit and avocados on lettuce in sunburst fashion. Pile cheese in center. Mix together olive oil, remaining lemon juice, sugar, salt and pepper. Pour over salad.

AVOCADO-ORANGE TOSS

6 ounces spinach, torn into bite-size pieces
2 oranges, pared and sectioned
1 avocado, sliced
2 green onions (with tops), thinly sliced
Lemon Dressing*
BAC*OS® Imitation Bacon

Toss spinach, oranges, avocado and onions with Lemon Dressing. Sprinkle with imitation bacon.   *6 to 8 servings*

*LEMON DRESSING

¼ cup vegetable oil
2 tablespoons lemon juice
¼ teaspoon salt
¼ teaspoon dried tarragon leaves

Shake all ingredients in tightly covered container.

PEACHTREE SALAD

⅔ cup salad oil
⅓ cup **HEINZ Wine Vinegar**
1 clove garlic, split
1 teaspoon sugar
½ teaspoon salt
⅛ teaspoon pepper
8 cups torn salad greens, chilled
1 cup finely chopped parsley
1 cup sliced fresh or canned peaches
½ cup broken pecans

Combine first 6 ingredients in jar. Cover; shake vigorously. Chill to blend flavors. Remove garlic and shake again before tossing with salad greens, parsley, peaches and nuts.

Makes 8 servings (about 8 cups)

FRUIT BOWL SALAD

2 red apples, cored and diced
1 pear, peeled, cored and diced
1 banana, peeled and sliced
1 cup diced celery
½ cup coarsely chopped walnuts
½ cup mayonnaise
2 tablespoons lemon juice
1½ teaspoons sugar
1½ teaspoons **LEA & PERRINS Worcestershire Sauce**

In a salad bowl combine apples, pear, banana, celery and walnuts. Mix remaining ingredients. Pour over salad; toss gently. Serve on lettuce-lined salad bowl, if desired. *Yield: 6 portions*

*May be prepared in advance of serving.

FRUIT SALAD WITH TANGY CHEESE DRESSING

Fruit:
Lettuce Leaves
1 (20-ounce) can pineapple slices in natural juices, reserving ¼ cup juice
1 (8¼-ounce) can pineapple slices in natural juices, drained
1 (16-ounce) can pear halves, drained
1 (16-ounce) can peach slices, drained
¾ pound red grapes

Dressing:
⅓ cup dairy sour cream
¼ cup **SNACK MATE Sharp Cheddar Pasteurized Process Cheese Spread**
¼ cup reserved pineapple juice
1 tablespoon lemon juice

Garnish:
2 tablespoons toasted slivered almonds or
1 tablespoon toasted sesame seeds

1. **Make Salad:** Cover individual salad plates or large serving platter with lettuce leaves. Arrange pineapple slices, pear halves, peach slices and grapes attractively on lettuce. Cover and chill.
2. **Make Dressing:** In medium bowl, using electric mixer at medium speed, beat together sour cream, **SNACK MATE Cheese**, pineapple juice and lemon juice. Cover and chill.
3. **To Serve:** Pour dressing over salad and sprinkle with toasted almonds or sesame seeds; or pass dressing separately.

Makes 6 servings

LAYERED FRUIT SALAD

2 cups (16 oz.) **BREAKSTONE'S® Smooth and Creamy Style Cottage Cheese**
1 (8¼ oz.) can crushed pineapple, drained
½ cup toasted coconut
2 cups banana chunks
2 cups red grape halves, seeded
2 cups nectarine or peach slices
2 cups pear slices
1 cup strawberry halves

Combine cottage cheese, pineapple and coconut; mix well. In 2-quart bowl, layer bananas, grapes, half of cottage cheese mixture, nectarines, pears and remaining cottage cheese mixture. Top with strawberries. *6 to 8 servings*

BANANA-NUT SALAD

1 tablespoon **JIF® Creamy Peanut Butter**
1 tablespoon honey
¼ cup mayonnaise or salad dressing
Bananas
Lemon juice
Shredded lettuce
Chopped peanuts

In small bowl, stir together the **JIF®** and honey. Blend in mayonnaise or salad dressing. Cut bananas in half lengthwise; dip in lemon juice. Arrange banana halves on shredded lettuce in salad dishes. Spread **JIF®** mixture on bananas; sprinkle with nuts.

WHEAT GERM FRUIT SALAD

2 cups creamed cottage cheese
½ cup **KRETSCHMER Wheat Germ With Brown Sugar & Honey**
¼ cup raisins *or* diced dates
¼ cup chopped walnuts
2 tsp. vanilla
2 tsp. sugar
2 apples, sliced
Lettuce leaves

Combine all ingredients *except* apples and lettuce. Mix well. Arrange apple slices in fan shape on lettuce leaves. Top with cheese mixture. *Makes 4 servings*

EXOTIC FRUIT SALAD

Coarsely grate some rind from 1 or 2 oranges; set aside. Pare oranges, discarding remaining rind. Slice oranges, then cut slices into halves. Toss gently with sliced bananas and pears, toasted **BLUE RIBBON® Slivered Almonds** and a little chopped semi-sweet chocolate. For each serving, place a crisp lettuce cup on a chilled salad plate; fill, mounding, with the fruit mixture. Dollop generously with a dressing made with dairy sour cream or imitation, a splash of sherry, a dash of salt and the reserved orange rind, all briskly stirred together with a fork. Sprinkle a little more chopped chocolate over dressing.

CRUZAN® SUNSHINE SALAD

2 tablespoons CRUZAN® White Rum
3 tablespoons lemon juice
½ cup salad oil
1 small garlic clove, crushed
½ teaspoon sugar
¼ teaspoon dried marjoram, crumbled
Salt and pepper, to taste
1 large ripe avocado, peeled and cubed
1 small sweet onion, very thinly sliced
1 large seedless orange, peeled and sliced

Combine first 7 ingredients in a bowl and stir to mix well. Add avocado and onion to bowl; toss gently. Cover and chill. Mix orange slices in just before serving.   *4 servings*

CHIQUITA® BANANA ORANGE MELODY SALAD

1 medium head romaine lettuce, torn into pieces
4 CHIQUITA® Bananas, sliced
2 oranges, sectioned
½ cup halved pitted dates
½ cup coarsely chopped walnuts

In salad bowl, arrange lettuce, CHIQUITA® Bananas, oranges and dates; toss with your favorite dressing and add walnuts.
Yield: Approximately 6 servings

BRANDY FIESTA SALAD

6 slices (1-inch thick) fresh pineapple, halved, peeled and cored
3 oranges, peeled and sliced
⅔ cup THE CHRISTIAN BROTHERS® Brandy
⅓ cup sugar
¼ cup water
¼ teaspoon salt
¼ cup white wine vinegar
2 cups shredded green cabbage
2 cups shredded red cabbage
Cilantro or watercress sprigs

Combine pineapple and orange slices in bowl; set aside. In 1-quart saucepan combine brandy, sugar, water and salt. Bring to boiling, stirring. Simmer 5 minutes. Remove from heat. Stir in vinegar. Pour over fruits. Cover and chill several hours, tossing occasionally. Mound cabbage in serving bowl. Arrange fruits over cabbage. Drizzle with brandy mixture. Garnish with cilantro.
Makes 6 servings

CUCUMBER FRUIT SALAD WITH PEANUT DRESSING

1 large CALAVO®-BURNAC EUROPEAN Cucumber—sliced thinly
1 small can well drained mandarin orange segments (or fresh orange slices may be used)
1 banana, sliced
1 avocado, sliced
Shredded coconut (optional)
Butter lettuce (Bibb, Buttercrunch)

Arrange cucumber, avocado and fruits on a lettuce-lined platter. Drizzle dressing over salad.   *Serves 4*
(Continued)

PEANUT DRESSING

½ cup peanuts
1 tsp. Champagne vinegar
⅛ tsp. curry
¼ cup mayonnaise
¼ cup sour cream
¼ cup chutney

Place all in blender or food processor. Blend until smooth.
Makes approximately 1¼ cups

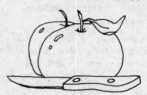

FRUIT ON CRISPY NOODLES

Curry Dressing*
2 bananas, sliced
1 can (16-ounces) sliced peaches, drained and cut into halves
1 red apple, cut into cubes
1 can (8-ounces) crushed pineapple in juice, well drained (reserve 2 tablespoons juice)
2 cups chow mein noodles
6 tablespoons BAC*Os® Imitation Bacon

Prepare Curry Dressing. Toss bananas, peaches, apple and pineapple. Arrange ⅓ cup chow mein noodles on each of 6 salad plates; top with fruit mixture. Sprinkle each with 1 tablespoon imitation bacon. Serve with dressing.   *6 servings*

*CURRY DRESSING

½ cup dairy sour cream
2 tablespoons reserved pineapple juice
1 tablespoon honey
½ teaspoon curry powder

Mix all ingredients.

Gelatin

VEGETABLE SEAFOOD ASPIC

2 pkgs. unflavored gelatin
4 cups S&W® "Spring" Vegetable Juice Cocktail
1 tsp. Worcestershire sauce
2-3 drops hot pepper sauce
½ cup finely chopped celery
¼ cup finely chopped green onion
¼ cup sliced black olives
1-6½ oz. can chunk light tuna, drained well
Sliced black olives and sour cream as desired for garnish

Dissolve gelatin in ½ cup vegetable juice cocktail. Heat the remaining 3½ cups vegetable juice cocktail, and combine gelatin mixture, Worcestershire sauce and hot pepper sauce with it. Blend well and refrigerate until partially set. Fold in remaining ingredients and pour into a 6 to 8 cup mold. Chill until firm. Unmold onto a bed of red leaf lettuce and decorate with sliced black olives and a dollop of sour cream. Serve with crusty French rolls, a wedge of cheese and iced tea.   *Serves 4-6*

SMITHFIELD HAM ASPIC SALAD

16 cups hot water
1 cup unflavored gelatin
3 cups **AMBER BRAND Deviled SMITHFIELD Ham**
1 cup chili sauce
12 hard-boiled eggs

Dissolve gelatin in hot water, stir in the **AMBER BRAND Ham**, chili sauce and pour into cup molds. Cut eggs in half, dividing the yolks; sink the divided egg-halves in the gelatin solution—when it is about set. Chill thoroughly, remove from molds, serve on lettuce with mayonnaise. *Serves 24*

MOLDED CLAM AND TOMATO RING
(Low Calorie)

2 envelopes unflavored gelatin
½ cup cold water
1 can (10½ oz.) minced clams
1½ teaspoons **LEA & PERRINS Worcestershire Sauce**
2¾ cups tomato juice
1 cup thinly sliced celery
¼ cup sliced scallions

Soften gelatin in water for 5 minutes. Drain clams, reserving liquid and clams separately. Add sufficient water to clam liquid to make ¾ cup. In a small saucepan heat clam liquid and **LEA & PERRINS** just to the boiling point. Pour over gelatin; stir to dissolve. Add tomato juice. Chill until mixture thickens to consistency of unbeaten egg white. Stir in reserved clams, celery, and scallions. Pour into a 5-cup ring mold. Chill until firm. Unmold onto serving platter.

Calorie Count: about 68 calories per serving

CHILLED LIME VEGETABLE MOLD

1¾ cups water
1 package (3-oz.) lime-flavored gelatin
2 tablespoons lemon juice
3 envelopes unflavored gelatin
2 cans (14½-oz. each) **SWANSON Ready-to-Serve Chicken Broth**
⅛ teaspoon garlic powder
Dash cayenne pepper
½ cup small cauliflowerets
½ cup chopped fresh tomatoes
½ cup chopped cucumber
2 tablespoons chopped green pepper
1 tablespoon finely chopped onion
Cucumber slices

To make lime layer, bring 1 cup water to boil. Pour over lime-flavored gelatin, stirring to dissolve. Add remaining water and 1 tablespoon lemon juice. Pour into 6-cup mold. Chill until slightly firm. Meanwhile, to make vegetable layer, sprinkle unflavored gelatin over ½ cup broth to soften. Place over low heat, stirring until gelatin is dissolved. Remove from heat; add remaining broth, lemon juice, garlic powder and cayenne. Chill until slightly thickened; fold in remaining ingredients. Spoon onto lime layer. Chill 4 hours or until firm. Unmold on salad greens. Garnish with cucumber slices. *Makes 6 cups, 8 servings*

VEGETABLE SALAD MOLD

1 (6-ounce) package lemon-flavored gelatin
2 cups boiling water
1 cup cold water
½ cup **HENRI'S BUTTERMILK FARMS® Original Dressing**
2 tablespoons lemon juice
¼ teaspoon dried dill weed
2 small carrots, shredded
1 medium green pepper, seeded and finely chopped
1 medium cucumber, peeled, seeded and finely chopped

1. In large mixing bowl, stir gelatin into boiling water until dissolved.
2. Add cold water, **HENRI'S BUTTERMILK FARMS® Original Dressing**, lemon juice, and dill weed. Mix well. Chill until partially set.
3. Fold carrots, green pepper and cucumber into gelatin mixture. Pour into a 5½-cup mold. Chill until firm.
4. Unmold and serve on bed of lettuce. *Makes 6 servings*

TOMATO ASPIC

2 envelopes unflavored gelatin
3 cups **CAMPBELL'S Tomato Juice**
2 tablespoons vinegar
½ teaspoon Worcestershire sauce
¼ teaspoon onion powder
Generous dash pepper

In saucepan, sprinkle gelatin over 1 cup cold juice to soften. Place over low heat, stirring until gelatin is dissolved. Remove from heat; add remaining juice, vinegar, and seasonings. Pour into 4-cup mold. Chill 4 hours or until firm. Unmold on salad greens. *Makes about 3 cups*

SNAP-E-TOM ASPIC

2 envelopes unflavored gelatin
1 teaspoon sugar
5 cans (6-oz. each) **SNAP-E-TOM Tomato Cocktail** or 3 (10-oz.) cans
1 teaspoon A.1. Steak Sauce
3 tablespoons lemon juice
½ teaspoon salt
Lettuce
Sour cream (or mayonnaise)

In a small saucepan combine gelatin and sugar. Slowly add 1 can **SNAP-E-TOM** and stir until well mixed. Cook over medium heat, stirring often, until gelatin dissolves. Remove from heat and stir in remaining cans of **SNAP-E-TOM, A.1.**, lemon juice and salt. Pour into 4-cup mold. Refrigerate until firm, at least 2 hours. Dip mold in lukewarm water, tap to loosen and unmold onto bed of lettuce. Serve with sour cream. *Serves 6-8*

VARIATION:

Add any or all of the following just after the gelatin has thickened, but before it is firm: ½ cup diced cucumber, ¼ cup sliced black olives, ½ cup cubed Jack cheese and/or ½ cup diced cooked ham, chicken, or shrimp.

COLESLAW SOUFFLÉ SALAD

1 pkg. (3-oz.) lemon flavored gelatin
1 cup hot water
½ cup cold water
2 tablespoons **REGINA White Wine Vinegar**
½ cup mayonnaise
½ teaspoon salt
¼ teaspoon white pepper
3 cups chopped cabbage
3 tablespoons minced green pepper
2 teaspoons minced fresh onion
½ teaspoon celery seed
Bibb or Boston lettuce

In medium bowl, dissolve gelatin in hot water. Mix in cold water, vinegar, mayonnaise, salt and pepper. Chill until firm around the edges. Beat until fluffy. Fold in remaining ingredients except lettuce. Pour into 4-cup mold. Chill until firm. Unmold on bed of lettuce.   *Serves 6*

GELATIN SURPRISE

1 pkg. (3 oz.) lime or lemon gelatin
3 oz. **ROQUEFORT Cheese**, crumbled
1 apple, peeled, cored and diced
¼ cup chopped nuts
Lettuce
Russian dressing

Prepare gelatin according to package directions. Chill until slightly thickened. Fold in cheese, apples and nuts. Pour into a 3-cup mold or 6 individual ½-cup molds. Chill until firm. Unmold on a bed of shredded lettuce and serve with Russian dressing.
                    Makes 4 to 6 servings

Favorite recipe from the **Roquefort Association, Inc.**

LINDSAY® OLIVE-NECTAR SALAD

½ cup **LINDSAY® Pitted Ripe Olives**
1 (3 oz.) package lime-flavored gelatin
1½ cups pear nectar
½ cup diced cucumber
Crisp lettuce
Green mayonnaise

Cut olives into wedges. Heat nectar to almost boiling. Stir in gelatin until dissolved. Cool, then chill until mixture thickens. Fold in olive wedges and cucumber. Spoon into individual molds; chill until firm. Turn out on crisp lettuce. Serve with Green Mayonnaise made by adding 1 tablespoon each chopped green onion and parsley to ½ cup mayonnaise. Garnish with pitted ripe olives.   *Serves 6*

RUBY BORSCHT SALAD

1 can (1 lb., 4 oz.) **DOLE® Crushed Pineapple**
1 package (6 oz.) wild raspberry gelatin
1½ cups boiling water
1 can (1 lb.) shoestring beets
3 tablespoons plain vinegar
1 teaspoon dill weed
Dash salt
1 cup chopped celery
Dairy sour cream

Drain pineapple reserving all syrup. Dissolve gelatin in boiling water. Stir in beets and all liquid, vinegar, dill, salt and reserved pineapple syrup. Chill until mixture thickens to consistency of unbeaten egg white. Fold in celery and pineapple. Pour into 2-quart mold. Chill firm. Top with sour cream and a sprinkle of dill weed to serve.   *Makes 8 servings*

CHRISTMAS FRUIT MOLD

2 packages (3-oz. each) or 1 package (6-oz.) **JELL-O®**
    Lemon Flavor Gelatin Dessert
2 cups boiling water
1 cup sherry wine or cherry wine*
½ cup cold water*
32 whole blanched almonds
¼ teaspoon *each* cinnamon and cloves
⅛ teaspoon allspice
1 cup chopped candied mixed fruit
½ cup light raisins
½ cup currants
½ cup drained maraschino or canned pitted sweet
    cherries, halved
½ cup coarsely chopped walnuts

Dissolve gelatin in boiling water. Stir in wine and cold water; pour ½ cup into 6-cup ring mold. Chill until set but not firm. Arrange almonds in single layer in decorative pattern on set gelatin. Pour another ½ cup of the gelatin mixture over the almonds. Chill again until set but not firm. Meanwhile, add spices, fruits and walnuts to remaining gelatin mixture; chill until thickened. Then spoon gently into mold. Chill until firm, about 4 hours. Unmold. Garnish with salad greens, if desired.

                    Makes about 6 cups or 12 servings

*Or use 1 bottle (12 fl. oz.) ginger ale and 1 teaspoon rum extract.

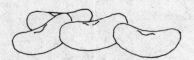

BANANA BERRY MOLD
(Low Calorie)

1 pkg. (47 grams) **ESTEE® Strawberry Gel**
1-10½ oz. can water or juice packed Mandarin orange
    sections
1 medium banana, sliced

Drain juice from mandarin oranges. Add water to juice to make two cups. Pour liquids into saucepan and heat to a boil. Empty **ESTEE® Strawberry Gel** into a bowl. Add boiled liquids to gel and stir until dissolved. Cool for 5 minutes. Gently stir in mandarin orange sections and sliced banana. Pour into a 3-cup mold. Chill until set.

NUTRITION INFORMATION

Calories	Cholesterol	Sodium
62	15g	5mg

DIABETIC EXCHANGE INFORMATION

Fruit
1½

SUNRISE MOLDED FRUIT SALAD

1 package (8-serving size) peach flavored gelatin
2 cups boiling water
1¾ cups cold water
1 cup **SUN·MAID® Fruit Bits**
2 (3-ounce) packages cream cheese, softened

Dissolve gelatin in boiling water. Add cold water. Set 1 cup aside. Pour remainder into a 9 × 5-inch loaf pan or 1½-quart mold and chill until almost set. Fold in fruit bits. Beat cream cheese; slowly add reserved gelatin until smooth and well blended. Pour over fruit-gelatin mixture. Chill until firm. Unmold and cut into 6 to 8 servings.

ORANGE-ALMOND MOLD

6-oz. can frozen orange juice concentrate
1 juice can water
3-oz. pkg. orange-flavored gelatin
1 cup lemon-lime carbonated beverage
11-oz. can mandarin oranges, drained
½ cup **FISHER® Slivered Almonds**

Heat orange juice and water to boiling; stir in gelatin until dissolved. Slowly add lemon-lime beverage; chill until thickened. Fold in orange sections and almonds. Pour into 4-cup mold. Chill until firm. *4 to 6 servings*

PEPPERMINT RASPBERRY SALAD

1 package raspberry gelatin (3-oz. size)
2 cups boiling water
4 bags **MAGIC MOUNTAIN™ Peppermint Spice Herb Tea**
1 (1 lb.) can pear halves, drained
1 (8¼-oz.) can crushed pineapple, drained
Sour cream, optional

In bowl, dissolve raspberry gelatin in boiling water. Add tea bags (remove tags), and steep five minutes. Remove tea bags and stir in crushed pineapple. Let cool. In cake pan, or gelatin mold, arrange pear halves, cut side up, in spoke pattern. Pour gelatin mixture over and let set till firm. Garnish with sour cream, if desired. *Serves 5-6*

MUFFIN PAN SALAD

1 package (3 oz.) **JELL-O® Lemon Flavor Gelatin Dessert**
½ teaspoon salt
¼ teaspoon celery salt
1½ cups boiling water
2 teaspoons vinegar
½ teaspoon prepared horseradish
1½ cups (about) fruit or vegetable combination*

Dissolve gelatin, salt and celery salt in boiling water. Add vinegar and horseradish. Place aluminum foil cupcake liners in muffin pan. Place salad ingredients in cups, filling each about ⅔ full. Then fill with gelatin mixture. Chill until firm, about 2 hours. Unmold carefully from foil cups. Serve with crisp salad greens, if desired. *Makes about 3 cups or 8 servings*

*SUGGESTED COMBINATIONS:

2 medium oranges, sectioned and diced and 1 small red onion, sliced into rings
1½ cups cooked mixed vegetables and 1 tablespoon grated onion
¾ cup *each* shredded zucchini and carrot and 2 tablespoons minced onion
1 cup cauliflower florets and ½ cup diced green pepper

SOUTHERN BELLE SALAD

1 can (16 oz.) pitted dark sweet cherries
1 pkg. (3 oz.) cherry gelatin
1 cup **COCA-COLA®**
2 tablespoons fresh lemon juice
1 pkg. (3 oz.) cream cheese
½ cup cut-up pecans or walnuts

Drain cherry juice. Bring ¾ cup of the juice to boiling; add to gelatin. Stir until dissolved. Stir in **COCA-COLA®** and lemon juice. Chill until gelatin mounds slightly. Cut cheese into very small pieces. Fold cheese, nuts and whole cherries into gelatin. Spoon into 7 individual molds. Chill until firm. *Makes 7 (½ cup) servings*

FROSTY GREEN SOUR CREAM MOLD

2 (3 oz.) packages lime flavored gelatin
2 cups boiling water
1 (20½ oz.) can, crushed pineapple, drained
½ pint (1 cup) sour cream
⅓ cup chopped pecans
1 (8 oz.) package **BORDO Imported Diced Dates**

Mix gelatin and water until gelatin is dissolved. Chill until thick, but not completely set. Whip with electric mixer or hand beater until frothy and light. Add sour cream and mix well. Fold in drained crushed pineapple, pecans and dates. Pour into lightly greased 6 cup mold. Chill until firm. *Serves 8-10*

MOLDED PINEAPPLE-ORANGE SALAD

1 package (6 oz.) orange flavored gelatin
2 cups boiling water
1 cup cold water
1 can (15¼ oz.) pineapple chunks, drained (reserve ½ cup pineapple juice)
½ cup prepared **HIDDEN VALLEY ORIGINAL RANCH® Salad Dressing**
1 cup finely chopped celery
1 can (11 oz.) mandarin orange segments, drained
½ cup finely chopped walnuts

Dissolve gelatin in boiling water. Add cold water and reserved pineapple juice. Chill until syrupy. Mix in remaining ingredients. Spoon into ungreased 2 quart mold. Chill until firm. *Makes 8 to 10 servings*

PEACH SAUTERNE SALAD

1 can (17 oz.) sliced peaches
2 packages (3 oz. each) or 1 package (6 oz.) **JELL-O® Peach Flavor Gelatin**
1½ cups sauterne wine
2 teaspoons lemon juice
1 medium apple, diced

Drain peaches, reserving syrup. Dice the peaches. Add water to syrup to make 2 cups; bring to a boil. Dissolve gelatin in boiling liquid. Stir in wine and lemon juice and chill until thickened. Fold in peaches and apple. Spoon into 5-cup mold. Chill until firm, about 4 hours. Unmold. Garnish with salad greens, if desired. *Makes 5 cups or 10 servings*

ROYAL PEAR SALAD

1 cup boiling water
1 package (6 ounces) raspberry-flavored gelatin
2 cups cold water
1 can (16 ounces) whole cranberry sauce
1 can (29 ounces) **STOKELY'S FINEST®** **Bartlett Pear Halves**, drained
½ cup chopped walnuts
½ teaspoon lemon juice

Stir gelatin into boiling water until dissolved. Add cold water and cranberry sauce. Stir to blend. Chill until almost set. Cut all but 3 pear halves into chunks; slice reserved pear halves and set aside. Stir pear chunks, nuts, and lemon juice into gelatin mixture. Pour into 6-cup mold. Chill at least 6 hours, or until firm. Unmold on bed of lettuce, garnish with sliced pears, and serve.

7 to 8 servings

RAINBOW GELATIN

1 package (3 oz.) cherry gelatin
1 jar (4½ oz.) **GERBER®** **Strained Beets**
1 package (3 oz.) lime gelatin
1 jar (4½ oz.) **GERBER®** **Strained Peas**
1 package (3 oz.) lemon gelatin
1 jar (4½ oz.) **GERBER®** **Strained Creamed Corn**
1 package (3 oz.) orange gelatin
1 jar (4¾ oz.) **GERBER®** **Strained Sweet Potatoes**

Dissolve cherry gelatin in 1½ cups boiling water. Add beets and chill in a 9 × 13 inch pan until set. While first layer is chilling, dissolve lime gelatin in 1½ cups boiling water, add peas and cool. When first layer is set, pour cooled lime gelatin mixture over first layer and chill until set. Repeat this procedure with lemon gelatin dissolved in 1½ cups boiling water and corn; orange gelatin dissolved in 1½ cups boiling water and sweet potatoes, until all layers are set. When completely set, cut in squares and serve.

Yield: 16-20 servings

CRANBERRY ORCHARD SALAD

1½ cups ground fresh cranberries
½ cup sugar
2 packages (3 oz. each) or 1 package (6 oz.) **JELL-O®** **Orange** or **Lemon Flavor Gelatin**
¼ teaspoon salt
2 cups boiling water
1½ cups cold water
1 tablespoon lemon juice
¼ teaspoon cinnamon
⅛ teaspoon cloves
1 orange, sectioned and diced
½ cup chopped walnuts or almonds*

Combine cranberries and sugar and set aside. Dissolve gelatin and salt in boiling water. Add cold water, lemon juice, cinnamon and cloves. Chill until thickened. Fold in the cranberries, orange and nuts. Spoon into 6-cup mold. Chill until firm, about 4 hours. Unmold. Garnish with salad greens, if desired.

Makes about 6 cups or 12 servings

*Or use ½ cup chopped celery.

ZESTY CRANBERRY-NUT MOLD
(Low Calorie/Low Fat)

1 pkg. (47 grams) **ESTEE®** **Orange Gel**
1½ cups low calorie cranberry juice
½ cup low calorie ginger ale
1 orange, peeled, seeded and chopped
¼ cup walnuts, chopped

Mix cranberry juice and ginger ale in saucepan and heat to a boil. Empty **ESTEE®** **Orange Gel** into medium bowl. Pour hot liquid over gel and stir until dissolved. Cool 5 minutes. Gently stir in orange and walnut pieces. Pour into 3-cup mold. Refrigerate until set.

Makes 6 servings, ½ cup per serving

NUTRITION INFORMATION

Calories	Carbohydrates	Protein	Fat
76	11g	1g	3g

DIABETIC EXCHANGE INFORMATION

Fruit	Fat
1	½

MOLDED FRUIT SALAD

1 3-oz. package fruit-flavored gelatin
2 cups hot water
½ cup **MARSHMALLOW FLUFF®**
1½ cups drained diced mixed fruit

Dissolve gelatin in hot water; stir in **FLUFF®**. Mix thoroughly, then chill until thickened and mounds when dropped from a spoon. Fold in fruit and turn into individual molds or custard cups. Chill until firm.

Makes 6 servings

APPLE BITS MOLD
(Low Calorie)

1 envelope unflavored gelatin
½ cup cold water
1 (12 oz.) can **DIET SHASTA®** **Strawberry**
¼ teaspoon salt
⅛ teaspoon cinnamon
⅛ teaspoon nutmeg
1 tablespoon lemon juice
¼ teaspoon artificial liquid sweetener
1 cup diced apple

Soften gelatin in water. Stir over hot water until dissolved. Add all remaining ingredients, except apple. Chill until mixture begins to thicken. Fold in apples. Spoon into individual molds or small ring mold and chill until firm. *Makes about 2½ cups (4 servings)*

SUNNY SIDE SALAD

1 pkg. lemon gelatin
¾ cup boiling water
2 cups **LUCKY LEAF®** **Apple Sauce**
⅓ cup chopped walnuts
¼ cup sliced olives

Dissolve lemon gelatin in hot water. Add apple sauce, nuts and sliced olives. Pour into rinsed 1 qt. salad mold (or individual molds). Chill until set. For added flavor, substitute **LUCKY LEAF®** **Apple Juice** for water in recipe.

SUNSHINE CITRUS MOLD
(Low Calorie/Low Fat/Low Sodium)

1 can (8 ounces) juice-packed crushed pineapple
2 cans (6½ ounces each) mandarin orange segments
2 envelopes unflavored gelatin
1 packet **SWEET 'N LOW®**
⅓ cup chopped walnuts
1 can (12 ounces) diet ginger ale, chilled

Drain fruit, reserving juice. In small saucepan, soften gelatin in juice, then heat and stir until gelatin is dissolved. Stir in **SWEET 'N LOW®**. Transfer to medium-size bowl and refrigerate about 45 minutes until chilled but not set. Stir in fruit and walnuts. Slowly pour ginger ale down side of bowl; stir gently until blended. Chill until partially set, about 45 minutes. Spoon into individual ½-cup molds. Chill till firm, about 1 hour. Unmold.   *8 servings*

Per Serving (½ cup): Calories: 71; Fat: 3g; Sodium: 3mg

BRANDIED FRUIT SALAD

1 cup (12 oz. can) pineapple chunks
1 cup halved fresh strawberries
½ cup California Brandy
1 (3 oz.) package lemon flavor gelatin
1 (3 oz.) package raspberry flavor gelatin
2 cups boiling water
3 tablespoons lemon juice
1 medium banana, sliced
½ cup sliced celery
2 tablespoons finely chopped preserved ginger
Lettuce
Sliced kiwi fruit
Whole strawberries

Drain pineapple thoroughly. Combine with halved strawberries and brandy, and let stand 20 minutes. Meanwhile, dissolve flavored gelatins in boiling water. Stir in lemon juice, and cool to room temperature. Add marinated fruits and brandy, and chill until slightly thickened. Add banana, celery and ginger. Turn into oiled 6-cup mold, and chill firm, at least 3 hours, (overnight for tall mold). At serving time, unmold, and garnish with lettuce, sliced kiwi and whole strawberries.

Makes 1 large salad, 6 to 8 servings

Favorite recipe from the **California Brandy Advisory Board**

SCARLETT O'HARA SALAD

1¼ cups **OCEAN SPRAY®** Cranberry Juice Cocktail
1 3 oz. pkg. cherry gelatin
½ cup **SOUTHERN COMFORT®**
3 Tbsp. lime or lemon juice
½ cup sugar
1 cup seedless grapes, halved
½ cup finely chopped celery
1 cup pitted canned Bing cherries
½ cup chopped walnuts or pecans

Heat cranberry juice; stir in gelatin till dissolved. Remove from heat. Add **SOUTHERN COMFORT®**, lime or lemon juice, and sugar. Chill until mixture begins to congeal. Fold in remaining ingredients. Chill until firm in lightly oiled mold. Unmold on lettuce.   *Serves 10*

Salad Dressings

MAYONNAISE
(Maionese)

1 whole egg
3 tablespoons lemon juice
½ teaspoon dry mustard
1 cup **BERTOLLI®** Olive Oil
Salt and pepper

Process egg, lemon juice and mustard in blender; add oil gradually, processing until thick. Season with salt and pepper. Refrigerate.
Makes 1 cup

DRESSINGS WITH DANISH BLUE CHEESE
VINAIGRETTE DRESSING

1½ tsp. Dijon-style mustard
¼ tsp. salt
½ tsp. freshly ground pepper
½ tsp. sugar
1 clove garlic, pressed
Dash cayenne pepper
⅓ cup wine vinegar
¾ cup vegetable oil
½ cup Danish Blue Cheese, crumbled

Combine all ingredients except Blue Cheese, in order given, blending well. Be sure to blend all ingredients well before adding Blue Cheese. Add Blue Cheese. Cover and chill to allow flavors to blend.

CREAMY DRESSING

¼ cup Danish Blue Cheese, crumbled
½ cup mayonnaise
½ cup dairy sour cream
⅓ cup milk
2 tsp. fresh lemon juice
1 tsp. minced green onion
Small clove garlic, pressed
Freshly ground pepper
Salt to taste

Combine all ingredients in order given, blending well. Cover and chill to allow flavors to blend.

VARIATION:
HERBED DRESSING

Prepare receipe for Creamy Dressing, adding ½ tsp. *each* dried tarragon and sweet basil and ¼ cup minced parsley.

Combine all ingredients in order given, blending well. Cover and chill to allow flavors to blend.

Favorite recipe from **Denmark Cheese Association**

SAVORY DRESSING

1 cup mayonnaise
¼ cup white wine vinegar
2 teaspoons celery seed
½ teaspoon TABASCO® Pepper Sauce
½ teaspoon sugar
¼ teaspoon salt

In small bowl combine all ingredients; mix well.

Yield: About 1¼ cups

FRENCH-STYLE BLUE CHEESE DRESSING

1½ cups CAMPBELL'S Tomato Juice
2 tablespoons salad oil
2 tablespoons crumbled blue cheese
1 tablespoon lemon juice
1 tablespoon finely chopped onion
1 small clove garlic, minced

In covered jar or shaker, combine ingredients; chill. Shake well before using. Serve on salad greens.   *Makes about 2 cups*

SWEET AND SOUR BLUE CHEESE DRESSING

1 can (6-ounces) V-8 Cocktail Vegetable Juice
⅔ cup mayonnaise
⅓ cup crumbled blue cheese
1 tablespoon brown sugar
1 tablespoon vinegar
1 teaspoon dry mustard
⅛ teaspoon Italian seasoning

In bowl, gradually stir V-8 Juice into mayonnaise; add remaining ingredients. Chill. Serve on salad greens.   *Makes 1½ cups*

CREAMY GREEN PEPPER DRESSING

1½ cups BEST FOODS®/HELLMANN'S® Real Mayonnaise
½ cup finely chopped green pepper
¼ cup finely chopped parsley
¼ cup finely chopped onion
¼ cup KARO® Light Corn Syrup
2 tablespoons cider vinegar
½ teaspoon salt
⅛ teaspoon pepper

In small bowl stir together real mayonnaise, green pepper, parsley, onion, corn syrup, vinegar, salt and ground pepper until well blended. Cover; refrigerate 2 hours to blend flavors.

Makes about 2¼ cups

HERB SALAD DRESSING
(Low Calorie)

1 packet BUTTER BUDS®, made into liquid
1 tablespoon distilled white vinegar
1 tablespoon lemon juice
¼ teaspoon garlic powder
¼ teaspoon oregano
¼ teaspoon tarragon
¼ teaspoon thyme
⅛ teaspoon freshly ground pepper

Combine all ingredients in small jar; cover and shake until well blended. Serve over your favorite tossed green salad.

About ⅔ cup

PER SERVING (1 tablespoon):   Calories: 5   Protein: trace
Carbohydrate: trace   Fat: 1g   Sodium: 93mg

FRUIT SALAD DRESSING

½ cup dairy sour cream
¼ cup SKIPPY® Creamy or Chunk Style Peanut Butter
¼ cup KARO® Dark Corn Syrup

Mix together sour cream, peanut butter and corn syrup. Serve over mixed fresh fruit salad.   *Makes 1 cup*

PIQUANT SALAD DRESSING

½ cup mayonnaise
½ cup fresh lemon juice
¼ cup SUE BEE® Honey
¼ teaspoon prepared mustard
Paprika
Extra seasonings if desired

Combine all ingredients in a jar or blender and mix well. Spoon over raw asparagus, cauliflower, tomatoes, cucumbers, or crisp lettuce wedges.   *Makes 1¼ cups*

ORANGE PINEAPPLE SALAD DRESSING

¼ teaspoon sugar
¼ teaspoon grated orange peel
1 cup SEALTEST® Cottage Cheese
½ cup SEALTEST® Sour Cream
Dash salt
½ cup unsweetened pineapple juice
½ teaspoon lemon juice
6 tablespoons canned crushed pineapple and syrup

Mix sugar and orange peel; set aside. Sieve cottage cheese; fold in sour cream. Add salt, pineapple and lemon juices, and crushed pineapple; blend well. Fold in orange peel. Chill.   *2¼ cups*

Minted Melon
Hiram Walker *(Hiram Walker & Sons, Inc.)*

Kielbasa Bites *(right)*, Sausage and
Horseradish Canapés *(left)*
Hillshire Farm® *(Kahn's and Company)*

Sticks Rumaki
Tyson® *(Tyson Foods, Inc.)*

Zesty Party Dip, Tasty Cheese Dip,
"Ketch" A Clam Dip
Heinz *(Heinz U.S.A.)*

Quick Chicken Soup with **New Mill®**
Kluski *(left)*, Beef Stroganoff a la **New
Mill®** Kluski *(right)*
New Mill® *(Ravarino & Freschi, Inc.)*

Meatball Soup Florentine *(middle)*, Dilled
Chicken and Cheese Ball *(bottom)*, Sweet
and Sour Blue Cheese Dressing *(top)*
Campbell's, Swanson, V-8 *(Campbell
Soup Company)*

Cheesy Vegetable Bisque *(front)*, Toasted
Jarlsberg Loaf *(back)*
Jarlsberg *(Norseland Foods Inc.)*

Fisherman's Wharf Cioppino
Bumble Bee®, Dole® *(Castle & Cooke
Foods)*

Brace of Birds Saronno
Amaretto di Saronno® *(Foreign Vintages, Inc.)*

Chicken Cacciatore
Prego *(Campbell Soup Company)*

Crispy Fried Chicken
Crisco® *(The Procter & Gamble Company)*

Turkey Breast a la Grecque
Louis Rich™ *(Louis Rich Co., Div. of Oscar Mayer Foods Corporation)*

Cheddar Cheese Bread *(top left)*, Roast Turkey with Prune Walnut Stuffing *(middle center)*, Green Bean Combo *(bottom left)*, Creamy Bacon Dip *(middle bottom)*, Festive Angel Torte *(bottom right)*
Chiffon®, **Seven Seas**® *(Anderson Clayton Foods)*

Meatballs in Meat Sauce
Bertolli® *(Bertolli U.S.A.)*

All American Pot Roast
Mazola®, **Argo**®/**Kingsford's**® *(Best Foods)*

New England Boiled Dinner
Domino® Brownulated® *(Amstar Corporation)*

Baked Ham Battilana *(right)*, Hamkebab *(left)*
Celebrity®, Excelsior™ *(Atalanta Corp.)*

Swiss Hamlets
Oscar Mayer *(Oscar Mayer Foods Corporation)*

Coconut-Crusted Sole with Sweet-Sour Sauce
(National Marine Fisheries Service)

Herb-Topped Fish Fillets
Premium, Fleischmann's *(Nabisco Brands Inc.)*

Filet of Sole En Croute
Pepperidge Farm® *(Pepperidge Farm, Inc.)*

Poached Farm Raised Catfish in Emerald Bay Sauce
(Catfish Farmers of America)

Beer-Boiled Shrimp
Coors® *(Adolph Coors Company)*

Pizza Casserole with **R•F®** Shelmacs
R•F® *(Ravarino & Freschi, Inc.)*

Pennsylvania Dutch Vegetable Skillet
French's® *(The R. T. French Company)*

Mandarin Chicken *(top left)*, Beef Stew *(top right)*, Taco Salad *(front)*
Henri's *(Henri's Food Products Co., Inc.)*

Diced Veal Stew
Provimi® *(Provimi, Inc.)*

Texas-Style Chili
Wyler's® *(Borden Inc.)*

Ham & Asparagus Quiche
Seven Seas® *(Anderson Clayton Foods)*

Spicy Southwestern Casserole *(left)*, Croissant Dogs *(center front)*, Taco Dogs *(top right)*
Perdue® *(Perdue Farms Inc.)*

Buck's County Beef Stew
Argo®/Kingsford's® *(Best Foods)*
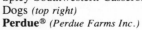

Buddig Corned Beef Hash *(right)*,
Buddig Omelet *(left)*
Buddig *(Carl Buddig and Company)*

''Creole'' Egg and Kidney Bean Quickie
Goya® *(Goya Foods, Inc.)*

Celebration Spaghetti
**Creamette®, Frigo®, California Olive
Industry** *(The Creamette Company)*

Fusilli Supreme *(back)*, Mostaccioli
Medley *(front)*
San Giorgio® *(San Giorgio-Skinner Co.)*

Christmas Fruit Mold *(front)*, Turkey with
Carrot Stuffing *(back)*
Jello®, Stove Top® *(General Foods Corp.)*

Majestic Layered Salad
(The Association for Dressings and Sauces)

Bird of Paradise Salad
Cape Granny Smith *(Cape Granny Smith
Apples)*

Tuna Salad Nicoise
Bumble Bee® *(Castle & Cooke Foods)*

Bacon **Stroh's** Burgers
Stroh's *(The Stroh Brewery Co.)*

Shazam Shamrock Pizza
Chef Boy-Ar-Dee® *(American Home Foods)*

All Star Hero
Nokkelost *(Norseland Foods Inc.)*

Party Pizza Variations
Bays® *(Bays Home Service Institute)*

Hawaiian French Toast
King's *(King's Hawaiian Bakery West, Inc.)*

Marinated Raw Shredded Carrots
Dante *(Atalanta Corporation)*

Onion Buttered Corn
Lipton® *(Thomas J. Lipton, Inc.)*

Quick Fruit-Nut Muffins
Wheatsworth, Planters *(Nabisco Brands Inc.)*

Coffee Can Bread *(top left)*, Bohemian Christmas Braid *(top right)*, Cheesy Mexican Bread *(bottom center)*
Pet® *(Pet Incorporated)*

Orange Prune Nut Loaf
Sunkist® *(Sunkist Growers, Inc.)*

Mrs. Frickholm's 4-Day Fruitcake
S&W® *(S&W Fine Foods, Inc.)*

Old-Fashioned Cake Roll *(front)*, Red Raspberry Jam *(back)*
Certo® *(General Foods Corporation)*

Cranberry Orange Cream Cheese Ice Cream Cake *(top)*, Cranberry Soufflé *(bottom)*
Ocean Spray® Cranorange® *(Ocean Spray Cranberries, Inc.)*

Chocolate Bundt® Cake *(top)*, Mighty Mini Chip Cookies *(middle)*, Easy Chocolate Ice Cream *(bottom)*
Hershey's® *(Hershey Foods Corporation)*

Strawberry Tunnel Cream Cake
Eagle® Brand, ReaLemon® *(Borden Inc.)*

Heavenly Vino Cake
Bertolli® *(Bertolli U.S.A.)*

Strawberry-Banana-Pineapple Flambé *(top)*, Fresh Strawberry Tarts *(middle)*, Strawberries with Misty Sauce in Meringue Shells *(bottom)*
Irish Mist®, Regina *(Heublein/Spirits Group)*

Saronno Sunglow Sundaes in Meringue
Amaretto di Saronno® *(Foreign Vintages Inc.)*

Deep Dish Blueberry Pie *(left)*, Pineapple Strawberry Pie *(right)*, Ginger Peach Lattice Pie *(left front)*
Argo®/Kingsford's®, Mazola® *(Best Foods)*

Chocolate Chiffon Squares *(bottom)*,
Choco-Berry Bavarian Cream *(top)*
Hershey's® *(Hershey Foods Corporation)*

Ambrosia Parfaits
Oreo *(Nabisco Brands Inc.)*

Rainbow Sherbet Roll
Betty Crocker® *(General Mills, Inc.)*

Chocolate-Peanut Butter Cups
Nestlé® *(The Nestlé Company, Inc.)*

Peanut Butter Jumbos
"M&M's"® *(M&M/Mars)*

Caramel Corn Clusters *(top right)*,
Crunchy Fruit Munch *(bottom right)*, **Jolly
Time**® Pop Corn Balls *(left)*
Jolly Time® *(American Pop Corn Company)*

Festive Punch
Smirnoff® *(Heublein/Spirits Group)*

Fresh Fruit Colada *(left)*, Piña Colada
Cooler *(right)*
Coco López®, **ReaLime**® *(Coco López
Imports, Inc.)*

Capistrano Coffee
(California Brandy Advisory Board)

Sandwiches & Pizza

Sandwiches

LITE-LINE® SANDWICH SPECIAL

2 cups finely shredded cabbage
½ cup shredded carrot
3 tablespoons bottled low calorie slaw dressing
4 slices very thin white bread, toasted
8 slices **BORDEN® LITE-LINE®** Pasteurized
  Process Cheese Product
½ pound thinly sliced cooked roast beef (trimmed of fat)
4 teaspoons prepared horseradish
Pimiento strips, optional

In medium bowl, combine cabbage, carrot and dressing; mix well. On each of 4 slices toast, place one slice cheese product, two ounces beef, one teaspoon horseradish, second slice cheese product; if desired, broil. Top with ½ cup cabbage mixture. Garnish with pimiento if desired. Refrigerate leftovers.

Makes 4 servings

1136 calories or 284 calories per serving

SWEET MUN-CHEE® MUFFINWICH

2 cups (8-ounces) shredded **SWEET MUN-CHEE®**
  Cheese
⅓ cup milk
½ cup chopped celery
¼ cup chopped green pepper
½ tablespoon finely chopped onion
1 tablespoon butter or margarine
2¼-ounce can mushroom slices, drained
2 tablespoons diced pimiento
3 hard-cooked eggs, coarsely chopped
5 English muffin halves, toasted

Combine cheese and milk in top of double boiler. Cook over hot water, stirring occasionally until well blended and smooth. Sauté celery, green pepper and onion in melted butter until tender. Add to sauce. Stir in mushrooms, pimiento and eggs. Heat. Serve ½ cup sauce over each muffin half. *Yield: 5 servings*

Note: For a quick meal, this sauce can be made ahead and refrigerated. Then reheat in a double boiler before serving.

SYRIAN CHICKEN SNACKS

1 can (4¾ ounces) **UNDERWOOD®** Chunky Chicken
  Spread
2 tablespoons chopped celery
2 tablespoons chopped onion
3 small loaves Syrian (pita) bread (3 inches in diameter)
½ cup shredded Cheddar cheese

In a bowl, mix together chunky chicken spread, celery and onion. Split bread in half horizontally to make 6 flat slices. Spread each with chicken mixture and top with shredded cheese. Broil 3 to 5 minutes, until filling is hot and cheese is melted. Cut into quarters.

Makes 24 snacks

ITALIAN CRISS-CROSS SANDWICHES

6 one-inch slices firm French bread
6 thin square slices of packaged ham
6 Tbsp. **SEVEN SEAS®** Creamy Italian Dressing
24 strips Swiss cheese (½ × 4-inch)
1 red delicious apple, cored and halved

Spread 1 tablespoon of Dressing all the way to the edge of each slice of bread. Broil 2 minutes or until lightly browned. Put a ham slice on each piece of bread. Cut apple halves into 9 slices each, and top every sandwich with 3 slices of apple. Add 4 strips of cheese per sandwich, laid diagonally across. Broil until bubbly and serve. *4-6 servings*

GOLDEN CLUB SANDWICH

6 **BAYS®** English Muffins, split
Butter, melted
24 slices of tomato (approximately same size as muffin) seasoned with salt and pepper
12 thin slices of onion (approximately same size as muffin)
1 pound sliced smoked salmon
12 fresh mushroom caps, thinly sliced
Lumpfish caviar (optional) or, black olive

Lightly toast muffins; brush with butter. Cover each with 1 slice tomato, 1 slice onion, 2 slices of smoked salmon (folded), another slice of tomato, and finish with thinly sliced mushrooms. Place in warm oven (300 degrees). Pour Cheese Sauce* over sandwich and top with 1 teaspoon lumpfish caviar or black olive slice.

Serves 6

*CHEESE SAUCE

In medium saucepan—bring 12 ounces beer to full boil. Combine 3 tablespoons cornstarch and ½ cup water; add to boiling beer; beat vigorously with a whip. Let mixture return to a full boil and continue stirring until it thickens. Reduce heat; add 1 pound grated Cheddar cheese. Stir mixture slowly. Do not let it boil. When cheese is melted, add a small amount of the sauce to 1 egg yolk; beat well, then add yolk mixture to rest of sauce. Beat well. Season to taste with cayenne pepper.

MUFFINS FANTASTIC

8 oz. small cooked shrimp
1½ cups diced cooked chicken
½ cup mayonnaise
¼ teaspoon salt
⅛ teaspoon pepper
½ cup finely chopped celery
12 slices **FISHER Cheese's SANDWICH-MATE®**
  Singles
6 English Muffins

Mix first 6 ingredients thoroughly. Split and toast muffins, top each half with 2 tablespoonfuls of shrimp/chicken mixture. Bake 10 minutes at 350°, then top muffins with **FISHER Cheese's SANDWICH-MATE®** Singles. Return to oven until slices melt.

Yield: 12 servings

MONTEREY MUFFIN MELT

6 **BAYS®** **English Muffins,** split and lightly toasted
4 ounces alfalfa sprouts
12 slices turkey breast
12 strips bacon, cooked crisp
2 large avocados, sliced
12 slices Monterey Jack or Swiss cheese
Dipping Sauce*

Lightly butter toasted muffin halves. Layer the following on muffins: about one tablespoon of alfalfa sprouts; one slice turkey breast; one slice bacon; 2-3 slices avocado and one slice cheese. Place under broiler until cheese melts or microwave on high for 15 seconds. Garnish with fresh fruit. Eat Monterey Melt Sandwich open-faced, dipping pieces into the sauce.   *Serves 6*

*DIPPING SAUCE

1 cup mayonnaise
2 tablespoons Dijon mustard
1 tablespoon sherry (optional)

Using a spatula, in a small bowl, combine mustard, mayonnaise and sherry.

BACON AND TOMATO RAREBIT

1 lb. **WILSON®** Bacon
2 tablespoons bacon drippings or margarine
2 tablespoons flour
⅛ teaspoon dry mustard
½ cup beer
½ cup milk
1 teaspoon Worcestershire sauce
2 cups shredded Cheddar cheese
1 large tomato
6 slices dark rye or pumpernickel bread, toasted
Sliced green onion

Cook bacon until crisp. Drain. Set aside 12 slices. Crumble remaining. Place 2 tablespoons bacon drippings in medium saucepan, over medium heat. Stir in flour and mustard until smooth. Stir in beer and milk. Cook, stirring constantly, until mixture thickens and comes to a full boil. Stir and boil 1 minute. Reduce heat. Stir in Worcestershire sauce and cheese until cheese is melted. Stir in crumbled bacon. Keep warm. Cut tomato in 6 slices. For each sandwich, place a slice of toast on a plate. Spoon ¼ cup cheese sauce over toast. Top with a slice of tomato and 2 slices bacon. Spoon remaining sauce evenly over the 6 sandwiches. Garnish with sliced green onion, if desired.   *Makes 6 servings*

ANTIPASTO SANDWICH

1 package (8 oz.) **OSCAR MAYER Hard Salami**
1 loaf (1 lb.) unsliced bread, about 10-inches long
1 head lettuce
6 to 8 oz. provolone or mozzarella cheese, sliced thin or cut into bite-size pieces
24 ripe olives
2 tomatoes, cut into wedges
Pickled mild Italian peppers
Italian salad dressing

Slice bread lengthwise into four flat pieces. Top each slice with lettuce. Arrange salami, cheese and olives on top. Garnish with tomato wedges and peppers. Serve with Italian salad dressing.
          Makes four open-faced servings

EASY CRAB SANDWICHES

1 package (6-ounces) snow crab or other crabmeat, fresh or frozen *or* 1 can (6½-ounces) crabmeat
1 cup shredded cheese
½ cup chopped celery
¼ cup chopped parsley
½ cup mayonnaise or salad dressing
1 tablespoon lemon juice
1 teaspoon Dijon-style mustard
⅛ teaspoon liquid hot pepper sauce
4 English muffins
¼ cup margarine or butter
8 sandwich-cut cheese slices

Thaw crabmeat if frozen. Drain canned crabmeat. Remove any remaining shell or cartilage. Combine crabmeat, cheese, celery and parsley. Combine mayonnaise, lemon juice, mustard, and liquid hot pepper sauce. Toss crabmeat mixture with dressing. Split and toast English muffins; spread muffins with margarine. Place approximately ¼ cup of crab mixture and one slice of cheese on each half of the English muffins. Broil about 4 inches from source of heat for 4 to 5 minutes until cheese is melted and crab mixture is heated.   *Makes 4 servings*

Note: To serve as an appetizer cut each muffin half into quarters.

Favorite recipe from **National Fisheries Institute, Inc.**

MEXICAN MELT

1 (6 inch diam.) corn tortilla (not fried)
1 slice (1 oz.) **KAHN'S® Cooked Ham,** cut into small pieces
1 oz. Cheddar cheese, grated
2 Tbsp. chopped green onion

Place tortilla in nonstick baking dish. Top with ham, cheese, and onion. Bake at 350° for 10-15 minutes or until cheese is melted.
          Makes 1 serving

Calories: 210 calories per serving

CRISPY TURKEY CHEESEWICHES

8 thin slices roasted **SWIFT PREMIUM® BUTTERBALL®** Turkey
¼ cup mayonnaise
1 tablespoon chopped parsley or freeze-dried chopped chives
½ stick (¼ cup) butter or margarine
¼ teaspoon sage leaves
8 slices bread
4 slices process American cheese

Combine mayonnaise and parsley. Cream together butter and sage leaves. Spread bread with mayonnaise mixture. Top 4 slices bread with turkey and cheese slices. Cover with remaining slices of bread, mayonnaise side down. Using about 1 tablespoon per sandwich, spread each side with butter-sage mixture. Brown slowly on both sides in skillet or griddle until crisp and cheese melts. Cut into halves to serve.   *Yield: 4 sandwiches*

MONTE CRISTO

1 package (6-oz.) **OSCAR MAYER Smoked Cooked Ham**
4 slices Swiss cheese, each 4 inches square
4 slices turkey breast
8 slices bread
Oil for frying
Confectioner's sugar
Raspberry jam
Toothpicks
Batter:
1½ cups flour
2 teaspoons baking powder
¼ teaspoon salt
2 eggs
1½ cups milk

Layer 2 slices ham, 1 slice cheese and 1 slice turkey on each of 4 slices of bread. Top with remaining bread slice. Press sandwich firmly together; cut into quarters. Secure with toothpicks. Heat oil to 375°F in heavy 3-quart saucepan or deep fat fryer.

BATTER:
To prepare batter: combine flour, baking powder and salt in medium bowl. Beat eggs and milk; stir into flour mixture until smooth.

Dip each sandwich in batter to coat well. Fry 3 minutes or until golden brown on both sides. Drain on paper towels. Remove toothpicks; sprinkle with sugar. Serve with jam.   *4 servings*

GRILLED RACHAEL

12 large slices dark rye bread
Mayonnaise or salad dressing
2 lb. **JENNIE-O® Brand Fully Cooked Turkey Breast**, thinly sliced
16 oz. jar or can sauerkraut, well drained
12 slices (12-oz.) Swiss cheese
Butter or margarine, softened

For each sandwich, use 2 slices bread, one-sixth of the turkey slices, one-third cup sauerkraut, and 2 slices cheese. Assemble sandwiches by spreading one side of each bread slice with mayonnaise. On six bread slices, layer turkey, sauerkraut, and cheese. Cover with remaining bread slices, mayonnaise side down. Spread top bread slice evenly with softened butter; place buttered side down in skillet. Butter other bread slice. Cover; grill slowly on each side.   *Makes 6 sandwiches*

Note: You may substitute other **JENNIE-O® Turkey Products** in this recipe.

ITALIAN MELT

2 slices (1 oz.) part-skim mozzarella cheese, divided
2 slices thin sliced diet bread
2 slices (2 oz.) **KAHN'S® Cooked Ham**
1 slice tomato, thinly sliced
Dash oregano
1 egg

Place 1 slice of cheese on one slice of bread. Add ham and tomato and season with oregano. Top with remaining slice of cheese and bread. In small bowl, mix egg with a few drops of water. Dip assembled sandwich into egg, turning, so that egg is absorbed into bread. Spray a nonstick skillet with nonstick cooking spray; heat over medium heat. Add the sandwich and cook, turning occasionally, until both sides are browned and cheese is melted.

Makes 1 serving

Calories: 300 calories per serving

FRENCH DIP SANDWICH

1 can **FRANCO-AMERICAN Au Jus Gravy**
4 servings thinly sliced cooked roast beef
4 servings French bread or long hard rolls, cut in half

1. In 10-inch skillet, combine gravy and beef. Over low heat, heat through, stirring occasionally.
2. To make sandwiches: Arrange beef on bread. Serve each sandwich with small bowl of gravy for dipping.

Makes 4 sandwiches

STEAK HOAGIES

6 shaved steaks
1 chopped onion
1 diced green pepper
1 chopped tomato
8 oz. **SORRENTO® Mozzarella or Shredded Mozzarella**
1 cup shredded lettuce
6 hot dog or hoagie rolls

Cook steak according to package directions. Brown onion and pepper until tender. Toast buns and place a cooked steak on each roll and top with slices of **SORRENTO® Mozzarella** or sprinkle on **Shredded Mozzarella** to taste. Place under broiler until cheese melts. Top each hoagie with onion, pepper, tomato and lettuce.   *Serves 6*

HOT AND HEARTY REUBEN SANDWICH

8 slices rye bread
½ cup **HENRI'S 1000 Island Dressing**
4 slices Swiss cheese
1 (12-ounce) can corned beef, sliced ⅛-inch thick
1 (8-ounce) can sauerkraut, well drained

1. Preheat oven to 350° F.
2. Spread one side of 4 slices of bread with 1 tablespoon of **HENRI'S 1000 Island Dressing**.
3. Top other 4 bread slices with one slice cheese, one slice corned beef and ¼ cup sauerkraut. Cover each with second slice of bread, dressing side down. Repeat with remaining ingredients.
4. Wrap each sandwich in aluminum foil. Bake 20 minutes. Serve immediately.   *Makes 4 sandwiches*

JIFFY HAMBURGERS

1 pound ground chuck
¼ cup chopped onion
2 tablespoons chili sauce
2 tablespoons **PLOCHMAN'S® Natural Stone Ground Mustard with Fresh Horseradish**
1 teaspoon instant beef bouillon granules
6 hamburger buns or English muffins

Combine first 5 ingredients. Spread a generous ¼ cup on hamburger bun halves or English muffin halves. Bake at 350° for 25 to 30 minutes.   *Yield: 6 servings*

GERMAN BURGERS

12 slices bacon
1 can (16-oz.) sauerkraut, rinsed and drained
¼ cup **A.1. Steak Sauce**
2 tablespoons dry minced onion
6 Basic Hamburgers,* cooked
12 slices rye bread with caraway seeds

Cook bacon until crisp. Drain, reserving ¼ cup drippings. To drippings add sauerkraut, **A.1.** and onion. Simmer, uncovered, 15 minutes. Serve hamburgers, topped with sauerkraut and bacon slices, on bread.   *Serves 6*

*BASIC HAMBURGERS

1½ lb. ground beef
¼ cup **A.1. Steak Sauce**

In medium bowl, lightly combine all ingredients. Form 6 patties to fit bread shape of your choice. Broil, barbecue or pan fry until cooked as desired.   *Makes 6*

GRANDMA'S BROILER BURGERS

1 (8-oz.) can of luncheon meat
4 slices of American cheese

Grind/Mix above ingredients together. Then add:

3 Tbsp. catsup
3 Tbsp. **COOKIES Taco Sauce and Dip**

Mix together, and spread on bun halves. Broil in oven until cheese melts. Watch closely. *Makes approximately 12-16 sandwiches*

CHEESE-STUFFED FRANKFURTERS

1 pound frankfurters (8 to 10)
OPEN PIT® Barbecue Sauce
2 to 3 slices process American cheese, cut in thin strips
8 to 10 bacon slices
8 to 10 frankfurter rolls, toasted

Slit frankfurters lengthwise to ¾-inch from each end. Spoon ¼ teaspoon barbecue sauce along slit in each; add 2 cheese strips to each. Wind a bacon slice around each frankfurter; secure with wooden picks at each end. Place on grill away from glowing coals. Brush with additional barbecue sauce and grill, turning and basting until bacon is cooked. Remove picks. Serve on rolls.

Makes 4 servings

SLOPPY DOGS
(Microwave Recipe)

1 pound ground beef
1 package (1.5-oz.) **DURKEE Sloppy Joe Seasoning Mix**
1 can (6-oz.) tomato paste
1¼ cups water
1 teaspoon **DURKEE Dry Mustard**
2 teaspoons **DURKEE RedHot! Sauce**
1 package (16-oz.) frankfurters
8-10 hot dog buns

In a 2½-quart casserole, crumble beef. Microwave on High 4-5 minutes, stirring halfway through cooking time; drain. Stir in seasoning mix, tomato paste and water. Microwave, covered, on High 4 minutes, stirring halfway through cooking time. Add mustard, hot sauce, and frankfurters. Microwave, covered, on High 6 minutes, stirring halfway through the cooking time. Serve on hot dog buns.   *Makes 8 to 10 servings*

TACO DOGS

8 **PERDUE**® Franks
8 taco shells
15-ounce can chili with beans
1 cup shredded Monterey Jack or Cheddar cheese
Taco sauce
1 cup shredded lettuce
½ cup diced tomato

Preheat oven to 350°. Split Franks in half lengthwise and grill or fry briefly. Place Franks in taco shells and top each with 2 tablespoons chili and 1 tablespoon cheese. Place tacos on baking sheet and bake at 350° for 15 minutes, or until chili is hot and cheese is melted. Top with taco sauce, lettuce, tomato and remaining cheese. Serve immediately.   *Serves 6-8*

HOTDOGS AZTECA®

1 pkg. **AZTECA**® Flour or Corn Tortillas
1 lb. hot dogs
1 (15-oz.) can of chili with beans
1 (8-oz.) pkg. American cheese slices

Bring **AZTECA**® Tortillas to room temperature. Preheat oven to 475°. Spread 1 heaping teaspoon of chili on each tortilla. Place slice of cheese on top of chili. Set hot dog in center of cheese. Roll up sides of tortilla and fasten with toothpicks. Bake approximately 10 minutes until cheese is melted and tortilla is crisp.

Serves 5-6

Note: For appetizers, slice in quarters.

CROISSANT DOGS

8 **PERDUE**® Franks
8-ounce package of crescent roll dough
2 tablespoons Dijon mustard
2 slices Swiss cheese, 7 × 4 inches
1 egg beaten with 1 tablespoon water
1½ teaspoons poppy seeds (optional)

Preheat oven to 375°. Pierce Franks all over with tines of fork. Divide crescent rolls and place on lightly floured surface. Working with one piece of dough at a time, fold tips of long side of triangle in to meet at center. Then stretch triangle lightly up toward point. Cut cheese slices in half, then diagonally to form four triangular pieces. Brush dough with thin layer of mustard, top with cheese, brush with mustard again. Roll Franks in the dough, starting at the bottom and rolling toward the point. Place on ungreased baking sheet so they are not touching. Brush lightly with egg wash and sprinkle with poppy seeds. Place in the middle of the oven for 15 to 20 minutes or until dough is golden brown.   *Serves 6-8*

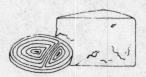

BEER BOILED BRATWURST

8 bratwurst, fully cooked in 4 cans **STROH'S** Beer
2 Tbsp. mustard
2 Tbsp. chopped onion
2 slices Cheddar cheese
8 slices bacon, partially cooked
Bottled barbecue sauce
8 hot dog buns, split and toasted

After cooking bratwurst, split lengthwise, cutting only ⅔ of the way through, and *almost* to ends. Spread inside of each bratwurst with mustard, then add a pinch of onion. Cut each slice of cheese into 4 strips, and place 1 strip inside each bratwurst. Wrap each with a strip of partially cooked bacon; secure with wooden picks. Grill over hot coals for 9 to 11 minutes, brushing with barbecue sauce. Turn often so bacon crisps evenly. Remove picks and serve bratwurst in toasted buns.

HERO SANDWICH

1 large loaf French or Italian Bread (2-3 feet long)
Mayonnaise
GREY POUPON Dijon Mustard
¼ lb. *each* sliced Genoa Salami, provolone cheese, and
   roast beef
½ lb. cole slaw, drained
1 small jar chopped fried peppers, drained
Romaine lettuce
¼ lb. *each* sliced Swiss cheese and turkey breast

Split bread lengthwise. Spread top side with mayonnaise. Spread bottom side with mustard. Place remaining ingredients, according to order, on bottom bread slice. Top with remaining bread slice. Slice as desired. Serve with radish fans and scallion curls, if desired.

ALL STAR HERO

1 large loaf Italian bread, split
3 tablespoons olive oil
2 tablespoons wine vinegar
¼ teaspoon basil, crushed
¼ teaspoon oregano, crushed
½ pound thinly sliced ham
2 ounces hard salami, thinly sliced
6 slices **NOKKELOST Cheese**, about 1 ounce each
1½ cups shredded lettuce
2 medium tomatoes, thinly sliced
1 medium purple onion, thinly sliced and separated
   into rings
2 sweet Italian sausage links, cooked and crumbled

Open bread. Combine oil, vinegar and seasonings. Sprinkle over bread. Arrange meats, cheese, lettuce, tomato and onion on bread. Top with sausage. *Serves: 6 to 8*

CRUNCHY TUNA STACKS

¾ cup mayonnaise or salad dressing
1 teaspoon curry powder
1 can (9¼-oz.) **CHICKEN OF THE SEA® Chunk
   Light Tuna**, drained and flaked
5 slices dark rye or pumpernickel bread, buttered
5 lettuce leaves
10 thin slices tomato
1 cup shredded carrot
⅓ cup sliced green onions with tops
5 green pepper rings
⅓ cup chopped cocktail peanuts

Combine mayonnaise and curry powder. Mix well. Stir in tuna.
   For sandwiches, top each bread slice with lettuce leaf, 2 tomato slices, 3 tablespoons carrot and 1 tablespoon onion. Divide and spread tuna mixture over onion layer. Garnish with green pepper ring and 1 tablespoon peanuts. If desired, sandwich may be topped with an additional bread slice. *Makes 5*

FRENCH TUNA HERO

⅔ cup **WISH-BONE® HERB CLASSICS™ Herbal
   French Dressing**
2 cans (7-oz. each) tuna, drained and flaked
⅓ cup chopped green pepper
1 loaf French or Italian bread (about 12 inches long),
   cut in half horizontally
2 tomatoes, thinly sliced
6 slices American cheese

Preheat oven to 350°. Combine ⅓ cup classic Herbal French Dressing, tuna and green pepper.
   Brush each bread half with remaining dressing, then equally top with tomatoes and tuna mixture. Wrap in foil and bake 30 minutes or until heated through. Unwrap and top with cheese; continue to bake until cheese is melted. *Makes about 6 servings*

BREADED OYSTER DOWNEASTER SANDWICH

1 (10-oz. pkg.) **BOOTH® Breaded Oysters**
3 oz. cream cheese
3 green onions, chopped
8 bacon slices, cooked until crisp
4 slices white bread, toasted
Salt and paprika

Fry oysters according to package directions. Blend cream cheese, salt and paprika to taste. Add onions. Spread cream cheese mixture on toast, top with oysters and bacon slices.

STAR-KIST® TUNA IN A PITA POCKET

1 can (6½- to 7-oz.) **STAR-KIST® Tuna**, drained, (use
   Chunk Light, Solid Light or **Solid White**, all in
   Natural Spring Water)
½ carrot, shredded
½ zucchini, shredded
1 small apple, cored, finely chopped
3 tablespoons sliced green onion
4 teaspoons reduced-calorie mayonnaise
1 teaspoon Dijon mustard
1 teaspoon poppy seeds
2 whole wheat pita breads (1-oz. each)

Combine tuna, carrot, zucchini, apple and onion. Combine mayonnaise, mustard and poppy seeds and toss lightly with tuna mixture. Cut pita bread in half; open to form pocket. Fill pocket with tuna mixture. Optional garnish: parsley, radish.
Makes 2 servings

DELI DELICIOUS

1 pkg. **TYSON® CHICK'N QUICK™ Swiss'n Bacon
   Patties**
4 pieces pita bread
Spicy brown mustard
4 slices cheese
Avocado, cucumber, lettuce, tomato, and sprouts

Prepare Swiss'n Bacon patties according to package directions. Coat inside of pita pockets with spicy brown mustard. Fill with prepared patties, cheese, lettuce, sprouts, and slices of avocado, cucumber, and tomato. Serve cold or heat in oven until cheese melts. Serve immediately. *Makes 4 servings*

COOKIN' GOOD™ POCKET SANDWICHES

2 cups of cooked, minced **COOKIN' GOOD™ Chicken**
8 slices of crisp, crumbled bacon
1-8 ounce container of sour cream
¼ cup mayonnaise
2 tablespoons minced onion
½ cup finely chopped celery (about 3-4 ribs)
½ cup black olives, sliced
½ teaspoon salt
½ teaspoon black pepper
¼ teaspoon poultry seasoning
2 tablespoons white wine or lemon juice
1 refrigerated can of biscuits (10-12 biscuits)
1 egg beaten

In a large mixing bowl combine mayonnaise, sour cream, celery, onion and spices, blend well after each addition. To this mixture add lemon juice, bacon and gradually add minced **COOKIN' GOOD™ Chicken** and olives. Tip: For ease in mincing **COOKIN' GOOD™ Chicken**, process in a blender or food processor according to manufacturer's directions. Blend mixture well.

On a floured pastry sheet or board, using a floured rolling pin, roll each biscuit to a 4-5 inch circle. Place ¼ cup of chicken mixture on each circle, fold in half and crimp edges with a fork to seal. Place pocket sandwiches on an ungreased cookie sheet. Brush with beaten egg and prick tops of sandwiches with a fork once or twice to allow steam to escape. Bake 375° for 12-15 minutes or until golden brown. Remove to a cooling rack. May be frozen for one month, properly wrapped. This salad can also be eaten cold on any type of bread or on a bed of lettuce.

Serves 4-6

FOOD PROCESSOR METHOD:
To prepare this recipe in a food processor continue adding ingredients. Process 1 minute to blend all ingredients.

Lunchbox tip: Place one or two frozen sandwiches in lunchbox—will be ready to eat by lunch time!

PITA BREAD PATTIES

Cut Pita bread in half. Spread inside pockets with barbecue sauce. Fill each pocket with a **FARMLAND FOODS, INC.™ Ham and Cheese Pattie**. Top each pattie with onion, tomato and pickle slice. Bake 15 minutes at 350°. MICROWAVE for 45 seconds on high.

THE CAMEL HUMP

4 pita breads
Sliced cooked ham
Sliced salami
2 tomatoes, sliced
2 Tbsp. feta cheese, crumbled
1 Tbsp. chopped ripe olives
Lettuce

Dressing:
¼ cup **PAUL MASSON® Rosé**
2 Tbsp. lemon juice
⅛ tsp. each oregano, garlic salt, turmeric and pepper

Fill each pocket bread with sliced meats, tomatoes, cheese, olives and lettuce.

Combine dressing ingredients and spoon over each sandwich before serving.

4 servings

GALLO® SALAME AND SPROUTS ONION BUNS

12 **GALLO® Italian Dry Salame Slices**
4 onion buns
Butter
8 ounces cream cheese
1 large tomato, sliced
1 avocado
¾ cup alfalfa sprouts

Split and butter onion buns. If desired, toast lightly. Spread bottom half with cream cheese. Cover with **GALLO® Salame** and sliced tomato. Peel and slice avocado and arrange on top. Scatter alfalfa sprouts over. Place tops of buns alongside.

Makes 4 servings

CRUNCHY CUCUMBER AND SALAMI

1 package (8-oz.) **OSCAR MAYER Salami**
4 round hard rolls, cut
1 cup low-fat cottage cheese
2 teaspoons horseradish
1 cucumber, thinly sliced
4 thin green pepper rings

Place 4 slices meat on bottom half of each roll. Combine cottage cheese and horseradish in bowl; spoon over meat. Top with cucumber slices and green pepper ring. Add top half of roll.

4 sandwiches

310 calories/sandwich

Note: This sandwich may be made a day ahead and refrigerated.

SIR THOMAS TOMATO

2 **THOMAS' English Muffins**, split, toasted
1 tablespoon mayonnaise
2 lettuce leaves
2 onion slices
1 tomato, sliced
2 hard-cooked eggs, sliced
2 bacon slices, cooked, crumbled

Spread muffin halves with mayonnaise. Arrange lettuce on bottom halves. Top with onion, tomato, egg, bacon, and remaining muffin halves.

Serves 2

SARA LEE CROISSANT CHEESE, AVOCADO, BACON FILLING

4 frozen **SARA LEE All-Butter Croissants**
4 slices (4-oz.) Cheddar cheese
4 slices (4-oz.) Swiss cheese
8 slices tomato, 2 medium
Alfalfa sprouts
8 slices bacon, cooked until crisp, optional
½ avocado, peeled, sliced

Cut frozen croissants in half lengthwise; leave together. Heat frozen croissants on ungreased baking sheet in preheated 325°F oven 9-11 minutes. Layer 1 slice each of Cheddar and Swiss cheeses on croissant bottom half. Top with 2 tomato slices; some alfalfa sprouts, if desired; 2 bacon slices, if desired; and several avocado slices. Top with remaining croissant half.

Makes 4 servings

SIR THOMAS SPAIN

4 **THOMAS'** English Muffins, split, toasted
3 eggs
8 green onions, minced fine
3 tablespoons minced green chilies OR 2 whole
  jalapeño peppers, seeded and minced if you like it
  hot
2 tablespoons butter or margarine

Beat the eggs with a fork in a small, deep bowl. Add onions and green chilies or jalapeño peppers. Heat butter or margarine in frying pan over medium high heat until bubbling. Pour in egg mixture, stir gently until cooked. Spoon on bottom muffin halves. Top with remaining muffin halves and serve immediately.

Serves 4

THE GLADIATOR

4 hard rolls, split
Spinach leaves
½ pound **WEAVER**® Sliced White Meat Chicken
  Roll
4 slices (4 oz.) provolone cheese
8 slices (4 oz.) hard salami
4 green pepper rings
¼ cup creamy Italian dressing

On rolls, layer spinach, chicken, cheese, salami and pepper. Drizzle with dressing.

4 servings

COUNTRY GARDEN HAMWICH

5 slices dark rye bread
Butter, softened
1 cucumber, thinly sliced
½ lb. **HORMEL** Cooked Ham Lunch Meat
2½ cups cole slaw
10 slices tomato
5 leaves lettuce
2 hard-cooked eggs, cut into wedges

Butter bread; place a leaf of lettuce on top of each slice. Arrange cucumbers on lettuce, then tomato slices. Place about ½ cup of cole slaw on top of each ham slice, then fold over and fasten with a toothpick. Use two ham rolls for each sandwich. Serve with deviled egg wedges as garnish.

SARA LEE CROISSANT CURRIED SHRIMP FILLING

4 frozen **SARA LEE** All-Butter Croissants
3 tablespoons butter
¼ cup chopped onion
¼ cup chopped celery
¾ teaspoon curry powder
¼ cup all-purpose flour
1½ cups half-and-half or milk
¼ teaspoon ground ginger
1 teaspoon lemon juice
⅓ cup light or dark raisins
10 ounces medium shrimp, cooked OR 1 can (6½-oz.)
  tuna, drained and flaked
Chopped peanuts OR sliced green onion tops, optional

Cut frozen croissants in half lengthwise; leave together. Heat frozen croissants on ungreased baking sheet in preheated 325°F oven 9-11 minutes. Sauté onion and celery in butter. Stir in curry powder; cook 1 minute. Stir in flour; heat until bubbly. Stir in half-and-half, ginger and lemon juice. Cook over low heat, stirring

until thickened. Stir in raisins and shrimp. Heat 2 to 3 minutes longer. Serve spooned over croissant bottom halves. Garnish with peanuts, if desired. Top with remaining croissant half.

Makes 4 servings

STACKED FRUIT-WITCHES

2 slices very thin whole wheat bread
Lettuce leaves
4 slices **BORDEN**® **LITE-LINE**® Swiss *or* Colby
  Flavor Pasteurized Process Cheese Product
1 small apple, cored and sliced
2 juice-packed pineapple slices, drained
¼ cup plain lowfat yogurt
2 teaspoons honey
¼ teaspoon poppy seed

On each bread slice, layer lettuce, **BORDEN**® **LITE-LINE**® Cheese Slices, apple and pineapple. In small bowl, combine yogurt and honey; spoon over each sandwich. Sprinkle with poppy seed. Serve immediately.

Makes 2 sandwiches

224 calories per serving

VARIATION:

LIGHT FRUIT PLATE

Arrange assorted fruit and **BORDEN**® **LITE-LINE**® Cheese Slices on lettuce.

Pizza

SHAZAM SHAMROCK PIZZA

1 package (15⅜-oz.) **CHEF BOY-AR-DEE**® Complete
  Cheese Pizza Mix

Preheat oven to 425°F. Prepare pizza dough according to package directions. Divide dough into 3 equal parts, reserving small amount for stem. Pat out three small circles approximately 5 inches in diameter. Arrange three circles on greased cookie sheet to shape shamrock leaves, shape stem and arrange. Sprinkle with cheese from package. Place topping on circle or leaves as desired. Bake 16 to 20 minutes.

TOPPINGS

½ cup coarsely chopped chicken livers
¼ cup chopped mushrooms
2 tablespoons butter or margarine
¼ cup chopped green onions (optional)

Sauté chopped chicken livers and mushrooms in butter until lightly browned. If green onions are used, toss with cooked chopped chicken livers or mushrooms.

¼ cup chopped tomatoes
¼ cup chopped avocado
¼ cup chopped green chillies, drained
¼ cup sour cream

Combine chopped tomatoes, avocados and green chillies. Garnish with sour cream.

6 slices bacon, cooked crisp, crumbled
1 cup sliced mushrooms, sautéed
½ cup sour cream

Combine cooked bacon and mushrooms. Garnish with sour cream.

BASIC AMERICAN PIZZA

1 cup warm water (105°F.-115°F.)
1 package **FLEISCHMANN'S Active Dry Yeast**
1 tablespoon sugar
2 teaspoons salt
2 tablespoons **PLANTERS Peanut Oil**
2¾ to 3¼ cups unsifted flour
1 can (6 oz.) tomato paste
½ cup water
½ teaspoon minced garlic
1 teaspoon oregano leaves, crushed
Dash ground black pepper
1½ cups shredded mozzarella cheese

Measure 1 cup warm water into large warm bowl. Sprinkle in **FLEISCHMANN'S Active Dry Yeast**; stir until dissolved. Stir in sugar, 1½ teaspoons salt, **PLANTERS Peanut Oil** and 1½ cups flour. Beat until smooth. Stir in enough additional flour to make a stiff dough. Turn out onto a lightly floured board. Knead until smooth and elastic, about 5 minutes. Place in greased bowl, turning to grease top. Cover; let rise in a warm place, free from draft, until doubled in bulk, about 45 minutes.

Meanwhile, combine tomato paste, water, garlic, remaining ½ teaspoon salt, oregano and pepper.

Punch dough down; divide in half. Shape each half into a ball; cover and let stand 10 minutes. Roll and stretch each half to a 14-inch circle. Place in 2 greased 12-inch pizza pans forming a standing rim of dough around edges. Let stand 10 minutes. Bake crusts at 375°F. for 8 to 10 minutes.

Spread half the prepared tomato sauce over each crust and sprinkle pies with cheese. Return pies to oven and continue baking for 15 to 20 minutes longer, or until cheese is very lightly browned. Cool slightly and cut into slices to serve.

Makes 2 (12-inch) pizzas

VARIATIONS:

For variety, one or more of the following toppings can be arranged on top of sauce before sprinkling pies with cheese: 1 pound crumbled, cooked and drained Italian sweet sausage, 1½ cups sliced fresh mushrooms, 1 small green pepper, cut in thin strips, ½ cup sliced pitted ripe olives, ¾ cup sliced marinated artichoke hearts, 1 can (2 oz.) anchovy fillets, drained and diced, ¼ pound sliced pepperoni or ¼ pound sliced hard salami.

WHOLE WHEAT CRUST

Substitute 1½ cups whole wheat flour for 1½ cups white flour, when adding flour to dissolved yeast

CHICAGO-STYLE DEEP DISH PIZZA

3¼ to 3¾ cups all-purpose flour
1 package **RED STAR® Instant Blend Dry Yeast**
1½ teaspoons salt
1¼ cups warm water
3 tablespoons oil

In large mixer bowl, combine 1½ cups flour, yeast and salt; mix well. Add warm water (120-130°) and oil to flour mixture. Blend at low speed until moistened; beat 3 minutes at medium speed. By hand, gradually stir in enough remaining flour to make a firm dough. Knead on floured surface, 3 to 5 minutes. Cover dough with plastic wrap and a towel. Let rest 20 minutes.

Prepare Pizza Sauce and Toppings*.

On lightly floured surface, roll dough to a 16-inch circle. Place in oiled 14-inch round deep dish pizza pan, pushing dough half-way up sides of pan. Cover; let rise in warm place until puffy, about 30 minutes.

(Continued)

Spread pizza sauce over dough. Sprinkle sausage over sauce; then arrange mushrooms, green pepper and onion over sausage. Sprinkle cheese on top. Bake at 425° for 20 to 25 minutes until edge is crisp and golden brown and cheese is melted.

Tip: This recipe has been developed for a 14-inch round deep dish pizza pan. The pizza could also be baked in a 13 × 9 × 2-inch cake pan. Roll dough to a 15 × 11-inch rectangle. Baking time may be slightly less.

*PIZZA SAUCE AND TOPPINGS

1 lb. pork sausage
1 can (8 oz.) tomato sauce
1 can (6 oz.) tomato paste
2 teaspoons sugar
1 to 1½ teaspoons oregano
1 teaspoon parsley flakes
½ to ¾ teaspoon basil
½ teaspoon salt
⅛ teaspoon garlic powder
⅛ teaspoon crushed red pepper
1 cup sliced mushrooms
⅓ cup diced green pepper (use part red pepper, if desired)
¼ cup chopped onion
1 package (8 oz.) **STELLA® Shredded Mozzarella Cheese**

In large skillet, lightly brown sausage; drain. Combine tomato sauce and paste with seasonings; simmer 10 to 15 minutes. Prepare other ingredients and set aside.   *One 14-inch Deep Dish Pizza*

FOOD PROCESSOR TRADITIONAL PIZZA

3 cups unsifted flour
2 tablespoons **PLANTERS Oil**
1 tablespoon sugar
1½ teaspoons salt
1 package **FLEISCHMANN'S Active Dry Yeast**
¼ cup warm water (105°F.-115°F.)
¾ cup very cold water (about)
¼ pound fresh mushrooms
1 medium green pepper
1 package (8 oz.) mozzarella cheese
1 can (6 oz.) tomato paste
½ cup water
1 teaspoon basil leaves, crushed, or ½ teaspoon oregano leaves, crushed
Few grains ground black pepper
¼ cup grated Parmesan cheese

With metal blade in place combine flour, **PLANTERS Oil**, sugar and 1 teaspoon salt in bowl; process 5-10 seconds to combine. Dissolve **FLEISCHMANN'S Active Dry Yeast** in warm water; pour through feed tube. Begin processing, pouring cold water through feed tube in a fast stream until ball forms, about 10-15 seconds. Continue processing for 60 seconds to knead dough.

Carefully remove dough from processor bowl. Shape into a ball and place in a greased bowl, turning to grease top. Cover; let rise in warm place, free from draft, until doubled in bulk, about 45 minutes.

With slicer disk in place, slice mushrooms. Coarsely chop green pepper with metal blade. Shred mozzarella cheese using shredder disk. Set ingredients aside.

(Continued)

Punch dough down; divide in half. Roll and stretch each half into a 13-inch circle. Place on ungreased 12-inch pizza pans, pressing around edge to form a standing rim of dough. Place a 9-inch pie plate over center of each pan. Bake at 350°F. for 10 minutes. Remove pie plate and bake about 5 minutes more.

Combine tomato paste, water, basil or oregano, remaining ½ teaspoon salt and pepper; spread mixture over crusts. Sprinkle half the mushrooms, green peppers, mozzarella cheese and Parmesan cheese over each pie. Bake at 425°F. for 15 minutes, or until done. Serve hot.

Makes two 12-inch pizzas

RHODES™ CHICAGO-STYLE DEEP DISH PIZZA

1 loaf RHODES™ White or Honey Wheat Dough,
  thawed
Olive oil or vegetable oil
Cornmeal
1 lb. bulk pork sausage, cooked and drained
1 can (1 lb. 20 oz.) peeled whole tomatoes, drained
1 teaspoon basil
1 teaspoon oregano
12 ounces mozzarella cheese, thinly sliced
1 green pepper, thinly sliced, optional
1 cup sliced ripe olives, optional
½ cup grated Parmesan cheese

Let dough rise in warm place 30 to 40 minutes. Grease 12-inch deep-dish pizza pan, 9x12-inch cake pan, or 12-inch oven-proof skillet. Sprinkle lightly with cornmeal. Pat out dough to fit bottom and up sides of pan. Prick with a fork and bake in a 425°F. oven for 7 minutes. Lightly mash tomatoes and mix with oregano and basil. Drizzle small amount of olive oil over partially baked crust. Arrange sliced mozzarella over crust. Add in layers; crumbled pork sausage, tomato mixture, green peppers and olives. Sprinkle Parmesan cheese over all. Bake at 425°F. 45 minutes. Let stand 5 minutes before serving.

BEER DRINKER'S DEEP-PAN PIZZA

Crust:
1 cup warm BUDWEISER® Beer
4 tablespoons olive or salad oil
1 tablespoon sugar
1½ teaspoons salt
1 package active dry yeast
2¾ to 3¼ cups all-purpose flour
2 tablespoons cornmeal

Topping:
10 to 12 ounces mozzarella cheese, shredded or thinly
  sliced
1 can (6 ounces) tomato paste
½ cup BUDWEISER® Beer
2 teaspoons oregano
1 teaspoon fennel seed (optional)
½ teaspoon sugar
¾ to 1 pound bulk pork or Italian sausage, broken up
½ cup grated Parmesan cheese

For crust, combine in a large bowl the warm **BUDWEISER® Beer**, 2 tablespoons oil, sugar, salt, and yeast. Add 1½ cups flour; beat until smooth. Stir in enough additional flour to make a fairly stiff dough. Turn dough out onto a lightly floured surface. Knead

until smooth and elastic (about 5 minutes). Place dough in a greased bowl, turning once to grease top. Cover and let rise in warm place (85°F) until double in bulk (about 1 hour). Punch dough down. (For 2 small pizzas, divide in half.) Using 2 tablespoons oil, coat a 14-inch round deep pizza pan. (Or use two 9-inch round cake pans). Sprinkle with cornmeal. Pat dough into pan, pinching up a rim around the edge. Cover and let rise in a warm place until double in bulk (about 30 minutes).

For topping, mix tomato paste, **BUDWEISER® Beer**, oregano, fennel seed, and sugar. Cover pizza dough evenly with mozzarella cheese; evenly spoon on tomato paste mixture. Sprinkle with sausage, then top with Parmesan cheese. Bake at 450°F 15 to 20 minutes, or until crust is browned and sausage is cooked.

Serves 4

DEEP DISH PIZZ-A-RONI

1 pkg. (8 oz.) GOLDEN GRAIN® Beef Flavor
  RICE-A-RONI®
2 Tbsp. butter or margarine
2¾ cups hot water
1 cup grated Cheddar cheese
1 cup spaghetti sauce
8 slices Jack cheese
2 Italian sausage, cooked and sliced
2 Tbsp. grated Parmesan cheese
1 can (2½ oz.) sliced mushrooms, drained

Prepare **RICE-A-RONI®** with butter and water, according to package directions. Let stand until all liquid is absorbed. Fold in Cheddar cheese. Spread into 10-inch pie plate. Bake at 450°F. for five minutes to set crust. Top with spaghetti sauce, sliced cheese, sausage, Parmesan, mushrooms. Top with additional sauce, if desired. Bake at 450°F. for 10 minutes or until lightly brown. Let stand 5 minutes before cutting into 8 wedges.

DEEP DISH MEXICAN PIZZA

2½ cups biscuit baking mix
½ cup yellow cornmeal
¾ cup water
1 pound lean ground beef
½ cup chopped onion
1 (8-ounce) can tomato sauce
1 (4-ounce) can chopped mild green chilies, drained
1 tablespoon WYLER'S® Beef-Flavor Instant
  Bouillon or 3 Beef-Flavor Bouillon Cubes
1 teaspoon chili powder
¼ teaspoon ground cumin
1 (16-ounce) can refried beans
1½ cups (6 ounces) shredded mild Cheddar or
  Monterey Jack cheese
Chopped tomato
Shredded lettuce
Sliced pitted ripe olives

Preheat oven to 425°. In medium bowl, combine biscuit mix, cornmeal and water; mix well. With floured hands, pat dough on bottom and up sides of greased 15x10-inch jellyroll pan. Bake 10 minutes; remove from oven. In large skillet, brown meat with onion; stir in tomato sauce, chilies, bouillon, chili powder and cumin. Cook and stir until bouillon dissolves. Spread beans evenly over baked crust; spoon meat mixture evenly over beans. Top with cheese. Bake 10 minutes. Garnish with tomato, lettuce and olives. Refrigerate leftovers.

Makes 8 to 10 servings

DEEP DISH PIZZA

Crust:
52 **RITZ Crackers**, finely rolled (about 2 cups crumbs)
¼ cup grated Parmesan cheese
¼ cup butter or margarine, softened
1 egg, slightly beaten
2 tablespoons cold water

Filling:
1 tablespoon butter or margarine
¼ cup coarsely chopped onion
¼ cup coarsely chopped green pepper
1 clove garlic, minced
1 (16-ounce) can whole peeled tomatoes, undrained, cut up
1 (6-ounce) can tomato paste
1 (4-ounce) can sliced mushrooms, drained
½ teaspoon basil
½ teaspoon marjoram
½ teaspoon oregano
4 ounces mozzarella cheese, grated (about 1 cup)
1 tablespoon grated Parmesan cheese

1. **Make Crust:** Preheat oven to 325° F.
2. In medium bowl, using fork or pastry blender, combine **RITZ Cracker** crumbs, Parmesan cheese and butter or margarine; mix in egg and water until thoroughly blended. Using back of large spoon, press onto bottom and sides of 9-inch pie plate to form crust. Bake 10 minutes.
3. **Make Filling:** In medium saucepan, over medium heat, melt butter or margarine; sauté onion, green pepper and garlic about 5 minutes, or until tender.
4. Add tomatoes, tomato paste, mushrooms, basil, marjoram and oregano; heat thoroughly. Spoon into crust; top with mozzarella cheese and Parmesan cheese. Bake 20 to 25 minutes, or until bubbly.
5. **To Serve:** Let stand 5 minutes; cut into wedges.

Makes 4 to 6 servings

MICROWAVE METHOD:
1. Prepare crust as in Step 2. Press into 9-inch microwave-proof pie plate. Microwave at 100% power 5 to 6 minutes, rotating ½ turn after 3 minutes, until crust is no longer moist.
2. In 3-quart microwave-proof bowl, microwave butter or margarine, onion, green pepper and garlic at 100% power 4 to 5 minutes, stirring after 3 minutes, until vegetables are tender. Stir in tomatoes, tomato paste, mushrooms, basil, marjoram and oregano; microwave at 100% power 5 minutes, stirring after 3 minutes.
3. Assemble pie as in Step 4; microwave at 100% power 3 minutes. Serve as in Step 5.

MARTHA WHITE PIZZA

¾ cup plus 1 tablespoon lukewarm water
1 cake or package yeast
2 cups sifted **MARTHA WHITE Plain Flour**
1 teaspoon salt
2 tablespoons shortening
Pizza Sauce*
Mozzarella cheese
Toppings of your choice

Dissolve yeast in water. Combine flour and salt; then cut in shortening, as for biscuits. Stir in water and yeast mixture. Turn dough out onto lightly floured board or pastry cloth and knead just until smooth. Place in a greased bowl and grease top. Cover and let rise in a warm place until light, about 1 hour. When light,

punch down and divide into 2 pieces for 12-inch pizzas or 4 pieces for 10-inch pizzas. Roll out about ¼-inch thick. Place rounds of dough on greased baking sheet or pizza pans. Crimp edges. Top with Pizza Sauce and mozzarella cheese. Add your favorite toppings. Bake at 400 degrees for about 20 minutes.

For very crisp crust: Bake pizza 10 minutes on pan, then slide pizza off pan directly onto oven rack and finish baking.

Makes 2 large or 4 small pizzas

Note: If using **MARTHA WHITE Self-Rising Flour**, omit salt.

*PIZZA SAUCE

1 6-ounce can tomato paste
1 8-ounce can tomato sauce
½ teaspoon salt
1 teaspoon Worcestershire sauce
1 teaspoon garlic salt
2 or 3 drops **TABASCO® Sauce**
½ teaspoon crushed thyme
1 teaspoon crushed oregano

Combine and mix well.

TWO STORY PIZZA

1 package (28⅞-oz.) **CHEF BOY-AR-DEE® Mix for 2 Complete Cheese Pizzas**
8 ounces grated mozzarella cheese
1 medium green pepper, diced
4 ounces fresh mushrooms, quartered
1 medium onion, chopped
½ pound browned ground beef
¼ cup chopped parsley

Preheat oven to 425°F. Prepare pizza dough according to package directions; divide in half. Grease fingers well; place dough-half in center of greased 13- or 14-inch pizza pan. Spread dough to edge of pizza pan. Bake for 5 minutes.

Meanwhile: roll or pat out remaining half of pizza dough on well-floured board into a 13- or 14-inch circle. Remove first crust from oven; sprinkle mozzarella cheese on top; then green pepper and mushrooms. Place second rolled crust on top of mushrooms. Pierce dough with fork. Seal the edges of the two pizza layers by pinching with fingers or pressing with floured fork; bring up sealed edges to sides of pan to hold sauce. Slowly pour pizza sauce from can over top crust. Sprinkle chopped onion on top; then browned ground beef; then grated cheese from package.

Bake approximately 20-25 minutes. Wait 3 minutes; sprinkle with chopped parsley. Slice. Serve wedges as pie.   *Serves 4 to 6*

DOUBLE DECKER PIZZA

1 loaf **RHODES™ Frozen Bread Dough**, thawed
2 green peppers, chopped
2 tomatoes, chopped
1 large onion, chopped
1¼ cups cut-up meat (salami, pepperoni, or cooked and drained sausage)
1 teaspoon Italian herbs (oregano, basil, marjoram)
½ teaspoon salt
1 cup shredded mozzarella cheese
½ cup grated Parmesan cheese
Softened butter or margarine
Sesame seeds

Cook green pepper, tomato and onion until onion is transparent. Add meat, herbs and salt; cook 5 minutes over low heat. Drain and cool.

Divide thawed dough into three equal parts. Roll each part into a rectangle 11 × 7-inches. Place one rectangle on a greased baking sheet. Spread with half the vegetable-meat mixture; sprinkle with half the mozzarella and Parmesan cheeses. Top with second rectangle of dough; repeat with remaining vegetable-meat mixture and cheese. Stretch third rectangle slightly; place on top. Pinch edges carefully together to seal. Brush top with butter; sprinkle with sesame seeds. Cover and let rise in a warm place about 1 hour.

Bake at 350°F. until a deep golden brown, about 40 to 45 minutes. Cut into slices. *Makes 6 to 8 servings*

PIZZA BURRITO MEXITALIAN

1 package (15⅜-oz.) **CHEF BOY-AR-DEE® Complete Cheese Pizza Mix**
1 can (4-oz.) chopped green chillies, drained well
1 can (16-oz.) refried beans
2 tablespoons chili seasoning mix
¼ teaspoon hot pepper sauce
8 ounces grated Cheddar cheese

Preheat oven to 425°F. Prepare dough according to package directions; mix in ½ can of green chillies (2 tablespoons). Combine refried beans, chili seasoning mix, hot pepper sauce and remaining green chillies.

Grease one 13- or 14-inch pizza pan or one 12 × 14-inch cookie sheet. Grease fingers well. Place dough in the center of pan. Spread dough to form 10 × 14-inch rectangle on cookie sheet or spread to edge of pizza pan. Pinch up sides of dough to hold sauce. Spread refried bean mixture over dough; top with pizza sauce from package. Sprinkle with grated cheese from package and grated Cheddar. Add ground beef topping. Bake 20 minutes.

Topping:
½ pound ground beef
1 onion, chopped
1 green pepper, cut in strips
1 medium tomato, chopped
¾ cup sliced ripe olives

Brown the ground beef; drain. Add chopped onion, green pepper strips, tomatoes and ripe olives; heat gently for 3 minutes.

TORTILLA PIZZAS

Salad oil
8 **VAN DE KAMP'S® Corn Tortillas**
2 lbs. ground chuck
1 medium onion, minced
1 garlic clove, minced
¼ lb. mushrooms, chopped
1 can (2¼ oz.) chopped ripe olives
1 can (6 oz.) tomato paste
1¼ cups water
1 tsp. salt
1 package taco seasoning mix
½ lb. shredded Cheddar or mozzarella cheese
Grated Parmesan or Romano cheese

In a skillet, heat about 1 inch of salad oil. Fry tortillas, turning occasionally until lightly browned, about 1 minute. Drain on paper towel. Cook ground meat, onion, garlic, and mushrooms in a frying pan until meat is browned. Add olives, tomato paste, water, salt, and seasoning mix, and cook over low heat, stirring occasionally for about 5 minutes more. Place tortillas flat on baking sheets. Top each tortilla with about 4 tablespoons of the meat mixture, then with 3 tablespoons of the Cheddar cheese. Sprinkle lightly with Parmesan cheese. Bake in 425°F. oven for 10 minutes, or until cheese melts. *Makes 8 tortilla pizzas*

BEEF PEPPER PIZZA

1 (12½-oz.) pkg. **APPIAN WAY® Pizza—Regular**
1 (2½-oz.) jar **ARMOUR STAR® Sliced Dried Beef,** shredded
1 2½-oz. jar sliced mushrooms, drained
1 green pepper, sliced into rings
1 cup (4 oz.) shredded mozzarella cheese

Heat oven to 425°. Prepare pizza dough according to package directions; cover with sauce. Sprinkle with dried beef, mushrooms, green pepper and cheese. Bake at 425°, 18 to 20 minutes or until crust is golden brown.

3 to 4 servings, or cut into small pieces and serve as appetizer snacks

PIZZA TURNOVER

⅓ cup chopped green pepper
¼ cup chopped onion
¼ cup tomato sauce
1 teaspoon dried oregano leaves
½ teaspoon dried basil leaves
2 cloves garlic, finely chopped
2 cups **BISQUICK® Baking Mix**
½ cup hot water
1 cup shredded mozzarella cheese (about 4 ounces)
¼ cup grated Parmesan cheese
1 package (3½-ounces) sliced pepperoni
Vegetable oil

Heat oven to 450°. Mix green pepper, onion, tomato sauce, oregano, basil and garlic; reserve. Mix baking mix and hot water until soft dough forms; beat vigorously 30 seconds. Roll dough, or pat dough with hand floured with baking mix, into 13-inch circle on ungreased cookie sheet. Top half of the circle with mozzarella cheese, tomato sauce mixture, Parmesan cheese and pepperoni to within 1 inch of edge. Fold dough over filling. Press edges together; roll ½-inch of pressed edges up and over; pinch to seal. (If edge of dough is dry, moisten with water.) Brush lightly with oil. Bake until golden brown, 15 to 20 minutes. Cool 5 minutes; cut into wedges. *4 servings*

Note: ¼ cup pizza sauce can be substituted for the tomato sauce, oregano, basil and garlic.

HIGH ALTITUDE DIRECTIONS (3500 to 6500 feet): Substitute boiling water for the hot water. Roll dough into 13-inch circle on cloth-covered board lightly floured with baking mix. Place circle of dough on ungreased cookie sheet.

LA PREFERIDA® MEXICAN PIZZA

2 oz. **LA PREFERIDA® Chorizo***
1 flour tortilla 10 in.
½ cup **LA PREFERIDA® Refried Beans**
2 Tbsp. **LA PREFERIDA® Enchilada Sauce**
10 slices **LA PREFERIDA® Jalapeños**
1 oz. Oaxaca cheese, grated**

Sauté Chorizo until cooked through. Spread tortilla first with Refried Beans, then Enchilada Sauce. Top with remaining ingredients. Place on lightly oiled baking sheet. Bake at 400 F. for 12 minutes. *Makes one 10 in.*

*Italian sausage may be substituted.
**Muenster cheese may be used as a substitute.

FALBO'S PIZZA

Dough: for 2-12 in. Crusts
1 pkg. dry yeast
¼ cup lukewarm water
⅔ cup lukewarm water
¾ tsp. salt
2 Tbsp. vegetable oil
1 tsp. sugar
About 3 cups flour

Dissolve yeast in ¼ cup of water. Blend water, salt, oil, sugar and dissolved yeast. Then add flour in small amounts and work in until the dough is smooth and only slightly sticky. Place in a lightly greased bowl, turn to coat the dough. Set in a warm place and allow to raise until double the original size (about 2 hours).

Punch down, divide into two balls. Roll out to fit each 12 inch pan or two 9½x13½ in. pans. Pans should be lightly greased.

Sauce and Topping for two Pizzas:
1½ cups tomato puree
½ cup water
¾ tsp. salt
⅛ tsp. black pepper
½ tsp. sweet basil
⅛ tsp. garlic salt
2 Tbsp. **FALBO'S Romano or Parmesan Cheese**
1 lb. **FALBO'S Mozzarella or Scamorza**, shredded
1 tsp. oregano

Combine puree, water, salt, pepper, basil, garlic and grated cheese. Spread ½ of the mixture on each pizza crust, cover with mozzarella and sprinkle with oregano. Bake in a preheated 500 degree oven on the bottom shelf for 10-20 min. or until the crust is crisp and the cheese is melted.

Note: Sausage should be put on raw and before the cheese. All other desired ingredients such as anchovies, mushrooms, etc. should also be put on before the cheese.

ZUCCHINI PIZZA

PAM® No-Stick Cooking Spray
½ cup chopped onion
Salt
4 cups coarsely grated zucchini
3 eggs
⅓ cup enriched all-purpose flour
½ cup grated Parmesan cheese
½ teaspoon basil leaves, crumbled
⅛ teaspoon pepper
½ cup grated skim milk
Mozzarella cheese
2 tomatoes, sliced
1½ cups zucchini slices
¼ cup pitted ripe olives, sliced

Spray medium-sized skillet with **PAM® No-Stick Cooking Spray** according to directions. Sauté onion about 5 minutes; set aside. Sprinkle salt lightly over grated zucchini on a large plate; let stand 15 minutes. With paper towel gently squeeze out any excess moisture from zucchini. In large bowl beat eggs, flour, Parmesan cheese, basil and pepper. Stir in mozzarella cheese, grated zucchini and onion; stir until well mixed.

Spray a 12-inch pizza pan with **PAM® No-Stick Cooking Spray** according to directions. Spread zucchini mixture to edges of pan. Bake in a 350°F oven 25 minutes or until very lightly browned and dry on top.　　　　　　　*(Continued)*

Overlap tomato slices and zucchini slices on surface of pizza. Garnish with olive slices. Bake about 8 minutes or until vegetables are just heated.　　　　　　　*Makes 6 servings*

Calories Per Serving: 160

MINI MEXICAN PIZZAS

1 jar (14 oz.) **RAGÚ'®** **Pizza Quick Sauce**, any flavor
3 English muffins, split and toasted
⅓ cup finely chopped onion
2 tablespoons minced jalapeños (optional)
1 cup (about 4 oz.) shredded Monterey Jack cheese
⅓ cup shredded lettuce
½ cup crushed corn chips
½ cup sliced black olives

Preheat oven to 350°F. Spoon 1½ tablespoons **RAGÚ'®** **Pizza Quick Sauce** on each muffin half. Evenly top with onion, jalapeños and cheese. Place pizzas on baking sheet and bake 15-20 minutes or until cheese melts. Top with lettuce, corn chips and black olives.　　　　　　　*Makes 6 pizzas*

EASY MINI PIZZAS

1 envelope **LIPTON® Golden Onion Soup Mix**
1 tablespoon finely chopped parsley
1 teaspoon oregano
⅛ teaspoon garlic powder
2 cans (8-oz. each) tomato sauce
½ cup water
6 English muffins, split and slightly toasted
Mozzarella cheese
Suggested Toppings—grated Parmesan cheese; sliced mushrooms; cooked Italian sausage; or chopped green pepper

Preheat oven to 425°. In medium saucepan, combine **LIPTON® Golden Onion Soup Mix**, parsley, oregano and garlic powder blended with tomato sauce and water. Simmer covered, stirring occasionally, 15 minutes. Spoon sauce onto muffin halves. Top with cheese and one of the Suggested Toppings. Bake 10 minutes.　　　　　　　*Makes 6 servings*

PARTY PIZZA VARIATIONS

6 **BAYS®** English Muffins, toasted
6 ounces spaghetti sauce (with meat)
Garlic salt
Powdered oregano
8 ounces mozzarella cheese, shredded

MUSHROOM PIZZA

Top toasted muffin half with 1 tablespoon spaghetti sauce. Sprinkle with garlic salt and oregano. Top with 1 tablespoon drained canned mushroom slices—then a scant ¼ cup mozzarella cheese. Broil till done.

PEPPERONI PIZZA

Top toasted muffin half with 1 tablespoon spaghetti sauce. Sprinkle with garlic salt and oregano. Top with three slices pepperoni sausage. Top with a scant ¼ cup mozzarella cheese. Broil till done.

PESTO PIZZA

Top toasted muffin half with 1 tablespoon spaghetti sauce. Then add 1½ teaspoons Pesto Sauce*. Sprinkle lightly with chopped walnuts. Then top with scant ¼ cup mozzarella cheese. Broil till done.　　　　　　　*(Continued)*

*EASY BLENDER PESTO SAUCE

1 cup basil leaves, loosely packed
1 clove garlic, peeled
½ teaspoon salt
⅓ cup walnut halves
½ cup grated Parmesan cheese
½ cup olive oil
1 tablespoon butter

Add all ingredients except ¼ of oil to a blender. Blend on low for 15 seconds; add the remaining oil in a thin stream (15-30 seconds more). Sauce should not be blended for more than 45 seconds total. A few parsley leaves can be added along with basil to deepen the color if desired. *Yield: one cup*

INSTANT PIZZA

1 package (6 muffins) **PEPPERIDGE FARM®** **English Muffins**
1 package brown and serve sausage, frozen
1½ cups prepared pizza sauce
1 package (8 ounces) mozzarella cheese, sliced
½ cup grated Parmesan cheese

Split English muffins and toast cut surfaces. Heat sausages and cut into slices. Place slices on English muffin halves. Spoon sauce over sausage slices. Top with mozzarella cheese slices and grated Parmesan cheese. Place under broiler and broil until cheese is melted and bubbly. *Makes 6 servings*

VARIATIONS:

Omit sausages and use any one of the following:

Sliced frankfurters
Chopped ham or leftover cooked meat loaf or chicken
Sliced olives or mushrooms
Anchovy fillets
Sautéed onions and green peppers

PIZZA MUFFINS

6 English muffins, split and toasted
¾ lb. ground beef
¼ cup minced onion
1 can (6-oz.) tomato paste
3 Tbsp. **A.1. Steak Sauce**
2 cups (½ lb.) grated sharp Cheddar cheese

In medium skillet cook beef until crumbly. Drain. Add onion and cook until softened. Mix in tomato paste and **A.1.** Spread muffins with meat mixture. Top with grated cheese. Place on baking sheet. Broil 2-4 minutes or until cheese is melted. *Makes 12 pizzas*

MINI-PIZZAS

2½ cups buttermilk biscuit mix
1 package active dry yeast
⅔ cup hot tap water
1 cup **PREGO Spaghetti Sauce**
1 cup shredded mozzarella cheese
½ cup sliced pepperoni

In large bowl combine biscuit mix and yeast; vigorously stir in water (dough may seem sticky). On floured surface, gently knead dough about 1 minute; let rest 10 minutes. Cut into quarters. On two ungreased baking sheets, pat each piece of dough into a 7-inch circle. Pinch up edges of dough to form rim. Bake at 425°F for 10 minutes. Remove from oven. Top each pizza with spaghetti sauce, cheese and pepperoni; sprinkle with seasonings as desired. Bake 5 minutes more or until crust is golden. *Makes 4 pizzas*

OPEN-FACE PIZZA SANDWICHES

2 cups **BISQUICK® Baking Mix**
½ cup cold water
1 pound ground beef
½ cup grated Parmesan cheese
¼ cup chopped onion
2 tablespoons chopped green pepper
1 teaspoon salt
1 teaspoon dried oregano leaves
⅛ teaspoon pepper
2 cans (6 ounces each) tomato paste
2 to 3 tomatoes, thinly sliced
8 slices mozzarella cheese (each about 4x4 inches), cut diagonally into halves

Heat oven to 450°. Mix baking mix and water until soft dough forms; beat vigorously 20 strokes. Divide dough into halves. Pat each half into rectangle, 16x4 inches, on greased cookie sheet with floured hands. Bake until light brown, 8 to 10 minutes.

Reduce oven temperature to 350°. Mix ground beef, Parmesan cheese, onion, green pepper, salt, oregano, pepper and tomato paste; spread over rectangles. Bake until beef is done, 20 to 25 minutes. Arrange tomatoes down center of each rectangle, overlapping edges; layer mozzarella cheese slices over tomatoes. Bake until cheese is melted, about 5 minutes longer.

About 6 servings

HIGH ALTITUDE DIRECTIONS (3500 to 6500 feet): Bake until beef is done, 25 to 30 minutes.

Pancakes, Waffles & Crêpes

Pancakes

QUICK PANCAKES

2 cups **ELAM'S® Pure Buckwheat Flour**
1 teaspoon baking powder
½ teaspoon baking soda
2½ cups milk
¼ cup cooking oil or melted shortening

Combine first 3 ingredients in bowl; mix well. Add milk and oil or melted shortening; stir until smooth. Stir batter down before using each time. For each pancake, pour about ¼ cup batter onto hot lightly greased griddle. Bake until top is covered with bubbles and edges look cooked. Turn and brown second side.
Yield: About 16 cakes, 4 inches in diameter

VARIATION:

BUTTERMILK PANCAKES

Follow recipe for Quick Pancakes and change as follows. Increase baking soda to 1½ teaspoons. Substitute 3 cups buttermilk or sour milk for 2½ cups sweet milk.
Yield: About 18 cakes, 4½ inches in diameter, 6 servings of 3 pancakes each

SOURDOUGH PANCAKES

1 cup warm low-fat milk
1 package active dry yeast (check the date on the package)
1 tablespoon **SWEETLITE™ Fructose**
2 eggs lightly beaten
¼ cup melted corn oil margarine
1 package **BATTER-LITE® Natural Sourdough Bread Mix**
1 teaspoon salt
1 cup white unbleached flour

1. Pour the warm milk into a large warm mixing bowl and sprinkle the yeast over the top of it. Stir until the yeast is dissolved, about 5 minutes.
2. Add the fructose, lightly beaten eggs and melted margarine and mix well.
3. Add the **BATTER-LITE® Natural Sourdough Bread Mix** and mix well.
4. Combine the salt and flour and add gradually to the liquid mixture.
5. Let the mixture sit in the bowl, covered, for 15 minutes.
6. Fry on a hot grill, using a ¼-cup measure to pour the batter onto the grill. Cook 3-4 minutes or until browned on each side.
Makes 13(4-inch) pancakes

VARIATIONS:

BUTTERMILK PANCAKES

Use warm buttermilk instead of warm low-fat milk. *(Continued)*

BLUEBERRY PANCAKES

Combine 1 cup unthawed frozen blueberries and 1 tablespoon unbleached white flour and add to the mixture after step 4.

HAMCAKES

Add 1 cup finely chopped ham to the mixture after step 4.

YOGURT BLENDER PANCAKES

1 egg
1 cup (8-ounces) **BORDEN® LITE-LINE® Plain Yogurt**
2 tablespoons vegetable oil
1 cup unsifted flour
1 tablespoon sugar
1 teaspoon baking powder
½ teaspoon baking soda
¼ teaspoon salt
¼ teaspoon ground cinnamon, optional
Blueberry Cinnamon Topping*

In blender container, blend egg, yogurt and oil until smooth. Add dry ingredients; blend until smooth. On lightly greased hot griddle, pour scant ¼ cup batter for each pancake. When pancake is covered with bubbles, turn over. Brown second side 1 to 2 minutes. Serve with butter and syrup or Blueberry Cinnamon Topping.
Makes about 10 pancakes

*BLUEBERRY CINNAMON TOPPING

1 cup (8-ounces) **BORDEN® LITE-LINE® Blueberry Yogurt**
2 tablespoons honey
¼ teaspoon ground cinnamon

In small saucepan, over *low heat*, combine ingredients. Warm mixture; *do not boil*. Serve over pancakes. *Makes 1 cup*

ROMAN MEAL® PANCAKES

1⅓ cups all-purpose flour
1 tablespoon baking powder
½ teaspoon salt
2 tablespoons sugar
2 tablespoons shortening
½ cup **ROMAN MEAL® Cereal**
1½ cups milk
2 eggs

Preheat griddle. In medium bowl stir together flour, baking powder, salt and sugar. Cut in shortening. Stir in cereal. Beat milk with eggs; add all at once to dry ingredients. Beat well. Pour batter by ¼-cup portions onto hot, lightly greased griddle. Bake until surface bubbles and edges lose their sheen. Turn and bake other side. Turn only once *Makes 15 pancakes, 5 inches in diameter*

VARIATIONS:

APPLE PANCAKES

Add ½ teaspoon cinnamon to dry ingredients and fold ¾ cup finely chopped apple into batter. Sprinkle with powdered sugar.
(Continued)

BACON PANCAKES

Fold ½ cup fried, crumbled bacon into batter.

HAWAIIAN PANCAKES

Slice bananas onto pancakes just after pouring batter on the griddle. Serve with crushed pineapple.

BLUEBERRY PANCAKES

Add ½ teaspoon lemon extract to liquid ingredients and fold ½ cup rinsed and drained blueberries into batter. Sprinkle with sifted brown sugar and serve with whipped topping.

CORNCAKES

Fold ¾ cup drained whole kernel corn into batter. Serve with bacon and maple syrup.

GRAHAM CRACKER PANCAKES

2 cups milk
1½ cups **SALERNO®** Graham Cracker Crumbs
¼ cup vegetable oil
2 eggs
⅔ cup all-purpose flour
2 tablespoons sugar
2 teaspoons baking powder
½ teaspoon baking soda
½ teaspoon salt
¼ teaspoon mace (optional)

Pour milk over graham cracker crumbs; let stand 5 minutes. With a fork, beat in oil, eggs and dry ingredients. Using about ¼ cup batter for each pancake, bake on a preheated hot griddle (400°) until golden brown on both sides, turning once.   *Makes 16*

BLINI WITH CAVIAR

2½ cups milk
¼ cup butter or margarine
3 cups sifted flour
3 Tbsp. sugar
1 tsp. salt
3 egg yolks
1 pkg. active dry yeast
¼ cup warm water (105-110°F.)
3 egg whites
½ cup melted butter or margarine
3½ to 4 oz. **ROMANOFF®** Caviar*
1½ cups sour cream

Bring milk and butter to just below boiling point. Cool. In large bowl, sift together flour, sugar and salt. Beat egg yolks until foamy. Alternately stir in milk and flour mixtures. Mix yeast with warm water, stir into batter. Cover and let rise in warm place one hour. Beat egg whites until stiff but not dry. Fold into batter. Cover; let rise until it reaches previous volume. Preheat lightly greased griddle. For each blini, drop a scant quarter-cup batter onto griddle. Lightly brown on both sides; keep warm. Each guest adds butter, caviar and sour cream to taste.

Makes about 36 blini

*****ROMANOFF®** Black Lumpfish or Whitefish Caviar** is suggested.

Waffles

OLD FASHIONED WAFFLES

2 cups **ELAM'S®** 3 in 1 Mix
2 cups milk
2 tablespoons honey
2 eggs
⅓ cup cooking oil or melted shortening

Measure mix into bowl; set aside. Combine milk, honey, eggs and oil or melted shortening; mix. Add liquids to mix; beat just until smooth. For each waffle, pour 1 cup batter into preheated, greased 9-inch square waffle iron. Spread over grid at once. Close iron and bake until done. Serve with applesauce, maple syrup, fresh fruit or preserves.   *Yield: 4 nine-inch waffles*

HARBORSIDE WAFFLES

2 cups unsifted flour
1 tablespoon baking powder
1 tablespoon sugar
½ teaspoon salt
1¼ cups milk
3 eggs, slightly beaten
¼ cup melted butter or margarine
1 cup shredded **FINLANDIA** Swiss Cheese

Combine dry ingredients; set aside. Blend milk, eggs and butter. Add to dry ingredients and beat until smooth. Fold in shredded cheese and blend thoroughly. Pour about 1 cup mixture into preheated waffle iron. Bake until done. Serve with additional shredded **FINLANDIA Cheese** and syrup. *Makes 3 to 4 servings*

BAYSHORE CHOCOLATE WAFFLES

1 bar (4-oz.) **GHIRARDELLI®** Semi-Sweet Chocolate
¼ cup butter or margarine
2 cups flour
3 teaspoons baking powder
Pinch nutmeg
Pinch cinnamon
Pinch ground cardamom
½ cup chopped pecans
3 eggs, separated
1½ cups milk
½ cup half-and-half
1 teaspoon vanilla
¼ teaspoon salt
¼ cup sugar

In heavy saucepan, break chocolate and melt with butter. Into large bowl, sift flour, baking powder, nutmeg, cinnamon, and cardamom; add nuts. Beat egg yolks with milk, half-and-half and vanilla. Mix liquid with dry ingredients, beating until smooth. Beat egg whites with salt until soft mounds form. Gradually add sugar, beating until stiff peaks form. Fold egg whites into batter. Preheat greased waffle iron. Bake waffles according to manufacturer's directions. Serve with warm Chocolate Maple Syrup*.

Makes 4 large waffles

*CHOCOLATE MAPLE SYRUP

In saucepan, combine 1 cup maple flavor syrup, 3 tablespoons **GHIRARDELLI® Ground Chocolate** and 2 tablespoons butter. Heat to boiling; blend with wire whip. Serve warm over pancakes.

GOLDEN BROWN WAFFLES

1⅓ cups all-purpose flour
2 tablespoons granulated sugar
1 tablespoon baking powder
½ teaspoon salt
⅔ cup **ROMAN MEAL® Cereal**
1½ cups milk
2 egg yolks
⅓ cup shortening, melted
2 stiffly beaten egg whites

Preheat waffle iron. Combine flour, sugar, baking powder, salt and cereal in medium-sized mixing bowl. Beat milk with egg yolks and shortening; add all at once to dry ingredients. Beat well. Fold in egg whites. Pour batter onto hot waffle iron.

Makes five 7-inch waffles

STRAWBERRY BELGIAN WAFFLES

4 frozen waffles
1 pint strawberries, hulled and halved
2 tablespoons confectioner's sugar
2 tablespoons orange juice (optional)
½ teaspoon grated orange-rind (optional)
1 cup thawed **BIRD'S EYE® COOL WHIP®
Non-Dairy Whipped Topping***

Toast waffles as directed on package and place on dessert dishes. Combine strawberries, sugar, orange juice and rind. Stir until sugar dissolves. Spoon onto waffles and top with whipped topping.

Makes 4 servings

*Or use 1 cup prepared **DREAM WHIP® Whipped Topping**.

SPICY APPLE WAFFLES

1¼ cups sifted all-purpose flour
2 teaspoons **CLABBER GIRL® Baking Powder**
½ teaspoon salt
1 teaspoon ground nutmeg
3 tablespoons sugar
2 tablespoons shortening
2 eggs, separated
1 cup milk
1½ cups pared, coarsely grated apple

Sift together flour, Baking Powder, salt, nutmeg, and sugar into a mixing bowl. Cut in shortening until mixture is fine. Beat together egg yolks and milk and add all at once to dry ingredients. Blend ingredients and beat just until smooth. Stir in apples. Beat egg whites until stiff but not dry. Fold into batter. Bake in waffle maker following manufacturer's directions.   *Yield: 4 servings*

French Toast

PARSLEY PATCH™ FRENCH TOAST

Mix together in a shallow dish:

2 eggs well beaten
¼ cup orange juice
1 tsp. **PARSLEY PATCH™ Salt Free BAKING
   BLEND**
1 tsp. vanilla

Dip whole wheat bread into batter mixture and brown in butter or margarine until toasted on both sides. Serve with your favorite syrup or preserves.

HAWAIIAN FRENCH TOAST

1 loaf **KING'S Hawaiian Bread***
4 eggs
½ cup milk
¼ cup sugar (optional)
½ teaspoon vanilla
⅛ teaspoon nutmeg
⅛ teaspoon cinnamon
Salad oil or butter

Slice bread crosswise so that each slice is about 1½ inches thick. Cut each slice into thirds, if desired. Combine remaining ingredients, except oil. Quickly dip slices (do not soak) in egg mixture and cook on hot oiled griddle until golden brown on both sides. Keep egg mixture stirred and spices well blended. For a delicate orange flavor, add the grated peel of one orange to egg mixture.

Makes six servings

*Best if bread is frozen or dry.

VARIATIONS:

STRAWBERRY OR BANANA TOAST

Prepare bread and egg mixture per Hawaiian French Toast recipe. With sharp knife, cut a pocket in cut edge of each third. Fill pockets with fresh strawberry or banana slices. Dip in egg mixture and cook as directed. Sprinkle with powdered sugar and top with additional strawberry or banana slices.

COMFORT® FRENCH TOAST

¾ cup butter or margarine, at room temperature
⅓ cup sugar
¾ teaspoon ground cinnamon
⅓ cup **SOUTHERN COMFORT®**
1 loaf French bread (26 to 30 inches long)
7 eggs
2 cups half-and-half *
¼ teaspoon salt
1 to 2 tablespoons butter or margarine
1 to 2 tablespoons vegetable oil

Cream butter until fluffy. Beat in sugar, cinnamon, and **SOUTHERN COMFORT®**. Slice bread lengthwise and spread thickly with butter mixture. Replace top. Cut into 1½-inch slices. Set slices, bottom crust down, in a 13 × 9-inch pan or casserole. Beat eggs with half-and-half and salt, just until frothy; pour into pan, coating top crusts. Refrigerate at least 2 hours, turning slices occasionally for even absorption.

Heat 1 tablespoon each butter and oil in heavy skillet. Over low heat sauté the coated bread until golden brown and cooked through. Add more butter and oil as needed. Serve warm with syrup.   *Serves 8*

*Light cream or milk may be substituted for half-and-half.

Crêpes

EASY TURKEY CREPES

Combine:

    4 cups cubed cooked turkey or chicken
    8 oz. cream cheese, softened
    2 Tbsp. finely minced onion
    1 small jar pimientos, chopped

Soften:

    8 AZTECA® Large Flour Tortillas per package
      directions

Place about ½ cup turkey filling on each tortilla, roll. Place lap side down in 13×9×2-inch pan.
Pour on:

    2 (10-oz.) cans enchilada sauce

Sprinkle with:

    ½ cup shredded Cheddar cheese

Bake 35 minutes at 350°.
Spoon on:

    ½ cup sour cream

ASPARAGUS CHEESE CRÊPES
(Low Calorie)

1 package (10-ounces) frozen cut asparagus
1 cup low-fat cottage cheese
2 tablespoons low-fat milk
1 tablespoon fresh lemon juice
1½ teaspoons minced onion flakes
½ teaspoon salt
8 Low-Calorie Crêpes*
Herb Butter Sauce**

Preheat oven to 350°F. Cook asparagus according to package directions; drain well. Chop into small pieces; place in medium-size bowl. In blender container, combine cottage cheese, milk, lemon juice, onion flakes, and salt. Cover and process at medium speed 20 to 30 seconds. Fold cottage cheese mixture into chopped asparagus. Fill crêpes with 2 rounded tablespoons of cheese mixture. Fold over and place in non-stick baking dish. Bake, covered, 15 to 20 minutes, or until heated throughout. Before serving, spoon about 1 tablespoon Herb Butter Sauce over each crêpe. *4 servings*

PER SERVING (2 crêpes): Calories: 200   Protein: 17g
   Carbohydrate: 30g   Fat: 4 g   Sodium: 615mg

*LOW-CALORIE CRÊPES

1 cup all-purpose flour
1¼ cups low-fat milk
1 packet BUTTER BUDS®
3 eggs
⅛ teaspoon salt

MIXER OR WHISK METHOD:
In medium bowl, combine all ingredients. Beat with electric mixer or whisk until smooth.

BLENDER METHOD:
Combine ingredients in blender container. Cover and process at medium speed about 1 minute. Scrape down sides with rubber spatula and blend for another 15 seconds, or until smooth.

(Continued)

Refrigerate 1 hour or more. If batter separates, stir gently before cooking. Cook on upside-down crêpe griddle or in traditional pan.
12 crêpes

PER SERVING (1 crêpe): Calories: 60   Protein: 3g
   Carbohydrate: 9g Fat: 1g Sodium: 70mg

By using BUTTER BUDS® instead of butter in this recipe, you have saved 63 calories and 23 mg cholesterol per serving.

**HERB BUTTER SAUCE
(Low Calorie)

1 packet BUTTER BUDS® made into liquid
2 tablespoons lemon juice
1 teaspoon parsley flakes
1 teaspoon dehydrated chives
½ teaspoon tarragon
⅛ teaspoon onion powder

Combine all ingredients in small saucepan and heat just until hot, mixing well. Spoon sauce over your favorite vegetable or meat crêpe. *½ cup sauce*

PER SERVING (1 tablespoon): Calories: 5   Protein: trace
   Carbohydrate: 1g   Fat: trace   Sodium: 110mg

By using BUTTER BUDS® instead of butter in this recipe, you have saved 188 calories and 70 mg cholesterol per serving.

CRÊPES CARL

Crêpe Batter:
1¼ cups milk
1 tablespoon melted butter
2 eggs
1 cup flour
¼ tablespoon salt

Sauce:
3 tablespoons butter
4 tablespoons flour
1½ cups milk
¼ cup white wine
1 cup half-and-half
¼ teaspoon salt
Freshly ground black pepper to taste
½ cup grated Swiss cheese
¼ cup grated Parmesan cheese

Filling:
2 tablespoons butter
4 scallions, finely chopped
4 mushrooms, thinly sliced
2 packages BUDDIG Smoked Sliced Chicken
  (shredded)
2 hard-boiled eggs, finely chopped
3 tablespoons finely chopped parsley
¼ teaspoon salt
Freshly ground black pepper to taste

Place all crêpe batter ingredients in blender and mix; or mix with wire whisk. Cook crêpes and set aside.
Make sauce by melting butter, then adding remaining ingredients one at a time. Set aside.
Prepare filling by sautéing scallions, mushrooms and chicken in butter. Remove from heat and add remaining ingredients. Then add enough sauce to hold filling together. Divide filling equally among crêpes. Place filling on one side of crêpe and then roll the crêpe like a cigar. Place crêpes in greased baking dish seam side down. Cover with remaining sauce. Bake in 375° oven for 30 minutes.
Yield: 16 crêpes

CRAB FILLED CREPES

1 (6-oz.) pkg. **WAKEFIELD®** Crabmeat
¼ cup butter or margarine
⅓ cup chopped green onions
1 cup thinly sliced celery
1 cup chopped mushrooms
3 tablespoons flour
1⅓ cups milk
⅓ cup grated Swiss cheese
¼ teaspoon salt
⅛ teaspoon pepper
Dash nutmeg
8 cooked crepes
Parmesan cheese (optional)

Thaw crabmeat, retain liquid and separate into chunks. In sauce-pan sauté onions, celery and mushrooms in butter or margarine for 2 to 3 minutes. Remove with slotted spoon and set aside. Stir flour into fat until smooth. Add milk and crab liquid, cook until thickened. Stir in cheese, salt, pepper and nutmeg. In small bowl toss together crab, onions, celery, mushrooms and ½ cup of sauce. Season to taste. Spread equal amount of filling across center of each crepe and roll up or fold over. Place in shallow baking pan and pour remaining sauce over the top. Sprinkle with Parmesan cheese if desired. Heat in 350° oven for 10 to 15 minutes.

Makes 8 crepes

CAVIAR CRÊPES

12 warm crêpes (recipe follows)
1 pint sour cream
1 cup (8 oz.) **ROMANOFF®** Caviar*
½ cup finely chopped scallions

When crêpes are ready, spread sour cream down middle of each. Sprinkle with caviar and scallions. Roll seamside down. Top with more sour cream, caviar and scallion.   *Makes 12*

CRÊPES

Use a mix, or this recipe. With rotary beater, beat 2 eggs, 2 tablespoons melted butter and 1 cup milk. Add ¾ cup flour and ½ teaspoon salt. Beat until smooth. Cover. Chill one hour. To make crêpe, melt a scant teaspoon butter in a seven-inch pan. Pour in about three tablespoons batter, swirl around bottom of pan. Cook over medium heat until sides begin to brown. With spatula, turn crêpe and brown other side. Stack, separating with foil; keep warm until all are prepared.   *Makes 12*

*****ROMANOFF®** Black Lumpfish or Whitefish Caviar suggested.

HIGH LINER® SEAFOOD CRÊPES

Crêpes:

¾ cup flour
1 Tbsp. sugar
½ tsp. salt
3 eggs
1 cup milk
1 Tbsp. melted butter

Beat eggs until just blended in large bowl. Sift flour, sugar, salt over eggs and beat in, just until smooth. Stir in milk and melted butter. Heat 8 inch fry pan and grease lightly. Pour ⅓ cup batter in; tilting pan to cover bottom. Cook 1-2 minutes—turn and cook 1 minute longer. Roll up and place on cookie sheet. Keep warm. Repeat with remaining batter, greasing pan before each.

(Continued)

Crêpes Filling:

1 - 16 oz. pkg. **HIGH LINER®** Fillets, cooked and flaked
1 - 12 oz. pkg. **HIGH LINER®** Frozen Shrimp, cooked
1 pkg. broccoli spears, cooked
⅓ cup onion, finely chopped
2 Tbsp. butter
3 Tbsp. flour
2 cups milk
¾ cup shredded Swiss cheese
⅓ cup grated Parmesan cheese
⅓ cup dry white wine
Slivered almonds

Sauté onions in butter. Blend in flour. Add milk, stirring constantly over medium heat until thickened. Add Swiss and Parmesan cheese. Stir until melted and add wine. To ½ cup sauce, gently fold in fillets and shrimp. Unroll crêpes. On each crêpe place 2 broccoli spears, with flowered ends protruding. Add 2 heaping tablespoons sauce mixture and re-roll. Place on lightly greased baking dish. Pour remaining sauce over all the rolled crepes and sprinkle with almonds. Bake in 350°F oven for 30 minutes.

Serves 6-8

MUSHROOM-SOLE CRÊPES AU GRATIN

1 can (3 oz.) **BinB®** Sliced Mushrooms, drained—reserving broth
1 lb. fillet of sole, cut in 1-inch strips
1 package (10 oz.) frozen chopped spinach, thawed and drained
2 tablespoons dry white wine
1 teaspoon lemon juice
Salt and pepper to taste
2 tablespoons butter or margarine
2 tablespoons flour
½ cup minced green onion
Milk
½ cup shredded Swiss cheese
½ cup shredded cheddar cheese
8 crêpes (use favorite recipe)

Wipe fish dry, place in shallow baking dish. Cover with wine, lemon juice and seasonings. In a saucepan, melt butter or margarine and sauté onions until tender; blend in flour. Add enough milk to broth to make 1¼ cups. Add cheese and cook over low heat until cheese is melted, stirring constantly. Pour off ½ cup and fold into fish and spinach. Add mushrooms to remaining sauce. Divide fish-spinach mixture into eighths. Fill each crepe and roll. Place in oiled shallow baking dish. Cover and heat in 350°F. oven for 20 minutes. For each serving, use two crepes and top with warm mushroom sauce.   *Makes 4 to 6 servings*

SALMON BLINTZES

1 can (7¾ ounces) salmon
1 cup cottage cheese
1 egg
2 tablespoons sugar
¾ teaspoon salt
¼ teaspoon cinnamon
12 Blintzes*
1 cup sour cream
½ cup cherry preserves (or strawberry preserves)

Drain and flake salmon. Add cottage cheese, egg, sugar, salt, and cinnamon. Mix thoroughly. Place about 2 tablespoonfuls of the salmon mixture on the browned side of each blintz. Spread the filling to within an inch of the edge. Fold the bottom edge of the blintz up about an inch over the filling. Fold the two sides of the blintz in about ¾ of an inch over the filling. Then finish rolling the blintz from the bottom. The blintzes may be made to this point and refrigerated until ready to use.

Place blintzes in a single layer in melted butter in a 10-inch fry pan. Fry at a moderate heat for 5 to 6 minutes or until brown. Turn carefully. Fry 5 to 6 minutes longer or until blintzes are brown. Drain on absorbent paper. Place 2 blintzes on a small plate. Top with sour cream and cherry preserves. *Makes 6 servings*

*BLINTZES

¾ cup all-purpose flour
¼ teaspoon salt
1 cup milk
2 eggs, beaten
Oil

Combine flour and salt. Combine milk and eggs. Add gradually to flour mixture. Stir until smooth. Pour 2 tablespoons of batter into lightly oiled 6-inch fry pan. Tip the fry pan so that the batter completely covers the bottom. Fry at a moderate heat for 3 to 4 minutes or until blintz is brown on the bottom and set on top. Remove from pan. *Makes 12 blintzes*

Favorite recipe from **National Marine Fisheries Service**

SHRIMP FILLED PANCAKES

8-10 thin pancakes
3-4 tablespoons butter
1¼ tablespoons flour
1¼ cups fish or vegetable stock
2 egg yolks
⅓ cup cream
¼ teaspoon salt
Dash of white pepper
1 tablespoon lemon juice
½ lb. shrimp
3 tablespoons chopped dill
4-6 tablespoons grated **FINLANDIA Swiss Cheese**

Blend 2 tablespoons melted butter and the flour in saucepan. Gradually add fish or vegetable stock stirring constantly and let simmer for a few minutes. Beat together cream and eggs. Stir a little of the hot sauce into this mixture. Add to the sauce, stirring vigorously. Let the sauce simmer, stirring constantly until it thickens. Remove from fire and add butter (1-2 tablespoons) in small pieces. Finally add seasoning, shrimp and dill.

Divide the mixture on each pancake. Roll the pancakes and arrange in a greased baking dish. Sprinkle with grated cheese and dot with butter. Bake in oven (375°) for about 10 minutes and serve as hors d'oeuvres. *Makes 4 servings*

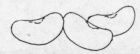

AMBROSIA CREPES

2 cans (13½ oz. each) pineapple tidbits, well drained
3 cups halved orange sections *OR* drained Mandarin orange segments
1 cup flaked coconut
1 cup dairy sour cream
20 crepes*

Combine all ingredients except crepes. Chill to blend flavors while preparing crepes. Spread scant ⅓ cup filling on each crepe and roll up. *Makes approx. 6 cups filling*
(Continued)

*BASIC CREPE RECIPE

6 tablespoons butter
6 eggs, slightly beaten
1 cup milk
1 cup water
1½ cups all-purpose flour
½ teaspoon salt

Melt butter in 10-inch omelet pan or 8-inch crepe pan. (Set aside skillet.) In bowl beat eggs, milk, water and melted butter together with rotary beater. Blend in flour and salt until mixture is smooth. On medium-high heat, heat buttered omelet pan until just hot enough to sizzle a drop of water. For each crepe pour scant ¼ cup batter in pan, rotating pan as batter is poured. Cook until lightly browned on bottom; remove from pan or, if desired, turn and brown other side.* Stack between sheets of paper toweling or waxed paper until ready to use. (Crepes may be frozen.) Spread scant ⅓ cup filling on each crepe; roll up. Serve 2-3 crepes per person. *Makes approx. 20 crepes*

*Crepes to be filled need only be browned on one side. Use unbrowned side for filling.

Note: Crepes should set to a thin lacy pancake almost immediately. If too much batter is poured into pan, pour off excess immediately. If there are holes, add a drop or two of batter for a patch.

Favorite recipe from the **American Egg Board**

STUFFED CREPES PINA COLADA

2 eggs
½ cup milk
½ cup water
2 Tbsp. unsalted butter
1 tsp. vanilla extract
¼ tsp. salt
1 tsp. sugar
1 cup flour

In blender, beat eggs until fluffy. Add remaining ingredients, except flour. Blend at medium speed 10 seconds. Add flour one tablespoon at a time, blending batter well after each addition. Let rest one hour or more. Spread batter as thinly as possible on hot crepe pan letting crepes brown well on one side. *Yields one dozen crepes*

Filling:

½ lb. cream cheese, softened
4 Tbsp. unsalted butter, softened
½ cup **COCO CASA® Pina Colada Mix**
1 egg yolk

Combine above ingredients; mix well. Chill until ready to serve.

Pina Colada Sauce:

½ cup **COCO CASA® Pina Colada Mix**
2 Tbsp. orange juice
2 Tbsp. butter, melted
1 tsp. grated orange rind

Combine above ingredients; mix well. Warm sauce before using.

To Serve: Place about 2 Tbsp. filling on each crepe, brown side down. Roll crepe cigarette fashion. Place in a well-buttered dish. Spoon sauce over crepes. Bake at 325° for 10 minutes. Set under hot broiler for 2 minutes until bubbly and browned.

Note: Crepes can be assembled ahead of time and chilled. Heat for serving.

DANISH CHERRY CREPES

1 21 ounce can cherry pie filling
2 large eggs
¼ cup sugar
¼ teaspoon salt
¾ cup **PETER HEERING Liqueur** (about)
1 cup heavy cream
1 tablespoon sugar
6 to 8 homemade crepes

Pour the pie filling into a strainer to drain off as much sauce as possible. Reserve both the sauce and the cherries. In the top of a double boiler, beat the eggs, sugar and salt until slightly thickened. Add ¾ cup of the cherry liquid to the egg mixture. Heat over boiling water until the mixture thickens stirring constantly. Remove from heat and add 3 tablespoons **PETER HEERING**. Set aside to cool. Beat heavy cream with sugar. Fold in one cup of the cream into the cooled cherry mixture. Add the cherries, reserving 6-8 for a garnish.

Take a warm crepe, spread the filling on the outside third and roll the crepe. Pour one tablespoon **PETER HEERING** over each crepe and garnish with some of the remaining whipped cream and a cherry. Repeat with remaining crepes.

Makes 6-8 crepes

BLUEBERRY CREPES

3 eggs (well beaten)
1 cup milk
1 cup all-purpose flour
½ tsp. salt
1 tsp. sugar
1 Tbsp. butter or margarine (melted)

Mix above ingredients well. Refrigerate 1-2 hours. Batter should be consistency of heavy cream; if too thick add a little more milk. Brush a 7- or 8-inch skillet with butter. Pour ⅛ cup batter at a time into skillet and turn and tip pan to form a thin film over the bottom. Turn after crepe has browned (15-20 seconds). Serve warm with **WILDERNESS® Blueberry Fruit Filling**. *Serves 6*

ALMOND CRÊPES MARTINIQUE

2 eggs
1 cup milk
1 cup flour
2 tablespoons melted butter
2 tablespoons granulated sugar
½ teaspoon salt
Melted butter (as needed for crêpe pan)
Lime-Ginger Sauce*
¼ cup chopped crystallized ginger
18 thin lime slices

Whisk eggs, then whisk in milk, flour, butter, sugar and salt. Cover and let stand 30 minutes. Heat a 5½-inch crêpe or frying pan until moderately hot; coat lightly with melted butter. Pour about 2 tablespoons batter into pan; tilt to cover entire bottom surface of pan. Cook until lightly browned. Turn and cook another minute or less, or until lightly browned. Repeat until all batter is used. If batter is too thick, thin with a little milk. For each serving, place a few tablespoons Lime-Ginger Sauce on an individual plate. One at a time, dip three crêpes in sauce and fold in quarters. Place on plate and garnish each crêpe with 1 teaspoon crystallized ginger and 1 lime slice. *Makes 6 servings*

*LIME-GINGER SAUCE

¾ cup butter or margarine
¾ cup firmly packed brown sugar
2 limes, grated and juiced
1 cup **BLUE DIAMOND®** Blanched Slivered Almonds, toasted

In medium skillet, melt butter. Add brown sugar. Cook and stir until sugar melts. Add lime juice, rind and almonds; stir until well mixed. Thin with a little hot water if sauce is too thick.

Vegetables

ALMOND VEGETABLE STIR-FRY

½ cup **BLUE DIAMOND**® **Whole Natural Almonds**
1 tablespoon vegetable oil
½ pound green beans, sliced 1-inch long and blanched
1 cup sliced mushrooms
4 green onions, sliced diagonally ½-inch long
1 tablespoon soy sauce
½ teaspoon fresh grated ginger or ⅛ teaspoon ground ginger
¼ teaspoon salt
1 clove garlic, minced or pressed

Toast almonds in hot oil, stirring constantly, about 5 minutes. Be careful not to burn. Add next 3 ingredients and cook, stirring constantly, 3 to 5 minutes or until mushrooms are just tender. Combine next 4 ingredients and stir into vegetables.

Makes 4 servings

VEGETABLE TAPESTRY

5 cups sliced crookneck squash (summer squash)
2 cups julienne carrots (2-inch lengths)
1 can (10¾-oz.) condensed cream of chicken soup
½ cup sour cream
¾ teaspoon **DURKEE Seasoned Salt**
1 can (2.8-oz.) **DURKEE French Fried Onions**

In 3-quart saucepan, bring 3 cups water to boil. Add squash and carrots; simmer 5 minutes; drain. Combine soup, sour cream, seasoned salt and ½ can French fried onions. Fold in hot vegetables. Pour mixture into 1½-quart casserole. Bake, uncovered, at 350° for 15 to 20 minutes. Top with remaining onions and bake 5 minutes longer.   *Makes 6 to 8 servings*

JARLSBERG VEGETABLE BAKE

1 medium eggplant, sliced
¼ cup oil
3 medium zucchini, sliced
1 cup sliced mushrooms
½ cup green pepper strips
½ cup sliced green onion
1 medium clove garlic, minced
1 cup halved cherry tomatoes
1 teaspoon salt
⅛ teaspoon pepper
2 cups shredded **JARLSBERG Cheese**

Sauté eggplant in oil in skillet, browning lightly on both sides; set aside. Sauté zucchini, mushrooms, green pepper, green onion and garlic several minutes. Add tomatoes, salt and pepper. Alternate layers of vegetables and cheese in shallow 1½-quart buttered baking dish. End with cheese. Bake at 350° F for 30 minutes.

Makes 6 servings

VEGETABLES ITALIANO

Chop:
    2 Tbsp. green onion
Drain, reserving liquid:
    1 can (16 oz.) **DEL MONTE Cut Green Beans**
Sauté onion in:
    1 Tbsp. butter or margarine
Add:
    1 can (8 oz.) **DEL MONTE Stewed Tomatoes**
    ⅛ tsp. thyme
    Dash pepper
Dissolve in reserved liquid:
    1½ tsp. cornstarch

Add to tomato-onion mixture. Cook over low heat, stirring constantly, until thickened. Add beans; heat.

TOFU-VEGETABLE SAUTÉ

1 tablespoon **HEALTH VALLEY**® **Safflower Oil**
½ cup chopped celery
½ cup chopped leeks or green onions
1 clove garlic, minced
1 10-ounce package **HEALTH VALLEY**® **Frozen Mixed Green Vegetables**
2 teaspoons arrowroot or whole wheat flour
2 tablespoons natural soy sauce (Tamari)
1 cup (½ can) **HEALTH VALLEY**® **Chicken Broth,** unsalted
1 cup (½ 10-ounce package) **HEALTH VALLEY**® **Hard Tofu,** cut into ½-inch cubes

Heat oil in a medium-size saucepan and lightly sauté the celery, leeks and garlic. Add vegetables (no need to thaw) and heat thoroughly. Mix arrowroot or flour, soy sauce and chicken broth, then add to vegetables. Bring to boiling and cook 5 to 8 minutes, or until thick. Add tofu and cook only until heated through. Serve the sauté over cooked **HEALTH VALLEY**® **Elbow Pasta** for a complete meal. Total Preparation Time: 20 minutes.

Yield: 4 servings

GRILLED VEGETABLE KABOBS

1 cup **PREGO Spaghetti Sauce**
3 tablespoons vinegar
2 tablespoons salad oil
⅛ teaspoon hot pepper sauce
4 cups assorted vegetables*

In large bowl combine spaghetti sauce, vinegar, oil and hot pepper sauce. Add vegetables; let stand 15 minutes, stirring occasionally. Thread vegetables on skewers. Place on rack in broiler pan. Preheat broiler as manufacturer directs. Broil kabobs 4 inches from heat for 7 minutes or until vegetables are tender-crisp, brushing with remaining sauce and turning often.

Makes 4 to 6 servings

*ASSORTED VEGETABLES—Choose from any of the following: green and red pepper chunks, fresh mushrooms, yellow or zucchini squash cut in 2-inch slices. Or cauliflowerets, carrot chunks, or whole small white onions, blanched for 5 minutes.

ORIENTAL STIR-FRY VEGETABLES

¼ cup soy sauce
1 teaspoon granulated sugar
¾ teaspoon ground ginger
1 cup **BLUE DIAMOND® Whole Natural Almonds**
3 tablespoons sesame seed or vegetable oil
2 stalks fresh broccoli, chopped
1 green pepper, diced
½ cup fresh mushrooms, sliced
½ cup red onion, chopped
1 cup snow peas

Combine soy sauce, sugar and ginger. Set aside. Heat 1 tablespoon of the oil in a large skillet. Add almonds, sauté over moderate heat until lightly roasted (about 3 to 5 minutes). Remove from skillet. Add remaining oil; heat. Add broccoli and pepper. Stir-fry about 2 minutes. Add mushrooms, onion and snow peas; stir-fry another minute. Return almonds to skillet; add soy mixture, cover and cook 2 minutes longer. Serve immediately.
Makes 5 to 6 servings

MARINADED VEGETABLES WITH DRESSING

2 pounds assorted fresh vegetables, cooked, such as green beans, cauliflowerets, broccoli flowerets and thinly sliced zucchini
1 cup **MAZOLA® Corn Oil**
⅓ cup white wine vinegar
1 clove garlic, minced
1 teaspoon salt
1 teaspoon sugar
¼ teaspoon pepper
1 cup plain yogurt
3 tablespoons reserved marinade
2 tablespoons chopped parsley
¼ teaspoon dried oregano leaves

Place vegetables in large shallow dish. In small bowl stir together corn oil, vinegar, garlic, salt, sugar and pepper. Pour over vegetables. Cover; refrigerate overnight. Drain vegetables, reserving marinade. Arrange vegetables on serving platter. In small bowl stir in 3 tablespoons marinade into yogurt. Add parsley and oregano. Serve dressing with vegetables.   *Makes 6 servings*

Note: Keep remaining marinade in a jar with tight-fitting cover in refrigerator. ¼ teaspoon curry may be substituted for oregano.

FRESH VEGETABLE MARINADE

1 can (10¾ ounces) **CAMPBELL'S Condensed Chicken Broth**
¼ cup vinegar
2 tablespoons salad oil
2 tablespoons dry vermouth
1 package (about 0.9 ounces) mild Italian salad dressing mix
2 cups thinly sliced sweet potatoes
2 cups thinly sliced zucchini squash
1 cup thinly sliced broccoli flowerets
1 cup thinly sliced cauliflowerets
1 cup thinly sliced fresh mushrooms
1 cup cherry tomatoes cut in half

To make marinade, combine broth, vinegar, oil, vermouth and salad dressing mix. Arrange vegetables in shallow dish; pour marinade over vegetables. Cover. Chill 6 hours or more; stir occasionally. With slotted spoon, arrange vegetables on platter.
Makes about 7 cups

LEMON MARINATED MUSHROOMS

¾ cup salad oil
¼ cup olive oil
½ cup **MINUTE MAID® 100% Pure Lemon Juice**
1 medium onion (chopped fine)
1 tsp. salt
¼ tsp. pepper
3 bay leaves
1 tsp. chopped parsley
1½ cups small fresh tiny mushrooms or 3 cans (4 oz.) button mushrooms

Mix all ingredients except mushrooms in a jar with screw top. Shake well. Add mushrooms. Let stand 12 hours or more.

SAVORY MARINATED VEGETABLES

1 can (10¾-ounces) **CAMPBELL'S Condensed Chicken Broth**
¼ cup vinegar
2 tablespoons dry vermouth
1 package (0.9-ounces) mild Italian salad dressing mix
2 tablespoons grated Parmesan cheese
2 cups diagonally sliced sweet potatoes or carrots
2 cups sliced cucumber
2 cups broccoli flowerets
1 cup cauliflowerets
1 cup thinly sliced fresh mushrooms
1 cup red pepper strips

1. Prepare marinade: In 13- by 9-inch baking dish, combine first five ingredients.
2. Arrange remaining ingredients in marinade, stirring to coat with marinade.
3. Cover; refrigerate 4 hours or overnight, stirring occasionally.
4. To serve: With slotted spoon arrange vegetables on platter.
Makes 8 cups or 8 servings

MARINATED TOMATOES AND MUSHROOMS

1 pint cherry tomatoes, halved
½ pint fresh mushrooms, sliced
3 green onions, sliced
¼ cup vegetable oil
1 tablespoon vinegar
1 teaspoon lemon juice
1 packet **ROMANOFF® MBT® Instant Vegetable Broth**
½ teaspoon Worcestershire sauce
4 drops **TABASCO® Sauce**

Combine tomatoes, mushrooms, and green onion in medium-sized bowl. Blend together the oil, vinegar, lemon juice, **MBT®**, Worcestershire, and **TABASCO®**. Pour over tomato mixture. Stir gently; cover and chill 1-2 hours.   *Makes 6 servings*
(about ½ cup each)

BOGGS® ACORN SQUASH

3 medium acorn squash, cut in half, seeded
Salt
3 tablespoons butter or margarine
½ cup **BOGGS® Cranberry Liqueur**
1 can (8-oz.) whole cranberry sauce

Place squash, cut side down, in shallow baking dish. Bake in preheated 400°F oven 35 minutes. Remove from oven. Invert squash. Sprinkle with salt. Place 1 teaspoon butter in each squash. Combine **BOGGS®** and cranberry sauce; spoon into squash cavity. Return to oven. Continue baking 30 minutes or until squash is tender.   *Serves 6*

ASPARAGUS VINAIGRETTE
(Asparagi alla "vinaigrette")

1¼ pounds asparagus
½ cup Vinaigrette Dressing*
1 tablespoon grated Parmesan cheese
2 cherry tomatoes, sliced
Sieved egg yolk

Cook asparagus in 1-inch boiling water until tender, about 8 minutes; drain. Heat Vinaigrette Dressing in saucepan until hot; pour over asparagus. Sprinkle with cheese. Garnish with tomato and egg yolk.   *Makes 4 servings*

*VINAIGRETTE DRESSING
(Salsa vinaigrette)

¾ cup **BERTOLLI® Olive Oil**
¼ cup **BERTOLLI® Red Wine Vinegar**
1 anchovy fillet, mashed (optional)
1 clove garlic, minced
½ teaspoon salt
¼ teaspoon pepper

Shake all ingredients in covered jar; refrigerate.

MARINATED ARTICHOKE HEARTS

2 packages (9 oz. each) frozen artichoke hearts
¾ cup **MAZOLA® Corn Oil**
⅓ cup tarragon vinegar
2 tablespoons finely chopped parsley
1 tablespoon finely chopped onion
1 teaspoon dry mustard
½ teaspoon salt
¼ teaspoon pepper
1 clove garlic, minced

Cook artichoke hearts according to package directions for minimum cooking period or just until tender crisp. Drain thoroughly. Mix together remaining ingredients. Pour over artichoke hearts; cover; chill overnight. Serve cold or heat artichoke hearts in marinade in 3-quart saucepan just until heated. Spoon into fondue pot or chafing dish. Hold over low heat during serving period.
                           Makes about 60 appetizer pieces

GREEN BEANS, ITALIAN-STYLE

1 package (9 oz.) frozen cut green beans, slightly thawed
1 can (1 lb.) stewed tomatoes
1 teaspoon cornstarch
1 teaspoon **LEA & PERRINS Worcestershire Sauce**
½ teaspoon basil leaves

In a small saucepan combine all ingredients. Bring to boiling point. Reduce heat; simmer until beans are tender.
                                    Yield: 6 portions

GREEN BEAN COMBO

2 (9-oz.) packages cut green beans
2 (3-oz.) cans sliced mushrooms, drained
½ cup **SEVEN SEAS® VIVA® Italian! Dressing**
2 tablespoons chopped pimiento

Cook green beans until crunchy. Drain. Mix with mushrooms, dressing, and pimiento. Season with salt and freshly ground pepper. Serve warm or chilled on lettuce. Garnish with onion.
                                         Serves 6

GREEN BEANS ITALIAN

3 Tbsp. **LAND O LAKES® Sweet Cream Butter**
½ cup (½ med.) onion, cut into ¼ inch rings
9-oz. pkg. frozen cut green beans, thawed, drained
2 Tbsp. sliced (⅛ inch) ripe olives
1 tsp. basil leaves
½ tsp. salt
⅛ tsp. garlic powder
½ cup (½ med.) cubed (½ inch) tomato

In 2-qt. saucepan melt butter. Stir in onion. Cook, uncovered, over med. heat, stirring occasionally, until crisply tender (3 to 5 min.). Stir in remaining ingredients *except* tomato. Cover; continue cooking, stirring occasionally, until vegetables are crisply tender (5 to 7 min.). Stir in tomato. Cover; continue cooking 1 min.   *Yield: 5 (½ cup) servings*

MICROWAVE METHOD:
In 1½-qt. casserole melt butter on high (40 to 50 sec.). Stir in onion. Cover; cook on high 2½ min. Stir in remaining ingredients *except* tomato. Cover; cook on high, stirring after ½ the time until vegetables are crisply tender (3 to 4 min.). Stir in tomato. Cover; cook on high 1 min. Let stand 1 min.

STIR FRY BEAN SPROUTS AND PEPPERS

2 tablespoons cooking oil
½ teaspoon salt
1 teaspoon minced fresh ginger root
2 fresh red chili or bell peppers *and* 2 sweet green peppers, cut into thin strips
1 can (8 oz.) **LA CHOY® Bean Sprouts**, rinsed and drained
¼ cup chicken stock
¼ teaspoon sugar
1 teaspoon sherry

Heat oil in wok or large skillet. Add salt and ginger, stirring. Add peppers; cook, stirring constantly, 2 minutes. Add bean sprouts; cook ½ minute more. Add stock and cook, covered, 2 or 3 minutes over medium heat. Stir in sugar and sherry. Serve.   *4 servings*

BAKED NAVY BEANS

2 cans **BUSH'S BEST** Navy Beans
¼ pound salt pork
5 sprigs parsley, minced or 1 teaspoon parsley flakes
1 medium onion, diced
1 clove garlic, crushed
¼ cup green pepper, chopped
¼ cup sweet red peppers, chopped
2 tablespoons maple syrup or molasses
6 tablespoons catsup

Combine all ingredients, including the liquid with the beans. Put into bean pot or casserole and bake, covered in 300° oven one hour. Remove the cover and bake one hour longer, adding a little water if necessary.   *Serves 6*

POLYNESIAN OVEN BAKED BEANS

2 Tbsp. olive oil
3 Tbsp. onion, chopped
2 cans (16 oz.) **S&W® Oven Baked Beans**
1 can (12 oz.) **S&W® Pineapple Chunks**, well drained
1 can (11 oz.) **S&W® Mandarin Oranges**, drained (optional)
1 can (3 oz.) deviled ham
½ cup chopped green peppers
¼ cup **S&W® Catsup**
½ tsp. salt, dash **TABASCO® Sauce**
2 Tbsp. brown sugar

Sauté onion in olive oil until transparent.
   Mix in 2 qt. casserole—oven-baked beans, onions and remaining ingredients.
   Bake uncovered at 375°F. for 30-35 minutes or until bubbly.
                                          Yield: 6-8 servings

BEANS ITALIANO

1 lb. dry navy beans
6 cups water
2 medium onions, grated
1 clove garlic, mashed
1 bay leaf
2 tablespoons fresh chopped parsley
½ teaspoon dill seed
Salt and pepper to taste
½ cup olive or vegetable oil
2 cups canned tomatoes, drained
3 small sweet pickles, chopped
½ cup green stuffed olives, chopped
1 cup celery, chopped
Grated cheese

Wash and sort beans. Combine beans and water in large saucepan. Bring to a boil and cook 2 minutes. Remove from heat, cover and let stand one hour. Add onion, garlic and seasonings; simmer about 2 hours until beans are tender, adding water if needed. Separately cook tomato, pickles, olives and celery in oil until tender. Mix vegetables and beans and pour mixture into 2½ quart casserole. Cover and bake at 275°F. about 2 hours. Uncover and sprinkle with grated cheese. Continue baking until cheese is browned.   *Makes 10-12 servings*

Favorite recipe from **Michigan Bean Commission**

BASIC RECIPE FOR PREPARING ALL DRIED BEANS

1 pound **BROWN'S BEST** Great Northerns, Pintos, Red Beans, Large Limas or Baby Limas
12 cups water
2 teaspoons salt

Wash beans thoroughly, removing any off-colored beans. Use a large heavy pot—approximately 3 times the amount of the water and beans. Bring the salted water to a boiling point. Add beans. Boil 2 minutes only. Cover. Remove from heat. Allow to stand 1 hour. Return to the heat and bring to a boil. Reduce the heat and simmer slowly until tender.

Note: It is suggested to always cook at least 1 lb. of **BROWN'S BEST Beans** at a time. If the recipe calls for less, the remainder can always be frozen to use at a later date.

PINTO BEAN CASSEROLE

¾ cup (about 5 ounces) dried pinto beans
1 quart cold water
½ teaspoon salt
1 clove garlic, pierced with a toothpick
1 bay leaf
4 ounces uncooked spinach noodles
1 tablespoon vegetable oil
½ cup diced celery
¼ cup chopped onion
½ teaspoon basil
½ teaspoon dry mustard
½ teaspoon thyme
¼ teaspoon sage
1 packet **BUTTER BUDS®**
¼ cup chopped pimiento
Freshly ground pepper to taste
¼ cup (1 ounce) grated mozzarella cheese

Pick over beans to remove any blemished ones. Wash in cold water. Drain. Soak in water overnight. Transfer beans and liquid to saucepan. Add salt, garlic, and bay leaf. Bring to a boil. Reduce heat and simmer, covered, until beans are tender, about 1 hour. Drain, reserving liquid from cooked beans. Cook noodles as directed on package. When tender, remove from heat, drain, and rinse noodles with cold water.

   Preheat oven to 350° F. Heat oil in large skillet. Add celery, onion, basil, mustard, thyme, and sage. Sauté until vegetables are tender, about 5 minutes. Measure 2 cups liquid from cooked beans. Add with **BUTTER BUDS®**, pimiento, and pepper to celery-onion mixture in skillet. Mix thoroughly. Remove garlic and bay leaf. Add beans and noodles. Mix well. Transfer mixture to non-stick baking dish. Sprinkle top with cheese. Cover with foil. Bake about 30 minutes, or until cheese melts.   *4 servings*

PER SERVING (1 cup):   Calories: 305   Protein: 12 gm
Carbohydrate: 46 gm   Fat: 5 gm   Sodium: 250 mg

RANCHERO BEANS

2 cans (1 pound each) **HEINZ Vegetarian Beans in Tomato Sauce**
⅓ cup **HEINZ Tomato Ketchup**
3 tablespoons chopped onion
1 tablespoon light brown sugar
1 tablespoon molasses or dark corn syrup
¼ teaspoon salt
⅛ to ¼ teaspoon hot pepper sauce
2 slices bacon, partially cooked

Combine all ingredients except bacon in a 1 quart casserole. Top with bacon. Bake, uncovered, in 375°F. oven, 1 hour, stirring occasionally. *Makes 4-6 servings (about 3½ cups)*

BROWN'S BEST PINTOS-MEXICAN DELICIOSO

2 cups **BROWN'S BEST Pintos** (prepare using Basic Recipe for Preparing All Dried Beans—see index)
1 lb. ground beef
4 tablespoons tomato sauce
1 tablespoon Mexican hot sauce
1 7 oz. can green chilies
1 cup stuffed green olives-sliced
¾ lb. shredded Cheddar cheese
1 tablespoon chili powder
Corn chips

Crumble beef in skillet, stir until lightly browned. Drain off fat. Add to cooked beans and mash with potato masher. Add sauces and green chilies, blend thoroughly. Turn into deep round casserole. Sprinkle olives around outer edge. Fill center with shredded cheese. Sprinkle chili powder over cheese. Bake uncovered, 350 degree oven 30 minutes or until cheese mixture is melted. Serve casserole on a warming plate with corn chips.

PICKLED BEETS
(Low Calorie)

3 pounds fresh beets
2 tsp. whole allspice
2 tsp. whole cloves
2 cinnamon sticks, broken in half
½ cup **SUPEROSE® Liquid Fructose**
4 cups cider vinegar
1 cup water

Cook the beets in salted water until tender. Cooking time depends greatly upon the size of the beets. Large beets require about 45 minutes. Remove the cooked beets from the heat and place under cold running water. Remove the beet skins by pressing the skin gently with your fingers under the running water. If you are using very small beets, leave them whole. Otherwise, slice them or cut them in strips or cubes as you desire and set aside.

Tie the spices securely in a piece of cheesecloth. Combine the **SUPEROSE® Liquid Fructose**, vinegar, water and spice bag in a large kettle or saucepan and bring to a boil. Add the beets and boil for 5 minutes. Remove the spice bag. Divide the beets evenly into five hot sterilized 8-ounce jars. Spoon the hot liquid over the beets, filling each jar. Seal the jars and place upside down to insure proper seal. *Makes 5 (8-ounce) jars beets*

Each ¼ cup contains approximately: 20 calories

Note: Save the juice from the pickled beets to color hard boiled eggs. Place peeled hard boiled eggs in the red liquid and marinate for 24 hours. They are particularly pretty used to decorate a baked ham at Easter.

BRUSSELS SPROUTS ROYALE

10-oz. pkg. baby brussels sprouts frozen in butter sauce
½ cup seedless green grapes
2 tablespoons sauterne
2 tablespoons **FISHER® Blanched Slivered Almonds**

Cook brussels sprouts according to package directions. Partially open pouch; drain butter sauce into small saucepan. Add grapes. Cook only enough to heat through. Remove from heat; add sauterne and almonds. Toss with brussels sprouts.

3 to 4 servings

ORIENTAL BROCCOLI

6 medium fresh broccoli stalks
Olive or vegetable oil
1 clove garlic, split
½ cup thinly sliced sweet red bell pepper
3 green onions with tops, sliced diagonally into ½-inch pieces
2-3 tablespoons **LA CHOY® Soy** or **Teriyaki Sauce**
Salt
Freshly ground black pepper
Toasted sesame seeds

Slice stem part of broccoli thin, discarding tougher portions of stalk. Separate flowerettes. In heavy frying pan, add enough oil to cover bottom; heat until hot. Add garlic and broccoli stems. Cover and cook quickly until partially tender, stirring occasionally. Add remaining broccoli, red bell pepper, and green onions and cook until just tender. Season with soy or teriyaki sauce and salt and pepper. Garnish with sesame seeds. *3 to 4 servings*

C & W BROCCOLI PUFF

1 (9-oz.) box **C & W Frozen Broccolettes**
1 (10¾-oz.) can condensed cream of mushroom soup
2 ounces sharp Cheddar cheese grated (½ cup)
¼ cup milk
¼ cup mayonnaise
1 beaten egg
¼ cup fine dry bread crumbs
1 tablespoon butter, melted

Cook frozen Broccolettes according to package directions, drain thoroughly. Place Broccolettes in buttered baking dish 8½ × 8½ × 2-inches. In separate bowl, stir together condensed soup and grated cheese. Gradually add mayonnaise, milk and beaten egg to soup mixture, stirring until well blended. Pour over Broccolettes. Combine bread crumbs and melted butter; sprinkle evenly over soup mixture. Bake at 350° for approximately 45 minutes, or until crumbs are lightly browned. *Serves 6*

RED CABBAGE WITH DICED APPLES
(Low Calorie)

4 cups thinly sliced red cabbage
1 green apple, peeled, cored and diced
¼ cup diced onion
2 tablespoons lemon juice
1 chicken-flavor bouillon cube
⅛ teaspoon allspice
Dash pepper
¾ cup water
2 packets **SWEET 'N LOW®**

Combine all ingredients except water and **SWEET 'N LOW®** in large saucepan. Add water. Cover and simmer 20 minutes, or until cabbage is tender. Stir in **SWEET 'N LOW®**. *6 servings*

PER SERVING (½ cup): Calories: 35 Protein 1 g
Carbohydrate: 8g Fat: trace Sodium: 175mg

MARINATED CAULIFLOWER

½ cup **HEINZ Salad or Wine Vinegar**
¼ cup salad oil
1 clove garlic, minced
1 teaspoon salt
Dash pepper
Dash paprika
1 small head cauliflower (about 1½ pounds), cut into
  bite-size pieces
1 small onion, thinly sliced
2 tablespoons chopped green pepper
1 tablespoon pimiento strips

Combine first 6 ingredients in jar; cover; shake well. In bowl, combine cauliflower and remaining ingredients. Pour marinade over vegetables. Cover; refrigerate overnight, stirring occasionally. Serve as a relish, appetizer or salad.

Makes about 4 cups

JAPANESE PICKLED CAULIFLOWER

1 medium size head of cauliflower
1 green pepper
½ cup very thinly sliced celery
¾ cup **COCA-COLA®**
6 tablespoons wine vinegar or white vinegar
¼ cup sugar
1½ teaspoons salt

Break off each floweret in cauliflower, wash and drain. Wash and remove seeds from green pepper; cut into thin 2-inch strips. In large bowl, combine cauliflower and green pepper. Cover with boiling water; let stand 2 minutes; drain thoroughly. Add celery. In small pan, heat **COCA-COLA®** with remaining ingredients. Pour over vegetables. Toss lightly with a fork, and pack into a 1-quart glass jar. Push down lightly so liquid covers vegetables. Cover and chill overnight. This keeps in the refrigerator for several days.

Makes about 1 quart

ORIENTAL CAULIFLOWER MEDLEY

⅓ cup **LAND O LAKES® Sweet Cream Butter**
10-oz. pkg. frozen cauliflower, thawed, drained
6-oz. pkg. frozen pea pods, thawed, drained
4-oz. can mushroom stems and pieces, drained
½ tsp. salt
¼ tsp. ginger
⅛ tsp. pepper
1 small tomato, cut into 10 wedges
2 Tbsp. sliced almonds, toasted

In 3-qt. saucepan melt butter. Stir in remaining ingredients *except* tomato and almonds. Cover; cook over med. heat, stirring occasionally, until vegetables are crisply tender (8 to 10 min.). Add tomato. Cover; continue cooking 1 min. Sprinkle with toasted almonds.

Yield: 6 (⅔ cup) servings

MICROWAVE METHOD:
In 2-qt. casserole melt butter on high (60 to 70 sec.). Stir in remaining ingredients *except* tomato and almonds. Cover; cook on high, stirring after ½ the time, until vegetables are crisply tender (3 to 4 min.). Add tomato. Cover; cook on high (1 to 1½ min.). Let stand 1 min. Sprinkle with toasted almonds.

CELERY MARSALA

1 stalk Florida Celery
2 tablespoons salad oil
½ cup minced onion
1 clove garlic, minced
¾ cup chicken broth or water
¾ teaspoon salt
1/16 teaspoon ground black pepper
2 egg yolks, beaten
¼ cup dry Marsala Wine

Trim stem ends of celery; cut off tops to within 6 inches from base. Cut stalk lengthwise in half; cut each half into thirds; set aside. In a large skillet heat oil. Add onion and garlic; sauté until golden. Add broth, salt, black pepper and reserved celery. Simmer, covered, about 25 minutes, or until celery is crisp-tender. Remove celery to warm serving dish. Mix egg yolks with Marsala. Stir in some of the hot pan liquid into yolk mixture. Then, stir yolk mixture into pan liquid. Cook and stir over low heat until sauce thickens. Spoon sauce over celery. *Yield: 6 portions*

Favorite recipe from **Florida Celery Committee**

MARINATED RAW SHREDDED CARROTS
(Carote all'Agro)

Wash 6 large carrots, then cut off the top and bottom ends. The outer ring of the carrot is darker in color and more tender. Use a swivel-action peeler to shred only the tender, darker part of each carrot into a bowl. Discard the inner cores of the carrots. Add the juice of 2 lemons, ¼ cup **DANTE Olive Oil**, and salt and freshly ground black pepper to taste to the shredded carrots. Mix well, cover the bowl tightly with aluminum foil, and refrigerate for at least 1 hour. When ready to serve, transfer the marinated carrots to a serving dish and sprinkle with the chopped leaves of 6 or 7 sprigs of Italian parsley. *6 servings*

TANGY CARROTS

1 pound carrots
½ cup **HENRI'S YOGONAISE® Reduced Calorie Dressing**
1 tablespoon chopped parsley
1 tablespoon dried, minced onion
1 tablespoon margarine
1½ teaspoons prepared horseradish

1. Peel and cut carrots into 2-inch sticks. Cook in small amount of water until tender. Drain.
2. Combine **HENRI'S YOGONAISE® Reduced Calorie Dressing**, parsley, onion, margarine and horseradish. Add to carrots. Stir to coat. Serve hot. *Makes 4 servings*

CHAMPAGNE GLAZED CARROTS

1½ pounds carrots, peeled, quartered lengthwise and
  cut into 2-inch lengths
1 cup beef stock
½ cup **KORBEL Blanc de Noirs Champagne**
Salt and pepper, to taste
6 tablespoons butter
2 tablespoons chopped fresh parsley

Combine all ingredients, except the parsley, in a saucepan. Cover, bring to a boil and then simmer, uncovered, for 25 to 30 minutes, or until the carrots are tender. When done, the liquid will have turned into a syrupy sauce. Before serving, sprinkle carrots with the parsley. *Serves 6*

PARSNIP AND CARROT CASSEROLE

½ lb. parsnips, cut into thin strips, 2 inches long
½ lb. carrots, cut into thin strips, 2 inches long
½ teaspoon salt
⅛ teaspoon pepper
1 tablespoon brown sugar
3 tablespoons **IRISH MIST®** Liqueur
2 tablespoons butter or margarine

Place parsnips and carrots in 1-quart casserole. Sprinkle with salt, pepper, brown sugar, and **IRISH MIST®**. Dot with butter. Cover. Bake in 325° F oven for 1 hour or until vegetables are tender-crisp. *Serves 6*

ONION BUTTERED CORN

½ cup **LIPTON®** Onion Butter*
8 ears corn

Place each ear of corn on large square of heavy-duty foil; spread with Onion Butter. Wrap, twisting ends; roast over hot coals about 25 minutes, turning frequently. *Makes 8 servings*

*LIPTON® ONION BUTTER

Blend 1 envelope **LIPTON®** Onion Soup Mix thoroughly with 1 container (8-oz.) whipped butter or soft margarine, or ½ pound butter or margarine. Store covered in refrigerator. *Makes about 1¼ cups*

CACTUS CORN

4 slices bacon
¼ cup green pepper strips
1 can (11 ounces) **CAMPBELL'S Condensed Cheddar Cheese Soup**
3 cups cooked whole kernel corn
½ cup drained chopped canned tomatoes

In saucepan, cook bacon until crisp; remove and crumble. Pour off all but 2 tablespoons drippings. Cook green pepper in drippings until tender. Add soup, corn and tomatoes. Heat; stir occasionally. Garnish with bacon. *Makes about 4 cups, 4 servings*

BAKED CORN CASSEROLE

1 (1-lb.) can whole kernel corn, drained
2 Tbsp. butter or margarine
2 Tbsp. flour
2 tsp. **BALTIMORE SPICE OLD BAY Seasoning**
¾ cup milk
1 tsp. sugar
1 egg, slightly beaten

Melt butter; blend in flour and **BALTIMORE SPICE OLD BAY**. Cook over low heat stirring until mixture is bubbly. Remove from heat and gradually add milk. Add sugar and heat to boiling, stirring constantly. Boil and stir 1 minute. Stir in egg and corn. Pour into an ungreased 1-quart casserole. Bake at 350° for 35-40 minutes. Garnish with cooked asparagus spears, pimiento strips and/or crumbled cooked bacon.

VARIATION:

For additional flavor, ¼ cup chopped and sautéed onion and/or green pepper or ¼ cup diced ham may be added to the casserole with the corn.

CREAMY CUCUMBER ANTIPASTO
(Low Calorie)

1 container (8 ounces) plain low-fat yogurt
2 tablespoons distilled white vinegar
2 tablespoons chopped fresh chives
2 teaspoons dillweed
1 teaspoon celery seed
2 packets **SWEET 'N LOW®**
½ teaspoon salt
½ teaspoon dry mustard
Dash freshly ground pepper
3 medium-size cucumbers, peeled and sliced thin

In a bowl, combine all ingredients except cucumbers. Mix thoroughly. Toss cucumber slices in dressing and marinate several hours in refrigerator. *8 servings*

PER SERVING (½ cup): Calories: 25 Protein: 2gm
Carbohydrate: 5gm Fat: trace Sodium: 160mg

EGGPLANT PARMESAN

1¾ pounds eggplant
⅓ cup oil
2 cups (1 pound) ricotta cheese
1⅓ cups (12-ounce can) **CONTADINA®** Italian Paste
1⅓ cups (1 can) water
½ cup fine dry bread crumbs
2 tablespoons Parmesan cheese

Peel eggplant; slice into ¼-inch slices. Fry on both sides, in oil, in large skillet until tender. (Add more oil if necessary.) Drain on paper towels. Place half of eggplant slices on bottom of 12 x 7½ x 2-inch baking dish. Spread half of ricotta cheese over eggplant. Combine Italian Paste and water; mix thoroughly. Pour half of mixture over ricotta. Combine bread crumbs and Parmesan cheese. Sprinkle half over top of Italian Paste mixture. Repeat layers. Bake in moderate oven (350° F.) 30 minutes or until sauce is bubbly. Cut in squares to serve. *Makes 6 servings*

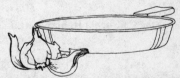

SARGENTO EGGPLANT PARMESAN

2 medium eggplant, peeled, cut into ½ inch slices
Salt
Flour for coating
Olive oil for frying
2 cups tomato sauce
8 oz. **SARGENTO Shredded Mozzarella Cheese**
½ cup **SARGENTO Grated Parmesan and Romano Blend Cheese**
3 Tbsp. butter

Cut eggplant into ½ inch slices. Sprinkle both sides lightly with salt and place between paper towels. Place a wooden board or heavy weight on top of eggplant and let stand at least 30 minutes. Rinse and pat dry with paper towels. Dip in flour and fry slices in olive oil until lightly brown.

Place a single layer of eggplant in a buttered dish. Cover with ⅓ of tomato sauce and also ⅓ of shredded Mozzarella and ⅓ of Parmesan and Romano cheese. Continue to layer eggplant, sauce, and cheeses for two more layers; end with Parmesan and Romano cheese. Dot with butter and bake at 400° degrees for 30 minutes. *Makes 4 servings*

EGGPLANT SZECHUAN STYLE

¼ cup salad oil
1 tablespoon minced pared fresh ginger or
  ¼ teaspoon powdered ginger
2 cloves garlic, minced
¼ pound ground pork
1 teaspoon sugar
½ teaspoon salt
¼ to ½ teaspoon **TABASCO® Pepper Sauce**
1 eggplant, pared and cut into 1-inch cubes
1 cup water
2 tablespoons soy sauce
1 tablespoon sherry
1 tablespoon cornstarch

Heat salad oil in large skillet or wok. Add ginger and garlic. Add pork and cook, stirring constantly, over high heat 2 minutes or until no longer pink. Add sugar, salt, **TABASCO®**, and eggplant. Cook and stir until eggplant is coated with oil. Mix water, soy sauce, sherry and cornstarch, and stir into skillet. Cover and cook 5 minutes over medium heat, or until eggplant is tender.

Yield: 4 to 6 servings

RATATOUILLE RELISH

¼ cup olive oil
1 medium eggplant, coarsely chopped
1 onion, chopped
1 can (28 ounces) Italian-style tomatoes, drained
¼ cup red wine vinegar
2 teaspoons sugar
½ teaspoon salt
¼ teaspoon pepper
10 pimiento-stuffed green olives, sliced

Heat oil in large skillet until hot. Stir in eggplant and onion. Cook, stirring constantly, until onion is transparent and eggplant is tender. Stir in remaining ingredients. Simmer, uncovered, 15 minutes. Cover and refrigerate up to 24 hours. Serve at room temperature.

Makes about 5 cups

Favorite recipe from the **California Iceberg Lettuce Commission**

MARINATED MUSHROOMS

Add 2 pounds very small mushrooms to Mild Garlic Marinade*. Marinate for several days in refrigerator. Stir or shake occasionally. Marinated mushrooms may be used as an appetizer, added to salads, or used as a garnish. Use Marinade as a salad dressing on fresh crisp greens.

*MILD GARLIC MARINADE

¼ cup **CRISCO® Oil**
3 tablespoons wine vinegar
⅓ cup tomato juice
1 teaspoon salt
1 teaspoon paprika
½ teaspoon black pepper
2 cloves garlic

Combine all ingredients in a screw-top jar and chill for several days in refrigerator. Remove garlic cloves and shake well before using.

About ¾ cup

CREOLE BROWNED OKRA

2 cans **TRAPPEY'S® Cut Okra**
2 tablespoons butter
2 tablespoons salad oil
1 cup chopped onion
2 cloves garlic, minced
½ teaspoon lemon juice
½ teaspoon **TRAPPEY'S® Pepper Sauce**
½ cup uncooked rice
Salt to taste

Drain okra well, rinse and chop. Heat butter and oil in skillet, stir in onions, cook until transparent. Turn heat very low, stir in chopped okra, garlic, lemon juice and **TRAPPEY'S® Pepper Sauce**. Continue cooking and stirring until mixture browns. Cook rice separately. Combine with okra, season to taste. Pour into casserole dish, heat in oven just before serving.   *Serves 4*

Note: Avoid iron pots and spoons in cooking okra. The iron is not harmful, but it blackens okra.

STUFFED ONIONS

8 large Spanish or Italian onions, boiled and drained
1 (10-oz.) pkg. frozen spinach, thawed and drained
1 cup mayonnaise
1 Tbsp. lemon juice
¼ cup **COFFEE RICH® Frozen Non-Dairy Creamer**
1 tsp. salt
1 (2-oz.) jar pimiento, drained

1. Remove centers from boiled onions. Chop and combine with spinach.
2. Fill onions with spinach mixture and place in flat, buttered 7 × 10-inch casserole.
3. Stir together mayonnaise, lemon juice, **COFFEE RICH®** and salt until smoothly blended. Stir in pimiento. Pour sauce over and around onions.
4. Bake in 350 degree oven until warmed through, about 30 minutes.

C & W BUTTERED ONIONS AND PEAS

In saucepan melt 2 tablespoons butter.
  Add:

1 (10-oz.) bag **C & W Frozen Small Whole Onions**
1 (10-oz.) box **C & W Frozen Petite Size Peas**
½ head iceberg lettuce, shredded
1 sprig thyme
2 sprigs parsley
½ teaspoon sugar
¼ teaspoon salt
Dash pepper

Stir to mix well. Cover pan *tightly* and allow to simmer on low heat. Moisture from lettuce should be sufficient, but you must stir occasionally, and can add a spoonful of water if necessary.

  Cook until onions are tender, about 30 minutes. Add 1½ tablespoons butter. Serve.   *Makes 4-6 servings*

POTATOES IN SALT SKINS

8 medium baking potatoes
4 tablespoons margarine or butter, softened
2½ tablespoons **MORTON® Kosher Salt**

About 45 Minutes Before Serving: Prepare outdoor grill for barbecuing. Rub each potato with ½ tablespoon margarine. Sprinkle with kosher salt. Wrap tightly in heavy-duty foil. Grill over medium coals 20 to 30 minutes until potatoes are fork tender, turning often. *Makes 8 servings*

OVEN BAKING VARIATION:

Prepare potatoes as above, but do not wrap in foil. Bake potatoes on baking sheet at 400°F for about 45 minutes, or until fork tender.

AU GRATIN POTATOES

7 large potatoes
2¼ Tbsp. flour
1 lb. **COUNTY LINE®** Colby Cheese, grated
Salt
1½ sticks butter
Pepper
3 cups milk
Paprika

Boil potatoes with skins, until soft. Thoroughly chill throughout. Peel and dice potatoes into small bite-size cubes. In buttered baking dish thoroughly mix potatoes and ¾ lb. of grated **COUNTY LINE®** Colby Cheese and salt and pepper. In saucepan mix flour, milk and one stick of butter over medium/low heat until thickened, then pour over the potatoes and mix. Evenly spread remaining grated cheese over mixture, pour ½ stick melted butter over cheese and sprinkle with paprika. Bake at 350° for 1 hour. *Serves 4 to 5*

CHILI CON QUESO POTATOES

1 package **BETTY CROCKER®** Au Gratin Potatoes
1 cup shredded process American cheese (about 4 ounces)
½ cup chili sauce
1 to 2 tablespoons diced hot jalapeño peppers
1 teaspoon Worcestershire sauce
3 or 4 drops red pepper sauce

Prepare potatoes as directed on package for Stove-Top Method. Stir in remaining ingredients; cook and stir 5 minutes longer. *6 servings*

MICROWAVE METHOD:
Mix potatoes, Sauce Mix and 3 cups boiling water in 3-quart round microwavable casserole. Cover with waxed paper and microwave on high (100%) 10 minutes; stir. Cover and microwave until potatoes are tender, 7 to 10 minutes. Stir in remaining ingredients. Cover and microwave until hot, 2 to 4 minutes longer.

HIGH ALTITUDE DIRECTIONS (3500 to 6500 feet): Prepare potatoes as directed in high altitude directions on package for Stove-Top Method. Continue as directed in recipe.

ESCALLOPED DILLY POTATOES

7 tablespoons margarine (divided)
1 cup dry bread crumbs
6 medium potatoes, peeled, thinly sliced
3 tablespoons flour
½ cup milk
½ cup **HENRI'S Creamy Dill Dressing**

1. Preheat oven to 350° F.
2. Melt 3 tablespoons margarine in small frypan. Add bread crumbs. Cook over medium heat until brown. Set aside.
3. Place potatoes in a greased 2-quart casserole.
4. Melt remaining 4 tablespoons margarine in small saucepan. Stir in flour. Gradually add milk and **HENRI'S Creamy Dill Dressing**. Cook until thickened.
5. Pour over potatoes. Mix gently to coat. Sprinkle crumb mixture over top. Cover.
6. Bake 1 hour 30 minutes. *Makes 6 (1-cup) servings*

TASTY SCALLOPED POTATOES

¾ cup thinly sliced celery
3 tablespoons chopped onion
3 tablespoons **MEADOW GOLD®** Butter
¼ cup all-purpose flour
¾ teaspoon salt
⅛ teaspoon pepper
2¼ cups **MEADOW GOLD®** Milk
3 cups thinly sliced cooked potatoes
¼ cup (1-ounce) shredded Cheddar cheese

In large skillet, cook celery and onion in butter until tender. Remove from heat; stir in flour, salt and pepper. Gradually add milk, mixing well. Stir over medium heat until thickened. In buttered 1½-quart casserole, alternate layers of potatoes and sauce, ending with sauce. Bake at 375° for 20 minutes. If using glass casserole, bake at 350°. Sprinkle cheese over top. Bake 3 to 4 minutes longer or until cheese has melted. *8 servings*

SWEET-AND-SOUR POTATO MEDLEY

2 slices bacon
2 cups water
1 tablespoon sugar
3 tablespoons vinegar
1 medium clove garlic, crushed
4 or 5 drops red pepper sauce
1 can (10¾ ounces) condensed cream of mushroom soup
1 package **BETTY CROCKER®** Au Gratin Potatoes
1 cup thinly sliced carrots
1½ cups frozen green peas
1 cup chopped tomato

Fry bacon in 10-inch skillet until crisp; drain and crumble. Stir water, sugar, vinegar, garlic, pepper sauce and soup into bacon fat in skillet. Stir in potatoes, Sauce Mix and carrots. Heat to boiling, stirring frequently; reduce heat. Cover and simmer, stirring occasionally, until potatoes are tender, about 25 minutes. Add peas; cook 5 minutes longer. Stir in tomato. Garnish with crumbled bacon. *6 servings*

HIGH ALTITUDE DIRECTIONS (3500 to 6500 feet): Decrease simmer time to 20 minutes. Add peas; cook 15 minutes longer.

MICROWAVE METHOD:
Place bacon in 2-quart round microwavable casserole. Cover loosely and microwave on high (100%) until crisp, 2 to 3 minutes; drain and crumble. Stir potatoes, 2¼ cups boiling water, the garlic and carrots into casserole. Cover with waxed paper and microwave 12 minutes. Stir in sugar, vinegar, pepper sauce, soup, Sauce Mix and peas. Cover and microwave until potatoes are tender, 4 to 7 minutes longer; stir in tomato. Garnish with crumbled bacon.

ANDALUSIAN POTATOES

¼ cup olive oil
1 onion, thinly sliced
1 clove garlic, minced
1½ cups dry sherry
1 bay leaf
4 medium potatoes (about 1⅓ pounds), peeled and
    sliced ½-inch thick
¼ cup minced green onions
Salt and pepper
¼ cup minced fresh parsley
Paprika

Heat olive oil in skillet and add onion and garlic. Cook until limp and add sherry and bay leaf. Bring to boil and add potatoes, green onions, salt and pepper to taste. Reduce heat to low and cook, covered, turning the potatoes occasionally, for 45 minutes or until they are tender. Sprinkle with minced fresh parsley and paprika. Remove bay leaf.   *Makes 8 servings*

Favorite recipe from **The Potato Board**

HOT CHINESE POTATOES

3 tablespoons vegetable oil
4 medium potatoes, halved lengthwise and thinly
    sliced (about 1⅓ pounds)
1 cup *each* carrots and celery, thinly sliced on the
    diagonal
½ cup green pepper strips (¼ x 2 inches)
½ cup sliced mushrooms
1 clove garlic, minced
½ cup water
2 tablespoons soy sauce
1½ teaspoons cornstarch
1 large tomato, cut in thin wedges
⅓ cup sliced green onions

In wok or large skillet heat 1½ tablespoons of the oil. Add potatoes; cook and stir over medium-high heat about 10 minutes until barely tender. Remove and keep warm. Add remaining oil to wok, then carrots, celery, pepper, mushrooms and garlic. Cook and stir 3 or 4 minutes until crisp-tender. In small bowl combine water, soy sauce and cornstarch. Return potatoes to wok with cornstarch mixture. Cook and stir about 2 minutes, just until sauce thickens and mixture is heated through. Spoon onto platter; garnish with tomato and onions.   *Makes 6 servings*

Favorite recipe from **The Potato Board**

BIG RED POTATO

1 baking potato
2 oz. lean ground beef
2 Tbsp. onion, chopped
½ clove garlic, minced
½ cup (2 oz.) **DARIGOLD Red Boy Cheese**, grated
¼ tsp. Italian seasoning
Salt and pepper

Scrub potato and bake in 425 degree oven for 1 hour. Meanwhile, sauté onion, garlic and beef in skillet to preferred doneness. Add seasonings. When potato is cooked, slice open and remove pulp, leaving only the shell. Place pulp, half of the **Red Boy Cheese** and all of the ground beef mixture into a bowl. Whip until blended. Stuff back into potato shell and top with remaining **Red Boy Cheese**. Bake in 300 degree oven for 15 minutes or until heated through and cheese is melted.   *Serves 1*

HASHED BROWN POTATOES

1½ pounds baking potatoes (about 4 medium), peeled
2 tablespoons chopped onion
¾ teaspoon salt
⅛ teaspoon pepper
3 tablespoons **Butter Flavor CRISCO®**

1. Shred potatoes into cold water; drain well. Combine with onion, salt and pepper in medium mixing bowl.
2. Melt **Butter Flavor CRISCO®** in large skillet. Add potatoes; spread evenly in pan. Cook over medium-high heat 13 to 15 minutes, or until golden brown and tender, turning potatoes with spatula after half the time.   *4 to 6 servings*

HASH BROWN POTATO BAKE

1 pound frozen hash brown potatoes (4½ cups)
⅔ cup (½ of 10¾-oz. can) condensed cream of chicken
    soup, undiluted
1 container (8-oz.) dairy sour cream
1 cup (4-oz.) shredded sharp Cheddar cheese
¼ cup finely chopped onion
½ teaspoon salt
¼ teaspoon ground black pepper
4 tablespoons butter or margarine, melted
3 cups **RICE CHEX®** Cereal crushed to 2 cups

Preheat oven to 350°. Butter shallow 1½-quart baking dish. In large bowl break up potatoes (need not thaw). Combine soup, sour cream, cheese, onion, salt and pepper. Add to potatoes. Mix thoroughly. Turn into baking dish. Combine butter and **CHEX** crumbs until evenly coated. Sprinkle over potato mixture. Bake 50-55 minutes or until potatoes are tender.   *Makes 6-8 servings*

STUFFED BAKED POTATOES

6 medium baking potatoes
½ lb. **WILSON®** Bacon
6 tablespoons butter
½ cup dairy sour cream
¼ cup milk
1 teaspoon salt
¼ teaspoon pepper
½ cup grated Parmesan cheese
4 green onions, sliced

CONVENTIONAL METHOD:
Heat oven to 350°F. Bake potatoes about 1 hour or until done. While potatoes are baking, cook bacon until crisp. Drain and crumble. Cut top quarter off potatoes. Scoop out the insides. Reserve shells. Mash potatoes until smooth. Beat in butter, sour cream, milk, salt, pepper and Parmesan cheese. Mix well. Stir in green onions and all but ¼ cup crumbled bacon. Spoon potato mixture back into shells. Place reserved bacon on top of potato mixture. Place on baking sheet. Bake in 400°F oven 20 minutes or until lightly browned. If desired, refrigerate until ½ hour before serving time. Bake 30 minutes or until heated through.
                    Makes 6 servings

MICROWAVE METHOD:
Bake potatoes at HIGH 16 to 17 minutes, rearranging twice. Stuff potatoes. Place on plate. Cook, uncovered at HIGH 5 minutes, giving dish a half turn once. If made ahead and refrigerated, cook, uncovered, at HIGH 8 minutes, giving dish a half turn once.

PIZZA STYLE TATER TOTS®

4 cups frozen **ORE-IDA® TATER TOTS®***
¼ tsp. salt
1 cup grated Cheddar cheese
⅓ cup **HEINZ Tomato Ketchup**
¼ tsp. Italian herb seasoning

1. Place frozen **TATER TOTS®** close together on lightly greased baking sheet and bake in oven at 450° F for 12-15 minutes until desired brownness. Remove from oven and sprinkle with salt and grated cheese.
2. Combine ketchup and Italian herbs; drizzle over **TATER TOTS®**. Bake another 5 minutes.   *Yield: 4-6 servings*

*May also be used with the following **ORE-IDA®** products:
TATER TOTS® with Bacon
TATER TOTS® with Onion

TATER TOTS® MEXICANA

3-4 cups frozen **ORE-IDA® TATER TOTS®***
1 can (16 ounce) stewed tomatoes
¼ tsp. oregano, crumbled
1 cup commercial sour cream
2 tablespoons milk
1 tablespoon chopped canned green chiles
½ tsp. salt
½ cup grated Cheddar cheese

1. Preheat oven to 375° F.
2. Turn frozen **TATER TOTS®** into 1½-quart shallow baking dish. Mix with tomatoes and oregano.
3. In small bowl, stir sour cream, milk, chiles and salt together. Spoon over top. Sprinkle with cheese.
4. Bake 25 minutes.   *Yield: 4-6 servings*

*May also be prepared with the following **ORE-IDA®** products:

TATER TOTS® with Bacon
TATER TOTS® with Onion

MICROWAVE METHOD:
Follow above recipe using these preparation directions:

1. Place microwave on high setting and set out a shallow microwave casserole dish.
2. In casserole dish combine tomatoes and oregano; mix in **TATER TOTS®**. In bowl mix together sour cream, milk, chiles and salt; spoon over top of **TATER TOTS®** mixture.
3. Microwave casserole 14-15 minutes or until center is hot and bubbly. Rotate dish twice during cooking. Sprinkle with cheese and let stand 5 minutes before serving.

DOMINO® CANDIED SWEET POTATOES

1 cup **DOMINO® BROWNULATED®** Sugar
Juice and grated rind of 1 navel orange
2 tablespoons butter or margarine
6 medium sweet potatoes or yams, parboiled, peeled and halved

In large skillet, combine sugar, grated rind, orange juice and butter. Heat, stirring occasionally, over moderate heat until blended and smooth. Add potatoes and simmer, uncovered, for 20 minutes. Baste and turn potatoes occasionally to glaze evenly.
Yield: 6 servings

CANDIED SWEET POTATOES

4 medium sweet potatoes, cooked and peeled
3 Tbsp. melted butter
½ cup light corn syrup
1 Tbsp. lemon juice
½ tsp. grated lemon rind

Cut sweet potatoes into crosswise slices ½-inch thick; place in greased 1-quart casserole. Combine remaining ingredients; mix well and pour over sweet potatoes. Bake at 375°F for 30 minutes.
Serves 4

Favorite recipe from **The Sweet Potato Council of the United States Inc.**

HERBED SWEET POTATO PUFFS

3 cups cooked mashed sweet potatoes
½ cup cornmeal
¼ cup all-purpose flour
2 Tbsp. butter or margarine melted
1 egg
2 Tbsp. grated onion
1 Tbsp. minced parsley
1 tsp. garlic salt
¾ tsp. each basil and marjoram, crushed
½ tsp. salt
Dash white pepper
¼ lb. Monterey Jack or Swiss cheese, cut into ½-inch cubes
Oil for deep frying

Combine all ingredients, except cheese and oil; beat until light and fluffy. Using teaspoons, shape into 1-inch balls. Bury a cheese cube in each ball, covering cheese completely. Arrange on cookie sheet until ready to deep fry.* Heat oil to 375°F; deep fry sweet potato balls, a few at a time, until deep golden brown. Drain and serve warm.   *Makes about 5½ to 6 dozen*

*These Herbed Sweet Potato Puffs can be prepared to this point, covered and refrigerated. Bring back to room temperature before frying.

Favorite recipe from **The Sweet Potato Council of the United States Inc.**

YAM SUNBURSTS

3 large oranges
2 cans (16-ounces each) **PRINCELLA®** Yams, drained
⅓ cup packed light brown sugar
¼ cup butter or margarine, melted
Toasted coconut, mint sprigs, maraschino cherries

Cut oranges into halves; squeeze, reserving ¼ cup juice. Carefully remove pulp from orange shells; make scalloped design on edges of orange shells, using small end of melon baller.

Beat yams until smooth; beat in reserved orange juice, the brown sugar and 3 tablespoons of the butter. Pipe yam mixture into orange shells, using pastry tube fitted with large star tip, or spoon mixture into shells. Brush edges of shells with remaining 1 tablespoon butter. Place filled shells in baking pan; bake at 350 degrees until hot through, 20 to 30 minutes. Garnish with coconut, mint or cherries.   *Makes 6 servings*

SPINACH ITALIENNE

2 packages frozen chopped spinach
1½ cups crushed **KEEBLER® HARVEST WHEAT Crackers**
3 eggs, beaten
1½ cups ricotta cheese
4 tablespoons butter
¾ cup milk
¼ teaspoon nutmeg or paprika
¼ teaspoon salt
½ cup grated Parmesan cheese
Dash of white pepper

Cook spinach according to package directions; drain thoroughly and while still hot, add ricotta cheese and stir over low heat until well blended. Add all other ingredients except **HARVEST WHEAT** cracker crumbs and Parmesan.

Place half of spinach mixture in a square pan which has been greased. Top with half of the **HARVEST WHEAT** cracker crumbs. Pour rest of spinach mixture over first layer. Top with cheese and remainder of crumbs.

Bake in 350° oven for 30 minutes until puffed and golden. Makes 6 large servings; use as a main dish or delicious vegetable combination. It also reheats well.

FRESH SPINACH PUFF

1 pound fresh spinach, well rinsed and coarse stems removed
¼ cup **Butter Flavor CRISCO®**
⅓ cup chopped onion
¼ cup all-purpose flour
¼ teaspoon dried dill weed
¼ teaspoon salt
⅛ teaspoon pepper
1 cup half-and-half
1 cup shredded Cheddar cheese
3 eggs, separated

1. Drop spinach into 2 quarts rapidly boiling water in large pan, return to boiling and boil 1 minute. Drain well; snip finely using kitchen shears. Press all excess moisture from spinach.
2. Lightly grease 1½-quart soufflé dish or casserole. Preheat oven to 350°.
3. Melt **Butter Flavor CRISCO®** in 2-quart saucepan. Add onion; cook and stir over medium heat until tender. Stir in flour and seasonings. Blend in half-and-half. Cook and stir over medium heat until mixture thickens and bubbles. Stir in cheese until melted. Remove from heat. Beat egg yolks slightly. Add small amount thickened sauce to yolks. Return to sauce, stirring to combine. Stir in spinach.
4. Beat egg whites until stiff, but not dry. Fold into spinach mixture. Pour into prepared dish. Bake at 350° 45 to 55 minutes or until knife inserted in center comes out clean. Serve immediately.
6 servings

VARIATION:
BROCCOLI PUFF

Substitute 1 bunch fresh broccoli for spinach. Rinse; trim ends and coarse outside leaves. Chop finely. Drop into 2 quarts rapidly boiling water in large pan, return to boiling and boil 7 minutes. Drain well.

BAKED TOMATOES, ITALIAN-STYLE

4 large tomatoes, peeled and chopped
1 small onion, chopped
½ cup parsley, chopped
2 slices stale white bread, crumbled
½ teaspoon salt
1 cup grated **LOCATELLI® Genuine Pecorino Romano Cheese**
2 tablespoons olive oil

Mix tomatoes, onion, parsley, bread, salt and ¾ cup cheese in a bowl. Brush olive oil over inside of shallow 10-inch casserole or 9-inch cake pan. Place tomato mixture in casserole and top with remaining cheese. Bake for 1 hour, uncovered, in 350° F oven.
Makes 4 to 6 servings, as a side dish

CHEESY-ROMAN TOMATOES

5 large tomatoes
¼ cup soft bread crumbs
¼ cup shredded **FISHER Cheese's PIZZA-MATE® Shreds**
1 Tbsp. butter or margarine—melted
Snipped parsley
Salt & pepper

Slice off tops of tomatoes. Cut zigzag edges; season with salt and pepper. Combine crumbs, **FISHER Cheese's PIZZA-MATE® Shreds** and butter; sprinkle over tomatoes. Garnish with parsley. Heat tomatoes on foil over hot coals, or bake at 375° till warmed through. Serve immediately.
Makes 5 servings

ZUCCHINI-STUFFED TOMATOES

1 cup (4-ounces) **P & R Rings,** uncooked
6 to 8 medium tomatoes
½ cup grated zucchini
1 cup cottage cheese
½ teaspoon basil
¼ teaspoon salt
⅛ teaspoon pepper

Cook Rings according to package directions; drain well. Cool. (Rinse with cold water to cool quickly; drain well.) Remove core from tomatoes; scoop pulp from tomatoes leaving a ½-inch shell. Combine ½ cup chopped tomato pulp, zucchini, cottage cheese, basil, salt and pepper in medium bowl; add cooled Rings and toss. Fill tomato shells; chill. Serve on lettuce leaves with wheat crackers, if desired.
6 to 8 servings

VARIATION:

Top tomatoes with shredded mozzarella cheese; place under broiler several minutes until cheese melts. Serve immediately.

DOROTHY'S STIR-FRY ZUCCHINI WITH PARMESAN CHEESE

4-5 medium zucchini
⅛ tsp. oregano
⅛ tsp. basil
½ tsp. **WITT'S Flavormost Seasoning**
1 Tbsp. grated Parmesan cheese
⅛ tsp. coarse ground black pepper (optional)

Cut zucchini in strips, and sauté in frying pan or wok, adding oregano, basil, **WITT'S Flavormost Seasoning,** and pepper (if desired). Sauté until tender. Just before turning off heat, stir in Parmesan cheese. Serve hot.
Serves 4

HERBED SQUASH MEDLEY
(Low Calorie/Low Cholesterol)

1 cup sliced zucchini squash
1 cup sliced yellow squash
1 cup sliced summer squash
2 tablespoons corn oil margarine
¼ teaspoon salt
½ teaspoon **SWEETLITE™ Liquid Fructose**
1 teaspoon sweet basil
¼ cup finely chopped parsley
¼ cup finely chopped chives or green onion tops

1. Place the squash in a steam basket above rapidly boiling water. Cover and steam for 3 minutes.
2. Immediately remove the squash from the heat and place under cold running water until they are at room temperature. This will preserve both the beautiful colors and the texture of the squash.
3. Melt the margarine in a large skillet.
4. Add all other ingredients and cook for 5 minutes over low heat.
5. Add the steamed squash to the herbed butter sauce and mix thoroughly.   *Makes 6 servings*

Each serving contains approximately:
   ½ vegetable exchange
   1 fat exchange
   58 calories
   0 mg. cholesterol

MEXICAN STUFFED ZUCCHINI

3 medium zucchini
1 can (10 oz.) **OLD EL PASO® Enchilada Sauce**
½ cup water
1 slice bacon, chopped
¼ cup chopped green pepper
1 can (4 oz.) **OLD EL PASO® Chopped Green Chilies**
1 small onion, chopped
1 cup chopped mushrooms
1 clove garlic, minced
½ cup canned corn
¼ cup sliced black olives
1½ cups cooked rice
1 cup **OLD EL PASO® Taco Sauce**
1 egg, beaten
¼ teaspoon salt
⅛ teaspoon pepper
½ cup grated dry Parmesan cheese

Preheat oven to 325°F. Slice the zucchini in half lengthwise and scoop out and discard seeds and pulp. Combine enchilada sauce and water in a large shallow baking dish. Then place the zucchini in the dish skin-side down and steam in oven under foil for 30 minutes or until tender. Meanwhile, sauté bacon; drain. Add green pepper, green chilies, onion, mushrooms, and garlic. Cook until onion is translucent. Remove from heat and add corn, olives, rice, taco sauce, egg, salt and pepper. Mix together. Scoop mixture into zucchini shells and top with cheese. Cover again with foil and bake until zucchini is tender, approximately 35 minutes.
Makes 6 servings

STIR GLAZED ZUCCHINI

2 small unpared zucchini
1 tsp. diet margarine
¼ tsp. garlic powder
Black pepper
1 envelope **ESTEE® Low Sodium Instant Cream of Tomato Soup Mix**
½ cup water
⅛ tsp. oregano
⅛ tsp. basil
½ tsp. dehydrated minced onion

Cut unpared zucchini into ½ inch thick slices, then sauté over medium-high heat in diet margarine and 1 tsp. water. Season with garlic powder and a dash of black pepper. Reduce heat to low and simmer, covered, for 2-3 minutes. In small bowl, mix 1 envelope **ESTEE® Low Sodium Instant Cream of Tomato Soup Mix** into ½ cup boiling water and stir to blend. Add oregano, basil, and dehydrated minced onion. Pour tomato soup mixture over zucchini, toss gently, and serve. Season to taste with **ESTEE® Salt-Free Vegetable Seasoning**.

Makes 2 servings, ½ cup per serving

NUTRITION INFORMATION

CAL	CHO	PRO	FAT	CHOL	NA
55	9g	3g	1g	0mg	50mg

ZUCCHINI BURGERS

1 cup shredded zucchini
½ cup (3-ounces) diced **COUNTY-LINE® Colby or Cheddar Cheese**
½ cup crushed saltine crackers (about 15 crackers)
⅓ cup regular toasted wheat germ
⅓ cup minced onion
2 eggs, beaten
½ teaspoon salt
1 to 2 tablespoons butter

Combine first 7 ingredients. Melt butter in large skillet. Drop zucchini mixture by tablespoonfuls into skillet. Cook over medium heat for 3 to 4 minutes on each side, or until well browned.

8 small burgers

Sauces & Relishes

Sauces

TENDERIZING MARINADE

3 cups water
3 cups cider vinegar
⅓ cup **DOMINO® Light or Dark Brown Sugar**
1 lemon, thinly sliced
4 onions, sliced
12 whole cloves
2 bay leaves
¼ teaspoon black pepper
1½ tablespoons salt

Combine all ingredients and keep at room temperature 2 hours. Add chuck, round, or rump roast. Cover bowl and refrigerate 2 to 3 days. Turn meat each day. Hold at room temperature 4 hours before roasting. Marinade can be kept in refrigerator and used again.

TERIYAKI MEAT MARINADE

½ cup soy sauce
¼ cup **DOMINO® Liquid Brown Sugar**
¼ cup dry sherry
1 teaspoon ground ginger
1½ lb. cubed beef, chicken, pork, or whole flank steak

Combine soy sauce, **DOMINO® Liquid Brown Sugar**, dry sherry, and ground ginger. Pour over meat. Refrigerate at least 4 hours. Baste meat with remaining sauce while barbecuing or broiling.

SAVORY BARBECUE SAUCE

1 can or bottle (12-ounces) **STROH'S Beer**
1 cup chili sauce
½ cup molasses
¼ cup prepared mustard
1 medium onion, chopped
Dash each Worcestershire sauce, salt and pepper

1. Put all ingredients into a saucepan. Simmer about 10 minutes. Add more beer or water if needed.
2. Store unused sauce in refrigerator.   *3 to 3¼ cups*

SPICY SAUCE FOR PORK OR CHICKEN

½ teaspoon ground cloves
2 teaspoons ground cinnamon
2 teaspoons ground ginger
½ teaspoon salt
1 tablespoon prepared mustard
¼ cup **DOMINO® Light or Dark Brown Sugar**
½ cup wine vinegar
1 cup pineapple juice

Combine all ingredients in saucepan and simmer 10 minutes. Baste pork or chicken frequently last half hour of roasting or last 15 minutes on the grill. Serve remaining sauce with cooked meat.
Makes about 1½ cups

ONIONY BARBECUE GLAZE

1 envelope **LIPTON® Onion Soup Mix**
1 jar (12 oz.) peach or apricot preserves
¾ cup chili sauce
2 tablespoons vinegar

In small bowl, blend all ingredients. Use as a glaze on chicken, chops, frankfurters, hamburgers, kabobs, ribs or steaks. Brush on during last half of cooking.   *Makes about 2½ cups glaze*

SPICY BARBECUE SAUCE

½ cup **SUE BEE® Honey**
¼ cup soy sauce
¼ cup lemon juice
2 tablespoons steak sauce (bottled)
1 teaspoon dry mustard
1 teaspoon ground ginger
⅛ teaspoon ground cloves

Combine ingredients in small saucepan. Bring to a boil and remove from heat.   *Makes about 1 cup*

TANGY BARBECUE SAUCE FOR MEAT OR POULTRY

3 cloves garlic, crushed
⅓ cup salad oil
½ cup wine vinegar
1 can (6 oz.) tomato paste
2 tablespoons lemon juice
¼ cup Worcestershire sauce
¼ cup **DOMINO® Light or Dark Brown Sugar**
1 teaspoon dry mustard
1 teaspoon oregano
1 teaspoon salt
¼ teaspoon pepper
1 cup beef bouillon
¼ teaspoon hot pepper sauce

Sauté garlic in oil until golden. Add remaining ingredients and simmer 15 minutes. Brush frequently on meat during roasting or last 15 minutes on a grill.   *Makes about 2¼ cups*

SWEET AND SOUR PINEAPPLE SAUCE

1 can (8½ oz.) unsweetened crushed pineapple
1 cup chicken broth
¼ cup white wine vinegar
¼ cup salad oil
2 tablespoons soy sauce
2 tablespoons chopped onion
1 clove garlic, crushed
¼ cup **DOMINO® Light or Dark Brown Sugar**
3 tablespoons lemon juice

Combine all ingredients in saucepan and simmer 15 minutes. Brush over chicken, spareribs or whitefish during roasting or last 15 minutes on the grill.   *Makes 2⅔ cups*

POLYNESIAN SAUCE

1 can (8¾ oz.) tropical fruit salad
1 can (6 oz.) **WELCH'S® Frozen Grape Juice Concentrate**, thawed
3 tablespoons honey
2 tablespoons lime juice
2 tablespoons heavy cream
1 tablespoon cornstarch
½ cup water
2 tablespoons grated coconut

Drain fruit; reserve liquid. In saucepan, combine liquid, **WELCH'S® Frozen Grape Juice**, honey, lime juice and heavy cream. Simmer 5 minutes to blend flavors. Dissolve cornstarch in water. Stir into sauce; cook, stirring until thickened and smooth. Add fruit and coconut just before serving. The perfect complement for chicken.

Makes about 2 cups sauce

THE INVENTIVE VEGETABLE SAUCE

Stir together until smooth:

1 Tbsp. **ARGO®/KINGSFORD'S® Corn Starch**
1 cup cold milk

Add:

2 Tbsp. margarine
¼ tsp. salt
⅛ tsp. pepper

Bring to boil, stirring constantly; boil 1 minute. Pour on cooked vegetables.

Makes 1 cup

VARIATIONS:

HERB/LEMON SAUCE

Add 2 Tbsp. lemon juice, 3 Tbsp. snipped fresh dill (or 1 tsp. dry), 1 Tbsp. chopped fresh parsley. Pour on cooked vegetables.

SOUR CREAM/CHEDDAR SAUCE

Add ½ cup dairy sour cream, ½ cup shredded Cheddar cheese. Stir over LOW heat until cheese melts. Do not boil! Pour on cooked vegetables.

SWISS SAUCE

Add 1 cup shredded Swiss cheese. Heat and stir until melted. Pour on cooked vegetables.

SASSY SEAFOOD SAUCE
(Low Calorie)

½ cup **DIA-MEL® Low Calorie Catsup**
1 tsp. lemon juice
1 tsp. horseradish

In a small bowl, mix **DIA-MEL® Low Calorie Catsup** with lemon juice and horseradish. Cover and chill until served. Use with shellfish and other seafood. Serve with **ESTEE® Unsalted Crackers**.

Makes 8 servings, 1 Tbsp. per serving

NUTRITION INFORMATION

CAL	CHO	PRO	FAT	CHOL	NA
6	1g				20mg

DIABETIC EXCHANGE INFORMATION

MILK	FRUIT	BREAD	MEAT	VEG	FAT
		1 TBSP. = FREE			

Relishes

QUICK CORN RELISH

1 package (16-ounces) **Frozen STOKELY'S® Chuckwagon Corn**
½ cup sugar
1 tablespoon cornstarch
½ cup white vinegar
⅓ cup water
1 teaspoon celery seed
1 teaspoon turmeric
½ teaspoon mustard seed
½ teaspoon dry mustard

Cook corn according to package directions; drain. In saucepan combine sugar and cornstarch; stir in vinegar and water. Add corn and remaining ingredients. Cook, stirring constantly, until thickened and bubbly, about 3 to 4 minutes. Cover and chill thoroughly.

About 1 pint

RED PEPPER RELISH

12 large red peppers, seeded and chopped
1 Tbsp. salt
2 cups cider vinegar
¼ cup **SEBASTIANI VINEYARDS Chenin Blanc Wine**
3 cups sugar

Place peppers in blender with wine. Chop fine and drain; mix with salt and let sit for 1 hour. Drain and combine with sugar and cider vinegar in large saucepan; simmer for 4 hours or until mixture reaches jam consistency. Relish can be put into small jars with lids and refrigerated, where it will keep for weeks.

GAZPACHO TOMATO RELISH

2¾ cups peeled, chopped tomatoes
1 green pepper, coarsely chopped
1 medium onion, coarsely chopped
1 tablespoon prepared horseradish
1 teaspoon salt
⅔ cup **HENRI'S Bacon 'n Tomato French Dressing**

1. Combine tomatoes, green pepper, onion, horseradish and salt. Let stand 1 hour.
2. Drain off excess liquid.
3. Stir in **HENRI'S Bacon 'n Tomato French Dressing**.
4. Chill.

Makes 2½ cups relish

CRANBERRY-WALDORF RELISH

2 cups fresh cranberries, finely chopped
½ cup sugar
2 apples, cored, diced (2 cups)
1 cup finely sliced celery
1 cup **BEST FOODS®/HELLMANN'S® Real Mayonnaise**

In medium bowl stir together cranberries and sugar. Cover; refrigerate at least 4 hours. Stir in apples and celery. Add real mayonnaise; stir until well mixed. Serve with poultry.

Makes 8 (½-cup) servings

Breads, Buns, Biscuits & More

Breads

GOLDEN HERB BREAD

1 loaf French or Italian bread
½ cup butter or margarine, softened
1 tablespoon **FRENCH'S® Prepared Yellow Mustard**
¼ teaspoon **FRENCH'S® Oregano Leaves**
¼ teaspoon **FRENCH'S® Dill Weed**
⅛ teaspoon **FRENCH'S® Garlic Powder**
½ cup Parmesan cheese
½ teaspoon **FRENCH'S® Paprika**

CONVENTIONAL METHOD:
Cut bread in 1-inch slices; arrange on cookie sheet. Combine butter, mustard, oregano, dill weed and garlic powder. Spread on bread. Combine cheese and paprika. Sprinkle on top of bread slices. Heat at 400° for 7 to 10 minutes.　*6 to 8 servings*

MICROWAVE METHOD:
Arrange on microwave baking sheet. Microwave on HIGH for 1 minute.

HOMEMADE WHEAT GERM HERB BREAD

5½-6½ cups unsifted **ROBIN HOOD® All Purpose Flour**
2 pkg. active dry yeast
⅓ cup sugar
1 tsp. salt
1 tsp. thyme leaves, crushed
1 tsp. marjoram leaves, crushed
1½ cups milk
½ cup water
½ cup butter or margarine
2 whole eggs
1 egg yolk
1⅓ cups **KRETSCHMER Wheat Germ, Regular** or **Brown Sugar & Honey**
1 egg white, beaten
1 Tbsp. **KRETSCHMER Wheat Germ, Regular** or **Brown Sugar & Honey**

Combine . . . . 3 cups flour, *undissolved* yeast, sugar, salt and herbs in large bowl. Stir well to blend.
Heat . . . . milk, water and butter together until warm to the touch (not scalding). Butter does not have to melt completely.
Add . . . . warm liquid to ingredients in bowl. Add eggs and egg yolk.
Blend . . . . with electric mixer at low speed until moistened. Beat at high speed for 3 minutes.
Stir in . . . . 1⅓ cups wheat germ with wooden spoon. Then gradually stir in just enough of remaining flour to make a soft dough which leaves sides of bowl. Turn out onto floured board.
Knead . . . . about 10 minutes or until smooth and elastic.
Place . . . . dough in large greased bowl, turning to coat all sides. Cover.　*(Continued)*

Let rise . . . . in warm, draft-free place about 1 hour or until doubled. Punch down. Divide in half.
Roll . . . . each half into a 12 × 8-inch rectangle.
Cut . . . . each rectangle into two 12-inch strips. Pinch edges of each strip together to make a rope. Twist 2 ropes together. Seal ends and tuck under.
Place . . . . in 2 well-greased 8½ × 4½ × 2½ or 9 × 5 × 3-inch loaf pans. Cover.
Let rise . . . . 30-40 minutes.
Brush . . . . lightly with egg white. Sprinkle with 1 tablespoon wheat germ.
Bake . . . . at 350° for 35-45 minutes until done. Cover loosely with foil last 5-10 minutes if crust browns too quickly.
Remove . . . . from pans immediately. Cool on rack.
Makes 2 loaves

WALNUT WHOLE WHEAT LOAF

1 cup **DIAMOND® Walnuts**
1¾ cups all-purpose flour
1 cup whole wheat flour
4 teaspoons baking powder
⅛ teaspoon baking soda
1 teaspoon salt
¼ teaspoon nutmeg
1 egg
¾ cup brown sugar, packed
1¼ cups milk
¼ cup shortening, melted
2 teaspoons grated orange peel

Chop walnuts and set aside. Stir together flours, baking powder, baking soda, salt and nutmeg. Beat egg; add brown sugar and beat well. Stir in milk, shortening and orange peel. Stir in dry mixture until all of flour is moistened. (Mixture may have small lumps.) Stir in walnuts. Turn into greased 9 × 5-inch loaf pan. Bake below oven center at 350 degrees F about 1 hour or until pick inserted in center comes out clean. Let stand 10 minutes, then turn out onto wire rack to cool.　*Makes 1 loaf*

SCOTTISH OATEN BREAD

2 cups all-purpose flour
1 cup old-fashioned rolled oats
½ cup sugar
2½ teaspoons baking powder
½ teaspoon baking soda
1 teaspoon salt
1 egg
3 tablespoons oil or melted shortening
½ teaspoon vanilla extract
1 cup **COCA-COLA®**
1 cup coarsely cut cooked prunes*
½ cup chopped walnuts

In large bowl, stir together flour, rolled oats, sugar, baking powder, baking soda and salt. With fork, beat egg with oil and vanilla until well blended and stir into flour mixture. Add **COCA-COLA®**, very well drained prunes and nuts and blend thoroughly with spoon. Turn into generously greased and lightly floured 9 × 5 × 3-inch loaf pan. If desired, garnish with prune halves. Bake at 350°F about 1 hour or until toothpick inserted in center comes out clean. Cool on rack 20 minutes before removing bread from pan. Store in foil overnight before slicing.

*½ lb. dried prunes = 1 cup cut-up cooked prunes.

SOUTHERN CORN BREAD

¼ cup vegetable shortening
2 cups white cornmeal
2 tablespoons all-purpose flour
2 teaspoons **CLABBER GIRL® Baking Powder**
1 teaspoon baking soda
1 teaspoon salt
2 cups buttermilk
1 egg

Melt shortening in a 9-inch iron skillet or a 9-inch square baking pan in the oven, brushing sides of pan with melted shortening.

Sift together dry ingredients. Combine egg and buttermilk and stir into the dry ingredients along with melted shortening. Pour batter into a hot pan. Bake in a 450° oven 20 to 25 minutes, or until browned. Cut in squares or wedges; serve hot with plenty of butter.

QUICK AND MOIST SOUR BREAD

5 cups unsifted self-rising flour
5 tablespoons sugar
1½ cups **BORDEN® Sour Cream**
1 (12-ounce) can beer
Melted butter

Preheat oven to 350°. In large bowl, combine flour and sugar. Add sour cream and beer alternately; mix well. Pour batter into greased 2-quart round baking dish. Bake 45 minutes; brush top with butter. Bake 15 to 20 minutes longer or until cake tester inserted completely into center comes out clean. Cool slightly. Serve warm, cool or toasted.   *Makes 1 loaf*

Tip: All-purpose flour may be substituted for self-rising flour. Add 2 tablespoons plus 2 teaspoons baking powder, 1 teaspoon baking soda and ½ teaspoon salt; stir into the flour and sugar. Proceed as directed. Baking time may require additional 5 to 10 minutes. Test for doneness.

SOURDOUGH BREAD

1 cup warm low-fat milk
1 package active dry yeast (check the date on the package)
2 tablespoons **SWEETLITE™ Fructose**
2 eggs lightly beaten
¼ cup melted corn oil margarine
1 package **BATTER-LITE® Natural Sourdough Bread Mix**
1 teaspoon salt
3 cups white unbleached flour
Melted corn oil margarine

1. Pour the warm milk into a large warm mixing bowl and sprinkle the yeast over the top of it. Stir until the yeast is dissolved, about 5 minutes.
2. Add the fructose, lightly beaten eggs and ¼ cup melted margarine and mix well.
3. Add the **BATTER LITE® Natural Sourdough Bread Mix** and mix well.
4. Combine the salt and flour. Add the flour mixture, ½ cup at a time, mixing thoroughly.
5. Place in a lightly oiled standard loaf pan. Place in a warm place and let rise until almost doubled in volume, approximately 1 hour (if the dough rises too much it will sink during baking). The oven of a gas stove or an electric oven with the light on provides enough warmth.
6. Brush lightly with melted margarine. Place in a preheated 400° oven for approximately 25-30 minutes or until a golden brown.

VARIATION:

Sprinkle with seeds (sesame, dill, cumin, poppy, etc.) just before placing in the oven to bake.   *Makes 1 standard loaf*

QUICK CHEESE BREAD

2 packages **MARTHA WHITE BIXMIX**
¾ cup water
2 eggs, beaten
2 teaspoons dry mustard
1½ cups grated sharp cheese
2 tablespoons butter or margarine

Heat oven to 350 degrees. Grease an 8½ × 4½ × 2½-inch loaf pan. Empty **BIXMIX** into large bowl. Stir in water and beat with wooden spoon until smooth. Add remaining ingredients except ½ cup cheese and butter. Mix thoroughly. Pour into pan. Sprinkle with remaining cheese and dot with butter. Bake 40 to 45 minutes. Cool in pan 10 minutes. Remove from pan and cool on rack before slicing.

CHEESY MEXICAN BREAD

2 packages active dry yeast
2½ teaspoons sugar
¼ cup warm water (110-115°)
1 small can (5.33 fl. oz.) **PET® Evaporated Milk**
⅓ cup water
3½-4 cups all-purpose flour
½ cup butter or margarine, softened
2 teaspoons salt
2 pounds (8 cups) shredded Muenster cheese
2 tablespoons butter, softened
1 egg
2 tablespoons ground coriander

Dissolve yeast and sugar in warm water. Combine evaporated milk and ⅓ cup water. Heat to 110°F. Add to yeast mixture. Slowly beat in flour, ½ cup butter and salt. Cover and let rise 1 hour or until doubled in size. Roll on floured board into a circle, about 20 inches in diameter. Combine cheese, 2 tablespoons butter, egg and coriander. Place in center of dough. Fold dough into center to cover cheese and pleat as you fold. It should now be about 9 inches in diameter. Gently slide greased cookie sheet under cheese filled loaf. Cover and let rise 1 hour. Bake in preheated 400°F oven for 30-35 minutes, until golden brown. Cool 15 minutes before serving. Slice in small wedges to serve.   *Makes 24 servings*

CHEDDAR CHEESE BREAD

1 cup milk, scalded
¾ cup SEVEN SEAS® Buttermilk Recipe Country Spice™ Dressing
¼ cup sugar
1½ teaspoons salt
2 tablespoons CHIFFON® Margarine
2 envelopes dry yeast dissolved in ½ cup warm water
2¼ cups grated sharp Cheddar cheese (approximately 9 oz.)
6 cups flour

Mix first five ingredients. When mixture is lukewarm, add dissolved yeast. Add grated cheese and flour, cup by cup to form dough. Knead, then rise till double. Shape into loaves, put into 9 × 5 × 2¾-inch pans and rise till double again. Bake at 350° F for 50 minutes. Brush with CHIFFON® after baking.   *2 loaves*

SHAWNEE HOLIDAY CHEESE BREAD

4¾–5¼ cups SHAWNEE'S Best All Purpose Flour
2 tsp. baking powder*
2 tsp. salt*
2 Tbsp. sugar
2 pkg. dry active yeast
¾ cup water
1¼ cups buttermilk
2 Tbsp. margarine
1 cup coarsely shredded Cheddar cheese
1 egg, slightly beaten
1 Tbsp. milk

Mix 1½ cups flour, sugar, salt, baking powder and yeast. Heat buttermilk, water and margarine in saucepan on low until liquids are very warm (120-130°). Slowly add to dry ingredients; beat 2 minutes at medium speed. Add 1 cup flour. Beat at high speed 2 minutes. Stir in cheese and enough flour for a stiff dough.

Place on lightly floured board; knead until smooth and elastic (7-10 minutes). Divide dough and shape into two round loaves. Place on greased baking sheets. Cover; let rise in warm place until doubled (approximately 1 hour).

Mix egg and milk; brush on loaves. Bake at 350° for 40-45 minutes. Cool on wire racks.

*Omit if using SHAWNEE'S Best Self-Rising Flour.

BOHEMIAN CASSEROLE BREAD

4¼ to 4¾ cups Bohemian rye and wheat flour
⅓ cup firmly packed brown sugar
2 teaspoons salt
1 teaspoon caraway seed
2 packages active dry yeast
1 cup real milk
1 cup water
2 tablespoons real butter
Real butter
Coarse salt

Combine 1½ cups flour, sugar, salt, caraway seed and yeast in large mixing bowl. Heat together milk, water and 2 tablespoons butter until very warm (120-130°F). Gradually add to dry ingredients; beat 2 minutes at medium speed of electric mixer, scraping bowl occasionally. Add ¾ cup flour. Beat 2 minutes at high speed, scraping bowl occasionally. Stir in enough additional flour to make stiff dough. Cover; let rise in warm place until doubled in bulk, about 45 minutes. Stir dough down. Cover; let rise again until doubled in bulk, about 20 minutes. Stir down. Place dough in

well-buttered 2½-quart round casserole. Place on bottom rack of oven. Bake in preheated 400°F oven 35 to 40 minutes or until done. Remove from pan. Brush with butter; sprinkle with coarse salt. Cool.   *Yield: 1 loaf*

Favorite recipe from American Dairy Association

HERB CASSEROLE BREAD

6 ounces (1½ four-ounce packages) TREASURE CAVE® Blue Cheese, crumbled
1 envelope active dry yeast
¼ cup warm water
¾ cup milk
1 tablespoon finely chopped onion
1 tablespoon butter or margarine
1 tablespoon sugar
½ teaspoon salt
1 tablespoon dill weed
2 teaspoons dried chopped parsley
2¼ cups sifted flour

Soften yeast in warm water. Scald milk. Add cheese, onion and butter. Stir until butter melts. Pour into large mixing bowl. Add sugar, salt, dill weed, parsley and 1 cup flour. Beat to blend. Add yeast and beat. Add remaining flour, beat to blend. Cover and let rise in warm place until doubled in bulk, about 45 minutes. Stir down and put into well-greased 1½-quart glass casserole. Let rise in warm place until doubled, about 30 minutes. Bake in 350°F oven 35 to 40 minutes. Cool.   *Yield: 1 loaf*

Note: Remove TREASURE CAVE® Blue Cheese from refrigerator about an hour before serving time to enhance the flavor.

DILLY CASSEROLE BREAD

2¼ cups all-purpose flour
1 package dry yeast
1 tablespoon dried minced onion
½ teaspoon dill weed
¾ cup warm water (120°-130° F)
⅔ cup HENRI'S Creamy Dill Dressing, room temperature
1 tablespoon margarine, melted
Salt

1. Combine flour, yeast, onion and dill weed in mixing bowl. Add warm water and HENRI'S Creamy Dill Dressing. Mix well.
2. Place in greased bowl, turning dough to grease top. Cover. Let rise 45 minutes.
3. Stir down, beat vigorously ½ minute. Turn into greased casserole. Let rise 30 minutes.
4. Preheat oven to 350° F.
5. Bake 45 minutes or until golden brown.
6. Brush with melted margarine. Sprinkle with salt. Serve warm.   *Makes 1 loaf*

OLD VIRGINIA SPOON BREAD

1 cup MARTHA WHITE Self-Rising Corn Meal
1½ cups boiling water
1 tablespoon butter
3 egg yolks, beaten
1 cup buttermilk
1 teaspoon sugar
¼ teaspoon soda
3 egg whites, beaten only enough to hold soft peaks

Heat oven to 375 degrees. Grease a 1½-quart casserole. Pour boiling water over corn meal. Stir to keep from lumping until cooled slightly. Add butter and egg yolks and stir until egg is thoroughly blended. Stir in buttermilk. Blend in sugar and soda. Fold in egg whites. Pour into greased casserole. Bake 45 to 50 minutes. Serve hot with butter.

HONEY-GRANOLA BRAID

1 (one-pound) loaf **BRIDGFORD Frozen Bread Dough**
¾ cup honey
2 cups granola cereal
¾ cup raisins

Let dough soften at room temperature (1 hour or more). Roll dough into 10 × 15-inch rectangle; place on greased cookie sheet. Mix granola, honey, and raisins; reserve ½ cup. Spread remaining filling in 4-inch strip lengthwise down center of dough. Cut slashes 1-inch apart along both 15-inch sides. Bring pieces together at center, overlapping ends and slanting them down for braided effect. Let rise in a warm place until doubled in size; bake for 20 minutes in preheated 375° oven. Spread remaining filling on top of baked braid. *Yield: 15 servings*

COFFEE CAN BREAD

1 package active dry yeast
½ cup warm water
⅛ teaspoon ginger
⅓ cup sugar, divided usage
1 tall can (13 fl. oz.) **PET® Evaporated Milk**
2 tablespoons vegetable oil
1 teaspoon salt
4 to 5 cups all-purpose flour

Dissolve yeast in water in a large mixing bowl; blend in ginger and 1 tablespoon sugar. Let stand in a warm place until mixture is bubbly, about 15 minutes. Stir in remaining sugar, evaporated milk, salt and oil. With mixer on low speed, beat in flour 1 cup at a time, beating well after each addition. Beat in last cup of flour with wooden spoon; until dough is very heavy and stiff but too sticky to knead. Place dough in a well-greased 2-pound coffee can. Cover with well-greased plastic can lid. Let stand in a warm place until lid pops off, about 1 to 1½ hours. Discard lid and bake in a 350°F oven for 55-60 minutes. Crust will be very brown; brush top lightly with butter. Let cool for 5-10 minutes on a wire rack; then loosen crust around edge of can with a thin knife, slide bread from can, and let cool in an upright position on rack.

TOASTED JARLSBERG LOAF

1 loaf unsliced white bread (1½-pound size)
2 cups shredded **JARLSBERG Cheese**
½ cup (1 stick) butter or margarine; softened
½ teaspoon garlic powder

Remove crust from bread. (Reserve for bread crumbs). Slice bread into 1-inch slices without slicing through the bottom of the loaf. Slice loaf in half lengthwise. Place on large sheet foil or baking sheet.

In bowl, combine 1½ cups cheese, butter and garlic powder. Spread between pieces of bread. Using foil, press loaf together. Sprinkle with remaining cheese. Bake at 400° F for 15 minutes until golden and cheese is melted. *Makes 8 servings*

Coffeecakes

COFFEECAKE SUPREME

1⅓ cups all-purpose flour
¾ teaspoon baking powder
¾ teaspoon baking soda
¼ teaspoon salt
⅓ cup soft butter or margarine
⅓ cup **DOMINO® BROWNULATED® Sugar**
⅓ cup **DOMINO® Granulated Sugar**
2 eggs
⅔ cup sour cream

Sift together flour, baking powder, baking soda, and salt. Cream butter and sugars together until fluffy. Add eggs and beat well. Alternately add flour mixture and sour cream, beating after each addition until blended. Spread batter into greased 9 × 9 × 2-inch square pan or 9 × 2-inch round pan. Bake at 350°F for 20 minutes; sprinkle Topping* over cake and continue to bake 15 minutes longer. Serve warm. *Yield: 1 cake*

*Topping:
½ cup **DOMINO® BROWNULATED® Sugar**
¾ teaspoon cinnamon
1 tablespoon flour
2½ tablespoons soft butter or margarine
½ cup chopped pecans or walnuts
½ cup shredded coconut
⅓ cup well drained crushed pineapple

Combine sugar, cinnamon, flour and butter or margarine. Mix in remaining ingredients.

MINCEMEAT COFFEECAKE

1 loaf **RHODES™ Frozen Bread Dough**, thawed
½ cup prepared mincemeat
⅓ cup orange marmalade or pineapple preserves
⅓ cup unsifted flour
2 tablespoons sugar
½ teaspoon ground cinnamon
2 tablespoons butter or margarine, softened
1 egg yolk plus 1 tablespoon water, beaten
Quick Icing*, optional

Let dough rise until almost doubled. Stretch and roll out dough to 18 × 8-inch rectangle. In small bowl, combine mincemeat and marmalade. Spread filling to within 1 inch of edge. Beginning with longest side, roll dough in jellyroll fashion; pinch along seam to seal. Form into ring; pinch open ends together. Place on greased baking sheet with seam side down. Cut slashes 1 inch apart and ⅔ of the way to center. Turn each slice on its side to show the filling. Cover; let rise until almost doubled in size.

In small bowl, combine flour, sugar and cinnamon. Cut in butter until mixture is crumbly. Brush dough with egg wash. Sprinkle with topping. Bake in a 350°F. oven for 25 minutes, checking halfway through for browning. If browning too fast, lightly cover with aluminum foil last half of baking. Remove to wire rack. Drizzle with Quick Icing, if desired. Serve warm.

*QUICK ICING

In small bowl, mix 1 cup confectioner's sugar with 1 tablespoon milk until smooth, thinning with more milk if necessary.

BOHEMIAN CHRISTMAS BRAID

1 package active dry yeast
¼ cup warm water (about 110°)
1 small can (5.33 fl. oz.) **PET® Evaporated Milk**
⅓ cup water
⅓ cup sugar
1½ teaspoons salt
1½ teaspoons lemon peel
1 teaspoon ground mace
2 tablespoons butter or margarine, softened
1 egg
4 cups flour
½ cup raisins
½ cup unblanched almonds, chopped
Almond Icing*
Pecan halves
Halved candied red cherries

In measuring cup add ¼ cup warm water and yeast. Let stand about 10 minutes. In large bowl stir together yeast mixture, evaporated milk, water, sugar, salt, lemon peel, mace, butter, egg and 1½ cups flour. As dough begins to leave sides of bowl, add the remaining 2½ cups of flour. Knead dough to form a soft, elastic ball. Place dough in greased bowl; turn to grease top. Cover and let rise in a warm place until doubled, about 1 hour.

Stir down dough, blending in raisins and chopped nuts. Turn out onto a board coated with about 2 tablespoons flour and knead lightly until smooth. Divide dough into 4 equal pieces. Shape 3 pieces into smooth ropes about 16-inches long. Place ropes side by side on a greased baking sheet and tightly braid; pinch ends to seal, then tuck underneath. Divide remaining dough into 3 pieces. Shape each into a smooth 10-inch long rope. Braid tightly; pinch ends to seal, then tuck underneath. Lightly moisten top of large braid with water and place smaller braid on top. Cover lightly and let rise in a warm place until almost doubled, about 30 minutes.

Bake in 350°F oven until well browned, about 25 to 30 minutes. Let cool on a wire rack about 10 minutes, then drizzle with icing and decorate with pecan halves and halved candied cherries.

*ALMOND ICING

Stir together ¾ cup sifted powdered sugar, 2 to 3 teaspoons milk and ⅛ teaspoon almond extract.

CRANBERRY-ALMOND BRAID

5¾ to 6¼ cups unsifted flour
¾ cup sugar
1 teaspoon salt
3 packages **FLEISCHMANN'S Active Dry Yeast**
½ cup (1 stick) margarine, softened
1 cup very warm water (120°F.-130°F.)
3 eggs (at room temperature)
Confectioners' sugar frosting
PLANTERS Sliced Almonds

Prepare Cranberry Filling* Refrigerate until ready to use. In a large bowl thoroughly mix 1¼ cups flour, sugar, salt and undissolved **FLEISCHMANN'S Active Dry Yeast.** Add softened margarine.

Gradually add very warm water to dry ingredients and beat 2 minutes at medium speed of electric mixer, scraping bowl occasionally. Add eggs and ¼ cup flour. Beat at high speed 2 minutes, scraping bowl occasionally. Stir in enough additional flour to make a soft dough. Turn out onto lightly floured board; knead until smooth and elastic, about 8 to 10 minutes.

Divide dough into 3 equal pieces. Roll one piece into a 12-inch square. Cut into 3 lengthwise strips, 12 × 4-inches each. Spread centers of strips with ⅓ prepared Cranberry Filling. Seal edges and ends very firmly forming long filled ropes. Braid ropes together. Pinch ends to seal; tuck underneath. Place on greased baking sheet. Cover tightly with plastic wrap; place in freezer. Repeat with remaining pieces of dough and filling. When firm, remove from baking sheets and wrap each braid with plastic wrap, then with aluminum foil. Keep frozen up to 4 weeks.

Remove from freezer; unwrap and place on ungreased baking sheets. Let stand covered loosely with plastic wrap at room temperature until fully thawed, about 2 hours. Let rise in warm place, free from draft, until more than doubled in bulk, about 1¾ hours.

Bake at 375°F. for 15 to 20 minutes, or until done. Remove from baking sheets and cool on wire racks. Frost with confectioners' sugar frosting and decorate with **PLANTERS Sliced Almonds.**   *Makes 3 loaves*

To bake without freezing: After shaping, let rise in a warm place, free from draft, until doubled in bulk, about 1 hour. Bake as directed above.

*CRANBERRY FILLING

Combine 1½ cups ground fresh cranberries, a large ground fresh orange and 1 cup firmly packed dark brown sugar in a saucepan. Bring to a boil; reduce heat and simmer until thickened, stirring occasionally.

RED STAR® BOHEMIAN CHRISTMAS BRAID

4½ to 5 cups all-purpose flour
2 packages **RED STAR® Instant Blend Dry Yeast**
½ cup sugar
2 teaspoons salt
2 teaspoons grated lemon rind
⅛ teaspoon mace
¾ cup milk
½ cup water
¼ cup shortening
2 eggs
½ to 1 cup raisins
½ cup chopped almonds

Preheat oven to 350°. In large mixer bowl, combine 2 cups flour, yeast, sugar, salt, lemon rind and mace; mix well. In saucepan, heat milk, water and shortening until warm (120-130°; shortening does not need to melt). Add to flour mixture. Add eggs. Blend at low speed until moistened; beat 3 minutes at medium speed. By hand, gradually stir in raisins, almonds and enough remaining flour to make a firm dough. Knead on floured surface until smooth and elastic, 5 to 8 minutes. Place in greased bowl, turning to grease top. Cover; let rise in warm place until double, about 1½ hours.

Punch down dough. Divide into 4 parts. On lightly floured surface, roll each of three parts to a 14-inch rope. On greased large cookie sheet, loosely braid from center to ends. Seal ends and tuck under loaf. With very sharp knife, make a ½-inch deep slash down the center of braid. Divide remaining dough into 3 pieces. Roll each piece to a 12-inch rope. Braid loosely from center to ends. Seal ends. Place in cut on larger braid. Press in lightly.

Cover; let rise in warm place until double, about 45 minutes. Bake at 350° for 40 to 45 minutes until golden brown. Remove from cookie sheet; cool. Drizzle with powdered sugar glaze and garnish with candied cherries and almonds, if desired.

1 large braid

SIMPLE STOLLEN

8-oz. pkg. cream cheese, softened
¼ cup sugar
1½ to 2 teaspoons rum flavoring
¼ cup chopped blanched almonds
½ cup raisins
¼ cup chopped maraschino cherries
2 (8-oz.) cans **PILLSBURY Refrigerated Quick Crescent Dinner Rolls**

Glaze:
1 cup powdered sugar
2 tablespoons milk
Candied red and green cherries, if desired

Heat oven to 375°F. In small bowl, beat cream cheese and sugar until fluffy. Stir in rum flavoring. Fold in almonds, raisins and cherries. Set aside.

Unroll the 2 cans of dough into 4 long rectangles on ungreased cookie sheet. Overlap long sides; firmly press perforations and edges to seal. Pat to form a 13×13-inch square. Spread cream cheese filling crosswise, in a 6-inch wide strip, down center of dough to within 1-inch of ends. Fold ends of dough 1-inch over filling. Bring sides of dough square over filling overlapping edges, forming a 6×11-inch loaf. Bake at 375°F. for 25 to 30 minutes or until light golden brown. Cool. Combine powdered sugar and milk; drizzle over top of cooled bread. Garnish with candied red and green cherries, if desired. Refrigerate leftovers.

12 to 14 slices

ZAGNUT® COFFEECAKE

2 cups biscuit mix
¾ cup packed brown sugar
¼ teaspoon cinnamon
¼ teaspoon nutmeg
¼ cup (½ stick) butter
⅔ cup buttermilk
1 egg, beaten
3 **ZAGNUT® Bars** (1¼ ounces each), chopped

Combine biscuit mix, brown sugar and spices; cut in butter until mixture resembles coarse bread crumbs. Reserve ⅔ cup for topping. Add buttermilk and egg to remaining mixture; mix well. Spread half of batter in buttered 9-inch square cake pan. Top with ⅓ of the candy. Spread with remaining batter. Sprinkle reserved crumb mixture over top. Bake at 350° for 35 minutes or until done. Top with remaining candy. Return to oven for 5 minutes or until candy is partially melted.

9 servings

PEANUTTY-ORANGE COFFEE LOAF

1 (one pound) loaf **BRIDGFORD Frozen Bread Dough**
⅓ cup brown sugar
⅓ cup peanut butter, crunchy or smooth style
3 Tbsp. orange juice
4 Tbsp. butter or margarine, melted
1 Tbsp. honey

Glaze:
⅓ cup peanut butter
3 Tbsp. honey
3 Tbsp. orange juice

Allow frozen bread dough to thaw to room temperature. On lightly floured board, roll dough out to 12″×14″ rectangle. Mix peanut butter, orange juice, honey, and brown sugar. Spread 2 Tbsp. butter on dough. Spread peanut butter mixture on top of butter. Beginning with 14 inch side, roll up in jelly roll fashion. Cut dough roll into 12 equal pieces. Place pieces, cut side up, in 8″×9″ cake pan greased with 1 Tbsp. butter. Baste tops of rolls with remaining butter. Let rise until dough fills the pan. Bake in preheated 350° oven 20-25 minutes, or until golden brown. Turn out of pan immediately onto serving platter. Mix ingredients for glaze. Spread glaze over top of loaf.

COFFEE COCONUT CAKE

1½ cups all-purpose flour
1 teaspoon baking soda
½ teaspoon salt
1 teaspoon ground cinnamon
¾ cup sugar
½ cup **KELLOGG'S® ALL-BRAN®** or **KELLOGG'S® BRAN BUDS®** Cereal
1 cup cold, strong coffee
¼ cup vegetable oil
1 tablespoon vinegar
½ teaspoon almond flavoring
½ cup flaked coconut

1. Stir together flour, soda, salt, cinnamon and sugar. Set aside.
2. Measure **KELLOGG'S® ALL-BRAN® Cereal** and coffee into large mixing bowl. Stir to combine. Let stand about 2 minutes or until cereal is softened. Stir in oil, vinegar, almond flavoring and ⅓ cup of the coconut. Add flour mixture, mixing until well combined. Spread evenly in greased 8 × 8 × 2-inch baking pan. Sprinkle remaining coconut over batter.
3. Bake at 350°F about 25 minutes or until cake tests done. Serve warm or cooled with whipped topping, if desired.

Yield: 9 servings

®Kellogg Company

PERFECT PEACH COFFEE CAKE

¾ cup **SUN•MAID®** or **SUNSWEET®** Dried Peaches
½ cup water
Crumb Topping*
2 cups buttermilk baking mix
¼ cup granulated sugar
2 tablespoons butter or margarine, melted
1 egg, beaten
¾ cup milk
1 teaspoon vanilla

Into a saucepan, cut peaches into ½-inch pieces; add water, bring to a boil, cover, simmer 5 minutes. Cool. Prepare Crumb Topping. Combine remaining ingredients; beat well. Spread into greased 8-inch square baking pan. Drain peaches and arrange over batter. Sprinkle evenly with Crumb Topping. Bake at 400 degrees F for 20 to 25 minutes or until cake tests done. Serve warm, cut into 9 squares.

*CRUMB TOPPING

Combine ¼ cup all-purpose flour with 2 tablespoons *each* granulated sugar and butter or margarine, and ⅛ teaspoon mace. Mix until crumbly.

CHOCOLATE CHIP COFFEE CAKE

½ cup milk
½ cup (1 stick) FLEISCHMANN'S Margarine
⅓ cup sugar
1 teaspoon salt
2 packages FLEISCHMANN'S Active Dry Yeast
½ cup warm water (105°F.-115°F.)
2 eggs, beaten (at room temperature)
3 cups unsifted flour
½ cup semi-sweet real chocolate morsels

Scald milk; stir in FLEISCHMANN'S Margarine, sugar and salt. Cool to lukewarm. Sprinkle FLEISCHMANN'S Active Dry Yeast into warm water in a large bowl. Stir until dissolved. Add lukewarm milk mixture, eggs and 2 cups flour. Beat at medium speed of electric mixer until smooth, about 15 seconds. Stir in remaining 1 cup flour and chocolate morsels until well blended, about 1 minute. Turn into a well greased 10-inch tube pan. Cover and let rise in warm place, free from draft, until doubled in bulk, about 1½ hours. Bake at 400°F. for 20 minutes; remove from oven and sprinkle with Coffee Cake Topping.* Return to oven and bake additional 15 minutes, or until done. Turn out of pan immediately and let cool on wire rack.

Makes 1 10-inch tube cake

FOOD PROCESSOR METHOD:
With metal blade in place combine flour, FLEISCHMANN'S Margarine, sugar and salt in bowl; process 5 to 10 seconds to combine. Dissolve FLEISCHMANN'S Active Dry Yeast in warm water; pour through feed tube. Add eggs. Begin processing, pouring cold milk through feed tube in a fast stream until ball forms, about 10-15 seconds. Continue processing for 30 seconds to knead batter. Mix in chocolate morsels.
  Carefully remove dough from processor bowl. Turn out into a well greased 10-inch tube pan. Let rise and bake as directed above.

*COFFEE CAKE TOPPING

⅓ cup unsifted flour
½ cup chopped PLANTERS Pecans
½ cup semi-sweet real chocolate morsels
⅓ cup sugar
¼ cup (½ stick) FLEISCHMANN'S Margarine
1½ teaspoons cinnamon

Combine topping ingredients and rub together with fingers, until crumbly. Sprinkle on top of dough last 15 minutes of cooking.

FOOD PROCESSOR METHOD:
With metal blade in place process PLANTERS Pecans for 3 to 5 seconds, until chopped. Add flour, chocolate morsels, sugar, FLEISCHMANN'S Margarine and cinnamon; process 5 seconds until crumbly.

CHEESE-FILLED COFFEE CAKE WREATH

1 frozen SARA LEE Butter Streusel Coffee Cake
½ cup ricotta cheese OR cottage cheese
1 tablespoon grated lemon peel
½ teaspoon lemon juice
2 tablespoons chopped candied cherries
3 red candied cherries, halved
3 green candied cherries, halved
About 2 tablespoons sliced almonds

Cut frozen Coffee Cake lengthwise into 2 layers. Beat together ricotta cheese, lemon peel and juice; spread on bottom layer.

(Continued)

Sprinkle on chopped cherries. Replace cake top; cut into 6 pieces. Arrange cherry halves and almonds on cake top to resemble a wreath. Heat in preheated 350° F. oven 15 minutes.

Makes 6 servings

SOLO® POPPY FORM CAKE

1 cup butter or margarine, softened
1½ cups sugar
1 (12½ oz.) can SOLO® Poppy Filling
4 eggs, separated
1 teaspoon vanilla extract
1 cup dairy sour cream
2½ cups all-purpose flour
1 teaspoon baking soda
1 teaspoon salt
Confectioners sugar

Preheat oven to 350°F. Grease and lightly flour a 9- or 10-inch tube pan. Cream butter or margarine and sugar together until light and fluffy. Add SOLO® Poppy Filling. Add egg yolks, one at a time, beating well after each addition. Add vanilla and sour cream. Sift together flour, baking soda, and salt; add to mixture gradually, beating well after each addition. Beat egg whites until stiff but not dry; fold in batter. Turn batter into prepared pan. Bake about 1 hour and 10 to 15 minutes, or until a cake tester inserted in center of cake comes out clean. Allow cake to cool about 5 minutes. Remove from pan. To decorate, sift confectioners sugar through a paper doily or a cutout on the top of the cake.

Quick Breads

CRAWFORD'S® NATURALLY SWEET BREAD

1⅓ cups sugar
4 Tbsp. butter
2 eggs, well beaten
1½ cups hot water
2 tsp. baking soda
1¼ cups chopped dates
1 cup CRAWFORD'S® The Healthy Sweetener
3 cups flour
1 cup chopped walnuts

Cream together sugar, butter and eggs. Add hot water, baking soda and dates. Blend in CRAWFORD'S® The Healthy Sweetener. Then gradually add flour and walnuts. Grease 2 loaf pans. Bake at 350° for 45 to 60 minutes. After baking, cover with foil for soft top, if desired.

MANDARIN ORANGE BREAD

4 eggs
1½ cups sugar
2½ cups flour
2 teaspoons salt
2 teaspoons soda
1½ cups 3-MINUTE BRAND® Oats
2 (11-ounces each) cans mandarin oranges, undrained
1 (3-ounce) package orange-flavored gelatin
1 cup chopped pecans

Combine eggs and sugar and beat until light, about 2 minutes. Sift flour, salt and soda. Add to egg mixture and blend until smooth, about 2 minutes longer. Add remaining ingredients and mix very well. Spoon into two greased and floured 9- by 5-inch loaf pans. Bake at 325 degrees for one hour. Remove from pans immediately. Allow to stand 24 hours before slicing.

Makes 2 loaves

ORANGE PRUNE NUT LOAF

1 **SUNKIST® California-Arizona Orange**, unpeeled
½ cup fresh squeezed orange juice
⅔ cup sugar
1 egg
1 tablespoon butter or margarine, melted
2 cups sifted flour
2½ teaspoons baking powder
1 teaspoon baking soda
½ teaspoon salt
1 cup pitted, chopped, canned prunes, well drained
1 cup chopped pecans or walnuts

Cut orange into large chunks. In electric blender, combine orange chunks and juice; blend until almost smooth. In large bowl, combine sugar, egg and butter; beat until smooth. Sift together flour, baking powder, soda and salt. To butter mixture, add dry ingredients and orange mixture, stirring until blended. Stir in prunes and nuts. Spoon into well greased 9 × 5 × 3-inch loaf pan. Bake at 300°F for 1 hour and 10 minutes or until toothpick inserted in center comes out clean. Cool 10 minutes; remove from pan. Cool on wire rack.

Makes 1 loaf

HOLIDAY APPLESAUCE NUT BREAD

1⅓ cups all-purpose flour
⅔ cup **ROMAN MEAL® Cereal**
½ cup sugar
2 tsp. baking powder
1 tsp. baking soda
½ tsp. cinnamon
¼ tsp. nutmeg
¼ tsp. cloves (optional)
½ cup chopped nuts
1 cup applesauce
⅓ cup vegetable oil
2 eggs
1 tsp. vanilla

CONVENTIONAL METHOD:
Combine dry ingredients, including nuts, in large mixing bowl. Beat applesauce, vegetable oil, eggs and vanilla in a small bowl. Stir into dry ingredients. Bake in greased 9 × 5 × 3-inch loaf pan at 350°F about 50 minutes, or until wooden pick inserted in center comes out clean. Cool in pan on rack 5 minutes. Remove from pan; cool completely.

MICROWAVE METHOD:
Mix as directed. Spread batter in greased 9 × 5 × 3-inch glass loaf pan. Microwave on Bake (70% power) 10 to 12 minutes, rotating once. Pick inserted in center should come out clean. Cool as directed.

DOMINO® BANANA BREAD

1½ cups all-purpose flour
1 teaspoon baking soda
1 teaspoon salt
⅓ cup shortening
¾ cup firmly packed **DOMINO® Light Brown Sugar**
2 eggs
1 cup (2-3) mashed ripe bananas
½ cup milk
½ cup walnuts, chopped

Sift flour, soda and salt together. Cream shortening and sugar thoroughly. Add eggs and bananas, beating until light. Alternately add flour mixture and milk. Beat after each addition until smooth. Add nuts. Pour batter into greased 9 × 5 × 3-inch loaf pan. Bake at 350°F 1 hour 5 minutes or until done. Remove pan, cool on rack. Wrap in foil or plastic wrap and store overnight before slicing.

Yield: 1 loaf

BANANA BREAD
(Low Calorie)

1 cup sifted all-purpose flour
¾ cup sifted whole-wheat flour
2 teaspoons baking powder
¼ teaspoon baking soda
¼ teaspoon salt
1 egg, well beaten
1 packet **BUTTER BUDS®**, mixed with ¼ cup hot water
¼ cup sugar
3 packets **SWEET 'N LOW®**
1 teaspoon vanilla
1 cup mashed bananas

Preheat oven to 350°F. In medium-size bowl, sift together flours, baking powder, baking soda, and salt. In separate bowl, combine egg, **BUTTER BUDS®**, sugar, **SWEET 'N LOW®**, vanilla, and bananas. Add dry ingredients, mix until moist. Turn into nonstick 9 × 5-inch loaf pan. Bake 1 hour, or until toothpick inserted in center comes out clean.

18 servings

PER SERVING (one ½-inch slice): Calories: 70 Protein: 2g
Carbohydrate: 15g   Fat: trace   Sodium: 135mg

Note: By using **BUTTER BUDS®** instead of butter in this recipe, you have saved 42 calories and 16 mg cholesterol per serving.

BANANA BRAN BREAD

⅓ cup shortening
⅔ cup honey
¾ cup **ELAM'S® Bran**
2 eggs
1 cup ripe banana pulp
1½ cups all-purpose flour
2¼ teaspoons baking powder

Thoroughly blend the first five ingredients in a bowl. Sift together and add the flour and baking powder. Pour into a greased 8½ × 4½ × 2½-inch loaf pan. Bake at 350°F for 1 hour or until done. Cool on wire rack.

PEACH NUT BREAD

1 cup **SUN·MAID®** or **SUNSWEET®** **Dried Peaches**
½ cup water
2½ cups all-purpose flour
3½ teaspoons baking powder
1 teaspoon salt
¾ teaspoon cardamom
⅓ cup butter or margarine, softened
⅓ cup granulated sugar
1 egg
1 cup milk
½ cup chopped **DIAMOND®** Walnuts

Cut peaches in small pieces. In small saucepan, combine peaches with water; bring to a boil, simmer 3 to 4 minutes. Set aside to cool. Sift together flour, baking powder, salt and cardamom. Cream together butter and sugar; beat in egg (mixture will appear slightly curdled). Blend in flour mixture alternately with milk. Stir in peaches and walnuts. Turn into greased 9 × 5-inch loaf pan. Bake below oven center at 350 degrees F about 60 minutes or until pick inserted in center comes out clean. Let stand in pan 10 minutes, then turn out onto wire rack to cool.   *Makes 1 loaf*

WALNUT ZUCCHINI BREAD

1 cup **AZAR®** Walnuts, coarsely chopped
4 eggs
1½ cups brown sugar, packed
¾ cup vegetable oil
3 cups unsifted unbleached flour
1½ teaspoons baking soda
¾ teaspoon baking powder
¾ teaspoon salt
2 teaspoons cinnamon
2 cups grated unpeeled zucchini
1 teaspoon vanilla

Preheat oven to 350°. Grease, flour large loaf pan. Beat eggs. Gradually beat in sugar, then oil. Combine dry ingredients, add to egg mixture alternately with zucchini. Stir in walnuts, vanilla. Turn into pan. Bake 1 hour. Let stand 15 minutes, turn out, cool.

CAN CAN DATE-NUT BREAD

1 (8 oz.) package **BORDO Imported Diced Dates**
¾ cup raisins
1 teaspoon baking soda
1 cup boiling water
2 tablespoons soft butter
1 cup sugar
1 teaspoon vanilla
1 egg
1⅓ cups flour
¾ cup chopped pecans

Place dates and raisins in covered bowl. Add soda and boiling water. Cover and let stand. Cream butter and sugar. Add vanilla. Add egg and beat well. Add flour, mix until moistened. Pour in fruit mixture, including liquid and pecans, and mix gently to prevent crushing the fruits.

Place a small amount of butter in the bottom of each of five empty condensed soup cans. Let the butter melt in the cans in the oven for a few minutes, before filling with batter. Then fill cans ⅔ full. Bake at 325° for 45 minutes or until cake tests done. Remove from can while warm.

If you prefer to make this recipe in a 9 × 5 inch loaf pan, butter the bottom of pan. Add batter. Bake at 350° for 45-55 minutes, or until cake tests done.

COCONUT BREAD

Brush 1 Tbsp. soft butter evenly on bottom and sides of three 3½-by 7-inch loaf pans. Sprinkle 1 Tbsp. flour in each pan. Tip pan side to side to spread evenly. Tap pan (upside down) to remove excess.

Into deep bowl, sift 5 cups flour, 2 cups sugar, 1 Tbsp. double-acting baking powder, ½ tsp. ground cinnamon, ¼ tsp. ground cloves, 1 tsp. salt. Add fine-grated meat from one **CALAVO®** Coconut. Mix well. Add 2 cups milk, ½ cup at a time, blending thoroughly. Stir in 4 Tbsp. melted butter. Spoon batter into pans, not more than ⅔ full. Bake 1 hour in 350 degree oven, or until bread pulls away from pan and top is crusty, golden brown. Cool 5 minutes. Turn bread out onto wire cake racks. Serve warm or cool.
Makes 3 loaves

Buns & Rolls

BATTERMIX DINNER ROLLS

¾ cup shortening
½ cup sugar
1 teaspoon salt
1 cup **ROMAN MEAL®** Cereal
⅔ cup boiling water
1 pkg. active dry yeast
⅔ cup lukewarm water
1 tablespoon molasses
1 egg
3 cups all-purpose flour

CONVENTIONAL METHOD:
Combine shortening, sugar, salt, cereal and boiling water in large mixing bowl. Stir until shortening melts. Cool to lukewarm. Soften yeast in warm water. Add dissolved yeast, molasses and egg to first mixture. Mix on medium speed until blended. Add ½ of flour while mixing on low speed; beat 2 minutes. Add enough remaining flour to make soft dough. Place in lightly greased bowl; cover and refrigerate overnight. Next day remove from refrigerator; form dough into rolls and place in greased muffin pans. Let rise in warm place until doubled (about 1 hour). Bake at 375°F 18 to 20 minutes.   *Makes 1½ dozen*

MICROWAVE METHOD:
Mix as directed. Follow the manufacturer's instructions for rising and baking of yeast breads as found in your microwave oven cookbook.

BUTTERMILK PAN ROLLS

2½ to 3 cups all-purpose flour
1 package **RED STAR®** Quick·Rise Yeast
2 tablespoons sugar
1 teaspoon salt
½ teaspoon soda
1 cup buttermilk
¼ cup water
¼ cup shortening

Preheat oven to 400°. In large mixer bowl, combine 1 cup flour, yeast, sugar, salt and soda; mix well. In saucepan, heat buttermilk, water and shortening until warm (120-130°; shortening does not need to melt). Add to flour mixture. Blend at low speed until moistened; beat 2 minutes at medium speed. By hand, gradually stir in enough remaining flour to make a soft dough. Knead on floured surface until smooth, about 2 minutes.   *(Continued)*

Press dough evenly into greased 9-inch square cake pan. Sprinkle top of dough lightly with flour. With table knife, cut dough into 12 rolls, cutting almost to bottom of pan. Cover; let rise in warm place about 20 minutes. Bake at 400° for 15 to 20 minutes until golden brown. Remove from pan. Break apart into rolls; serve warm. *12 rolls*

SPEEDY PECAN ROLLS

3½ to 4 cups all-purpose flour
2 packages **RED STAR® Quick•Rise Yeast**
1 teaspoon salt
¾ cup water
½ cup milk
2 tablespoons honey
2 tablespoons butter or margarine
1 egg
2 tablespoons butter or margarine, softened

Filling:
⅓ cup sugar
1 tablespoon cinnamon

Topping:
½ cup packed brown sugar
¼ cup butter or margarine
3 tablespoons honey
½ cup pecans

Preheat oven to 375°. In large mixer bowl, combine 2 cups flour, yeast and salt; mix well. In saucepan, heat water, milk, honey and 2 tablespoons butter until warm (120-130°; butter does not need to melt). Add to flour mixture. Add egg. Blend at low speed until moistened; beat 3 minutes at medium speed. By hand, gradually stir in enough remaining flour to make a soft dough. Knead on floured surface until smooth and elastic, about 5 minutes. Place in greased bowl, turning to grease top. Cover; let rise in warm place about 20 minutes.

Prepare Filling: Combine ⅓ cup sugar and 1 tablespoon cinnamon; set aside.

Prepare Topping: Sprinkle brown sugar in well-greased 13 × 9-inch cake pan. Cut ¼ cup butter into small pieces and sprinkle evenly over brown sugar. Drizzle with honey. Sprinkle nuts on top.

Punch down dough. On lightly floured surface, roll dough to a 15 × 12-inch rectangle. Spread with softened butter; sprinkle Filling over dough. Starting with shorter side, roll up tightly. Pinch edge to seal. Cut into 12 slices. Place on Topping in pan. Cover; let rise in warm place about 20 minutes. Bake at 375° for 25 to 30 minutes until golden brown. Cool in pan 1 minute; invert onto rack. Cool. *12 rolls*

CHERRY & NUT SWIRLS

2 packages (8 oz. each) cream cheese, softened
⅓ cup sugar
2 egg yolks
½ teaspoon vanilla extract
1 cup chopped **PLANTERS Pecan Pieces**
1 cup chopped red candied cherries
5¾ to 6¼ cups unsifted flour
¾ cup sugar
1 teaspoon salt
3 packages **FLEISCHMANN'S Active Dry Yeast**
1 cup water
½ cup (1 stick) margarine
3 eggs (at room temperature)
1 tablespoon margarine, melted

Beat together cream cheese and ⅓ cup sugar. Add egg yolks and vanilla; beat well. Add **PLANTERS Pecan Pieces** and cherries; beat until cheese mixture becomes pink in color. Refrigerate until ready to use.

In a large bowl thoroughly mix 1¾ cups flour, ¾ cup sugar, salt and undissolved **FLEISCHMANN'S Active Dry Yeast.**

Combine water and margarine in a saucepan. Heat over low heat until very warm (120°F.-130°F.). Margarine does not need to melt. Gradually add to dry ingredients and beat 2 minutes at medium speed of electric mixer, scraping bowl occasionally. Add eggs and ¾ cup flour. Beat at high speed 2 minutes, scraping bowl occasionally. Stir in enough additional flour to make a soft dough. Turn out onto lightly floured board; knead until smooth and elastic, about 8 to 10 minutes.

Divide dough into 3 equal pieces. Roll out one piece to a 12 × 10-inch rectangle. Spread ⅓ of prepared cheese filling over dough to within ½-inch of the long ends. Roll up like a jelly roll from long end. Cut into 12 1-inch thick slices. Place rolls on baking sheet and cover with plastic wrap. Place in freezer. Repeat with remaining dough and filling. When rolls are frozen, place in plastic bags in groups of twelve. Freeze up to 4 weeks.

For 1 dozen rolls remove 1 bag from freezer; unwrap. Loosely cover and let stand at room temperature until fully thawed, about 1 hour and 15 minutes. With palm of hand, flatten rolls out to 2½-inch circles. Place on greased baking sheet. Cover; let rise in warm place, free from draft, until doubled in bulk, about 1 hour and 30 minutes.

Brush with melted margarine. Bake at 350°F. for 12 to 15 minutes, or until done. Let cool 10 minutes before removing from baking sheet. Continue cooling on wire rack. Decorate as desired. *Makes 3 dozen*

To bake without freezing: After shaping rolls, cover and let rise in a warm place, free from draft, until doubled in bulk, about 1 hour and 15 minutes. Bake as directed above.

CINNAMON ROLLS

3 cups all-purpose flour
1½ cups **ROMAN MEAL® Cereal**
⅓ cup nonfat dry milk
⅓ cup sugar
2 teaspoons salt
1 pkg. active dry yeast
⅓ cup vegetable oil
1¼ cups very warm water (115° to 120°F)
2 eggs, beaten
2 tablespoons butter or margarine, melted
2 tablespoons sugar
2 teaspoons cinnamon
½ cup raisins

In large bowl blend 2 cups flour, ¾ cup cereal, the dry milk, ⅓ cup sugar, salt and yeast. Add oil and water; beat 60 strokes. Cover; let rise in warm place 45 minutes. Beat in eggs; add remaining flour and cereal. On floured board, knead until dough feels springy (about 5 minutes), adding just enough flour to hands and board to prevent sticking. Return dough to greased bowl, turning once to grease top. Cover; let rise until doubled (about 45 minutes). On floured board roll dough to 24 × 12-inch rectangle. Brush with butter; sprinkle with remaining sugar, cinnamon and raisins. Roll up as for jelly roll; seal edges. Cut in 24 sections (about 1 inch each). Place cut side down in well-greased 13 × 9 × 2-inch baking pan. Cover; let rise until doubled. Bake at 400° F until well browned, about 35 minutes. Remove from pan. Frost with powdered sugar glaze.

PINEAPPLE PECAN ROLLS

3½ to 4 cups all-purpose flour
1 package **RED STAR® Instant Blend Dry Yeast**
2 tablespoons sugar
1 teaspoon salt
¾ cup milk
¼ cup water
¼ cup shortening
1 egg
½ cup plus 3 tablespoons pineapple preserves
2 tablespoons butter, softened
¼ cup brown sugar
⅓ cup pecans, chopped

Topping:
½ cup brown sugar
⅓ cup butter or margarine
2 tablespoons corn syrup
½ cup pecans, chopped

In large mixer bowl, combine 1½ cups flour, yeast, sugar and salt; mix well. In saucepan, heat milk, water and shortening until warm (120-130°; shortening does not need to melt). Add to flour mixture. Add egg. Blend at low speed until moistened; beat 3 minutes at medium speed. By hand, gradually stir in ½ cup pineapple preserves and enough remaining flour to make a soft dough. Knead on floured surface until smooth and elastic, about 5 minutes. Place in greased bowl, turning to grease top. Cover; let rise in warm place until light and doubled, about 45 minutes.

In small saucepan, combine Topping ingredients. Heat until butter melts. Stir and pour into ungreased 13 × 9-inch pan; spread evenly.

Punch down dough. On lightly-floured surface, roll or pat to 18 × 9-inch rectangle. Spread with softened butter and 3 tablespoons preserves. Sprinkle with brown sugar and pecans. Starting with longer side, roll up tightly, pressing dough into roll with each turn. Pinch edges to seal. Cut into eighteen 1-inch slices. Place in prepared pan. Cover; let rise in warm place until doubled, about 45 minutes. Bake at 350° for 25 to 30 minutes. Cover pan with foil and invert onto rack. Cool 1 minute. Remove pan; cool.

18 Rolls

OVERNIGHT CINNAMON ROLLS

2 packages active dry yeast
½ cup warm water (105 to 115°)
2 cups lukewarm milk (scalded then cooled)
⅓ cup sugar
⅓ cup vegetable oil or shortening
3 teaspoons baking powder
2 teaspoons salt
1 egg
6½ to 7½ cups **GOLD MEDAL® All-Purpose Flour***
4 tablespoons margarine or butter, softened
½ cup sugar
1 tablespoon plus 1 teaspoon ground cinnamon
Powdered Sugar Frosting (recipe follows)

Dissolve yeast in warm water in large bowl. Stir in milk, ⅓ cup sugar, the oil, baking powder, salt, egg and 2 to 3 cups of the flour. Beat until smooth. Mix in enough remaining flour to make dough easy to handle. Turn dough onto well-floured surface; knead until smooth and elastic, 8 to 10 minutes. Place in greased bowl; turn greased side up. Cover; let rise in warm place until double, about 1½ hours. (Dough is ready if indentation remains when touched.)

(Continued)

Grease 2 rectangular pans, 13x9x2 inches. Punch down dough; divide into halves. Roll 1 half into rectangle, 12x10 inches. Spread with 2 tablespoons of the margarine. Mix ½ cup sugar and the cinnamon; sprinkle half the sugar-cinnamon mixture over rectangle. Roll up, beginning at 12-inch side. Pinch edge of dough into roll to seal. Stretch roll to make even.

Cut roll into twelve 1-inch slices. Place slightly apart in 1 pan. Wrap pan tightly with heavy-duty aluminum foil. Repeat with remaining dough. Refrigerate at least 12 hours but no longer than 48 hours. (To bake immediately, do not wrap. Let rise in warm place until double, about 30 minutes.) Heat oven to 350°. Remove foil from pans. Bake until golden, 30 to 35 minutes. Frost with Powdered Sugar Frosting while warm.   *2 dozen rolls*

*If using self-rising flour, omit baking powder and salt.

POWDERED SUGAR FROSTING

Mix 1 cup powdered sugar, 1 tablespoon milk and ½ teaspoon vanilla until smooth and of spreading consistency.

Frosts 1 pan of rolls

Note: Unbleached flour can be used in this recipe.

Note: If larger rolls are desired, roll dough into rectangles, 10x9 inches. Cut each roll into 9 slices. Place in greased square pans 9x9x2 inches.   *18 rolls*

SOURDOUGH CINNAMON ROLLS

1 cup warm low-fat milk
1 package active dry yeast (check the date on the package)
1 teaspoon vanilla extract
½ cup **SWEETLITE™ Fructose**
¼ cup melted corn oil margarine
2 eggs lightly beaten
1 package **BATTER-LITE® Natural Sourdough Bread Mix**
1 teaspoon salt
3½ cups unbleached white flour
Melted corn oil margarine
1 tablespoon cinnamon
½ cup **SWEETLITE™ Fructose**
1 package **FROSTLITE™ White Frosting Mix**

1. Pour the warm milk into a large warm mixing bowl and sprinkle the yeast over the top of it. Stir until the yeast is dissolved, about 5 minutes

2. Add vanilla, ½ cup fructose, lightly beaten eggs and ¼ cup melted margarine and mix well.

3. Add the **BATTER-LITE® Natural Sourdough Bread Mix** and mix well.

4. Combine the salt and flour. Add 3 cups of the flour mixture, ½ cup at a time, mixing thoroughly. Turn onto a floured board and knead the dough, adding the remaining flour mixture until the dough is no longer sticky and is easy to handle, and still a soft dough.

5. Roll out approximately 14″ x 14″ and ½″ thick. Brush with melted margarine.

6. Combine the cinnamon and ½ cup fructose and sprinkle generously over the dough.

7. Form into an even long roll. Cut into slices approximately 1″ wide and place each slice onto a lightly oiled cookie sheet. Place on the pan so that the sides touch.

(Continued)

8. Let rise in a warm place until doubled in volume, about 45 minutes. The oven of a gas stove or an electric oven with the light on provides the right warmth.

9. Preheat the oven to 375°. Bake for 20-25 minutes. Remove from the oven.

10. Prepare the **FROSTLITE**™ **White Frosting Mix** according to package directions. Spread evenly over the tops of the rolls while they are still warm.　　　*Makes 20 cinnamon rolls*

VARIATION:
PECAN ROLLS

Add ½ cup finely chopped pecans after step 6, sprinkling them evenly over the cinnamon-fructose mixture just before forming the roll.

SWEET BRANDY BUNS

½ cup **THE CHRISTIAN BROTHERS**® **Brandy**
½ cup diced candied orange peel
½ cup golden raisins
3½ to 4 cups flour
2 packages active dry yeast
¾ cup milk (approximately)
¼ cup vegetable shortening
¼ cup sugar
1 teaspoon salt
2 eggs
Sugar Topping (recipe follows)

In bowl mix brandy, orange peel and raisins; cover and set aside several hours. In large bowl combine 1½ cups of the flour and the yeast. Drain fruit mixture over measuring cup (there should be about ¼ cup liquid). Add enough milk to make 1 cup. Reserve fruit. In small saucepan combine milk mixture, shortening, sugar and salt. Heat to 120 degrees. Add to flour mixture. Beat with electric mixer at low speed 1 minute. Add eggs and beat at medium speed 3 minutes, scraping sides of bowl as needed. Stir in fruit and another 1½ cups of the flour. Turn onto floured board and knead about 8 minutes, adding the remaining flour as needed to make a satiny, non-sticky dough. Form into a ball and place in a greased bowl, turning to coat top. Cover and let rise in a warm place about 1½ hours until dent remains when poked with finger. Meanwhile, prepare Sugar Topping. Punch dough down and form into 12 equal balls. Place, spaced apart, on greased baking sheets. With heel of hand, flatten each ball to a 3-inch circle. Between lightly floured hands, form 1 tablespoon of the topping mixture into a ball. Pat into a 2½-inch circle and place on 1 of the dough circles. Repeat with the remaining topping mixture. With sharp knife cut through topping to make designs. Cover and let rise in warm place until almost doubled, about 1½ hours. Bake in 375 degree oven about 15 minutes until lightly browned and hollow sounding when tapped. Serve warm or at room temperature.
Makes 12 buns

SUGAR TOPPING

In small bowl combine ⅔ cup flour and ½ cup sugar. Cut in ¼ cup softened butter or margarine until mixture resembles coarse meal. Mix in 1 egg yolk to blend thoroughly.

QUICK BANANA KOLATCHEN

¼ cup finely chopped pecans
¼ cup brown sugar
¼ teaspoon cinnamon
1 can refrigerated crescent dinner rolls
1 tablespoon softened butter or margarine
2 **CHIQUITA**® **Bananas**, peeled and cut in quarters crosswise
1 teaspoon lemon juice
2 tablespoons honey
½ cup confectioner's sugar (about)
1-2 teaspoons hot water

Mix pecans with brown sugar and cinnamon. Unroll crescent dough, separate into 4 rectangles and place on ungreased baking pan. Spread each rectangle with a little softened butter and sprinkle with nut mixture. Place bananas crosswise on the rectangles, 2 pieces to each rectangle. Mix lemon juice and honey and drizzle over the bananas. Bring dough up around bananas and seal by pinching all edges together.

Bake at 400° for 12 to 15 minutes or until golden brown. Stir confectioner's sugar into hot water and spread on tops of hot buns. Sprinkle with extra chopped nuts if desired. Serve warm.
Makes 4 generous buns

SOLO® KOLACKY

1 cup butter or margarine, softened
1 (8-ounce) package cream cheese, softened
1 tablespoon milk
1 tablespoon sugar
1 egg yolk, well beaten
1½ cups all-purpose flour
½ teaspoon baking powder
1 (#1 can) **SOLO**® **Cake and Pastry Filling**
Confectioners sugar

Cream butter or margarine, cream cheese, milk, and sugar together. Add egg yolk. Sift together flour and baking powder. Add to creamed mixture and blend well. Refrigerate for several hours or overnight. Preheat oven to 400°F. Turn dough out on a lightly floured board and roll to a ¼-inch thickness. Cut with a cookie cutter and make a depression with thumb or spoon in center of each. Place 1 teaspoon **SOLO**® **Cake and Pastry Filling** into each center. Bake 10 to 12 minutes, or until lightly browned. Sprinkle with confectioners sugar before serving.

About 3 dozen

HOT CROSS BUNS

1 pound loaf **BRIDGFORD Frozen Bread Dough**
¾ cup raisins
2 cups sifted confectioners' sugar
½ teaspoon cinnamon
Milk

Let frozen loaf thaw at room temperature about 1 to 2 hours until soft. On floured board, knead raisins into dough using more flour if necessary. Cut and shape into 20 rolls. Place 10 rolls into each of two 9″ pie pans. Let rise in a warm place until doubled in volume. Bake the rolls in a 350°F. oven for 20 to 25 minutes or until golden brown. While hot, glaze with a mixture of 1 cup confectioners' sugar and ½ teaspoon cinnamon mixed with 4 teaspoons milk. Cool rolls 5 to 10 minutes. Mix together remaining confectioners' sugar and enough milk (2 or 3 teaspoons) to make a stiff mixture. Using a pastry tube, make a cross on each roll.

KOLACHE
(koh-lotch-eh)

3 to 3½ cups all-purpose flour
1 package **RED STAR® Instant Blend Dry Yeast**
¼ cup sugar
1 teaspoon salt
¾ cup milk
¼ cup water
¼ cup butter or margarine
1 egg
1 tablespoon butter

In large mixer bowl, combine 1½ cups flour, yeast, sugar and salt; mix well. In saucepan, heat milk, water and butter until warm (120-130°; butter does not need to melt). Add to flour mixture. Add egg. Blend at low speed until moistened; beat 3 minutes at medium speed. By hand, gradually stir in enough remaining flour to make a soft dough. Knead on floured surface until smooth and elastic, about 3 minutes. Place in greased bowl, turning to grease top. Cover; let rise in warm place until light and doubled, about 1 hour.

Punch down dough. Divide into 2 parts. On lightly floured surface, roll each half to a 12-inch square. Cut each square into nine 4-inch squares. Spoon Filling (recipe follows) in center of each square. Fold one corner to the center. Moisten corner of dough with water. Fold opposite corner over and seal. Place on greased cookie sheets. Cover; let rise in warm place until almost double, about 15 minutes. Brush with butter. Bake at 375° for 12 to 15 minutes until golden brown. Remove from cookie sheets. Serve warm or cold.　　　　　*18 Kolaches*

FILLING VARIATIONS:

PRUNE ORANGE FILLING

1 cup prunes (¾ cup puréed)
⅓ cup orange marmalade
⅓ cup chopped nuts
1 teaspoon lemon juice

In small saucepan, cover prunes with water. Cook until tender. Remove seeds. Purée prunes in blender. In small bowl, blend prunes, marmalade and nuts. Add lemon juice. Use about 1 tablespoon filling for each Kolache.
Filling for 18 Kolaches Makes 1½ cups

CREAM CHEESE RAISIN FILLING

2 packages (3 oz. each) cream cheese, softened
2 tablespoons sugar
1 egg
1 teaspoon lemon rind
¼ cup golden raisins, chopped

In small mixer bowl, combine cream cheese, sugar, egg and lemon rind. Beat until smooth and creamy. Stir in raisins. Use about 2 teaspoons filling for each Kolache.
Filling for 18 Kolaches Makes 1 cup

APRICOT ALMOND FILLING

1 cup dried apricot halves
⅓ cup packed brown sugar
⅓ cup chopped almonds
½ teaspoon cinnamon

In small saucepan, cover apricot halves with water. Cook over medium heat until water is absorbed and apricots are tender. Purée apricots in blender. In small bowl, combine apricots, brown sugar, almonds, and cinnamon. Use about 2½ teaspoons filling for each Kolache.　　*Filling for 18 Kolaches Makes 1¼ cups*
(Continued)

CRANBERRY ORANGE FILLING

⅔ cup canned (ready-to-serve) cranberry orange relish
⅓ cup vanilla wafer crumbs
¼ cup chopped nuts
Dash cinnamon

In small bowl, combine ingredients. Use about 2 teaspoons filling for each Kolache.　　*Filling for 18 Kolaches Makes 1 cup*

CHINESE BREADS WITH SPICED BEEF FILLING

2 loaves (1 lb. each) frozen bread dough, thawed and allowed to rise once (or prepare basic yeast dough bread recipe)
1 tablespoon cooking oil
1 lb. lean ground beef
1 can (8 oz.) **LA CHOY® Bamboo Shoots**, rinsed, drained, and diced
3 tablespoons tomato paste
2 teaspoons mild curry powder
1 tablespoon **LA CHOY® Soy Sauce**
½ teaspoon salt
2 green onions, chopped fine
1 egg white, beaten
1 teaspoon water
¼ teaspoon sugar

Heat oil in skillet over medium high heat. Add beef and bamboo shoots; cook, stirring constantly, until meat is browned, about 5 minutes. Drain off excess fat. Add tomato paste, curry powder, soy sauce, salt, blending well. Stir in green onion. Chill mixture thoroughly, covered.

Meanwhile, cut out 24 four-inch squares waxed paper. Divide yeast dough into 24 balls; pat each out into a 4-inch round, somewhat thicker at the center than at the edges. Place 2 tablespoons filling in center of each circle. Gather dough up around filling and twist to seal. Place each filled bread on a square of waxed paper placed on baking sheet (allow at least two inches between each bread). Allow breads to rise uncovered 45 minutes to 1 hour.

Combine egg white, water, and sugar, brush over each bread. Bake in preheated 375 degree oven for 20 to 25 minutes, or until breads are golden. Serve hot.　　*24 individual buns*

Biscuits

LIGHT, TASTY BISCUITS

2 cups all-purpose flour
2½ teaspoons **CLABBER GIRL® Baking Powder**
½ teaspoon salt
⅓ cup shortening
¾ cup milk
Butter or margarine

Sift together flour, **CLABBER GIRL® Baking Powder** and salt. Cut in shortening with fork until mixture resembles coarse corn meal. Add milk and blend lightly with fork only until flour is moistened and dough pulls away from sides of bowl. Turn out on lightly floured board. Knead lightly (30 seconds) and roll ¾-inch thick. Place on lightly greased pan and brush tops of biscuits with butter or margarine. Bake at 475° for 12 to 15 minutes.

BISCUITS

2 cups sifted all-purpose flour
3 teaspoons baking powder
1 teaspoon salt
⅓ cup **CRISCO® Shortening**
¾ cup milk

Preheat oven to 425°. Combine flour, baking powder and salt in bowl. Cut in **CRISCO®** using pastry blender or two knives until mixture resembles coarse meal. Add milk; stir with fork until blended. Transfer dough to lightly floured surface. Knead gently 8 to 10 times. Roll dough ½-inch thick. Cut with floured 2-inch round cutter. Bake on ungreased baking sheet at 425° for 12 to 15 minutes.   *12 to 16 biscuits*

FREEZER BISCUITS

2 cups sifted flour
4 tsp. baking powder
½ tsp. cream of tartar
½ tsp. salt
2 Tbsp. sugar
½ cup shortening
1 egg, unbeaten
⅔ cup milk

Sift flour, baking powder, salt, sugar and cream of tartar into bowl. Add shortening to the flour mixture and blend together until of corn meal consistency. Pour milk into flour mixture slowly, add the egg. Stir to a stiff dough. Knead 5 times on lightly floured surface. Roll to ½-inch thickness. Cut with 1½-inch cutter. Bake on an aluminum cookie sheet for 10 to 15 minutes at 450° F. Freeze them after they have been rolled out and cut, on a tray. After frozen, put in container, bake as usual either thawing first or putting them into the oven right from the freezer.

Favorite recipe from **Oregon Wheat Commission**

BAKING POWDER BISCUITS

2 cups all-purpose flour
1 tablespoon baking powder
½ teaspoon baking soda
½ teaspoon salt
⅔ cup **HENRI'S BUTTERMILK FARMS® Original Dressing**
⅓ cup milk

1. Preheat oven to 350° F.
2. Combine dry ingredients. Add **HENRI'S BUTTERMILK FARMS® Original Dressing** and milk. Stir with fork.
3. Knead in bowl 10 times.
4. On floured board, roll dough ½-inch thick. Cut out biscuits and place on ungreased baking sheet. Bake 18 to 20 minutes. Serve hot.   *Makes 10 biscuits*

DEVILED HAM BISCUITS

1 package biscuit mix, prepared
6 tsp. **AMBER BRAND Deviled SMITHFIELD Ham**
2 Tbsp. mayonnaise
½ tsp. horseradish
½ tsp. prepared mustard

Roll biscuit dough into a rectangular sheet about ¼ inch thick. Combine ham, mayonnaise, horseradish, and mustard and spread on dough. Roll the dough in cinnamon-roll fashion and cut into slices ½ inch thick. Place on a greased baking sheet or in a shallow pan. Bake in a hot oven (425°F.) 20 minutes or until brown.

TANGY APRICOT SUGAR BISCUITS

2 tablespoons sweetened powdered lemonade-flavor drink mix
2 tablespoons sugar
10-oz. can **HUNGRY JACK® Refrigerated Flaky Biscuits**
3 tablespoons margarine or butter, melted
30 (approximately ⅓ cup) miniature marshmallows
¼ cup apricot preserves
2 tablespoons chopped nuts

Heat oven to 375°F. Grease 9-inch round cake or pie pan. Combine lemonade mix and sugar. Separate dough into 10 biscuits. Dip 1 side of each biscuit in melted margarine, then in sugar mixture. Place rolls sugar-side-up in prepared pan. Sprinkle remaining sugar over top of biscuits. With thumb, make imprint in center of each biscuit; fill each with 3 marshmallows. Combine apricot preserves and nuts; spoon 1 teaspoonful over marshmallows on each roll. Bake at 375°F for 17 to 24 minutes or until golden brown. Remove from pan immediately.   *10 rolls*

NUTRITION INFORMATION PER SERVING
SERVING SIZE:

		PERCENT U.S. RDA	
1 roll		PER SERVING	
Calories	160	Protein	2
Protein	2 g	Vitamin A	2
Carbohydrate	25 g	Vitamin C	4
Fat	6 g	Thiamine	6
Sodium	330 mg	Riboflavin	4
Potassium	35 mg	Niacin	4
		Calcium	*
		Iron	4

*Contains less than 2% of the U.S. RDA of this nutrient.

Muffins

MEXICAN MUFFINS

1½ cups **BISQUICK® Baking Mix**
½ cup yellow cornmeal
½ cup cream-style corn
1 tablespoon sugar
2 tablespoons milk
¼ teaspoon chili powder
1 egg
1 can (4 ounces) whole green chilies, drained, seeded and chopped
1 jar (2 ounces) diced pimientos, drained

Heat oven to 400°. Line 12 medium muffin cups, 2½ x 1¼ inches, with paper baking cups. Mix all ingredients; beat vigorously 30 seconds. Fill muffin cups about ⅔ full. Bake until golden brown and wooden pick inserted in center comes out clean, 20 to 25 minutes.   *12 muffins*

VARIATION:

MEXICAN CORN BREAD

Grease round pan, 9 x 1½ inches. Pour batter into pan. Continue as directed.

HIGH ALTITUDE DIRECTIONS (3500 to 6500 feet): Heat oven to 425°. Stir 2 tablespoons **GOLD MEDAL® All-Purpose Flour** into baking mix. Bake about 20 minutes.

BEST-EVER BRAN MUFFINS

1 cup water
3 cups whole bran cereal
½ cup shortening
1¼ cups sugar
2 eggs
2½ cups all-purpose flour
2½ teaspoons baking soda
1½ teaspoons salt
1 teaspoon **DURKEE Ground Cinnamon**
½ teaspoon **DURKEE Ground Allspice**
⅛ teaspoon **DURKEE Ground Cloves**
2 cups buttermilk
½ cup raisins or currants

Pour water over *2 cups* bran cereal; stir and set aside. In a large bowl, cream shortening and sugar; beat in eggs. Combine remaining 1 cup bran and remaining dry ingredients; blend into creamed mixture alternately with buttermilk. Stir in soaked bran and raisins. Fill greased muffin pans ⅔ full and bake at 400° for 15 to 20 minutes. Batter can be stored in sealed container in refrigerator for up to 1 month. *Makes about 2 dozen muffins*

QUICK FRUIT-NUT MUFFINS
(Food Processor Recipe)

1 large ripe pear (about 5 ounces), washed, cored and cut into eighths *or* 1 large apple (about 5 ounces), washed, cored and cut into eighths*
20 **WHEATSWORTH Stone Ground Wheat Crackers***
1 cup **PLANTERS Pecan Halves***
1½ cups flour
½ cup granulated sugar
½ teaspoon baking soda
¼ teaspoon baking powder
3 eggs
⅔ cup **PLANTERS Peanut Oil**
1 teaspoon lemon juice
½ teaspoon vanilla extract

Place steel blade in food processor bowl; add pear or apple. Process 1 minute, until finely chopped. Add **WHEATSWORTH Stone Ground Wheat Crackers**, **PLANTERS Pecans**, flour, sugar, baking soda and baking powder; process until well combined and nuts are chopped. Using tube, add eggs, **PLANTERS Peanut Oil**, lemon juice and vanilla extract. Process until well combined, 1 to 2 minutes. Spoon into 12 greased or paper-lined 2½-inch muffin cups. Bake at 350°F until toothpick inserted in center comes out clean, 30 to 35 minutes. Remove from muffin cups; serve immediately. *Makes 1 dozen*

*If food processor is not available, coarsely grate fruit, finely crush crackers and coarsely chop pecans. Combine all ingredients in large bowl and mix well.

OLD FASHIONED CORNMEAL MUFFINS

⅓ cup all-purpose flour
3 tablespoons sugar
1 teaspoon baking powder
½ teaspoon soda
½ teaspoon salt
1 cup yellow cornmeal
1½ cups **MEADOW GOLD® Sour Cream**
1 egg, beaten
2 tablespoons **MEADOW GOLD® Butter**, melted

Mix together flour, sugar, baking powder, soda and salt. Stir in cornmeal. Combine sour cream, egg and butter; add to dry ingredients. Stir just until blended. Fill greased muffin-pan cups ¾ full. Bake at 400° for 25 minutes. *12 muffins*

SOUR CREAM GEMS

2 eggs
¼ cup granulated sugar
1 cup dairy sour cream
2 cups buttermilk baking mix
½ teaspoon nutmeg
½ teaspoon grated lemon peel
⅔ cup **SUN·MAID® Seedless Golden Raisins**

Beat together well eggs and sugar. Mix in sour cream. Stir in baking mix, nutmeg and peel until just moistened. Fold in raisins. Spoon batter evenly into 12 greased 2¾-inch muffin cups. Bake at 375 degrees F about 15 minutes, or until lightly browned and pick inserted in center comes out clean. *Makes 12 muffins*

PAPAYA MUFFINS

3 eggs
½ cup oil
¾ cup sugar
1½ teaspoons vanilla
½ cup grated carrots
½ cup grated soft **CALAVO® Papaya** (If papaya is too soft, dice in ¼-inch chunks)
¾ cup sweetened applesauce
2 cups flour
½ teaspoon baking powder
½ teaspoon baking soda
½ teaspoon cinnamon
½ teaspoon nutmeg
½ teaspoon salt
½ cup chopped walnuts or pecans
2 teaspoons sugar (for topping)
¼ teaspoon cinnamon (for topping)

Preheat oven to 325°F. In large mixing bowl on low speed, blend eggs, oil, ¾ cup sugar and vanilla. Add grated carrots, papaya and applesauce; mix well.

Add flour, baking powder, baking soda, ½ teaspoon cinnamon, nutmeg and salt. Blend just until ingredients are mixed; fold in chopped nuts.

Fill 12 oiled, individual muffin tins with batter. Mix remaining sugar and cinnamon and sprinkle over batter.

Bake muffins for 30 minutes or until they are golden brown and tops are cracked. Allow bread to rest in pan(s) for 10 minutes before removing to cooling rack. *Makes 12 muffins*

Odds & Ends

ITALIAN BREADSTICKS

1¼ cups **BISQUICK® Baking Mix**
1 tablespoon sugar
2 tablespoons firm margarine or butter
¼ cup cold water
1 egg, beaten
Sesame seed, poppy seed or garlic salt

Heat oven to 400°. Mix baking mix and sugar; cut in margarine thoroughly with fork. Stir in water until dough cleans side of bowl and rounds up into a ball. Turn dough onto surface floured with baking mix. Gently roll in baking mix to coat; shape into ball. Knead 5 times. Roll into rectangle, about 12 × 8 inches. Cut crosswise into about ½-inch strips. Place strips about 1-inch apart on lightly greased cookie sheet. Brush with egg; sprinkle with sesame seed. Bake until golden brown, 9 to 12 minutes. Cool slightly; carefully remove from cookie sheet.

About 2 dozen breadsticks

HIGH ALTITUDE DIRECTIONS (3500 to 6500 feet): Heat oven to 425°. Bake 7 to 9 minutes.

HUSH PUPPIES

¾ cup **SHAWNEE'S Best White Corn Meal**
¾ cup **SHAWNEE'S Best All Purpose Flour**
1 tsp. salt
1 Tbsp. baking powder
1 onion, chopped
1 cup milk
1 egg, beaten
Cooking oil

Mix dry ingredients and add onion. Beat milk into egg. Add liquid to dry ingredients and stir to moisten thoroughly. Drop by teaspoonfuls into hot deep fat. Fry 2-3 minutes, turning once. Drain on paper towels and serve hot. *Makes 6-8 servings*

POPPY SEED POPOVERS

PAM® No-Stick Cooking Spray
1 cup enriched all-purpose flour
½ teaspoon salt
1 tablespoon shortening
3 eggs
1 cup reconstituted nonfat dry milk
Poppy seeds

Coat eight 6-ounce custard cups with **PAM® No-Stick Cooking Spray** according to directions; set aside.

Into mixing bowl sift flour and salt. With pastry blender or two knives, cut in shortening. In small bowl beat eggs slightly; beat in milk. Add to flour mixture. With egg beater, beat until smooth. Fill cups ½ full. Sprinkle each with poppy seeds. Place cups on cookie sheet. Bake in 375°F oven about 50 minutes or until richly browned. Serve at once. *Makes 8 popovers*

Calories Per Serving: 119

Stuffings

WALNUT AND MUSHROOM STUFFING

¾ cup **AZAR® Chopped Walnuts**
¾ cup chopped onion
½ pound fresh mushrooms, sliced, or 2 cans (4-oz. each) sliced mushrooms, drained
¾ cup butter
3 quarts (1½ loaves) soft bread cubes
¾ teaspoon salt
½ teaspoon pepper
2 teaspoons rubbed sage
½ teaspoon marjoram
½ to 1 cup chicken stock

Slowly cook onion and mushrooms in butter until lightly browned, pour over bread cubes and toss to blend. Add walnuts, salt, pepper, sage, marjoram, and enough broth to moisten; mix lightly. This amount of stuffing is ample for an 18- to 20-pound turkey. If you use a smaller turkey, the extra dressing can bake in a greased casserole at 350° for 35 minutes.

DATE NUT STUFFING

3 to 4 small Florida oranges
3 cups **PEPPERIDGE FARM® Herb Seasoned Stuffing Mix**
¾ cup dates, chopped
⅓ cup pecans, chopped
⅓ cup raisins
6 tablespoons butter
¾ cup water

Using a sharp knife cut around center of each orange in a zig-zag pattern. Pull halves apart and scoop out centers. (Use to make orange juice). Mix stuffing with dates, pecans and raisins. Heat butter with water. Toss with stuffing. Stuff orange halves with ½ cup stuffing each. Cover with foil and bake in a 350°F oven 20 minutes. *Yield: 6 to 8 servings*

Favorite recipe from **Florida Department of Citrus**

LOW SALT POULTRY SEASONING

2 tablespoons **DURKEE Leaf Sage**
1 tablespoon **DURKEE Leaf Thyme**
1 tablespoon **DURKEE Instant Chopped Onion**
½ teaspoon **DURKEE Ground Cumin**
¼ teaspoon **DURKEE Garlic Powder**

Place all spices in blender container. Blend 1 minute on high speed. Store in airtight container. Use in your favorite stuffing recipe; 1 teaspoon of seasoning for each quart of bread cubes or rice. *Makes about ¼ cup*

.62 mg. sodium per tsp.

LOW-CALORIE VEGETABLE STUFFING
(Low Calorie)

1 pound fresh mushrooms, sliced
3 cups (8 or 9 stalks) sliced, celery
2 cups (3 medium-size) peeled, cored, and chopped apples
½ pound finely shredded cabbage
1 cup (1 large) chopped onion
½ cup fresh bread crumbs
2 packets **BUTTER BUDS®**
1 teaspoon sage
Freshly ground pepper to taste
2 egg whites, beaten

In large bowl, combine mushrooms, celery, apples, cabbage and onion. In separate bowl, combine bread crumbs, **BUTTER BUDS®**, sage, and pepper; toss to mix well. Stir into vegetables. Fold in beaten egg whites. Lightly stuff neck and body cavities of turkey. Tuck wing tips between the wing and body to prevent overcooking. Tie wings and legs to body with string to hold in place during cooking. (Bake extra stuffing in small casserole, about 30 minutes, along with turkey.) *Approximately 8 cups*

PER SERVING (¾ cup):	Calories: 60	Protein: 3g
Carbohydrate: 12g	Fat: trace	Sodium: 255mg

Note: By using **BUTTER BUDS®** instead of butter in this recipe, you have saved 150 calories and 56 mg cholesterol per serving.

Cakes & Frostings

Cakes

ANGEL FOOD CAKE

1 cup **DOMINO®** Confectioners 10-X Sugar
½ teaspoon salt
1 cup sifted cake flour
1½ cups (11-12) egg whites, room temperature
1 teaspoon vanilla extract
¼ teaspoon almond extract
1½ teaspoons cream of tartar
1¼ cups **DOMINO®** Superfine Sugar

Sift confectioners sugar, salt and flour together twice. Set aside for later use.

Combine egg whites and extracts in large mixing bowl. Sprinkle cream of tartar on mixture. Beat at highest speed until whites stand in peaks but are not dry. Reduce speed.

Gradually beat Superfine sugar into whites, sprinkling 1 tablespoonful at a time on meringue and beating about 15 seconds for each addition. With large whisk, fold spoonfuls of flour mixture into meringue slowly and gently. Continue folding *only* long enough to blend batter completely.

Turn into ungreased 10-inch tube pan. Bake in moderate oven 350°F about 35 minutes or until cake springs back when touched lightly. Invert pan on funnel or suspend over cooking rack. Allow to hang until cool. Remove by running sharp thin-bladed knife around side of pan with one long steady stroke.

Yield: one 10-inch cake

HEAVENLY COCONUT CAKE

Preheat oven to 325°. Grease and flour a tube pan. Sprinkle ½ cup chopped walnuts or pecans, mixed with ⅓ cup flaked coconut, on bottom and sides of pan. Combine the following ingredients:

1 (18.5 oz.) box yellow cake mix
1 small (3⅝ oz.) box instant vanilla pudding
4 eggs
½ cup cooking oil
½ cup water
½ cup **COCO CASA®** Cream of Coconut

Beat 2 minutes with electric mixer. Bake about 1 hour. Remove from oven and punch holes on top of hot cake in pan. Pour half Coconut Sauce* mixture over cake. When cake cools, remove from pan, turn over and cover with other half Coconut Sauce mixture. Sprinkle with flaked coconut.

*COCONUT SAUCE

4 oz. butter
⅓ cup sugar
2 Tbsp. water
3 Tbsp. **COCO CASA®** Cream of Coconut

Boil butter, sugar and water for 1 minute. Remove from flame and mix in **Cream of Coconut**.

BLOW-AWAY SPONGE CAKE
(Low Calorie/Low Fat)

½ cup cornstarch
2 tablespoons all-purpose flour
1 teaspoon baking powder
3 eggs
⅓ cup sugar
4 packets **SWEET 'N LOW®**
2 cups Delicious Whipped Topping*
12 medium-size fresh strawberries

Preheat oven to 375°F. Spray two 8-inch round layer pans with non-stick coating agent. Sift together cornstarch, flour, and baking powder. In separate deep bowl, beat eggs with electric mixer until foamy. Beat in sugar and **SWEET 'N LOW®** gradually, and continue beating 5 minutes or until mixture is very thick and lemon colored. Gently fold in dry ingredients, a few tablespoons at a time, mixing carefully and thoroughly. Turn mixture into prepared pans. Place in oven and reduce heat to 350°F. Bake 15 minutes, or until cake begins to shrink from sides of pan and top springs back when lightly pressed with finger. Let stand 1 or 2 minutes. Loosen sides and turn onto cooling rack. When cool, fill and frost with Delicious Whipped Topping. Top with strawberries.

Per Serving (¹⁄₁₂ of cake): Calories: 85; Fat: 2g

Note: There's no need to spray with a non-stick coating agent if you own non-stick 8-inch layer pans.

*DELICIOUS WHIPPED TOPPING
(Low Calorie/Low Fat/Low Sodium)

¾ cup plain low-fat yogurt
½ cup part-skim ricotta cheese
1 teaspoon vanilla
2 packets **SWEET 'N LOW®**

In small deep bowl, beat yogurt and ricotta cheese with electric mixer until smooth and creamy. Add vanilla and **SWEET 'N LOW®** and continue beating until mixture is thoroughly blended. Mixture will keep in refrigerator several days. Rewhip before serving. Serve as frosting on cakes and as topping on pies or fruit desserts.

About 2 cups

Per Serving (2 tablespoons): Calories: 15; Fat: 1g; Sodium: 15mg

DELLA ROBBIA CAKE

1 package **DUNCAN HINES®** Deluxe Angel Food Cake Mix
1½ teaspoons grated lemon peel
6 tablespoons sugar
1½ tablespoons cornstarch
1 cup water
½ teaspoon vanilla extract
1 tablespoon lemon juice
Few drops red food coloring
6 canned cling peach slices
6 medium strawberries

Mix cake as directed on package except add grated lemon peel along with the cake flour mixture (red "B" packet). Bake and cool as directed.

Combine sugar, cornstarch, and water in a small saucepan. Cook over medium high heat until mixture thickens and clears. Remove from heat; add vanilla extract, lemon juice, and red food coloring. Alternate peach slices with strawberries around top of cake. Pour prepared glaze over fruit and top of cake. Refrigerate uncovered at least 1 hour. Store cake in refrigerator.

12 to 16 servings

MAGIC MUFFIN CAKE

6 eggs, separated
½ cup sugar
½ lemon, grate rind; then juice
1 teaspoon vanilla
2 **BAYS® English Muffins** ground to crumb texture in blender or food processor (approximately 1⅓ cups)
1 cup ground nuts
½ teaspoon ground cinnamon
¼ teaspoon ground cloves
¼ teaspoon allspice
¼ teaspoon salt
Pinch cream of tartar
Frosting*

Preheat oven to 350°. Butter and flour Bundt® pan or 9"x13" pan. In bowl, beat ¼ cup of the sugar and egg yolks until light yellow. Add rind, lemon juice and vanilla. In another bowl, combine English muffin crumbs with ground nuts, cinnamon, cloves and allspice. Stir half of crumb/nut mixture into egg yolk mixture. Beat egg whites until foamy; add salt and cream of tartar; continue beating until firm; add remaining ¼ cup sugar and continue beating until stiff peaks form. Fold stiff egg whites along with remaining crumb mixture into yolk/crumb mixture. Pour into prepared pan and bake for 30 minutes. Frost Bundt® cake while slightly warm to help frosting flow in a decorative pattern.

*FROSTING

1 cup confectioners' sugar
½ teaspoon cinnamon
⅛ teaspoon nutmeg
½ teaspoon vanilla
1 tablespoon corn syrup
1½ tablespoons water

Combine all ingredients. Beat until smooth.

BUSY DAY CAKE

Sift into mixing bowl:
2¼ cups sifted cake flour
3 teaspoons **CLABBER GIRL® Baking Powder**
1 teaspoon salt
1½ cups sugar

Add:
½ cup high-grade vegetable shortening (room temperature)
⅔ cup milk
1 teaspoon vanilla

Beat 2 minutes at medium speed in cake mixer, or 200 strokes by hand. Add 2 unbeaten eggs and ½ cup milk. Beat again as before. Divide batter into 2 greased and floured 9-inch cake pans. Bake in a 350°F (moderate) oven about 30 minutes, or until done. Cool before frosting as desired. *Yield: 2 (9-inch) layers*

WALNUT DELIGHT CAKE

1 package (2-layer size) yellow cake mix
1 cup chopped **DIAMOND® Walnuts**
4 eggs, separated
Pinch salt
1 cup granulated sugar
¼ teaspoon salt
½ cup granulated sugar
2 tablespoons orange-flavored liqueur
2 tablespoons orange juice
1 teaspoon grated lemon peel
1½ cups whipping cream
1 teaspoon vanilla
DIAMOND® Walnut pieces

Prepare cake mix according to package directions. Spoon into two greased and floured 9-inch layer cake pans. Sprinkle walnuts *evenly* over both layers. Beat egg whites with pinch salt until foamy; add 1 cup sugar gradually and beat until stiff. (This should be a hard meringue as for a torte, not a soft meringue as for a pie.) Spread evenly over both layers to within 1 inch of edge of pans, but *do not* seal. Bake at 350 degrees F for 35 to 40 minutes. (This is 10 minutes more than the package directions call for.) Cool in pans 5 minutes; turn out onto wire rack to complete cooling.

FILLING:

Beat egg yolks and ¼ teaspoon salt until thick and lemon-colored. Gradually beat in the ½ cup sugar and continue beating until very thick. Stir in orange-flavored liqueur, orange juice and peel. Cook over hot water, stirring constantly, 5 to 8 minutes or until thick. Cool. With meringue-side up, put layers together with filling.

FROSTING:

Whip cream with vanilla until stiff. Spread and swirl over cake. Decorate with walnut pieces. *Makes one 9-inch layer cake*

Measuring Hints: If a recipe calls for "1 cup chopped walnuts," measure the walnuts *after* chopping. If a recipe calls for "1 cup walnuts, chopped," measure the walnuts *before* chopping.

AMARETTO CUSTARD CAKE

1 package (18½ oz.) yellow cake mix
1 package (3 oz.) custard mix
2 eggs
1¼ cups milk
¼ cup **HIRAM WALKER Amaretto** or Amaretto & Cognac
¼ teaspoon nutmeg

Heat oven to 350° Grease and flour 12-cup Bundt® cake pan. Beat all ingredients in large bowl on low speed, scraping bowl constantly, 1 minute. Beat on medium speed, scraping bowl occasionally, 2 minutes. Pour into pan. Bake until wooden pick inserted in middle comes out clean, 40 to 45 minutes. Cool 15 minutes; remove from pan. Drizzle with glaze.*

*GLAZE

1½ cups powdered sugar
2 tablespoons **HIRAM WALKER Amaretto** or Amaretto & Cognac
2 tablespoons milk or light cream
Dash of nutmeg
Dash of salt

Mix all ingredients until glaze is smooth and of drizzling consistency.

WHEAT GERM ALMOND CAKE

1 cup unsifted **ROBIN HOOD® All Purpose Flour**
¾ cup **KRETSCHMER Wheat Germ**, Regular or
 Brown Sugar & Honey
⅓ cup sugar
¼ tsp. salt
½ cup butter or margarine
2 Tbsp. milk
⅔ cup raspberry *or* apricot preserves

Batter:
1 cup ground natural almonds (¾ cup whole almonds)
½ cup **KRETSCHMER Wheat Germ**, Regular or
 Brown Sugar & Honey
½ cup unsifted **ROBIN HOOD® All Purpose Flour**
¼ tsp. salt
6 eggs, separated
¾ cup sugar
1 tsp. vanilla
½ tsp. almond extract

Combine 1 cup flour, ¾ cup wheat germ, ⅓ cup sugar and ¼ teaspoon salt in bowl. Stir well to blend. Cut in butter until mixture looks like coarse meal. Stir in milk. Press mixture evenly onto bottom and 2 inches up sides of 9-inch springform pan. Bake at 400° for 10 minutes. Remove from oven. Reduce temperature to 350°. Spread preserves over baked pastry.

BATTER:
Combine ground almonds, ½ cup wheat germ, ½ cup flour and ¼ teaspoon salt on wax paper. Stir well to blend. Beat egg yolks with ¾ cup sugar until thick and smooth. Beat in flavorings. Add blended dry ingredients, mixing until well-blended.

 Beat egg whites until stiff peaks form. Fold half the whites into egg mixture. Fold in remaining whites. Pour into pastry shell. Bake at 350° for 60-65 minutes until cake tester inserted in center comes out clean. Cool for 1 hour. Remove sides of pan. Spread with Almond Glaze*. *Makes 12-16 servings*

*ALMOND GLAZE

¼ cup butter or margarine
¼ cup sugar
2 Tbsp. light corn syrup
2 tsp. unsifted **ROBIN HOOD® All Purpose Flour**
½ cup sliced natural almonds

Melt butter in small saucepan. Stir in sugar, corn syrup and flour. Heat to boiling, stirring constantly. Remove from heat. Stir in almonds.

BRANDY PUDDING CAKE

2 tablespoons butter for pan
⅓ cup finely chopped almonds
1 tablespoon sugar
1 (18½ ounce) package yellow cake mix
1 (3¾ ounce) package vanilla instant pudding mix
4 large eggs
⅓ cup California Brandy
⅔ cup water
½ cup butter, softened
1 tablespoon grated orange peel
Brandy Orange Glaze*

Butter 10-inch fluted tube cake pan well, using 2 tablespoons butter. Sprinkle with almonds and sugar. Combine cake mix, pudding mix, eggs, brandy, water and softened butter. Blend on low speed of electric mixer until moistened. Beat at medium speed

for 2 minutes, scraping bowl frequently, until batter is smooth and well blended. Stir in orange peel. Turn into prepared pan. Bake below oven center in moderate oven (350 degrees F) 40 to 45 minutes, until pick inserted in center comes out clean. Remove from oven and let stand in pan 15 minutes, then invert onto wire rack to cool. When cold, drizzle with Brandy Orange Glaze.
 Makes 1 large cake

*BRANDY ORANGE GLAZE

Melt 2 tablespoons butter. Stir in 1 tablespoon *each* California Brandy and orange juice, 1½ teaspoons grated orange peel and 1 cup sifted powdered sugar. *Makes ½ cup*

Favorite recipe from the **California Brandy Advisory Board**

VELVET CREAM CAKE

1 package **BETTY CROCKER®** any flavor **Creamy
 Frosting Mix**
1½ cups whipping cream
1 teaspoon vanilla
1 package **BETTY CROCKER® SUPERMOIST®** any
 flavor **Cake Mix**
Glaze*
2 tablespoons finely chopped pistachio nuts or walnuts

Mix 2 cups of the frosting mix (dry), the whipping cream and vanilla in small mixer bowl; refrigerate 1 hour. Bake cake mix in 2 round pans, 9x1½ inches, as directed on package; cool. Split cake to make 4 layers. (To split, mark side of cake with wooden picks and cut with sharp pointed knife.) Beat frosting mixture on low speed until blended. Beat on high speed until soft peaks form, about 3 minutes. Fill each cake layer with 1 cup frosting mixture. Spread Glaze over top; sprinkle with nuts. Store in refrigerator.

*GLAZE

Mix remaining frosting mix and 2 tablespoons boiling water. Beat on high speed until smooth, 2 to 3 minutes. If necessary, stir in 1 to 2 teaspoons additional water until of desired consistency.

CREAMY CAKE KAHLÚA®

¼ pound butter, unsalted
3 oz. or ½ cup of almonds, finely chopped
⅓ cup sugar
1 egg yolk
½ tsp. vanilla
7 Tbsp. **KAHLÚA® Coffee Liqueur**
1 pint whipping cream
18 lady fingers (36 halves)
2 tsp. powdered sugar

Combine butter, almonds, sugar, egg yolk, vanilla and 2 tablespoons **KAHLÚA®** in the bowl of an electric mixer and beat mixture for 15 minutes.

 In a shallow dish, combine ⅓ cup cream and 1 tablespoon **KAHLÚA®**. Rapidly dip each ½ lady finger in the cream and **KAHLÚA®** mixture, making sure not to soak the lady fingers. Place 12 lady fingers on a serving tray side-by-side to form the first layer. Spread half of the butter and almond mixture over the lady finger layer. Place a second layer of 12 dipped lady fingers on the butter mixture and spread remaining butter mixture on the second layer of lady fingers. Top with the third layer of 12 dipped lady fingers. This now resembles a loaf-shaped cake. *(Continued)*

Combine remaining cream, **KAHLÚA®** and powdered sugar and whip until stiff. Frost cake with whipped cream, top and sides. Place toothpicks in cake on top and gently cover with plastic wrap. Refrigerate overnight.

CHOCOLATE FANS
(The crowning touch)

4 oz. semi-sweet chocolate
2 Tbsp. **KAHLÚA®** Coffee Liqueur

Combine chocolate and **KAHLÚA®** in the top of a double boiler, over simmering water. Stir continually until chocolate has melted. Cover a cookie sheet with wax paper and draw two eight-inch circles on the paper. Spread the chocolate evenly inside the circles approximately ¼ inch thick. Chill in refrigerator until hard. Remove from refrigerator and allow to rest for a few minutes. Measure eight equal wedges and cut the chocolate. Arrange the wedges or fans on the top of the cake.   *Serves 6-8*

HERSHEY'S® DEEP, DARK CHOCOLATE CAKE

1¾ cups unsifted all-purpose flour
2 cups sugar
¾ cup **HERSHEY'S®** Cocoa
1½ teaspoons baking soda
1½ teaspoons baking powder
1 teaspoon salt
2 eggs
1 cup milk
½ cup vegetable oil
2 teaspoons vanilla
1 cup boiling water

Combine dry ingredients in large mixing bowl. Add remaining ingredients except boiling water; beat at medium speed 2 minutes. Remove from mixer; stir in boiling water (batter will be thin). Pour into two greased and floured 9-inch or three 8-inch layer pans or one 13 × 9-inch pan. Bake at 350° for 30 to 35 minutes for layers, 35 to 40 minutes for 13 × 9-inch pan, or until cake tester (inserted in center) comes out clean. Cool 10 minutes on rack. Remove from pans; cool completely. Top with your favorite frosting.

ROCKY ROAD CAKE

1 cup chopped walnuts
1 cup seedless raisins (optional)
1 cup miniature marshmallows
1 package (6-oz.) semisweet chocolate pieces
1 package (18½-oz.) devil's food cake mix (with pudding in the mix)
4 eggs
1 cup **BEST FOODS®/HELLMANN'S® Real Mayonnaise**
1 cup water

Grease and flour 12-cup fluted tube pan. In small bowl stir together nuts, raisins, marshmallows and chocolate pieces. In large bowl with mixer at low speed beat cake mix, eggs, Real Mayonnaise and water just until blended. Increase speed to medium; beat 2 minutes. Stir in nut mixture. Pour into prepared pan. Bake in 350°F oven 50 minutes or until cake tester inserted in center comes out clean. Cool in pan on wire rack 15 minutes. Remove and cool on wire rack. If desired, dust with confectioner's sugar.   *Makes 1 cake*

OUR FAVORITE DEVIL'S FOOD CAKE

1 cup **DOMINO®** Granulated Sugar
¾ cup firmly packed **DOMINO®** Light Brown Sugar
¼ lb. (½ cup) soft butter or margarine
3 oz. unsweetened chocolate, melted
3 egg yolks
¼ cup water
1 teaspoon vanilla extract
2 cups sifted cake flour
½ teaspoon salt
1 teaspoon baking soda
1 cup milk
3 egg whites, stiffly beaten

Cream sugars and butter. Add melted chocolate. Beat yolks; add water and extract and blend. Gradually add yolk mixture to chocolate mixture; beat until light and fluffy. Sift together flour, salt and baking soda. Alternately add flour mixture and milk, blending well after each addition. Beat egg whites until stiff but not dry, fold into batter.

Turn into two greased and floured 9-inch round cake pans or one greased and floured 13×9×2-inch pan. Bake layers or loaf in moderate oven 350°F about 30-35 minutes or until cake springs back when touched lightly. Turn out on cooling rack.

Yield: two 9-inch layers or one 13×9×2-inch loaf

TOLL HOUSE® BUNDT® CAKE

Nut Topping:
¼ cup butter, softened
2 measuring tablespoons sugar
⅔ cup finely chopped nuts

Cake:
2¾ cups all-purpose flour
2 measuring teaspoons baking soda
1 measuring teaspoon salt
1 measuring tablespoon vinegar
Whole milk
1 cup butter, softened
1 cup firmly packed brown sugar
1 measuring tablespoon vanilla extract
4 eggs
One 12-oz. pkg. (2 cups) **NESTLÉ® TOLL HOUSE®** Semi-Sweet Chocolate Mini-Morsels

TOPPING:
Preheat oven to 375°F. In small bowl, combine butter, sugar and nuts; mix until crumbly. Spoon into well greased and floured 10-inch fluted tube pan. Chill in refrigerator while you prepare cake batter.

CAKE:
In small bowl, combine flour, baking soda and salt; set aside. Place vinegar in 1 cup liquid measure; fill with milk to 1 cup line; set aside. In large mixer bowl, combine butter, brown sugar and vanilla extract; beat at medium speed until light and fluffy, (about 3-5 minutes). Add eggs, one at a time, beating well after each addition. Turn mixer to low. Gradually add flour mixture, one third at a time, alternately with milk. Remove bowl from mixer. Gently fold in **NESTLÉ® TOLL HOUSE®** Semi-Sweet Chocolate Mini-Morsels with a rubber spatula. Pour into prepared pan. Bake at 375°F 50 minutes. Check for doneness by inserting toothpick in center. When it comes out clean, cake is done. Cake is a dark golden brown when baked. Loosen edges of cake with spatula. *Immediately* invert on cooling rack. Cool cake completely.   *Makes: one 10-inch tube cake*

CHOCOLATE CHIFFON CAKE

2 squares unsweetened chocolate
¼ cup water
4 egg yolks
¾ cup sugar
1 cup SALERNO® Graham Cracker Crumbs
1 teaspoon baking soda
½ teaspoon baking powder
½ teaspoon salt
¼ cup water
¼ cup oil
1 teaspoon vanilla
4 egg whites
¼ teaspoon cream of tartar
¼ cup sugar

Melt chocolate with water over low heat; cool to lukewarm. In small bowl of mixer, beat egg yolks with ¾ cup sugar until thick and lemon colored, about 2 minutes. Add graham cracker crumbs, baking soda, baking powder, salt, water, oil, vanilla and chocolate mixture. Beat at low speed until blended, then at medium speed for 5 minutes. With clean beaters, beat egg whites and cream of tartar in large bowl of mixer until foamy. Gradually add sugar while beating at high speed. Beat until stiff peaks form. Fold ¼ of egg whites into chocolate mixture to lighten. Fold chocolate mixture into remaining egg whites. Pour into ungreased 10 inch tube pan. Bake in preheated 325° oven 45 to 50 minutes. Invert; cool. Run a spatula around edge and center tube; remove from pan. Serve with ice cream.

BLACK FOREST CHERRY CAKE

1 (18.5-ounce) pkg. chocolate cake mix (do not use cake mix with pudding added)
2 (21-ounce) cans THANK YOU® Brand Cherry Pie Filling
¼ cup oil
3 eggs

Grease and flour a 12-cup **Bundt**® pan. Preheat oven to 350°. Combine cake mix, 1 can of pie filling, oil and eggs; beat well with mixer until batter is smooth. Pour in prepared pan. Bake 45-50 minutes or until cake springs back from light touch. Cool in pan 25 minutes, invert onto rack to finish cooling. Decorate and serve with one 21-ounce can Cherry Pie Filling and whipped cream.

CHOCOLATE BUNDT® CAKE

1¾ cups unsifted all-purpose flour
1¾ cups sugar
¾ cup HERSHEY'S® Unsweetened Cocoa
1½ teaspoons baking soda
1 teaspoon salt
⅔ cup butter or margarine, softened
1½ cups dairy sour cream
¼ cup milk
2 eggs
1 teaspoon vanilla
Cocoa Glaze*
Chopped nuts, optional

Combine flour, sugar, cocoa, baking soda and salt in large mixer bowl. Add butter, sour cream, milk, eggs and vanilla; blend on low speed. Beat three minutes on medium speed. Pour batter into a well-greased and floured 10- or 12-cup Bundt® pan. Bake at 350° for 60 to 65 minutes or until cake tester inserted into cake comes out clean. Cool 10 minutes; remove from pan. Cool completely on wire rack. Prepare Cocoa Glaze; glaze cake and garnish with chopped nuts, if desired.   *12 servings*

*COCOA GLAZE

3 tablespoons butter
2 tablespoons HERSHEY'S® Unsweetened Cocoa
3 tablespoons milk
1 cup confectioner's sugar
½ teaspoon vanilla

Melt butter in small saucepan over low heat; add cocoa and stir until smooth. Add milk stirring until well blended. Remove from heat; whisk or beat in confectioner's sugar and vanilla until smooth. Spoon onto inverted cake allowing some to drizzle down sides.

FUDGE SWIRL CAKE
(Low Calorie)

1 box ESTEE® Chocolate Cake Mix
1 box ESTEE® White Cake Mix
Water

Preheat oven to 350°F. Lightly grease and flour one 13×9×2-inch pan, or spray with non-stick vegetable spray. Prepare each ESTEE® Cake Mix in separate bowls, according to package directions. Spoon batter into pan, alternating ½ cup of each, until all of the batter is utilized. Run a knife through the batter once, in a zig-zag motion, to make a swirled design. Bake at 350°F for 25 minutes. Frost with a double batch of Fudgy Fructose Frosting* when completely cooled.

Makes 24 servings, 2×2-inch per serving

NUTRITION INFORMATION

Calories	Carbohydrates	Protein	Fat	Cholesterol	Sodium
80	17g	1g	1g		12mg

DIABETIC EXCHANGE INFORMATION
Bread
1

*FUDGY FRUCTOSE FROSTING
(Low Calorie)

½ cup ESTEE® Granulated Fructose
⅓ cup skim milk
1 square unsweetened baker's chocolate, broken into small pieces
3 tsp. cornstarch
1 Tbsp. margarine
½ tsp. vanilla

Mix fructose, milk, and cornstarch together in small saucepan until starch is dissolved. Add chocolate and cook over medium heat until chocolate melts and mixture thickens and bubbles. Remove from heat. Add vanilla and margarine and stir until creamy. Spread over cake. One serving Fudge Swirl Cake with frosting:

NUTRITION INFORMATION

Calories	Carbohydrates	Protein	Fat	Cholesterol	Sodium
145	28g	2g	3g		18mg

DIABETIC EXCHANGE INFORMATION

Fruit	Bread	Fat
1	1	½

BANANA CHOCOLATE CAKE

2¼ cups flour
1 teaspoon baking powder
1 teaspoon salt
¾ teaspoon baking soda
1½ cups sugar
⅔ cup margarine
2 eggs
2 ounces unsweetened chocolate, melted
1 teaspoon vanilla
1 cup mashed, ripe bananas
½ cup **HENRI'S Creamy Slaw Dressing**

1. Preheat oven to 350° F.
2. Sift flour, baking powder, salt and baking soda.
3. Cream sugar and margarine until light and fluffy. Add eggs, one at a time. Beat well after each addition.
4. Blend in chocolate and vanilla.
5. Add dry ingredients alternately with bananas and **HENRI'S Creamy Slaw Dressing**. Mix well after each addition.
6. Pour into 2 greased 9-inch layer cake pans or a 9 × 13 × 2-inch pan. Bake 30-35 minutes. Cool.
7. Use Grand Fudge Frosting* for icing.

Makes 1 cake

*GRAND FUDGE FROSTING

¼ cup margarine
2 ounces unsweetened chocolate
3 cups sifted confectioner's sugar
¼ cup **HENRI'S Creamy Slaw Dressing**
2 tablespoons warm water
½ teaspoon vanilla

1. Melt margarine and chocolate in saucepan over low heat. Transfer to medium bowl.
2. Add sugar, **HENRI'S Creamy Slaw Dressing**, water and vanilla. Beat until smooth and creamy.
3. Spread on cake.

Frosts 2 (9-inch) layer cakes or 30 cupcakes

CHOCOLATE PEANUT RIPPLE CAKE

Cake:
1 pkg. **PILLSBURY PLUS Fudge Marble Cake Mix**
1 cup dairy sour cream
½ cup creamy peanut butter
¼ cup water
3 eggs
½ cup chopped peanuts

Frosting:
1 can **PILLSBURY Ready To Spread Chocolate Fudge Frosting Supreme**
2 tablespoons creamy peanut butter
1 tablespoon chopped peanuts

Heat oven to 350°F. Grease and flour two 8 or 9-inch round cake pans. In large bowl, blend cake mix (reserve marble pouch), sour cream, ½ cup peanut butter, water and eggs until moistened. Beat 2 minutes at highest speed. Fold in ½ cup chopped peanuts. Pour three-fourths of batter into prepared pans.

To the remaining batter add marble pouch and 2 tablespoons water; blend well. Spoon randomly over yellow batter. Swirl with spoon in a folding motion, turning pan while folding.

Bake at 350°F. for 35 to 45 minutes or until toothpick inserted in center comes out clean. Cool in pans 15 minutes; then remove. Cool completely.

Blend frosting with 2 tablespoons peanut butter. Spread small amount (about ⅓ cup) between cake layers. Frost sides and top with remaining frosting. Garnish with 1 tablespoon chopped peanuts.

12 servings

HIGH ALTITUDE—Above 3500 Feet: Add 3 tablespoons flour to dry cake mix. Bake at 375°F. for 30 to 35 minutes.

CHOCOLATE CHIFFON SQUARES

1½ cups unsifted cake flour or 1¼ cups unsifted all-purpose flour
1 cup sugar
½ cup **HERSHEY'S® Unsweetened Cocoa**
¾ teaspoon baking soda
½ teaspoon salt
½ cup vegetable oil
1 cup buttermilk or sour milk*
2 egg yolks
2 egg whites
½ cup sugar
Berry Whipped Cream (recipe follows)

Combine flour, 1 cup sugar, cocoa, baking soda and salt in large mixer bowl. Add oil, buttermilk or sour milk and egg yolks; beat until smooth. Beat egg whites in small mixer bowl until foamy; gradually add ½ cup sugar, beating until very stiff peaks form. Gently fold egg whites into chocolate batter. Pour into greased and floured 13 × 9 × 2-inch oblong pan. Bake at 350° for 30 to 35 minutes or until cake springs back when lightly touched in center. Cool in pan on wire rack. Just before serving, frost with Berry Whipped Cream. Cut into squares and garnish with additional sliced, sweetened strawberries or chocolate curls. Refrigerate any remaining cake.

About 12 servings

*To sour milk: Use 1 tablespoon vinegar plus milk to equal 1 cup.

BERRY WHIPPED CREAM

1 cup heavy cream
½ cup Strawberry Purée*
1 teaspoon vanilla
Red food color (optional)

Whip heavy cream until stiff. Gently fold in strawberry purée, vanilla and 2 or 3 drops red food color, if desired.

*STRAWBERRY PURÉE

Sweeten 2 cups sliced strawberries; allow to stand. Drain well; mash or purée about 1 cup berry halves in blender to equal ½ cup. Reserve remainder for garnish.

CHOCOLATE WINE CAKE

½ cup butter or margarine
1½ cups sugar
4 eggs
1 teaspoon vanilla
1¾ cups flour
2 teaspoons baking soda
¼ teaspoon salt
4 tablespoons cocoa
¼ cup milk
¼ cup **HOLLAND HOUSE® Red Cooking Wine**

Cream butter or margarine and sugar in a large mixing bowl. Add eggs, one at a time, beating constantly. Add vanilla. In a separate bowl, combine dry ingredients and add to creamed mixture. Blend in milk and red wine. Bake in a greased 9 × 13-inch pan in a 350° oven for about 30 minutes.

Serves 6 to 8

PEANUT BUTTER FUDGE MARBLE CAKE

1 pkg. PILLSBURY PLUS Fudge Marble Cake Mix
3 eggs
⅓ cup oil
1 cup water
⅓ cup peanut butter
½ cup chopped FISHER® Peanuts

Glaze:

1 cup powdered sugar
2 tablespoons cocoa
1 tablespoon peanut butter
2 tablespoons butter or margarine, softened
1 teaspoon vanilla
2 to 3 tablespoons water

Heat oven to 350°F. Grease (not oil) and flour 12-cup fluted tube pan. In large bowl, blend first 6 ingredients until moistened. Beat 2 minutes at highest speed. Pour ¾ of batter into pan. To remaining batter add marble pouch and 2 tablespoons water, blend well. Pour chocolate batter on top of yellow batter in pan. Marble batter using a spoon or knife using a swirling motion. Bake at 350°F for 35 to 45 minutes or until toothpick inserted in center comes out clean. Cool upright in pan 25 minutes; turn onto serving plate. Cool completely.

GLAZE:
Blend glaze ingredients in small bowl until smooth. If needed add a few more drops of water to make glaze consistency. Spoon over cool cake.   *10-inch ring cake*

SARONNO WINTER WONDERLAND CAKE

1 package chocolate cake mix
⅓ cup AMARETTO DI SARONNO® Liqueur
2 cups heavy cream
2 tablespoons confectioner's sugar
¼ cup AMARETTO DI SARONNO® Liqueur
1 (6-ounce) package of semisweet real chocolate morsels

Pour cake mix into large bowl. Substitute ⅓ cup AMARETTO DI SARONNO® for ⅓ cup of the liquid called for in cake mix directions. Add liquid to cake mix with eggs as directed on package. Prepare and bake in two 8×8×2-inch greased cake pans, following package directions. Cool in pans 10 minutes. Remove from pans; cool completely on wire racks. Even off tops if necessary.

In chilled deep bowl, beat cream and confectioner's sugar until almost stiff; add ¼ cup AMARETTO DI SARONNO® and continue beating until stiff. Place one cake layer on serving plate. Spread with about 1 cup of cream. Top with second layer. Frost top and sides with remaining cream. Chill several hours.

Melt chocolate morsels over hot water until smooth. Spread in a ¼-inch thick layer on foil and chill until firm enough to cut. With different sized cookie cutters, cut out trees from chocolate. If you don't have tree-shaped cookie cutters, a pattern may be cut out of cardboard and traced on the chocolate with a sharp knife. Chill trees until completely hardened. Just before serving, place trees on top of cake or along the sides.   *Makes one 8-inch cake*

CHRISTMAS RAINBOW CAKE

2 baked (8- or 9-inch) white cake layers, cooled
1 package (3 oz.) JELL-O® Brand Raspberry Flavor Gelatin
1 package (3 oz.) JELL-O® Brand Lime Flavor Gelatin
2 cups boiling water
1 container (8 oz.) BIRDS EYE® COOL WHIP® Non-Dairy Whipped Topping, thawed

Place cake layers, top sides up, in two clean 8- or 9-inch layer pans; prick each cake with utility fork at ½-inch intervals. Meanwhile, dissolve each flavor gelatin separately in 1 cup of the boiling water and carefully spoon each flavor over one of the cake layers. Chill 3 to 4 hours. Dip one cake pan in warm water for 10 seconds; then unmold cake layer onto serving plate. Top with about 1 cup of the whipped topping. Unmold second cake layer and carefully place on first layer. Frost top and sides with remaining whipped topping. Chill. Garnish as desired.

BRANDIED YULETIDE CAKE

1 package (1-pound 3-ounces) yellow cake mix
1 package (4-ounces) instant vanilla pudding
4 eggs
½ cup California brandy
¾ cup oil
½ cup orange juice
½ cup finely chopped pecans

Blend all ingredients except nuts; beat at medium speed about five minutes. Grease 10-inch tube or Bundt® pan; sprinkle with nuts. Pour batter into pan; bake at 325 degrees for one hour or until done. Cool five minutes; remove from pan. Decorate with candied fruit, if desired.   *Makes 12 to 16 servings*

Favorite recipe from **California Brandy Advisory Board**

HELEN HILAND'S WHEATENA® APPLE CAKE

1 cup finely chopped pecans
½ cup sugar
1 teaspoon cinnamon
2 tablespoons WHEATENA®, uncooked
1 cup grated apples, well packed
½ cup butter or margarine
1 cup sugar
3 eggs
3 cups sifted flour
3 teaspoons baking powder
1 teaspoon soda
¼ cup WHEATENA®, uncooked
¾ cup sour cream

Combine first 4 ingredients; set aside. Grate apples. Cream butter with sugar; add eggs, one at a time, and cream until light. Sift flour, baking powder and soda together; add WHEATENA®. Add dry ingredients to creamed mixture alternately with apples and sour cream. Spoon ½ the batter into well greased 10-inch tube pan. Sprinkle with ½ the nut mixture; cover with remaining batter and top with remaining nut mixture. Bake in preheated 375°F. oven 50 to 55 minutes, or until tests done. Cool slightly before removing from pan.   *Makes one 10-inch tube cake*

APPLE PIE CAKE

1 pkg. spice cake mix
2 cans **LUCKY LEAF®** Apple Pie Filling
2 Tbsp. lemon juice, plus enough **LUCKY LEAF®** Apple
   Juice to make 1 cup liquid or 1 cup water

Sprinkle ½ box cake mix into greased oblong 13″ × 9″ baking dish. Pour on 2 cans **LUCKY LEAF® Apple Pie Filling**, then remaining cake mix. Mix apple juice and lemon juice and carefully distribute over top. Bake at 350° for 1 hour.

Makes 10 servings

APPLESAUCE CAKE

1 cup **FEATHERWEIGHT®** Corn Flour
¾ cup sugar
¾ tsp. baking soda
¾ tsp. salt
¼ tsp. each cinnamon, nutmeg, cloves, allspice
¼ cup shortening
¾ cup **FEATHERWEIGHT®** Applesauce
1 egg

Sift dry ingredients together and place in mixing bowl. Add shortening and one half of the applesauce and mix well. Add remainder of applesauce and egg and mix well. Pour batter into greased cake pan (approx. 8″ × 8″). Bake at 350°F. for 35 minutes.

VARIATION:

Fold in ⅓ cup each of chopped dates, raisins, and nuts. Sprinkle with topping of ¼ cup nuts and one tablespoon sugar.

BANANA RUM CAKE
(Torta Al Ron)

2¼ to 2¾ cups unsifted all purpose flour
1 cup sugar
1 package active dry yeast
1 teaspoon salt
¼ cup milk
½ cup butter or margarine
3 eggs (at room temperature)
1 cup mashed **CHIQUITA®** Bananas (2 to 3 bananas)
¼ cup water
¼ cup orange juice
¼ cup rum
⅔ cup (approximately) apricot jam
Glacé cherries, blanched whole almonds, if desired
   for garnish

Combine ½ cup flour with ½ cup sugar, yeast and salt in a large bowl. Heat milk with butter until warm. Butter does not need to be completely melted. Add gradually to flour mixture. Beat at medium speed of mixer for 2 minutes. Scrape sides of bowl several times. Add another ½ cup flour, eggs and mashed bananas and beat another 2 minutes at high speed of mixer. Scrape sides of bowl several times. Gradually stir in enough of the remaining flour to make a thick batter. (It should hold its shape when lifted with spoon.)

Cover and let set in a warm place about 1 hour or until bubbly. Stir down batter. Turn into a well greased and floured 2-quart Turk's head, ring mold, or **Bundt®** cake pan. Cover and let rise in a warm place about 1½ hours or until doubled in bulk. Bake in 350°F oven 30 to 35 minutes. Unmold on rack and let cool. Meanwhile boil remaining ½ cup sugar and water together for 1 minute. Cool. Add orange juice and rum. *(Continued)*

Place cooled cake on a serving plate. Carefully pour rum sauce over cake. Let set until all sauce is absorbed. Spread apricot jam over cake. If desired, the cake may be garnished with glacé cherries and blanched almonds.

Makes 1 ring mold or 12 servings

Note: If any cake is left over, it should be stored loosely covered, at room temperature. It will keep this way for several days. Leftover cake may also be frozen. Freeze, then wrap in moisture-proof freezer paper. Label, date and return to freezer. Storage time, about 30 days.

BANANA POUND CAKE

1 package (17 ounce) pound cake mix
1 cup mashed ripe **CHIQUITA®** Bananas
2 eggs
½ cup chopped nuts, optional

Preheat oven to 325°. Generously grease and flour a 9-inch loaf pan.

Omit milk or water called for in package directions. Combine mix, bananas and eggs and beat 3 minutes at medium speed on electric mixer or 450 strokes by hand. Fold in nuts. Spoon into 9-inch loaf pan and bake 1¼ hours or until golden brown and cake springs back when lightly touched on top. Cool in pan for thirty minutes. Turn out on rack and cool. Store cake in plastic wrap.

COLOMBIAN FRESH BANANA CAKE WITH SEA FOAM FROSTING

1 pkg. (18½ oz.) yellow cake mix*
⅛ teaspoon baking soda
2 eggs
¾ cup **COCA-COLA®**
1 cup (2 to 3) mashed ripe bananas
2 teaspoons lemon juice
⅓ cup finely chopped nuts, optional

In large mixing bowl combine mix, baking soda and eggs. Measure **COCA-COLA®**, stir briskly until foaming stops, and add to batter. Blend ingredients just until moistened, then beat at high speed of electric mixer for 3 minutes, scraping bowl often. Combine mashed bananas with lemon juice. Add to cake batter with nuts. Beat 1 minute at medium speed and turn into a generously greased and lightly floured 13 × 9 × 2-inch pan. Bake at 350°F about 40 minutes or until cake tests done. Cool on rack 15 minutes, remove cake from pan and turn right side up on rack to finish cooling.

*Do not use mix with pudding added or which requires oil.

SEA FOAM FROSTING

2 egg whites (¼ cup)
1½ cups firmly packed light brown sugar
⅛ teaspoon cream of tartar or 1 tablespoon light corn
   syrup
⅓ cup **COCA-COLA®**
1 teaspoon vanilla extract
Dash salt

In top of double boiler, combine all ingredients except vanilla and beat 1 minute at high speed of electric mixer. Place over boiling water (water should not touch bottom of top part); beat on high speed about 7 minutes until frosting forms peaks when beater is raised. Remove from boiling water (for smoothest frosting, empty into large bowl). Add vanilla and continue beating on high speed until thick enough to spread, about 2 minutes. Spread on sides and top of cold banana cake.

MOTHER'S DAY DATE DESSERT

Date-Nut Loaf:

2 Tbsp. butter
½ cup honey
1 egg
1 tsp. grated lemon peel
2 tsp. lemon juice
1½ cups unbleached white flour
¼ tsp. salt
⅛ tsp. baking soda
1 tsp. baking powder
½ cup buttermilk
1 cup chopped pitted SUN WORLD® Dates
½ cup chopped walnuts

Banana Topping:

1 egg
2 Tbsp. sugar
2 Tbsp. skim milk
1 tsp. lemon juice
½ chopped banana
1 cup whipped low-calorie dessert topping

Preheat oven to 350 degrees. Cream the butter and slowly beat in the honey. Beat in the egg, lemon peel and lemon juice. Combine the flour, salt, baking soda and baking powder and add alternately with the buttermilk to the batter. Fold in the dates and walnuts. Pour the mixture into a greased 9 × 5 × 3 inch pan. Bake 50 to 60 minutes or until done.

Cool the date-nut loaf and top with the following: In small saucepan beat egg, sugar and milk. Cook and stir over low heat until mixture thickens slightly. Add lemon juice while stirring. Cool thoroughly. Add chopped bananas and fold in whipped topping. Chill and serve as topping for date-nut loaf.

CARROT CAKE

1½ cups unsifted all-purpose flour
1½ teaspoons CALUMET® Baking Powder
½ teaspoon salt
1 cup butter or margarine, softened
¾ cup granulated sugar
¾ cup firmly packed light brown sugar
3 eggs
¼ cup milk
1 teaspoon vanilla
2 cups POST® FRUIT & FIBER® Whole Wheat and Bran Cereal with Apples and Cinnamon
2 cups grated carrots

Mix flour with baking powder and salt. Cream butter. Gradually beat in sugars and continue beating until light and fluffy. Add eggs, one at a time, beating well after each addition. Add milk and vanilla (mixture will appear curdled). Stir in flour mixture, blending well. Add cereal and carrots. Spread in greased and floured 13 × 9-inch pan. Bake at 350° for 25 to 30 minutes, or until top springs back when lightly pressed. Cool in pan 10 minutes. Remove from pan and finish cooling on rack. Frost with Cream Cheese Frosting*.

*CREAM CHEESE FROSTING

Cream 3 tablespoons butter or margarine with 1 package (3 oz.) cream cheese, softened, until well blended. Add 2 cups sifted confectioner's sugar and 2 teaspoons milk alternately in small amounts, beating well after each addition. Blend in ½ teaspoon vanilla.   *Makes about 1½ cups*

CARROT CAKE–LOW CALORIE

1 cup whole wheat flour
1 tsp. baking powder
¾ tsp. baking soda
¼ tsp. salt
1 tsp. ground cinnamon
¼ cup corn oil
¼ cup SUPEROSE® Liquid Fructose
2 eggs lightly beaten, or ⅓ cup liquid egg substitute
2 carrots, scraped and grated (1 cup)
1 tsp. freshly grated orange peel
2 small oranges peeled and very finely chopped
¼ cup chopped walnuts

Preheat the oven to 350°. Lightly grease the sides of an 8½-inch square cake pan. Cut wax paper to fit the bottom of the pan. If using a Teflon® pan, put wax paper on the bottom but it is not necessary to grease the sides.

Combine the flour, baking powder, soda, salt and cinnamon in a large mixing bowl. In another bowl, combine the oil, SUPEROSE® Liquid Fructose and eggs and mix well. (Always measure the oil in a measuring cup before the SUPEROSE® Liquid Fructose. Then the fructose does not stick to the measuring cup.) Add the liquid ingredients to the dry ingredients and again mix well. Add the grated carrots, grated orange peel, chopped oranges and chopped walnuts and mix well. Pour the batter into the cake pan and bake in a 350° oven for approximately 35 minutes. Cool to room temperature and cover so the cake will not get dry. If you are keeping the cake for more than one day, store it in the refrigerator to preserve freshness.   *Makes 16 servings*

Each serving contains approximately: 94 calories

WHEAT GERM CARROT CAKE

2 cups unsifted ROBIN HOOD® All Purpose Flour
1½ cups KRETSCHMER Wheat Germ, Regular or Brown Sugar & Honey
3 tsp. baking powder
1½ tsp. salt
1½ tsp. cinnamon
¾ tsp. nutmeg
2 cups packed brown sugar
1½ cups cooking oil
4 eggs
1½ tsp. vanilla
3 cups grated carrots
1 Tbsp. grated orange rind
1 cup raisins
¾ cup finely chopped pecans

Combine . . . . . flour, wheat germ, baking powder, salt and spices on wax paper. Stir well to blend.
Beat . . . . sugar, oil, eggs and vanilla together in large bowl.
Add . . . . carrots and orange rind, mixing well.
Stir in . . . . blended dry ingredients, then raisins and pecans.
Spread . . . . in greased and floured 10-inch Bundt® pan.
Bake . . . . at 350° for 60-70 minutes until wooden pick inserted in center comes out clean.
Cool . . . . in pan 10 minutes. Remove from pan. Cool on rack.
Serve . . . . with Cream Cheese Sauce*
Makes 12-16 servings
(Continued)

*CREAM CHEESE SAUCE

2 pkg. (3 oz. each) cream cheese
2 Tbsp. softened butter or margarine
1 tsp. vanilla
1 cup unsifted powdered sugar

Cream . . . . cheese, butter and vanilla together thoroughly.
Add . . . . sugar gradually, beating until creamy. (Add milk if necessary for creamy consistency.)
Makes 1 1/3 cups

ORANGE CHIFFON CAKE

2¼ cups SOFTASILK® Cake Flour or 2 cups GOLD MEDAL® All-Purpose Flour*
1½ cups sugar
3 teaspoons baking powder
1 teaspoon salt
½ cup vegetable oil
5 egg yolks (with SOFTASILK® Flour) or 7 egg yolks (with GOLD MEDAL® Flour)
¾ cup cold water
2 tablespoons grated orange peel
1 cup egg whites (7 or 8)
½ teaspoon cream of tartar
Orange or Lemon Butter Frosting (recipe follows)

Heat oven to 325°. Mix flour, sugar, baking powder and salt in bowl. Make a well and add in order: oil, egg yolks, water and orange peel. Beat with spoon until smooth. Beat egg whites and cream of tartar in large bowl on high speed until stiff peaks form. Pour egg yolk mixture gradually over beaten whites, gently folding with rubber spatula just until blended. Pour into ungreased tube pan, 10x4 inches. Bake until top springs back when touched lightly, about 1¼ hours. Invert pan on heatproof funnel; let hang until cake is cold. Frost with Orange or Lemon Butter Frosting.

*If using self-rising flour, omit baking powder and salt.

ORANGE OR LEMON BUTTER FROSTING

⅓ cup margarine or butter, softened
3 cups powdered sugar
1 tablespoon plus 2 teaspoons grated orange or lemon peel
About 3 tablespoons orange or lemon juice

Beat all ingredients until of spreading consistency.

ORANGE CAKE
(No Cholesterol)

1½ cups sifted flour
1 cup sugar
2 teaspoons baking powder
¼ teaspoon salt
½ cup MAZOLA® Corn Oil
2 teaspoons grated orange rind
½ cup orange juice
4 egg whites, stiffly beaten

Grease and flour bottom of 8 × 4 × 3-inch loaf pan. In large mixer bowl stir together flour, sugar, baking powder and salt. Add corn oil, orange rind and juice. With mixer at medium speed beat until smooth. Fold in egg whites. Turn into pan. Bake in 350°F. oven 1 hour or until cake springs back when touched. Cool 10 minutes. Remove from pan, cool on wire rack.
Makes 8 servings

Cholesterol: 0 mg per serving

E-Z-BAKE ORANGE CAKE

¾ cup shortening
1¼ cups sugar
8 egg yolks
1 orange, juice and grated rind
2½ cups E-Z-BAKE Flour
½ teaspoon salt
3 teaspoons baking powder
¾ cup milk

HAND-MIXING METHOD:
Cream shortening and sugar until fluffy. Beat yolks until thick and lemon colored. Add to creamed mixture and beat smooth. Then add orange juice and rind. Add sifted dry ingredients alternately with milk. Beat thoroughly. Bake in a greased and floured pan in moderate oven (350° F.) 50 to 60 minutes. After baking, let cake stand a few minutes before removing from pan.

ELECTRIC-MIXER METHOD:
Measure shortening into bowl. Add flour, resifted with sugar, salt, leavening and three-fourths of the milk. Beat 2 minutes at low to medium speed, frequently scraping down sides of bowl and beater. Add unbeaten eggs, remaining milk and flavoring, and beat another 2 minutes. For best results, have all ingredients at room temperature.

YELLOW ICING

2 cups sugar
½ cup water
¼ cup white corn syrup
4 egg yolks
¼ teaspoon salt
1 teaspoon lemon juice
½ teaspoon orange rind
1 teaspoon orange juice
2 tablespoons cream
½ cup coconut

Cook sugar, water and corn syrup until mixture spins long double threads. Beat yolks until thick and lemon colored. Add salt and pour syrup over eggs in continuous stream, beating continuously until cool and fudgelike. Add cream, fruit juices and orange rind. Frost cake. If icing gets too stiff, thin with a little sweet cream. Sprinkle with coconut before frosting sets.

ORANGE CHIFFON LAYER CAKE

2 egg whites
⅓ cup sugar
2 cups sifted cake flour
1 cup sugar
3 teaspoons baking powder
1 teaspoon salt
½ cup orange juice
½ cup skim milk
½ cup PURITAN® Oil
2 egg yolks

Preheat oven to 350°.
In a small bowl beat egg whites with ⅓ cup sugar until thick and glossy but not stiff. Set aside. Combine flour, 1 cup sugar, baking powder and salt in a large mixing bowl. Add orange juice, milk, PURITAN® Oil, and egg yolks. Mix at medium speed for 3 minutes; scrape bottom and sides of bowl often. Fold egg whites into batter until well-blended. Pour into two greased and floured 8 × 1½-inch layer pans. Bake at 350° for 25 to 30 minutes until center springs back when touched lightly. Cool 10 to 20 minutes, then remove from pans.
Makes two 8-inch layers

PEACHES 'N' CREAM POUND CAKE

½ cup dairy sour cream
1 tablespoon orange liqueur OR orange juice
1 cup sliced sweetened fresh peaches, strawberries, OR nectarines
½ cup fresh blueberries
6 slices, each ½-inch thick, **SARA LEE Pound Cake**, thawed

Stir together sour cream and liqueur. Fold in fruit. Spoon about ¼ cup fruit mixture over each Pound Cake slice.

Makes 6 servings

PEACH UPSIDE-DOWN CAKE

1 (16-oz.) can **S&W® Natural Style Peaches**
3 Tbsp. butter
½ cup brown sugar
4 maraschino cherries, halved
¼ cup sliced almonds
⅓ cup shortening
½ cup granulated sugar
1 egg
1 tsp. vanilla
1 cup sifted flour
1¼ tsp. baking powder
⅛ tsp. salt

Preheat oven to 350°. Drain peaches, reserving juice. Melt butter in 8 × 8 × 2-inch square baking pan in preheated oven. Blend in brown sugar and 1 Tbsp. reserved juice. Arrange peaches, cherries and almonds in pan. Add water if necessary to remaining juice to make ½ cup.

Cream together shortening and granulated sugar until light and fluffy. Add egg and vanilla and beat until blended. Sift together remaining dry ingredients. Add to creamed mixture alternately with the ½ cup reserved juice, beating after each addition. Spread over peach mixture in pan. Bake at 350° for 40-45 minutes. Cool in pan 5 minutes. Invert on plate and serve warm.   *Serves 8*

PINEAPPLE CARROT CAKE

3 cups flour
2 teaspoons baking soda
1 teaspoon nutmeg
1 teaspoon cinnamon
½ teaspoon **MORTON® Table Salt**
1½ cups oil
2 cups sugar
3 eggs
2 cups finely grated raw carrots (about 3 large carrots)
1 can (8 ounces) crushed pineapple, undrained
2 teaspoons vanilla
1 cup chopped nuts

Glaze:

1 cup confectioners' sugar
2 teaspoons water
¼ teaspoon orange extract

Day Before Serving or Early in Day: To make cake: Combine flour, baking soda, nutmeg, cinnamon, and table salt. Set aside. In large mixing bowl, mix oil and sugar. Add eggs, one at a time, beating well after each addition. Add half the dry ingredients; beat until well mixed. Stir in carrots, pineapple and vanilla. Beat in remaining dry ingredients. Stir in nuts. Pour into greased and floured Bundt® pan. Bake at 350°F. for 70 minutes, or until wooden pick inserted in center comes out clean. Cool cake in pan

10 minutes. Remove from pan and cool completely.

To make glaze: Mix confectioners' sugar, water, and orange extract. If glaze is too thick, add a few more drops of water. Drizzle over cooled cake. Transfer to cake dish or large round platter.

Just Before Serving: Cut into thin slices.

Makes 20 to 24 servings

PINEAPPLE UPSIDE-DOWN CAKE

2 tablespoons margarine or butter
¼ cup packed brown sugar
1 can (8¼ ounces) sliced pineapple, drained
1½ cups **BISQUICK® Baking Mix**
½ cup granulated sugar
1 egg
½ cup milk or water
2 tablespoons shortening
1 teaspoon vanilla

Heat oven to 350°. Heat margarine in square pan, 8 × 8 × 2 inches, or round layer pan, 9 × 1½ inches, in oven until melted. Sprinkle brown sugar over margarine. Arrange pineapple slices on sugar mixture. Decorate with maraschino cherries and walnut or pecan halves if desired.

Beat remaining ingredients in large bowl on low speed, scraping bowl constantly, 30 seconds. Beat on medium speed, scraping bowl occasionally, 4 minutes. Pour batter over pineapple. Bake until wooden pick inserted in center comes out clean, 35 to 40 minutes. Immediately invert pan on heatproof serving plate; leave pan over cake a few minutes. Serve warm and, if desired, with sweetened whipped cream.   *9 to 12 servings*

HIGH ALTITUDE DIRECTIONS (3500 to 6500 feet): Heat oven to 375°. Use square pan, 9 × 9 × 2 inches. Add 2 tablespoons all-purpose flour; increase liquid to ⅔ cup.

GOLDEN BEAUTY PRUNE CAKE

1 cup snipped cooked **SUNSWEET® Prunes**
½ cup butter or margarine
1 cup granulated sugar
½ cup brown sugar, packed
1 teaspoon vanilla
2 large eggs, beaten
2½ cups sifted all-purpose flour
¾ teaspoon baking powder
¾ teaspoon soda
¾ teaspoon salt
½ teaspoon cinnamon
¼ teaspoon nutmeg
¼ teaspoon cloves
1 cup buttermilk
Mocha Frosting*

Cook prunes by package directions; drain and snip. Cream butter with sugars and vanilla until light and fluffy. Beat in eggs. (Mixture may appear slightly curdled.) Resift flour with baking powder, soda, salt and spices. Blend into creamed mixture alternately with buttermilk, beginning and ending with flour mixture. Fold in prunes. Turn into two well greased, 8-inch layer cake pans. Bake in oven center at 375°F. for about 30 minutes, until cakes test done. Remove from oven; let stand 10 minutes, then turn out onto wire racks to cool. When cold, spread Mocha Frosting between layers and on top and sides of cake.   *Makes one 8-inch cake*

(Continued)

*MOCHA FROSTING

Dissolve 1 teaspoon instant coffee powder in ¼ cup milk. Combine with ⅓ cup soft butter or margarine, and 1 pound powdered sugar, sifted. Beat until smooth, adding a few drops more milk if needed for good spreading consistency.

CALIFORNIA SUNSHINE CAKE

Cake:
1½ cups BLUE RIBBON® Finely Chopped Almonds
1 pkg. PILLSBURY PLUS Yellow Cake Mix
1 cup water
⅓ cup oil
1 teaspoon almond extract, if desired
3 eggs

Filling:
12-oz. pkg. (about 2 cups) pitted prunes
½ cup amaretto or orange juice

Frosting:
1½ cups whipping cream
3 tablespoons sugar
2 teaspoons amaretto or vanilla extract

Garnish:
Whole pitted prunes and BLUE RIBBON® Whole Blanched Almonds, toasted* or Amaretto Almonds**

CAKE:
Heat oven to 350° F. Grease and flour two 8 or 9-inch round cake pans. To prepare top layer of cake, sprinkle ½ cup chopped almonds in bottom of *one* prepared pan. In large bowl, blend all cake ingredients except almonds at low speed; beat 2 minutes at *highest speed.* Stir in remaining 1 cup almonds. Pour batter into prepared pans. Bake at 350° F. for 30 to 40 minutes or until toothpick inserted in center comes out clean. Cool cake in pans 15 minutes then invert layers on cooling racks. Cool completely.

FILLING:
In electric blender container, combine about half of each of the filling ingredients. Blend until almost smooth, turning blender on and off and scraping sides of container as needed. Repeat with remaining ingredients; set aside.

FROSTING:
In small bowl, whip cream until foamy. Gradually add sugar and *2 teaspoons* amaretto; continue whipping until stiff peaks form. Stir ½ cup whipped cream into prune filling. Spread prepared prune filling between cake layers, keeping almond side on top. Frost sides of cake with remaining whipped cream; garnish with prunes and almonds. Store cake loosely covered in refrigerator.
Makes 12 servings

*TOASTED ALMONDS

Spread almonds in an ungreased baking pan or skillet. Place in a 350° F. oven or over medium-low heat on a range top for about 10 minutes, until almonds are a light golden brown; stir once or twice to assure even browning. Note that almonds will continue to brown slightly after being removed from the heat.

**AMARETTO ALMONDS

Heat oven to 300° F. Oil one cookie sheet. In small bowl, combine *½ cup blanched whole almonds* and *4 teaspoons amaretto*; arrange in single layer on prepared pan. Bake at 300° F. for 20 to 25 minutes, tossing often, until glazed and lightly browned; cool.

HIGH ALTITUDE—Above 3500 feet: Add 3 tablespoons flour to dry cake mix. Bake at 375° F. for 25 to 35 minutes.

TOWERING STRAWBERRY SHORTCAKE

10-oz. can HUNGRY JACK® Refrigerated Flaky Biscuits
2 tablespoons margarine or butter, melted
2 to 4 tablespoons sugar
1 pint (2 cups) fresh strawberries, sliced and sweetened
1 cup whipping cream, whipped or 2 cups whipped topping
Whole strawberries

Heat oven to 400°F. Grease a cookie sheet. Separate dough into 10 biscuits. Gently press 2 biscuits together for each shortcake. Dip top and sides of each in margarine; then in sugar. Place on prepared cookie sheet. Bake at 400°F. for 12 to 16 minutes or until golden brown. Cool slightly; split and fill with strawberries and whipped cream. Top with additional whipped cream and garnish with whole strawberry. *5 servings*

STRAWBERRY SHORTCAKES

2 pints strawberries, sliced
⅔ cup sugar
Shortcakes*
¾ cup chilled whipping cream

Sprinkle strawberries with sugar; let stand 1 hour. Bake Shortcakes. Beat whipping cream in chilled bowl until stiff. Split shortcakes; spoon strawberries between halves and over tops. Top with whipped cream. *6 servings*

*SHORTCAKES

2⅓ cups BISQUICK® Baking Mix
½ cup milk
3 tablespoons sugar
3 tablespoons margarine or butter, melted

Heat oven to 425°. Mix all ingredients until soft dough forms. Gently smooth dough into ball on lightly floured cloth-covered board. Knead 8 to 10 times. Roll dough ½ inch thick. Cut with floured 3-inch cutter. Place on ungreased cookie sheet. Bake until golden brown, 10 to 12 minutes.

STRAWBERRY TUNNEL CREAM CAKE

1 (10-inch) prepared angel food cake
1 (8-ounce) package cream cheese, softened
1 (14-ounce) can EAGLE® Brand Sweetened Condensed Milk (NOT evaporated milk)
⅓ cup REALEMON® Lemon Juice from Concentrate
1 teaspoon almond extract
2 cups sliced fresh strawberries
3 to 4 cups frozen non-dairy whipped topping, thawed *or* sweetened whipped cream
Additional fresh strawberries, optional

Cut 1-inch slice crosswise from top of cake; set aside. With sharp knife, cut around cake 1 inch from center hole and 1 inch from outer edge, leaving cake walls 1-inch thick. Remove cake from center, leaving 1-inch thick base on bottom of cake. Reserve cake pieces. In large mixer bowl, beat cheese until fluffy. Beat in sweetened condensed milk until smooth. Stir in REALEMON® and extract; mix well. Stir in reserved torn cake pieces and strawberries. Fill cavity of cake with strawberry mixture; replace top slice of cake. Chill 3 hours or until set. Garnish with whipped topping and additional strawberries if desired. Refrigerate leftovers.
Makes one 10-inch cake

STRAWBERRY SPICED SHORTCAKE

6 frozen **SARA LEE Individual Cinnamon Raisin Danish**
½ cup whipping cream
1 tablespoon confectioners' sugar
2 packages (10-oz. each) frozen strawberries, thawed and drained

Warm Danish according to package directions. While Danish are warming, whip cream, gradually adding confectioners' sugar. Beat until stiff peaks form. TO SERVE TWO LAYER SHORT-CAKES: place 3 warm Danish on 3 plates, spoon about 1 table-spoon strawberries on each Danish. Top each serving with about 2 tablespoons of whipped cream. Repeat layers once. Makes 3 servings. OR TO SERVE SINGLE LAYER SHORTCAKES: place warm Danish on 6 plates, spoon about 1 tablespoon strawberries on each Danish. Top with whipped cream.

Makes 6 servings

PEANUT BUTTER SPICE CAKE

½ cup butter or margarine, softened
1 cup smooth or crunchy peanut butter
2 cups firmly-packed **COLONIAL® Light Golden Brown Sugar**
2 eggs
2½ cups unsifted flour
2 teaspoons baking soda
1 teaspoon salt
1 teaspoon ground cinnamon
¼ teaspoon ground cloves
2 cups applesauce
Peanut Butter Frosting*

Preheat oven to 350°. In large mixer bowl, cream together butter, peanut butter and sugar; beat in eggs. Combine dry ingredients. Add alternately with applesauce to sugar mixture, beating well after each addition. Pour into 2 greased 9-inch round cake pans. Bake 35 to 40 minutes or until cake springs back when lightly touched. Cool. Fill and frost with Peanut Butter Frosting.

Makes one 9-inch 2-layer cake

*PEANUT BUTTER FROSTING

½ cup smooth or crunchy peanut butter
1 cup firmly-packed **COLONIAL® Light Golden Brown Sugar**
⅓ cup milk
3 cups **COLONIAL® Confectioners' Sugar**

In medium saucepan, melt peanut butter over very low heat. Blend in brown sugar and milk. Remove from heat; stir in confectioners' sugar.

Makes about 2½ cups

HARVARD BEET SPICE CAKE

½ cup (1 stick) butter
1¼ cups sugar
2 eggs
1 jar (16 ounces) **AUNT NELLIE'S® Sweet Sour Harvard Beets**
2¼ cups sifted all-purpose flour
4 teaspoons baking powder
1 teaspoon soda
1½ teaspoons allspice
1 teaspoon cinnamon
¼ teaspoon cloves
1 cup coarsely chopped walnuts
Confectioners' sugar

In large mixing bowl, beat butter with sugar until light and fluffy. Add eggs; beat until well mixed. Blend beets in electric food blender until smooth. Sift together dry ingredients. Add alternately with beets to butter mixture, mixing well after each addition. Fold in walnuts. Turn batter into greased and lightly floured 9-cup Bundt® pan. Bake at 350° for 55 to 60 minutes, or until cake tests done. Cool on rack for 30 minutes before removing from pan. Sift confectioners' sugar over top of cooled cake.

SPICE CAKE WITH BUTTERMILK GLAZE

1 cup chopped cooked **SUNSWEET® Pitted Prunes**
½ cup butter or margarine, softened
1 cup granulated sugar
½ cup brown sugar, packed
1 teaspoon vanilla
2 eggs
2½ cups all-purpose flour
¾ teaspoon baking powder
¾ teaspoon baking soda
¼ teaspoon salt
1½ teaspoons cinnamon
1 teaspoon nutmeg
½ teaspoon cloves
1 cup buttermilk
Buttermilk Glaze*

Cook prunes by package directions; drain and chop. Cream together well butter, sugars and vanilla. Beat in eggs. (Mixture may appear curdled.) Sift flour with baking powder, soda, salt and spices. Blend into creamed mixture alternately with buttermilk. Fold in prunes. Turn into well-greased 9 × 13-inch baking pan. Bake at 375 degrees F about 35 minutes or until top of cake springs back when lightly touched. Let cake stand in pan while preparing Buttermilk Glaze.

*BUTTERMILK GLAZE

In a small saucepan, combine 1 cup granulated sugar, ½ cup buttermilk, 3 tablespoons corn syrup and ½ cup butter or margarine. Bring mixture to a rolling boil; cook for 5 minutes. Stir in ½ teaspoon baking soda and boil 1 minute longer. Remove from heat and stir in 2 teaspoons vanilla. Pour evenly over warm cake in pan. Allow glaze to be absorbed into cake before cutting.

FESTIVE FRUIT CAKE

2 cups miniature marshmallows
1 small can (⅔ cup) **PET® Evaporated Milk**
6 tablespoons orange juice
1 cup chopped **FUNSTEN Pecans**
1 cup candied mixed fruit
¾ cup diced dates
¾ cup raisins
¼ cup candied cherries
4 cups graham cracker crumbs
1 teaspoon cinnamon
1 teaspoon nutmeg
½ teaspoon cloves

In a 3-quart saucepan, heat marshmallows, evaporated milk and orange juice until marshmallows melt completely. Combine remaining ingredients. Stir into melted marshmallow mixture. Press firmly into a 5- to 6-cup ring mold or loaf pan lined with waxed paper. Cover tightly. Chill at least two days before serving.

Makes 3 lb.

Note: Festive Fruit Cake can be stored in a tightly covered container in a cool place for about 3 months or freeze and keep for 4 to 6 months.

10-MINUTE FRUITCAKE RING

1 package (8 ounces) pitted dates
1 jar (8 ounces) maraschino cherries, well drained
1 cup dried apricots
1 cup walnuts in whole pieces
¾ cup unsifted all-purpose flour
¼ cup sugar
½ teaspoon baking powder
¼ teaspoon salt
3 eggs
½ cup GRANDMA'S® Unsulphured Molasses
1 teaspoon vanilla

In large bowl, mix together dates, drained cherries, apricots and nuts. Mix together flour, sugar, baking powder and salt; add to fruit mixture and mix well. Beat eggs; beat in molasses and vanilla. Add to fruit and dry ingredients; stir until dry ingredients are completely moistened. Spoon into very well greased 6-cup ring mold. Bake in 300°F. oven 1 hour. Cool for 5 to 10 minutes, then turn cake out of pan onto wire rack. Cool.

Yield: 1 fruitcake

HEAVENLY VINO CAKE
(Torta "Paradiso" con vino)

2 cups all-purpose flour, sifted
2½ tablespoons cornstarch
1½ cups sugar
1 tablespoon baking powder
1 teaspoon ground cinnamon
½ teaspoon ground nutmeg
¼ teaspoon ground allspice
¼ teaspoon ground cloves
1 teaspoon salt
¾ cup BERTOLLI® Soave Wine
½ cup vegetable shortening
1 tablespoon dark molasses
1½ teaspoons vanilla
¼ cup milk
2 eggs
Almond Frosting*
Sliced almonds

Mix dry ingredients in large bowl. Mix in wine, shortening, molasses and vanilla; beat at medium speed 2 minutes. Mix in milk and eggs; beat 2 minutes. Pour into 2 greased and floured 9-inch round cake pans. Bake at 350° for 25 minutes, or until cake springs back when touched. Cool in pans 10 minutes; remove and cool on racks. Frost with Almond Frosting and decorate with almonds.

*ALMOND FROSTING
(Crema alla mandoria)

1 package (3 ounces) cream cheese, softened
¼ cup butter, softened
1 box (1 pound) powdered sugar
3 tablespoons milk
1 cup finely ground almonds

Beat cream cheese and butter in bowl until fluffy. Beat in sugar and milk; stir in almonds.

MRS. FRICKHOLM'S 4-DAY FRUITCAKE

For 3 days, soak ⅓ cup S&W® Seedless Raisins, ¼ cup S&W® Candied Orange Peel, ¼ cup S&W® Glacé Pineapple Wedges, ⅓ cup S&W® Glacé Cake Mix, 3 red and 3 green S&W® Glacé Cherries, sliced, in ½ cup brandy. The third day, preheat oven to 375° and drain the fruits, saving the brandy.

Cream ¾ cup softened butter with ¾ cup sugar and beat until fluffy. Whip in 3 eggs, 1 tsp. vanilla, 1 tsp. cardamom and the brandy from the fruit. Sift in 2 cups flour and 1 Tbsp. baking powder. Stir. Lightly dredge fruits in flour and mix them into batter with ⅓ cup chopped pecans. Turn into greased and lightly floured 9×5-inch loaf pan.

Bake 10 minutes at 375°; then 45-55 minutes at 325°. Let cake cool 10-15 minutes and remove from pan. Cool on rack. Sift powdered sugar over the top. Cover cooled cake with foil and let flavors steep in it 1 more day before serving. *Serves 12*

BOURBON PECAN POUND CAKE

½ pound butter
2½ cups sugar
6 eggs
3 cups sifted cake flour
2 teaspoons baking powder
1 teaspoon salt
1 teaspoon ground nutmeg
1 cup sour cream
½ cup bourbon
1½ cups coarsely chopped pecans
Glaze:
2 cups sifted confectioner's sugar
1 tablespoon bourbon
2 tablespoons water

Combine butter and sugar in bowl of electric mixer and blend until light and fluffy. Add eggs one at a time, beating constantly.

Sift together flour, baking powder, salt, and nutmeg. Blend sour cream and bourbon. Alternately add flour and sour cream mixtures to batter. Add pecans.

Grease bottom and sides of tube or Bundt® pan. Pour in batter and bake at 325° F for about one hour and 30 minutes. Test cake frequently after first hour and 15 minutes for doneness. Let cake cool in pan for 15 minutes before turning out on wire rack.

GLAZE:
To prepare glaze, combine sugar and bourbon. Stir, while gradually adding water. Add only enough water to make a pourable glaze, without allowing mixture to become too thin. Pour glaze over top of warm cake and let dribble down sides.

Favorite recipe from **National Pecan Marketing Council**

BAILEYS CAKE

1 angel food cake
½ cup to ⅔ cup BAILEYS Irish Cream Liqueur
Sliced almonds
2 teaspoons vanilla
3 cups whipping cream
½ cup confectioner's sugar

Bake almonds in 325° oven 15 to 20 minutes. Cool. Slice the top 1¼ inches from the angel food cake. Remove cake center, leaving 1-inch walls inside.

Whip cream until stiff. Add vanilla and confectioner's sugar. Slowly mix in **BAILEYS**. Fill cake with ⅔ of cream mixture. Set top in place and frost with remaining cream mixture. Sprinkle toasted almonds on top and freeze until serving time. If cake is to be stored in freezer, cover tightly *after* outside has become firm.

ROYAL COURVOISIER® POUND CAKE

    2¼ cups flour
    1 teaspoon baking powder
    ¼ teaspoon salt
    2 sticks (1 cup) butter
    1 cup sugar
    6 egg yolks, lightly beaten
    1 teaspoon vanilla extract
    ⅓ cup water
    6 egg whites

Butter and line bottom of a 9-inch loaf pan with waxed paper. Sift flour, baking powder and salt twice. Cream the butter and add sugar gradually; beat until light and fluffy. Add the egg yolks and continue beating until mixture is very light. Gradually sift in flour, a little at a time, beating well. Stir in vanilla and water. Beat egg whites until stiff. Fold into flour mixture. Pour the batter in the prepared pan. Bake in a preheated 300°F. oven for 1¼ hours. Meanwhile, make the Orange COURVOISIER® Sauce*.

*ORANGE COURVOISIER® SAUCE

    ⅓ cup sugar
    1½ tablespoons cornstarch
    1 cup orange juice
    3 tablespoons butter
    1 tablespoon grated orange rind
    ½ cup COURVOISIER® Brandy
    ¼ cup sliced almonds

Mix sugar and cornstarch in a small saucepan; add juice. Cook for five minutes over medium heat, stirring constantly. Add butter and stir until melted. Add orange rind and COURVOISIER®. Pour half the sauce over cake while sauce is still warm. Sprinkle with almonds. Pass the remaining sauce as the cake is served.

Makes 6 to 8 servings

BRANDY CAKE DE LOS REYES

    Brandied Fruits and Syrup (recipe follows)
    2 cups chopped pecans
    1 cup flaked coconut
    ½ cup THE CHRISTIAN BROTHERS® Brandy
    3½ cups sifted flour
    1½ teaspoons baking powder
    ½ teaspoon salt
    8 eggs
    2 cups butter or margarine, softened
    1½ cups granulated sugar
    ½ cup packed brown sugar
    1 teaspoon vanilla
    ¼ cup toasted blanched almonds
    Powdered sugar

Prepare Brandied Fruits and Syrup at least 24 hours and up to 1 week in advance; set aside. In 1-quart bowl combine pecans, coconut and brandy. Toss and set aside. Combine flour, baking powder and salt; set aside. With electric mixer at high speed beat eggs until light and lemon-colored, about 5 minutes; set aside. In large bowl cream butter, sugars and vanilla with mixer at medium speed, until light and fluffy, about 5 minutes. Add eggs. Beat 2 minutes. Gradually add flour mixture, beating at low speed just to blend. Stir in pecan mixture to blend thoroughly. Turn into greased and floured 10 x 4-inch tube pan. Smooth top. Bake in 350 degree oven about 1 hour 20 minutes until pick inserted into center comes out clean. If needed, cover with aluminum foil to prevent over-browning. Cool in pan on rack 20 minutes. Remove from pan and place on serving plate top side up. Drain Brandied Fruits;

reserve syrup. While still warm brush exposed surfaces of cake several times with syrup, reserving about 3 tablespoons. Arrange fruits and almonds on top of cake. Drizzle with remaining syrup. Just before serving, dust with powdered sugar. To serve place some of the fruits on each plate and accompany with a slice of cake.

Makes 24 servings

BRANDIED FRUITS AND SYRUP

In glass or plastic container with tight-fitting lid combine 1 cup dried pear halves, ⅔ cup dried apricot halves and ½ cup candied red cherries; set aside. In 1-quart saucepan combine 1 cup sugar, ¾ cup THE CHRISTIAN BROTHERS® Brandy and ¼ cup water. Stir and bring to boiling over medium heat. Simmer 5 minutes. Pour over fruits; stir. Cover and let stand at room temperature.

GLAZED PISTACHIO RUM CAKE

    1 cup margarine or butter
    1 cup firmly packed brown sugar
    1 cup granulated sugar
    2 tsp. grated lemon rind
    4 eggs
    3 cups sifted all-purpose flour
    ½ tsp. baking soda
    ½ tsp. baking powder
    ¼ tsp. salt
    ½ tsp. cinnamon
    ½ tsp. ground cloves
    ¾ cup buttermilk
    ½ cup rum
    ½ cup shelled California Pistachios, chopped

Measure margarine, brown sugar, granulated sugar and lemon rind into large mixing bowl. Beat until smooth and creamy. Add eggs, one at a time, beating well after each addition.

In small mixing bowl, stir together flour, baking soda, baking powder, salt, cinnamon and cloves. Add flour mixture and buttermilk, alternately to the margarine mixture. Stir in rum and California Pistachios.

Pour batter into a well-greased 10-inch tube pan or a Bundt® pan. Bake at 325°F for 50 minutes or until wooden pick inserted in center comes out clean. Cool on wire rack 10 minutes. Turn out of pan and glaze* while hot.

*GLAZE

    2 Tbsp. margarine or butter
    ¼ cup rum
    2 cups sifted powdered sugar
    ½ cup shelled California Pistachios, chopped

To prepare glaze, melt margarine in small saucepan. Remove from heat. Stir in rum and powdered sugar. Mix well. Stir in California Pistachios. Drizzle over top of warm cake.

Favorite recipe from **California Pistachio Commission**

KAHLÚA® PARTY CRUNCH CAKE

    1¼ cups sifted cake flour
    1½ cups sugar
    ½ cup egg yolks (6 large)
    2 tablespoons KAHLÚA® Coffee Liqueur
    2 tablespoons water
    1 tablespoon lemon juice
    1 cup egg whites (8 large)
    1 teaspoon cream of tartar
    1 teaspoon salt
    KAHLÚA® Crunch*
    KAHLÚA® Cream**

Sift flour with ¾ cup sugar into small bowl of mixer. Make a well in center and add egg yolks, **KAHLÚA**®, water and lemon juice. Beat to smooth batter. Beat egg whites in large mixer bowl with cream of tartar and salt. Beat to very fine foam. Gradually add remaining ¾ cup sugar, 2 tablespoons at a time, continuing to beat to firm meringue. Pour batter slowly over meringue folding in with rubber scraper until blended (do not stir). Turn batter into ungreased tube pan, 10 x 4 inches. Bake in moderate oven (350 degrees F) 50 to 55 minutes, or until top springs back when lightly touched. Turn pan upside down, placing tube over neck of a bottle. Let stand until cold. Prepare **KAHLÚA**® Crunch. Remove cake from pan and cut horizontally into 4 even layers. Reassemble layers with about *half* **KAHLÚA**® Cream between. Spread remainder over sides and top. Cover cake generously with crushed **KAHLÚA**® Crunch, pressing gently over cream with hands. Mark cutting lines on top, and down the side of cake with knife. Refrigerate until served.   *Makes 16 servings*

*KAHLÚA® CRUNCH

Measure 1½ cups sugar, 2 tablespoons water, ¼ cup **KAHLÚA**®, and ¼ cup white corn syrup into narrow, deep pan such as top of double boiler. Stir, then bring to boil and cook to 310 degrees F (hard crack stage). Remove from heat and add 3 teaspoons soda (free from lumps). Mixture will foam rapidly when soda is added. Stir briskly just until mixture thickens, but do not break down foam with excessive stirring. Turn out into ungreased 9-inch square pan; do not stir. Let stand until cold. Knock out of pan and crush with rolling pin to coarse crumbs.

**KAHLÚA® CREAM

Beat 2 cups whipping cream with 2 tablespoons **KAHLÚA**® and 1 tablespoon sugar until stiff.

FROZEN TIA MARIA® MOUSSE CAKE

Crust:
3 cups (12 ounces) chocolate wafer crumbs
1 stick (½ cup) plus 2 tablespoons butter, melted

Mousse:
8 ounces semisweet chocolate broken into pieces
¼ cup boiling water
½ cup sugar, divided
4 egg yolks, extra large
½ cup **TIA MARIA**® liqueur
4 egg whites, extra large
¼ teaspoon cream of tartar
2 cups heavy cream

Additional TIA MARIA® for sauce

CRUST:
Preheat the oven to 375°F. Lightly butter the sides of a 9 × 3-inch spring form pan. Mix the wafer crumbs and melted butter. Press the mixture firmly against the bottom and sides of the pan. Bake for 8 minutes. Let cool.

MOUSSE:
Melt chocolate pieces with ¼ cup sugar and the boiling water in the top of a double boiler. Remove from heat, beat in egg yolks. Return and cook over hot water for 1 minute. Add **TIA MARIA**®, blend thoroughly and set aside to cool completely. Beat egg whites with cream of tartar until stiff; add remaining ¼ cup sugar gradually and beat until stiff peaks form. Fold into chocolate gradually. Whip cream and fold into the mixture; blend well.

ASSEMBLY:
Set a small shot glass in the center of the baked springform pan.* Spoon in the mousse mixture around the glass and fill the shell.

(Continued)

Smooth out the top, cover with plastic wrap and freeze several hours or overnight. Decorate the cake with chocolate shavings, if desired. Or if time permits, make attractive chocolate leaves by painting the underside of fresh leaves (ivy or rose are good choices) with melted semisweet chocolate. Place leaves on saucer and freeze. When ready to serve, remove the springform sides from the cake. Slide onto a serving plate. Peel away the green leaves from the chocolate and arrange on top of cake. Fill the center shot glass with **TIA MARIA**® and serve as a sauce for each piece of cake.   *Serves 10 to 12*

*If desired, a chocolate cup can be made or purchased to replace shot glass.

HARVEY WALLBANGER CAKE

1 box orange cake mix (about 18½ oz.)
1 box (3¾ oz.) instant vanilla pudding mix
4 eggs
½ cup vegetable oil
5 oz. **LIQUORE GALLIANO**®
2 oz. vodka
5 oz. orange juice
1 cup confectioners sugar

Combine cake mix and pudding in a large bowl. Blend in eggs, oil, 4 oz. **LIQUORE GALLIANO**®, 1 oz. vodka, and 4 oz. orange juice. Mix batter until smooth and thick. Pour into a greased and floured 10″ **Bundt**® pan.* Bake at 350° for 45 minutes. Let cool in pan 10 minutes, then remove and place on rack. Have glaze ready to spoon on while cake is still warm.

GLAZE:
Combine confectioners sugar, remaining **LIQUORE GALLIANO**®, vodka and orange juice. Blend until very smooth.

*Or use two greased and floured 9″ cake pans. Bake at 350° for 30 minutes.

DOUBLE CHOCOLATE CHEESECAKE

1 cup chocolate cookie crumbs
3 tablespoons butter or margarine, melted
2 envelopes unflavored gelatin
⅔ cup sugar
1⅓ cups diluted **MILNOT**® (⅔ cup **MILNOT**® and ⅔ cup water)
2 eggs, slightly beaten
2 cups (12-oz.) chocolate chips
2 cups cottage cheese, sieved or blended
1 cup **MILNOT**®

Pour melted butter over chocolate crumbs. Press firmly over bottom of 10-inch springform pan. Mix gelatin and sugar; blend in diluted **MILNOT**® and eggs. Cook over low heat, stirring constantly; continue cooking until gelatin dissolves and mixture thickens slightly. Remove from heat; stir in chocolate chips until melted. Chill 30 minutes, then blend in cheese. Chill until mixture mounds when dropped from a spoon.
    Chill **MILNOT**® then whip until it holds stiff peaks; fold into chocolate mixture. Pour into springform pan over crust. Chill until firm (3 or more hours). Cut into wedges. Garnish with whipped **MILNOT**® topping, grated chocolate, etc.

OREO DOUBLE CHOCOLATE CHEESECAKE

Crust:
¼ cup butter or margarine
25 **OREO Chocolate Sandwich Cookies**, crushed
Filling:
2 (8-ounce) packages cream cheese, at room temperature
6 eggs, separated, at room temperature
4 (1-ounce) squares semi-sweet chocolate, melted
2 teaspoons vanilla extract
½ cup sugar
Decoration:
1 (1-ounce) square semi-sweet chocolate
Chocolate curls

1. **MAKE CRUST:**
In medium saucepan, over low heat, melt butter or margarine; remove from heat; stir in **OREO** crumbs. Press evenly onto bottom and sides of 9-inch spring-form pan; refrigerate while preparing filling.

2. **MAKE FILLING:**
In large bowl, with electric mixer at medium speed, beat cream cheese until light and fluffy; beat in egg yolks, melted chocolate and vanilla extract until smooth, about 3 minutes; set aside.

3. In another large bowl, with electric mixer at high speed, beat egg whites until soft peaks form; gradually add sugar, beating until stiff peaks form. Using rubber spatula, gently fold beaten egg whites, ⅓ at a time, into cream cheese mixture. Pour into crust; freeze 4 hours.

4. **MAKE CHOCOLATE LOOP DECORATION:**
In small saucepan, over low heat, melt 1 (1-ounce) square semi-sweet chocolate; remove from heat; let cool to room temperature.

5. On 11 × 8½-inch sheet of white paper, draw 1 (6-inch) circle; on outside of circle, draw 12 (1-inch) circles, spaced evenly around circle. Place on cookie sheet; cover with wax paper, securing wax paper edges under cookie sheet.

6. Using No. 1 decorating tip, pipe melted chocolate onto wax paper over outline (or drizzle chocolate, a little at a time, from teaspoon); freeze until firm, about 30 minutes.

7. **TO SERVE:**
Remove sides of pan; carefully remove wax paper from Chocolate Loop Decoration; set on frozen cheesecake. Garnish with chocolate curls. *Makes 10 to 12 servings*

INDIVIDUAL CHOCOLATE CHEESECAKES

Graham Crumb Shells*
3 ounces cream cheese, softened
2 tablespoons sugar
⅓ cup **HERSHEY'S® Semi-Sweet Chocolate Mini Chips**
1 egg
½ teaspoon vanilla

Prepare Graham Crumb Shells; set aside. Soften cream cheese in small mixer bowl; beat in sugar. Place Mini Chips in small bowl and melt by setting in pan of hot water or place in microwave on high for 1 minute; stir until completely melted; add to cream cheese mixture. Beat in egg and vanilla until well blended. Spoon into crumb shells filling cups ¾ full; bake at 350° for 20 to 25 minutes or until set. Cool completely. To serve, top with dollop of sour cream or whipped topping and garnish with fresh fruit, if desired. *2 servings*
(Continued)

*GRAHAM CRUMB SHELLS

Combine ¼ cup graham cracker crumbs, 2 teaspoons sugar and 1 tablespoon melted butter in small bowl; pat into bottom and ½-inch up sides of four paper-lined muffin cups or two (6-ounce) custard cups or small ramekins.

BLUE CHEESE CAKE

4 ounce package **TREASURE CAVE®** Blue Cheese, crumbled
2 cups graham cracker crumbs
⅓ cup melted butter or margarine
2 teaspoons sugar
¼ teaspoon cinnamon
19 ounces (two 8-ounce packages and one 3-ounce package) cream cheese
4 eggs
1 cup sugar
4 teaspoons vanilla
1 pint dairy sour cream
2 packages (10 ounces each) frozen strawberries

Blend crumbs, butter, 2 teaspoons sugar and cinnamon. Pat into bottom and sides of 9 × 3-inch springform pan. Bake 5 minutes in 425°F oven. Remove; cool. Beat blue and cream cheeses until smooth. Add eggs one at a time, beating well after each addition. Gradually add 1 cup sugar. Add 2 teaspoons vanilla and whip until smooth. Pour into pan. Bake in 325°F oven 1 hour. Remove and increase oven temperature to 425°F. Whip sour cream with remaining vanilla. Spread over cake. Return to oven for 15 minutes. Chill. Spoon strawberries over individual servings. *Yield: 16 two-inch wedges*

CAPPUCCINO CHEESECAKE

1 envelope **KNOX® Unflavored Gelatine**
⅓ cup sugar
¾ cup boiling water
1 cup (8 oz.) sour cream
1 package (8 oz.) cream cheese, softened
⅓ cup coffee liqueur
1 teaspoon vanilla extract
½ cup chopped pecans or walnuts
Zwieback Crumb Crust*

In large bowl, mix unflavored gelatine with sugar; add boiling water and stir until gelatine is completely dissolved. With electric mixer, add sour cream, cream cheese, liqueur and vanilla, one at a time, beating well after each addition. Fold in nuts. Turn into prepared crust; chill until firm. *Makes about 8 servings*

*ZWIEBACK CRUMB CRUST

In small bowl, combine 1 cup zwieback cracker crumbs, 2 tablespoons sugar and 3 tablespoons melted butter or margarine. Press into 9-inch pie pan; chill.

INDIVIDUAL CHEESECAKES

8 **NILLA Wafers**
2 (3-ounce) packages cream cheese, softened
⅓ cup **SNACK MATE Sharp Cheddar Pasteurized Process Cheese Spread**
2 eggs
½ cup granulated sugar
1 teaspoon lemon juice
1 (20-ounce) can blueberry or cherry pie filling

1. Preheat oven to 350°F. Line 8 (2½-inch) cupcake pans or muffin tins with paper liners. Place one **NILLA Wafer** in bottom of each.
2. In medium bowl, with electric mixer at medium speed, beat together cream cheese and **SNACK MATE Cheese** 2 minutes. Add eggs, sugar and lemon juice; beat an additional 3 minutes. (Mixture will not be smooth.)
3. Fill each cupcake liner with ¼-cup cheesecake mixture. Bake 30 minutes; place on wire rack to cool completely. Top each cheesecake with a little blueberry or cherry pie filling; refrigerate additional pie filling for later use.

Makes 8 individual cheesecakes

MICROWAVE METHOD:
1. Line 9 (6-ounce) microwave-proof custard cups with a double layer of paper liners. Proceed as in Steps 1 and 2.
2. Fill each cup with a scant ¼-cup cheesecake mixture. Arrange filled cups in a circle in microwave oven. Microwave at 100% power 5 to 6 minutes, re-arranging position of cups after 2 minutes. Cool and top with pie filling as in Step 3.

KAHLÚA® CHEESECAKE

Zwieback Crust*
2 envelopes unflavored gelatin
½ cup **KAHLÚA® Coffee Liqueur**
½ cup water
3 eggs, separated
¼ cup sugar
⅛ tsp. salt
2 (8 oz.) packages cream cheese
1 cup whipping cream
Shaved or curled semi-sweet chocolate

Prepare Zwieback Crust. In top of double boiler, soften gelatin in **KAHLÚA®** and water. Beat in egg yolks, sugar and salt. Cook over boiling water, stirring constantly, until slightly thickened. Beat cheese until fluffy. Gradually beat in **KAHLÚA®** mixture; cool. Beat egg whites until stiff but not dry. Beat cream stiff. Fold egg whites and cream into cheese mixture. Pour into prepared pan. Chill 4 or 5 hours, or overnight. Remove from refrigerator 15 minutes before serving. Decorate with shaved or curled chocolate. (To add flavor, spoon a little **KAHLÚA®** over each serving.)

Makes 12 servings

*ZWIEBACK CRUST

Blend 1½ cups fine Zwieback crumbs, and ⅓ cup **each** sugar and melted butter together. Press firmly over bottom and half way up sides of a 9-inch springform pan. Bake in a moderate oven (350 degrees F) 8 to 10 minutes. Cool.

RED, WHITE 'N' BLUE CHEESE CAKE

1 frozen **SARA LEE Cream Cheese Cake**
1 cup halved fresh strawberries
½ cup fresh blueberries
2 tablespoons currant jelly

Thaw cheese cake out of package at room temperature 30 minutes; cut into 6 pieces. Thaw cheese cake an additional 30-45 minutes. Arrange strawberry halves around top edge. Pile blueberries in center leaving white area between strawberries and blueberries. Melt jelly, cool to lukewarm; carefully spoon just over strawberries and blueberries.

Makes 6 servings

WILDERNESS® BLUEBERRY CHEESECAKE

Crust:
2 cups graham cracker crumbs
1½ tsp. flour
1½ tsp. confectioner's sugar
½ cup margarine, melted

Filling:
2 pkg. (8-oz. each) cream cheese, softened
¾ cup sugar
2 tsp. vanilla
2 eggs, beaten

Topping:
1 pint sour cream
2 Tbsp. sugar
½ tsp. vanilla
1 can (21-oz.) **WILDERNESS® Blueberry Fruit Filling**

CRUST:
Combine crumbs, flour, and confectioner's sugar; stir in melted margarine. Press crust mixture firmly on bottom and sides of ungreased 9-inch square baking dish.

FILLING:
Cream softened cream cheese and beat in sugar until smooth. Add vanilla and beaten eggs. Spread filling over crust and bake at 350 degrees for 15 to 20 minutes, until set.

TOPPING:
To prepare topping, blend sour cream, sugar and vanilla. Remove cake from oven and spoon mixture over cake immediately. Return cake to oven for 15 minutes more. Cool cake; spread **WILDERNESS® Blueberry Fruit Filling** over sour cream topping. Cover and refrigerate before serving. *Serves 12*

VARIATION:

Substitute Cherry or any other **WILDERNESS® Fruit Filling**.

LOW CAL CHEESECAKE

1 cup graham cracker crumbs
¾ cup sugar, divided
¼ cup butter or margarine, softened
1 container (15 ounces) small curd cottage cheese
4 eggs
½ cup evaporated skim milk
3 Tablespoons lemon or orange juice
1 teaspoon lemon or orange peel
¼ teaspoon salt
¼ cup flour
1 package (10 ounces) **Frozen STOKELY'S® Red Raspberries, in Syrup**, thawed

Preheat oven to 300° F. Grease lightly a spring-form pan. Mix cracker crumbs, ¼ cup sugar and butter. Press into bottom of prepared pan. In blender mix until smooth cheese, eggs, milk, remaining sugar, lemon juice, lemon peel, and salt. Add flour and blend a few seconds. Pour over cracker crumbs. Bake 1 hour or until firm. Cool completely before removing side of pan. Pour raspberries over cheesecake and serve at once.

Makes 14 servings

Note: Canned fruit may be substituted for raspberries.

FRUIT CHEESECAKE DESSERT

1 package **BETTY CROCKER® SNACKIN' CAKE®**
   Applesauce Raisin, Banana Walnut, Butter Pecan,
   Coconut Pecan or **Date Nut Cake Mix**
1 egg
1 cup dairy sour cream
¼ cup lemon juice
1 can (14 ounces) sweetened condensed milk
1 can (21 ounces) fruit pie filling

Heat oven to 375°. Grease bottom only of rectangular pan, 13 × 9 × 2-inches. Prepare cake mix as directed on package except—add egg with the water and mix in bowl. Pour into pan. Mix sour cream, juice and milk until smooth. Drop mixture by large spoonfuls onto batter in pan. Spread pie filling over top. Bake until edges are golden brown and sour cream mixture is set, about 35 minutes. Spoon into dessert dishes.   *About 14 servings*

VARIATION:

CHOCOLATE CHEESECAKE DESSERT

Use **Chocolate Fudge Chip** or **German Chocolate Coconut Pecan Cake Mix** and cherry pie filling.

CHERRY CHEESECAKE MINIATURES

8 oz. cream cheese, softened
2 eggs
1¼ cups (14 oz.) sweetened condensed milk
1 tsp. vanilla
1 tsp. lemon juice (optional)
¼ tsp. salt
24 vanilla wafers
2¼ cups (21 oz.) cherry pie filling
2 Tbsp. almond flavor liqueur

In bowl beat cream cheese until fluffy. Add eggs, milk, vanilla, lemon juice and salt, beating until well combined. Insert 24 cupcake liners into muffin pan, place one vanilla wafer, flat side down, on bottom of each liner. Divide mixture into 24 portions, filling each cup ⅔ full with batter. Bake at 350°F. for 15-20 minutes or until filling is puffed and set. (Filling will settle to original volume when cool.) Top with cherry pie filling flavored with liqueur (optional); chill before serving. Must be refrigerated.
      Approx. Yield: 24 miniature cheesecakes

Favorite recipe from the **Western New York Apple & New York Cherry Growers**

GRANNY APPLE CHEESECAKE

Crust:

1¼ cups graham cracker crumbs
¼ cup butter or margarine, melted
2 tablespoons sugar
¼ teaspoon ground cinnamon

Apple-Cheese Filling:

2 envelopes unflavored gelatine
¾ cup sugar, divided
1 cup low-fat milk
2 eggs, separated
1 tablespoon lemon juice
½ teaspoon grated lemon peel
¼ teaspoon salt
2 cups (1 pound) small curd cottage cheese
2 large **CAPE GRANNY SMITH Apples**, pared, cored and shredded (2 cups)

CRUST:

In small bowl, combine graham cracker crumbs, butter, sugar and cinnamon; mix well. Press firmly into a 9-inch spring-form pan, covering bottom and 1¼ inches up sides. Chill 1 hour.

APPLE-CHEESE FILLING:

In medium saucepan, combine gelatine with ½ cup sugar. Stir in milk, egg yolks, lemon juice, lemon peel and salt. Cook over low heat, stirring constantly with wire whisk, until gelatine dissolves. Remove from heat. In large bowl beat cottage cheese until smooth. Gradually beat in gelatine mixture. Stir in shredded apples. Chill, stirring occasionally, until mixture mounds slightly when dropped from a spoon. In small bowl, beat egg whites until foamy. Gradually add remaining ¼ cup sugar, beating until stiff peaks form. Fold into apple-cheese mixture. Pour into prepared cake pan. Chill overnight or 8 to 12 hours until firm.   *Yield: 12 servings*

CREAMY FRUIT 'N' NUT CHEESECAKE

¼ cup margarine or butter, melted
1 cup graham cracker crumbs
¼ cup sugar
2 (8-ounce) packages cream cheese, softened
1 (14-ounce) can **EAGLE® Brand Sweetened Condensed Milk** (NOT evaporated milk)
1 envelope unflavored gelatin
¼ cup **REALEMON® Lemon Juice from Concentrate**
1⅓ cups (one-half 28-ounce jar) **NONE SUCH® Ready-to-Use Mincemeat**
½ cup chopped nuts
1 tablespoon grated lemon rind
1 cup (½ pint) whipping cream, whipped
Sour cream and nuts, optional

Combine margarine, crumbs and sugar; pat firmly on bottom of 9-inch springform or 9-inch square baking pan. Chill. In large mixer bowl, beat cheese until fluffy. Add sweetened condensed milk; beat until smooth. In small saucepan, soften gelatin in **REALEMON®**. Over low heat, dissolve gelatin completely. Add to cheese mixture with mincemeat, nuts and rind; mix well. Thoroughly fold in whipped cream. Turn into prepared pan. Chill 3 hours or until set. Garnish with sour cream and nuts if desired. Refrigerate leftovers.   *Makes one 9-inch cake*

SOUR CREAM LEMON CHEESECAKE

1 package **DUNCAN HINES® Pudding Recipe Lemon Cake Mix**
3 eggs
2 tablespoons flour
1 tablespoon plus 1 teaspoon **CRISCO® Oil** or **PURITAN® Oil**
2 cartons (8 ounces each) dairy sour cream
½ cup sugar
1 teaspoon lemon juice
1 cup milk
2 drops yellow food coloring
1 can (21 ounces) blueberry pie filling

Preheat oven to 300°. Measure out 1½ cups dry cake mix; set aside. Stir together remaining dry cake mix, 1 egg, flour, and oil in large bowl. Press this crumb mixture evenly into bottom and three-quarters of the way up the sides of a 13 × 9 × 2-inch pan.

In same bowl, blend sour cream, sugar, 2 eggs, reserved cake mix, and lemon juice 1 minute at low speed. Gradually add milk and food coloring while beating 2 minutes at medium speed. Pour into crumb crust. Bake at 300° for 45 to 50 minutes, or until center

Cakes & Frostings   263

is firm. Do not overbake. Cool at room temperature 1 hour. Top with blueberry pie filling or your favorite pie filling and refrigerate.   *One 13 × 9-inch cake*

CASSATA CAKE

2 lb. container **SORRENTO® Whole Milk Ricotta**
1 cup sugar
1 oz. maraschino or any favorite liqueur
½ tsp. vanilla
2 Tbsp. shredded chocolate
¼ cup chopped candied fruit
1 baked sponge cake, split in 3 layers
½ cup heavy cream, whipped for frosting

Beat ricotta, sugar, liqueur & vanilla until smooth. Add chocolate & fruit. Spread between layers of cake. Chill 1 hour. Spread whipped cream over top & sides of cake and decorate with chocolate or nuts.

RAINBOW SHERBET ROLL

1 package **BETTY CROCKER® White Angel Food** or **Lemon Chiffon Cake Mix**
1½ cups raspberry sherbet
1½ cups orange sherbet
1½ cups lime sherbet

Heat oven to 350°. Line jelly roll pan, 15½ × 10½ × 1-inch, with waxed paper. Prepare cake mix as directed on package except—spread half of the batter in pan. Spread remaining batter in ungreased loaf pan, 9 × 5 × 3-inches. Bake until top springs back when touched lightly in center, jelly roll pan 20 to 25 minutes, loaf pan 45 to 50 minutes.

Cool jelly roll pan 10 minutes. Loosen cake from edges of pan; invert on towel sprinkled with powdered sugar. Carefully remove waxed paper. Trim off stiff edges if necessary. While hot, carefully roll cake and towel from narrow end. Cool on wire rack. Invert loaf pan to cool. Remove cake from pan; freeze for future use.

Unroll cake; remove towel. Beginning at narrow end, spread raspberry sherbet on ⅓ of cake, orange sherbet on next ⅓ of cake and lime sherbet on remaining cake. Roll up carefully. Place roll, seam side down, on aluminum foil, 18 × 12-inches. Wrap securely in foil; freeze until firm, at least 6 hours. Remove from freezer 15 minutes before serving. Cut roll into ¾-inch slices.   *12 servings*

MINT CHOCOLATE ICE CREAM CAKE

Crust:
32 **OREO Chocolate Sandwich Cookies**
¼ cup butter or margarine

Filling:
½ gallon mint chocolate-chip ice cream, slightly softened
1 quart chocolate ice cream, slightly softened

Garnish:
½ cup heavy cream, whipped
3 tablespoons chocolate syrup

1. **MAKE CRUST:**
In large plastic bag, using rolling pin, crush 18 **OREO Cookies**; set aside. In medium saucepan, over low heat, melt butter or margarine; remove from heat; stir in **OREO** crumbs. Press evenly onto bottom of 9-inch spring-form pan; stand remaining 14 whole **OREO Cookies** around sides. Refrigerate 15 minutes.

2. **MAKE FILLING:**
Spread ½ mint chocolate-chip ice cream over cookie crumbs; freeze until firm, about 15 minutes. Top with chocolate ice cream, spreading to cover completely; freeze until firm, about 15 minutes. Spread remaining mint chocolate-chip ice cream over entire surface; freeze until firm, about 4 hours.

3. **TO SERVE:**
In small bowl, using rubber spatula, gently fold together whipped cream and chocolate syrup. Remove sides of pan. Using No. 5A meringue tip, pipe whipped cream around edge and in center of cake.   *Makes 14 servings*

SEVEN-LAYER ICE CREAM CAKE

Using a packaged cake mix, bake a 9-inch square white cake. When cold, cut cake in half, making 2 rectangles; split each into two layers. Spread one layer with **BREYERS® Chocolate Ice Cream**; one with **BREYERS® Butter Almond Ice Cream**; one with **BREYERS® Natural Strawberry Ice Cream**. Put one layer on top of the other, with a cake layer on top; pressing into shape. Wrap and freeze. Before serving, let thaw in refrigerator for about 1 hour. Slice and serve with chocolate sauce or thawed frozen strawberries.

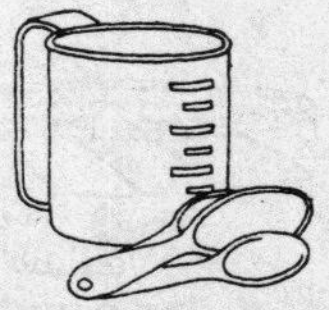

BLACK FOREST ICE CREAM CAKE

1 quart **FRIENDLY® Golden Vanilla** or **Burgundy Cherry Ice Cream**, softened
1¾ cups unsifted all-purpose flour
2 cups sugar
¾ cup **HERSHEY'S® Cocoa**
2 teaspoons baking soda
1 teaspoon baking powder
1 teaspoon salt
2 eggs
1 cup strong black coffee
1 cup buttermilk or sour milk*
½ cup vegetable oil
1 teaspoon vanilla
3 cups whipped cream
1 cup cherry pie filling

Firmly pack **FRIENDLY® Ice Cream** into a foil-lined 9-inch round cake pan. Cover; freeze about 2 hours. Combine flour, sugar, cocoa, baking soda, baking powder and salt in large mixer bowl. Add eggs, coffee, buttermilk, oil and vanilla. Beat on medium speed 2 minutes (batter will be thin). Pour batter into greased and floured 9-inch round cake pans. Bake at 350° for 30 to 35 minutes or until cake tester comes out clean. Cool 10 minutes; remove from pans and cool completely. Place 1 cake layer upside down on serving plate; top with **FRIENDLY® Ice Cream** unmolded from cake pan. Place second cake layer, top side up, over **FRIENDLY® Ice Cream** layer. Gently spread whipped cream on top and sides of cake. With decorator's tube or spoon, make border of whipped cream around edge of top layer of cake. Fill center with cherry pie filling. Cover and freeze at least 1 hour before serving.

*To sour milk: Use 1 tablespoon vinegar plus milk to equal 1 cup.

CRANBERRY ORANGE CREAM CHEESE ICE CREAM CAKE

1 cup graham cracker crumbs
3 tablespoons sugar
½ teaspoon ground cinnamon
3 tablespoons butter or margarine, melted
2 packages (8 ounces each) cream cheese
1 quart vanilla ice cream
1 cup **OCEAN SPRAY® CRANORANGE®** Cranberry Orange Relish
½ cup heavy cream, whipped (optional)

Combine crumbs, sugar, cinnamon and butter in small bowl; blend well. Press firmly over the bottom and sides of a buttered 8-inch springform pan; chill.

Beat cream cheese in large bowl until soft and fluffy. Soften ice cream in a chilled large bowl; beat into cream cheese until just blended. Ripple relish through ice cream-cheese mixture into prepared pan—¼ of the ice cream-cheese mixture and 3½ tablespoons cranberry orange relish at a time, until ⅔ of a cup of the relish and all of the ice cream-cheese mixture is used. Smooth top with a spatula and cover with plastic wrap. Freeze overnight or until firm.

Remove dessert from freezer ½ hour before serving. Spread remaining ⅓ cup cranberry orange relish over top. If desired, decorate with whipped cream piped through a pastry bag fitted with a small star tip.   *Makes 12 servings*

SPICY APPLESAUCE ICE CREAM ROLL

3 eggs
1 cup sugar
1 can (16½ ounces) **STOKELY'S FINEST®** **Applesauce**, divided
1 cup all-purpose flour
1 teaspoon baking powder
1 teaspoon cinnamon, divided
¼ teaspoon nutmeg
¼ teaspoon salt
Confectioners sugar
1 quart vanilla ice cream, slightly softened

Preheat oven to 375°F. Line greased 15 × 10 × 1-inch jelly-roll pan with waxed paper; grease paper. In small mixing bowl, beat eggs at high speed with electric mixer 5 minutes. Gradually beat in sugar and ½ cup applesauce (reserving remaining applesauce for topping). Sift together flour, baking powder, ¾ teaspoon cinnamon, nutmeg, and salt; blend into egg mixture using low speed of mixer. Spread batter in prepared pan and bake 15 minutes, or until cake is lightly browned and springs back when pressed with fingers. Sprinkle clean dish towel with confectioners sugar. Immediately invert cake onto prepared towel. Remove waxed paper; roll cake and towel from narrow end; cool completely. Unroll cake, trim edges if desired, remove from towel, spread with softened ice cream, and reroll. Wrap tightly in foil or plastic film and freeze. Blend reserved applesauce with remaining ¼ teaspoon cinnamon; chill. When ready to serve, cut roll into 8 or 10 slices. Top each slice with applesauce mixture.   *8 to 10 servings*

OLD-FASHIONED CAKE ROLL

⅔ cup unsifted cake flour
¾ teaspoon double-acting baking powder
¼ teaspoon salt
4 eggs (at room temperature)
¾ cup granulated sugar
1 teaspoon vanilla
2 tablespoons butter or margarine, melted
Confectioner's sugar
1 cup Red Raspberry Jam*

Mix flour with baking powder and salt. Beat eggs in large bowl at high speed of electric mixer or with hand beater, adding granulated sugar gradually and beating until mixture becomes fluffy, thick and light colored, about 5 minutes. Gradually fold in flour mixture; add vanilla and butter. Pour into a 15 × 10-inch jelly roll pan which has been greased, lined on bottom with paper, and greased again. Bake at 400° for 13 minutes. Turn out onto cloth sprinkled with confectioner's sugar. Quickly remove paper and trim off crisp edges. Starting with short side, roll cake with cloth. Cool on a rack about 30 minutes. Unroll, remove cloth and spread with jam. Roll cake again, leaving the end underneath. Sprinkle with confectioner's sugar or spread with a glaze, if desired.

Note: Cooled, rolled cake may be frozen; thaw, fill and roll. Or freeze filled cake; thaw and serve.

IN HIGH ALTITUDE AREAS, use large *cold* eggs, increase flour to *1 cup minus* 1 tablespoon and add 2 tablespoons water.

*RED RASPBERRY JAM

2 cups prepared fruit (about 1 qt. fully ripe red raspberries)
4 cups (1¾ lb.) sugar
2 tablespoons lemon juice
1 pouch **CERTO®** **Fruit Pectin**

First prepare the containers. Use only containers 1 pint or less in size that have tight-fitting lids. Wash, scald and drain containers and lids; or use automatic dishwasher with really hot (150° or higher) rinse water.

Then prepare the fruit. Thoroughly crush, one layer at a time, about 1 quart red raspberries. (Sieve ½ of the pulp to remove some of the seeds, if desired.) Measure 2 cups into a large bowl or pan.

Then make the jam. Thoroughly mix sugar into fruit; let stand 10 minutes. Add lemon juice to fruit pectin in small bowl. Stir into fruit. Continue stirring *3 minutes*. (A few sugar crystals will remain.) Ladle quickly into containers. Cover at once with tight lids. Let stand at room temperature 24 hours; then store in freezer. If jam will be used within 2 or 3 weeks, it may be stored in the refrigerator.   *Makes 4⅔ cups or about 6 (8 fl. oz.) containers*

GRAPE PINWHEELS

Shortening or butter
Flour
¾ cup sifted cake flour
¾ teaspoon baking powder
⅛ teaspoon salt
2 eggs, at room temperature
½ cup sugar
¼ cup **SMUCKER'S Low Sugar Orange Marmalade**
¼ teaspoon almond extract
Confectioners' sugar
⅔ cup **SMUCKER'S Low Sugar Grape Spread**
¼ cup slivered almonds, toasted and ground

Grease a 15½ × 10½ × 1-inch jelly-roll pan with shortening or butter; dust with flour to coat evenly; invert pan to remove any excess flour. Place cake flour, baking powder and salt in a sifter or sieve. Beat eggs in a medium bowl with electric mixer at high speed until pale yellow. Gradually beat in sugar until mixture is thick and double in volume, about 10 minutes. Beat in Orange Marmalade and extract. Sift flour mixture, ¼ at a time, over egg mixture; with rubber spatula, gently fold in. Spread batter evenly in prepared pan. Bake in a preheated 375°F. oven for 12 to 14 minutes or until cake springs back when lightly touched. Sift confectioners' sugar lightly over a clean cloth towel. Invert cake onto towel. Cut cake crosswise in half to form two rectangles. Place one cake rectangle with the long edge along one edge of the towel and roll up towel with cake. Place other cake rectangle along opposite end of towel and roll up. Cool cake rolls on a wire rack. When cool, unroll each half and spread with ⅓ cup of the Grape Spread; sprinkle with 2 tablespoons ground almonds. Reroll cake firmly without towel. Cut rolls crosswise into ½-inch slices. Arrange on a serving plate. *Makes about 3 dozen*

SWEET POTATO CAKE ROLL

Cake:
1 package (12 ounces) **MRS. PAUL'S® Candied Sweet Potatoes**, thawed and diced
3 eggs
1 cup sugar
1 teaspoon lemon juice
¾ cup flour
1 teaspoon baking powder
2 teaspoons cinnamon
1 teaspoon ginger
½ teaspoon nutmeg
½ teaspoon salt
1 cup chopped walnuts

Filling:
6 ounces cream cheese, softened
¼ cup butter, softened
1 cup confectioners' sugar
½ teaspoon vanilla extract

Preheat oven to 375° F. Grease a 10½ × 15½ × 1 inch jelly roll pan and line the bottom and sides with wax paper. Grease the paper. Beat eggs on high speed of electric mixer for 5 minutes. Gradually beat in sugar. Add candied sweet potatoes and lemon juice and beat until smooth. In a small bowl, combine flour, baking powder and spices. Gradually add to the sweet potato mixture, beating the batter until smooth. Spread in prepared pan. Sprinkle batter with chopped walnuts. Bake for 15 minutes. Dust a clean dish towel with confectioners' sugar. As soon as the cake comes out of the oven, reverse onto towel. While cake is hot, carefully peel off wax paper. Then, starting at the narrow end, roll towel and cake together. Place on a rack to cool.

Prepare filling by combining cream cheese, butter, confectioners' sugar and vanilla. Beat until smooth. When cake is cool, unroll and spread filling evenly over cake. Roll cake back up, using the towel as a guide. Chill. *Serves 12*

CHOCOLATE CUPCAKES

Cupcakes:
1 package Chocolate Pudding in the Cake Mix
½ cup **HENRI'S YOGOWHIP™ Reduced Calorie Dressing**

1. Preheat oven to 350° F.
2. Prepare cake according to package directions substituting **HENRI'S YOGOWHIP™ Reduced Calorie Dressing** for 1 egg and ⅓ cup oil.
3. Pour into greased muffin pans. Bake according to package directions.

Makes 24 cupcakes

Frosting:
¼ cup butter or margarine, room temperature
1 (8-ounce) package cream cheese, softened
1 teaspoon vanilla
1 pound confectioner's sugar

1. Cream butter and cream cheese until light and fluffy.
2. Add vanilla and mix well. Add sugar. Beat until smooth.

GUITTARD® BLACK BOTTOM CUPCAKES

#1 Mixture:
Combine
    6 ounces cream cheese
    2 beaten eggs
    ¼ tsp. salt, ⅔ cup sugar
Beat well, stir in
    12 ounce pkg. **GUITTARD® Semi-Sweet Chocolate Chips**
Set above aside.

#2 Mixture:
Sift together
    3 cups flour
    ½ cup unsweetened cocoa
    2 tsp. baking soda
    2 cups sugar
    1 tsp. salt
Add
    2 cups water
    ⅔ cup cooking oil
    2 Tbsp. vinegar
    2 tsp. vanilla
Beat well together.

Fill 36 large cupcake liners with #2 mixture a little more than half. Drop one teaspoon #1 mixture on top of each. Bake at 350 degrees for 25 minutes.

JIF® PEANUT BUTTER CUPCAKES

1 cup packed brown sugar
½ cup **JIF® Peanut Butter**
¼ cup butter or margarine, softened
2 eggs
1 teaspoon vanilla
1½ cups sifted all-purpose flour
2 teaspoons baking powder
½ teaspoon salt
½ cup milk
1 6-ounce package (1 cup) semisweet chocolate pieces or ¾ cup jelly

Preheat oven to 350°. Cream brown sugar, **JIF®**, and butter. Beat in eggs and vanilla. Mix flour, baking powder, and ½ teaspoon salt. Add to creamed mixture alternately with milk, mixing till blended.

Spoon a rounded tablespoonful of batter into greased muffin pans or paper bake cups in muffin pans. Place 10 to 12 chocolate pieces or 2 teaspoons jelly in center of each spoonful of batter. Top with a second tablespoonful of batter. Bake in 350° oven about 25 minutes or till done. *Makes 18*

GHOST 'N GOBLIN CUPCAKES

⅓ cup butter or margarine
¾ cup sugar
1 egg
½ teaspoon vanilla
1¾ cups all-purpose flour
2½ teaspoons baking powder
½ teaspoon salt
¾ cup milk
½ cup finely crushed hard candies (lemon, cinnamon, lime or orange)
Assorted candies (licorice whips, gumdrops, jelly beans, candy corn, chocolate morsels, marshmallows, candy-coated chocolate)

In small bowl of electric mixer cream butter and sugar. Beat in egg and vanilla until smooth. Sift together flour, baking powder and salt. Blend flour mixture and milk alternately into creamed mixture. Stir in crushed candy. Place 2½-inch paper liners in muffin cups. Fill cups half full with batter. Bake in 375°F oven 20 minutes, or until cupcakes test done. Cool. Top with your favorite frosting, and decorate as funny faces using assorted candies.

Yield: 18 cupcakes

Favorite recipe from **National Confectioners Association**

Frostings

HERSHEY'S® CHOCOLATE BUTTERCREAM FROSTING

6 tablespoons butter or margarine (softened)
¾ cup **HERSHEY'S® Cocoa**
2⅔ cups unsifted confectioner's sugar
⅓ cup milk
1 teaspoon vanilla

Cream butter in small mixer bowl. Add cocoa and confectioner's sugar alternately with milk; beat to spreading consistency (additional tablespoon milk may be needed). Blend in vanilla.

About two cups frosting

BROILED-FLUFF® FROSTING

⅓ cup butter or margarine, melted
1 cup **MARSHMALLOW FLUFF®**
⅛ tsp. salt
1 cup shredded coconut
½ cup chopped walnuts

Combine all ingredients; spread over the top of *hot* cake. Broil slowly, about 2 minutes until golden brown.

Makes enough to frost one 9-inch square cake

CREAM CHEESE FROSTING

2 tablespoons soft butter or margarine
2 (3-oz.) packages cream cheese
1 lb. **DOMINO® Confectioners 10-X Sugar**
2-3 teaspoons milk
1 teaspoon vanilla

Cream butter and cheese together. Add sugar alternately with milk. Beat until blended. Add vanilla.

Yield: frosting for two 9-inch round layers

VARIATION:

CHOCOLATE CREAM CHEESE FROSTING

Add 2 squares unsweetened chocolate, melted.

CHOCOLATE SOUR CREAM FROSTING

1 (12-oz.) package semi-sweet chocolate chips
¾-1 cup heavy sour cream
1 lb. **DOMINO® Confectioners 10-X Sugar**
1 teaspoon vanilla extract

Melt chocolate over hot water. Remove. Add one-third of sugar, beating until blended. Alternately add remaining sugar and sour cream, beating until smooth. Add vanilla.

Yield: frosting for two 9-inch round layers

LACY TOPPING FOR CAKE OR GINGERBREAD

Place openwork paper doily on cake; sift **DOMINO® Confectioners 10-X Sugar** onto cake. Lift doily from cake, leaving fancy design.

Pies

CHOCOLATE CRUMB CRUST

1½ cups of **MALT-O-MEAL® Puffed Rice Cereal**
1 package (6 oz.) semi-sweet chocolate morsels
¼ cup of butter
½ cup toasted coconut

Place cereal in a shallow baking dish and bake in 350° oven for 10 minutes; chop coarsely. Combine chocolate morsels and butter; cook over very low heat, stirring constantly until chocolate is melted. Blend cereal and coconut into melted chocolate. Press firmly and evenly against bottom and sides of a 9 inch pie pan. Chill before filling with your favorite pudding or ice cream.

Makes one 9 inch chocolate crust

DOUBLE CHOCOLATE PIE

2 packages (4-serving size) **JELL-O® Brand Chocolate, Chocolate Fudge or Milk Chocolate Flavor Pudding and Pie Filling**
3½ cups milk
2 tablespoons butter or margarine
⅓ cup **BAKER'S® Semi-Sweet Chocolate Flavored Chips***
1 baked 9-inch pie shell, cooled

Combine pie filling mix, milk, butter and chips in saucepan. Cook and stir over medium heat until mixture comes to a *full* bubbling boil. Remove from heat. Cool 5 minutes, stirring twice. Pour into shell; place plastic wrap on surface of filling and chill 3 hours. Garnish with thawed frozen whipped topping and sprinkle with chocolate curls or grated chocolate, if desired.

*Or use 2 squares **BAKER'S® Semi-Sweet Chocolate**.

CHOCOLATE COCONUT MERINGUE PIE

1 cup sugar
¼ cup **ARGO®/KINGSFORD'S® Corn Starch**
⅛ teaspoon salt
2½ cups milk
3 egg yolks, slightly beaten
2 squares (1 oz. each) unsweetened chocolate, cut-up
1⅓ cups flaked coconut, divided
1 teaspoon vanilla
3 egg whites
1 baked (9-inch) pastry shell

In 2-quart saucepan stir together ⅔ cup of the sugar, corn starch and salt. Gradually stir in milk until smooth. Stir in egg yolks until well blended. Stir in chocolate. Stirring constantly, bring to boil over medium-low heat and boil 1 minute. Remove from heat. Stir in 1 cup of the coconut and vanilla. Cover surface with waxed paper or plastic wrap; cool completely. Spoon into pastry shell. In small bowl with mixer at high speed beat egg whites until foamy. Gradually beat in remaining ⅓ cup sugar until stiff peaks form. Spread some meringue around edge of filling first, touching crust all around; then fill in center. Sprinkle remaining ⅓ cup coconut over meringue. Bake in 350°F oven 15 to 20 minutes or until lightly browned. Cool at room temperature away from drafts.

Makes 8 servings

SILKY CHOCOLATE PIE

Crust:
1 cup vanilla wafer crumbs
½ cup **KRETSCHMER Wheat Germ**, Regular or Brown Sugar & Honey
2 Tbsp. sugar
⅓ cup butter or margarine, melted

Filling:
1 pkg. (6 oz.) semi-sweet chocolate pieces
¼ cup softened butter or margarine
1 pkg. (8 oz.) cream cheese, softened
½ cup sugar
1 tsp. vanilla
2 eggs

CRUST:
Combine vanilla wafer crumbs, wheat germ and 2 tablespoons sugar in 9-inch pie plate. Stir well to blend. Add ⅓ cup melted butter. Mix well. Press onto bottom and sides of pie plate. Bake at 350° for 5-8 minutes until lightly browned. Cool.

FILLING:
Melt chocolate pieces in small saucepan over low heat. Cool. Cream ¼ cup butter and cream cheese in small mixing bowl until light and fluffy. Gradually add ½ cup sugar. Beat in chocolate mixture and vanilla. Add eggs, one at a time, beating at high speed for 3-5 minutes after each addition. Spread evenly into cooled crust. Refrigerate several hours or overnight. Serve with whipped cream, nuts or shaved chocolate if desired.

Makes 10-12 servings

CHOCOLATE PIE WITH PRETZEL CRUST

1 13-ounce package **ROLD GOLD® Brand Pretzels**
3 tablespoons sugar
½ cup butter or margarine, melted

Crush pretzels very fine in blender or between waxed paper. Add sugar and butter or margarine. Mix thoroughly. Press ½ of mixture in 9" pie plate. Bake at 350°F. for 8 minutes. Cool.
    Pour in CHOCOLATE FILLING* and top with remaining pretzel mixture. Chill.

*CHOCOLATE FILLING

⅔ cup sugar
4 tablespoons cornstarch
2½ cups milk
3 3-ounce squares unsweetened chocolate, cut in small pieces
3 egg yolks, slightly beaten
1 teaspoon vanilla extract

Combine sugar, cornstarch, milk and chocolate in top of double boiler. Cook over boiling water until thickened, stirring constantly. Cover and cook 15 minutes. Stir part of hot chocolate mixture into egg yolks. Add to chocolate mixture. Mix thoroughly. Cool. Add vanilla extract and mix thoroughly.

CHOCOLATE-CHIFFON PIE

1 envelope unflavored gelatin
½ cup cold water
3 1-oz. squares unsweetened chocolate
1 cup **MARSHMALLOW FLUFF®**
½ cup milk
2 egg yolks, slightly beatened
½ tsp. vanilla extract
2 egg whites, at room temperature, beaten until stiff
½ cup heavy or whipping cream
1 graham cracker-crumb crust
¼ cup chopped nuts

In medium saucepan combine gelatin and water; let stand 1 minute. Over low heat, heat, stirring constantly, until gelatin is completely dissolved. Melt chocolate in double-boiler and stir in **FLUFF®** and milk. Add egg yolks and vanilla; mix well. Add dissolved gelatin. Chill. When thickened to the consistency of unbeaten egg whites, beat with mixer until foamy. Fold in beaten egg whites. Beat heavy or whipping cream until soft peaks form. Fold into chiffon mixture. Turn into pie crust. Sprinkle with nuts and chill until set.   *Makes 6-8 servings*

COCOA BAVARIAN PIE

9-inch crumb crust or baked pastry shell
1 envelope unflavored gelatin
1 cup milk
⅔ cup sugar
⅓ cup **HERSHEY'S®** Unsweetened Cocoa
2 tablespoons butter
⅔ cup milk
1 teaspoon vanilla
1 cup heavy cream
Garnish: Dessert topping, fresh fruit

MICROWAVE METHOD:
Prepare pie shell; set aside. Sprinkle gelatin onto 1 cup milk in medium micro-proof bowl; allow to soften a few minutes. Microwave on high 1 to 2 minutes or until gelatin is dissolved. Combine sugar and cocoa; whisk into gelatin mixture. Microwave on high 2 to 3 minutes or until mixture boils, stirring after 2 minutes. Remove from microwave; add butter and stir until melted. Blend in ⅔ cup milk and vanilla. Cool; chill, stirring occasionally, until almost set. Whip cream until stiff peaks form. Blend in whipped cream, pour into pie shell. Chill until firm. Garnish with dessert topping and fresh fruit, if desired.

CONVENTIONAL METHOD:
Sprinkle gelatin onto 1 cup milk in saucepan; allow to soften a few minutes. Add sugar and cocoa; cook on medium heat, stirring constantly, until mixture boils. Remove from heat and complete as in preceding recipe.

CHOCOLATE PIE
(Low Calorie/Low Sodium)

1 baked 9-inch pie shell (or graham cracker crumb crust)
2 envelopes **FEATHERWEIGHT®** Chocolate Pudding
3 cups skim milk
1 envelope **FEATHERWEIGHT®** Whipped Topping

Place bottom of double boiler containing water on high heat. Place 3 cups skim milk in top of double boiler. Add contents of Chocolate Pudding envelopes. Mix well and stir until simmer point (185°-195°F.) is reached. Continue stirring for 3 minutes.

Pour pudding mixture into baked pie crust, saving back ½ cup, and chill until partially set.   *(Continued)*

Prepare: Whipped Topping as directed on package.
Blend: 1 cup of Whipped Topping into remaining ½ cup of pudding. Pour into partially set pie. Chill until set (about 4 hours) then garnish with remaining Whipped Topping.

Approx.	Calories	Protein (Grams)	Fat (Grams)	Carbohydrate Grams	Sodium (Mgs)
⅛ section of pie with pastry crust-					
	165	5	8	18	195
With graham cracker crumb crust-					
	180	4	7	24	215

CHOCOLATE-PEANUT BUTTER PIE

1 package (21.5 ounces) **BETTY CROCKER®** Fudge Brownie Mix
½ cup chopped peanuts
Peanut Butter-Cream Cheese Filling*
1 square (1 ounce) semi-sweet chocolate, melted and cooled

Heat oven to 350°. Grease pie plate, 10 × 1½ inches. Prepare brownies as directed on package. Spread dough in pie plate; sprinkle with peanuts. Bake until center is set, 30 to 35 minutes; cool. Prepare Peanut Butter-Cream Cheese Filling. Spoon into pie shell. Refrigerate until chilled, about 3 hours. Drizzle with chocolate. Refrigerate any remaining pie.   *16 servings*

*PEANUT BUTTER-CREAM CHEESE FILLING

¼ cup sugar
⅓ cup peanut butter
1 tablespoon milk
1 package (8 ounces) cream cheese, softened
½ cup chilled whipping cream

Mix sugar, peanut butter, milk and cream cheese in large bowl until smooth. Beat whipping cream in chilled small bowl until stiff; fold into cream cheese mixture.

BUTTER CRUNCHY ESPRESSO PIE

Crust:

½ package pie crust mix
1 square (1 oz.) unsweetened chocolate, ground in rotary grater
¼ cup lumpfree light brown sugar
¾ cup finely chopped walnuts
1 teaspoon vanilla extract mixed with 1 tablespoon water

Start this pie as much as 2 days and at least 8 hours before serving: Stir together pie crust mix, grated chocolate, sugar and nuts with fork, eliminating lumps. Drizzle vanilla mixture over; stir and toss with fork as if making regular pastry. Fit a 12-inch square of aluminum foil into 9-inch oven glass pie plate, letting corners hang out. Line with pastry, pressing firmly in place. Bake in center of oven at 375°F. for 15 minutes. Cool. Freeze 45 to 60 minutes. Remove crust gently from plate; coax off aluminum foil. Return crust to plate. During this time, prepare filling.

Filling:

1 square (1 oz.) unsweetened chocolate, melted
1 stick (½ cup) softened butter
½ cup lumpfree light brown sugar
¼ cup granulated sugar
1 tablespoon instant **MEDAGLIA D'ORO®** Espresso Coffee
2 eggs

Cool chocolate. With portable electric mixer, beat butter until fluffy. Gradually beat in sugars and continue to beat 2 or 3 minutes. Scrape bowl occasionally. Add cooled chocolate and coffee; beat well. Add 1 egg at a time, beating 2 to 3 minutes after each. Pour into prepared crust. Chill 5 or 6 hours, up to 2 days. Shortly before serving, prepare topping*

Serve in wedges to 8 to 10

*TOPPING

Whip together 1 cup heavy cream, 1 tablespoon instant **MEDA-GLIA D'ORO® Espresso Coffee** and ¼ cup confectioners' sugar until soft standing peaks form. Use to decorate top of pie attractively. If desired, sprinkle with grated chocolate. Refrigerate.

FLUFFY FROZEN PEANUT BUTTER PIE

Peanut Butter Crust*
1¼ cups **REESE'S® Peanut Butter Chips**
1 package (3 ounces) cream cheese, softened
½ cup milk
½ cup confectioner's sugar
2 cups frozen non-dairy whipped topping, thawed

Prepare Peanut Butter Crust; set aside. In top of double boiler over hot water, melt peanut butter chips; cool slightly. Beat cream cheese until smooth; gradually add milk, blending well. Beat in sugar and melted peanut butter chips until smooth; fold in whipped topping. Spoon into prepared crust. Cover; freeze until firm.

*PEANUT BUTTER CRUST

¾ cup **REESE'S® Peanut Butter Chips**
1 cup vanilla wafer or graham cracker crumbs
5 tablespoons butter or margarine

Chop peanut butter chips in blender or food processor, or with nut chopper; in 9-inch pie pan, combine chips and crumbs. Drizzle with melted butter or margarine; mix well. Press onto bottom and up sides of pie pan; freeze.

CALAVO® COCONUT CREAM PIE

Mix 1 box (4¾ oz.) vanilla pudding. Cool slightly. Add 1 cup fresh shredded **CALAVO® Coconut**. Pour into baked 9-inch pie shell. Cool. Cover with meringue made of 3 stiffly beaten egg whites, 6 tablespoons sugar. Sprinkle ½ cup shredded coconut on meringue. Bake in moderate oven (300°) for 12-15 minutes.

COCONUT CREAM PIE

1 (9-inch) baked pastry shell
¾ cup flaked coconut
½ cup milk
¼ cup cornstarch
Dash salt
1 (15-ounce) can **COCO LÓPEZ® Cream of Coconut**
2 egg yolks, beaten
1 cup (½ pint) whipped cream, whipped

Toast ¼ cup coconut; set aside. In medium saucepan, combine milk, cornstarch and salt, stirring until cornstarch dissolves. Add cream of coconut and egg yolks. Over medium heat, cook and stir until mixture is very thick and smooth; remove from heat. Stir in untoasted coconut; cool. Chill thoroughly. Fold in whipped cream. Turn into prepared pastry shell. Garnish with toasted coconut. Chill at least 3 hours. Refrigerate leftovers.

Makes one 9-inch pie

FRESH COCONUT CREAM PIE

10-inch baked pie shell
6 ounces **COCO CASA® Cream of Coconut**
¼ cup milk
10 ounces mini-marshmallows
3 cups heavy cream, whipped stiff
2 cups coconut flakes (fresh or canned)

Mix Cream of Coconut with milk. Add marshmallows. Cook over low heat until marshmallows melt. Cool in bowl and refrigerate 1 hour or until mixture starts to jell. Beat jelled mixture until frothy with electric mixer. Carefully, fold in whipped cream. Blend in 1 cup flaked coconut by hand. Pour into baked pie shell. Sprinkle remaining cup of flaked coconut (toast if desired) over pie and refrigerate at least 6 hours before serving.

RHUBARB CREAM PIE

3 cups rhubarb pieces (1-inch or less)
2 eggs, beaten
3 tablespoons water
1 can (14-oz.) **DAIRY SWEET™ Sweetened Condensed Milk**
¼ teaspoon nutmeg
1 unbaked pastry crust (deep 9-inch)

Spread rhubarb over crust. Beat eggs and water until frothy; stir in **DAIRY SWEET™** and nutmeg. Pour mixture over rhubarb. Bake in 400° oven 15 minutes; reduce heat to 350° and bake 35 minutes longer or until custard is set. Serve at room temperature or chilled.

CLARK® BAR WHIPPED CREAM PIE

1 (9-inch) Vanilla Wafer Crumb Crust*
16 marshmallows, quartered
⅓ cup milk
3 **CLARK® Bars**, finely chopped
1 teaspoon vanilla
1 cup whipping cream, whipped

Combine marshmallows and milk in top of double boiler. Heat over boiling water until marshmallows are melted. Cool. Fold in candy, vanilla and whipped cream. Pour into crumb crust. Chill thoroughly. Garnish with sweetened whipped cream and coarsely chopped candy.

Makes 6 servings

*VANILLA WAFER CRUMB CRUST

1⅓ cups finely crushed vanilla wafer crumbs
⅓ cup melted butter

Combine ingredients. Press onto bottom and sides of buttered 9-inch pie pan. Bake at 375° for 5-8 minutes. Cool.

FROZEN MACAROON PIE

1 (9-inch) baked pastry shell, cooled or graham cracker crumb crust
1 pint orange sherbet, softened
1 cup (½ pint) whipping cream
½ cup firmly-packed **COLONIAL® Light Golden Brown Sugar**
1 cup coarsely crushed crisp macaroon cookies
¾ cup toasted coconut
½ cup chopped toasted almonds

Spread sherbet in bottom of pastry shell. Freeze while preparing topping. In small mixer bowl, beat cream, slowly adding sugar, until stiff; fold in cookies, ½ cup coconut and the almonds. Spread on top of sherbet; garnish with remaining coconut. Freeze until firm.

Makes one 9-inch pie

BUTTERSCOTCH CHIFFON PIE IN CHOCOLATE CRUST

Crust:
⅔ cup semi-sweet chocolate chips or 4-oz. bar sweet chocolate
3 tablespoons butter
⅔ cup finely chopped walnuts or pecans*
1 cup crisp rice cereal

Melt chocolate and butter over hot water; stir until smooth. Remove. Add nuts and cereal, mixing well. Line 9-inch pie plate with foil. Spread chocolate mixture evenly on bottom and sides of pie plate. Chill until firm. Remove pie shell, peel off foil. Replace chocolate shell in pie plate. Chill until filling is made.

*If desired, the crust can be made with 1⅔ cups rice cereal and omit the nuts.

Filling:
1 envelope unflavored gelatin
¼ cup cold milk
1 cup milk, heated to boiling
¼ cup **DOMINO® BROWNULATED®** Sugar
1 teaspoon vanilla
2 egg whites
¼ teaspoon salt
¼ cup **DOMINO® BROWNULATED®** Sugar
½ cup heavy cream, whipped

In medium bowl, mix gelatin with cold milk; let stand 3 minutes. Add boiling milk; stir until gelatin is dissolved. Add ¼ cup sugar and vanilla; mix until sugar is dissolved. Chill until mixture begins to mound. Beat egg whites with salt and ¼ cup sugar until stiff. Fold into gelatin mixture. Fold in whipped cream. Pour into chocolate crust; chill until firm, about 2 hours. Garnish with sweetened whipped cream and chocolate curls or nuts, if desired.

Yield: one 9-inch pie

LIME CHIFFON PIE

Pastry:
1⅓ cups sifted all-purpose flour
½ teaspoon salt
½ cup **CRISCO®** Shortening
2 to 3 tablespoons cold water

Preheat oven to 425°. Combine flour and salt in mixing bowl. Cut in **CRISCO®** with pastry blender or 2 knives until mixture is uniform (mixture should be fairly coarse). Sprinkle with water, 1 tablespoon at a time; toss lightly with fork. When all water has been added, work dough into firm ball. Press into flat circle with smooth edges. Roll out on lightly floured surface into a circle about ⅛-inch thick and about 1½ inches larger than inverted pie plate. Gently ease dough into 9-inch pie plate, taking care not to stretch dough. Trim ½-inch beyond edge of plate. Fold under to make double thickness around rim. Flute edge of pastry as desired. Prick bottom and sides of shell with fork. Bake at 425° 10 to 15 minutes or until lightly browned. Cool.

Filling:
1 envelope unflavored gelatin
¼ cup cold water
4 eggs, separated
⅔ cup sugar
2 teaspoons grated lime peel
½ cup lime juice
¼ teaspoon salt
2 to 3 drops green food color
½ cup sugar

Sprinkle gelatin over cold water to soften. Beat egg yolks slightly in small saucepan. Stir in ⅔ cup sugar, lime peel and juice and salt. Cook over medium heat, stirring constantly, 6 to 8 minutes or until mixture is slightly thickened. Remove from heat, add softened gelatin; stir until gelatin is dissolved. Mix in food color a drop at a time. Chill in refrigerator or bowl of ice water until mixture mounds slightly when dropped from a spoon, about 25 to 40 minutes. Beat egg whites until frothy. Add ½ cup sugar gradually, beating constantly until stiff peaks form. Spread over thickened gelatin; fold whites into gelatin. Spoon into pastry shell; chill until firm.

One 9-inch pie

LEMON CHIFFON PIE
(Low Calorie/Low Fat)

1 envelope unflavored gelatin
¾ cup sugar, divided
½ cup water
¼ cup lemon juice
2 eggs, separated
1 packet **BUTTER BUDS®**
1 teaspoon grated lemon peel
1 8-inch Low-Sodium Pie Crust*
Lemon slices

In top of double boiler, combine gelatin and ½ cup sugar. Beat in water, lemon juice, and egg yolks. Heat, stirring constantly, until hot. Remove ½ cup of hot mixture to small bowl and slowly beat in **BUTTER BUDS®**, mixing well. Put **BUTTER BUDS®** mixture back into double boiler. Cook, stirring constantly, until mixture thickens and coats a metal spoon. Remove from heat and add lemon peel. Cool slightly. Chill until thickened but not firm. Beat egg whites until foamy; gradually add remaining sugar, beating until stiff. Fold egg whites into chilled gelatin mixture. Pour into 8-inch pie crust. Garnish with lemon slices. Chill several hours, until firm.

Note: By using **BUTTER BUDS®** instead of butter in this recipe, you have saved 94 calories and 35 mg cholesterol per serving.

Per Serving (⅛ of pie): Calories: 105; Fat: 1g

*LOW-SODIUM PIE CRUST

1 cup sifted all-purpose flour
1 packet **BUTTER BUDS®**
¼ teaspoon cinnamon
⅛ teaspoon mace
1 teaspoon sesame seeds
2 tablespoons plus 1 teaspoon vegetable oil
2 to 3 tablespoons ice water

Blend flour with **BUTTER BUDS®**, cinnamon, mace, and sesame seeds. Add oil gradually, mixing into flour with a fork. When all of the oil has been added, work mixture lightly between fingertips until mixture is the size of small peas. Gradually add just enough ice water until dough is moist enough to hold together. Do not overwork dough. Form into a ball and roll out on floured surface with floured rolling pin, to a circle 1 inch larger than inverted 8- or 9-inch pie pan. Carefully transfer pastry to pie plate. Press dough into bottom and sides of pan, gently patting out air pockets. Preheat oven to 450°F. Prick bottom and sides of pastry with fork. Bake 8 to 10 minutes, or until lightly golden brown. Cool before using.

Per Serving (⅛ of crust): Calories: 95; Fat: 4g

LEMON LIGHT YOGURT PIE

Crust:
1⅔ cups finely crushed **QUAKER® 100% Natural Cereal**, original (about 2 cups cereal)
⅓ cup firmly packed brown sugar
¼ cup butter or margarine, melted

Filling:
1 envelope unflavored gelatin
⅓ cup plus 2 tablespoons granulated sugar
¼ teaspoon salt
2 eggs, separated
1 cup water
1 8-oz. carton (1 cup) lemon flavored yogurt

Heat oven to 350°F. For crust, combine all ingredients, mixing well. Reserve ¼ cup cereal mixture for topping; press remaining mixture onto bottom and side of greased 9-inch pie plate. Bake at 350°F. for 8 to 10 minutes or until golden brown. Press bottom and side of crust into place with spoon while still warm, if necessary. Cool.

For filling, thoroughly mix gelatin, ⅓ cup sugar and salt in saucepan. Beat together egg yolks and water; stir into gelatin mixture. Cook over medium heat just until mixture comes to a boil, stirring constantly. Pour mixture into bowl; chill, stirring occasionally, until mixture mounds slightly when dropped from a spoon. Beat egg whites at medium speed on electric mixer until foamy. Beat at high speed while gradually adding remaining 2 tablespoons sugar, until stiff peaks form. Fold beaten egg whites and yogurt into gelatin mixture. Pour into prepared crust. Sprinkle with reserved cereal mixture; chill 3 to 4 hours or until firm. Garnish with lemon slices and mint leaves, if desired.

Makes 9-inch pie

FLUFFY ORANGE-LEMON PIE

Crust:
¾ cup **KELLOGG'S® ALL-BRAN®** or **KELLOGG'S® BRAN BUDS® Cereal**
¾ cup finely chopped nuts
¼ cup margarine or butter, melted
3 tablespoons sifted confectioner's sugar

Filling:
1 can (5.3 oz., ⅔ cup) evaporated milk
Water
1 can (11 oz., 1⅓ cups) mandarin orange segments, drained, reserving syrup
1 package (3 oz.) lemon flavor gelatin dessert

1. Crush **KELLOGG'S® ALL-BRAN® Cereal** to crumbs. Stir in nuts, margarine and sugar. Press mixture evenly in 9-inch glass pie plate to form crust.
2. Bake at 375°F for 6 to 8 minutes or until lightly browned. Cool completely. Chill.
3. Pour evaporated milk into small bowl of electric mixer. Place in freezer until ice crystals form around edge.
4. Meanwhile, add water to reserved mandarin orange syrup to measure 1¼ cups liquid. Bring to boil in small saucepan. Add gelatin, stirring until dissolved. Pour into large bowl of electric mixer. Chill until slightly thickened.
5. Beat thickened gelatin until frothy. Add orange segments, reserving some for garnish. Beat well. Beat milk until soft peaks form. Fold into gelatin mixture. Pour into cereal crust. Chill until firm. Garnish with reserved orange segments.

® Kellogg Company

Yield: 8 servings

PEACH CHIFFON PIE

1 envelope unflavored gelatin
1¼ cups **DR PEPPER®**
¼ teaspoon salt
½ cup sugar
3 eggs, separated
1 tablespoon lemon juice
¼ cup sugar
1¼ cups drained canned sliced peaches, diced
1 (9-inch) baked pie shell

Combine gelatin with **DR PEPPER®**. Set aside. Combine salt, ½ cup sugar and beaten egg yolks in top of double boiler. Stir in gelatin mixture. Cook and stir over hot water until slightly thickened. Add lemon juice. Chill until partially set, stirring occasionally. Beat egg whites until foamy. Add ¼ cup sugar gradually, beating until stiff peaks are formed. Fold in gelatin mixture. Then fold in peaches. Chill until mixture mounds when dropped from a spoon. Pour into cold pie shell. Chill until firm. Serve plain or garnish with whipped cream and additional sliced peaches.

Yield: 1 (9-inch) pie

GLAZED FRESH FRUIT PIE

½ cup sugar
3 tablespoons **ARGO®/KINGSFORD'S® Corn Starch**
1½ cups apple juice
1 teaspoon grated lemon rind
¼ cup lemon juice
4 cups cut-up apples
1 cup orange sections
1 cup green grapes, halved
Cookie Crust Pastry*

In 2-quart saucepan mix sugar and corn starch. Gradually stir in apple juice until smooth. Stirring constantly, bring to boil over medium heat and boil 1 minute. Remove from heat, stir in lemon rind and juice. Cool completely. Gently fold in fruit. Turn into pastry shell. Refrigerate 4 hours or until set.

Makes 8 servings

*COOKIE CRUST PASTRY

Stir ¼ cup **MAZOLA® Corn Oil Margarine** to soften; mix in ¼ cup sugar and 1 egg yolk. With pastry blender gradually mix in 1 cup flour until crumbs form. Press firmly into bottom and sides of 9-inch pie plate. Bake in 400°F oven about 10 minutes or until edge is browned. Cool.

PEANUT BUTTER-ICE CREAM TARTS

½ cup whipping cream
1 quart vanilla ice cream
½ cup **JIF® Crunchy Peanut Butter**
8 baked tart shells

Whip cream till soft peaks form. Stir ice cream to soften. Quickly fold **JIF®** and whipped cream into softened ice cream. Spoon into tart shells. Freeze about 5 hours or till firm. Remove from freezer 10 minutes before serving. If desired, sprinkle with chopped peanuts.

Makes 8 servings

FRUIT GLACÉ PIE

1 **KEEBLER® READY-CRUST® Graham Cracker Pie Crust**
1 package (3 ounces) cream cheese, softened
2 tablespoons honey
1 medium banana, sliced
2 cups prepared mixed fruit: sliced peaches, seedless grapes, blueberries, strawberries, sweet cherries (pitted and halved), melon (cut in ½-inch pieces), canned pineapple chunks (well-drained), canned mandarin orange sections (well-drained)
1 package (4-serving size) peach flavor gelatin
¾ cup boiling water
2 cups ice cubes

Beat cream cheese and honey until smooth and creamy. Spread on bottom and sides of crust, covering completely. Chill while preparing fruit. Wash and drain fresh fruit; pat dry. Cut or slice large pieces. Layer banana slices in bottom of crust. Arrange mixed fruit decoratively on top. Prepare gelatin using quick-set method as follows: Dissolve gelatin using only ¾ cup boiling water; add ice cubes and stir until gelatin is thickened, about 3-4 minutes. Remove unmelted ice. Spoon gelatin over fruit to glaze. Do not overfill. Chill pie until set, about 1 hour.

Note: To use frozen fruit, prepare as follows:

Layer banana slices in bottom of crust. Prepare gelatin using quick-set method by dissolving gelatin in ¾ cup boiling water; add a 10 oz. package of frozen mixed fruit and stir until thickened, about 3-4 minutes. Pour into crust. Chill pie until set, about 1 hour.

NO-BAKE FRESH FRUIT TART

8 ozs. cream cheese, softened
1 tablespoon grated orange rind
2 tablespoons orange juice
½ cup **DOMINO® Confectioners 10-X Powdered Sugar**
8-inch ready-to-fill crumb crust or 6 individual crumb tart shells (bought)
2 to 3 cups fresh whole berries, seedless green grapes, pitted sweet cherries, sliced peaches, nectarines, plums, etc.

Beat cheese, rind, juice, and sugar together until fluffy. Fill pie crust or tart shells with cheese mixture. Chill thoroughly. Top with fruit. Add 1 tablespoon lemon juice to peaches or nectarines to prevent discoloration. Sift more sugar generously over fruit.

Yields 6 servings

Note: For an especially festive tart, stand berries with tips up, or use circles of different fruits. Green grapes, strawberries, and blueberries make a festive combination.

VARIATION:

BUSY COOKS' DESSERT

A simple crustless version of the No-Bake Fresh Fruit Tart. Mix the cheese, rind, 4 tablespoons juice, and sugar as directed. Keep at room temperature. Arrange one or more fruits in dessert dishes, chill. At serving time sprinkle fruit with more sugar and top with cheese sauce. Garnish with grated orange rind if desired.

BASIC MARGARINE PASTRY (SINGLE CRUST)

1¼ cups unsifted flour
⅛ teaspoon salt
½ cup **MAZOLA® Corn Oil Margarine**
2 tablespoons cold water

In medium bowl mix flour and salt. With pastry blender or 2 knives cut in margarine until fine crumbs form. (Do not be afraid of overmixing.) Sprinkle water over mixture while tossing to blend well. Press dough firmly into ball with hands. (If mixture seems crumbly, work with hands until it will hold together.) Flatten dough slightly and on lightly floured surface roll out to 12-inch circle. Fit loosely into 9-inch pie plate. Trim ½-inch beyond rim of plate. Flute edge.

VARIATION:

BASIC MARGARINE PASTRY (DOUBLE CRUST)

Use 2 cups minus 2 tablespoons unsifted flour, ¼ teaspoon salt, ⅔ cup corn oil margarine, and 3 tablespoons cold water. Prepare as in Single Crust, divide dough almost in half. Flatten larger portion slightly. On lightly floured surface roll out to 12-inch circle. Fit loosely into 9-inch pie plate. Trim dough ½-inch beyond rim of pan. Fill as desired. Roll out remaining dough for top crust or for lattice strips. For Double Crust, cut slits to permit steam to escape during baking and place over filling. Trim ½-inch beyond rim of pan. Fold edges of both crusts under; seal and flute. For lattice top, see directions in Blueberry Lattice Pie, and Ginger Peach Lattice Pie (See Index).

GINGER PEACH LATTICE PIE

1 recipe Basic Margarine Pastry (Double Crust) (See Index)
¾ cup sugar
3 tablespoons **ARGO®/KINGSFORD'S® Corn Starch**
6 cups peeled pitted sliced peaches (about 12)
1 tablespoon lemon juice
1 teaspoon grated fresh ginger or ¼ teaspoon ground ginger

Line 9-inch pie plate with one-half pastry rolled to ⅛-inch thickness, allowing 1-inch overhang. In large bowl stir together sugar and corn starch. Toss with peach slices, lemon juice and ginger until well coated. Turn into pie plate. Roll remaining pastry into 12-inch circle. Cut into 10 (½-inch) strips with pastry wheel or knife. Place 5 of the strips over filling. Weave lattice crust with remaining strips by folding back alternate strips as each cross strip is added. Fold trimmed edge of lower crust over ends of strips; seal and flute. Sprinkle top of pastry lightly with sugar before baking. Bake in 425°F oven 40 to 50 minutes or until bubbly and crust is brown.

Makes 1 (9-inch) pie

VARIATION:

DEEP DISH GINGER PEACH PIE

Follow recipe for Ginger Peach Lattice Pie eliminating bottom pastry. Turn peach mixture into 9-inch regular or deep dish pie plate or 1½-quart casserole dish. Roll out Basic Margarine Pastry (Single Crust) (See Index) 1-inch larger than pie plate. Cut slits in top for steam to escape. Cover pie with pastry. Flute edges. Bake in 425°F oven 30 to 35 minutes or until crust is brown.

Makes 1 (9-inch) pie

DEEP DISH BLUEBERRY PIE

¾ cup sugar
3 tablespoons **ARGO®/KINGSFORD'S® Corn Starch**
2 pints fresh blueberries (about 6 cups)
1 teaspoon grated lemon rind
1 recipe Basic Margarine Pastry (Single Crust) (See Index)

In large bowl stir together sugar and corn starch. Add blueberries and lemon rind; toss to coat well. Turn into 9-inch regular or deep dish pie plate or 1½-quart casserole dish. Roll out pastry 1 inch larger than pie plate. Cut slits in top for steam to escape. Cover pie with pastry. Flute edges. Bake in 425°F oven 30 to 35 minutes or until bubbly and crust is brown. *Makes 1 (9-inch) pie*

VARIATION:

BLUEBERRY LATTICE PIE

Follow recipe for Deep Dish Blueberry Pie. Use 1 recipe Basic Margarine Pastry (Double Crust) (See Index). Line 9-inch pie plate with one-half pastry rolled to ⅛-inch thickness, allowing 1-inch overhang. Turn blueberry mixture into pie plate. Roll remaining pastry into 12-inch circle. Cut into 10 (½-inch) strips with pastry wheel or knife. Place 5 of the strips over filling. Weave lattice crust with remaining strips by folding back alternate strips as each cross is added. Fold trimmed edge of lower crust over ends of strips; seal and flute. Sprinkle top of pastry lightly with sugar before baking. Bake in 425°F oven 35 to 45 minutes or until bubbly and crust is browned. *Makes 1 (9-inch) pie*

APPLE SNOW PIE

Crust:
1 Stay Fresh Pack **NABISCO** or **HONEY MAID Graham Crackers**, finely rolled (about 1⅔ cups)
¼ cup granulated sugar
⅓ cup butter or margarine, softened

Filling:
1 envelope unflavored gelatin
¼ cup water
3 eggs, separated
⅓ cup granulated sugar
1½ cups unsweetened applesauce
1 tablespoon lemon juice
1½ teaspoons lemon rind

Garnish:
¾ cup seedless green grapes, halved
1 (4⅝-ounce) can **SNACK MATE American Pasteurized Process Cheese Spread**

1. MAKE CRUST:
Preheat oven to 375°F. In medium bowl, using fork or pastry blender, combine graham cracker crumbs and sugar; blend in butter or margarine. Using back of large spoon, press mixture firmly into 9-inch pie plate to form crust. Bake 8 minutes; let stand on wire rack to cool.

2. MAKE FILLING:
In small saucepan, sprinkle gelatin over water; let stand 5 minutes to soften. Heat gently over very low heat, stirring to dissolve. In small bowl, beat egg yolks with a little hot gelatin mixture; return mixture to saucepan. Heat gently 30 seconds, stirring constantly.

3. In large bowl, with electric mixer at high speed, beat egg whites until soft peaks form. Gradually add sugar, 2 tablespoons at a time, beating until egg whites are stiff.

4. In medium bowl, blend applesauce, lemon juice and lemon

rind; stir in egg-yolk mixture. Using a rubber spatula, gently fold in egg-white mixture. Spoon evenly into pie shell; chill 3 to 4 hours or until firm.

5. TO GARNISH:
Decorate top of pie with alternating circles of grape halves and **SNACK MATE Cheese** rosettes. *Makes 6 to 8 servings*

APPLE CUSTARD PIE

1 (9-inch) unbaked pie shell with a high fluted rim, or a regular 10-inch pie shell
1 can (21-oz.) **WILDERNESS® Apple Fruit Filling**
2 Tbsp. brown sugar
3 eggs
2 cups whipping cream

Spoon half the can of Apple Fruit Filling over bottom of unbaked pie shell. Sprinkle with 1 Tbsp. of the brown sugar. Add remaining Apple Fruit Filling; sprinkle with remaining 1 Tbsp. brown sugar. Beat eggs until thick and lemon colored; add 1 cup of the cream and blend thoroughly. Pour egg mixture over the Apple Fruit Filling. Bake at 400°F for 30-35 minutes, or until custard sets. Whip remaining 1 cup of cream; sweeten to taste. Serve with warm pie.

STREUSEL APPLE TART

1 (6-ounce) package (2 cups) **SUN·MAID® Dried Apple Chunks**, medium chopped
1 cup apple juice
1 egg
1 cup dairy sour cream
½ cup granulated sugar
2 tablespoons all-purpose flour
1 teaspoon grated orange peel
1 (9-inch) unbaked pie shell
Streusel Topping*

In a medium saucepan, bring apples and juice to a boil; reduce heat to low. Cook, stirring until liquid is absorbed. Cool. In a medium bowl, stir together beaten egg, sour cream, sugar, flour and orange peel. Fold in apples. Pour into pie shell and sprinkle with Streusel Topping. Bake at 450 degrees F for 10 minutes; lower heat to 350 degrees F and bake 25 to 30 minutes longer or until browned. *Makes 8 servings*

*STREUSEL TOPPING
Combine ½ cup all-purpose flour, ⅓ cup packed brown sugar, and ½ teaspoon cinnamon. Cut in ¼ cup butter or margarine, softened. Stir in ⅓ cup finely chopped **DIAMOND® Walnuts**.

OPEN FACE APPLE PIE

1 one pound loaf **BRIDGFORD Frozen Bread Dough**
5 medium apples peeled, stewed, and sweetened or one (21-oz.) can apple pie filling
½ stick butter or margarine, melted
4 Tablespoons sugar
2 Tablespoons cinnamon
¼ cup chopped nuts

Let frozen bread thaw and rise in loaf pan until 1 inch above pan. Knead down; roll out to rectangle 9 × 12 inches. Spread apples on dough; pour butter over apples. Sprinkle cinnamon, sugar, and nuts over apples. Roll in jelly roll fashion. Cut 1-inch pieces and place flat side down in greased baking pan, 9 × 12 inches. Bake in 350° oven for 45 minutes. *Yield: 12 servings*

FRENCH APPLE PECAN PIE

1 (9-inch) baked pie shell
1 can (21-oz.) **WILDERNESS**® **French Apple Fruit Filling**
½ cup all-purpose flour
½ cup brown sugar
½ tsp. cinnamon
4 Tbsp. butter or margarine
¼ cup chopped pecans

Pour French Apple Fruit Filling in baked pie shell. Combine flour, brown sugar and cinnamon; cut in butter with a fork until well blended. Sprinkle over French Apple Fruit Filling. Top with chopped pecans. Bake at 350°F for 25-30 minutes.

APPLE PIE

1 recipe double crust pastry*
¾ cup sugar
1 tablespoon **ARGO**®/**KINGSFORD'S**® **Corn Starch**
1 teaspoon ground cinnamon
2 pounds apples, peeled, cored, sliced (about 6 cups)
1 tablespoon lemon juice
1 tablespoon **MAZOLA**® **Corn Oil Margarine**

Line 9-inch pie plate with one-half pastry rolled to ⅛-inch thickness, allowing 1-inch overhang. In large bowl stir together sugar, corn starch and cinnamon. Toss with apple slices and lemon juice until coated. Turn into pie plate. Dot with margarine. Roll remaining pastry to 12-inch circle. Make several slits to permit steam to escape. Cover pie with pastry; seal and flute edge. Bake in 425°F oven 50 minutes or until crust is golden and apples are tender.
Makes 1 (9-inch) pie

*DOUBLE CRUST PASTRY

½ cup **MAZOLA**® **Corn Oil**
¼ cup skim milk
2 cups unsifted flour
1 teaspoon salt

In measuring cup stir together corn oil and milk. In large bowl stir together flour and salt. Add corn oil mixture stirring constantly with fork. With hands form into ball. Divide dough almost in half. Flatten larger portion slightly. Roll into 12-inch circle between 2 sheets waxed paper. Peel off top paper. Place dough in 9-inch pie pan, paper side up. Peel off paper; fit pastry loosely into pan. Fill as desired. Trim dough ½-inch beyond rim of pan. Roll out remaining dough between 2 sheets waxed paper. Place over filling. Peel off paper; cut slits to permit steam to escape. Trim ½-inch beyond rim of pan. Fold edges of both crusts under; seal and flute. Bake pie according to filling used.

VARIATIONS:

APPLE CRESCENTS

Follow recipe for Apple Pie. Use 2 recipes double crust pastry. Omit margarine. On lightly floured surface roll out pastry ¼ at a time to ⅛-inch thickness. Cut each ¼ into 3 (7-inch) circles. Place ½ cup filling on one-half of each circle. Fold dough over filling to form crescent. Seal edge with fork; cut slits in top. Place on cookie sheets. Bake in 425°F oven 15 minutes or until browned.
Makes 12

APPLE CRANBERRY PIE

Follow recipe for Apple Pie. Increase corn starch to 2 tablespoons. Omit lemon juice. Toss 1 cup cranberries, halved, with apple slices. Turn into pastry-lined pie plate. Dot with margarine. Roll remaining pastry into 12-inch circle. Cut into 10 (½-inch) strips with pastry wheel or knife. Place 5 of the strips across filling. Weave lattice crust with remaining strips by folding back alternate strips as each cross strip is added. Fold trimmed edge of lower crusts over ends of strips; seal and flute. Sprinkle top of pastry lightly with sugar before baking. Bake in 400°F oven 15 minutes. Reduce heat to 350°F and bake 45 minutes longer or until bubbly and apples are tender.

APPLE BLUEBERRY PIE

Follow recipe for Apple Pie. Use 1¾ pounds apples (5 cups sliced). Increase corn starch to 3 tablespoons. Toss apples with 1 cup blueberries. Turn into pastry-lined pie plate. Dot with margarine. Continue as directed for Apple Pie.

To freeze uncooked pie: Follow recipe for Apple or Apple Cranberry Pie. Add 1 additional tablespoon corn starch to pie filling. Follow recipe cutting steam slits in pastry, as directed. (If frozen without slits, cutting frozen pie breaks pastry and frozen pie will have to be cooked slightly, then slits cut.) Wrap unbaked pie in plastic wrap or bag, foil or other moisture vapor-proof material. Seal with tape, label and freeze. Frozen unbaked pie may be held in freezer up to 4 months. Bake as directed in recipe for Apple or Apple Cranberry Pie, increasing time 15 to 20 minutes. If edge of pie begins to brown too much, cover with a strip of foil.

CALIFORNIA DREAMING AVOCADO PIE

1 **KEEBLER**® **READY-CRUST**® **Graham Cracker Pie Crust**
1 3-oz. package lemon gelatin
1 8-oz. container vanilla yogurt
1 11-oz. can mandarin oranges, drained
2 tablespoons sliced almonds
2 ripe avocados, peeled and mashed

Prepare gelatin according to package instructions. Refrigerate until slightly thickened (egg white consistency); add yogurt and refrigerate until firm, about 30 minutes. Add avocados to mixture. Beat with electric mixer until mixture is fluffy, fold in oranges, reserving 10 for garnish, and refrigerate until mixture is spoonable. Mound into pie crust and garnish with sliced almonds and remaining oranges.
Serves 8

PEACHES AND CREAM PIE

1 (9-inch) **BANQUET**® **Deep Dish Frozen Pie Crust Shell**
1 (9-inch) **BANQUET**® **Frozen Pie Crust Shell**
5 to 6 medium peaches, sliced (about 4 cups)*
1 cup sugar, divided
5 tablespoons flour
⅛ teaspoon salt
½ cup dairy sour cream
¼ teaspoon cinnamon

Thaw frozen deep dish pie crust at room temperature for 10 minutes. Pop other frozen pie crust out of foil pan. Place upside down on waxed paper to thaw, about 10 minutes. Spread sliced peaches in bottom of deep dish pie crust. Place all but 2 tablespoons sugar in small mixing bowl. Add flour, salt and sour cream; stir until smooth. Spread evenly over peaches.

Flatten thawed pie crust on waxed paper by gently pressing down. Place on top of pie. Crimp edges to seal. Combine cinnamon and remaining 2 tablespoons sugar. Sprinkle on top of pie. Cut several 1-inch slits in top crust. Place a 2-inch strip of foil around crimped edges to prevent over browning. Bake pie on cookie sheet in 400°F oven for 40 to 45 minutes, until golden brown. Cool 30 minutes before serving.　　*Makes 6 servings*

*Substitution: Use 2 cans (1 lb. ea.) sliced peaches, drained or 1 bag (20 oz.) sliced frozen peaches for fresh sliced peaches.

APRICOT PINEAPPLE PIE

1 (8¼-ounce) can crushed pineapple, undrained
⅔ cup granulated sugar
2 teaspoons cornstarch
1 tablespoon butter or margarine
1½ cups drained, cooked **SUN • MAID®** or
　SUNSWEET® Dried Apricots, cut in quarters
1 (8-inch) unbaked pastry shell and strips for lattice
　top*

In a medium saucepan, combine pineapple, sugar, cornstarch and butter. Heat to boiling, stirring often; remove from heat and stir in apricots. Turn into pastry-lined 8-inch pie pan. Top with lattice pastry strips. Flute edge, building up a rim. Bake at 425 degrees F for 35 to 40 minutes or until well browned. Cool before cutting.
Makes one 8-inch pie

*Recipe for 9-inch pie shell is enough for 8-inch shell and lattice strips.

TROPICAL FRUIT PIE

¼ cup margarine or butter, melted
1 (7-ounce) package flaked coconut (about 2⅔ cups)
1 envelope unflavored gelatin
1 (8-ounce) can crushed pineapple in juice, well
　drained, reserving liquid
¾ cup **COCO LÓPEZ® Cream of Coconut**
¼ cup light Puerto Rican rum
2 (3-ounce) packages cream cheese, softened
1 cup (½ pint) whipping cream, stiffly whipped
Fruit slices

Preheat oven to 350°. In 9-inch pie plate, mix together margarine and coconut. Reserving 2 tablespoons coconut, press remainder firmly on bottom and up side of plate. Bake 15 minutes or until edge is golden. Cool thoroughly. Toast remaining coconut; set aside. In small saucepan, sprinkle gelatin over reserved pineapple liquid to soften. Cook and stir over low heat until dissolved. Stir together gelatin mixture, cream of coconut and rum. In large mixer bowl, beat cheese until smooth and fluffy. Add rum mixture; beat until smooth. Stir in pineapple. Fold in whipped cream. Chill 20 to 25 minutes. Turn into prepared crust. Garnish with remaining coconut and fruit. Chill thoroughly, about 3 hours. Refrigerate leftovers.　　*Makes one 9-inch pie*

PINEAPPLE STRAWBERRY PIE

1 cup sugar
¼ cup **ARGO®/KINGSFORD'S® Corn Starch**
3 cups sliced strawberries
2 cups cubed fresh pineapple
1 unbaked (9-inch) pastry shell
½ cup unsifted flour
⅓ cup sugar
⅓ cup corn oil margarine
⅓ cup shredded coconut

In large bowl stir together sugar and corn starch. Add strawberries and pineapple; toss to coat. Turn into pastry shell. In medium bowl stir together flour and sugar. With pastry blender or 2 knives, cut

in margarine until coarse crumbs form. Stir in coconut. Sprinkle evenly over pie. Bake in 425°F oven 35 to 40 minutes or until bubbly and crust is brown.　　*Makes 1 (9-inch) pie*

STRAWBERRIES 'N CREAM PIE

18 to 20 brown edge cookies or vanilla or chocolate
　wafers
3 pints vanilla or strawberry ice cream
1 jar (12 ounces) *well chilled* **CRYSTAL® Strawberry**
　Preserves
1 cup thinly sliced fresh strawberries, *chilled*

Line bottom and sides of a buttered 9-inch pie plate with cookies or wafers. Chill in freezer. Spoon 1½ pints of ice cream over wafers. Drizzle ½ of the preserves over ice cream and spoon remaining ice cream over top. Store in freezer until 1 to 2 hours before serving time. Remove pie from freezer. Combine remaining preserves and berries and spoon over pie. Return to freezer until serving time.　　*Yield: One 9-inch pie, about 8 servings*

STRAWBERRY MARBLE PIE

Crust:
1¼ cups graham cracker crumbs
¼ cup sugar
¼ cup butter or margarine (softened)
Filling:
1 package (8-oz.) cream cheese (softened)
2 packages (1½-oz. each) whipped topping mix
1 cup powdered sugar
1 can (21-oz.) **WILDERNESS® Strawberry Fruit**
　Filling

Mix crust ingredients. Press firmly in bottom of a 10-inch pie plate. Bake at 375° F for 8 minutes. Cool.
　Blend softened cream cheese and powdered sugar together. Whip topping mix according to directions on package. Blend cheese mixture and whipped topping together. Gently fold in Strawberry Fruit Filling only until marbleized. Pile high in baked pie shell. Refrigerate at least 8 hours before serving.

JOY CHOY PIE

3 egg whites
¼ teaspoon cream of tartar
1 cup sugar
1 teaspoon vanilla
1 cup **LA CHOY® Chow Mein Noodles**, crushed
1 cup chopped pecans
1 pint fresh strawberries, sliced, OR
　1 package (10 oz.) frozen sliced strawberries,
　partially thawed
1 cup whipping cream, whipped, sweetened

Beat egg whites until frothy. Add cream of tartar and beat until stiff but not dry. Add sugar a tablespoon at a time; continue to beat until stiff peaks form. Fold in vanilla. Gradually fold in chow mein noodles and pecans. Spoon into well-buttered 9-inch pie pan. Spread over bottom and sides of pie pan to form a shell. Bake at 325 degrees for 25 to 30 minutes. Cook completely on wire cake rack. Fill center with strawberries. Top with whipped cream.
6 servings

MILE HIGH RASPBERRY PIE

1 baked (9-inch) pastry or crumb pie shell
1 (10-oz.) package frozen raspberries or 2 cups fresh
    raspberries plus ¼ cup sugar
2 egg whites at room temperature
1 cup sugar
1 Tbsp. lemon juice
Dash of salt
1 cup heavy cream, whipped
½ tsp. almond extract

Thaw frozen raspberries, reserving a few for garnish. Combine raspberries, sugar, egg whites, lemon juice and salt. Beat for 15 minutes or until stiff. Fold in whipped cream and almond extract. Mound in prepared pastry shell. Freeze until firm. Garnish with reserved raspberries.

Favorite recipe from **Oregon Caneberry Commission**

RASPBERRY PARADISE PIE

3 egg whites
¼ teaspoon baking powder
¼ teaspoon salt
¼ teaspoon cream of tartar
1 cup sugar
¾ cup 3-MINUTE BRAND® Oats
½ cup finely chopped walnuts
½ teaspoon vanilla
10-ounce package frozen raspberries, thawed
1 tablespoon cornstarch
Whipped Cream
Shredded Coconut

Beat egg whites with baking powder, salt and cream of tartar until nearly stiff. Add sugar gradually, beating until very stiff but not dry. Combine oats and walnuts and blend into egg whites. Fold in vanilla. Spoon into an 8 or 9-inch pie pan, making the meringue thicker around the edges, leaving a depression in the center for the filling. Bake at 325 degrees for 25 minutes, or until lightly browned. Cool.

Drain raspberries and place juice in a small saucepan. Carefully blend in cornstarch and cook over medium heat until juice is thickened. Cool slightly and then blend in the berries. Spoon mixture into the cooled meringue shell. Cover with whipped cream and garnish with coconut. Refrigerate several hours before serving.

DELUXE PECAN PIE

3 eggs
1 cup KARO® Light or Dark Corn Syrup
1 cup sugar
2 Tbsp. margarine, melted
1 tsp. vanilla
⅛ tsp. salt
1 cup pecans
1 unbaked (9-inch) pastry shell

In medium bowl with mixer at medium speed beat eggs slightly. Beat in next 5 ingredients. Stir in pecans. Pour into pastry shell. Bake in 350°F oven 55 to 65 minutes or until knife inserted halfway between center and edge comes out clean. Cool.

Makes 1 (9-inch) pie

Favorite recipe from **National Pecan Marketing Council**

MISS MARTHA'S CHESS PIE

1⅓ cups sugar
⅓ cup butter or margarine
1 tablespoon MARTHA WHITE Self-Rising Corn
    Meal
⅓ cup coffee cream
1 teaspoon white vinegar
3 whole eggs
1 teaspoon vanilla extract

Make 8-inch pastry shell*; do not bake, and refrigerate until filling is made. Cream sugar and butter together until light and fluffy. Add corn meal, cream and vinegar. Add eggs, one at a time, beating after each addition. Blend in vanilla. Pour into chilled, unbaked pastry shell. Bake 350° F 50 minutes. Pie should be well browned and a knife inserted about 1-inch from the edge should come out clean. Pie will be shaky in the center but will set when it cools. Let cool 1½ to 2 hours.

*Pastry:
1 cup and 1 tablespoon sifted MARTHA WHITE
    Plain Flour
½ teaspoon salt
⅓ cup shortening
About 3 tablespoons water

Place sifted flour and salt into a bowl and cut one half of the shortening in until particles look fine and mealy. Cut in remaining half of shortening until particles are in the size of big green peas. Sprinkle water over the mixture and stir with a fork until it cleans the sides of the bowl. Shape into a ball. Flatten dough out and roll into a circle about ¾-inch larger than pie pan. Fit into pan and pick with a fork dipped in flour.   *8-inch pie*

TOM'S® PEANUT CRUNCH PIE

1 unbaked 9-inch pastry shell
¼ cup sugar
1 tablespoon quick-cooking tapioca
¼ teaspoon salt
1 cup dark corn syrup
¼ cup water
3 eggs
½ teaspoon vanilla
2 tablespoons butter or margarine
1 cup TOM'S® Toasted Peanuts, coarsely chopped

Prepare pastry shell but do not bake. Blend sugar, tapioca, and salt in a medium-size saucepan. Stir in corn syrup and water. Bring to a boil, stirring constantly. Boil 4 minutes. Beat eggs slightly in a bowl. Pour hot syrup slowly into eggs, stirring vigorously. Stir in vanilla and butter. Cool. Scatter chopped peanuts over bottom of pastry shell. Add cooled pie filling. Bake in a hot oven (450°F.) for 8 minutes. Reduce heat to moderately low (325° F.) and bake for 25 to 35 minutes, or until a silver knife inserted in the center comes out clean. Serve warm, or cool and top with sweetened whipped cream.

AMBROSIA PIE

1 (9-inch) unbaked pastry shell
1 (9-ounce) package NONE SUCH® Condensed
    Mincemeat
1 cup water
2 eggs, beaten
1 (16-ounce) container BORDEN® Sour Cream
2 tablespoons sugar
1 teaspoon vanilla extract
2 tablespoons chopped nuts

Preheat oven to 425°. In small saucepan, break mincemeat into small pieces; add water. Boil briskly 1 minute. Cool. Pour mincemeat into pastry shell. Bake 20 minutes. In small bowl, combine eggs, sour cream, sugar and vanilla. Pour over mincemeat; sprinkle with nuts. Return to oven 8 to 10 minutes or until sour cream mixture is set. Cool. Chill thoroughly before serving. Refrigerate leftovers.   *Makes one 9-inch pie*

MINCE PIE

4 medium apples, cored, pared and chopped (1 quart)
¾ cup sweet orange marmalade
½ cup dark seedless raisins
3 teaspoons **KITCHEN BOUQUET®**
1 teaspoon cinnamon
½ teaspoon cloves
⅛ teaspoon salt
½ cup chopped walnuts
1 tablespoon brandy (optional)
½ teaspoon vanilla
1 (9 inch) baked pie shell
½ cup flour
⅓ cup brown sugar (packed)
¼ cup butter

Combine apples, orange marmalade, raisins, **KITCHEN BOU-QUET**, cinnamon, cloves and salt in saucepan. Bring to a boil. Reduce heat and simmer uncovered 10 minutes, stirring occasionally. Remove from heat. Stir in walnuts, brandy and vanilla. Turn into pie shell. Combine flour and sugar in mixing bowl. Mix in butter with fork or by pinching with fingertips until moist and crumbly. Sprinkle over pie. Bake in 400° oven for 20 minutes or until light golden brown on top. Serve warm or cool. Dollop with whipped cream, if desired.   *Makes 1 (9 inch) pie*

SWEET POTATO PIE WITH ALMOND CRUNCH TOPPING

1 pound fresh orange sweet potato; cooked and mashed to yield about 1¼ cups
½ cup brown sugar
2 tablespoons maple syrup
½ teaspoon cinnamon
½ teaspoon ginger
¼ teaspoon cloves
¼ teaspoon allspice
Pinch of salt
2 eggs
1 can (5.3 ounces) evaporated milk
1 unbaked 9-inch pie shell
Almond Crunch Topping*
Sweetened whipped cream, if desired

In large bowl combine sweet potato, sugar, syrup, cinnamon, ginger, cloves, allspice, salt, eggs and milk; blend well. Carefully pour into pie shell. Bake in 375° F oven for 35 minutes. Remove from oven, sprinkle with Almond Crunch Topping and return to oven. Bake 10 minutes longer.   *Makes one 9-inch pie*

*ALMOND CRUNCH TOPPING

Combine ¼ cup all-purpose flour, ¼ cup brown sugar, 2 tablespoons softened butter, ½ teaspoon cinnamon and dash nutmeg. Stir in ⅓ cup chopped almonds.

Favorite recipe from **The Sweet Potato Council of the United States Inc.**

SOUTHERN YAM PECAN PIE

1 (16-oz.) can **TRAPPEY'S® SUGARY SAM®** Mashed Yams
½ cup brown sugar
¼ cup granulated sugar
¼ cup cornstarch
1 egg yolk
¼ cup margarine, softened
1 tablespoon grated orange rind
¼ teaspoon salt
½ teaspoon cinnamon
½ teaspoon nutmeg
½ cup chopped pecans
1 (9-inch) unbaked pie shell

Preheat oven to 350° F. Blend yams, sugars (brown and granulated), cornstarch, egg yolk, margarine, orange rind, salt and spices in blender until smooth. Pour into unbaked pie shell. Sprinkle top with chopped pecans. Bake for 50 minutes. Garnish with dessert topping, if desired.

GRANOLA-BRANDY PIE

Granola Pastry*
1 cup dark corn syrup
½ cup sugar
¼ cup brandy
¼ cup margarine or butter, melted
3 eggs
1 teaspoon vanilla
¼ teaspoon salt
2 cups **NATURE VALLEY®** Granola
Sweetened whipped cream

Heat oven to 375°. Prepare Granola Pastry. Beat corn syrup, sugar, brandy, margarine, eggs, vanilla and salt with hand beater. Stir in granola. Pour into pastry-lined pie plate. Cover edge with 2- to 3-inch strip of aluminum foil to prevent excessive browning; remove foil during last 10 minutes of baking. Bake until set, 40 to 45 minutes. Serve with sweetened whipped cream.

*GRANOLA PASTRY

Prepare pastry for 9-inch One-Crust Pie as directed on package of **BETTY CROCKER®** **Pie Crust Mix or Sticks** except stir in ½ cup **NATURE VALLEY®** Granola (toasted oat mixture), crushed, before mixing in water.

GRASSHOPPER PIE

2 Tbsp. butter
14 **HYDROX®** Cookies
32 large marshmallows
½ cup milk
4 Tbsp. **LEROUX** Green Creme de Menthe
2 Tbsp. **LEROUX** White Creme de Cacao
1 cup whipped cream
½ cup shaved chocolate

Melt butter, stir into crushed **HYDROX®** Cookies; use for crust (press into 9-inch pie plate). Melt marshmallows in milk over hot water; remove from water, let cool. Stir in **LEROUX Green Creme de Menthe** and **LEROUX White Creme de Cacao**. Fold in whipped cream, pour into pie shell. Freeze; serve frozen. Sprinkle shaved chocolate over top.

PRALINE® EGGNOG PIE

1 9-inch graham cracker crust
2 envelopes **KNOX® Unflavored Gelatine**
¼ cup sugar
3 egg yolks
2 cups prepared eggnog
¼ cup **PRALINE® Liqueur**
1 tablespoon rum
½ teaspoon vanilla extract
1 cup (½ pt.) whipping or heavy cream, whipped
Ground nutmeg
Whole berry cranberry sauce, drained

In medium saucepan, mix unflavored gelatine with sugar; blend in egg yolks beaten with 1 cup eggnog. Let stand 1 minute. Stir over low heat until gelatine is completely dissolved, about 5 minutes. Stir in remaining eggnog, liqueur, rum and vanilla. Pour into large bowl and chill, stirring occasionally, until mixture mounds slightly when dropped from spoon.

Fold in whipped cream. Turn into prepared crust; sprinkle with nutmeg. Chill until firm. Garnish with cranberry sauce.

Makes about 8 servings

ARROW® GRASSHOPPER PIE

3 tablespoons melted butter (or margarine)
21 chocolate wafers, crushed
36 marshmallows
¾ cup milk
5 tablespoons **ARROW® Creme de Menthe**
2 tablespoons **ARROW® White Creme de Cacao**
1½ cups heavy cream

In medium bowl, combine butter and crushed wafers. Press crumb mixture on bottom and up sides of 9 inch pie plate. Bake 5 minutes in preheated 375°F. oven. Cool. In 2 quart saucepan, melt marshmallows in milk over low heat, stirring constantly. Mix in liqueurs. Cool until slightly thickened. Beat cream until it mounds slightly. Fold into marshmallow mixture. Pour into pie shell. Freeze. Garnish with whipped cream and mint leaves, if desired.

Serves 8

MAI TAI PIE

2 cups flaked coconut
¼ cup butter, melted
1 can (1 lb., 4 oz.) **DOLE® Crushed Pineapple**
Water
2 envelopes plain gelatin
½ cup sugar
½ teaspoon salt
1 teaspoon lime peel
1 tablespoon lime juice
3 eggs, separated
½ cup dark Jamaican rum
2 tablespoons **COINTREAU Liqueur**
½ pint whipping cream
Twisted lime slices
Stemmed maraschino cherries

Combine coconut and melted butter, tossing with a fork to combine. Press into a 9-inch glass pie plate on bottom and sides. Bake in a preheated 300° F. oven 25 minutes until well browned. Cool.

(Continued)

Meanwhile, drain pineapple well reserving all syrup. Add water to syrup to make 1½ cups liquid. Sprinkle gelatin over liquid in a small saucepan. Stir in sugar, salt, lime peel and juice. Heat mixture to boiling, stirring constantly until sugar is dissolved. Remove from heat. Beat egg yolks until foamy. Gradually pour hot mixture over eggs, beating constantly. Stir in rum and **COINTREAU**. Chill mixture about 40 minutes to consistency of unbeaten egg white. Beat egg white until stiff peaks form. Fold into gelatin mixture until well blended. Whip cream until stiff. Fold cream and pineapple into gelatin mixture. Turn into pie shell. Chill two hours before cutting. Garnish with twisted lime slices and cherries to serve.

Makes 1 (9-inch) pie

MARGARITA PIE

½ cup margarine or butter
1¼ cups finely crushed **WISE® Mini Pretzels**
¼ cup sugar
1 (14-ounce) can **EAGLE® Brand Sweetened Condensed Milk** (NOT evaporated milk)
⅓ cup **REALIME® Lime Juice from Concentrate**
2 to 3 tablespoons tequila
2 tablespoons triple sec or other orange-flavored liqueur
1 cup (½ pint) **BORDEN® Whipping Cream**, whipped
Additional whipped cream and pretzels for garnish, optional

In small saucepan, melt margarine; stir in pretzel crumbs and sugar. Mix well. Press crumbs on bottom and up side of buttered 9-inch pie plate; chill. In large bowl, combine **EAGLE® Brand**, **REALIME®**, tequila and triple sec; blend well. Fold in whipped cream. Turn into prepared crust. Freeze or chill until firm (4 hours in freezer; 2 hours in refrigerator). Before serving, garnish with whipped cream and pretzels if desired. Refrigerate or freeze leftovers.

Makes one 9-inch pie

COFFEE LIQUEUR PIE

1 **PET-RITZ® Regular Pie Crust Shell**, baked
1 small can (5.33 fl. oz.) **PET® Evaporated Milk**
½ cup semi-sweet chocolate pieces
2 cups miniature marshmallows
⅓ cup chopped almonds, toasted*
⅓ cup coffee liqueur
1 container (12 oz.) **PET® WHIP Non-Dairy Whipped Topping**, thawed
Maraschino cherries

Combine evaporated milk and chocolate pieces in heavy 1-quart saucepan. Cook over low heat, stirring occasionally, until chocolate melts completely and mixture thickens. Stir in marshmallows until melted. Remove from heat. Add almonds. Pour into a 2-quart bowl and refrigerate until cool (about 20 to 30 minutes), stirring twice. Add coffee liqueur. Fold in whipped topping. Spoon into baked pie shell. Freeze several hours until firm. Remove from freezer 10 minutes before serving for ease in cutting. If desired, garnish with additional **PET® WHIP**, chopped almonds and maraschino cherries.

Makes 8 servings

*To toast almonds: Place almonds on baking sheet in preheated 350°F oven, stirring frequently until almonds are lightly toasted, about 10 minutes.

PIÑA COLADA RIBBON PIE

1 box (8½ ounces) chocolate wafers, finely crushed
¼ cup butter or margarine, melted
1 can (16 ounces) crushed pineapple, with juice
5 teaspoons cornstarch
⅔ cup plus 1 tablespoon **CocoRibe®** **Coconut Rum**, divided
1 quart vanilla ice cream, softened slightly
1 cup (½ pint) heavy cream

In small bowl, mix wafer crumbs with melted butter. Reserve 2 tablespoons crumb mixture. Press remaining crumb mixture into a 9-inch pie plate. Freeze 30 minutes.

Measure 2 tablespoons pineapple juice from crushed pineapple. In small cup, blend pineapple juice with cornstarch. In saucepan, combine pineapple and juice and cornstarch mixture. Bring to a boil, stirring constantly; cook 1 minute. Remove from heat, stir in ⅔ cup **CocoRibe®**; chill in refrigerator.

Spread 2 cups softened ice cream in prepared pie shell. Return to freezer for 30 minutes. Spread half of the pineapple mixture over top of frozen ice cream, return to freezer for 30 minutes. Repeat layering process with ice cream and pineapple filling. Before serving, combine remaining 1 tablespoon **CocoRibe®** with heavy cream. Beat until soft peaks form. Decorate pie with whipped cream, sprinkle with reserved crumbs. Slice with warm knife. *Yield: 10 servings*

Note: For easier slicing, pie should be tempered at room temperature for 15 minutes. Or, place in refrigerator for 30 minutes.

ORANGE DRAMBUIE® PIE

2 tablespoons cornstarch
1 cup orange juice
5 egg yolks
¼ cup sugar
1 envelope unflavored gelatin
1 tablespoon butter
⅓ cup **DRAMBUIE®** **Liqueur**
¾ cup heavy cream
9-inch prebaked pie shell
2 very small navel oranges
½ cup orange marmalade or apricot jelly

Mix cornstarch with ½ cup orange juice in a medium size bowl. Add the egg yolks and sugar; beat well. Pour remaining ½ cup juice in a medium saucepan. Sprinkle on gelatin, and bring to a boil, stirring until gelatin is dissolved. Remove from heat. Gradually stir a few spoons of hot juice into the egg yolk mixture. Then combine both mixtures in the saucepan. Return to heat and cook 3 minutes more stirring constantly. Remove from the heat and stir in the butter until melted; add **DRAMBUIE®**.

Cool rapidly over ice, then place in refrigerator until completely cool. Whip cream until thick; fold the cream into the cooled mixture and pour into pie shell. Melt the marmalade over low heat. Slice the oranges, unpeeled, into very thin rounds. Dip each slice in melted jelly. Starting at the outside arrange the slices on top of the pie, overlapping each slice, and covering the entire top. Refrigerate until ready to serve. *Makes 6 to 8 servings*

REGAL CHEESECAKE PIE

Crumb Crust:
2 cups fine vanilla wafer or graham cracker crumbs
6 tablespoons butter or margarine, melted
¼ cup sugar

Filling:
12 ounces cream cheese, softened
⅔ cup sugar
3 eggs
1 can (11 ounces) **CAMPBELL'S Condensed Cheddar Cheese Soup**
2 tablespoons lemon juice
1 teaspoon grated lemon rind
1 teaspoon vanilla extract
¼ teaspoon almond extract

Topping:
1 cup sour cream
¼ cup sugar
1 teaspoon grated lemon rind
1 teaspoon vanilla extract

TO MAKE CRUST:
Combine crumbs, butter and sugar. Press firmly into 10-inch pie plate. Chill for 1 hour.

TO MAKE FILLING:
In mixing bowl, blend cream cheese until smooth. With medium speed of electric mixer, blend sugar and eggs alternately into cream cheese. Blend in *1 cup* soup. Stir in lemon juice, rind and flavorings. Pour into chilled piecrust. Bake at 350°F. for 50 minutes. Meanwhile, for topping, blend remaining soup with sour cream, sugar, lemon rind and vanilla. Spread on pie. Bake 5 minutes more. Cool; chill. Garnish chilled cheesecake with the following fruit topping.

GOLDEN PEACH SURPRISE

Drain 1 can (about 16 ounces) sliced cling peaches, reserving 2 tablespoons syrup. Arrange peaches on cheesecake pie. In saucepan, combine reserved syrup, 2 teaspoons cornstarch, ½ cup peach preserves and ⅛ teaspoon almond extract. Cook over low heat, stirring until thickened. Cool. Spoon on cheesecake; chill.

ELEGANT CHEESE PIE

2 envelopes **DREAM WHIP®** **Whipped Topping Mix**
1 cup milk
1 cup (½ pint) sour cream
1 teaspoon vanilla
1 package (8-oz.) cream cheese, softened
1 package (4-serving size) **JELL-O®** **Vanilla Flavor Instant Pudding and Pie Filling**
1 baked 9-inch graham cracker crumb crust, cooled

Combine whipped topping mix, ½ cup of the milk, the sour cream and vanilla in mixer bowl. Blend; then beat on high speed of electric mixer for 2 to 3 minutes or until mixture will form soft peaks. Measure 1 cup and set aside. Add cream cheese to remaining topping mixture and beat until smooth. Add remaining milk and the pie filling mix. Blend on low speed for about 1 minute, scraping sides of bowl occasionally. Spoon into crust and spread measured mixture over the top. Chill at least 4 hours.

CREAMY CHEESE PIE
(Low Calorie)

Pie:
2 tsp. corn oil margarine
4 graham cracker squares
2 cups low fat cottage cheese
¼ cup **SUPEROSE® Liquid Fructose**
2 tsp. vanilla
1 tsp. freshly grated lemon peel
1 tsp. lemon juice

Topping:
1 cup sour cream
2 Tbsp. **SUPEROSE® Liquid Fructose**
1½ tsp. vanilla extract

PIE:
Preheat the oven to 375°. Rub the 2 teaspoons of margarine evenly over the entire surface of a 9-inch pie plate. Put the four graham cracker squares in a plastic bag and roll them with a rolling pin until they are fine crumbs. Sprinkle the graham cracker crumbs evenly over the greased pie plate, pressing them down with your fingers to make certain they stick to the surface.

Put the cottage cheese and all other pie ingredients in a blender and blend until completely smooth. Pour the cottage cheese mixture into the pie shell. Spread it out evenly in the pie plate. Place in the center of a 375° oven and cook for 15 minutes.

TOPPING:
While the pie is cooking, combine the topping ingredients in a mixing bowl and mix thoroughly. Remove the pie from the oven and spread the topping evenly over the top of the pie. Place the pie back in the center of the 375° oven and continue cooking for 10 more minutes. Remove the pie from the oven and cool on a rack until room temperature. Refrigerate until cold before serving.

Just before serving the pie, rub the outside of the pie plate with a warm damp towel. This softens the margarine in the crust, making it less likely to stick to the bottom of the pie plate.

Makes 16 servings

Each serving contains approximately: 79 calories

FLUFFY BERRY CHEESE PIE

CRISCO® Pastry for single-crust 9-inch pie*
1 cup miniature marshmallows
½ cup milk
1 package (3 ounces) strawberry-flavored gelatin
½ cup water
1 package (3 ounces) cream cheese, softened
1 package (10 ounces) frozen strawberries, thawed
½ cup whipping cream

Line 9-inch pie plate with pastry; bake and cool. In saucepan, heat miniature marshmallows and milk over medium-low heat, stirring frequently, till marshmallows are melted; set aside. In small saucepan, combine strawberry-flavored gelatin and water. Heat and stir till gelatin is dissolved. Combine marshmallow mixture and gelatin; gradually beat into the softened cream cheese. Drain thawed strawberries, reserving syrup. Add water to syrup to equal ¾ cup liquid. Stir strawberry syrup into gelatin mixture; chill till mixture is partially set. Whip gelatin mixture; fold in strawberries. Whip the cream; fold into the whipped gelatin mixture. Chill again till mixture mounds when spooned. Pile strawberry mixture into the baked pastry shell. Chill 3 to 4 hours or till filling is set. Garnish with dollops of additional whipped cream and strawberries, if desired.

(Continued)

*CRISCO® PASTRY FOR SINGLE-CRUST PIE

1⅓ cups sifted flour
½ teaspoon salt
½ cup **CRISCO® Shortening**
2 to 3 tablespoons water

In mixing bowl, combine flour and salt. Cut in **CRISCO®** with pastry blender or two knives until mixture is uniform (mixture should be fairly coarse). Sprinkle with water, a tablespoon at a time; toss lightly with fork. When all water has been added, work dough into a firm ball.

Press dough into a flat circle with smooth edges. On lightly floured board or pastry cloth, roll dough to a circle ⅛ inch thick and about 1½ inches larger than inverted pie plate. Gently ease dough into the pie plate, being careful not to stretch the dough. Trim ½ inch beyond edge of pie plate. Fold under to make double thickness around rim. Flute edge of pastry as desired.

To bake without filling: Preheat oven to 425°. Prick bottom and sides of crust with fork. Bake 10 to 15 minutes or till lightly browned.

To bake with filling: Preheat oven to temperature stated in recipe. Do not prick dough. Bake according to recipe directions.

FRUITED DANISH CHEESE PIE

1 9-inch graham cracker crust
1 lb. Danish Natural Cream Cheese with Peach, softened
¼ cup milk
¼ cup orange flavored liqueur
½ cup heavy cream
Orange or Pineapple slice

In mixing bowl, beat cream cheese with milk and liqueur. Pour into crust. Bake in preheated 350 degree oven for 25 minutes. (Center will look soft). Cool; then chill thoroughly. Garnish with whipped cream and fruit slice. Cut into wedges.

Makes 6 to 8 servings

Favorite recipe from the **Denmark Cheese Association**

FRIENDLY® ICE CREAM PIE™

Cocoa Crumb Crust*
½ gallon **FRIENDLY® Butter Crunch** or Strawberry Ice Cream
Classic Chocolate Fudge Sauce**

Prepare Cocoa Crumb Crust. Evenly spread half the **FRIENDLY® Ice Cream** into frozen pie shell. Top with scoops of remaininug **FRIENDLY® Ice Cream**. Wrap; freeze until firm. Serve topped with Classic Chocolate Fudge Sauce.

*COCOA CRUMB CRUST

Combine 1½ cups vanilla wafer crumbs (about 45 vanilla wafers), ⅓ cup **HERSHEY'S® Cocoa** and ⅓ cup confectioners' sugar in a bowl. Stir in 6 tablespoons melted butter or margarine. Press mixture onto bottom and side of 9-inch pie pan; freeze.

**CLASSIC CHOCOLATE FUDGE SAUCE

Combine 1 cup sugar and 6 tablespoons **HERSHEY'S® Cocoa** in saucepan; blend in ¾ cup evaporated milk. Add ¼ cup butter or margarine and ⅛ teaspoon salt. Cook, stirring constantly until mixture begins to boil. Remove from heat; add vanilla. Serve warm over **FRIENDLY® Ice Cream Pie™** or other desserts.

2 cups sauce

FANTASY RICE PIE

1½ cups cottage cheese
½ cup milk
1 package (3¾ ounces) lemon instant pudding and pie filling
1½ cups chilled, cooked UNCLE BEN'S® CONVERTED® Brand Rice
1 (8 or 9-inch) graham cracker pie crust
½ cup sour cream
Fresh strawberry slices or other fruit for garnish

Beat cottage cheese using an electric mixer until fairly smooth. Add milk and pudding mix; beat until well blended. Stir in rice. Spoon into prepared crust. Chill. Spread sour cream over top before serving. Garnish with fruit.   *Makes 6 servings*

HEAVENLY HASH PIE

1½ cups finely crushed gingersnaps
¼ cup sugar
¼ cup butter or margarine, melted
½ of ½ gallon SEALTEST® Heavenly Hash Ice Cream, softened
Whipped cream (optional)

Measure crumbs into medium-sized mixing bowl. Toss with sugar and melted butter until well mixed. With back of spoon, press mixture to bottom and sides of 8 inch pie plate, leaving small rim. Place in moderate oven (375°) for 8 minutes. Remove to wire rack to cool completely. Spread softened Heavenly Hash ice cream evenly into prepared crust. Freeze until firm. At serving time, garnish with whipped cream if desired.

Makes 4 to 6 servings

FROSTY MINT ICE CREAM PIES

Pie Shells:
1 pkg. PILLSBURY PLUS Chocolate Mint, Devil's Food or Dark Chocolate Cake Mix
¼ cup PILLSBURY Ready-To-Spread Chocolate Fudge Frosting Supreme
¾ cup water
¼ cup oil

Filling:
6 cups (1½ quarts) mint chocolate chip or your favorite ice cream, softened

Heat oven to 350°F. Generously grease bottom, sides and rim of two 9-inch pie pans or round cake pans.* In large bowl, blend all shell ingredients at low speed until moistened; beat 2 minutes at *highest* speed. Spread half of batter (2¼ cups) in bottom of each pan. Do *not* spread up sides of pan. Bake at 350°F. for 25 to 30 minutes; DO NOT OVERBAKE. Cakes will collapse to form shells. Cool completely.

In large bowl, blend ice cream until smooth; spread evenly in center of each shell leaving a ½-inch rim. If desired, heat remaining frosting just until softened. Drop by spoonfuls on top of ice cream; swirl with knife. Freeze at least 2 hours. Store in freezer. Wrap frozen pies airtight to avoid freezer burn.

Makes 2 pies, 12 servings

*Tip: Do *not* use 8-inch pie or cake pans.

HIGH ALTITUDE—Above 3500 Feet: No change.

APRICOT TART SARONNO

1½ cups unsifted all-purpose flour
½ teaspoon salt
⅓ cup butter or margarine
3 tablespoons AMARETTO DI SARONNO® Liqueur
1 egg yolk

Filling:
1 jar (12 ounces) apricot preserves
¼ cup AMARETTO DI SARONNO® Liqueur
Grated rind and juice of 1 orange
1½ tablespoons cornstarch
2 cans (17 ounces each) apricot halves, drained
¼ cup sliced almonds, toasted
1 pint vanilla ice cream
¼ cup AMARETTO DI SARONNO® Liqueur

In a bowl, mix flour and salt. Cut in butter or margarine until particles are very fine. Stir in AMARETTO DI SARONNO® and egg yolk. Knead dough until a smooth ball is formed. Roll out dough to a 14-inch round. Place dough in an ungreased 11-inch flan pan with 1-inch sides. Fold excess dough down into shell. Prick bottom with the tines of a fork. Bake in a preheated hot oven (425° F) for 12 to 15 minutes, or until golden brown. Cool.

FILLING:
In a saucepan, mix apricot preserves, AMARETTO DI SARONNO®, orange rind and juice and cornstarch. Stir over low heat until mixture bubbles and thickens. Cool to room temperature. Spread a thin layer of apricot mixture over bottom of pie shell. Arrange apricot halves, rounded side up, in pie shell. Spoon remaining glaze over apricots. Sprinkle edge of tart with sliced almonds.

In a bowl, mix ice cream and AMARETTO DI SARONNO® until smooth and creamy. Cut tart into wedges and serve each wedge topped with ice cream mixture. Serve at once.

Makes 1 (11-inch) tart

ICE CREAM PUMPKIN PIES

2 pints vanilla ice cream, softened
2 nine-inch packaged graham cracker crumb crusts
1 can (16 oz.) LIBBY'S® Solid Pack Pumpkin
1½ cups sugar
1 teaspoon ground cinnamon
½ teaspoon ground ginger
¼ teaspoon ground cloves
½ teaspoon salt
1 teaspoon vanilla
2 cups whipping cream
Glazed Almonds*

Spread one pint ice cream in the bottom of each crumb crust; place in freezer while making filling. In a large bowl, combine pumpkin, sugar, spices, salt and vanilla; mix well. Beat 1 cup of the cream until stiff; fold into pumpkin mixture until no streaks of white remain. Top each pie with half of the pumpkin mixture. Freeze until solid, at least 4 hours. Wrap well with foil for longer storage. To serve, remove from freezer 20 minutes before cutting. To garnish: whip ½ cup cream for each pie; spoon in a ring on pie; sprinkle with Glazed Almonds.   *Yields 2 nine-inch pies*

*GLAZED ALMONDS

In a small heavy skillet, combine 1 cup slivered blanched almonds and ¼ cup sugar. Place over medium heat, stirring constantly and rapidly to prevent burning as sugar begins to melt and turn color. When almonds are caramel color, remove from heat; spread on greased baking sheet. Break apart when cool.

BLUEBOTTOM ICE CREAM PIE
(No Bake Type)

3 cups (one 16-oz. bag) **STILWELL Frozen Blueberries**
¾ cup sugar
½ cup water
2 Tbsp. cornstarch
1 pint vanilla ice cream
1 **STILWELL** or **PREMIUM PAK Graham Cracker Pie Crust** (no-bake)

Combine blueberries and sugar. Mix water and cornstarch and stir into blueberries. Cook at a simmer until filling is thickened. (Reserve one cup of the mixture for decorating the top.) Cool.

Spoon blueberry filling into Graham Cracker Crust. Spoon softened ice cream over blueberry filling. Drizzle reserved blueberry filling over ice cream. Freeze. Remove 30 minutes before serving to thaw. Cut into wedges and serve.

ICE CREAM SUNDAE PIE

1 **KEEBLER® READY-CRUST® Chocolate-Flavored Pie Crust**
2 pints ice cream*
1 cup hot fudge sauce, heated
¼ cup chopped nuts
Whipped cream or topping
Maraschino cherries

Allow ice cream to soften or stir with a spoon until pliable. Spoon into crust. Cover and freeze until firm, about 3 hours. Serve pie wedges with hot fudge sauce, nuts, whipped cream or topping and cherries.

*ICE CREAM VARIATIONS

2 pints of the same flavor such as peppermint, pistachio nut, fruit flavors, or chocolate. Or use two flavors such as chocolate and peppermint, mint-chocolate chip, fruit or nut ice creams.

FROST ON THE PUMPKIN PIE

1½ cups gingersnap cookie crumbs
¼ cup butter or margarine, melted
1 cup canned pumpkin
¼ cup packed brown sugar
2 teaspoons **DURKEE Pumpkin Pie Spice**
1 quart butter pecan ice cream, softened

Mix together gingersnap crumbs and melted margarine. Press mixture firmly against bottom and sides of 9-inch pie pan. Bake at 350° for 5 to 7 minutes. Cool. In small saucepan, combine pumpkin, sugar and pumpkin pie spice. Cook slowly until mixture is heated through; cool. Fold pumpkin mixture into softened ice cream. Pour into cooled gingersnap crust. Freeze pie 4 to 6 hours or overnight. Garnish with whipped cream.

Makes 6 to 8 servings

PUMPKIN ICE CREAM PIE

2 **ZAGNUT® Bars** (1.75 ounces each), crushed
⅔ cup graham cracker crumbs
3 tablespoons butter, melted
1 cup canned pumpkin
⅓ cup packed dark brown sugar
½ teaspoon cinnamon
¼ teaspoon nutmeg
⅛ teaspoon ground cloves
1 quart vanilla ice cream, softened
1 cup whipping cream, whipped
1 **ZAGNUT® Bar** (1.75 ounces), coarsely chopped

In bowl, combine first 3 ingredients; mix well. Press mixture firmly into bottom and along sides of 9-inch pie plate. Chill 1 hour. In large bowl, combine pumpkin, sugar and spices. Add softened ice cream; mix well. Pour into chilled crust. Freeze until firm. Remove from freezer 5 minutes before serving. Spread whipped cream over top. Sprinkle with crushed **ZAGNUT® Bar.**

8 servings

STRAWBERRY WINE PIE

Heat 1 cup **ALMADÉN Mountain Nectar Vin Rosé** to boiling; pour over 1 package (3 oz.) strawberry-flavored gelatin in a large bowl, stirring to dissolve. Add 1 pint softened vanilla ice cream, stirring until ice cream melts and mixture begins to set. Fold in 1 basket strawberries, rinsed and cut in halves. Spread in a cooled baked 9-inch Graham Cracker Crust* Chill until firm. Garnish with whipped cream and whole berries.   *Makes 8 servings*

*GRAHAM CRACKER CRUST

Mix 1 cup graham cracker crumbs, ¼ cup ground almonds, 3 tablespoons sugar and ¼ cup melted butter or margarine. Press crumb mixture evenly and firmly into a 9-inch pie pan. Bake in 400° oven for 6 to 8 minutes until browned.

Cookies, Candy & Snacks

Cookies

PINWHEEL COOKIES

1 cup firmly packed **DOMINO® Light Brown Sugar**
¼ teaspoon salt
¼ lb. (½ cup) butter or margarine
1 egg
1 teaspoon vanilla extract
2 cups all-purpose flour
1 teaspoon baking powder
2 tablespoons cocoa

Cream sugar, salt and butter or margarine thoroughly. Beat egg and extract into creamed ingredients until light and fluffy. Sift together flour and baking powder. Gradually stir into creamed mixture. Divide dough in half.

Roll half of dough on lightly floured waxed paper to form 9 × 12 inch rectangle ⅛-inch thick; set aside. Blend cocoa into unrolled dough; roll second rectangle from chocolate dough.

Turn chocolate layer onto butterscotch rectangle; remove waxed paper. Trim rough edges. Roll two layers of dough like jelly roll. Wrap in waxed paper; chill until firm.

Slice ⅛-inch cookies with sharp knife; place on lightly greased cookie sheet. Bake in moderate oven 350°F 8-10 minutes or until brown. Remove to cooling rack.

Yield: about 6 dozen pinwheels

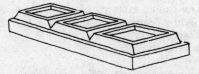

CHOCOLATE CRINKLES
(Low Calorie)

2 cups sifted all-purpose flour
2 teaspoons baking powder
1 cup sugar
¼ cup vegetable oil
1 packet **BUTTER BUDS®**, mixed with ¼ cup hot water
4 ounces unsweetened baking chocolate, melted and cooled
2 teaspoons vanilla
3 eggs

Sift together flour and baking powder; set aside. In separate bowl, combine sugar, oil, **BUTTER BUDS®**, chocolate, and vanilla. Beat in eggs. Add dry ingredients and beat until well blended. Cover; chill several hours until firm enough to handle. Preheat oven to 350°F. Spray cookie sheets with non-stick coating agent. Using 1 tablespoon dough for each cookie, shape into balls and place on cookie sheets. Bake 15 to 17 minutes.

4 dozen cookies

PER SERVING (1 cookie):	Calories: 60	Protein: 1g
Carbohydrate: 9g	Fat: 3g	Sodium: 35mg

Note: By using **BUTTER BUDS®** instead of butter in this recipe, you have saved 16 calories and 6 mg cholesterol per cookie.

CHOCOLATE FINGER COOKIES

⅔ cup butter or margarine
1 cup sugar
2 eggs
2 teaspoons vanilla
2½ cups unsifted all-purpose flour
½ cup **HERSHEY'S® Unsweetened Cocoa**
½ teaspoon baking soda
¼ teaspoon salt
Chocolate Glaze*
Chopped nuts (optional)
Garnish: Candied cherries

Cream butter or margarine and sugar in large mixer bowl until light and fluffy. Add eggs and vanilla; blend well. Combine dry ingredients; gradually add to creamed mixture, blending thoroughly. Shape heaping teaspoonful of dough into 3-inch long fingers 1-inch wide; place on ungreased cookie sheet. Bake at 350° for 8 to 10 minutes or until set, but not hard. Cool slightly; remove from cookie sheet onto wire rack. Prepare Chocolate Glaze; glaze and sprinkle with chopped nuts, if desired. Garnish with cherry half.

Yield: 2½ dozen cookies

*CHOCOLATE GLAZE

Combine 2 tablespoons butter and 2 tablespoons water in small saucepan; bring to boil. Remove from heat; immediately stir in 3 tablespoons unsweetened cocoa until well blended. Add 1 cup confectioner's sugar and ½ teaspoon vanilla. Beat until smooth. (If too thick, add 1 to 2 teaspoons water).

SNAPPY TURTLE COOKIES

1½ cups **PILLSBURY'S BEST® All Purpose or Unbleached Flour**
½ to ¾ cup firmly packed brown sugar
¼ teaspoon salt
¼ teaspoon soda
½ cup butter or margarine, softened
¼ teaspoon vanilla and/or ¼ teaspoon maple flavoring, if desired
1 egg
1½ to 2 cups **FISHER® Pecan Halves**

Frosting:

1 square (1-oz.) unsweetened chocolate
1 tablespoon butter or margarine
3 tablespoons milk
1½ cups powdered sugar

(Lightly spoon flour into measuring cup; level off.) In large bowl, combine first eight ingredients (except pecan halves); blend well. Chill dough. Heat oven to 350°F. On greased cookie sheets, arrange pecan halves in groups of three or five to resemble head and legs of a turtle. Shape dough into 1-inch balls; press lightly onto nuts. (Tips of pecans must show when cookie is baked.) Bake 10 to 15 minutes until bottom is lightly browned. Cool.

FROSTING:
In small saucepan, heat first three Frosting ingredients, stirring constantly until chocolate melts. Remove from heat. Add powdered sugar; blend until smooth. Frost tops of cookies generously.

2 to 2½ dozen cookies

HIGH ALTITUDE: No Change.

CHOCOLATE FUDGIES

½ cup **Butter Flavor CRISCO®**
2 packages (1-ounce each) unsweetened baking
   chocolate, melted
1 cup sugar
1 egg
1 teaspoon vanilla
1 cup all-purpose flour
1 teaspoon baking powder
¼ teaspoon salt
¼ cup semi-sweet mini-chocolate chips
¼ cup finely ground pecans

1. Preheat oven to 375°.
2. Blend **Butter Flavor CRISCO®** and melted chocolate in large mixing bowl. Blend in sugar, egg and vanilla. Mix in flour, baking powder and salt. Stir in mini-chocolate chips and nuts.
3. Drop by rounded teaspoonfuls 2 inches apart onto ungreased baking sheet. Bake at 375° 6 to 7 minutes. Remove to cooling rack after 2 minutes.   *3½ to 4 dozen cookies*

CHOCOLATE CRISPIES

1 cup all-purpose flour
½ measuring teaspoon baking powder
½ measuring teaspoon baking soda
½ measuring teaspoon salt
½ cup butter, softened
½ cup firmly packed brown sugar
½ cup sugar
1 egg
2 envelopes (2-oz.) **NESTLÉ® CHOCO-BAKE**
½ cup quick oats, uncooked
½ cup shredded coconut

Preheat oven to 350°F. In small bowl, combine flour, baking powder, baking soda and salt; set aside. In large bowl, combine butter, brown sugar, sugar and egg; beat until creamy. Blend in **NESTLÉ® CHOCO-BAKE**. Add flour mixture, oats and coconut; mix until well blended. Drop by rounded measuring teaspoonfuls onto ungreased cookie sheets. Bake at 350°F 10-12 minutes.   *Makes: 3 dozen (2-inch) cookies*

SACHERTORTE COOKIES

1 cup margarine or butter, softened
4½ oz. pkg. instant chocolate pudding and pie filling mix
1 egg
2 cups **PILLSBURY'S BEST® All Purpose Flour**
3 tablespoons sugar
½ cup apricot or cherry preserves
½ cup semi-sweet chocolate chips
3 tablespoons margarine or butter, melted

Heat oven to 325°F. In large bowl, cream margarine and pudding mix until light and fluffy; beat in egg. Lightly spoon flour into measuring cup; level off. Gradually add flour at low speed until well mixed and dough forms. Shape into 1-inch balls, roll in sugar. Place 2 inches apart on ungreased cookie sheets. With thumb, make imprint in center of each cookie. Bake at 325°F. for 15 to 18 minutes or until firm to touch. Remove from cookie sheets immediately. Cool. Fill each imprint with ½ teaspoon preserves. In small saucepan, blend chocolate chips and margarine over low heat until chocolate melts, stirring constantly. Drizzle ½ teaspoon over each cookie.   *48 cookies*

HIGH ALTITUDE—Above 3500 Feet: Bake at 350°F. for 12 to 15 minutes.

CHOCOLATE PEANUT BUTTER COOKIES

Preheat oven to 375°.
Cream together until smooth . . .

   ¾ cup butter (softened)
   ½ cup sugar
   ½ cup firmly packed brown sugar
   ½ cup creamy peanut butter

Beat and add. . .

   1 egg and 1 tsp. vanilla extract

Mix together and add gradually . . .

   1¼ cups unsifted flour
   ½ tsp. baking soda
   ½ tsp. salt

Stir in. . . .

   1 pkg. (2 cups) **GUITTARD® Real Chocolate Maxi Chips**
   ½ cup chopped peanuts

Drop batter by well-rounded teaspoon onto ungreased cookie sheet. Flatten to 2-inch diameter. Bake 8-10 minutes in 375° oven.
          Yield: 2½ dozen

WORLD'S GREATEST CHOCOLATE CHIP COOKIES

1 cup **AZAR® Chopped Walnuts** or **Pecans**
1½ cups semi-sweet chocolate morsels
2 teaspoons grated orange peel
1 cup butter
½ cup granulated sugar
1 cup dark or light brown sugar
1 teaspoon vanilla extract
2 eggs, lightly beaten
2 cups flour
1 teaspoon baking soda
½ teaspoon salt

Preheat oven to 375°. Mix butter, sugars, and vanilla. Cream well. Add eggs. Beat until thoroughly blended. Sift together the flour, baking soda and salt. Add to the creamed mixture. Continue beating. Fold in the chocolate morsels and nuts. Add grated orange peel. Lightly butter a cookie sheet. Drop about 2 tablespoons of the mixture onto the cookie sheet, keeping the drops about 2 inches apart. Flatten slightly on top. Place in the oven and bake about 12 minutes.   *Makes 2 dozen*

FAVORITE CHOCOLATE CHIP COOKIES

1¼ cups all-purpose flour
½ teaspoon baking soda
½ teaspoon salt
⅔ cup soft butter or margarine
¾ cup **DOMINO® BROWNULATED® Sugar**
1 teaspoon water
½ teaspoon vanilla extract
1 egg
1 cup (6-oz.) chocolate chips
½ cup chopped walnuts, peanuts, or pecans

Sift together flour, soda, and salt. Combine shortening, sugar, water and extract; mix well. Beat in egg. Add flour mixture; beat until smooth. Stir in chocolate chips and nuts. Drop from teaspoon onto lightly greased cookie sheets. Bake at 375° F 10-12 minutes or until lightly browned.   *Yield: 3½ dozen cookies*

MIGHTY MINI CHIP COOKIES

½ cup butter or margarine, softened
½ cup shortening
¾ cup packed light brown sugar
¾ cup sugar
2 eggs
1 teaspoon vanilla
2¼ cups unsifted all-purpose flour
1 teaspoon baking soda
½ teaspoon salt
1½ cups **HERSHEY'S® Semi-Sweet Chocolate Mini Chips**
1 cup chopped nuts, optional

Cream butter or margarine, shortening, brown sugar and sugar until well blended. Add eggs and vanilla; beat until light and fluffy. Combine flour, baking soda and salt. Gradually add to creamed mixture until well combined. Stir in **Mini Chips** and nuts. Drop by rounded teaspoonfuls onto ungreased cookie sheet. Bake at 375° for 8 to 10 minutes or until lightly browned. Cool slightly before removing from cookie sheet to wire rack.

About 6 dozen (2½-inch) cookies

SIERRA NUGGETS · COUNTRY STYLE CHOCOLATE CHIP COOKIES

1 cup butter (softened)
1 cup brown sugar
1½ cups white sugar
1 Tbsp. milk
1½ tsp. vanilla
2 eggs
1 cup fresh corn flakes (crumbled)
3 cups oatmeal
1½ cups flour
1¼ tsp. baking soda
½ tsp. mace
1 tsp. salt
1½ tsp. cinnamon
¼ tsp. nutmeg
⅛ tsp. powdered cloves
4 oz. coconut
1 pkg. (2 cups) **GUITTARD® Chocolate Drops**
1 cup walnuts or pine nuts (chopped)

Preheat oven to 350°. Cream together butter and sugars. Add milk and vanilla. Beat in eggs. Stir in cornflakes and oatmeal. Sift together flour, baking soda, mace, salt, cinnamon, nutmeg and cloves. Add to mixture and mix thoroughly. Stir in coconut, chocolate and nuts. Drop by well rounded teaspoon onto greased cookie sheets. Bake 10 minutes at 350°.

Yield: Approx. 8 dozen

REESE'S® COOKIE

1 cup shortening or ¾ cup butter or margarine
1 cup of sugar
½ cup packed light brown sugar
1 teaspoon vanilla
2 eggs
2 cups unsifted all-purpose flour
1 teaspoon baking soda
1 cup **HERSHEY'S® Semi-Sweet Chocolate Chips**
1 cup **REESE'S® Peanut Butter Chips**

Cream shortening or butter or margarine, sugar, brown sugar and vanilla until light and fluffy. Add eggs and beat well. Combine flour and baking soda; add to creamed mixture. Stir in **HER-**SHEY'S® Semi-Sweet Chocolate Chips and REESE'S® Peanut Butter Chips. Drop by teaspoonful onto ungreased cookie sheet. Bake at 350° for 10-12 minutes or until light brown. Cool slightly before removing from cookie sheet.

About 5 dozen 2½-inch cookies

Note: Or substitute one cup of **REESE'S® Peanut Butter Chips** in your favorite chocolate chip cookie recipe.

CHOCOLATE CHIP COOKIES

2¼ cups sifted flour
1 tsp. baking soda
1 tsp. salt
1 cup softened butter or shortening
¾ cup **US Granulated Sugar**
¾ cup **US Light Brown Sugar**, firmly packed
1 tsp. vanilla
½ tsp. water
2 eggs
12 oz. chocolate chips
¾ cup chopped nuts (optional)

Preheat oven to 375°F. Sift together flour, baking soda and salt; set aside. Combine butter, sugars, vanilla and water and beat until creamy. Beat in eggs. Add flour mixture and mix well. Stir in chocolate chips and nuts. Drop by rounded teaspoonfuls onto greased cookie sheets. Bake at 375°F for 10 to 12 minutes.

Makes about 6 dozen (2½-inch) cookies

Note: For softer cookies use butter in place of shortening and shorten baking time.

PEANUT POLKA DOTTIES

1½ cups **3-MINUTE BRAND® Oats**
½ tsp. salt
14 oz. can sweetened condensed milk
½ tsp. vanilla
½ cup crunchy peanut butter
1 cup (6-oz.) semi-sweet chocolate chips

Combine oats, salt, milk and vanilla. Blend in peanut butter and chocolate chips. Press mixture into a greased 8 × 8-inch baking pan. Bake at 350° F for 35 minutes. Cut in bars to serve.

PEANUT BUTTER CHOCOLATE CHIP COOKIES

½ cup peanut butter
½ cup butter or margarine, softened
½ cup packed brown sugar
¼ cup sugar
1 teaspoon vanilla
1 egg
1 tablespoon water
1 cup unsifted flour
½ teaspoon salt
½ teaspoon baking powder
¾ cup chopped peanuts
1 package (6-oz.) **GHIRARDELLI® Semi-Sweet Chocolate Chips**

Cream peanut butter with butter, adding brown sugar, sugar, vanilla, egg and water. Stir flour with salt and baking powder. Gradually add dry ingredients to creamed mixture. Stir in peanuts and Chocolate Chips. Drop by teaspoon onto ungreased baking sheet. To flatten cookies, crisscross with fork. Bake at 350°F for 10-12 minutes. Cool on rack.

Makes 5 dozen cookies

PEANUT BUTTER JUMBOS

1 cup butter or margarine
1 cup peanut butter
1 cup granulated sugar
1 cup firmly packed brown sugar
2 eggs
2 cups flour
1 teaspoon baking soda
1 cup "M&M's"® Plain or Peanut Chocolate Candies
½ cup raisins, if desired

Beat together butter, peanut butter and sugars until light and fluffy; blend in eggs. Gradually add combined flour and soda; mix well. Stir in candies and raisins. Drop dough by level ¼ cup measure onto greased cookie sheet about 3 inches apart. Press 3 to 4 additional candies into each cookie, if desired. Bake at 350°F for 14 to 16 minutes or until edges are golden brown. Cool on cookie sheet 3 minutes; remove to wire rack to cool thoroughly.

Makes about 2 dozen (4-inch) cookies

PEANUT BUTTER CRACKLES

1½ cups unsifted flour
1 teaspoon baking soda
¼ teaspoon salt
¾ cup MAZOLA® Corn Oil Margarine
¼ cup SKIPPY® Creamy or Super Chunk Peanut Butter
1 cup sugar
1 egg
1 teaspoon vanilla
Sugar (optional)

In small bowl stir together flour, baking soda and salt. In large bowl with mixer at medium speed beat together margarine and peanut butter until smooth. Beat in 1 cup sugar until blended. Beat in egg and vanilla. Reduce speed to low; add flour mixture and beat well. If necessary, chill dough. Shape into ¾-inch balls. Roll in sugar and place on ungreased cookie sheets. Bake in 375°F oven 10 to 12 minutes or until lightly browned. Cool on wire rack.

Makes about 5 dozen

PEANUT BUTTER DATE COOKIES

4 cups sifted all-purpose flour
1 teaspoon baking powder
¼ teaspoon baking soda
1 teaspoon salt
½ teaspoon ground cinnamon
¼ teaspoon ground nutmeg
1 cup SUPERMAN™ Crunchy Peanut Butter
1 cup butter or margarine
1 cup packed brown sugar
⅔ cup granulated sugar
2 eggs
1 cup chopped dates

Sift together flour, baking powder, soda, salt, and spices. Cream peanut butter and butter. Gradually stir in sugars and beat until light and fluffy. Beat in eggs, one at a time; then mix in flour mixture. Stir in dates. Shape into 4 rolls, each about 8 inches long. Wrap with waxed paper or plastic wrap. Chill thoroughly. Cut into thin slices, place on ungreased baking sheet, and bake at 400° for 5 to 8 minutes.

Makes 7 dozen

Note: Unbaked dough may be stored in refrigerator for several weeks.

ALMOND BUTTER COOKIES

2¼ cups BLUE DIAMOND® Blanched Whole Almonds, lightly toasted, divided
1¼ cups all-purpose flour
¼ cup granulated sugar
1 cup butter, softened
1 teaspoon vanilla

Finely grind 1½ cups almonds in food processor or blender. Mix together flour, sugar, and ground almonds; with fingers work in butter and vanilla until soft dough forms. Chill about 1 hour.

Shape dough into 1-inch balls. Press one whole almond into center of cookie. Bake on ungreased cookie sheet at 350°F, 12 to 15 minutes or until lightly browned. Cool on wire rack.

Makes about 5 dozen cookies

DOMINO® CHINESE ALMOND COOKIES

¾ cup shortening (half butter or margarine if desired)
½ cup DOMINO® Granulated Sugar
1½ teaspoons almond extract
2¼ cups all-purpose flour
1½ teaspoons baking powder
¼ teaspoon salt
⅔ cup ground almonds
2 eggs
1 tablespoon water
24 whole blanched almonds

Cream shortening and sugar. Add almond extract. Beat in 1 egg. Sift together flour, baking powder, and salt; add to creamed mixture. Stir in ground almonds; mixing thoroughly. Shape into 24 balls; place 2 inches apart on lightly greased cookie sheet. Flatten to 2½ inches in diameter. Combine remaining egg and water, brush tops of cookies. Place a whole almond on each cookie. Bake at 375°F for 12 to 14 minutes until golden. Cool on racks.

Makes 2 dozen cookies

CHINESE ALMOND COOKIES

½ lb. HAIN® Safflower Oil Margarine
2½ cups unbleached pastry flour
½ tsp. baking soda
1½ tsp. salt
½ cup honey
1 egg, slightly beaten
2 tsp. almond extract
60 blanched almonds

Cut margarine into sifted dry ingredients. Add honey, egg and extract and blend well. Shape into 1-inch balls and place on ungreased cookie sheet. Flatten cookies and press one almond into the center of each. Bake 12 to 15 minutes at 350 degrees F. Turn out on wire screen to cool.

Yield: 5 dozen

NO-BAKE COOKIES

¼ cup butter or margarine
⅓ cup peanut butter
¼ cup maple flavored syrup
2 tablespoons firmly packed brown sugar
3 cups coarsely crushed QUAKER® 100% Natural Cereal, original (about 3½ cups cereal)

Combine all ingredients except cereal in 1-qt. saucepan; bring to a boil. Simmer over medium heat about 3 minutes, stirring constantly. Pour over cereal; mix well. Press into greased 8-inch square baking pan. Chill until firm; cut into bars. Store in refrigerator. *Makes 8-inch square pan of no-bake cookies*

GIANT OATMEAL COOKIES

1¼ cups all-purpose flour
½ teaspoon soda
½ teaspoon salt
1 cup firmly packed brown sugar
¾ cup butter or margarine
2 eggs
1 teaspoon vanilla
2½ cups **QUAKER**® Oats (quick or old fashioned, uncooked)
One 6-oz. pkg. (1 cup) semi-sweet chocolate pieces
½ cup chopped nuts

Heat oven to 350°F. Grease 2 large cookie sheets. In small bowl, combine flour, soda and salt; mix well. In large bowl, beat together sugar and butter until light and fluffy; blend in eggs and vanilla. Add flour mixture; mix well. Stir in oats, chocolate pieces and nuts. Divide dough in half. Spread each half to ¾-inch thickness on prepared cookie sheets. Bake 17 to 20 minutes or until lightly browned. Decorate with candles, if desired.

Makes two 11-inch cookies

VARIATION:

Drop dough by rounded tablespoonfuls onto greased cookie sheets. Bake 10 to 12 minutes.

Makes about 3 dozen 2½-inch cookies

SNICKER DOODLES

1 cup shortening
½ cup sugar
½ cup brown sugar
1 egg
1 cup **3-MINUTE BRAND**® Oats
2 cups sifted flour
½ tsp. salt
1 tsp. soda
2 tsp. sugar
1 tsp. cinnamon

Cream shortening and sugars. Add egg and oats and beat well. Sift flour, salt and soda and blend into first mixture. Chill dough. Roll into balls the size of small walnuts. Dip in a mixture of the sugar and cinnamon. Bake on ungreased baking sheet at 375°F for 15 minutes or until golden brown.

BUTTERSCOTCH REFRIGERATOR COOKIES

1¼ cups **ELAM'S**® Pastry Flour
1 cup **ELAM'S**® Unbleached White Flour With Wheat Germ
1 teaspoon baking powder
½ cup butter
¾ cup honey
1 teaspoon vanilla
½ teaspoon almond extract
1 egg
1 cup very finely chopped pecans

Combine first 3 ingredients in bowl; mix and reserve. Cream together butter, honey, vanilla and almond extract until soft and smooth. Add egg; beat until fluffy. Blend in dry ingredients; mix well. Stir in chopped nuts. Shape into a roll about 12 inches long.

(Continued)

Roll up tightly in a sheet of waxed paper or plastic film. Chill several hours or overnight. Cut into thin slices, about ⅛-inch thick. Place 1 inch apart on ungreased baking sheets. Bake in moderate oven (375°F) until done and lightly browned, about 8 minutes. *Yield: 7 to 8 dozen cookies, about 2½ inches in diameter*

BUTTERSCOTCH CRISPIES

1½ cups sifted flour
¼ teaspoon salt
1¼ teaspoons baking powder
½ cup butter or shortening
⅔ cup brown sugar
1 teaspoon vanilla
1 egg
¾ cup crushed **JAYS Potato Chips**

Sift flour once, then measure; add salt and baking powder and sift together three times. Cream shortening and sugar together until light and fluffy. Add vanilla and egg and beat well. Gradually add flour, mixing well after addition. Add potato chips. Shape in a two-inch roll and wrap in wax paper. Chill overnight in refrigerator. Cut in ⅛ inch slices. Bake on ungreased cooky sheet in moderately hot 375 degree oven for 10 to 12 minutes or until lightly browned. Keep cookies in tightly covered can or jar.

Makes 4 dozen

BROWN SUGAR DROP COOKIES

1 egg
1 cup brown sugar, firmly packed
1 tsp. vanilla
½ cup unsifted all-purpose flour
¼ tsp. soda
¼ tsp. salt
1½ cups **DIAMOND**® Walnuts, chopped medium fine

In small mixer bowl beat egg till it is light and fluffy (about 3 min. at high speed). Add sugar and vanilla and stir till smooth. Quickly stir in flour, soda and salt. Blend in walnuts chopped medium fine. By teaspoonfuls, drop onto greased and floured cookie sheet 2 inches apart. Bake at 350°F., 7-9 min. Or just till cookies start to brown at edge. Do not overbake. Remove immediately to cooling rack. *Makes about 4 dozen 2-inch cookies*

GINGERSNAPS

¾ cup shortening
¾ cup sugar
½ cup **GRANDMA'S**® Unsulphured Molasses
1 egg
2¼ cups sifted all-purpose flour
1½ teaspoons baking soda
¼ teaspoon salt
1 teaspoon cinnamon
½ teaspoon ginger
⅛ teaspoon ground cloves
Granulated sugar (about ¼ cup)

Cream together shortening and sugar until light and fluffy. Add molasses and egg; mix well. Sift in flour, baking soda, salt and spices. Mix well. Place in freezer 1 hour or chill in refrigerator 2 hours. Form into approximately 1-inch balls; roll in granulated sugar. Bake on greased baking sheets in 375°F. oven 10 to 12 minutes. *Yield: Approximately 4 dozen*

CRACKLE-TOP MOLASSES COOKIES

2½ cups all-purpose flour
2 teaspoons baking soda
1½ teaspoons **DURKEE Ground Mustard**
½ teaspoon **DURKEE Ground Allspice**
¼ teaspoon salt
¼ cup shortening
½ cup butter or margarine
1 cup packed brown sugar
1 egg
¼ cup molasses
1 teaspoon **DURKEE Vanilla Extract**
1 teaspoon **DURKEE Imitation Lemon Extract**
Sugar

Combine flour, soda, mustard, allspice and salt; set aside. Cream together shortening, butter and brown sugar until light and fluffy. Add egg, molasses, and extracts; blend well. Gradually add dry ingredients to creamed mixture, stirring until well combined. Cover and chill dough at least 1 hour.

Shape into 1-inch balls; dip tops into sugar. Place balls, sugared side up, about 2-inches apart on greased baking sheet. Bake at 375° for 10 to 12 minutes or until no imprint remains when cookies are lightly touched with finger. Remove from baking sheet, cool on rack.　*Makes 4 dozen cookies*

HERMITS

½ cup shortening
½ cup brown sugar, packed
½ cup granulated sugar
1 egg
¼ cup orange juice
1½ cups all-purpose flour
½ teaspoon baking soda
½ teaspoon salt
1 teaspoon allspice
¼ teaspoon mace
1 cup **SUN • MAID® Seedless Raisins**
½ cup chopped **DIAMOND® Walnuts**

Cream together shortening and sugars; beat in egg and juice. Sift together flour, soda, salt and spices; add to creamed mixture, beating well. Fold in raisins and walnuts. Drop by rounded tablespoonfuls onto greased baking sheet. Bake at 350 degrees F about 12 minutes, or until lightly browned.　*Makes about 36 cookies*

LEMON GINGER SHORTBREAD COOKIES

½ cup **MAZOLA® Corn Oil Margarine**, softened
⅔ cup unsifted flour
⅓ cup **ARGO®/KINGSFORD'S® Corn Starch**
¼ cup confectioner's sugar
1 teaspoon grated lemon rind
⅛ teaspoon ground ginger

In medium bowl place margarine, flour, corn starch, sugar, lemon rind and ginger. With pastry blender or fork combine until crumbly and well mixed. With hands form into 1-inch balls. Place 2 inches apart on ungreased cookie sheet. Bake in 350° oven 15 minutes, or until very lightly browned.　*Makes 20 cookies*

Note: Cookies may be lightly pressed with cookie stamp before baking.

LEMON THINS

½ lb. (2 sticks) **DARIGOLD Butter**
1 cup white sugar
1 **DARIGOLD Egg**
1¾ cups flour
¼ teaspoon salt
Juice and rind of 1 lemon

Cream **DARIGOLD Butter** and sugar. Add egg, flour, salt and lemon. Roll into a roll 2″ thick and 12″ long. Place in refrigerator to chill. Slice thin and bake in 375 degree oven on greased cookie sheets 8 to 10 minutes or until edges turn light brown.

ORANGE CREAM SANDWICHES

1 (8-ounce) package cream cheese, softened
1 (14-ounce) can **EAGLE® Brand Sweetened Condensed Milk** (NOT evaporated milk)
1 (6-ounce) container frozen unsweetened orange juice concentrate, thawed
1 cup (½ pint) whipping cream, whipped
48 **NABISCO Old Fashion Ginger Snaps**

In large mixer bowl, beat cheese until fluffy. Beat in sweetened condensed milk until smooth. Stir in juice concentrate. Fold in whipped cream. Fill 24 paper-lined muffin cups ½ to ⅔ full with mixture. Top each with a ginger snap, bottom side down. Freeze 4 hours or until firm. Let stand at room temperature 5 to 10 minutes; remove paper liner and top with remaining ginger snaps, top side up. Press together gently. To store, wrap sandwiches individually in aluminum foil and return to freezer.　*Makes 24 servings*

"LADY BE GOOD" FINGERS

1 teaspoon soft butter
½ teaspoon grated orange or lemon rind
½ cup **DOMINO® Confectioners 10-X Powdered Sugar**
2 teaspoons orange or lemon juice
1 dozen lady fingers, split

Blend butter and rind. Alternately add sugar and juice, mixing until smooth. Spread a thin layer of fruit glaze between lady fingers. Sprinkle with more sugar. Serve at once, or store in air tight container.

RALSTON® CRESCENTS

1 cup butter or margarine
1 cup sifted confectioner's sugar
2 teaspoons vanilla
2 cups all-purpose flour*
½ teaspoon salt
1 cup **Instant RALSTON®** OR ¾ cup **Regular RALSTON®**
Confectioner's sugar

Preheat oven to 325°. Cream butter. Add sugar gradually. Mix well. Add vanilla. Stir together flour, salt and **RALSTON®**. Add to creamed mixture. Mix well.

Shape dough into 1-inch balls or crescents. Place on ungreased baking sheet. Bake about 15 minutes or until edges are light brown. Roll in confectioner's sugar while still warm.
　Makes about 7 dozen

*Stir flour; then spoon into measuring cup.

PERNOD® CRESCENTS

1 cup butter or margarine, softened
6 Tbsp. confectioners' sugar
1 egg yolk
3 Tbsp. PERNOD® Liqueur
⅓ cup finely chopped walnuts
¼ tsp. salt
2½ cups all-purpose flour
Glaze*
Walnuts, finely chopped

Beat butter, sugar, egg yolk and **PERNOD®** until light and fluffy. Stir in walnuts, salt and flour. Gather mixture and form into a ball. Cover and refrigerate about 1 hour. Heat oven to 325°. Shape dough into 1-inch balls. Shape into crescent shapes. Bake on greased baking sheets until firm and light brown around edges, 20 to 25 minutes. Cool on wire racks. Brush glaze over cookies and sprinkle immediately with nuts. Flavor of cookies will mellow after being stored 2 to 3 days.   *Makes about 4 dozen*

*PERNOD® GLAZE

½ cup confectioners' sugar
PERNOD® Liqueur

Mix about ½ cup confectioners' sugar with enough **PERNOD®** to make a spreadable glaze.

MACADAMIA MACAROONS

2 egg whites (at room temperature)
2 teaspoons coffee liqueur
½ teaspoon pure vanilla extract
¼ teaspoon salt
⅔ cup sugar
1 can (3½-oz.) flaked coconut (¾ cup)
¼ cup chopped MAUNA LOA® Macadamia Nuts

Preheat oven to 250°F. In large bowl of an electric mixer beat egg whites with liqueur, vanilla extract and salt until soft peaks form. Gradually add sugar; continue to beat until stiff peaks form. Fold in coconut. Drop by teaspoonfuls 2 inches apart on greased baking sheets. Sprinkle with macadamia nuts. Bake until browned and crisp, about 1 hour. Cool on wire racks.   *Yield: about 2 dozen*

HOLIDAY CUTOUTS

1 cup butter or margarine
1 cup light brown sugar
1 egg, unbeaten
1½ cups quick cooking oats, uncooked
2¼ cups all-purpose flour
1 teaspoon soda
½ teaspoon salt
1 teaspoon vanilla
¼ cup DR PEPPER®
Preserves or jelly (your favorite flavor)

Cream fat, add sugar and beat until light and fluffy. Add egg and beat again. Add oats and mix well. Sift together flour, salt and soda and add alternately with the **DR PEPPER®** to which has been added the vanilla. Divide into 4 or 5 portions and chill several hours.

Then, roll out to ⅛-inch thickness. Cut into rounds with 2-inch round cutter. Using a small cookie cutter, cut an opening in the center of ½ of the rounds. Place the whole rounds on ungreased cookie sheet. Top each with about ½ teaspoon of your favorite preserves or jelly. Top with the cutout cookie. Seal the edges with fork dipped in flour. Bake in 375 degrees F oven 12 to 15 minutes until nicely browned. Remove to cooling rack.   *Yield: 6 dozen*

VARIATION:

If you are in a hurry, drop by teaspoonfuls onto the ungreased cookie sheet. Make thumb print on each and fill with preserves or jelly.

HOLIDAY COOKIES
(Low Calorie)

1 cup sifted all-purpose flour
¼ teaspoon baking powder
⅛ teaspoon salt
¼ cup margarine
¼ cup sugar
1 egg
¾ teaspoon vanilla
4 packets SWEET 'N LOW®

In medium-size bowl, sift together flour, baking powder, and salt. In separate bowl, cream margarine; add sugar gradually and continue creaming until light. Add egg, vanilla, and **SWEET 'N LOW®**, beat well. Thoroughly stir in dry ingredients. Refrigerate one hour.

Preheat oven to 400°F. Spray cookie sheets with non-stick coating agent. Roll dough into ¾-inch balls. Place 2 inches apart on prepared cookie sheets; press flat with base of floured glass. Flute edges with fork. Bake 6 to 8 minutes, or until brown.
2½ dozen cookies

| PER SERVING (1 cookie): | Calories: 35 | Protein: 1g |
| Carbohydrate: 5g | Fat: 2 g | Sodium: 30 mg |

EASTER NEST COOKIES

½ cup shortening
½ cup sugar
½ cup GRANDMA'S® Unsulphured Molasses
1 egg, well beaten
2½ cups unsifted flour
1½ teaspoons baking powder
¾ teaspoon baking soda
½ teaspoon salt
¼ teaspoon ground cinnamon
¼ teaspoon ground nutmeg
2 cups shredded coconut, divided
1 cup chopped walnuts
½ cup milk
1 cup canned buttercream frosting
Food coloring
Jelly beans

In large bowl cream shortening and sugar; beat in molasses and egg. In medium bowl sift together flour, baking powder, baking soda, salt, cinnamon, and nutmeg. Stir in 1 cup coconut and walnuts. Add dry ingredients alternately with milk to creamed mixture. Measure ¼ cup dough for each cookie. Spread on lightly greased cookie sheets. Bake in a 375°F oven 10 to 12 minutes or until lightly browned. Cool. In a small bowl combine remaining 1 cup coconut with a few drops food coloring. Mix to blend color. Spread a thin layer of frosting over each cookie. Press a ring of coconut around cookie edge. Arrange jelly beans in center.
Yield: 18 large cookies, about 4½ inches each

SANTA'S WHISKERS

1 cup butter or margarine
1 cup sugar
1 teaspoon DURKEE Almond Extract
2½ cups all purpose flour
¾ cup finely chopped DURKEE Maraschino Cherries
    (1-10 oz. jar)
½ cup finely chopped pecans
¾ cup DURKEE Flaked Coconut

Cream butter and sugar, blend in extract. Stir in flour, cherries, and nuts. Form in 2 rolls, each 2 inches in diameter and 8 inches long. Roll in coconut. Wrap and chill several hours or overnight. Slice ¼ inch thick; place on ungreased cookie sheet. Bake at 375° for 12 minutes or until edges are golden.   *Makes about 5 dozen*

FRANGELICO® SCROLLS

1 cup flour
½ cup sugar
¼ teaspoon salt
¼ cup light corn syrup
½ cup butter
3 Tbsp. FRANGELICO® Liqueur
¼ cup finely chopped hazelnuts
½ cup heavy cream, whipped with 1 tsp. sugar &
    2 Tbsp. FRANGELICO®

Mix flour, sugar & salt together. Heat corn syrup just to boil. Turn off heat; add butter, stirring until it melts. Slowly add flour-sugar mixture, FRANGELICO®, nuts. Drop heaping teaspoonfuls on buttered baking sheet—*no more than 6 at a time.* Bake in 300°F. oven for 8-10 minutes. Wait one minute; lift each cookie off baking sheet; immediately roll around handle of wooden spoon. Cool. Before serving, fill each scroll with whipped cream.

ROMAN MEAL® SPICE DROPS

½ cup shortening
1½ cups brown sugar, packed
3 eggs, slightly beaten
¼ cup milk
1 tsp. vanilla
1⅓ cups sifted flour
1½ tsp. baking powder
½ tsp. salt
1 tsp. each of cinnamon, nutmeg and cloves
2 cups ROMAN MEAL® Cereal
1 cup raisins
1 cup chopped nuts (optional)

Cream shortening and sugar. Blend in eggs, milk and vanilla. Add flour sifted with baking powder, spices and salt; mix thoroughly. Add cereal, raisins and nuts. Drop from teaspoon about 2 inches apart onto cookie sheet. Bake 10-12 minutes at 375°F.
Makes 4-5 dozen cookies

SNOW BALLS

1 cup (2 sticks) butter
½ cup sifted confectioners' sugar
2 cups sifted cake flour
1 tablespoon milk
1 teaspoon vanilla
3 CLARK® Bars (1¼ ounces each), chopped
Sifted confectioners' sugar

Beat butter and confectioners' sugar until creamy and fluffy. Add flour, milk and vanilla; mix well. Stir in candy. Chill thoroughly. Shape into 1-inch balls. Place 2 inches apart on ungreased cookie sheet. Bake at 375° for 12 to 15 minutes. While still warm, sprinkle with confectioners' sugar.   *3 dozen*

FIRESIDE PUMPKIN COOKIES

1 cup butter or margarine
½ cup light brown sugar, firmly packed
½ cup granulated sugar
1 cup LIBBY'S® Solid Pack Pumpkin
1 egg
1 teaspoon vanilla
2 cups sifted flour
1 teaspoon baking soda
1 teaspoon baking powder
1 teaspoon ground cinnamon
½ teaspoon salt
1 cup chopped walnuts
1 cup snipped dates

Preheat oven to 350°F. In a large bowl, beat butter and sugars together until fluffy. Add pumpkin, egg and vanilla; mix well. Sift flour, baking soda, baking powder, cinnamon and salt together. Add to pumpkin mixture and stir to mix well. Stir in nuts and dates. Drop batter by heaping teaspoonfuls onto ungreased baking sheets, 1 inch apart. Bake at 350° for 15 minutes or until tops are golden and centers firm to the touch. Remove from baking sheets and cool on wire racks.   *Yields about 4 dozen 2-inch cookies*

HAWAIIAN DROP COOKIES

2 cups sifted all-purpose flour
2 teaspoons CLABBER GIRL® Baking Powder
½ teaspoon salt
⅔ cup shortening
1¼ cups sugar
½ teaspoon vanilla extract
½ teaspoon almond extract
1 egg
¾ cup well-drained, crushed pineapple
½ cup finely chopped shredded coconut

Sift together flour, Baking Powder, and salt. Cream shortening, sugar, and extracts thoroughly. Beat in egg until mixture is fluffy. Blend in pineapple and dry ingredients. Drop by teaspoonfuls on ungreased cooky sheet 3 inches apart. Sprinkle with coconut. Bake in a 325°F (slow) oven about 20 minutes. Cookies are better stored for 24 hours.   *Yield: 4½ dozen (2½-inch) diameter cookies*

PRIZE COOKIES

1 cup shortening
1½ cups sugar
3 eggs
3 cups unsifted flour
1 teaspoon baking soda
½ teaspoon salt
1⅓ cups (one-half 28-ounce jar) NONE SUCH®
    Ready-to-Use Mincemeat

Preheat oven to 375°. In large mixer bowl, beat shortening and sugar until fluffy. Add eggs, beating until smooth. Stir together dry ingredients; gradually add to shortening mixture. Mix well. Stir in mincemeat. Drop by rounded teaspoonfuls, 2 inches apart, onto greased baking sheets. Bake 8 to 10 minutes or until lightly browned. *Makes about 6½ dozen cookies*

Note: For a less moist and more crisp cookie, substitute 1 (9-ounce) package **NONE SUCH® Condensed Mincemeat**, crumbled, for ready-to-use mincemeat.

ROSE'S CINNAMON SNACK COOKIES

6 tea bags **CELESTIAL SEASONINGS® Cinnamon Rose™** (Contents)
¼ cup hot water
½ cup margarine
¾ cup honey
1 egg
¼ cup unsulfured molasses
½ teaspoon salt
1½ teaspoons baking soda
2¾ cups whole wheat flour
½ cup buttermilk

Empty tea bags into a small container. Add the hot water. Stir and allow to stand 15 minutes.

Mix margarine, honey, egg and molasses together thoroughly. Add salt, soda, **Cinnamon Rose™** and 1 cup flour. Alternate buttermilk and remaining flour. Chill for 2 hours—until mixture holds shape. Put teaspoonsful about 2″ apart on greased baking sheets. Bake at 400°F for 10 minutes.

Makes 4 dozen cookies

CHEESE COOKIE CRISPS

1 cup unsifted **ROBIN HOOD® All Purpose Flour**
½ tsp. baking powder
1 cup flaked coconut
½ cup softened butter or margarine
½ cup (4-oz.) **KAUKAUNA® Port Wine Cold Pack Cheese Food***
¾ cup sugar
½ tsp. vanilla
½ cup finely crushed corn flakes

Combine . . . . flour and baking powder on wax paper. Stir to blend. Mix in coconut.

Cream . . . . butter, cheese, sugar and vanilla thoroughly.

Add . . . . blended dry ingredients to creamed mixture. Mix well.

Refrigerate . . . . dough 1 hour. Shape into 1-inch balls.

Roll . . . . in corn flake crumbs. Place on ungreased baking sheets.

Flatten . . . . balls with bottom of glass dipped in remaining crumbs.

Bake . . . . at 350° for 12-14 minutes.

Let stand . . . . 1 minute before removing from baking sheet. Cool on rack.

Makes 3 dozen cookies

VARIATION:

***KAUKAUNA® Sharp Cheddar Cold Pack Cheese Food** may be substituted for **Port Wine Cold Pack Cheese Food**.

Bars

TOLL HOUSE® DOUBLE CHOCOLATE BROWNIES

¾ cup *unsifted* flour
¼ measuring teaspoon baking soda
¼ measuring teaspoon salt
⅓ cup butter
¾ cup sugar
2 measuring tablespoons water
One (12-oz.) pkg. (2 cups) **NESTLÉ® Semi-Sweet Real Chocolate Morsels**, divided
1 measuring teaspoon vanilla extract
2 eggs
½ cup chopped nuts

Preheat oven to 325°F. In small bowl, combine flour, baking soda and salt; set aside. In small saucepan, combine butter, sugar and water; bring *just to a boil*. Remove from heat. Add 6-oz. (1 cup) **NESTLÉ® Semi-Sweet Real Chocolate Morsels** and vanilla extract. Stir until morsels melt and mixture is smooth. Transfer to large bowl. Add eggs, one at a time, beating well after each addition. Gradually blend in flour mixture. Stir in remaining 1 cup **NESTLÉ® Semi-Sweet Real Chocolate Morsels** and nuts. Spread into greased 9-inch square baking pan. Bake at 325°F 30-35 minutes. Cool completely. Cut into 2¼-inch squares.

Makes: Sixteen 2¼-inch squares

GHIRARDELLI® FROSTED CHOCOLATE BROWNIES

⅓ cup butter or margarine, softened
1 cup sugar
2 eggs
½ tsp. vanilla
½ tsp. salt
4 sections (2-oz.) **GHIRARDELLI® Unsweetened Baking Chocolate**
½ cup unsifted flour
½ cup chopped walnuts

By hand, lightly cream butter with sugar. Mix in eggs, vanilla, salt. Stir in melted chocolate. Add flour, mixing until smooth, then add nuts. Spread into greased 8- or 9-inch square pan. Bake at 350° F for 20-25 minutes. For extra fudgy brownies, use 8-inch pan or less baking time. For cake-like brownies, use 9-inch pan or longer baking time. Cool in pan. Frost with half recipe Dark Chocolate Frosting.* Cut into squares. *Makes 20-25 squares*

*DARK CHOCOLATE FROSTING

4 sections (2-oz.) **GHIRARDELLI® Unsweetened Baking Chocolate**
¼ cup butter
¼ cup milk
Pinch salt
2½ cups powdered sugar
½ tsp. vanilla

In heavy saucepan on low heat, melt broken chocolate with butter, milk, salt. Stir constantly until thick and smooth. Remove from heat. Mix in sugar and vanilla. Beat until thick enough to spread.

Frosts 9×13-inch cake

FROSTED FUDGIE BROWNIES

Brownies:
1 cup sugar
2 eggs
½ cup butter, softened
2 envelopes (2-oz.) NESTLÉ® CHOCO-BAKE
1 measuring teaspoon vanilla extract
⅔ cup *unsifted* flour
½ measuring teaspoon baking powder
½ measuring teaspoon salt
½ cup chopped nuts

Fudge Frosting:
1 egg yolk
2 measuring tablespoons butter, melted
1 envelope (1-oz.) NESTLÉ® CHOCO-BAKE
1 measuring teaspoon milk
½ measuring teaspoon vanilla extract
1 cup sifted confectioners' sugar

BROWNIES:
Preheat oven to 350°F. In small bowl, combine sugar, eggs, butter, NESTLÉ® CHOCO-BAKE and vanilla extract; beat until creamy. Add flour, baking powder and salt; mix well. Add nuts. Spread into greased 8″ square baking pan. Bake at 350°F for 30 minutes.
Cool completely. Spread with Fudge Frosting. Cut into 2″ squares.

FUDGE FROSTING:
In small bowl, combine egg yolk, butter, NESTLÉ® CHOCO-BAKE, milk and vanilla extract; mix until well blended. Gradually add confectioners' sugar; beat until creamy.
Makes: sixteen 2″ squares and ¾ cup frosting

MARBLED BROWNIES

⅓ cup MAZOLA® Corn Oil Margarine
⅓ cup sugar
⅓ cup KARO® Light Corn Syrup
1 egg
1 cup unsifted flour
½ teaspoon baking powder
½ teaspoon salt
2 squares (1-oz. each) semisweet chocolate, melted
1 package (3-oz.) cream cheese

Grease 9×9×2-inch baking pan. In large bowl with mixer at medium speed beat margarine and sugar until well mixed. Beat in corn syrup and egg. Stir together flour, baking powder and salt. At low speed beat flour mixture into margarine mixture until combined. Stir ½ cup of batter into melted chocolate. Add cream cheese to batter remaining in bowl; beat until smooth. Turn into prepared pan. With metal spatula swirl chocolate mixture through cream cheese mixture. Bake in 350°F oven 40 minutes. Cool. Cut into bars.   *Makes 16*

RICOTTA BROWNIES

1 cup SORRENTO® Whole Milk Ricotta
1 cup margarine
4 squares unsweetened chocolate
2½ cups sugar
1 cup chopped nuts
1 cup flour
½ tsp. salt
2 tsp. vanilla
4 eggs

In heavy saucepan, melt margarine and chocolate. With wire whisk, beat in 2 cups sugar and 3 eggs until blended. Stir in flour, salt, 1 tsp. vanilla and nuts. Spread in greased 13×9-inch pan. Beat ricotta, ½ cup sugar, 1 tsp. vanilla and 1 egg till smooth—3 minutes. Drop by spoonfuls on top of chocolate mixture. Swirl with knife to marbleize. Bake at 350° 40-45 minutes.

BROWNIES
(Cake Type)

½ cup shortening
2 ounces unsweetened chocolate
1 cup DOMINO® Granulated Sugar
¾ teaspoon salt
2 eggs
1 teaspoon vanilla extract
¾ cup all-purpose flour
½ teaspoon baking powder
½ cup chopped pecans or walnuts

Melt shortening and chocolate in top of double boiler over simmering water. Remove from heat; cool. Cream chocolate mixture, sugar and salt thoroughly. Beat eggs into creamed mixture, one at a time, until light and smooth. Add extract.

Sift together flour and baking powder; stir into creamed ingredients, blending well. Add nuts; mix briefly. Spread batter into greased 8-inch square pan. Bake in moderate oven 350°F 20-25 minutes or until done. Remove to cooling rack. When cool, cut 2-inch squares. Store in airtight container with waxed paper between layers.
Yield: 16 brownies

PEANUT FUDGE BROWNIES

¾ cup (1½ sticks) butter
1½ cups granulated sugar
1½ teaspoons vanilla
3 eggs
1½ cups all-purpose flour
½ cup unsweetened cocoa
½ teaspoon each: baking powder, salt
1 square (1 ounce) unsweetened chocolate
1½ tablespoons each: butter, creamy peanut butter
1 cup confectioners' sugar
2 to 3 tablespoons hot tap water
2 CLARK® Bars (1.75 ounces each), coarsely chopped

In saucepan, melt butter; cool slightly. Blend in granulated sugar and vanilla. Beat in eggs, one at a time. Combine flour, cocoa, baking powder and salt. Add to butter mixture; mix well. Pour into greased 13 × 2-inch pan. Bake at 350° for 25 to 30 minutes. Cool on rack. In saucepan over low heat, melt chocolate, butter and peanut butter. Remove from heat. Blend in confectioners' sugar and enough hot water to make a pourable glaze. Pour over brownies, spreading evenly with spatula. Sprinkle crushed CLARK® Bars over top. When glaze has set, cut into bars.   *3 dozen*

SUPREME LAYER BARS

2½ cups quick-cooking or old-fashioned oats
¾ cup all-purpose flour
¾ cup packed brown sugar
½ teaspoon baking soda
¾ cup margarine or butter, melted
1 package BETTY CROCKER® Supreme Fudge Brownie Mix
½ cup chopped nuts
Chocolate-Cream Cheese Frosting*

Heat oven to 350°. Grease bottom only of rectangular pan, 13 × 9 × 2-inches. Mix oats, flour, brown sugar and baking soda; stir in margarine. Reserve 1 cup oat mixture. Press remaining oat mixture in pan. Bake 10 minutes; cool 5 minutes. Prepare brownies as directed on package; stir in nuts. Spread dough over baked oat mixture; sprinkle with reserved oat mixture. Bake 25 to 30 minutes; cool. Spread with Chocolate-Cream Cheese Frosting. Cut into bars, about 2 × 1-inch.   *48 brownies*

*CHOCOLATE-CREAM CHEESE FROSTING

> 2 cups powdered sugar
> 1 teaspoon vanilla
> 1 ounce melted unsweetened chocolate (cool)
> 1 package (3-ounces) cream cheese, softened
> 1 to 2 teaspoons milk

Mix all ingredients until smooth and of spreading consistency.

CHEESECAKE BROWNIES

> 1 package (8-ounces) cream cheese, softened
> 1⅓ cups sugar
> 3 eggs
> ⅔ cup **CHIFFON®** Margarine
> 6 tablespoons unsweetened cocoa
> ¾ cup all-purpose flour
> ½ teaspoon baking powder
> ½ teaspoon salt
> 1 teaspoon vanilla

Mix cream cheese with ⅓ cup sugar and 1 egg until light and fluffy. Set aside. Cream **CHIFFON®** with remaining sugar; then beat in two eggs, one at a time, until light and fluffy; then add cocoa. Stir in a mixture of flour, baking powder and salt until blended. Add vanilla. Spoon half chocolate mixture into greased 8 × 8 × 2-inch or 9 × 9 × 2-inch baking pan. Spoon cheese mixture over chocolate layer. Add remaining chocolate by teaspoonfuls to cover cream cheese, spreading carefully. Bake at 350° for about 30 to 40 minutes depending on size of pan. Do not overbake. Cool. Cut into squares.   *Makes 36 squares*

CHOCOLATE CHEESECAKE BARS

> 1 package (18½ oz.) chocolate cake mix
> ½ cup **BEST FOODS®/HELLMANN'S®** Real Mayonnaise
> 12 ounces cream cheese, softened
> ½ cup sugar
> 2 eggs
> 1 package (6 oz) semisweet chocolate pieces, melted
> 1 teaspoon vanilla

In large bowl stir together cake mix and Real Mayonnaise until coarse crumbs form. Press evenly onto bottom and up sides of 15½ × 10½ × 1-inch jelly roll pan. In large bowl with mixer at medium speed beat cream cheese until smooth. Gradually beat in sugar. Add eggs, one at a time, beating well after each. Beat in chocolate and vanilla until smooth. Spread evenly over crust. Bake in 350°F oven 30 to 35 minutes or until set. Cool on wire rack. Refrigerate several hours. Cut into bars.
          Makes 75 (1 × 2-inch) bars

FUDGE-FILLED BARS

> 2 cups quick oats, uncooked
> 1½ cups flour
> 1 cup chopped nuts
> 1 cup firmly packed light brown sugar
> 1 teaspoon baking soda
> ¾ teaspoon salt
> 1 cup butter or margarine, melted
> 2 tablespoons vegetable shortening
> 1½ cups **"M&M's"®** Plain Chocolate Candies
> 1 can (14-oz.) sweetened condensed milk

Combine oats, flour, nuts, sugar, soda and salt; mix well. Add butter; mix until dry ingredients are thoroughly moistened and mixture resembles coarse crumbs. Reserve 1½ cups; press remaining crumb mixture evenly onto bottom of greased 15½ × 10½-inch jelly roll pan. Bake at 375°F for 10 minutes.
  Melt shortening in heavy saucepan until warm. Add 1 cup candies; continue cooking over very low heat, stirring constantly with metal spoon and pressing candies with back of spoon to break up. (Chocolate mixture will be almost melted and pieces of color coating will remain.) Remove from heat; stir in condensed milk, mixing well. Spread over partially baked crust to within ½-inch of edge.
  Combine reserved crumb mixture and remaining candies; sprinkle evenly over chocolate mixture, pressing in lightly. Continue baking about 20 minutes or until golden brown. Cool thoroughly; cut into bars.   *Makes one 15½ × 10½-inch pan of bars*

CHOCOLATE SCOTCHEROOS

> 1 cup light corn syrup
> 1 cup sugar
> 1 cup peanut butter
> 6 cups **KELLOGG'S® RICE KRISPIES®** Cereal
> 1 pkg. (6 oz., 1 cup) semi-sweet chocolate morsels
> 1 pkg. (6 oz., 1 cup) butterscotch morsels

1. Measure corn syrup and sugar into large saucepan. Cook over medium heat, stirring frequently, until sugar dissolves and mixture begins to boil. Remove from heat. Stir in peanut butter. Mix well. Add **KELLOGG'S® RICE KRISPIES®** Cereal. Stir until well coated. Press mixture into buttered 13 × 9 × 2-inch pan. Set aside.
2. Melt chocolate and butterscotch morsels together in small saucepan over low heat, stirring constantly. Spread evenly over cereal mixture. Let stand until firm. Cut into 1 × 2-inch bars to serve.   *Yield: 48 bars*

® Kellogg Company

CHOCO-RAISIN SQUARES

> ⅓ cup butter or margarine, softened
> 1 cup brown sugar, packed
> 2 eggs
> 1¼ cups all-purpose flour
> 1¼ teaspoons baking powder
> ⅛ teaspoon salt
> ¾ cup **SUN · MAID®** Seedless Raisins
> ½ cup semi-sweet chocolate pieces

Beat together butter, sugar and eggs until light. Combine flour with baking powder and salt; stir into beaten mixture. Add raisins and chocolate. Spread mixture in a greased 9-inch square pan; bake at 350 degrees F about 30 minutes, or until center tests done. Cool on a wire rack. Cut into squares.

CRUMB TOP CHOCO-PEANUT BUTTER BARS

⅔ cup **PETER PAN® Peanut Butter, Creamy**
6 ounces (1 cup) semi-sweet chocolate pieces
1½ cups quick oats, uncooked
1¼ cups flour
½ teaspoon baking soda
½ teaspoon salt
1 stick (½ cup) butter, softened
1 cup packed brown sugar
1 egg
1 teaspoon vanilla

Grease a 13 by 9 by 2-inch pan. Over hot, not boiling, water melt the chocolate pieces. In a small bowl combine the oats, flour, baking soda and salt. In a large bowl combine and blend until creamy the butter, brown sugar and peanut butter. Add the egg and vanilla and mix well. Gradually add the flour-oat mixture and beat until well mixed. Pour ¾ of the dough into a greased baking pan. Spread with melted chocolate. Then dot chocolate with remaining dough. Bake in 350°F. oven 25 minutes. When slightly cooled, cut into 2 by 1-inch bars.

Yield: 48 bars, 2 by 1 inch

GOLDEN MERINGUE DESSERT BARS

Crust:
⅔ cup butter, softened
⅓ cup light brown sugar, packed
2 egg yolks
1 teaspoon vanilla
1½ cups flour

Filling:
1 can (1 lb., 4 oz.) **DOLE® Crushed Pineapple**
1 cup dried apricots, cut up
½ cup sugar
3 tablespoons cornstarch
1 teaspoon grated orange peel
¼ teaspoon ground nutmeg

Orange Meringue:
3 egg whites
¼ teaspoon cream of tartar
⅔ cup sugar
½ teaspoon grated orange peel

CRUST:
Beat butter and brown sugar until light and fluffy. Beat in egg yolks and vanilla. Fold in flour until blended. Pat into a 9-inch square glass baking pan. Bake in a preheated 350° F. oven 15 minutes until lightly browned. Place on wire rack to cool.

FILLING:
Drain pineapple, reserving all syrup. Pour syrup over apricots in a small saucepan. Cook over medium heat, stirring occasionally for about ½ hour until all liquid is absorbed. Stir in sugar, pineapple, cornstarch, orange peel and nutmeg. Cook stirring constantly until mixture boils and becomes clear. (This will be very thick.) Remove from heat and cool slightly. Spread over crust.

ORANGE MERINGUE:
Beat egg whites to soft peaks. Add cream of tartar and beat in sugar gradually until stiff peaks form. Beat in orange peel. Spread over warm filling.

Bake in a 350° F. oven 18 to 20 minutes until golden. Cool before cutting.   *Makes 16 bars*

BLONDIES

1½ cups firmly packed **DOMINO® Dark Brown Sugar**
1 teaspoon salt
¼ lb. (½ cup) butter or margarine, melted
2 eggs
1 teaspoon vanilla extract
1½ cups all-purpose flour
1¼ teaspoons baking powder
1 cup chopped nuts
DOMINO® Confectioners 10-X Sugar

Cream sugar with salt and melted butter or margarine thoroughly. Beat eggs into creamed mixture, one at a time, until light and smooth. Add extract.

Sift together flour and baking powder; stir into creamed ingredients, blending well. Add nuts; mix briefly. Spread batter into greased 11×7-inch pan. Bake in moderate oven, 350°F, 30-35 minutes or until done.

While warm, cut 1½×2½-inch bars and roll in confectioners sugar. Remove to cooling rack. Store in airtight container with waxed paper between layers. Roll in confectioners sugar again if necessary before serving.   *Yield: 16 blondies*

APRICOT BARS

Filling:
1 package (6 oz.) dried apricots
½ teaspoon cinnamon
⅛ teaspoon ground cloves
⅔ cup packed brown sugar

Crumb Mixture:
½ cup butter or margarine, softened
¾ cup packed brown sugar
1¼ cups all-purpose flour*
¼ teaspoon salt
¼ teaspoon baking soda
¾ cup **Instant** or **Regular RALSTON®**

FILLING:
In 1-quart saucepan combine apricots and spices. Add just enough water to cover. Simmer, covered, 15 minutes or until tender. Drain. Mash apricots with fork. Add sugar. Mix thoroughly. Cool.

CRUMB MIXTURE:
Preheat oven to 400°. Butter 9-inch square baking pan. Cream together butter and sugar. Stir together remaining ingredients. Add to creamed mixture. Mix well to form coarse crumbs. Pack ⅔ of crumb mixture into pan. Spread with cooled filling. Sprinkle with remaining crumbs. Pack lightly. Bake about 20 minutes or until top is lightly browned. Cool. Cut into bars. For a delicious dessert, cut into larger pieces and top with ice cream.   *Makes 24*

*Stir flour; then spoon into measuring cups.

APRICOT COOKIE BARS

1 cup all purpose flour
½ cup solid shortening (part butter or margarine)
¼ cup brown sugar
1 egg (well beaten)
½ tsp. baking powder
1 can (21-oz.) **WILDERNESS® Apricot Fruit Filling**

Cream shortening and sugar together. Add well beaten egg. Sift flour, measure, then sift with baking powder.

Blend sifted dry ingredients into creamed mixture. Spread evenly over bottom of lightly greased 9×9-inch pan. Spread can of Apricot Fruit Filling over this. Top with the following:

(Continued)

Topping:

2 eggs (well beaten)
1 cup sugar
3 Tbsp. butter or margarine (melted)
1½ cups coconut
½ cup chopped walnuts

Add sugar to well beaten eggs. Stir in remaining ingredients. Drop by spoonfuls over Apricot Fruit Filling and with table knife spread evenly. Bake at 350° F for 30-35 minutes. Cool. Cut into bars.

APPLE BROWNIES

⅔ cup butter
2 cups brown sugar
2 eggs
1 tsp. vanilla
½ cup nuts
2 cups flour
2 tsp. baking powder
¼ tsp. salt
1 cup chopped apples
Powdered sugar

Cream butter and sugar. Add eggs and vanilla. Mix well. Add flour, baking powder and salt. Stir well. Stir in apples and nuts. Bake in well greased pan (12×9×3-inches). Bake for 30-35 minutes at 350°. When cooled, sprinkle powdered sugar over the top with flour sifter, then serve.

Favorite winning recipe from **Michigan Apple Committee**

FIG DAINTIES

3 eggs
1 cup brown sugar, packed
1 teaspoon vanilla
1 tablespoon butter or margarine, softened
2 cups SUN·MAID® or BLUE RIBBON® Dried Figs, finely chopped
1 cup all-purpose flour
2 teaspoons baking powder
⅛ teaspoon *each* salt and cinnamon
1 cup DIAMOND® Walnuts, coarsely chopped
Powdered sugar

Beat eggs well; add sugar, vanilla, butter and figs; combine thoroughly. Sift together flour, baking powder, salt and cinnamon; beat into fig mixture. Stir in walnuts. Spread batter into greased 15×10-inch baking pan. Bake at 350 degrees F about 20 to 25 minutes, or until lightly browned and top springs back when touched lightly. Cool in pan. Dust with powdered sugar and cut into 1×2½-inch bars.   *Makes 60 bars*

ORANGE PEANUT BUTTER BARS

1 cup SKIPPY® Creamy or Chunk Style Peanut Butter
⅔ cup MAZOLA® Corn Oil Margarine
1 teaspoon vanilla
1½ cups firmly packed light brown sugar
3 eggs
1¼ cups unsifted flour
½ teaspoon salt
¾ cup sifted confectioners sugar
1 teaspoon grated orange rind
4 teaspoons orange juice

Grease 13 × 9 × 2-inch baking pan. Mix together peanut butter, margarine and vanilla in large bowl; beat with electric mixer on medium speed until well blended. Beat in sugar until light and fluffy. Beat in eggs, 1 at a time. Stir in flour and salt just until well blended. Spread batter in prepared pan. Bake in 350°F. (moderate) oven about 30 minutes or until center springs back when lightly touched. Remove from oven. Cool slightly on wire rack. Stir together confectioners' sugar, orange rind and juice until smooth. Drizzle orange glaze over warm cookies in pan; swirl with bowl of spoon to make a random pattern. Cut into 36 (3 × 1-inch) bars.

VARIATION:

CHOCOLATE SWIRL TOPPING

Follow recipe for Orange Peanut Butter Bars as directed. Melt ¼ cup semisweet chocolate pieces with 1 tablespoon MAZOLA® Corn Oil Margarine over simmering water in top of double boiler. Drizzle over the orange glaze for a black and orange pattern. When cool, cut into bars.

ORANGEOLA BARS

1¼ cups (about ⅓ package) HEALTH VALLEY® ORANGEOLA® Cereal
¼ cup HEALTH VALLEY® SPROUTS 7™ Cereal
⅓ cup finely ground walnuts or pecans
2 tablespoons fresh or dried grated coconut
Dash of nutmeg
2 tablespoons HEALTH VALLEY® Clover Honey
½ teaspoon vanilla
2 egg whites, beaten stiff

Preheat oven to 275°F. and butter a 6½×11×2-inch baking pan. In a mixing bowl, combine ORANGEOLA®, SPROUTS 7™, nuts, coconut and nutmeg. Add honey and vanilla and mix thoroughly (it might be necessary to use your hands to do this). Then fold in egg whites and allow mixture to stand 2 to 3 minutes. Spread or press into prepared pan and bake in preheated oven for 20 minutes. Remove from oven, cut into 20 or 24 bars and transfer immediately to glass or china plate to cool. *Yield: 20 or 24 bars*

LEMONY BARS

Base:

1 cup all-purpose flour*
¾ cup sugar
½ teaspoon baking powder
¼ teaspoon salt
2 cups RICE CHEX® Cereal crushed to ½ cup
½ cup butter or margarine

Topping:

2 eggs, beaten
¾ cup sugar
2 tablespoons all-purpose flour
¼ teaspoon baking powder
4 teaspoons lemon juice
1 teaspoon grated lemon peel
Confectioner's sugar

Preheat oven to 350°. Grease 9-inch square baking pan. To prepare Base, combine flour, sugar, baking powder and salt. Stir in CHEX® Crumbs. Cut in butter until very fine crumbs. Press mixture firmly into bottom of pan. Bake 12 minutes.

Meanwhile, prepare Topping. Combine all ingredients except confectioner's sugar. Mix until well blended. Pour over hot base. Return to oven for additional 15-20 minutes or until top is set but not browned. Cool. Sprinkle with confectioner's sugar. Cut into bars.   *Makes 24*

*Stir flour; then spoon into measuring cup.

PUMPKIN BARS

⅓ cup sugar
⅓ cup oil
3 eggs
15-oz. can (2 cups) pumpkin
1 pkg. **PILLSBURY PLUS Yellow Cake Mix**
3 teaspoons pumpkin pie spice*
1 can **PILLSBURY Ready To Spread Cream Cheese
    Frosting Supreme**
Walnut halves

Heat oven to 350°F. Grease and flour 15 × 10-inch jelly roll pan. In large bowl, beat sugar, oil, eggs and pumpkin 1 minute at highest speed. Add cake mix and spice; blend until moistened. Beat 2 minutes at highest speed. Pour into prepared pan.

Bake at 350°F. for 25 to 35 minutes or until toothpick inserted in center comes out clean. Cool completely. Frost cooled bars. Garnish with walnut halves. Store in refrigerator.   *36 bars*

*Tip: Two teaspoons cinnamon, ½ teaspoon ginger, ½ teaspoon cloves and ½ teaspoon nutmeg can be used in place of pumpkin pie spice.

HIGH ALTITUDE—Above 3500 Feet: Bake at 350°F. for 30 to 35 minutes.

RASPBERRY-WALNUT SHORTBREAD BARS

Shortbread Base*
⅓ cup raspberry jam
2 eggs
½ cup brown sugar, packed
1 teaspoon vanilla
2 tablespoons all-purpose flour
⅛ teaspoon salt
⅛ teaspoon baking soda
1 cup chopped **DIAMOND® Walnuts**

Prepare Shortbread Base. Sprinkle evenly over bottom of greased 9-inch square pan and press firmly in an even layer. Bake at 350 degrees F about 20 minutes or just until edges become tinged with brown. Remove from oven and spread jam evenly over shortbread. Beat together eggs, brown sugar and vanilla; stir in flour, salt and soda; add walnuts. Pour evenly over jam layer and spread to corners of pan. Return to oven and bake 20 minutes longer or until top is set. Cool in pan; cut into bars.

*SHORTBREAD BASE

Combine 1¼ cups all-purpose flour with ½ cup granulated sugar; cut in ½ cup butter or margarine, softened, until mixture is like fine meal.

SOUTHERN PECAN BARS

1 cup **PILLSBURY'S BEST® All Purpose** or
    Unbleached Flour
⅓ cup firmly packed brown sugar
¼ cup margarine or butter, softened
¼ cup **FISHER® Finely Chopped Pecans**
¼ teaspoon baking powder

Topping:
¼ cup firmly packed brown sugar
2 tablespoons flour
½ teaspoon salt
¾ cup corn syrup
1 teaspoon vanilla
2 eggs
¾ cup **FISHER® Chopped Pecans**

Heat oven to 350°F. In large bowl, combine first 5 ingredients; mix at low speed until crumbly. Press crumb mixture into ungreased 13 × 9-inch pan. Bake 10 to 12 minutes at 350°F until light brown; remove from oven.

In same bowl, combine all Topping ingredients except pecans; beat at medium speed until well blended. Pour over partially-baked crust. Sprinkle with pecans. Bake at 350°F for 20 to 25 minutes until golden brown. Cool; cut into bars. Store loosely covered.   *2 to 3 dozen bars*

GRANNY'S RAISIN BARS

1 cup dark raisins
½ cup water
2 cups all-purpose flour
½ teaspoon baking powder
½ teaspoon baking soda
¼ teaspoon salt
¾ teaspoon **DURKEE Ground Cinnamon**
¾ teaspoon **DURKEE Ground Allspice**
¼ teaspoon **DURKEE Ground Nutmeg**
½ cup butter or margarine
1 cup packed brown sugar
1 egg
2 teaspoons **DURKEE Imitation Maple Flavor**
1 teaspoon **DURKEE Vanilla Extract**
Orange Frosting*

In saucepan, combine raisins and water. Bring to a boil; reduce heat and simmer, covered 5 minutes. Remove from heat; cool completely. Combine flour, baking powder, soda, salt and spices; set aside. Cream together butter and brown sugar until light. Beat in egg. Blend in maple flavor, vanilla and cooled raisin mixture. Gradually stir in flour mixture. Spread dough in greased 10 × 15-inch jelly roll pan. Bake at 350° for 18 to 20 minutes or until golden brown. Cool. Frost with Orange Frosting.
Makes about 48 bar cookies

*ORANGE FROSTING

Combine 2 cups powdered sugar, ¼ teaspoon **DURKEE Ground Allspice**, 1 tablespoon melted butter or margarine and 2 tablespoons orange juice. Stir until smooth. Add more orange juice, if necessary, to reach spreading consistency.

TOFFEE NUT BARS

¼ cup (½ stick) butter, softened
½ cup packed light brown sugar
1 cup sifted all-purpose flour

Beat butter, sugar and flour until well blended. Press into buttered 13 × 9 × 2-inch pan. Bake at 350° for 5 minutes. Cool.

Topping:
2 eggs, beaten
1 cup packed light brown sugar
1 teaspoon vanilla
2 tablespoons flour
1 teaspoon baking powder
½ teaspoon salt
½ cup moist flaked coconut
½ cup chopped nuts
⅔ cup **MILK DUDS®**
Confectioner's sugar

Beat together eggs, brown sugar and vanilla. Add dry ingredients. Stir in coconut, nuts and **MILK DUDS®**. Spread over baked crust. Bake at 350° for 15 minutes more or until topping is golden brown. Cool. Sift confectioner's sugar over top. Cut into 30 bars.

OATMEAL TOFFEE BARS

½ cup butter, melted
10 oz. pkg. coconut almond or coconut pecan frosting mix
2 cups 3-MINUTE BRAND® Oats
¼ cup milk
1 cup (6-oz.) semi-sweet chocolate chips

Combine first four ingredients and mix well. Press into a greased 9×9-inch baking pan. Bake at 350° F for 20 to 25 minutes or until lightly browned. Immediately sprinkle chocolate chips over the top. Allow chips to melt and then spread. Cool and cut into bars.

CHEWY GRAHAM BARS

3 eggs
1½ cups graham cracker crumbs
¾ cup brown sugar, packed
½ teaspoon grated orange peel
½ teaspoon vanilla
⅛ teaspoon salt
1 cup SUN•MAID® Fruit Bits

Combine all ingredients and mix well. Spread evenly into a greased 9-inch square pan. Bake at 350 degrees F about 25 minutes or until browned and center springs back when lightly touched. Cool in pan. Cut into bars.

Candy

QUICK CHOCOLATE FUDGE

¼ cup MAZOLA® Corn Oil Margarine
3 squares (1-oz. each) unsweetened chocolate
½ cup KARO® Light Corn Syrup
1 tablespoon water
1 teaspoon vanilla
1 pound confectioner's sugar
1 cup chopped nuts or miniature marshmallows or raisins

Grease 8×8×2-inch baking pan. In 2-quart saucepan melt margarine and chocolate over low heat. Stir in corn syrup, water and vanilla. Remove from heat. Add confectioner's sugar and nuts. Stir until mixture is well blended and smooth. Turn into prepared pan. Cool. Cut into squares. *Makes 1¾ pounds*

VARIATIONS:

QUICK BROWN SUGAR FUDGE

Follow recipe for Quick Chocolate Fudge. Omit chocolate and water. Melt ½ cup firmly packed brown sugar with margarine. Use dark corn syrup.

STUFFED FRUIT

Prepare Quick Chocolate Fudge. Stuff into dried fruit.

Note: Store covered in refrigerator.

SARONNO FUDGE

4 cups sugar
2 cups (1 pint) half-and-half
⅔ cup AMARETTO DI SARONNO® Liqueur
¼ teaspoon salt

In a large saucepan, combine all ingredients. Brush the sides of the pan with butter or margarine. Stir over moderate heat until sugar is dissolved. Bring to a boil and cook without stirring until 238°F on a candy thermometer, or until a small amount forms a soft ball when dropped into water. Remove from heat and let stand until 140° F. Beat with a spoon until mixture begins to thicken slightly (mixture will still be shiny). Pour quickly into a foil-lined 8-inch square pan. Let stand until hard and cool. Use foil to remove from pan and cut with a sharp knife into 1-inch squares.

Makes 1 (8-inch) pan

FOOLPROOF CHOCOLATE FUDGE

3 (6-ounce) packages semi-sweet chocolate morsels
1 (14-ounce) can EAGLE® Brand Sweetened Condensed Milk (NOT evaporated milk)
Dash salt
1½ teaspoons vanilla extract
½ cup chopped nuts, optional

In heavy saucepan, over low heat, melt morsels with EAGLE® Brand. Remove from heat; stir in remaining ingredients. Spread evenly into wax paper-lined 8-inch square pan. Chill 2 to 3 hours or until firm. Turn fudge onto cutting board; peel off paper and cut into squares. Store loosely covered at room temperature.

Makes about 1¾ pounds

VARIATION:

ROCKY ROAD FUDGE

Omit 1 (6-ounce) package semi-sweet chocolate morsels, salt, vanilla and nuts. In saucepan, melt morsels with EAGLE® Brand and 2 tablespoons margarine. In large bowl, combine 2 cups dry roasted peanuts and 1 (10½-ounce) package miniature marshmallows. Pour chocolate mixture into nut mixture; mix well. Spread into wax paper-lined 13x9-inch pan. Chill 2 hours.

CREAMY CHOCOLATE FUDGE

1 jar marshmallow cream*
1½ cups sugar
⅔ cup evaporated milk
¼ cup butter
¼ measuring teaspoon salt
One 11½-oz. pkg. (2 cups) NESTLÉ® Milk Chocolate Morsels
One 6-oz. pkg. (1 cup) NESTLÉ® Semi-Sweet Real Chocolate Morsels
½ cup chopped nuts
1 measuring teaspoon vanilla extract

In large saucepan, combine marshmallow cream, sugar, evaporated milk, butter and salt; bring to *full boil* over moderate heat, stirring constantly. *Boil 5 minutes*, stirring constantly over moderate heat. Remove from heat. Add NESTLÉ® Milk Chocolate Morsels and NESTLÉ® Semi-Sweet Real Chocolate Morsels; stir until morsels melt and mixture is well blended. Stir in nuts and vanilla extract. Pour into aluminum foil-lined 8″ square pan. Chill in refrigerator until firm (about 2 hours).

*5 oz.—10 oz. jar *Makes: 2½ lbs. candy*

PISTACHIO MICROWAVE FUDGE

1 pound powdered sugar
⅔ cup cocoa
¼ teaspoon salt
¼ cup milk
2 teaspoons vanilla
¼ teaspoon pistachio flavoring (optional)
½ cup butter or margarine
½ cup chopped shelled Pistachios from California

In large microwave-proof bowl, combine powdered sugar, cocoa and salt. Stir in milk and flavorings; mix well. Place butter on top. Microwave at HIGH 2 minutes. Beat until smooth; stir in pistachios. Spread in foil-lined or buttered 8 × 8 × 2-inch baking pan. Chill about 1 hour or until firm. Cut into 36 pieces.

Note: Pistachio Microwave Fudge may be sprinkled with 1 to 2 tablespoons finely chopped shelled Pistachios from California before chilling.

Favorite recipe from **California Pistachio Commission**

CHOCOLATE ALMOND BARK

One 11½-oz. pkg. (2 cups) NESTLÉ® Milk
  Chocolate Morsels
1 measuring tablespoon vegetable shortening
½ cup raisins
½ cup chopped toasted almonds, divided

CONVENTIONAL METHOD:
Combine over hot (not boiling) water, **NESTLÉ® Milk Chocolate Morsels** and vegetable shortening. Heat until morsels are melted and mixture is smooth. Remove from heat and stir in raisins and half the almonds. Spread into waxed paper-lined 13" × 9" × 2" baking pan*. Sprinkle remaining almonds on top. Chill in refrigerator until ready to serve, at least 30 minutes. Before serving, break into bite-size pieces. *Makes 1-lb. candy*

*Make waxed paper long enough so that candy can be easily lifted out of the pan.

MICROWAVE METHOD:
To melt, in a 4-cup glass measuring cup, add **NESTLÉ® Milk Chocolate Morsels**. Microwave on high 2 minutes; stir. Microwave on high 1 minute longer. Stir until chocolate is smooth. *Makes: 1 cup melted chocolate*

CHOCOLATE-PEANUT BUTTER CUPS

Chocolate Cups:
One 11½-oz. pkg. (2 cups) NESTLÉ® Milk
  Chocolate Morsels
2 measuring tablespoons vegetable shortening
24 paper gem size candy liners

Peanut Butter Filling:
¾ cup creamy peanut butter
¾ cup sifted confectioner's sugar
1 measuring tablespoon butter, melted

CHOCOLATE CUPS

Combine over hot (not boiling) water, **NESTLÉ® Milk Chocolate Morsels** and vegetable shortening. Stir until morsels melt and mixture is smooth. Coat inside of 24 candy liners using 1 measuring teaspoon chocolate mixture for each. Keep remaining chocolate over very low heat to remain melted and smooth. Place candy liners in palm of hand; rotate gently using rubber spatula to push chocolate up sides. *(Continued)*

Place coated liners in gem pans. Chill in refrigerator until firm (about 30 minutes). Using slightly rounded measuring teaspoonfuls, shape Peanut Butter Filling into balls. Place 1 ball in each cup and press lightly with fingers to flatten. Spoon 1 level measuring teaspoonful melted chocolate mixture on top and smooth over. Return to refrigerator and chill until firm (about 45 minutes) or until hardened. Keep refrigerated until serving.

PEANUT BUTTER FILLING

In small bowl, combine peanut butter, confectioner's sugar and butter. Mix until well blended. *Makes: 24 cups*

CHOCOLATE NUT CUPS

1 cup HERSHEY'S® Semi-Sweet Chocolate Mini
  Chips
1 cup peanut butter chips
2 tablespoons vegetable oil
1 cup salted peanuts

Combine chocolate chips, peanut butter chips and vegetable oil in top of double boiler. Place over hot water, stirring until chips are completely melted and well blended. Remove from heat; stir in peanuts. Cool slightly; drop by teaspoonfuls into decorative nut cups. Garnish with additional peanuts, peanut butter chips or sprinkle with finely chopped peanuts. Chill until firm. Store in covered container in refrigerator. *About 4 dozen cups*

ROCKY ROAD CANDY

1 pkg. (10-oz.) GHIRARDELLI® Milk Chocolate
  Blocks
1½ cups miniature marshmallows
½ cup chopped walnuts

Melt broken chocolate in double boiler over 1 inch simmering water, stirring constantly or MICROWAVE on medium, 2-3 minutes. Remove from heat. (Chocolate should not be too hot, 100-120°F). Stir in marshmallows and walnuts. Pour into buttered 9 × 5-inch loaf pan. Chill until firm. Remove candy and cut into squares. *Makes 18 pieces*

TURTLES

Whole pecans
1 cup PET® Evaporated Milk
¼ cup butter
1 cup sugar
1 cup dark corn syrup
¼ teaspoon salt
1 teaspoon vanilla
1 package (6-oz.) semi-sweet chocolate pieces

In small saucepan, heat butter and evaporated milk until butter is melted. In separate 2-quart saucepan, cook sugar, corn syrup and salt over medium heat until it reaches firm-ball stage (244°F), stirring often. Slowly stir in hot milk mixture so that sugar mixture does not stop boiling. Stirring constantly, cook mixture until candy reaches firm-ball stage again. Remove pan from heat and stir in vanilla. Cool caramel to room temperature.

On waxed paper, arrange 4 pecans per turtle and place 1 heaping teaspoon of cooled caramel on each. Let cool until firm. Melt semi-sweet chocolate pieces on top of a double boiler. Spread chocolate on top to cover caramel. Let cool until hardened.

Note: To give chocolate a shiny, hard coating, add 1 to 2 tablespoons melted parafin wax to chocolate.

CHOCOLATE COVERED CHERRIES

3 tablespoons butter
¼ cup **PET® Evaporated Milk**
1 teaspoon vanilla
¼ teaspoon salt
3 to 4 cups powdered sugar, sifted
48 maraschino cherries, drained
1 package (6-oz.) semi-sweet chocolate pieces

Melt butter over low heat. Stir in evaporated milk, vanilla and salt. Remove from heat and gradually stir in sifted powdered sugar. Turn out onto a board, lightly sprinkled with powdered sugar; work with hands until smooth. Cover cherries completely by shaping about 2 teaspoons fondant around each cherry. Melt semi-sweet chocolate in double boiler. Drop fondant covered cherries into melted chocolate to cover. Remove from chocolate with two forks. Place on waxed paper to cool.

Note: To give chocolate a shiny, hard coating, add 1 to 2 table-spoons melted parafin wax to chocolate.

WATERFORD CREAM™ TRUFFLES

6 ounces unsweetened chocolate
½ cup butter
¼ cup **WATERFORD CREAM™ Liqueur**
1 tablespoon instant coffee
1 to 1½ cups sifted confectioner's sugar
1 cup finely chopped pecans or walnuts

Melt chocolate and butter in the top part of a double boiler set over simmering water. Remove from heat and stir in **WATERFORD CREAM™**, instant coffee and confectioner's sugar until a thick mixture. Cover and chill overnight. Shape 1-inch balls of the mixture by rolling in the palm of the hand. Roll in nuts. Chill until ready to serve. Remove from refrigerator 1 hour before serving.
Makes 48

MICROWAVE PRALINES
(Microwave Recipe)

2 cups brown sugar, firmly packed
1 cup **MILNOT®**
⅛ teaspoon salt
3 tablespoons butter or margarine
1½ cups pecans
1 teaspoon vanilla or maple flavoring

Mix sugar, **MILNOT®**, and salt in 3-quart casserole. Stir in butter. Microwave on full power, uncovered, for 5 minutes; stir and turn. Return to oven and continue on high for another 5 minutes; stir and test for soft ball stage. If further cooking is needed, check at 30-second intervals until done. Allow to cool 1 minute; add vanilla. Beat until creamy (about 3 minutes); stir in pecans, and drop from teaspoon onto waxed paper. Allow to cool at room temperature. *Makes 36 two-inch pralines*

CANE-FEST PRALINES

2 cups **IMPERIAL Granulated Sugar**
1 teaspoon soda
1 cup buttermilk
⅛ teaspoon salt
2 tablespoons butter or margarine
2½ cups pecan halves

In large (3½ quart) heavy saucepan combine **IMPERIAL Granulated Sugar**, soda, buttermilk and salt. Cook over high heat about 5 minutes (or to 210°F. on candy thermometer); stir often and scrape bottom of pan. Mixture will foam up. Add butter or margarine and pecans. Over medium heat, continue cooking, stirring constantly and scraping bottom and sides of pan until candy reaches soft ball stage (234°F. on candy thermometer). Remove from heat and cool slightly, about 2 minutes. Beat with spoon until thick and creamy. Drop from tablespoon onto sheet of aluminum foil or waxed paper. Let cool.
Makes about 20 pralines, 2" in diameter

BRANDY PIÑATA PRALINES

2 cups granulated sugar
1 cup packed brown sugar
½ cup **THE CHRISTIAN BROTHERS® Brandy**
½ cup whipping cream
¼ cup butter or margarine
2 cups salted peanuts

In 3-quart saucepan stir sugars, brandy, cream and butter over medium heat to dissolve sugars. Bring to boiling and cook without stirring until mixture reaches 234 degrees on candy thermometer. Remove from heat. Add peanuts and beat 2 to 3 minutes just until mixture begins to look opaque. Spoon immediately onto baking sheets lined with waxed paper, to form 3-inch patties. Cool; peel off paper and store in airtight container.
Makes 18 pralines (about 1½ pounds)

PECAN BRITTLE

2 cups sugar
3 cups broken pecans
¾ cup white corn syrup
¼ cup water
3 teaspoons baking soda

Combine all ingredients, except baking soda, in heavy pan or skillet and cook over medium heat, stirring constantly, until candy thermometer registers 290°. Stir in baking soda quickly—mixture will foam up. Pour onto greased cookie sheet and spread out with spatula. Allow to cool thoroughly—about two hours, then break into pieces. Store in airtight containers.
Makes about 1¼ pounds

Favorite recipe from **National Pecan Marketing Council**

DREAMY DIVINITY

3½ cups **DOMINO® Granulated Sugar**
⅔ cup water
⅔ cup light corn syrup
⅓ teaspoon salt
3 egg whites, stiffly beaten
1½ teaspoons vanilla extract
Candied cherries, food colorings, chopped nuts, optional

Combine sugar, water, corn syrup and salt in saucepan. Place over heat, stirring constantly until sugar dissolves. Wipe crystals from side of pan as necessary. Boil, without stirring, to 265°F or hard ball stage.

Gradually beat hot syrup into beaten egg whites. Add extract. Tint desired color with food coloring. Continue beating until candy holds shape. Drop from teaspoons onto buttered surface. Garnish as desired. When firm, store in airtight container.
Yield: 50 pieces (1½ lb.) divinity

PECAN MINT BALLS

1 cup **RICHARDSON Butter Mints** (about 72), finely crushed
1 cup (2 sticks) butter
2 cups sifted all-purpose flour
½ teaspoon salt
2 teaspoons vanilla
1 cup finely chopped pecans
Confectioners' sugar

Beat crushed mints and butter until creamy and fluffy. Add flour, salt and vanilla; mix well. Stir in pecans. Shape into 1-inch balls. Bake on ungreased cookie sheet at 325° for 10 to 12 minutes, or until lightly browned. Remove to rack to cool. Sprinkle with sifted confectioners' sugar.   *5 dozen*

BRANDY BALLS

3½ cups vanilla wafer crumbs
1 cup powdered sugar
1 cup chopped **FUNSTEN Pecans**
2 tablespoons cocoa
⅓ cup **PET® Evaporated Milk**
⅓ cup brandy
3 tablespoons light corn syrup

Combine all ingredients. Mix well. Shape into balls. Roll in finely chopped nuts or powdered sugar.   *Makes 3 dozen*

PUMPKIN DANDIES

1 cup **LIBBY'S® Solid Pack Pumpkin**
1 cup sugar
1¼ cups flaked coconut, lightly packed
½ teaspoon ground cinnamon
¼ teaspoon ground nutmeg
Finely chopped walnuts or peanuts
Red and green candied cherries, optional

In a large heavy saucepan, combine pumpkin, sugar, coconut and spices; mix well. Cook over medium-high heat, stirring constantly, for about 15 to 20 minutes. Candy is done when it becomes very thick and leaves the side of pan, forming a ball in center as you stir. Turn mixture out onto a buttered baking sheet; cover loosely with foil or plastic wrap; let cool completely. Lightly butter hands and shape candy into balls; roll in chopped nuts. Top each with a candied cherry half if desired. Cover and store in refrigerator.   *Yields about 2½ dozen candies*

VARIATION:

For a crunchier candy, stir 1 cup crushed 100% natural cereal into cooked candy before cooling and shaping.

CANDY APPLES

8 medium red apples
8 flat wooden skewers or spoons
2 cups sugar
1 cup **KARO® Light Corn Syrup**
½ cup water
¼ cup red cinnamon candies
10 drops red food color (optional)

Wash and dry apples; remove stems and insert skewers into stem ends. In heavy 2-quart saucepan stir together sugar, corn syrup and water. Stirring constantly, cook over medium heat until mixture boils and sugar is dissolved. Continue cooking, without stirring, until temperature reaches 250°F on candy thermometer or until

small amount of mixture dropped into very cold water forms a ball which is hard enough to hold its shape, yet plastic. Add cinnamon candies and continue cooking until temperature reaches 285°F on candy thermometer or until small amount of mixture dropped into very cold water separates into threads which are hard, but not brittle. Remove from heat. Stir in food color.

Hold each apple by its skewer and quickly twirl in syrup, tilting pan to cover apple. Remove from syrup; allow excess to drip off, then twirl to spread syrup smoothly over apple. Place on lightly greased cookie sheet to cool. (If mixture hardens before all apples are dipped, stir over low heat just until mixture is melted.) Store in cool place.   *Makes 8*

VARIATION:
CRUNCHY APPLES

Follow recipe for Candy Apples. Before cooling roll bottom quarter of apples in slightly crushed corn flakes or shredded coconut.

CHOCOLATE-CARAMEL APPLES

5 medium apples
5 wooden sticks or skewers
4 boxes (1.61 ounces each) **MILK DUDS®**
1 tablespoon milk
2 teaspoons butter
¾ teaspoon vanilla
¾ cup finely chopped walnuts

Wash and dry apples; remove stems. Insert stick into stem end of each apple; set aside. In saucepan, heat **MILK DUDS®**, milk, butter and vanilla over low heat, stirring constantly, until candy has melted and mixture is smooth. Remove from heat. Dip apples into candy mixture, one at a time, turning to coat evenly. Allow excess candy mixture to drip back into pan. Roll coated apples in nuts. Transfer to buttered cookie sheet. Let stand until firm.   *5 apples*

Snacks

GLAZED SALTED ALMONDS

1 egg white
1 tablespoon butter or margarine, melted
2 cups **FISHER® Blanched Almonds**
Salt
Grated Parmesan cheese

Heat oven to 375°F. In medium bowl beat egg white until foamy. Gradually add butter; stir in nuts. Spread nut mixture in 13 × 9-inch baking pan; sprinkle lightly with salt and Parmesan cheese to taste. Bake at 375°F for 15 to 20 minutes, stirring often, until heated and glazed.   *2 cups*

SPIRITED PECANS

1½ cups sugar
½ cup **AMARETTO DI SARONNO® Liqueur**
3 cups pecan halves

In a saucepan, combine sugar and **AMARETTO DI SARONNO®**. Bring to a boil and boil until 238° F on a candy thermometer, or until a small amount forms a soft ball when dropped into cold water. Stir in pecans and keep stirring until sugar syrup becomes cloudy and grainy. Spread out on a cookie sheet and let harden. Separate into small pieces. Store in an airtight container in a cool dry place.   *Makes about 1 quart*

SPICED PECANS

Melt one stick butter or margarine in skillet. Add 2 cups whole pecan halves. Cook 20 minutes on low heat, stirring occasionally. Drain on paper towels. Mix in paper bag:

    1½ cups confectioners sugar
    1 tablespoon ground cloves
    1 tablespoon cinnamon
    1 tablespoon nutmeg

Add warm nuts to mixture in bag and shake to coat. Buttered pecans, which are prepared by omitting the seasonings in the above recipe, are delicious when served as a garnish on all kinds of dessert.

Favorite recipe from **National Pecan Marketing Council**

SNACKING-GOOD NUTS

    ⅓ cup **CRISCO®** Shortening
    1½ teaspoons chili powder
    1 teaspoon Worcestershire sauce
    ½ teaspoon cayenne pepper
    ½ teaspoon garlic salt
    2 cups cashews
    2 cups pecans

Preheat oven to 300°. In 11×7×1½-inch baking pan, melt the **CRISCO®** in the 300° oven. When melted, stir in the chili powder, Worcestershire sauce, cayenne, and garlic salt. Add the cashews and pecans and toss to coat the nuts. Spread nuts evenly in the baking pan. Bake at 300° for 20 to 25 minutes, stirring once or twice. Sprinkle the nuts with additional salt, if desired.
                    Makes about 4 cups nuts

APRICOT MUNCH-MIX

Heat together 2 tablespoons *each* butter or margarine and honey until butter melts. In a 9×13-inch baking pan, combine 6 cups puffed corn cereal *or* popped corn, ¾ cup *each* coarsely chopped **DIAMOND®** Walnuts, cut up **SUN•MAID®** or **SUN-SWEET®** Dried Apricots, and a dash salt. Drizzle with butter mixture and toss well. Bake at 275 degrees F about 25 minutes, stirring occasionally, until Munch-Mix is evenly coated. Cool; stir to loosen mixture.

CRUNCHY FRUIT MUNCH

    3 quarts freshly popped **JOLLY TIME®** Pop Corn
    2 cups natural cereal with raisins
    ¾ cup dried apricots, chopped
    ¼ teaspoon salt
    ⅓ cup butter or margarine
    ¼ cup honey

Preheat oven to 300 degrees F. Combine first four ingredients in large baking pan; set aside. In small saucepan, combine butter or margarine and honey. Cook over low heat until butter or margarine is melted. Pour over pop corn mixture, tossing lightly until well coated. Place in oven. Bake 30 minutes, stirring occasionally. Store in tightly covered container up to 2 weeks.
                    Makes 3 quarts

GREEK DATES

    ½ cup **SUE BEE®** Honey
    ½ cup chopped toasted almonds
    ½ cup chopped walnuts
    ½ cup diced orange peel
    1 pound pitted dates
    Granulated sugar

Mix honey, nuts and orange peel. Stuff dates with mixture, and roll in sugar. To preserve freshness, wrap dates individually in plastic wrap.

CHEESE STICKS

    2 sticks pie crust mix (or 1 pkg. double crust pie mix)
    1 cup shredded sharp natural cheddar cheese
    1 Tbsp. **BALTIMORE SPICE OLD BAY Seasoning**

Prepare pie crust according to package instructions, mixing in cheese and **OLD BAY**. Roll dough on lightly floured surface to 12″ × 8″ rectangle. Cut into 3″ × ½″ strips. Bake on lightly greased baking sheet at 425° for 10-12 minutes.

NUTTY GARLIC SNACKS

    ¾ cup finely chopped nuts
    ½ to 1½ teaspoons garlic salt
    10-oz. can **HUNGRY JACK®** Refrigerated Flaky
      Biscuits
    1 egg, slightly beaten
    1½ cups roasted peanuts or nuts, if desired

Heat oven to 375°F. Combine chopped nuts and garlic salt. Separate dough into 10 biscuits; cut each into 4 pieces. Roll each biscuit piece into a ball; dip top and sides in beaten egg, then in nut mixture. Place on ungreased cookie sheets. Bake at 375°F. for 9 to 12 minutes or until light golden brown; cool. If desired, toss snacks with roasted peanuts to serve.   *40 snacks*

Tip: To make ahead, prepare, cover and refrigerate up to 2 hours; bake as directed.

High Altitude—Above 3500 Feet: No change.

NUTRITION INFORMATION PER SERVING			
SERVING SIZE: ¹⁄₁₀ of recipe		Percent U.S. RDA	
Calories	150	Per Serving	
Protein	4 g	Protein	6%
Carbohydrate	15 g	Vitamin A	*
Fat	8 g	Vitamin C	*
Sodium	390 mg	Thiamine	8%
Potassium	70 mg	Riboflavin	6%
		Niacin	4%
		Calcium	*
		Iron	4%

*Contains less than 2% of the U.S. RDA of this nutrient.

PILLSBURY BAKE-OFF® recipe

HOTSY TOTSY SNACK MIX

    2 cans (2.8-oz. each) **DURKEE French Fried Onions**
    2 can (1½-oz. each) **DURKEE Potato Sticks**
    3 cups broken pretzel sticks
    1 can (12-oz.) salted nuts (2 cups)
    ¼ cup grated Parmesan cheese
    ½ cup butter or margarine, melted
    2 to 3 tablespoons **DURKEE RedHot! Sauce**

In a large roasting pan, stir together first 5 ingredients. Combine melted butter and hot sauce; toss with French Fried Onion mixture. Bake at 250° for 1 hour, stirring every 15 minutes.
                    Makes approximately 2½ quarts

CINNAMON MUNCH

⅓ cup sugar
1¼ teaspoons cinnamon
4 tablespoons butter or margarine
4 cups **CORN** or **RICE CHEX**® Cereal OR 3 cups
   BRAN or **WHEAT CHEX**® Cereal

Combine sugar and cinnamon. Set aside. In large skillet melt butter over low heat. Add **CHEX**®. Heat and stir gently until all pieces are coated. Continue to heat and stir 5-6 minutes. Sprinkle half the cinnamon-sugar mixture evenly over **CHEX**®. Stir to bring unsugared pieces to top. Sprinkle with remaining cinnamon-sugar. Heat and stir 1 minute longer. Spread on absorbent paper to cool.
Makes 3-4 cups

TOASTY O'S SNACK MIX

3 cups **MALT-O-MEAL**® Toasty O's Cereal
½ cup pretzel sticks, broken
2 cups miniature shredded wheats, cut in half
½ cup nuts or peanuts
6 Tbsp. Butter or margarine, melted
1 Tbsp. Worcestershire sauce
½ tsp. garlic powder
½ tsp. onion salt

In a small bowl, combine **Toasty O's Cereal**, shredded wheat, pretzels, and nuts. To the melted butter add Worcestershire sauce, garlic powder, and onion salt. Pour gradually over cereal mixture stirring constantly to blend evenly. Spread in shallow baking pan. Bake in a 250° oven for 45 minutes or until lightly toasted. Stir occasionally, let cool. To keep fresh, store in an airtight container.

CHINATOWN MUNCH

2 cups **MALT-O-MEAL**® Puffed Rice
¾ cup roasted salted peanuts
¾ cup sesame sticks
½ cup roasted, salted sunflower seeds
3 tablespoons salad oil
1½ tablespoons soy sauce
¼ teaspoon ground ginger

Combine Puffed Rice, peanuts, sesame sticks and sunflower seeds in a large bowl. Blend oil, soy sauce and ginger. Toss with Puffed Rice mixture. Spread on a rimmed baking sheet. Bake in a 250°F oven for 30 minutes. Store in an airtight container.
Makes about 4 cups

TERIYAKI TRAIL MIX

⅓ cup **KIKKOMAN** Teriyaki Sauce
2 tablespoons vegetable oil
1 cup pecan halves
1 cup walnut halves
2 cups toasted oat cereal (like **CHEERIOS**®)
1 cup shredded coconut
¾ cup sunflower seeds
½ cup blanched slivered almonds
1 cup raisins

Combine teriyaki sauce and oil in large bowl; stir in pecans and walnuts until thoroughly coated. Let stand 10 minutes; stir occasionally. Add next 4 ingredients; toss together to combine and coat thoroughly. Turn out onto large shallow baking pan or cookie sheet; spread mixture out evenly. Bake at 250°F. 15 minutes. Remove from oven and stir gently. Bake 15 minutes longer. Remove from oven; stir in raisins and let stand in pan until thoroughly cooled. Store in tightly covered container.

ON THE RUN TRAIL MIX

3 cups **QUAKER**® 100% Natural Cereal
⅔ cup chopped walnuts
⅓ cup firmly packed brown sugar
¼ cup butter or margarine
3 tablespoons honey
1 tablespoon grated orange peel

Heat oven to 325°F. Combine cereal and nuts in large bowl. Combine brown sugar, butter and honey in small saucepan; cook over low heat, stirring occasionally until smooth. Stir in orange peel. Pour over cereal mixture; mix well. Spread into lightly greased 13 × 9-inch baking pan. Bake at 325°F. for 20 to 22 minutes or until golden brown, stirring occasionally. Remove mixture to ungreased cookie sheet or aluminum foil; cool completely. Break into pieces. Store in tightly covered container.
Makes about 6 cups

SUGAR PUFF TRAIL MIX

2 cups **MALT-O-MEAL**® Sugar Puffs
2 cups broken nuts*
1 cup shaved unsweetened coconut
1 cup raisins
1 cup date pieces

Toss all ingredients together. Store in an airtight container.
*Walnuts, pecans, brazil nuts, peanuts or a combination.

VARIATION:

Dried apricots, peaches, figs, prunes, dried papaya or dried pineapple, cut up, may be substituted for raisins and dates.

JOLLY TIME® PARTY MIX

2 quarts popped **JOLLY TIME**® Pop Corn
2 cups slim pretzel sticks
2 cups cheese curls
¼ cup butter or margarine
1 tablespoon Worcestershire Sauce
½ teaspoon garlic salt
½ teaspoon seasoned salt

In a shallow baking pan, mix popped corn, pretzel sticks and cheese curls. Melt butter or margarine in small saucepan and stir in seasonings. Pour over dry mixture and mix well. Bake at 250 degrees F. for 45 minutes, stirring several times.
Makes 2½ quarts

Note: 1 cup dry roasted peanuts may be added.

PERKY PARTY MIX

1½ cups "M&M's"® Plain or Peanut Chocolate
   Candies
3 cups thin pretzel sticks, broken in half
3 cups bite-size Cheddar cheese crackers
1½ cups raisins

Combine all ingredients. Serve as a snack.
Makes about 8 cups mix

MEXICAN PICK-UP STICKS

2 cans (3 oz. each) **DURKEE** French Fried Onions
1 can (7 oz.) **DURKEE** Potato Sticks
2 cups Spanish peanuts
⅓ cup butter or margarine, melted
1 pkg. (1⅛ oz.) **DURKEE** Taco Seasoning Mix

Combine first three ingredients and place in a 9 × 13-inch baking dish. Drizzle with melted butter; stir to combine. Sprinkle with Taco seasoning and mix well. Bake at 250° for 45 minutes. Stir every 15 minutes. *Makes approximately 2 quarts*

SUPER SIMPLE GRANOLA

3 cups **3-MINUTE BRAND® Oats** (we prefer Old Fashioned)
½ cup raisins
½ cup sunflower nuts
½ cup slivered almonds
½ cup chopped pecans
½ cup wheat germ
½ cup coconut
½ cup vegetable oil
⅓ cup honey

Combine all ingredients except oil and honey in a large mixing bowl. Mix oil and honey together; pour over oat mixture. Mix well. Spread into two 15×10×1-inch baking pans. Bake in a 300°F oven about 20 minutes, stirring once. Remove from pan when cool. Store in a tightly covered container.
Makes about 6 cups

GRANOLA SNACK

½ cup creamy or crunchy peanut butter
¼ cup honey
¼ cup vegetable oil
2 tablespoons firmly packed brown sugar
1 (9-ounce) package **NONE SUCH® Condensed Mincemeat**
2 cups quick-cooking oats
1 cup dry-roasted peanuts

Preheat oven to 250°. In large saucepan, combine peanut butter, honey, vegetable oil and sugar; blend well. Break mincemeat into small pieces; add to peanut butter mixture. Boil briskly 1 minute, stirring constantly. Remove from heat. Add oats and peanuts; mix well. Spoon into 13 × 9-inch baking pan. Bake 45 minutes, stirring after 15 minutes and 30 minutes. Cool. Break into chunks. Store in tightly covered container. *Makes 6½ cups*

Tip: To refreshen Granola Snack, place on baking sheet and bake at 250° for 10 minutes. Cool.

CRUNCHY GRANOLA

4 cups rolled oats
⅓ cup wheat germ
⅓ cup shredded coconut
⅓ cup nonfat dry milk
1 cup slivered almonds
1 cup raisins
⅓ cup oil
¾ cup **DOMINO® Liquid Brown Sugar**
1 teaspoon vanilla

Preheat oven to 350°F. Spread the rolled oats in an ungreased 13 × 9-inch pan. Heat oats in oven for 10 minutes. Combine wheat germ, coconut, dry milk, almonds and raisins with oats in baking pan. Add oil, **DOMINO® Liquid Brown Sugar** and vanilla. Bake at 350°F for 20 to 25 minutes, stirring often to brown evenly. Cool. Stir mixture until crumbly. Store in tightly covered container in refrigerator. *Makes about 6 cups*

FRIED PASTA CROUTONS

2 cups **SAN GIORGIO® Shell Macaroni, Ditalini, Twirls,** etc.
Cooking oil
¼ cup grated Parmesan cheese
¼ teaspoon garlic salt

Cook pasta according to package directions; drain well. Dry on paper towel. Fry pasta, ½ cup at a time, in deep fat fryer or in deep oil in fry pan at 375° for about 2 minutes or until golden brown. Stir to separate. Drain on paper towels. While hot, toss with Parmesan cheese and garlic salt or herbs as suggested below. Cool. Store in airtight container. Use in salads or as garnish for casseroles.

VARIATIONS:

- Substitute ¼ teaspoon onion salt for garlic salt.
- Omit cheese and sprinkle hot pasta pieces with onion salt or garlic salt.
- Fry pasta, do not season. Use as dipper for your favorite dips and sauces.

CRISPY SNACKS

2 quarts water
2 teaspoons salt
1 tablespoon oil
3⅔ cups **AMERICAN BEAUTY® CURLY-RONI®** or 1¾ cups **ELBO-RONI®**
Oil for deep frying
Seasoning

Choose one of the following:
½ cup grated Parmesan cheese combined with
    2 teaspoons Italian seasoning
    2 teaspoons Mexican seasoning
    2 teaspoons seasoned salt
    2 teaspoons onion salt

Boil water in large deep pot with salt and 1 tablespoon oil (to prevent boiling over). Add **CURLY-RONI®**, stir to separate. Cook uncovered after water returns to a full rolling boil for 10 to 11 minutes. Stir occasionally. Drain and rinse under hot water. Pat dry with paper towels.

In medium saucepan or deep fryer, heat oil to 375°F. Fry cooked **CURLY-RONI®**, ½ cup at a time, for 2 to 3 minutes until crispy and slightly golden. Do not overcook. Stir to separate while frying. Spread on paper towels to drain; separate if necessary. Sprinkle with desired seasoning. *8 servings*

High Altitude—Above 3500 Feet: Cooking times may need to be increased slightly for **CURLY-RONI®**. Heat oil to 360°F. and fry 2½ to 3½ minutes.

NUTRITION INFORMATION PER SERVING			
SERVING SIZE: ⅛ of recipe		PERCENT U.S. RDA	
Calories	155	PER SERVING	
Protein	7g	Protein	10
Carbohydrate	22g	Vitamin A	—
Fat	4g	Vitamin C	—
Sodium	413mg	Thiamin	9
Potassium	69mg	Riboflavin	8
		Niacin	5
		Calcium	11
		Iron	5

Nutritional information does not include the oil used for frying.

SUPER SNACKS

On a Toasted BAYS® English Muffin Half:

- spread with butter; sprinkle generously with Parmesan cheese; add garlic powder to taste; broil until cheese is bubbling.
- spread generously with softened cream cheese and top with strawberry jam.
- spread with softened cream cheese; top with slice of smoked salmon; sprinkle with lemon juice, chopped onion and capers (optional).
- spread with chunky style peanut butter; top with crumbled bacon.
- top with slice of Cheddar or American cheese; add one tablespoon chutney; broil until cheese melts.
- top with 3 tablespoons refried beans, then shredded, spiced "taco cheese"; broil until cheese is bubbling. For more spice, sprinkle chili powder on mixture before broiling.

PARTY PIZZAS

4 English muffins
1 package LAWRY'S® Extra Rich & Thick Spaghetti Sauce Mix
1 can (1 lb.) tomatoes, cut in pieces
1 clove garlic, crushed
½ cup grated Cheddar or Parmesan cheese
2 tablespoons minced anchovy fillets or 1 pound crumbled cooked pork sausage (optional)

Split the muffins in half using fork. Broil to a light brown. Meanwhile, combine the **Extra Rich & Thick Spaghetti Sauce Mix**, tomatoes and crushed garlic. Stir thoroughly. Bring to a boil. Cover and simmer 20 minutes. Place 2 tablespoons sauce on each muffin half. Sprinkle with the cheese and anchovy or sausage, if desired. Broil until bubbling and brown. Cut each muffin half in fourths and serve hot.   *Makes 32 pieces*

PASTRAMI PIZZAS

2 cups biscuit baking mix
½ cup cold water
1 cup pizza sauce
1 cup shredded mozzarella cheese
1 package BUDDIG Smoked Sliced Pastrami

Stir baking mix and water to a soft dough. Form dough into a ball on floured board and knead 5 times. Roll dough into a 15 × 9 inch rectangle. Cut into 3-inch squares; pinch edges to form rims. Spread each square with 1 tablespoon sauce; sprinkle with 1 tablespoon cheese and 1 tablespoon shredded pastrami. Bake on ungreased baking sheet 10 to 12 minutes in 425° oven.
Yield: 15 pizzas

POPCORN . . . GONE NUTS!

3 quarts popped SUPER POP Popcorn
1¼ cups pecan halves
⅔ cup sliced almonds
1 cup butter or margarine
1⅓ cups sugar
½ cup light corn syrup
2 teaspoons vanilla

Combine popcorn and nuts in large bowl; set aside. Combine butter, sugar, and corn syrup in heavy 2-quart saucepan. Bring to a boil. Cook, stirring constantly, to 300°F on candy thermometer.
(Continued)

Remove from heat. Stir in vanilla. Quickly pour syrup mixture over popcorn mixture; gently stir to coat evenly. Spread on a buttered baking sheet to cool. When mixture has cooled completely, break into serving-size pieces.

NACHO-CHEESE POPCORN

⅓ cup cooking oil
3 or 4 dried chilies
1 large clove garlic, cut into quarters
1 teaspoon cumin seed
⅓ cup popcorn
3 tablespoons hot oil
⅓ cup Parmesan cheese
1 teaspoon paprika
½ teaspoon salt

Place cooking oil, chilies, garlic and cumin seed in a small saucepan. Cook over low heat for 3 minutes; let stand 10 minutes. Strain. Use 3 tablespoons of seasoned oil for popping corn; reserve the rest. This makes about 2½ quarts popped popcorn.

Pour remaining oil over popped popcorn, tossing to coat. Mix Parmesan cheese, paprika and salt. Sprinkle over popped popcorn, tossing to mix.   *Makes 2½ quarts*

Note: A larger amount of hot oil may be made and stored for future use.

Favorite recipe from **The Popcorn Institute**

FAVORITE CARAMEL CORN

3¾ quarts (15 cups) popped SUPER POP Popcorn
2 cups packed brown sugar
1 cup butter or margarine
½ cup light corn syrup
½ teaspoon salt
1 teaspoon baking soda

Divide popped popcorn between two 13 × 9 × 2-inch baking pans. Combine brown sugar, butter, corn syrup, and salt in heavy saucepan. Cook, stirring occasionally, till bubbly around edges. Continue cooking over medium heat 5 minutes more.

Remove from heat. Stir in baking soda. Pour over popcorn; gently stir to coat popcorn. Bake in a 200°F oven for 1 hour, stirring every 15 minutes.

JOLLY TIME® POP CORN BALLS

1 cup granulated sugar or firmly packed brown sugar
⅓ cup light or dark corn syrup
⅓ cup water
¼ cup (½ stick) butter or margarine
½ teaspoon salt
1 teaspoon vanilla
2 quarts popped JOLLY TIME® Pop Corn

Keep pop corn warm in a 250 degree F oven. In a 2-quart saucepan, stir together sugar, corn syrup, water, butter and salt. Cook over medium heat, stirring constantly until mixture comes to a boil. Attach candy thermometer to pan. Continue without stirring until mixture reaches 270 degrees F or until a small amount dropped into very cold water separates into hard, but not brittle, threads. Remove from heat. Add vanilla and stir only enough to mix it through hot syrup. Pour syrup slowly over popped corn, mixing it with a fork. When cool enough to handle but still quite warm, form into balls or shape as desired.

CARAMEL CORN CLUSTERS

1 package of caramels (about 28)
¼ cup sugar
¼ cup water
2 quarts popped **JOLLY TIME®** Pop Corn
1 cup peanuts

Combine caramels, sugar and water in saucepan. Cook over low heat, stirring constantly until mixture is smooth and comes to a full boil; continue to stir constantly while mixture boils gently for 5 minutes.

Combine pop corn and peanuts in large baking pan. Pour caramel sauce over pop corn mixture and quickly toss, using two forks until pop corn and peanuts are well coated. Spread mixture on lightly greased cookie sheets. Let stand until cold, then break into clusters.

NUTTY CARAMEL POPCORN

12 cups popped corn
1½ cups salted peanuts
1⅓ cups sugar
¾ cup **KARO®** Light Corn Syrup
½ cup **MAZOLA®** Corn Oil Margarine
½ teaspoon baking soda
1 teaspoon vanilla

In large shallow roasting pan toss together popcorn and nuts. Bake in 300°F oven while preparing syrup mixture. In heavy 2-quart saucepan stir together sugar, corn syrup and margarine. Stirring constantly, cook over medium heat until mixture comes to boil and sugar is dissolved. Continue cooking, without stirring, until temperature reaches 280°F on candy thermometer or until a small amount of mixture when dropped into very cold water, forms a ball hard enough to hold its shape, yet plastic. Remove from heat; stir in baking soda. Stir in vanilla. Slowly pour over popped corn mixture, stirring to coat well. Spread out to cool. Break into pieces. Store in tightly covered container.

Makes about 12 cups

BEEF JERKY

1 beef flank steak (1 to 1½ pounds)*
Soy Sauce
Garlic salt
Pepper

Freeze steak partially for easy slicing. Trim off all visible fat. Using a sharp knife, cut the flank steak, WITH THE GRAIN, into strips approximately ⅛-inch wide and the length of the steak. Dip strips into soy sauce and place them flat and close together on a wire rack or racks, and place over a shallow pan. Sprinkle lightly with garlic salt and pepper. Turn and sprinkle other side. "Bake" in very slow oven, 140°F to 150°F for 8 to 10 hours or until dried and chewy. It should dry out, not cook. Store in tightly covered container.

*Use round steak as a substitute for flank.

Favorite recipe from **Iowa Beef Industry Council**

MERKT'S FRIES

MERKT'S Cheddar Cheese Spread
French Fries

In small saucepan over low heat, melt cheese. Pour over hot french fries. Serve as snack, party treat or with dinner.

Desserts

CHOCOLATE FONDUE DESSERT

6 squares (6 ounces) GHIRARDELLI® Milk
   Chocolate Blocks*
1 bar (4 ounces) GHIRARDELLI® Semi-Sweet
   Chocolate*
½ cup vanilla ice cream
3 Tbsp. liqueur (any flavor) or sweet wine
Chilled fresh fruit: strawberries, bananas, pineapple,
   pears, grapes, oranges

Fondue may be prepared in a fondue pot, heavy saucepan or double boiler. Break chocolate into small pieces. Melt chocolate with ice cream and liqueur stirring constantly for a smooth sauce or MICROWAVE all ingredients on medium for 2-3 minutes, stirring 3 times to blend ingredients. Cool sauce slightly before serving. If sauce is too hot, chocolate will run off fruit.

This dessert may be prepared in advance and kept warm in a double boiler. At dessert time, serve a bowl of chocolate fondue surrounded by cubes of chilled fresh fruit. Guests use forks to dip fruit. *Makes about 1 cup sauce*

*Any type GHIRARDELLI® Milk Chocolate and Semi-Sweet Chocolate may be substituted in this recipe.

Note: Left-over fondue may be used for a sauce over ice cream. Thin with milk or cream to desired consistency.

FESTIVE ANGEL TORTE

1 package angel food cake mix
1½ cups sifted powdered sugar
10 tablespoons CHIFFON® Margarine
1 egg
¾ teaspoon rum extract
½ cup toasted coconut
½ cup toasted chopped almonds
⅔ cup apricot preserves
2 cups sweetened whipped cream or non-dairy topping
Toasted sliced almonds

Prepare cake as directed on package. Cool. Beat sugar, CHIFFON®, egg and extract until light and fluffy (2-5 minutes). Stir in coconut and almonds. Slice cake crosswise into four 1-inch layers. Spread filling on three layers. Stack. Add top layer. Spread preserves on top and sides of cake; then whipped cream. Decorate with sliced almonds all over and more preserves drizzled on top.

MARITA'S LINZERTORTE

1¾ cups CERESOTA or HECKERS Unbleached
   Flour, sifted
½ teaspoon baking powder
½ cup sugar
¼ teaspoon (⅛ if salted butter is used) salt
½ teaspoon cinnamon
Dash (less than ⅛ teaspoon) cloves
1½ cups raw filbert nuts, finely ground and measured
   after grinding
1 egg, separated
1¼ sticks butter (or margarine)
5-6 tablespoons raspberry jam
1 teaspoon milk

Sift flour, baking powder, sugar, salt and spices into a large bowl. Mix in the nuts. Add the white of egg and half the yolk (reserve remaining half), and mix. Cut in butter until the mixture resembles a coarse meal.

Working the dough with your hands, press it into a ball. (If it gets sticky, put it in the refrigerator for a little while.) Take about ¾ of the dough and, again with your hands, press it into a 9″ pie pan, working it up the sides like a pie shell. Spread jam over the center, and not quite to the edges.

On a lightly floured board, press out the remaining piece of dough with your hands to about ¼″ thickness. (It's easier to work this with your hands than with a rolling pin because it's a very crumbly dough.)

Cut out strips about ¾″ wide and criss-cross them lattice fashion over the jam. Make one thin rope out of the remaining strips and circle the top edge with it. Score with a spoon handle, press it with your thumbprint, or decorate it however you'd like.

Mix the remaining half egg yolk with milk, and brush it on the pastry.

Bake in a preheated 350° oven for about 35 mintues, or until browned.

CHOCOLATE MERINGUE TORTE

8 egg whites
1¼ cups sugar
2 cups finely-chopped toasted pecans
3 pints BREYERS® Chocolate Ice Cream, softened*
½ cup heavy cream
¼ cup cocoa
2 tablespoons sugar

Grease and flour four baking sheets. Trace an 8-inch circle on each. Beat egg whites until foamy. Gradually add sugar and continue beating to stiff peaks. Fold in pecans. Divide mixture evenly among pans; spread evenly on each circle. Bake at 325°F. 30 minutes or until golden. Cool on pan for 10 minutes. Remove to racks and cool completely.

Place one meringue on serving platter. Spread with 1 pint ice cream. Repeat with two more layers. Place remaining meringue on top. Freeze 6 hours or overnight. Remove from freezer 10 minutes before serving. Combine cream, cocoa and sugar. Whip to soft peaks. Force through pastry tube on top of torte.

Makes one 8-inch torte

*Soften ice cream until easily scooped

PACIFIC GINGER TORTE

1 can (1 lb., 4 oz.) DOLE® Crushed Pineapple
1 package (14.5 oz.) gingerbread mix
½ cup dairy sour cream
1 large banana, sliced
2 tablespoons lemon juice
½ pint whipping cream
1 teaspoon vanilla
¼ cup powdered sugar
½ cup chopped walnuts

Drain pineapple reserving ½ cup syrup. Blend reserved pineapple syrup into gingerbread mix. Beat in sour cream. Pour into two greased 8-inch round cake pans. Bake in a preheated oven 350° F. 20 to 25 minutes until it tests done. Turn out onto wire racks to cool. Meanwhile slice banana into lemon juice and toss to coat each slice well. Whip cream with vanilla and sugar until stiff. Place one layer gingerbread on serving plate. Spread with half whipped cream. Arrange banana slices around edge. Spoon half of drained pineapple into center. Top with remaining gingerbread layer. Spread with remaining whipped cream. Ring edge with walnuts, spoon remaining pineapple into center.

Makes 8 to 10 servings

"CARNIVAL" APRICOT-DATE TORTE

1 (17 oz.) can **S&W® Peeled Apricots,** drained and cut in quarters
1 cup **S&W® Apricot Nectar**
⅔ cup chopped **S&W® Pitted Dates**
½ cup brown sugar
1 Tbsp. cornstarch
1 Tbsp. lemon juice
1 cup all-purpose flour
1 tsp. baking powder
¼ tsp. salt
½ cup butter or margarine
½ cup sugar
3 egg yolks
1 tsp. vanilla
½ cup chopped **S&W® Pecans**

Meringue:
3 egg whites
¼ tsp. cream of tartar
1 cup brown sugar
1 tsp. vanilla
½ cup chopped **S&W® Pecans**

In saucepan combine apricots, apricot nectar, dates, brown sugar and cornstarch. Cook over medium heat until slightly thickened. Add lemon juice and cool. Sift together flour, baking powder and salt. Cream butter and sugar. Add egg yolks and vanilla. Beat well. Add dry ingredients and pecans and spread in a 12 × 8 well-greased pan. Pour cooled apricot-date mixture over dough. Beat egg whites and cream of tartar until soft mounds form. Gradually add sugar and beat until stiff. Fold in vanilla and pecans. Cover filling with meringue. Bake at 300° for 50 to 60 minutes.

GRAHAM CRACKER TORTE

1 can (22 oz.) **WILDERNESS® Lemon Fruit Filling**
1 cup sugar
½ cup butter or margarine
2 eggs (separated)
1 cup milk
¾ cup coconut
2¼ cups graham cracker crumbs
2 tsp. baking powder
1 package (1½ oz.) whipped topping mix

Cream sugar and butter together. Beat egg yolks. Add beaten egg yolks, milk and ½ cup of the coconut to creamed mixture. Blend in graham cracker crumbs and baking powder. Beat egg whites until stiff, fold into graham cracker mixture, pour into two 8-inch or 9-inch square greased and floured Teflon® pans. Bake at 350°F for 25-30 minutes. Cool.

Put layers together with ½ can Lemon Fruit Filling. Frost with mixture of prepared whipped topping and remaining Lemon Filling. Sprinkle top with remaining ¼ cup coconut–toasted. Refrigerate 2-3 hours.

CHERRY TORTE

1 frozen **SARA LEE Chocolate Cake** (single layer)
1 teaspoon cherry brandy
1 can (5 oz.) vanilla pudding
1 cup canned cherry pie filling
Confectioner's sugar

Cut frozen cake lengthwise into 2 layers. Sprinkle cherry brandy on bottom layer. Spread on pudding then spoon on cherry pie filling. Replace cake top. Chill. Sprinkle with confectioner's sugar just before serving.

Makes 6 servings

TURKEY TORTE

Pour ½ cup **WILD TURKEY LIQUEUR®** into 8-inch pie plate or saucer. Dip 14 full-size graham crackers in liqueur. Spread ¾ cup apricot preserves on top of 13 crackers. Place on top of each other. Omit preserves from top cracker. In medium saucepan melt 1 package (12 oz.) semisweet chocolate bits with 1 can (14 oz.) sweetened condensed milk. Stir in 1 Tbsp. instant coffee. Cool. Spread top and sides of graham layers. Garnish with almonds. Chill several hours or overnight.

APRICOT LINZER TORTE

1 cup butter
¼ tsp. salt
2 cups sifted flour
1 cup ground blanched almonds
½ tsp. cinnamon
¼ tsp. allspice
1 tsp. cocoa
Juice and grated rind of ½ lemon
1 heaping cup confectioner's sugar
1 to 1½ cups **SIMON FISCHER Apricot Butter**

Mix all ingredients except Apricot Butter in electric mixer. When thoroughly mixed, knead until smooth; chill. Roll two-thirds of the dough ¼″ thick and line either a torte pan or an 8″ spring form pan, forming a good edge with the dough. Spread generously with Apricot Butter. Roll remaining dough into strips ¼″ wide and place criss-cross over Apricot Butter, making a lattice topping. Place 1 wide strip around cake edge to hold filling secure. Brush dough with slightly beaten egg white. Bake in moderate oven, 350 degrees, 45 to 55 minutes. When cool, fill squares formed by lattice topping with more Apricot Butter so it looks plump and fat, sprinkle with additional powdered sugar. Serve warm or cold.

ARROW® MOCHA MOUSSE

1½ cups milk
1 envelope unflavored gelatin
½ cup **ARROW® Coffee Flavored Brandy**
1 egg
¼ cup sugar
⅛ teaspoon salt
1 cup (6 ounces) semi-sweet chocolate morsels
1 cup heavy cream

In small saucepan, heat milk and gelatin to boiling point, stirring to dissolve gelatin. Pour into blender with remaining ingredients except cream. Process until smooth. Add cream. Process at low speed until well blended. Pour into a 1½ quart mold. Chill until firm.

Serves 8

MOCHA MOUSSE

Melt 8 squares (8 ounces) of semi-sweet chocolate in ⅔ cup brewed **MEDAGLIA D'ORO® Espresso Coffee**, stirring constantly over low heat until smooth. Cool. Whip 2 cups of heavy cream until mounded. Gradually beat in ½ cup of granulated sugar. Fold into chocolate coffee mixture. Chill.

Makes 8 servings

CHOCOLATE MOCHA MOUSSE

1 envelope unflavored gelatin
¼ cup cold water
1 (15-ounce) can **COCO LÓPEZ® Cream of Coconut**
3 tablespoons unsweetened cocoa
¼ cup coffee-flavored liqueur
2 cups (1 pint) whipping cream, whipped
Chocolate curls or mocha candy beans

In medium saucepan, sprinkle gelatin over water; let stand 1 minute. Add cream of coconut and cocoa; over medium heat, cook and stir until well blended. Chill until mixture begins to thicken. Fold in coffee liqueur and whipped cream. Spoon into individual serving dishes. Chill thoroughly. Garnish with chocolate curls.

Makes 8 to 10 servings

DUBOUCHETT MOCHA MOUSSE

8 Tbsp. liqueur—half **DuBOUCHETT Dark Creme de Cacoa,** half **DuBOUCHETT Coffee Brandy**
2 Tbsp. water
⅔ cup sugar
Pinch of salt
1 egg, beaten
2 Tbsp. sifted confectioners sugar
1 pint heavy cream, stiffly whipped

Cook 6 Tbsp. of the liqueur with next 3 ingredients until syrup will spin a thread (230°). Slowly add syrup and remaining liqueur to beaten egg, beating constantly. Cook in double boiler, stirring constantly, about 5 minutes, or until thickened. Cool mixture, then refrigerate until cold. Blend well, and fold liqueur mixture and sugar into whipped cream. Put mixture in fancy 1 qt. mold and freeze.

Serves 4

SUPER CHOCOLATE MOUSSE

One 12-oz. pkg. (2 cups) **NESTLÉ® Semi-Sweet Real Chocolate Morsels**
1 cup sugar, divided
¼ cup water
¼ cup brandy
4 egg yolks, beaten
1½ cups heavy cream
1 measuring tablespoon vanilla extract
6 egg whites

Garnish (optional):
Whipped cream

In large heavy gauge saucepan, combine **NESTLÉ® Semi-Sweet Real Chocolate Morsels**, ½ cup sugar, water and brandy. Cook over low heat until morsels melt and mixture is smooth; stirring constantly. Bring *just to a boil* over low heat; stirring occasionally. Remove from heat; set aside. In large bowl, gradually beat melted chocolate mixture into beaten egg yolks, using a wire whisk. Beat until smooth. Chill chocolate mixture over ice bath for about 10 minutes or until mixture mounds from spoon; stirring occasionally.* In small chilled bowl, beat heavy cream and vanilla extract until stiff peaks form; set aside. In large bowl, beat egg whites

until soft peaks form. Gradually add remaining ½ cup sugar, beating until stiff peaks form. Gradually fold a small amount of beaten egg whites into chilled chocolate mixture. Then fold in remaining egg whites. Fold in whipped cream. Pour into 8-cup soufflé dish. Chill in refrigerator several hours. Garnish with rosettes of whipped cream piped through decorative tube, if desired. Refrigerate until ready to serve.

Makes: about 15-16 servings

*Chocolate mixture sets up quickly. It is necessary to see that chocolate does not solidify on the bottom and sides of bowl.

LOW SODIUM CHOCOLATE MOUSSE

1 pkg. (12 oz.) semi-sweet chocolate pieces
½ cup boiling water
2 teaspoons **ANGOSTURA® Aromatic Bitters**
4 egg yolks
4 egg whites, stiffly beaten

In a blender, combine chocolate pieces, boiling water, **ANGOSTURA®** and egg yolks. Whirl until smooth and cool to room temperature. Beat egg whites in a bowl until stiff. Fold in chocolate mixture. Spoon mixture into serving dishes. Chill for several hours. Serve with demi-tasse.

Serves 6

Per serving: Sodium 37 mg; Calories 325

CHOCOLATE MOUSSE
(Low Calorie/Low Fat)

1 envelope unflavored gelatin
2 tablespoons unsweetened cocoa
2 eggs, separated
2 cups low-fat milk, divided
5 packets **SWEET 'N LOW®**
1½ teaspoons vanilla

In medium-size saucepan, mix gelatin and cocoa. In separate bowl, beat egg yolks with 1 cup milk. Blend into gelatin mixture. Let stand 1 minute to soften gelatin. Stir over low heat until gelatin is completely dissolved, about 5 minutes. Add remaining milk, **SWEET 'N LOW®**, and vanilla. Pour into large bowl and chill, stirring occasionally, until mixture mounds slightly when dropped from spoon. In separate large bowl, beat egg whites until soft peaks form; gradually add gelatin mixture and beat until doubled in volume, about 5 minutes. Chill until mixture is slightly thickened. Turn into dessert dishes or 1-quart bowl and chill until set.

8 servings

Per Serving (½ cup): Calories: 65; Fat: 3g

GHIRARDELLI® CHOCOLATE MOUSSE

1 bar (4 oz.) **GHIRARDELLI® Semi-Sweet Chocolate**
2 Tbsp. water
2 eggs, separated
Pinch salt
⅓ cup sugar
¾ cup whipping cream

In heavy saucepan on low heat, melt broken chocolate with water, stirring constantly. Beat egg yolks until thick. Stirring quickly, add yolks to chocolate; remove from heat. Beat egg whites with salt, gradually adding sugar and beating until stiff peaks form. Fold chocolate into whites. Whip cream and fold into chocolate mixture. Pour into small stemmed glasses. Chill several hours or overnight. Each serving may be topped with whipped cream and chocolate curls, if desired.

Makes 6 (½ cup) servings

FROZEN PEACH MOUSSE

1 cup mashed fresh peaches (or canned, frozen)
¼ teaspoon mace
1 teaspoon grated lemon rind
1 cup heavy cream, whipped
2 egg whites
¼ teaspoon salt
⅓ cup **DOMINO® BROWNULATED®** Sugar

Fold peaches, mace, and lemon rind into whipped cream. Beat egg whites with salt and sugar until stiff. Fold into creamed mixture. Pour mousse into ice cube tray; freeze at lowest temperature until firm. About 1½ hours. *Makes 5 to 6 servings*

BRANDY APRICOT MOUSSE

1 (16 oz.) can apricot halves
1 (6 oz.) can apricot nectar
1 envelope unflavored gelatin
4 large eggs, separated
½ cup sugar
¼ teaspoon salt
⅓ cup California brandy
1 cup whipping cream

Drain apricot halves. Set aside 3 halves for decoration. Turn remaining halves into blender, and blend to a puree (or force through a strainer). Turn nectar into top of double boiler and sprinkle with gelatin. Let stand 5 minutes to soften. Beat egg yolks lightly, and add to nectar, along with ¼ cup sugar and salt. Set over boiling water. Cook 5 to 10 minutes, stirring constantly, until mixture thickens and coats back of spoon. Remove from heat and stir in pureed apricots and brandy. Cool until mixture begins to thicken and jell. Beat egg whites to a fine foam. Gradually beat in remaining ¼ cup sugar, continuing to beat to a stiff meringue. With same beater, beat cream stiff. Fold meringue and cream into gelatin mixture. Turn into a soufflé dish 6 inches diameter, 3 inches deep (about 5 cups capacity), fitted with a foil or waxed paper collar extending at least 1 inch above the rim of dish. Chill until firm, at least 3 hours. At serving time, remove collar and decorate top with reserved apricot halves. *Makes 6 to 8 servings*

Favorite recipe from the **California Brandy Advisory Board**

TWENTY-MINUTE MOUSSE

2 envelopes **KNOX® Unflavored Gelatine**
½ cup cold water
1 cup boiling water
2 cups (1 pt.) sherbet, any flavor
1 container (9 oz.) frozen whipped topping, thawed

In large bowl, sprinkle unflavored gelatine over cold water; let stand 1 minute. Add boiling water and stir until gelatine is completely dissolved. With wire whip or rotary beater, blend in sherbet until melted, then whipped topping. Spoon into dessert dishes; chill 15 minutes. *Makes about 8 servings*

BÉNÉDICTINE MOUSSE

6 egg yolks, room temperature
¾ cup **BÉNÉDICTINE** Liqueur
2 cups heavy cream
Pecan halves for garnish

Place egg yolks in the container of a blender; process at low speed. In a small saucepan, heat **BÉNÉDICTINE** until it comes to a full rolling boil. Pour hot liqueur in a steady stream into the egg yolks, with the blender motor running. Process until the mixture becomes a thick custard. Chill. Beat heavy cream until stiff. Remove 1 cup. Fold chilled **BÉNÉDICTINE** mixture into whipped cream. Pour into 8 serving dishes. Garnish with reserved whipped cream and pecan halves. *Serves 8*

BLACK FOREST SOUFFLÉ

1 can (16 oz.) sour pitted cherries, drained
5 tablespoons cherry brandy or brandy
4 squares (1 oz. ea.) semi-sweet chocolate
2 envelopes **KNOX® Unflavored Gelatine**
¾ cup sugar
3 eggs, separated
2 cups milk
1½ teaspoons vanilla extract
2 cups (1 pt.) whipping or heavy cream

Reserve ½ cup cherries. Chop remaining cherries and marinate in 2 tablespoons brandy. Make enough chocolate curls for garnish (about ¼ oz. chocolate); reserve.

In medium saucepan, mix unflavored gelatine with ½ cup sugar; blend in egg yolks beaten with milk. Let stand 1 minute. Stir over low heat until gelatine is completely dissolved, about 5 minutes. Add remaining chocolate (about 3¾ oz.) and continue cooking, stirring constantly, until chocolate is melted. With wire whip or rotary beater, beat mixture until chocolate is blended. Stir in remaining brandy and vanilla. Pour into large bowl and chill, stirring occasionally, until mixture mounds slightly when dropped from spoon.

In large bowl, beat egg whites until soft peaks form; gradually add remaining sugar and beat until stiff. Fold into gelatine mixture. In medium bowl, whip 1½ cups cream; fold into gelatine mixture with chopped cherries and brandy. Turn into 1-quart soufflé dish with 3-inch collar; chill until set. Remove collar; garnish with remaining cream, whipped, reserved cherries and chocolate curls. *Makes about 10 servings*

CRANBERRY SOUFFLÉ

½ cup sugar
2 envelopes unflavored gelatin
1 cup milk
6 egg yolks, slightly beaten
1 cup **OCEAN SPRAY®** Cranberry Juice Cocktail
6 egg whites
½ teaspoon cream of tartar
½ cup sugar
¼ cup orange-flavored liqueur
1 cup heavy cream, whipped
½ cup **OCEAN SPRAY® CRANORANGE®** Cranberry Orange Relish

Fold long piece of waxed paper in half lengthwise. Tie and tape securely around the outside of 1-quart soufflé dish to form collar and hold soufflé mixture above dish until it sets. Combine ½ cup sugar, gelatin, milk, and egg yolks in saucepan. Cook, over medium heat, stirring constantly, until mixture just comes to boiling; do not boil. Remove from heat; cool. Add cranberry juice cocktail. Chill until mixture mounds slightly. Beat egg whites and cream of tartar until foamy; gradually beat in ½ cup sugar; continue to beat until meringue forms stiff, glossy peaks. Fold meringue into chilled gelatin mixture; fold in liqueur and whipped cream. Fold in relish. Turn mixture into prepared dish. Chill 3-4 hours or until set. Just before serving, carefully peel off collar. Decorate with additional whipped cream if desired. *Makes 8 servings*

COOL CHOCOLATE SOUFFLÉ

2 envelopes unflavored gelatin
½ cup water
6 egg yolks
¾ cup milk
3 tablespoons butter or margarine
1½ teaspoons vanilla
1½ cups (1-pound can) **HERSHEY'S**® **Chocolate Syrup**
6 egg whites
¼ teaspoon cream of tartar
⅓ cup sugar
1 cup heavy cream (*NOT* whipped topping)

MICROWAVE METHOD:

Measure length of aluminum foil to go around 1-quart soufflé dish; fold in half lengthwise. Butter one side of collar; tape securely to outside of dish (buttered side in) allowing collar to extend 4 inches above rim of dish. Set aside. Soften gelatin in water in small bowl a few minutes. Slightly beat egg yolks in large micro-proof bowl; add milk, gelatin mixture, and butter or margarine. Microwave on medium-high (⅔ power) for 3 to 4 minutes, stirring once, just until mixture is very hot and coats a spoon. DO NOT BOIL. Blend in vanilla and chocolate syrup. Press plastic wrap onto surface. Cool; chill, stirring occasionally, until mixture mounds from spoon. Beat egg whites with cream of tartar in large mixer bowl until foamy; gradually add sugar, beating until stiff peaks form. Fold egg whites into chocolate mixture. Whip cream; fold in. Pour into prepared dish; cover and chill overnight. Just before serving, carefully remove foil collar. Garnish with dessert topping and fresh fruit, if desired.   *12 to 14 servings*

CONVENTIONAL METHOD:

Soften gelatin in water in medium saucepan; add milk, egg yolks and butter. Cook, stirring constantly, until mixture coats a spoon but does not boil. Remove from heat and complete as in preceding recipe.

PUMPKIN CHIFFON SOUFFLÉ

1 package (6¾ ounces) **PEPPERIDGE FARM**® **BORDEAUX Cookies** (crisp rectangular cookies)
2 tablespoons butter or margarine, melted
¾ cup brown sugar
2 envelopes unflavored gelatin
½ teaspoon cinnamon
½ teaspoon nutmeg
½ teaspoon allspice
¼ teaspoon ginger
¼ teaspoon salt
1 cup milk
4 eggs, separated
1 can (29 ounces) pumpkin
⅓ cup sugar
½ pint whipping cream

Reserve 10 cookies. Crush remaining cookies to make crumbs and mix with melted butter. Combine brown sugar, gelatin, cinnamon, nutmeg, allspice, ginger and salt in saucepan. Add milk to egg yolks and beat; stir in pumpkin. Add to brown sugar mixture, cook over low heat, stirring until gelatin is completely dissolved and mixture thickens slightly. Chill, stirring occasionally until mixture mounds slightly when dropped from a spoon. Beat egg whites until

soft peaks form. Gradually add sugar, beating after each addition, until stiff. Fold into cooled pumpkin mixture. Beat whipping cream until stiff and fold into pumpkin mixture. Pour just enough pumpkin filling into a 2-quart heat-resistant glass soufflé dish to cover the bottom. Stand reserved 10 cookies around sides of dish, spacing evenly. Carefully add remaining filling, keeping cookies pressed around sides of dish. Sprinkle reserved cooky crumb mixture over top of soufflé. Chill 4 hours or overnight.

8 to 10 servings

MARGARITA SOUFFLÉ

1 can (20 oz.) **DOLE**® **Sliced Pineapple in Juice**
½ cup water
1 package (3 oz.) lime flavored gelatin
¼ teaspoon salt
4 eggs, separated
2 tablespoons lime juice
½ teaspoon grated lime peel
¼ cup tequila
¼ cup triple sec liqueur
1½ cups heavy cream, whipped

Drain pineapple reserving juice. Heat juice and water to boil. Stir in gelatin and salt until dissolved. Beat egg yolks well. Slowly add to warm mixture, stirring constantly. Cook over low heat, stirring, 3 to 4 minutes. Remove from heat and let cool. Stir in lime juice, peel, tequila and triple sec. Chill until mixture mounds on spoon. Beat egg whites until stiff peaks form. Fold into gelatin mixture. Fold in whipped cream. Place 7 pineapple slices on edge around sides of 1½-quart clear glass soufflé dish. Make a wax paper collar to extend 2 inches above rim of dish; brush with oil. Gently pour gelatin mixture into prepared dish. Chill until firm, 4 hours or overnight. Garnish with remaining 3 slices of pineapple and lime slices, if desired. Remove collar to serve.

Makes 6 to 8 servings

BRANDIED PINK APPLE SOUFFLÉ

1¼ cups apple juice
2 tablespoons red cinnamon candies
2 large or 3 medium cooking apples (about 1¼ lb.)
½ cup sugar
½ cup California brandy
2 tablespoons lemon juice
1 envelope unflavored gelatin
3 large egg whites
⅛ teaspoon salt
Brandy Custard Sauce*

Combine 1 cup apple juice and cinnamon candies in large skillet and heat slowly until candies dissolve. Meanwhile, pare, core and slice apples. Add ¼ cup *each* sugar and brandy to skillet along with the lemon juice, and stir until sugar dissolves and mixture reaches a boil. Add apples and simmer about 10 minutes, just until tender and translucent, turning once. Remove apples with slotted spoon, saving syrup. Set aside a few apple slices to decorate top of soufflé. Blend or sieve remainder to make 1 cup. Sprinkle gelatin over remaining ¼ cup apple juice to soften. Turn the rosy cooking syrup into measuring cup. Add more apple juice or water, if needed, to measure ½ cup. Combine with softened gelatin, set over boiling water, and heat until gelatin dissolves. Remove from heat and stir in remaining ¼ cup brandy and the blended apple.

(Continued)

Cool until mixture begins to thicken and jell.

Beat egg whites with salt to soft peaks. Gradually beat in remaining ¼ cup sugar, beating to a stiff meringue. Fold into apple mixture. Chill a few minutes, until mixture mounds on a spoon. Turn into serving bowl, and chill firm. At serving time, decorate with reserved apple slices. Serve with Brandy Custard Sauce.

Makes about 6 servings (about 1 quart)

*BRANDY CUSTARD SAUCE

Beat 3 egg yolks lightly in top of double boiler. Stir in 1¼ cups half-and-half (thin cream), 3 tablespoons sugar, 1 teaspoon cornstarch and ⅛ teaspoon salt. Set over boiling water, and cook, stirring constantly, until mixture thickens and coats back of spoon. Remove from heat, and stir in 2 tablespoons California brandy and ½ teaspoon vanilla. Chill before serving.

Makes about 1½ cups

Favorite recipe from **California Brandy Advisory Board**

SOUFFLÉ NORMANDE

3 cups sliced pared apples
1 tablespoon lemon juice
⅓ cup **BLUE BONNET® Margarine**
½ cup sugar
¼ cup **LEMON HART Golden Jamaica Rum**

Soufflé Mixture:

5 eggs, separated (at room temperature)
½ cup sugar
3 tablespoons **BLUE BONNET® Margarine**, melted
3 tablespoons flour
¼ teaspoon salt
1 cup milk
1 teaspoon vanilla extract

Sprinkle apple slices with lemon juice. In large skillet melt ⅓ cup **BLUE BONNET® Margarine**. Sauté apples in margarine until tender, about 8 minutes. Pour ½ cup sugar over apples, and stir gently for a few minutes, until the sugar caramelizes. Pour **LEMON HART Rum** over apples, set aflame, and shake the pan until the flame goes out. Set aside.

SOUFFLÉ MIXTURE:
In small deep bowl, beat egg yolks until thick and lemon colored. Gradually beat in ¼ cup sugar. Combine 3 tablespoons melted **BLUE BONNET® Margarine**, flour and salt in heavy saucepan. Gradually add milk. Cook over low heat, stirring constantly, until smooth and thick, about 5 minutes. Slowly beat hot mixture into beaten egg yolks. Stir in vanilla extract. Cool slightly. Beat egg whites until frothy; slowly beat in remaining ¼ cup of sugar and continue to beat to make stiff meringue. Fold a quarter of the egg whites into the egg yolk mixture; then fold all back lightly and evenly into the remaining egg whites.

Place sautéed apples in bottom of 2-quart soufflé dish; top with soufflé mixture. With spatula, make a slight indentation around top of soufflé, 1-inch from edge. Bake at 350°F. for about 35 to 40 minutes, or until fairly firm. Serve immediately.

Makes 6 to 8 servings

PEACH BAVARIAN CREAM

1 package (16 ounces) **Frozen STOKELY'S® Sliced Peaches**, thawed
1 cup boiling water
1 envelope unflavored gelatin
1 package (3 ounces) peach-flavored gelatin
1 cup whipping cream, whipped

Drain peaches, reserving liquid. Reserve a few slices for garnish and cut remaining peaches into pieces. Pour boiling water over gelatins, stirring until gelatin dissolves. Add enough water to reserved peach liquid to equal 1 cup; add to gelatin, stir to blend. Chill until almost set. Meanwhile, fold a 30-inch piece of foil lengthwise into a 3-inch-wide strip. Tape paper collar around outside of a 1-quart soufflé dish. Beat gelatin with mixer until foamy. Add peach pieces. Reserve 2 Tablespoons whipped cream for garnish; fold remainder into gelatin-peach mixture. Pour into soufflé dish. Chill until firm. Garnish with reserved peach slices and reserved whipped cream.

4 servings

MOCHA SPANISH CREAM
(Low Calorie)

1 envelope unflavored gelatin
¼ cup cold water
2 eggs, separated
1½ cups low-fat milk, scalded
1 teaspoon instant decaffeinated coffee
½ teaspoon vanilla
6 packets **SWEET 'N LOW®**, divided

In small bowl, soften gelatin in cold water. In top of double boiler, beat egg yolks; blend in milk. Cook, stirring constantly, over hot water until mixture thickens slightly. Add softened gelatin and coffee; stir until dissolved. Remove from heat. Stir in vanilla and 3 packets **SWEET 'N LOW®**. Chill until mixture is consistency of unbeaten egg whites.

In large bowl, beat egg whites with electric mixer until foamy. Add remaining **SWEET 'N LOW®**. Beat until stiff. Fold chilled custard mixture into egg whites. Pour into serving dishes. Chill until set.

4 servings

PER SERVING (½ cup): Calories: 105 Protein: 9gm
Carbohydrate: 7gm Fat: 5gm Sodium: 90mg

CHOCO-BERRY BAVARIAN CREAM

10-ounce package frozen, sliced strawberries, thawed or 1½ cups sweetened sliced strawberries
2 envelopes unflavored gelatin
½ cup sugar
1 cup **HERSHEY'S® Semi-Sweet Chocolate Mini Chips**
2¼ cups milk
1 teaspoon vanilla
1 cup heavy cream
Strawberry Cream*
Garnish: Fresh strawberries

Drain strawberries; reserve syrup. Add water to syrup to equal ¾ cup. Stir gelatin into liquid; set aside. Chill drained berries. Combine sugar, Mini Chips and ½ cup milk in saucepan. Stir constantly over low heat until mixture is smooth and very hot. Add gelatin mixture, stirring until gelatin is completely dissolved. Remove from heat; add remaining milk and vanilla. Pour into bowl; chill until mixture mounds from a spoon, stirring occasionally during chilling. Whip cream until stiff; fold into chocolate mixture. Pour into oiled 5- or 6-cup mold; chill until firm. Unmold and garnish with Strawberry Cream and additional fresh strawberries.

8 to 10 servings

*STRAWBERRY CREAM

Mash or purée reserved strawberries from Bavarian Cream recipe to equal ½ cup. Whip 1 cup heavy cream with 1 teaspoon vanilla until stiff. Fold in strawberry purée and 2 or 3 drops red food color.

About 2 cups topping

CREAMY FRUIT FROST

1 (3 oz.) package cream cheese, softened
1 (12 oz.) container non-dairy whipped topping
1 (21 oz.) can **WILDERNESS® Cherry Fruit Filling**
1 (11 oz.) can mandarin oranges, drained
1 (8 oz.) can pineapple chunks, drained

Stir softened cream cheese into non-dairy whipped topping. Gradually add **WILDERNESS® Cherry Fruit Filling**, blending well. Fold drained mandarin oranges and pineapple chunks into cherry mixture.

Pour into 8-cup mold and freeze overnight or until firm. Unmold and serve as a salad or dessert.   *Makes 10 servings*

SNOWY COCONUT CHEESE DESSERT

2 envelopes unflavored gelatin
½ cup cold water
1½ cups boiling water
2 (16-ounce) containers **BORDEN® Cottage Cheese**
1 (14-ounce) can **EAGLE® Brand Sweetened Condensed Milk** (NOT evaporated milk)
1 (3½-ounce) can flaked coconut (1⅓ cups)
Fresh or canned fruit

In large bowl, sprinkle unflavored gelatin over cold water; let stand 1 minute. Add boiling water and stir until gelatin is dissolved. Add cheese, sweetened condensed milk and coconut; mix well. Turn into 2-quart mold or 12-cup fluted tube pan. Chill 4 hours or until firm. Unmold. Serve with fruit. Garnish as desired. Refrigerate leftovers.   *Makes 12 servings*

VANILLA CREME SNOW
(Low Calorie)

1 envelope unflavored gelatin
1 (12 oz.) can **DIET SHASTA® Creme Soda**
1 teaspoon artificial liquid sweetener
1 tablespoon vanilla
2 egg whites
Dash salt

Soften gelatin in ¼ cup **DIET SHASTA®**. Heat remaining soda, add softened gelatin, stirring until dissolved. Add sweetener and vanilla. Chill and when mixture begins to thicken, fold in egg whites beaten until stiff with salt. Spoon into sherbet glasses or individual molds. Chill firm.   *Makes 6 to 8 servings*

8 calories per serving

FRUIT BAVARIAN

1 package (3 oz.) flavored gelatin (use 6 oz. for heavy fruit)*
4 tablespoons sugar
1 cup boiling water
1 cup cold fruit juice
2 cups fresh, frozen, or canned fruit (Do not use fresh or frozen pineapple or kiwi fruit.)
⅔ cup **MILNOT®**, whipped

Dissolve gelatin and sugar in boiling water, add cold juice, and chill until it is slightly thickened. Beat until fluffy; add fruit. Fold stiffly whipped **MILNOT®** into fruit mixture. Pour into prepared mold (approx. 6 cups). Chill several hours or overnight until well set.   *Yield: approx. 9 servings*

*Note: Strawberry or raspberry especially good.

TORTONI MOLD

1 (14-ounce) can **EAGLE® Brand Sweetened Condensed Milk** (NOT evaporated milk)
3 egg yolks, beaten*
¼ cup light rum
2 teaspoons vanilla extract
⅔ cup coconut macaroon crumbs (about 5 large cookies)
½ to ¾ cup toasted slivered almonds
⅓ cup chopped maraschino cherries
2 cups (1 pint) **BORDEN® Whipping Cream**, whipped
Additional maraschino cherries, toasted slivered almonds and mint leaves for garnish, optional

In large bowl, combine all ingredients except whipped cream and garnish; mix well. Fold in whipped cream. Pour into lightly oiled 1½-quart mold; cover with aluminum foil. Freeze 6 hours or until firm. Using a hot cloth on outside of mold, unmold onto serving plate. Garnish with cherries, almonds and mint leaves if desired. Return leftovers to freezer.   *Makes 12 to 15 servings*

*Use only Grade A clean, uncracked eggs.

LITE FRUIT WHIP

2 cans (16 oz. each) **DEL MONTE Lite Fruit Cocktail** or **Chunky Mixed Fruits**
1 cup **DEL MONTE Unsweetened Orange Juice**, chilled
1 pkg. (3 oz.) orange or lemon-flavored gelatin
Rind of one lemon, grated
Juice of one lemon
1 tsp. vanilla extract
2 egg whites, room temperature

Drain fruit reserving ⅔ cup liquid. Add ½ cup orange juice to reserved liquid; heat to boiling. Add gelatin; dissolve completely. Stir in remaining orange juice, lemon rind, lemon juice and vanilla. Chill until slightly thickened. Add egg whites and beat with electric mixer until double in size and creamy (8 to 10 minutes). In serving bowl, spread half the fruit. Top with gelatin mixture; chill until firm. Top with remaining fruit and serve.   *6 to 8 servings*

LIGHT-AS-MIST APPLE CREAM

1 envelope unflavored gelatin
¼ cup cold water
1½ cups light cream
½ cup sugar
⅛ teaspoon salt
1 cup sour cream
1 cup applesauce
¼ cup **JOHNNIE WALKER RED** Scotch

Soften gelatin in cold water in small saucepan. Stir in light cream, sugar and salt. Cook, stirring, over low heat until gelatin and sugar dissolve. Remove from heat; beat in sour cream until smooth. Stir in applesauce and **JOHNNIE WALKER RED**. Pour into 4 serving dishes. Garnish as desired. Chill until set.

KOOL FREEZE

1 can (13-oz.) **MILNOT**®
⅔ cup sugar
1 pkg. unsweetened drink mix powder
1 to 2 cups fruit pieces (optional)

Whip **MILNOT**® until it holds stiff peaks. Whip in the sugar; then whip in the powder. Fold in fruit, if used. Spoon into flat 8 × 8-inch pan. Freezes smoothly without stirring.

PATRIOTIC ANGEL DESSERT

4 cups strawberries, sliced
2 cups blueberries
3 Tbsp. **HIRAM WALKER Apricot Flavored Brandy**
3 Tbsp. **HIRAM WALKER Triple Sec Liqueur**
¼ cup sugar
5 eggs, separated
¾ cup sugar
2 Tbsp. lemon juice
1 Tbsp. grated orange rind
2 Tbsp. **HIRAM WALKER Apricot Flavored Brandy**
2 Tbsp. **HIRAM WALKER Triple Sec Liqueur**
1 cup whipping cream, whipped
1 10-inch angel food cake, torn into 2-inch pieces
Toasted sliced almonds

Mix first five ingredients and chill. Beat egg yolks and ¾ cup sugar in top of double boiler until thick and lemon-colored. Add lemon juice. Heat over simmering water, stirring constantly, until mixture thickens and coats the spoon. (Do not boil.) Add orange rind, 2 tablespoons **Apricot Flavored Brandy** and 2 tablespoons **Triple Sec**. Cool. Beat egg whites until soft peaks form and fold into egg yolk mixture. Fold in whipped cream.

In *large* glass bowl layer half the cake pieces, half the fruit mixture and half the mousse mixture. Repeat layers. Garnish with almonds. Refrigerate several hours. *10 to 12 servings*

FLOATING ISLAND

1 egg, separated
⅛ teaspoon cream of tartar
2 tablespoons sugar
1¾ cups milk
3 eggs
¼ cup sugar
¼ teaspoon salt
1 tablespoon orange juice concentrate, optional
½ teaspoon vanilla or lemon extract

In small mixing bowl beat egg white and cream of tartar at high speed until foamy. Add 2 tablespoons sugar beating constantly until sugar is dissolved* and white is glossy and stands in soft peaks.

In 8-inch fry pan or saucepan heat milk over low heat until simmering. Drop 4 meringues, using about ⅓ cup each, onto milk. Simmer, uncovered, until firm, about 5 minutes. Remove meringues from milk and drain on absorbent paper. Chill while preparing custard. Reserve milk.

In medium saucepan beat eggs and egg yolk. Stir in ¼ cup sugar and salt. Gradually blend reserved milk into egg mixture. Cook, stirring constantly, over low heat until mixture thickens slightly and coats a metal spoon. Remove from heat. Stir in orange juice and vanilla. Pour into serving dishes. Top custard with meringues to serve. Serve warm or chilled.

*Rub just a bit of meringue between thumb and forefinger to feel if sugar is dissolved. *4 servings*

Favorite recipe from the **American Egg Board**

OEUF A' LA NEIGE MANTO

2 eggs, separated
4 tablespoons sugar
2 cups milk
½ cup **METAXA**® **Manto Liqueur**
¼ cup sugar
2 egg yolks

Beat egg whites until foamy. Gradually add 4 tablespoons sugar, beating until stiff peaks form.

In a medium saucepan, combine milk, 2 tablespoons **METAXA**® **Manto Liqueur** and ¼ cup sugar. Cook over medium heat to a gentle simmer. Shape tablespoonfuls of egg white mixture into the shape of eggs. Slide into simmering milk mixture. Cook 3 meringue "eggs" 2 minutes; gently turn over and cook 2 minutes more. Remove with a slotted spoon and set aside to drain, then chill. Repeat to make 6 meringue "eggs."

Strain milk mixture, measuring out 1½ cups. Place 4 egg yolks in the top of a double boiler. Gradually beat in 1½ cups milk mixture. Cook, stirring constantly, over hot (not boiling) water until custard coats a metal spoon, about 7 to 9 minutes. Cool slightly. Stir in remaining 6 tablespoons liqueur. Chill.

To serve, float meringue "eggs" in custard sauce. Garnish with grated orange rind if desired. *Makes 6 servings*

ITALIAN DELIGHT

1 3-ounce package lady fingers
¼ cup **HOLLAND HOUSE**® **Marsala Cooking Wine**
2 eggs, separated
½ cup granulated sugar
1 cup ricotta or cream cheese
5 ounces chocolate bits
30 macaroons, crushed

Sprinkle lady fingers with Marsala. In a mixing bowl, beat egg yolks with sugar and cheese until ingredients thicken. In a separate bowl, beat egg whites with an electric beater or whisk until stiff. Fold the chocolate bits and macaroons into the egg whites. Line a 1-quart glass bowl with the lady fingers. Fold egg yolk and egg white mixtures together and place in mold. Freeze overnight. Unmold and serve. *Serves 6*

VANILLA PUDDING SURPRISE

Crust:
1¾ cups granola
¼ cup melted **HAIN**® **Safflower Margarine**
2 Tbsp. light honey
2 medium bananas, sliced

Filling:
1 pkg. **HAIN**® **Vanilla Pudding and Pie Filling Mix**
8 oz. sour cream

CRUST:
Mix granola, margarine and honey in bowl. In 8-inch square baking pan, spread granola mixture. Arrange 1½ of the sliced bananas over granola mixture. (Save ½ banana for top garnish.)

FILLING:
Make Vanilla Pudding according to package directions. Pour into bowl. Add 8 oz. of sour cream and mix well. Pour over bananas and refrigerate 3 hours or overnight. Garnish with dry granola and bananas. *Makes 6 servings*

COCOA PUDDING

¼ cup **HERSHEY'S®** **Cocoa**
⅔ cup sugar
3 tablespoons cornstarch
¼ teaspoon salt
2¼ cups milk
2 tablespoons butter
1 teaspoon vanilla

Combine cocoa, sugar, cornstarch and salt in medium saucepan; gradually blend milk into dry ingredients. Cook over medium heat, stirring constantly, until mixture boils; boil and stir one minute. Remove from heat; blend in butter and vanilla. Pour into individual serving dishes. Chill. Garnish as desired.

4 to 5 servings

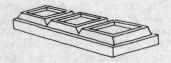

KAHLÚA® CHOCOLATE VELVET

⅓ cup **KAHLÚA®** **Coffee Liqueur**
½ teaspoon instant coffee granules
1 teaspoon vanilla
2 (1 oz.) squares unsweetened chocolate
4 (1 oz.) squares semi-sweet chocolate
5 large eggs, separated
¼ teaspoon cream of tartar
⅓ cup superfine sugar

Measure **KAHLÚA®**, coffee granules, vanilla and chocolate into 1-quart saucepan. Place directly over *low* heat (*or*, set pan in shallow pan of hot water over low heat). Stir now and then until chocolate melts and mixture is smooth and thick. Meanwhile, beat egg yolks well in small mixer bowl. Beat in chocolate mixture. When mixture is cool, beat egg whites with cream of tartar to soft peaks.

Gradually beat in sugar to make meringue. Beat *half* the meringue into chocolate mixture until smooth. Fold in remaining meringue. Turn into 1-quart serving dish (or individual dishes). Cover and chill until firm. If desired, decorate with whipped cream and white *or* semi-sweet chocolate curls.*

Makes 8 servings (1 quart)

*CHOCOLATE CURLS

Draw a vegetable peeler across surface of warm 1-oz. semi-sweet chocolate square. Chocolate should be slightly warmer than room temperature.

SCRUMPTIOUS DESSERT

¼ lb. margarine or butter
2 tablespoons sugar
1 cup flour
1 (8 oz.) package cream cheese
⅔ cup powdered sugar
2 (8 oz.) cartons of whipped topping
1 can **THANK YOU®** **Brand Chocolate Pudding**
1 can **THANK YOU®** **Brand Vanilla Pudding**

1. Cream margarine and sugar, add flour, mix well. Bake in 9 × 13 × 2 inch baking pan in 350° oven. Cool.
2. Mix cream cheese, sugar, and one carton of whipped topping until creamy. Spread on baked crust.
3. Mix chocolate and vanilla pudding. Spread over cheese mixture. Spread remaining whipped topping over top. Chill.

CHOCOLATE PUDDING MIX

4 cups nonfat dry milk powder
2⅔ cups sugar
1⅓ cups **ARGO®/KINGSFORD'S®** **Corn Starch**
1 cup unsweetened cocoa
½ teaspoon salt

In large bowl stir together dry milk, sugar, corn starch, cocoa and salt until well mixed. Store in tightly covered container at room temperature.   *Makes about 7 cups*

Note: Stir pudding mix before each use.

CHOCOLATE PUDDING

1 cup Chocolate Pudding Mix
2 cups water
1 tablespoon **MAZOLA®** **Corn Oil Margarine**
½ teaspoon vanilla

In medium saucepan stir together pudding mix and water until well mixed. Stirring constantly, bring to boil over medium heat and boil 1 minute. Stir in margarine and vanilla. Pour into individual serving dishes. Cover; refrigerate.

Makes 4 (½ cup) servings

VARIATIONS:

MOCHA PUDDING

Follow recipe for Chocolate Pudding. Substitute 1 cup strong black coffee for 1 cup of the water.

CHOCO-PEPPERMINT PUDDING

Follow recipe for Chocolate Pudding. Add ¼ teaspoon peppermint extract with margarine and vanilla. Top chilled pudding with ¼ cup crushed peppermint candy.

NUTTY CHOCOLATE PUDDING

Follow recipe for Chocolate Pudding. Mix ¼ cup **SKIPPY®** **Creamy** or **Super Chunk Peanut Butter** with the water until smooth. Top chilled pudding with ¼ cup chopped peanuts.

LEMON PUDDING
(Low Calorie)

1 envelope unflavored gelatin
½ cup boiling water
1 tablespoon lemon juice
½ teaspoon grated lemon rind
¼ cup cold water
1 envelope Vanilla **ALBA '77**
6 oz. net weight of **WEIGHT WATCHERS®** **Vanilla Frozen Dessert** (approx. 1¼ cups)

Stir gelatin into boiling water until dissolved. Mix in lemon juice and rind; cool slightly. In mixing bowl, beat **ALBA '77** with cold water until frothy. Add **WEIGHT WATCHERS®** **Frozen Dessert** and beat on high speed with electric mixer. Slowly pour in gelatin mixture while continuing to beat until mixture is fluffy. Pour into dessert glasses and serve at once.

Calories: Each serving equals about 146

WEIGHT WATCHERS® members should omit for each serving: ½ cup skim milk, ½ serving milk substitute, 1 serving non-citrus fruit and 1 serving extras from their menu plan.

RICH CHOCOLATE PUDDING

2¾ cups milk
¼ cup **MALT-O-MEAL®**
2 squares unsweetened chocolate
2 egg yolks
½ cup sugar
¼ tsp. salt
¼ tsp. cinnamon
½ cup chopped nuts
¾ tsp. vanilla

In medium saucepan, heat milk. Add **MALT-O-MEAL®** gradually. Cook until thickened. Add chocolate; stir until melted and blended. Cook at low heat for 10 minutes, stirring occasionally. Combine remaining ingredients in a small bowl. Add slowly to cooked mixture and continue cooking for 2 minutes. Pour into greased 1 quart casserole and bake at 350° for 15 minutes. Serve warm.   *4 to 6 servings*

LEMON REFRIGERATOR DESSERT

22 gingersnaps or graham crackers
¼ cup butter (or margerine)
1 can **LUCKY LEAF®** Lemon Pie Filling
¾ cup water
½ cup evaporated milk, chilled
1 Tbsp. lemon juice

Crush gingersnaps or graham crackers and mix with softened butter. Spread ½ crumbs in 9″ square baking pan. Mix pie filling with water until well blended. Whip evaporated milk until fluffy. Add lemon juice. Continue beating until stiff. Fold into lemon mixture. Pour over crumbs in pan. Top with remaining crumbs. Chill in freezer compartment at least 1 hour.

MEXICAN PUDDING

Spoon into dessert dishes:
    4 cans (5 oz. each) **DEL MONTE PUDDING CUP Lemon Cream Pudding**

Place in freezer to chill.

Toast:
    ¼ cup chopped nuts

Garnish each serving with ground cinnamon and toasted chopped nuts.

PEPPERMINT RICE CLOUD

1 bag **SUCCESS®** Rice
1 cup milk
1½ cups miniature marshmallows
⅓ cup crushed peppermint candy
½ cup heavy cream
1 tablespoon sugar
1 teaspoon vanilla
Chocolate sauce

Cook bag of rice according to package directions. Drain bag and pour out water.   *(Continued)*

In same saucepan, empty the rice and add the milk, marshmallows, and candy. Cook and stir over medium heat for 5 minutes, or until marshmallows and candy melt. Remove from heat and cool.

Whip cream, gradually adding sugar and vanilla. Beat until stiff peaks form.

Fold whipped cream into cooled rice mixture. Pour into serving dish and chill. Garnish with Chocolate sauce, if desired.

Makes 6 servings (about ½ cup each)

LEMON PUDDING WITH A TWIST

2 envelopes unflavored gelatin
⅓ cup fresh lemon juice
1 (12 oz.) can **DIET SHASTA®** Creme Soda
1½ teaspoons grated lemon peel
2 cups buttermilk
1½ teaspoons artificial sweetener
4 or 5 drops yellow food coloring
Fresh strawberries for decoration

Combine gelatin and lemon juice in blender top. Heat **DIET SHASTA®** Creme Soda to boiling. Pour over gelatin and whirl until dissolved. Blend in remaining ingredients. Pour into serving dishes. Chill until set. Garnish each serving with a fresh berry.

Makes about 1 quart

HYDROX® BUTTERSCOTCH PUDDING

1 package butterscotch pudding mix
18 **HYDROX®** Cookies

Prepare butterscotch pudding as package directs. Place 1 **HYDROX®** Cookie in the bottom of each of six 6-ounce custard cups. Pour enough hot pudding over the cookies to cover them. Repeat, alternating cookies and pudding until cookies and pudding are all used. Chill at least 4 hours, or overnight. Serve in custard cups topped with whipped cream, or unmold into dessert dishes and serve with light cream, maple syrup or whipped cream.

Yield: 6 servings

PEACHY LEMON PUDDING

2 egg yolks
1 tablespoon **HEALTH VALLEY®** BEST BLEND Oil
⅓ cup **HEALTH VALLEY®** Clover Honey
½ cup **HEALTH VALLEY®** SPROUTS 7™ Cereal
¼ cup lemon juice
1 cup chopped **HEALTH VALLEY®** Peach Halves, with juice
½ cup **HEALTH VALLEY®** PLAIN SOY MOO® (soy milk)
2 egg whites, beaten stiff

Preheat oven to 350°F. In a medium-size bowl, beat egg yolks lightly, then add oil and honey. Stir in cereal, lemon juice, peaches and soy milk. Fold in egg whites. Pour into 5 ungreased individual custard cups. Place cups in baking pan and pour hot water into the pan around the cups to a level of about halfway up the sides of the cups. Bake in preheated oven for about 35 minutes. Serve warm or cold. As the pudding bakes, the egg whites will rise to form a golden brown meringue.   *Yield: 5 servings*

EXTRA NICE RICE PUDDING
(Low Calorie/Low Cholesterol)

1 pkg. (53 grams) **ESTEE® Vanilla Pudding**
2 cups skim milk
1 cup cooked rice
¼ cup raisins (optional)
¼ tsp. cinnamon
¼ tsp. vanilla

Prepare **ESTEE® Vanilla Pudding** with skim milk as directed on package. Cool 5 minutes. Stir in rice, raisins, and vanilla. Pour into individual serving dishes. Sprinkle top of each with cinnamon. Refrigerate until served.

Makes 6 servings, ½ cup per serving

NUTRITION INFORMATION
Calories	Carbohydrates	Protein	Cholesterol	Sodium
92	20g	4g	1mg	44mg

DIABETIC EXCHANGE INFORMATION
Bread
1½

RICE WITH MILK PUDDING
(Arroz con Leche)

1 envelope **KNOX® Unflavored Gelatine**
½ cup sugar
3 eggs
2 cups milk
1 teaspoon vanilla extract
2 cups cooked rice
1 cup (½ pt.) whipping or heavy cream, whipped
½ cup diced mixed candied fruit

In large saucepan, mix unflavored gelatine with sugar; blend in eggs beaten with milk. Let stand 1 minute. Stir over low heat until gelatine is completely dissolved, about 5 minutes. Stir in vanilla and rice. Pour into large bowl and chill, stirring occasionally, until mixture mounds slightly when dropped from spoon.

Fold in whipped cream and fruit. Turn into 6-cup mold or bowl; chill until firm. Garnish with maraschino cherries. Serve, if desired, with caramel or fruit sauce.

Makes about 12 servings

UPSIDE DOWN NOODLE PUDDING

¼ cup parve margarine, softened
½ cup light brown sugar
8 slices canned pineapple, well drained
2 eggs
¼ cup cooking oil or melted parve margarine
¼ cup sugar
½ teaspoon salt
½ teaspoon cinnamon
1 tablespoon lemon juice
½ teaspoon grated lemon rind
8 ounces (5½ to 6 cups) **MUELLER'S® Fine Egg Noodles**
½ cup finely cut dried fruits (apricots, prunes, dates, etc.)
½ cup raisins
½ cup chopped nuts

Prepare a 9-inch ring mold or 9-inch square pan by spreading with margarine to coat thoroughly; sprinkle with brown sugar. Cut pineapple slices in half; arrange in a design on sugar mixture. In large bowl, beat eggs and oil with sugar, salt, cinnamon, lemon juice and rind. Meanwhile, cook noodles 5 to 6 minutes; drain and stir into egg mixture. Add dried fruits, raisins and nuts; toss to distribute throughout. Carefully spoon into prepared pan so as not to dislodge pineapple slices. Bake at 350°F. for 40 to 50 minutes or until set and golden brown. Let stand 5 minutes; loosen with spatula and invert over warm serving dish.   *6 to 8 servings*

Note: A good side dish with chicken or beef. Or, as dessert with Pineapple* or Wine Sauce.**

*PINEAPPLE SAUCE

1 egg, separated
1 cup pineapple juice drained from canned pineapple
1 tablespoon lemon juice
1 tablespoon grated lemon rind

In top of double boiler, beat egg yolk; stir in pineapple juice, lemon juice and rind. Place over hot water; cook, stirring constantly until thickened. Cool. Beat egg white until stiff but not dry; fold into sauce.   *Makes about 1½ cups sauce*

Note: For an extra treat, just before serving, fold in cut up fruits or berries (drain first if using canned).

**WINE SAUCE

¼ cup sugar
2 tablespoons cornstarch
½ cup water
1 cup sweet red wine
1 teaspoon lemon juice

In small pan, combine sugar and cornstarch; stir in water to form a smooth paste. Cook over low heat, stirring constantly until thickened. Blend in wine and lemon juice. Cook 2 minutes, stirring constantly; do not boil.   *Makes about 1¼ cups sauce*

PASTINA APPLE/RAISIN PUDDING

3 ounces of **RONZONI® Egg Pastina**
1 egg (beaten)
¼ cup sugar
1 cup milk
½ teaspoon vanilla
½ medium apple (diced or chopped)
½ cup raisins
1 tablespoon butter
½ teaspoon cinnamon

Cook pastina as per directions on package. Then blend all ingredients and pour into a 1-quart baking dish. Bake 20 minutes at 350°. Can be served warm or cold, with cream topping if desired.

Serves 4 to 6

OLD-FASHIONED AMBROSIA PUDDING

2 eggs, beaten
¼ cup sugar
2 (16 oz.) cans **S&W® Natural Style Fruit Cocktail**, drained (reserve juice)
4 bananas, sliced and sprinkled with lemon juice
1 (16 oz.) pkg. miniature marshmallows
1 (13.5 oz.) can **S&W® Crushed Pineapple**, drained (reserve juice)
1 (3½ oz.) can shredded coconut
½ pint whipping cream, whipped

Cook eggs, sugar and reserved juices in double boiler until thick. Stir with wire whip. Cool. Fold into whipped cream. Meanwhile combine fruit cocktail, sliced bananas, marshmallows, crushed pineapple and shredded coconut in large mixing bowl. Blend whipped cream mixture into fruit. Cover and refrigerate at least overnight.

Serves 12-15

CUSTARD NOODLE PUDDING

2 quarts water
2 teaspoons salt
1 tablespoon oil
3 eggs
2 cups milk
1 cup sugar
1½ teaspoons vanilla
4 cups **AMERICAN BEAUTY® Fine Egg Noodles**
¼ cup raisins
1 teaspoon nutmeg
Whipping cream, if desired

Heat oven to 350°F. Boil water in large deep pot with salt and oil (to prevent boiling over). Add noodles; stir to separate. Cook uncovered after water returns to a full rolling boil for 4 to 5 minutes. Stir occasionally. Drain and rinse under cold water.

Grease 13×9-inch pan. In large bowl, beat eggs. Add milk, sugar and vanilla. Stir in cooked noodles and raisins. Turn mixture into prepared pan. Sprinkle nutmeg over top. Cover and bake at 350°F. for 55 to 60 minutes or until knife inserted near center comes out clean. Serve with whipped cream, if desired.

8 to 10 servings

High Altitude—Above 3500 Feet: Cooking times may need to be increased slightly for noodles; no additional changes.

NUTRITION INFORMATION PER SERVING
SERVING SIZE: ⅒ of recipe

		PERCENT U.S. RDA	
Calories	244	PER SERVING	
Protein	7 g	Protein	10
Carbohydrate	42 g	Vitamin A	6
Fat	6 g	Vitamin C	—
Sodium	78 mg	Thiamine	9
Potassium	149 mg	Riboflavin	11
		Niacin	5
		Calcium	8
		Iron	6

BAYS® ENGLISH MUFFIN BREAD PUDDING

4 **BAYS® English Muffins**, cubed
2 tablespoons unsalted butter
4 cups milk, scalded
4 eggs
1½ teaspoons vanilla extract
¾ cup sugar
½ cup raisins
1½ teaspoons ground cinnamon
¼ teaspoon ground clove
¼ cup sugar

Preheat oven to 350°. Place large roasting pan with ½ inch water in oven during preheating to prepare water bath for pudding. Grease a 1½ quart **Pyrex®** pan; set aside. Place cubed muffins and butter in a bowl. Pour scalded milk over and stir to combine well. Let soak for 15 minutes, stirring occasionally. In another bowl, combine eggs, vanilla extract, sugar and raisins. Beat well to mix. Add the egg mixture to the muffin and milk mixture; stir well. Pour into prepared pan. In a small bowl, combine cinnamon, cloves and

sugar. Sprinkle this mixture over the pudding. Bake in water bath for 1 hour or until the pudding is puffed and an inserted knife comes out clean. Let pudding cool for another hour or until warm. Serve with whipped cream or plain cream.

Serves 8

MACAROON PEASANT PUDDING

½ cup uncooked medium **WOLFF'S® Kasha**
1 Tbsp. melted butter or margarine
2 cups milk, scalded
2 eggs, separated
¼ cup light or unsulphured molasses
2 Tbsp. sugar
½ tsp. salt
¼ tsp. ginger
¼ tsp. nutmeg
¼ tsp. cinnamon
½ cup raisins or diced mixed fruit

Mix together kasha and melted butter. Scald milk in saucepan; stir in kasha and cook over low heat for 15-20 minutes or until kasha is tender. Beat egg yolks until lemon-colored. Add small amount of hot mixture to egg yolks, then combine egg yolks with kasha. Add molasses, sugar, salt, and spices. Stir in raisins or fruit. Beat egg whites until they form soft peaks, then gently fold in. Bake pudding in well-oiled 1-quart casserole at 325°F for 35-45 minutes or until pudding is puffy and no longer runny in center. Serve warm with whipped topping, stirred custard, or "pour" cream.

Makes 6 servings

MICROWAVE METHOD:
Kasha/milk mixture may be micro-cooked on medium power for 8-9 minutes in large measuring pitcher or bowl. Pudding may be "baked" in microwave oven on medium power for 10-15 minutes or until set. Pudding may be micro-cooked in 3-4 minutes if baked in individual custard-size cups. Arrange cups in circular pattern, turning once after 1 minute. Do not oil casserole or custard cups if micro-cooking.

RUM FLAN

1¼ cups sugar, divided usage
4 eggs
2 cups **PET® Evaporated Milk**
2 cups milk
2 tablespoons dark rum or 1 tablespoon rum flavoring
¼ teaspoon salt

Preheat oven to 350°F. In skillet place ½ cup sugar over low heat, watching carefully, allow sugar to melt and turn brown (caramelize). Pour caramelized sugar into flan pan, or 2-quart casserole, or soufflé dish. Rotate until bottom is covered. Beat eggs and remaining ¾ cup sugar in large mixing bowl. Add evaporated milk, milk, rum and salt. Mix well. Pour milk mixture into mold. Place the mold in a large pan. Pour warm water into the larger pan halfway up the sides of the mold. Bake about 1 hour and 45 minutes to 2 hours, or until knife inserted halfway into flan comes out clean (do not pierce bottom). Chill for several hours. Unmold.

Makes 6-8 servings

CLASSIC ALMOND FLAN

¼ cup firmly packed light brown sugar
¾ cup (3 ounces) blanched slivered almonds, toasted
1 (14-ounce) can **EAGLE® Brand Sweetened Condensed Milk** (NOT evaporated)
1 cup (½ pint) whipping cream
5 eggs
½ teaspoon almond extract
Additional toasted almonds, optional

Preheat oven to 325°. In 8-inch round layer cake pan, sprinkle sugar; set aside. In blender container, grind nuts; add sweetened condensed milk, ½ cup cream, eggs and extract. Blend thoroughly. Pour into pan. Set in larger pan of hot water, 1-inch deep. Bake 40 to 45 minutes or until knife inserted near center comes out clean. Chill thoroughly (about 3 hours); turn out of pan. Beat remaining cream for garnish; top with additional toasted almonds if desired. Refrigerate leftovers.   *Makes 8 to 10 servings*

CHOCOLATE FLAN

1 frozen **SARA LEE Chocolate Cake** (single layer)
½ cup water
1 teaspoon lemon juice
2 sliced bananas
⅓ cup orange marmalade, melted

Cut frozen Cake lengthwise into 2 layers. Place top cake half on serving plate, frosting up, stack on remaining layer. Dip bananas in mixture of water and lemon juice; drain. Arrange bananas in overlapping design on cake top. Drizzle marmalade over bananas. Thaw at room temperature about 30 minutes.
Makes 6-8 servings

HOT FUDGE SAUCE

1 pkg. (10 oz.) **GHIRARDELLI® Milk Chocolate Blocks**
⅓ to ½ cup milk
1 teaspoon vanilla

In heavy saucepan, break chocolate into hot milk. Stir constantly until sauce is smooth; add vanilla. Serve warm over ice cream.
Makes 1¼ cups sauce

MICROWAVE METHOD:
Melt chocolate with milk in measuring cup for 3-4 minutes, stirring twice; add vanilla.

CUSTARD FROTH

4 egg yolks
½ cup dry white wine
¼ cup sugar
1 tablespoon orange-flavored liqueur (**COINTREAU**)
2 egg whites
2 tablespoons sugar
Strawberries, blueberries or cake, optional

Beat together with rotary beater egg yolks, wine, ¼ cup sugar and liqueur in 3-quart heavy saucepan. Cook at simmering, not boiling, while beating *constantly* with rotary beater. Cook until thick and foamy, about 10 minutes. Set pan in a bowl of ice water. Beat until thoroughly cold. (Unless beaten until cold, mixture will collapse and separate.) Beat egg whites with two tablespoons sugar until stiff but not dry. Fold into custard mixture. Serve immediately alone or over fresh strawberries, if desired.
Makes approximately 7 cups

Favorite recipe from **American Egg Board**

DROSTE® CHOCOLATE CUSTARD SAUCE

⅓ cup sugar
2 tablespoons unsifted flour
1 cup milk
2 egg yolks
1½ teaspoons butter
¼ cup **DROSTE® Bittersweet Chocolate Liqueur**
¼ cup heavy cream, whipped
Assorted fresh fruit

Combine sugar and flour in a medium saucepan. Gradually beat in milk. Cook over medium high heat, stirring constantly, until mixture comes to a full boil. Reduce heat to low and cook 1 minute. Stir a small amount of hot milk mixture into egg yolks, then stir yolks into milk mixture in saucepan. Cook 1 minute more, stirring constantly. Remove from heat; stir in butter. Cool mixture thoroughly. Just before serving stir in **DROSTE® Bittersweet Chocolate Liqueur**; fold in whipped cream. Serve over assorted fresh fruit.   *Makes 1½ cups*

CHOCOLATE CUSTARD
(*Low Calorie*)

2 cups reconstituted **ALBA Instant Non-Fat Dry Milk**
3 envelopes **ALBA '66 Hot Cocoa Mix**
3 eggs
½ teaspoon vanilla

In a small bowl, combine milk, **ALBA '66**, eggs and vanilla. Stir until **ALBA** is completely dissolved. Pour mixture into 5 custard cups. Set cups in a baking pan. Pour hot water into pan to a 1 inch level. Bake in oven preheated to 350°F for 30 minutes. Turn off heat. Allow custard to stand in oven 15 minutes. Remove from oven, cool to room temperature, cover with plastic wrap and chill.

Calories: Each serving contains approximately 119

BAKED CEREAL CUSTARD

1 tall can (1⅔ cups) **PET® Evaporated Milk**
1 cup water
1 cup **HEARTLAND® Natural Cereal**, Raisin Variety
2 eggs
¼ cup sugar
¼ teaspoon salt
¼ teaspoon nutmeg
1 teaspoon vanilla

1. Heat evaporated milk, water and cereal to boiling.
2. Beat eggs. Add sugar, salt, nutmeg and vanilla.
3. Gradually stir in hot cereal mixture.
4. Pour into 1½-quart casserole dish. Place casserole dish into a baking dish with an inch of water.
5. Bake in 325°F oven for 1 hour or until knife inserted near edge comes out clean. Serve warm with cream or ice cream.
Makes 6 servings, ½ cup each

HONEY CUSTARD

3 eggs
¼ teaspoon salt
¼ cup **SUE BEE® Honey**
2 cups milk, scalded
Nutmeg

Beat eggs slightly; add salt. Blend honey into hot milk. Stir milk mixture slowly into beaten eggs. Pour into five custard cups. Sprinkle nutmeg over top. Arrange custard cups in shallow pan of hot water. Bake at 325° for about 30 minutes or until knife inserted in center of custard comes out clean. *Makes five servings*

CHOCOLATE-DIPPED FRUIT

One (11½-oz.) pkg. (2 cups) **NESTLÉ® Milk Chocolate Morsels**
¼ cup vegetable shortening
Fresh strawberries
Mandarin orange slices, drained
Pineapple chunks, drained
Maraschino cherries, drained
Bananas, cut into ¾-inch slices

Melt over hot (not boiling) water, **NESTLÉ® Milk Chocolate Morsels** and shortening; stir until morsels melt and mixture is smooth. Remove from heat but keep chocolate over hot water.* (If chocolate begins to set, return to heat. Add 1-2 measuring teaspoons shortening; stir until smooth.) Dip pieces of fruit into chocolate mixture, shaking off excess chocolate. Place on foil-lined cookie sheets. Chill in refrigerator 10-15 minutes until chocolate is set. Gently loosen from foil with metal spatula. Chocolate-Dipped Fruit may be kept at room temperature up to 1 hour. If chocolate becomes sticky, return to refrigerator.
Makes: 1 cup melted chocolate

*To make in electric fondue pot or skillet, set at low temperature. Combine **NESTLÉ® Milk Chocolate Morsels** and shortening. Stir until morsels melt and mixture is smooth. Keep heat set at low. Proceed as directed.

TANGY COCONUT FRUIT DIP

1½ cups **COCO CASA® Cream of Coconut**
1 can (6 oz.) frozen concentrated lemonade, thawed and undiluted
Assorted bite-size fruit pieces such as strawberries, pineapple, bananas, apples, pears, melon, mandarin orange sections, etc.

In a bowl, mix cream of coconut and lemonade. Stir until well blended. Chill. Place bowl on platter surrounded with pieces of fruit. Spear fruits on skewers or fondue forks and dip into cream of coconut mixture. *Makes about 2½ cups*

VARIATIONS:

Substitute frozen concentrated orange juice, pink lemonade, pineapple juice or limeade for a variety of tastes and colors.

DESSERT FRUIT TACO

2 cups melon balls or cubes (cantaloupe, watermelon, honeydew)
2 cups strawberries, washed, hulled and halved
2 cups pineapple chunks
1 cup seedless green grapes, halved
1 orange, peeled, sectioned and sliced into ½-inch pieces
1 banana, peeled and sliced
1 kiwi, peeled and sliced
½ cup fresh raspberries
1 box (10 shells) **LAWRY'S® Super Taco Shells***
¼ cup powdered sugar
¼ teaspoon cinnamon
Shredded coconut, to garnish

Combine all fruit in large bowl; chill. Sift together powdered sugar and cinnamon. Heat Taco Shells according to package directions. Lightly sift sugar mixture over inside and outside of heated Taco Shells. Fill each shell with 1 cup mixed fruit; garnish with coconut. *Makes 10 Super Tacos*

*May use **LAWRY'S® Taco Shells**, regular size. Fill regular shells with ⅓ cup mixed fruit.

GINGER CREAM DIP

1 cup **BREAKSTONE'S® Sour Cream**
2 tablespoons honey
½ teaspoon grated orange rind
⅛ teaspoon ground ginger

Combine ingredients; mix well. Chill. Serve with fruit. *1 cup*

FRUIT POPS

1 envelope **KNOX® Unflavored Gelatine**
⅓ cup sugar
1 cup fruit juice, heated to boiling (NOT fresh or frozen pineapple juice)
½ cup water
1 tablespoon lemon juice
1 cup pureed fresh ripe berries, peaches, sweet cherries, apricots, nectarines or plums

In large bowl, mix **KNOX® Unflavored Gelatine** with sugar; add hot juice and stir until gelatine is completely dissolved. Stir in remaining ingredients. (Add more sugar if extra tart fruit is used.) Pour into 6 (5 oz.) paper cups; freeze until partially frozen. Insert wooden ice cream sticks; freeze until firm. Remove from freezer 5 minutes before serving. Peel off paper cup. *Makes 6 fruit pops*

PER SERVING: (Based on orange juice)—80 calories; 1 g protein; 17 g carbohydrate; 0 g fat; less than 5 mg sodium

WISCONSIN BAKED APPLES

6 large baking apples (about 4 pounds)
½ cup **DROMEDARY Chopped Dates**
¼ cup chopped walnuts
½ teaspoon ground cinnamon
2 tablespoons butter or margarine
1 cup water
1 (4⅝-ounce) can **SNACK MATE Cheddar** or **American Pasteurized Process Cheese Spread**

1. Preheat oven to 350°F.; lightly grease 2-quart shallow baking dish. Slice ½ inch from top of each apple; core each apple to within ½ inch of bottom.
2. In medium bowl, combine **DROMEDARY Dates**, walnuts and cinnamon; spoon into apple centers. Dot top of filling with butter or margarine.
3. Place apples in baking dish; add water. Bake, uncovered, 40 to 50 minutes, basting occasionally. Apples should be tender when pierced with cake tester. Cool slightly; top with swirl of **SNACK MATE Cheese**. *Makes 6 servings*

MICROWAVE METHOD:

1. Prepare apples as directed in Steps 1 and 2. Place in 2-quart microwave-proof shallow baking dish. *Do not* add water.
2. Microwave, uncovered, at 100% power 16 to 18 minutes, rotating a half turn every 4 minutes. Apples should be tender when pierced with cake tester. Cool and serve as in Step 3.

BRANDIED FRUIT

1 cup water
1 cup sugar
1 cup LAIRD'S Applejack

Combine water and sugar; bring to a boil and add **LAIRD'S Applejack**. Cool. Serve over any desired combination of fresh or canned fruit.

ROQUEFORT APPLE DESSERT

4 medium-sized red apples
1 tablespoon lemon juice
1½ oz. **ROQUEFORT Cheese**, crumbled
¼ cup French dressing
¼ cup chopped walnuts
2 tablespoons seedless raisins

Cut slice from top of each apple; reserve. Remove cores. Scoop out pulp, leaving ¼-inch shells. Brush shells with lemon juice. Dice apple pulp. Combine diced apple and remaining ingredients; toss lightly. Fill apple shells with walnut mixture. Replace apple tops.

Serves 4

Favorite recipe from the **Roquefort Association, Inc.**

BUSHMILLS' APPLES

6 large tart apples
⅓ cup golden raisins
½ cup boiling water
Nutmeg
6 Tbsp. **OLD BUSHMILLS Irish Whiskey**
½ cup butter
⅓ cup super fine sugar
1 Tbsp. lemon juice
½ cup cider
6 Tbsp. sliced almonds
Red coloring (optional)
Whipped Cream and whole almonds for garnish

Peel, core and gently pierce apples. Place them in a 13 × 9 × 2 inch baking dish. Soak raisins in ½ cup boiling water for 5 min. Place 1 Tbsp. butter in the bottom of each cavity. Add a dash of nutmeg, 2 tsp. sugar, 2 tsp. raisins, 1 Tbsp. almonds and 1 Tbsp. **OLD BUSHMILLS Irish Whiskey** to each apple. Sprinkle the apples with remaining sugar and raisins. Melt remaining 2 Tbsp. butter and mix with cider, lemon juice and a few drops of red coloring, if desired. Spoon this mixture over apples, cover with foil and bake at 350° for 45 min., basting every 15 minutes. Time can fluctuate by size of apples. Do not overbake or apples will break down into a puree. Top each apple with a large dollop of whipped cream and a whole almond. Serve warm.

APPLE FRITTERS

BUTTER FLAVOR CRISCO® for frying
1½ cups all-purpose flour
3 tablespoons sugar
2 tablespoons cornstarch
1½ teaspoons baking powder
½ teaspoon salt
¼ teaspoon ground allspice
¾ cup milk
2 eggs, slightly beaten
1 tablespoon **Butter Flavor CRISCO®**, melted
2 cups finely chopped apples (about 2 medium)

1. Heat 2 inches **Butter Flavor CRISCO®** to 375°F in deep-fat fryer or deep saucepan. Combine flour, sugar, cornstarch, baking powder, salt, allspice, milk, eggs and 1 tablespoon melted **Butter Flavor CRISCO®** in medium mixing bowl. Stir with fork or wire whisk until just blended. Fold in apples.
2. Drop batter by level measuring tablespoonfuls into hot shortening. Fry a few at a time 2 to 4 minutes, or until golden brown, turning 1 or 2 times. Drain on paper towels. Serve warm with maple syrup. Keep warm in single layer on paper towels in 175° oven, if desired.

3 to 4 dozen fritters

VARIATION:

CORN FRITTERS

Follow the recipe above, omitting sugar, cornstarch and allspice. Substitute 1 cup canned or frozen whole kernel corn, thawed, for the apples.

APPLE YAM DELIGHT

Topping:
¾ cup dark brown sugar
4 Tbsp. all purpose flour
¾ cup instant rolled oats
⅓ cup butter or margarine

1 (17 oz.) can **PRINCELLA® YAMS** cut to bite size
1 (16 oz.) jar chunky style apple sauce
1 tsp. ground cinnamon

TOPPING:
Mix together rolled oats, flour and brown sugar. Cut in butter until evenly mixed and crumbly.

Arrange a little less than half of the apple sauce in a 6 × 10 × 2-inch baking dish. Sprinkle with ½ teaspoon cinnamon. Spoon 3 tablespoons of the topping over the apple sauce base. Evenly arrange the **PRINCELLA® Yams**. Add the remaining apple sauce to cover yams. Sprinkle with remaining ½ teaspoon cinnamon. Add the rest of the topping and spread evenly. Bake at 350°F until heated throughout (30-40 minutes). Serve hot, plain, or top with whipped cream or vanilla ice cream.

INDIVIDUAL APPLE-OAT CRISP

Base:
1 cup thin apple slices
1 tablespoon firmly packed brown sugar
1 teaspoon all-purpose flour
½ teaspoon lemon juice

Topping:
⅓ cup **QUAKER® Oats** (quick or old fashioned, uncooked)
1 tablespoon firmly packed brown sugar
1 tablespoon chopped almonds
1 teaspoon all-purpose flour
¼ teaspoon cinnamon
⅛ teaspoon nutmeg
Dash of salt
2 tablespoons butter or margarine, melted

FOR BASE:
Heat oven to 375°F. Combine all ingredients, mixing well. Place in small individual baking dish.

FOR TOPPING:
Combine dry ingredients; mix well. Add butter; mix until crumbly. Sprinkle over fruit mixture. Bake about 20 minutes or until apples are tender and topping is golden brown.

Makes 1 serving

Note: Recipe may easily be doubled to make 2 servings.

MICROWAVE METHOD:

Prepare 1 serving as recipe directs. Cook at HIGH 4½ to 5½ minutes, rotating dish ¼ turn after 3 minutes of cooking.

SPICY APPLESAUCE
(Low Calorie)

1 cooking apple (peeled or unpeeled)
⅓ cup **Sugar Free DR PEPPER®**
Dash of cinnamon and cloves

Cut up and remove core of apple and place in saucepan; add **Sugar Free DR PEPPER®**. Cook over low heat until tender. If peeled, stir until sauce consistency. If unpeeled, put through colander, ricer, or food strainer. Add spices and serve hot or cold.

Yield: One serving (½ cup)

Calories: 71 per serving

FRESH BRANDIED APRICOTS

¼ cup water
¼ cup sugar
½ stick cinnamon
½ cup brandy
1 pound fresh apricots

Combine water, sugar and cinnamon in small saucepan. Bring to boil; simmer, uncovered, about 5 minutes. Remove cinnamon stick; add brandy and simmer about 1 minute. Pour over apricots. Cover and chill overnight.　　　　*Makes 4 to 6 servings*

Favorite recipe from the **California Apricot Advisory Board**

BANANAS WITH MEXICAN CHOCOLATE SAUCE
(A Dessert Fondue)

½ cup light cream
½ teaspoon instant coffee (dry granules)
2 bars (4 ounces each) sweet cooking chocolate
½ cup coffee liqueur
Chilled **CHIQUITA® Bananas**
Pound cake squares

Heat cream in dessert size fondue pot over medium to low heat. Dissolve coffee in cream. Break chocolate into squares and heat and stir in cream until melted and blended. Stir in coffee liqueur. Continue to keep hot over low heat.

　Cut peeled bananas into 1-inch slices. Spear on fondue fork and dip into sauce. Spear cake squares on fork and dip into sauce.

Makes 2 cups

Note: Sauce adheres better to cold bananas than those at room temperature. Place fruit in refrigerator at least an hour before peeling and serving. Allow one banana per person.

BANANA MARSHMALLOW TREATS

16 graham cracker squares
¼ cup creamy peanut butter
1 small banana, peeled, sliced thin
8 **FIRESIDE Regular Marshmallows**

Arrange 8 graham cracker squares on cookie sheet; spread each with 1½ teaspoons peanut butter. Overlap 3 banana slices on top of peanut butter; put marshmallow in center. Broil 4-inches from heat, until marshmallows are lightly browned. Top with remaining crackers, pressing gently until marshmallow spreads.　　*8 treats*

BANANA SPLIT DESSERT

1½ cups **SALERNO® Graham Cracker Crumbs**
6 tablespoons melted butter or margarine
2 cups unsifted confectioner's sugar
½ cup (1 stick) butter, softened
2 eggs
1 teaspoon vanilla
3 medium bananas
1 can (1 lb. 13 oz.) crushed pineapple, well drained
½ pint (1 cup) whipping cream, whipped
1 tablespoon confectioner's sugar
¼ cup chopped nuts
¼ cup chopped maraschino cherries, drained

Combine graham cracker crumbs and melted butter; press into bottom of 13 × 9-inch pan. In small bowl of mixer, beat confectioner's sugar with softened butter, eggs and vanilla together at low speed to blend. Beat at medium speed 3 minutes. Spread over crumbs. Peel and slice bananas; arrange on cream layer. Spoon pineapple over bananas. Combine whipped cream and 1 tablespoon sugar; spread on top. Sprinkle with chopped nuts and cherries. Cover and refrigerate several hours. If desired, drizzle with chocolate sauce before serving.　*Makes 12 servings*

BANAN' CRUZAN®

3 tablespoons butter
1 can (8 oz.) crushed pineapple
¼ cup brown sugar, packed
4 firm-ripe bananas, halved lengthwise
¼ cup **CRUZAN® Gold Rum**, warmed
1 pint vanilla ice cream

Melt butter in a large skillet or chafing dish pan. Add undrained pineapple and sugar. Heat just to boil, stirring often. Add banana halves, cut side down, and heat about 3 minutes, basting with pan juices. Ignite **CRUZAN® Rum** and pour into pan. When flames go out, serve bananas and sauce topped with ice cream.

4 servings

BRANDIED GRAPES WITH SOUR CREAM

2 tablespoons lemon juice
½ cup honey
1 pound seedless grapes
2 tablespoons **JACQUIN'S Cognac**
Sour cream

Wash grapes, remove stems and place in bowl. Mix honey, **JACQUIN'S Cognac** and lemon juice; pour over grapes. Stir to mix well and refrigerate overnight. Serve grapes in dessert bowls, topped with a spoonful of sour cream.　　*Serves 4*

SMIRNOFF® MELON BALLS

6 cups melon balls (cantaloupe, watermelon, honeydew, etc.)
⅓ cup **SMIRNOFF® Vodka**

In medium bowl, combine melon and vodka. Chill several hours, stirring occasionally. Garnish with sliced lime.　　*Serves 6*

TEXAS GRAPEFRUIT PARFAIT

½ cup **TEXAS RUBY RED Grapefruit Juice**
1 envelope unflavored gelatin
½ cup **IMPERIAL Brown Sugar**
2 cups light cream (half-and-half)
1 to 2 teaspoons lemon juice, according to taste
2 egg whites
2 tablespoons **IMPERIAL Brown Sugar**
4 **TEXAS RUBY RED Grapefruits**

Cut grapefruit in halves and section. Set sections aside and let drain. Squeeze grapefruit halves for juice. Combine grapefruit juice and gelatin in small saucepan and stir; let stand 1 minute. Warm over low heat just until gelatin is dissolved; add ½ cup **IMPERIAL Brown Sugar** and stir to dissolve sugar. Stir in cream and lemon juice and transfer to large mixing bowl. Chill thoroughly (about 1½ to 2 hours); while chilling stir occasionally, until mixture begins to thicken. Meanwhile, in medium bowl, beat egg whites to soft peak stage; gradually add the 2 tablespoons **IMPERIAL Brown Sugar** and beat until stiff peaks form. Fold into chilled mixture. Transfer to chilled parfait or wine glasses alternately with grapefruit sections. Chill until serving time.

Makes eight, 6-oz. servings

Favorite recipe from the **Texas Citrus Industry**

FROSTED MANDARIN MELON

1 11-oz. can **GEISHA® Brand Japanese Mandarin Oranges**, drained
1 large honeydew melon
1 banana, fluted, sliced
Sliced strawberries
1 8-oz. package softened cream cheese
2 tablespoons blue cheese spread (optional)
¼ cup heavy cream
Toasted coconut, slivered almonds or chopped walnuts (optional)

Carefully cut peel from melon. Cut top from melon; scoop out inside seeds. Stand melon on serving platter (it may be necessary to slice off some of the bottom, so melon stands level). Fill center of melon with Mandarin Orange segments and other fruits of your choice. Put on melon top. Combine cheeses and cream until smooth and spreadable. Frost melon with cheese. Sprinkle with nuts. Chill about 2 hours. Garnish with more fruit. It is not hard to serve—just cut wedges and spoon on some of the fruit.

Makes 6 to 8 servings

VARIATION:

If you don't want to bother frosting the fruit, just spoon mixed fruit over wedges of melon and top with fluff of cheese; sprinkle with nuts.

LITE MELON MERINGUE

2 small honeydews or cantaloupes
4 egg whites
2 tsp. sugar
2 cups plain yogurt or ice milk
1 can (16 oz.) **DEL MONTE Lite Sliced Peaches** or **Sliced Pears**, drained

Cut melons in half. Seed. Whip egg whites with sugar until stiff. Fill melon halves with yogurt and place peach slices on top edge in pinwheel fashion. Top with meringue. Bake at 450°F., 2 to 3 minutes, until lightly browned.
4 servings

MANTO MELON FREEZE

4 cups 1-inch cubes ripe cantaloupe
1 envelope unflavored gelatin
⅓ cup **METAXA® Manto Liqueur**
2 tablespoons lemon juice
¼ cup boiling water
1 cup heavy cream
¼ cup sugar

Puree cantaloupe in food processor or blender. Soften gelatin in **METAXA® Manto Liqueur** and lemon juice. Stir in boiling water. Stir gelatin mixture into pureed cantaloupe.

Beat heavy cream with sugar until stiff peaks form. Fold into cantaloupe mixture. Place in freezer, stirring occasionally as mixture begins to freeze. Freeze 3 to 4 hours until very firm. Allow mixture to stand at room temperature about 5 minutes before serving. Scoop into individual dessert dishes; garnish as desired.
Makes 8 servings

FROSTED ORANGES SARONNO

2 cups water
¾ cup sugar
Grated rind and juice of 1 lemon
½ cup **AMARETTO DI SARONNO® Liqueur**
2 egg whites, stiffly beaten
6 large oranges
½ cup flaked coconut
⅓ cup **AMARETTO DI SARONNO® Liqueur**
1 egg white, beaten until foamy
Granulated sugar

In a saucepan, combine water and sugar. Bring mixture to a boil and boil for 5 minutes. Remove from heat and stir in lemon rind and juice and **AMARETTO DI SARONNO®**. Pour mixture into a freezer container and freeze until mushy. Pour mixture into a bowl and beat until smooth. Fold in beaten egg whites. Replace in container, cover and freeze until hard. With a sharp knife, slice ⅓ off the top of each orange. With knife, cut out pulp of orange, leaving shell whole. Remove membrane from pulp, cut into sections, and place in a bowl. Fold in coconut and **AMARETTO DI SARONNO®**. Chill. Brush outside of orange shell and top of orange with slightly beaten egg white. Dip into granulated sugar until well coated. Let dry at room temperature until crusty. When ready to serve, fill orange shell with orange mixture. Spoon **AMARETTO DI SARONNO®** ice on top of filled shell. Replace top of orange and serve garnished with fresh mint sprigs, if desired. Serve at once.
Makes 6 servings

FLORIO® MARSALA POACHED PEARS

¾ cup sugar
⅔ cup water
½ cup **FLORIO® Sweet Marsala Wine**
4 ripe pears, peeled

Combine sugar, water and **FLORIO® Sweet Marsala** in a medium saucepan. Bring to a boil over medium high heat, stirring to dissolve sugar. Reduce heat to low. Set pears in simmering liquid. Cover and cook until tender, about 15 to 20 minutes. Remove pears from pan with a slotted spoon and chill. Increase heat to medium high; reduce liquid in pan until thickened to syrup consistency. Chill.

To serve, place each pear in a serving dish. Spoon 2 tablespoons caramel sauce around each pear. Garnish with whipped cream if desired.
Makes 4 servings

PEACH HAY STACKS

¼ cup crushed shredded wheat
2 tablespoons butter or margarine, melted
2 tablespoons brown sugar
2 tablespoons shredded coconut
2 tablespoons chopped pecans
¼ teaspoon cinnamon
1 can (16 ounces) STOKELY'S FINEST® Cling
Peach Halves, well drained

Combine shredded wheat, butter, brown sugar, coconut, pecans, and cinnamon; mix well. Place peach halves, cut side up, in 11 × 8 × 2-inch pan. Spoon shredded wheat mixture into center of each peach half. Broil 3 minutes, or until lightly toasted. Serve at once.

6 servings

BAKED PEACH MERINGUE
(Low Calorie/Low Sodium)

1-16 oz. can water or juice packed peach halves
6 tsp. DIA-MEL® Grape Jelly
1 egg white
⅛ tsp. cream of tartar
2 Tbsp. ESTEE® Granulated Fructose

Preheat oven to 350°F. Drain juice from peaches. Arrange 6 peach halves, cut side up, in ungreased square baking pan. Fill each peach half with 1 tsp. of DIA-MEL® Grape Jelly. To prepare meringue, beat egg white and cream of tartar in small bowl until frothy. Slowly add ESTEE® Fructose and continue beating until soft peaks form. Cover each peach half with meringue. Bake for 20 minutes or until tops are lightly browned.

Makes 6 servings, 1 peach half per serving

NUTRITION INFORMATION
Calories	Carbohydrates	Protein	Sodium
40	10g	1g	9mg

DIABETIC EXCHANGE INFORMATION
Fruit
1

BAKED BOSC PEARS ON THE HALF SHELL

3 fresh Bosc pears
Choice of Fillings*
½ cup water
½ cup brown sugar
1 tablespoon butter
½ teaspoon cinnamon

Halve and core pears. Fill centers with desired filling. Combine remaining ingredients. Bring to a boil and pour over pears. Bake at 350 degrees 45 minutes, basting frequently with syrup.

Makes 6 servings

*RAISIN FILLING

Combine ¼ cup raisins and 2 tablespoons chopped nuts.

*DATE FILLING

Combine ⅓ cup snipped dates, 2 tablespoons chopped nuts and ½ teaspoon grated orange peel.

*MINCEMEAT FILLING

Combine ½ cup prepared mincemeat with 1 tablespoon rum or brandy.

Favorite recipe from the Oregon-Washington-California Pear Bureau

MINTED PEARS

1 can (1 lb.) pear halves, drained
1 pkg. (3 ozs.) lime gelatin
½ cup boiling water
½ cup ASPEN™ Glacial Liqueur

Arrange pear halves in broiling dish. Dissolve gelatin in water. Add ASPEN™, stir. Pour over pears. Broil, basting frequently, until liquid bubbles, about 15 minutes. Serve warm or chilled.

Yield: 4 servings

AMBROSIA PARFAITS

20 OREO Chocolate Sandwich Cookies, finely rolled
(about 2 cups crumbs)
2 (8-ounce) cartons low-fat, vanilla-flavored yogurt
2¼ cups fresh pineapple chunks (about half of a
medium-size pineapple, fresh)
1 (3½-ounce) can flaked coconut (about 1⅓ cups)
3 medium oranges

Sprinkle 1 tablespoon OREO Chocolate Sandwich Cookie crumbs evenly in 6 (10-ounce) wine or dessert glasses.

In medium bowl, blend yogurt, pineapple chunks and coconut. Spread about ⅓ cup evenly over crumbs in each glass to form layer.

Sprinkle 2 tablespoons cookie crumbs over each yogurt layer to cover. Peel and section 3 oranges; arrange segments evenly in each glass on top of cookie crumb layer.

Top orange layer with all but 3 teaspoons remaining crumbs; cover with remaining yogurt mixture, using approximately ¼ cup per glass. Sprinkle top of each lightly with half teaspoon of remaining cookie crumbs. Chill at least 30 to 60 minutes before serving. Garnish with orange peel curl. Serve immediately.

Note: If fresh fruit is out-of-season or unavailable, use 1 (20-ounce) can pineapple chunks in natural juice, drained, and 1 (16-ounce) can mandarin orange segments, drained.

Makes 6 servings

STRAWBERRY RIBBON LOAF

2 (3 ounce) packages strawberry gelatin
1 jar (15 ounce) applesauce
18 double SUNSHINE® Honey Graham Crackers
1 envelope DREAM WHIP® Whipped Topping Mix
3 tablespoons confectioners' sugar
1 cup fresh strawberries

Combine gelatin and applesauce in a small mixing bowl, stirring until well blended. Place 2 double crackers end to end, on a platter; spread with ¼ cup applesauce mixture. Repeat layers, ending with crackers. Prepare whipped topping as directed on package, adding confectioners' sugar before beating; spread over top and sides of loaf. Chill 30 minutes. Garnish with strawberry halves.

Yield: 10 servings

STRAWBERRIES AMARETTO

1 quart strawberries, washed and hulled
AMARETTO from GALLIANO® Liqueur
1 cup finely granulated sugar

Divide berries between 4 dessert dishes. Sprinkle each serving of berries with about 1 oz. AMARETTO from GALLIANO®. Provide a small cup of finely granulated sugar with each dish for dipping berries.

Serves 4

FRESH STRAWBERRY TARTS

1½ quarts fresh strawberries
½ cup **IRISH MIST**® Liqueur
4 teaspoons cornstarch
½ cup currant jelly
8 baked tart shells

In small saucepan, crush 1 cup strawberries. Stir in **IRISH MIST**®, cornstarch and jelly. Cook over medium heat, stirring constantly, until jelly is melted. Cool. Place 1 tablespoon glaze in bottom of each tart shell. Fill with strawberries. Pour remaining glaze over strawberries. Chill. Top with **IRISH MIST**® Whipped Cream*, if desired. *Serves 8*

*IRISH MIST® WHIPPED CREAM

½ cup heavy cream
2 tablespoons **IRISH MIST**® Liqueur

Beat cream and **IRISH MIST**® until stiff. Spoon on strawberry tarts.

STRAWBERRIES WITH MISTY SAUCE IN MERINGUE SHELLS

Meringue Shells:
3 egg whites
1½ teaspoons **REGINA** White Wine Vinegar
¾ cup sugar
½ teaspoon vanilla

Strawberries:
⅓ cup **IRISH MIST**® Liqueur
3 tablespoons lemon juice
6 cups sliced fresh strawberries

Sauce:
2 eggs, separated
½ cup sugar
2 tablespoons **IRISH MIST**® Liqueur

MERINGUE SHELLS:
In large mixing bowl, beat egg whites and vinegar until foamy. Gradually add sugar, continuing to beat until stiff but not dry. Mix in vanilla. Cover cookie sheet with brown paper. Shape 8 individual meringue shells on paper. Bake in preheated 275° F oven 40-45 minutes or until firm. Cool. Remove from paper.

STRAWBERRIES:
Combine **IRISH MIST**® and lemon juice. Drizzle mixture over strawberries. Chill, gently stirring occasionally.

SAUCE:
For sauce, beat egg whites until soft peaks form. Gradually add ¼ cup sugar, and continue beating until stiff. Set aside. Beat egg yolks with remaining sugar and **IRISH MIST**® until thickened. Fold two mixtures together. Chill.

Spoon strawberries in meringue shells. Top with sauce.

STRAWBERRIES, ROMANOFF STYLE

1 pint strawberries, sliced and sweetened*
2 tablespoons brandy
1½ tablespoons orange liqueur
2 cups (1 pint) vanilla ice cream
1¾ cups thawed **BIRDS EYE**® **COOL WHIP**® **Non-Dairy Whipped Topping**

Combine strawberries, brandy and liqueur. Mash ice cream with a fork until smooth but still frozen. Fold in whipped topping and serve over berries. *Makes 6 servings*

*Or use 2 packages (10 oz. each) **BIRDS EYE**® **Quick Thaw Strawberries**, thawed.

Note: Ice cream mixture may be stored up to 30 minutes in freezer before serving.

FROSTY STRAWBERRY DESSERT

Crust:
1¼ cups crushed cinnamon/sugar graham crackers, about 8 whole crackers
¼ cup plus 1 tablespoon soybean oil mayonnaise

Combine graham cracker crumbs and mayonnaise. Press mixture on bottom and sides of 9″ glass pie plate. Bake 8 to 10 minutes until slightly browned and cookie-like. Cool thoroughly.

Filling:
½ cup soybean oil mayonnaise
2 tablespoons frozen lemonade concentrate, slightly thawed
1 (10 oz.) package frozen strawberries, thawed
1 pint vanilla ice cream, softened

In a large mixing bowl, combine mayonnaise, lemonade, and strawberries. Beat with electric mixer until berries are thoroughly crushed. Add ice cream and beat just until combined. Pour into cooled crust and freeze until firm. *Makes 6 to 8 servings*

Favorite recipe from the **American Soybean Association**

POTEET STRAWBERRY PYRAMID

1 cup **IMPERIAL** Granulated Sugar
1 cup heavy cream
2 cups sour cream
Shiny decorative fresh leaves
1 pint whole strawberries (fresh or frozen)
Raspberries, (fresh or frozen)
IMPERIAL 10X Powdered Sugar

Combine **IMPERIAL Granulated Sugar** and heavy cream; gently combine this mixture with sour cream. Chill until thickened. Arrange decorative leaves in circle on serving plate. Put about ½ cup of cream in center and begin arranging strawberries around edges and in center of cream. Add more cream and more strawberries on top of first layer and continue to build into tapering tower. When ready to serve, drizzle mashed, sweetened raspberries over top of chilled strawberry pyramid. Dust with **IMPERIAL 10X Powdered Sugar**. *Serves 6 to 8*

SWEET FRUIT CRISP

3 tablespoons granulated sugar
2 tablespoons all-purpose flour
¼ teaspoon **MORTON LITE SALT**® Brand*
1 (16- to 20-ounce) package frozen dark sweet cherries or blueberries**
2 tablespoons lemon juice
2 tablespoons unsalted butter or margarine
½ cup all-purpose flour
¾ teaspoon **MORTON LITE SALT**® Brand
½ cup quick oats
⅓ cup firmly packed brown sugar
¼ cup melted unsalted butter or margarine

In saucepan, combine granulated sugar, 2 tablespoons flour and ¼ teaspoon **MORTON LITE SALT® Brand**. Add fruit and lemon juice. Cook and stir over medium heat just until sauce comes to a boil. Add 2 tablespoons butter. Remove from heat, stirring just until butter melts. Pour fruit mixture into a 9-inch pie plate or into six (6-ounce) custard cups (use a scant ½ cup for each custard cup).

In mixing bowl, combine remaining ½ cup flour and ¾ teaspoon **MORTON LITE SALT® Brand** with oats and brown sugar. With fork, mix in ¼ cup melted butter until crumbly. Sprinkle crumbly mixture over top of fruit (use about ¼ cup for each custard cup). Place custard cups on baking sheet.

Bake at 375°F for 25 minutes. Serve warm or cooled, with ice cream or whipped cream if desired.   *Makes 6 servings*

*Contains only half the sodium of table salt.
**To substitute *canned* fruit, use 1 (15- to 17-ounce) can dark sweet cherries or blueberries, undrained.

BLUEBERRY-CHERRY BROWN BETTY

1 package **BETTY CROCKER® Wild Blueberry Muffin Mix**
½ cup quick-cooking oats
¼ cup packed brown sugar
1 teaspoon ground cinnamon
½ cup firm margarine or butter
1 can (16 ounces) pitted red tart cherries, drained
1 teaspoon grated lemon peel
¼ cup chopped nuts

Heat oven to 400°. Drain and rinse blueberries included with package. Mix muffin mix, oats, brown sugar and cinnamon in medium bowl. Cut in margarine until mixture is crumbly. Sprinkle half of the crumbly mixture evenly in ungreased round pan, 9 × 1½ inches, or square pan, 8 × 8 × 2 inches. Arrange cherries on crumbly mixture; sprinkle lemon peel and blueberries over cherries. Sprinkle with remaining crumbly mixture and the nuts. Bake until golden brown, 30 to 35 minutes. Serve warm and, if desired, with sweetened whipped cream.   *9 servings*

MIMOSA MACEDOINE

4 Florida oranges, peeled and sectioned (2 cups)
1 cup pineapple chunks
1 cup red grapes
1 cup strawberry halves
3 kiwi, peeled and thinly sliced
1 cup Florida orange juice
1 cup **KORBEL Champagne**

Combine fruit in medium bowl. Cover. Chill several hours. Spoon into serving dishes. In a small pitcher combine orange juice and champagne. Pour over fruit. Serve immediately.

Yield: 6 servings

Favorite recipe from **Florida Department of Citrus**

LEMON HONEY COMPOTE

1 (11-ounce) package (2 cups) **SUNSWEET® Dried Mixed Fruit**
2 cups water
1 stick cinnamon
3 lemon slices
2 tablespoons lemon juice
⅓ cup honey

In a saucepan, combine all ingredients *except* honey. Heat to boiling, lower heat and simmer 15 minutes. Stir in honey; cook 5 minutes longer. Cool before serving.   *Makes 4 to 6 servings*

DRIED FRUITS AND APPLE IN WINE

PAM® No-Stick Cooking Spray
1½ cups dried apricots
1½ cups pitted dates
¾ cup dry white wine
2 red delicious apples, cubed

Coat kitchen shears with **PAM® No-Stick Cooking Spray** according to directions. Cut apricots and dates into 4 or 5 pieces. Place in shallow bowl. Cover with wine and chill at least 3 hours or until wine is absorbed. To serve, layer apricots, dates and apples in parfait glasses.   *Makes 6 servings*

Total Calories: 1,698
Per Serving: 283

HOT & SPICY FRUIT COMPOTE
(Low Calorie)

1 (16 oz.) can **S&W® NUTRADIET® Blue Label Cling Peaches** (sliced), drained
1 (16 oz.) can **S&W® NUTRADIET® Blue Label Apricots** (halves), drained
1 (15¼ oz.) can **S&W® NUTRADIET® Blue Label Sliced Pineapple**, drained
1 cup orange juice
2 tsp. lemon juice
½ tsp. grated orange peel
¼ tsp. grated lemon peel
½ tsp. ginger
¼ tsp. rum extract
4-5 whole cloves
Pinch salt

In a 1½-quart casserole with lid, combine drained fruit. Blend together remaining ingredients and pour over fruit. Bake, covered, at 350° for 20 minutes.   *Serves 8*

Each Serving Equals Approximately:
1½ fruit exchanges
60 calories
15 g carbohydrate
0 g fat
0 g protein

FRESH CHERRY AND PINEAPPLE COMPOTE

½ cup sugar
1 cup water
2 (two-inch) sticks whole cinnamon
½ teaspoon fresh lemon juice
2 cups fresh pineapple wedges
2 cups fresh pitted sweet cherries
1½ cups fresh cantaloupe balls

Boil first 4 ingredients together in a covered saucepan 5 minutes. Add pineapple wedges and cherries. Heat thoroughly. Chill. Just before serving, add cantaloupe balls.   *Yield: 6 servings*

Favorite recipe from **The American Spice Trade Association**

TIPPERARY FRUIT COMPOTE WITH MISTY SAUCE

⅓ cup **IRISH MIST®** Liqueur
3 tablespoons lemon juice
6 cups cut-up fresh fruit

Sauce:
2 eggs, separated
½ cup sugar
2 tablespoons **IRISH MIST®** Liqueur

Combine **IRISH MIST®** and lemon juice. Drizzle mixture over fruit. Chill, gently stirring occasionally. For sauce, beat egg whites until soft peaks form. Gradually add ¼ cup sugar, beating until stiff. Set aside. Beat egg yolks with remaining sugar and **IRISH MIST®** until thickened. Fold two mixtures together. Chill. Serve fruit topped with sauce.   *Serves 8*

FRUIT COMPOTE
(Low Calorie)

1 (12 oz.) can **DIET SHASTA®** Citrus Mist
1 cup diced fresh pineapple
2 cups diced apple
½ cup diced pear
Dash salt
1 cinnamon stick
½ cup diced or sectioned orange

Combine **DIET SHASTA®** with pineapple, apple, pear, salt and cinnamon. Simmer 5 minutes. Remove from heat, discard cinnamon and add orange. Serve warm or cold.
                  Makes 4 or 5 servings

Calories: 132 calories per serving

THREE-FRUIT COMPOTE

1 can (1 pound, 1 ounce size) peaches
1 can (1 pound, 1 ounce size) apricots
1 can (1 pound, 1 ounce size) Bing cherries
1 cup **GIROUX®** Grenadine Syrup
Grated rind and juice ½ lemon

Drain syrup from all three fruits. Combine fruits with all remaining ingredients in a suitable serving dish. Chill. *Serves about 6*

MACEDONIA DI FRUTTA

1 ripe pineapple, cut into chunks
1 (16 oz.) package frozen cherries or other berries
¾ lb. green and/or red grapes
1 lb. fresh fruits in season (such as peaches, plums, nectarines) or frozen mixed fruit, sliced
1 cup **THE CHRISTIAN BROTHERS®** Napa Rosé or Chablis
¼ cup apple jelly

In a large shallow bowl, combine fruit with rosé or chablis. Chill 4 hours, turning fruit once or twice. Melt jelly in saucepan; brush over fruit to glaze.   *Makes 4 to 6 servings*

FROSTY FRUIT COMPOTE

1 can (11 oz.) mandarin oranges, drained
1 can (20 oz.) pineapple chunks, drained
½ cup **BOGGS** Cranberry Liqueur
Coconut

Mix oranges, pineapple and **BOGGS**. Place in freezer 2 hours or until fruits begin to get icy. Spoon into individual dessert dishes and sprinkle with coconut. Serve immediately.
                  Makes 4-6 servings

MINTY ORANGE GRAPE COMPOTE
(Low Calorie)

⅓ cup honey or light corn syrup
2 tablespoons fresh squeezed lemon juice
1 to 2 tablespoons chopped fresh mint
2 **SUNKIST®** oranges, peeled, sliced into cartwheels, quartered
2 cups seedless green grapes

In bowl, combine honey, lemon juice, and mint. Add orange pieces and grapes; stir well. Chill at least 2 hours, stirring occasionally. Garnish with fresh mint sprigs, if desired.
                   Makes 6 servings

Calories: about 115 per ½ cup serving

SPICED FRUIT MEDLEY
(Low Calorie)

1 teaspoon unflavored gelatin
1 (12 oz.) can **DIET SHASTA®** RedBerry
1 cinnamon stick
½ treaspoon whole allspice
¼ teaspoon powdered ginger
⅛ teaspoon artificial liquid sweetener
⅔ cup diced fresh pear
1 cup sliced fresh nectarine or peaches
1½ cups diced fresh apple
Vanilla Meringues*

Soften gelatin in 2 tablespoons **DIET SHASTA®**. Pour remaining soda into saucepan. Add spices, sweetener and fruits. Bring to a boil, lower heat and simmer 5 minutes. Add gelatin, stirring until dissolved. Chill. Serve plain or topped with Vanilla Meringues.
                    Makes 4 servings

Note: Whole spice may be removed before chilling, if desired. Leaving them in gives a more pronounced spice flavor.

112 calories per serving

*VANILLA MERINGUES

Beat 1 egg white with ⅛ teaspoon cream of tartar until stiff. Beat in ¼ teaspoon artificial liquid sweetener and ½ teaspoon vanilla extract. Spoon 4 mounds on cooky sheet. Bake in a hot oven (425°F) for 5 minutes.

4 calories per serving

BLUEBERRY COBBLER

1 qt. fresh or dry-pack frozen blueberries, rinsed and
    drained
½ cup granulated sugar
1 tablespoon cornstarch
½ teaspoon grated lemon peel
1 teaspoon lemon juice
¼ teaspoon **ANGOSTURA® Aromatic Bitters**
¼ teaspoon cinnamon
1 cup unsifted all-purpose flour
1 tablespoon granulated sugar
1½ teaspoons baking powder
2 teaspoons grated orange rind
¼ teaspoon salt
3 tablespoons shortening
⅓ cup milk
1 egg

In medium saucepan combine blueberries, ½ cup sugar, cornstarch, lemon peel, lemon juice, **ANGOSTURA® Bitters** and
cinnamon. Cook over medium heat, stirring constantly, until mixture just starts to bubble. Lower heat and simmer about 5 minutes
or until mixture has thickened, stirring frequently. In mixing bowl
thoroughly combine flour, sugar, baking powder, orange rind and
salt. Cut in shortening until mixture resembles coarse crumbs. In
small bowl combine milk and egg. Beat slightly to combine. Pour
all at once into flour mixture and stir just until all flour is moistened. Transfer hot blueberries to 2-quart baking dish. Drop heaping tablespoons of biscuit dough into fruit. Bake at 400° F. 20 to
25 minutes or until biscuits are browned. Serve with whipped
cream or ice cream, if desired.   *Yield: 4 to 6 servings*

CHERRY COBBLER

1 can (16 oz) red sour cherries packed in water
½ cup sugar
1 tablespoon corn starch
1 tablespoon **MAZOLA® Corn Oil Margarine**
1 teaspoon lemon juice
3 drops red food coloring
1 recipe Biscuit Dough*

Drain cherries reserving ¾ cup juice. In small saucepan mix
together juice, sugar and corn starch. Cook over medium heat
stirring constantly until mixture comes to a boil and boils 1
minute. Stir in margarine, lemon juice and food coloring. Remove
from heat. Add cherries. Pour hot cherry mixture into 10″ × 6″ ×
2″ baking dish. Drop Biscuit Dough by teaspoonfuls onto hot
cherry mixture. Bake in 400°F oven 20 to 30 minutes or until
Biscuit Dough is golden.   *Makes 6 servings*

*BISCUIT DOUGH

1 cup unsifted flour
1 tablespoon sugar
2 teaspoons baking powder
¼ teaspoon salt
¼ teaspoon nutmeg
¼ cup **MAZOLA® Corn Oil**
⅓ cup milk

Stir together flour, sugar, baking powder, salt and nutmeg. Stir in
corn oil. Add milk and mix well.

SPICY PEAR COBBLER

2 Tbsp. cornstarch
½ tsp. nutmeg
2-16 oz. cans **S&W® Natural Style Bartlett Pears**,
    drained (reserve juice)
½ cup **S&W® Seedless Raisins**
½ cup **S&W® Shelled Walnuts**, chopped
1 Tbsp. butter
1½ cups all-purpose flour
3 Tbsp. sugar
2 tsp. baking powder
¼ tsp. salt
6 Tbsp. butter
¾ cup milk
1 egg, beaten

Combine cornstarch and nutmeg; blend in the reserved juice using
a wire whip to eliminate any lumps. Cook over medium heat until
thick and bubbly. Remove from heat. Stir in pears, raisins, walnuts and butter. Turn hot pear mixture into 7 x 11″ baking pan.
Meanwhile, prepare topping by sifting together flour, sugar, baking powder and salt. Cut in butter until mixture resembles coarse
crumbs. Combine milk with beaten egg. Add to dry mixture and
stir just to moisten. Spoon on pear mixture in 8 portions. Bake at
400° for 20-25 minutes or until top is golden brown. Serve with
cream or ice cream.   *Serves 8*

CHIQUITA® FROZEN YOGURT BANANA DESSERT

⅔ cup sugar
½ cup orange juice
4 large ripe **CHIQUITA® Bananas**
2 teaspoons lemon juice
1 cup plain yogurt
2 egg whites

1. Combine sugar and orange juice in saucepan. Heat and stir
until sugar is dissolved. Set aside to cool.
2. Slice bananas into blender container, add lemon juice. Whirl
until bananas are pulp. Add yogurt blending well. With motor
running, add orange juice mixture.
3. Pour into 9″ × 9″ flat pan and place in freezer for about two
hours or until mixture is frozen to a slush.
4. Break up frozen mixture and put in mixer bowl. Beat until
smooth adding egg whites one at a time. Continue beating until
light and fluffy.
5. Return to pan and freeze until firm; about 1 hour.
          Yield: 9-12 servings

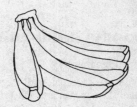

HONEY-YOGURT SUNDAES

Spread 2 cartons (6 ounces each) **YOPLAIT® Breakfast Yogurt
Citrus Fruits Yogurt** in ice-cube tray. Freeze until firm, at least
2 hours.
    Remove frozen yogurt from freezer 10 minutes before serving.
Heat ¼ cup honey until warm. Spoon frozen yogurt into dishes.
Pour 1 tablespoon honey over each serving. Sprinkle each with
small amount ground coffee.   *4 servings*

FRESH YOGURT SUNDAE

1 cup **DANNON® Plain Yogurt**
2 Tbsp. honey
2 Tbsp. chopped almonds
Chopped dates

Put yogurt into chilled sherbet cup. Pour honey over yogurt, sprinkle with almonds and dates.   *Makes 1 serving*

VIRGINIA DARE'S CREME DE MENTHE PARFAITS

Scoop vanilla ice cream into parfait glass. Add **VIRGINIA DARE Creme De Menthe Syrup**. Top with whipped cream and a maraschino cherry. Other delicious and colorful varieties: Use **VIRGINIA DARE Creme De Maraschino**, **Claret**, **Chocolate Mint**, **Strawberry-Raspberry** or **Melba**. For a formal dinner, use Rum, Brandy or Sherry Sauces.

TROPICAL PARFAITS

1 (14-ounce) can **EAGLE® Brand Sweetened Condensed Milk** (NOT evaporated milk)
¼ cup reconstituted lime juice
1 (8-ounce) container plain yogurt
1 (8-ounce) can crushed pineapple, drained, reserving 2 tablespoons liquid
3 tablespoons margarine or butter
¾ **NABISCO Old Fashion Ginger Snap Crumbs** (about 20 cookies)
½ cup flaked coconut
2 to 3 drops green food coloring

In small bowl, combine sweetened condensed milk and lime juice; mix well. Stir in yogurt, reserved pineapple liquid, crushed pineapple and food coloring; set aside. In small saucepan, melt margarine, stir in crumbs and coconut. Layer filling and coconut mixture in parfait or dessert glasses, topping with coconut mixture. Chill in freezer 30 to 45 minutes or 2 hours in refrigerator before serving. Garnish as desired. Refrigerate leftovers.
        Makes 4 to 6 parfaits

CARA MIA™ CREAM PUFFS

1 cup water
½ cup (1 stick) butter
1⅓ cups unsifted flour
4 eggs
⅓ cup sugar
2 cups milk
½ cup **CARA MIA™ Amaretto Cream Liqueur**
4 egg yolks
1 cup whipped cream

Heat water and butter in a saucepan until the water is boiling and margarine has melted. Lower heat and add 1 cup flour all at once. Beat vigorously until mixture leaves sides of the pan. Remove from heat. Add whole eggs, one at a time, beating well after each addition. Continue beating until mixture is smooth. Drop mixture on a lightly greased baking sheet to form 12 puffs, dividing the mixture evenly. Bake at 400°F. for about 35 to 40 minutes, or until done. Remove puffs from baking sheet and cool on wire racks.

Combine remaining ⅓ cup flour with sugar in a medium saucepan. Mix in milk. Bring to a boil over medium high heat, stirring constantly. Reduce heat to medium low and cook 1 minute.

Beat together **CARA MIA™ Amaretto Cream Liqueur** and

egg yolks. Stir ⅓ cup hot mixture in saucepan into yolk mixture, then add yolk mixture to saucepan, stirring constantly. Cook and stir 1 minute more over low heat. Pour mixture into a medium heat-proof bowl and place plastic directly on top to prevent skin from forming. Chill well. Fold whipped cream into chilled mixture. Refrigerate until thick and mounding. To serve, cut off tops of puffs and scoop out soft insides. Fill each puff with about ⅓ cup prepared filling.   *Makes 1 dozen*

CREAM PUFFS

1 cup sifted **E-Z-BAKE Flour**
1 cup boiling water
½ cup butter or margarine
4 eggs

Sift and measure flour. Bring water and butter to a rolling boil. Add all the flour and stir continuously with a wooden spoon until mixture clears the pan and forms into a ball (about 1 minute). Cool. Add unbeaten eggs one at a time, beating to a smooth paste after each addition. Continue beating until mixture looks velvety. Drop by spoonfuls onto baking sheet, forming 12 mounds—3 inches apart.

Bake in hot oven (450° F.) 15 minutes. Reduce heat to 350° F. and continue baking 30 to 35 minutes more. When baked, cool away from drafts. To fill, remove tops with a sharp knife. Scrape out any flecks of soft dough. Fill puffs with sweetened and flavored whipped cream or soft custard. Replace tops. Sprinkle with powdered sugar.

VENETIAN CREAM™ PUFFS

8 cream puff shells
1½ cups milk
6 egg yolks
⅔ cup sugar
⅓ cup flour
¾ cup **VENETIAN CREAM™ Liqueur**
½ cup whipping cream

Bring milk to a boil and set aside. Place egg yolks in a bowl and beat 50 strokes with wire whisk. Add sugar and continuously beat until mixture becomes lighter in color. Add flour and mix well. Place reserved milk on heat, add the **VENETIAN CREAM™** and the egg mixture and slowly bring to a boil, stirring continuously. After the whole mixture thickens, remove from the heat, cover it with plastic and let it cool. Whip the cream and fold into the mixture. Stuff the puff shells. Sprinkle top of the shells with confectioners' sugar or chocolate sauce.

RICOTTA FILLED PUFFS

Puffs:
½ cup shortening
⅛ teaspoon salt
1 cup sifted all-purpose flour
3 eggs
1 cup boiling water
Filling:
1 container (15 oz.) **MIGLIORE® Ricotta**
¼ cup confectioners sugar
1 teaspoon vanilla
¼ teaspoon lemon rind

Preheat oven to 450°. Add shortening and salt to 1 cup boiling water; stir over medium heat until mixture boils. Lower heat, add flour all at once and stir vigorously until mixture leaves sides of pan. Remove from heat and add 1 egg at a time, beating thoroughly after each addition. Shape on ungreased cookie sheet, using 1 teaspoon to 1 tablespoon paste per puff (depending on size desired). A pastry bag may be used. Bake 20 minutes, reduce oven temperature to 350° and bake about 20 minutes longer. Remove from oven and place on rack to cool.

Combine ricotta, confectioners sugar, vanilla and lemon rind. Blend well. Cut tops from puffs, fill with ricotta mixture, replace tops and sprinkle with confectioners sugar.

ROQUEFORT PUFF PASTRY

Thaw 2 packages (12 shells) frozen puff pastry shells. Separate each shell into 2 layers. Mash 8 oz. **ROQUEFORT Cheese** until creamy. Spread 1 tablespoon of the cheese evenly on 12 of the bottom rounds. Cover cheese with top rounds. Place on an ungreased cookie sheet. Bake in a preheated hot oven (400°F.) for 30 to 35 minutes. Serve hot. *Makes 12 servings*

Favorite recipe from the **Roquefort Association, Inc.**

SUNNY PAPAYA CRESCENTS

2 (8-ounce) packages refrigerated crescent rolls
2 tablespoons butter or margarine, melted
½ teaspoon cinnamon
¾ cup finely chopped walnuts
1 ripe **CALAVO® Papaya**, peeled, sliced lengthwise
½ cup powdered sugar
1 tablespoon milk
Chopped walnuts for garnish (optional)

Heat oven to 375° F. Separate dough into individual triangles; lightly brush with butter. Sprinkle buttered dough with cinnamon and chopped nuts. Place a papaya slice on each triangle; roll dough to enclose papaya; place on ungreased cookie sheet. Bake 15 minutes or until rolls are browned. Combine powdered sugar and milk; drizzle over hot rolls. Serve immediately. If desired, sprinkle on additional chopped walnuts. *Makes 16 crescents*

CRISPY CHOCOLATE RING

¼ cup butter or margarine
½ cup **DOMINO® Golden Light Brown Sugar**, firmly packed
⅓ cup peanut butter
1 envelope (1 ounce) pre-melted unsweetened chocolate flavor
3 cups crisp rice cereal or cornflakes

Melt butter in medium saucepan. Add sugar, stirring well. Add peanut butter and chocolate flavor; stir until well blended. Stir in cereal; mix until cereal is well coated. Pack mixture into well buttered 8-inch ring mold or individual ring molds. Chill until firm. Unmold by running spatula around inside of mold. Serve with ice cream balls if desired. *Makes 6 to 8 servings*

DUBONNET TORTONI

¾ cup sugar
¼ cup water
5 egg yolks, beaten
⅜ cup **DUBONNET Rouge Aperitif Wine**
2 cups heavy cream, whipped

In saucepan combine sugar and water. Bring to a boil and boil for 5 minutes. Stir into egg yolks and stir over hot, but not boiling water, until custard is thick. Stir in **DUBONNET Rouge** and fold in heavy cream. Freeze in home freezer. *Makes 5 cups*

STANFORD COURT ALMOND DACQUOISE

1½ cups **BLUE RIBBON® Ground Toasted Almonds**
1¼ cups sugar
1½ tablespoons cornstarch
6 egg whites
¼ teaspoon cream of tartar
⅛ teaspoon salt
1 teaspoon vanilla
¼ teaspoon almond extract
Amaretto Butter Cream**
½ cup sliced natural almonds, toasted*
BLUE RIBBON® Whole Natural (unblanched) **Almonds**, toasted
Cinnamon

In bowl combine ground almonds, 1 cup of the sugar and the cornstarch. Mix thoroughly; set aside. Butter and flour 2 baking sheets; mark a 9-inch circle in the center of each. In large bowl beat egg whites until foamy. Add cream of tartar and salt. Beat at high speed until whites form soft peaks. Gradually add the remaining ¼ cup sugar while beating at high speed until mixture forms stiff peaks. Beat in vanilla and almond extract. With rubber spatula quickly and gently fold in ground almond mixture, ¼ at a time. Spoon evenly onto baking sheets to fill circles completely. (Mixture will be about ¾ inch high.) Gently smooth tops with spatula. Bake on middle rack of preheated 250 degree oven about 2 hours until layers are dried, lightly browned and lift easily from baking sheets. Cool on wire racks. Place one layer on serving plate and cover evenly with ⅔ of the Amaretto Butter Cream to within ½ inch of edge. Sprinkle with ½ of the sliced almonds. Place remaining layer on top. Spoon remaining Amaretto Butter Cream into pastry bag fitted with ⅜-inch star tip. Pipe rosettes onto top layer. Garnish with the remaining sliced almonds and the whole almonds. Dust with cinnamon. With sharp knife cut into wedges to serve immediately or refrigerate no more than 2 hours before serving. *Makes 12 servings*

*To toast almonds, spread in an ungreased baking pan or skillet. Place in a 350-degree oven or over medium-low heat on the stove top for 5-10 minutes (depending on the form of almonds that you are using) or until almonds are a light golden brown, stir once or twice to assure even browning. Note that almonds will continue to brown slightly after being removed from the heat.

**AMARETTO BUTTER CREAM

3 egg yolks
1¼ cups powdered sugar
¾ cup milk
1½ cups sweet (unsalted) butter, softened
3 tablespoons amaretto (almond-flavored liqueur)
1 teaspoon almond extract

In medium bowl beat egg yolks and powdered sugar until thick and lemon-colored. In medium saucepan heat milk just to boiling. Beat into yolk mixture to blend thoroughly. Pour into saucepan. Place over medium heat and stir constantly about 10 minutes until slightly thickened. (Do not allow mixture to boil.) Pour back into bowl and beat until cool. At high speed beat in butter a tablespoon at a time. Beat amaretto and almond extract into butter mixture to blend thoroughly. If desired, Amaretto Butter Cream may be prepared in advance. Cover and refrigerate. Before assembling dessert, return to room temperature and beat until smooth. *Makes about 3 cups*

CANNOLI ALLA SICILIANA

Shells:
2 cups all-purpose flour
2 tablespoons shortening
1 teaspoon sugar
¼ teaspoon salt
¾ cup Marsala, Burgundy or Chablis wine
Vegetable oil

Filling:
3 cups **POLLY-O® RICOTTA**
½ cup confectioner's sugar
¼ teaspoon cinnamon
½ square unsweetened chocolate, grated,
   or ½ tablespoon cocoa (optional)
½ teaspoon vanilla
3 tablespoons chopped citron peel
3 tablespoons chopped candied orange peel
6 glacé cherries, cut up

To make cannoli shells it is necessary to have 3 or 4 metal tubes, preferably made from very light tin, about 7-inches long and 1⅛-inches in diameter. The edges should not be soldered.

SHELLS:
Combine flour, shortening, sugar and salt, and wetting gradually with wine, knead together with fingers until rather hard dough or paste is formed. Form into ball, cover with cloth and let stand about 1 hour. Cut dough in half and roll half of dough into a thin sheet about ¼-inch thick. Cut into 4-inch squares. Place a metal tube diagonally across each square from one point to another, wrapping dough around tube by overlapping the two points and sealing overlapping points with a little egg white. Meanwhile heat vegetable oil in large deep pan for deep frying. Drop one or two tubes at a time into hot oil. Fry gently until dough is a golden brown color. Remove from pan, let cool and gently remove shell from metal tube. Set shells aside to cool. Repeat procedure until all shells are made.

FILLING:
Mix ricotta thoroughly with sifted dry ingredients. Add vanilla and fruit peel. Mix and blend well. (A little grated pistachio may be added if desired.) Chill in refrigerator before filling shells. Fill cold cannoli shells; smooth filling evenly at each end of shell. Decorate each end with a piece of glacé cherry and sprinkle shells with confectioner's sugar. Refrigerate until ready to serve.

10-12 cannoli

SUPER SCOOPS

Place 1 qt. ice cream in mixing bowl to soften; let stand about 5 minutes or until slightly soft. Beat with wooden spoon until thick and of spoonable consistency. Add ingredients as per flavor desired; mix until well blended. Return to original ice cream container; freeze overnight or until firm. Serve in cones or dessert dishes. *Makes 1 qt. flavored ice cream**

VARIATIONS:

VIBRANT VANILLA

Add ½ to ¾ cup chopped **"M&M's"® Plain Chocolate Candies**, frozen, to softened vanilla ice cream; mix well. Freeze as directed above. (**Variation:** Add ¼ teaspoon orange or lemon extract.)

PERKY PISTACHIO

Add ½ to ¾ cup chopped **"M&M's"® Plain Chocolate Candies**, frozen, ¼ teaspoon almond extract and 8 to 10 drops green food coloring to softened vanilla ice cream; mix well. Freeze as directed above. *(Continued)*

PEANUT BUTTER CHIP

Add 2 tablespoons creamy peanut butter to softened vanilla ice cream; mix until well blended. Fold in ½ to ¾ cup chopped **"M&M's"® Plain Chocolate Candies**, frozen. Freeze as directed above.

HEAVENLY HASH

Add ¾ cup marshmallow creme to softened chocolate ice cream; mix until marbled. Fold in 1 cup chopped toasted almonds and ¾ to 1 cup chopped **"M&M's"® Plain Chocolate Candies**, frozen. Freeze as directed above.

*Note: All recipe ingredients double easily to make ½ gal. flavored ice cream.

VANILLA ICE CREAM

2 eggs
⅓ cup sugar
1½ cups milk
1 cup heavy cream
⅔ cup **KARO® Light Corn Syrup**
1½ teaspoons vanilla

In large bowl with mixer at medium speed beat eggs until light and frothy. Gradually add sugar, beating until sugar is dissolved. Add milk, cream, corn syrup and vanilla, beating until blended. Pour into 9×5×3-inch loaf pan. Freeze about 3 hours or until firm. Turn into large mixer bowl. With mixer at low speed beat until smooth but not melted. Return to loaf pan. Freeze several hours or until firm. *Makes 1 quart*

VARIATIONS:

BANANA ICE CREAM

Follow recipe for Vanilla Ice Cream. Reduce milk to 1 cup and vanilla to 1 teaspoon. Mix 1 cup mashed banana and 2 teaspoons lemon juice. Stir into ice cream mixture before first freezing.

LEMON ICE CREAM

Follow recipe for Vanilla Ice Cream. Increase sugar to ½ cup. Substitute ½ cup lemon juice for ½ cup of the milk. Substitute 1 teaspoon grated lemon rind for the vanilla.

PEACH ICE CREAM

Follow recipe for Vanilla Ice Cream. Reduce milk to 1 cup and vanilla to 1 teaspoon. Place 2 cups sliced peeled peaches and ¼ cup **KARO® Light Corn Syrup** in blender container; cover. Blend on high speed 30 seconds or until smooth. Stir into ice cream mixture before first freezing.

PINEAPPLE ICE CREAM

Follow recipe for Vanilla Ice Cream. Reduce milk to 1 cup and vanilla to 1 teaspoon. Place 1 can (8 oz.) pineapple in own juice and 1 teaspoon lemon juice in blender container; cover. Blend on high speed 30 seconds or until smooth. Stir into ice cream mixture before first freezing.

RASPBERRY ICE CREAM

Follow recipe for Vanilla Ice Cream. Reduce milk to 1 cup and vanilla to 1 teaspoon. Place 1 package (10 oz.) frozen raspberries in syrup, thawed, in blender container; cover. Blend on high speed 30 seconds or until smooth. Stir into ice cream mixture before first freezing. *(Continued)*

STRAWBERRY ICE CREAM

Follow recipe for Vanilla Ice Cream. Reduce milk to 1 cup and vanilla to 1 teaspoon. Place 1 package (10 oz.) frozen strawberries in syrup, thawed, in blender container; cover. Blend on high speed 30 seconds or until smooth. Stir into ice cream mixture before first freezing.

AMARETTO ICE CREAM

1 can (14 oz.) sweetened condensed milk
2 egg yolks, beaten
¼ cup **HIRAM WALKER Amaretto Liqueur**
¼ teaspoon almond extract
2 cups whipping cream, whipped
½ cup sliced almonds, toasted and chopped

Mix sweetened condensed milk, egg yolks, Amaretto and almond extract in large bowl. Fold in whipped cream and almonds. Pour into foil-lined loaf pan, 9x5x3 inches. Cover and freeze until firm, about 8 hours. Thaw slightly before serving. Serve with sweetened fresh strawberries.

DRY SACK® PEACH ICE CREAM

2 medium peaches, peeled and chopped
¼ cup **DRY SACK® Sherry**
1 tablespoon sugar
⅛ teaspoon ground ginger
1 quart vanilla ice cream, softened

Combine peaches, **DRY SACK® Sherry**, sugar and ginger; mix thoroughly. Cover and chill one hour. Stir into softened vanilla ice cream. Cover and freeze until firm. Scoop prepared ice cream into chilled bowls and serve immediately. *Makes 4½ cups*

QUICK BANANA ICE CREAM

2 large ripe **CHIQUITA® Bananas**
1 pint vanilla ice cream, softened

Slice bananas into a medium bowl (1½ quart) and beat with an electric mixer or rotary beater until smooth. Beat in softened vanilla ice cream a fourth of a pint at a time. Spoon into ice cube tray and freeze until firm (about 1 hour). *Makes 3 cups*

VARIATION:

BANANA-NUT

Fold ½ cup chopped pecans into mixture before freezing.

AMARETTO DELIGHT

6 to 8 large scoops of ice cream in assorted flavors
2 cups fresh fruit in season
AMARETTO from GALLIANO® Liqueur
Strawberries
Whipped Cream

Heap ice cream in stemmed serving dish. Spoon fruit around scoops of ice cream. Pour about 1 ounce **AMARETTO from GALLIANO®** over each scoop of ice cream. Garnish with strawberries and whipped cream. *Serves 6 to 8*

EASY CHOCOLATE ICE CREAM

1⅓ cups (14-ounce can) sweetened condensed milk
⅔ cup **HERSHEY'S® Chocolate Syrup**
2 cups heavy cream

Stir together sweetened condensed milk and chocolate syrup in large bowl. Whip heavy cream until stiff; fold in. Cover; freeze until firm, stirring occasionally during the first hour.
About 1½ quarts

FROSTY FRUIT SHERBETS

1 envelope unflavored gelatin
½ cup milk
3 cups cubed cantaloupe
1 cup **KARO® Light Corn Syrup**

In small saucepan sprinkle gelatin over milk. Stir over low heat until dissolved. Place in blender container with cantaloupe and corn syrup; cover. Blend on high speed 30 seconds. Pour into 9 × 9 × 2-inch pan. Cover; freeze overnight. Soften slightly at room temperature, about 15 minutes. Spoon into large bowl. With mixer at low speed, beat until smooth, but not melted. Pour into 4-cup mold or freezer container. Cover; freeze about 4 hours or until firm. Unmold or soften at room temperature for easier scooping. *Makes about 4 cups*

VARIATIONS:

BLUEBERRY SHERBET

Follow recipe for Frosty Fruit Sherbets. Omit cantaloupe. Use 3 cups whole blueberries. *Makes about 3½ cups*

HONEYDEW SHERBET

Follow recipe for Frosty Fruit Sherbets. Omit cantaloupe. Use 3 cups cubed honeydew melon. *Makes about 4 cups*

NECTARINE SHERBET

Follow recipe for Frosty Fruit Sherbets. Omit cantaloupe. Use 3 cups cubed nectarines and 1 tablespoon lemon juice.
Makes about 4 cups

PAPAYA SHERBET

Follow recipe for Frosty Fruit Sherbets. Omit cantaloupe. Use 3 cups cubed papaya and 1 tablespoon lemon juice.
Makes about 4 cups

PEACH SHERBET

Follow recipe for Frosty Fruit Sherbets. Omit cantaloupe. Use 3 cups cubed peaches and 1 tablespoon lemon juice.
Makes about 4 cups

PINEAPPLE SHERBET

Follow recipe for Frosty Fruit Sherbets. Omit cantaloupe. Use 3 cups cubed pineapple. *Makes about 4 cups*

STRAWBERRY SHERBET

Follow recipe for Frosty Fruit Sherbets. Omit cantaloupe. Use 3 cups whole strawberries. *Makes about 3½ cups*

WATERMELON SHERBET

Follow recipe for Frosty Fruit Sherbets. Omit cantaloupe. Use 3 cups cubed watermelon. *Makes about 4 cups*

RASPBERRY-PEACH SHERBET

Follow recipe for Frosty Fruit Sherbets. Omit cantaloupe. Use 2 cups sliced peaches and 1 cup raspberries.

TORTONI FRANGELICO®

1 quart pistachio ice cream, slightly softened
½ cup heavy cream, whipped
⅓ cup FRANGELICO® Liqueur
⅓ cup macaroon crumbs

Turn ice cream into large chilled bowl; fold in whipped cream, FRANGELICO®, macaroon crumbs. Spoon into chilled dessert dishes. Freeze until firm. (Garnish with macaroon crumbs if desired.)   *6 to 8 servings*

CREAMY LEMON SHERBET

1 cup sugar
2 cups (1 pint) BORDEN® Whipping Cream whipped
½ cup REALEMON® Lemon Juice From Concentrate
Few drops yellow food coloring

In medium bowl, combine sugar and cream, stirring until dissolved. Stir in REALEMON® and food coloring. Pour into 8-inch square pan or directly into sherbert dishes. Freeze 3 hours or until firm. Remove from freezer 5 minutes before serving. Return leftovers to freezer.   *Makes about 3 cups*

VARIATION:

LIME SHERBET

Substitute REALIME® Lime Juice From Concentrate for REALEMON® and green food coloring for yellow.

NAPA SHERBET

1 envelope plain gelatine
½ cup cold water
2 cups THE CHRISTIAN BROTHERS® Napa Rosé
¾ cup sugar
¼ cup lime juice, freshly squeezed
1 package (10 oz.) frozen raspberries

Mix gelatine and water; let stand to soften gelatine. Meanwhile, heat wine until piping hot but not boiling. Stir in sugar to dissolve. Stir in gelatine mixture until dissolved. Mix in lime juice and raspberries. Place in freezer until softly frozen. Turn into mixer bowl. Beat vigorously just until frothy and berries are evenly blended. Freeze solid.   *Makes 1 quart*

COUPES NAPOLÉON

2 seedless oranges
3 tablespoons MANDARINE NAPOLÉON Brandy
1 pint lemon sherbet, slightly softened

Halve oranges and lift out segments, using the tip of a grapefruit spoon. Clean out inside of shells and refrigerate. Marinate orange segments in MANDARINE NAPOLÉON. Stir 3 tablespoons of marinade into softened sherbet, then pile into reserved orange shells. Freeze until firm. Garnish with orange segments.   *4 servings*

KIWI EMERALD ICE

1 pound NEW ZEALAND Kiwifruit (about 5 to 6 medium)
1 cup sugar
1 cup water
¼ cup lemon juice

Peel and quarter kiwifruit. Beat with electric mixer until coarsely mashed. Measure 1½ cups mashed fruit; stir in sugar and let stand

10 to 15 minutes to dissolve sugar. Stir in water and lemon juice. Pour mixture into 8-inch cake pan; freeze until mixture is just firm but not hard. Turn into mixing bowl; beat at high speed until smooth. Return to freezer; freeze firm. To serve: remove from freezer and let stand 10 to 15 minutes to soften slightly. Scoop or spoon into individual serving dishes.   *Makes about 3½ cups*

Favorite recipe from the New Zealand Kiwifruit Authority

DRY SACK® CITRUS ITALIAN ICE

1 cup water
¼ cup sugar
2 cups orange juice
¾ cup lemon juice
½ cup lime juice
3 tablespoons DRY SACK® Sherry

Combine water and sugar in a saucepan; heat over low heat until sugar dissolves. Combine orange, lemon and lime juices, DRY SACK® Sherry and prepared sugar-water mixture in a large metal bowl. Freeze until crystals form around edges and over top of mixture, about 1½ hours. Beat well with a spoon or hand beater. Continue freezing and beating until mixture is icy and mounding. Serve in chilled dessert glasses and garnished with fresh fruit or mint leaves if desired.   *Makes 6 cups*

LEMON ICE

1½ cups water
1 cup sugar
½ cup BERTOLLI® Soave Classico Wine
Grated rind of 4 lemons
¾ to 1 cup lemon juice

Heat water and sugar to boiling in saucepan; boil 3 minutes. Cool. Mix all ingredients. Freeze in 9-inch pan until firm, about 3 hours.   *8 servings*

ICE CREAM IGLOO WITH PETER PAN® SAUCE

Ice Cream Mold:
2 pints vanilla ice cream
1 pint chocolate ice cream
1 pint strawberry ice cream
2 cups (1 pint) whipping cream
4 tablespoons sugar
2 tablespoons toasted peanuts, chopped

Sauce:
½ cup sugar
14-ounce can sweetened condensed milk
2 teaspoons vanilla
1 cup PETER PAN® Peanut Butter
¼ cup milk

MOLD:
Line a 2½-quart mixing bowl with plastic wrap. Crisscross 2 strips of plastic wrap, extending strips over sides of bowl for ease of unmolding.

Soften vanilla ice cream to spreading consistency. Line bottom and sides of bowl with vanilla ice cream, leaving a well in center of bowl. Cover bowl with plastic wrap. Freeze for 1 hour. Repeat process for chocolate ice cream, again leaving well in the center. Cover and freeze for 1 hour. Repeat process for strawberry ice cream, leaving a center well. Cover and freeze 1 hour.

Whip 1 cup whipping cream and 2 tablespoons sugar; fold in peanuts. Fill the well with whipped cream mixture. Cover with plastic wrap and freeze 1 to 2 hours.

Whip remaining whipping cream and sugar. Invert mold onto a platter. Remove bowl and plastic wrap. Frost with whipped cream. Freeze for 30 minutes. Serve with warm sauce.

Yield: 10 to 12 servings

SAUCE:

Caramelize sugar in a heavy 2-quart saucepan over medium heat, stirring constantly. Remove from heat and slowly pour in condensed milk. Mixture will foam. Continue stirring.

Return pan to low heat. Stir to blend condensed milk and caramelized sugar mixture. Remove from heat; add vanilla. Add peanut butter; stir until peanut butter melts. Pour in milk. Stir and serve warm.

Yield: 2½ cups sauce

TOLL HOUSE® TREATWICHES

2¼ cups all purpose flour
1 measuring teaspoon baking soda
1 measuring teaspoon salt
1 cup butter, softened
¾ cup sugar
¾ cup firmly packed brown sugar
1 measuring teaspoon vanilla extract
2 eggs
One (12-oz.) pkg. (2 cups) NESTLÉ® TOLL
    HOUSE® Semi-Sweet Chocolate Morsels
1 cup chopped nuts
1 quart ice cream, softened

Preheat oven to 375°F. In small bowl, combine flour, baking soda and salt; set aside. In large bowl, combine butter, sugar, brown sugar and vanilla extract; beat until creamy. Beat in eggs. Gradually add flour mixture; mix well. Stir in **NESTLÉ® TOLL HOUSE® Semi-Sweet Chocolate Morsels** and nuts. Drop by rounded measuring tablespoonfuls onto ungreased cookie sheets. Press dough into about 2-inch circles. Bake at 375°F 10-12 minutes. Cool 1 minute; remove from cookie sheets. Cool completely.

Spread 2-3 measuring tablespoons ice cream onto bottom of one cookie. Top with another cookie. Repeat with remaining cookies. Wrap each ice cream sandwich in aluminum foil or plastic wrap. Freeze until ready to serve.

Makes: twenty-one (3-inch) ice cream sandwiches

COLORFUL ICE CREAMWICHES

¾ cup butter or margarine
¾ cup creamy peanut butter
1¼ cups firmly packed light brown sugar
1 egg
1 teaspoon vanilla
1¼ cups flour
1 teaspoon baking soda
¼ teaspoon salt
1⅔ cups chopped "M&M's"® Plain Chocolate
    Candies
3 pints vanilla or chocolate ice cream, slightly softened

Beat together butter, peanut butter and sugar until light and fluffy; blend in egg and vanilla. Add combined flour, soda and salt; mix well. Stir in 1 cup candies. Shape dough to form 1¼-inch balls; place on lightly greased cookie sheet about 3 inches apart. Flatten dough to ¼-inch thickness. Sprinkle with remaining chopped candies; press in lightly. Bake at 350°F for 10 to 12 minutes or until edges are lightly browned. Cool on cookie sheet about 3 minutes; remove to wire rack to cool thoroughly. For each ice cream sandwich, spread about ⅓ cup ice cream onto bottom of cooled cookie. Top with second cookie; press together lightly. Wrap in foil; freeze.

Makes about 14 ice cream sandwiches

PEPPERMINT FROSTED FLOAT

½ to ¾ cup finely crushed peppermint stick candy
3 cups chilled milk
1 pint vanilla ice cream
Peppermint sticks, whole

In container of electric blender combine crushed candy and milk. Cover. Process until candy is dissolved. Divide ice cream into 4 glasses. Fill glasses with milk mixture. Garnish with peppermint sticks.

Yield: 4 servings

Favorite recipe from **National Confectioners Association**

SARONNO SUNGLOW SUNDAES IN MERINGUES

6 egg whites (¾ cup) at room temperature
2 cups sugar
1½ teaspoons lemon juice
1 quart vanilla ice cream
2 cups apricot preserves
⅔ cup AMARETTO DI SARONNO® Liqueur

Beat egg whites until stiff. Gradually beat in sugar, 1 tablespoon at a time, until mixture is stiff and glossy. Beat in lemon juice. Spoon 12 (¼ cup) mounds on a foil-lined cookie sheet. Spread each mound into a 3-inch round. Place remaining meringue into a large pastry bag with a large star tip and pipe an edge around rounds until all meringue is used. Bake in a preheated very slow oven (275° F) for 1 hour, or until shells are hard in the center. Cool thoroughly before removing from foil.

In a bowl, mix ice cream, ½ cup of the preserves and ⅓ cup of the **AMARETTO DI SARONNO®**. Mix quickly and place in freezer to harden. Mix remaining apricot preserves with remaining **AMARETTO DI SARONNO®**. When ready to serve, spoon ice cream into meringue shells and top with sauce. Serve at once. If desired, garnish with chocolate flowers.* *Makes 12 servings*

*To prepare chocolate flowers, melt 4 ounces semi-sweet chocolate over hot water and cool. Place into a pastry bag with a fine writing tip. Pipe flowers out on foil. Chill for several hours, then remove from foil and place on ice cream.

APPLE DANISH A LA MODE

6 frozen SARA LEE Individual Apple Danish
½ cup caramel topping
1 tablespoon rum
1 pint vanilla ice cream

Warm Danish according to package directions. While Danish are warming, stir together caramel topping and rum. Place Danish on plates; top each with scoop of ice cream. Pour about 1 tablespoon rum sauce over each serving. *Makes 6 servings*

PRALINE® CHERRY CRUNCH

Crumble 1 pecan shortbread cookie and line bottom of demi-snifter. Add 2 to 3 tablespoons canned cherry pie filling. Top with 3 to 4 vanilla ice cream balls. Drizzle with **PRALINE® Liqueur**. Garnish with cookie crumbs and whole cherry.

BANANA FLAMBÉ

SWIFT'S® Vanilla Ice Cream
3 tablespoons **SWIFT'S BROOKFIELD® Butter**
½ cup brown sugar
2 bananas
⅛ teaspoon cinnamon
3 drops brandy or rum flavoring
Sugar cubes
Lemon extract

Melt butter and brown sugar in a chafing dish. Cut each banana lengthwise and then crosswise into 4 pieces. Sauté until tender. Add cinnamon and flavoring; stir. Dip sugar cubes into lemon extract, place on top of sauce, and touch with a lighted match. (The cubes will flame for 1 to 2 minutes.) Spoon hot sauce over vanilla ice cream. Top with salted nuts, if desired.

Yield: 4 servings

STRAWBERRY—BANANA—PINEAPPLE FLAMBÉ

3 tablespoons butter (or margarine)
2 tablespoons sugar
3 tablespoons brown sugar
1 can (8 oz.) pineapple chunks, drained
1 banana, thickly sliced
⅔ cup **IRISH MIST® Liqueur**
1 pint fresh strawberries, sliced
Vanilla ice cream

Melt butter in chafing dish or medium skillet. Mix in sugars. Add pineapple and banana. Stir to coat with syrup. Heat until bubbly. Add **IRISH MIST®**. Ignite carefully. When flame dies, mix in strawberries. Serve over vanilla ice cream.   *Serves 6*

STRAWBERRY ICE CREAM FRUIT BOWL

1 angel food cake
1 quart **BREYERS® Strawberry Ice Cream**
2 1-lb. cans fruit cocktail
Whipped cream (optional)

Tear half of the cake into 2-inch pieces with fingers or forks. Save remaining half for future use. Drain fruit cocktail and fold into softened ice cream. Mix in angel food cake pieces. Turn mixture into a 6-cup bowl that has been rinsed in cold water. Freeze for 5-6 hours or overnight. To serve, dip bowl in hot water for the count of 8; turn out onto a serving platter. If desired, garnish with piped whipped cream and fresh fruit.   *Makes 10 servings*

Note: diced fresh fruit or frozen mixed fruit (thawed and drained) may be used instead of canned.

STRAWBERRY CREAM CHARLOTTE

3 pints fresh California strawberries, washed and stemmed
1 tablespoon lime or lemon juice
2 envelopes unflavored gelatine
½ cup sugar
4 eggs, separated
1¼ cups milk*
4 ounces semisweet chocolate, melted
12 ladyfingers, split
1 cup **BLUE RIBBON® Sliced Natural Almonds**, toasted
1 cup (½ pint) whipping or heavy cream, whipped
Whipped cream (recipe follows)

Slice enough strawberries to equal 5 cups; reserve remaining strawberries for garnish. In blender or food processor, puree 3 cups sliced strawberries. Combine with lime juice; set aside. In medium saucepan, mix unflavored gelatine with ¼ cup sugar; blend in egg yolks beaten with milk. Let stand 1 minute. Stir over low heat until gelatine is completely dissolved, about 5 minutes; stir in pureed strawberries. Pour into large bowl and chill, stirring occasionally, until mixture mounds slightly when dropped from spoon.

Meanwhile, prepare pan; spread melted chocolate over rounded sides of ladyfingers. Sprinkle with almonds, pressing gently to coat. Stand ladyfingers, coated side out, against sides of 9-inch springform pan. In large bowl, beat egg whites until soft peaks form; gradually add remaining sugar and beat until stiff. Fold egg whites, then whipped cream and remaining 2 cups sliced strawberries into gelatine mixture. Turn into prepared pan; chill until firm. Garnish with reserved strawberries, halved, and whipped cream.

Makes about 12 servings

*VARIATION:

Substitute ¼ cup almond-flavored liqueur for ¼ cup of the milk.

CHEF'S SECRET WHIPPED CREAM

Unflavored gelatine is the ''secret'' to fluffy whipped cream that won't wilt so quickly when used as a topping for strawberry shortcakes or other desserts. In small saucepan, mix ½ teaspoon unflavored gelatine with 1 tablespoon cold water. Let stand 1 minute. Stir over medium heat until gelatine is completely dissolved, about 1 minute. Pour into small bowl. Quickly stir in 1 cup heavy or whipping cream and beat until stiff; chill.

BLUEBERRY PEACH CHARLOTTE

17-18 slices firm white bread
1½ quarts **SEALTEST® Peach Ice Cream**
4 cups blueberries
1 cup sugar
2 tablespoons cornstarch
½ cup water
1 teaspoon cinnamon

To make sauce, combine cornstarch, sugar and water in saucepan. Cook over medium heat until thickened. Stir in blueberries and cinnamon. Cook until blueberries are soft and sauce is thick. Cool.

Cut crusts off bread and cut slices into three pieces. Line bottom and sides of a 2-quart soufflé dish with bread slices, fitting together so there are no empty spaces. Spoon in ⅓ of blueberry sauce and cover with half of the softened ice cream, about 3 cups. Add another layer of bread slices and another ⅓ sauce. Cover with remaining 3 cups of ice cream, and another layer of bread. Finish with remaining sauce. Freeze for 24 hours. Before serving, remove from freezer and let stand at room temperature. Run knife around outer edge of dish and turn upside down on serving platter. If desired, garnish with whipped cream and sprinkle with fresh blueberries. *12 servings*

CHERRIES JUBILEE

1 cup cherry juice from canned cherries
2 tsp. cornstarch
¼ cup LEROUX Cherry Liqueur
2½ cups canned pitted Bing cherries
½ cup LEROUX Deluxe Brandy, warmed
1 qt. vanilla ice cream

Put juice in saucepan and bring to a boil. Mix cornstarch and liqueur until smooth, add to juice and cook slowly, stirring constantly until thickened and clear. Add cherries and cook 2 minutes longer. Pour brandy over cherries; ignite. Spoon through cherries until flame dies. Serve at once over vanilla ice cream. *Serves 6*

MINIATURE BAKED ALASKAS

2 RAFFETTO® Grand Marnier Brandied Peaches
4 3-inch baked tart shells
2 egg whites
¼ cup sugar
½ pint vanilla ice cream

Carefully cut each peach in half and place one half in the bottom of each baked tart shell. Beat egg whites until stiff. Gradually beat in sugar, 1 tablespoonful at a time until meringue is stiff and shiny. Divide ice cream between peach halves. Cover ice cream and peaches with a layer of meringue, being careful to cover ice cream completely. Place on a baking sheet and bake in very hot preheated 450° oven 3 to 4 minutes or just until meringue is lightly browned. Remove from oven and serve immediately. *4 servings*

Note: These can be prepared and held in the freezer, then baked at the last minute just before serving. Or they can be lightly browned, then frozen and served frozen.

BAKED ALASKA IN PATTY SHELLS

Vanilla ice cream
1 package (10 oz.) frozen PEPPERIDGE FARM® Patty Shells, baked
Meringue*

Preheat oven to 450°. Bake Patty Shells according to package directions. Place baked Patty Shells on bread board or cookie sheet. Fill each Patty Shell with ice cream. Cover the ice cream and Patty Shell completely with meringue. Bake in 450° oven for five minutes or until delicately browned. Serve immediately.

*MERINGUE

Beat the whites of two eggs until frothy. Gradually beat in four tablespoons granulated sugar. Continue beating until stiff. Flavor with ¼ teaspoon vanilla.

BAKED ALASKA

Sponge angel food or pound loaf cake
1 quart LOUIS SHERRY® Ice Cream (your favorite flavor)
4 egg whites
⅛ teaspoon cream of tartar
⅛ teaspoon salt
½ cup sugar
½ teaspoon vanilla

Cover two thicknesses of corrugated cardboard, 8 × 6 inches, with aluminum foil. Cut enough ½″ thick slices of cake to construct a rectangle 7 × 5 inches. Place cake on foil and freeze.

Let egg whites stand at room temperature for 1 hour. Beat egg whites until frothy. Add cream of tartar and salt; continue beating until soft peaks form when beater is slowly raised. Gradually beat in sugar, 2 tablespoons at a time, beating well after each addition. Add vanilla and continue beating for about 3 minutes.

Place ice cream on cake base. Quickly spread ice cream and cake with meringue, spreading down onto foil all around to seal completely. Make swirls on top and sides. Place the Alaska on a cookie sheet and bake at 500° for about 3 minutes or until meringue is light brown. Remove to chilled platter. Serve at once. *Serves 12 to 16*

Beverages

Nonalcoholic — Cold

MORNING PICK-ME-UP
(Low Calorie)

2 cans (6 ounces each) **V-8 Low Sodium Cocktail
  Vegetable Juice**, chilled
⅓ cup apple juice, chilled
Lemon slices

In 2-cup measuring cup, combine **V-8 Low Sodium Cocktail
Vegetable Juice** and apple juice. Pour into chilled glasses. Garnish with lemon slices.   *Makes 1⅔ cups or 2 servings*

> Per serving: Calories 59
> Sodium 60 mg.

VEGETABLE CITRUS COCKTAIL

1 (46-oz.) can **S&W® "Spring" Vegetable Juice
  Cocktail**
1 (6-oz.) can frozen concentrated orange juice
1 cup cold water
1 tsp. crushed basil leaves
1 tsp. lemon juice

Blend all ingredients together in a 2-quart container. Chill thoroughly, and serve in stemmed glasses. Garnish with a lemon
wheel or an orange wedge.   *Serves 8-10*

PICK-ME-UP

1 part **SNAP-E-TOM Tomato Cocktail**
1 part beef broth (or chicken broth)

Mix both ingredients and serve either hot or cold. If desired, serve
with lemon slices and/or dollops of sour cream.

PIÑA COLADA COOLER

1 cup pineapple juice
½ cup **COCO LÓPEZ® Cream of Coconut***
2½ cups ice

In blender container, combine ingredients; blend until smooth.
Serve immediately garnished as desired.   *Makes 4 servings*

*You may use **COCO LÓPEZ® Pina Colada Mix** in banana
or strawberry.

HAWAIIAN BUTTERMILK COOLER

2 cups **MEADOW GOLD® Buttermilk**
1½ cups pineapple juice
½ cup frozen concentrated orange juice

Combine above ingredients in blender, mixing until smooth. Serve
chilled.   *3 to 4 servings*

TWO-FRUIT LIME COOLER
(Low Calorie)

1 (12-oz.) can **DIET SHASTA® Lemon-Lime**
½ cup chopped fresh pineapple
1 cup chopped cantaloupe
2 tablespoons lemon juice
Dash salt

Whirl all ingredients together in blender until smooth.
        Makes about 2½ cups

55 calories per serving

PINK LEMONADE

Mix together the juice of ½ lemon, strained, and 1 tablespoon of
GIROUX® Grenadine Syrup. Pour into a glass of cracked ice.
Add carbonated or plain water.

FRESH FRUIT COLADA

2 cups cut-up fresh fruit*
¾ cup **COCO LÓPEZ® Cream of Coconut**
2 teaspoons **REALIME® Lime Juice from
  Concentrate**
1½ cups ice

In blender container, combine ingredients; blend until smooth.
Serve immediately garnished as desired.   *Makes 2 servings*

*Suggested fruits: banana, strawberries, melon, peaches, or
blueberries.

JOGGER'S NOG

1 cup **OCEAN SPRAY® Grapefruit Juice**, chilled
¼ cup plain yogurt
½ banana
1 egg
2 tablespoons honey

In a blender container, combine all ingredients. Whirl at top speed
until smooth and blended. Pour in a tall glass and serve at once.
        Makes 1 serving

CREAMY EGGNOG

6 eggs
⅔ cup sugar
¼ teaspoon salt
2 tall cans (13 fl. oz. each) **PET® Evaporated Milk**
2 cups heavy cream
4 tablespoons vanilla
2 to 3 tablespoons rum flavoring or ½ cup rum
Nutmeg or cinnamon

Beat eggs, sugar, and salt in 3-quart mixing bowl. Mix in evaporated milk, cream, vanilla and rum. Chill. Pour into punch bowl.
Sprinkle with nutmeg or cinnamon.   *Makes 2 quarts*

CHIQUITA® BA-NOG-ANANA

3 large eggs
3 tablespoons honey
1 ripe **CHIQUITA® banana**
1 cup half & half cream
1 teaspoon rum flavoring
6½ oz. sparkling water (if desired)*
Nutmeg

Combine eggs with honey and sliced bananas in blender at high speed until smooth. Blend in cream and rum flavoring. Pour over ice. Sprinkle with nutmeg and serve.　　　*Yield: 3 cups*

*This nog is good diluted with sparkling water for those watching calories.

HOLIDAY APRICOT NOG
(Low Calorie)

1 (8-oz.) can **S&W® NUTRADIET® White Label**
　Apricots (halves), undrained
⅔ cup non-fat dry milk
1 tsp. vanilla extract
4-6 ice cubes
Pinch nutmeg

Place apricots, dry milk and vanilla extract in the blender. Blend for 15-20 seconds; add ice cubes, one at a time and blend after each addition. Serve in mugs or high-ball glasses and sprinkle with nutmeg.　　　*Serves 2*

　Each serving equals approximately:
　　1 fruit exchange
　　1 milk exchange
　　120 calories
　　22 g carbohydrate
　　Trace of Fat
　　8 g protein

MARASCHINO CHERRY PINK EGG NOG

4 eggs
1⅔ cups water
⅓ cup red maraschino cherry syrup
⅔ cup nonfat dry milk solids
3 tablespoons sugar
¾ teaspoon rum extract
½ cup ice water
½ cup nonfat dry milk solids
½ cup red maraschino cherries

In electric blender, combine eggs, 1⅔ cups water, cherry syrup, ⅔ cup milk solids, sugar and rum extract. Blend until well mixed and frothy. Chill until serving time. In small bowl, combine ½ cup water and ½ cup milk solids, beat until stiff. Fold into egg mixture. Stir in cherries.　*Makes about 1½ quarts (6 servings)*

Favorite recipe from **Oregon Regional Sweet Cherry Commission**

LIME SODA

　¼ cup **REALIME® Reconstituted Lime Juice**
3 tablespoons sugar
2 scoops lime sherbet
Club soda, chilled

In tall glass, stir together **REALIME®** and sugar until sugar dissolves. Add sherbet; fill glass with club soda. Stir. Serve immediately.　　　*Makes 1 serving*

VANILLA MILKSHAKE
(Low Calorie)

⅓ cup instant non-fat dry milk
1 cup ice water
2 packets **SWEET 'N LOW®**
1 teaspoon vanilla

Combine all ingredients in blender container. Cover and process at high speed about 30 seconds, or until frothy.　　*1 serving*

VARIATIONS:

Substitute 1 teaspoon instant coffee granules for vanilla. Substitute 1 teaspoon cocoa powder for vanilla. Add ½ cup fresh fruit before processing.

　PER SERVING (1 cup):　Calories: 88　Protein: 8g
　Carbohydrate: 13g　　Fat: trace　Sodium: 120mg

YOUR BASIC SHAKE
(Low Calorie)

1 (12-oz.) can **DIET SHASTA®** (any flavor)
⅓ cup instant nonfat dry milk
½ cup fresh fruit*
⅛ teaspoon artificial sweetener (or to taste)
½ teaspoon vanilla extract
Salt to taste
¼ teaspoon extract**
1 cup coarsely crushed ice (about 12 cubes)

Combine all ingredients in top of blender. Whirl at high speed until frothy and blended.　　*Makes about 1 quart*

*Your choice to complement soda flavor used, such as strawberries, raspberries, blueberries, oranges, pineapple, cantaloupe or rhubarb (cooked).
**Your choice to complement soda and fruit flavors, such as lemon, almond, strawberry, pineapple, rum or brandy extracts.

　46 calories per serving

CREAM SHAKE

In a tall glass blend in . . . 1 carton of your favorite **BORDEN® LITE-LINE® Fruit Yogurt** and 1 large scoop **BORDEN® Vanilla Ice Cream**. Top with additional ice cream if desired.

AMBROSIA SHAKE

2 cups boiling water
6 **LIPTON® Almond Pleasure Herbal Tea Bags**
¼ cup sugar
2 medium bananas
2 cups (1 pt.) vanilla ice cream
1½ cups ice cubes (about 9 to 11)
1 can (8 oz.) crushed pineapple in natural juice,
　drained
Flaked coconut

In teapot, pour boiling water over **Almond Pleasure Herbal Tea Bags**; cover and brew 5 minutes. Remove tea bags; stir in sugar and cool.
　In blender, combine tea, bananas and ice cream; process at high speed until blended. Add ice cubes, one at a time; process at high speed until blended. Top with pineapple, coconut, and, if desired, additional ice cream.　　*Makes about 4 servings*

NAPOLI FRUIT SHAKE

Combine in blender container:
2 cups DEL MONTE Pineapple-Grapefruit Juice Drink
1 can (8 oz.) DEL MONTE Fruit Cocktail
2 cups vanilla ice cream

Cover and blend until smooth. Garnish with nutmeg.

MOCHA FLOAT

2½ cups milk, scalded
2½ cups hot coffee
SEALTEST® Heavenly Hash Ice Cream

Combine milk and coffee; chill. Gradually add to 1 cup ice cream stirring until smooth. Place scoop of ice cream in each glass; fill with coffee mixture. Garnish with whipped cream, if desired.

6 to 8 servings

BRAZILIAN ICED CHOCOLATE

2 squares (1 oz. each) unsweetened chocolate
¼ cup sugar
1 cup double strength hot coffee
2½ cups milk
1½ cups COCA-COLA®
Whipped cream or ice cream

Melt chocolate in top of double boiler over hot water. Stir in sugar. Gradually stir in hot coffee, mixing thoroughly. Add milk and continue cooking until all particles of chocolate are dissolved and mixture is smooth, about 10 minutes. Pour into jar, cover and chill. When ready to serve, stir in chilled **COCA-COLA®**. Serve over ice cubes in tall glasses. For a beverage, top with whipped cream. For a dessert, add a scoop of vanilla ice cream.

Makes 5 cups

FIZZLER-ON-THE-ROCKS

Pour **SUNSWEET® Prune Juice** into ice cube trays and freeze. Use to chill carbonated beverages you serve—sparkling cider, ginger ale, colas, lemon-lime or orange-flavored sodas.

VERY BERRY STRAWBERRY

2 cups water
5 BIGELOW Cinnamon Stick® Tea Bags (or 6 level tsp. Cinnamon Stick® Instant Tea)
1 pkg. (16-oz.) frozen strawberries, partially thawed (or 2 pints fresh strawberries, chopped in food processor)
1 qt. frozen strawberry yogurt
2 cups club soda
6 fresh strawberries

To prepare **Cinnamon Stick®** tea base:
Tea bags: Place **Cinnamon Stick® Tea Bags** in warmed teapot. Pour in 2 cups freshly boiled water. Cover. Steep 7 minutes. Discard tea bags. Stir. Let cool.

Instant tea: Dissolve **Cinnamon Stick® Instant Tea** in 2 cups cold water.

Pour **Cinnamon Stick®** tea base into 3 qt. pitcher. At serving time, add strawberries to tea base. Stir. Then stir in yogurt and club soda. Pour into chilled glasses. Garnish with fresh strawberry in each glass. Serve immediately.

Serves six

"CONSTANT COMMENT"® PUNCH

4 cups boiling water
4 BIGELOW "Constant Comment"® Teabags
2 cans (6-ounces each) frozen lemonade
2 cans (6-ounces each) frozen orange juice
2 quarts ginger ale or 2 bottles (750 ml each) champagne
1 jar cherries (optional)
1 can (12-ounces) crushed pineapple with juice
2 pints orange *ice* sherbet

In saucepan, bring water to boil; add tea, cover, steep for 5 minutes. Remove teabags. Cool tea; then chill. Just before serving time, combine remaining ingredients with tea into a punch bowl.

Makes about 5 quarts

Note: For a more festive punch, substitute champagne for ginger ale.

FRUITED TEA COOLER

1 cup LIPTON® Lemon Flavored Iced Tea Mix with NutraSweet™
1½ quarts water
¼ cup lime juice
1½ cups sliced fresh fruit
Club soda, chilled

In large pitcher, combine all ingredients except soda. Serve with ice; add splash of soda.

Makes about 8 servings

SUNBURST C™ PUNCH

6 CELESTIAL SEASONINGS® Sunburst C™ Teabags
2 cups boiling water
¼ cup honey
1 cup orange juice
2 cups ice cubes
2 cups chilled sparkling water
Paper thin orange wheels (optional)

Brew tea in boiling water for 5 minutes. Remove teabags. Stir in honey, then add orange juice and ice cubes. Stir until thoroughly chilled. Add sparkling water. Float paper thin orange wheels on top of punch.

Makes 6 servings

CINNAMONY STRAWBERRY PUNCH

1 package strawberry gelatin (3-oz. size)
3 cups boiling water
8 bags MAGIC MOUNTAIN™ Sweet Cinnamon Spice Herb Tea
1 small can frozen limeade
3 canfuls cold water
1 quart ginger ale

Dissolve gelatin in boiling water, in bowl or quart jar. Stir or shake to be sure granules are totally dissolved. Drop eight bags **Sweet Cinnamon Spice Herb Tea** into hot mixture. (Remove tags before adding). Steep 10 minutes. Remove tea bags. In separate container, dissolve limeade in water. Add gelatin mixture and stir to blend. Chill till ready to serve.

To serve: fill punch bowl with ice, or use ice block. (To prevent dilution of punch, use ice cubes or ice frozen in milk cartons made of double strength **Sweet Cinnamon Spice Herb Tea**.) Pour punch mixture over ice. Add ginger ale just before serving. Garnish with whole strawberries.

Serves 14

ROSY CITRUS PUNCH

6 cups Florida orange juice, chilled
3 cups Florida grapefruit juice, chilled
2 tablespoons grenadine
1 tablespoon honey
2 Florida oranges, thinly sliced
1 bottle (23-ounces) sparkling water, chilled

In a large bowl combine orange juice, grapefruit juice, grenadine and honey. Stir to dissolve honey. Add orange slices. Before serving, add sparkling water.

Yield: About 3 quarts, 24 (4-ounce) servings

Favorite recipe from **Florida Department of Citrus**

THE PARTY PLEASER

¾ cup **LIPTON**® Lemon Flavored Iced Tea Mix with NutraSweet™
4 cups water
3 cups cranberry juice cocktail
1 bottle (28-oz.) ginger ale, chilled

In punch bowl, combine lemon flavored iced tea mix, water and cranberry juice; chill. Just before serving, add ginger ale. Serve in ice-filled glasses. *Makes about 35 (5-oz.) servings*

Nonalcoholic — Hot

EASY HOT CHOCOLATE MIX

1 cup **GHIRARDELLI**® Ground Chocolate
1½ cups nonfat dry milk

Mix Ground Chocolate with dry milk. Store dry mixture in can or heavy plastic bag. To make hot chocolate, fill each mug half full of chocolate mix. Stir in boiling water. Top with marshmallows, if desired. *Makes 8 servings*

HOT DR PEPPER®

DR PEPPER®
Thin lemon slices

Pour **DR PEPPER**® into saucepan. Heat to simmering temperature, about 180 degrees F or just below boiling point. (The beverage will appear to be boiling long before it is hot due to the carbonation.) Place a thin slice of fresh lemon in bottom of cup and pour steaming hot **DR PEPPER**® over it.

Serve at once. This drink will be hot—sipping hot—or should be about 170 degrees F when ready to drink.

Note: A fresh slice of lemon is required to give the proper taste of Hot **DR PEPPER**®.

HERSHEY'S® FAVORITE HOT COCOA

SINGLE SERVING: Combine 1 heaping teaspoon **HERSHEY'S**® **Cocoa**, 2 heaping teaspoons sugar and dash salt in mug; add 2 teaspoons milk and stir until smooth. Heat 1 cup milk; fill mug. Stir and serve.

FOUR SERVINGS: Combine ⅓ cup **HERSHEY'S**® **Cocoa**, ½ cup sugar, dash salt in saucepan; blend in ⅓ cup hot water. Bring to boil over medium heat, stirring constantly; boil and stir 2 minutes. Add 1 quart milk; stir and heat. Do NOT boil. Remove from heat; add ¾ teaspoon vanilla. Beat with rotary beater until foamy. *About 1 quart or 4 servings*

"CONSTANT COMMENT"® SPICED FRUIT TODDY

2 cups water
5 **BIGELOW "Constant Comment"® Teabags**
½ cup orange juice
1 cup apple juice
¼ tsp. cinnamon
2 tablespoons sugar

In saucepan, bring water to boil; add tea, cover, steep for 7 minutes. Remove teabags. Stir in orange juice, apple juice, and sugar. Sprinkle cinnamon in slowly while heating to serving temperature. Pour into heated mugs. Garnish with a cinnamon stick or apple slice. *Makes 4-6 servings*

HOT JUICE/CIDER

6 cups apple juice/cider
1-2 sticks cinnamon
½ tsp. whole cloves

Heat in saucepan until simmer or perk in coffee pot putting spices in coffee pot basket.

VARIATIONS:

Add a twist of lemon or add 1 can (6-oz.) frozen lemonade concentrate or eliminate spices and add ⅛ cup red cinnamon candies.

Favorite recipe from **Michigan Apple Committee**

MEXICANO OLÉ

1½ cups strong hot coffee
4 teaspoons sugar
¼ teaspoon **DURKEE Ground Cinnamon**
2 tablespoons **DURKEE Chocolate Extract**

Combine all ingredients and pour into small cups. Top with spicy whipped topping.* *Makes 3 to 4 servings*

*SPICY WHIPPED TOPPING

1 cup frozen whipped topping, thawed
¼ teaspoon **DURKEE Ground Cinnamon**
⅛ teaspoon **DURKEE Ground Nutmeg**

Combine all ingredients.

Alcoholic — Cold

CHAMPAGNE FLOAT

6 tall float glasses
½ gallon French vanilla ice cream
2 cups fresh raspberries (or substitute sliced strawberries)
1 bottle **KORBEL Extra Dry Champagne**

Alternate layers of ice cream and raspberries in the float glasses until they are ¾ full. Fill the remaining ¼ with Champagne. *Serves 6*

BEEFED-UP BLOODY MARY

2 cans (12 ounces *each*) **CAMPBELL'S Tomato Juice**
1 can (10½-ounces) **CAMPBELL'S Condensed Beef
  Consommé**
2 tablespoons lemon juice
1 tablespoon Worcestershire Sauce
Dash celery salt
Dash hot pepper sauce
1 cup vodka
Crushed ice

1. In 1½-quart pitcher, combine all ingredients except ice. Cover and refrigerate until chilled.
2. To serve: Stir mixture; pour over ice into six (10-ounce) highball glasses. Garnish with lemon wedges, if desired. Serve immediately. *Makes 5½ cups or 6 servings*

BLOODY BULLSHOT

In 8-oz. glass, pour 1½ oz. **SMIRNOFF® Vodka** over ice. Add dash *each* celery salt, Worcestershire sauce and hot sauce. Fill glass with 1½ oz. beef broth and 3½ oz. tomato juice. Garnish with scallion curl.

PICKLE SWIZZLES

Cut **CLAUSSEN Pickle** halves lengthwise into thirds and use the pickle sticks as swizzles.

BRANDY ALEXANDER

1 oz. **LEROUX Creme de Cacao (brown)**
1 oz. heavy cream
1 oz. **LEROUX Deluxe Brandy**

Shake with ice and strain.

CAMPARI® SPARKLER

A glass of **ALMADÉN Champagne.**
A splash of **CAMPARI®.**
A sliver of lemon peel.

CocoRibe® COLADA

4 ounces pineapple juice
3 ounces **CocoRibe® Coconut Rum**
3 small scoops vanilla ice cream

Combine all ingredients in container of electric blender. Cover. Blend until smooth and frothy. Serve in cocktail glass. Garnish with pineapple chunk and fresh mint. *Yield: 1 serving*

FRANGELICO® FRAPPE

¾ oz. **FRANGELICO® Liqueur**
¾ oz. vodka
Crushed ice
¾ oz. vanilla ice cream, softened
¾ oz. cream
Ground nutmeg

Place all ingredients in a shaker cup, and shake. Pour into champagne glass and garnish with nutmeg.

Note: Also good with a squirt of **KAHLÚA®** or **TIA MARIA®** when the amount of **FRANGELICO®** is increased to 1¼ oz.

CHOCOLATE MINT FLIP

6 cups water
6 **BIGELOW Plantation Mint® Tea Bags** (or 6 rounded tsp. **Plantation Mint® Instant Tea**)
3 rounded Tbsp. sugar
12 Tbsp. chocolate syrup
6 Tbsp. chocolate flavored liqueur
1 qt. chocolate chip ice cream
12 Tbsp. club soda
Optional garnish: 6 sprigs of fresh mint

To prepare **Plantation Mint®** tea base:
  Tea bags: Place tea bags in warmed teapot. Pour in 6 cups freshly boiled water. Cover. Steep 7 minutes. Discard tea bags. Add sugar. Stir. Let cool.
  Instant tea: Dissolve **Plantation Mint® Instant Tea** and sugar in 6 cups cold water.
  Pour **Plantation Mint®** tea base into 2 qt. pitcher. Add chocolate syrup and liqueur. Stir. Chill. Stir again, and pour into 6 stemmed glasses. Add 1 scoop of ice cream and 2 Tbsp. club soda to each glass. Garnish with mint sprig—serve with spoon and a straw. *Serves six*

CRANBERRY CORDIAL

1½ cups **OCEAN SPRAY® Cranberrry Juice Cocktail**
¼ cup sugar
½ cup vodka

In a saucepan, mix together cranberry juice cocktail and sugar. Bring to a boil; boil for 10 minutes. Cool. Stir in vodka and pour into bottles. Chill until ready to serve. *Makes about 2 cups*

COFFEE CORDIAL ON THE ROCKS

3 tablespoons **SANKA® Brand Instant 97% Caffeine Free Coffee**
¼ cup sugar
3 cups cold water
¼ cup brandy or rum
Crushed ice or ice cubes
6 strips orange peel

Measure coffee and sugar into pitcher. Add water and brandy; stir until coffee and sugar are dissolved. Pour over crushed ice in old-fashioned glasses. Twist strips of peel, on skewer, if desired; add to each glass. *Makes about 3 cups or 6 servings*

COFFEE FRANGELICO®

¾ oz. **KAHLÚA® Coffee Liqueur**
2 tsp. **FRANGELICO® Liqueur**
¾ oz. vodka
3 oz. crushed ice

Combine **KAHLÚA®, FRANGELICO®** and vodka. Stir well. Pour over ice and serve in old fashioned glass.

BAILEYS IRISH ICED COFFEE

Fill a glass with ice, and pour cool coffee so the glass is ⅔ full. Fill glass with **BAILEYS Irish Cream Liqueur** and top with whipped cream.

BRANDIED MEXICAN CHOCOLATE

1 cup instant chocolate-flavored beverage powder
1 teaspoon ground cinnamon
¾ cup water
3 cups half and half
2 cups **THE CHRISTIAN BROTHERS®** Brandy
¾ cup amaretto
Cinnamon sticks

In large bowl whisk together chocolate beverage powder, ground cinnamon and water until smooth. Stir in half and half, brandy and amaretto. Cover and chill. Stir before serving. Ladle over ice into stemmed glasses. Or, heat just to boiling; pour into small cups. Serve with cinnamon stick stirrers.

Makes 12 servings (about 4½ ounces each)

FINNEGAN'S FIZZ

2-3 ounces **WATERFORD CREAM™** Liqueur
2 ounces club soda or seltzer

Add a few ice cubes in a chilled 8-ounce highball glass. Pour in **WATERFORD CREAM™**. Add splash of club soda; stir well. Add remaining soda and stir quickly. Serve with straws.

FIREFLY

In cocktail glass, pour 1½ oz. **SMIRNOFF®** Vodka over ice. Add 4 oz. grapefruit juice and generous dash of grenadine to make firefly glow.

FRAPPE FANTASTIQUE

Into champagne glass of shaved ice, pour 1 oz. **LEROUX White Creme de Menthe**, 1 oz. **LEROUX Brown Creme de Cacao**.

GRASSHOPPER

1 oz. **MILNOT®**
1 oz. creme de cacao (white)
1 oz. creme de menthe (green)
⅓ cup crushed ice

Blend for 15 seconds on low speed. Serve in chilled glass.

TEA MINT JULEP

1 oz. **LEROUX Spearmint Schnapps**
6 oz. hot tea

Pour **LEROUX Spearmint Schnapps** into a mug or stemmed glass, fill with hot tea, flavor with sugar and lemon to taste.

"THE BIG APPLE" MANHATTAN

In cocktail shaker with ice, blend 2 oz. **LEROUX Apple Flavored Brandy** and 1 oz. Sweet Vermouth with dash of bitters. Serve in cocktail glass garnished with unpeeled apple slice.

PINK SLIPPER

½ cup cream of coconut
⅓ cup **REALIME®** Reconstituted Lime Juice
⅓ cup light rum
2 tablespoons grenadine syrup
4 cups ice cubes

In blender container, combine cream of coconut, **REALIME®**, rum and grenadine; blend well. Gradually add ice, blending until smooth. Serve immediately. Garnish as desired.

Makes about 4 cups

PINK SQUIRREL

1½ oz. **LEROUX Creme de Noya**
1½ oz. **LEROUX White Creme de Cacao**
1½ oz. light cream

Shake with ice cubes.

FROZEN MARGARITA

1½ oz. **TWO FINGERS®** Tequila
½ oz. **HIRAM WALKER Triple Sec Liqueur**
½ oz. lime juice

Combine in blender with cracked ice. Serve in on-the-rocks glass with salted rim.

CUERVO® MARGARITA

1½ oz. **JOSE CUERVO®** Tequila
1½ oz. **ARROW®** Triple Sec Liqueur
1 oz. lemon juice (or lime juice)

Mix ingredients, shake with shaved ice and serve in salt-rimmed glass.*

*To prepare salt rim on glass, dip edge of glass ½ inch deep into lime juice, then into coarse salt. Let dry at room temperature.

THE ROSE'S® MARGUERITA

Mix 1½ oz. White Tequila, 1 oz. **ROSE'S®** Lime Juice, ½ oz. Triple Sec. Shake with crushed ice and strain into Marguerita glass edged with salt. For an easy way to edge the glass, pour ½ oz. **ROSE'S®** Lime Juice into a saucer, dip glass edge into the **Lime Juice**, then dip into another saucer of Marguerita salt.

GALLIANO MARGARITA

½ oz. **LIQUORE GALLIANO®**
1½ oz. Tequila
2 oz. Sweet and Sour Mix, or Margarita Mix
(1 oz. fresh lime or lemon juice may also be used)

Blend or shake with ice and pour into champagne glass. Salt rim if desired.

OLD FASHIONED

1 jigger rye whiskey
2 dashes **ANGOSTURA®** Aromatic Bitters
1 tablespoon **GIROUX®** Grenadine Syrup
1 ice cube
Garnish: orange and lemon slices, maraschino cherry, twist of lemon rind

Combine all ingredients except garnish and stir well. Add one of the above garnishes.

SHAGGY DOG

Combine:

3 ice cubes in old fashioned glass
1 jigger gin
2 jiggers **DR PEPPER®**
½ jigger grenadine
Dash of lemon juice

Serve with lemon twist.

SIDEWINDER

2 ounces **WATERFORD CREAM™ Liqueur**
¾ ounce **FINLANDIA® Vodka**
½ ounce triple sec
Melon ball, strawberry, pineapple chunk

Shake liquid ingredients briskly with ice. Strain into chilled old fashioned glass over fresh ice cube. Thread fruit on bamboo skewer and place in glass, fruit end up.

KIRSCH SLING

To 1 oz. **LEROUX Kirschwasser** and 2 oz. **BOODLES British Gin** add ½ oz. **CLARISTINE Liqueur** and the juice of 1 lemon. Sugar to taste, add a dash of bitters, pour into iced tea glass with ice and add club soda.

SMITH & KEARNS

1 oz. **MILNOT®**
1 oz. **KAHLÚA® Coffee Liqueur**
2 oz. club soda

Blend ingredients. Serve over ice in chilled glass.

APRICOT SOURBALL

Pack an on-the-rocks glass with ice, add 1½ oz. **HIRAM WALKER Apricot Flavored Brandy**. Top with juices of half a lemon and half an orange. Stir.

SPRITZER

½ cup dry white wine, chilled
1 tablespoon **GIROUX® Grenadine Syrup**
Carbonated water to fill glass
Ice cubes

To an 8-ounce glass add ingredients and stir gently.

CELLA SPRITZER

4 oz. **CELLA Lambrusco Italian Light Red Wine**
4 oz. club soda
Lemon twist

Serve with ice.

CUERVO® SUNRISE (ORIGINAL)

1½ oz. **JOSE CUERVO® Tequila**
½ oz. lime juice
3 oz. orange juice
½ oz. grenadine

Shake ingredients together; serve in tall glass of ice. Garnish with lime.

TEQUILA SUNRISE

1½ ounces tequila
4 ounces orange juice
¾ ounce **GIROUX® Grenadine Syrup**
Ice cubes

Pour tequila and orange juice over ice. Stir. Add **GIROUX® Grenadine**. Let it sink to the bottom. Watch the sunrise.

8-ounce glass

STINGER

1 part **LEROUX White Creme de Menthe**, 2 parts **LEROUX Deluxe Brandy**. Shake over ice. Strain.

TOASTED ALMOND

Mix 2 ounces **LEROUX Coffee Amaretto** and 2 ounces milk together over ice cubes in an old fashioned on-the-rocks glass.

BANANA SPLIT

1½ oz. **HIRAM WALKER Swiss Chocolate Almond Liqueur**
½ oz. **HIRAM WALKER Creme de Banana Liqueur**
3 oz. cream

Blend with cracked ice and pour into on-the-rocks glass.

CHERRY DOUBLER

Add 1½ oz. **LEROUX Cherry Flavored Brandy** to your favorite cherry-flavored soda, serve in tall glass with ice and fresh mint.

BAILEYS CHOCOLATE CHIPPER

Pour **BAILEYS Irish Cream Liqueur** over crushed ice and top with shaved chocolate.

CRANBERRY SLUSH

In blender, crush 1 cup ice cubes. Add 2 oz. **BOGGS® Cranberry Liqueur**, 1 oz. lemon juice and 1 teaspoon sugar. Blend. Pour in stemmed glass.

COMFORT® COOLER

2 oz. **SOUTHERN COMFORT®**
½ large fresh lime
2 oz. fresh grapefruit juice

Pour **SOUTHERN COMFORT®** over crushed ice in a tall cooler glass. Add juice of lime and grapefruit juice, stirring gently. Mellow for half minute as frost builds on glass. Add a thick plastic straw and float a maraschino cherry on top.

PINEAPPLE BRANDY FROST

1½ ounces California brandy
2 tablespoons undiluted frozen pineapple juice concentrate
½ cup finely crushed ice
2 scoops (⅔ cup) lemon sherbet
Pineapple spear

Combine brandy and pineapple juice concentrate in blender jar and blend smooth. Add ice, and blend until ice is very fine. Add sherbet and blend smooth. Pour into 12-ounce glass and garnish with pineapple spear. *Makes 1 serving*

Favorite recipe from **California Brandy Advisory Board**

CHENIN BLANC HIGHBALL

Fill an 8-ounce glass with 4 ounces of **ALMADÉN Chenin Blanc Wine**. Add 2 ounces soda water and 2 ounces orange juice. Garnish with a maraschino cherry.

WHITE WINE COOLER
(Rinfrescante al vino bianco)

½ cup black currant liqueur
3 cups BERTOLLI® Soave Wine
2 cups crushed ice
Sparkling water

Pour 2 tablespoons liqueur in 4 tall glasses; tilt glasses to coat with liqueur. Pour wine into glasses; stir gently. Add ice; top with sparkling water. *Makes 4 servings*

BEER COCKTAILS

BLACK VELVET

Fill a tall glass with half **COORS®** and half champagne.

SHANDYGAFF

Fill a tall glass with half **COORS®** and half ginger ale.

RED BEER

Fill a tall glass with half **COORS®** and half tomato juice.

BEER BUSTER

Add a jigger of gin or vodka to a cold, tall glass of **COORS®**. Add a dash or two of bottled hot pepper sauce.

INDIBEER

Fill a tall glass with half **COORS®** and half orange juice; season with a little curry powder.

BOILERMAKER

Serve a jigger of rye whiskey alongside a cold, tall glass of **COORS®**.

CUP OF GOLD

Spike a cold, tall glass of **COORS®** with a jigger of gin or vodka, a jigger of lime juice, and a little superfine sugar.

BLOODY BULL IN ICE

Combine 3 cups tomato juice, 2 teaspoons Worcestershire sauce, and several dashes bottled hot pepper sauce; pour into ice cube tray. Place a quartered lemon slice into each cube section of tray. Freeze. To serve, fill tall glass with frozen cubes; pour in **COORS®** to fill glass.

LAGER AND LIME

Stir 1 to 2 tablespoons lime juice into a cold, tall glass of **COORS®**.

CRANBERRY SANGRIA

6 cups (48 ounces) OCEAN SPRAY® Cranberry Juice Cocktail
3 cups red sweet wine
1 orange, sliced
1 lemon, sliced
Sugar to taste

In a tall pitcher, mix together cranberry juice cocktail, wine and sliced fruits. Sweeten to taste. Chill several hours to blend flavors. Serve in large wine glasses with fruit. *Makes 12 servings*

SANGAREE COCKTAIL

3 oz. PAUL MASSON® Madeira Wine
1½ oz. lemon and orange juice, combined
Slice of orange
Crushed ice

Fill a twelve-ounce glass with crushed ice. Add Madeira and fruit juice. Stir to mix and garnish with orange slice.

SANGRIA

1 bottle red wine
½ cup sugar
½ cup lemon juice
1 orange, thinly sliced
1 lemon, thinly sliced
1 oz. ARROW® Triple Sec Liqueur
1 oz. brandy
1 bottle (7-oz.) club soda, chilled

Combine all ingredients, except club soda, in pitcher. Chill. Just before serving add club soda. *Serves 4*

LIGHT SANGRIA

5 cups SOUVERAIN® Chardonnay
2 cups chilled club soda
¼ cup DRY SACK® Sherry
½ cup sugar
1 orange, thinly sliced
1 lemon, thinly sliced
1 apple, cut in wedges
6 maraschino cherries with stems

In a large pitcher combine **SOUVERAIN® Chardonnay**, club soda, **DRY SACK® Sherry** and sugar; stir until sugar dissolves. Mix in orange, lemon, apple and cherries. Serve chilled with ice cubes if desired. *Makes 2 quarts*

FIVE ALIVE™ SANGRIA

1 orange, thinly sliced
1 lemon, thinly sliced
1 lime, thinly sliced
½ cup granulated sugar
1 bottle (5th) TAYLOR® California Cellars Chablis
1 carton (32 oz.) SNOW CROP® FIVE ALIVE™ Fruit Beverage
½ cup apricot brandy

Place the sliced fruit in large pitcher. Add the sugar and mash with spoon to release juice from fruit. Add the wine, **FIVE ALIVE™** and brandy. Mix well and chill. Serve over ice, if desired, and garnish with additional fruit slices.
Makes 16 servings (about ½ cup each)

SANGRIA CUP

¼ cup **LIPTON® 100% Instant Tea** Powder
½ cup sugar
1 bottle (⅘ qt.) rosé wine
1 cup sliced strawberries
1 orange, sliced
½ lemon, sliced
2 bottles (7 oz. ea.) club soda, chilled

In large pitcher, mix 100% instant tea powder with sugar. Stir in wine and fruit. Just before serving, add soda. Serve with ice.
Makes about 5 servings

WHITE SANGRIA

1 cup sugar
1 (8-ounce) bottle **REALIME® Lime Juice from Concentrate**, chilled
1 (750mL) bottle sauterne, chilled
2 tablespoons orange-flavored liqueur
1 (32-ounce) bottle club soda, chilled
Orange slices, optional

In pitcher, dissolve sugar in **REALIME®**; stir in sauterne and orange-flavored liqueur. Just before serving, add club soda and orange slices. Serve over ice.   *Makes about 2 quarts*

SPICED RUM PUNCH

750 ml **CAPTAIN MORGAN Spiced Rum**
6 oz. pineapple juice
Juice of 6 oranges
Juice of 6 lemons
¾ cup powdered sugar
1½ quarts ginger ale

Combine in a large bowl and stir well. Chill with a block of ice. Garnish with orange and lemon slices and maraschino cherries.
Makes approximately 22 servings

FESTIVE PUNCH

1 can (6-oz.) frozen grapefruit juice concentrate
1 can (12-oz.) apricot nectar
½ cup sugar
2 cups **SMIRNOFF® Vodka 100°**, chilled
1 bottle (32-oz.) club soda, chilled
Fresh mint leaves

Combine grapefruit juice concentrate, apricot nectar and sugar. Stir until sugar is dissolved. In punch bowl, pour juice mixture over ice. Add vodka and club soda. Garnish with mint leaves. If desired, a few mint leaves may be crushed in small amount of juice mixture and added to punch.   *Makes 16 servings*

LAMBRUSCO BOWL
(Coppa di Lambrusco)

1 scoop vanilla ice cream
1 scoop raspberry sherbet
½ cup fresh or thawed frozen raspberries
½ cup **BERTOLLI® Lambrusco Wine**
½ cup grape soda

Process all ingredients in blender until smooth; pour into glass or bowl. Add 1 scoop vanilla ice cream. Serve with 2 straws.
Makes 2 servings

FESTIVE CHAMPAGNE PUNCH

2 cups **SEBASTIANI VINEYARDS Champagne**
1 (13½-oz.) can pineapple, chunks or crushed
2 small cans frozen pink lemonade, thawed
1 large bottle soda water
½ cup maraschino cherry syrup

Combine all ingredients and chill well.
Recipe will serve about 15

EGG NOG

3 eggs, separated
¼ cup sugar
½ cup **DUNPHY'S Cream Liqueur**
1½ cups heavy cream
Nutmeg
Orange peel

Beat together egg yolks and sugar until thick and lemon colored. Gradually beat in **DUNPHY'S Cream Liqueur** and heavy cream. Beat egg whites until stiff peaks form; fold into yolk mixture. Chill before serving. Sprinkle with nutmeg and garnish with orange peel to serve.   *Makes 4 servings*

Note: Recipe can be doubled or tripled to make larger quantities.

ESPRESSO EGGNOG

Separate 3 eggs. In a large mixing bowl, beat the yolks, adding ¾ cup sugar gradually, until mixture is light-colored. Add 2 cups of half-and-half, then 2 cups of cooled **MEDAGLIA D'ORO® Espresso Coffee**. Beat egg whites stiff, but not dry. Fold gently into yolks. Gently stir in 1 cup of brandy and 1 cup of coffee-flavored liqueur. Transfer to a punch bowl. Float scoops of coffee ice cream (one pint in all). Garnish with dusting of cinnamon and ¼ cup of shaved chocolate.   *Makes 8 to 12 servings*

Alcoholic — Hot

BRANDY HOT TODDY

1 jigger light rum
1 jigger **PAUL MASSON® Brandy**
1 teaspoon sugar
Hot water
Lemon and cloves

Combine the sugar, rum and brandy in a glass. Fill with hot water. Stir and top with lemon and clove.

CAPISTRANO COFFEE

1½ oz. California brandy
1 teaspoon chocolate syrup
1 teaspoon brown sugar
¼ teaspoon vanilla
Dash cinnamon
6 oz. hot coffee
Sweetened whipped cream

Stir brandy, chocolate syrup, sugar, vanilla and cinnamon together in 10-ounce serving glass or cup. Pour in hot coffee. Top with sweetened whipped cream.   *Serves 1*

Favorite recipe from **California Brandy Advisory Board**

BRANDY EGGNOG

1 egg
1 teaspoon sugar
⅔ jigger rum
⅔ jigger **PAUL MASSON®** Brandy
Hot milk
Nutmeg

In a preheated highball glass mix together egg and sugar. Add rum and brandy, then fill with hot milk. Sprinkle nutmeg over top.

HEARTY TODDY

Put 1 clove, bit of cinnamon stick and lemon twist in mug. Add a jigger of **LEROUX Irish Moss**. Fill with boiling water.

CAPPUCINO
(Tosca Cafe)

1 oz. **PAUL MASSON®** Brandy
½ tsp. sugar
½ tsp. cocoa powder
2 oz. Italian roast coffee
2 oz. half-and-half
Whipped cream (optional)
Ground cinnamon (optional)

Combine sugar and cocoa; put in warmed glass or mug. Pour in coffee and half-and-half. Add brandy. (If desired, top with whipped cream and cinnamon.)

AMARETTO DI AMORE® EXPRESSO

1 oz. **AMARETTO DI AMORE®** Liqueur
6 oz. hot expresso coffee
Sliver of orange or lemon peel
Sugar

Stir **AMARETTO DI AMORE®** into hot expresso coffee. Serve with a sliver of orange or lemon peel and sugar.   *2 servings*

ESPRESSO CREMA

Place 1 tablespoon of Irish Cream Liqueur in a heatproof mug or demitasse cup. Fill with hot **MEDAGLIA D'ORO®** Espresso **Coffee** and top with whipped cream.

COFFEE ROYALE

For each drink, place 1 jigger of **KORBEL Brandy** in a heat-proof glass or mug. Fill with hot, black coffee and sweeten to taste with sugar. Top with a float of whipped cream.

JOHN JAMESON IRISH COFFEE

Put 1 teaspoon of brown sugar in a stemmed glass or mug. Fill to within an inch of the brim with hot black coffee. Add 1½-oz. **JOHN JAMESON Irish Whiskey** and stir. Top off with lightly whipped cream. (Float it in gently over the back of a spoon.)

HOT CHOCOLATE WOWEE

Just add 1 oz. **LEROUX Creme de Cacao (brown)** to your favorite hot chocolate recipe and top with marshmallow or whipped cream.

LACED BRAZILIAN MOCHA

¼ cup instant coffee
1 square (1-oz.) unsweetened chocolate cut up
¾ cup hot water
¼ cup sugar
Dash of salt
1 cup milk
1 cup light cream
¼ cup **BÉNÉDICTINE Liqueur**
Sweetened whipped cream

Combine instant coffee and chocolate in a deep saucepan. Add hot water; stir until chocolate is melted. Stir in sugar and salt. Bring mixture to a boil. Gently boil mixture about 5 minutes, stirring frequently.

Scald milk and cream. Stir into chocolate mixture. Remove from heat. Stir in **BÉNÉDICTINE**. Beat with rotary beater until frothy. Serve immediately topped with sweetened whipped cream.   *Serves 4*

COCOA CARA MIA™

2 tablespoons sugar
1 tablespoon unsweetened cocoa
1 cup milk
½ cup **CARA MIA™ Amaretto Cream Liqueur**
Whipped cream
2 cinnamon sticks

Combine sugar and cocoa in a medium saucepan. Beat in milk with a wire whip. Cook over medium high heat until just boiling, stirring constantly. Remove from heat. Stir in **CARA MIA™ Amaretto Cream Liqueur**. Pour into two 6-oz. serving cups. Garnish with whipped cream and cinnamon sticks.
       Makes 2 servings

MULLED WINE

1 bottle (750 ml) **SEBASTIANI VINEYARDS Zinfandel Wine**
2 cups apple juice
1 cup orange juice
1-2 cinnamon sticks
1 orange
Approximately 2 dozen cloves
1 Tbsp. honey

Stud orange with cloves and bake at 350°F for 30 minutes or in MICROWAVE set to *High* for 5 minutes. Combine all ingredients, including orange, in saucepan and simmer—do not boil—for about 15 minutes. Remove orange and cinnamon sticks before serving in cups or mugs.

BRANDY MULLED CIDER

2½ cups apple cider
1½ cups California brandy
¼ cup sugar
1 tablespoon lemon juice
¼ teaspoon ground cardamom
3 sticks cinnamon

In a saucepan combine apple cider, brandy, sugar, lemon juice, cardamom, and cinnamon. Heat until just simmering but do not boil. Remove from heat and cool. Pour with cinnamon into an attractive decanter or carafe and cork tightly.
       Makes about one quart

Favorite recipe from **California Brandy Advisory Board**

Acknowledgments

The Editors of CONSUMER GUIDE® wish to thank the companies and organizations listed for use of their recipes. For further information contact the following:

A.1., *see* Heublein Inc.

Ac'cent International, Inc.
Pet Incorporated
Pet Plaza, 400 S. Fourth St.
St. Louis, MO 63166

Adolph's®, *see* Chesebrough-Pond's Inc.

Alaska Seafood Marketing Institute, *see* Pacific Kitchens

Alba, *see* Heinz U.S.A.

Almadén Vineyards
P.O. Box 5010
San Jose, CA 95150

Amaretto Di Amore®, *see* Wile, Julius, Sons & Co., Inc.

Amaretto Di Saronno®—Foreign Vintages, Inc.
95 Madison Avenue
New York, NY 10016

Amaretto from Galliano®, *see* "21" Brands, Inc.

Amber Brand Smithfield, *see* Smithfield Ham and Products Co., The

American Beauty®, *see* Pillsbury Company, The

American Dairy Association
6300 N. River Rd.
Rosemont, IL 60018

American Egg Board
1460 Renaissance
Park Ridge, IL 60068

American Soybean Association
777 Craig Rd.
St. Louis, MO 63141

American Spice Trade Association, The
580 Sylvan Avenue
Englewood Cliffs, NJ 07632

Anderson Clayton Foods
P.O. Box 226165
Dallas, TX 75080

Angostura International Ltd.
1745 Elizabeth Ave.
Rahway, NJ 07065

Appian Way®, *see* Armour and Company

Argo®/Kingsford's®, *see* Best Foods

Armanino Farms of California
1945 Carroll Ave.
San Francisco, CA 94124

Armour and Company
111 W. Clarendon
Phoenix, AZ 85077

Arrow®, *see* Heublein Spirits Group

Aspen™—Spar, Inc.
803 Jefferson Highway
New Orleans, LA 70152

Association for Dressings and Sauces, The
5775 Peachtree-Dunwoody Road
Atlanta, GA 30342

Atalanta Corp.
17–25 Varick St.
New York, NY 10013

Aunt Nellie's Foods Inc.
P.O. Box 67
Clyman, WI 53016

Austin Nichols & Co. Inc.
1290 Avenue of the Americas
New York, NY 10104

Azar Nut Company
6975 Commerce Avenue
El Paso, TX 79915

Azteca Corn Products Corp.
4850 S. Austin
Chicago, IL 60638

Azumaya Inc.
1575 Burke Avenue
San Francisco, CA 94124

B&B, *see* Wile, Julius, Sons & Co., Inc.

B&M®, *see* Underwood, Wm., Company

Bac∗Os®, *see* General Mills, Inc.

Baileys—The Paddington Corporation
1290 Avenue of the Americas
New York, NY 10104

Baker's®, *see* General Foods

Baltimore Spice Company, The
P.O. Box 5858
Baltimore, MD 21208

Banana Bunch, The
40 W. 57th St.
New York, NY 10019

Banquet Foods Corp.
P.O. Box 70
Ballwin, MO 63011

Batterlite Whitlock Inc.
P.O. Box 259
Springfield, IL 62705

Bays Home Service Institute
500 N. Michigan Ave.
Chicago, IL 60611

Beatrice Confections
503 Martindale St.
Pittsburgh, PA 15212

Bell, William G., Co., The
167 Moore Rd.
East Weymouth, MA 02189

Bénédictine, *see* Wile, Julius, Sons & Co., Inc.

Bernstein's, *see* Nalley's Fine Foods

Bertolli U.S.A.
P.O. Box 931
So. San Francisco, CA 94080

Best Foods
Englewood Cliffs, NJ 07632

Betty Crocker®, *see* General Mills, Inc.

Bigelow, R. C., Inc.
15 Merwin St.
Norwalk, CT 06856

BinB®, *see* Pillsbury Company, The

Birds Eye®, *see* General Foods

Bisquick®, *see* General Mills, Inc.

Blue Diamond®—California Almond Growers Exchange
P.O. Box 1768
Sacramento, CA 95808

Blue Ribbon® Almonds—Continental Nut Company
P.O. Box 400
Chico, CA 95927

Blue Ribbon Rice—American Rice, Inc.
P.O. Box 2587
Houston, TX 77252

Bob Evans Farms
3776 S. High St.
Columbus, OH 43207

Boggs®, *see* Heublein Spirits Group

Bolla, *see* Garneau, Jos., Co.

Boodles, *see* General Wine & Spirit Co.

Booth Fisheries Corp.
2 North Riverside Plaza
Chicago, IL 60606

Borden Inc.
180 E. Broad St.
Columbus, OH 43215

Bordo Products Company
2825 Sheffield Ave.
Chicago, IL 60657

Bran Chex®, *see* Ralson Purina Co.

Breakstone's®, *see* Kraft Inc.-Dairy Group

Breyers®, *see* Kraft Inc.-Dairy Group

Bridgford Foods Corp.
1308 N. Patt St.
Anaheim, CA 92801

Brilliant Seafood, Inc.
315 Northern Ave.
Boston, MA 02210

Broadcast®, *see* John Morrell & Co.

Bronte Champagne & Wines Co., Inc.
930 W. Eight Mile Rd.
Detroit, MI 48220

Brown's Best—Kelley Bean Co.
P.O. Box 457
Morrill, NE 69358

Buckingham Corporation, The
620 Fifth Ave.
New York, NY 10020

Bud of California®, *see* Castle & Cooke Foods

Buddig, Carl, and Company
11914 S. Peoria St.
Chicago, IL 60643

Budweiser®—Anheuser-Busch, Inc.
One Busch Place
St. Louis, MO 63118

Bumble Bee®, *see* Castle & Cooke Foods

Bush Brothers & Company
Dandridge, TN 37725

Butter Buds®, *see* Cumberland Packing Corp.

Butterball®, *see* Swift & Company

Buttery Flavored Sesame Snack Cracker, *see* Nabisco Brands Inc.

C&W—California & Washington Co.
1575 Old Bayshore Highway
Burlingame, CA 94010

Calavo Growers of California
Box 3486, Terminal Annex
Los Angeles, CA 90051

California Apricot Advisory Board
1280 Boulevard Way
Walnut Creek, CA 94595

California Artichoke Advisory Board
P.O. Box 747
Castroville, CA 95012

California Avocado Commission
17620 Fitch, 2nd Floor
Irvine, CA 92714

California Brandy Advisory Board
426 Pacific Avenue
San Francisco, CA 94133

California Iceberg Lettuce Commission
P.O. Box 3354
Monterey, CA 93940

California Olive Industry
516 N. Fulton Street
Fresno, CA 93728

California Pistachio Commission
5118 East Clinton
Fresno, CA 93727

Calumet®, *see* General Foods

Campbell Soup Co.
Campbell Place
Camden, NJ 08101

Cape Granny Smith Apples
Dudley, Anderson, Yutzy
40 West 57th Street, Suite 1900
New York, NY 10016

Captain Morgan, *see* Seagram, Joseph E., & Sons, Inc.

Cara Mia Artichokes, *see* California Artichoke Advisory Board

Cara Mia™ Liqueur, *see* Wile, Julius, Sons & Co., Inc.

Castle & Cooke Foods
P.O. Box 3928
San Francisco, CA 94119

Catfish Farmers of America
P.O. Box 34
Jackson, MS 39205

Celebrity Foods, Inc.
17 Varick Street
New York, NY 10013

Celestial Seasonings
1780 55th St.
Boulder, CO 80301

Cella, *see* Garneau, Jos., Co.

Ceresota/Heckers, *see* Standard Milling Co.

Certo®, *see* General Foods

Chambord, *see* Jacquin, Charles, et Cie., Inc.

Chef Boy-Ar-Dee®—American Home Foods
685 Third Ave.
New York, NY 10017

Chesebrough-Pond's Inc.
Trumbull Industrial Park
Trumbull, CT 06611

Chicken of the Sea®, *see* Ralston Purina Co.

Chieftain Wild Rice Co.
Route 7
Hayward, WI 54843

Chiffon®, *see* Anderson Clayton Foods

Chilli Man®, *see* Milnot Company

China Beauty®—Great China Food Products Co.
2520 S. State
Chicago, IL 60616

China Bowl Trading Co., Inc.
80 Fifth Ave.
New York, NY 10011

Chiquita Brands, Inc.
15 Mercedes Dr.
Montvale, NJ 07645

Christian Brothers®, *The*—Fromm and Sichel, Inc.
P.O. Box 7448
San Francisco, CA 94120

Clabber Girl®—Hulman & Co.
P.O. Box 150
Terre Haute, IN 47808

Claristine, *see* General Wine & Spirit Co.

Clark®, *see* Beatrice Confections

Claussen, *see* Oscar Mayer Foods
Corporation

Clicquot Yellow Label, *see* Garneau,
Jos., Co.

Clorox Company
1221 Broadway
Oakland, CA 94623

Coca-Cola Company, The
310 North Avenue
Atlanta, GA 30303

Coca-Cola Company, The
Foods Division
P.O. Box 2079
Houston, TX 77001

Coco Casa®, *see* Holland House Brands Co.

Coco López Imports, Inc.
3655-B Old Court Rd.
Pikesville, MD 21208

CocoRibe®—National Distillers and Chemical
Corporation
99 Park Avenue
New York, NY 10016

Coffee Rich®—Rich Products Corp.
1150 Niagara St.
Buffalo, NY 14240

Colgin, Richard, Co., Inc.
149 Yorktown
Dallas, TX 75221

Colonial Club—Paramount Distillers
3116 Berea Road
Cleveland, OH 44111

Colonial Sugars, Inc.
P.O. Box 1646
Mobile, AL 36633

Contadina Food, Inc.
Sub. of Carnation Company
5045 Wilshire Blvd.
Los Angeles, CA 90036

Cookies Food Products, Inc.
Wall Lake, IA 51466

Cookin' Good™—Showell Farms
P.O. Box 58
Showell, MD 21862

Coors, Adolph, Company
Golden, CO 80401

Corn Chex®, *see* Ralston Purina Co.

Country Pride Foods Ltd.
422 N. Washington
El Dorado, AR 71730

Country Smoked Meats, Inc.
Apple Creek Road
Wooster, OH 44691

County Line Cheese Company, Inc.
Route 2
Auburn, IN 46706

Courvoisier®, *see* Taylor, W. A., & Co.

Crawford's®, *see* Shaffer, Clarke & Co., Inc.

Creamette Co., The
428 North First St.
Minneapolis, MN 55401

Crisco®, *see* Procter & Gamble
Company, The

Cruzan®, *see* Schenley Affiliated
Brands Corp.

Crystal®—Baumer Foods, Inc.
P.O. Box 19166
New Orleans, LA 70179

Cumberland Packing Corp.
2 Cumberland Street
Brooklyn, NY 11205

Dairy Sweet™, *see* Milnot Company

Dannon Company, Inc., The
22-11 38th Ave.
Long Island City, NY 11101

Dante, *see* Atalanta Corp.

Darigold—Consolidated Dairy Products Co.
635 Elliott Avenue W.
Seattle, WA 98109

Del Monte Corporation
1 Market Plaza
San Francisco, CA 94105

Deming's, *see* Peter Pan Seafoods, Inc.

Denmark Cheese Association
4415 W. Harrison
Hillside, IL 60162

Dia-Mel®, *see* Estee Corp., The

Diamond®, *see* Sun-Diamond Growers of
California

Dinty Moore®, *see* Hormel, Geo. A., & Co.

Dole®, *see* Castle & Cooke Foods

Domino®—Amstar Corporation
1251 Avenue of the Americas
New York, NY 10020

Doritos®, *see* Frito-Lay, Inc.

Dorman, N., & Co.
125 Michael Drive
Syosset, NY 11791

Double Q, *see* Peter Pan Seafoods, Inc.

Drambuie®, *see* Taylor, W. A., & Co.

Dream Whip®, *see* General Foods

Dromedary, *see* Nabisco Brands Inc.

Droste®, *see* Wile, Julius, Sons & Co., Inc.

Dr Pepper Company
P.O. Box 225086
Dallas, TX 75265

Dry Sack®, *see* Wile, Julius, Sons &
Co., Inc.

Dubonnet, *see* Schenley Affiliated

DuBouchett, *see* Schenley Affiliated

Dubuque Royal, *see* Royal Ham

Duncan Hines®, *see* Procter & Gamble
Company, The

Dunphy's, *see* Wile, Julius, Sons & Co., Inc.

Durkee Foods
16651 Sprague Road
Strongsville, OH 44136

Eagle® Brand, *see* Borden Inc.

Eatwell®, *see* Star-Kist Foods, Inc.

Eckrich, Peter, & Sons, Inc.
P.O. Box 388
Fort Wayne, IN 46801

Elam Mills
2625 Gardner Road
Broadview, IL 60153

Empire Kosher Foods, Inc.
Mifflintown, PA 17059

Enrico's—Ventre Packing Co., Inc.
373 Spencer
Syracuse, NY 13204

Escort, *see* Nabisco Brands Inc.

Estee Corp., The
169 Lackawanna Ave.
Parsippany, NJ 07054

Excelsior™, *see* Atalanta Corp.

E-Z-Bake—Acme Evans Co.
902 W. Washington Ave.
Indianapolis, IN 46204

Falbo, S., Cheese Co., Inc.
1931 N. 15th Ave.
Melrose Park, IL 60160

Farm Fresh Catfish Co.
P.O. Box 85
Hollandale, MS 38748

Farmland Foods, Inc.
6910 N. Holmes
Kansas City, MO 64116

Featherweight®—Chicago Dietetic
Supply, Inc.
405 E. Shawmut Ave.
La Grange, IL 60525

Fiesta Foods, Inc.
310 W. Mockingbird
Dallas, TX 75247

Figaro Co., The
111 Manufacturing St.
Dallas, TX 75207

Filippo Berio—Berio Importing Corp.
109 Montgomery Ave.
Scarsdale, NY 10583

Fin Brand—Finsilver Seafoods
16400 N. Park Place
Southfield, MI 48037

Finlandia Cheese, *see* Atalanta Corp.

Finlandia® Vodka, *see* Buckingham
Corporation, The

Firebrand®, *see* Swift & Company

Fireside—Doumak Illinois, Inc.
2491 Estes Avenue
Elk Grove Village, IL 60007

Fisher Cheese Co.
P.O. Box 409
Wapakoneta, OH 45895

Fisher Nut Company
P.O. Box 43434
St. Paul, MN 55164

Five Alive™, *see* Coca-Cola Company, The,
Foods Division

Fleischmann's Yeast, *see* Nabisco
Brands, Inc.

Florida Celery Committee
P.O. Box 20067
Orlando, FL 32814

Florida Department of Citrus
P.O. Box 148
Lakeland, FL 33802

Florida Department of Natural Resources
Bureau of Marketing & Extension Services
3900 Commonwealth Boulevard
Tallahassee, FL 32303

Florida Lime Administrative Committee
Produce Marketing Association
700 Barksdale Road
Newark, DE 19711

Florida Tomato Exchange
P.O. Box 20635
Orlando, FL 32814

Florio®, *see* Wile, Julius, Sons & Co., Inc.

Food and Wines from France
24 E. 21st St.
New York, NY 10010

Foulds Inc.
520 E. Church St.
Libertyville, IL 60048

Franco-American, *see* Campbell Soup Co.

Frangelico®—William Grant & Sons, Inc.
130 Fieldcrest Ave.
Edison, NJ 08837

French, R. T., Co.
One Mustard Street
Rochester, NY 14609

Friendly
1855 Boston Road
Wilbraham, MA 01905

Frigo Cheese Corp.
Lena, WI 54139

Frito-Lay, Inc.
P.O. Box 35034
Dallas, TX 75235

Frostlite™, *see* Batterlite Whitlock Inc.

Funsten, *see* Pet Incorporated

Furman Canning Co.
R.D. #2
Northumberland, PA 17857

Gallo Salame
250 Brannan St.
San Francisco, CA 94107

Garneau, Jos., Co., The
P.O. Box 1080
Louisville, KY 40201

Gebhardt Mexican Foods
P.O. Box 7130, Station A
San Antonio, TX 78285

Geisha® Brand—Nozaki America, Inc.
1 World Trade Center
New York, NY 10048

General Foods
250 North Street
White Plains, NY 10625

General Mills, Inc.
9200 Wayzata Blvd.
Minneapolis, MN 55440

General Wine & Spirit Co.
95 East Algonquin Road
Des Plaines, IL 60016

Gerber Products Company
445 State Street
Fremont, MI 49412

Ghirardelli Chocolate Co.
1111-139th Avenue
San Leandro, CA 94578

Gillnettersbest, *see* Peter Pan Seafoods, Inc.

Giroux®, *see* Iroquois Grocery Products, Inc.

Gold Medal®, *see* General Mills, Inc.

Gold Seal, *see* Seagram, Joseph E., &
Sons, Inc.

Golden Dipt Company
100 E. Washington
Millstadt, IL 62260

Golden Grain Macaroni Co.
1111-139th Avenue
San Leandro, CA 94578

Golden Prairie—Iowa Pork Industries, Inc.
5738 Olson Highway
Minneapolis, MN 55422

Goya Foods, Inc.
100 Seaview Dr.
Secaucus, NJ 07094

Grandma's®—Duffy-Mott Co., Inc.
370 Lexington Ave.
New York, NY 10017

Green Giant®, *see* Pillsbury Company, The

Grey Poupon, *see* Heublein Inc.

Guittard Chocolate Company
10 Guittard Rd.
Burlingame, CA 94010

Hain Pure Food Co.
P.O. Box 54841 Terminal Annex
Los Angeles, CA 90054

Hamburger Helper®, *see* General Mills, Inc.

Harvest Brand®, *see* National Oats
Company Inc.

Hawaiian Ginger Growers Association
25 Aupuni St.
Hilo, HI 96720

Health Valley Natural Foods
700 Union Street
Montebello, CA 90640

Heartland®, *see* Pet Incorporated

Heinz U.S.A.
P.O. Box 57
Pittsburgh, PA 15230

Hellmann's®, *see* Best Foods

Henri's Food Products Co. Inc.
2730 W. Silver Spring Dr.
Milwaukee, WI 53209

Herb-Ox®—The Pure Food Co.
Box N
Mamaroneck, NY 10543

Hershey Foods Corp.
19 East Chocolate Avenue
Hershey, PA 17033

Heublein Inc.
Grocery Products Group
Farm Springs Road
Farmington, CT 06032

Heublein Spirits Group
330 New Park Avenue
Hartford, CT 06101

Hi Ho Crackers®, *see* Sunshine Biscuits, Inc.

Hidden Valley Original Ranch®, *see* Clorox Company

High Liner®—National Sea Products Ltd.
555 Burnham Thorpe Rd.
Etobicoke, Ontario Canada M9C 2Y3

High Sea®, *see* Robinson Canning Company, Inc.

Hillshire Farm®, *see* Kahn's and Company

Hiram Walker & Sons, Inc.
P.O. Box 33006
Detroit, MI 48232

Hoffman's®, *see* Anderson Clayton Foods

Holland House Brands Co.
P.O. Box 336
Ridgefield, NJ 07657

Holly Farms Poultry Industries, Inc.
P.O. Box 88
Wilkesboro, NC 28697

Honey Maid, *see* Nabisco Brands Inc.

Hormel, Geo. A., & Co.
P.O. Box 800
Austin, MN 55912

House of Tsang®—Tsang and Ma International
1306 Old County Road
Belmont, CA 94002

Humpty Dumpty, *see* Peter Pan Seafoods, Inc.

Hungry Jack®, *see* Pillsbury Company, The

Hunt-Wesson Kitchens
1645 W. Valencia Dr.
Fullerton, CA 92634

Hydrox®, *see* Sunshine Biscuits, Inc.

Ideal Macaroni Co.
26001 Richmond Rd.
Bedford Heights, OH 44146

Imperial Sugar Company
7606 Burns Run
Dallas, TX 75248

International Multifoods
Box 2942
Minneapolis, MN 55402

Iowa Beef Industry Council
P.O. Box 451
Ames, IA 50010

Irish Mist®, *see* Heublein Spirits Group

Iroquois Grocery Products, Inc.
P.O. Box 3856
Stamford, CT 06905

JAC Creative Foods, Inc.
514 Towne Avenue
Los Angeles, CA 90013

Jacquin, Charles, et Cie., Inc.
2633 Trenton Ave.
Philadelphia, PA 19125

James River Smithfield, *see* Smithfield Ham and Products Co., The

Jarlsberg, *see* Norseland Foods Inc.

Jays Foods, Inc.
825 E. 99th St.
Chicago, IL 60628

Jell-O®, *see* General Foods

Jennie-O Foods, Inc.
P.O. Box 778
Willmar, MN 56201

Jeno's
525 Lake Avenue South
Duluth, MN 55802

Jif®, *see* Procter & Gamble Company, The

Jimmy Dean Meat Company, Inc.
1341 W. Mockingbird Ln.
Dallas, TX 75247

Joan of Arc Co.
2231 W. Altorfer Dr.
Peoria, IL 61615

John Jameson, *see* Seagram, Joseph E., & Sons, Inc.

John Morrell & Co.
191 Waukegan Rd.
Northfield, IL 60093

Johnnie Walker Red, *see* Somerset Importers, Ltd.

Jolly Time®—American Pop Corn Company
Box 178
Sioux City, IA 51102

Jose Cuervo®, *see* Heublein Spirits Group

Kahlúa®—Maidstone Wine & Spirits, Inc.
70 Universal City Plaza, Suite 465
Universal City, CA 91608

Kahn's and Company
3241 Spring Grove Ave.
Cincinnati, OH 45225

Karo®, *see* Best Foods

Kaukauna®, *see* International Multifoods

Keebler Company
One Hollow Tree Lane
Elmhurst, IL 60126

Kellogg Company
Battle Creek, MI 49016

Kikkoman International, Inc.
50 California St.
San Francisco, CA 94111

King Oscar—Chr. Bjelland & Co., Inc.
89 Millburn Ave.
Millburn, NJ 07041

King's Hawaiian Bakery West, Inc.
P.O. Box 6396
Torrance, CA 90504

Kingsford's®, *see* Best Foods

Kitchen Bouquet®, *see* Clorox Company

Knox®, *see* Lipton, Thomas J., Inc.

Koops'—Holland Mills, Inc.
625 N. Sacramento Blvd.
Chicago, IL 60612

Korbel, F., & Bros., Inc.
13250 River Rd.
Guerneville, CA 95466

Kraft Inc.-Dairy Group
P.O. Box 7830
Philadelphia, PA 19101

Krakus, *see* Atalanta Corp.

Kretschmer, *see* International Multifoods

Kubla Khan Food Co.
3617 S.E. 17th Ave.
Portland, OR 97242

La Choy Food Products
901 Stryker Street
Archbold, OH 43502

La Cocina®, *see* Fiesta Foods, Inc.

La Fiesta™, *see* Fiesta Foods, Inc.

La Preferida, Inc.
3400 W. 35th St.
Chicago, IL 60632

La Rosa, V., & Sons, Inc.
40 Jacksonville Rd.
Warminster, PA 18974

La Sauce®, *see* Armour and Company

Laird's Applejack, *see* Taylor, W. A., & Co.

Land O'Lakes, Inc.
P.O. Box 116
Arden Hills, MN 55440

Lawry's Foods, Inc.
570 West Avenue 26
Los Angeles, CA 90065

Lea & Perrins, Inc.
1501 Pollitt Drive
Fair Lawn, NJ 07410

Leafy Greens Council
503 S. Oak Park Avenue
Oak Park, IL 60304

Lemon Hart, *see* Wile, Julius, Sons & Co., Inc.

Leroux, *see* General Wine & Spirit Co.

Leslie Salt Co.
7200 Central Avenue
Newark, CA 94560

Libby, McNeill & Libby, Inc.
200 S. Michigan Ave.
Chicago, IL 60604

Lindsay International Inc.
5327 W. Hillsdale Drive
Visalia, CA 93277

Lipton, Thomas J., Inc.
800 Sylvan Avenue
Englewood Cliffs, NJ 07632

Liquore Galliano, *see* "21" Brands, Inc.

Locatelli®—The Ambriola Company Inc.
Two Burma Road
Jersey City, NJ 07305

Louis Rich Company
Div. of Oscar Mayer Foods Corp.
P.O. Box 7188
Madison, WI 53707

Louisiana Brand, *see* Robinson Canning Company, Inc.

Lucky Leaf®—Knouse Foods Cooperative, Inc.
Peach Glen, PA 17306

M&M/Mars
High Street
Hackettstown, NJ 07840

Madeline's—Herbs for Seasoning
Route 1, Box 57
Amana, IA 52203

Magic Mountain™, *see* Iroquois Grocery Products, Inc.

Maine Department of Marine Resources
State House—Station 21
Augusta, ME 04333

Malt-O-Meal Co.
1520 TCF Tower
Minneapolis, MN 55402

Mandarine Napoléon, *see* Somerset Importers, Ltd.

Manischewitz, B., Company, The
340 Henderson St.
Jersey City, NJ 07302

Manwich®, *see* Hunt-Wesson Kitchens

Marshmallow Fluff®—Durkee-Mower, Inc.
P.O. Box 470
Lynn, MA 01903

Martha White Foods Inc.
P.O. Box 58
Nashville, TN 37202

Marukan Vinegar (U.S.A.) Inc.
7755 E. Monroe St.
Paramount, CA 90723

Mauna Loa Macadamia Nut Corp.
1833 Kalakaua Ave., Suite 200
Honolulu, HI 96815

Mazola®, *see* Best Foods

Meadow Gold®—Beatrice Foods Co.
Two North LaSalle St.
Chicago, IL 60602

Medaglia D'Oro®—S.A. Schonbrunn & Co., Inc.
21 Grand Avenue
Palisades Park, NJ 07650

Merkt Enterprises, Inc.
8125 199th Avenue
Bristol, WI 53104

Merlino Macaroni Co.
8247 South 194th St.
Kent, WA 98032

Metaxa®, *see* Wile, Julius, Sons & Co., Inc.

Michigan Apple Committee
2726 E. Michigan Avenue
Lansing, MI 48912

Michigan Bean Commission
P.O. Box 22037
Lansing, MI 48909

Migliore—Scheps Cheese
Box 8099
Haledon, NJ 07538

Milk Duds®, *see* Beatrice Confections

Milnot Company
P.O. Box 190
Litchfield, IL 62056

Minute®, *see* General Foods

Minute Maid®, *see* Coca-Cola Company, The, Foods Division

Morton Thiokol, Inc.
110 N. Wacker Dr.
Chicago, IL 60606

Mr. Turkey®—Bil-Mar Foods, Inc.
8300 96th Ave.
Zeeland, MI 49464

Mrs. Paul's Kitchens, Inc.
5830 Henry Avenue
Philadelphia, PA 19128

Mueller, C. F., Company
180 Baldwin Avenue
Jersey City, NJ 07306

Nabisco Brands Inc.
East Hanover, NJ 07936

Nalley's Fine Foods
3303 S. 35th
Tacoma, WA 98411

National Confectioners Association
36 S. Wabash
Chicago, IL 60603

National Duckling Council
503 S. Oak Park Avenue
Oak Park, IL 60304

National Fisheries Institute, Inc.
111 East Wacker Drive
Chicago, IL 60601

National Hot Dog & Sausage Council
400 W. Madison
Chicago, IL 60606

National Live Stock & Meat Board
444 N. Michigan Avenue
Chicago, IL 60611

National Marine Fisheries Service
9450 Koger Blvd.
St. Petersburg, FL 33702

National Oats Company Inc.
1515 H Avenue NE
Cedar Rapids, IA 52402

National Pecan Marketing Council
741 Piedmont Avenue
Atlanta, GA 30308

National Pork Producers Council
P.O. Box 10383
Des Moines, IA 50306

Nature Valley®, *see* General Mills, Inc.

Nestlé Company, Inc., The
100 Bloomingdale Road
White Plains, NY 10605

New Mill® Kluski, *see* Ravarino & Freschi, Inc.

New Zealand Kiwifruit Authority
55 Union Street
San Francisco, CA 94111

Nilla, *see* Nabisco Brands Inc.

Nokkelost, *see* Norseland Foods Inc.

None Such®, *see* Borden Inc.

Norbest, Inc.
P.O. Box 1529
Salt Lake City, UT 84110

Norseland Foods Inc.
100 Prospect St.
Stamford, CT 06901

Ocean Spray Cranberries, Inc.
Water Street
Plymouth, MA 02360

Old Bushmills, *see* Garneau, Jos., Co.

Old Canadian, *see* Swift & Company

Old El Paso®, *see* Pet Incorporated

Old London®, *see* Borden Inc.

Open Pit®, *see* General Foods

Oregon Beef Council
1000 N.E. Multnomah St.
Portland, OR 97232

Oregon Caneberry Commission
635 Capitol St., N.E.
Salem, OR 97310

Oregon Regional Sweet Cherry Commission
635 Capitol St., N.E.
Salem, OR 97310

Oregon-Washington-California Pear Bureau,
see Pacific Kitchens

Oregon Wheat Commission
P.O. Box 400
Pendleton, OR 97801

Ore-Ida Foods, Inc.
220 W. Parkcenter Blvd.
Boise, ID 83707

Oreo, *see* Nabisco Brands Inc.

Ortega, *see* Heublein Inc.

Oscar Mayer Foods Corporation
P.O. Box 7188
Madison, WI 53707

P&R, *see* San Giorgio-Skinner, Inc.

Pacific Kitchens
300 Elliott Avenue West
Seattle, WA 98119

Pam®—Boyle-Midway
685 Third Ave.
New York, NY 10017

Parsley Patch, Inc., The
P.O. Box 2043
Santa Rosa, CA 95405

Paul Masson®, *see* Seagram, Joseph E., &
Sons, Inc.

Pepperidge Farm, Inc.
Norwalk, CT 06856

Perdue Farms Inc.
Salisbury, MD 21801

Pernod®, *see* Austin Nichols & Co. Inc.

Pet Incorporated
Pet Plaza, 400 S. Fourth St.
St. Louis, MO 63166

Peter Heering, *see* Taylor, W. A., & Co.

Peter Pan®, *see* Swift & Company

Peter Pan Seafoods, Inc.
1220 Dexter Horton Building
Seattle, WA 98104

Pickle Packers International
One Pickle & Pepper Plaza
St. Charles, IL 60174

Pillsbury Company, The
608 2nd Avenue South
Minneapolis, MN 55402

Planters, *see* Nabisco Brands Inc.

Plochman Inc.
2743 West 36th Place
Chicago, IL 60632

Polka, *see* Atalanta Corp.

Polly-O®—Pollio Dairy Products Corp.
25 Harbor Park Drive
Port Washington, NY 11050

Pompeian, Inc.
4201 Pulaski Highway
Baltimore, MD 21224

Popcorn Institute, The
111 E. Wacker Drive
Chicago, IL 60601

Post® Fruit & Fiber®, *see* General Foods

Potato Board, The
1385 S. Colorado Blvd. #512
Denver, CO 80222

Potato Buds®, *see* General Mills, Inc.

Praline®, *see* Hiram Walker & Sons, Inc.

Prego, *see* Campbell Soup Co.

Premium, *see* Nabisco Brands Inc.

Premium Pak, *see* Stilwell Foods, Inc.

Princella®, *see* Joan of Arc Co.

Procter & Gamble Company, The
301 E. 6th St.
Cincinnati, OH 45202

Progresso Quality Foods
354 W. Passaic Street
Rochelle Park, NJ 07662

Provimi, Inc.
450 N. Sunnyslope Rd., Suite 250
Brookfield, WI 53005

Puritan®, *see* Procter & Gamble
Company, The

Quaker Oats Company, The
Merchandise Mart Plaza
Chicago, IL 60654

Raffetto®, *see* Iroquois Grocery
Products, Inc.

Ragu®, *see* Chesebrough-Pond's Inc.

Ralston Purina Co.
Checkerboard Square
St. Louis, MO 63164

Rath Packing Company, The
P.O. Box 330
Waterloo, IA 50704

Ravarino & Freschi, Inc.
4651 Shaw Blvd.
St. Louis, MO 63100

Ready-Crust®, *see* Keebler Company

ReaLemon®, *see* Borden Inc.

ReaLime®, *see* Borden Inc.

Red Cross®, *see* Ravarino & Freschi, Inc.

Red Star®, *see* Universal Foods Corporation

Redpack—California Canners and Growers
3100 Ferry Building
San Francisco, CA 94106

Reese's®, *see* Hershey Foods Corp.

Regina, *see* Heublein Inc.

R•F®, *see* Ravarino & Freschi, Inc.

Rhode Island Seafood Council
3 Robinson Street
Wakefield, RI 02879

Rhodes™—Dakota Bake-N-Serv, Inc.
Box 688
Jamestown, ND 58401

Rice-A-Roni®, *see* Golden Grain
Macaroni Co.

Rice Chex®, *see* Ralston Purina Co.

Richardson, Thos. D., Co.
Atlantic and I Street
Philadelphia, PA 19134

Ritz, *see* Nabisco Brands Inc.

Robin Hood®, *see* International Multifoods

Robinson Canning Company, Inc.
500 Louisiana St.
Westwego, LA 70094

Rold Gold®, *see* Frito-Lay, Inc.

Roman Meal Co.
2101 S. Tacoma Way
Tacoma, WA 98409

Romanoff®, *see* Iroquois Grocery
Products, Inc.

Ronzoni Macaroni Co. Inc.
50-02 Northern Blvd.
Long Island City, NY 11101

Roquefort Association, Inc.
41 East 42nd Street
New York, NY 10017

Rosarita Mexican Foods Co.
310 South Extension Rd.
Mesa, AZ 85201

Rose, L., & Co.
1200 High Ridge Road
Stamford, CT 06905

Royal Ham—FDL Foods Inc.
P.O. Box 898
Dubuque, IA 52001

Rus-Ettes—Idaho Frozen Foods
P.O. Box 128
Twin Falls, ID 83301

S&W Fine Foods, Inc.
P.O. Box 5580
San Mateo, CA 94402

Salerno-Megowen Biscuit Co.
7777 N. Caldwell
Niles, IL 60648

San Giorgio-Skinner, Inc.
One Chocolate Avenue
Hershey, PA 17033

Sanka®, *see* General Foods

Sara Lee, Kitchens of
500 Waukegan Rd.
Deerfield, IL 60015

Sargento Cheese Company, Inc.
P.O. Box 360
Plymouth, WI 53073

Schenley Affiliated Brands Corp.
888 Seventh Avenue
New York, NY 10106

Seagram, Joseph E., & Sons, Inc.
375 Park Avenue
New York, NY 10152

Sealtest®, *see* Kraft Inc.-Dairy Group

Sebastiani Vineyards
389 Fourth Street East
Sonoma, CA 95476

Sesame Wheats, *see* Nabisco Brands Inc.

Seven Seas®, *see* Anderson Clayton
Foods

Shaffer, Clarke & Co., Inc.
1445 E. Putnam Avenue
Old Greenwich, CT 06870

Shake 'N Bake®, *see* General Foods

Shasta Beverages
26901 Industrial Blvd.
Hayward, CA 94545

Shawnee Milling Company
P.O. Box 1567
Shawnee, OK 74801

Shoal Lake Wild Rice Ltd.
Keewatin, Ontario Canada P0X 1C0

Simon Fischer—Globe Products Co., Inc.
P.O. Box 1927
Clifton, NJ 07015

Sizzlean®, *see* Swift & Company

Skinner®, *see* San Giorgio-Skinner, Inc.

Skippy®, *see* Best Foods

Smirnoff®, *see* Heublein Spirits Group

Smithfield Ham and Products Co., The
Smithfield, VA 23430

Smucker, J. M., Company, The
Strawberry Lane
Orrville, OH 44667

Snack Mate, *see* Nabisco Brands Inc.

Snap-E-Tom, *see* Heublein Inc.

Snow Crop® Five Alive™, *see* Coca-Cola
Company, The, Foods Division

Sociables, *see* Nabisco Brands Inc.

Softasilk®, *see* General Mills, Inc.

Solo®—Sokol and Company
5315 Dansher Road
Countryside, IL 60525

Somerset Importers, Ltd.
1114 Avenue of the Americas
New York, NY 10036

Sorrento Cheese Co., Inc.
2375 So. Park Avenue
Buffalo, NY 14220

Soup Starter™, *see* Swift & Company

South African Rock Lobster Service Corp.
450 Seventh Ave.
New York, NY 10123

Southern Comfort
1220 N. Price Rd.
St. Louis, MO 63132

Souverain®, *see* Wile, Julius, Sons &
Co., Inc.

Spam®, *see* Hormel, Geo. A., & Co.

Standard Milling Co.
1009 Central St.
Kansas City, MO 64141

Star-Kist Foods, Inc.
582 Tuna Street
Terminal Island, CA 90731

Stella®, *see* Universal Foods Corporation

Stilwell Foods, Inc.
P.O. Box 432
Stilwell, OK 74960

Stokely-Van Camp, Inc.
941 N. Meridian St.
Indianapolis, IN 46206

Stokes Canning/Ellis Foods
1575 Alcott St.
Denver, CO 80204

Stove Top®, *see* General Foods

Stroh Brewery Company, The
One Stroh Drive
Detroit, MI 48226

Success®—Rivinia Foods Inc.
P.O. Box 2636
Houston, TX 77001

Sue Bee®—Sioux Honey Association
P.O. Box 388
Sioux City, IA 51102

Sun-Diamond Growers of California
1320 El Capitan Dr.
San Ramon, CA 94583

Sun•Maid®, *see* Sun-Diamond Growers of
California

Sun World, Inc.
5544 California Avenue
Bakersfield, CA 93309

Sunkist Growers, Inc.
P.O. Box 7888
Van Nuys, CA 91409

Sunshine Biscuits, Inc.
245 Park Avenue
New York, NY 10017

Sunsweet®, *see* Sun-Diamond Growers of
California

Super Pop, *see* National Oats Company Inc.

Superman™—Sunnyland Refining Co.
P.O. Box 457
Birmingham, AL 35234

Superose®, *see* Batterlite Whitlock Inc.

Swanson, *see* Campbell Soup Co.

Sweet Mun-chee®, *see* Swift & Company

Sweet 'N Low®, *see* Cumberland Packing
Corp.

Sweet Potato Council of the United States
Inc., The
5023 Iroquois Street
College Park, MD 20740

Sweetlite™, *see* Batterlite Whitlock Inc.

Swift & Company
1919 Swift Drive
Oak Brook, IL 60521

Tabasco®—McIlhenny Co.
Avery Island, LA 70513

Table Trim®, *see* John Morrell & Co.

Tater Tots®, *see* Ore-Ida Foods, Inc.

Taylor, W. A., & Co.
825 South Bayshore Dr.
Miami, FL 33131

Taylor's—John W. Taylor Packing Co., Inc.
Hallwood, VA 23359

Tennessee Pride®—Odom Sausage Co., Inc.
1201 Neely's Bend Road
Madison, TN 37115

Texas Ruby Red—Texas Citrus Advertising,
Inc.
P.O. Box 2497
McAllen, TX 78501

Thank You® *Brand*—Michigan Fruit Canners
P.O. Box 68
Benton Harbor, MI 49022

Thomas, S. B., Inc.
930 N. Riverview Drive
Totowa, NJ 07512

3-Minute Brand®, *see* National Oats
Company Inc.

Tia Maria®, *see* Taylor, W. A., & Co.

Tom's Foods
P.O. Box 60
Columbus, GA 31994

Trappey's, B. F., Sons, Inc.
P.O. Drawer 400
New Iberia, LA 70560

Treasure Cave®, *see* Swift & Company

Treet®, *see* Armour and Company

Triscuit, *see* Nabisco Brands Inc.

Tuna Helper®, *see* General Mills, Inc.

Tuna Research Foundation Inc.
1101 17th St., N.W.
Washington, DC 20036

"21" Brands, Inc.
75 Rockefeller Plaza
New York, NY 10019

Two Fingers®, *see* Hiram Walker &
Sons, Inc.

Tyson Foods, Inc.
2210 W. Oaklawn Dr.
Springdale, AR 72764

Uncle Ben's Foods
P.O. Box 1752
Houston, TX 77001

Underwood, Wm., Company
Pet Incorporated
Pet Plaza, 400 S. Fourth St.
St. Louis, MO 63166

Universal Foods Corporation
433 E. Michigan
Milwaukee, WI 53201

U.S. Brands Corporation
4411 S. Park Avenue
Buffalo, NY 14219

Usinger, Fred, Inc.
1030 N. Third Street
Milwaukee, WI 53203

Van Camp's®, *see* Stokely-Van Camp, Inc.

Van De Kamp's Frozen Foods
13100 Arctic Circle
Santa Fe Springs, CA 90670

Veg-All®—The Larsen Company
520 N. Broadway
Green Bay, WI 54305

V-8, *see* Campbell Soup Co.

Venetian Cream™, *see* Taylor, W. A., & Co.

Vienna Sausage Mfg. Co.
2501 N. Damen Avenue
Chicago, IL 60647

Virginia Dare Extract Co., Inc.
882 Third Avenue
Brooklyn, NY 11232

Wakefield Seafoods Corp.
1450 114th Ave., S.E.
Bellevue, WA 98004

Wasa®, *see* Shaffer, Clarke & Co., Inc.

Washington State Potato Commission, *see*
Pacific Kitchens

Waterford Cream™, *see* Buckingham
Corporation, The

Weaver, Victor F., Inc.
403 S. Custer Ave.
New Holland, PA 17557

Weight Watchers®—Foodways National Inc.
P.O. Box 41
Boise, ID 83707

Welch Foods Inc.
Westfield, NY 14787

Wesson®, *see* Hunt-Wesson Kitchens

Western New York Apple & New York
Cherry Growers Association
7645 Main Street Fishers
Victor, NY 14564

Wheat Chex®, *see* Ralston Purina Co.

Wheatena®, *see* Standard Milling Co.

Wheatsworth, *see* Nabisco Brands Inc.

Wild Turkey Liqueur®, *see* Austin Nichols &
Co. Inc.

Wilderness Foods
P.O. Box 989
Traverse City, MI 49685

Wile, Julius, Sons & Co., Inc.
One Hollow Lane
Lake Success, NY 11042

Wilson Foods Corp.
4545 N. Lincoln Blvd.
Oklahoma City, OK 73105

Wise®, *see* Borden Inc.

Wish-Bone®, *see* Lipton, Thomas J., Inc.

Witt, F. W., & Company, Inc.
1106 S. Bridge St.
Yorkville, IL 60560

Wolf Brand Products
2929 Carlisle St.
Dallas, TX 75204

Wolff's®—The Birkett Mills
Penn Yan, NY 14527

Woody's®, *see* Anderson Clayton
Foods

Wright, E. H., Co., Inc.
783 Old Hickory Blvd.
Brentwood, TN 37027

Wyler's®, *see* Borden Inc.

Yoplait®, *see* General Mills, Inc.

Zagnut®, *see* Beatrice Confections

Index